C00 46550755

D0300874

East Coast Australia

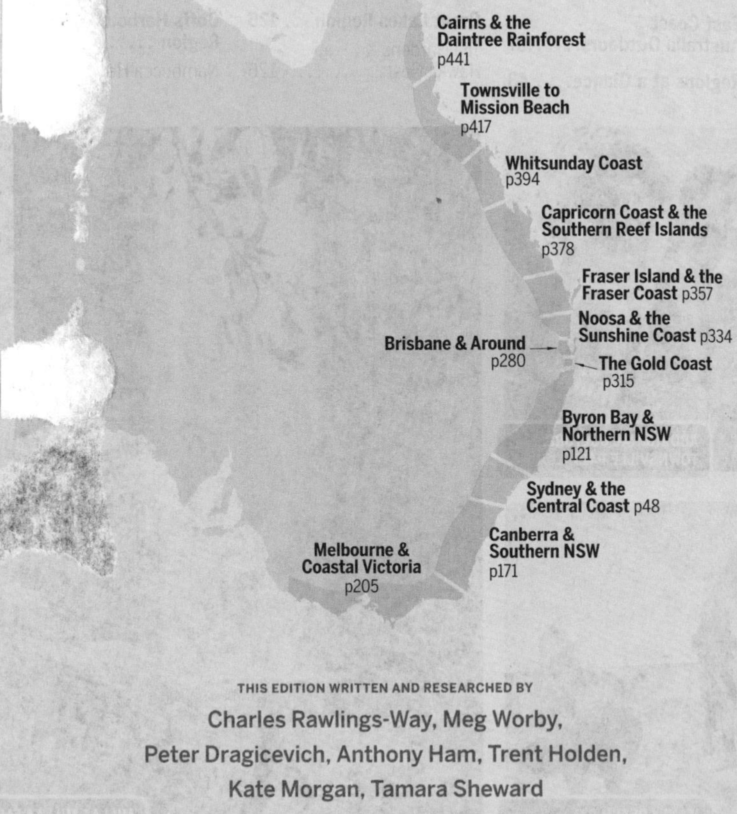

Cairns & the
Daintree Rainforest
p441

Townsville to
Mission Beach
p417

Whitsunday Coast
p394

Capricorn Coast & the
Southern Reef Islands
p378

Fraser Island & the
Fraser Coast p357

Noosa & the
Sunshine Coast p334

Brisbane & Around
p280

The Gold Coast
p315

Byron Bay &
Northern NSW
p121

Sydney & the
Central Coast p48

Melbourne &
Coastal Victoria
p205

Canberra &
Southern NSW
p171

THIS EDITION WRITTEN AND RESEARCHED BY

Charles Rawlings-Way, Meg Worby,
Peter Dragicevich, Anthony Ham, Trent Holden,
Kate Morgan, Tamara Sheward

Contents

PLAN YOUR TRIP

ON THE ROAD

ABORIGINAL CULTURE, TOWNSVILLE P419

PAUL DYMOND / GETTY IMAGES ©

ANTHONY ONG / GETTY IMAGES ©

MANLY BEACH P71

PETE ATKINSON / GETTY IMAGES ©

MILLAA MILLAA FALLS
P459

Contents

MELBOURNE P206

ON THE ROAD

WILSONS PROMONTORY P265

PETER WALTON PHOTOGRAPHY / GETTY IMAGES ©

Contents

KANGAROOS, MURRAMARANG NATIONAL PARK P192

Welcome to East Coast Australia

Picture-perfect beaches, rainforests, hip cities and the Great Barrier Reef: just a few of our favourite things along Australia's East Coast.

Into the Wild

More than 18,000km end to end, Australia's East Coast is a rippling ribbon of beaches and rampant wildlife. Offshore, the astonishing Great Barrier Reef is a 2000km-long hypercoloured haven for tropical marine life. Also here are hundreds of islands, from craggy nature reserves to palm-studded paradises. Fringing the land are brilliant beaches, with Australia's best surf breaks peeling into the shore. Inland are bewitching national parks with lush rainforests, jagged peaks and native critters that rate from cute and cuddly (koalas) to downright fearsome (saltwater crocs).

Action Stations

Traversing the East Coast is an exercise in, well, exercise! The sun is shining and the locals are outdoors, running, swimming, surfing, cycling, skating, snorkelling and hiking. Why not join in? Explore the Great Barrier Reef, the most photogenic underwater landscape on earth. Rampage down some white-water rapids, kayak across a lagoon, or set sail through a tropical archipelago. Propel yourself up a mountain, through a national park or alongside a rushing river. Or just head for the beach, where the locals let it all hang out, as democratic as sand.

City Scenes

Home to Indigenous Australians for millennia, Australia's East Coast is also where modern Australia kicked off. The first European settlement was in Sydney, and the city remains a honey-pot lure for anyone looking for a good time. Sassy and ambitious yet unpretentious, Sydneysiders eat, drink, shop and party with hedonistic abandon. To the south, Melbourne is Australia's arts and coffee capital – a bookish, Euro-tinged town with a bohemian soul. Wrapped around river bends, boomtown Brisbane is a glam patchwork of inner-city neighbourhoods. And don't forget Australia's capital, Canberra – so much more than a political filing cabinet!

Eat, Drink & Be Merry

Australia's big East Coast cities lift the lid on a rich culinary experience, with fantastic cafes, sprawling food markets and world-class restaurants. After dark, moody wine bars, student-filled speakeasies and boisterous Aussie pubs provide plenty of excuses to raise a glass. Beyond the cities, foodie delights range from fish and chips straight off the fishing boats to degustation dinners, paired perfectly with luscious wines from the Hunter and Yarra Valleys. The hardest part is deciding what to try first...

Why We Love East Coast Australia

By Charles Rawlings-Way & Meg Worby, Authors

Growing up in modest southern Australian towns, the lure of the East Coast, with its beaches and big cities, was ever-present for us both. Melbourne enticed with bookshops, bars and urban soul; Sydney lured with city-slicker cool and warm waves to splash around in. Towns such as Byron Bay, Noosa and Port Douglas held near-mythical status, demanding to be explored at the first opportunity. And we haven't stopped exploring since! South to north or north to south, travelling the East Coast is Australia's essential road trip.

For more about our authors, see p536.

For more about our authors, see p536.

Above: Cape Byron (p155), mainland Australia's most easterly point

East Coast Australia

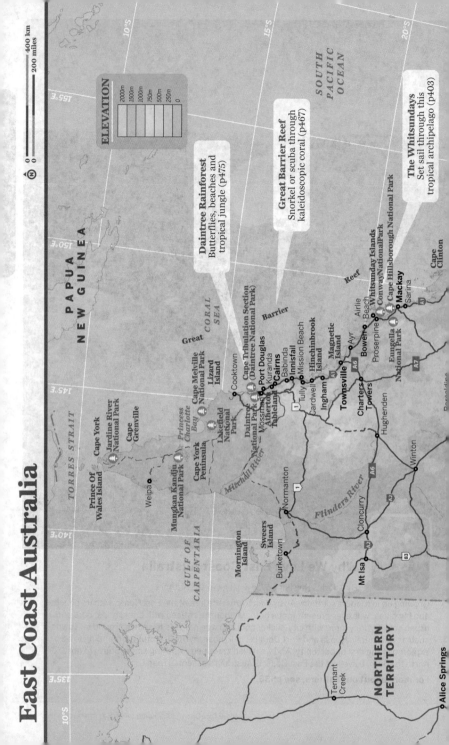

Daintree Rainforest
Butterflies, beaches and tropical jungle (p475)

Great Barrier Reef
Snorkel or scuba through kaleidoscopic coral (p467)

The Whitsundays
Set sail through this tropical archipelago (p403)

ELEVATION
2000m
1500m
1000m
750m
500m
250m
0

0 — 400 km
0 — 200 miles

PAPUA NEW GUINEA

TORRES STRAIT

Prince Of Wales Island

Cape York
Jardine River National Park

Cape Grenville

Cape York Peninsula

Mungkan Kandju National Park

Princess Charlotte Bay

Lakefield National Park

Cape Melville National Park

Lizard Island

Cooktown

Cape Tribulation Section (Daintree National Park)

Daintree National Park — Mossman
Port Douglas
Kuranda
Atherton Tableland
Cairns
Babinda
Innisfail
Tully
Mission Beach
Cardwell
Hinchinbrook Island
Ingham
Magnetic Island
Townsville
Ayr
Charters Towers
Bowen
Proserpine
Airlie Beach
Whitsunday Islands
Conway National Park
Cape Hillsborough National Park
Mackay
Sarina
Eungella National Park

CORAL SEA

Great Barrier Reef

SOUTH PACIFIC OCEAN

Cape Clinton

GULF OF CARPENTARIA

Mornington Island

Sweers Island

Burketown

Normanton

Mitchell River

Flinders River

Cloncurry

Hughenden

Winton

Mt Isa

NORTHERN TERRITORY

Tennant Creek

Alice Springs

Weipa

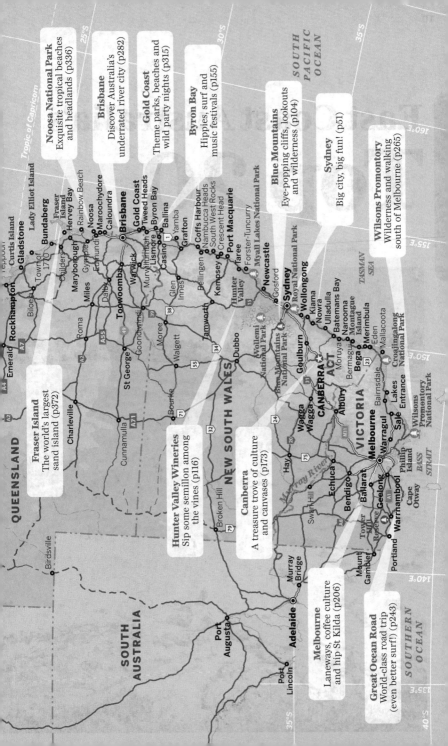

Noosa National Park
Exquisite tropical beaches and headlands (p336)

Brisbane
Discover Australia's underrated river city (p282)

Gold Coast
Theme parks, beaches and wild party nights (p315)

Byron Bay
Hippies, surf and music festivals (p155)

Blue Mountains
Eye-popping cliffs, lookouts and wilderness (p104)

Sydney
Big city, big fun! (p51)

Wilsons Promontory
Wilderness and walking south of Melbourne (p265)

Fraser Island
The world's largest sand island (p372)

Hunter Valley Wineries
Sip some semillon among the vines (p116)

Canberra
A treasure trove of culture and canvases (p173)

Melbourne
Laneways, coffee culture and hip St Kilda (p206)

Great Ocean Road
World-class road trip (even better surf!) (p243)

QUEENSLAND

NEW SOUTH WALES

VICTORIA

SOUTH AUSTRALIA

SOUTH PACIFIC OCEAN

TASMAN SEA

BASS STRAIT

SOUTHERN OCEAN

Birdsville
Charleville
Cunnamulla
Roma
St George
Charleville
Miles
Dalby
Goondiwindi
Moree
Walgett
Bourke
Broken Hill
Hay
Swan Hill
Murray Bridge
Port Augusta
Port Lincoln
Adelaide
Mount Gambier
Portland
Warrnambool
Cape Otway
Tower Hill Reserve
Geelong
Ballarat
Bendigo
Echuca
Wagga Wagga
Albury
Bairnsdale
Sale
Warragul
Melbourne
Phillip Island
Lakes Entrance
Mallacoota
Eden
Merimbula
Bega
Bermagui
Narooma
Montague Island
Moruya
Batemans Bay
Ulladulla
Nowra
Kiama
Wollongong
Sydney
Canberra
Goulburn
Dubbo
Tamworth
Glen Innes
Warwick
Toowoomba
Maryborough
Gympie
Nambour
Caloundra
Maroochydore
Noosa
Rainbow Beach
Hervey Bay
Fraser Island
Bundaberg
Lady Elliot Island
Gladstone
Curtis Island
Rockhampton
Emerald
Biloela
Townof 1770
Gin Gin
Childers
Murwillumbah
Lismore
Casino
Grafton
Yamba
Ballina
Byron Bay
Tweed Heads
Gold Coast
Brisbane
Coffs Harbour
Nambucca Heads
South West Rocks
Crescent Head
Port Macquarie
Taree
Forster-Tuncurry
Myall Lakes National Park
Newcastle
Gosford
Hunter Valley
Bellingen
Kempsey
Wauchope
Murray River
Wilsons Promontory National Park
Croajingalong National Park
Lakes National Park
Wollemi National Park
Blue Mountains National Park
Royal National Park

ACT

Tropic of Capricorn

25°S
30°S
35°S
40°S

135°E
140°E
150°E
155°E
160°E

East Coast Australia's
Top 20

Sydney

1 The big-ticket sights are all here – the Sydney Opera House (p54), the Rocks (p51) and Sydney Harbour Bridge (p51) top most people's lists – but to really catch Sydney's vibe, spend a day at the beach. Stake out a patch of sand, lather yourself in sunscreen and plunge into the surf at Bondi Beach (p64); or hop on a harbour ferry from Circular Quay to Manly (p71) for a swim, a surf or a walk along the sea-sprayed promenade to Shelley Beach. *Ahhh,* this is the life! Left: Bondi Beach (p64)

Great Barrier Reef

2 The Great Barrier Reef (p467) lives up to its reputation. Stretching more than 2000km along the Queensland coastline, it's a complex ecosystem populated with dazzling coral, languid sea turtles, gliding rays, timid reef sharks and 1500 species of colourful tropical fish. Whether you dive on it, snorkel over it, explore it via scenic flight or glass-bottom boat, linger in an island resort or camp on a remote coral-fringed atoll, this vivid undersea kingdom and its 900 coral-fringed islands is unforgettable.

CHRISTINE WEHRMEIER / GETTY IMAGES ©

JEFF HUNTER / GETTY IMAGES ©

PETER HENDRIE / GETTY IMAGES ©

Sailing the Whitsunday Islands

3 You can hop around an entire archipelago of tropical islands in this seafaring life and never find anywhere with the sheer tropical beauty of the Whitsundays (p403). Travellers of all monetary persuasions launch yachts from party town Airlie Beach and drift between these lush green isles in a slow search for paradise (you'll probably find it in more than one place). Wish you were here?

Left: Whitehaven Beach (p415)

Daintree Rainforest

4 Lush green rainforest tumbles down towards brilliant white-sand coastline in the ancient, World Heritage–listed Daintree Rainforest (p475). Upon entering the forest – home to 3000 or so plant species including fan palms, ferns and mangroves – you'll be enveloped by birdsong, the buzz of insects and the constant commentary of frogs. Continue exploring via wildlife-spotting tours, mountain treks, interpretive boardwalks, tropical-fruit orchard tours, canopy walks, 4WD trips, horse riding, kayaking and cruises.

Indigenous Far North Queensland

5 The human history of Far North Queensland (p441) is as dramatic as its natural surrounds. Indigenous people have called the region's rainforests and beaches home for more than 40,000 years, and a boom in Aboriginal-led tours and experiences makes it easier than ever for visitors to see it all through native eyes. Throw a spear, make a boomerang, sample bush tucker, interpret rock art, go on a rainforest walk, dig the didgeridoo: a world of new – yet incredibly old – adventures awaits. Bottom right: Laura Aboriginal Dance Festival (p25)

Byron Bay

6 Byron Bay (just Byron to its mates; p155) is one of the enduring icons of Australian culture. Families on school holidays, surfers and sunseekers from around the globe gather here, drawn to Australia's most easterly point by fabulous restaurants, a laid-back ethos, surf beaches and an astonishing range of activities. This is one of the most beautiful stretches of coast in the country, and the town's infectious, hippie vibe will put a smile on your dial.

Melbourne's Laneways

7 Once the sole domain of garbage bins, rats, drug addicts and adult cinemas, the maze-like bluestone laneways threading through downtown Melbourne (p206) have been transformed into city hot spots. Home to some of the best street art in the world, here you can discover secret works by Banksy and local artists' canvasses, en route to the city's swankiest basement restaurants, divey rock bars and secret stairways leading up to rooftop cocktail bars. Bottom: Centre Place

RICHARD I'ANSON / GETTY IMAGES ©

JENNY JONES / GETTY IMAGES ©

Brisbane

8 If you've never been to Australia's river city (or, like many Aussies, you haven't been in a while), you're in for a big surprise! Billing itself as 'Australia's new World City', Brisbane (p282) has shed its redneck overtones in favour of a simmering coffee culture, great bookshops, fabulous museums and festivals, and a hip small-bar scene that, per capita, is as good as Melbourne's and Sydney's. The inner-city neighbourhoods each have a distinct flavour: follow the bends of the Brisbane River and spend some time exploring each one. Left: South Bank Parklands (p283)

Blue Mountains

9 The views from Katoomba's Echo Point and Blackheath's Govetts Leap in the Blue Mountains (p104) are so utterly good you'll find yourself pushing to the front of the crowd then pushing your camera's memory card to the limit. After the photo shoot, hike a trail into the magnificent Jamison Valley or Grose Valley, accompanied by the scent of eucalyptus oil, a fine mist of which issues from the dense tree canopy and gives these World Heritage–listed mountains their name.

Noosa National Park

10 Cloaking the headland beside the stylish resort town of Noosa itself, Noosa National Park (p336) features a string of perfect bays fringed with sand and pandanus trees. Surfers come here for the long, rolling waves; walkers make the trip for the unspoilt natural vibes. Lovely hiking trails criss-cross the park: our pick is the scenic coastal trail to Hell's Gates on which you might spy sleepy koalas in the trees around Tea Tree Bay, and dolphins swimming off the rocky headland.

RICHARD I'ANSON / GETTY IMAGES ©

Fraser Island

11 Fraser Island (p372) is an ecological wonderland created by drifting sand, where wild dogs roam free and lush rainforest grows on sand. It's a primal island utopia, home to a profusion of wildlife including the purest strain of dingo in Australia. The best way to explore the island is in a 4WD – cruising up the seemingly endless Seventy-Five Mile Beach and bouncing along sandy inland tracks. Tropical rainforest, pristine freshwater pools and beach camping under the stars will bring you back to nature. Bottom: Champagne Pools (p375)

CHRISTOPHER GROENHOUT / GETTY IMAGES ©

Great Ocean Road

12 Jutting out of turbulent waters, the Twelve Apostles on the Great Ocean Road (p243) are one of Victoria's defining sights – but it's the 'getting there' road trip that doubles their impact. Take it slow along roads that curl beside Bass Strait beaches, then whip inland through rainforests and quaint towns. The Great Ocean Road doesn't stop at the Twelve Apostles: further along is maritime treasure Port Fairy and hidden Cape Bridgewater. For the ultimate in slow travel, hike the Great Ocean Walk from Apollo Bay to the Apostles. Top: Twelve Apostles (p253)

Hunter Valley Wineries

13 Picture this: a glass-fronted pavilion overlooking gently rolling hills covered with row after row of grape-heavy vines. Inside, you're sipping a glass of golden-hued semillon and pondering a delectable lunch menu of top-quality local produce. Make your choice, settle back, slide into a glass of earthy shiraz and thoroughly enjoy your meal. It's the stuff of which travel memories are made: all of this could be yours in New South Wales' premier wine district, the Hunter Valley (p116).

TONY LIU PHOTOGRAPHY / GETTY IMAGES ©

ANDREW WATSON / GETTY IMAGES ©

Wildlife-Watching

14 Head to Phillip Island southeast of Melbourne for a parade of adorable little penguins (p259) and fur seals cavorting along the rocky shore, or into tropical Far North Queensland for otherworldly cassowaries (p438) and dinosaur-like crocodiles. In between, you'll find a panoply of extraordinary animals found nowhere else on earth: koalas, kangaroos, wombats and platypuses. There's also great whale-watching (p359) along the coast in season (May to October), plus the laughter of kookaburras.
Left: Sleeping koala

Bridge Climbing

15 Vertigo not an issue? Make a beeline for Sydney's iconic Harbour Bridge or Brisbane's Story Bridge and scale their steely heights. Once only the domain of bridge painters and trespassing daredevils, Sydney's big arch can now be tackled by anyone on a BridgeClimb (p75). Story Bridge Adventure Climb (p289) is a newer experience but no less mesmerising. And it's not just about the sublime city views – the bridges themselves are amazing structures! Top right: Sydney Harbour BridgeClimb

Canberra's Museums & Galleries

16 Though Canberra (p173) is only a century old, Australia's capital has always been preoccupied with history. So it's not surprising that the major drawcards here are lavishly endowed museums and galleries that focus on recounting and interpreting the national narrative. Institutions such as the National Gallery of Australia (p173), National Museum of Australia (p174), National Portrait Gallery (p175) and Australian War Memorial (p174) offer visitors a fascinating insight into the country's history and culture. Bottom right: National Museum of Australia

Wilsons Promontory

17 Victoria's southernmost point and finest coastal national park, Wilsons Promontory (p265) is heaven for bushwalkers, wildlife-watchers, surfers and photographers. The scenery here is out of this world: even a short detour from the park base at Tidal River will access swathes of white-sand beaches and bays. But with more than 80km of marked walking trails, the best of the Prom requires some legwork. Serious hikers should tackle the three-day Great Prom Walk, staying a night in gloriously isolated lighthouse keepers' cottages.

Gold Coast

18 Brash, trashy, hedonistic, over-hyped... Queensland's Gold Coast (p315) is all of these things, but if you're looking for a party, bring it on! Beyond the fray is the beach – an gorgeous coastline of clean sand, warm water and peeling surf breaks. The bronzed gods of the surf, Australia's surf life-savers, patrol the sand and pit their skills against one another in surf carnivals – events involving ocean swimming, beach sprints and surf boat racing. Also here are Australia's biggest theme parks – rollercoaster nirvana!

Bottom: Surfers Paradise (p317)

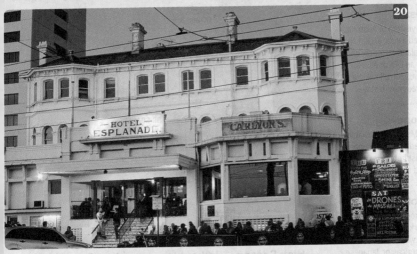

Montague Island

19 Montague Island (p195) is one of wild Australia's most underrated destinations. Offshore from Narooma, bald, boulder-strewn Montague is a haven for nesting seabirds, including a mere 10,000 little penguins. Indigenous sacred sites, an unusual granite lighthouse and guided eco-tours set Montague apart from the mainland by more than the 9km boat ride it takes to get here. Diving (spot some grey nurse sharks!), seal-watching and occasional pods of passing whales all add to the island's appeal.

St Kilda

20 With its raffish beachside ambience, art deco architecture, palm trees, rattling trams and seedy history, St Kilda (p217) has long been one of Melbourne's most charismatic inner-city suburbs. Wander along Acland St ducking into bookshops and cake bakeries, or grab a beer and see a live band at the Esplanade Hotel (the Espy; p234), a sticky-carpet breeding ground for local talent for decades. There are some not-so-obvious secrets here too: a penguin colony, outdoor movies and some fab waterfront restaurants.

Need to Know

For more information, see Survival Guide (p505)

Currency
Australian dollar ($)

Language
English

Visas
All visitors to Australia need a visa, except New Zealanders. Apply online for an ETA or eVisitor visa, each allowing a three-month stay.

Money
ATMs widely available. Credit cards accepted at most hotels, restaurants and shops.

Mobile Phones
European phones will work in Australia's network, but most American or Japanese phones will not. Use global roaming or a local SIM card and prepaid account.

Time
Australia's East Coast is on Australian Eastern Standard Time (AEST), which is GMT/UCT plus 10 hours.

When to Go

Desert, dry climate
Dry climate
Tropical climate, wet & dry seasons
Warm to hot summers, mild winters

CAIRNS
GO Apr–Sep

WHITSUNDAYS
GO May–Oct

BRISBANE
GO Jul–Nov

SYDNEY
GO Nov–Mar

MELBOURNE
GO Dec–Apr

High Season
(Dec–Feb)

➡ Summertime: hot and humid up north, warm and dry down south.

➡ Prices rise 25% for big-city accommodation.

➡ Unsafe swimming north of Agnes Water November to May (due to jellyfish).

Shoulder
(Sep–Nov & Mar–May)

➡ Warm sun, clear skies, shorter queues.

➡ Spring flowers (October); autumn colours in Victoria (April).

➡ Local business people unstressed by summer crowds.

Low Season
(Jun–Aug)

➡ Cool rainy days and low accommodation prices down south.

➡ Tropical high season: mild days, low humidity, pricey beds.

➡ Good Great Barrier Reef visibility.

Useful Websites

Lonely Planet (www.lonelyplanet.com/australia) Destination information, hotel bookings, traveller forum and more.

Tourism Australia (www.australia.com) Government tourism site with visitor info.

Queensland Holidays (www.queenslandholidays.com.au) Queensland coverage.

Visit NSW (www.visitnsw.com) New South Wales information.

Tourism Victoria (www.visitvictoria.com) Victoria's official site.

Coastalwatch (www.coastalwatch.com) Surf reports.

Important Numbers

Country code	☑61
International access code	☑0011
Emergency (ambulance, fire, police)	☑000
Directory assistance	☑1223
Reverse charges	☑1800-REVERSE (738 3773)

Exchange Rates

Canada	C$1	$0.99
China	Y1	$0.18
Euro zone	€1	$1.53
Japan	¥100	$1.08
New Zealand	NZ$1	$0.95
South Korea	W100	$0.10
UK	UK£1	$1.84
USA	US$1	$1.10

For current exchange rates see www.xe.com.

Daily Costs

Budget: Less than $100

➡ Dorm bed: $25–35 a night

➡ Double room in a hostel: from $80

➡ Simple pizza or pasta meal: $10–15

➡ Short bus or tram ride: $4

Midrange: $100–$280

➡ Double room in a midrange hotel: $100–200

➡ Breakfast or lunch in a cafe: $20–40

➡ Short taxi ride: $25

➡ Car hire per day: from $35

Top End: More than $280

➡ Double room in a top-end hotel: from $200

➡ Three-course meal in a classy restaurant: from $80

➡ Adventure activities: sailing the Whitsundays from $300 per night, diving course $650

➡ Domestic flight Sydney to Melbourne: from $100

Opening Hours

Opening hours vary from state to state – following is a general guide:

Banks 9.30am–4pm Monday to Thursday, until 5pm Friday

Bars 4pm–late

Cafes 7am–5pm

Pubs 11am–midnight

Restaurants noon–2.30pm and 6pm–9pm

Shops 9am–5pm Monday to Saturday

Supermarkets 7am–8pm; some 24 hours

Arriving in Australia

Sydney Airport (p517)

AirportLink trains to central Sydney every 10 minutes, 4.50am to 12.40am. Prebooked shuttle buses service city hotels. A taxi into the city costs $40 to $50 (30 minutes).

Melbourne Airport (p517)

SkyBus services (24-hour) to central Melbourne every 10 to 30 minutes. A taxi into the city costs around $40 (25 minutes).

Brisbane Airport (p517)

Airtrain trains to central Brisbane every 15 to 30 minutes, 5.45am to 10pm. Prebooked shuttle buses service city hotels. A taxi into the city costs $35 to $45 (25 minutes).

Getting Around

Australia's East Coast is over 18,000km long! Getting from A to B requires some thought.

Car Travel at your own tempo, explore remote areas and visit regions with no public transport. Hire cars in major towns; drive on the left.

Plane Fast-track your holiday: affordable, frequent, fast internal flights. Carbon-offset flights if you're feeling guilty.

Bus Reliable, frequent long-haul services around the country (not always cheaper than flying).

Train Slow, expensive, infrequent...but the scenery is great! Opt for a sleeper carriage rather than an 'overnighter' seat.

For much more on **getting around**, see p517

If You Like...

Beaches

Bondi Beach (p64) Essential Sydney: carve up the surf or laze around and people-watch.

Wilsons Promontory (p265) Victoria's premier coastal wilderness, with deserted beaches.

Fraser Island (p372) The world's largest sand island is basically one big beach.

Whitehaven Beach (p415) The jewel of the Whitsundays, with powdery white sand and crystal-clear waters.

Cape Tribulation (p476) The rainforest sweeps down to smooch the reef at these empty stretches of sand.

Indigenous Culture

Blue Mountains Walkabout (p107) Aboriginal-guided day tours take you through the Blue Mountains in Sydney's backyard.

Koorie Heritage Trust (p209) A great place to discover southeastern Aboriginal culture.

Kuku-Yalanji Dreamtime Walks (p474) Guided walks through Queensland's Mossman Gorge with knowledgable Indigenous guides.

Ingan Tours (p434) Aboriginal-operated rainforest tours in tropical north Queensland.

Tjapukai Cultural Park (p444) Interactive tours and vibrant performances in Cairns by local Tjapukai people.

Pubs & Live Music

Tote (p234) The battered old Tote remains an essential Melbourne rock room.

Corner Hotel (p234) Legendary live-music venue in Richmond, Melbourne.

Zoo (p306) Grungy, alternative and unfailingly original: the best spot in Brisbane for rock acts on the rise.

Coolangatta Hotel (p331) Beach-side beer barn on the Gold Coast with live bands, DJs and surfers aplenty.

Family Fun

Gold Coast Theme Parks (p323) Water parks, aquatic shows and plenty of heart-starting roller coasters.

Phillip Island (p259) The world-famous Penguin Parade, with large seal colonies not far away.

Australia Zoo (p344) Spend a full day at massive Australia Zoo, Queensland's wildlife temple.

Daydream Island Resort (p413) Unlike many Whitsun-days resorts, this one welcomes kids with open arms.

Sea Life Sydney Aquarium (p61) Underwater wonders at Sydney's Darling Harbour.

Scenic Journeys

Sail the Whitsundays (p406) Set sail into this magical Queensland archipelago.

Great Ocean Road (p243) A sinewy 243km strip of tarmac between ocean and cliffs: one of the world's classic road trips.

Cairns to Kuranda (p460) Sail above the rainforest on a

IF YOU LIKE...WINE REGIONS

Take a day out of your schedule to explore the wine regions around Melbourne – the **Yarra Valley** (p500), **Mornington Peninsula** (p242) and **Bellarine Peninsula** (p239) – or the **Hunter Valley** (p116), a day trip from Sydney.

cable car to Kuranda, then take the scenic old-fashioned railway back.

Waterfall Way (p140) Wiggle your way through Bellingen steeply up to Dorrigo on this eye-popping NSW drive.

East Gippsland Rail Trail (p276) Hop on a bike or hike this scenic 97km former railway line in Victoria.

Art Galleries

Gallery of Modern Art (p283) A challenging, thought-provoking, kid-centric and downright weird modern-art gallery in Brisbane.

National Gallery of Australia (p173) Australia's premier collection of fine art, including fabulous Indigenous works.

National Gallery of Victoria International (p209) Home to travelling exhibitions par excellence: queue up with the rest of Melbourne.

Art Gallery of NSW (p55) This old stager keeps things hip with ever-changing exhibitions and excellent kids' programs.

Ian Potter Centre: NGV Australia (p206) The Australian-art branch of Melbourne's NGV, with a superb Indigenous collection.

(Above) Skyrail Rainforest Cableway (p460), Kuranda

(Below) Penguins, Phillip Island (p258)

Month by Month

January

January yawns into action as Australia recovers from its Christmas hangover, but then everyone realises: 'Hey, it's summer!'. Heat and humidity along the coast; monsoonal rains up north.

☆ Big Day Out

(www.bigdayout.com) This touring one-day rock festival visits Sydney, Melbourne and the Gold Coast. It features a huge line-up of big-name international artists (think Metallica, Pearl Jam, Arcade Fire) and plenty of home-grown talent. Much moshing, sun and beer.

⭐ Australia Day

(www.australia-day.com) Australia's 'birthday' (when the First Fleet landed in 1788) is 26 January: Australians celebrate with picnics, barbecues, fireworks and, increasingly, nationalistic chest-beating. In less mood to celebrate are Indigenous Australians, who refer to it as 'Invasion Day'.

⭐ Sydney Festival

(www.sydneyfestival.org.au) 'It's big' says the promo material. Indeed, sprawling over three summer weeks, this fab affiliation of music, dance, talks, theatre and visual arts – much of it free and family-focussed – is an artistic behemoth.

⭐ Midsumma

(www.midsumma.org.au) Melbourne's gay, lesbian and transgender festival starts in mid-January with the music- and dance-fuelled outdoor Midsumma Carnival, followed by three weeks of events, including theatre, exhibitions, cabaret, film, live music and socio-political debates.

☆ Australian Open Tennis

(www.australianopen.com) Held at Melbourne Park in late January, the Australian Open draws tennis fanatics from around the planet as the world's best duke it out on the courts.

February

February is usually Australia's warmest month: hot and sticky up north as the wet season continues, but divine in Victoria. Everywhere else, locals go back to work, to the beach or to the cricket.

⭐ Sydney Gay & Lesbian Mardi Gras

(www.mardigras.org.au) A month-long arts festival running deep into March, culminating in a flamboyant parade along Sydney's Oxford St that attracts 300,000 spectators. Gyms empty out, solariums darken, waxing emporiums tally their profits. After-party tickets are gold.

March

Heat and humidity ease down south – crowds dissipate and resort prices drop. Meanwhile, high temps and general irritability prevail in the north. Harvest time in the vineyards.

☆ Australian Formula One Grand Prix

(www.grandprix.com.au) Melbourne's normally tranquil Albert Park explodes with four days of rev-head action in late March. The 5.3km street circuit around the lake is known for its smooth, fast surface.

April

Autumn brings golden colours to Victoria and cooler, mild temperatures to NSW. Up north it's the end of the wet season: smiling faces and warm, pleasant weather. Pricey Easter accommodation.

☆ Byron Bay Bluesfest

(www.bluesfest.com.au) Music erupts over the Easter weekend when 20,000 festival goers swamp Byron Bay to hear blues-and-roots bands from all over the world (Ben Harper, Santana, Bonnie Raitt). Held on Tyagarah Tea Tree Farm, 11km north of Byron. Some folks camp.

May

Days grow noticeably cooler down south; beach days are unlikely anywhere south of the Gold Coast. You can find good deals on accommodation all around.

🎭 Noosa Food & Wine Festival

(www.noosafoodandwine. com.au) One of Australia's best regional culinary fests, with cooking demonstrations, wine tasting, cheese exhibits, feasting on gourmet fare and live concerts at night. Over three days in mid-May.

🎭 Sydney Writers' Festival

(www.swf.org.au) Books, words, and books full of words: for one week in May, Sydney hosts 300-plus novelists, essayists, poets, historians and philosophers – from Australia and beyond – who read their work, run workshops and host edifying panel discussions.

🎭 Biennale of Sydney

(www.biennaleofsydney. com.au) Held in evennumbered years between May and August, Sydney's Biennale showcases the work of hundreds of contemporary artists and is the country's largest visual arts event. Expect tours, talks, screenings and cutting-edge exhibitions; most events are free.

June

The south shivers into winter, while tourist season kicks into high gear in the warm, clear tropical north, with stinger-free beaches. Migrating whales cavort off the coast (until November).

🎭 Laura Aboriginal Dance Festival

(www.lauradancefestival. com) Sleepy Laura, 330km north of Cairns in Far North Queensland, hosts the largest traditional Indigenous gathering in Australia. Communities come together for dance, song and ceremony. The Laura Races and Rodeo happen the following weekend.

July

Pubs with open fires, cosy coffee shops and empty beaches down south; packed markets, tours and accommodation up north. Bring warm clothes for anywhere south of Brisbane. Don't miss 'MIFF'.

☆ Melbourne International Film Festival

(MIFF; www.miff.com.au) Right up there with Toronto and Cannes, MIFF has been running since 1952 and has grown into a wildly popular event; tickets sell like piping-hot chestnuts. Myriad short films, feature-length spectaculars and documentaries flicker across inner-city screens.

August

August is when southerners, sick of winter's grey-sky drear, head to Queensland for some sun. A good time to explore Far North Queensland before things start to heat up again.

🎭 Cairns Festival

(www.cairns.qld.gov.au/ festival) Running for three weeks from late August into September, this massive art-and-culture fest brings a stellar program of music, theatre, dance, comedy, film, Indigenous art and public exhibitions to Cairns. Lots of outdoor events.

✬✬ Hervey Bay Whale Festival

(www.herveybaywhalefestival.com.au) One of the world's best whale-watching towns pays homage to its favourite cetacean in this popular early-August event. Attractions include an illuminated evening street parade, a kids' festival and free seafront concerts.

September

Winter ends and spring returns, bringing wildflowers and brighter spirits in the south. Weather generally remains mild across the country. Football finishes and the spring horse-racing carnival begins.

✬✬ Brisbane Festival

(www.brisbanefestival.com.au) One of Australia's largest, most diverse arts festivals runs for 22 days in September. An impressive schedule includes concerts, plays, dance and fringe events. It finishes off with 'Riverfire', an elaborate fireworks show over the Brisbane River.

☆ Australian Rules Football Grand Final

(www.afl.com.au) The pinnacle of the Aussie Rules football season is this high-flying spectacle in Melbourne, watched (on TV) by millions. At half-time everyone's neighbourhood BBQ moves into the local park for a little amateur kick-to-kick.

October

The weather avoids extremes everywhere: a good time to go camping or hit some vineyards. After the football and before the cricket, sports fans twiddle their thumbs.

✬✬ Melbourne Festival

(www.melbournefestival.com.au) This annual arts festival offers some of the best of opera, theatre, dance and visual arts from around Australia and the world. It starts in early October and runs to early November.

🏃 Coolangatta Gold

(www.sls.com.au/coolangattagold) The epic Coolangatta Gold is a gruelling test of surf-lifesaving endurance: a 23km surf-ski paddle, 3.5km swim and various beach runs = 41.5km of arduousness. The event is open to the public, so anyone can enter (see the very B-grade 1984 movie of the same name for inspiration).

November

Northern beaches may close due to 'stingers' – jellyfish in the shallows north of Agnes Water. The surf-lifesaving season flexes its muscles on beaches everywhere.

☆ Melbourne Cup

(www.melbournecup.com) On the first Tuesday in November, Australia's (if not the world's) premier horse race chews up the Melbourne turf. The whole country does actually pause to watch the 'race that stops a nation'.

December

Ring the bell, school's out! Holidays begin a week or two before Christmas. Cities are packed with shoppers and the weather is hot. Up north, monsoon season is underway: afternoon thunderstorms bring pelting rain.

☆ Tropfest

(www.tropfest.com.au) The world's largest short-film festival happens in Sydney's grassy Centennial Park in early December, with live satellite links to outdoor locations in Melbourne, Canberra and Surfers Paradise. To inspire creativity, a compulsory prop must appear in each entry (eg kiss, sneeze, balloon).

☆ Sydney to Hobart Yacht Race

(www.rolexsydneyhobart.com) Pack a picnic and join the Boxing Day (26 December) crowds along Sydney's waterfront to watch the start of the world's most arduous open-ocean yacht race (628 nautical miles to Hobart in Tasmania!).

☆ Sydney Harbour Fireworks

(www.sydneynewyearseve.com) A fantastic way to ring in the New Year: join the crowds overlooking the harbour as fireworks light up the night sky. There's a family display at 9pm; the main event erupts at midnight.

Itineraries

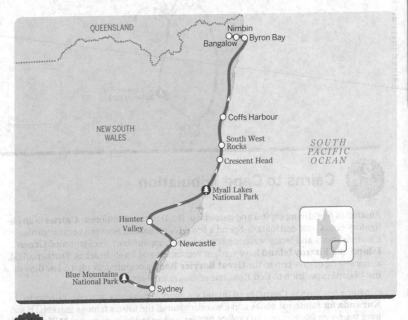

1 WEEK — Sydney to Byron Bay

Kick start your East Coast tour in **Sydney**, checking out the big-ticket sights, seeing Bondi Beach, bar hopping, shopping and shuffling between restaurants. Don't miss a seaside stroll along the Bondi to Coogee Clifftop Walk. Dart inland to explore the **Blue Mountains**: misty Katoomba has a cache of art-deco architecture, and the Three Sisters is the range's quintessential lookout. Alternatively, a couple of days shunting around the bends of the **Hawkesbury River** on a houseboat is a sure-fire stress remedy.

Next stop is the arts- and surf-loving city of **Newcastle**. Thirsty? Detour inland to the hedonistic vineyards of **Hunter Valley** (super semillon). Back on the coast, explore the eye-popping scenery and pristine beaches of **Myall Lakes National Park**.

Northern New South Wales basks in subtropical glory. Surf the excellent breaks at **Crescent Head** and swim in the sea at photogenic **South West Rocks**. At **Coffs Harbour**, the Big Banana awaits: one of the many 'big' landmarks the East Coast proffers for your kitsch confusion. **Byron Bay** is inescapable – a chilled-out beach town where surfers, hipsters and hippies share the sands. Meditating in Byron's verdant hinterland is the alt-stoner haven of **Nimbin** and affluent, laid-back **Bangalow** – both worthy day trips.

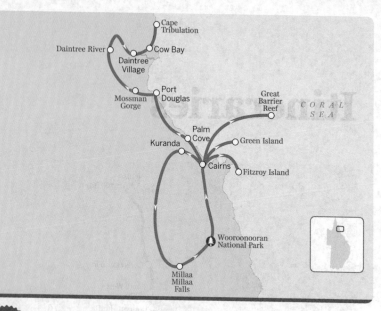

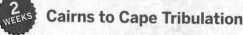

2 WEEKS Cairns to Cape Tribulation

Australia's reef-diving capital and gateway to the Daintree Rainforest, **Cairns** is an obligatory East Coast destination. Spend a few days pinballing between botanic gardens, hip restaurants and buzzy watering holes. A short hop offshore, reef-trimmed **Green Island** and **Fitzroy Island** have verdant vegetation and lovely beaches. Further afield, a snorkelling or dive trip to the **Great Barrier Reef** is essential, or plan a few days on a live-aboard expedition to Cod Hole, one of Australia's best dive spots.

After a few days in Cairns, head inland via gondola cableway or scenic railway to **Kuranda** for rainforest walks and a wander around the town's famous markets. If you have your own wheels you can explore further: swing by the picturesque **Millaa Millaa Falls** and take a rainforest hike in spectacular **Wooroonooran National Park**.

Back down at sea level, treat yourself to a night in a plush resort at **Palm Cove**, just north of Cairns. An hour further north is **Port Douglas**, an uptempo holiday hub with fab eateries, bars and a beaut beach. It's also a popular base for boat trips to the outer reef. Next stop is **Mossman Gorge**, where lush lowland rainforest surrounds the photogenic Mossman River. Take a guided walk and cool off in a waterhole.

Further north is the **Daintree River** where you can go on a crocodile-spotting cruise, then stop for lunch at **Daintree Village**. Afterwards, continue back to the river, where you'll cross by vehicle ferry to the northern side. From here continue driving north (easy does it – this is cassowary country!) to the Daintree Discovery Centre – a great place to learn about this magnificent jungle wilderness. The beach at nearby **Cow Bay** is perfect for a few hours of beachcombing.

Last stop is **Cape Tribulation**, a magnificent natural partnership between rainforest and reef. Spend a few nights taking in the splendour at one of the upmarket lodges tucked into the rainforest.

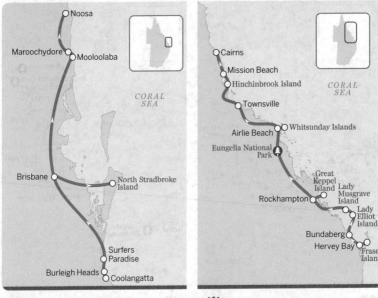

3 DAYS Brisbane, the Gold Coast & Sunshine Coast

A day in Queensland's river-city capital of **Brisbane** will deliver a lot of surprises. Infused with self confidence, this semi-tropical boomtown is dappled with brilliant bars, cafes and bookshops (the pillars of civilised society). Don't miss the arty GOMA and Brisbane Powerhouse on the riverbanks.

Just an hour to the south, the **Gold Coast** exhibits the flip-side of Queensland's soul: beachy, brassy and boozy. The hub of the action here is **Surfers Paradise**, with its palpable after-dark sexiness. More relaxed and surf-centric are **Burleigh Heads** just to the south, and **Coolangatta** on the NSW border.

If time is your amigo, tack on a few days roaming the beaches on **North Stradbroke Island** in Moreton Bay. Otherwise, truck north to the unpretentious Sunshine Coast towns of **Mooloolaba** and **Maroochydore**. Another half-hour north is **Noosa**, a classy resort town with sublime beaches, a lush national park and top-flight restaurants.

1 WEEK Hervey Bay to Cairns

About 2½ hours north of Noosa is amiable **Hervey Bay**, famed for whale watching. Eyeball some massive mammals, then explore the huge dunes and crystalline lakes on **Fraser Island**. Not far north, sip Australia's favourite rum in **Bundaberg**.

Get a taste of Queensland's coral wonders at **Lady Musgrave Island** or **Lady Elliot Island**, then don a big hat and devour a steak at 'beef city' **Rockhampton**. Offshore, if you have time to unwind for a few days, the trails and beaches on **Great Keppel Island** are pure tropical-beach bliss.

Spot a platypus in peaceful **Eungella National Park**, then wheel into busy **Airlie Beach**, gateway to the azure waters and white-sand beaches of the **Whitsunday Islands**: sail, dive, snorkel, unwind at a resort or camp on an uninhabited atoll.

Vibrant **Townsville** is next with a surprising eating and drinking scene. If you have time, don't miss hiking the Thorsborne Trail on **Hinchinbrook Island**. Recover at **Mission Beach**, where the rainforest meets the sea. End your epic road trip in **Cairns**: shout yourself a trip to the Great Barrier Reef and a seafood feast.

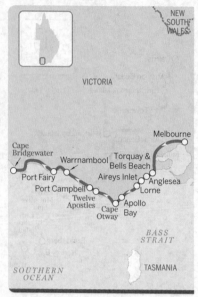

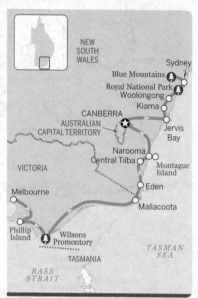

⭐3 DAYS Melbourne & the Great Ocean Road

Melbourne has enough to keep visitors engaged for months – bars, galleries, live music, shopping, Australian Rules football... But the Great Ocean Road beckons: a classic Aussie road trip.

Start in the surfing mecca of **Torquay** and check the swell at **Bells Beach**, then head to family-focussed **Anglesea** for a surf lesson and a riverside picnic. **Aireys Inlet** is next: tour the lighthouse, then spend the night in the surprisingly cosmopolitan resort town of **Lorne**.

West of here, the Great Ocean Road gets wiggly and seriously scenic, winding between the sea and the rainforest-clad Otway Ranges. Unwind in the artsy village of **Apollo Bay**, then swing by **Cape Otway** to see some koalas and the lighthouse.

Next up is Port Campbell National Park and its famed **Twelve Apostles**; count them from the clifftops, then spend a night in **Port Campbell** to get a real feel for the area. Scan for whales off the **Warrnambool** coast, then continue west to quaint, rather Irish-feeling **Port Fairy**. If there's time, tiny **Cape Bridgewater** is worth a visit.

⭐10 DAYS Melbourne to Sydney

Kick off in big-smoke **Melbourne** – all coffee-scented laneways and street art – before exploring **Phillip Island**, where penguins, seals and surfers frolic in the brine. Next stop is **Wilsons Promontory** with its fab bushwalks and beaches. Truck northeast through the forests, farms and the Gippsland Lakes district to **Mallacoota**, a low-key Victorian seaside town.

Entering south-coast NSW, **Eden** is famed for whale watching, and don't miss historic **Central Tilba**. Continue to **Narooma**, with its solid surf. From here, catch a ferry to **Montague Island**, an important Aboriginal site and nature reserve. Tracking north, detour inland to Australian capital **Canberra** to see Parliament House and Australia's best museums.

Back on the coast, **Jervis Bay** offers beaches, dolphins and national parks. Heading north, zip through pretty **Kiama**, then **Woolongong** to the Grand Pacific Drive. Just south of Sydney are the cliffs of the **Royal National Park**.

Welcome to **Sydney**: tour the Sydney Opera House, catch a harbour ferry and swim at Bondi Beach. Leave time for the awe-inspiring scenery of the **Blue Mountains**.

Plan Your Trip

Your Reef Trip

The Great Barrier Reef, stretching over 2000km from just south of the Tropic of Capricorn (near Gladstone) to just south of Papua New Guinea, is the most extensive reef system in the world, and made entirely by living organisms. There are numerous ways to see the magnificent spectacle of the Reef. Diving and snorkelling are the best methods of getting up close and personal with the menagerie of marine life and dazzling corals. You can also surround yourself with fabulous tropical fish without getting wet on a semi-submersible or glass-bottomed boat, which provide windows to the underwater world below.

When to Go

High season is from June to December. The best overall visibility is from August to January.

From December to March northern Queensland (north of Townsville) has the wet season, bringing oppressive heat and abundant rainfall; from July to September it's drier and cooler.

Anytime is generally good to visit the Whitsundays. Winter (June to August) can be pleasantly warm, but you will occasionally need a jumper. South of the Whitsundays, summer (December to March) is hot and humid.

Southern and central Queensland experience mild winters – pleasant enough for diving or snorkelling in a wetsuit.

Picking Your Spot

There are many popular and remarkable spots from which to access the Reef but bear in mind that individual areas change over time, depending on the weather or any recent damage.

Best Wildlife Experiences

Sea turtles hatching on Lady Elliot Island or Heron Island; looking out for reef sharks, turtles and rays while kayaking off Green Island; spotting koalas on Magnetic Island; and Fraser Island wildlife.

Best Snorkelling Experiences

Head to Knuckle, Hardy and Fitzroy Reefs, Magnetic Island or the Whitsunday Islands.

Best Views from Above

Scenic chopper or plane ride from Cairns, Hamilton and the Whitsunday Islands. Skydiving over Airlie Beach.

Best Sailing Experiences

Sailing from Airlie Beach through the Whitsunday Islands; exploring Agincourt Reef from Port Douglas.

Useful Websites

Dive Queensland (www.divequeensland.com.au)

Great Barrier Reef Marine Park Authority (www.gbrmpa.gov.au)

Queensland Department of National Parks (www.nprsr.qld.gov.au)

Mainland Gateways

There are several mainland gateways to the Reef, all offering slightly different experiences or activities. Here's a brief overview, ordered from south to north.

Agnes Water & Town of 1770 are small towns and good choices if you want to escape the crowds. Tours head to Fitzroy Reef Lagoon, one of the most pristine sections of the Reef, where visitor numbers are still limited. The lagoon is excellent for snorkelling but also spectacular viewed from the boat.

Gladstone is a slightly bigger town but still a relatively small gateway. It's an exceptional choice for avid divers and snorkellers, being the closest access point to the southern or Capricorn reef islands and innumerable cays, including Lady Elliot Island.

Airlie Beach is a small town with a full rack of sailing outfits. The big attraction here is spending two or more days aboard a boat and seeing some of the Whitsunday Islands' fringing coral reefs. Whether you're a five- or no-star traveller, there'll be a tour to match your budget.

Townsville is a renowned gateway among divers. A four- or five-night live-aboard around the numerous islands and pockets of the Reef is a great choice. In particular, Kelso Reef and the wreck of the SS *Yongala* are teeming with marine life. There are also a couple of day-trip options on glass-bottomed boats. **Reef HQ**, which is basically a version of the Reef in an aquarium, is also here.

Mission Beach is closer to the Reef than any other gateway destination. This small, quiet town offers a few boat and diving tours to sections of the outer reef. Although the choice isn't huge, neither are the crowds.

Cairns is the main launching pad for Reef tours with a bewildering number of operators offering relatively inexpensive day trips on large boats to intimate five-day luxury charters. The variety covers a wide section of the Reef, with some operators going as far north as Lizard Island. Inexpensive tours are likely to travel to inner, less pristine reefs. Scenic flights also operate out of Cairns.

Port Douglas is a swanky resort town and a gateway to the Low Isles and Agincourt Reef, an outer ribbon reef featuring crystal-clear water and stunning corals. Diving, snorkelling and cruising trips tend to be classier, pricier and less crowded than in Cairns. You can also take a scenic flight from here.

Cooktown is close to Lizard Island but the town and its tour operators shut down between November and May for the wet season.

Islands

Speckled throughout the Reef are a profusion of islands and cays that offer some of the most stunning access to the Reef. Here is a list of some of the best islands, travelling from south to north.

For more information on individual islands, take a look at areas around the Whitsunday Coast, Capricorn Coast, Townsville to Mission Beach, Cairns and Port Douglas to Cooktown.

Lady Elliot Island has a coral cay that is awe-inspiring for birdwatchers, with some 57 species living on the island. Sea turtles also nest here and it's possibly the best location on the Reef to see manta rays. It's also a famed diving spot. There's a resort here, but you can also visit Lady Elliot on a day trip from Bundaberg.

Heron Island is a tiny, tranquil coral cay sitting amid a huge spread of reef. It's a diving mecca, but the snorkelling is also good and it's possible to do a reef walk from here. Heron is a nesting ground for green and loggerhead turtles and home to some 30 species of birds. The sole resort on the island charges accordingly.

Hamilton Island, the daddy of the Whitsundays, is a sprawling family-friendly resort laden with infrastructure. While the atmosphere isn't exactly intimate, there is a wealth of tours going to the outer reef. It's also a good place to see patches of the Reef that can't be explored from the mainland.

Hook Island is an outer Whitsunday island surrounded by reefs. There is excellent swimming and snorkelling here, and the island offers good bushwalking. There's affordable accommodation on Hook and it's easily accessed from Airlie Beach, making it a top choice for those on a budget.

Orpheus Island is a national park and one of the Reef's most exclusive, tranquil and romantic hideaways. This island is great for snorkelling – you can step right off the beach and be surrounded by the Reef's colourful marine life. Clusters of fringing reefs also provide plenty of diving opportunities.

Green Island is another of the Reef's true coral cays. The fringing reefs here are considered to be among the most beautiful surrounding any island, and the diving and snorkelling are quite spectacular. Covered in dense rainforest, the entire island is a national park. Bird life is abundant.

Reef Highlights

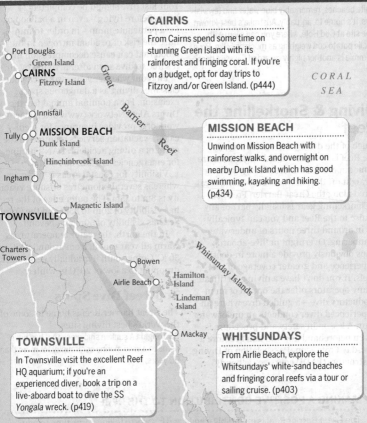

0 ——— 200 km
0 ——— 120 miles

CORAL SEA

CAIRNS

From Cairns spend some time on stunning Green Island with its rainforest and fringing coral. If you're on a budget, opt for day trips to Fitzroy and/or Green Island. (p444)

MISSION BEACH

Unwind on Mission Beach with rainforest walks, and overnight on nearby Dunk Island which has good swimming, kayaking and hiking. (p434)

TOWNSVILLE

In Townsville visit the excellent Reef HQ aquarium; if you're an experienced diver, book a trip on a live-aboard boat to dive the SS *Yongala* wreck. (p419)

WHITSUNDAYS

From Airlie Beach, explore the Whitsundays' white-sand beaches and fringing coral reefs via a tour or sailing cruise. (p403)

TOWN OF 1770

Head to the Town of 1770 and day trip out to Lady Musgrave Island for semi-submersible coral-viewing, plus snorkelling or diving in a pristine blue lagoon. (p379)

Port Douglas
Green Island
CAIRNS
Fitzroy Island
Innisfail
Tully
MISSION BEACH
Dunk Island
Hinchinbrook Island
Ingham
Magnetic Island
TOWNSVILLE
Charters Towers
Bowen
Airlie Beach
Hamilton Island
Lindeman Island
Mackay
Tropic of Capricorn
Emerald
Rockhampton
Great Keppel Island
Gladstone
TOWN OF 1770
Bundaberg
Hervey Bay
Maryborough
Fraser Island
Miles
Noosa

Great Barrier Reef
Whitsunday Islands

Lizard Island is remote, rugged and the perfect place to escape civilisation. It has a ring of talcum-white beaches, remarkably blue water and few visitors. It's home to, arguably, Australia's best-known dive site at Cod Hole, where you can swim with docile potato cod weighing as much as 60kg. Pixie Bommie is another highly regarded dive site here.

Diving & Snorkelling the Reef

Much of the diving and snorkelling on the Reef is boat-based, although there are some superb reefs accessible by walking straight off the beach of some islands scattered along the Great Barrier. Free use of snorkelling gear is usually part of any cruise to the Reef and you can typically fit in around three hours of underwater wandering. Overnight or 'live-aboard' trips obviously provide a more in-depth experience and greater coverage of the reefs. If you don't have a diving certificate, many operators offer the option of an introductory dive – a guided dive where an experienced diver conducts an underwater tour. A lesson in safety and procedure is given beforehand and you don't require a five-day Professional Association of Diving Instructors (PADI) course or a 'buddy'.

Key Diving Details

Your last dive should be completed 24 hours before flying – even in a balloon or for a parachute jump – in order to minimise the risk of residual nitrogen in the blood that can cause decompression injury. It's fine to dive soon after arriving by air.

Find out whether your insurance policy classifies diving as a dangerous sport exclusion. For a nominal annual fee, the Divers Alert Network (www.diversalertnetwork.org) provides insurance for medical or evacuation services required in the event of a diving accident. DAN's hotline for emergencies is ☏919 684 9111.

Visibility for coastal areas is 1m to 3m whereas several kilometres offshore visibility is 8m to 15m. The outer edge of the reef has visibility of 20m to 35m and the Coral Sea has visibility of 50m and beyond.

In the north, the water temperature is warm all year round, from around 24°C to 30°C. Going south it gradually gets cooler, dropping to a low of 20°C in winter.

Top Reef Dive Spots

The Great Barrier Reef is home to some of the world's best diving sites.

SS Yongala A sunken shipwreck that has been home to a vivid marine community for more than 90 years.

MAKING A POSITIVE CONTRIBUTION TO THE REEF

The Great Barrier Reef is incredibly fragile and it's worth taking some time to educate yourself on responsible practices while you're there.

➡ No matter where you visit, take all litter with you – even biodegradable material like apple cores – and dispose of it back on the mainland.

➡ It is an offence to damage or remove coral in the marine park.

➡ If you touch or walk on coral you'll damage it and get some nasty cuts.

➡ Don't touch or harass marine animals.

➡ If you have a boat, be aware of the rules in relation to anchoring around the reef, including 'no anchoring areas' to avoid coral damage.

➡ If you're diving, check that you are weighted correctly before entering the water and keep your buoyancy control well away from the reef. Ensure that equipment such as secondary regulators and gauges aren't dragging over the reef.

➡ If you're snorkelling (and especially if you are a beginner) practice your technique away from coral until you've mastered control in the water.

➡ Hire a wetsuit rather than slathering on sunscreen, which can damage the reef.

➡ Watch where your fins are – try not to stir up sediment or disturb coral.

➡ Do not enter the water near a dugong, including when swimming or diving.

➡ Note that there are limits on the amount and types of shells that you can collect.

TOP SNORKELLING SITES

Some nondivers may wonder if it's really worth going to the Great Barrier Reef 'just to snorkel'. The answer is a resounding yes. Much of the rich, colourful coral lies just underneath the surface (as coral needs bright sunlight to flourish) and is easily accessible. Here's a round-up of the top snorkelling sites:

➡ Fitzroy Reef Lagoon (Town of 1770)

➡ Heron Island (Capricorn Coast)

➡ Great Keppel Island

➡ Lady Elliot Island (Capricorn Coast)

➡ Lady Musgrave Island (Capricorn Coast)

➡ Hook Island (Whitsundays)

➡ Hayman Island (Whitsundays)

➡ Lizard Island (Cairns)

➡ Border Island (Whitsundays)

➡ Hardy Reef (Whitsundays)

➡ Knuckle Reef (Whitsundays)

➡ Michaelmas Reef (Cairns)

➡ Hastings Reef (Cairns)

➡ Norman Reef (Cairns)

➡ Saxon Reef (Cairns)

➡ Green Island (Cairns)

➡ Opal Reef (Port Douglas)

➡ Agincourt Reef (Port Douglas)

➡ Mackay Reef (Port Douglas)

Cod Hole Go nose-to-nose with a potato cod.

Heron Island Join a crowd of colourful fish straight off the beach.

Lady Elliot Island 19 highly regarded dive sites.

Pixie Bommie, Delve into the after-five world of the Reef by taking a night dive.

Boat Excursions

Unless you're staying on a coral-fringed island in the middle of the Great Barrier Reef, you'll need to join a boat excursion to experience the Reef's real beauty. Day trips leave from many places along the coast, as well as from island resorts, and typically include the use of snorkelling gear, snacks and a buffet lunch, with scuba diving an optional extra. On some boats a marine biologist presents a talk on the Reef's ecology.

Boat trips vary dramatically in passenger numbers, type of vessel and quality – which is reflected in the price – so it's worth getting all the details before committing. When selecting a tour, consider the vessel (motorised catamaran or sailing ship), the number of passengers (from six to 400), what extras are offered and the destination. The outer reefs are usually more pristine. Inner reefs often show signs of damage from humans, coral bleaching and coral-eating crown-of-thorns starfish. Some operators offer the option of a trip in a glass-bottomed boat or semi-submersible.

Many boats have underwater cameras for hire – although you'll save money by hiring these on land (or using your own waterproof camera or underwater housing). Some boats also have professional photographers on board who will dive with you and take high-quality shots of you in action.

Live-Aboards

If you're eager to do as much diving as possible, a live-aboard is a good option as you'll do three dives per day, plus some night dives, all in more remote parts of the Great Barrier Reef. Trip lengths vary from one to 12 nights. The three-day/three-night voyages, which allow up to 11 dives, are among the most common.

Check out the various options as some boats offer specialist itineraries following marine life, such as minke whales or coral spawning, or offer trips to remote spots like the far northern reefs, Pompey Complex, Coral Sea Reefs or Swain Reefs.

It's recommended to go with operators who are Dive Queensland members: this ensures they follow a minimum set of guidelines. Ideally, they are also accredited by **Ecotourism Australia** (www.ecotourism. org.au).

Popular departure points for live-aboard dive vessels, along with the locales they visit are:

Bundaberg The Bunker Island group, including Lady Musgrave and Lady Elliot Islands, possibly Fitzroy, Llewellyn and rarely visited Boult Reefs or Hoskyn and Fairfax Islands.

1770 Bunker Island group.

Gladstone Swain and Bunker Island groups.

Mackay Lihou Reef and the Coral Sea.

Airlie Beach The Whitsundays, Knuckle Reef and Hardy Reef.

Townsville *Yongala* wreck, plus canyons of Wheeler Reef and Keeper Reef.

Cairns Cod Hole, Ribbon Reefs, the Coral Sea and the far northern reefs.

Port Douglas Osprey Reef, Cod Hole, Ribbon Reefs, Coral Sea and the far northern reefs.

Dive Courses

In Queensland there are numerous places where you can learn to dive, take a refresher course or improve your skills. Dive courses are generally of a high standard, and all schools teach either PADI or Scuba Schools International (SSI) qualifications. Which certification you choose isn't as important as choosing a good instructor, so be sure to seek local recommendations and meet with the instructor before committing to a program.

A popular place to learn is Cairns, where you can choose between courses for the budget-minded (four-day courses from around $490) that combine pool training and reef dives, to more intensive courses that include reef diving on a live-aboard (five-day courses including three-day/two-night live-aboard start from $700).

Other places where you can learn to dive, and then head out on the Reef include Airlie Beach, Bundaberg, Hamilton Island, Magnetic Island, Mission Beach, Port Douglas and Townsville.

Camping on the Great Barrier Reef

Pitching a tent on an island is a unique and affordable way to experience the Great Barrier Reef. Campers enjoy an idyllic tropical setting at a fraction of the price of the five-star island resort that may be located down the road from the camp ground. Camp site facilities range from virtually nothing to showers, flush toilets, interpretive signage and picnic tables. Most islands are remote, so ensure you are adequately prepared for medical and general emergencies.

Wherever you stay, you'll need to be self-sufficient, bringing your own food and water (5L per day per person). Weather can often prevent planned pick ups, so have enough supplies to last an extra four days in case you get stranded.

Camp only in designated areas, keep to marked trails and take out all that you brought in. Fires are banned so you'll need a gas stove or similar.

National park camping permits need to be booked in advance online through Queensland Department of National Parks (www.nprsr.qld.gov.au). Our top picks:

Whitsunday Islands Nearly a dozen beautifully sited camping areas, scattered on the islands of Hook, Whitsunday and Henning.

Capricornia Cays Camping available on three separate coral cays including Masthead Island, North West Island and Lady Musgrave Island – a fantastic, uninhabited island that's limited to a maximum of 40 campers.

Dunk Island Equal parts resort and national park with good swimming, kayaking and hiking.

Fitzroy Island Resort and national park with short walking trails through bush and coral just off the beaches.

Frankland Islands Coral-fringed island with white-sand beaches off Cairns.

Lizard Island Stunning beaches, magnificent coral and abundant wildlife, but visitors mostly arrive by plane.

Orpheus Island Secluded island (accessible by air) with pretty tropical forest and superb fringing reef.

Abseiling, Glass House Mountains National Park (p343)

Plan Your Trip

East Coast Australia Outdoors

A cavalcade of ancient rainforests, islands and craggy ranges, plus the Great Barrier Reef, the East Coast is tailor made for outdoor action. Scuba diving and snorkelling are daily indulgences, while the surfing here is world-class. There is also whale watching, sailing and many other watery pursuits. On dry land you can go hiking or rock climbing. For an adrenaline rush, try abseiling or skydiving.

Top Activities

Best Hiking

Blue Mountains

Dorrigo National Park

Wilsons Promontory

Croajingolong National Park

Springbrook National Park

Best Wildlife-Watching

Penguins on Phillip Island

Whales off Hervey Bay

Cassowaries in the Daintree rainforest

Sea turtles at Mon Repos

Crocodiles in the Daintree River

On the Land

Hiking

The East Coast is laced with brilliant bushwalks (hikes) of every length, standard and difficulty. Coastal and hinterland national parks and state forests – many easily accessible from the cities – provide some of the best opportunities.

Bushwalking (hiking) happens year-round here. Summer is the most popular time in the southeast. In much of Queensland, the best time to hike is from April to September before things get too hot.

GREAT WALKS OF QUEENSLAND

The Great Walks of Queensland is a $16.5-million project to create a world-class set of walking tracks, and includes magical hikes through the Whitsundays, Sunshine Coast hinterland, Fraser Island and Gold Coast hinterland. For complete details on the 10 Great Walks, including track descriptions, maps and camp site bookings, visit www.nprsr.qld.gov.au/experiences/great-walks.

Where to Walk

Prime hiking terrain includes the Blue Mountains, Ku-ring-gai Chase National Park and Royal National Park in New South Wales; Wilsons Promontory National Park, Croajingolong National Park and along the Great Ocean Road coast in Victoria; and Hinchinbrook Island, Springbrook National Park and D'Aguilar Range National Park in Queensland. For peak baggers, Wooroonooran National Park, south of Cairns, contains Queensland's highest peak, Mt Bartle Frere (1622m).

Or, if you'd rather mix a surf and a soy latte in with your hike, within Sydney itself are the brilliant semi-urban Bondi to Coogee Coastal Walk and Manly Scenic Walkway.

Resources

Pick up Lonely Planet's *Walking in Australia,* which details 60 countrywide walks of varying lengths. The *Take a Walk* series (www.takeawalk.com.au) includes titles covering the Blue Mountains, southeast Queensland and Victoria's national parks. The *Tropical Walking Tracks* series (www.footloosebooks.com.au) covers the tropical north.

Local bushwalking information:

Bushwalking NSW (www.bushwalking.org.au)

Bushwalking Queensland (www.bushwalkingqueensland.org.au)

Bushwalking Victoria (www.bushwalkingvictoria.org.au)

Cycling & Mountain Biking

Cyclists along the East Coast have access to plenty of routes and can go touring for days or weekends, or even do multiweek trips. The landscape is (mostly) un-mountainous, and the sun is often shining. Or you can just rent a bike for a few hours in a city.

Rates charged by rental outfits for road or mountain bikes range from $10 to $15 per hour and $25 to $50 per day. Security deposits range from $50 to $200, depending on the rental period. See www.bicycles.net.au for links to state and territory cycling organisations. For more information, see Lonely Planet's *Cycling Australia.*

Wildlife Watching

Native wildlife is one of Australia's top selling points. National parks along the East Coast are the best places to meet the residents, although many species are noc-

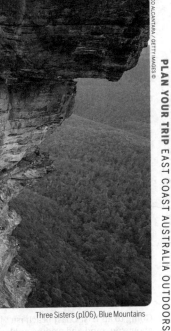

PACO ALCANTARA / GETTY IMAGES ©

Three Sisters (p106), Blue Mountains

turnal (bring a torch). Australia is also a bird-watching nirvana, with a wide variety of habitats and species, particularly water birds. Most Aussies will be utterly surprised to learn that Canberra, in the ACT, has the richest bird life of any Australian capital city.

In NSW there are 120 bird species in Dorrigo National Park, while Border Ranges National Park is home to a quarter

SAILING

After surfing, sailing is the number-one ocean activity on Australia's East Coast. It has its own affluent marina culture and its own migratory patterns: during the winter, the yachties migrate north, following the warmer weather.

Where to Set Sail

In NSW, Sydney Harbour and boats are inextricably and historically intertwined: this is one of the world's great nautical cities. The easiest way to get out there is on a ferry – hop a ride to Manly or Balmain and see the sea. There are also harbour cruises and yacht charters available. Beyond Sydney, Port Stephens, Jervis Bay and Ballina are busy sailing centres.

In Queensland, the postcard-perfect Whitsunday Islands are magical for a sail. You can join a full- or multiday cruise, or charter your own craft in Airlie Beach. You can also explore the Great Barrier Reef and some of the islands off the Far North Queensland coast on board a chartered boat or cruise from Cairns or Port Douglas.

In Victoria, city-based yachties gravitate to the sailing clubs around Port Phillip Bay. Other popular boating areas include the sprawling Gippsland Lakes and Mallacoota Inlet near the NSW border.

of all of Australia's bird species. Koalas are a dime a dozen around Port Macquarie.

In Victoria, Wilsons Promontory National Park teems with wildlife (wombats sometimes seem to outnumber people); and don't miss the penguins on Phillip Island.

In Queensland, Cape Tribulation is the place for birds; Magnetic Island for koalas; Fraser Island for dingoes; Hervey Bay for whales; Mon Repos near Bundaberg for sea turtles; and the Daintree rainforest for crocodiles and cassowaries.

Abseiling, Canyoning & Rock Climbing

NSW's Blue Mountains, especially around Katoomba, are fantastic for rock climbing, abseiling (rappelling) and canyoning, with numerous professional outfits able to set you up with equipment, training and climbing trips. In Victoria, Wilsons Promontory is another prime rock-climbing locale.

On the Water

Going to an East Coast beach isn't just about sun, sand and wading ankle deep in the water: there are plenty of more active pursuits. We've detailed the key ones following, but you can also try **jet skiing** in Cairns, Southport on the Gold Coast (Queensland) and in Batemans Bay (NSW), and **parasailing** on Sydney Harbour, Victoria's Mornington Peninsula, and in Queensland at Cairns, Rainbow Beach and the Gold Coast beaches. Try **stand-up paddleboarding** in NSW at Manly and Cronulla in Sydney, Jervis Bay and Newcastle; in Queensland at Noosa and on the Gold Coast; and in Victoria on the

---

AQUATIC HIGHLIGHTS
....
➡ Diving and snorkelling on the Great Barrier Reef

➡ Surfing at Bondi Beach, Byron Bay or Noosa

➡ Sailing the Whitsundays

➡ Kayaking at North Stradbroke Island

➡ Catching a ferry on Sydney Harbour

Mornington Peninsula and at Melbourne's St Kilda.

Surfing

The southern half of the East Coast is jam-packed with sandy surf beaches and point breaks. North of Agnes Water in Queensland, the Great Barrier Reef shields the coast from the ocean swells. If you're keen to learn, you'll find plenty of good waves, board hire and lessons available – notably in Sydney and Byron Bay in New South Wales, the Gold Coast in Queensland, and along the Great Ocean Road in Victoria.

Where to Surf

The East Coast is one long *Endless Summer,* with myriad surf breaks peeling into the shore. Our picks:

New South Wales
➡ Bondi Beach
➡ Byron Bay
➡ Crescent Head

Queensland
➡ The Superbank
➡ Burleigh Heads
➡ North Stradbroke Island

Victoria
➡ Bells Beach
➡ Point Leo, Flinders, Rye and Portsea
➡ Torquay and numerous spots along the Great Ocean Road

Diving & Snorkelling

Even if the Great Barrier Reef weren't just off the East Coast, the diving and snorkelling here would still be world-class. Coral reefs, rich marine life (temperate, subtropical and tropical species) and shipwrecks paint an enticing underwater picture.

Diving is possible year-round, although in Queensland avoid the wet season (December to March), when floods can impair visibility and stingers (jellyfish) are present (November to May, north of Agnes Water).

Dive Courses

Every major town along the East Coast has a dive school, but standards vary – do some research before signing up. Budget outfits tend to focus on shore dives; pricier outfits

Top: Surf lifesaver training, Cronulla (p62)

Bottom: Sailing boats, Port Phillip Bay, Melbourne (p206)

CHRISTOPHER GROENHOUT / GETTY IMAGES ©

BUNGEE JUMPING & SKYDIVING

Brave? Lose a bet? Just plain crazy? Cairns is the place to try bungee jumping, with multiperson 'jungle swings' for those not willing to go it alone. If you'd rather jump out of a plane, sign up for some skydiving at Byron Bay, Caloundra, Surfers Paradise, Brisbane, Airlie Beach, Mission Beach or Cairns. Most folks start with a 9000ft jump, with around 30 seconds of free fall – or up the ante to 14,000ft with up to a minute of pant-wetting plummeting.

sometimes run multiday live-aboard boat tours. Multiday PADI open-water courses cost anywhere from $400 to $800; one-day introductory courses start at around $200.

For certified divers, renting gear and going on a two-tank day dive costs between $150 and $200. Mask, snorkel and fin hire from a dive shop costs around $30 to $50.

Where to Get Wet

In NSW you can dive all along the coast, including Sydney, Byron Bay, Jervis Bay, Coffs Harbour and Narooma. With the Great Barrier Reef a day trip offshore, Queensland is a divers' paradise: most diving and snorkelling trips set sail from Cairns and Port Douglas. You can also organise dive trips at North Stradbroke Island, Moreton Island, Mooloolaba, Rainbow Beach and Bundaberg. In Victoria try Port Campbell on the Great Ocean Road and Bunurong Marine Park in Gippsland.

Kayaking & Canoeing

Kayaks and canoes let you paddle into otherwise inaccessible areas, poking your nose into dense mangroves and estuaries, river gorges, secluded island beaches and remote wilderness inlets. In NSW you can kayak on Sydney Harbour and at Byron Bay, Coffs Harbour, Port Stephens and Jervis Bay. In Queensland head for Mission Beach, Magnetic Island, Noosa and the Whitsundays. In Victoria you can kayak around Melbourne itself (on the Yarra River), plus there are operators running trips around Apollo Bay, Phillip Island, Wilsons Promontory and Gippsland.

White-Water Rafting

In Queensland, the mighty Tully, North Johnstone and Russell Rivers between Townsville and Cairns are renowned white-water rafting locations. The Tully is the most popular of the three, with 44 rapids graded 3 to 4. In Victoria head for the Snowy River; in NSW try the class 2 and 3 rapids on the scenic Goolang River near Coffs Harbour. Full-day rafting trips cost around $200.

Regions at a Glance

Sydney & the Central Coast

Beaches
Food
Wilderness

Sydney Surf

Sydney's surf beaches are outstanding. Bondi is the name on everyone's lips, but the waves here get crowded. Head south to Maroubra or Cronulla or north to Manly for more elbow room.

Sydney 'Mod Oz'

Modern Australian, or 'Mod Oz', is the name of the culinary game here – a pan-Pacific fusion of styles and ingredients with plenty of local seafood. Serve it up with a harbour view and you've got a winning combo.

National Parks

This region has some of the best national parks in Australia. Around Sydney there's Royal National Park, with fab walks and beaches; waterways and wildlife in Ku-ring-gai Chase National Park; and vast tracts of native forest in Wollemi National Park in the Blue Mountains.

p48

Byron Bay & Northern New South Wales

Nightlife
Surfing
Small Towns

Drinking in Byron

Byron Bay has bars and pubs for every day of the week, be it beer barns, live-music pubs or classy wine bars. Just name your poison!

North Coast Surf

The water is warm, and perfect point breaks are rolling in at legendary north-coast surf spots like the Pass in Byron Bay and Lennox Head.

Nimbin & Bangalow

A short detour into the Byron Bay hinterland are some beaut small towns: wander through the smoke haze in hippie Nimbin or have a pub lunch in classy (but unpretentious) Bangalow.

p121

Canberra & Southern New South Wales

History & Culture
Beaches
Politics

Canberra's Museums

Choose among the National Gallery, with its magnificent Indigenous art; imaginative exhibits at the National Museum; the moving War Memorial; and the impressive National Portrait Gallery.

South Coast Beaches

Southern NSW offers impressive stretches of wide white sand with reliable surf and (best of all) no one else's footprints.

Parliament House

Attend Question Time at Parliament House, or visit Old Parliament House and check out the Museum of Australian Democracy.

p171

Melbourne & Coastal Victoria

Bushwalking
Food
Beaches

Hiking Wilsons Prom

Wilsons Promontory National Park offers everything from short jaunts along the beach to multiday circuits covering the whole peninsula.

Eating in Melbourne

Melbourne is a foodie's paradise: produce markets, eat streets, arty cafes and sassy restaurants, all infused with the ebullient multiculturalism that defines this big southern city.

Great Ocean Road

The water is chilly, but this stretch of coast hosts some of the prettiest beaches in the country, from the big breaks at Bells Beach to Lorne's gentle bay and the swells around Port Campbell.

p205

Brisbane & Around

Food
Neighbourhoods
Nightlife

Cafe Culture

Brisbane is hot and humid, but that doesn't mean the locals can't enjoy a steaming cup of java. Cool cafes abound, plus a clutch of quality local bean roasters.

Brisbane's West End

Brisbane is a tight-knit web of distinct neighbourhoods: our fave is the bohemian West End, where you'll find bookshops, bars, live-music rooms and myriad cheap eats.

Brisbane's Small Bars

It's taken a while, but Brisbane has joined in on the Australia-wide boom in small speakeasies, down laneways and in compact shopfronts across town.

p280

The Gold Coast

Surfing
Nightlife
Wilderness

Surfers Paradise

They don't call it Surfers Paradise for nothing! The beach here is one of the best places in Australia to learn to surf, or head for the more challenging breaks around Burleigh Heads and Kirra.

Clubs, Pubs & Bars

All along the Gold Coast – from the throbbing clubs in Surfers Paradise to the brawling surf-side pubs in Coolangatta – you'll never be far from a cold beer.

National Parks

Ascend into the Gold Coast hinterland to discover some brilliant national parks: Springbrook, Lamington and Tamborine feature waterfallls, hikes and constant native birdsong.

p315

Noosa & the Sunshine Coast

Surfing
Food
Nature

Sunshine Coast Surf

The relaxed surfer ethos of the Sunshine Coast permeates the streets and beaches, with reliable breaks and warm waves right along the coast.

Noosa Dining Scene

You know you're *really* on holiday when you wake up and the choice of where to have breakfast, lunch and dinner is the most important item on the day's agenda. Welcome to Noosa!

Noosa National Park

Bathed by the South Pacific, with photogenic beaches reaching up to hillsides awash with dense subtropical bush, accessible Noosa National Park is perfect for bushwalking.

p334

Fraser Island & the Fraser Coast

Islands
Marine Life
Small Towns

Fraser Island

Sandy Fraser Island hosts a unique subtropical ecosystem that's pretty darn close to paradise. A day tour merely whets the appetite; camp overnight and wish upon a thousand shooting stars.

Whale Watching

Off Hervey Bay, migrating humpback whales breach, blow and tail-slap. When they roll up alongside the boat with one eye above the water, you've got to wonder who's watching who.

Rainbow Beach & Childers

One on the coast and one inland, these two little towns are absolute beauties: Rainbow Beach for its magnificent cliffs, and Childers for its country vibe and historic architecture.

p357

Capricorn Coast & the Southern Reef Islands

Diving & Snorkelling
Islands
Accessible Outback

Southern Reef

Book a snorkelling cruise out to the reef or a bunk on a live-aboard dive vessel. Or base yourself on an island for full immersion in this technicolour underwater world.

Lady Elliot Island

Tiny, coral-ringed Lady Elliot is superb for snorkelling, with reefs directly off the beach. The resort is eco-attuned, and the flight here is like a scenic tour.

Rockhampton

Just 40km from the coast, Australia's 'beef capital' gives visitors a true taste of the bush, with buckin' broncos and big hats. Further west, cattle-station stays offer full immersion into outback livin'.

p378

Whitsunday Coast

Islands
Sailing
Nightlife

The Whitsundays

With 74 tropical beauties to choose from, the Whitsunday Islands archipelago is truly remarkable. There are plenty of ways to experience the islands: bushwalking, kayaking or just lounging around on a yacht.

Island-hopping

The translucent seas around the Whitsundays would seem incomplete without the snow-white billows of sails in the picture. Climb aboard a yacht and find your perfect island.

Airlie Beach

The main jumping-off point for trips around the Whitsundays, Airlie Beach is a party town full of party people. Join the thirsty throngs in the bars after dark.

p394

Townsville to Mission Beach

Coastline
Nature
Architecture

Beaut Beaches

Between Townsville's palm-shaded Strand and Flying Fish Point near Innisfail, this stretch of coastline shelters vast, sandy expanses such as Mission Beach through to intimate coves like Etty Bay.

National Parks

Hiking, camping, swimming and picnicking opportunities abound in the region's national parks, plus flightless prehistoric-looking cassowaries roam the rainforest.

Historic Buildings

Architecture in the region includes the gold-rush era streetscapes of Charters Towers, beautiful 19th-century buildings in Townsville, and Australia's highest concentration of art deco edifices in Innisfail.

p417

Great Barrier Reef

Marine Life
Diving & Snorkelling
Islands

Coral & Fish

Believe the hype: the World Heritage–listed Great Barrier Reef is home to an absolutely mind-blowing spectrum of colourful coral and fish of all shapes, sizes and demeanours.

Reef Day Trips

Don't delay – book yourself onto a diving or snorkelling trip out to explore the reef. Cairns and Port Douglas offer multiple operators that can take you there for the day (or longer).

Castaway Cays

Play castaway for a day: studded along the 2000km spine of the reef are myriad sandy cays, islands and atolls, most with no one else on them.

p467

Cairns & the Daintree Rainforest

Nightlife
Food
Indigenous Culture

Cairns After Dark

There are so many backpackers and international tourists in Cairns that it's sometimes hard to spot a local. You can usually find one or two in the city's fun, boisterous pubs and bars.

Regional Produce

Many of the Atherton Tableland's farms, orchards and plantations can be visited on tours. Or simply taste the good stuff at regional restaurants.

Daintree Tours

Several Aboriginal-led tour companies can take you on a cultural journey through the timeless Daintree rainforest, offering an insight into its rich Indigenous heritage.

p441

On the Road

Sydney & the Central Coast

Best Places to Eat

➡ Quay (p90)
➡ Subo (p114)
➡ Mr Wong (p91)
➡ Muse Kitchen (p119)
➡ Messina (p93)

Best Places to Stay

➡ Thistle Hill (p119)
➡ Broomelea (p108)
➡ Adge Apartment Hotel (p80)
➡ Sydney Harbour YHA (p76)
➡ Blue Mountains YHA (p108)

Why Go?

Chances are Sydney will be your introduction to Australia's East Coast and there simply isn't a better one. The city's spectacular harbour setting, sun-kissed beaches and sophisticated sheen make it unique in Australia, and its outdoorsy population endows it with a confident charm that every city yearns for but few achieve.

It would be reasonable to assume that the areas surrounding Sydney would be content to bask in the reflected and undeniably golden glow of the metropolis, but that's not the case. Each has its own delights. The Blue Mountains offers magnificent bush-clad vistas and opportunities to snuggle in front of log fires; Newcastle has surf beaches in profusion; and the Hunter Valley has leafy country roads scattered with producers of fine wine, chocolate and cheese. All three are endowed with world-class restaurants that rival even those in the big smoke.

When to Go

Sydney

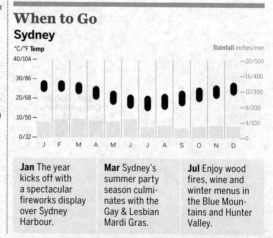

Jan The year kicks off with a spectacular fireworks display over Sydney Harbour.

Mar Sydney's summer party season culminates with the Gay & Lesbian Mardi Gras.

Jul Enjoy wood fires, wine and winter menus in the Blue Mountains and Hunter Valley.

Indigenous Culture

When the First Fleet arrived, this part of the coast was home to the Eora, Dharug, Ku-ring-gai, Gundungurra and Awabakal peoples. Each had its own language, laws and identity, and the people lived a semi-nomadic life, moving within their territories to fish, hunt and gather plants.

The land formed the basis for their spiritual life and Dreaming (belief system), which is why its appropriation by the British had such catastrophic consequences. As well as loss of land and disruption to millennia-old ways of life, the local people suffered foreign diseases, kidnappings, incarceration and wholesale massacres.

Ancient Aboriginal rock paintings or engravings can still be seen on the Manly Scenic Walkway and in the Ku-ring-gai Chase, Blue Mountains and Brisbane Waters National Parks. The Australian Museum, Art Gallery of NSW, Museum of Sydney, Rocks Discovery Museum and Kalkari Discovery Centre all have exhibits relating to Aboriginal life and culture.

EcoTreasures (p76), Blue Mountains Walkabout (p107) and Waradah Aboriginal Centre (p106) all provide a hands-on introduction to Aboriginal culture. The Royal Botanic Gardens (p54), Blue Mountains Botanic Garden (p107) and Taronga Zoo (p70) offer Aboriginal-themed tours.

EARLY COLONIAL SITES

The most recent Australian additions to the World Heritage list are 11 places that are collectively known as the Australian Convict Sites. Four of these sites are in this part of NSW: Hyde Park Barracks Museum in central Sydney; Cockatoo Island on the Parramatta River; Old Government House in Parramatta; and the Great North Rd, which connects Sydney to the Hunter Valley.

These sites are among many dating back to early colonial times which can be visited. History buffs should consider purchasing a Ticket Through Time (www.hht.net.au/visiting/ticket_through_time; adult/child $30/15), which gives access to 12 Sydney properties managed by the Historic Houses Trust, including Susannah Place, Justice & Police Museum, Government House, Hyde Park Barracks, Museum of Sydney, Elizabeth Bay House and Vaucluse House. The pass is valid for three months and available online or at most properties.

Great Surfing Spots

→ Cronulla, south of Botany Bay, Sydney

→ Dee Why, Northern Beaches, Sydney

→ Narrabeen, Northern Beaches, Sydney

→ Merewether Beach, Newcastle

→ Bar Beach, Newcastle

TOP TIP

MyMulti passes, the Family Funday Sunday pass and Pensioner Excursion passes can save you money when travelling on public transport. Off-peak daily return train tickets also offer good value.

Fast Facts

→ Telephone area code 02

→ Population 5.2 million

→ Number of patrolled surf beaches 70

Advance Planning

→ Check events calendars for regions you'll be visiting.

→ Book accommodation well in advance, particularly for the summer months.

→ It always pays to book ahead for weekend sittings at Sydney restaurants, but top places should be booked weeks in advance.

Resources

→ New South Wales (www.visitnsw.com.au)

→ NSW National Parks & Wildlife Service (NPWS; www.nationalparks.nsw.gov.au)

→ City of Sydney (www.cityofsydney.nsw.gov.au)

→ Sydney Morning Herald (www.smh.com.au)

→ Time Out Sydney (www.au.timeout.com/sydney)

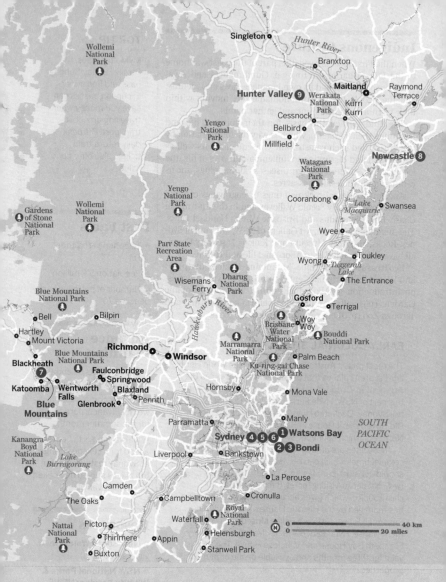

Sydney & the Central Coast Highlights

1 Hopping aboard one of Sydney's harbour ferries and heading to **Watsons Bay** (p55).

2 Whiling away the day on the golden sands of **Bondi Beach** (p64).

3 Enjoying the dramatic coastal scenery of the **Bondi to Coogee Clifftop Walk** (p74).

4 Eating and drinking your way through hip **Surry Hills** (p91).

5 Attending a performance at the **Sydney Opera House** (p97).

6 Strolling the leafy paths of the **Royal Botanic Gardens** (p54) with Sydney Harbour sparkling below.

7 Following a bush trail under dense and ancient forest canopies in the **Blue Mountains** (p104).

8 Hopping from beach to bar to restaurant in laid-back **Newcastle** (p110).

9 Broadening your palate and waistline in the **Hunter Valley** (p116).

SYDNEY

POP 4.4 MILLION

Sun-kissed, sophisticated and supremely self-confident, Sydney is the show pony of Australian cities. Built around one of the most beautiful harbours in the world, its myriad attractions include three of Australia's most emblematic sights – Sydney Harbour Bridge, Sydney Opera House and Bondi Beach. This is the country's oldest, largest and most diverse city, home to magnificent galleries, even more magnificent beaches and an edgy multiculturalism that injects colour and vitality into its inner neighbourhoods and outer suburbs.

History

What is now Greater Sydney is the ancestral home of at least three distinct Aboriginal peoples, each with their own language. Ku-ring-gai was generally spoken on the northern shore, Dharawal along the coast south of Botany Bay, and Dharug from the harbour to the Blue Mountains. The coastal area around Sydney is the ancestral home of the Eora people (which literally means 'from this place'), who were divided into clans such as the Gadigal and the Wangal.

In 1770 Lieutenant (later Captain) James Cook dropped anchor at Botany Bay. The ship's arrival alarmed the local people, and Cook noted in his journal: 'All they seem'd to want was for us to be gone'. In 1788 the British came back, this time for good. Under the command of naval captain Arthur Phillip, the 'First Fleet' included a motley crew of convicts, marines and livestock. They also brought with them European diseases such as smallpox, which devastated the Eora people (only three of the Gadigal clan are said to have survived).

Armed resistance was led by Indigenous warriors including Pemulwuy (c 1750–1802), a member of the Dharug-speaking Bidjigal clan from around Botany Bay, and Musquito (c 1780–1825), an Eora man from the north shore of Port Jackson. The resistance fighters were eventually crushed and the British colony wrested control.

Early Sydney bumbled through near starvation and rum-fuelled political turmoil, but by the early 1800s it was a bustling port with new houses, warehouses and streets. Over the course of the 19th century, inroads were made into the vast interior of the continent and the city expanded rapidly. The 20th century saw an influx of new migrants from Europe (especially after WWII), Asia and the Middle East, changing the dynamics of the city as it spread westwards and became the multicultural metropolis that it is today.

⊙ Sights

⊙ The Rocks & Circular Quay

Sydney Cove carries the weight of Sydney iconography, with the Harbour Bridge and the Opera House abutting each point of its horseshoe. The site of Australia's first European settlement is unrecognisable from the squalid place it once was, where ex-convicts, sailors and whalers boozed and brawled in countless harbourside pubs and nearly as many brothels and opium dens. The open sewers and squalid alleyways of the Rocks have been transformed into an 'olde worlde' tourist trap, while the Circular Quay promenade serves as a backdrop for buskers of mixed merit and locals disgorging from harbour ferries.

The Rocks remained a commercial and maritime hub until shipping services left Circular Quay in the late 1800s. A bubonic plague outbreak in 1900 continued the decline. Construction of the Harbour Bridge in the 1920s brought further demolition, entire streets disappearing under the bridge's southern approach. It wasn't until the 1970s that the Rocks' cultural and architectural heritage was recognised and the ensuing tourism-driven redevelopment saved many old buildings.

Beyond the Argyle Cut (Map p56; Argyle St; ⓡ Circular Quay), an impressive tunnel excavated by convicts, is Millers Point, a charming district of early colonial homes.

★ Sydney Harbour Bridge   BRIDGE
(Map p56; ⓡ Circular Quay) Sydneysiders adore their giant 'coathanger'. Opened in 1932, this majestic structure spans the harbour at one of its narrowest points. The best way to experience the bridge is on foot – don't expect much of a view crossing by car or train. Staircases climb up to the bridge from both shores, leading to a footpath running the length of the eastern side. You can climb the southeastern pylon to the Pylon Lookout (Map p56; ☏ 02-9240 1100; www.pylonlookout. com.au; adult/child \$11/6.50; ☺ 10am-5pm), or ascend the great arc on the wildly popular BridgeClimb (p76).

Sydney

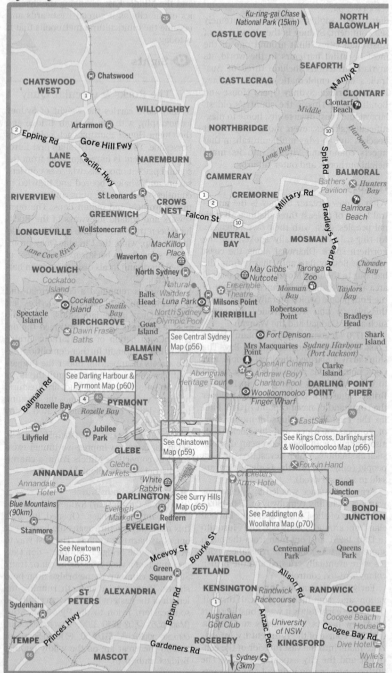

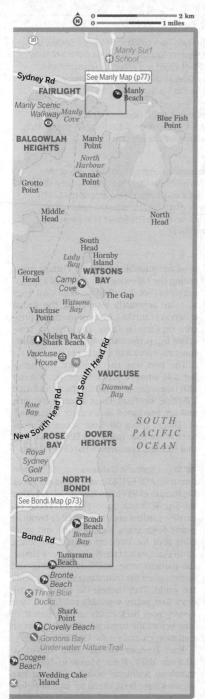

Sydney Observatory
OBSERVATORY

(Map p56; ☑02-9921 3485; www.sydneyobservatory.com.au; Watson Rd; ⊙10am-5pm; 🚇Circular Quay) **FREE** Built in the 1850s, Sydney's copper-domed, Italianate observatory squats atop pretty **Observatory Hill**, overlooking the harbour. Inside is a collection of vintage apparatus, including Australia's oldest working telescope (1874). Also on offer are audiovisual displays, including Aboriginal sky stories, and a virtual-reality **3D Theatre** (adult/child $8/6; ⊙2.30pm & 3.30pm daily, plus 11am & noon Sat & Sun). Bookings are essential for night-time stargazing sessions.

Susannah Place Museum
MUSEUM

(Map p56; ☑02-9241 1893; www.hht.net.au; 58-64 Gloucester St; adult/child $8/4; ⊙tours 2pm, 3pm & 4pm; 🚇Circular Quay) Dating from 1844, this diminutive terrace of four houses and a shop selling historical wares is a fascinating time capsule of life in the Rocks since colonial times. After you watch a documentary about the people who lived here, a guide will take you through the claustrophobic homes, which are decorated to reflect different periods in their histories.

Rocks Discovery Museum
MUSEUM

(Map p56; ☑02-9240 8680; www.rocksdiscovery museum.com; 2-8 Kendall Lane; ⊙10am-5pm; 🚇Circular Quay) **FREE** Divided into four chronological displays – Warrane (pre-1788), Colony (1788–1820), Port (1820–1900) and Transformations (1900 to the present) – this excellent museum digs deep into the Rocks' history and leads you on an artefact-rich tour. Sensitive attention is given to the Rocks' original inhabitants, the Gadigal people.

Cadman's Cottage
HISTORIC BUILDING

(Map p56; www.nationalparks.nsw.gov.au; 110 George St; 🚇Circular Quay) Built in 1816 on a now-buried beach for the government coxswain, Cadman's Cottage is the inner city's oldest house. The Sydney Water Police detained criminals here in the 1840s and it was later converted into a home for retired sea captains. At the time of writing it was closed for the foreseeable future, so you may need to constrain your interest to the exterior.

Museum of Contemporary Art
GALLERY

(Map p56; ☑02-9245 2400; www.mca.com.au; 140 George St; ⊙10am-5pm Fri-Wed, to 9pm Thu; 🚇Circular Quay) **FREE** One of Australia's best and most challenging galleries, the MCA is a showcase for Australian and international contemporary art. The fab Gotham City–style

SYDNEY IN...

Two Days

Start at the Anzac Memorial and walk through Hyde Park (p58) to St Mary's Cathedral (p58) and Hyde Park Barracks (p58). Cut through the Domain to the Art Gallery of NSW (p55) and then loop around Mrs Macquaries Point (p55) and enter the Royal Botanic Gardens (p54). Follow the waterline to Sydney Opera House (p54) and continue along the Circular Quay promenade. That evening head to hip Surry Hills for dinner and a drink.

Spend your second day soaking up the sun and scene at Bondi (p64). After a dip, follow the coastal walk to Coogee. Freshen up for a trashy night out in Kings Cross. Start with dinner in Potts Point before exploring the famously seedy strip.

Four Days

On day three, spend the morning exploring the historic buildings and museums of the Rocks. After lunch, take the scenic ferry ride from Circular Quay to Watsons Bay. Check out the views from the Gap, then continue on to Camp Cove and loop around the South Head Heritage Trail. Watch the sunset from the Watsons Bay Hotel before heading back.

Spend day four in the inner city, exploring Martin Pl, the Pitt Street Mall shopping strip and Chinatown and finishing up in Darling Harbour.

art deco building bears the wounds of a redevelopment that has grafted on additional gallery space and a rooftop cafe–sculpture terrace. Volunteer-led guided tours are offered at 11am and 1pm daily, with extra tours at 7pm on Thursday and 3pm on weekends.

Customs House HISTORIC BUILDING
(Map p56; ☑02-9242 8555; www.cityofsydney. nsw.gov.au/customshouse/thelibrary; 31 Alfred St; ⊙10am-7pm Mon-Fri, 11am-4pm Sat & Sun; @☜; ☒Circular Quay) FREE This handsome harbourside edifice (1885) contains the three-level **Customs House Library** (Map p56; ☑02-9242 8555; ⊙10am-7pm Mon-Fri, 11am-4pm Sat & Sun), with a great selection of international newspapers and magazines, internet access and interesting temporary exhibitions. Look for the swastikas in the tiling of the lobby and the 1:500 model of the inner city displayed under the glass floor.

Justice & Police Museum MUSEUM
(Map p56; ☑02-9252 1144; www.hht.net.au; cnr Albert & Phillip Sts; adult/child $10/5; ⊙10am-5pm Sat & Sun; ☒Circular Quay) Occupying the former Water Police Station (1858), this mildly unnerving museum documents the city's dark and disreputable past through old police photographs and an often macabre series of exhibitions.

★**Sydney Opera House** NOTABLE BUILDING
(Map p56; ☑02-9250 7111; www.sydneyopera-house.com; Bennelong Point; ☒Circular Quay) Designed by Danish architect Jørn Utzon, this World Heritage–listed building is Australia's most recognisable landmark. Visually referencing the billowing white sails of a seagoing yacht (but described by some local wags as more accurately resembling the sexual congress of turtles), it's a commanding presence on Circular Quay. The complex comprises five performance spaces where dance, concerts, opera and theatre are staged.

The best way to experience the building is to attend a performance, but you can also take a one-hour guided tour (adult/child $35/25; ⊙9am-5pm). These depart half-hourly and are conducted in a variety of languages. There's also a two-hour 'access all areas' backstage tour (per person $155; ⊙7am daily) that includes breakfast in the Green Room.

★**Royal Botanic Gardens** GARDENS
(Map p56; ☑02-9231 8111; www.rbgsyd.nsw.gov.au; Mrs Macquaries Rd; ⊙7am-8pm Oct-Feb, to 5.30pm Mar-Sep; ☒Circular Quay) ✿FREE These expansive gardens are the inner city's favourite picnic destination, jogging route and snuggling spot for loved-up couples. Bordering Farm Cove, east of the Sydney Opera House, the gardens were established in 1816 and feature plant life from Australia and around the world. They include the site of the colony's first paltry vegetable patch, but their history goes back much further than that; long before the convicts arrived this was an initiation ground for the Gadigal people.

Free 1½-hour guided walks depart at 10.30am daily. From March to November there's an additional hour-long tour at 1pm on weekdays. Book ahead for an Aboriginal Heritage Tour (Map p52; ☑02-9231 8134; adult/

child $37/17; ⊙10am Fri), which covers local history, traditional plant uses and bush-food tastings.

Government House
HISTORIC BUILDING

(Map p56; ☑02-9931 5222; www.hht.net.au; Macquarie St; ⊙grounds 10am-4pm, tours 10.30am-3pm Fri-Sun; ⍿Circular Quay) FREE Encased in English-style grounds within the Royal Botanic Gardens, this Gothic sandstone mansion served as the home of NSW's governors from 1846 to 1996. The governor, who now resides in Admiralty House on the North Shore, still uses it for weekly meetings and hosting visiting heads of state and royalty. The interior can only be visited on a guided tour; collect your ticket from the gatehouse.

Mrs Macquaries Point
PARK

(Map p52; Mrs Macquaries Rd; ⍿Circular Quay) Adjoining the Royal Botanic Gardens but officially part of the Domain, Mrs Macquaries Point forms the northeastern tip of Farm Cove and provides beautiful views over the bay to the Opera House and city skyline. It was named in 1810 after Elizabeth, Governor Macquarie's wife, who ordered a seat chiselled into the rock from which she could view the harbour.

⦿ The Domain, Macquarie Street & Hyde Park

The Domain
PARK

(Map p56; www.rbgsyd.nsw.gov.au; Art Gallery Rd; ⍿St James) Administered by the Royal Botanic Gardens, the Domain is a large, grassy tract east of Macquarie St, set aside by Governor Phillip in 1788 for public recreation.

Phillip's intent rings true: today's lunchtime workers use the space to work up a sweat or eat their lunch. Large-scale public events are also held here.

Sculptures dot the park, including a reclining Henry Moore figure and Brett Whiteley's *Almost Once* (1991) – two giant matches, one burnt – rising from the ground near the Art Gallery of NSW.

★Art Gallery of NSW
GALLERY

(Map p66; ☑02-9925 1744; www.artgallery.nsw.gov.au; Art Gallery Rd; ⊙10am-5pm Thu-Tue, to 9pm Wed; ⍾; ⍿St James) FREE With its classical Greek frontage and modern rear end, this much-loved institution plays a prominent and gregarious role in Sydney society. Blockbuster international touring exhibitions arrive regularly and there's an outstanding permanent collection of Australian art, including a substantial Indigenous section.

The gallery also plays host to a lively line-up of lectures, concerts, screenings, celebrity talks and children's activities. A range of free guided tours is offered on different themes and in various languages; enquire at the desk or check the website.

State Library of NSW
LIBRARY

(Map p56; ☑02-9273 1414; www.sl.nsw.gov.au; Macquarie St; ⊙9am-8pm Mon-Thu, 10am-5pm Fri-Sun; ⍾; ⍿Martin Pl) FREE Amongst the State Library's over five million tomes are James Cook's and Joseph Banks' journals and William Bligh's log from the HMAV *Bounty*. It's worth dropping in to peruse the grand atrium and the temporary exhibitions in the galleries. The main reading room is a temple of knowledge clad in milky marble.

SYDNEY & THE CENTRAL COAST SYDNEY

WORTH A TRIP

WATSONS BAY

The narrow peninsula ending in South Head is one of Sydney's most sublime spots and it's easily reached by ferry from Circular Quay. Watsons Bay was once a small fishing village, as evidenced by the tiny heritage cottages that pepper the suburb's narrow streets (and now cost a fortune). On the ocean side is the Gap, a dramatic cliff-top lookout gazing over the crashing surf.

Facing the harbour immediately north of Watsons Bay is Camp Cove, a small swimming beach popular with families. At the northern end of the beach, the South Head Heritage Trail kicks off, leading into a section of Sydney Harbour National Park. It passes old battlements and a path heading down to Lady Bay (popular with nudists and gay men), before continuing on to the candy-striped Hornby Lighthouse and the sandstone Lightkeepers' Cottages (1858) on South Head itself.

Before you get back on the ferry, tradition demands that you sit in the beer garden at Watsons Bay Hotel at sunset and watch the sun fall behind the disembodied Harbour Bridge, jutting up above Bradleys Head.

Central Sydney

N

0 —————— 400 m
0 —————— 0.2 miles

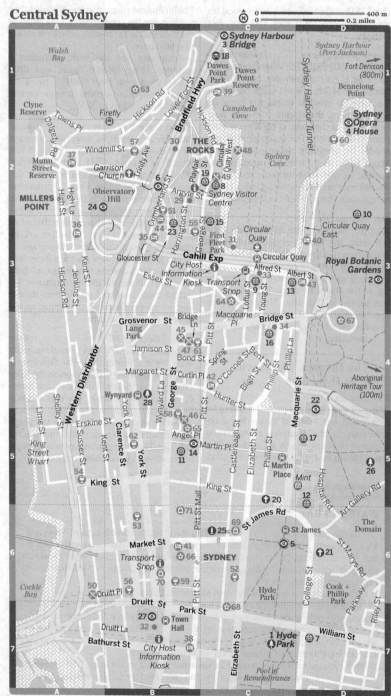

Walsh Bay

SYDNEY & THE CENTRAL COAST SYDNEY

C Sydney Harbour
3 Bridge

18

Dawes
Point
Park

Dawes
Point
Reserve

39

*Sydney Harbour
(Port Jackson)*

Fort Denison
(800m)

Bennelong
Point

*Campbells
Cove*

Sydney Harbour Tunnel

**Sydney
Opera
4 House**

60

Clyne
Reserve

Firefly

63

Towns Pl

Hickson Rd

Lower Fort St

Bradfield Hwy

Hickson Rd

30

**THE
ROCKS**

Circular Quay West

48

*Sydney
Cove*

Dalgety Rd

Windmill St

57

Trinity Ave

Cumberland St

6

Playfair St

Argyle St

19

49

8

Sydney Visitor
Centre

10

Munn
Street
Reserve

37

High La

High St

Garrison
Church

Observatory
Hill

24

29

51

Cumberland St

Harrington St

George St

55

15

First
Fleet
Park

31

Circular
Quay

Circular Quay
East

40

**MILLERS
POINT**

36

44

23

35

Gloucester St

Cahill Exp

City Host
Information
Kiosk

Essex St

Transport
Shop

64

Alfred St

33

9

Lotus St

Young St

Circular Quay

Albert St

13

43

*Royal Botanic
Gardens*

2

67

Kent St

Jenkins St

Hickson Rd

Grosvenor St

Lang
Park

Jamison St

45

47 61

Bridge
Ln

Pitt St

Bond St

Spring St

*Macquarie
Pl*

O'Connell St

Bent St

Bridge St

34

16

Phillip La

Margaret St

George St

Curtin Pl

42

Hunter St

Bligh St

Phillip St

Macquarie St

*Aboriginal
Heritage Tour
(100m)*

Shelley St

Lime St

*King
Street
Wharf*

Erskine St

Sussex St

Kent St

Clarence St

York La

Wynyard

28

58

46

65

Angel Pl

14

11

Martin Pl

Pitt St

Castlereagh St

Elizabeth St

22

17

Western Distributor

62

York St

54

King St

54

Martin
Place

Mint

12

26

53

Pitt St Mall

71

69

25

St James Rd

20

King St

St James

5

21

Market St

41

66

*Transport
Shop*

70

59

50

Druitt Pl

56

Pitt St

SYDNEY

52

Hyde
Park

College St

St Marys Rd

Cook +
Phillip
Park

*The
Domain*

Art Gallery Rd

Parkway

Riley St

*Cockle
Bay*

Druitt St

Park St

68

27

32

**Town
Hall**

38

City Host
Information
Kiosk

Bathurst St

Druitt La

Elizabeth St

1 **Hyde
Park**

7

William St

*Pool of
Remembrance*

Central Sydney

Parliament House   HISTORIC BUILDING
(Map p56; ☑02-9230 2111; www.parliament.nsw.
gov.au; 6 Macquarie St; ⊙9am-5pm Mon-Fri;
🚇Martin Pl) **FREE** Built as part of the Rum
Hospital in 1816, this has been home to the
Parliament of New South Wales since 1829,
making it the world's oldest continually operating parliament building. Its venerable
frontage now blends into a modern addition
on the eastern side.

You need to pass through a metal detector
to access the inner sanctum, where you can
check out art exhibitions in the lobby and
the historical display in the wood-panelled
Jubilee Room. On nonsitting days both assembly chambers are open, but when parliament is sitting, you're restricted to the
Public Gallery.

Hyde Park Barracks Museum   MUSEUM
(Map p56; ☑02-8239 2311; www.hht.net.au; Queens Sq, Macquarie St; adult/concession $10/5; ⊙10am-5pm; ℝSt James) Convict architect Francis Greenway designed this decorously Georgian structure as convict quarters. Between 1819 and 1848, 50,000 men and boys did time here, most of whom had been sentenced by British courts to transportation to Australia for property crime. It later became an immigration depot, a women's asylum and a law court. These days it's a fascinating (if not entirely cheerful) museum, focusing on the barracks' history and the archaeological efforts that helped reveal it.

St James' Church   CHURCH
(Map p56; ☑02-8227 1300; www.sjks.org.au; 173 King St; ⊙10am-4pm Mon-Fri, 9am-1pm Sat, 7.15am-4pm Sun; ℝSt James) Built from convict-made bricks, Sydney's oldest church (1819) is widely considered to be Francis Greenway's masterpiece. It was originally designed as a courthouse, but the brief changed and the cells became the crypt. Check out the dark-wood choir loft, the sparkling copper dome, the crypt and the stained-glass 'Creation Window'.

St Mary's Cathedral   CHURCH
(Map p56; ☑02-9220 0400; www.stmaryscathedral.org.au; St Marys Rd; crypt $5; ⊙6.30am-6.30pm; ℝSt James) Built to last, this 106m-long Gothic Revival–style Catholic cathedral was begun in 1868, but the 75m-high sandstone spires weren't added until 2000. The crypt has a mosaic floor inspired by the Celtic-style illuminations of the *Book of Kells*.

★Hyde Park   PARK
(Map p56; Elizabeth St; ℝSt James & Museum) Formal but much-loved Hyde Park has manicured gardens and a tree-formed tunnel running down its spine that looks particularly pretty at night, illuminated by fairy lights. The park's northern end is crowned by the Archibald Memorial Fountain (Map

p56), featuring Greek mythological figures, while at the other end, the shallow Pool of Remembrance fronts the Anzac Memorial (Map p59; www.rslnsw.com.au; ⊙9am-5pm; ℝMuseum) FREE, commemorating the soldiers of the Australian and New Zealand Army Corps (Anzacs) who served in WWI.

◉ City Centre

Museum of Sydney   MUSEUM
(MoS; Map p56; ☑02-9251 5988; www.hht.net.au; cnr Phillip & Bridge Sts; adult/child $10/5; ⊙10am-5pm; ⊛; ℝCircular Quay) Built on the site of Sydney's first Government House, this small, somewhat fragmented museum uses artefacts and audiovisual installations to explore the city's people, places, cultures and evolution.

Martin Place   SQUARE
(Map p56; ℝMartin Pl) Lined with imposing edifices, long, lean Martin Pl was closed to traffic in 1971, forming a terraced pedestrian mall. Near the George St end you'll find the Cenotaph, commemorating Australia's war dead. As iconic in its time as the Opera House, GPO Sydney (Map p56; www.gposydney.com; 1 Martin Pl) is a beautiful colonnaded Victorian palazzo that was once Sydney's main post office. It has since been gutted, stabbed with office towers and transformed into the Westin hotel, swanky shops, restaurants and bars.

Sydney Tower Eye   TOWER
(Map p56; ☑02-9333 9222; www.sydneytowereye.com.au; 100 Market St; adult/child $26/15, Skywalk adult/child $69/45; ⊙9am-10pm; ℝSt James) The 309m-tall Sydney Tower (1981) offers unbeatable 360-degree views from the observation level 250m up and even better ones for the daredevils braving the Skywalk on its roof. The visit starts with *The 4D Experience* – a short 3D film giving you a bird's-eye view of city, surf, harbour and what lies beneath the water, accompanied by mist sprays and bubbles.

Town Hall   NOTABLE BUILDING
(Map p56; ☑02-9265 9189; www.cityofsydney.nsw.gov.au/sydneytownhall; 483 George St; ⊙8am-6pm Mon-Fri; ℝTown Hall) Mansard roofs, sandstone turrets, wrought-iron trimmings and over-the-top balustrades: the High Victorian exterior of the Town Hall (built 1869–89) is something to behold. Inside, the elaborate chamber room and the wood-lined concert hall are almost as impressive (the concert

---

ℹ **COMBO TICKETS**

Sea Life (p61), Wild Life (p61), Madame Tussauds (p61), Sydney Tower Eye (p58) and Manly Sea Life Sanctuary (p71) are all owned by the same company. You'll save on admission by purchasing a combo ticket (two/three/four attractions $65/70/80) and even more by booking online. If you visit Manly first, there are further discounts.

Chinatown

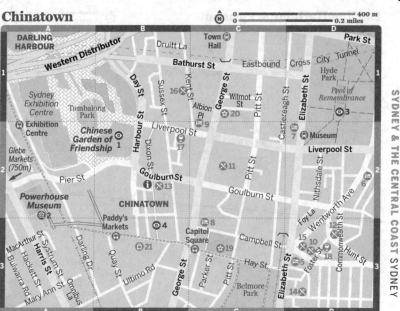

0   400 m
0   0.2 miles

Chinatown

hall has a humongous 8000-pipe organ and
hosts free monthly lunchtime concerts).

Chinatown   NEIGHBOURHOOD
(Map p59; www.chinatown.com.au/eng; ⏺ Town Hall)
Wedged into the Haymarket district, Chinatown is a tight nest of restaurants, shops and
aroma-filled alleys. No longer just Chinese,
the area is truly pan-Asian. On the lunar new

year half of Sydney tries to squish into these
lanes. Dixon St is the heart and soul of Chinatown: a narrow pedestrian mall with ornate
dragon gates (*paifang*) at either end.

◉ Darling Harbour & Pyrmont

Dotted between the flyovers and fountains of
Sydney's purpose-built tourist hub (opened

Darling Harbour & Pyrmont

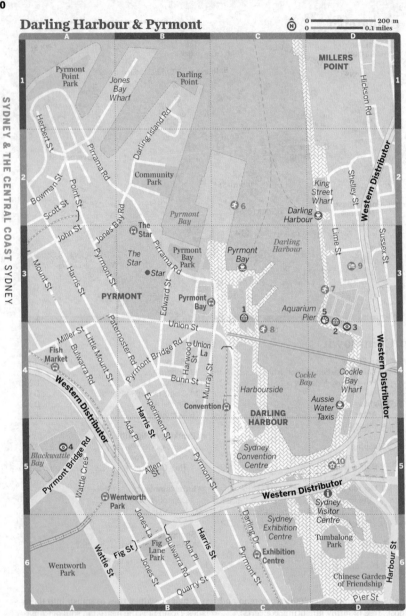

for the bicentennial in 1988) are some of the city's highest-profile paid attractions. Every other inch of this former dockland is given over to bars and restaurants. In Pyrmont, on the western shore, the Star casino complex has had an expensive do-over, yet it remains like such establishments the world over: big and soulless beneath a thin veneer of glamour.

If you are after a slice of real Sydney life you won't find it here, but it's still worth allocating an hour to go on a walkabout around the area.

Darling Harbour & Pyrmont

Sea Life Sydney Aquarium AQUARIUM
(Map p60; ☎02-8251 7800; www.sydneyaquarium. com.au; Darling Harbour; adult/child $38/24; ◷9am-8pm; ⓡTown Hall) 🐟 As well as regular wall-mounted tanks and ground-level enclosures, this impressive complex has two large pools that you can walk through, safely enclosed in perspex tunnels, as an intimidating array of sharks and rays pass overhead. The aquarium's two dugongs were rescued when washed up on Queensland beaches. After attempts to return them to the wild failed, the decision was made to keep them here. As sad as that may be, it offers a fascinating and rare opportunity to get close to these large marine mammals. Other highlights include platypuses, moon jellyfish, sea dragons and the colourful finale of the complex, the two-million-litre Great Barrier Reef tank.

Wild Life Sydney Zoo ZOO
(Map p60; ☎02-9333 9245; www.wildlifesydney. com.au; Darling Harbour; adult/child $38/24; ◷9am-5pm Apr-Sep, to 8pm Oct-Mar; ⓡTown Hall) Complementing its sister and neighbour Sea Life, this complex houses a collection of Australian native reptiles, butterflies, spiders, snakes and mammals (including kangaroos and koalas). The nocturnal section is particularly good, bringing out the extrovert in the quolls, potoroos, echidnas and possums. As interesting as Wild Life is, it's not a patch on Taronga Zoo. Still, it's worth considering as part of a combo with Sea Life or if you're short on time.

Madame Tussauds MUSEUM
(Map p60; www.madametussauds.com/sydney; Darling Harbour; adult/child $38/24; ◷9am-8pm; ⓡTown Hall) In this celebrity-obsessed age, it's not surprising that these waxwork dummies are just as popular now as when the eponymous madame lugged her macabre haul of French revolution death masks to London in 1803. Where else do mere mortals get to strike a pose with Hugh Jackman and cosy up to Kylie? On its own it's hard to justify the price, but it's worth considering as an add-on if you're planning to visit Sea Life, Wild Life or Sydney Tower.

★**Chinese Garden of Friendship** GARDENS
(Map p59; ☎02-9240 8888; www.chinesegarden. com.au; Harbour St; adult/child $6/3; ◷9.30am-5pm; ⓡTown Hall) Built according to Taoist principles, this tranquil garden was designed by architects from Guangzhou (Sydney's sister city) for Australia's bicentenary in 1988. Paths twist around pavilions, waterfalls, ponds and lush plant life.

Australian National Maritime Museum MUSEUM
(Map p60; ☎02-9298 3777; www.anmm.gov.au; 2 Murray St; adult/child $7/3.50; ◷9.30am-5pm; ⓡPyrmont Bay) Beneath an Utzon-like roof (a low-rent Opera House?), the Maritime Museum sails through Australia's inextricable relationship with the sea. Exhibitions range from Aboriginal canoes to surf culture, to the navy. The 'big ticket' ($25/15 per adult/child) includes entry to the vessels moored outside, including a submarine, a destroyer, an 1874 square rigger and, when it's not sailing elsewhere, a replica of James Cook's *Endeavour*.

Sydney Fish Market MARKET
(Map p60; ☎02-9004 1100; www.sydneyfishmarket.com.au; Bank St; ◷7am-4pm; ⓡFish Market) This piscatorial precinct on Blackwattle Bay shifts over 15 million kilograms of seafood annually, and has retail outlets, restaurants, a sushi bar, an oyster bar and a highly regarded cooking school. Chefs, locals and overfed seagulls haggle over mud crabs, Balmain bugs, lobsters and slabs of salmon at the daily fish auction, which kicks off at 5.30am. Check it out on a behind-the-scenes **tour** (☎02-9004 1108; adult/child $25/10; ◷6.40am Mon, Thu & Fri).

Ultimo & Chippendale

★ Powerhouse Museum
MUSEUM

(Map p59; ☑02-9217 0111; www.powerhouse-museum.com; 500 Harris St; adult/child $12/6; ☉10am-5pm; ⒭Paddy's Markets) A short walk from Darling Harbour, this science and design museum whirs away inside the former power station for Sydney's defunct tram network. High-voltage interactive demonstrations wow school groups with the low-down on how lightning strikes, magnets grab and engines growl. It's a huge hit with kids but equally popular with adults, touching on subjects such as fashion and furniture design.

White Rabbit
GALLERY

(Map p52; www.whiterabbitcollection.org; 30 Balfour St; ☉10am-6pm Thu-Sun; ⒭Redfern) FREE If you're an art lover or a bit of a Mad Hatter, this particular rabbit hole will leave you grinning like a Cheshire Cat. There are so many works in this private collection of cutting-edge, contemporary Chinese art that only a fraction can be displayed at one time.

Newtown

The inner west is a sociological stew of students, goths, urban hippies, artists and Mediterranean immigrants. At its heart is Sydney University, a bastion of old-world architecture that dominates the surrounding suburbs. Southwest of the university, Newtown shadows sinuous King St, lined with interesting boutiques, secondhand-clothes stores, bookshops, yoga studios, pubs, cafes and Thai restaurants. It's definitely climbing the social rungs, but Newtown is still free thinking and idiosyncratic. Glebe, on the other side of the university, is similar but quieter.

Surry Hills

Sydney's hippest neighbourhood bears absolutely no resemblance to the beautiful hills of Surrey, England, from which it takes its name. And these days it also bears little resemblance to the tightly knit, working-class community so evocatively documented in Ruth Park's classic Depression-era novels. The rows of Victorian terrace houses remain, but they're now home to a mishmash of inner-city hipsters, foodies and gay guys who rarely venture beyond the excellent local pubs and eateries.

Brett Whiteley Studio
GALLERY

(Map p65; ☑02-9225 1881; www.brettwhiteley.org; 2 Raper St; ☉10am-4pm Fri-Sun; ⒭Central) FREE Acclaimed local artist Brett Whiteley (1939–92) lived fast and without restraint. His hard-to-find studio (look for the signs on Devonshire St) has been preserved as a gallery for some of his best work. At the door is a miniature of his famous sculpture *Almost Once*, which you can see in the Domain.

Darlinghurst

Immediately east of the city, Darlinghurst is synonymous with Sydney's vibrant and visible gay community. The shabby lower end of Oxford St has traditionally been Sydney's sequinned mile, and while it has seen better days, it is still home to most of the city's gay venues as well as the Mardi Gras parade.

Sydney Jewish Museum
MUSEUM

(Map p66; ☑02-9360 7999; www.sydneyjewish-museum.com.au; 148 Darlinghurst Rd; adult/child $10/6; ☉10am-4pm Sun-Thu, to 2pm Fri; ⒭Kings Cross) Created largely as a Holocaust memorial, this museum examines Australian Jewish history, culture and tradition from the time of the First Fleet (which included 16 known Jews) to the immediate aftermath of WWII (when Australia became home to the largest number of Holocaust survivors per capita after Israel) to the present day. Allow enough time (at least two hours) to take it all in. Free 45-minute tours leave at noon on Monday, Wednesday, Friday and Sunday.

WORTH A TRIP

CRONULLA

Cronulla is a beach suburb south of Botany Bay, its long surf beach stretching beyond the dunes to the Botany Bay refineries. It can be an edgy place (captured brilliantly in the '70s cult novel *Puberty Blues*), with dingy fish-and-chip shops, insomniac teens and a ragged sense of impending 'something', which in 2005 erupted into racial violence. That said, the beach is beautiful and the surf excellent and it's the only ocean beach that's easy to reach by train.

Newtown

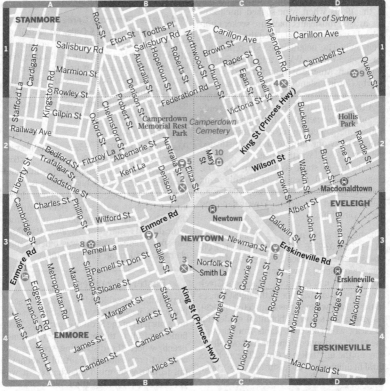

Australian Museum MUSEUM

(Map p56; 02-9320 6000; www.australianmuseum.net.au; 6 College St; adult/child $17/9; 9.30am-5pm; Museum) This natural-history museum, established just 40 years after the First Fleet dropped anchor, has endeavoured to shrug off its museum-that-should-be-in-a-museum feel by jazzing things up a little. Hence dusty taxidermy has been interspersed with video projections and a terrarium with live snakes, while dinosaur skeletons cosy up to life-size re-creations. Yet it's the most old-fashioned section that is arguably the most interesting – the hall of bones and the large collection of crystals and precious stones.

Woolloomooloo, Kings Cross & Potts Point

Crowned by a huge illuminated Coca-Cola sign (Map p66) – Sydney's equivalent of LA's iconic Hollywood sign – 'the Cross' has long

been the home of Sydney's vice industry. In the 19th and early 20th centuries the suburb was home to grand estates and stylish apartments, but it underwent a radical change in the 1930s when wine-soaked intellectuals, artists, musicians, pleasure-seekers and ne'er-do-wells rowdily claimed the streets for their own. The neighbourhood's reputation was sealed during WWII and the Vietnam War, when American sailors based at the nearby Garden Island naval base flooded the Cross with a tide of shore-leave debauchery.

Although the streets retain an air of seedy hedonism, the neighbourhood has recently undergone something of a cultural renaissance. Sleazy one minute and sophisticated the next, it's well worth a visit.

Standing in stark contrast are the gracious, tree-lined avenues of neighbouring Potts Point and Elizabeth Bay, filled with well-preserved Victorian, Edwardian and art deco buildings.

Elizabeth Bay House HISTORIC BUILDING
(Map p66; ☎02-9356 3022; www.hht.net.au; 7 Onslow Ave; adult/concession $8/4; ⊙11am-4pm Fri-Sun; ⓡKings Cross) Now dwarfed by 20th-century apartments, Alexander Macleay's Greek Revival mansion was one of the finest houses in the colony when it was completed in 1839. Its grounds – a sort of botanical garden for Macleay, who collected plants from around the world – extended from the harbour all the way up the hill to Kings Cross. The architectural highlight is an exquisite entrance saloon with a curved and cantilevered staircase.

Woolloomooloo Finger Wharf NOTABLE BUILDING
(Map p52; Cowper Wharf Rd; ⓡKings Cross) A former wool and cargo dock, this Edwardian wharf faced oblivion for decades before a 2½-year trade-union 'green ban' on the site in the late 1980s saved it. It received a sprucing up in the late 1990s and has emerged as one of Sydney's most exclusive eating, drinking, sleeping and marina addresses.

⊙ Paddington & Woollahra

Paddington is an elegant area of beautifully restored terrace houses and steep, leafy streets where fashionable folks drift between designer shops, restaurants, art galleries and bookshops. Its main artery is Oxford St, extending from nearby Darlinghurst. The best time to visit is on Saturday, when the markets are effervescing. Neighbouring Woollahra is upper-crust Sydney

at its finest: leafy streets, mansions, wall-to-wall BMWs and antique shops.

Paddington Reservoir Gardens PARK
(Map p70; cnr Oxford St & Oatley Rd; ☐380) ✦ Opened to much architectural acclaim in 2008, this park makes use of Paddington's long-abandoned 1866 water reservoir, incorporating the brick arches and surviving chamber into an interesting green space featuring a sunken garden, a pond, a boardwalk and lawns.

Centennial Park PARK
(Map p70; ☎02-9339 6699; www.centennialparklands.com.au; Oxford St; ⓡBondi Junction) Scratched out of the sand in 1888 in grand Victorian style, Sydney's biggest park is a rambling 189-hectare expanse full of horse riders, joggers, cyclists and in-line skaters. Among the wide formal avenues, ponds and statues is the domed **Federation Pavilion** (Map p70) – the spot where Australia was officially proclaimed a nation (on 1 January 1901).

⊙ Eastern Beaches

Improbably good-looking arcs of sand framed by jagged cliffs, the Eastern Beaches are a big part of the Sydney experience. Most famous of all is the broad sweep of Bondi Beach, where the distracting scenery and constant procession of beautiful bods never fail to take your mind off whatever it was you were just thinking about...

★Bondi Beach BEACH
(Map p73; Campbell Pde; ☐380) Definitively Sydney, Bondi is one of the world's great beaches: ocean and land collide, the Pacific arrives in great foaming swells and all people are equal, as democratic as sand. It's the closest ocean beach to the city centre (8km away), has consistently good (though crowded) waves, and is great for a rough-and-tumble swim (the average water temperature is a considerate 21°C). The unique flavour of Bondi has been greatly influenced by the Jewish, British and Kiwi immigrants who populated it before it became hip. Housing prices on Bondi's strangely treeless slopes have skyrocketed, but the beach remains a priceless constant.

If the sea's angry, try the ocean pools at either end of the beach. **Bondi Pavilion** (Map p73; www.waverley.nsw.gov.au; Queen Elizabeth Dr; ☐380) FREE has changing rooms, lockers and a gelato shop. Ice-cream vendors also strut the sand in summer. At the beach's northern end there's a grassy spot with barbecues.

Surry Hills

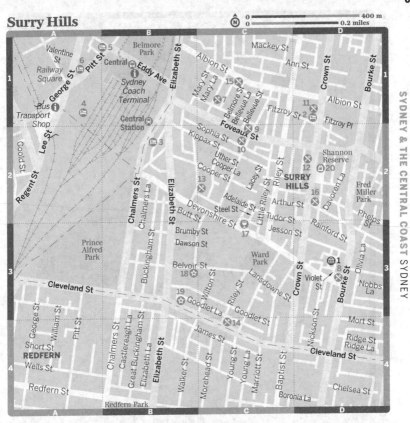

Surry Hills

★ **Tamarama Beach**   BEACH
(Map p73; Pacific Ave; 🚌361) Surrounded by
high cliffs, Tamarama has a deep tongue of
sand with just 80m of shoreline. Diminutive,
yes, but ever-present rips make Tamarama

Kings Cross, Darlinghurst & Woolloomooloo

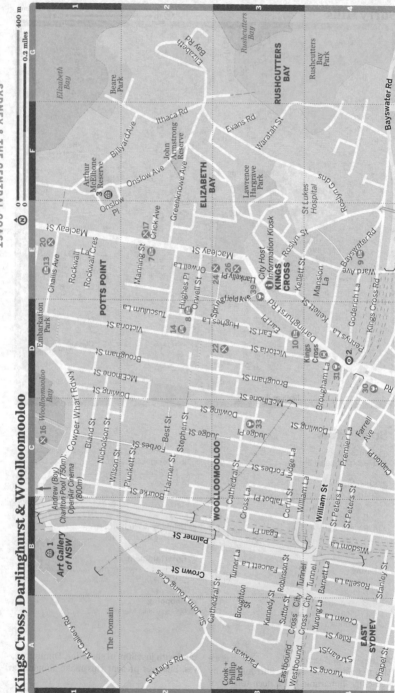

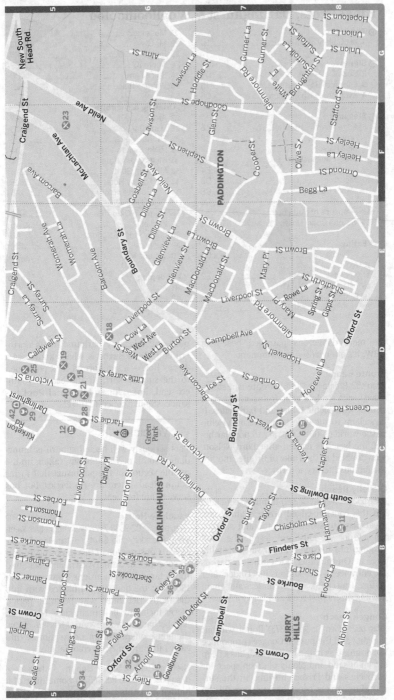

Kings Cross, Darlinghurst & Woolloomooloo

the most dangerous patrolled beach in NSW; it's often closed to swimmers.

Bronte Beach BEACH
(Map p52; Bronte Rd; 🚍378) Bronte is a steep-sided beach stretching up from a grassy park strewn with picnic tables and barbecues. It lays claim to the oldest surf-lifesaving club in the world (1903). Contrary to popular belief, the beach is named after Lord Nelson, who doubled as the Duke of Bronte, and not the famous literary sorority.

Clovelly Beach BEACH
(Map p52; Clovelly Rd; 🚍339) It might seem odd, but this concrete-edged ocean channel is a great place to swim, sunbathe and snorkel. It's safe for the kids, and despite the swell surging into the inlet, underwater visibility is great. On the other side of the car park is the entrance to the Gordons Bay Underwater Nature Trail (p68), a 500m underwater chain guiding divers past reefs and kelp forests.

Coogee Beach BEACH
(Map p52; Arden St; 🚍372-373) Bondi without the glitz and the posers, Coogee (pronounce the double *o* as in the word 'took') has a deep sweep of sand and plenty of green space for barbecues and Frisbee hurling. In the surrounding streets beery backpackers fill the

pubs and takeaway parlours. At its northern end, **Giles Baths** is what's known as a 'bogey hole' – a semiformal rock pool open to the surging surf. At the beach's southern end, **Ross Jones Memorial Pool** has sandcastle-like concrete turrets.

◉ Vaucluse

This seriously well-heeled suburb is immediately south of Watsons Bay, taking up the middle section of the peninsula that forms South Head. There are no ferries, but bus services are frequent.

Vaucluse House HISTORIC BUILDING
(Map p52; ☏02-9388 7922; www.hht.net.au; Wentworth Rd; adult/child $8/4; ⊙11am-4pm Fri-Sun; 🚍325) Construction of this imposing, turreted specimen of Gothic Australiana, set amid 10 hectares of lush gardens, commenced in 1805, but the house was tinkered with into the 1860s. Decorated with beautiful period pieces including Bohemian glass, heavy oak 'Jacobethan' furniture and Meissen china, the house offers visitors a rare glimpse into early (albeit privileged) colonial life.

Nielsen Park & Shark Beach PARK, BEACH
(Map p52; Vaucluse Rd; 🚍325) Something of a hidden gem, this gorgeous harbourside park

with a sandy beach was once part of the then 206-hectare Vaucluse House estate. Secluded beneath the trees is Greycliffe House, a gracious 1851 Gothic sandstone pile (not open to visitors), which serves as the headquarters for Sydney Harbour National Park. Despite the beach's ominous name, there's really nothing to worry about – there's a shark net to put paranoid swimmers at ease. Visit on a weekday when it's not too busy: just parents with kids, retirees and people taking sickies from work.

⊙ Harbour Islands

Cockatoo Island   ISLAND
(Map p52; ☑02-8969 2100; www.cockatooisland. gov.au; ⌷Cockatoo Island) Studded with photogenic industrial relics, convict architecture and art installations, fascinating Cockatoo Island (Wareamah) opened to the public in 2007 and now has regular ferry services, a cafe and a bar. Information boards and audio guides ($5) explain the island's time as a prison, shipyard and naval base.

Fort Denison   ISLAND, FORTRESS
(Map p52; www.fortdenison.com.au; ferry & tour adult/child $38/29; ⊙tours 10.45am, 12.15pm & 2.30pm) Called Mat-te-wan-ye (rocky island) by the Gadigal people, in colonial times the small fortified island off Mrs Macquaries Point was a site of suffering used to isolate recalcitrant convicts (it was nicknamed 'Pinchgut' for its meagre rations). Fears of a Russian invasion during the mid-19th-century Crimean War led to its fortification. It now has a cafe.

Captain Cook Cruises (p76) runs ferries to the island from Darling Harbour and Circular Quay about seven times a day, but to access the Martello tower you'll need to prebook a tour through the NPWS (☑02-9253 0888; www.nationalparks.nsw.gov.au).

⊙ Lower North Shore

At the northern end of the Harbour Bridge are the unexpectedly tranquil waterside suburbs of Milsons Point and McMahons Point. Both command astonishing city views. Just east of the bridge is the stately suburb of Kirribilli, home to Admiralty House and Kirribilli House, the Sydney residences of the governor general and prime minister respectively.

East of here are the upmarket suburbs of Neutral Bay, Cremorne and Mosman,

known for their coves, harbourside parks and 'ladies who lunch'. A great coastal walk stretches from Cremorne Point, past Mosman Bay and into a section of Sydney Harbour National Park hugging Bradleys Head.

Luna Park   AMUSEMENT PARK
(Map p52; ☑02-9922 6644; www.lunaparksydney.com; 1 Olympic Dr; single-ride tickets $10, ride pass $20-50; ⊙11am-10pm Fri & Sat, 10am-6pm Sun, 11am-4pm Mon; ⌷Milsons Point/Luna Park) A demented-looking clown face forms the entrance to this amusement park overlooking Sydney Harbour. It's one of a number of original 1930s features, including the Coney Island funhouse, a pretty carousel and the nausea-inducing rotor. You can pay as you go, or buy a height-based unlimited-ride pass (cheaper if purchased online). Hours are extended during school and public holidays.

Mary MacKillop Place   MUSEUM, CHURCH
(Map p52; ☑02-8912 4878; www.marymackillopplace.org.au; 7 Mount St; adult/child $8/5; ⊙10am-4pm; ⌷North Sydney) This museum tells the story of St Mary of the Cross (aka Mary MacKillop), Australia's only Catholic saint. She was a dedicated and outspoken educator who prevailed over conservative hierarchical ideals, despite being excommunicated for six months. You'll find her tomb inside the chapel.

May Gibbs' Nutcote   MUSEUM
(Map p52; ☑02-9953 4453; www.maygibbs.com. au; 5 Wallaringa Ave; adult/child $9/3.50; ⊙11am-3pm Wed-Sun; ⌷Neutral Bay) Spanish Mission–style Nutcote (1925) is the former home of author May Gibbs, who wrote the much-loved Australian children's book Snugglepot & Cuddlepie. It's now restored to its 1930s glory and houses a museum devoted to her life and work. Cheery volunteer guides will show you around, and there are beautiful gardens, a tearoom and a gift shop. It's a five-minute walk from the wharf.

Taronga Zoo   ZOO
(Map p52; ☑02-9969 2777; www.taronga.org.au; Bradleys Head Rd; adult/child $44/22; ⊙9.30am-5pm; ⌷Taronga Zoo) 🖉 A 12-minute ferry ride from Circular Quay, Taronga Zoo has 75 hectares of harbour hillside full of kangaroos, koalas and similarly hirsute Australians. The zoo's 4000 critters have million-dollar harbour views but seem blissfully unaware of the privilege.

Highlights include the nocturnal platypus habitat, the Great Southern Oceans section

Paddington & Woollahra

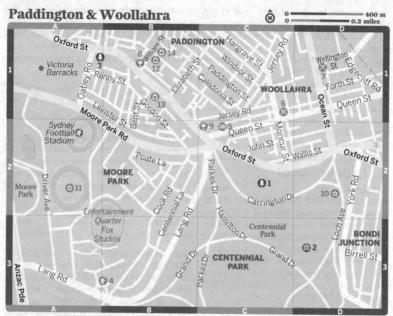

Paddington & Woollahra

and the Asian elephant display. Feedings and 'encounters' happen throughout the day. Twilight concerts jazz things up in summer, and you can even sign up for a 'Roar and Snore' overnight camping experience.

Tours include **Nura Diya** (☎02-9978 4782; 90min tour adult/child $99/69; ◷9.45am Mon, Wed & Fri), where Indigenous guides introduce you to native animals and share Dreaming stories about them, while giving an insight into traditional Aboriginal life; advance bookings essential.

From the wharf, the Sky Safari cable car or a bus will whisk you up to the entrance. A Zoo Pass (adult/child/family $51/25/143) from Circular Quay includes return ferry rides, the bus or cable-car ride to the top and zoo admission.

Balmoral Beach   BEACH
(Map p52; The Esplanade; ☐245) The beachy enclave of Balmoral faces off with Manly across Middle Harbour, and has some good restaurants and a beaut swimming beach. Split in two by an unfeasibly picturesque rocky outcrop, Balmoral attracts picnicking North Shore families. Swimmers migrate to the shark-netted southern end.

◎ Manly

Laid-back Manly clings to a narrow isthmus abutting North Head, Sydney Harbour's northern gatepost. The suburb's unusual name comes from Governor Phillip's description of the physique of the Indigenous people he met here; his Excellency was clearly indulging in an early example of the very Sydney habit of body scrutinising.

The Corso connects Manly's ocean and harbour beaches; here surf shops, burger joints, juice bars and pubs are plentiful. The refurbished Manly Wharf has classier pubs and restaurants, and there are some good cafes scattered around the backstreets.

In summer, allocate a day to walking and splashing about. In winter, it's worth heading over for a quick look around, if only for Sydney's best ferry journey. Don't bother staying after dark – there are much better eateries and bars elsewhere.

★ Manly Beach   BEACH

(Map p77; ⛴Manly) Sydney's second most famous beach stretches for nearly two golden kilometres, lined by Norfolk Island pines and scrappy midrise apartment blocks. The southern end of the beach, nearest the Corso, is known as South Steyne, with North Steyne in the centre and Queenscliff at the northern end; each has its own surf-lifesaving club.

Manly Sea Life Sanctuary   AQUARIUM

(Map p77; ☎02-8251 7877; www.manlysealifesanc-tuary.com.au; West Esplanade; adult/child $24/12; ⊙10am-5.30pm, last admission 4.45pm; ⛴Manly) This ain't the place to come if you're on your way to Manly Beach for a surf. Underwater glass tunnels enable you to become alarmingly intimate with 3m grey nurse sharks. Reckon they're not hungry? **Shark Dive Xtreme** (☎02-8251 7878; introductory/certified dives $270/195) enables you to enter their world.

Upstairs, the residents of the penguin enclosure have lawless amounts of fun. Manly has one of the last mainland colonies of little penguins in Australia, and this display aims to educate people about these cute-as-a-button critters (don't fret, none of these little guys were taken from the wild).

Manly Scenic Walkway   OUTDOORS

(Map p52; www.manly.nsw.gov.au/attractions/walking-tracks/manly-scenic-walkway/; ⛴Manly) This epic walk has two major components: the 10km western stretch between Manly and Spit Bridge, and the 9.5km eastern loop to North Head. Either download a map or pick one up from the information centre near the wharf.

The western section traces the coast past million-dollar harbour-view properties and then through a rugged 2.5km section of Sydney Harbour National Park that remains much as it was when the First Fleet sailed in. After crossing the Spit Bridge you can either bus back to Manly (buses 140, 143 or 144) or into the city (176 to 180).

The eastern loop is known as the North Head Circuit Track, and takes between three and four hours. From the wharf, follow Eastern Esplanade and Stuart St to Spring Cove, head into the North Head section of Sydney Harbour National Park, and make your way through the bush to the spectacular Fairfax Lookout on North Head (approximately 45 minutes in total). From the lookout, walk the Fairfax Loop (1km, 30 minutes) and then head back via the Cabbage Tree Bay Walk, which follows the sea-sprayed shoreline back to Manly Beach via picturesque Shelly Beach and tiny Fairy Bower Beach.

◎ Northern Beaches

The 20km stretch of coast between Manly and well-heeled Palm Beach has been called the most impressive urban surfing landscape in the world, and the locals who swim and catch the waves at Dee Why, Collaroy, Narrabeen, Mona Vale, Newport, Bilgola, Avalon, Whale and Palm Beaches would be quick to agree.

Driving is by far the best way to explore, but if that's not an option and you still feel the need to make a *Home & Away* pilgrimage, bus L90 will get you from Railway Sq to Palm Beach in just under two hours.

Whale Beach   BEACH

(Whale Beach Rd; 🚌L90) Sleepy Whale Beach, 3km south of Palm Beach, is well worth seeking out – a paradisaical slice of deep, orange sand flanked by steep cliffs; good for surfers and families.

Palm Beach   BEACH

(Ocean Rd; 🚌L90) Lovely Palm Beach is a meniscus of bliss, famous as the setting for TV soap *Home & Away*. The 1881 **Barrenjoey Lighthouse** punctuates the northern tip of the headland in an annexe of Ku-ring-gai Chase National Park. You'll need some decent shoes for the steep 20-minute hike, but the views across Pittwater are worth the effort.

Ku-ring-gai Chase National Park PARK

(www.nationalparks.nsw.gov.au; per car per day $11, landing fee by boat adult/child $3/2) This spectacular expanse of wilderness sits across Pittwater from the narrow peninsula containing Palm Beach and stretches for a vast 150 sq km, forming Sydney's northern boundary. On display is that classic Sydney cocktail of bushland, sandstone outcrops and water vistas, plus walking tracks, horse-riding trails, picnic areas and Aboriginal rock engravings.

The park has over 100km of shoreline and several through roads (enter from Bobbin Head Rd, North Turramurra; Ku-ring-gai Chase Rd off the Pacific Hwy, Mt Colah; or McCarrs Creek Rd, Terrey Hills). **Palm Beach Ferries** (☑02-9974 2411; www.palmbeachferries.com.au; adult/child $7.50/3.70; ◷9am-6pm Sat-Thu, to 8pm Fri) leaves Palm Beach Wharf on the hour, heading to the Basin, which has a camping ground and a shark-netted swimming area.

The volunteer-run **Kalkari Discovery Centre** (☑02-9472 9300; Ku-ring-gai Chase Rd; ◷9am-5pm) FREE, 2.5km from the Mt Colah entrance, has displays on local fauna and Aboriginal culture. The road descends from Kalkari to the **Bobbin Inn Visitor Centre** (☑02-9472 8949; Bobbin Head; ◷10am-4pm), where there's a cafe and a mangrove boardwalk.

Elevated sections of the park offer glorious water views over Cowan Creek, Broken Bay and Pittwater. Best of all is **West Head**, which has views across Pittwater to Barrenjoey Lighthouse. Normally elusive, lyrebirds are conspicuous here during their mating season (May to July).

West Head Rd also gives access to Aboriginal engravings and handprints: from the Resolute picnic area it's 100m to some faint ochre handprints at Red Hands Cave. Another 500m along Resolute Track is an engraving site. A 3km loop from here takes in Resolute Beach and another engraving site. The Basin Track makes an easy stroll to some well-preserved engravings; the Echidna Track (off West Head Rd) has boardwalk access to engravings.

🏃 Activities

Diving & Snorkelling

Sydney's best shore dives are at Gordons Bay and Shark Point, Clovelly, and Ship Rock, Cronulla. Other destinations include North Bondi, Camp Cove and Bare Island. Popular boat-dive sites are Wedding Cake Island off Coogee, Sydney Heads, and off Royal National Park.

Dive Centre Manly DIVING

(Map p77; ☑02-9977 4355; www.divesydney.com.au; 10 Belgrave St; ◷9am-6pm; 🚌Manly) A two-day learn-to-dive PADI adventure costs $445, guided shore dives cost $95/125 for one/two dives (run daily), and boat dives cost $175 (Friday to Sunday).

Dive Centre Bondi DIVING

(Map p73; ☑02-9369 3855; www.divebondi.com.au; 198 Bondi Rd; ◷9am-6pm Mon-Fri, 7.30am-6pm Sat & Sun; 🚌380) Offers PADI Discover Scuba Diving courses and boat dives (both $225).

Sailing

James Craig Square-Rig Sailing Adventure SAILING

(Map p60; ☑02-9298 3888; www.shf.org.au; Wharf 7, Pyrmont; adult/child $150/50; 🚌Pyrmont Bay) The *James Craig* is a hulking three-masted iron barque built in England in 1874 that's normally moored at the Maritime Museum. It sails out beyond the heads roughly twice monthly (bookings essential). Trips include morning tea, lunch and a sea shanty or three.

Sailing Sydney SAILING

(Map p60; ☑02-9660 9133; www.sailingsydney.net; Wharf 9, King St Wharf; 🚇Wynyard) Sail around the harbour on an America's Cup yacht (2½ hours, adult/child $129/99); on Wednesday the yacht runs in a Sydney Harbour Yacht Club fleet race (three hours, $169/139 per adult/child).

EastSail SAILING

(Map p52; ☑02-9327 1166; www.eastsail.com.au; d'Albora Marina, New Beach Rd, Rushcutters Bay; 🚌Edgecliff) Nobody ever said that yachting was a cheap sport. Take the two-day Start Yachting course for $575, or arrange a charter.

Sydney by Sail SAILING

(Map p60; ☑02-9280 1110; www.sydneybysail.com; 2 Murray St, Darling Harbour; 🚌Pyrmont Bay) Departing daily from outside the Maritime Museum, Sydney by Sail offers three-hour harbour cruises (adult/child $195/85), six-hour coastal sailing adventures (adult/child $195/120) and weekend-long introductory sailing courses ($595).

Surfing

On the south side, get tubed at Bondi, Tamarama, Coogee, Maroubra and Cronulla. The North Shore is home to a dozen gnarly surf beaches between Manly and Palm Beach, including Curl Curl, Dee Why, Narrabeen, Mona Vale and Newport.

Bondi

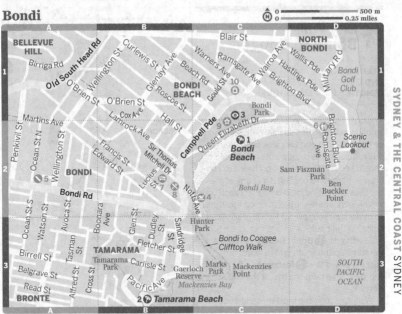

Bondi

Let's Go Surfing   SURFING

(Map p73; ☑02-9365 1800; www.letsgosurfing.
com.au; 128 Ramsgate Ave; board and wetsuit
hire 1hr/2hr/day/week $25/30/50/150; ☐380)
You can hire gear or learn to surf with this
well-established school at North Bondi. It
caters to practically everyone, with classes
for grommets aged seven to 16 (1½ hours
$49) and adults (two hours $89, women-
only classes available); private tuition is also
available (1½ hours $175). North Bondi is a
great beach for learners.

Manly Surf School   SURFING

(Map p52; ☑02-9977 6977; www.manlysurfschool.
com; North Steyne Surf Club; ☻Manly) Offers
two-hour group surf lessons year-round
(adult/child $70/55), as well as private tui-
tion. Also runs surf safaris up to the Northern Beaches, including two lessons, lunch,
gear and city pick-ups ($99).

Swimming

There are 100-plus public swimming pools
in Sydney, and many beaches have protected
rock pools. Harbour beaches offer sheltered
and shark-netted swimming, but nothing
beats the ocean waves. Always swim within

City Walk
Bondi to Coogee

START BONDI BEACH
END COOGEE BEACH
LENGTH 6KM; TWO TO THREE HOURS

Arguably Sydney's most famous, most popular and best walk, this coastal path shouldn't be missed. Both ends are well connected to bus routes, as are most points in between should you feel too hot and bothered to continue – although a cooling dip at any of the beaches en route should cure that (pack your swimmers). There's little shade on this track, so make sure you dive into a tub of sunscreen before setting out.

Starting at ❶**Bondi Beach** (p64) take the stairs up the south end to Notts Ave, passing above the ❷**Icebergs** (p75) pool complex. Step onto the trail at the end of Notts Ave.

Walking south, the blustery sandstone cliffs and grinding Pacific Ocean couldn't be more spectacular (watch for dolphins, whales and surfers). Small but perfectly formed ❸**Tamarama** (p68) has a deep reach of sand, totally disproportionate to its width.

Descend from the cliff tops onto ❹**Bronte Beach** (p68) and take a dip or hit a beachy cafe for a coffee, a chunky lunch or a quick snack. Cross the sand and pick up the path on the other side.

Some famous Australians are among the subterranean denizens of the amazing cliff-edge ❺**Waverley Cemetery**. On a clear day this is a prime vantage point for whale watchers.

Duck into the sunbaked Clovelly Bowling Club for a beer or a game of bowls, then breeze past the cockatoos and canoodling lovers in ❻**Burrows Park** to sheltered ❼**Clovelly Beach** (p68), a fave with families.

Follow the footpath up through the car park, along Cliffbrook Pde, then down the steps to the upturned dinghies lining ❽**Gordons Bay** (p68), one of Sydney's best shore-dive spots.

The trail continues past ❾**Dolphin Point** then lands you smack-bang on glorious ❿**Coogee Beach** (p68).

the flagged lifeguard-patrolled areas and never underestimate the surf.

North Sydney Olympic Pool
SWIMMING

(Map p52; ☑ 02-9955 2309; www.northsydney.nsw.gov.au; 4 Alfred St South; adult/child $7.10/3.50; ☉ 5.30am-9pm Mon-Fri, 7am-7pm Sat & Sun; ☒ Milsons Point/Luna Park) Next to Luna Park and with extraordinary harbour views. Facilities include a 50m outdoor pool, a 25m indoor pool, a gym ($19 with pool and sauna access), a crèche ($4.20 per hour) and a cafe.

Wylie's Baths
SWIMMING

(Map p52; ☑ 02-9665 2838; www.wylies.com.au; Neptune St; adult/child $4.50/1; ☉ 7am-7pm Oct-Mar, to 5pm Apr-Sep) On the rocky coast south of Coogee Beach, this superb seawater pool (1907) is more targeted to swimmers than splashabouts. After your swim, take a yoga class ($15), enjoy a massage or have a coffee at the kiosk, which has magnificent ocean views.

Andrew (Boy) Charlton Pool
SWIMMING

(Map p52; ☑ 02-9358 6686; www.abcpool.org; 1c Mrs Macquaries Rd; adult/child $6/4.50; ☉ 6am-7pm mid-Sep–Apr; ☒ Martin Pl) Sydney's best saltwater pool – smack bang next to the harbour – is a magnet for water-loving gays, straights, parents and fashionistas. Serious lap swimmers rule the pool, so maintain your lane if you're not so serious.

Dawn Fraser Baths
SWIMMING

(Map p52; ☑ 02-9555 1903; www.lpac.nsw.gov.au/Dawn-Fraser-Baths/; Elkington Park, Fitzroy Ave; adult/child $4.60/$3.20; ☉ 7.15am-6.30pm Oct-Apr; ☒ Balmain West) This late-Victorian seawater pool (1884) offers a small beach at low tide and yoga classes ($14) during summer.

Bondi Icebergs Swimming Club
SWIMMING

(Map p73; ☑ 02-9130 4804; www.icebergs.com.au; 1 Notts Ave; adult/child $5.50/3.50; ☉ 6.30am-6.30pm Fri-Wed) The city's most famous pool commands the best view in Bondi and has a cute little cafe.

Other Activities

Natural Wanders
KAYAKING

(Map p52; ☑ 0427 225 072; www.kayaksydney.com; tours $65-150) Offers exhilarating morning tours around the Harbour Bridge, Lavender Bay, Balmain and Birchgrove.

Centennial Parklands Equestrian Centre
HORSE RIDING

(Map p70; ☑ 02-9332 2809; www.cpequestrian.com.au; 114-120 Lang Rd, Centennial Park; escorted park rides from $70; ☒ 372-374 & 391-397) Take a one-hour, 3.6km horse ride around tree-lined Centennial Park, Sydney's favourite urban green space. Five stables within the centre conduct park rides – check the website for details.

☞ Tours

Most tours can be booked at the Sydney Visitor Centres.

Bike Buffs
CYCLING TOUR

(☑ 0414 960 332; www.bikebuffs.com.au; adult/child $95/70) Offers daily four-hour, two-wheeled tours around the harbourside sights (including jaunts over the Harbour Bridge). It also hires bikes (per half-day/day/week $35/60/295).

Bonza Bike Tours
CYCLING TOUR

(Map p56; ☑ 02-9247 8800; www.bonzabiketours.com; 30 Harrington St; ☒ Circular Quay) These bike boffins run a 2½-hour Sydney Highlights tour (adult/child $99/79) and a four-hour Sydney Classic tour (adult/child $119/99). Other tours tackle the Harbour Bridge and Manly.

Sydney Architecture Walks
WALKING TOUR, CYCLING TOUR

(Map p56; ☑ 0403 888 390; www.sydneyarchitecture.org; adult/concession walk $35/25, cycle $120/110) These bright young archi-buffs run a five-hour cycling tour and five themed two-hour walking tours (The City; Utzon & the Sydney Opera House; Harbourings; Art, Place & Landscape; Modern Sydney).

I'm Free
WALKING TOUR

(Map p56; www.imfree.com.au) **FREE** These tours are nominally free but in reality are run by enthusiastic young guides for tips. There's a three-hour tour of the city departing from the anchor beside Sydney Town Hall at 10.30am and 2.30pm, and a 1½-hour tour of the Rocks departing from Cadman's Cottage at 6pm. No bookings taken – just show up and look for the guide in a bright green T-shirt.

Peek Tours
WALKING TOUR

(Map p56; ☑ 0420 244 756; www.peektours.com.au; ☉ 10.30am & 2.30pm; ☒ Circular Quay) **FREE** Gather outside the Customs House to join a 'free' three-hour walking tour; look for the red T-shirt. The guides work for tips, so pay what you think is a fair rate.

BridgeClimb
WALKING TOUR

(Map p56; ☑ 02-8274 7777; www.bridgeclimb.com; 3 Cumberland St; adult $198-318, child $148-208;

Circular Quay) Don a headset, a safety cord and a dandy grey jumpsuit and you'll be ready to embark on an exhilarating climb to the top of Sydney's famous Harbour Bridge.

Real Sydney Tours   BUS TOUR
(0412 876 180; www.realsydneytours.com.au; 1-3 passengers from $465, additional passengers from $135) Private minibus tours around Sydney or to further-flung destinations such as the Blue Mountains or the Hunter Valley.

EcoTreasures   CULTURAL TOUR, SNORKELLING
(0415 121 648; www.ecotreasures.com.au) Small group tours include Manly Snorkel Walk & Talk (90 minutes; adult/child $55/35) and longer excursions to the Northern Beaches and Ku-ring-gai Chase National Park, including Aboriginal Heritage Tours lead by Indigenous guides.

Captain Cook Cruises   CRUISE
(Map p56; 02-9206 1111; www.captaincook.com.au) As well as ritzy lunch and dinner cruises, this crew offers the aquatic version of a hop-on/hop-off bus tour, stopping at Watsons Bay, Taronga Zoo, Circular Quay, Luna Park and Darling Harbour.

🎉 Festivals & Events

Sydney Festival   ARTS
(www.sydneyfestival.org.au) Sydney's premier arts and culture festival features three weeks of music, theatre and visual art every January.

Big Day Out   MUSIC
(www.bigdayout.com) The biggest event on the alt-rock calendar, this touring festival hits Sydney Olympic Park on Australia Day (26 January).

Chinese New Year   CULTURE
(www.sydneychinesenewyear.com) Three-week Chinatown-based celebration featuring food, fireworks, dragon dancers and dragon-boat races. Actual dates vary according to the phases of the moon, but it's in January or February.

Sydney Gay & Lesbian Mardi Gras   GAY & LESBIAN
(www.mardigras.org.au) A three-week festival culminating in a massive parade and party on the first Saturday in March.

Biennale of Sydney   CULTURE
(www.biennaleofsydney.com.au) High-profile festival of art and ideas held between March and June in even-numbered years.

Royal Easter Show   AGRICULTURE
(www.eastershow.com.au) Twelve-day agricultural show and funfair at Sydney Olympic Park.

Vivid Sydney   CULTURE
(www.vividsydney.com) A three-week festival of 'light, music and ideas' brightens up Sydney during May and June with light installations and multicoloured buildings.

National Rugby League Grand Final   SPORT
(www.nrl.com) The two teams left standing in the National Rugby League (NRL) meet to decide who's best on the Sunday of the October long weekend.

Tropfest   FILM
(www.tropfest.com) The world's largest short-film festival is enjoyed from picnic blankets in Centennial Park in December.

Sydney to Hobart Yacht Race   SPORT
(www.rolexsydneyhobart.com) On 26 December Sydney Harbour is a sight to behold as hundreds of boats crowd its waters to farewell the yachts competing in this gruelling race.

New Year's Eve   FIREWORKS
(www.sydneynewyearseve.com) The biggest party of the year, with a flamboyant firework display on the harbour.

🛏 Sleeping

Sydney offers a huge quantity and variety of accommodation, with solid options in every price range. Even so, the supply shrivels up under the summer sun, particularly around weekends and big events. All but the smallest hotels vary their prices from day to day, depending on occupancy. Friday and Saturday tend to be the most expensive nights, while Sunday is usually the cheapest. Rates skyrocket over the busy Christmas–New Year period.

🏨 The Rocks & Circular Quay

⭐ **Sydney Harbour YHA**   HOSTEL **$**
(Map p56; 02-8272 0900; www.yha.com.au; 110 Cumberland St; dm/r from $44/148; ❄ @ ⛆; Circular Quay) Any qualms about the higher-than-usual prices will be shelved the moment you head up to the roof terrace of this custom-built YHA and see Circular Quay laid out before you. All of the rooms, including the dorms, have private bathrooms.

Manly

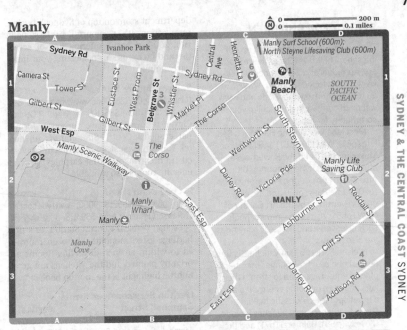

N 0 — 200 m
0 — 0.1 miles

SYDNEY & THE CENTRAL COAST SYDNEY

Lord Nelson Brewery Hotel PUB **$$**
(Map p56; ☏02-9251 4044; www.lordnelsonbrew-ery.com; 19 Kent St; r from $180; ❄️🛜; 🚇Circular Quay) Pulling beers since 1841, this boutique sandstone pub has eight upstairs rooms with exposed stone walls and dormer windows. Most are spacious and have en suites, but there are also cheaper, smaller rooms with shared facilities.

Bed & Breakfast Sydney Harbour B&B **$$**
(Map p56; ☏02-9247 1130; www.bbsydneyhar-bour.com.au; 142 Cumberland St; r with/without bathroom $250/165; ❄️🛜; 🚇Circular Quay) This well-located century-old guesthouse manages to squeeze in some Opera House views, despite being hemmed in by high-rise hotels. The rooms vary wildly in size and facilities; some are suitable for family groups.

Park Hyatt HOTEL **$$$**
(Map p56; ☏02-9256 1234; www.sydney.park.hy-att.com; 7 Hickson Rd; r from $795; 🅿️❄️@🛜🏊; 🚇Circular Quay) Luxury meets location at Sydney's poshest hotel, facing the Opera House across Circular Quay. A recent renovation has freshened up the rooms. The service levels and facilities are second to none.

Manly

Top Sights
1 Manly Beach..C1

Sights
2 Manly Sea Life Sanctuary....................A2

Activities, Courses & Tours
3 Dive Centre Manly................................B1

Sleeping
4 101 Addison Road................................D3
5 Quest Manly...B2

Drinking & Nightlife
6 Hotel Steyne...C1

Pullman Quay Grand Sydney Harbour APARTMENT **$$$**
(Map p56; ☏02-9256 4000; www.pullmanhotels.com; 61 Macquarie St; apt from $472; 🅿️❄️🛜; 🚇Circular Quay) With the Opera House as its neighbour, the building dimissively referred to as 'the Toaster' has a scorching-hot location – so much so that it might burn a hole right through your wallet. The well-designed contemporary apartments within have balconies, bath tubs and bedrooms angled for the views.

SYDNEY FOR CHILDREN

Organised kids activities ramp up during school holidays (December to January, April, July and September). Check www.sydneyforkids.com.au, www.au.timeout.com/sydney/kids and www.webchild.com.au/sydneyschild/your-community for listings.

Most kids love Darling Harbour's Sea Life (p61), Wild Life (p61) and Maritime Museum (p61), and the Powerhouse Museum (p62) in neighbouring Ultimo. Also worth considering are Taronga Zoo (p70), Luna Park (p69) and the children's events run by the Art Gallery of NSW (p55). Visits to swimming pools, surfing lessons, and horse or pony rides are also popular.

Nielsen Park (p69) in Vaucluse is the perfect choice if the younger members of your entourage need to stretch their legs and burn up some energy. It's also a great spot for sandcastle building. Other toddler-friendly beaches include Clovelly (p68), Balmoral (p71) and the pool at North Bondi (p64).

Langham HOTEL $$$
(Map p56; ✆02-8248 5200; www.sydney.langham-hotels.com; 89-113 Kent St; r from $350; P ❋ @ ❋; ⓡWynyard) At the time of writing, the luxurious Observatory Hotel had only recently been subsumed into the Langham group. By the time you're reading this the rooms are likely to have been freshened up, although we'll be surprised if they alter the fabulous indoor pool.

Sir Stamford HOTEL $$$
(Map p56; ✆02-9252 4600; www.stamford.com.au; 93 Macquarie St; r from $365; P ❋ ❋ ❋; ⓡCircular Quay) Going for a stiff-upper-lip, old-world ambience, Sir Stamford leaves a grand first impression with its red-carpet entry, waist-coated staff, glittering chandeliers and gilt-framed portraits. The rooms themselves are a little dated, but comfortable nonetheless.

🏠 City Centre

Wake Up! HOSTEL $
(Map p65; ✆02-9288 7888; www.wakeup.com.au; 509 Pitt St; dm $36-42, s $98, d with/without bathroom $128/108; ❋@❋; ⓡCentral) Flash-packers sleep soundly in this converted 1900

department store on top of Sydney's busiest intersection. It's a colourful, professionally run, 250-bed hostel offering lots of activities and no excuse for neglecting your inner party animal.

Railway Square YHA HOSTEL $
(Map p65; ✆02-9281 9666; www.yha.com.au; 8-10 Lee St; dm/r from $36/109; @❋❋; ⓡCentral) Clever renovations have turned a former parcel shed at Central Station into a hip hostel. You can even sleep in dorms in converted train carriages (bring earplugs). Private en-suite rooms also available.

Sydney Central YHA HOSTEL $
(Map p65; ✆02-9218 9000; www.yha.com.au; 11 Rawson Pl; dm/r from $39/118; P ❋@❋❋; ⓡCentral) ✦ Near Central Station, this 1913 heritage-listed monolith has been renovated to within an inch of its life. Rooms are brightly painted and the kitchens are great, but the highlight is the rooftop pool.

Meriton Serviced Apartments Campbell Street APARTMENT $$
(Map p59; ✆02-9009 7000; www.staymsa.com/campbell; 6 Campbell St; apt from $172; ❋❋❋; ⓡCentral) Forget its most famous project, Wembley Stadium, Meriton is known in Sydney as the builder of swanky but somewhat soulless apartment complexes. The newest and best, the Campbell St incarnation offers roomy studio and one-bedroom units with plenty of mod cons (including laundry facilities) but no views to speak of.

Meriton Serviced Apartments Kent Street APARTMENT $$
(Map p59; ✆02-8263 5500; www.staymsa.com/kent; 528 Kent St; apt from $195; ❋❋❋; ⓡTown Hall) Each of the studio to three-bedroom apartments in this modern tower has laundry facilities and a full kitchen complete with a dishwasher. Not that you'll want to cook, with Chinatown at your feet.

Hyde Park Inn HOTEL $$
(Map p59; ✆02-9264 6001; www.hydeparkinn.com.au; 271 Elizabeth St; r from $171; P ❋@❋; ⓡMuseum) Right on the park, this relaxed place offers studio rooms with kitchenettes, deluxe rooms with balconies and full kitchens, and some two-bedroom apartments. All have flat-screen TVs with cable access.

Meriton Serviced Apartments Pitt Street APARTMENT $$
(Map p56; ✆02-8263 7400; www.staymsa.com/pitt; 329 Pitt St; apt from $185; P ❋❋❋; ⓡTown

Hall) This huge tower (42 floors above ground) offers Smeg appliances and spectacular views. BYO soul.

QT Sydney
BOUTIQUE HOTEL $$$

(Map p56; ✐02-8262 0000; www.qtsydney. au; 49 Market St; r from $380; ❋❂; ✦St James) Nothing's being kept on the QT at this new boutique hotel. The theatrical decor and gregarious staff perfectly suit the location in the historic State Theatre buildings, and quirky touches such as the DIY martini kit in every room deserve applause.

Radisson Blu Plaza
HOTEL $$$

(Map p56; ✐02-8214 0000; www.radissonblu.com/ plazahotel-sydney; 27 O'Connell St; r from $302; P❋@❂; ✦Martin Pl) Would-be Clark Kents will feel right at home in this wedge-shaped sandstone building, built for the hardened hacks of the *Sydney Morning Herald* in the 1920s. The rooms are spacious, if a little generic, with marble bathrooms and all the typical big-hotel comforts.

Adina Apartment Hotel
Sydney Harbourside
APARTMENT $$$

(Map p60; ✐02-9249 7000; www.adinahotels.com. au; 55 Shelley St; apt from $305; P❋❂❂; ❂Darling Harbour) A newish low-rise development just off King St Wharf where all apartments but the studios have full kitchens, laundry facilities and balconies. There is also a pool, a gym and a sauna.

Surry Hills

Bounce
HOSTEL $

(Map p65; ✐02-9281 2222; www.bouncehotel.com. au; 28 Chalmers St; dm/r from $37/149; ❋@❂; ✦Central) ✿ Bounce positions itself 'where budget and boutique meet', and we're pleased to concur. All dorms and rooms are air-conditioned, female-only dorms have private bathrooms, beds have inner-spring mattresses and bathrooms are sleek. Chuck another prawn on the roof terrace's barbie and soak up those skyline views.

Big Hostel
HOSTEL $

(Map p59; ✐02-9281 6030; www.bighostel.com; 212 Elizabeth St; dm $30-34, s/d $85/110; ❋@❂; ✦Central) Mr Big has snazzy communal areas, clean bathrooms and a cool rooftop terrace. Elizabeth St's dark hollows aren't Sydney's most salubrious spaces, but Central Station is just across the road.

Hotel Stellar
HOTEL $$

(Map p59; ✐02-9264 9754; www.hotelstellar. com; 4 Wentworth Ave; r from $169; P❋@❂; ✦Museum) It may now be a Best Western, but this converted Victorian office building has a boutique feel and plenty of character. Rooms have recently been freshened up and they all have kitchenettes.

★ Adge Apartment Hotel
APARTMENT $$$

(Map p66; ✐02-8093 9888; www.adgehotel.com. au; 222 Riley St; apt from $374; ❋❂; ✦Museum)

WORTH A TRIP

HAWKESBURY RIVER

Less than an hour from Sydney, the tranquil Hawkesbury River flows past honeycomb-coloured cliffs, historic townships and riverside hamlets into bays and inlets and between a series of national parks, including Ku-ring-gai Chase and Brisbane Water.

The **Riverboat Postman** (✐0400 600 111, 02-9985 9900; www.riverboatpostman. com.au; Brooklyn Public Wharf, Dangar Rd; adult/child/senior $50/15/44; ⏱10am Mon-Fri), Australia's last operating mail boat, departs from Brooklyn Wharf and chugs 40km up the Lower Hawkesbury as far as Marlow, returning to Brooklyn at 1.15pm. Senior citizens form the bulk of the passenger list, drawn by the views, morning tea and ploughman's lunch (all inclusive). Regular trains run from Sydney's Central Station to Brooklyn's Hawkesbury River Station (one way adult/child $6.80/3.40, one hour).

Upstream from Brooklyn, a narrow forested waterway diverts from the Hawkesbury and peters down to the chilled-out river town of **Berowra Waters**, where a handful of businesses, boat sheds and residences cluster around the free, 24-hour ferry across Berowra Creek.

Even more remote, the riverside hamlet of **Wisemans Ferry** is most easily accessed by river but can be reached by a pretty road that winds along the north bank of the river from the Central Coast, through Dharug National Park. Largely unsealed but photogenic roads run north from Wisemans Ferry to tiny **St Albans**.

Providing a clever hipster-friendly boutique twist on the ubiquitous apartment hotel, the Adge offers 12 idiosyncratic but extremely comfortable two-bedroom apartments, all bedecked with garishly striped carpets, espresso machines and colourful retro fridges.

Adina Apartment Hotel Sydney, Crown Street APARTMENT **$$$**
(Map p65; ☑ 02-8302 1000; www.adinahotels.com. au; 359 Crown St; apt from $250; P☀@☎☲; ☒Central) As one of the main pastimes in Surry Hills is eating out, you may find the well-equipped kitchenette of your slick, spacious apartment doesn't get a lot of use – the Adina building alone is home to three exalted eateries. The gym, sauna and leafy pool area are popular over Mardi Gras.

Darlinghurst

Manor House BOUTIQUE HOTEL **$$**
(Map p66; ☑ 02-9380 6633; www.manorhouse. com.au; 86 Flinders St; r $145-250, ste $215-230; P☀☎☲; ☒Central) Sashay from Taylor Sq into this time-tripping 1850s mansion, complete with extravagant chandeliers, moulded ceilings, Victorian tiling and fountains tinkling in the garden. Even an ugly green carpet and dated bathrooms don't detract from the character. It's filled to the gills around Mardi Gras time.

Medusa BOUTIQUE HOTEL **$$$**
(Map p66; ☑ 02-9331 1000; www.medusa.com.au; 267 Darlinghurst Rd; r from $215; ☀@☎; ☒Kings Cross) Medusa's dusky pink exterior hints at the luscious decor inside, where small colour-saturated rooms with large beds open onto a courtyard with a water feature. If your hair turns into snakes, Medusa is pet-friendly.

Woolloomooloo, Kings Cross & Potts Point

Blue Parrot HOSTEL **$**
(Map p66; ☑ 02-9356 4888; www.blueparrot.com. au; 87 Macleay St; dm $35-42; @☎; ☒Kings Cross) Polly want a cracker, little hostel? Behind the shocking blue-and-mustard-painted bricks is a well-maintained, social little place with a lazy courtyard strung with hammocks. There are no private rooms, just dorms sleeping between four and 10 people.

Eva's Backpackers HOSTEL **$**
(Map p66; ☑ 02-9358 2185; www.evasbackpackers.com.au; 6-8 Orwell St; dm/r from $32/85; ☀☎; ☒Kings Cross) Eva's distinguishes itself as one of Sydney's cleanest hostels. Dorms are of a reasonable size and have lockers; a few have private bathrooms and air-conditioning. Additional drawcards include free breakfast and wi-fi, and a fab rooftop terrace.

Jackaroo HOSTEL **$**
(Map p66; ☑ 02-9332 2244; www.jackaroohostel. com; 107-109 Darlinghurst Rd; dm $33-35, r with/ without bathroom $90/80; @☎; ☒Kings Cross) Jackaroo passes muster as the least trashy place on Sydney's most trashy strip. Try to nab a rear-facing room, but pack earplugs regardless. The vibe is bright, bustling and (extremely) youthful.

Hotel 59 B&B **$$**
(Map p66; ☑ 02-9360 5900; www.hotel59.com.au; 59 Bayswater Rd; s $99, d $130-140; ☀☎; ☒Kings Cross) Hotel 59 is good bang for your buck, with nouveau-Med rooms and smiley staff. The cafe downstairs does whopping cooked breakfasts (included in the price) for those barbarous Kings Cross hangovers. Two-night minimum.

Victoria Court Hotel B&B **$$**
(Map p66; ☑ 02-9357 3200; www.victoriacourt. com.au; 122 Victoria St; r from $150; ☀☎; ☒Kings Cross) Chintzy charm reigns supreme at this well-run B&B, which has 25 rooms in two three-storey 1881 brick terrace houses. The more expensive rooms are larger and have balconies.

Simpsons of Potts Point BOUTIQUE HOTEL **$$$**
(Map p66; ☑ 02-9356 2199; www.simpsons hotel.com; 8 Challis Ave; r from $235; P☀@☎; ☒Kings Cross) An 1892 red-brick villa at the quiet end of a busy cafe strip, the perennially popular Simpsons looks to yesteryear for decorative flourishes. Rooms are comfortable and impeccably clean.

Paddington & Woollahra

Kathryn's on Queen B&B **$$**
(Map p70; ☑ 02-9327 4535; www.kathryns.com. au; 20 Queen St; r $180-260; ☀; ☒380) This grandiose 1888 Victorian terrace at the top end of Woollahra's gilded mile offers two rooms dotted with antiques and tastefully decorated in cream and white. Choose between the en-suite attic room or the 1st-floor room with a balcony overlooking the street.

(Continued on page 89)

KIMBERLEY COOLE / GETTY IMAGES © ARCHITECT: JØRN UTZON

This Is Sydney

The shimmering harbour may be the city's most famous asset, but Sydney's glorious beaches and sybaritic nightlife are equally alluring. This is a destination with a perfect balance of outdoor and indoor, natural and contrived – one that miraculously manages to be even more than the sum of its magnificent parts.

Contents

Above Sydney Opera House (p54)

S. GREG PANOSIAN / GETTY IMAGES ©

1. Sydney Harbour Bridge (p51) **2.** Luna Park (p69)
3. Sydney Harbour ferry

Sydney Harbour

It's called the Harbour City for good reason. Few places on earth are as defined by their geographical form as Sydney, and even fewer incorporate such a spectacular water feature.

Visitors have been writing odes to the harbour's beauty ever since the First Fleet landed here on 26 January 1788. Few have done it justice, though. After all, how can any writing match the exultation of a ferry trip across shimmering blue waters or the satisfaction of an afternoon spent lazing in a sheltered sandy cove?

Everything here revolves around the water – suburbs, recreation, traffic, even the collective consciousness.

At the heart of the city is Circular Quay, from where the city's famous flotilla of green-and-yellow ferries do five-minute dashes across to Milsons Point and Kirribilli, speedy sails to the Middle Harbour and majestic processions past the Opera House, Fort Denison and the Heads to the popular day-tripper destination of Manly.

To the east of Circular Quay, a genteel ribbon of suburbs unfurls, characterised by mansions, money and conservative mindsets. Harking west are former working-class neighbourhoods such as Balmain and Birchgrove that have been reinvented as arty residential enclaves.

Across the iconic Sydney Harbour Bridge is the somewhat stolid North Shore, residential location of choice for the city's conservative middle classes, whose leafy villas stretch from Neutral Bay to Manly. Traffic snarls are the norm here, as is the aspiration to own a yacht for weekend jaunts on the harbour.

An altogether different Sydney is found to the south, where a ring of trendy inner-city neighbourhoods surround the central business district and give the harbour a buzzing urban edge.

Sydney Harbour

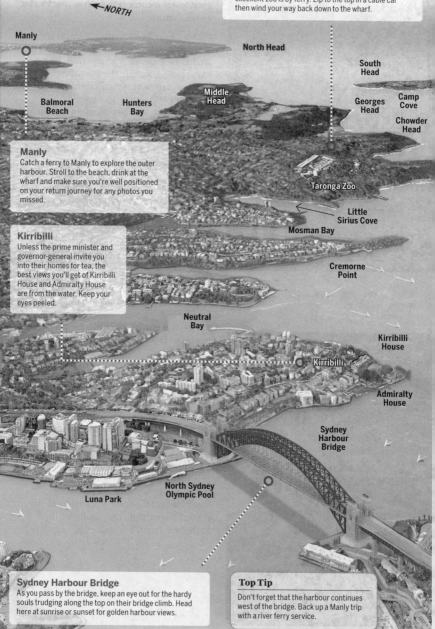

← NORTH

Manly

North Head

South Head

Balmoral Beach

Hunters Bay

Middle Head

Georges Head

Camp Cove

Chowder Head

Taronga Zoo
Even if you've hired a car, the best way to reach this excellent zoo is by ferry. Zip to the top in a cable car then wind your way back down to the wharf.

Taronga Zoo

Manly
Catch a ferry to Manly to explore the outer harbour. Stroll to the beach, drink at the wharf and make sure you're well positioned on your return journey for any photos you missed.

Little Sirius Cove

Mosman Bay

Cremorne Point

Kirribilli
Unless the prime minister and governor-general invite you into their homes for tea, the best views you'll get of Kirribilli House and Admiralty House are from the water. Keep your eyes peeled.

Neutral Bay

Kirribilli House

Kirribilli

Admiralty House

Sydney Harbour Bridge

Luna Park

North Sydney Olympic Pool

Sydney Harbour Bridge
As you pass by the bridge, keep an eye out for the hardy souls trudging along the top on their bridge climb. Head here at sunrise or sunset for golden harbour views.

Top Tip
Don't forget that the harbour continues west of the bridge. Back up a Manly trip with a river ferry service.

Watsons Bay
Imagine Watsons Bay as the isolated fishing village it once was as you pull into its sheltered wharf. Stroll around South Head for views up the harbour and over ocean-battered cliffs.

Fort Denison
Known as Pinchgut, this fortified speck was once a place of fearsome punishment. The bodies of executed convicts were left to hang here as a grisly warning to all; the local Aborigines were horrified.

PETE DRAGICEVICH ©

Ferries
Circular Quay is the hub for state-run Sydney Ferries; nine separate routes leave from here, journeying to 38 different wharves.

Vaucluse Bay

Watsons Bay

Macquarie Lighthouse

Shark Bay

Shark Island

Rose Bay

Point Piper

Bradleys Head

Double Bay

Darling Point

Clark Island

Garden Island

Naval Base

Elizabeth Bay

Fort Denison

Mrs Macquaries Point

Potts Point

Woolloomooloo Finger Wharf

Sydney Opera House

Government House

Farm Cove

Royal Botanic Gardens

Circular Quay

The Rocks

Sydney Opera House
You can clamber all over it and walk around it, but nothing beats the perspective you get as your ferry glides past the Opera House's dazzling sails. Have your camera at the ready.

Circular Quay
Circular Quay has been at the centre of Sydney life since the First Fleet dropped anchor here in 1788. Book your ferry ticket, check the indicator boards for the correct pier and get onboard.

Beaches

In Sydney, nothing beats a day at the beach. Sun, sand and surf dominate the culture for six months of every year, and locals wouldn't have it any other way.

The city's magnificent string of ocean beaches stretches north from the Royal National Park to Palm Beach, luring surfers, scenesters, swimmers and sunbathers onto their golden sands and into the powerful waves of the South Pacific Ocean.

There's none of that horrible European habit of privatising the beach here. Lay down a towel and you've claimed a personal patch of paradise for as long as you want it. Some locals enjoy a quick dip before or after work, while the lucky ones stay on the sand for the whole day – everyone makes the most of the time they have.

Ocean Beaches

Serious surfers head to Cronulla in the south; Maroubra, Bronte, Tamarama and North Bondi in the east; and Curl Curl, Narrabeen, Queenscliff, Harbord (Freshwater) and Manly on the Northern Beaches. Of these, Bronte and Manly are also popular with swimmers, joining Coogee, Clovelly, Bondi, Bilgola, Whale and Palm as regular entries on 'Best Beaches' lists. Each of these beaches has a devoted crew of regulars – families flock to Clovelly, Bronte and Whale Beach, while bronzed singles strut their stuff at Coogee and Palm Beach. The best-known beaches – Bondi and Manly – host an incongruous mix of pasty-skinned foreigners, weather-wizened surf gurus, grommets (beginner surfers) and geriatric locals who have been perfecting their body-surfing techniques for more than

1. Bondi Icebergs Swimming Club (p75) **2.** Surfers, Bondi Beach (p64)

half a century. Always crowded, these two beaches showcase the most endearing and eclectic aspects of Sydney's character, and shouldn't be missed.

Ocean Pools

Those who find surf off-putting should take advantage of Sydney's famous ocean pools. There are 40 man-made ocean pools up and down the coast, the most popular of which are Wylie's Baths, Giles Baths and the Ross Jones Memorial Pool in Coogee; the Bondi Icebergs Swimming Club; and the pool at Fairy Bower Beach in Manly.

Harbour Beaches & Pools

Lady Bay at South Head and Shark Beach at Nielsen Park in Vaucluse are the best of the harbour beaches (note that Lady Bay is a nude beach). There are netted swimming enclosures or pools at Cremorne Point on the North Shore and Balmoral Beach on the Middle Harbour.

BEACHES BY NEIGHBOURHOOD

➡ **Sydney Harbour** Lots of hidden coves; the best are near the Heads.

➡ **Bondi to Coogee** High cliffs frame a string of surf beaches, and an excellent coffee is always a short walk away.

➡ **Northern Beaches** A steady succession of spectacular surf beaches stretching for nearly 30km.

New Year's Eve fireworks (p76), Sydney Harbour

After Dark

In the early years of the colony, enjoying a beaker or two of rum was the only form of entertainment available to Sydneysiders. Today, the situation couldn't be more different.

The festival calendar is a good case in point. The year kicks off with a frenzy of fireworks over Circular Quay and doesn't calm down for months. No sooner has the Sydney Festival, with its associated openings and events, finished than the biggest party of all kicks off: the famous Sydney Gay & Lesbian Mardi Gras. Winter brings fashion, literature, film and art to the fore, with opening nights, cocktail parties and literary soirées

dominating everyone's datebooks. And then there's a slight hiatus until summer works its magic and everyone takes to the city's streets to make the most of daylight savings' long days and blissfully balmy nights.

Whatever your inclination, Sydney will indulge it. You can attend the theatre or the opera, drink in a beer garden or rooftop bar, take in a jazz performance or a drag show, watch films under the stars or club late into the night.

Put simply, this is a town that well and truly lives up to its hype when it comes to partying. So make your plans, dress sexy and get ready to paint the town red. You'll be in excellent company when you do.

(Continued from page 80)

Arts
HOTEL **$$**

(Map p66; ☎02-9361 0211; www.artshotel.com.au; 21 Oxford St; r from $174; **P ✱ @ 🛜 ☰**; ☐380) Popular with gay travellers, this 64-room hotel has simple rooms in a handy location on the Paddington–Darlinghurst border. There's heavy-duty glazing on the Oxford St frontage, while the rear rooms face a quiet lane. The brick-paved courtyard has a solar-heated pool.

🛏 Eastern Beaches

Coogee Beach House
HOSTEL **$**

(Map p52; ☎02-9665 1162; www.coogeebeachhouse.com; 171 Arden St; dm/r $38/95; **@ 🛜**;

☐ 372-374) Our favourite of the beach hostels has four- to six-bed dorms and private rooms (all with shared bathrooms), a barbecue terrace and a homely living room for rainy days. Freebies include a simple breakfast and use of bodyboards and surfboards.

Bondi Beach House
GUESTHOUSE **$$**

(Map p73; ☎0417 336 444; www.bondibeachhouse.com.au; 28 Sir Thomas Mitchell Rd; s $110-135, d $160-280, ste $300; **✱ 🛜**; ☐380) Tucked away in a tranquil pocket near the beach, this charming place offers a real home-away-from-home atmosphere. Six of the nine rooms have private bathrooms. DIY breakfast supplies are provided.

GAY & LESBIAN SYDNEY

Gays and lesbians have migrated to Oz's Emerald City from all over Australia, New Zealand and the world, adding to a community that is visible, vocal and an integral part of the city's social fabric. Locals will assure you that things aren't as exciting as they once were, but Sydney is still indisputably one of the world's great queer cities.

Darlinghurst and Newtown have traditionally been the gayest neighbourhoods, although all of the inner suburbs have a higher than average proportion of gay and lesbian residents. Most of the gay venues are on the Darlinghurst section of Oxford St.

The biggest event on the calendar is the famous Mardi Gras (p76), which includes a three-week festival, a parade that attracts up to half a million spectators, and a vast dance party.

Free gay media includes the **Star Observer** (www.starobserver.com.au), **SX** (www.gaynewsnetwork.com.au) and **LOTL** (www.lotl.com).

Arq (Map p66; ☎02-9380 8700; www.arqsydney.com.au; 16 Flinders St; admission free-$25; ⊙9pm-late Thu-Sun; ▢Museum) If Noah had to fill his ark with groovy gay clubbers, he'd head here with a big net. This flash club has a cocktail bar, a recovery room and two dance floors with high-energy house, drag shows and a hyperactive smoke machine.

Oxford Hotel (Map p66; ☎02-8324 5200; www.theoxfordhotel.com.au; 134 Oxford St; ⊙10am-4am Sun-Thu, to 6am Fri & Sat; 🛈; ▢Museum) Over the course of 30 years and numerous facelifts the Oxford has remained the locus of beer-swilling gay blokedom.

Imperial Hotel (Map p63; www.theimperialhotel.com.au; 35 Erskineville Rd; admission free-$15; ⊙3pm-midnight Sun-Thu, to 5am Fri & Sat; ▢Erskineville) The art deco Imperial is legendary as the setting for *The Adventures of Priscilla, Queen of the Desert*. The front bar is a lively place for pool-shooting and cruising, with the action shifting to the cellar club late on the weekends. But it's in the cabaret bar that the legacy of *Priscilla* is kept alive.

Palms on Oxford (Map p66; ☎02-9357 4166; 124 Oxford St; ⊙8pm-1am Thu & Sun, to 3am Fri & Sat; ▢Museum) No one admits to coming here, but the lengthy queues prove them liars. In this underground dance bar, the heyday of Stock Aitken Waterman never ended. It may be uncool, but if you don't scream when Kylie hits the turntables you'll be the only one.

Midnight Shift (Map p66; ☎02-9358 3848; www.themidnightshift.com.au; 85 Oxford St; admission free-$10; ⊙4pm-late Mon-Fri, 2pm-late Sat & Sun; ▢Museum) The grande dame of the Oxford St gay scene, the Shift boasts two quite distinct venues. Downstairs the bar attracts an unpretentious mix of blokes, twinks and bears, and has a musical mandate ranging from top 40 to camp classics. Upstairs is a serious club (open from 10pm Friday and Saturday), with grinding beats and lavish drag productions.

Dive Hotel

BOUTIQUE HOTEL $$

(Map p52; ☑02-9665 5538; www.divehotel.
au; 234 Arden St; r from $190; ᴾ❄️📶; ♨️372-374)
Plenty of hotels don't live up to their name
('grand', 'palace' and 'central' are often less
than literal) – and thankfully neither does
this one. The 14 rooms are spacious and
come with kitchenettes. Light breakfast
included.

🛏️ Manly

101 Addison Road

B&B $$

(Map p77; ☑02-9977 6216; www.bb-manly.com; 101
Addison Rd; s/d $165/185; ᴾ📶; 🚢Manly) At the
risk of sounding like a Victorian matron, the
only word to describe this 1880 cottage on
a quiet street is 'delightful'. Two rooms are
available, but only single-group bookings
(of up to four people) are taken – meaning
you'll have free rein of the antique-strewn
accommodation, including a private lounge.

Quest Manly

APARTMENT $$$

(Map p77; ☑02-9976 4600; www.questmanly.com.
au; 54a West Esplanade; apt from $300; ᴾ❄️📶;
🚢Manly) Superbly located for all of Manly's
beachy delights as well as for a speedy es-
cape to the city (the ferry couldn't be closer),
the Quest's smart, self-contained apart-
ments are a great option. It's worth paying
extra for a harbour view.

🛏️ Other Neighbourhoods

Cockatoo Island

CAMPGROUND $

(Map p52; ☑02-8898 9774; www.cockatooisland.
gov.au; camp sites from $45, 2-bed tents from $145,
houses $595; 🚢Cockatoo Island) Catch the ferry
(20 minutes from Circular Quay) and stay
amid the convict and industrial detritus of
Cockatoo Island. You can pitch your own
tent; 'glamp' in a pre-pitched two-person tent
complete with made-up beds; or rent one of
two beautifully restored, self-contained Fed-
eration houses (sleeping 10). Ferries don't
run much past 10pm.

Lane Cove River Tourist Park

CAMPGROUND $

(☑02-9888 9133; www.lcrtp.com.au; Plassey Rd,
Macquarie Park; unpowered/powered camp sites
per 2 people $37/39, cabins from $135; ᴾ@📶🏊;
🚉North Ryde) 🌿 Have a back-to-nature expe-
rience in the heart of Sydney, staying in this
national-park camp site 14km northwest of
the city centre (but only a 15-minute walk
from North Ryde station). There are caravan
and camping sites, cabins and a pool to cool
off in when the city swelters.

Tara Guest House

B&B $$

(Map p63; ☑02-9519 4809; www.taraguesthouse.
com.au; 13 Edgeware Rd, Enmore; d with/without
bathroom $205/175; 📶; 🚉Newtown) You could
imagine Scarlett O'Hara and Rhett Butler
trading insults beneath the high ceilings of
this 1886 mansion, if it weren't for the eclectic art scattered about and the steady stream
of traffic outside (pack earplugs). Frankly,
my dears, you won't give a damn that only
one of the four bedrooms has an en suite –
that's all part of the period charm.

🍴 Eating

Sydney's cuisine celebrates the city's place
on the Pacific rim, marrying the freshest local ingredients with the flavours of Asia, the
Americas and, of course, the colonial past.
The top restaurants are properly pricey, but
eating out needn't be expensive. There are
plenty of ethnic eateries where you can grab
a cheap and tasty pizza or bowl of noodles.

🍴 The Rocks & Circular Quay

Sailors Thai Canteen

THAI $$

(Map p56; ☑02-9251 2466; www.sailorsthai.com.
au; 106 George St; mains $17-29; ⊙noon-4pm &
5.30-10pm; 🚉Circular Quay) Wedge yourself
into Sailors' long communal table and order
from the fragrant menu of Thai street-food
classics. Downstairs the vibe is more formal
and the prices higher ($65 for four courses).

★ Quay

MODERN AUSTRALIAN $$$

(Map p56; ☑02-9251 5600; www.quay.com.au;
Level 3, Overseas Passenger Terminal; 3/4 courses
$130/150; ⊙noon-2.30pm Tue-Fri, 6-10pm daily;
🚉Circular Quay) Quay is shamelessly guilty
of breaking the rule that good views make
for bad food. Sydney's top restaurant never
rests on its laurels, consistently delivering
the exquisite, adventurous cuisine that has
landed it on the prestigious World's Top 50
Restaurants list. And the view? Like dining
in a postcard.

🍴 City Centre

Din Tai Fung

CHINESE $

(Map p59; www.dintaifung.com.au; Level 1, World Sq,
644 George St; dishes $7-19; ⊙11.30am-2.30pm
& 5.30-9pm; 🚉Museum) It also does noodles
and buns, but it's the dumplings that made
this Taiwanese chain famous, delivering an
explosion of fabulously flavoursome broth
as you bite into their delicate casings. Come
early, come hungry, come prepared to share

your table. It also has stalls in the Star casino and Westfield Sydney (p99) food courts.

Mamak
MALAYSIAN $

(Map p59; www.mamak.com.au; 15 Goulburn St; mains $6-17; ⊙ 11.30am-2.30pm & 5.30-10pm Mon-Thu, to 2am Fri & Sat; ⒭ Town Hall) Get here early if you want to score a table without queuing, because this eat-and-run Malaysian joint is one of the most popular cheapies in the city. The satays are cooked over charcoal and are particularly delicious when accompanied by a flaky golden roti.

★ Mr Wong
CHINESE $$

(Map p56; ✆ 02-9240 3000; www.merivale.com.au/mrwong; 3 Bridge Lane; mains $18-38; ⊙ noon-3pm & 5.30-11pm; ⒭ Wynyard) Dumpling junkies shuffle down a dirty lane and into the bowels of an old warehouse for a taste of Mr Wong's deliciously addictive Cantonese fare. There's a dark-edged glamour to the cavernous basement dining room; despite seating for 240, there are often queues out the door.

Sepia
JAPANESE, FUSION $$$

(Map p56; ✆ 02-9283 1990; www.sepiarestaurant.com.au; 201 Sussex St; mains $56, degustation $165; ⊙ noon-3pm Fri & Sat, 6-10pm Tue-Sat; ⒭ Town Hall) There's nothing washed out or brown-tinged about Sepia's food: Martin Benn's picture-perfect creations are presented in glorious technicolour, with each taste worth a thousand words. A Japanese sensibility permeates the boundary-pushing menu.

Est.
MODERN AUSTRALIAN $$$

(Map p56; ✆ 02-9240 3000; www.merivale.com.au/est; Level 1, 252 George St; mains $58-59, 4-course dinner $150, degustation $175; ⊙ noon-2.30pm Mon-Fri, 6-10pm Mon-Sat; ⒭ Wynyard) Pressed-tin ceilings, huge columns, oversized windows and modern furniture make the interior design almost as interesting as the food. This is Sydney fine dining at its best; thick wallet and fancy threads a must. Seafood fills around half of the slots on the menu.

Tetsuya's
FRENCH, JAPANESE $$$

(Map p59; ✆ 02-9267 2900; www.tetsuyas.com; 529 Kent St; degustation $210; ⊙ noon-3pm Sat, 6-10pm Tue-Sat; ⒭ Town Hall) Down a clandestine security driveway, Tetsuya's is for those seeking a culinary journey rather than a simple stuffed belly. Settle in for 10-plus courses of French- and Japanese-inflected food from the creative genius of Japanese-born Tetsuya Wakuda. Book way ahead.

Felix
FRENCH $$$

(Map p56; ✆ 02-9240 3000; www.merivale.com/felix; 2 Ash St; mains $30-38; ⊙ noon-3pm Sun-Fri, 5.30-10.30pm daily; ⒭ Wynyard) Waiters bustle about in black ties and long aprons in this *très traditionnel* French bistro, with Parisian subway tiles on the walls and a solid list of tried-and-true classics on the menu. If you feel the urge to work off your coq au vin in *le discothèque* later, Ivy is upstairs.

Newtown

Black Star Pastry
BAKERY, CAFE $

(Map p63; www.blackstarpastry.com.au; 277 Australia St; mains $7-10; ⊙ 7am-5pm; ⒭ Newtown) Wise folks follow the black star to pay homage to excellent coffee, a large selection of sweet things and a few very good savoury things (gourmet pies and the like). There are only a couple of tables; it's more a snack-and-run or picnic-in-the-park kind of place.

Campos
CAFE $

(Map p63; ✆ 02-9516 3361; www.camposcoffee.com; 193 Missenden Rd; pastries $4; ⊙ 7am-4pm; ⒭ Macdonaldtown) Trying to squeeze into crowded Campos, king of Sydney's bean scene, can be a challenge. Bean fiends come from miles around – hat-wearing students, window-seat daydreamers and doctors on a break from the hospital – all gagging for a shot of 'Campos Superior' blend. Food is limited to tasty pastries.

Bloodwood
MODERN AUSTRALIAN $$

(Map p63; www.bloodwoodnewtown.com; 416 King St; mains $25-32; ⊙ 5-10pm Mon, Wed & Thu, noon-10pm Fri-Sun; ⒭ Newtown) Relax over a few drinks and a progression of globally inspired and beautifully constructed shared plates at this popular bar-bistro. The decor is industrial-chic and the vibe is alternative – very Newtown. It doesn't take bookings.

Surry Hills

Spice I Am
THAI $

(Map p59; www.spiceiam.com; 90 Wentworth Ave; mains $12-19; ⊙ 11.30am-3.30pm & 5.45-10pm Tue-Sun; ✈; ⒭ Central) Once the preserve of expat Thais, this little red-hot chilli pepper now has queues out the door for its fragrant, flavoursome, authentic food. It's been so successful that the owners have opened an upmarket version in **Darlinghurst** (Map p66; 296-300 Victoria St; mains $18-30; ⊙ 11.30am-3.30pm & 5.45-10.30pm; ✈; ⒭ Kings Cross).

Reuben Hills
CAFE $

(Map p65; www.reubenhills.com.au; 61 Albion St; mains $12-16; ☺7am-4pm; ▣Central) An industrial fitout and Latin American menu await at Reuben Hills, where hipsters serve fantastic coffee to media types. Alongside tasty tacos and *baleadas* (Honduran filled tortillas), the menu lists cooked breakfasts (served all day) and 'really fucking great fried chicken'.

El Loco
MEXICAN $

(Map p65; ☑02-9254 8088; www.merivale.com.au/elloco; 64 Foveaux St; mains $10-17; ☺noon-midnight Mon-Thu, to 3am Fri & Sat, to 10pm Sun; ▣Central) As much as we lament the passing of live rock at the Excelsior Hotel, we have to admit that the hip Mexican cantina that's taken over the band room is pretty darn cool. The food's tasty, inventive and, at $5 per taco, fantastic value.

Le Monde
CAFE $

(Map p65; www.lemondecafe.com.au; 83 Foveaux St; mains $9-16; ☺6.30am-4pm Mon-Fri, 7.30am-4pm Sat; ▣Central) Some of Sydney's best breakfasts are served among the demure dark wooden walls of this small streetside cafe. Top-notch coffee and a terrific selection of tea will gear you up to face the world.

Bourke Street Bakery
BAKERY, CAFE $

(Map p65; ☑02-9669 1011; www.bourkestreetbakery.com.au; 633 Bourke St; items $5-9; ☺7am-6pm; ▣355) Teensy BSB sells a tempting array of pastries, cakes, bread and sandwiches, along with sausage rolls with near-legendary status in these parts. There are a few tables inside, but on a fine day you're better off on the street.

Single Origin Roasters
CAFE $

(Map p59; ☑02-9211 0665; www.singleorigin.com.au; 60-64 Reservoir St; mains $13-17; ☺6.30am-4pm Mon-Fri; ▣Central) ✒ Unshaven graphic artists roll cigarettes at the little outdoor tables in the bricky hollows of deepest Surry Hills, while inside impassioned, bouncing-off-the-walls caffeine fiends prepare their beloved brews, along with a tasty selection of cafe fare.

MoVida
SPANISH $$

(Map p65; ☑02-8964 7642; www.movida.com.au; 50 Holt St; tapas $5-11, raciones $14-30; ☺noon-late Mon-Fri, 2pm-late Sat) A Sydney incarnation of a Melbourne legend, MoVida serves top-notch tapas and *raciones* (larger shared plates) and a great selection of Spanish wines. Book well ahead for a table or get in early for a seat by the bar.

Porteño
ARGENTINE $$

(Map p65; ☑02-8399 1440; www.porteno.com.au; 358 Cleveland St; sharing plates $12-46; ☺6-10pm Tue-Sat; ▣; ▣Central) Lamb and suckling pig are spit-roasted for eight hours before the doors open at this acclaimed and extremely hip restaurant. Bring a huge appetite and the biggest posse you can muster; the dishes are designed for sharing and it only takes bookings for five or more (smaller parties should arrive early to avoid queuing).

Bodega
TAPAS $$

(Map p65; ☑02-9212 7766; www.bodegatapas.com; 216 Commonwealth St; tapas $12-26; ☺noon-2pm Fri, 6-10pm Tue-Sat; ▣Central) Plundering the cuisines of Spain and South America, Bodega has a casual vibe, good-lookin' staff and a funky matador mural. Tapas dishes vary widely in size and price. Wash 'em down with Hispanic wine, sherry, port or beer and plenty of Latin gusto.

Bar H
CHINESE $$

(Map p59; ☑02-9280 1980; www.barhsurryhills.com; 80 Campbell St; dishes $10-40; ☺6-11pm Tue-Sat; ▣Museum) The pork buns and wontons served at this sexy, shiny, black-walled corner eatery are a revelation. Larger dishes – pork belly, steamed fish and roast duck – are just as good.

House
THAI $$

(Map p59; ☑02-9280 0364; www.spiceiam.com; 202 Elizabeth St; mains $11-20; ☺11.30am-10.30pm; ▣Central) On a sticky Sydney night, House's lantern-strung courtyard really feels like Southeast Asia, not least because of the constant passing traffic and the chicken embryo on the menu. Specialising in the street food of the Issan region of northeast Thailand, the food is deliciously authentic – and when they say spicy, believe them.

Toko
JAPANESE $$

(Map p65; ☑02-9357 6100; www.toko.com.au; 490 Crown St; dishes $9-33; ☺noon-3pm Tue-Fri, 6-11pm Mon-Sat; ▣Central) Toko dishes up superb modern Japanese *otsumami* (tapas) such as soft-shell crab, eggplant with miso and meaty options from the *robata* (charcoal grill). Settle into a communal table and expect to spend around $30 on food – more if you're a sashimi junkie.

Longrain
THAI $$$

(Map p59; ☑ 02-9280 2888; www.longrain.com; 85 Commonwealth St; mains $33-44; ⊗ noon-2.30pm Fri, 6-11pm daily; ☒ Central) Devotees flock here to feast on Longrain's fragrant modern Thai dishes and to sip delicately flavoured and utterly delicious cocktails. Sit at shared tables or at the bar.

Marque
MODERN AUSTRALIAN $$$

(Map p65; ☑ 02-9332 2225; www.marquerestaurant.com.au; 355 Crown St; degustation $160; ⊗ noon-3pm Fri, 6.30-10pm Mon-Sat; ☒ Central) It's Mark Best's delicious, inventive, beautifully presented food that has won Marque various awards in recent years; it's certainly not the somewhat stuffy ambience or the insipid decor. There's an excellent-value, three-course set lunch on Friday ($45).

✗ Darlinghurst

★ Messina
ICE CREAM $

(Map p66; www.gelatomessina.com; 241 Victoria St; 2 scoops $6; ⊗ noon-11pm; ☒ Kings Cross) Join the queues of people who look like they never eat ice cream at the counter of Sydney's most extraordinary gelato shop. The 'Creative Department' next door serves gelato cakes masquerading as burgers and toadstools. You'll find additional branches in the cafe court below Star casino and in Surry Hills (Map p65; 389 Crown St; ⊗ noon-11pm; ☒ Central).

Popolo
ITALIAN $$

(Map p66; ☑ 02-9361 6641; www.popolo.com.au; 50 McLachlan Ave; breakfast $10-15, mains $19-29; ⊗ 6-10.30pm Mon, noon-10.30pm Tue-Fri, 8am-10.30pm Sat & Sun; ☒ Kings Cross) Handsome, thickly accented, authentically arrogant Italian waiters glide about distributing delicious pizza, pasta and, on the weekends, inventive breakfasts to an adoring clientele. It's set back from a luxury-car dealership (naturally) on its own sunny square – or should that be piazza.

bills
CAFE $$

(Map p66; www.bills.com.au; 433 Liverpool St; breakfast $13-21, lunch $19-26; ⊗ 7.30am-3pm; ☒ Kings Cross) Bill Granger almost single-handedly introduced the Sydney craze for stylish brunching. This sunny corner cafe with its newspaper-strewn communal table was the original, but there are other branches in Woollahra (Map p70; 118 Queen St; ⊗ 7.30am-5pm; ☒ 389) and Surry Hills (Map p65; 359 Crown St; ⊗ 7am-10pm; ☒ Central).

Buffalo Dining Club
ITALIAN $$

(Map p66; www.buffalodiningclub.com.au; 116 Surrey St; mains $18-19; ⊗ noon-11pm Wed-Sun; ☒ Kings Cross) Describing itself as a 'mozzarella bar', this tiny but massively popular eatery limits its output to high-quality antipasto plates and three types of pasta. The kitchen takes up a good half of the space, leaving room for a communal table and a scattering of two-seaters; expect to queue.

A Tavola
ITALIAN $$

(Map p66; ☑ 02-9331 7871; www.atavola.com.au; 348 Victoria St; mains $24-38; ⊗ 6-10pm Mon-Sat; ☒ Kings Cross) At this classy pasta joint, the menu only has a handful of dishes, but you can be confident that they will all be fantastic. Before each service starts, the long communal marble table doubles as the main pasta-making workbench.

✗ Woolloomooloo, Kings Cross & Potts Point

Room 10
CAFE $

(Map p66; 10 Llankelly Pl; mains $9-14; ⊗ 7am-4pm Mon-Sat, 9am-2pm Sun; ☒ Kings Cross) If you're wearing a flat cap, sprouting a beard and obsessed by coffee, chances are you'll recognise this tiny room as your spiritual home in the Cross. The food's limited to sandwiches, salads and such – tasty and uncomplicated.

Ms G's
ASIAN $$

(Map p66; ☑ 02-9240 3000; www.merivale.com/msgs; 155 Victoria St; mains $21-29; ⊗ 5-11pm Mon-Thu & Sat, noon-3pm & 5-11pm Fri, 1-9pm Sun; ☒ Kings Cross) Offering a cheeky, irreverent take on Asian cooking (hence the name – geddit?), Ms G's is nothing if not an experience. It can be loud, frantic and painfully hip, but the adventurous combinations of pan-Asian and European flavours have certainly got Sydney talking.

Apollo
GREEK $$

(Map p66; ☑ 02-8354 0888; www.theapollo.com.au; 44 Macleay St; mains $18-38; ⊗ 6-10.30pm Mon-Thu, noon-11pm Fri & Sat, noon-9.30pm Sun; ☒ Kings Cross) An exemplar of modern Greek cooking, this taverna has a fashionably rough-edged decor, a well-priced menu of share plates and a bustling vibe. Starters are particularly impressive, especially the pitta bread hot from the oven and the wild weed and cheese pie.

Wilbur's Place
EUROPEAN **$$**

(Map p66; www.wilbursplace.com; 36 Llankelly Pl; brunch $9-18, dinner $24; ⊙8am-3pm Sat, 5-9.30pm Tue-Sat; ⬚Kings Cross) With limited bench seating inside and a few tables on the lane, tiny Wilbur's is an informal spot for a quick bite on what's become the Cross' coolest eating strip. Expect simple, straightforward food that is expertly assembled.

Fratelli Paradiso
ITALIAN **$$**

(Map p66; www.fratelliparadiso.com; 12-16 Challis Ave; breakfast $11-14, mains $21-31; ⊙7am-11pm Mon-Sat, to 5pm Sun; ⬚Kings Cross) This underlit trattoria has them queuing at the door (especially on weekends). The intimate room showcases seasonal Italian dishes cooked and served with Mediterranean zing: lots of busy black-clad waiters, lots of Italian chatter, lots of oversized sunglasses. No bookings.

Aki's
INDIAN **$$**

(Map p66; ✆02-9332 4600; www.akisindian.com. au; 1/6 Cowper Wharf Rd; mains $21-36; ⊙noon-10pm Sun-Fri, 6-10.30pm Sat; ⬚⬚; ⬚Kings Cross) The first cab off the rank as you walk onto Woolloomooloo's wharf is Aki's. And you need walk no further: this is beautifully presented, intuitively constructed high-Indian cuisine, supplemented by a six-page wine list showcasing local and international drops.

✗ Paddington & Woollahra

Chiswick Restaurant
MODERN AUSTRALIAN **$$**

(Map p70; ✆02-8388 8688; www.chiswickrestaurant.com.au; 65 Ocean St; mains $28-35; ⊙noon-2.30pm & 6-10pm; ⬚389) There may be a celebrity at centre stage (TV regular Matt Moran), but the real star of this show is the pretty kitchen garden, which wraps around the dining room and dictates what's on the menu. Meat from the Moran family farm and local seafood feature prominently too.

Four in Hand
GASTROPUB **$$$**

(Map p52; ✆02-9362 1999; www.fourinhand.com. au; 105 Sutherland St; mains $39; ⊙noon-2.30pm & 6.30pm-late Tue-Sun; ⬚Edgecliff) You can't go far in Paddington without tripping over a beautiful old pub with amazing food. This is the best of them, famous for its slow-cooked and nose-to-tail meat dishes.

✗ Eastern Beaches

Three Blue Ducks
CAFE **$$**

(Map p52; www.threeblueducks.com; 141-143 Macpherson St; breakfast $16-22, lunch $22-30, dinner shared plates $17; ⊙7am-3pm Sun-Tue, 7am-3.30pm & 6-11pm Wed-Sat; ⬚378) ✔ These ducks are a fair waddle from the water, but that doesn't stop queues forming outside the graffiti-covered walls for weekend brunches. The adventurous owners have a strong commitment to using local, organic and fair-trade ingredients whenever possible.

Bondi Trattoria
ITALIAN **$$**

(Map p73; ✆02-9365 4303; www.bonditrattoria. com.au; 34 Campbell Pde; breakfast $9-21, lunch $16-26, dinner $19-36; ⊙8am-late; ⬚380) For a Bondi brunch, you can't go past the trusty 'Trat'. Tables spill out onto Campbell Pde for those hungry for beach views, while inside there's a trad trat feel: wooden tables and the obligatory Tuscan mural and black-and-white photography. As the day progresses, pizza, pasta and risotto dominate the menu.

♟ Drinking & Nightlife

Pubs are an integral part of the Sydney social scene, and you can down a schooner (the NSW term for a large glass of beer) at elaborate 19th-century edifices, cavernous art deco joints, modern and minimalist recesses, and everything in between. Bars are generally more stylish and urbane, sometimes with a dress code.

There's a thriving live-music scene, but good dance clubs are strangely thin on the ground.

♟ The Rocks & Circular Quay

Opera Bar
BAR, LIVE MUSIC

(Map p56; www.operabar.com.au; lower concourse, Sydney Opera House; ⊙11.30am-midnight Sun-Thu, to 1am Fri & Sat; ⬚Circular Quay, ⬚Circular Quay, ⬚Circular Quay) Right on the harbour with the Opera House on one side and the Harbour Bridge on the other, this perfectly positioned terrace manages a very Sydney marriage of the laid-back and the sophisticated. There's live music from 8.30pm weekdays and 2.30pm on weekends.

Hero of Waterloo
PUB, LIVE MUSIC

(Map p56; www.heroofwaterloo.com.au; 81 Lower Fort St; ⊙9.30am-11.30pm Mon-Sat, noon-10pm Sun; ⬚Circular Quay) Enter this rough-hewn 1843 sandstone pub to meet some locals, chat up the Irish bar staff and grab an earful of the swing, folk, bluegrass and Celtic bands (Friday to Sunday).

Lord Nelson Brewery Hotel   PUB, BREWERY
(Map p56; ☑02-9251 4044; www.lordnelson.com.au; 19 Kent St; ◷11am-11pm; ⓡCircular Quay) Built in 1836 and converted into a pub in 1841, this atmospheric sandstone boozer is one of three claiming to be Sydney's oldest. The on-site microbrewery cooks up its own natural ales (try the Old Admiral).

Australian Hotel   PUB
(Map p56; www.australianheritagehotel.com; 100 Cumberland St; ⓡCircular Quay) Not only is this pub architecturally notable (c 1913), it also boasts a bonza selection of fair-dinkum Ocker beer and wine. Keeping with the antipodean theme, the kitchen fires up pizza topped with kangaroo and saltwater crocodile ($17 to $26).

Fortune of War   PUB, LIVE MUSIC
(Map p56; www.fortuneofwar.com.au; 137 George St; ◷9am-late Mon-Fri, 11am-late Sat, 11am-midnight Sun; ⓡCircular Quay) This 1828 drinking den retains much of its original charm and, by the looks of things, some of the original punters, too. There's live music on Thursday, Friday and Saturday nights and on weekend afternoons.

🍴 City Centre

★ Baxter Inn   BAR
(Map p56; www.thebaxterinn.com; 152-156 Clarence St; ◷4pm-1am Mon-Sat; ⓡTown Hall) Yes, it really is down that dark lane and through that unmarked door (it's easier to find if there's a queue; otherwise look for the bouncer lurking nearby). Whisky's the main poison and the moustached barmen know their stuff.

Palmer & Co   BAR
(Map p56; www.merivale.com.au/palmerandco; Abercrombie Lane; ◷5pm-late Sat-Wed, noon-late Thu & Fri; ⓡWynyard) Another self-consciously hip member of Sydney's speakeasy brigade, this 'legitimate importer of bracing tonics and fortifying liquids' attracts a cashed-up, fashionable clientele.

Grandma's   COCKTAIL BAR
(Map p56; www.grandmasbarsydney.com; Basement, 275 Clarence St; ◷3pm-late Mon-Fri, 5pm-late Sat; ⓡTown Hall) Billing itself as a 'retrosexual haven of cosmopolitan kitsch and faded granny glamour', Grandma's hits the

mark. A stag's head greets you on the stairs and ushers you into a tiny subterranean world of parrot wallpaper and tiki cocktails.

Stitch   BAR
(Map p56; www.stitchbar.com; 61 York St; ◷4pm-midnight Mon-Wed, noon-2am Thu & Fri, 4pm-2am Sat; ⓡWynyard) The finest exemplar of Sydney's penchant for ersatz speakeasys, Stitch is accessed via swinging doors at the rear of what looks like a tailor's workshop. Hidden beneath is a surprisingly large but perpetually crowded space decorated with sewing patterns and wooden Singer cases.

Good God Small Club   BAR, CLUB
(Map p59; www.goodgodgoodgod.com; 55 Liverpool St; admission front bar free, club varies; ◷5pm-late Wed-Sat; ⓡTown Hall) In a defunct underground taverna near Chinatown, Good God's rear danceteria hosts everything from live indie bands to Jamaican reggae, '50s soul, rockabilly and tropical house music. Its success lies in the focus on great music rather than glamorous surrounds.

Establishment   BAR
(Map p56; www.merivale.com/establishmentbar; 252 George St; ◷11am-late Mon-Sat, noon-10pm Sun; ⓡWynyard) Establishment's cashed-up crush proves that the art of swilling cocktails after a hard city day is not lost. Sit at the majestic marble bar or in the swish courtyard, or be absorbed by a leather lounge.

Hemmesphere   BAR
(Map p56; ☑02-9240 3100; www.merivale.com.au/hemmesphere; Level 4, 252 George St; ◷noon-late Mon-Fri, 6pm-late Sat; ⓡWynyard) This is pure Sydney: a gentlemen's-club vibe with a whiff of Ottoman Empire opulence. Melt into a deep leather chair, order a cocktail and wait for someone famous to show up.

Ivy   BAR, CLUB
(Map p56; ☑02-9254 8100; www.merivale.com/ivy; Level 1, 330 George St; ◷noon-late Mon-Fri, 8.30pm-late Sat; ⓡWynyard) Hidden down a laneway off George St, Ivy is a scarily fashionable complex of bars, restaurants, discreet lounges...even a swimming pool. It's also Sydney's most hyped venue; expect lengthy queues of suburban kids teetering on unfeasibly high heels, waiting to shed up to $40 on a Saturday for entry to Sydney's hottest club night, Pacha.

Marble Bar   BAR, LIVE MUSIC
(Map p56; www.marblebarsydney.com.au; Basement, Hilton Hotel, 488 George St; ◷4pm-midnight

Sun-Thu, to 2am Fri & Sat; 🚇 Town Hall) Built for a staggering £32,000 in 1893, this marble-lined underground bar is one of the best places in town for putting on the ritz (even if this is the Hilton). Musos play anything from jazz to funk from Thursday to Saturday.

Chinese Laundry CLUB
(Map p56; www.merivale.com; cnr King & Sussex Sts; club $15-25; ⊙10pm-late Fri & Sat; 🚇 Wynyard) On Friday night they crank up the bass at this dance club underneath the Slip Inn. On Saturday there's a roster of international and local electro, house and techno DJs.

Bambini Wine Room WINE BAR
(Map p56; www.bambinitrust.com.au; 185 Elizabeth St; ⊙3-10pm Mon-Fri, 5.30-11pm Sat; 🚇 St James) Don't worry, this bar doesn't sell wine to *bambini* – it's a very grown-up, European affair. The tiny dark-wood-panelled room is the sort of place where you'd expect to see Oscar Wilde holding court in the corner.

🍴 Newtown

Midnight Special BAR, LIVE MUSIC
(Map p63; www.facebook.com/MidnightSpecial-Newtown; 44 Enmore Rd; ⊙5pm-midnight) Band posters and paper lanterns decorate the black walls of this groovy little bar. Musicians take to the tiny stage on Wednesday and Sunday.

Courthouse Hotel PUB
(Map p63; 202 Australia St; ⊙10am-midnight Mon-Sat, to 10pm Sun; 🚇 Newtown) A cool old pub with a great beer garden where everyone from pool-playing goth lesbians to magistrates can feel right at home.

🍴 Surry Hills

Tio's Cerveceria BAR
(Map p59; 4-14 Foster St; ⊙4pm-midnight Mon-Sat, to 10pm Sun; 🚇 Museum) Tio likes tequila. Heaps of different types. And wrestling, Catholic kitsch and *Day of the Dead* paraphernalia. Surry Hills skaters, beard-wearers and babydoll babes love him right back.

Shakespeare Hotel PUB
(Map p65; www.shakespearehotel.com.au; 200 Devonshire St; 🚇 Central) A classic Sydney pub (1879) with art nouveau–tiled walls, skuzzy carpet, the horses on the TV and cheap bar meals. Not a hint of glitz or interior design. Perfect!

Cricketers Arms Hotel PUB
(Map p52; www.cricketersarmshotel.com.au; 106 Fitzroy St; ⊙3pm-midnight Mon-Fri, 1pm-midnight Sat, 1-10pm Sun; 🚌 339) A favourite haunt of arts students, turntable fans and locals of all persuasions. There are open fires for when you need warming up.

Hotel Hollywood PUB
(Map p59; 🖉 02-9281 2765; www.facebook.com/hotel.hollywood.sydney; 2 Foster St; ⊙4-10pm Sun, 4pm-midnight Mon, noon-midnight Tue & Wed, noon-3am Thu & Fri, 4pm-3am Sat; 🚇 Museum) A mixed crowd of Surry Hillbillies gets down to serious beer business in the art deco pub that time forgot.

🍴 Darlinghurst

Shady Pines Saloon BAR
(Map p66; www.shadypinessaloon.com; Shop 4, 256 Crown St; ⊙4pm-midnight; 🚇 Museum) With no sign or street number on the door and entry from a shady back lane (look for the white door before Bikram Yoga on Foley St), this subterranean honky-tonk bar caters to the urban boho. Sip whisky and rye with the good ole hipster boys amid Western memorabilia and taxidermy.

Eau-de-Vie COCKTAIL BAR
(Map p66; www.eaudevie.com.au; 229 Darlinghurst Rd; ⊙6pm-1am; 🚇 Kings Cross) Take the door marked 'restrooms' at the back of the Kirketon Hotel's main bar and enter this sophisticated black-walled speakeasy, where a team of dedicated shirt-and-tie-wearing mixologists concoct the sorts of beverages that win best-cocktail gongs.

Victoria Room COCKTAIL BAR
(Map p66; 🖉 02-9357 4488; www.thevictoriaroom.com; Level 1, 235 Victoria St; ⊙6pm-midnight Tue-Fri, noon-2am Sat, noon-midnight Sun; 🚇 Kings Cross) Claim a chesterfield and relax over an expertly prepared cocktail at this sultry, Raj-style drinking den. Book ahead for high tea ($45 to $65) on weekend afternoons.

Hinky Dinks COCKTAIL BAR
(Map p66; www.hinkydinks.com.au; 185 Darlinghurst Rd; ⊙5pm-midnight Mon-Fri, 3pm-midnight Sat, 1-10pm Sun; 🚇 Kings Cross) Everything's just hunky dory in this little cocktail bar styled after a 1950s milkshake parlour. Try the Hinky Fizz, an alcohol-soaked strawberry sorbet served in a waxed-paper sundae cup.

Pocket BAR
(Map p66; www.pocketsydney.com.au; 13 Burton St; ⏰4pm-midnight; 🚇Museum) Sink into the corner Pocket's comfy leather couches, order a drink and chat about the day's adventures accompanied by a decade-defying indie soundtrack. Pop-art murals and exposed brickwork add to the ambience.

Oxford Art Factory BAR, LIVE MUSIC
(Map p66; www.oxfordartfactory.com; 38-46 Oxford St; cover varies; ⏰various; 🚇Museum) Indie kids party against an arty backdrop at this two-room multipurpose venue modelled on Warhol's NYC creative base. There's a gallery, bar and performance space that often hosts international acts and DJs. Check the website for what's on.

Darlo Bar PUB
(Map p66; ☎02-9331 3672; www.darlobar.com.au; 306 Liverpool St; ⏰10am-midnight Mon-Sat, noon-midnight Sun; 🚇Kings Cross) The Darlo's triangular retro room is a magnet for thirsty urban bohemians, fluoro-clad ditch diggers and architects with a hankering for pinball or pool.

Woolloomooloo, Kings Cross & Potts Point

Old Fitzroy Hotel PUB
(Map p66; www.oldfitzroy.com.au; 129 Dowling St; ⏰11am-midnight Mon-Sat, 3-10pm Sun; 🚇Kings Cross) Islington meets Melbourne in the back streets of Woolloomooloo: this unpretentious theatre pub is a decent old-fashioned boozer in its own right.

Kings Cross Hotel PUB, CLUB
(Map p66; www.kingscrosshotel.com.au; 244-248 William St; ⏰noon-3am; 🚇Kings Cross) With five floors above ground and one below, this grand old pub is a hive of boozy entertainment that positively swarms on weekends. Best of all is FBi Social, an alternative radio station–led takeover of the 2nd floor, bringing with it an edgy roster of live music. The roof bar has awesome city views.

Sugarmill BAR
(Map p66; www.sugarmill.com.au; 33 Darlinghurst Rd; ⏰10am-midnight; 🚇Kings Cross) For a bloated Kings Cross bar, Sugarmill is actually pretty cool. Columns and high pressed-tin ceilings hint at its bankery past, while the band posters plastered everywhere do their best to dispel any lingering capitalist vibes. As the night progresses the party moves upstairs to the rooftop bar and Kit & Kaboodle nightclub.

Paddington & Woollahra

Wine Library WINE BAR
(Map p70; www.wine-library.com.au; 18 Oxford St; ⏰11.30am-11.30pm Mon-Sat, to 10pm Sun; 🚌380) An impressive range of wines by the glass, a smart-casual ambience and a Mediterranean-inclined bar menu make this the most desirable library in town.

10 William Street WINE BAR
(Map p70; www.10williamst.com.au; 10 William St; ⏰5pm-midnight Mon-Thu, noon-midnight Fri & Sat; 🚌380) This *minuscolo* slice of *la dolce vita* on the fashion strip serves excellent imported wines and equally impressive food.

Eastern Beaches

Icebergs Bar BAR
(Map p73; www.idrb.com; 1 Notts Ave; ⏰noon-midnight Tue-Sat, to 10pm Sun; 🚌380) The hanging chairs, comfortable sofas and ritzy cocktails are fab, but the view looking north across Bondi Beach is the absolute killer.

Manly

Hotel Steyne PUB
(Map p77; ☎02-9977 4977; www.steynehotel.com.au; 75 The Corso; ⏰9am-3am Mon-Sat, to midnight Sun; ⛴Manly) Boasting numerous bars over two levels, this landmark pub accommodates everyone from sporty bogans to clubby kids to families. Live bands and DJs entertain.

☆ Entertainment

Pick up the Metro section in Friday's *Sydney Morning Herald* for comprehensive entertainment details. Tickets for most shows can be purchased directly from venues or through the **Moshtix** (☎1300 438 849; www.moshtix.com.au), **Ticketmaster** (Map p56; ☎136 100; www.ticketmaster.com.au) or **Ticketek** (Map p56; ☎132 849; www.ticketek.com.au) ticketing agencies.

Live Music & Comedy

★ Sydney Opera House PERFORMING ARTS
(Map p56; ☎02-9250 7777; www.sydneyoperahouse.com; Bennelong Point; 🚇Circular Quay) The glamorous jewel at the heart of Australian performance, with five main stages. As well as theatre and comedy, there are performances by companies such as **Opera Australia**

(www.opera-australia.org.au), the **Australian Ballet** (www.australianballet.com.au), the **Sydney Symphony Orchestra** (www.sydney symphony.com) and the **Australian Chamber Orchestra** (www.aco.com.au).

State Theatre   PERFORMING ARTS
(Map p56; ☑02-9373 6655; www.statetheatre. com.au; 49 Market St; ☒St James) The beautiful 2000-seat State Theatre is a lavish, gilt-ridden, chandelier-dangling palace. It hosts the Sydney Film Festival, concerts, comedy, opera, musicals and the odd celebrity chef.

City Recital Hall   CLASSICAL MUSIC
(Map p56; ☑02-8256 2222; www.cityrecitalhall. com; 2 Angel Pl; ☺box office 9am-5pm Mon-Fri; ☒Martin Pl) Based on the classic configuration of 19th-century European concert halls, this custom-built 1200-seat venue boasts near-perfect acoustics. Catch top-flight companies such as **Musica Viva** (www.mva.org.au) and the **Australian Brandenburg Orchestra** (www.brandenburg.com) here.

Sydney Conservatorium of Music   CLASSICAL MUSIC
(Map p56; ☑02-9351 1222; www.music.usyd.edu. au; Conservatorium Rd; ☒Circular Quay) This historic venue showcases the talents of its students and their teachers. Choral, jazz, operatic and chamber concerts happen from March to November, along with free lunchtime recitals on Wednesday at 1pm.

Metro Theatre   PERFORMING ARTS
(Map p59; ☑02-9550 3666; www.metrotheatre. com.au; 624 George St; ☒Town Hall) Easily Sydney's best venue to catch local and alternative international acts in well-ventilated, easy-seeing comfort. Other offerings include comedy, cabaret and dance parties.

Enmore Theatre   PERFORMING ARTS
(Map p63; ☑02-9550 3666; www.enmoretheatre. com.au; 130 Enmore Rd; ☺box office 9am-6pm Mon-Fri, 10am-4pm Sat; ☒Newtown) Originally a vaudeville playhouse, the elegantly wasted 2500-capacity Enmore now hosts touring musicians and comedians.

Basement   JAZZ
(Map p56; ☑02-9251 2797; www.thebasement.com. au; 7 Macquarie Pl; ☒Circular Quay) Once solely a jazz venue, the Basement now hosts international and local musicians working in many disciplines and genres. Dinner-and-show tickets net you a table by the stage, guaranteeing a better view than the standing-only area by the bar.

Vanguard   LIVE MUSIC
(Map p63; ☑02-9557 9409; www.thevanguard. com.au; 42 King St; ☒Macdonaldtown) This intimate, purpose-built space showcases everything from burlesque to blues, country to world. Most seats are reserved for dinner-and-show.

Annandale Hotel   LIVE MUSIC
(Map p52; ☑02-9550 1078; www.annandalehotel. com; 17 Parramatta Rd; ☒435-440) At the forefront of Sydney's live-music scene, the Annandale coughs up alt-rock, metal, punk and electronica.

Theatre

Sydney Theatre Company   THEATRE
(STC; Map p56; ☑02-9250 1777; www.sydneytheatre.com.au; Pier 4/5, 15 Hickson Rd; ☺box office 9am-8.30pm Mon-Fri, 11am-8.30pm Sat, 2hr before show Sun; ☒Wynyard) Sydney's premier theatre company performs at its Walsh Bay base and in the Drama Theatre at the Sydney Opera House.

Belvoir Street Theatre   THEATRE
(Map p65; ☑02-9699 3444; www.belvoir.com.au; 25 Belvoir St; ☒Central) In a quiet corner of Surry Hills, this intimate venue is the home of the often-experimental and consistently excellent Company B.

Capitol Theatre   PERFORMANCE VENUE
(Map p59; ☑1300 558 878; www.capitoltheatre. com.au; 13 Campbell St; ☒Central) Lavishly restored, this 1920s theatre is home to long-running musicals and the occasional big-name concert.

Ensemble Theatre   THEATRE
(Map p52; ☑02-9929 0644; www.ensemble.com. au; 78 McDougall St; ☒North Sydney) The long-running Ensemble presents work by overseas and Australian playwrights, often with well-known Australian actors.

Dance

Sydney Dance Company   DANCE
(SDC; Map p56; ☑02-9221 4811; www.sydneydancecompany.com; Pier 4/5, 15 Hickson Rd; ☒Wynyard) Australia's number-one contemporary-dance company has been staging wildly modern, sexy, sometimes shocking works for more than 30 years.

Bangarra Dance Theatre   DANCE
(Map p56; ☑02-9251 5333; www.bangarra.com. au; Pier 4/5, 15 Hickson Rd; ☒Wynyard) Bangarra is hailed as Australia's finest Aboriginal performance company, conjuring a fusion

of contemporary themes and Indigenous traditions.

Cinema

OpenAir Cinema
CINEMA

(Map p52; www.stgeorgeopenair.com.au; Mrs Macquaries Rd; tickets $35; ☉ Jan & Feb; ⓡ Circular Quay) Right on the harbour, the outdoor three-storey screen here comes with surround sound, sunsets, skyline and swanky food and wine. Most tickets are purchased in advance, but a limited number of tickets go on sale at the door each night at 6.30pm – check the website for details.

Bondi Openair Cinema
CINEMA

(Map p73; www.openaircinemas.com.au; Dolphin Lawn, next to Bondi Pavilion; tickets $17-40; ☉ Jan & Feb; ⓑ 380) Enjoy open-air screenings by the sea, with live bands providing pre-screening entertainment. Bookings advisable.

Moonlight Cinema
CINEMA

(Map p70; www.moonlight.com.au; Belvedere Amphitheatre, cnr Loch & Broome Aves; adult/child $18/14; ☉ Dec-Mar; ⓡ Bondi Junction) Take a picnic and join the bats under the stars in magnificent Centennial Park; enter via Woollahra Gate on Oxford St. A mix of new-release blockbuster, art house and classics is programmed.

IMAX
CINEMA

(Map p60; ☎ 02-9281 3300; www.imax.com.au; 31 Wheat Rd; adult/child from $31/23; ☉ sessions 10am-9pm; ⓡ Town Hall) It's big bucks for a 45-minute movie, but everything about IMAX is big, and this is the biggest IMAX in the world. The eight-storey screen shimmers with kid-friendly documentaries (sharks, butterflies etc) as well as blockbuster features, many in 3D.

Spectator Sports

National Rugby League
SPECTATOR SPORT

(NRL; www.nrl.com) Rugby League is king in NSW, and Sydney is considered one of the world capitals for the code. The season runs from March to October, with home games for Sydney's nine teams held at stadiums throughout the city.

Australian Football League
SPECTATOR SPORT

(AFL; www.afl.com.au) From March right through to September, local favourites the **Sydney Swans** (www.sydneyswans.com.au) compete in the national competition, with home games at the **Sydney Cricket Ground** (SCG; Map p70; ☎ 02-9360 6601; www.sydneycricketground.com.au; Driver Ave; ⓑ 372-374 & 391-397).

The **Greater Western Sydney Giants** (www.gwsgiants.com.au) are based at Sydney Olympic Park.

Cricket
SPECTATOR SPORT

(www.cricket.com.au) The cricket season runs from October to March, with the SCG hosting interstate Sheffield Shield and sell-out international test, Twenty20 and 50-over matches.

🛍 Shopping

Sydneysiders head cityward – particularly to Pitt Street Mall – if they have something special to buy or when serious retail therapy is required. Paddington has traditionally been Sydney's premier fashion enclave, although it's now facing stiff competition from the giant Westfield malls in Pitt St and Bondi Junction. Newtown's King St has come into its own as one of the city's most interesting strips, especially for vintage boutiques and bookshops.

🛍 City Centre

Queen Victoria Building
SHOPPING CENTRE

(QVB; Map p56; www.qvb.com.au; 455 George St; ☉ 11am-5pm Sun, 9am-6pm Mon-Wed, Fri & Sat, 9am-9pm Thu; ⓡ Town Hall) Unbelievably, this High Victorian masterpiece (1898) was repeatedly slated for demolition before it was restored in the mid-1980s. Occupying an entire city block on the site of the city's first markets, the QVB is a Venetian Romanesque temple to the gods of retail, boasting nearly 200 shops on five levels.

Strand Arcade
SHOPPING CENTRE

(Map p56; www.strandarcade.com.au; 412 George St; ☉ 9.30am-5.30pm Mon-Wed & Fri, 9am-8pm Thu, 9am-4pm Sat, 11am-4pm Sun; ⓡ St James) Constructed in 1891, the Strand competes with the QVB for the title of the city's most beautiful shopping centre. It has a particularly strong range of Australian designer fashion, and is home to Strand Hatters, a Sydney institution.

Westfield Sydney
MALL

(Map p56; www.westfield.com.au/sydney; cnr Pitt St Mall & Market St; ☉ 9.30am-6.30pm Wed & Fri, to 9pm Thu; ⓡ St James) The city's newest and most glamorous shopping mall is a bafflingly large complex gobbling up Sydney Tower and a fair chunk of Pitt Street Mall. The 5th-floor food court is excellent and on level three there's a branch of RM Williams, 'the bush outfitters', stocking everything you'll need to pull off that Crocodile Dundee look.

David Jones DEPARTMENT STORE
(Map p56; www.davidjones.com.au; 86-108 Castlereagh St; ⓡ St James) In two enormous city buildings, DJs is Sydney's premier department store. The Castlereagh St store has women's and children's clothing; Market St has menswear, electrical goods and a highbrow food court.

Newtown

Better Read Than Dead BOOKS
(Map p63; ⌨ 02-9557 8700; www.betterread.com.au; 265 King St; ⏱ 9.30am-9pm; ⓡ Newtown) This might be our favourite Sydney bookshop, and not just because of the pithy name and

the great selection of Lonely Planet titles. Nobody seems to mind if you waste hours perusing the beautifully presented aisles.

Darlinghurst

Artery ART
(Map p66; ⌨ 02-9380 8234; www.artery.com.au; 221 Darlinghurst Rd; ⏱ 10am-5pm; ⓡ Kings Cross) Step into a world of mesmerising dots and swirls at this small gallery devoted to Aboriginal art; its motto is 'ethical, contemporary, affordable'.

Paddington & Woollahra

Ariel BOOKS
(Map p66; ⌨ 02-9332 4581; www.arielbooks.com.au; 42 Oxford St; ⏱ 9am-midnight; ⍰ 380) Furtive

---

MARVELLOUS MARKETS

Heading to the local market is a popular weekend diversion. Many inner-city suburbs have markets in the grounds of local schools and churches, and these sell everything from organic food to designer clothing. You'll inevitably encounter some tragic hippy paraphernalia, appalling art and overpriced tourist tat, but there are often exciting purchases to be made, too.

The best markets include the following:

Paddington Markets (Map p70; www.paddingtonmarkets.com.au; 395 Oxford St; ⏱ 10am-4pm Sat; ⍰ 380) Originating in the 1970s when it was drenched in the scent of patchouli oil, this market is considerably more mainstream these days but still worth checking out for its new and vintage clothing, creative crafts and jewellery. Expect a crush.

Paddy's Markets (Map p59; www.paddysmarkets.com.au; 9-13 Hay St; ⏱ 9am-5pm Wed-Sun; ⓡ Central) Cavernous, 1000-stall Paddy's is the Sydney equivalent of Istanbul's Grand Bazaar, but swap the hookahs and carpets for mobile-phone covers, One Direction T-shirts and made-in-China koala backpacks. Pick up a VB singlet for Uncle Bruce or wander the aisles in capitalist awe.

Bondi Markets (Map p73; www.bondimarkets.com.au; Bondi Beach Public School, Campbell Pde; ⏱ farmers market 9am-1pm Sat, general market 10am-4pm Sun; ⍰ 380) On Sunday when the kids are at the beach, their school fills up with Bondi characters rummaging through tie-dyed secondhand clothes, books, beads, earrings, aromatherapy oils, candles, old records and more.

Eveleigh Market (Map p52; www.eveleighmarket.com.au; 243 Wilson St; ⏱ farmers market 8am-1pm Sat, artisans market 10am-3pm 1st Sun of month; ⓡ Redfern) Over 70 regular stallholders sell their home-grown produce at Sydney's best farmers' market, which is held in a heritage-listed railway workshop in the Eveleigh railyards. While here, you can also visit the CarriageWorks arts and cultural precinct (www.carriageworks.com.au).

Glebe Markets (Map p52; www.glebemarkets.com.au; Glebe Public School, cnr Glebe Point Rd & Derby Pl; ⏱ 10am-4pm Sat; ⓡ Glebe) Sydney's dreadlocked, shoeless, bohemian contingent beats an aimless course to this crowded hippyish market for secondhand threads and ethnic food.

Surry Hills Markets (Map p65; www.shnc.org/markets; Shannon Reserve, Crown St; ⏱ 7am-4pm 1st Sat of month; ⓡ Central) There's a chipper community vibe at this monthly market, with mainly locals renting stalls to sell/recycle their old stuff: clothes, CDs, books and sundry junk. Bargains aplenty.

artists, architects and students roam Ariel's aisles late into the night. 'Underculture' is the thrust here – glossy art, film, fashion and design books, along with kids' books, travel guides and literature.

Corner Shop CLOTHING
(Map p70; ☑02-9380 9828; www.thecornershop. com.au; 43 William St; ⊙10am-6pm; ☒380) This treasure trove of a women's boutique is stocked with a healthy mix of casual and high end, with some jewellery for good measure.

Poepke CLOTHING
(Map p70; www.poepke.com; 47 William St; ⊙10am-6pm Mon-Sat, noon-5pm Sun; ☒380) One of Paddington's more interesting women's boutiques, stocking a range of Australian and international designers.

ℹ Information

EMERGENCY
In the event of an emergency, call ☑000 for police, ambulance or fire brigade.
Lifeline (☑13 11 14; www.lifelinesydney.org; ⊙24hr) Round-the-clock phone-counselling services, including suicide prevention.
Police Stations For a searchable list of all police stations in NSW, go to www.police.nsw. gov.au and look for the 'your police' tab.
Rape Crisis Centre (☑1800 424 017; www. nswrapecrisis.com.au; ⊙24hr) Offers 24-hour counselling.

INTERNET ACCESS
The vast majority of hotels and hostels offer their guests internet access; it's increasingly offered for free, although you'll still have to pay in many hostels and top hotels. Libraries are a good bet for free wi-fi and bookable terminals.

MEDICAL SERVICES
Kings Cross Clinic (☑02-9358 3066; www. kingscrossclinic.com.au; 13 Springfield Ave; ⊙9am-6pm Mon-Fri, 10am-1pm Sat; ☒Kings Cross) General and travel medical services.
St Vincent's Hospital (☑02-8382 1111; www. stvincents.com.au; 390 Victoria St; ⊙emergency 24hr; ☒Kings Cross)
Sydney Hospital (☑02-9382 7111; www. seslhd.health.nsw.gov.au/SHSEH; 8 Macquarie St; ⊙emergency 24hr; ☒Martin Pl)

TOURIST INFORMATION
City Host Information Kiosk (www.cityofsydney.nsw.gov.au; George St) Town Hall; Circular Quay (Map p56; cnr Pitt & Alfred Sts; ⊙9am-5pm; ☒Circular Quay); Haymarket (Map p59; Dixon St; ⊙11am-7pm; ☒Town Hall); Kings

Cross (Map p66; cnr Darlinghurst Rd & Springfield Ave; ⊙9am-5pm; ☒Kings Cross) Helpful staff supply maps, brochures and information.
Manly Visitor Information Centre (Map p77; ☑02-9976 1430; www.manlyaustralia.com.au; Manly Wharf; ⊙10am-2pm Mon-Fri, to 4pm Sat & Sun; ☒Manly) Has free pamphlets covering the Manly Scenic Walkway and other Manly attractions.
Sydney Visitor Centres (☑02-8273 0000; www.sydneyvisitorcentre.com) The Rocks (Map p56; ☑02-9240 8788; www.therocks.com; 1st fl, cnr Argyle & Playfair Sts; ⊙9.30am-5.30pm; ☎; ☒Circular Quay); Darling Harbour (Map p60; www.darlingharbour.com; Palm Grove, behind IMAX; ⊙9.30am-5.30pm; ☒Town Hall) Both branches have a wide range of brochures, and staff can book accommodation, tours and attractions.

ℹ Getting There & Away

AIR
Also known as Kingsford Smith Airport, Sydney Airport (p517) has separate international (T1) and domestic (T2 and T3) sections, 4km apart on either side of the runway. Each has left-luggage services, ATMs, currency-exchange bureaux and rental-car counters.
Airlines flying to other East Coast destinations are listed below.
Brindabella Airlines (☑1300 66 88 24; www. brindabellaairlines.com.au) Flies to/from Newcastle.
Jetstar (☑13 15 38; www.jetstar.com.au) Flies to/from Melbourne, Ballina, the Gold Coast, Brisbane, the Sunshine Coast, Hamilton Island, Townsville and Cairns.
Qantas (☑13 13 13; www.qantas.com.au) Flies to/from Melbourne, Canberra, Port Macquarie, Coffs Harbour, the Gold Coast, Brisbane, Gladstone and Cairns.
Regional Express (Rex; ☑13 17 13; www.rex. com.au) Flies to/from Merimbula, Moruya, Newcastle, Taree, Ballina and Lismore.
Tigerair (☑02-8073 3421; www.tigerairways. com/au/en) Flies to/from Melbourne, Coffs Harbour, the Gold Coast, Brisbane, Mackay and Cairns.
Virgin Australia (☑13 67 89; www.virginaustralia. com) Flies to/from Melbourne, Canberra, Port Macquarie, Coffs Harbour, Ballina, the Gold Coast, Brisbane, the Sunshine Coast, Hervey Bay, Mackay, Hamilton Island, Townsville and Cairns.

BUS
Long-distance bus services arrive at **Sydney Coach Terminal** (Map p65; ☑02-9281 9366; Eddy Ave; ⊙6am-6pm Mon-Fri, 8am-6pm Sat

& Sun; 🚉 Central), underneath Central Station. Major operators are listed below.

Firefly (Map p56; ☎ 1300 730 740; www. fireflyexpress.com.au) Melbourne (from $60, 12 to 14 hours, two daily) and Canberra ($50, 4¼ hours, daily).

Greyhound (☎ 1300 473 946; www.greyhound. com.au) Melbourne ($105, 12 to 14 hours, two daily), Canberra (from $26, 4½ hours, four daily), Newcastle ($30, 2¾ hours, two daily), Byron Bay (from $95, 12 to 14 hours, three daily) and Brisbane (from $105, 17 hours, four daily).

Murrays (☎ 13 22 51; www.murrays.com.au) Canberra (from $26, 3½ hours, 14 daily).

Port Stephens Coaches (☎ 02-4982 2940; www.pscoaches.com.au) Port Stephens ($39, three hours, daily).

Premier Motor Service (☎ 13 34 10; www.pre-mierms.com.au) Melbourne ($85, 17¾ hours, daily), Wollongong ($18, two hours, two daily), Coffs Harbour ($66, 8½ hours, daily), Byron Bay ($92, 14 hours, daily) and Brisbane ($95, 17½ hours, daily).

TRAIN

NSW TrainLink (☎ 13 22 32; www.nswtrainlink. info) connects Sydney's Central Station with destinations including Melbourne ($111, 11 hours, two daily), Canberra ($48, 4¼ hours, two daily), Coffs Harbour ($81, nine hours, three daily), Grafton ($88, 10 hours, three daily) and Brisbane ($111, 14½ hours, daily).

Sydney's local train network, run by **Sydney Trains** (☎ 13 15 00; www.sydneytrains.info), includes regular services to NSW destinations such as Kiama (2½ hours), Wollongong (1¾ hours), Katoomba (two hours), Gosford (1½ hours) and Newcastle (three hours); all of these cost $8.40.

ⓘ Getting Around

TO/FROM THE AIRPORT

Taxi Allow $50 for a taxi to Circular Quay.

Shuttle Airport shuttles head to hotels and hostels in the city centre, and some reach surrounding suburbs and beach destinations. Operators include **Sydney Airporter** (☎ 02-9666 9988; www.kst.com.au; adult/child $15/10), **Super Shuttle** (☎ 02-9697 2322; www.signa-turelimousinessydney.com.au; airport hotels $6), **Airport Shuttle North** (☎ 1300 505 100; www.airportshuttlenorth.com; to Manly 1/2/3 people $41/51/61) and **Manly Express** (☎ 02-8068 8473; www.manlyexpress.com.au; to Manly 1/2/3 people $35/50/60).

Train Trains from both the domestic and international terminals, connecting into the main train network, are run by **Airport Link** (www.airportlink.com.au; to city $17; ⊙ 5am-

midnight). They're frequent (every 10 minutes), quick (13 minutes to Central) and easy to use, but airport tickets are charged at a hefty premium. If there are a few of you it's cheaper to catch a cab.

Bus The cheapest option to Bondi Junction is the 400 bus ($4.60, 1¼ hours).

BOAT

Water taxis are a fast way to shunt around the harbour (Circular Quay to Watsons Bay in as little as 15 minutes). Companies will quote on any pick-up point within the harbour and the river, including private jetties, islands and other boats.

Aussie Water Taxis (Map p60; ☎ 02-9211 7730; www.aussiewatertaxis.com; Cockle Bay Wharf) The smallest seats 16 passengers. Can be rented per hour or point to point. Has discounted per-person prices from Darling Harbour, including Circular Quay ($15), Luna Park ($15), Fish Market ($20) and Taronga Zoo ($25).

H2O Taxis (☎ 1300 426 829; www.h2owater-taxis.com.au) Up to eight people from Circular Quay to Fort Denison $80; to Cockatoo Island $90.

Water Taxis Combined (☎ 02-9555 8888; www.watertaxis.com.au) Fares based on up to four passengers; add $10 per person for additional passengers. Sample fares: Circular Quay to Watsons Bay $110; to Rose Bay $105; Mosman to Woolloomooloo $80. Time-based cruises are $200 per half-hour for up to 16 people.

Yellow Water Taxis (☎ 02-9299 0199; www.yellowwatertaxis.com.au) Set price for up to four passengers, then $10 per person for additional people. Sample fares from King Street Wharf: Circular Quay and Fort Denison $83; Taronga Zoo $105; Cockatoo Island $121; Watsons Bay $127.

CAR & MOTORCYCLE

➧ Avoid driving in central Sydney if you can: there's a confusing one-way-street system, parking's elusive and expensive (even at hotels), and parking inspectors, tolls and tow-away zones proliferate. Conversely, a car is handy for accessing Sydney's outer reaches (particularly the beaches) and for day trips.

➧ All of the major international car-rental companies have offices at Sydney Airport and other locations. The main city hub for rental cars is William St, Darlinghurst. Reliable local operators include **Bayswater Car Rental** (☎ 02-9360 3622; www.bayswatercarrental. com.au), cut-price **Ace Rentals** (☎ 02-8338 1055; www.acerentalcars.com.au) and, for campervans, **Jucy Rentals** (☎ 1800 150 850; www.jucy.com.au).

➧ There are hefty tolls on most of Sydney's motorways and major links (including the Harbour Bridge, Harbour Tunnel, Cross City Tunnel and Eastern Distributor). The tolling system is electronic, meaning that it's up to you to organise an electronic tag or visitors pass through any of the following websites: www.roam.com.au, www.roamexpress.com.au or www.myetoll.com.au. Note that some car-hire companies now supply eTags.

PUBLIC TRANSPORT

Sydneysiders love to complain about their public-transport system, but visitors should find it surprisingly easy to navigate. The train system is the linchpin, with lines radiating out from Central Station. Ferries head all around the harbour and up the river to Parramatta; light rail is useful for Pyrmont and Glebe; and buses are particularly useful for getting to the beaches.

Bus

Sydney Buses (☑131 500; www.sydneybuses.info) runs the local bus network. Regular buses run between 5am and midnight, when NightRide buses take over. Bus routes starting with an X indicate limited-stop express routes; those with an L have limited stops.

There are Transport Shops selling bus tickets and offering route information at **Circular Quay** (Map p56; cnr Alfred & Loftus Sts; ⊘7am-7pm Mon-Fri, 8.30am-5pm Sat & Sun), **Wynyard Park** (Map p56; Carrington St; ⊘7am-7pm Mon-Fri; ☒Wynyard), the **Queen Victoria Building** (Map p56; York St; ⊘7am-7pm Mon-Fri) and

Railway Square (Map p65; cnr George & Lee Sts; ⊘7am-7pm Mon-Fri). Tickets can also be purchased at numerous newsagents, corner stores and supermarkets throughout the city.

Fares depend upon the number of 'sections' you traverse; tickets range from $2.20 to $4.60. Pay the driver as you enter (correct change minimises annoyance), or dunk prepaid tickets in the green ticket machines. You're best to purchase your tickets in advance as increasing numbers of services are 'prepay only'. If you'll be catching buses a lot (but not trains or ferries), consider a prepaid 10-ride TravelTen ticket (sections 1-2/3-5/6+ $18/29/37).

Route 555 is a free service that heads up and down George St from Circular Quay to Central Station.

Ferry

Most **Sydney Ferries** (☑131 500; www.sydney-ferries.info) operate between 6am and midnight. The standard single fare for most harbour destinations is $5.80; boats to Manly, Sydney Olympic Park and Parramatta cost $7.20. If you're staying near a ferry wharf and don't think you'll be using buses or trains much, consider a prepaid 10-ride MyFerryTen ticket ($47). If you're heading to Taronga Zoo by ferry, consider the all-inclusive ZooPass (adult/child $52/26).

Manly Fast Ferry (☑02-9583 1199; www.manlyfastferry.com.au; adult/child $9/6) and **Sydney Fast Ferries** (☑02-9818 6000; www.sydneyfastferries.com.au; adult/child

---

INTEGRATED PASSES

All of the state's public and many of its private services are gathered together under the umbrella of NSW Transport (☑131 500; www.131500.com.au). The website has an excellent journey planner, where you can plug in your requirements and then let the system spit out a range of options.

A smart-card system called Opal (www.opal.com.au) is gradually being rolled out across the various public-transport modes. It allows you to add money to the card and then touch it on electronic readers as you commence and end your trip. Advantages include slightly cheaper single journeys and daily charges capped at $15 ($2.50 on Sunday).

MyMulti passes allow unlimited travel on trains (except the airport stations), light rail, buses and government ferry services. You can purchase these at bus/ferry/train ticket offices as well as many newsagents and convenience stores. Options include the following:

➡ **MyMulti DayPass** ($21) Covers the entire system.

➡ **MyMulti1** (per week/month $44/168) Includes all buses, light rail and ferries but only Zone 1 trains. This pass is the best option for most travellers.

➡ **MyMulti2** (per week/month $52/199) As above, but includes trains to places like Olympic Park and Parramatta.

➡ **MyMulti3** (per week/month $61/238) As above, but includes trains to Cronulla, the Blue Mountains and the stations on the fringes of Royal National Park.

➡ **Family Funday Sunday** If you're related and have at least one adult and one child in your party, all of you can travel anywhere within the network on Sunday for a day rate of $2.50 per person.

$9.50/5.50) both offer boats that blast from Circular Quay to Manly in 18 minutes.

Light Rail

Metro Light Rail (MLR; ☎131 500; www.131500.com.au; zone 1 $3.50, 1&2 $4.50) heads from Central to Lilyfield (via Chinatown, Darling Harbour, Pyrmont and Glebe) every 10 to 15 minutes from 6am to 11pm. There's a 24-hour service from Central to the Star, with late-night trains every 30 minutes.

Train

Sydney has a large suburban railway web with relatively frequent services, although there are no lines to the northern or eastern beaches. Trains run from around 5am to 1am – check timetables for your line. A short inner-city one-way trip on Sydney Trains (p102) costs $3.60. Purchase your ticket in advance from an automated machine or counter at the station. On weekends and after 9am Monday to Friday you can buy an off-peak return ticket for not much more than a standard one-way fare.

TAXI

Metered taxis are easy to flag down in the city and the inner suburbs, except for at 'change-over' times (3pm and 3am). Flagfall is $3.50; the fare thereafter is $2.14 per kilometre. There's a 20% surcharge between 10pm and 6am, and additional charges for bookings ($2.40) and tolls. For more on Sydney's taxis, see www.nswtaxi. org.au.

Big, reliable operators:

Legion Cabs (☎13 14 51; www.legioncabs. com.au)

Premier Cabs (☎13 10 17; www.premiercabs. com.au)

RSL Cabs (☎02-9581 1111; www.rslcabs. com.au)

Taxis Combined (☎13 33 00; www.taxiscombined.com.au)

BLUE MOUNTAINS

POP 75,700

A region with more than its fair share of natural beauty, the Blue Mountains was an obvious choice for Unesco World Heritage status. The slate-coloured haze that gives the mountains their name comes from a fine mist of oil exuded by the huge eucalypts that form a dense canopy across the landscape of deep, often inaccessible valleys and chiselled sandstone outcrops.

The foothills begin 65km inland from Sydney, rising to an 1100m-high sandstone plateau riddled with valleys eroded into the stone over thousands of years. There

are eight connected conservation areas in the region, including the **Blue Mountains National Park** (www.nationalparks.nsw.gov.au/ Blue-Mountains-National-Park), which has some truly fantastic scenery, excellent bushwalks (hikes), Aboriginal engravings and all the canyons and cliffs you could ask for. **Wollemi National Park** (www.nationalparks.nsw. gov.au/Wollemi-National-Park), north of the Bells Line of Rd, is NSW's largest forested wilderness area, stretching all the way to the Hunter Valley.

Although it's possible to visit on a day trip from Sydney, we strongly recommend that you stay at least one night so that you can explore a few of the towns, do at least one bushwalk and eat at some of the excellent restaurants. The hills can be surprisingly cool throughout the year, so bring warm clothes.

◉ Sights

◉ Glenbrook

Arriving from Sydney, the first of the Blue Mountains towns you will encounter is unassuming Glenbrook. From here, you can drive or walk into the lower reaches of the national park; this is the only part of the park where vehicle entry fees apply ($7). Six kilometres from the park entrance gate is the **Mt Portal Lookout** with panoramic views into the Glenbrook Gorge, over the Nepean River and back to Sydney.

Red Hands Cave ARCHAEOLOGICAL SITE
Less a cave than an alcove, this Aboriginal shelter is decorated with hand stencils dating from between 500 and 1600 years ago. It's an easy, 7km return walk southwest of the Glenbrook Visitor Centre (p109).

◉ Wentworth Falls

As you head into the town of Wentworth Falls, you will get your first real taste of Blue Mountains scenery: with views to the south opening out across the majestic Jamison Valley.

Falls Reserve WATERFALL, PARK
The falls that lend the town its name launch a plume of droplets over a 300m drop. This is the starting point of a network of walking tracks, which delve into the sublime **Valley of the Waters**, with waterfalls, gorges, woodlands and rainforests.

Blue Mountains

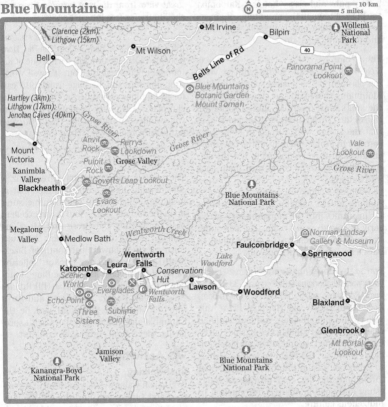

👁 Leura

Leura is the Blue Mountains' prettiest town, fashioned around undulating streets, well-tended gardens and sweeping Victorian verandahs. Leura Mall, the tree-lined main street, offers rows of country craft stores and cafes for the daily tourist influx.

Sublime Point   LOOKOUT
(Sublime Point Rd) South of Leura, this sharp, triangular outcrop narrows to a dramatic lookout with sheer cliffs on each side. We prefer it to Katoomba's more famous Echo Point, mainly because it's much, much quieter. On sunny days cloud shadows dance across the vast blue valley below.

Everglades   GARDENS
(📞 02-4784 1938; www.everglades.org.au; 37 Everglades Ave; adult/child $10/4; ☉10am-4pm) National Trust–owned Everglades was built in the 1930s. While the house is interesting, it's

the magnificent garden created by Danish 'master gardener' Paul Sorenson that's the main drawcard.

Leuralla NSW Toy &
Railway Museum   MUSEUM, GARDENS
(📞 02-4784 1169; www.toyandrailwaymuseum.com.au; 36 Olympian Pde; adult/child $14/6, gardens only $10/5; ☉10am-5pm) The art deco mansion that was once home to HV 'Doc' Evatt, the first UN president, is jam-packed with an incredible array of collectables – from grumpy Edwardian baby dolls to *Dr Who* figurines, to a rare set of Nazi propaganda toys. Railway memorabilia is scattered throughout the handsome gardens.

👁 Katoomba

Swirling, otherworldly mists, steep streets lined with art deco buildings, astonishing valley views and a quirky miscellany of restaurants, buskers, artists, homeless people, bawdy pubs and classy hotels – Katoomba, the biggest town in the mountains, manages to be bohemian and bourgeois, embracing and menacing all at once.

Echo Point
LOOKOUT

(Echo Point Rd) Echo Point's clifftop viewing platform is the busiest spot in the Blue Mountains thanks to the views it offers of the area's most essential sight: a rocky trio called the Three Sisters. The story goes that the sisters were turned to stone by a sorcerer to protect them from the unwanted advances of three young men, but the sorcerer died before he could turn them back into humans.

Warning: Echo Point draws vast, serenity-spoiling tourist gaggles, their idling buses farting fumes into the mountain air – arrive early or late to avoid them. The surrounding parking is expensive ($4.40 per hour), so park a few streets back and walk.

Waradah Aboriginal Centre
CULTURAL CENTRE

(www.waradahaboriginalcentre.com.au; 33-37 Echo Point Rd; show adult/child $12/7; ☉9am-5pm) Located in the World Heritage Plaza, this gallery and shop displays some exceptional examples of Aboriginal art alongside tourist tat like painted boomerangs and didgeridoos. However, the main reason to visit is to catch one of the 15-minute shows. Held throughout the day, they provide an interesting and good-humoured introduction to Indigenous culture.

Scenic World
CABLE CAR

(☑02-4780 0200; www.scenicworld.com.au; cnr Violet St & Cliff Dr; adult/child $35/18; ☉9am-5pm) Take the glass-floored Skyway gondola out across the gorge and then ride what's billed as the steepest railway in the world down the 52-degree incline to the Jamison Valley floor. From here you can wander a 2.5km forest boardwalk (or hike the 12km, six-hour return track to the Ruined Castle rock formation) before catching a cable car back up the slope.

Blue Mountains Cultural Centre
GALLERY

(www.bluemountainsculturalcentre.com.au; 30 Parke St; adult/child $5/free; ☉10am-5pm; ☎) It's a captivating experience to walk through the World Heritage display, with a satellite image of the Blue Mountains beneath your feet, mountain scenery projected on the walls and ceiling, and bush sounds surrounding you. The neighbouring gallery hosts interesting exhibitions and there's a

great view from the roof terrace. Drop into the library for free internet access.

Paragon
NOTABLE BUILDING

(65 Katoomba St; ☉11am-3.30pm Sun-Thu, 11am-9.30pm Fri, 10am-10.30pm Sat) It's not one of Katoomba's better eateries, but it's well worth dropping into this heritage-listed 1916 cafe for its fabulous period decor. The handmade chocolates are pretty good too. Make sure you wander through to the Great Gatsby-esque mirrored cocktail bar at the rear.

◎ Blackheath

The crowds and commercial frenzy fizzle considerably 10km north of Katoomba in neat, petite Blackheath. The town measures up in the scenery stakes, and it's an excellent base for visiting the Grose and Megalong Valleys. East of town are Evans Lookout (turn off the highway just south of Blackheath) and Govetts Leap Lookout, offering views of the highest falls in the Blue Mountains. To the northeast, via Hat Hill Rd, are Pulpit Rock, Perrys Lookdown and Anvil Rock. To the west and southwest lie the Kanimbla and Megalong Valleys, with spectacular views from Hargraves Lookout.

🏃 Activities

Bushwalking

For tips on walks to suit your level of experience and fitness, call into the NPWS' Blue Mountains Heritage Centre in Blackheath or the information centres in Glenbrook or Katoomba. All three sell a variety of walk pamphlets, maps and books.

Note that the bush here is dense and that it can be easy to become lost – there have been deaths as a consequence. Always leave your name and walk plan with the Katoomba police or at the NPWS centre. The police, NPWS and information centres all offer free personal locator beacons and it's strongly suggested you take one with you, especially for longer hikes. Remember to carry clean drinking water and plenty of food.

The two most popular bushwalking areas are the Jamison Valley, south of Katoomba, and the Grose Valley, northeast of Katoomba and east of Blackheath. The Golden Stairs Walk (Glenraphael Dr, Katoomba) is a less-congested route to the Ruined Castle than the track leading from Scenic World. To get there, continue along Cliff Dr from Scenic World for 1km and look for Glenraphael Dr on your left. It quickly becomes rough and

WORTH A TRIP

BELLS LINE OF ROAD

This stretch of road between North Richmond and Lithgow is the most scenic route across the Blue Mountains and is highly recommended if you have your own transport. It's far quieter than the highway and offers bountiful views.

Bilpin, at the base of the mountains, is known for its apple orchards. If you're passing through at lunch or dinner time make a beeline for the Apple Bar (02-4567 0335; www.applebar.com.au; 2488 Bells Line of Rd; mains $25-33; noon-3pm Mon, noon-3pm & 6-10pm Fri-Sun), a cool-looking place that serves local cider and excellent pizzas and grills from its wood-fired oven. The Bilpin Markets are held at the district hall every Saturday from 10am to midday.

Midway between Bilpin and Bell, the Blue Mountains Botanic Garden Mount Tomah (02-4567 3000; www.rbgsyd.nsw.gov.au; 9.30am-5.30pm) FREE is a cool-climate annexe of Sydney's Royal Botanic Gardens where native plants cuddle up to exotic species, including some magnificent rhododendrons.

To access Bells Line from central Sydney, head over the Harbour Bridge and take the M2 and then the M7 (both have tolls). Exit at Richmond Rd, which becomes Blacktown Rd, then Lennox Rd, then (after a short dog-leg) Kurrajong Rd and finally Bells Line of Road.

---

unsealed. Watch out for the signs to the Golden Stairs on the left after a couple of kilometres. It is a steep, exhilarating trail down into the valley (about 8km, five hours return).

One of the most rewarding long-distance walks is the 45km, three-day Six Foot Track from Katoomba along the Megalong Valley to Cox's River and on to the Jenolan Caves. It has camp sites along the way.

Cycling

The mountains are also a popular cycling destination, with many people taking their bikes on the train to Woodford and then cycling downhill to Glenbrook, a ride of two to three hours. Cycling maps are available from the visitor centres.

Adventure Activities & Tours

Blue Mountains Adventure Company ADVENTURE SPORTS
(02-4782 1271; www.bmac.com.au; 84a Bathurst Rd, Katoomba; 8am-7pm) Abseiling from $150, abseiling and canyoning combo from $195, canyoning from $195, bushwalking from $150 and rock climbing from $195.

River Deep Mountain High ADVENTURE SPORTS
(02-4782 6109; www.rdmh.com.au; 2/187 Katoomba St, Katoomba) Offers abseiling (from $130), canyoning (from $150) and canyoning and abseiling packages ($180), plus a range of hiking, mountain-biking and 4WD tours.

Australian School of Mountaineering ADVENTURE SPORTS
(02-4782 2014; www.asmguides.com; 166 Katoomba St, Katoomba) Abseiling/canyoning/bushcraft/rock climbing from $165/180/195/195.

High 'n' Wild Mountain Adventures ADVENTURE SPORTS
(02-4782 6224; www.highandwild.com.au; 3/5 Katoomba St, Katoomba) Guided abseiling/rock climbing/canyoning from $125/159/180.

Tread Lightly Eco Tours WALKING TOUR
(02-4788 1229; www.treadlightly.com.au) Has a wide range of day and night walks ($65 to $135) that emphasise the region's ecology.

Blue Mountains Walkabout CULTURAL TOUR
(0408 443 822; www.bluemountainswalkabout.com; tour $95) Full-day Indigenous-owned and -guided adventurous trek with a spiritual theme; starts at Faulconbridge train station and ends at Springwood station.

Festivals & Events

Yulefest FESTIVAL
(www.yulefest.com) Out-of-kilter Christmas-style celebrations between June and August.

Winter Magic Festival FESTIVAL
(www.wintermagic.com.au) This one-day festival, held at the winter solstice in June, sees Katoomba's main street taken over by market stalls, costumed locals and performances.

Leura Gardens Festival
GARDENS

(www.leuragardensfestival.com; all gardens $20, single garden $5) Green-thumbed tourists flock to Leura during October, when 10 private gardens are open to the public.

🛏 Sleeping

There's a good range of accommodation in the Blue Mountains, but you'll need to book ahead during winter and for every weekend during the year (Sydneysiders love coming here for romantic weekends away). Leafy Leura is your best bet for romance, while Blackheath is a good base for hikers; both are better choices than built-up Katoomba, although the latter has excellent hostels.

🛏 Leura

★ Broomelea
B&B $$

(☑ 02-4784 2940; www.broomelea.com.au; 273 Leura Mall; r $175-195; @ 🛜) The consummate romantic Blue Mountains B&B, this fine Edwardian house offers four-poster beds, manicured gardens, cane furniture on the verandah, an open fire and a snug lounge. There's also a self-contained cottage for families.

Greens of Leura
B&B $$

(☑ 02-4784 3241; www.thegreensleura.com.au; 24-26 Grose St; s/d from $145/165; @ 🛜) On a quiet street parallel to the Mall, this pretty timber house set in a lovely garden offers five rooms named after English writers (Browning, Austen etc). All are individually decorated; some have four-poster beds and spas.

🛏 Katoomba

★ Blue Mountains YHA
HOSTEL $

(☑ 02-4782 1416; www.yha.com.au; 207 Katoomba St; dm $30, d with/without bathroom $112/99; @ 🛜) Behind the austere brick exterior of this popular 200-bed hostel are dorms and family rooms that are comfortable, light-filled and spotlessly clean. Facilities include a lounge (with an open fire), a pool table, an excellent communal kitchen and an outdoor space with barbecues.

No 14
HOSTEL $

(☑ 02-4782 7104; www.no14.com.au; 14 Lovel St; dm $28, r with/without bathroom $85/75; @ 🛜) Resembling a cheery share house, this small hostel has a friendly vibe and helpful managers. There's no TV, so guests actually tend to talk to each other. A basic breakfast and internet access are included in the rates.

Flying Fox
HOSTEL $

(☑ 02-4782 4226; www.theflyingfox.com.au; 190 Bathurst Rd; camp sites per person $20, dm $29-32, r $88; 🛜) The owners are travellers at heart and have endowed this unassuming hostel with an endearing home-away-from-home feel. There's no party scene here – just mulled wine and Tim Tams in the lounge, free breakfasts and a weekly pasta night.

Shelton-Lea
B&B $$

(☑ 02-4782 9883; www.sheltonlea.com; 159 Lurline St; r $140-210; 🛜) This homely mountain cottage has been tweaked to create three bedrooms, each with its own sitting area and kitchenette. There's a hint of art deco in the decor and lots of frilly furnishings.

Lilianfels
HOTEL $$$

(☑ 02-4780 1200; www.lilianfels.com.au; Lilianfels Ave; r from $269; ❋ @ 🛜) Right next to Echo Point and enjoying spectacular views, this luxury resort has 85 guest rooms, the region's top-rated restaurant (Darley's; three courses $125) and an indulgent array of facilities including spa, heated indoor and outdoor pools, tennis court, billiards/games room, library and gym.

🍴 Eating & Drinking

🍴 Wentworth Falls

Nineteen23
MODERN AUSTRALIAN $$$

(☑ 02-4757 3311; www.nineteen23.com.au; 1 Lake St; 5/7 courses $55/70; ⊙ 6-10pm Thu & Fri, noon-3pm & 6-10pm Sat & Sun) Wearing its 1920s ambience with aplomb, this elegant dining room is a particular favourite with loved-up couples happy to gaze into each other's eyes over a lengthy degustation. While the food isn't particularly experimental, it's beautifully cooked and bursting with flavour.

🍴 Leura

Leura Garage
MEDITERRANEAN $$

(☑ 02-4784 3391; www.leuragarage.com.au; 84 Railway Pde; lunch $17-28, shared plates $13-33; ⊙ noon-late Thu-Mon) If you were in any doubt that this hip cafe-bar was once a garage, the suspended mufflers and stacks of old tyres press the point. At dinner the menu shifts gears to rustic shared plates served on wooden slabs, including deli treat–laden pizza.

Cafe Madeleine
CAFE $$

(www.josophans.com.au; 187a Leura Mall; mains $12-18; ⊙ 9am-5pm) The sister to a chocolate shop, Madeleine excels in sweet treats such as chocolate-drenched waffles, cakes and hot chocolates. Mind you, the eggy breakfasts and French-influenced savoury dishes are also excellent.

Silk's Brasserie MODERN AUSTRALIAN **$$$**
(📞 02-4784 2534; www.silksleura.com; 128 Leura Mall; mains lunch $24-39, dinner $35-39; ☺noon-3pm & 6-10pm) A warm welcome awaits at Leura's long-standing fine diner. Despite its contemporary approach, it's a brasserie at heart, so the serves are generous and flavoursome. Save room for the decadent desserts.

Alexandra Hotel PUB
(www.alexandrahotel.com.au; 62 Great Western Hwy) The Alex is a gem of an old pub. Join the locals at the pool table or listening to DJs and live bands on the weekend.

✖ Katoomba

Sanwiye Korean Cafe KOREAN **$**
(📞 0405 402 130; 177 Katoomba St; mains $10-16; ☺11am-9.30pm Tue-Sun) In the sea of overpriced mediocrity that is the Katoomba dining scene, this tiny place distinguishes itself with fresh and tasty food made with love by the Korean owners.

Fresh CAFE **$**
(www.freshcafe.com.au; 181 Katoomba St; mains $9-18; ☺8am-5pm; 🚲) 🍃 The rainforest-alliance, fair-trade coffee served at this diminutive cafe attracts a devoted local following. Excellent all-day breakfasts are popular, too.

True to the Bean CAFE **$**
(123 Katoomba St; waffles $3-6; ☺7am-4pm; 🛜) The Sydney obsession with single-estate coffee has made its way to Katoomba's main drag in the form of this tiny espresso bar. Food is limited to the likes of bircher muesli and waffles.

ℹ Information

Blue Mountains Heritage Centre (📞 02-4787 8877; www.nationalparks.nsw.gov.au/Blue-Mountains-National-Park; end of Govetts Leap Rd, Blackheath; ☺9am-4.30pm) The extremely helpful, official NPWS visitor centre.

Glenbrook Information Centre (📞 1300 653 408; www.bluemountainscitytourism.com.au; Great Western Hwy; ☺8.30am-4pm)

Echo Point Visitors Centre (📞 1300 653 408; www.visitbluemountains.com.au; Echo Point, Katoomba; ☺9am-5pm) A sizeable centre with can-do staff.

ℹ Getting There & Around

To reach the Blue Mountains by road, leave Sydney via Parramatta Rd. At Strathfield detour onto the toll-free M4, which becomes the Great Western Hwy west of Penrith and takes you to all of the Blue Mountains towns. It takes approximately 1½ hours to drive from central Sydney to Katoomba. A scenic alternative is the Bells Line of Road (p107).

Blue Mountains Bus (📞 02-4751 1077; www.bmbc.com.au; fares $2.20-4.60) Connects the main towns.

Blue Mountains Explorer Bus (📞 1300 300 915; www.explorerbus.com.au; 283 Bathurst Rd, Katoomba; adult/child $38/19; ☺9.45am-5pm) Offers hop-on, hop-off service on a Katoomba–Leura loop. Leaves from Katoomba station every 30 to 60 minutes.

Trolley Tours (📞 1800 801 577; www.trolleytours.com.au; 76 Bathurst St, Katoomba; adult/child $25/15; ☺9.45am-4.45pm) Runs a hop-on, hop-off bus barely disguised as a trolley, looping around 29 stops in Katoomba and Leura.

Sydney Trains (📞 13 15 00; www.sydneytrains.info; adult/child $8.40/4.20) Trains on the Blue Mountains line depart Sydney's Central Station approximately hourly for Glenbrook, Springwood, Faulconbridge, Wentworth Falls, Leura, Katoomba and Blackheath; allow two hours for Katoomba.

CENTRAL COAST
POP 373,000

After struggling through the traffic of Sydney's northern suburbs, you can choose whether to motor straight up the freeway to Newcastle or meander along the Central Coast. Truth be told, neither route will be a highlight of your trip, but if you've got time to kill there are some pleasant diversions along the coastal road.

The largest town in the area is hilly **Gosford**, which serves as the transport and services hub for the surrounding beaches. East of Gosford, the coast is heavily populated. **Terrigal** has a beautiful crescent-shaped beach with good surf and a bustling town centre.

A series of saltwater 'lakes' spreads north up the coast between Bateau Bay and Newcastle, the largest of which, **Lake Macquarie**, covers four times the area of Sydney Harbour.

◉ Sights

Australian Reptile Park   ZOO
(www.reptilepark.com.au; adult/child $26/14; ⊙9am-5pm) Well signposted from the freeway west of Gosford, this zoo offers a chance to get up close to koalas and pythons, watch funnel-web spiders being milked (for the production of antivenin) and learn about the plight of the Tasmanian devil (the park serves as a breeding park).

Brisbane Water National Park   PARK
(www.nationalparks.nsw.gov.au/brisbane-water-national-park; vehicle access at Girrakool & Somersby Falls picnic areas $7) Rambling trails run through rugged sandstone in this national park bordering the Hawkesbury River southwest of Gosford. It's known for its spring wildflowers and for its Aboriginal rock art. The Bulgandry Aboriginal Engraving Site is situated 3km south of the Central Coast Hwy on Woy Woy Rd. A favourite retreat for actors, writers and other luvvies is the pretty village of Pearl Beach, on the southeastern edge of the park. For more on the Hawkesbury, see p79.

Bouddi National Park   PARK
(☑02-4320 4200; www.nationalparks.nsw.gov.au/bouddi-national-park; vehicle access $7, tent sites per 2 people $20-28) Southeast of Gosford, Bouddi National Park extends from the north head of Broken Bay to MacMasters Beach, 12km south of Terrigal. Short walking trails lead to isolated beaches, including lovely Maitland Bay. The park is in two sections on either side of Putty Beach. There are camp sites at Little Beach, Putty Beach and Tallow Beach; book ahead. Only the Putty Beach site has drinkable water and flush toilets.

🛏 Sleeping & Eating

Tiarri   MOTEL $$
(☑02-4384 1423; www.tiarriterrigal.com.au; 16 Tiarri Cres, Terrigal; r/ste $145/170) Our pick of the places to stay is this unusual boutique motel in a quiet street on the slopes above Terrigal. The rooms are modern, clean and comfortable; the upstairs ones open onto a little bush-shaded terrace.

Pearls on the Beach   MODERN AUSTRALIAN $$$
(☑02-4342 4400; www.pearlsonthebeach.com.au; 1 Tourmaline Ave, Pearl Beach; mains $38; ⊙noon-2.30pm & 6-10pm Thu-Sun) Occupying a wooden cottage right by the water at Pearl Beach, this highly rated restaurant offers contemporary fare in stylish surrounds.

Reef   MODERN AUSTRALIAN $$$
(☑02-4385 3222; www.reefrestaurant.com.au; The Haven, Terrigal; mains $37-42; ⊙noon-3pm & 6-10pm Tue-Sat, noon-3pm Sun) The seafood-heavy menu does a good job of stealing attention away from the spectacular beach views at this white-linen place at the southern end of Terrigal beach. Downstairs, the Cove Cafe offers a more relaxed and less pricey alternative.

ℹ Information

Central Coast Visitor Centre (☑02-4343 4444; www.visitcentralcoast.com.au; The Avenue, Kariong; ⊙9am-5pm Mon-Fri, 9.30am-3.30pm Sat & Sun)

Gosford Visitor Centre (☑02-4343 4444; 200 Mann St; ⊙9.30am-4pm Mon-Fri, to 1.30pm Sat)

The Entrance Visitor Centre (☑02-4333 1966; Marine Pde; ⊙9am-5pm)

Lake Macquarie Visitor Centre (☑02-4921 0740; www.visitlakemac.com.au; 228 Pacific Hwy, Swansea; ⊙9am-5pm)

ℹ Getting There & Around

Train Gosford is a stop on the Newcastle and Central Coast line, with frequent trains from Sydney and Newcastle (both adult/child $8.40/4.20, 1½ hours). Trains also stop at Wondabyne within Brisbane Waters National Park upon request (rear carriage only).

Bus Local buses connecting the various towns and beaches are operated by Busways (☑02-4368 2277; www.busways.com.au) and Redbus (☑02-4332 8655; www.redbus.com.au).

NEWCASTLE

POP 308,000

Sydney may possess the glitz and the glamour, but the state's second-largest city has down-to-earth larrikin charm instead. Newcastle is the kind of place where you can grocery shop barefoot and go surfing in your lunch hour. This easygoing, 'no worries' attitude is a product of Newcastle's rough-and-tumble past, shaped by a cast of convicts, coal miners and steelworkers.

The city is still one of the largest coal-export harbours in the world, but it's undergoing something of a cultural renaissance. Rejuvenation projects are breathing new life into the waterfront and an eclectic and innovative arts scene is injecting colour and culture into the streets.

Swim or surf at the first-rate beaches, explore the heritage architecture in the CBD and window shop along funky Darby St – Newcastle is easily worth a day or two of your time.

◉ Sights

◉ City Centre

Christ Church Cathedral CHURCH
(www.newcastlecathedral.org.au; 52 Church St; ⊙7am-6pm) Although relatively squat, Newcastle's hilltop Anglican cathedral (built 1892 to 1979) dominates the skyline in the way that European cathedrals once did. Inside there are lots of interesting features to discover, helpfully described on a self-guided-tour brochure.

Pre-Raphaelite fans should seek out the stained-glass window by Edward Burne-Jones and William Morris. However, the cathedral's greatest treasure is a gold chalice and remembrance book set with precious stones, made from jewellery donated by locals who lost loved ones in WWI.

Lock Up ARTS CENTRE
(☑02-4925 2265; www.thelockup.info; 90 Hunter St; ⊙10am-4pm Wed-Sun) FREE These days, artists in residence, rather than prisoners, are incarcerated in this former police station (1861). There's a contemporary art gallery, artists' studios and an interesting law-and-order museum within the creepy, cramped, heritage-listed cells.

Newcastle Art Gallery GALLERY
(☑02-4974 5100; www.nag.org.au; 1 Laman St; ⊙10am-5pm Tue-Sun) FREE NAG's permanent collection includes works by revered Australian artists and there are often interesting temporary exhibitions to peruse.

◉ Newcastle East

★Fort Scratchley HISTORIC SITE
(☑02-4974 5033; www.fortscratchley.com.au; Nobbys Rd; tour adult/child $15/7.50; ⊙10am-4pm Wed-Mon, last tour 2.30pm) FREE Constructed during the Crimean War to protect the city from possible invasion, this recently restored fort, perched high above Newcastle Harbour, was one of the few gun installations in Australia to fire in anger during WWII. On 8 June 1942, a Japanese submarine suddenly surfaced, raining shells on the city. Fort Scratchley returned fire, eliminating the threat after just four rounds. Learn all about it on a guided tour of the fort and its underground tunnels.

Nobby's Head WATERFRONT
Originally an island, this headland at the entrance to Newcastle's harbour was joined to the mainland by a stone breakwater built by convicts between 1818 and 1846; many of those poor souls were lost to the wild seas during its construction. The walk along the spit towards the lighthouse and meteorological station is exhilarating, with waves crashing and joggers jostling your elbows.

◉ Honeysuckle Precinct

Newcastle Museum MUSEUM
(☑02-4974 1400; www.newcastlemuseum.com.au; Workshop Way; ⊙10am-5pm Tue-Sun) FREE The city's flagship museum occupies the restored Honeysuckle rail workshops on the foreshore and focuses on the social history and industrial heritage of the city. Many of the exhibits are of the whizz-bang modern sort, designed for those with short attention spans.

Maritime Centre MUSEUM
(☑02-4929 2588; www.maritimecentrenewcastle. org.au; Lee Wharf, 3 Honeysuckle Dr; adult/child $10/5; ⊙10am-4pm Tue-Sun) Learn all about Newcastle's nautical heritage at this museum in the same restored wharf building that houses the visitor centre.

⃛ Activities

Swimming & Surfing

At the east end of town, the needs of surfers and swimmers are sated at **Newcastle Beach**, but if you're irrationally paranoid about sharks, the concrete **ocean baths** are a mellow alternative, encased in wonderful multicoloured 1922 architecture. There's a shallow pool for toddlers and a compelling backdrop of heaving ocean and chugging cargo ships. Surfers should goofy-foot it to **Nobby's Beach**, just north of the baths – the fast left-hander known as the Wedge is at its northern end.

South of Newcastle Beach, below King Edward Park, is Australia's oldest ocean bath, the convict-carved **Bogey Hole**. It's an atmospheric place to splash about when the surf's crashing over its edge. The most popular surfing breaks are at **Bar Beach** and **Merewether Beach**, further south.

The city's famous surfing festival, **Surfest** (www.surfest.com), takes place in March.

Newcastle

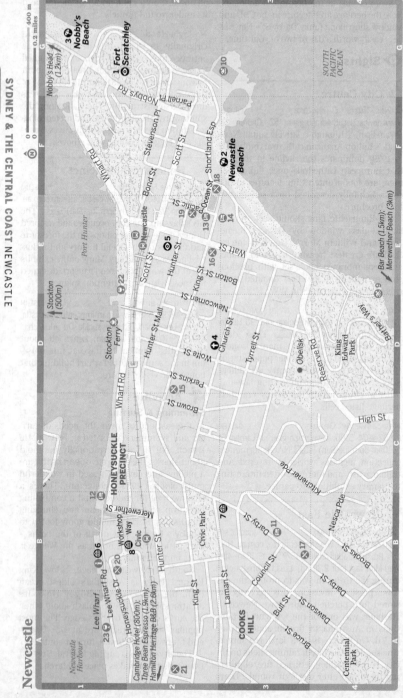

Newcastle Harbour

Lee Wharf

Lee Wharf Rd

Honeysuckle Dr

Cambridge Hotel (800m);
Three Bean Espresso (1.9km);
Hamilton Heritage B&B (2.6km)

HONEYSUCKLE PRECINCT

Workshop Way

Merewether St

Civic Park

COOKS HILL

King St

Laman St

Council St

Bull St

Dawson St

Bruce St

Centennial Park

Brooks St

Darby St

Nesca Pde

Kitchener Pde

High St

Brown St

Perkins St

Hunter St

Wharf Rd

Stockton Ferry

Stockton (500m)

Port Hunter

Newcastle

Scott St

Hunter St

King St

Bolton St

Watt St

Newcomen St

Church St

Tyrrell St

Wolfe St

Obelisk

Reserve Rd

King Edward Park

Bathers Way

Bar Beach (1.5km);
Merewether Beach (3km)

Hunter St Mall

Bond St

Scott St

Stevenson Pl

Wharf Rd

Parnell Pl

Nobbys Rd

Nobby's Head (1.2km)

Nobby's Beach

Fort Scratchley

Newcastle Beach

Ocean St

Shortland Esp

Atlantic St

SOUTH PACIFIC OCEAN

Newcastle

Walking & Cycling

The visitor centre has plenty of brochures outlining self-guided themed tours of the city. These include the *Bather's Way*, which leads between Nobby's and Merewether Beaches and is dotted with signs describing Indigenous, convict and natural history, and the *Newcastle East Heritage Walk*, which heads past colonial highlights in the city centre. The *Newcastle by Design* brochure outlines a short stroll down and around Hunter St, covering some of the inner city's interesting architecture.

🛏 Sleeping

Newcastle Beach YHA   HOSTEL $
(☑02-4925 3544; www.yha.com.au; 30 Pacific St, Newcastle East; dm/s/d $36/60/87; @🛜) This heritage-listed building is a bikini strap away from Newcastle Beach. Inside, it's a bit like an English public school (without the humiliating hazing rituals), featuring grand spaces and high ceilings. There's also free bodyboard use, surfboard hire, free pub meals and a free barbecue on Thursday night.

Stockton Beach Holiday Park CAMPGROUND $
(☑02-4928 1393; www.stocktonbeach.com; 3 Pitt St, Stockton; sites/cabins from $34/75; ❄@🛜) 🏊 The beach is at your doorstep (or should that be tent flap?) at this tourist park behind the dunes in Stockton. Cabins range from bunkhouse units to smart self-contained villas. Park yourself here and catch the ferry to explore Newcastle.

Crown on Darby   APARTMENT $$
(☑02-4941 6777; www.crownondarby.com.au; 101 Darby St, Cooks Hill; apt from $155; P❄🛜) If giant TV screens and comfy beds are your yardstick for good accommodation, consider this brand-new complex of 38 apartments on Newcastle's coolest street. The studios are bigger than your average hotel room and have kitchenettes, while the one-bedrooms have full kitchens and living rooms with sofa beds.

Hamilton Heritage B&B   B&B $$
(☑02-4961 1242; www.accommodationinnewcastle.com.au; 178 Denison St, Hamilton; s $95-120, d $140-170; ❄🛜🐾) It's all florals and frills in this Federation-era home near the Beaumont St cafe strip. The three rooms (including a family room sleeping up to six) have old-fashioned en suites and tea- and coffee-making facilities. Pet friendly.

Novotel Newcastle Beach   HOTEL $$$
(☑02-4032 3700; www.novotel.com; 5 King St, Newcastle East; r from $287) What the Novotel's rooms lack in size they make up for in style. There's no pool, but the beach is just across the road, and there is a small gym.

Crowne Plaza   HOTEL $$$
(☑02-4907 5000; www.crowneplaza.com.au/newcastle; cnr Merewether St & Wharf Rd, Honeysuckle Precinct; ste from $240; P❄@🛜🏊) It's a large, generic, modern hotel, but it's right on the waterfront and all the rooms are spacious suites. The service is excellent and the pool is a real plus.

✗ Eating

Darby and Beaumont are the main eat streets and there are also plenty of cafes and restaurants along the waterfront. The **Newcastle City Farmers Market** (www.newcastle cityfarmersmarket.com.au; Griffiths Rd, Broadmeadows; ⊙8am-1pm Sun) is held at Newcastle Showground most Sundays.

Estabar CAFE $
(61 Shortland Esplanade, Newcastle East; mains $10-15; ⊙6.30am-6pm) Start the day with breakfast at this sun-drenched cafe overlooking Newcastle Beach – although there's no rush as it's served all day. When the temperature soars, drop by for gelato.

Bocados SPANISH $$
(✆02-4925 2801; www.bocados.com.au; 25 King St, Newcastle; tapas $11-20, raciones $22-33; ⊙noon-3pm Wed-Sat, 6pm-late Tue-Sun) Only a castanet click away from Newcastle Beach, Bocados has a menu featuring *tapas* (small plates) and *raciones* (larger plates) that trawl the Iberian peninsula for their inspiration. There are plenty of Spanish drops on the menu.

Sprout Dining MEDITERRANEAN $$
(✆02-4023 3565; www.sproutcatering.com.au; 1/2 Honeysuckle Dr, Honeysuckle Precinct; mains $27-32; ⊙6-9pm Wed & Thu, noon-2pm & 6-9pm Fri & Sat, noon-2pm Sun) The menu changes weekly at this casually elegant bistro, but it always features an array of delicious house-made pasta. Crowd-pleasing mains and desserts are complemented by a good range of regional wines.

Merewether Surfhouse CAFE, RESTAURANT $$
(✆02-4918 0000; www.surfhouse.com.au; Henderson Pde, Merewether; mains cafe $15-20, bar $19, restaurant $26-35; ⊙7am-late) Watch the action on Merewether Beach from one of the many spaces in this newly built, architecturally notable complex. You can enjoy quality pub grub in the top-floor terrace bar, sophisticated Mod Oz dishes in the adjoining restaurant, breakfast and light lunches in the cafe downstairs, or a $10 pizza from the beach promenade.

Three Bean Espresso CAFE $$
(146 Beaumont St, Hamilton; mains $15-21; ⊙7am-5pm Mon-Fri, to 3pm Sat) ✍ This bustling cafe is a prime brunching spot. Innumerable variations of eggs are the main attraction, and both the coffee and the cakes are excellent.

Delucas Pizza PIZZERIA $$
(✆02-4929 3555; 159 Darby St, Cooks Hill; pizza $25; ⊙5pm-late Tue-Sun) Delicious pizza and old-school decor make this Newcastle's most popular pizzeria. The pasta's good, too.

★Subo MODERN AUSTRALIAN $$$
(✆02-4023 4048; www.subo.com.au; 551d Hunter St, Newcastle West; 2 courses $58; ⊙6-10pm Wed-Sun) Gorgeous looking and exquisite tasting Japanese- and French-influenced cuisine graces the plates at this innovative restaurant down the shabby end of Hunter St. The stylish dining room really is tiny, so book well in advance.

Restaurant Mason FRENCH $$$
(✆02-4926 1014; www.restaurantmason.com; 3/35 Hunter St, Newcastle; mains breakfast $18-21, lunch $20-36, dinner $35-42; ⊙noon-3.30pm & 6pm-late Tue-Fri, 8am-3pm & 6pm-late Sat & Sun; ✍) There's a summery feel to this modern French restaurant, with tables placed under the plane trees outside and a main dining space that opens to the elements. Dishes make the most of fresh local produce.

Bacchus MODERN AUSTRALIAN $$$
(✆02-4927 1332; www.bacchusnewcastle.com.au; 141 King St, Newcastle; mains $44; ⊙6-11pm Tue-Sat) A decadent Roman god has transformed this former Methodist mission into a very atmospheric place to splurge (not purge – this isn't ancient Rome, after all). The surrounds are extremely elegant, dishes are assured and the wine list is excellent.

🍸 Drinking & Nightlife

Honeysuckle Hotel PUB
(www.honeysucklehotel.com.au; Wharf C, Honeysuckle Dr, Honeysuckle Precinct; ⊙10am-11pm) The deck at this waterfront place, located in a cavernous but cool converted warehouse, is a perfect spot for a sundowner. Live Latin bands play under the rafters in the Rum Bar from Thursday to Saturday, and there's often live music downstairs on the weekends too.

Brewery BAR
(www.qwb.com.au; 150 Wharf Rd, Newcastle; ⊙10.30am-midnight Sun, to 10pm Mon, Tue & Thu, to 3am Wed, Fri & Sat) Perched on Queens Wharf, the Brewery's views and outdoor tables are sought after by office workers and uni students alike. DJs take to the decks on Wednesday student nights and live bands kick off on weekends.

Cambridge Hotel LIVE MUSIC
(www.yourcambridge.com; 789 Hunter St, Newcastle West) This backpacker favourite launched Silverchair, Newcastle's most famous cultur-

WORTH A TRIP

NEWCASTLE NATURE RESERVES

The **Hunter Wetlands Centre** (☎02-4951 6466; www.wetlands.org.au; 412 Sandgate Rd, Shortland; adult/child $10/5; ☺9am-4pm) 🖉 is home to over 200 bird and animal species. You can explore via canoe ($10 for two hours) or dip in a net and examine the results under a magnifying glass. Bring mosquito repellent if you don't want to contribute to the ecosystem in ways you hadn't intended. To get there, take the Pacific Hwy towards Maitland and turn left at the cemetery, or catch the train to Sandgate and walk (10 minutes).

Blackbutt Reserve (☎02-4904 3344; www.newcastle.nsw.gov.au/recreation/blackbutt_reserve; Carnley Ave, Kotara; parking per hr $1.50; ☺park 7am-7pm, wildlife exhibits 10am-5pm) **FREE** sits in a tract of bushland a short walk from Kotara train station. The council-run reserve has plenty of walking trails, picnic areas and enclosures filled with native critters: koalas, wallabies, wombats and a cacophonic chorus of birds.

al export, and continues to showcase touring national bands and local acts.

ⓘ Information

As well as the public libraries, you can access free wi-fi in Hunter St Mall, the Honeysuckle Precinct, Hamilton's Beaumont St and Newcastle Airport.

John Hunter Hospital (☎02-4921 3000; www.health.nsw.gov.au; Lookout Rd, New Lambton Heights) Has 24-hour emergency care.

Visitor Information Centre (☎02-4929 2588; www.visitnewcastle.com.au; Lee Wharf, 3 Honeysuckle Dr; ☺10am-4pm Tue-Sun)

ⓘ Getting There & Away

AIR

Newcastle Airport (☎02-4928 9800; www.newcastleairport.com.au) is at Williamtown, 23km north of the city.

Brindabella Airlines (☎1300 66 88 24; www.brindabellaairlines.com.au) Flies to/from Sydney and Canberra.

Jetstar (☎13 15 38; www.jetstar.com.au) Flies to/from Melbourne, the Gold Coast and Brisbane.

QantasLink (☎13 13 13; www.qantas.com.au) Flies to/from Brisbane.

Regional Express (Rex; ☎13 17 13; www.rex.com.au) Flies to/from Sydney and Ballina.

Virgin Australia (☎13 67 89; www.virgin-australia.com) Flies to/from Brisbane and Melbourne.

BUS

Nearly all long-distance buses stop behind Newcastle train station.

Busways (☎02-4983 1560; www.busways.com.au) At least two buses daily to Tea Gardens ($21, 1½ hours), Hawks Nest ($21, 1¾ hours), Bluey's Beach ($25, two hours), Forster ($31, 3¼ hours) and Taree ($34, four hours).

Greyhound (☎1300 473 946; www.greyhound.com.au) Two daily coaches to/from Sydney ($30, 2¾ hours), Port Macquarie ($55, four hours), Coffs Harbour ($76, seven hours), Byron Bay ($124, 10 to 11½ hours) and Brisbane ($153, 14½ hours).

Port Stephens Coaches (☎02-4982 2940; www.pscoaches.com.au; adult/child $4.60/2.30) Regular buses to Anna Bay (1¼ hours), Nelson Bay (1½ hours), Shoal Bay (1½ hours) and Fingal Bay (two hours).

Premier Motor Service (☎13 34 10; www.premierms.com.au) Daily coaches to/from Sydney ($34, three hours), Port Macquarie ($47, 3¾ hours), Coffs Harbour ($58, six hours), Byron Bay ($71, 11 hours) and Brisbane ($76, 14½ hours).

Rover Coaches (☎02-4990 1699; www.rover-coaches.com.au) Four buses to/from Cessnock ($7, 1¼ hours) on weekdays and two on Saturday; no Sunday service.

TRAIN

Sydney Trains (p102) has regular services to Gosford ($8.40, 1½ hours) and Sydney ($8.40, three hours). A line also heads to the Hunter Valley; Branxton ($6.60, 50 minutes) is the closest stop to wine country.

ⓘ Getting Around

TO/FROM THE AIRPORT

➡ Port Stephens Coaches (p115) has frequent buses stopping at the airport en route between Newcastle ($4.60, 40 minutes) and Nelson Bay (one hour).

➡ A taxi to Newcastle city centre costs about $60.

Fogg's Airport Shuttle (☎02-4950 0526; www.foggsshuttle.com.au)

Hunter Valley Day Tours (☎02-4951 4574; www.huntervalleydaytours.com.au) Provides shuttles to Newcastle ($35 for one person, $45 for two), the Hunter Valley ($125 for one or two people), Lake Macquarie and Port Stephens.

BUS
Newcastle has an extensive network of **local buses** (☑ 13 15 00; www.newcastlebuses.info). There's a fare-free bus zone in the inner city between 7.30am and 6pm. Other fares are time-based (one hour/four hours/all day $3.60/7/11); tickets can be purchased from the driver. The main depot is next to Newcastle train station.

FERRY
The Stockton ferry (adult/child $2.50/1.20) leaves every half-hour from Queens Wharf from 5.15am to about 11pm.

TRAIN
Services leaving Newcastle station stop at Hamilton, Wickham and Civic before branching out to either Sydney or the Hunter Valley. Travel between these stations costs $3.60.

HUNTER VALLEY

A filigree of narrow country lanes criss-crosses this verdant valley, but a pleasant country drive isn't the main motivator for visitors – sheer decadence is. The Hunter is one big gorge fest: fine wine, boutique beer, chocolate, cheese, olives, you name it. Bacchus would surely approve.

Going on the philosophy that good food and wine will inevitably up the odds for nookie, the region is a popular weekender for Sydney couples. Every Friday they descend, like a plague of Ralph Lauren polo shirt–wearing locusts. Prices leap up accordingly.

The oldest wine region in Australia, the Hunter is known for its semillon and shiraz. Vines were first planted in the 1820s and by the 1860s there were 20 sq km under cultivation. However, the wineries gradually declined and it wasn't until the 1960s that winemaking again became an important industry. If it's no longer the crowning jewel of the Australian wine industry, it still turns in some excellent vintages.

The Hunter has an important ace up its sleeve: these wineries are attitude-free and welcoming of viticulturists and novices alike. Staff will rarely give you the evil eye if you leadenly twirl your glass once too often, or don't conspicuously savour the bouquet. Even those with only a casual interest in wine should consider visiting – it's a lovely area, and a great direction to turn to if the weather drives you from the beaches.

◉ Sights

Most attractions lie in an area bordered to the north by the New England Hwy and to the south by Wollombi/Maitland Rd, with the main wineries and restaurants on or around Broke Rd in Pokolbin (population 694). The main town in the area is Cessnock (population 13,700), to the south. Wine Country Dr heads straight up from Cessnock to Branxton (population 1830). Note, the bottom half of this route is sometimes labelled Allandale Rd and the top end Branxton Rd.

To the northwest there are further vineyards around Broke (population 636) and Singleton (population 14,000).

Wineries
The valley's 140-plus wineries range from small, family-run affairs to big commercial operations. Most offer free tastings, although some charge a small fee.

Check out the free *Hunter Valley Visitors Guide* at the information centre at Pokolbin and use its handy map to plot your course.

Audrey Wilkinson Vineyard   WINERY
(www.audreywilkinson.com.au; 750 DeBeyers Rd, Pokolbin; ☉10am-5pm) First planted in 1866, it's worth visiting more for its interesting historic display and views than for its tasting room.

Brokenwood   WINERY
(www.brokenwood.com.au; 401-427 McDonalds Rd, Pokolbin; ☉9.30am-5pm) One of the Hunter's most acclaimed wineries.

Macquariedale Estate   WINERY
(www.macquariedale.com.au; 170 Sweetwater Rd, Rothbury; ☉10am-5pm) ⏺ A boutique winemaker that's certified organic and biodynamic. The estate also grows garlic and olives.

McWilliams Mount Pleasant   WINERY
(www.mountpleasantwines.com.au; 401 Marrowbone Rd, Pokolbin; ☉10am-5pm) Guided winery tours at 11am daily ($5).

Pooles Rock Wines   WINERY
(www.poolesrock.com.au; DeBeyers Rd, Pokolbin; ☉10am-5pm) A big player, producing the midpriced Cockfighter's Ghost range as well as its excellent flagship wines.

Small Winemakers Centre   WINERY
(www.smallwinemakerscentre.com.au; 426 McDonalds Rd, Pokolbin; ☉10am-5pm) Acts as a cellar door for a handful of boutique winemakers. After a tasting, drop into the attached **Australian Regional Food Store** for a snack.

Tamburlaine
WINERY

(www.tamburlaine.com.au; 358 McDonalds Rd, Pokolbin; ⊙9am-5pm) 🌱 Certified organic winemaker with a rustic cellar door.

Tempus Two
WINERY

(www.tempustwo.com.au; 2144 Broke Rd, Pokolbin; ⊙10am-5pm) This huge architecturally interesting place is a favourite with tour buses, which descend upon its tasting room, Japanese restaurant and Smelly Cheese Shop. Boutique producer Meerea Park has set up a tasting room here, which is worth seeking out, especially when Tempus Two's own cellar door is heaving.

Tower Estate
WINERY

(www.towerestatewines.com; cnr Halls & Broke Rds, Pokolbin; ⊙10am-5pm) Established by one of Australia's major wine industry figures, the late Len Evans, this classy winery is part of a package of sophisticated accommodation and eating options.

Wyndham Estate
WINERY

(☑02-4938 3444; www.wyndhamestate.com; 700 Dalwood Rd, Dalwood; ⊙9.30am-4.30pm) 🌱 Established in 1828, this winery is known for its shiraz. It's also home to the Olive Tree restaurant and hosts Opera in the Vineyards.

Other Attractions

Hunter Valley Gardens
GARDENS

(www.hvg.com.au; Broke Rd, Pokolbin; adult/child $25/15; ⊙9am-5pm) This 24-hectare garden has impressive floral and landscape displays. Popular annual events include *Snow Time* in July and the *Christmas Lights Spectacular*, Australia's biggest such display.

The neighbouring Pokolbin Village complex has restaurants, shops, a children's playground and aqua golf.

🚗 Tours

If no one's volunteering to stay sober enough to drive, there are plenty of winery tours available. Some operators will collect you in Sydney or Newcastle for a lengthy day trip. Staff at visitor centres and accommodation providers should be able to arrange a booking that suits your needs.

Hunter Valley Boutique Wine Tours
WINERY TOUR

(☑0419 419 931; www.huntervalleytours.com.au) Small tours from $65 per person for a half day and from $99 for a full day including lunch.

Aussie Wine Tours
WINERY TOUR

(☑0402 909 090; www.aussiewinetours.com.au) You can determine your own itinerary if you take one of these private, chauffeur-driven tours.

Wine Rover
WINERY TOUR

(☑02-4990 1699; www.rovercoaches.com.au) Coaches will pick you up in Cessnock or Pokolbin ($55), Branxton ($65) or Newcastle ($70) for a day spent visiting wineries.

⭐ Festivals & Events

During the warm months superstars regularly drop by for weekend concerts at the bigger vineyards. If there's something special on, accommodation books up well in advance. Check what's on at www.winecountry.com.au.

A Day on the Green
MUSIC

(www.adayonthegreen.com.au) Concert series at Bimbadgen Estate during summer.

Lovedale Long Lunch
FOOD

(www.lovedalelonglunch.com.au) Seven wineries and chefs team up to serve lunches accompanied by music and art; third weekend of May.

Hunter Valley Wine & Food Month
WINE, FOOD

(www.huntervalleyuncorked.com.au) In June.

Jazz in the Vines
MUSIC

(www.jazzinthevines.com.au) At Tyrrell's vineyard in October.

Opera in the Vineyards
OPERA

(www.operainthevineyards.com.au) At Wyndham Estate in October.

🛌 Sleeping

Prices shoot up savagely on Friday and Saturday nights and two-night minimum stays are common. Many places don't accept children.

Hunter Valley YHA
HOSTEL $

(☑02-4991 3278; www.yha.com.au; 100 Wine Country Dr, Nulkaba; dm $29-33, r with/without bathroom $88/77; @🞍🞍) Each February this newish, custom-built hostel is packed to the rafters with working-holidaymakers picking fruit on the vineyards. The reward at the end of a long day is a pool and plenty of bonhomie around the barbecue and outdoor pizza oven. The rooms can get stiflingly hot, though.

⭐ Thistle Hill
B&B $$

(☑02-6574 7217; www.thill.com.au; 591 Hermitage Rd, Pokolbin; r/cottages from $190/330; 🞍🞍🞍) This idyllic 25-acre property features rose

SYDNEY & THE CENTRAL COAST HUNTER VALLEY

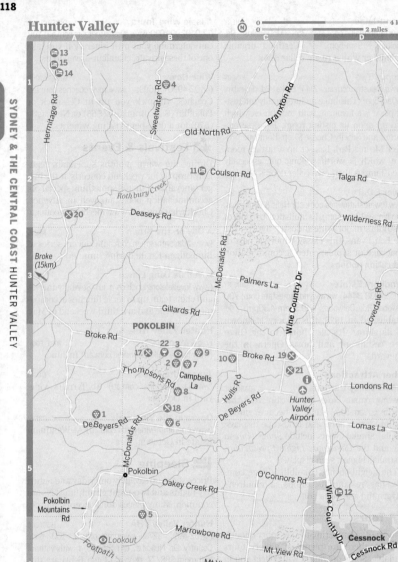

gardens, a lime orchard, a vineyard, a self-contained cottage sleeping up to five and a luxurious guesthouse with six double rooms. Rooms and common areas have an elegant French provincial sensibility.

Splinters Guest House B&B $$

(☏ 02-6574 7118; www.splinters.com.au; 617 Hermitage Rd, Pokolbin; r/cottages from $190/240; ✳ 🛜 ⌨) Gregarious owner Bobby Jory runs this tranquil B&B with great élan, spoiling guests with treats such as gourmet break-

SYDNEY & THE CENTRAL COAST HUNTER VALLEY

fasts, port and chocolates in rooms, and wine and cheese on the terrace. There are three smart doubles with comfortable beds, and two rustic self-catering cottages.

Buffs at Pokolbin CABIN $$
(☑ 02-4998 7636; www.buffsatpokolbin.com.au; 47 Coulson Rd, Pokolbin; 1-/2-bedroom cottages from $180/280; 🆚🐾🏊) Set on a tranquil 100-acre property where kangaroos hop under the gum trees, Buffs' four spotlessly clean, self-contained cottages are as comfortable as they are keenly priced. It's a fantastic choice for families and couples alike.

Spicers Vineyards Estate RESORT $$$
(☑ 02-6574 7229; www.spicersgroup.com.au; 555 Hermitage Rd, Pokolbin; ste $395-495; 🆚🛜🏊) Marketing itself as 'the ultimate intimately unique wine country estate', Spicers offers 12 modern suites with king-size beds, lounge areas (with open fireplace) and bathrooms (with spa bath). Facilities include the **Restaurant Botanica**, a day spa and a pool.

🍴 Eating

Bookings are recommended midweek and essential on weekends. Don't expect any bargains – those on a tight budget should self-cater. Many wineries have restaurants.

⭐ **Muse Kitchen** EUROPEAN $$
(☑ 02-4998 7899; www.musedining.com.au; Keith Tulloch Winery, cnr Hermitage & Deasys Rds, Pokolbin; mains $25-36; ⏰ noon-3pm Wed-Sun, 6-9pm Sat) The relaxed daytime incarnation of the Hunter's top restaurant serves delicious croque monsieurs and fancy burgers, but most of the menu is given over to substantial mains with

a French or Italian bent. A set tasting menu is offered on Saturday night ($75).

Enzo CAFE $$
(www.enzohuntervalley.com.au; cnr Broke & Ekerts Rds, Pokolbin; mains breakfast $15-29, lunch $22-30; ⏰ 9am-4pm) Claim a table by the fireside in winter or in the garden in summer to enjoy the rustic, generously sized dishes served at this popular Italian-inflected cafe. Combine your visit with a tasting at neighbouring David Hook Wines.

Muse Restaurant MODERN AUSTRALIAN $$$
(☑ 02-4998 6777; www.musedining.com.au; 1 Broke Rd, Pokolbin; 2-/3-course meal $75/95; ⏰ 6.30-10pm Wed-Fri, noon-3pm & 6.30-10pm Sat, noon-3pm Sun; 🅿) Shaped like a big barrel with its 'lid' permanently propped open, the Hungerford Hill winery complex stands sentinel at the entry to Broke Rd. Inside, the area's highest rated restaurant offers sophisticated contemporary fare and first-rate service. Vegetarians get their own menu (two courses $60).

Bistro Molines FRENCH $$$
(☑ 02-4990 9553; www.bistromolines.com.au; 749 Mt View Rd, Mt View; mains $38-42; ⏰ noon-3pm Thu-Mon, 7-9pm Fri & Sat) Set in the Tallavera Grove winery, this French restaurant has a sensational, seasonally driven menu that is nearly as impressive as the view over the vines.

Margan MODERN AUSTRALIAN $$$
(☑ 02-6579 1102; www.margan.com.au; 1238 Milbrodale Rd, Broke; mains breakfast $18, lunch $36-38, 3-/4-/5-course tasting menu $65/80/95; ⏰ noon-3pm & 6-9.30pm Fri & Sat, 9-10.30am & noon-3pm Sun) 🌿 Live up to the area's name and go for broke when it comes to ordering from

the tempting array of dishes on offer at this vineyard restaurant. Much of the produce is sourced from its kitchen garden; the rest comes from local providores whenever possible.

Providores

**Hunter Valley Smelly
Cheese Shop**   DELI $

(www.smellycheese.net.au; Tempus Two Winery, 2144 Broke Rd, Pokolbin; mains $9-16; ⊙10am-5pm) Along with the desirables filling the climate-controlled cheese room, this place sells antipasto picnic platters ($40), all-day breakfasts, pies, pizzas and filled baguettes. There's another branch at Pokolbin Village.

**Hunter Valley Cheese
Company**   CHEESE SHOP $

(www.huntervalleycheese.com.au; McGuigans Winery, 447 McDonalds Rd, Pokolbin; ⊙9am-5.30pm) Staff will chew your ear about cheesy comestibles all day long, especially during the daily 11am cheese talk. There's a bewildering variety of styles available for purchase.

**Hunter Valley Chocolate
Company**   CHOCOLATE SHOP $

(www.hvchocolate.com.au; Peterson House, Broke Rd, Pokolbin; ⊙9am-5pm) Sells a tempting array of locally made chocolate, fudge and other treats. While you're here, pop in for a tasting at Peterson House next door – the only producer of sparkling wine in the Hunter.

Hunter Olive Centre   DELI $

(www.pokolbinestate.com.au; 298 McDonalds Rd, Pokolbin; ⊙9am-5pm) Hidden behind Pokolbin Estate Vineyard, this stone cottage offers dozens of things to try on little squares of bread – oil, tapnade, chutney, jam etc.

🍷 Drinking

Harrigan's   PUB

(www.harrigans.com.au; Broke Rd, Pokolbin; ⊙9am-10pm) A comfortable Irish pub with beef-and-Guinness pies on the menu and live bands most weekends.

Wollombi Tavern   PUB

(www.wollombitavern.com.au; Great North Rd, Wollombi; ⊙10am-late) Located at the Wollombi crossroads, this fabulous little pub is the home of Dr Jurd's Jungle Juice, a dangerous brew of port, brandy and wine. On weekends, the tavern is a favourite pit stop for motorbike clubs (the non-scary sort).

ℹ Information

Hunter Valley Visitor Centre (⊘02-4991 4535; www.huntervalleyvisitorcentre.com.au; 455 Wine Country Dr; ⊙9am-5pm) The visitor centre has a huge stock of leaflets and info on valley accommodation, attractions and dining.

ℹ Getting There & Away

BUS

Rover Coaches (⊘02-4990 1699; www.rovercoaches.com.au) Has four buses heading between Newcastle and Cessnock ($7, 1¼ hours) on weekdays and two on Saturday; no Sunday service. Other buses head to Cessnock from the train stations at Morisset ($3.60, one hour, two daily) and Maitland ($3.60, 50 minutes, frequent).

TRAIN

Sydney Rail has a line through the Hunter Valley from Newcastle ($6.60, 50 minutes). Branxton is the closest station to the vineyards, although only Maitland has bus services to Cessnock.

ℹ Getting Around

Exploring without a car can be challenging. The YHA hostel hires bikes, as do **Grapemobile** (⊘02-4998 7660; www.grapemobile.com.au; 307 Palmers Lane, Pokolbin; hire per 2/8hr $20/25; ⊙10am-6pm) and **Hunter Valley Cycling** (⊘0418 281 480; www.huntervalleycycling.com.au; 266 DeBeyers Rd, Pokolbin; hire per 1/2 days $35/45).

The **Vineyard Shuttle** (⊘02-4991 3655; www.vineyardshuttle.com.au; per person $15) offers a door-to-door service between Pokolbin accommodation and restaurants.

Byron Bay & Northern New South Wales

Includes ➡

Why Go?

Beach towns and national parks leapfrog each other all the way up this stupendous stretch of coast. Inland, lush farmland and ancient tracts of World Heritage–listed rainforest do the same.

Providing a buffer between New South Wales' big cities to the south and Queensland's built-up Gold Coast, the North Coast offers an altogether quieter and simpler way of life. In cute little towns throughout the region dyed-in-the-wool country types rub shoulders with big-city escapees and post-hippie alternative lifestylers – if you're looking for fresh local produce, a top-notch meal or a psychic reading, you shouldn't be disappointed. And if you're searching for a surf break, rest assured that there will be an awesome one around the very next corner.

Nowhere on the East Coast conjures up the beach–nature–good times vibe quite like Byron Bay. Those who visit seldom go home complaining – if they go home at all.

Best Places to Eat

➡ No 2 Oak St (p140)

➡ Beachwood Cafe (p151)

➡ Stunned Mullet (p133)

➡ Jaaning Tree (p138)

➡ Sugar Beat (p170)

Best Places to Stay

➡ Elindale House (p165)

➡ Aabi's at Byron (p159)

➡ Crystal Creek Rainforest Retreat (p170)

➡ Lily Pily (p140)

➡ Grey Gum Lodge (p167)

When to Go
Byron Bay

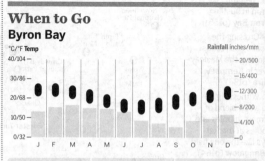

Jun & Jul
Winter brings migrating whales, lanterns to Lismore and rockers to Byron Bay.

Sep–Nov
Returning whales, blooming jacarandas and Byron Bay's Surf Fest.

Dec–Feb
Life's a beach, Tropical Fruits in Lismore and Byron gets the blues.

Byron Bay & Northern New South Wales Highlights

① Laying claim to your own stretch of empty beach in coastal wilderness such as **Myall Lakes National Park** (p126).

② Delving into the ancient World Heritage–listed Gondwana rainforest in **Dorrigo National Park** (p141).

③ Getting more closely acquainted with whales and dolphins in a cruise from **Port Stephens** (p123).

④ Marvelling at the pre-European landscape stretching endlessly from **Crowdy Head** (p128).

⑤ Enjoying the charm of pretty hinterland villages such as **Bellingen** (p139).

⑥ Watching the whales spout and the dolphins surf from atop beautiful Cape Byron in bustling **Byron Bay** (p155).

⑦ Cruising the bucolic back roads following the Macleay River in **Kempsey Shire** (p134).

⑧ Witnessing the weird blend of farmers, hippies and foodies at market days like the one held in **Bangalow** (p164).

ℹ Getting There & Around

AIR

There are domestic airports at Taree, Port Macquarie, Coffs Harbour, Grafton, Ballina and Lismore. Additionally, Newcastle Airport is handy for Port Stephens, and Gold Coast Airport is only 4km from Tweed Heads.

BUS

Greyhound and Premier both have coach services linking Sydney and Brisbane via the Pacific Hwy. Other companies cover smaller stretches along the way.

TRAIN

NSW TrainLink services between Sydney and Brisbane stop at Wingham, Taree, Nambucca Heads, Coffs Harbour and Grafton.

PORT STEPHENS

POP 64,800

This sheltered harbour is about an hour's drive north of Newcastle, occupying a submerged valley that stretches more than 20km inland. Framing its southern edge is the narrow **Tomaree Peninsula**, blessed with near-deserted beaches, national parks and an extraordinary sand-dune system. The main centre, **Nelson Bay**, is home to both a fishing fleet and an armada of tourist vessels, the latter trading on the town's status as the 'dolphin capital of Australia'.

Just east of Nelson Bay, and virtually merged with it, is slightly smaller **Shoal Bay**, with a long beach that's great for swimming (but only in the morning, as winds come up in the afternoon). The road ends a short drive south from here at **Fingal Bay**, with another lovely beach on the fringes of Tomaree National Park. The park stretches west around clothing-optional **Samurai Beach**, a popular surfing spot, and **One Mile Beach**, a gorgeous semicircle of the softest sand and bluest water favoured by those in the know: surfers, beachcombers, idle romantics.

The park ends at the surfside village of **Anna Bay**, which has as a backdrop the incredible **Worimi Conservation Lands**. Gan Gan Rd connects Anna Bay, One Mile Beach and Samurai Beach with Nelson Bay Rd.

◉ Sights

Worimi Conservation Lands   OUTDOORS
(www.worimiconservationlands.com; 3-day entry permit $10) Located at Stockton Bight, these are the longest moving sand dunes in the southern hemisphere, stretching over 35km. In the heart of it, it's possible to become so surrounded by shimmering sand that you'll lose sight of the ocean or any sign of life. At the far western end of the beach, the wreck of the *Sygna* founders in the water.

Thanks to the generosity of the Worimi people, whose land this is, you're able to roam around (provided you don't disturb any Aboriginal sites) and drive along the beach (4WD only; permit required). Get your permits from the visitor centre or National Parks & Wildlife Service (NPWS) office in Nelson Bay, the Anna Bay BP or the 24-hour Metro service station near the Lavis Lane entry.

Tomaree National Park   PARK
(www.nationalparks.nsw.gov.au/tomaree-national-park) This wonderfully wild expanse harbours several threatened species, including the spotted-tailed quoll and powerful owl. If you keep your eyes peeled, you're bound to spot a koala or wallaby.

At the eastern end of Shoal Bay there's a short walk to the surf at unpatrolled **Zenith Beach** (beware of rips and strong undercurrents), or you can tackle the **Tomaree Head Summit Walk** (1km, one hour return) and be rewarded by stunning ocean views. Ask at the NPWS office about longer treks, including the coastal walk from Tomaree Head to Big Rocky.

Nelson Head Lighthouse Cottage   HISTORIC BUILDING
(Lighthouse Rd, Nelson Bay; ⊙10am-4pm) **FREE** Built in 1875, this restored building has a tearoom and a small museum with displays on the area's history. The views of Port Stephens are suitably inspiring.

🏃 Activities & Tours

Imagine Cruises   CRUISE
(☑02-4984 9000; www.imaginecruises.com.au; Dock C, d'Albora Marinas, Nelson Bay) 🚢 Trips include 3½-hour Sail, Swim, Snorkel & Dolphin Watch trips (adult/child $60/30, December to March), 90-minute Dolphin Watch cruises ($26/14, November to May), three-hour Whale Watch cruises ($60/25, May to mid-November) and two-hour Seafood Dinner cruises ($39/20, October to May).

Moonshadow   CRUISE
(☑02-4984 9388; www.moonshadow.com.au; 35 Stockton St, Nelson Bay) 🚢 Dolphin watching

(adult/child $21/11, year-round; $26/14 including boom-netting, Christmas to Easter), whale watching ($60/25, May to November) and dinner cruises ($69/26).

Dolphin Swim Australia
OUTDOORS

(📞 1300 721 358; www.dolphinswimaustralia.com.au; 5hr trip $269; ⊙ Sat & Sun Oct-Easter) It's impossible to keep up with dolphins if you're swimming, so on this trip you hang on to a rope and get towed through the water.

Port Stephens Surf School
SURFING

(📞 0411 419 576; www.portstephenssurfschool.com.au; 2hr/2-/3-day lessons $60/110/165) Surf lessons, stand-up paddleboarding and board hire (one hour/two hours $17/28).

Port Stephens Ecosports
KAYAKING

(📞 0405 033 518; www.portstephensecosports.com.au; kayak/paddleboard/surf-ski hire per hr $25/30/40) Offers a range of kayak excursions, including hour-long mini tours (adult/child $30/20), 1½-hour sunset tours ($35/25) and 2½-hour discovery tours ($45/35).

Port Stephens 4WD Tours
TOUR

(📞 02-4984 4760; www.portstephens4wd.com.au; 35 Stockton St) Offers a 1½-hour Beach & Dune tour (adult/child $49/29), a three-hour Sygna Shipwreck tour (adult/child $85/47) and a sandboarding experience ($26/19). They're tied in with Moonshadow, so cruise combos are available.

Oakfield Ranch
OUTDOORS

(📞 0429 664 172; www.oakfieldranch.com.au; Birubi Pt car park, James Patterson St, Anna Bay) Twenty-minute camel rides along the beach on weekends and public holidays.

🛏 Sleeping

Samurai Port Stephens YHA
HOSTEL $

(📞 02-4982 1921; www.samuraiportstephens.com; Frost Rd, Anna Bay; dm $35, d $91-123; 🛜 ⛱) These attractively furnished, wooden-floored cabins are arranged around a swimming pool and set in koala-populated bushland dotted with Asian sculpture. There's a bush kitchen with BBQs and a ramshackle games shed with pool table.

Melaleuca Surfside Backpackers
HOSTEL $

(📞 02-4981 9422; www.melaleucabackpackers.com.au; 2 Koala Pl, One Mile Beach; camp sites/dm/d from $20/32/100; @🛜) Architect-designed wooden cabins are set amid peaceful scrub inhabited by koalas and kookaburras at this friendly, well-run place. There's a welcoming

lounge area and kitchen, and the owners offer sandboarding and other day trips.

Beaches Serviced Apartments
APARTMENT $$

(📞 02-4984 3255; www.beachesportstephens.com; 12 Gowrie Ave, Nelson Bay; apt from $160; ❄️ 🛜 ⛱) You'll find all the comforts of home (including full kitchens and laundry facilities) in these beautifully kept apartments, ranging in size from studio to three-bedroom. There's a pretty palm-lined pool too.

Wanderers Retreat
APARTMENT $$

(📞 02-4982 1702; www.wanderersretreat.com; 7 Koala Pl, One Mile Beach; cottages from $145; ❄️ ⛱) 🍃 Guests can make like Robinson Crusoe in one of the three luxury treehouses at this tranquil retreat. For those who prefer to keep their feet on the ground, there's a range of cottages and a four-bedroom house with a hot tub.

Bali at the Bay
APARTMENT $$$

(📞 02-4981 5556; www.baliatthebay.com.au; 1 Achilles St, Shoal Bay; apt $260-300; ❄️) Two exceedingly beautiful self-contained apartments – full of flower-garlanded Buddhas and carved wood – do a good job of living up to the name here. The bathrooms are exquisite and spa treatments are available.

🍴 Eating

Red Ned's Gourmet Pie Bar
FAST FOOD $

(www.redneds.com.au; 17-19 Stockton St, Nelson Bay; pies $6; ⊙ 6.30am-5pm) Pie maker Barry Kelly learnt his trade in top-shelf international hotels and his philosophy is simple: he gets a kick out of watching people stare goggle-eyed at his specials board (anyone for crocodile in mushroom and white-wine sauce?).

Sandpipers
MODERN AUSTRALIAN $$

(📞 02-4984 9990; www.sandpipersrestaurant.com.au; 81 Magnus St, Nelson Bay; mains $29-32; ⊙ 5.30-10pm Mon-Sat) A strong Asian influence comes through on the menu of this upmarket but informal restaurant in the Nelson Bay shops. Soft-shell crab is light and delicious, pork belly is perfectly crispy, and satay beef is beautifully tender. Or you can opt for a simple chicken breast or freshly caught fish-of-the-day.

Point
SEAFOOD $$$

(📞 02-4984 7111; www.thepointrestaurant.com.au; Ridgeway Ave, Soldiers Point; mains lunch $16-40, dinner $36-40; ⊙ noon-3pm Tue-Sun,

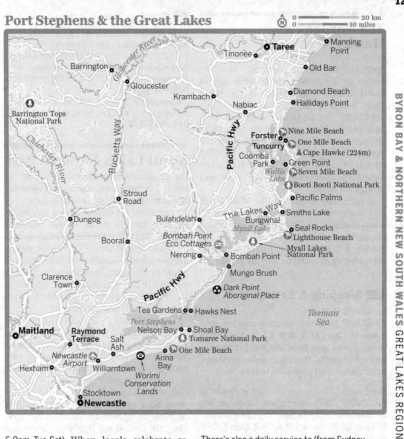

6-9pm Tue-Sat) When locals celebrate romantic milestones, this restaurant on the marina at Soldiers Point is their number-one choice. Views from the balcony and glassed-in dining room are lovely, and the menu has loads of tempting dishes, not all of them seafood.

ℹ Information

NPWS Office (☑ 02-4984 8200; www.national-parks.nsw.gov.au; 12b Teramby Rd, Nelson Bay; ⊙ 8.30am-4.30pm Mon-Fri)

Visitor Information Centre (☑ 02-4980 6900; www.portstephens.org.au; 60 Victoria Pde, Nelson Bay; ⊙ 9am-5pm) Has interesting displays on the marine park.

ℹ Getting There & Around

Port Stephens Coaches (☑ 02-4982 2940; www.pscoaches.com.au) regularly zips around Port Stephens' townships heading to Newcastle and Newcastle Airport ($4.60, 1½ hours).

There's also a daily service to/from Sydney ($39, four hours) stopping at Anna Bay, Nelson Bay and Shoal Bay.

Both **Port Stephens Ferry Service** (☑ 0412 682 117; www.portstephensferryservice.com.au) and the **MV Wallamba** (☑ 0408 494 262) chug from Nelson Bay to Tea Gardens and back two to three times a day (adult/child/bicycle return $20/10/2).

GREAT LAKES REGION

Despite its somewhat grand name, this compact area is an unassuming kind of place, easily missed if you barrel straight up the Pacific Hwy. It takes its name from a series of lakes that hug the coast all the way to the regional centre of Forster-Tuncurry. The joy here is forsaking the highway for leafy roads through national parks.

Tea Gardens & Hawks Nest

POP 2430 & 1120

Sporting the most quaintly evocative names on the coast, this tranquil pair of towns straddles the mouth of the Myall River, linked by the graceful, curved Singing Bridge. Tea Gardens has a quiet, laidback charm; it's a river culture here, older and genteel. At Hawks Nest it's all about the beaches. Jimmy's Beach fronts a glasslike stretch of water facing Nelson Bay, while Bennett's Beach looks to the ocean and Broughton Island.

A great way to explore the Myall River and surrounding waterways is by kayak. Lazy Paddles (✆ 0412 832 220; www.lazypad dles.com.au; tours adult/child $50/35, hire per 2/4/10hr $40/55/65) offers two-hour historical and nature tours, as well as kayaks for hire.

🛏 Sleeping & Eating

Hawks Nest Motel MOTEL $$
(✆ 02-4997 1166; www.hawksnestmotel.com.au; 5 Yamba St; r from $120; ❋ 🕸 ☎) Updated with new carpets, new furniture and bright photographic prints, this older-style two-storey brick motel is an appealing option.

Boatshed CAFE, RESTAURANT $$
(✆ 02-4997 0307; www.teagardensboatshed.com. au; 110 Marine Dr, Tea Gardens; mains breakfast $10-17, lunch $18-30, dinner $34-40; ☉ 8.30am-2.30pm daily, 6-9pm Wed-Sat) You'll have to cope with a few shrieks from the local pelicans while you devour your meal at this former boat shed right on the water. And it's no wonder they're miffed about missing out – everything's delicious. The coffee is good and the deck is a lovely spot for a sunset drink.

Benchmark on Booner INTERNATIONAL $$
(✆ 02-4997 2980; www.benchmarkrestaurant.com. au; 100 Booner St, Hawks Nest; mains $16-32) It's a bit more upmarket and adventurous than you'd expect for a restaurant attached to a bar attached to a motel in a small town. The floor staff are overworked and the menu could do with a proofreader, but the pizza is delicious.

ℹ Information

Tea Gardens Visitor Centre (✆ 02-4997 0111; www.teagardens.nsw.au; 245 Myall St; ☉ 10am-4pm)

ℹ Getting There & Around

While only 5km from Nelson Bay as the cockatoo flies, the drive here necessitates returning to the Pacific Hwy via Medowie and then doubling back – a distance of 81km. The alternative for foot passengers and cyclists are the ferries from Nelson Bay (p125).

Busways (✆ 02-4983 1560; www.busways. com.au) has at least two buses to/from Newcastle daily ($21, 90 minutes).

Myall Lakes National Park

On an extravagantly pretty section of the coast, this large national park (www.nationalparks.nsw.gov.au/Myall-Lakes-National-Park; vehicle admission $7) incorporates a patchwork of lakes, islands, dense littoral rainforest and beaches. The lakes support an incredible quantity and variety of bird life, including bowerbirds, white-bellied sea eagles and tawny frogmouths. There are paths through coastal rainforest and past beach dunes at Mungo Brush in the south, perfect for spotting wildflowers and dingoes.

The best beaches and surf are in the north around beautiful, secluded Seal Rocks, a bushy hamlet hugging Sugarloaf Bay. It has a great beach, with emerald-green rock pools and golden sand. Take the short walk to the Sugarloaf Point Lighthouse for epic ocean views. There's a water-choked gorge along the way and a detour to lonely Lighthouse Beach, a popular surfing spot. The path around the lighthouse leads to a lookout over the actual Seal Rocks – islets where Australian fur seals can sometimes be spotted. Humpback whales swim past Seal Rocks during their annual migration and can often be seen from the shore.

Offshore, Broughton Island is uninhabited except for muttonbirds, little penguins and an enormous diversity of fish species. The diving is tops and the beaches are incredibly secluded. Moonshadow (p123) runs full-day trips to the island from Nelson Bay on Sunday between October and Easter (more frequently over the summer school holidays), which include snorkelling and boom-net rides (adult/child $85/45).

🛏 Sleeping

Seal Rocks Holiday Park CAMPGROUND $
(✆ 02-4997 6164; www.sealrocksholidaypark.com. au; Kinka Rd, Seal Rocks; camp sites/cabins from $35/80; ☎) Offers a range of budget accom-

modation styles including grassed camping and caravan sites that are right on the water.

NPWS Campgrounds

CAMPGROUND **$**

(📞1300 072 757; www.nationalparks.nsw.gov.au/Myall-Lakes-National-Park; Broughton Island per 2 people $30, others per adult/child $10/5) There are 19 basic campgrounds dotted around the park; only some have drinking water and flush toilets. At the time of writing, the only one requiring advance bookings was Broughton Island, although there are plans to change this; check the website for details.

Sugarloaf Point Lighthouse

COTTAGES **$$$**

(📞02-4997 6590; www.sealrockslighthouseaccommodation.com.au; cottages from $390; 🗋) Watch the crashing waves and wildlife from one of three fully renovated, heritage lighthouse-keeper's cottages. Each is self-contained and has queen bed, iPod dock, DVD player and barbecue.

Bombah Point Eco Cottages

COTTAGES **$$$**

(📞02-4997 4401; www.bombah.com.au; 969 Bombah Point Rd; d $220-275; 🗋) 🏊 Set amongst the trees in the heart of the national park, these attractive, architect-designed, self-contained cottages sleep either five or six guests. The 'Eco' in the name is well deserved: sewage is treated on site using a bioreactor system, electricity comes courtesy of solar panels and filtered rainwater tanks provide water.

ⓘ Getting There & Around

From Hawks Nest scenic Mungo Brush Rd heads through the park to Bombah Broadwater, where the Bombah Point ferry ($6 per car) makes the five-minute crossing every half-hour from 8am to 6pm. Continuing north, a 10km section of Bombah Point Rd heading to the Pacific Hwy at Bulahdelah is unsealed.

The Lakes Way leaves the Pacific Hwy 5km north of Buladelah and shadows the northern edge of Myall Lake and Smiths Lake before continuing on to Pacific Palms and Forster-Tuncurry. Seal Rocks Rd branches off the Lakes Way at Bungwahl.

Pacific Palms

POP 664

Nestled between Myall Lakes and Booti Booti National Parks, Pacific Palms is one of those places that well-heeled city dwellers slink off to on weekends. If you're camping in either of the parks you might find yourself here when the espresso cravings kick in – there are a couple of excellent cafes.

Most of the houses cling to Blueys Beach or Boomerang Beach, both long stretches of golden sand that are popular with surfers. The most popular swimming beach (and the only one that's patrolled) is Elizabeth Beach.

🛏 Sleeping & Eating

Mobys Beachside Retreat

RESORT **$$**

(📞02-6591 0000; www.mobysretreat.com.au; 4 Red Gum Rd, Boomerang Beach; apt from $180; ✳🗋🗋) Directly opposite Boomerang Beach, this holiday resort crams 75 self-contained holiday apartments with sleek decor and excellent amenities into a relatively small area. A tennis court and a children's playground are on site, as well as a popular restaurant.

Twenty by Twelve

CAFE **$**

(207 Boomerang Dr; mains $7-17; ⏰7.30am-3pm; 🗋) Camping is all very well, but try getting a coffee like this out of a billycan! It also sells light meals, local organic produce and delicious deli treats.

Pacific Palms Recreation Club

PUB **$$**

(www.pprc.com.au; 3957 The Lakes Way; mains $13-21; ⏰11am-late) Known universally as 'the Recky', this is one of those sign-in clubs with cheap booze, a bistro, bingo and occasional live music. There's plenty of seafood on the menu and cheap midweek meal deals (rump steaks, fish and chips, roasts).

ⓘ Information

Visitor Centre (📞02-6554 0123; www.pacificpalmscoast.info; Boomerang Dr; ⏰10am-1pm Thu-Mon, extended hours summer; 🗋)

ⓘ Getting There & Away

At least two **Busways** (📞02-4997 4788; www.busways.com.au) buses stop at Blueys Beach daily, en route to Newcastle ($25, two hours) and Taree ($14, one hour).

Booti Booti National Park

This 1567-hectare national park stretches along a skinny peninsula with Seven Mile Beach on its eastern side and Wallis Lake on its west. The park's $7 vehicle-entry charge doesn't apply to the Lakes Way, which passes straight through the heart of it. The northern section of the park is swathed in coastal rainforest and topped by 224m Cape Hawke. At the Cape Hawke headland there's

ABORIGINAL MID- & NORTH-COAST NEW SOUTH WALES

The area from the Tomaree Peninsula to Forster and as far west as Gloucester is the land of the **Worimi** people. Very little of it is now in their possession, but in 2001 the sand dunes of the Stockton Bight were returned to them, creating the Worimi Conservation Lands. **Dark Point Aboriginal Place** in Myall Lakes National Park has been significant to the Worimi for around 4000 years. Local lore has it that in the late 19th century it was the site of one of many massacres at the hands of white settlers, when a community was herded onto the rocks and pushed off.

Heading north you then enter **Birpai** country, which includes Taree and Port Macquarie. The Sea Acres Rainforest Centre (p131) has a section devoted to the local people, and Birpai guides lead bush-tucker tours from here.

After travelling through the lands of the **Dainggatti** people (roughly equivalent to Kempsey Shire) you then enter **Gumbainggir** country, which stretches up to the Clarence River. Places such as Nambucca Heads still have a sizeable Aboriginal community. The Jaaning Tree (p138) restaurant in Nambucca Heads offers an opportunity to sample contemporary Indigenous cuisine, as does the cafe at the Yarrawarra Aboriginal Cultural Centre (p147). Nearby, Red Rocks is the site of another 19th-century massacre.

The northern part of the NSW coast and much of the Gold Coast is the domain of the **Bundjalung** nation, including their sacred mountain Wollumbin Mt Warning (p169). Tours run by Aboriginal Cultural Concepts (p153) offer an introduction to Bundjalung life. The **Minjungbal Aboriginal Cultural Centre** (☑02-5524 2109; www.facebook.com/MinjungbalMuseum; Kirkwood Rd; adult/child $15/7.50; ☺10am-3pm Mon-Wed) at Tweed Heads is also worth visiting.

a **viewing platform**, well worth the sweat of climbing the 420-something steps.

You won't really be darkening the door of a church if you visit the **Green Cathedral**, as there is no door. This interesting space (consecrated in 1940) consists of wooden pews under the palm trees, looking to the lake.

There's self-registration camping at the **Ruins** (camp sites per adult/child $10/7), at the southern end of Seven Mile Beach.

ℹ️ Information

NPWS Office (☑02-6591 0300; www.nationalparks.nsw.gov.au/booti-booti-national-park; The Ruins; ☺8.30am-4.30pm)

GREATER TAREE

Heading north, the Pacific Hwy swings inland to **Taree** (population 17,800), a large, unassuming town serving the farms of the fertile Manning Valley. Heading up the valley, the nearby town of **Wingham** (population 4520) combines English county cuteness with a rugged lumberjack history – an intriguing combination.

In the other direction, at the mouth of the Manning River, is the sprawling beach town of **Harrington** (population 2260), sheltered by a spectacular rocky breakwater and watched over by pelicans. It's a leisure-orientated place, popular with both holiday-makers and retirees – 48% of the population is over the age of 60.

Crowdy Head (population 221) is a small fishing village 6km northeast of Harrington at the edge of Crowdy Bay National Park. It was named when Captain Cook witnessed a gathering of Aboriginal people on the headland in 1770. The views from the 1878 **lighthouse** stretch out to the limitless ocean, down to the deserted beaches and back to the apparent wilderness of the coastal plain and mountains. It's as if Cook had never arrived at all.

Even if you don't drive through the national park it's worth leaving the Pacific Hwy at Kew and taking the coastal route to Port Macquarie via Ocean Dr. After stopping at the North Brother lookout you'll pass through **Laurieton** (population 1930). Turn left here and cross the bridge to **North Haven** (population 1600), an absolute blinder of a surf beach. Continuing north the road passes **Lake Cathie** (pronounced çat-eye), a shallow body of water that's perfect for kids to have a paddle in.

◉ Sights

Wingham Brush Nature Reserve   FOREST
(Isabella St, Wingham) A boardwalk traverses this idyllic patch of rainforest, home to giant,

otherworldly Moreton Bay figs and flocks of flying foxes. If you look closely enough you might spot an osprey or a diamond python.

Crowdy Bay National Park PARK
(www.nationalparks.nsw.gov.au/crowdy-bay-national-park; vehicle admission $7) Known for its rock formations and rugged cliffs, this 100-sq-km national park backs onto a long and beautiful beach that sweeps from Crowdy Head north to Diamond Head. There's a picturesque 4.8km (two-hour) loop track over the Diamond headland. The roads running through the park are unsealed and full of potholes, but the dappled light of the gum trees makes it a lovely drive.

Dooragan National Park PARK
(www.nationalparks.nsw.gov.au/dooragan-national-park) Immediately north of Crowdy Bay National Park, on the shores of Watson Taylor's Lake, this little national park is dominated by North Brother Mountain. A sealed road leads to the lookout at the top, which offers incredible views up and down the coast.

🛏 Sleeping

NPWS Campgrounds CAMPGROUND $
(02-6588 5555; camp sites per adult/child $10/5) Of the Crowdy Bay National Park campgrounds, Diamond Head is the most popular and best equipped (flush toilets and gas barbecues), while Kylie's Hut is the most rudimentary. Crowdy Gap, by the beach in the southern part of the park, is cheaper (adult/child $5/3). You'll need to bring drinking water for all of them.

Bank Guest House B&B $$
(02-6553 5068; www.thebankandtellers.com.au; 48 Bent St, Wingham; s/d from $160/170; ✳ 🛜) A friendly place offering stylish rooms in a 1920s bank manager's residence, as well as a pet-friendly room in the rear garden.

🍴 Eating

Bent on Food CAFE $$
(www.bentonfood.com.au; 95 Isabella St, Wingham; mains $10-25; ◷ 8am-5pm Mon-Fri, to 3pm Sat & Sun) It's worth stopping in Wingham just to call into this excellent little cafe, which serves sophisticated cooked meals and delicious baked goods. It also sells its own range of olive oils and chutneys, as well as other local products such as cheese.

Harrington Hotel PUB $$
(02-6556 1205; 30 Beach St, Harrington; mains $15-26) When not playing golf or fishing, the Harrington locals hang out at this spacious pub, sipping beer on the large waterside terrace. The expansive bistro has glorious water views and excellent food.

ℹ Information

Manning Valley Visitor Information Centre (02-6592 5444; www.manningvalley.info; 21 Manning River Dr, Taree; ◷9am-4.30pm)

ℹ Getting There & Away

Taree Airport (TRO; 02-6553 9863; 1 Lansdowne Rd, Cundletown) is 5km northeast of central Taree. **Regional Express** (Rex; 13 17 13; www.regionalexpress.com.au) has flights to/from Sydney and Grafton.

NSW TrainLink (13 22 32; www.nswtrainlink.info) trains stop at Wingham and Taree, heading to/from Sydney ($57, 5¼ hours, three daily), Nambucca Heads ($36, three hours, three daily), Coffs Harbour ($39, 3½ hours, three daily), Grafton ($48, five hours, three daily) and Brisbane ($103, nine hours, daily).

PORT MACQUARIE

POP 41,500

Pleasure has long replaced punishment as the main purpose of Port Macquarie. Formed in 1821 as a place of hard labour for those convicts who reoffended after being transported to Sydney, it was the third town to be established on the Australian mainland. These days, though, Port, as it's commonly known, is overwhelmingly holiday focused, making the most of its position at the entrance to the subtropical coast, its beautiful surf beaches and its laid-back coffee culture.

◉ Sights

Port is blessed with awesome beaches. Surfing is excellent at **Town**, **Flynn's** and **Lighthouse** beaches, all of which are patrolled in summer. The rainforest runs down to the sand at **Shelly** and **Miners** beaches, the latter of which is an unofficial nude beach.

It's possible to walk all the way from the Town Wharf to Lighthouse Beach. Along the way, the **breakwater** at the bottom of town has been transformed into a work of community guerrilla art. The elaborately painted rocks range from beautiful memorials for lost loved ones to 'party hard'-type inanities.

Port Macquarie

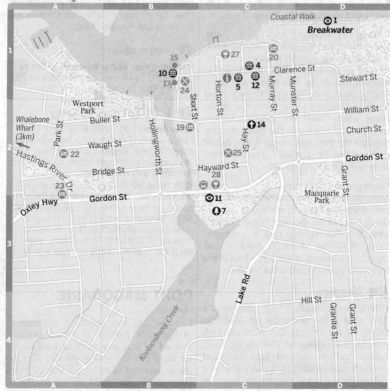

Port Macquarie

Sea Acres Rainforest Centre
PARK

(www.nationalparks.nsw.gov.au/sea-acres-national-park; Pacific Dr; adult/child $8/4; ⊘9am-4.30pm) This 72-hectare pocket was recently declared a national park, protecting the state's largest stand of coastal rainforest. It's alive with birds, goannas, brush turkeys and, so as to be truly authentic, mosquitoes (insect repellent is provided).

The centre has an excellent cafe and, downstairs, audiovisual displays about the local Birpai people. The highlight is the wheelchair- and pushchair-accessible 1.3km-long boardwalk through the forest. Fascinating one-hour guided tours by knowledgeable volunteers are included in the price. Call ahead for times of bush-tucker tours led by Aboriginal guides ($15).

Kooloonbung Creek Nature Park
PARK

(Gordon St) FREE Encompassing 50 hectares of bush and wetland, this park is home to many bird species. A series of walking trails and wheelchair-accessible boardwalks heads through mangroves and casuarina forest. It also includes the Port Macquarie Historic Cemetery (Gordon St).

Billabong Koala & Wildlife Park
ZOO

(www.billabongkoala.com.au; 61 Billabong Dr; adult/child $23/13; ⊘9am-5pm) Make sure you time your visit to be here for the 'koala patting' (10.30am, 1.30pm and 3.30pm). The park has a koala-breeding centre, although if this facility is anything to go by, koala dating requires a lot of sitting around looking stoned. There are heaps of other Australian critters here, too, as well as monkeys and snow leopards. The park is just west of the intersection of the Pacific and Oxley Hwys.

Port Macquarie Historical Museum
MUSEUM

(www.port-macquarie-historical-museum.org.au; 22 Clarence St; adult/child $5/2; ⊘9.30am-4.30pm Mon-Sat) An 1836 house has been transformed into this surprisingly interesting little museum. Aboriginal and convict history are given due regard before more eclectic displays take over, including a 'street of shops' and a display of beautiful old clothes (including a whole section on underwear).

Courthouse
HISTORIC BUILDING

(31-35 Clarence St; adult/child $2/50c; ⊘10am-3pm Mon-Fri, to 1pm Sat) One of Port's loveliest colonial buildings, the courthouse was used from its opening in 1869 right up until 1986.

Koala Hospital
WILDLIFE RESERVE

(www.koalahospital.org.au; Lord St; admission by donation; ⊘8am-4.30pm) Koalas living near urban areas are at risk from traffic and domestic animals, and between 200 and 300 end up in this shelter each year. You can walk around the open-air enclosures any time of the day, but you'll learn more during the tours (3pm). Some of the longer-term patients have signs detailing their stories. Check the website for details of volunteer opportunities.

Roto House
HISTORIC BUILDING

(www.nationalparks.nsw.gov.au/macquarie-nature-reserve; Lord St; admission by gold-coin donation; ⊘10am-4.30pm) Located next to the Koala Hospital in Macquarie Nature Reserve, this lovely Victorian villa (1890) has interesting displays about its original owners.

Glasshouse ARTS CENTRE

(www.glasshouse.org.au; cnr Clarence & Hay Sts) This civic and architectural showpiece (opened 2009) was built on the site of convict overseers' cottages; artefacts from the original buildings are on display in the foyer and basement. The environmentally conscious structure houses the **regional art gallery** (⊙10am-4pm Tue-Sun) **FREE**, a 600-seat theatre and the tourist information centre.

St Thomas' Anglican Church CHURCH

(www.pmqang.org; 50 Hay St; admission by gold-coin donation; ⊙9.30am-noon & 2-4pm Mon-Fri) This 1824 convict-built church is one of Australia's oldest still-functioning churches. It still has its box pews and crenulated tower, aping the Norman churches of southern England.

Maritime Museum MUSEUM

(www.maritimemuseumcottages.org.au; 6 William St; adult/child $5/2; ⊙10am-4pm) The old pilot station (1882) above Town Beach has been converted into a small maritime museum. There's an even smaller extension of the museum in the 1890s **Pilot's Boatshed** (⊙10am-2pm) **FREE** at the Town Wharf.

Observatory OBSERVATORY

(www.pmobs.org.au; William St; adult/child $8/5; ⊙7.30pm Wed & Sun, 8.15pm during daylight saving) For those looking for answers beyond the horizon, sneak a peek through the telescope at the astronomical observatory on one of its public viewing and presentation nights.

Tacking Point Lighthouse LIGHTHOUSE

(Lighthouse Rd) This little lighthouse (1879) commands a headland offering immense views along the coast. It's a great spot to watch the waves rolling in to long, beautiful Lighthouse Beach.

🏃 Activities

Port Macquarie Surf School SURFING

(02-6584 7733; www.portmacquariesurfschool.com.au; lessons from $40) Offers a wide range of lessons for all ability levels.

Soul Surfing SURFING

(02-6582 0114; www.soulsurfing.com.au; classes from $50) A surf school that's particularly good for beginners.

👉 Tours

Port Venture Cruises CRUISE

(1300 795 577; www.portventure.com.au; Town Wharf; adult/child from $20/12) Twilight, lunch and 'eco-history' cruises with dolphin watch-

ing included. It also runs whale-watching cruises from mid-May to mid-November ($50).

Port Macquarie Cruise Adventures CRUISE

(0414 897 444; www.cruiseadventures.com.au; Town Wharf; cruises from $10) Offers dolphin-watching, whale-spotting, lunch, sunset and everglades cruises.

Port Macquarie Hastings Heritage WALKING TOUR

(0447 429 016; www.pmheritage.com.au; per person $29; ⊙9.30am Wed-Sat) Two-and-a-half-hour walking tours through Port's history, leaving from the Glasshouse. There's an additional 90-minute cemetery tour ($19) at 2pm Wednesday to Saturday.

🛏 Sleeping

Ozzie Pozzie YHA HOSTEL $

(02-6583 8133; www.ozziepozzie.com; 36 Waugh St; dm/s/d from $31/66/88; @🛜🏊) In an unusual compound made up of three converted suburban houses, this hostel has clean rooms and a laid-back atmosphere. There's a range of activities on offer, along with pool and table-tennis tables, free bodyboards and bike hire ($5 per day).

Port Macquarie Backpackers HOSTEL $

(02-6583 1791; www.portmacquariebackpackers.com.au; 2 Hastings River Dr; dm/s/d from $27/62/76; @🛜🏊) This heritage-listed house has pressed-tin walls, colourful murals and a leafy backyard with a small pool. Traffic can be noisy, but the freebies (including wi-fi, bikes and bodyboards) compensate.

Observatory HOTEL $$

(02-6586 8000; www.observatory.net.au; 40 William St; r/apt from $145/169; ❄🛜🏊) Rooms and apartments are comfortable and well equipped at this friendly hotel opposite Town Beach; many have balconies overlooking the water. You won't have to stray far from your room for the beach or a good meal.

Mantra Quayside APARTMENT $$

(02-6588 4000; www.mantraquayside.com.au; cnr William & Short Sts; apt from $180; ❄🛜🏊) Head up to the roof of this central midrise block for a BBQ, a splash about in the heated lap pool, or simply to soak in the views. Studios have kitchenettes and access to a free communal laundry, while one- and two-bedrooms are fully self-contained.

Beachport
B&B $$

(📞 0423 072 669; www.beachportbnb.com.au; 155 Pacific Dr; r from $126; ❋ 🛜) In this excellent B&B the two downstairs rooms open onto private terraces, while the spacious upstairs unit has its own small dining-living room. Fruit, cereal and bread is provided for a do-it-yourself breakfast and the Rainforest Cafe is just across the road if you fancy an espresso.

Northpoint Apartments
APARTMENT $$

(📞 02-6583 8333; www.northpointapartments. com.au; 2 Murray St; apt from $179; ❋ 🛜 ⊠) Some of these large, classy and contemporary one-to three-bedroom apartments have fabulous sea views, although you'll save $55 if you're prepared to go without.

Eastport Motor Inn
MOTEL $$

(📞 02-6583 5850; www.hwmotel.com.au; cnr Lord & Burrawan Sts; r from $129; ❋ 🛜 ⊠) At the cheaper end of the non-hostel scale, this three-storey motel has smallish, clean and well-equipped rooms with comfortable beds and crisp linen. Wi-fi is free.

Eating

Rainforest Cafe
CAFE, FRENCH $

(📞 02-6582 4444; www.rainforestcafe.com.au; Sea Acres Rainforest Centre, Pacific Dr; mains breakfast $10-15, lunch $8-22; ⊙ 9am-4pm; 🅿) 🎗 You may be surrounded by lush foliage, but don't expect bush tucker: the talented chef is as French as they come. The focus is on healthy sandwiches and salads, and heavenly cakes and pastries.

Cedro
CAFE $

(72 Clarence St; mains $10-19; ⊙ 7.30am-2.30pm Tue-Fri, to 12.30pm Sun) On a sunny day you can sit on the street between the palm trees, order the generous house breakfast, sip a grunty coffee and plan your next move: the beach or another coffee stop?

Milkbar
CAFE $

(40 William St; mains $9-16; ⊙ 7.30am-3pm Mon-Fri, to noon Sat & Sun) A casually chic cafe on the ground floor of the Observatory hotel, Milkbar is known for its homemade icy poles, single-origin coffee and surfer clientele.

★ Stunned Mullet
MODERN AUSTRALIAN $$$

(📞 02-6584 7757; www.thestunnedmullet.com.au; 24 William St; mains $36-39; ⊙ noon-2.30pm & 6-8.30pm) Australian idiom lesson: to 'look like a stunned mullet' is to wear an expression of bewilderment. It's exactly the sort of look you might adopt while struggling to choose among the delicious Mod Oz menu items and extensive wine-list offerings at Port's best restaurant.

Fusion 7
FUSION $$$

(📞 02-6584 1171; www.fusion7.com.au; 124 Horton St; mains $35; ⊙ 6-9pm Tue-Sat) Chef-owner Lindsey Schwab worked in London with the father of fusion cuisine, Peter Gordon, but returned to Port to be closer to his family. Local produce features prominently and desserts are particularly delicious.

Whalebone Wharf
SEAFOOD $$$

(📞 02-6583 2334; www.whalebonewharf.com.au; 269 Hastings River Dr; mains $28-39; ⊙ noon-3pm & 6-10pm) Grab a seat on the deck overlooking the river and tuck into a plate of chilli Moreton Bay bugs (flathead lobster), blue swimmer crab linguine or fish and chips. Cocktails and desserts are also good.

🍷 Drinking & Nightlife

Beach House
BAR

(www.ktgroup.com.au/the-beach-house; 1 Horton St; ⊙ 7.30am-10pm Sun, to midnight Mon-Thu, to late Fri & Sat) The enviable position right on the grassy water's edge makes this place perfect for lazy afternoon drinks. As the wee hours draw near, folk fasten their beer goggles and mingle on black-leather couches inside. DJs and live bands crank up on weekends.

Finnian's
PUB

(www.finnians.com.au; 97 Gordon St; ⊙ 11am-late) The backpacker's boozer of choice, this Irish tavern near the bus depot cranks up the party atmosphere on Friday and Saturday with live music from 8pm.

ℹ Information

Port Macquarie Base Hospital (📞 02-5524 2000; www.mnclhd.health.nsw.gov.au; Wrights Rd)

Visitor Information Centre (📞 02-6581 8000; www.portmacquarieinfo.com.au; The Glasshouse, cnr Hay & Clarence Sts; ⊙ 9am-5.30pm Mon-Fri, to 4pm Sat & Sun)

ℹ Getting There & Around

AIR

Port Macquarie Airport (PQQ; 📞 02-6581 8111; www.portmacquarieairport.com.au; Oliver Dr) is 5km from the centre of town; a taxi will cost $18 to $20 and there are regular local bus services.

QantasLink (📞13 13 13; www.qantas.com.au) Flies to/from Sydney.

Virgin Australia (📞13 67 89; www.virginaustralia.com) Flies to/from Sydney and Brisbane.

BUS

Regional buses depart from **Port Macquarie Coach Terminal** (Gordon St).

Busways (📞02-6583 2499; www.busways.com.au) Busways runs local bus services and heads as far afield as North Haven ($12, one hour), Port Macquarie Airport ($4.80, 28 minutes) and Kempsey ($14, one hour).

Greyhound (📞1300 473 946; www.greyhound.com.au) Two daily buses head to/from Sydney ($72, 6½ hours), Newcastle ($55, four hours), Coffs Harbour ($36, 2½ hours), Byron Bay ($74, six hours) and Brisbane ($116, 10 hours).

New England Coaches (📞02-6732 1051; www.newenglandcoaches.com.au) Two coaches per week to/from Dorrigo ($70, 3½ hours), Bellingen ($60, 2¾ hours), Coffs Harbour ($50, two hours), Nambucca Heads ($40, 1¼ hours) and Kempsey ($30, 35 minutes).

Premier (📞13 34 10; www.premierms.com.au) Daily coach to/from Sydney ($60, 6½ hours), Newcastle ($47, 3¾ hours), Coffs Harbour ($47, 2¼ hours), Byron Bay ($66, 7½ hours) and Brisbane ($67, 11 hours).

KEMPSEY SHIRE

Kempsey Shire, north of Port Macquarie, takes in the large agricultural town of Kempsey and the farms of the Macleay Valley, but the real attractions for visitors are the gorgeous surf beaches of the Macleay Coast.

If you've got the time for a scenic detour, leave the highway at Kempsey and take Crescent Head Rd to the coast. From Crescent Head, the partly unsealed road to Gladstone edges leafy Hat Head National Park before following the Belmore River to its junction with the Macleay River. From here it's a pretty drive to South West Rocks following the Macleay, its banks lined with dense reeds, old farmhouses and vintage shacks built on stilts.

Kempsey

POP 10,400

Two absolute icons of Australiana came from Kempsey – the Akubra hat and the late country-music legend Slim Dusty – but the town certainly couldn't be accused of cashing in on them. The Akubra factory is closed to the public and a long-proposed **Slim Dusty Heritage Centre** (www.slimdustycentre.com.au; Old Kempsey Showgrounds) was still at least a year off completion at the time of research (check online for the latest).

Until then, the only moderately interesting attraction on offer is the **Kempsey Museum** (www.kempseymuseum.org; South Kempsey Park, Lachlan St; adult/child $4/2; ⊙10am-4pm), which honours the memory of the sheep shearers, lumber whackers, cattle pokers and all the others who made the Macleay Valley an agricultural paradise. It shares space with the **Kempsey Visitor Centre** (📞02-6563 1555; www.macleayvalleycoast.com.au; Pacific Hwy; ⊙9am-5pm).

🛈 Getting There & Around

BUS

Local bus services are run by Busways (p134). Services extend to Port Macquarie, Crescent Head and South West Rocks.

Greyhound has coaches to/from Sydney ($88, 5¾ to 7½ hours, four daily), Port Macquarie ($9, 50 minutes, two daily), Coffs Harbour ($25, 1¾ hours, four daily), Byron Bay ($65, 4¾ to 6½ hours, four daily) and Brisbane ($110, nine to 10½ hours, three daily).

Premier has a daily coach to/from Sydney ($63, seven hours), Port Macquarie ($18, 45 minutes), Coffs Harbour ($40, 1½ hours), Byron Bay ($59, seven hours) and Brisbane ($67, 10 hours).

New England Coaches has two services per week to/from Dorrigo ($65, three hours), Bellingen ($55, 2¼ hours), Coffs Harbour ($40, 1¼ hours), Nambucca Heads ($30, 45 minutes) and Port Macquarie ($30, 35 minutes).

TRAIN

Three NSW TrainLink (p129) trains head to/from Sydney ($85, seven hours), Nambucca Heads ($12, one hour), Coffs Harbour ($19, 1¾ hours) and Grafton ($36, three hours) daily and one continues to Brisbane ($95, 7¼ hours).

Crescent Head

POP 979

It's in this sleepy little beachside hideaway, 18km southeast of Kempsey, that the longboard (aka the Malibu surfboard) gained prominence in Australia during the 1960s. Today many come just to watch the longboard riders surf the epic waves of **Little Nobby's Junction**. There's also good shortboard riding off Plomer Rd. Untrammelled **Killick Beach** stretches 14km north.

🛏 Sleeping & Eating

Local agency **Point Break Realty** (📞02-6566 0306; www.crescentheadholidayaccommodation. com.au; 4 Rankine St) specialises in holiday rentals.

Surfari HOSTEL, MOTEL $
(📞02-6566 0009; www.surfaris.com; 353 Loftus Rd; dm/r from $30/100; @🛜🐾) These guys started the original Sydney–Byron surf tours and have now based themselves in Crescent Head because 'the surf is guaranteed every day'. The rooms are clean and comfortable with some wicked wall murals. Surf-and-stay packages are a speciality. It's located 3.5km out of town, on the road to Gladstone.

Sun Worship Eco Apartments APARTMENT $$$
(📞1300 664 757; www.sunworship.com.au; 9 Belmore St; apt from $205; 🛜) 🏄 Stay in guilt-mitigated luxury in one of five rammed-earth villas featuring sustainable design, including flow-through ventilation, solar orientation and solar hot water. They're spacious too.

Crescent Head Tavern PUB $$
(www.crescentheadtavern.com.au; 2 Main St; mains $12-30; ⊙noon-2pm & 5.30-7.30pm) The local pub has cold beer, a sun-soaked deck and good food – what else could you want? There's a massive menu of burgers, steaks, pizza and pies to choose from.

❶ Getting There & Away

Busways (📞02-6562 4724; www.busways. com.au) buses run between Crescent Head and Kempsey ($14, 25 minutes) two to three times a day; no Sunday services.

Hat Head National Park

Covering almost the entire coast from Crescent Head to South West Rocks, this 74-sq-km national park (vehicle entry $7) protects scrubland, swamps and some amazing beaches, backed by one of the largest dune systems in NSW.

The wonderfully isolated beachside village of **Hat Head** (population 326) sits at its centre. At the far end of town, behind the holiday park, a picturesque wooden footbridge crosses the aqua-green Korogoro Creek estuary. The water is so clear you can see fish darting around.

The best views can be had from **Smoky Cape Lighthouse**, at the northern end of

WORTH A TRIP

GLADSTONE

It's worth stopping at gorgeous riverside Gladstone (population 387) for a zip around the **Macleay Valley Community Art Gallery** (www. kempsey.nsw.gov.au/gallery/; 5 Kinchela St; 10.30am-4pm Thu-Sun) **FREE** and a drink at the **Heritage Hotel** (www. heritagehotel.net.au; 21 Kinchela St; mains from $16; ⊙10am-midnight Mon-Sat, to 9pm Sun), an excellent old pub with an oasislike beer garden.

the park; during the annual whale migration it's a prime place to spot whales from.

🛏 Sleeping

Hat Head Holiday Park CAMPGROUND $
(📞02-6567 7501; www.mvcholidayparks.com.au; Straight St; sites/cabins from $35/121) An old-fashioned family-orientated holiday park close to the beach and footbridge.

NPWS Camp Sites CAMPGROUND $
(www.nationalparks.nsw.gov.au/hat-head-national-park; camp sites per adult/child $5/3) You can camp at Hungry Gate, 5km south of Hat Head, or at Smoky Cape, just below Smoky Cape Lighthouse. Both operate on a first-in basis; neither takes bookings. Non-flush toilets and a barcecue area are provided; you'll need to bring water with you.

Smoky Cape Lighthouse B&B, COTTAGE $$$
(📞02-6566 6301; www.smokycapelighthouse.com; Lighthouse Rd; s/d from $150/220, cottages per 2 nights from $500) Romantic evenings can be spent gazing out to sea and hearing the wind whip around the lighthouse-keeper's building, just a few metres from the lighthouse itself.

South West Rocks

POP 4820

One of many pretty seaside towns on this stretch of coast, South West Rocks has spectacular beaches and enough interesting diversions to distract you for a day or two.

The lovely curve of **Trial Bay**, stretching east from the township, takes its name from the *Trial*, a boat that sank here during a storm in 1816 after being stolen by convicts fleeing Sydney. The eastern half of the bay is now protected by **Arakoon National Park**, centred on a headland that's popular with kangaroos, kookaburras and campers. On its eastern flank, Little Bay Beach is a small grin of sand sheltered from the surf by a rocky barricade. It's a great place for a swim with the kangaroos looking on. It's also the starting point for some good walks.

Sights & Activities

Trial Bay Gaol
MUSEUM

(☑02-6566 6168; www.nationalparks.nsw.gov.au/arakoon-national-park/; Cardwell St; adult/child $7.50/5; ☺9am-4.30pm) Occupying Trial Bay's eastern headland, this imposing structure was built between 1877 and 1886 to house convicts brought in to build a breakwater to protect boats taking shelter in the bay. Nature had other ideas and the breakwater washed away. The prison subsequently fell into disuse, aside from a brief interlude in WWII when men of German and Austrian heritage were interned here. Today it contains a museum devoted to its chequered history. It's a 4km beach walk from South West Rocks.

Diving
DIVING

The South West Rocks area is great for divers, especially Fish Rock Cave, south of Smoky Cape. South West Rocks (☑02-6566 6474; www.southwestrocksdive.com.au; 5/98 Gregory St) and Fish Rock (☑02-6566 6614; www.fishrock.com.au; 134 Gregory St) dive centres both offer dives (1-/2-day double boat dives $130/250) and accommodation.

Sleeping

Horseshoe Bay Holiday Park
CAMPGROUND $

(☑02-6566 6370; www.mvcholidayparks.com.au; 1 Livingstone St; camp sites/cabins from $49/99) Planted a hop and a skip from both the main street and the beach, this caravan park gets extremely busy during the summer holidays.

Trial Bay Gaol Campground
CAMPGROUND $

(☑02-6566 6168; Cardwell St; camp sites from $28) Behind the gaol, this NPWS campground affords generous beach views from most sites and ever-present kangaroos. Amenities include drinking water, flush toilets and coin-slot hot showers and gas barbies.

Heritage
B&B $$

(☑02-6566 6625; www.heritageguesthouse.com.au; 21-23 Livingstone St; s $115, d $120-175; ❈ ☎) This renovated 1880s house has old-fashioned rooms, some with spa baths. Choose from the simpler rooms downstairs or the more lavish

versions upstairs with ocean views. A simple do-it-yourself breakfast is provided.

Rockpool Motor Inn
MOTEL $$

(☑02-6566 7755; www.rockpoolmotorinn.com.au; 45 McIntyre St; r from $140; ❈ ☎) There's a slightly corporate vibe to this modern block, fronted by palm trees, but the rooms are smartly furnished and the restaurant isn't bad either.

Eating & Drinking

Trial Bay Kiosk
CAFE $$

(☑02-6566 7100; www.trialbaykiosk.com.au; Cardwell St; mains breakfast $10-16, lunch & dinner $18-28; ☺8am-2.30pm daily, 5.30-9.30pm Fri & Sat) Sit on the terrace and soak up the views from this upmarket cafe near the gaol. At lunchtime the menu wanders into bistro territory, traversing the likes of steak and mash, risotto and fish and chips.

Seabreeze Beach Hotel
PUB

(www.seabreezebeachhotel.com.au; Livingstone St; ☺noon-8.30pm) Catering to families, sports fans and surfers in equal measure, this big hotel serves scrubbed-up pub nosh on pleasant decks. Watch for the $12 daily meal deals.

Surf Life Saving Club
PUB

(www.swrslsc.org.au; ☺3-10pm Thu-Sun) The best place for a beer or an unpretentious meal with an ocean view.

Information

Visitor Information Centre (☑02-6566 7099; www.macleayvalleycoast.com.au; 1 Ocean Ave; ☺9am-4pm)

Getting There & Away

Busways (☑02-6562 4724; www.busways.com.au) has buses to/from Kempsey two or three times daily Monday to Saturday ($14, 46 minutes).

COFFS HARBOUR REGION

As well as a stretch of beautiful beaches, there are some quaint towns hiding in the Coffs hinterland.

Nambucca Heads

POP 6220

Nambucca Heads is languidly strewn over a dramatically curling headland interlaced with the estuaries of the Nambucca River. It's a

Nambucca Heads

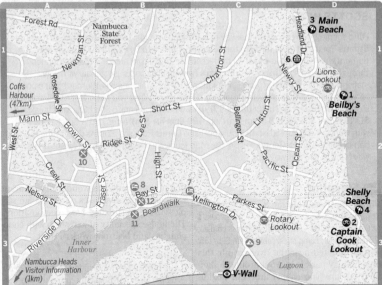

N 0 — 400 m
   0 — 0.2 miles

BYRON BAY & NORTHERN NEW SOUTH WALES NAMBUCCA HEADS

Nambucca Heads

◉ Top Sights
1 Beilby's Beach....................................D1
2 Captain Cook Lookout D3
3 Main Beach...D1
4 Shelly Beach......................................D3
5 V-Wall C3

◉ Sights
6 Headland Historical Museum...............D1

🛏 Sleeping
7 Marcel Towers B2
8 Riverview Boutique Hotel B2
9 White Albatross Caravan & Holiday
    Resort C3

🍴 Eating
10 Bookshop Café A2
11 Jaaning Tree......................................B3
12 Matilda's B3

spacious, sleepy and relatively unspoilt place with one of the coast's prettiest foreshores, enhanced for walkers with boardwalks edging the mangroves. The ocean breezes put people to bed early here; the streets are mostly rolled up by 10pm weeknights.

Nambucca (pronounced nam-*buk*-a) means 'many bends' and the river valley was ruled by the Gumbainggir people until European timber cutters arrived in the 1840s. There are still strong Aboriginal communities in Nambucca Heads and up the valley in Bowraville.

◉ Sights & Activities

Beaches　　　　　　　　　　　　　BEACH
Of the numerous viewpoints, **Captain Cook Lookout**, set on a high bluff, is the place to ponder the swath of beaches. A road here leads down to **Shelly Beach**, which has tidepools but isn't particularly shelly. Going north, it blends into **Beilby's Beach** and then **Main Beach**, which is the only one that's patrolled.

★ V-Wall　　　　　　　　　　　　LANDMARK
As at Port Macquarie, Nambucca's bent breakwater has been blanketed with mostly well-mannered graffiti by locals and travellers.

Headland Historical Museum　MUSEUM
(www.here.com.au/museum; Liston St; adult/child $3/50c; ☉2-4pm Wed, Sat & Sun) Above Main Beach, this museum has local-history exhibits, including a collection of over 1000 photos.

WORTH A TRIP

SCOTTS HEAD

For a scenic 17km detour on the way to Nambucca Heads, take Tourist Drive 14 towards Stuarts Point and drive through the eucalyptus forest to Grassy Head, a tiny settlement with a gorgeous beach of butterscotch sand. From here the road continues through leafy Yarriabini National Park (www.nationalparks.nsw.gov.au/yarriabini -national-park) to Scotts Head (population 820), a small beach settlement that's popular with surfers and retirees in almost equal measure. While you're here, it's well worth stopping at Taverna Six (02-6569 7191; www.tavernasix.com; 6 Short St; mains breakfast $13-16, dinner $26-28; 8.30am-1pm daily, 6.30-9pm Tue-Sun), a cosy little Greek eatery with wonderful food and Nana Mouskouri and Demis Roussos albums decorating the bamboo-lined walls. Continuing on, the road follows a stream lined by tall trees on its way back to the highway.

Sleeping

White Albatross Caravan & Holiday Resort CAMPGROUND $
(02-6568 6468; www.whitealbatross.com.au; 52 Wellington Dr; camp sites/cabins from $75/135; ※ ⊛ ⊜) Located near the river mouth, this large holiday park is laid out around a sheltered lagoon. The cabins are kept fastidiously clean and have full kitchens.

Riverview Boutique Hotel GUESTHOUSE $$
(02-6568 6386; www.riverviewlodgenambucca. com.au; 4 Wellington Dr; s/d from $129/139; ※ ⊜) Built in 1887, this former pub was for many years one of the few buildings on the rise of a hill overlooking the foreshore. Today the old two-storey wooden charmer has eight stylish rooms (with fridges); some have blissful views.

Marcel Towers APARTMENT $$
(02-6568 7041; www.marceltowers.com.au; 12-14 Wellington Dr; d from $120; ※ @ ⊜) It's worth paying the extra $10 for an ocean view in this tidy block of holiday apartments, although all of the units have views over the estuary. If the views lead to inspiration, the complex has row boats for you to borrow.

Eating

Bookshop Café CAFE $
(cnr Ridge & Bowra Sts; meals $9-14; 8am-5pm; ⊜) The porch tables here are *the* place in town for breakfast. As the day progresses, there are cakes, slices, sandwiches and salads to sample. The fruit smoothies are excellent.

★ **Jaaning Tree** MODERN AUSTRALIAN $$
(02-6569 4444; www.jaaningtree.com.au; 1 Wellington Dr; mains $25-35; 6-9pm Wed & Thu, noon-3pm & 6-9pm Fri & Sat, noon-3pm Sun) Right on the waterfront, this wonderful restaurant is all about creative takes on Australian staples using surprising food combinations. The house speciality of kangaroo with chocolate jus and beetroot works a treat.

Matilda's SEAFOOD $$
(02-6568 6024; Wellington Dr; mains $25-35; 6-9pm Mon-Sat) Boasting 'fair dinkum cuisine', this cute little shack juggles good old-fashioned beachfront character with fresh seafood and capable service. Steaks and vegie dishes round out the menu. BYO.

Information

Nambucca Heads Visitor Information (02-6568 6954; www.nambuccatourism.com.au; cnr Riverside Dr & Pacific Hwy; 9am-5pm)

Getting There & Around

BUS

Long-distance buses stop at the visitor centre.

Busways (02-6568 3012; www.busways. com.au) Six buses to/from Bellingen and Coffs Harbour on weekdays (both $11.90, 1¼ hours), and one or two on Saturday.

Greyhound (1300 473 946; www.greyhound. com.au) Two coaches daily to/from Sydney ($97, eight hours), Port Macquarie ($21, 1¾ hours), Coffs Harbour ($13, 45 minutes), Byron Bay ($58, 4½ hours) and Brisbane ($103, 8¼ hours).

New England Coaches (02-6732 1051; www. newenglandcoaches.com.au) Two coaches per week to/from Dorrigo ($50, two hours), Bellingen ($40, 1½ hours), Coffs Harbour ($35, 35 minutes), Kempsey ($30, 45 minutes) and Port Macquarie ($40, 1¼ hours).

Premier (13 34 10; www.premierms.com.au) Daily coach to/from Sydney ($63, eight hours), Port Macquarie ($38, 1¾ hours), Coffs Harbour ($34, 40 minutes), Byron Bay ($58, 5¾ hours) and Brisbane ($63, 9¼ hours).

TRAIN

NSW TrainLink (☑13 22 32; www.nswtrainlink. info) Three daily trains to/from Sydney ($95, eight hours), Wingham ($36, three hours), Kempsey ($12, one hour) and Coffs Harbour ($7, 40 minutes), and one to Brisbane ($89, 6¼ hours).

Bellingen
POP 3040

Buried in foliage on a hillside above the Bellinger River, this gorgeous town dances to the beat of its own bongo drum, attracting a populace of artists, academics and those drawn to a more organic lifestyle. Thick with gourmet cuisine and accommodation, it is, as one visitor rightly stated, hippie without the dippy.

The wide river valley was part of the extensive territory of the Gumbainggir people until cedar cutters arrived in the 1840s. The first European settlement here was at Fernmount, about 5km east, but the administrative centre of the region was eventually moved to Bellingen. Until tourism boomed at Coffs Harbour in the 1960s, Bellingen was the most important town in this area. River craft were able to reach here until the 1940s, when dredging was discontinued. In 1988 it found a new claim to fame as the setting of Peter Carey's Booker Prize–winning novel *Oscar and Lucinda*.

◉ Sights

Bellingen Island　　　WILDLIFE RESERVE
(www.bellingen.com/flyingfoxes) This little semi-attached island on the Bellinger River (it's only completely cut off when the river is in flood) is home to a huge colony of grey-headed flying foxes. At dusk they fly out in their thousands to feed; it's an impressive sight, best seen from the bridge in the centre of town. If you fancy a closer look, a steep path leads onto the island from Red Ledge Lane, on the northern bank. The best months to visit are from October to January, when the babies are being born and nursed.

Bellingen Museum　　　MUSEUM
(☑02-6655 0382; www.bellingenmuseum.org.au; Hyde St; adult/child $3/free; ⊙10am-2pm Mon-Fri) One of those places run by enthusiastic volunteers whom you suspect hang out there even when it's closed. It has an odd collection of local ephemera: old photos, cameras, clothes, tools etc.

🏃 Activities

Bellingen Canoe Adventures　　CANOEING
(☑02-6655 9955; www.canoeadventures.com.au; 4 Tyson St, Fernmount; hire per hr/day $15/55) Guided day trips on the Bellinger River (adult/child $90/60), including full-moon tours (adult/child $25/20).

Valery Trails　　　HORSE RIDING
(☑02-6653 4301; www.valerytrails.com.au; 758 Valery Rd, Valery; 2hr ride adult/child $65/55) A stable of over 75 horses and plenty of acreage to explore; located 15km northeast of town.

🎉 Festivals & Events

Camp Creative　　　ARTS
(www.campcreative.com.au; ⊙mid-Jan) Five-day carnival of the arts.

Bellingen Jazz Festival　　MUSIC
(www.bellingenjazzfestival.com.au; ⊙mid-Aug) A strong line-up of jazz names performs over a long weekend.

🛏 Sleeping

Bellingen YHA　　　HOSTEL $
(☑02-6655 1116; www.yha.com.au; 2 Short St; dm $33, r without/with bathroom $80/105; @ 🖥) A tranquil, engaging atmosphere pervades this renovated weatherboard house, and once you see the views from the broad verandah you'll understand why it's so popular. They'll even pick you up from the bus stop and train station in Urunga if you call ahead.

Federal Hotel　　　HOTEL $
(☑02-6655 1003; www.federalhotel.com.au; 77 Hyde St; dm/s/d with shared bathroom $40/65/80; 🖥) This beautiful old pub has renovated weatherboard rooms, some of which open onto a balcony facing the main street. Downstairs there's a lively pub scene that includes food and live music.

Bellingen Riverside Cottages　　CABIN $$
(☑02-6655 9866; www.bellingenriversidecottages. com.au; 224 North Bank Rd; cottages from $145; ❄) These polished mountain cabins have cosy interiors with country furnishings and big, sun-sucking windows. Timber balconies overlook the river, which you can tackle on a complimentary kayak. Your first night includes a sizeable brekkie hamper.

Bellingen River Family Cabins　　CABIN $$
(☑02-6655 0499; www.bellingencabins.com.au; 850 Waterfall Way; cabins $140) Two large two-bedroom cabins overlook the wide river valley on this family farm 4km east of Bellingen.

The units are well equipped and sleep up to six; extras include complimentary use of canoes and kayaks.

Koompartoo Retreat
CHALET $$

(☑02-6655 2326; www.koompartoo.com.au; cnr Rawson & Dudley Sts; d $165-185; ✸) Ferns hang over the wide balconies of the four chalets at this tropical retreat close to town. Each is constructed from local hardwoods and blends right into the hillside. Kitchenettes let you show off your romantic prowess at the cooker.

Bellingen Valley Lodge
MOTEL $$

(☑02-6655 1599; www.bellingenvalleylodge.com.au; 1381 Waterfall Way; s/d from $100/110; ✸✸) 🖉 Large motel-style rooms (all with valley views) and a pleasant rural setting make this a fine choice, 1km from Bellingen. On the downside, the walls are thin and the air-conditioning units are clunky old rattlers.

★ Lily Pily
B&B $$$

(☑02-6655 0522; www.lilypily.com.au; 54 Sunny Corner Rd; r from $260; ✸☎) Set on a knoll, this beautiful architect-designed complex has three bedrooms overlooking the river. It's a high-end place designed to pamper with champagne on arrival, lavish breakfasts served until noon, luxurious furnishings and more. It's 3km south of the centre.

🍴 Eating & Drinking

Atelier
DELI $

(www.fullerfresh.com.au; 905 Waterfall Way, East End; snacks $7.50; ☺7am-7pm; ☎) Attached to a big fruit-and-vegetable store on the eastern approach to town, this deli-cafe sells a tempting array of baked goods, such as pies, pastries and cakes. There's free wi-fi too.

Vintage Espresso
CAFE $

(62 Hyde St; snacks $6; ☺7.30am-4.30pm Mon-Fri, 9am-1.30pm Sat; ☎) Sip excellent coffee amid the eclectic curios of this vintage shop. One side is clothes-tastic, the other is a nudge at nostalgia with old books and records, used furniture and '70s kitchenware. Thankfully, the muffins and cakes are not preloved.

Little Red Kitchen
PIZZERIA $

(111 Hyde St; mains $10-18; ☺noon-2pm & 5-9pm Thu-Tue; 🖉) This brightly lit place serves up pizza with a wide range of toppings. Tasty and good value.

Tuckshop Bellingen
CAFE $

(63 Hyde St; mains $9-16; ☺7.30am-2.30pm Mon-Sat) If only all tuck shops were like this. This incy-wincy cafe serves great coffee and a delicious line-up of breakfast and lunch options, including lots of salads.

Bellingen Gelato Bar
ICE CREAM $

(www.bellingengelato.com.au; 101 Hyde St; ☺10am-6pm Wed-Sun) A 1950s America–styled cafe with sensational homemade ice cream.

★ No 2 Oak St
MODERN AUSTRALIAN $$$

(☑02-6655 9000; www.no2oakst.com.au; 2 Oak St; mains $40-44; ☺6.30-9.30pm Wed-Sat) The bounty of local produce is celebrated at this lauded restaurant where Ray Urquart works his kitchen magic. There's nothing gimmicky about the menu, just top-notch classic cooking using the very best ingredients. Book ahead.

No 5 Church St
BAR, CAFE

(www.5churchstreet.com; 5 Church St; mains $16; ☺11am-10pm Wed-Fri, 8am-10pm Sat, 8am-4pm Sun; ☎) Morphing effortlessly between cafe

---

THE WATERFALL WAY

Once you've travelled the 40km from the Pacific Hwy through Bellingen to Dorrigo, there's still another 125km of the Waterfall Way to go before you reach Armidale. Should you press on, these are the highlights:

➡ Fifty kilometres past Dorrigo (2km west of Ebor) there's a right turn for Ebor Falls in **Guy Fawkes River National Park** (www.nationalparks.nsw.gov.au/guy-fawkes-river-national-park).

➡ The Waterfall Way then edges **Cathedral Rock National Park** (www.nationalparks.nsw.gov.au/cathedral-rock-national-park). On the left after 8km is Point Lookout Rd, which leads to **New England National Park** (www.nationalparks.nsw.gov.au/new-england-national-park), another section of the Gondwana Rainforests World Heritage Area (p152).

➡ After another 28km, look for the left turn to the 260m-high Wollomombi Falls, a highlight of **Oxley Wild Rivers National Park** (www.nationalparks.nsw.gov.au/oxley-wild-rivers-national-park).

and bar, Bellingen's coolest venue stages an often edgy roster of live music. Pull up a pew at the communal table or snuggle into one of the couches and make yourself at home.

🔒 Shopping

Markets   MARKET
On the third Saturday of the month the **community market** (www.bellingenmarkets.com.au; Bellingen Park, Church St) is a regional sensation, with more than 250 stalls. On the second and fourth Saturday of the month there's a **growers' market** (www.bellingen-growersmarket.com; Bellingen Showgrounds, cnr Hammond & Black Sts; ⊘8am-1pm).

Old Butter Factory   ARTS & CRAFTS
(www.theoldbutterfactory.com.au; 1 Doepel St; ⊘9am-5pm) A little piece of local history, this interesting complex houses craft, gift and homeware shops, a gallery, opal dealers and a cafe.

Emporium Bellingen   CLOTHING
(www.emporiumbellingen.com.au; 73-75 Hyde St) Occupying the main street's most impressive building (built in 1909 to house the Hammond & Wheatley department store), this beautifully presented boutique has a good range of clothes for men and women.

Heartland Didgeridoos   MUSIC, CLOTHING
(www.heartlanddidgeridoos.com.au; 2/25 Hyde St; ⊘10am-4.30pm Mon-Sat) Didgeridoos and hemp clothing may be modern hippie clichés, and although this shop sells both, it has a stellar reputation for producing high-quality instruments. In fact, that might be interstellar – the first didg in space came from here.

Bellingen Book Nook   BOOKS
(25 Hyde St; ⊘10am-4pm Tue-Sat) Secondhand books are stacked to the ceiling in this tiny bookworm cave.

ℹ️ Information

Waterfall Way Information Centre (☎02-6655 1522; www.coffscoast.com.au; 29-31 Hyde St; ⊘9am-5pm) Stocks brochures on scenic drives, walks and an arts trail.

ℹ️ Getting There & Away

From Bellingen the Waterfall Way climbs steeply for 29km to Dorrigo – it's a spectacular drive.
Busways (☎02-6655 7410; www.busways.com.au) Five or six buses to/from Nambucca Heads and Coffs Harbour on weekdays (both $11.90, 1¼ hours), and two on Saturday.

New England Coaches (☎02-6732 1051; www.newenglandcoaches.com.au) Two to three coaches per week to/from Dorrigo ($35, 45 minutes), Coffs Harbour ($30, 50 minutes), Nambucca Heads ($40, 1½ hours), Kempsey ($55, 2¼ hours) and Port Macquarie ($60, 2¾ hours).

Dorrigo National Park

From Bellingen the Waterfall Way climbs up the escarpment to Dorrigo. The drive passes plunging torrents and provides a teaser for the lush vistas of Dorrigo National Park.

Stretching for 119 sq km, this beautiful park is part of the Gondwana Rainforests World Heritage Area (p152). It's home to a huge diversity of vegetation and over 120 species of bird. The **Rainforest Centre** (☎02-9513 6617; www.nationalparks.nsw.gov.au/Dorrigo-National-Park; Dome Rd; adult/child $2/1; ⊘9am-4.30pm; ☎), at the park entrance, has displays and a film about the park's ecosystems, and can advise you on which walk to tackle. It even provides free wi-fi and a charging station for phones and cameras. It's also home to the excellent **Canopy Cafe** (www.canopycafedorrigo.com; mains $14-19; ⊘9am-4.30pm) and the **Skywalk**, a viewing platform that juts over the rainforest and provides vistas over the valleys below. On a fine day you can see the ocean.

Starting from the centre, the **Wonga Walk** is a two-hour, 6.6km-return walk on a bitumen track through the depths of the rainforest. Along the way it passes a couple of very beautiful waterfalls, one of which you can walk behind.

It's well worth driving down to the **Never Never Picnic Area**, set in the warm temperate forest in the middle of the park, where there are further walks and waterfalls (2km of the approach road is unsealed).

Dorrigo

POP 1080
Arrayed around the T-junction of two wider-than-wide streets, Dorrigo is a pretty little place. One gets the sense that this might be the next Bellingen in terms of food and wine, but it hasn't quite happened yet.

The town's main attraction is the **Dangar Falls**, 1.2km north of town, which cascades over a series of rocky shelves before plummeting into a basin. You can swim here if you have a yen for glacial bathing.

🛏 Sleeping

Hotel Motel Dorrigo   HOTEL **$**
(☑ 02-6657 2016; www.hotelmoteldorrigo.com.au;
cnr Cudgery & Hickory Sts; dm $35, r without/with
bathroom from $70/95; ❋ @) The charm of this
pub's exterior is not echoed in the bar or the
dining room. Upstairs, the renovated bedrooms are fine, for the price, but not all have
bathrooms. Motel units face the rear car park.

Mossgrove   B&B **$$**
(☑ 02-6657 5388; www.mossgrove.com.au; 589 Old
Coast Rd; r $185) Set on 2.5 hectares, 8km from
Dorrigo, this lovely Federation home has
two upmarket rooms, a guest lounge and a
bathroom, all tastefully renovated to suit the
era. A continental breakfast is included; an
extra $35 will get you something hot.

🍴 Eating & Drinking

Thirty Three on Hickory   EUROPEAN **$$**
(☑ 02-6657 1882; www.thirtythreeonhickory.com.
au; 33 Hickory St; mains $17-23; ⊙ 5-9pm Thu-Sat,
noon-6pm Sun) This gorgeous 1920s weatherboard cottage has stained-glass windows,
tasteful antiques and a blossoming garden.
The menu ranges from pizza to hearty bistro
fare, served in style with white tablecloths,
sparkling silverware and a cosy wood fire.

Red Dirt Distillery   DISTILLERY, CAFE
(☑ 02-6657 1373; www.reddirtdistillery.com.au; 51-
53 Hickory St; ⊙ 10am-4pm Mon-Fri, to 2pm Sat &
Sun) David Scott, the owner of the Red Dirt
Distillery, gets creative with a range of vodka
and liqueurs made with, for example, spuds
grown in Dorrigo's red dirt. Buy a bottle,
plus some of his deli snacks and you're talking picnic, or sit in for an antipasto platter.

ℹ Information

Dorrigo Information Centre (☑ 02-6657 2486;
www.dorrigo.com; 36 Hickory St; ⊙ 10am-3pm)

ℹ Getting There & Away

Two to three New England Coaches (p141) buses
per week head to/from Bellingen ($35, 45 min-
utes), Coffs Harbour ($40, 1½ hours), Nambucca
Heads ($50, two hours), Kempsey ($65, three
hours) and Port Macquarie ($70, 3½ hours).

Coffs Harbour

POP 24,600

Where other coastal towns have the ready-
made aesthetic of a main street slap-bang on
the waterfront, Coffs has an inland city centre, and much of the town seems to turn its
back on the sea. And yet, Coffs has a string
of fabulous beaches and a preponderance
of water-based activities, action sports and
wildlife encounters, making it hugely popular with families, backpackers and 'middle
Australians' drawn to the cultural beacon
that is the Big Banana.

Originally called Korff's Harbour, the
town was settled by Europeans in the 1860s.
The jetty was built in 1892 to load cedar and
other logs. Bananas were first grown in the
area in the 1880s, but no one made much
money from them until the railway came to
town in 1918. Banana growing reached its
peak in the 1960s and these days tourism is
the mainstay of the local economy.

The town is split into three areas: the
jetty area, the commercial centre and the
beaches. South of Coffs is Sawtell, a sprawl
of housing developments fronting some
fabulous surf beaches.

⊙ Sights

Coff's biggest attraction is the beach. **Park
Beach** is a long, lovely stretch of sand
backed by dense shrubbery and sand dunes
that conceal the buildings beyond. **Jetty
Beach** is somewhat more sheltered. **Diggers Beach**, reached by turning off the
highway near the Big Banana, is popular
with surfers, with swells averaging 1m to
1.5m. Naturists let it all hang out at **Little
Diggers Beach**, just inside the northern
headland.

★ **Muttonbird Island**   ISLAND
(www.nationalparks.nsw.gov.au/Muttonbird-Is-
land-Nature-Reserve) The Gumbainggir people knew this island as Giidany Miirlarl,
meaning Place of the Moon. It was joined
to Coffs Harbour by the northern breakwater in 1935. The walk to the top (quite
steep at the end) provides sweeping vistas
along the coast. From late August to early
April this eco treasure is occupied by some
12,000 pairs of wedge-tailed shearwaters,
with cute offspring visible in December
and January.

★ **North Coast Regional
Botanic Garden**   GARDENS
(www.ncrbg.com; Hardacre St; admission by donation; ⊙ 9am-5pm) Immerse yourself in the
subtropical surrounds of the greenhouses,
sensory gardens and stands of lush rainforest. There are sections devoted to such exotic places as Africa, China and Queensland.

The 6km **Coffs Creek Walk** passes by, starting opposite the council chambers on Coff St and finishing near the ocean.

Bunker Cartoon Gallery GALLERY
(www.coffsharbour.nsw.gov.au; John Champion Way; adult/child $2/1; ☺10am-4pm Mon-Sat) Displays rotating selections from its permanent collection of 18,000 cartoons in a WWII bunker.

Coffs Harbour Regional Gallery GALLERY
(www.coffsharbour.nsw.gov.au; Rigby House, cnr Coff & Duke Sts; ☺10am-4pm Tue-Sat) FREE Exhibits regional art and touring exhibitions.

Big Banana AMUSEMENT PARK
(www.bigbanana.com; 351 Pacific Hwy; combo pass adult/child $33/27; ☺9am-4.30pm) Built in 1964, the Big Banana started the craze for 'Big Things' in Australia (just so you know who to blame). Admission is free, with charges for associated attractions such as ice skating, toboggan rides, the waterpark, plantation tours and the irresistably named 'World of Bananas Experience'.

Solitary Islands Aquarium AQUARIUM
(www.solitaryislandsaquarium.com; Bay Dr, Charlesworth Bay; adult/child $10/6; ☺10am-4pm Sat & Sun) On the weekends when the students are at the beach, this small aquarium belonging to Southern Cross University's Marine Science Centre is open to the public. Tanks provide close encounters with species of fish, coral and octopus that frequent the waters of the Solitary Islands Marine Park, which stretches north from Coffs. Kids might find the lengthy video a little dry, but at least you won't find any captive marine mammals here.

🏃 Activities & Tours

Canoes, kayaks and stand-up paddleboards can be hired from Mangrove Jack's cafe (p146). Keen hikers should pick up a copy of the *Solitary Islands Coastal Walk* brochure from the visitor centre ($2).

Jetty Dive DIVING
(☑02-6651 1611; www.jettydive.com.au; 398 Harbour Dr) The Solitary Islands Marine Park is a meeting place of tropical waters and southern currents, making for a wonderful combination of corals, reef fish and seaweeds. This dive shop offers spectacular diving and snorkelling trips (double boat dives $60), PADI certification ($459) and, from June to October, whale watching (adult/child $59/49).

Spirit of Coffs Harbour CRUISE
(☑02-6650 0155; www.gowhalewatching.com.au; Coffs Harbour Marina; per person $45; ☺9.30am May-Nov) Whale-watching trips on an 18.3m catamaran.

Coffs City Skydivers SKYDIVING
(☑02-6651 1167; www.coffsskydivers.com.au; Coffs Harbour airport; tandem jumps $229-495) Satisfies all urges to fling yourself from a plane.

East Coast Surf School SURFING
(☑02-6651 5515; www.eastcoastsurfschool.com.au; Diggers Beach; lessons from $55) A particularly female-friendly outfit run by former pro surfer Helene Enevoldson.

Lee Winkler's Surf School SURFING
(☑02-6650 0050; www.leewinklerssurfschool.com.au; Park Beach; from $50) One of the longest-standing surf schools in Coffs.

Coffs Jet Ski JET-SKIING
(☑0418 665 656; www.coffsjetskihire.com.au; Park Beach; 15/30/60min from $60/100/160) Hires jet skis from the beach.

Liquid Assets ADVENTURE TOUR
(☑02-6658 0850; www.surfrafting.com; 38 Marina Dr) half-day tours from $60) Offers a suite of watery tours and activities, including kayaking, white-water rafting, surfing and platypus spotting.

🎉 Festivals & Events

Pittwater to Coffs Harbour Regatta SPORT
(www.pittwatertocoffs.com.au) Starts in Sydney on 2 January and finishes here, with further short races on the 5th and 6th.

Sawtell Chilli Festival FOOD
(www.sawtellchillifestival.com.au) Early July.

Gold Cup Carnival SPORT
(www.coffsracingclub.com.au) Coffs' premier horse race; early August.

Coffs Harbour International Buskers & Comedy Festival MUSIC
(www.coffsharbourbuskers.com) Held over eight days in late September.

🛏 Sleeping

Motels cluster in two spots: out on the Pacific Hwy by the visitor centre where they can suck in road-trippers, and down by Park Beach where they can lure beachgoers. There's no real reason to stay out by the highway.

Coffs Harbour

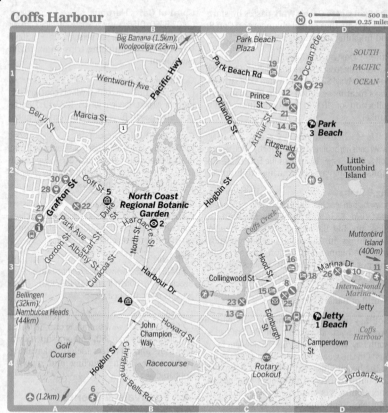

Coffs Harbour

⊙ Top Sights

1 Jetty Beach	D4
2 North Coast Regional Botanic Garden	B3
3 Park Beach	D2

⊙ Sights

| 4 Bunker Cartoon Gallery | B3 |
| 5 Coffs Harbour Regional Gallery | B2 |

✦ Activities, Courses & Tours

6 Coffs City Skydivers	A4
7 Coffs Creek Walk	C3
Coffs Jet Ski	(see 3)
8 Jetty Dive	C3
9 Lee Winkler's Surf School	D2
10 Liquid Assets	D3
11 Spirit of Coffs Harbour	D3

⊟ Sleeping

12 Adrift by the Beach	C1
13 Aussitel Backpackers	C3
14 Bosuns Inn Motel	C2

15 Caribbean Motel	C3
16 Coffs Harbour YHA	C3
17 Observatory Apartments	C4
18 Pacific Marina Luxury Apartments	D3
19 Pacific Property Management	C1
20 Park Beach Holiday Park	C2

✦ Eating

21 Cafe Aqua	C1
22 Cocoa	A2
Crying Tiger	(see 8)
Fiasco	(see 18)
23 Mangrove Jack's	C3
24 O.P 81	D1
25 Old John's	C3
Urban Espresso Lounge	(see 8)
26 Yknot Bistro	D3

⊜ Drinking & Nightlife

27 Coast Hotel	A2
28 Coffs Hotel	A2
29 Hoey Moey	D1
30 Plantation Hotel	A2

One of many holiday-apartment agents is **Pacific Property Management** (☑02-6652 1466; www.coffsaccommodation.com.au; 101 Park Beach Rd).

Coffs Harbour YHA
HOSTEL $

(☑02-6652 6462; www.yha.com.au; 51 Collingwood St; dm $30-33, r $86; @✳) With service and amenities like these, it's a wonder hotels don't go out of business. The dorms are spacious, the private rooms have bathrooms, and the TV lounge and kitchen are immaculate. You can hire surfboards and bikes.

Bosuns Inn Motel
MOTEL $

(☑02-6651 2251; www.motelcoffsharbour.com; 37 Ocean Pde; r $85-95; ✳✳) The friendly owners keep everything shipshape at this well-priced motel across the road from Park Beach. Blue trim and furnishings add a vaguely nautical flavour amid all the brickwork, and there's a nice pool at the rear.

Park Beach Holiday Park
CAMPGROUND $

(☑02-6648 4888; www.coffsholidays.com.au; Ocean Pde; camp sites/cabins from $35/87; @✳) This place is massive and ideally located at the beach. Kids are well catered for with a jumping pillow, a playground and a pool with a lighthouse slide and colourful seahorse fountains.

Aussitel Backpackers
HOSTEL $

(☑02-6651 1871; www.aussitel.com; 312 Harbour Dr; dm/d $27/70; @✳✳) Don't be put off by the exterior, which manages to be forbidding despite being bright orange. This capacious brick house has homely dorms and a shady courtyard. Surfboards, stand-up paddleboards, kayaks, canoes and snorkelling gear are free to borrow.

Observatory Apartments
APARTMENT $$

(☑02-6650 0462; www.theobservatory.com.au; 30-36 Camperdown St; apt from $150; ✳✳✳) The studio, two- and three-bedroom apartments in this attractive modern complex are bright and airy, with chef-friendly kitchens. They all have balconies with ocean views and some have spa baths.

Adrift by the Beach
APARTMENT $$

(☑02-6652 2087; www.adriftbythebeach.com.au; 5 Boultwood St; apt from $125; ✳✳✳) These well-priced, brick, motel-style, two- and three-bedroom apartments stretch in a lazy L around a pool. They all have kitchens, but only some have washing machines (there's a communal laundry for the rest).

Caribbean Motel
MOTEL $$

(☑02-6652 1500; www.caribbeanmotel.com.au; 353 Harbour Dr; r/apt from $128/158; ✳✳✳) Close to the jetty, this 24-unit motel has been tastefully renovated and offers a breakfast buffet (at an extra charge). The best rooms have balconies, views and spa baths, and there are great-value one-bedroom suites with kitchenettes.

Pacific Marina Luxury Apartments
APARTMENT $$$

(☑02-6651 7955; www.pacificmarina.com.au; 22 Orlando St; apt from $290; ✳✳✳) These large, modern, self-contained apartments are in one of the best locations in town, close to shops, restaurants and the beach.

✗ Eating

Cafe Aqua
CAFE $

(☑02-6652 5566; www.cafeaqua.com.au; 57 Ocean Pde; mains $10-19; ⊙7am-3pm) This excellent cafe near Park Beach whips up substantial breakfasts and Mediterranean-influenced dishes for lunch, including delicious mezze plates.

Cocoa
CAFE $

(35 Harbour Dr; mains $11-19; ⊙7am-6pm) The bright and gleaming modern decor, on-to-it service and excellent breakfasts make this town-centre cafe a hot spot for Coffs' business set and pram brigade. Seasonal specials are chalked up weekly.

Old John's
CAFE $

(www.facebook.com/oldjohns; 358 Harbour Dr; mains $10-17; ⊙7am-4pm Mon & Tue, to 11pm Wed-Sun) The friendly hipster staff may not have the whole service thing nailed, but this very cool shabby-chic eatery serves excellent food. And at $15 for an evening pasta and a glass of wine, you can't really complain.

O.P 81
CAFE $

(www.facebook.com/O.P81Cafe; 81 Ocean Pde; mains breakfast $8-10, lunch $15; ⊙7am-2pm Tue-Sun) One of the few eateries along motel-cluttered Ocean Pde, O.P 81 has modern decor, tasty food, serious coffee and a big front deck.

Fiasco
ITALIAN $$

(☑02-6651 2006; www.fiascorestaurant.com.au; 22 Orlando St; mains $19-37; ⊙6-9pm Tue-Sat) Fiasco doesn't come close to living up to its name. Classic Italian fare is prepared in an open kitchen using produce from the best local suppliers and herbs from its garden. If you're not overly hungry, grab a snack at the bar.

Mangrove Jack's
CAFE $$

(☑ 02-6652 5517; www.mangrovejackscafe.com. au; Promenade Centre, Harbour Dr; mains breakfast $9-16, lunch $15-25, dinner $24-30; ⊙ 7.30am-3pm Sun & Mon, 7.30am-3pm & 5-9.15pm Tue-Sat; 🛜) Wonderfully located on a quiet bend of Coffs Creek, Mangrove Jack's uses almost exclusively local produce, has Coopers on tap, and offers tasty cafe fare during the day and more substantial dinner options at night.

Urban Espresso Lounge
CAFE $$

(www.urbanespressolounge.com.au; 384a Harbour Dr; mains $13-23; ⊙ 7am-4pm) A stylish little outpost on the main dining strip, Urban opens out onto the street and is at once classy and casual. The food and service rarely miss a beat and terrific coffee rounds out a great package.

Yknot Bistro
PUB $$

(☑ 02-6651 1741; www.yknotbistro.com.au; 30 Marina Dr; mains breakfast $13-18, lunch $17-30, dinner $21-33; ⊙ 7am-2.30pm & 6-8.30pm) Part of the Coffs Harbour Yacht Club, this busy eatery serves pub-style seafood, steaks and pasta. Best of all, it has an ocean view – rare in Coffs. The dining room is huge and there's plenty of outdoor seating.

Crying Tiger
THAI $$

(☑ 02-6650 0195; www.facebook.com/TheCryingTigerThaiRestaurant; 382 Harbour Dr; mains $19-25; ⊙ 5.30-9pm; 🖉) There'll be no tears before bedtime for Thai food fans at this fragrant restaurant – unless they're spice induced. The menu is full of classic Thai dishes and you can turn the chilli gauge as high or low as you like. It also offers cooking classes.

🍸 Drinking & Nightlife

See Thursday's edition of the **Coffs Harbour Advocate** (www.coffscoastadvocate.com. au) for listings. Clubs change names with the seasons.

Hoey Moey
PUB

(www.hoeymoey.com.au; 84 Ocean Pde; ⊙ 10am-late; 🛜) The massive inner beer garden gives a good indication of how much this place kicks off in summer. Pool competitions, live music (Wednesday to Sunday), quiz nights and crab racing fill up the week.

Coffs Hotel
PUB

(www.coffsharbourhotel.com; cnr Grafton & West High Sts; ⊙ 11am-late) Irish pub with bands, several bars and DJs. Head around the side to Ye Olde Bottle Shop cocktail bar for a more boutique experience.

Plantation Hotel
PUB

(www.plantationhotel.com.au; 88 Grafton St; ⊙ 11am-late) Better than most giant booze barns, the Plantation has live bands and DJs until late at night, but beer and steaks are the mainstays.

Coast Hotel
PUB

(www.coasthotel.com.au; 2 Moonee St; ⊙ 11am-late) Formerly the Old Fitzroy Hotel, this place has been purpose-renovated to supply lovers of a lazy afternoon with a beer garden. It has landscaped decking and cool breakaway areas so you can kick back on a couch if the mood takes you. Entertainment includes lots of live music and a Tuesday trivia night.

ℹ️ Information

Visitor Information Centre (☑ 02-6648 4990; www.coffscoast.com.au; cnr McLean St & Pacific Hwy; ⊙ 9am-5pm)

ℹ️ Getting There & Away

AIR

Coffs Harbour Airport (CFS; ☑ 02-6648 4767; www.coffscoast.com.au/airport; Airport Dr) is 3km southwest of town.

Brindabella Airlines (☑ 1300 668 824; www. brindabellaairlines.com.au) Flies to/from Brisbane.

QantasLink (☑ 13 13 13; www.qantas.com.au) Flies to/from Sydney.

Tigerair (☑ 02-8073 3421; www.tigerair.com. au) Flies to/from Sydney.

Virgin Australia (☑ 13 67 89; www.virgin-australia.com) Flies to/from Sydney and Melbourne.

BUS

Long-distance and regional buses leave from a shelter adjacent to the visitor centre.

Busways (☑ 02-6652 2744; www.busways. com.au) At least five buses to/from Nambucca Heads and Bellingen on weekdays (both $11.90, 1¼ hours), and at least one on Saturday.

Greyhound (☑ 1300 473 946; www.greyhound. com.au) Coaches to/from Sydney ($66, 8½ hours, daily), Port Macquarie ($36, 2½ hours, two daily), Nambucca Heads ($13, 45 minutes, two daily), Byron Bay ($45, 3½ hours, four daily) and Brisbane ($81, seven hours, three daily).

New England Coaches (☑ 02-6732 1051; www. newenglandcoaches.com.au) At least two coaches per week to/from Dorrigo ($40, 1½ hours), Bellingen ($30, 50 minutes), Nambucca Heads ($35, 35 minutes), Kempsey ($40, 1¼ hours) and Port Macquarie ($50, two hours).

Premier (☑13 34 10; www.premierms.com.au) Daily coach to Sydney ($66, 8½ hours), Port Macquarie ($47, 2¼ hours), Nambucca Heads ($34, 40 minutes), Byron Bay ($50, five hours) and Brisbane ($59, 8½ hours).

Ryans Bus Service (☑02-6652 3201; www. ryansbusservice.com.au) Buses to/from Woolgoolga ($13, one hour, six on weekdays, two on Saturday) and Grafton ($25, two hours, two on weekdays).

TRAIN

NSW TrainLink (☑13 22 32; www.nswtrainlink. info) Three trains head to/from Sydney ($81, nine hours), Kempsey ($19, 1¾ hours), Nambucca Heads ($7, 40 minutes) and Grafton ($17, 1¼ hours) daily, and one continues to Brisbane ($85, 5½ hours).

ⓘ Getting Around

Busways, Ryans and **Sawtell** (☑02-6653 3344; www.sawtellcoaches.com.au) run local bus routes; Sawtell has regular services to the airport.

Coffs District Taxis (☑13 10 08; www.coffs taxis.com.au) operates a 24-hour service.

Woolgoolga
POP 4720

About 25km north of Coffs, Woolgoolga is a good option for a beachy small-town stop. It's known for its surf-and-Sikh community – even if you're just driving by on the highway you're sure to notice the impressive **Guru Nanak Temple**, a Sikh *gurdwara* (place of worship).

🛏 Sleeping

Woolgoolga Beach Caravan Park   CAMPGROUND $
(☑02-6648 4711; www.coffscoastholidayparks. com.au; 55 Beach St; camp sites/cabins from $35/87; 🛜) Right on the beach but surprisingly quiet at night.

Solitary Islands Lodge   B&B $$
(☑02-6654 1335; www.solitaryislandslodge.com. au; 3 Arthur St; r $160; 🛜) You can while away the hours gazing out to sea from any of the three immaculate guest rooms in this modern hilltop house; two of them have their own balconies. The charming hosts stock the rooms with ingredients for a continental breakfast.

Waterside Cabins   CABIN $$
(☑02-6654 1644; www.watersidecabins.com.au; Hearnes Lake Rd; cabins from $113; ✳ ✱) Located just off the highway, south of the town, these stylish two- and three-bedroom units are part of a large complex of cabin-style residences. The four rental cabins are in a leafy spot near the lake; there's a walkway to the beach.

🍴 Eating

Rustic Table   ITALIAN $$
(☑02-6654 1645; 53 Beach St; mains breakfast & lunch $10-16, dinner $18-28; ⊘7am-1pm Sun, to 3pm Mon & Tue, to 10pm Wed-Sat) If the Holy Goat coffee doesn't completely wake you up,

BYRON BAY & NORTHERN NEW SOUTH WALES WOOLGOOLGA

WORTH A TRIP

RED ROCK

Red Rock (population 310) is a sleepy village set between a beautiful beach and a glorious fish-filled river inlet. It takes its name from the red-tinged rock stack at the headland, but the local Gumbainggir people know it by a more sombre name: Blood Rock. In the 1880s a detachment of armed police slaughtered the inhabitants of an Aboriginal camp, chasing the survivors to the headland, where they were driven off. The Blood Rock Massacres are commemorated by a simple plaque, and the area is considered sacred.

The **Yarrawarra Aboriginal Cultural Centre** (☑02-6640 7100; www.yarrawarra. org; 170 Red Rock Rd, Corindi Beach) has an interesting art gallery and a bush-tucker cafe, where you can try kangaroo and lemon-myrtle damper. It also holds bush-medicine tours and art classes for groups; call ahead if you're interested in joining one.

Accommodation (including some flash permanently pitched tents) is available at **Red Rock Caravan Park** (☑02-6649 2730; www.redrock.org.au; 1 Lawson St; camp sites/ cabins from $33/110; 🛜).

On weekdays Ryans has occasional buses to/from Woolgoolga ($11, 15 minutes) and Grafton ($20, 50 minutes).

the garrulous waiters certainly will. Delicious, seasonal Italian classics are chalked up on the blackboard daily. On Friday and Saturday evenings there's live music.

Bluebottles Brasserie CAFE $$
(☑02-6654 1962; 53 Beach St; mains breakfast $12-17, lunch $14-23, dinner $24-30; ☺7.30am-3pm Sun-Thu, till late Fri & Sat) Tables spill out onto the street at this corner eatery, which feels much more like a cafe than the name suggests. Listen out for the live jazz sessions.

❶ Getting There & Away

Ryans (p147) has infrequent buses to/from Coffs Harbour ($13, one hour), Red Rock ($11, 15 minutes) and Grafton ($21, 1½ hours). Coaches on the Pacific Hwy route stop here.

CLARENCE COAST

North of Woolgoolga the Pacific Hwy leaves the coast and skirts Yuraygir National Park on its way to the small city of Grafton on the Clarence River. This is the start of the Northern Rivers region, which stretches all the way to the Queensland border. It's an area defined as much by its beaches and clement weather as it is by its three major waterways (the Clarence, Richmond and Tweed Rivers).

Yuraygir National Park

The 535-sq-km Yuraygir National Park (vehicle entry $7) covers the 60km stretch of coast north from Red Rock, and is an important habitat for the endangered coastal emu. The isolated beaches are best discovered on the Yuraygir Coastal Walk, a 65km waymarked walk from Angourie to Red Rock following a series of tracks, trails, beaches and rock platforms, and passing through the villages of Brooms Head, Minnie Water and Wooli. It's best walked north to south with the sun at your back. Walkers can bush-camp at basic campgrounds (www.nationalparks.nsw.gov.au/Yuraygir-National-Park; adult/child $10/5) along the route; only some have drinking water. The visitor centres stock walk guides ($2).

Wooli (population 493) occupies a long isthmus within the southern half of the park, with a river estuary on one side and the ocean on the other. This only adds to its isolated charm. In early October it hosts the Australian National Goanna Pulling Championships (www.goannapulling.com.au), where participants squatting on all fours attach leather harnesses to their heads and engage in a cranial tug-of-war. Fret not: no actual goannas are involved.

If you fancy settling in for a few days' fishing, kayaking and lazing on the beach, Solitary Islands Marine Park Resort (☑02-6649 7519; www.solitaryislandsresort.com.au; 383 North St; camp sites/cabins from $34/140; ❀❧) ⋒ has a range of tidy cabins in a scrubby riverside setting.

Grafton

POP 16,600
Grafton is a mildly interesting apparition from an uncomplicated past. Nestled into a quiet bend of the Clarence River, the city's charming grid of wide streets has grand pubs and some splendid old houses. In late October the streets are awash with the purple flowers of the Brazilian jacaranda tree. Susan Island, in the middle of the river, is home to a large colony of fruit bats; their evening fly-past is an impressive sight.

Don't be fooled by the franchises along the highway: the main part of town is reached by an imposing 1932 double-decker (road and rail) bridge.

◉ Sights

Victoria Street HISTORIC BUILDING
Victoria St is the city's main heritage precinct, with some fine examples of 19th-century architecture, including the courthouse (1862) at number 47, the Anglican Cathedral (commenced 1884) on the corner of Duke St and Roches Family Hotel (1871) at number 85.

Grafton Regional Gallery GALLERY
(☑02-6642 3177; www.graftongallery.nsw.gov.au; 158 Fitzroy St; admission by donation; ☺10am-4pm Tue-Sun) Occupying an impressive 1880 house, this small gallery has an interesting collection of NSW landscape paintings and displays regular special exhibitions.

Clarence River Historical Society MUSEUM
(www.clarencehistory.org.au; 190 Fitzroy St; adult/child $3/1; ☺1-4pm Tue-Thu & Sun) Based in pretty Schaeffer House (1903), this little museum displays treasures liberated from attics across town.

✨ Festivals & Events

July Racing Carnival SPORT
(www.crjc.com.au) A week-long carnival culminating in the Grafton Cup, the richest horse-racing event in country Australia.

Jacaranda Festival FLOWERS
(www.jacarandafestival.org.au) For two weeks from late October, the longest-running floral festival in Australia paints the town mauve.

🛏 Sleeping

Gateway Village CAMPGROUND **$**
(☑02-6642 4225; www.thegatewayvillage.com.au; 598 Summerland Way; camp sites/cabins from $29/120; ❄@🛜🐕) Putting the 'park' back into holiday park, this attractive complex on the northern approach to town has manicured gardens with avenues of palms and an ornamental lake filled with water-lilies.

Annies B&B B&B **$$**
(☑0421 914 295; www.anniesbnbgrafton.com; 13 Mary St; s/d $145/160; ❄🛜🐕) This beautiful Victorian house on a leafy corner has private rooms with an old-fashioned ambience, set apart from the rest of the family home. A continental breakfast is provided.

🍴 Eating & Drinking

Limonata ITALIAN **$$**
(☑02-6643 1010; www.dukestreet.com.au; 1 Duke St; mains lunch $14-20, dinner $20-27; ⊙8am-3pm Sat & Sun, 5-9pm Wed-Sat) Wood-fired pizzas, delicious pasta, occasional live jazz and a riverside location make this the best of Grafton's eateries by quite some way.

Roches Family Hotel HOTEL
(☑02-6642 2866; www.roches.com.au; 85 Victoria St) Breaking the rule that regional pubs need to be cavernous and starkly lit, this historic corner hotel is a cosy spot for a drink or reasonably priced bite. It's worth calling in just for a peek at the beer-can collection and the croc in the public bar.

ℹ Information

Clarence River Visitor Information Centre
(☑02-6642 4677; www.clarencetourism.com; cnr Spring St & Pacific Hwy; ⊙9am-5pm; 🛜) South of the river.

NPWS Office (☑02-6641 1500; Level 4, 49 Victoria St)

ℹ Getting There & Around

AIR

Clarence Valley Regional Airport (GFN; ☑02-6643 0200; www.clarence.nsw.gov.au) is 12km southeast of town. **Regional Express** (Rex; ☑13 17 13; www.rex.com.au) flies to/from Sydney and Taree.

BUS

Busways (☑02-6642 2954; www.busways.com.au) Runs local services including four to eight buses to Maclean (one hour), Yamba (1¼ hours) and Angourie (1½ hours) daily; all $12.

Greyhound (☑1300 473 946; www.greyhound.com.au) Coaches to/from Sydney ($128, 10½ hours, three daily), Nambucca Heads ($30, 2½ hours, two daily), Coffs Harbour ($16, one hour, three daily), Byron Bay ($27, three hours, three daily) and Brisbane ($60, 6½ hours, three daily).

Northern Rivers Buslines (☑02-6626 1499; www.nrbuslines.com.au) One bus to/from Maclean ($9.70, 43 minutes) and Lismore ($9.70, three hours) on weekdays.

Premier (☑13 34 10; www.premierms.com.au) Daily coach to/from Sydney ($67, 9½ hours), Nambucca Heads ($34, 1¾ hours), Coffs Harbour ($34, one hour), Byron Bay ($47, 4¼ hours) and Brisbane ($52, 7½ hours).

Ryans Bus Service (☑02-6652 3201; www.ryansbusservice.com.au) Weekday buses to/from Woolgoolga ($21, 1½ hours), Red Rocks ($20, 1½ hours) and Coffs Harbour ($25, two hours).

TRAIN

NSW TrainLink (☑13 22 32; www.nswtrainlink.info) Three trains head to/from Sydney ($103, 10 hours), Kempsey ($36, three hours), Nambucca Heads ($27, two hours) and Coffs Harbour ($17, 1¼ hours) daily, and one continues to Brisbane ($67, 4¼ hours). There's also a daily coach to Maclean ($9.22, 35 minutes), Yamba ($14, 1¼ hours), Ballina ($30, three hours), Lennox Head ($34, 3½ hours) and Byron Bay ($36, 3¾ hours).

Grafton to Yamba

The delta between Grafton and the coast is a patchwork of farmland in which the now sinuous and spreading Clarence River forms more than 100 islands, some very large. Here you'll see the first of the sugar-cane plantations and Queenslander-style houses – wooden structures perched on stilts and with high-pitched roofs to allow air circulation in the hot summers. The burning of the cane fields (May to December) adds a smoky tang to the air.

WORTH A TRIP

MUSEUM OF INTERESTING THINGS

What is Russell Crowe's *Gladiator* costume doing sitting alongside Johnny Cash's gold albums and Don Bradman's cricket bats in an old wooden barn in tiny Nymboida, 40km southwest of Grafton? The answer: this is where Crowe stashes his considerable collection of boys' toys. The New Zealand–born superstar grew up in nearby Nana Glen, where his parents still live.

As well as movie, music and sporting memorabilia, the **museum** (☑02-6649 4126; adult/child $5/2.50; ☉11am-3pm Wed-Fri & Sun, 10am-5pm Sat) has vintage motorbikes and artefacts from local pioneering history, a nod to the days when horse-drawn Cobb & Co coaches stopped here on the woolpack road from Armidale to Grafton.

The adjoining **Coaching Station Inn** (☑02-6649 4126; www.coachingstation.com; 3970 Armidale Rd; s/d $110/140, mains $15-18; ☉10am-8pm; ❋ ☎) is a great old roadside pub offering good-value meals and tidy accommodation in a log-clad motel block. Don't get too excited, though: aside from the photos that dot the inn's main bar, you're not likely to see the man himself. Then again, the barman reckons he sometimes pops in unannounced. After all, 'it's only 11 minutes by chopper from his mum and dad's house'.

It's worth taking a small detour from the Pacific Hwy to **Ulmarra** (population 435), a heritage-listed town with a river port. The **Ulmarra Hotel** (www.ulmarrahotel.com.au; 2 Coldstream St) is a quaint old corner pub with a wrought-iron verandah and a greener-than-green beer garden that stretches down to the river.

Maclean (population 2600) is a picturesque little riverside town that takes its Scottish heritage seriously, even wrapping its lampposts in tartan. Stroll the riverfront, check out the shops and have a cold one at one of the old hotels. Ask at the very helpful **Clarence Coast Visitor Information Centre** (☑02-6645 4121; www.clarencetourism.com; cnr Cameron St & Pacific Hwy; ☉9am-5pm; ☎), at the edge of town, about picturesque driving routes in the area.

Yamba & Angourie

POP 6040 & 184

The sleepy little fishing town of Yamba is slowly growing in popularity amongst those who favour a relaxed pace of life with access to great beaches and some excellent eateries. Its neighbour Angourie, 5km to the south, is a tiny, chilled-out place that has long been a draw for experienced surfers. In 2007 it became the first beach on the North Coast to be declared a National Surfing Reserve.

◉ Sights

Beaches BEACH

Surfing for the big boys and girls is at **Angourie Point**, but Yamba's beaches have something for everyone else. **Main Beach** is the busiest, with an ocean pool, banana palms and a grassy slope for those who don't want to get sandy. **Convent Beach** is a sunbaker's haven and **Turner's**, protected by the breakwall, is ideal for surf lessons. You can sometimes spot dolphins along the long stretch of **Pippi Beach**.

A walking and cycling track wends along Yamba's coastline. The prettiest bit is from Pippi Beach around Lovers Point to Convent Beach. The Yuraygir Coastal Walk (p148) begins in Angourie.

Angourie Blue Pools SPRING

(The Crescent) These springwater-fed water holes are the remains of the quarry used for the breakwall. The daring climb the cliff faces and plunge to the depths. The saner can slip silently into the water, surrounded by bush, only metres from the surf. From time to time algal blooms render swimming unsafe.

Bundjalung National Park PARK

(www.nationalparks.nsw.gov.au/Bundjalung-National-Park; vehicle entry $7) Stretching for 25km along the coast north of the Clarence River to South Evans Head, this national park is largely untouched and most of it is best explored with a 4WD. However, the southern reaches can be easily reached from Yamba via the passenger-only **Clarence River Ferry** (☑02-6646 6423; www.clarenceriverferries .com; adult/child $7.20/3.60; ☉at least 4 times daily) to Iluka. This section of the park includes Iluka Nature Reserve, a stand of rainforest facing Iluka Beach that's part of the Gondwana Rainforests World Heritage Area. On the other side of Iluka Bluff the literally named Ten Mile Beach unfurls.

Yamba River Markets
MARKET

(www.surfingthecoldstream.com.au; Ford Park, River St; ⊙9am-2pm) Held by the Clarence River on the fourth Sunday of the month, featuring locally produced food and craft.

🏃 Activities

Yamba Kayak
KAYAKING

(☑02-6646 0065; www.angourie.me; 3/5hr $70/90) Half- and full-day adventures are the speciality, with forays into nearby wilderness areas.

Yamba-Angourie Surf School
SURFING

(☑02-6646 1496; www.yambaangouriesurfschool.com.au; 2hr/3-day lessons $50/120) Lessons are run by former Australian surfing champion Jeremy Walters.

Clarence River Ferries
CRUISE

(☑0408 664 556; www.clarenceriverferries.com; ⊙11am-3pm) As well as the regular ferries, it runs a live-music cruise on Sunday (adult/child $30/15) and a Harwood Island cruise on Wednesday and Friday (adult/child $20/10). There's a licensed bar where you can purchase sandwiches and cheese platters.

Xtreme Cycle & Skate
BICYCLE RENTAL

(☑02-6645 8879; 34 Coldstream St, Yamba; bike hire per half-/full day $20/25)

🛏 Sleeping

Yamba YHA
HOSTEL $

(☑02-6646 3997; www.yha.com.au; 26 Coldstream St; dm $30-34, r $80; @🛜🏊) This welcoming, family-run, purpose-built hostel has a popular bar and restaurant downstairs, and a barbecue area with a tiny pool on the roof. Both the double rooms and some of the four-share dorms have their own bathrooms.

Blue Dolphin Holiday Resort
CAMPGROUND $

(☑02-6646 2194; www.bluedolphin.com.au; Yamba Rd; camp sites/cabins from $37/105; ❄@🛜🏊) The units range from simple cabins to luxurious houses at this big holiday park on the approach to Yamba. There's plenty to keep the kids happy, with two pool complexes (one with water slides), a jumping pillow and a playground.

Yamba Beach Motel
MOTEL $$

(☑02-6646 9411; www.yambabeachmotel.com.au; 30 Clarence St; r $149-199; ❄🛜🏊) You'll be hard pressed to find a motel better than this anywhere in NSW. The rooms have large flat-screen TVs, extremely comfortable beds, bath sheets and quality toiletries. There's also a small pool shaped like a parmesan wedge, an excellent cafe that will deliver meals to your room, and a beach just down the hill.

Clubyamba
APARTMENTS $$

(☑0427 461 981; www.clubyamba.com.au; 14 Henson Lane; apt $125-160; 🛜) Struggle up the hill and then collapse into one of four brightly painted contemporary apartments and two sea-view suites. There's also an architecturally designed one-bedroom townhouse near the river. All are luxurious options.

Surf Motel
MOTEL $$

(☑02-6646 2200; www.yambasurfmotel.com.au; 2 Queen St; r $120-180; ❄🛜) On a bluff overlooking Yamba's main beach, this modern place has eight spacious rooms with kitchenettes. Some have balconies too. Aside from the surf, it's blissfully quiet.

🍴 Eating

Pie & Pea
CAFE, BAKERY $

(11 Yamba St, Yamba; pies $5-8; ⊙6am-3pm Mon-Thu, to late Fri-Sun) Ratcheting the humble pie shop up a notch, this cool cafe bakes and serves a big range of gourmet meat pies, including a breakfast version (bacon, egg and cheese). There's also banana bread, muffins, scones, waffles and, in the evenings, kebabs.

★Beachwood Cafe
TURKISH $$

(☑02-6646 9781; www.beachwoodcafe.com.au; 22 High St, Yamba; mains breakfast $13-16, lunch $18-22; ⊙7am-2pm Tue-Sun) Cookbook author Sevtap Yüce steps out of the pages to deliver her *Turkish Flavours* to the plate at the wonderful little Beachwood Cafe. Most of the tables are outside, where the grass verge has been commandeered for a kitchen garden.

Frangipan
MEDITERRANEAN $$

(☑02-6646 2553; 11-13 The Crescent, Angourie; mains $30; ⊙6.30-10pm Tue-Sat) Surfing memorabilia overlooks a classy dining area where hearty meals such as crispy-skinned salmon and beef-cheek pappardelle are served with a complementary glass of wine. In summer it opens for Sunday breakfast.

🍷 Drinking & Entertainment

Pacific Hotel　　　　　　　　　　PUB
(📞 02-6646 2466; www.pacifichotelyamba.com.au;
18 Pilot St, Yamba) Check out the views from
this appealing pub overlooking the ocean.
There's regular live music and DJ nights,
and the food's good too.

Yamba Bowling Club　　　　LIVE MUSIC
(📞 02-6646 2305; www.yambabowlingclub.com.
au; 44 Wooli St) The biggest thing in town is
this brightly lit club, which we suspect does
rather better out of its poker machines than
it does out of lawn bowling. Still, if there's
anything major happening in town (live
music, comedy etc), it's probably happening here.

ⓘ Getting There & Away

Busways (📞 02-6645 8941; www.busways.
com.au) Four to eight buses from Yamba to
Angourie ($3.30, nine minutes), Maclean
($8.90, 19 minutes) and Grafton ($12, 1¼
hours) daily.
Greyhound (📞 1300 473 946; www.greyhound.
com.au) Has a daily coach to/from Sydney
($139, 11½ hours), Coffs Harbour ($28, two
hours), Byron Bay ($15, 2¼ hours), Surfers
Paradise ($41, five hours) and Brisbane ($46,
6¼ hours).
NSW TrainLink (📞 13 22 32; www.nswtrainlink.
info) Has a daily coach to Maclean ($7, 30
minutes), Grafton ($14, 1¼ hours), Lennox Head
($19, 2½ hours), Ballina ($17, 2¼ hours) and
Byron Bay ($20, three hours).

BALLINA & BYRON SHIRES

Where back-to-nature meets life's-a-beach,
this laid-back stretch of coast offers a mix
of family-friendly and party-hearty destinations. The beachy towns of Ballina and Lennox Head are less buzzy options than the
tourist Babylon of Byron Bay to the north.

Ballina

POP 16,000

At the mouth of the Richmond River, Ballina
is spoilt for white sandy beaches and crystal-
clear waters. In the late 19th century it was a
rich lumber town; a scattering of impressive
wooden buildings dating from that time can
still be found on its sleepy backstreets. These
days Ballina is best known as a quieter, more
family-friendly alternative to nearby Byron
Bay – although Ballina has over three times
the permanent population of Byron.

⊙ Sights

Beaches　　　　　　　　　　BEACH
Just across the bridge at the east of the main
strip is calm **Shaws Bay Lagoon**, a popular
place for family splashes. Despite its name,
nearby **Shelly Beach** is white, sandy and
patrolled. **South Ballina Beach** is a good
excursion option via the car ferry on Burns
Point Ferry Rd.

**Ballina Naval & Maritime
Museum**　　　　　　　　　　MUSEUM
(📞 02-6681 1002; www.ballinamaritimemuseum.
org.au; 8 Regatta Ave; adult/child $5/2; ⊙ 9am-
4pm) In the 19th century Ballina was the
third biggest port in NSW, and following
WWII many ex-navy personnel took jobs in
the shipyards here. Their presence is honoured through extensive text-heavy displays
about WWII naval battles. Perhaps more interesting for landlubbers is the actual balsa-
wood raft that sailed across the Pacific from
Ecuador as part of the Las Balsas expedition
that docked in Ballina in 1973.

GONDWANA RAINFORESTS OF AUSTRALIA

Spread between 41 distinct sites (including 16 national parks) in the north of NSW and
the southernmost parts of Queensland, this Unesco World Heritage List–inscribed
area is the world's largest expanse of subtropical rainforest. In evolutionary terms it's
a time capsule, representing ecosystems that have existed since before the breakup
of Gondwana, the ancient super-continent that once included Australia, New Zealand,
Antarctica, South America, Africa and India. It's thought that Gondwana started to break
up around 80 million years ago, with Australia separating from Antarctica around 45
million years ago.

To journey into the Jurassic, visit Iluka Nature Reserve (p150), Dorrigo National Park
(p141), New England National Park (p140), Nightcap National Park (p167), Wollumbin
National Park (p169) or Border Ranges National Park (p168).

Big Prawn

LANDMARK

(507 River St) Ballina's big prawn was very nearly thrown on the barbie in 2009 after the local council approved its demolition, but no one had the stomach to dispatch it. After a 5000-signature pro-prawn petition and a $400,000 restoration in 2013, the 9m, 35-tonne, 14-year-old crustacean is looking as tasty as it ever has. Although for that money you'd expect it to tap dance at the very least.

🏃 Activities

Ballina Boat Hire

BOATING

(☑ 0402 028 767; www.ballinaboathire.com.au; rear 268 River St; per half day $90) Has tinnies for fishing, barbecue boats and catamarans for the more adventurous.

Summerland Surf School

SURFING

(☑ 0428 824 393; www.summerlandsurfschool. com.au; 2hr lesson $50) Based south of Ballina in Evans Head.

Kool Katz

SURFING

(☑ 02-6685 5169; www.koolkatzsurf.com; 2hr lesson $49) Surf lessons at Shaws Bay, Shelly Beach or Lennox Head.

👉 Tours

Richmond River Cruises

CRUISE

(☑ 02-6687 5688; www.rrcruises.com.au; Regatta Ave; adult/child $30/15) Chugs up the Richmond River on two-hour morning- and afternoon-tea cruises every Sunday, and on request on Wednesday and Saturday. The visitor centre takes bookings.

Aboriginal Cultural Concepts

CULTURAL TOUR

(☑ 0405 654 280; www.aboriginalculturalconcepts. com; half-/full-day tours per person $80/160; ⊘ 10am-2pm Wed-Sat) Get an Indigenous insight into the local area on heritage tours exploring mythological sights along the Bundjalung coast. Regular tours require a minimum of four people, but tailored tours are also available.

🛏 Sleeping

Ballina Travellers Lodge

MOTEL $

(☑ 02-6686 6737; www.ballinatravellerslodge.com. au; 36-38 Tamar St; r without/with bathroom from $65/99; ❋ 🛜 🌀) If you opt for a budget room you won't get a car park and you'll need to share a diligently maintained ablutions block, but in all other respects you'll enjoy the same level of comfort and style as the motel rooms.

Shaws Bay Holiday Park

CARAVAN PARK $

(☑ 02-6686 2326; www.northcoastholidayparks. com.au; 1 Brighton St; camp sites/cabins from $38/134; ❋ @ 🛜) Well kept and well positioned, this low-key park is right on the lagoon and an easy walk from the centre. As well as camping and caravan sites, there's a range of self-contained units including three flash villas.

Ballina Palms Motor Inn

MOTEL $$

(☑ 02-6686 4477; www.ballinapalms.com; cnr Bentinck & Owen Sts; s/d $110/120; ❋ 🛜 🌀) With its lush garden setting and tidy rooms, this well-kept brick place is our pick of Ballina's motels. The rooms aren't overly large, but they all have kitchenettes, iPod docks and snazzy furnishings.

Ballina Heritage Inn

MOTEL $$

(☑ 02-6686 0505; www.ballinaheritageinn.com.au; 229 River St; s/d from $120/125; ❋ 🛜 🌀) Near the centre of town, this tidy inn has neat, bright and comfortable rooms that are a significant leap up in quality from the other motels on this strip.

Ballina Manor

HOTEL $$$

(☑ 02-6681 5888; www.ballinamanor.com.au; 25 Norton St; r $165-290; ❋ 🛜) This grand old dame of hospitality was once a school but has since been converted into a luxurious guesthouse, filled to the hilt with restored 1920s furnishings. All rooms are indulgent: the best room has a four-poster bed and spa bath.

🍴 Eating & Drinking

Beanz

FAST FOOD $

(222 River St; mains $8-11; ⊘ 11am-4pm; 🍴) If you prefer your fast food healthy and served with plenty of good humour, check out this friendly little salad bar on the main strip. The menu is limited to tasty felafel wraps, burgers and salads, and while there are plenty of vegetarian options, it also serves chicken and salmon.

Ballina Gallery Cafe

CAFE $$

(☑ 02-6681 3888; www.ballinagallerycafe.com.au; 46 Cherry St; mains breakfast $10-18, lunch $14-26; ⊘ 7.30am-3pm Wed-Sun) Ballina's former council chambers have been put to good use as the town's best cafe. An interesting selection of cooked meals is offered with a side serve of contemporary art inside, and there are further tables on the verandah.

Evolution Espresso Bar CAFE, BAR **$$**
(4 Martin St; mains breakfast & lunch $12-18, dinner $24-26; ⊙7am-4pm Sun-Thu, to late Fri & Sat; 🛜) During the day this cool little cafe is a reliable spot for coffee, cake and free wi-fi, or an afternoon tipple on the deck. On Friday and Saturday nights it morphs into a bistro-bar.

La Cucina di Vino ITALIAN **$$**
(🖉02-6618 1195; 2 Martin St; mains $22-35; ⊙5-9pm Mon & Tue, 11am-3pm & 5-9pm Wed-Sun) Water views and an open corner locale make this chic Italian restaurant beneath the Ramada hotel an excellent venue for a long lunch or dinner. There's pizza too (from $16).

Fleur's Restaurant MODERN AUSTRALIAN **$$$**
(🖉02-6681 1699; www.fleursrestaurant.com.au; 305 River St; dishes $16-23; ⊙6-9pm Mon-Sat) You'd never expect such a formal dining room to be lurking in a budget chain hotel, and you'd never expect it to be turning out such interesting, beautifully presented cuisine.

🛍 Shopping

During the daylight-saving months there's a weekly **Twilight Market** (Fawcett Park; ⊙4-8pm Thu Oct-Mar), while the **Ballina Missingham Farmers' Market** (Kingsford Smith Dr; ⊙6am-noon Sun) takes place year-round. The big one is **Ballina Markets** (Canal Rd; ⊙7am-1pm Sun), held on the third Sunday of each month.

ℹ Information

Ballina Airport Services Desk (Ballina Airport; ⊙10.45am-noon & 3.15-5pm Tue, Thu & Sat, 3.15-5pm Mon, Wed, Fri & Sun) An outpost of the information centre; opening hours are synched with flights.

Ballina Visitor Information Centre (🖉02-6686 3484; www.discoverballina.com; 6 River St; ⊙9am-5pm)

ℹ Getting There & Around

AIR

Ballina Byron Gateway Airport (BNK; 🖉02-6681 1858; www.ballinabyronairport.com.au; Southern Cross Dr) is 5km north of the centre of town. A taxi to the centre of Ballina should cost roughly $12 to $15 and there are regular Blanch's buses and shuttle services.

Jetstar (🖉13 15 38; www.jetstar.com.au) Flies to/from Sydney and Melbourne.

Regional Express (Rex; 🖉13 17 13; www.regionalexpress.com.au) Flies to/from Sydney.

Virgin Australia (🖉13 67 89; www.virginaustralia.com) Flies to/from Sydney.

AIRPORT SHUTTLES

Byron Easy Bus (🖉02-6685 7447; www.byronbayshuttle.com.au) Scheduled door-to-door service from the airport to Lennox Head ($15, 15 minutes), Byron Bay ($18, 40 minutes) and Bangalow ($24, 50 minutes). Also shuttles from town to Gold Coast Airport ($42, 1¾ hours) and Brisbane Airport ($62, four hours).

Steve's Tours Airport Express (🖉0414 660 031; www.stevestours.com.au) Airport to Byron Bay (from $20).

Xcede (🖉02-6620 9200; www.xcede.com.au) Airport to Byron Bay ($20).

Byron Bay Airbus (🖉0400 247 287; www.byronbayairbus.com.au) Town centre to Gold Coast Airport ($75).

BUS

Blanch's (🖉02-6686 2144; www.blanchs.com.au) Local buses, including services to Lennox Head ($6.40, 15 minutes), Bangalow ($7.60, 30 minutes), Byron Bay ($9.60, 55 minutes) and Mullumbimby ($10, 1½ hours).

Greyhound (🖉1300 473 946; www.greyhound.com.au) Has at least two coaches daily to/from Sydney ($147, 12½ hours), Nambucca Heads ($52, four hours), Coffs Harbour ($38, three hours), Byron Bay ($6, 45 minutes) and Brisbane ($40, 4½ hours).

Northern Rivers Buslines (🖉02-6626 1499; www.nrbuslines.com.au) Eight buses to Lismore on weekdays and three on weekends ($9.70, 1¼ hours).

NSW TrainLink (🖉13 22 32; www.nswtrainlink.info) Daily coaches to/from Grafton ($30, three hours), Yamba ($17, 2¼ hours), Lismore ($6.92, 45 minutes), Murwillumbah ($15, 1½ hours) and Tweed Heads ($20, two hours).

Premier (🖉13 34 10; www.premierms.com.au) Daily coach to/from Sydney ($92, 13¼ hours), Port Macquarie ($66, seven hours), Nambucca Heads ($52, 5¼ hours), Coffs Harbour ($47, 4½ hours) and Brisbane ($36, 4½ hours).

CAR & MOTORCYCLE

The airport has plenty of car-hire desks. If you're driving to Byron Bay, take the coast road through Lennox Head. It's much prettier than the Pacific Hwy and less busy.

Lennox Head

POP 5770

A protected National Surfing Reserve, Lennox Head's picturesque coastline has some of the best surf on the coast, including long right-hander breaks. Its village atmosphere makes it a laid-back alternative to its boisterous neighbour Byron, 17km north.

⦿ Sights

Seven Mile Beach BEACH
Lovely Seven Mile Beach starts at the township and stretches north. The best place for a dip is near the surf club, at the northern end of town adjacent to Lake Ainsworth.

Lake Ainsworth LAKE
Lying just inshore from the beach, this freshwater lake is tinged brown by tannins leeching from the tea trees along its banks. Don't fret: they're supposedly beneficial to the skin. The **Lennox Head Lakeside Market** (⊙8am-2pm Sun) is held on the foreshore on the second and fifth Sundays of the month.

Pat Morton Lookout LOOKOUT
This lookout on Lennox Head itself, immediately south of the turn-off to the town, is a great spot for whale watching in winter.

🏃 Activities

Wind & Water WINDSURFING, SURFING
(☑0419 686 188; www.windnwater.net; 1hr lesson from $80) Offers windsurfing, kitesurfing and board surfing lessons on Lake Ainsworth and Seven Mile Beach.

Seabreeze Hang Gliding ADVENTURE SPORTS
(☑0428 560 248; www.seabreezehanggliding.com) Leap off Lennox Head or Cape Byron on a tandem flight, or learn how to go it solo.

🛏 Sleeping & Eating

Real-estate agency **Professionals** (☑02-6687 7579; www.lennoxheadaccom.net.au; 72 Ballina St) has a large range of holiday rentals.

Lennox Head Beach House YHA HOSTEL $
(☑02-6687 7636; www.yha.com.au; 3 Ross St; dm/s/d $34/55/82; @) Only 100m from the beach, this place has immaculate rooms and a great vibe. For $5 you can use the surfboards, sailboards and bikes.

Lake Ainsworth Holiday Park CAMPGROUND $
(☑02-6687 7249; www.northcoastholidayparks.com.au; Pacific Pde; camp sites/cabins from $37/89; 🛜) By the lake and near the beach, this family-friendly holiday park has a wide range of units, from basic cabins without bathrooms to a deluxe villa sleeping six.

Lennox Point Holiday Apartments APARTMENT $$
(☑02-6687 5900; www.lennoxholidayapartments.com; 20-21 Pacific Pde; apt from $195; ❄🛜▨) Gaze at the surf from your modern apartment and, when the mood takes you, borrow a board from reception. The one-bedroom apartments are the same size as the two-bedrooms, so they feel more spacious.

Cafe Marius LATIN AMERICAN $$
(www.cafemarius.com.au; 90-92 Ballina St; mains $15-22; ⊙7am-3pm) Hip dudes with interesting facial hair serve a delicious selection of Latin American and Spanish treats in this licensed cafe. The fish tacos are delicious.

ⓘ Getting There & Away

Blanch's (☑02-6686 2144; www.blanchs.com.au) Regular buses to/from Ballina Byron Gateway Airport ($6.40, 30 minutes), Ballina ($6.40, 15 minutes), Byron Bay ($7.60, 35 minutes) and Mullumbimby ($10, one hour).

Northern Rivers Buslines (☑02-6626 1499; www.nrbuslines.com.au) One or two buses to/from Lismore on weekdays ($9.70, one hour).

Byron Bay
POP 4960

The reputation of this famous beach town precedes it to such an extent that first impressions may leave you wondering what all the fuss is about. The beaches are great, but then again there are spectacular beaches all along this coast. What makes Byron special is the singular vibe of the town itself. It's here that coastal surf culture flows into the hippie tide washing down from the hinterland, creating one great barefooted, alternative-lifestyle mash-up.

The town centre is low-rise, funky and relaxed – in short, everything that the overdeveloped towns across the border in Queensland are not. Developers would cheerfully turn Byron into a Surfers Paradise given the chance, but locals are dedicated to preserving its essential small-town soul.

Of course Byron does get crowded and it also attracts its fair share of off-the-leash teens and drug casualties. Yet its unique vibe has a way of converting even the most cynical with its long, balmy days, endless beaches, reliable surf breaks, fine food, raucous nightlife and ambling milieu. A weekend turns into a week, a week into a month... Before you know it, dreadlocks are a serious consideration.

⦿ Sights

★ Cape Byron State Conservation Park PARK
(www.nationalparks.nsw.gov.au/cape-byron-state-conservation-area) James Cook named Cape

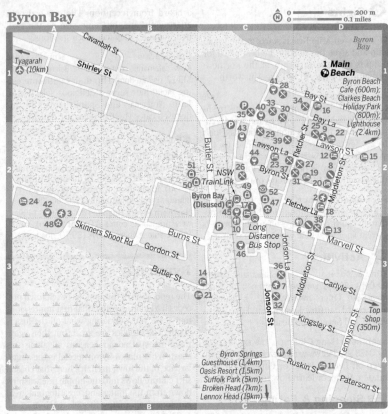

Byron Bay

Byron, mainland Australia's most easterly point, after renowned navigator John Byron, grandfather of the poet Lord Byron. (Later bureaucrats assumed it was the grandson who'd been honoured and planned out streets named after fellow poets such as Jonson, Burns and Shelley.)

The views from the summit are spectacular, rewarding those who have climbed up from the **Captain Cook Lookout** (Lighthouse Rd) on the **Cape Byron Walking Track**. Ribboning around the headland, the track dips and (mostly) soars its way to the **lighthouse** (Lighthouse Rd; ☺10am-4pm) **FREE**. Along the way, look out for dolphins (year-round) and migrating whales during their northern (June to July) and southern (September to November) migrations. You're also likely to encounter brush turkeys and wallabies. Allow about two hours for the entire 3.7km loop.

Inside the 1901 lighthouse there are maritime and nature displays, but if you want to venture to the top you'll need to take one of the volunteer-run tours, which operate from around 10am to 3pm (gold-coin donation). There's also a cafe here and self-contained accommodation in the lighthouse keeper's cottages.

You can drive right up to the lighthouse and pay $7 for the privilege of parking (or nothing at all if you chance upon a park in the small lot 300m below).

Beaches
BEACH

West of the town centre, **Belongil Beach** avoids the worst of the crowds and is unofficially clothing optional. At its eastern end is the **Wreck**, a powerful right-hander surf break.

Immediately in front of town, lifesaver-patrolled **Main Beach** is as good for people-watching as it is for swimming. Stretching east it merges into **Clarkes Beach**. The most

Byron Bay

popular surf break is the **Pass** near the eastern headland.

Around the rocks is **Watego's Beach**, a wide crescent of sand with turquoise surf. Another 400m brings you to **Little Watego's**, another lovely patch of sand directly under rocky Cape Byron.

Tallow Beach is an amazing sandy stretch that extends for 7km south from Cape Byron. This is the place to flee the crowds. Much of the beach is backed by **Arakwal National Park**, but the suburb of **Suffolk Park** sprawls along the sand near its southern end. **Kings Beach** is a popular gay beach, just off Seven Mile Beach Rd past the Broken Head Holiday Park.

✘ Activities

Adventure sports abound in Byron Bay and most operators offer a free pick-up service from local accommodation. Surfing and diving are the biggest draws.

Surfing

Most hostels provide free boards to guests, or you can rent equipment.

Black Dog Surfing   SURFING
(☑02-6680 9828; www.blackdogsurfing.com; 11 Byron St; 3½hr lesson $60) Intimate group lessons including women's and kids' courses. Highly rated.

Style Surfing   SURFING
(☑02-6685 5634; www.stylesurfingbyronbay.com; 3½hr lesson $60) Surfing and stand-up paddleboarding lessons.

Surfing Byron Bay   SURFING
(☑02-6685 7099; www.gosurfingbyronbay.com; 84 Jonson St; 2½hr lesson $49) Surfing lessons for adults and kids, plus a 'surf yoga' combo.

Byron Bay Surf School   SURFING
(☑1800 707 274; www.byronbaysurfschool.com; 3½hr lesson $65) Lessons and surf camps.

Mojosurf Adventures
SURFING

(☑1800 113 044; www.mojosurf.com; 9 Marvell St; 1/2 lessons $69/119, 2-/3-day trips $280/445) Lessons and epic surf safaris.

Soul Surf School
SURFING

(☑1800 089 699; www.soulsurfschool.com.au; 4hr lesson $59) Half-day to five-day courses for beginners.

Diving

About 3km offshore, **Julian Rocks Marine Reserve** is a meeting point for cold southerly and warm northerly currents, attracting a profusion of marine species including three types of turtle. You might spot leopard sharks and manta rays in summer, and grey nurse sharks in winter.

Sundive
DIVING, SNORKELLING

(☑02-6685 7755; www.sundive.com.au; Middleton St; snorkelling tour $55) Two to three expeditions to Julian Rocks daily, plus various courses.

Dive Byron Bay
DIVING

(☑02-6685 8333; www.byronbaydivecentre.com. au; 9 Marvell St; ☺9am-5pm) Rentals, sales, PADI courses from $550, dives from $95.

Flying & Other Airborne Pursuits

Byron Bay Ballooning
BALLOONING

(☑1300 889 660; www.byronbayballooning.com. au; Tyagarah Airfield; adult/child $325/175) Sunrise flights including breakfast.

Skydive Byron Bay
SKYDIVING

(☑02-6684 1323; www.skydivebyronbay.com; Tyagarah Airfield; tandem flights from $299) Hurtle to earth from 14,000ft.

Byron Airwaves
HANG-GLIDING

(☑02-6629 0354; www.byronair.com) Tandem hang-gliding ($145) and courses ($1500).

Byron Bay Microlights
MICROLIGHTING

(☑0407 281 687; www.byronbaymicrolights.com. au; Tyagarah Airfield; 15-/30-/45-minute flight $100/180/245) Whale watching ($180) and scenic flights ($100).

Byron Gliding
GLIDING

(☑02-6684 7627; www.byrongliding.com; Tyagarah Airfield; flights from $120) Scenic flights over the coast and hinterland.

Alternative Therapies

Byron is an alternative-therapy heartland, offering a diverse range of treatments claiming to heal the body and mind.

Be Salon & Spa
DAY SPA

(☑0413 432 584; www.besalonspa.com.au; 14 Middleton St; 30-minute massage $60) Manicures, pedicures, facials and waxing offered alongside psychic readings, massage, 're-balancing' and naturopathy.

Buddha Gardens
DAY SPA

(☑02-6680 7844; www.buddhagardensdayspa. com.au; 1 Skinners Shoot Rd; massage from $120; ☺10am-6pm) Balinese-style day spa.

Relax Haven
MASSAGE

(☑02-6685 8304; www.relaxhaven.com.au; 107 Jonson St; ☺10am-6.30pm) Floatation tanks (one hour $65), massage (one hour $79), kinesiology, 'quantum hypnotherapy' and 'theta energy healing'.

Other

Go Sea Kayaks
KAYAKING

(☑0416 222 344; www.goseakayakbyronbay. com.au; adult/child $69/59) 🌿 If you don't see a whale, turtle or dolphin, you can go again for free. Tours have an Aboriginal dimension.

Circus Arts
CIRCUS ARTS

(☑02-6685 6566; www.circusarts.com.au; 17 Centennial Circuit; half-day/day $40/70) Learn trapeze, tightrope and juggling skills; there are holiday classes for kids.

Surf & Bike Hire
BICYCLE RENTAL

(☑02-6680 7066; www.byronbaysurfandbikehire. com.au; 31 Lawson St; ☺9am-5pm) Rents bikes ($20 per day), surfboards ($25 per day) and other active gear.

👉 Tours

Mountain Bike Tours
MOUNTAIN BIKING

(☑0429 122 504; www.mountainbiketours.com. au; half-day/day $75/125) 🌿 Environmentally aware bike tours into the rainforest and along the coast.

Vision Walks
WILDLIFE TOUR

(☑02-6685 0059; www.visionwalks.com; night tour adult/child $99/75, other tours from $45/28) A variety of tours enable you to see all manner of creatures in their natural habitat, including nocturnal animals (on the Night Vision Walk) and hippies (on the Hippie Trail Hinterland Tour).

Byron Bay Wildlife Tours
WILDLIFE TOUR

(☑0429 770 686; www.byronbaywildlifetours.com; adult/child $70/35; ☺Nov-Mar) If you don't spot seven different mammal species you'll get your money back.

Byron Bay Adventure Tours   WALKING TOUR, HIKING
(☑1300 120 028; www.byronbayadventuretours.com.au; day tour $109) Day walks and overnight tours to Mt Warning.

🎊 Festivals & Events

Byron Bay Bluesfest   MUSIC
(www.bluesfest.com.au; Tyagarah Tea Tree Farm) Held over Easter, this jam attracts high-calibre international performers and local heavyweights.

Splendour in the Grass   MUSIC
(www.splendourinthegrass.com; North Byron Parklands) Three-day festival featuring big-name indie artists in late July.

Byron Bay Writers' Festival   CULTURE
(www.byronbaywritersfestival.com.au) In early August, this festival gathers together top-shelf writers and literary followers from across Australia.

Byron Bay Surf Festival   SPORT
(www.byronbaysurffestival.com) Three-day, late-October celebration of surf culture.

🛏 Sleeping

Book well in advance for January or during any of the annual music festivals. If you're not 17, Schoolies Week at the end of November is one to avoid. During these periods, places taking one-night-only bookings are rare.

Booking services include **Byron Bay Accom** (☑02-6680 8666; www.byronbayaccom.net).

Clarkes Beach Holiday Park   CAMPGROUND $
(☑02-6685 6496; www.northcoastparks.com.au/clarkes; off Lighthouse Rd; camp sites/cabins from $42/140; ✳🤖) The tightly packed cabins and shady tent sites at this holiday park sit within an attractive bush setting, close to the beach and the lighthouse.

Aquarius   HOSTEL $
(☑02-6685 7663; www.aquarius-backpackers.com.au; 16 Lawson St; dm/d/motel r from $23/60/130; ✳@🤖) This motel-style backpackers has plenty of communal space – including a bar and cafe – ensuring that those going it solo can find mates. Motel rooms have kitchenettes and some have spa baths.

Cape Byron YHA   HOSTEL $
(☑02-6685 8788; www.yha.com.au; cnr Middleton & Byron Sts; dm $38-40, d without/with bathroom

$135/145; ✳@🤖) 🌿 Modern, tidy and close to the town centre, this two-storey complex is gathered around a palm-lined heated pool. Only one of the private rooms has an en suite, so book ahead.

Nomads Arts Factory Lodge   HOSTEL $
(☑02-6685 7709; www.nomadsworld.com/artsfactory; Skinners Shoot Rd; camp sites/dm/d from $10/34/70; @🤖) 🌿 For an archetypal Byron experience, bunker down at this ramshackle hippie-esque hostel set by a picturesque swamp. Choose from colourful six- to 10-bed dorms, a cottage, tepees or wagons. Couples can opt for aptly titled 'cube' rooms, island-retreat canvas huts or the pricier love shack with bathroom.

⭐ **Aabi's at Byron**   GUESTHOUSE $$
(☑02-6680 9519; www.guesthousesbyronbay.com.au; 17 Ruskin St; r from $175; ✳🤖) 🌿 Statues of Hindu deities watch over the pool at this gorgeous contemporary complex, making a nice change from the Buddhas that typically swarm around Byron. Rooms are luxurious, plus there's a shared kitchen, lounge, BBQ and spa pool.

Bamboo Cottage   GUESTHOUSE $$
(☑0414 187 088; www.byron-bay.com/bamboocottage; 76 Butler St; s/d without bathroom $129/149, d with bathroom $169, apt $240; 🤖) Featuring global charm and a tropical setting, Bamboo Cottage treats guests to Asian- and Pacific Island–inflected rooms in a home-away-from-home atmosphere. It's on the quiet side of the tracks.

Byron Springs Guesthouse   GUESTHOUSE $$
(☑0457 808 101; www.byronsprings.com.au; 2 Oodgeroo Garden; s/d without bathroom from $75/110, d with bathroom $150; 🤖) Polished floorboards, white linen and a leafy setting make this a good choice if you like to be removed from the throng. A continental breakfast is included in the rates.

Byron Central Apartments   APARTMENT $$
(☑02-6685 8800; www.byroncentral.com; 5-7 Byron St; apt $129-230; ✳🤖) Hidden within a town-centre commercial block, this complex has a pleasant set of apartments grouped around a swimming pool. The 'deluxe' units have loft bedrooms, new furnishings and full kitchens.

Bay Beach Motel   MOTEL $$
(☑02-6685 6090; www.baybeachmotel.com.au; 32 Lawson St; r/apt from $155/250; ✳🤖) Unpretentious but smart, this white-brick motel is

close to town and the beach, but not so close that partygoers keep guests awake.

Byron Bay Side Central Motel
MOTEL $$
(☑02-6685 6004; www.byronbaysidemotel.com.au; 14 Middleton St; d/f from $145/180; ❋ ☎) These uninspiring but tidy motel units have small kitchenettes, laundry facilities and secure underground parking in a central location. There's free wi-fi, but the signal struggles to reach the outlying rooms.

Hibiscus Motel
MOTEL $$
(☑02-6685 6195; www.hibiscusmotel.com.au; 33 Lawson St; d $165; ❋ ☎) Basic but central and sparkling clean, with friendly owners. There's wi-fi, but you'll need to pay for it.

Glen-Villa Resort
RESORT $$
(☑02-6685 7382; www.glenvillaresort.com.au; Butler St; cabins from $100; ❋ @ ☎ ☲) Targetting couples via a strict two-person-per-booking rule (party groups and families should look elsewhere), this holiday park is clean, comfortable and secure. It's tucked away in the backstreets and blissfully quiet.

Nomads
HOSTEL $$
(☑02-6680 7966; www.nomadsworld.com; 1 Lawson Lane; dm $50-60, d $160-190; ❋ @ ☎) Byron's biggest (and priciest) backpackers packs a punch with its glossy designer-led decor and funky furniture. The dorm rooms are comfortable, but they're not half as good as the king rooms, which have bathroom, fridge and plasma television.

Byron at Byron
RESORT $$$
(☑02-6639 2000; www.thebyronatbyron.com.au; 77-97 Broken Head Rd; ste from $335; ❋ ☎ ☲) ✦ Set within subtropical rainforest 4km south of town, this 92-suite resort offers a luxurious way to get back to nature. When you're not lounging by the infinity pool, take the 10-minute stroll to Tallow Beach via a series of wonderful boardwalks.

Oasis Resort
APARTMENT $$$
(☑02-6685 7390; www.byronoasis.com.au; 24 Scott St; apt from $220; ❋ ☎ ☲) Away from the town centre, this compact resort is engulfed by palms and has sizeable apartments with big balconies. Even better are those sitting atop the tree canopies with outdoor spa and ocean view.

Atlantic
HOTEL $$$
(☑02-6685 5118; www.atlanticbyronbay.com.au; 13 Marvell St; r $200-225; ❋ ☎) Designery white rooms open on to tropical gardens within

this pretty little enclave of weatherboard cottages. The accommodation ranges from hotel-style rooms to studio apartments with kitchens to a gorgeous polished-aluminium Airstream caravan on the back lawn.

Beach Suites
APARTMENT $$$
(☑02-6680 9944; www.beachsuites.com.au; 20 Bay St; ste $350-490, apt $1200-1700; ❋ ☎ ☲) The most luxurious option in the town centre, this apartment-hotel has slickly styled suites and apartments, all of which have kitchenettes and their own BBQ. Some of the beachfront studios have plunge pools, while the lavish penthouses have full kitchens and rooftop decks.

✖ Eating

OzyMex
MEXICAN $
(www.byronbaychilli.com; 8 Jonson St; mains $7-13; ☺10am-8pm) There's only bench seating for five people at this super-popular Mexican place, so order your spicy treats and hotfoot it to the beach. The fish tacos ($4) make for a tasty snack.

Top Shop
CAFE $
(65 Carlyle St; mains $10-14; ☺6.30am-5pm) Off the tourist strip on the hill east of town, Top Shop is the top choice of locals seeking coffee and cake. The menu stretches to the likes of fish and chips, BLATs and burgers.

Espressohead
CAFE $
(Middleton St; mains $10-18; ☺7.30am-3pm) Caffeine fiends flock to this place to sip the excellent coffee while soaking up the morning sun. Lunch options include bagels, pasta and salads.

Mary Ryan's
CAFE $
(www.maryryan.com.au; 21-25 Fletcher St; mains $8-18; ☺7.30am-4pm) Snuggled up to the ABC Centre, this bookshop cafe serves a healthy selection of salads and a somewhat less healthy array of cakes.

Twisted Sista
CAFE $
(4 Lawson St; mains $9-20; ☺7am-5pm) Bounteous baked goods include huge muffins, calorific cakes and overstuffed sandwiches on beautiful bread. Tuck in to them at one of the outdoor tables.

Blue Olive
DELI $
(27 Lawson St; mains $10-13; ☺10am-5.30pm Tue-Sat, to 4pm Sun) Fine cheeses, deli items and light meals; enjoy the beautifully prepared

MULLUMBIMBY & BRUNSWICK HEADS

These two intriguing towns straddle the Pacific Hwy 18km north of Byron Bay, with Mullumbimby 6km inland and Brunswick Heads 2km off the highway, on the coast.

A pyramid-shaped mountain acts as a backdrop for Mullumbimby (aka Mullum, population 3170), an attractive town lined with lazy palms, tropical architecture and a cosmopolitan spread of cafes, bistros and pubs. Of these, one of the goodies is Milk & Honey (02-6684 1422; 59a Station St; mains $15-24; 5-9pm Tue-Sat), an artisan pizza joint that wood-fires thin-crust wonders with a changing line-up of toppings. Walk it off on a leafy trail along the Brunswick River. The four-day Mullum Music Festival (www.mullummusicfestival.com) at the end of November is the prime time to visit. There's also a weekly Farmers' Market (www.mullumfarmersmarket.org.au; Mullumbimby Showground, 51 Main Arm Rd; 7-11am Fri) and Community Markets (www.mullumbimbymuseum.org.au/markets.html; Stuart St; 7.30am-2pm Sat) on the third Saturday of the month.

Beautiful Brunswick Heads (population 1450) reaps a bounty of fresh oysters and mud crabs from its peaceful Brunswick River inlets and beaches. Byron Bay Eco Cruises & Kayaks (0410 016 926; www.byronbaycruises.com.au; Boat Harbour; 1½hr cruise $25) allows you to get better acquainted with the mangrove-lined waterways on guided kayak tours and boat cruises.

The 1940s Hotel Brunswick (02-6685 1236; www.hotelbrunswick.com.au; Mullumbimbi St; s/d without bathroom $55/85) is a destination unto itself, with a magnificent beer garden that unfurls beneath flourishing poincianas. There's live music on weekends, decent pub rooms and a menu that includes burgers and pizza (mains $17 to $27). Similarly laudable but easy to miss beneath a motel, Fatbelly Kaf (02-6685 1100; www.fatbellykaf.com; 26 Tweed St; mains $15-22; 6-9pm Tue-Thu, noon-2pm & 6-9pm Fri-Sun) is a Greek restaurant that brings feta fetishists and dolmades adorers from afar.

Brunswick Heads has its Riverside Market (Memorial Park, Fawcett St; 7.30am-2pm Sat) on the first Saturday of the month. For further information on local attractions and accommodation, call into the Brunswick Heads Visitor Information Centre (www.brunswickheads.org.au; 7 Park St; 9.30am-4.30pm Mon-Fri, 10am-2pm Sat & Sun).

Blanch's (p154) has buses to Mullumbimby from Ballina ($10, 1½ hours), Lennox Head ($10, one hour) and Byron Bay ($6.40, 25 minutes). On weekdays Northern Rivers Buslines (p164) heads to Mullumbimby from Byron Bay (20 minutes), and to both towns from Bangalow (40 minutes) and Lismore (1¼ hours); all cost $9.70. NSW Train-Link (p164) coaches stop in both towns, heading to Lismore ($12, one hour), Ballina ($7, one hour) and Tweed Heads ($14, 1¼ hours).

foods at shady pavement tables or decamp to the beach.

Italian at the Pacific
ITALIAN $$

(02-6680 7055; www.italianatthepacific.com.au; 2 Bay St; mains $28-36; 6-10pm) Adjoining the raucous Beach Hotel, this informal but chic Italian restaurant offers only a limited selection of pasta and larger dishes, but what it does do, it does well. Try the slow-cooked lamb-shank lasagne – it might just be the best you've ever tasted.

One One One
MEDITERRANEAN $$

(02-6680 7388; www.facebook.com/oneoneonebyronbay; 111 Jonson St; mains $12-18; 6.30am-3pm Mon-Wed, to 9pm Thu-Sat, to 1pm Sun;) Regional produce is married to the flavours of the Mediterranean (every-

thing from Moroccan to Greek to Spanish) at this cool cafe on the main strip. The menu is mostly vegetarian, although the select few seafood and meat dishes are excellent.

Byron Beach Cafe
CAFE $$

(02-6685 8400; www.byronbeachcafe.com.au; Lawson St; mains breakfast $15-22, lunch & dinner $25-33; 7.30am-5pm Sun-Wed, to 9pm Thu-Sat) The covered verandah of this slick cafe right on Clarkes Beach is ideal for a lazy brunch with ocean views. There are loads of interesting breakfast options and the menu gets more restaurant-like as the day progresses.

Dip
CAFE $$

(21 Fletcher St; mains breakfast $8-19, lunch $13-18; 7am-3pm) Tables spill out onto the street

from this cute little licensed cafe. The breakfast options are excellent.

Targa
ITALIAN $$

(☑02-6680 9960; www.targabyronbay.com; 11 Marvell St; mains lunch $13-18, dinner $22-35; ☺7am-3pm Sun-Wed, to 10pm Thu-Sat) This lovely Italian cafe and wine bar is just far enough removed from the main-street clamour. The vibe is casual for breakfast and lunchtime, while dinner is a slightly more serious affair. The food is delicious at any time.

St Elmo
SPANISH $$

(☑02-6680 7426; www.stelmodining.com; cnr Fletcher St & Lawson Lane; dishes $14-26; ☺4pm-late Mon-Thu, noon-late Fri-Sun) Perch on a designer stool and sup a cocktail prepared by the extremely fit, bronzed and accented bar staff. Or settle in for dinner; the shared plates make great date fodder. Celebrate Sunday afternoon with live music and $10 cocktails.

Orient Express
ASIAN $$

(☑02-6680 8808; 1/2 Fletcher St; mains $17-35; ☺5.30-9.30pm Mon-Thu, 11am-9.30pm Fri-Sun) Decked out like a Chinese teahouse complete with a large wooden Buddha, this atmospheric eatery plunders gainfully from the cuisines of Southeast Asia and the Far East. Settle in for an afternoon yum-cha session.

Orgasmic
MIDDLE EASTERN $$

(11 Bay Lane; mains $15-25; ☺10am-10pm; ☑) Plop your bum on a cube cushion at this alley eatery that's one step above a felafel stall. Takeaways include big mezze plates, ideal for quick picnics.

Byronian
CAFE $$

(58 Jonson St; mains breakfast $10-20, lunch $15-20; ☺8am-3pm) This stalwart has been churning out coffee since 1978 and it's still going strong. There's a good breakfast selection and an interesting range of cooked lunches, best enjoyed on the covered front terrace.

Lemongrass
VIETNAMESE $$

(Lawson Arcade, 17 Lawson St; mains $15-20; ☺5.30-9.30pm) Spilling out onto a terrace set back from the street, Lemongrass serves up all your favourite Vietnamese dishes, from rice-paper rolls to *pho bo* (beef noodle soup).

Kinoko
JAPANESE $$

(www.kinoko.com.au; 23 Jonson St; mains $15-25; ☺10am-9pm) Choo-choo-choose something from the sushi train or let the Japanese chef slice up a plate of fresh sashimi.

Byron at Byron Restaurant
MODERN AUSTRALIAN $$$

(☑02-6639 2111; www.thebyronatbyron.com.au; 77-97 Broken Head Rd; mains $37-40; ☺6-9pm) Byron's swishest eatery occupies a glass pavilion within the luxurious Byron at Byron resort. The food is sophisticated without being modish or overly complicated, contenting itself with highlighting the region's tastiest produce.

Petit Snail
FRENCH $$$

(☑02-6685 8526; www.thepetitsnail.com.au; 5 Carlyle St; mains $31-45; ☺6.30-9.30pm Wed-Sat; ☑) At this intimate side-street restaurant, French staff serve up traditional Gallic fare such as steak tartare, duck confit and lots of *fromage*. There's outdoor dining on the verandah. Vegetarians get their own menu (mains $21 to $25).

Rae's Fish Cafe
SEAFOOD $$$

(☑02-6685 5366; www.raesonwategos.com; 8 Marine Pde, Watego's Beach; mains $38; ☺noon-3pm & 6-11.30pm) There's nothing even vaguely cafe-like about this upmarket terrace restaurant, where the sound of the surf provides an accompaniment to your witticisms. The menu changes daily but always surprises with its unconventional pairings of ingredients.

🍷 Drinking & Nightlife

Byron's reputation as a feel-good party town took a hit when it was rated the third-worst place for booze-fuelled street violence in NSW. At the time of writing there were moves afoot to ban shots, introduce lockouts and force bars to call last drinks at midnight. You may find all or some of these restrictions in place when you visit.

For entertainment listings, check out the gig guide in Thursday's Byron Shire News (www.byronnews.com.au) or tune into Bay 99.9 FM.

★ Byron Bay Brewing Co
BREWERY, PUB

(www.byronbaybrewery.com.au; 1 Skinners Shoot Rd; ☺4pm-late Tue-Fri, noon-late Sat & Sun) Having made the transition from pig barn to booze barn, this large complex is Byron's coolest venue. Surfboards hang from the walls, while in the tropical courtyard Buddha heads peer out from the shade of a giant fig tree. Entertainment includes live music, DJs and trivia nights.

Balcony
BAR
(www.balcony.com.au; Level 1, 3 Lawson St; ⊙8am-11pm) 🍴 With its verandah poking out amid the palm trees, this bar-restaurant is a fine place to park yourself. Choose from stools, chairs or sofas while working through a cocktail list that will make you giddy just looking at it.

Railway Friendly Bar
PUB
(www.therailsbyronbay.com; Jonson St; ⊙11am-late) This indoor-outdoor pub (aka the Rails) draws everyone from lobster-red British tourists to acid-sozzled hippies and high-on-life earth mothers. The front beer garden, conducive to boozy afternoons, has live music most nights.

Woody's Surf Shack
BAR
(www.woodysbyronbay.com; The Plaza, 90-96 Jonson St; ⊙8pm-3am Mon-Sat) Traditionally the last stop of the night, there's now a lockout for this clubby bar, so if you fancy shooting pool until 3am you'll need to get in before 1.30am.

Great Northern
PUB
(www.thenorthern.com.au; 35-43 Jonson St; ⊙noon-late) You won't need your fancy duds at this brash and boisterous pub. It's loud and beery, with live music most nights. Soak up the booze with a wood-fired pizza.

Beach Hotel
PUB
(www.beachhotel.com.au; cnr Jonson & Bay Sts; ⊙11am-late) It's all about the beer garden at this mammoth pub opposite the beach. There's live music and DJs some nights.

Cocomangas
CLUB
(www.cocomangas.com.au; 32 Jonson St; ⊙9pm-late Wed-Sat) Byron's longest-standing nightclub, with regular backpacker nights. No entry after 1.30am.

Lala Land
CLUB
(www.lalalandbyronbay.com.au; 6 Lawson St; ⊙9pm-3am) This is one of Byron Bay's better nightclubs.

☆ Entertainment

Pighouse Flicks
CINEMA
(02-6685 5828; www.pighouseflicks.com.au; 1 Skinners Shoot Rd; tickets $10-14) Attached to Byron Bay Brewing Co, this 135-seat cinema shows classic reruns and art-house flicks.

Byron Community Centre
THEATRE
(02-6685 6807; www.byroncentre.com.au; 69 Jonson St) A 250-seat venue that stages theatre and touring concerts.

🛍 Shopping

Central Byron has surprisingly good shopping. You'll find everything from upmarket boutiques to hippie stores draped in dreamcatchers.

Markets include a weekly **Farmers' Market** (www.byronfarmersmarket.com.au; Butler St Reserve; ⊙8-11am Thu) and **Artisan Market** (www.byronmarkets.com.au; Railway Park, Jonson St; ⊙4-9pm Sat Nov-Mar), and the **Byron Community Market** (www.byronmarkets.com.au; Butler St Reserve; ⊙8am-2pm Sun) on the first Sunday of the month.

Planet Corroboree
ARTS & CRAFTS
(www.planetcorroboree.com.au; 69 Jonson St; ⊙10am-6pm) Sells a variety of Aboriginal art and souvenirs.

ℹ Information

Bay Centre Medical (02-6685 6206; www.byronmed.com.au; 6 Lawson St; ⊙8am-5pm Mon-Fri, to noon Sat)

Byron District Hospital (02-6685 6200; www.ncahs.nsw.gov.au; cnr Wordsworth & Shirley Sts; ⊙24hr) Has an emergency department.

Byron Visitor Centre (02-6680 8558; www.visitbyronbay.com; Stationmaster's Cottage, 80 Jonson St; admission by gold-coin donation; ⊙9am-5pm) Ground zero for tourist information, last-minute accommodation and bus bookings. The helpful staff can get a little overwhelmed by demand at times.

ℹ Getting There & Away

For shuttle services from Ballina Byron Gateway Airport, see p154. Coaches stop on Jonson St near the tourist office.

Blanch's (02-6686 2144; www.blanchs.com.au) Regular buses to/from Ballina Byron Gateway Airport ($9.60, one hour), Ballina ($9.60, 55 minutes), Lennox Head ($7.60, 35 minutes), Bangalow ($6.40, 20 minutes) and Mullumbimby ($6.40, 25 minutes).

Brisbane Byron Express (1800 626 222; www.brisbane2byron.com) Two daily buses to/from Brisbane ($38, two hours) and Brisbane Airport ($54, three hours); only one on Sunday.

Byron Bay Express (www.byronbayexpress.com.au; one way/return $30/55) Five buses a day to/from Gold Coast Airport (1¾ hours) and Surfers Paradise (2¼ hours).

Byron Easy Bus (02-6685 7447; www.byron-bayshuttle.com.au) Minibus service to Ballina Byron Gateway Airport ($18, 40 minutes), Gold Coast Airport ($39, two hours), Brisbane ($40, 3½ hours) and Brisbane Airport ($54, four hours).

Greyhound (1300 473 946; www.greyhound.com.au) Coaches to/from Sydney (from $95, 12 to 14 hours, three daily), Port Macquarie ($74, six hours, two daily), Nambucca Heads ($58, 4½ hours, two daily), Coffs Harbour ($45, 3½ hours, four daily) and Brisbane ($37, four hours, four daily).

Northern Rivers Buslines (02-6626 1499; www.nrbuslines.com.au) Weekday buses to/from Lismore (1½ hours), Bangalow (30 minutes) and Mullumbimby (20 minutes); all $9.70.

NSW TrainLink (13 22 32; www.nswtrainlink.info; Jonson St) Locals still lament the loss of their train service in 2004. TrainLink coaches can be booked at the old train station. Destinations include Grafton ($36, 3¾ hours), Yamba ($20, three hours), Ballina ($7, 41 minutes), Lismore ($9.22, one hour) and Murwillumbah ($9.22, one hour).

Premier (13 34 10; www.premierms.com.au) Daily coach to/from Sydney ($92, 14 hours), Port Macquarie ($66, 7½ hours), Nambucca Heads ($58, 5¾ hours), Coffs Harbour ($50, five hours) and Brisbane ($30, 3½ hours).

Getting Around

Byron Bay Taxis (02-6685 5008; www.byronbaytaxis.com.au; 24hr)

Earth Car Rentals (02-6685 7472; www.earthcar.com.au; 1 Byron St)

Hertz (02-6680 7925; www.hertz.com.au; 5 Marvell St)

Bangalow

POP 1520

Beautiful Bangalow's character-laden main street has interesting stores, fine eateries and an excellent pub. The best time to visit is during the monthly **Bangalow Market** (www.bangalowmarket.com.au; Bangalow Showgrounds; 9am-3pm 4th Sun of month), but it's well worth making the 14km trip from Byron at any time. There's also a small weekly **farmers market** (www.byronfarmersmarket.com.au; Byron Hotel carpark, 1 Byron St; 8-11am Sat) and a well-regarded **cooking school** (02-6687 2799; www.leahroland.com).

Sleeping

Bangalow Guesthouse   B&B $$
(02-6687 1317; bangalowguesthouse.com.au; 99 Byron St; r $165-245;) This stately old wooden villa sits on the river's edge, ensuring guests see platypuses and oversized lizards as they take on breakfast. It's the stuff of B&B dreams.

Possum Creek Eco Lodge   BUNGALOW $$
(02-6687 1188; www.possumcreeklodge.com.au; Cedarvale Rd; bungalows from $198;) Set within farmland about 4km north of Bangalow, this complex has three well-spaced self-contained houses with views across the lush valleys. The 'eco' in the name includes water-conservation technologies and solar power.

Eating & Drinking

Pantry 29   FAST FOOD $
(www.pantry29.com.au; 29 Byron St; mains $8-9; 8am-4pm) Serves tasty wraps, salads, rolls, smoothies and gelato.

Utopia   CAFE $$
(02-6687 2088; www.utopiacafe.com.au; 13 Byron St; mains $14-26; 8.30am-4pm;) Open, airy and hung with interesting art, this long cafe has free wi-fi and a good selection of magazines to divert you while you wait for your morning coffee and cooked brekkie. The sweets are to die for.

Town   MODERN AUSTRALIAN $$$
(02-6687 2555; www.townbangalow.com.au; 33 Byron St; meals $85; 7-9.30pm Thu-Sat) Upstairs (Uptown, if you will) is one of northern NSW's best restaurants, serving a five-course set menu artfully constructed from seasonal local produce. Head **Downtown** (33 Byron St; mains $14-17; 8am-3pm) for perfect breakfasts, light lunches, cakes and coffee.

Bangalow Hotel   PUB
(www.bangalowhotel.com.au; 1 Byron St; 10am-midnight Mon-Sat, noon-10pm Sun) Bangalow's much-loved pub has regular live music, pool comps and trivia nights. Sit on the deck and order gourmet burgers from the pub menu, or reserve a table at the classy but cool **Bangalow Dining Rooms** (02-6687 1144; www.bangalowdining.com; mains $17-36; noon-3pm & 5.30-9pm).

Getting There & Away

Byron Easy Bus operates shuttles to/from Ballina Byron Gateway Airport.

Blanch's (02-6686 2144; www.blanchs.com.au) Weekday buses to/from Ballina ($7.60, 30 minutes) and Byron Bay ($6.40, 20 minutes).

NSW TrainLink (13 22 32; www.nswtrainlink.info) Daily coaches to/from Murwillumbah ($14, 1¼ hours), Tweed Heads ($17, two hours),

Burleigh Heads ($20, 1½ hours) and Surfers Paradise ($22, two hours).

Northern Rivers Buslines (☑ 02-6626 1499; www.nrbuslines.com.au) Weekday buses to/from Lismore (1¼ hours), Byron Bay (30 minutes), Brunswick Heads (30 minutes) and Mullumbimby (40 minutes); all $9.70.

LISMORE & THE TWEED RIVER REGION

Away from the coast, the lush scenery, organic markets and alternative lifestyles make this one of Australia's most intriguing and appealing regions – for locals and visitors alike. In fact the post-hippie rural lifestyle out here has become so mainstream that the epicentre of Nimbin is almost a theme park.

Twenty-three million years ago, a giant shield volcano burst forth here, gifting the landscape its mysterious contours. Erosion has taken its toll and all that remains is the lava plug (the peculiarly shaped Wollumbin Mt Warning) and the giant ring of jagged ridges that outlines the caldera.

Lismore

POP 27,500

Lismore, the commercial heart of the Northern Rivers region, manages to sit alongside the Wilson River without paying it terribly much attention. Rather, the city's liberal supply of heritage buildings prefer to gaze at each other across broad thoroughfares. A thriving artistic community, students from Southern Cross University, and a larger than average gay and lesbian presence add to the town's eclecticism, but it's still a little rough around the edges. It's an interesting place to visit, but most travellers prefer to stay on the coast or venture further into the hinterland.

◉ Sights & Activities

Lismore Regional Gallery   GALLERY
(www.lismoregallery.org; 131 Molesworth St; ◷ 10am-4pm Tue, Wed & Fri, to 6pm Thu, to 2pm Sat & Sun) **FREE** Lismore's diminutive gallery has just enough space for two temporary exhibitions, but they're usually excellent.

Koala Care Centre   WILDLIFE RESERVE
(www.friendsofthekoala.org; Rifle Range Rd; adult/family $5/10; ◷ tours 10am & 2pm Mon-Fri, 10am Sat) This worthy centre takes in sick, injured

and orphaned koalas; visits are only possible by guided tour at the designated times. To see koalas in the wild, head to **Robinson's Lookout** (Robinson Ave, Girard's Hill), immediately south of the town centre.

Walks   WALKING
The **Wilson River Experience Walk** starts in the city centre and skirts the river for 3km. Along the way you'll pass a bush-tucker garden, nurturing plants that once formed the daily diet of the local Widjabal clan.

In the suburb of Goonellabah, 6km east of the centre, the **Birdwing Butterfly Walk** has been planted with vines to attract the rare insect. You might also spot platypuses in the Tucki Tucki Creek, especially at dawn or sunset. To get here, take the Bruxner Hwy and turn right on Kadina St.

✸✸ Festivals & Events

Lismore Lantern Parade   PARADE
(www.lanternparade.com) Over 25,000 people line the streets to watch giant illuminated creatures glide past on the Saturday closest to the winter solstice (June).

Tropical Fruits   GAY & LESBIAN
(www.tropicalfruits.org.au) This legendary New Year's bash is country NSW's biggest gay and lesbian event. The main New Year's Eve party is followed by a pool party and recovery party the following day. There are also events at Easter and on the Queen's Birthday holiday (June).

🛏 Sleeping

★**Elindale House**   B&B $$
(☑ 02-6622 2533; www.elindale.com.au; 34 Second Ave; s/d $135/150; ❈ ⊛) Any chintziness is tempered with modern art at this excellent gay-friendly B&B in a characterful wooden house. The four rooms all have their own bathrooms and some have hefty four-poster beds.

Lismore Gateway   MOTEL $$
(☑ 02-6621 5688; www.lismoregatewaymotel.com.au; 99 Ballina Rd; r/apt from $139/450; ❈ ⊛ ⊛) It calls itself a motel, but this brand-new complex is decidedly hotel-like, with its well-staffed reception, in-house restaurant, inoffensive decor and large, comfortable rooms. For a place fronting the highway, surprisingly little traffic noise penetrates the rooms.

Lismore Wilson Motel
MOTEL **$$**

(☑ 02-6622 3383; www.lismorewilsonmotel.com. au; 119 Ballina Rd; r $105-145; ❈ 🛜) Better than your average motel, the Lismore Wilson has large, well-kept rooms and offers extra services such as cooked breakfasts, evening meals and cot hire. Some rooms have spa baths.

✖ Eating

Goanna Bakery & Cafe
BAKERY, CAFE **$**

(www.goannabakery.com.au; 171 Keen St; mains $11-17; ⊗8am-5.30pm Mon-Fri, 8.30am-3pm Sat & Sun; ☑) As well as baking organic sourdough bread and a delectable array of sweet things, this cavernous bakery-cafe serves a good selection of vegetarian and vegan meals (although smoked salmon seems to have snuck in).

Lismore Pie Cart
FAST FOOD **$**

(cnr Magellan & Molesworth Sts; ⊗6am-5pm Mon-Fri, to 2pm Sat) A local institution serving homemade meat pies, mash, mushy peas and gravy.

Palate at the Gallery
MODERN AUSTRALIAN **$$**

(☑ 02-6622 8830; www.palateatthegallery.com; 133 Molesworth St; mains breakfast $10-20, lunch $16-29, dinner $26-32; ⊗10am-2.30pm Tue & Wed, 10am-2.30pm & 6-9pm Thu & Fri, 8am-2pm & 6-9pm Sat, 8am-2pm Sun; 🛜) Grafted on to the side of the gallery, this slick pavilion has French doors that open out onto a sunny, shrub-lined terrace. It morphs seamlessly from swish daytime cafe to Lismore's top night-time restaurant, offering delicious dishes throughout.

Fire in the Belly
ITALIAN **$$**

(☑ 02-6621 4899; www.fireinthebelly.com.au; 109 Dawson St; mains $14-23) A red dragon curls around the wood-burning oven as brave souls fearlessly extract delicious gourmet pizza from its innards. The menu is rounded out with pasta, risotto and a traditional osso bucco.

🛍 Shopping

Lismore has more markets than anywhere else in the region, with a weekly organic market (www.tropo.org.au; Lismore Showground; ⊗7.30-11am Tue), produce market (www.farmersmarkets.org.au; Magellan St; ⊗3.30-6.30pm Thu) and farmers market (⊗8-11am Sat), and a car boot market (Lismore Shopping Sq, Uralba St; ⊗8am-2pm Sun) every first and third Sunday.

Noah's Arc
BOOKS

(www.noahsarcbookstore.com.au; 66 Magellan St; ⊗9am-5.30pm Mon-Fri, 9.30am-1pm Sat) Stocks a large selection of secondhand and rare books in a heritage building.

ℹ Information

Lismore Visitor Information Centre (☑ 02-6626 0100; www.visitlismore.com.au; cnr Molesworth & Ballina Sts; ⊗9.30am-4pm) Has interesting displays on the rainforest and local history. Kids dig the nearby Heritage Park playground and skate park.

ℹ Getting There & Around

AIR

Lismore Regional Airport (LSY; ☑ 02-6622 8296; www.lismore.nsw.gov.au; Bruxner Hwy) is 3km south of the city. **Regional Express** (Rex; ☑ 13 17 13; www.regionalexpress.com.au) flies to/from Sydney.

BUS

Buses stop at the **Lismore City Transit Centre** (cnr Molesworth & Magellan Sts).

Northern Rivers Buslines (☑ 02-6622 1499; www.nrbuslines.com.au) Local buses plus services to/from Grafton (three hours), Ballina (1¼ hours), Lennox Head (one hour), Bangalow (1¼ hours) and Byron Bay (1½ hours); all $9.70.

NSW TrainLink (☑ 13 22 32; www.nswtrainlink.info) Coaches to/from Byron Bay ($9.25, one hour), Ballina ($6.95, 45 minutes), Mullumbimby ($12, one hour), Brunswick Heads ($14, 1½ hours) and Brisbane ($41, three hours).

Waller's (☑ 02-6622 6266; www.wallersbus.com) At least three buses on weekdays to/from Nimbin ($9, 30 minutes).

Nimbin

POP 468

Welcome to Australia's hippie capital, an intriguing little place that struggles under the weight of its own clichés. Psychedelic swirls brighten every wall of the main street and the smell of marijuana smoke is inescapable, as are the persistent young pot dealers who make a living from the bus tours that barrel up from Byron daily.

It's hard to know what to make of it all, especially if you're only here for the day – stay overnight to get a more rounded impression. Once the buses depart, the touts back off and the village is left to the locals. Genuine remnants of the peace-and-love generation remain, but many have abandoned Nimbin to live an alternative lifestyle in farms and villages in the surrounding hinterland.

◉ Sights

Nimbin Museum MUSEUM
(www.nimbinmuseum.com; 62 Cullen St; admission by donation $2) An interpretive and expressionistic museum that's far more a work of art than of history.

Nightcap National Park PARK
(www.nationalparks.nsw.gov.au/Nightcap-National-Park) The spectacular waterfalls, sheer cliff walls and dense rainforest in 80-sq-km Nightcap National Park are perhaps expected from somewhere with the highest annual rainfall in NSW. It's part of the Gondwana Rainforests World Heritage Area (p152) and home to many species including the wompoo fruit dove, masked owl and red-legged pademelon (similar to a wallaby).

From Nimbin, a 10km drive via Tuntable Falls Rd and Newton Dr leads to the edge of the park and then on to Mt Nardi (800m). The **Historic Nightcap Track** (16km, 1½ days), which was stomped out by postal workers in the late 19th century, runs from here to **Rummery Park**, a well-provided picnic spot and campground. **Peate's Mountain Lookout**, just on from Rummery Park, offers a panoramic view all the way to Byron. A largely unsealed but very scenic road leads from the Channon to the Terania Creek Picnic Area, where an easy track heads to **Protestor Falls** (1.4km return).

🛏 Sleeping

There are dozens of local farms happy to host volunteers willing to yank weeds and perform other chores; contact Willing Workers on Organic Farms (www.wwoof.com.au) for more information.

★ Grey Gum Lodge GUESTHOUSE $
(☎02-6689 1713; www.greygumlodge.com; 2 High St; r $75-120; @🛜) The valley views from the front verandah of this palm-draped wooden Queenslander-style house are gorgeous. All the rooms are comfortable, tastefully furnished and have their own bathrooms. It's gay-friendly too.

Nimbin Rox YHA HOSTEL $
(☎02-6689 0022; www.nimbinrox.com; 74 Thornburn St; tepees/dm/d from $26/28/68; @🛜🏊) Backing onto fields on the edge of town, this laid-back hostel has friendly managers, hammocks strung from the trees, a tepee out

THE NIMBIN STORY

Until the 1970s, Nimbin was an unremarkable village like so many others in the Northern Rivers region. That changed forever in May 1973 when the Aquarius Festival was held here, drawing large numbers of students, hippies and devotees of sustainable living and alternative lifestyles. After the 10-day festival ended, some of the attendees stayed on in an attempt to live out the ideals expressed during the festival – and Nimbin hasn't been the same since.

Another landmark in Nimbin's history came in 1979 with the Terania Creek Battle, a four-week stand-off between environmentalists and logging companies. It was the first major conservation battle of its kind in Australia and the victory by conservationists is often credited with ensuring the survival of NSW's vast tracts of rainforest. Protestor Falls in what is now Nightcap National Park is named in their honour.

the back, a heated swimming pool and regular marsupial visitors.

Rainbow Retreat Backpackers HOSTEL $
(☎02-6689 1262; www.rainbowretreat.net; 75 Thorburn St; camp sites/dm/s/d $15/25/40/60, cabins from $120) Very basic, but totally in the age-of-Aquarius spirit, this back-to-the-bush retreat has a set of brightly coloured cabins, a guesthouse enveloped by banana palms, camp sites and a thoroughly chilled-out vibe.

Nimbin Backpackers at Granny's Farm HOSTEL $
(☎02-6689 1333; www.nimbinbackpackers.com; 112 Cullen St; camp sites/dm/s $15/25/40, d $50-80; 🛜🏊) Nimbin's backpackers of longest standing has some nice rooms but a basic outside toilet block and a slightly shabby kitchen. Camping is by the creek and there's a saltwater swimming pool.

🍴 Eating & Drinking

Rainbow Cafe CAFE $
(☎02-6689 1997; 64a Cullen St; mains $8-15; ⊙7.30am-5pm) Murals cover the walls of this thumping Nimbin institution, which serves generously proportioned breakfasts, burgers and salads. You might spot a rosella or a kookaburra in the leafy courtyard.

Nimbin Hotel
PUB $

(☑02-6689 1246; www.nimbinhotel.com.au; Cullen St; mains $11-18; ☉11am-10pm) This classic local boozer has a vast covered back porch overlooking a valley. At the rear is the good Hummingbird Bistro, serving up everything from a 'tree-hugger's salad' to curries and grilled barramundi. There's live music most weekends and backpacker rooms upstairs.

🛍 Shopping

Despite the general reluctance to be pinned down on exact opening times, perhaps for fear of ruining Nimbin's freewheelin' image, most places open from 10am to 5pm.

Nimbin Market
MARKET

(www.facebook.com/NimbinMarkets; Nimbin Community Centre; ☉9am-2.30pm Sun) Nimbin's rainbow tribe comes out on market days, held on the fourth and fifth Sundays of the month.

Hemp Embassy
SPECIALIST

(www.hempembassy.net; 51 Cullen St) Part head shop, part political centre, this place raises consciousness about marijuana legalisation, as well as providing all the tools and fashion items you'll need to attract police attention. The embassy organises the Mardi-Grass festival (www.nimbinmardigrass.com) each May.

Nimbin Candle Factory
CRAFT

(☑02-6689 1010; www.nimbincandles.com.au; ☉9am-5pm Mon-Fri) Situated by the bridge on the Murwillumbah side of town, the Old Butter Factory now incubates various little businesses. The candle factory sells hand-dipped paraffin candles shaped like marijuana leaves, pyramids, wizards and unicorns.

Nimbin Artists Gallery
ARTS & CRAFTS

(www.nimbinartistsgallery.org; 49 Cullen St; ☉10am-5pm) Local artists and craftspeople display and sell their wares here.

ℹ Information

Nimbin Visitor Information Centre (☑02-6689 1388; www.visitnimbin.com.au; 46 Cullen St; ☉10am-4pm)

ℹ Getting There & Around

BUS

Gosel's (☑02-6677 9394) Two buses on weekdays to Uki ($13, 40 minutes) and Murwillumbah ($15, one hour).

Waller's (☑02-6622 6266; www.wallersbus. com) At least three buses on weekdays to/ from Lismore ($9, 30 minutes).

SHUTTLES & TOURS

Various operators offer day tours and shuttles to Nimbin from Byron Bay, sometimes with stops at surrounding sights. Most leave at 10am or 11am and return around 5pm or 6pm.

Grasshoppers (☑0438 269 076; www.grass-hoppers.com.au; return incl BBQ lunch $49)

Happy Coach (☑02-6685 3996; return $25)

Jim's Alternative Tours (☑0401 592 247; www.jimsalternativetours.com; tours $40)

OFF THE BEATEN TRACK

BORDER RANGES NATIONAL PARK

The vast Border Ranges National Park (www.nationalparks.nsw.gov.au/border-ranges-national-park; vehicle entry $7) covers 317 sq km on the NSW side of the McPherson Range, which runs along the NSW–Queensland border. It's another part of the Gondwana Rainforests World Heritage Area (p152) and it's estimated that representatives of a quarter of all bird species in Australia can be found here.

The eastern section of the park can be explored on the 44km Tweed Range Scenic Drive (gravel and usable in dry weather), which loops through the park from Lillian Rock (midway between Uki and Kyogle) to Wiangaree (north of Kyogle on Summerland Way). The signposting on access roads isn't good (when in doubt take roads signposted to the national park), but it's well worth the effort.

The road runs through mountain rainforest, with steep hills and lookouts over the Tweed Valley to Wollumbin Mt Warning and the coast. The short walk out to the Pinnacle Lookout is a highlight and one of the best places to see Wollumbin against a rising sun. At Antarctic Beech there is a forest of 2000-year-old beech trees. From here, a walking track (about 5km) leads down to rainforest, swimming holes and a picnic area at Brindle Creek.

TWEED HEADS

Conjoined with Coolangatta, Tweed Heads is bisected by the state border, meaning that there are some roads where one side is officially in NSW and the other is in Queensland. At Point Danger, the towering Captain Cook Memorial straddles them both and offers wonderful views up and down the coast.

Before you cross into the Sunshine State, check out the Minjungbal Aboriginal Cultural Centre (p128), set in a grove of old gum trees on the Tweed River. The scant historical displays are interesting, but better still is the free Walk on Water loop, which follows boardwalks through the mangroves to a rare surviving Bora ring – a circle of raised earth that was once used for community gatherings.

Uki

POP 214

Uki (pronounced 'uke-eye') is a sleepy village tucked alongside the surging Tweed River, under the numinous peak of Wollumbin Mt Warning. Although not as self-consciously hippyish as Nimbin, it does have more than its fair share of holistic health and organics shops, testimony to the enduring effect of the Aquarius Festival in this part of the hinterland. Alternative lifestylers can be spotted at the weekly Farmers' Market (Uki Hall; ⊘8am-12.30pm Sat) and the Uki Butterfly Bazaar (Uki Village Buttery; ⊘8am-2pm Sun), held on the third Sunday of each month.

◉ Sights

Wollumbin National Park PARK
(www.nationalparks.nsw.gov.au/wollumbin-national-park) Northwest of Uki, 41-sq-km Wollumbin National Park surrounds Wollumbin Mt Warning (1156m), the most dramatic feature of the hinterland, towering over the valley. Its English name was given by James Cook in 1770 to warn seafarers of offshore reefs. Its far older Aboriginal name, Wollumbin, means 'cloud catcher' or 'weather maker'.

The summit is the first part of mainland Australia to be touched by sunlight each day, a drawcard that sees many make the trek to the top. You should be aware that, under the law of the local Bundjalung people, only certain people are allowed to climb the sacred mountain; they ask you not to climb it, out of respect for this. Instead, you can get an artist's impression of the view from the 360-degree mural at the Murwillumbah Visitor Information Centre.

Wollumbin is part of the Gondwana Rainforests World Heritage Area (p152). Look out for the Albert's lyrebird on the Lyrebird Track (300m return).

🛏 Sleeping & Eating

Mt Warning B&B Retreat B&B $
(☑02-6679 5259; www.mtwarningretreat.com.au; 73 Mt Warning Rd; camp sites/yurts/cabins $15/80/125, r $80-95; ❄️ 🐾) Near the beginning of the leafy road to Mt Warning, this beautiful property abuts the Tweed River. It's wonderfully isolated, making the tent sites, yurt and cabins in the garden a popular choice. The three B&B rooms in the 100-year-old house share a bathroom.

A View of Mt Warning B&B $$
(☑02-6679 5068; www.mtwarningview.com; 28 Glenock Rd; s/d $145/165; ❄️🐾) Looking like a spaceship that has landed on a hill and attempted a Spanish Mission camouflage, this unusual octagonal house has four B&B rooms, all with the views promised by its name. It's located off Uki Rd, 3km north of the village.

Mavis's Kitchen EUROPEAN $$
(☑02-6679 5664; www.maviseskitchen.com.au; 64 Mt Warning Rd; mains $24-28; ⊘11am-3pm Wed, Thu & Sun, 11am-3pm & 5.30-9pm Fri & Sat) 🐾 The setting is sublime: a two-storey wooden Queenslander house surrounded by gorgeous gardens, gazing at Wollumbin Mt Warning. The country-style menu makes the most of the homegrown produce from the impressive organic kitchen garden.

ⓘ Getting There & Away

Gosel's buses on the Nimbin–Murwillumbah route stop here on weekdays.

Murwillumbah

POP 8530

Sitting pretty on the banks of the wide Tweed River, Murwillumbah is a scenic spot and well worth the detour off the Pacific Hwy. Between here and the coast, the fertile river valley wears a lush green coat of sugar cane and banana palms. Gazing inland, the mist-shrouded rim of an ancient volcanic caldera looms in the distance. Art deco buildings line the town centre, and while it's still an old-fashioned country town, it has excellent cafes and a tangible whiff of hippiedom.

◉ Sights

Tweed River Regional Art Gallery   GALLERY
(www.tweed.nsw.gov.au/artgallery; 2 Mistral Rd; ⊙10am-5pm Wed-Sun) FREE This exceptional gallery is an architectural delight and home to some of Australia's finest, including a new extension devoted to acclaimed Lismore-born painter Margaret Olley (1923–2011).

Tropical Fruit World   GARDENS
(☑02-6677 7222; www.tropicalfruitworld.com.au; Duranbah Rd; adult/child $44/25; ⊙10am-4pm) North of town under the Big Avocado, this fruity theme park–plantation claims to have the world's largest collection of rare and tropical fruit – 500 varieties. It offers guided tractor tours, tastings, boat rides, native critters, a petting zoo and a miniature train.

🛏 Sleeping

Mount Warning-Murwillumbah YHA   HOSTEL $
(☑02-6672 3763; www.yha.com.au; 1 Tumbulgum Rd; dm/d from $33/72) 🌿 This former river-captain's home overlooking the water now houses a colourful waterfront hostel with eight-bed dorms. There's free ice cream at night plus canoe and bike hire.

★ Crystal Creek Rainforest Retreat   LODGE $$$
(☑02-6679 1591; www.ccrr.com.au; Brookers Rd, Upper Crystal Creek; d $395-675) A blissful 19km drive northwest of Murwillumbah leads to this luxurious, secluded retreat in the shadow of the caldera. The timber bungalows have open fires, spa baths, massive TVs, full kitchens and elevated balconies.

🍴 Eating

★ Sugar Beat   CAFE $
(☑02-6672 2330; www.sugarbeatcafe.com.au; 6-8 Commercial Rd; mains $7-17; ⊙7.30am-5pm Mon-Fri, to 2pm Sat; 🌿) Sit by the sunny window, settle into a corner of the long bench or take in the scene from one of the pavement tables. Food choices include tasty cafe-style fusion fare and locally famous baked goods.

Modern Grocer   CAFE, DELI $
(☑02-6672 5007; www.themoderngrocer.com; 3 Wollumbin St; mains $8-11; ⊙8.30am-5pm Mon-Fri, to 2pm Sat) The deli counter has goodies fit to turn picnics into gluttonous feasts, but at its heart this is a very cool, very laid-back cafe. Sit yourself at the communal table and tuck into a cooked breakfast, sandwich or wrap.

🛍 Shopping

The weekly **Caldera Farmers' Market** (www.murwillumbahfarmersmarket.com.au; Murwillumbah Showground, 37 Queensland Rd; ⊙7-11am Wed) has produce, food stalls and music. The **Cottage Market** (Knox Park; ⊙8am-1pm Sat) is held on the first and third Saturday of the month, and the **Showground Market** (www.murwillumbahshowground.com; Murwillumbah Showground; ⊙8am-1pm Sun) is on the fourth Sunday.

ℹ Information

Murwillumbah Visitor Information Centre (☑02-6672 1340; www.tweedtourism.com.au; cnr Alma St & Tweed Valley Way; ⊙9am-4.30pm) Has national park info and passes, a great rainforest display, a Kombi van protruding from the wall (in honour of the Terania Creek protesters) and a gallery devoted to works focussing on the natural environment. There's also a 20m wraparound mural of the views from the sacred peak of Wollumbin Mt Warning.

ℹ Getting There & Away

Gosel's (☑02-6677 9394) Two buses on weekdays to Nimbin ($15, one hour) via Uki.

Greyhound (☑1300 473 946; www.greyhound.com.au) Daily coach to/from Byron Bay ($13, one hour), Coolangatta ($9, 10 minutes), Surfers Paradise ($20, one hour), Southport ($22, 1¼ hours) and Brisbane ($34, 2¼ hours).

NSW TrainLink (☑13 22 32; www.nswtrainlink.info) Coaches to/from Lismore ($19, two hours), Ballina ($15, 1½ hours), Bangalow ($14, 1¼ hours), Byron Bay ($9.25, one hour) and Brisbane ($22, 1½ hours).

Premier (☑13 34 10; www.premierms.com.au) Daily coaches to/from Sydney ($92, 14¾ hours), Port Macquarie ($66, 7½ hours), Coffs Harbour ($52, 6¼ hours), Byron Bay ($12, one hour) and Brisbane ($25, 1¾ hours).

Canberra & Southern New South Wales

Includes ➡

Best Places to Eat

➡ Caveau (p183)

➡ Ottoman (p178)

➡ Cupitt's Winery & Restaurant (p192)

➡ Bannisters Restaurant (p192)

➡ Bluewave Seafoods (p200)

Best Places to Stay

➡ Lighthouse keepers' cottages (p196)

➡ Paperbark Camp (p191)

➡ Post & Telegraph B&B (p195)

➡ Bermagui Beach Hotel (p200)

➡ Diamant Hotel (p178)

Why Go?

Come with us on a journey into three very important aspects of Australian culture. It begins in the modern city of Canberra, the nation's capital and the repository of the national story: no other Australian city has better museums, better art galleries or, yes, more kangaroos.

A short distance away, the raw natural beauty of Australia's eastern shore is everywhere in evidence, showcasing the Aussie love of wilderness from Royal National Park down to Ben Boyd National Park. En route, watch for poignant landmarks in Australia's Indigenous history.

And then there's the Aussie passion for the beach and all that goes with it – sometimes-nondescript towns with good restaurants, friendly pubs and activities from surf schools and skydiving to sea cruises. Throw in historic settlements such as Berry and Central Tilba and you'll find ample reason to linger en route between Sydney and Melbourne.

When to Go
Canberra

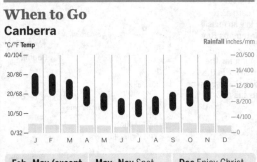

Feb–May (except Easter) Sun's still shining and kids are back at school.

May–Nov Spot whales along the coast.

Dec Enjoy Christmas Aussie-style on the coast – seafood for lunch and beach cricket.

Canberra & Southern New South Wales Highlights

1 Having kangaroos call in at your camp site in **Murramarang National Park** (p192).

2 Exploring stunning **Booderee National Park** (p190) with local Indigenous guides.

3 Hanging out with the seals and penguins at **Montague Island** (p195).

4 Leaving snowy-white footprints on the beaches of **Jervis Bay** (p189).

5 Marvelling at the architectural splendour of Canberra's **Parliament House** (p173).

6 Watching whales pass by the postcard-pretty coastline around **Eden** (p203).

7 Returning to the charming, wood-panelled past at **Central Tilba** (p198).

8 Learning to surf like an Aussie at **Batemans Bay** (p193).

9 Admiring the Australiana in the **National Museum of Australia** (p174).

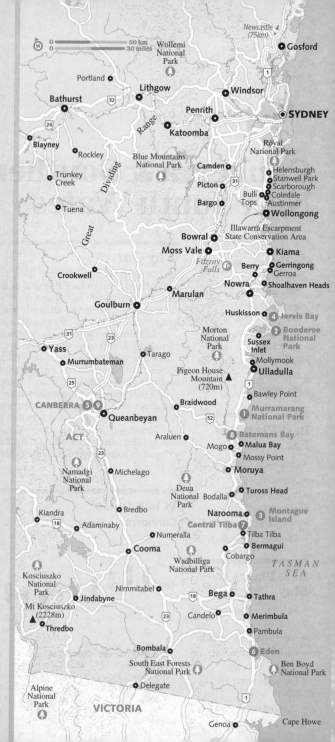

ℹ Getting There & Around

AIR

The region's main airport is in Canberra and smaller airports are at Moruya and Merimbula.

BUS

Coaches run between Canberra and the capital cities, and from the capital cities along the coast.

CAR & MOTORCYCLE

The quickest route between Canberra and the coast is the Kings Hwy. The Princes Hwy winds its way from Wollongong in the north to Eden in the south and is the main route for exploring the coast no matter which direction you're coming from. It passes through the bigger towns of Batemans Bay, Narooma and Merimbula. Smaller roads that bypass sections of the highway are a good way of accessing coastal and hinterland villages.

TRAIN

Trains run between Canberra and Sydney. There are no direct trains between Canberra and Melbourne.

CANBERRA

POP 355,596

A hyperplanned city, Canberra is big on architectural symbolism and low on spontaneity, but there's a lot going on behind the slightly sterile exterior. And if you want a crash course in Australian history, culture and politics, this is your town. Its fine art galleries and wonderful museums offer a window into the Australian soul, and its political institutions provide fascinating insights into how this marvellous modern democracy works. There's also a limited but often excellent choice of restaurants and cafes and the lively bar scene is fuelled by the city's university students. During parliamentary sitting weeks the town hums with the business of national politics.

Unfortunately, the city is totally geared towards the car – it's difficult to explore by public transport and almost impossible to do so on foot. You really need wheels (two or four) to do it and its scenic natural surrounds justice.

Canberra came about because the fierce rivalry between Sydney and Melbourne in 1901 meant neither could become the new nation's capital. Thus it was that a small chunk was carved out of New South Wales' Limestone Plains somewhere between the two cities as a compromise; this new city was officially named Canberra in 1913 and it took over from Melbourne as the seat of national government in 1927.

◉ Sights

Most of Canberra's significant buildings, museums and galleries are scattered around Lake Burley Griffin. You can easily walk here from Civic, Manuka or Kingston.

★**Parliament House**   NOTABLE BUILDING
(☑02-6277 5399; www.aph.gov.au; ☺from 9am Mon & Tue, from 8.30am Wed & Thu sitting days, 9am-5pm non-sitting days) **FREE** Opened in 1988 after a 10-year, $1.2-billion construction project, the national parliament building is dug into Capital Hill, its roof covered in grass and topped by an 81m-high flagpole. The rooftop lawns are easily accessible, encompass 23 hectares of landscaped gardens, and provide superb 360-degree views of the city. Underneath is a complex of five buildings that incorporate 17 courtyards, a striking entrance foyer, a Great Hall, the House of Representatives, the Senate and 2300km of corridors. Much of it can be visited on a free guided tour (30 minutes on sitting days, 45 minutes on non-sitting days). These set off at 10am, 1pm and 3pm daily.

Visitors are welcome to self-navigate and watch parliamentary proceedings from the public galleries. Tickets for Question Time (2pm on sitting days) in the House of Representatives are free but must be booked through the **Sergeant-at-Arms** (☑02-6277 4889); tickets aren't required for the Senate chamber. See the website for a calendar of sitting days.

★**National Gallery of Australia**   GALLERY
(☑02-6240 6502; www.nga.gov.au; Parkes Pl, Parkes; ☺10am-5pm) **FREE** On entering this impressive gallery, you will be confronted with one of its most extraordinary exhibits, an Aboriginal Memorial from Central Arnhem Land that was created for the nation's bicentenary in 1988. The work of 43 artists, this 'forest of souls' presents 200 hollow log coffins (one for every year of European settlement) and is one of the gallery's many works by Aboriginal and Torres Strait Islander people.

Also on show is Australian art from the colonial to the contemporary period and three galleries showcasing art from the Indian subcontinent, Southeast Asia and China, Japan and Central Asia. Together, these form the country's most important and comprehensive collection of Asian art. There's also a notable collection of Pacific art and a collection of European and American works with a few knockout pieces.

There's a ground-floor cafe and a gallery shop, while behind the building is a somewhat scruffy sculpture garden and a restaurant (open noon to 2pm Wednesday to Sunday).

Consider taking advantage of a free guided tour – check the website for details. Note that visiting exhibitions usually attract an admission fee.

National Museum of Australia MUSEUM
(📞 02-6208 5000; www.nma.gov.au; Lawson Cres, Acton Peninsula; admission to permanent collection free, guided tours adult/child/family $10/5/25; ⊙ 9am-5pm) FREE Dismantling and analysing a national identity is a laudable endeavour, and this museum makes a valiant effort to do just that. Cluttered with exhibits, it makes a point of avoiding standard curatorial conventions such as organising exhibits chronologically, which some visitors will find exhilarating and others will find annoying – kids tend to love it. Exhibits focus on environmental change, Indigenous culture, national icons and more. Don't miss the introductory film, shown in the small rotating **Circa Theatre** at the start of the exhibition route.

Bus 7 runs here from Civic. There's also a free bus on weekends and public holidays, departing regularly from 10.30am from platform 7 in the Civic bus interchange along Alinga St, East Row and Mort St.

★ **Australian War Memorial** MUSEUM
(📞 02-6243 4211; www.awm.gov.au; Treloar Cres, Campbell; ⊙ 10am-5pm) FREE The War Memorial provides a fascinating insight into how war has forged Australia's national identity, and in so doing delivers Canberra's most rewarding museum experience. Entry is via a **Commemorative Courtyard** where the names of the nation's war dead are memorialised on a roll of honour. Over the years family members have attached bright-red paper poppies to the names of their fallen relatives, imparting a melancholic beauty. These poppies of remembrance reference those that flowered on the battlegrounds of Belgium, France and Gallipoli in the spring of 1915.

Behind the courtyard is the mosaic-encrusted **Hall of Memory**. This is home to the **Tomb of the Unknown Australian Soldier**, which represents all Australians who have given their lives during wartime.

Inside the museum are halls dedicated to WWI, WWII and conflicts from 1945 to the present day. There's also an aircraft hall with plenty of exhibits that provides a perfect introduction to the sound-and-light shows that are staged in the massive and hugely impressive **Anzac Hall**. The most exciting of the shows are *Striking by Night*, a recreation of a night operation over Berlin in 1943 that is staged on the hour; and *Over the Front: the Great War in the Air*, which kicks off at a quarter past the hour.

Free volunteer-led 90-minute guided tours leave from the **Orientation Gallery** next to the main entrance at 10am, 10.15am, 10.30am, 11am, noon, 1pm, 1.30pm, 2pm, 2.30pm and 3pm; 45-minute tours leave at 10.45am and 1.15pm. Alternatively, purchase the *Self-Guided Tour* leaflet with map ($5).

The memorial's **Terrace Cafe** (📞 02-6230 4349; Treloar Cres, Australian War Memorial; breakfast $6-17, lunch $9-20; ⊙ 8.30am-4.30pm) occupies an attractive glass pavilion next door to the main building. It serves decent food and coffee in indoor and outdoor spaces.

Museum of Australian Democracy MUSEUM
(📞 02-6270 8222; www.moadoph.gov.au; Old Parliament House, 18 King George Tce, Parkes; adult/concession/family $2/1/5; ⊙ 9am-5pm) It was the seat of government from 1927 to 1988, so this building offers visitors a whiff of bygone parliamentary activity alongside its exhibits. These won't be particularly meaningful for non-Aussies, but all those who have studied Australian history or followed the histrionics and high jinx in Canberra over the decades will be transported back to many significant events in the relatively short life of its parliamentary democracy. Displays cover Australian prime ministers, the roots of global and local democracy, and the history of local protest movements. You can also visit the old Senate and House of Representatives chambers, the parliamentary library and the prime minister's office.

The lawn in front of Old Parliament House is home to the **Aboriginal Tent Embassy** – an important site in the struggle for equality and representation for Indigenous Australians. **Reconciliation Place**, where artwork represents the nation's commitment to the cause of reconciliation between Indigenous and non-Indigenous Australians, is down on the shore of Lake Burley Griffin.

★ **National Portrait Gallery** GALLERY
(☎02-6102 7000; www.portrait.gov.au; King Edward Tce, Parkes; ☺10am-5pm) FREE This gallery tells the story of Australia through its faces – from wax cameos of Aboriginal people to colonial portraits of the nation's founding families and contemporary works such as Howard Arkley's DayGlo portrait of musician Nick Cave.

The purpose-built building was designed by architect Richard Johnson of Sydney firm Johnson Pilton Walker, and all of its spaces – from exhibition rooms to the lovely terrace cafe – work extremely well.

National Film &
Sound Archive MUSEUM, CINEMA
(☎02-6248 2000; www.nfsa.gov.au; McCoy Circuit, Acton; ☺9am-5pm Mon-Fri, 10am-5pm Sat & Sun) FREE Set in a delightful art deco building, this archive preserves Australian moving-picture and sound recordings for posterity. The *Sights + Sounds of a Nation* exhibition is great to visit if the place is quiet but incredibly frustrating when it's busy, as there is no soundproofing around the audiovisual exhibits. There are also temporary exhibitions, talks and film screenings in the Arc Cinema (adult/concession $10/8; ☺2pm & 7pm Thu, 2pm, 4.30pm & 7.30pm Sat, 2pm & 4.30pm Sun). There are plans for a cafe in the complex.

Lake Burley Griffin LANDMARK
The 35km shore of this lake is home to most of the city's cultural institutions and to a high proportion of its leisure activities. It is named after American architect Walter Burley Griffin who, with the help of his wife and fellow architect Marion, won an international competition to design Australia's new capital city in 1911.

Built in 1970 to mark the bicentenary of Cook's landfall, the Captain Cook Memorial Water Jet near Regatta Point flings a 6-tonne column of water up into the air. There is also a skeleton globe at the point on which Cook's three great voyages are traced.

On Aspen Island is the 50m-high National Carillon, a gift from Britain on Canberra's 50th anniversary in 1963. The tower has 55 bronze bells, weighing from 7kg to 6 tonnes each, making it one of the world's largest musical instruments. Daily recitals are held – check the monthly schedule at www.nationalcapital.gov.au.

Australian National Botanic
Gardens GARDENS
(☎02-6250 9540; www.anbg.gov.au; Clunies Ross St, Acton; ☺8.30am-5pm year-round, to 8pm Sat & Sun Jan, visitors centre 9.30am-4.30pm) FREE Devoted to the growth, study and promotion

A LONG WEEKEND IN CANBERRA

Saturday
After checking into your hotel, get your fill of Australian art, stopping by the National Gallery of Australia (p173) and the National Portrait Gallery. Wander west along Lake Burley Griffin's foreshore, past the High Court and National Library (p177), ending your walk with high tea at the historic Hyatt Hotel (p179). Take in a classic or a modern masterpiece at the Arc Cinema (p175) before a late dinner at Ottoman (p178) or Italian & Sons (p179).

Sunday
Have brunch at Silo Bakery (p179), then head to the National Museum of Australia (p174), where you'll learn all you need to know about the country's fascinating Indigenous and post-colonial histories. If you have a car, take the afternoon to explore some of the region's excellent wineries (see www.canberrawines.com.au for details). Otherwise, jump on a bicycle and cycle around the lake before exploring nearby Yarralumla, with its collection of quirky embassy buildings. Reward yourself with dinner at Sage Dining Room (p180).

Monday
If today's a sitting day, book a ringside seat at the only game in town – Parliamentary Question Time. On your way to the 2pm session, drop into the Museum of Australian Democracy at Old Parliament House and bone up on some political history before lunching in the pleasant courtyard cafe. Before leaving town, be sure to visit the moving and informative War Memorial.

Canberra

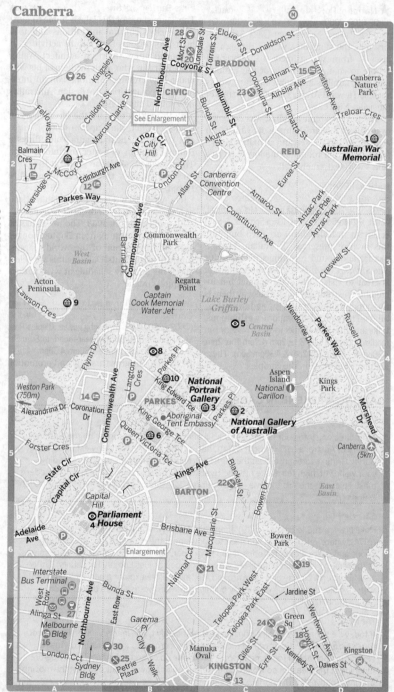

Canberra

of Australian floral diversity, these gardens are spread over 90 hectares on Black Mountain's lower slopes. Self-guided trails include the **Joseph Banks Walk**, which showcases colourful plants to illustrate the diversity of Australian flora. There's also a 90-minute return trail branching from the main path near the eucalypt lawn (peppered with 600 species of this quintessential Aussie tree) and leading into the higher areas of the gardens before continuing into the **Black Mountain Nature Park** and on to the summit.

The **visitor centre** is the departure point for free volunteer-led **guided walks** at 11am and 2pm. On weekends, a 12-seater electric bus leaves the visitor centre on a **Flora Explorer Tour** (adult/child $6/3; ⊙1pm Sat & Sun).

National Library of Australia   LIBRARY
(☑02-6262 1111; www.nla.gov.au; Parkes Pl, Parkes; ⊙Treasures Gallery 10am-5pm, reading room 9am-9pm Mon-Thu, 9am-5pm Fri, 1.30-5pm Sun) **FREE** This library has accumulated over six million items since being established in 1901, most of which can be accessed in the reading rooms. Don't miss the new **Treasures Gallery**, where artefacts such as Captain Cook's *Endeavour* journal and Captain Bligh's list of mutineers are among the regularly refreshed display – free 40-minute volunteer-led tours are held at 11.30am daily.

National Zoo & Aquarium   ZOO, AQUARIUM
(☑02-6287 8400; www.nationalzoo.com.au; 999 Lady Denman Dr, Yarralumla; adult/student & senior/child/family $38/31/21.50/105, tour weekends/weekdays $135/110; ⊙10am-5pm) Nestled behind Scrivener Dam, this zoo and aquarium is home to a roll call of fascinating animals. Book ahead to cuddle a cheetah ($175), have an up-close-and-relatively-personal encounter with a red panda, white lion or giraffe ($50), or take a **tour** behind the scenes to hand feed the lions, tigers and bears ($120). Bus 81 from the Civic interchange stops close by on weekends only.

Questacon   MUSEUM
(☑02-6270 2800; www.questacon.edu.au; King Edward Tce, Parkes; adult/child & concession/family $23/17.50/70; ⊙9am-5pm) This hands-on science and technology centre is a child magnet due to its lively, educational and just-plain-fun interactive exhibits. Kids can explore the physics of sport, athletics and fun parks, cause tsunamis and take shelter from cyclones and earthquakes. Exciting science shows, presentations and puppet shows are included in the admission price.

★ Festivals & Events

National Multicultural Festival   CULTURE
(www.multiculturalfestival.com.au) Celebrated in February.

CANBERRA & SOUTHERN NEW SOUTH WALES CANBERRA

Royal Canberra Show　　　　AGRICULTURAL SHOW
(www.rncas.org.au/showwebsite/main.html) The country meets the city at the end of February.

National Folk Festival　　　　ARTS, CULTURE
(www.folkfestival.asn.au) One of the country's largest folk festivals is held each Easter.

Floriade　　　　FLOWER SHOW
(www.floriadeaustralia.com) Held in September or October, Canberra's headline festival is dedicated to the city's spectacular spring flowers.

🛏 Sleeping

Canberra's accommodation is busiest during parliamentary sitting days. At this time, hotels charge peak rates midweek but drop rates on weekends. Peak rates also apply during the Floriade festival.

Canberra City YHA　　　　HOSTEL $
(☑02-6248 9155; www.yha.com.au; 7 Akuna St, Civic; dm $30-39, d & tw $110, f $175; ✳@🛜♨) School groups dominate the guest register of this well-run hostel. Most rooms and dorms use shared bathrooms, although the family rooms have private facilities. Dorms have bunks and lockers and private rooms have tea-and-coffee-making facilities. Services and amenities include bike hire, a small indoor pool, a sauna, a self-catering kitchen, an outdoor terrace (that hosts a BBQ on Friday) and a cafe.

Victor Lodge　　　　GUESTHOUSE $
(☑02-6295 7777; www.victorlodge.com.au; 29 Dawes St, Kingston; with shared bathroom s $89, d & tw $106; ✳🛜) This place is very handy to the Kingston cafes and shops. The rooms are compact and comfortable. There's linen provided, use of a commercial kitchen, a barbecue area, continental breakfasts and bicycle hire, plus a helping hand if you need info on local attractions.

★Diamant Hotel　　　　BOUTIQUE HOTEL $$
(☑02-6175 2222; www.8hotels.com.au; 15 Edinburgh Ave, Civic; r $160-320, apt $350-650; P✳🛜) Located in the up-and-coming New Acton precinct near Civic, the Diamant has a sheen of Sydney-style sophistication. Eight types of rooms and apartments occupy a handsome 1926 apartment block, all totally renovated and featuring amenities including iPod docks, B&O CD players and spacious bathrooms with rain showers. Service is solicitous and facilities include a gym and the popular Library Bar and Bicicletta Restaurant.

Blue & White Lodge　　　　B&B $$
(☑02-6248 0498; www.blueandwhitelodge. com.au; 524 Northbourne Ave, Downer; s/d from $95/110; ✳🛜) The Hellenic columns and Mediterranean colour scheme at this impeccable B&B pay tribute to the friendly owners' Greek roots. The comfortable rooms, some with shared bathrooms, are neat as a pin and come with a delicious cooked breakfast for $15.

University House　　　　HOTEL $$
(☑02-6125 5211; www.anu.edu.au/unihouse; 1 Balmain Cres, Acton; s without bathroom $99, d & tw with bathroom $144-159, apt $190; P✳🛜) This 1950s-era building, with furniture and ambience to match, resides in the bushy grounds of the Australian National University (ANU) and is favoured by research students, visiting academics and the occasional politician. The spacious rooms and two-bedroom apartments are basic but comfortable enough. There is also a pleasant rear courtyard, a restaurant and a cafe.

KANGAROOS IN CANBERRA

Canberra is one of the best places in Australia to see kangaroos in the wild, although in some places they're so close they can almost seem semi-tame. At last count, the national capital was home to an estimated 340,000 kangaroos. Some of the best places include Weston Park on the shores of Lake Burley Griffin northwest of Parliament House, Government House, Mt Ainslie (take the path leading up the mountain behind the Australian War Memorial) and Namadgi National Park. In 2013 a rare, pure-white albino was spotted in Namadgi.

But Canberra's growing roo population is not without its problems. Collisions with vehicles are not uncommon and in 2013 a kangaroo attacked an Australian politician who was out jogging (no, it wasn't a disgruntled voter in disguise...). Arguing that some populations represent a nuisance and a threat to the public, Canberra's authorities carry out an annual cull of Australia's most recognisable national symbol.

Mercure Canberra
HOTEL **$$**

(☑ 02-6243 0000; www.accorhotels.com; cnr Ainslie & Limestone Aves, Braddon; standard d $159-209, superior $189-269; ❀ 🖳) The main wing of this busy business hotel occupies a 1927 National Trust–listed building very close to the War Memorial. Later additions have been built around a garden courtyard and house the best of the rooms – opt for a superior room with balcony if possible.

Quest
APARTMENT **$$**

(☑ 02-6224 2222; www.questapartments.com.au; 28 West Row, Civic; studio from $164, 1-/2-bed apt from $174/294; ❀ 🖳) These apartments are spick and span and right in the heart of town – easy walking distance to the National Museum and all the bars, theatres and eateries of Civic. Each comes with a comfortable lounge, big TV, spacious balcony and modern kitchenette.

★ East Hotel
HOTEL **$$$**

(☑ 1800 816 469, 02-6295 6925; www.easthotel.com.au; 69 Canberra Ave, Kingston; studio r $265-320, apt $315-270; 🅿 ❀ @ 🖳) Cleverly straddling the divide between boutique and business, this new hotel offers thoughtfully planned and stylishly executed spaces. The foyer is home to a multimedia installation, bank of Apple Macs, lounge area (complete with excellent magazine selection) and cafe; next door is the chic Ox Eatery and a bar.

Hyatt Hotel Canberra
LUXURY HOTEL **$$$**

(☑ 02-6270 1234; www.canberra.park.hyatt.com; 120 Commonwealth Ave, Yarralumla; r $250-700, ste $695-1200; 🅿 ❀ @ 🖳 ⛱) Spotting visiting heads of state is a popular activity in the foyer of Canberra's most luxurious and historic hotel. Rooms are large, recently refurbished and extremely well equipped, and facilities include indoor pool, spa, sauna and gym.

✗ Eating

Most restaurants are in Civic, Kingston, Manuka and Griffith, and there's a fantastic Asian strip on Woolley St in Dickson. Many of the city's sights have excellent eateries – try the War Memorial.

★ Silo Bakery
BAKERY, CAFE **$**

(☑ 02-6260 6060; http://silobakery.com.au; 36 Giles St, Kingston; breakfast $3.50-22, lunch $12-24; ⊙ 7am-4pm Tue-Sat) Why can't this place open a branch where we live? If it did, we'd be there all the time! Its sourdough bread, pies, pastries and tarts are perfect breakfast temptations, and an assortment of filled baguettes, rustic mains and cheese platters keep the customers happy at lunch. Good coffee and a thoughtful list of wines by the glass complete an almost perfect package. Book for lunch.

★ Lanterne Rooms
MALAYSIAN **$$**

(☑ 02-6249 6889; http://lanternerooms.chairmangroup.com.au; Shop 3, Blamey Pl, Campbell; mains $28-36; ⊙ noon-2.30pm & 6-10.30pm Tue-Fri, 6-10.30pm Sat) It may be located in a scruffy shopping centre in Campbell, but that's the only suburban trait apparent in this atmosphere-laden eatery. Serving expertly cooked Nyonya dishes in a colourful interior that references Penang farmhouses from the colonial era, it's sophisticated and welcoming in equal measure.

Brodburger
BURGERS **$**

(☑ 02-6162 0793; www.brodburger.com.au; Glassworks Bldg, 11 Wentworth Ave, Kingston; burgers $13-20; ⊙ 11.30am-3pm & 5.30pm-late Tue-Sat, noon-4pm Sun) Like all purveyors of authentic hamburgers should, Kingston-based Brodburger started life as a no-frills lakeside caravan takeaway. It has since moved up in the world, but the flame-grilled burgers are as good as ever. It does salmon, chicken and lamb versions, but we can't go past the Brodeluxe (one with the lot).

Italian & Sons
ITALIAN **$$**

(☑ 02-6162 4888; www.italianandsons.com.au; Shop 7, 7 Lonsdale St, Braddon; mains $24-29; ⊙ 6-10pm Mon, noon-2.30pm & 6-10pm Tue-Fri, 6-10pm Sat) As hip as Canberra gets, this bustling trattoria serves thin-crust pizzas, perfectly al dente pastas and one dish of the day to an appreciative and loyal clientele. Book ahead.

Tosolini's
ITALIAN **$$**

(☑ 02-6247 4317; www.tosolinis.com.au; cnr London Circuit & East Row, Civic; mains $24-37; ⊙ 7.30am-late) Well-worn Tosolini's has been keeping workers and shoppers replete and happy for decades, and shows no sign of losing its somewhat stolid allure. Toasted panini, bruschetta and focaccias are popular at lunch, but mamma-style pastas take centre stage for dinner.

★ Ottoman
TURKISH **$$$**

(☑ 02-6273 6111; www.ottomancuisine.com.au; cnr Broughton & Blackall Sts, Barton; mains $30-36, 7-course degustation menu $80; ⊙ noon-2.30pm & 6-10pm Tue-Fri, 6-10pm Sat) A whimsically designed glass pavilion in the middle of Barton is a surprising location for this simply splendid Turkish restaurant, which is a favourite destination for Canberra's power-brokers. There are plenty of traditional dishes on the menu (mezes, dolma, kebabs), but most are given a cunning Mod Oz twist by chef Erkin Esen. The wine list is well priced and thoughtfully constructed, and service is exemplary.

Sage Dining Room FRENCH $$$
(☑02-6249 6050; www.sagerestaurant.net.au; Batman St, Braddon; 2-/3-course meal $60/75; ◎5.30-10pm Tue-Fri, noon-2.30pm & 5.30-10pm Sat) In the Gorman House Arts Centre, Sage is the home kitchen of French chef Clement Chauvin, who once graced the kitchen at London's Claridges and Maison Pic in France. Subtle French plays on local ingredients make for exquisite tastes.

Malamay CHINESE $$$
(☑02-6162 1220; http://malamay.chairmangroup .com.au; Burbury Hotel, 1 Burbury Cl, Barton; mains $33-37, lunch banquet $52, dinner banquet $68.50; ◎noon-2.30pm & 6-10.30pm Tue-Fri, 6-10.30pm Sat) The spicy flavours of Sichuan cuisine entice at this new restaurant. A glamorous interior fitout references Shanghai c 1930 and is a perfect setting in which to enjoy a (mandatory) set banquet.

🍸 Drinking & Nightlife

Pubs and bars are mostly concentrated in Civic, but there are also some in the northern suburbs of Dickson and O'Connor and across the lake in Kingston. During summer, when the university students are out of town, the bar scene pretty well collapses.

ANU Union Bar PUB
(☑02-6125 2446; www.anuunion.com.au; Union Crt, Acton; gigs $5-20; ◎gigs from 8pm) A mainstay of Canberra's music scene, the Uni Bar (on the ANU campus) has energetic live music bouncing off its walls and into the ears of sozzled students up to three times a week during the semester. Significant student discounts usually apply to gigs. It's also a good place for a game of pool and a drink.

Knightsbridge Penthouse COCKTAIL BAR
(☑02-6262 6221; www.knightsbridgepenthouse. com.au; 34 Mort St, Braddon; ◎5pm-midnight Tue & Wed, 4pm-1am Thu, 4pm-3am Fri & Sat) Its name may make it sound like an upmarket brothel, but this gin joint is a lot classier than that. It meets its self-stated aim of 'purveying good times', offering an arty, gay-friendly atmosphere and serving excellent cocktails.

Phoenix PUB
(☑02-6247 1606; www.lovethephoenix.com; 23 East Row, Civic; ◎noon-1am Mon-Wed, noon-3am Thu-Sat) Regulars don't think twice about coming back to this pub after rising from the ashes of the night before. It's a staunch supporter of new local musicians, and has a mellow atmosphere, rustic decorations and armchairs that incline you towards pondering life for the night.

Benchmark Wine Bar WINE BAR
(☑02-6262 6522; www.benchmarkwinebar.com. au; 65 Northbourne Ave, Civic; ◎11.30am-3pm & 5pm-late Mon-Fri, 5pm-late Sat) All-day tapas, a tasty brasserie menu and an annually adjusted wine menu listing over 500 bottles are the hallmarks here. Book if you're coming for dinner.

Little Brussels Belgian Beer Cafe PUB
(☑02-6260 6511; http://belgiumbeercanberra. com.au; 29 Jardine St, Kingston; ◎noon-10pm Mon & Sun, to 11pm Tue-Thu, to midnight Fri & Sat) Serving over 40 Belgian beers and offering a menu replete with Belgian dishes (mussels, anyone?), this is the place to quench a thirst and educate a palate.

ℹ Information

Canberra & Region Visitors Centre (☑02-6205 0044, 1300 554 114; www.visitcanberra. com.au; 330 Northbourne Ave, Dickson; ◎9am-5pm Mon-Fri, to 4pm Sat & Sun) Head to this centre north of Civic for a wealth of information about the city and the region. There's also a City Information Booth (◎10am-4pm Mon-Sat) near Garema Pl in Civic, but it's only open from September to April.

ℹ Getting There & Away

AIR

Canberra Airport (☑02-6275 2226; www. canberraairport.com.au) is serviced by three airlines:

Brindabella Airlines (☑1300 668 824; www. brindabellaairlines.com.au) Services Newcastle (70 minutes) and Albury (45 minutes).

Qantas (☑13 13 13, TTY 1800 652 660; www. qantas.com.au; Northbourne Ave, Jolimont Centre, Civic) Heads to Brisbane (95 minutes), Sydney (50 minutes), Melbourne (one hour), Adelaide (1¾ hours) and Perth (four hours).

Virgin Australia (☑13 67 89; www.virgin australia.com.au) Connects Canberra to all state capitals.

BUS

The interstate bus terminal is at the Jolimont Centre, which has free phone lines to the visitor centre.

Greyhound Australia (☑1300 4739 46863; www.greyhound.com.au; ⊙Jolimont Centre branch 6am-9.30pm) Has frequent services to Sydney ($36 to $42, 3½ to 4½ hours) and Melbourne ($75 to $85, nine hours).

Murrays (☑13 22 51; www.murrays.com.au; ⊙Jolimont Centre branch 7am-7pm) Has daily services to Sydney ($33 to $39, 3½ hours), Batemans Bay ($28, 2½ hours), Narooma ($42, 4½ hours) and Wollongong ($42, 3½ hours), as well as the ski fields.

CAR & MOTORCYCLE

The quickest route between Canberra and the coast is the Kings Hwy, passing through grazing land before descending the nearly sheer cliffs of the escarpment in a steep, winding, but extremely beautiful road through Mongo National Park to Batemans Bay (150km).

If you're fast-tracking it to Sydney (280km), take the Federal then the Hume Hwy. For Melbourne (660km), take the Barton Hwy and then the Hume. For the Victorian coast, take the Monaro Hwy to Lakes Entrance (420km).

TRAIN

Kingston train station (Wentworth Ave) is the city's rail terminus (take bus 35 or 39 from Civic). Seats are booked at the station's **CountryLink travel centre** (☑02-6295 1198, 13 22 32; ⊙6am-5pm Mon-Sat, 10.30am-5.30pm Sun). Trains run to/from Sydney ($48, 4½ hours, two daily). There are no direct trains to Melbourne – instead you take a CountryLink coach to Yass and transfer to the train, but the trip takes a couple of hours longer than a direct bus with Murrays or Greyhound.

ⓘ Getting Around

TO/FROM THE AIRPORT

Canberra Airport is 7km southeast of the city. A taxi to the city costs around $35. The **Airport Express** (☑1300 368 897; www.royalecoach. com.au; one way/return $12/20) runs between the airport and the city (20 minutes).

BUS

Canberra's public-transport provider is **ACT Internal Omnibus Network** (Action; ☑13 17 10; www.action.act.gov.au), with routes that crisscross the city.

You can buy single-trip tickets (adult/concession $4.20/2.10), but a better deal is a daily ticket (adult/concession $8/4). Prepurchase tickets from Action agents (including the visitor centre and some newsagents) or buy them from the driver.

TAXI

Canberra Elite Taxis (☑13 22 27; www.canberracabs.com.au)

Cabxpress (☑02-6260 6011; www.cabxpress.com.au)

WOLLONGONG

POP 245,942

The 'Gong', 80km south of Sydney, is the envy of many cities. Sure, it has restaurants, bars, arts, culture and entertainment, that's easy enough. But it also enjoys a laid-back beachside lifestyle. Just to rub it in, Sydney is easily accessible by local rail.

There are 17 patrolled beaches and a spectacular sandstone escarpment that runs from the Royal National Park south past Wollongong and Port Kembla. Grand Pacific Dr makes the most of the landscape and the whole combination makes for a host of outdoor activities: excellent surf, safe beaches, bushwalks and sky-high adventures to name a few. Our only complaint? Distant factories belching out smoke scar the middle distance along the main town beaches.

⊙ Sights

Belmore Basin
HARBOUR, PORT

Wollongong's fishing fleet is based here at the southern end of the harbour. The basin was cut from solid rock in 1868. There's a fishing cooperative and an **old lighthouse** (built 1872) on the point. Nearby, on the headland, is the newer **Breakwater Lighthouse**.

Science Centre & Planetarium
MUSEUM

(☑02-4283 6665; http://sciencecentre.uow.edu.au/; Squires Way, Fairy Meadow; adult/child $13/9; ⊙10am-4pm) Quizzical kids of all ages can indulge their senses here. It's operated by the University of Wollongong and covers everything from dinosaurs to electronics. Planetarium shows ($4 per person) run through the day.

Wollongong Botanic Gardens
GARDENS

(61 Northfields Ave, Keiraville) **FREE** Utterly serene and beautiful, this is a great spot to wind down with a picnic lunch. The gardens represent a range of habitats including tropical, temperate and woodland.

Nan Tien Buddhist Temple
BUDDHIST

(☑02-4272 0600; www.nantien.org.au; Berkeley Rd, Berkeley; ⊙9am-5pm Tue-Sun) Just south of the city, Nan Tien is the largest Buddhist temple in the southern hemisphere. The custodians encourage visitors to contemplate the 10,000 Buddhas and participate in meditations and cultural activities. Dress appropriately (no shorts, singlets or flip-flops) and remove your shoes before entering.

Wollongong City Gallery GALLERY
(www.wollongongcitygallery.com; cnr Kembla & Burelli Sts; ⊗10am-5pm Tue-Fri, noon-4pm Sat & Sun) FREE An excellent place displaying a permanent collection of modern Australian, Indigenous and Asian art, and diverse temporary exhibits.

🏃 Activities

Beaches BEACH
North Beach generally has better surf than **Wollongong City Beach** (and you can't see the belching smoke). The harbour itself has beaches that are good for children. Other beaches run north up the coast, including the surfer magnets of **Bulli**, **Sandon Point**, **Thirroul** (where DH Lawrence lived during his time in Australia; the cottage where he wrote *Kangaroo* still stands) and pretty **Austinmer**.

Pines Surfing Academy SURFING
(☑0410 645 981; http://pinessurfingacademy.com.au; North Beach; 3-day course $120, board hire 1/3hr $20/30; ⊗mid-Dec-late Jan) Summer-only surf lessons.

Sydney Hang Gliding Centre ADVENTURE SPORTS
(☑0400 258 258; www.hanggliding.com.au; tandem flights from $220; ⊗7am-7pm) A bird's-eye view of the coastline is perhaps the best. Sydney Hang Gliding Centre has tandem flights from breathtaking Bald Hill at Stanwell Park.

Cockatoo Run SCENIC RAILWAY
(☑1300 653 801; www.3801limited.com.au; adult/child/family $60/50/175; ⊗10.50am mostly Sun & Thu) Board a heritage tourist train that travels inland across the Southern Highlands to Moss Vale. The route traverses the escarpment, coursing through dense rainforest along the way.

Peter Sheppard's Cookery School COOKING COURSE
(☑02-4226 4855; www.caveau.com.au/school; 122-124 Keira St; 3/5hr classes $99/180) Operating out of Caveau, the South Coast's best restaurant, these cooking classes run according to demand. The shorter version involves learning to cook three courses, while the five-hour version of the class is more advanced.

🛏 Sleeping

Coledale Beach Camping Reserve CAMPGROUND $
(☑02-4267 4302; www.coledalebeach.com.au; Beach Rd; unpowered/powered sites from $25/32) Small and right on the beach about 20 minutes north of the city centre, this is one of the best urban camping spots on the coast. Campers can wake to great surf, with a chance of having dolphins and southern right and humpback whales for company.

Keiraleagh HOSTEL $
(☑02-4228 6765; www.backpack.net.au; 60 Kembla St; dm/s/d from $20/50/75; @☜) This rambling heritage house is clogged with atmosphere, with pressed-metal ceilings, roses in the cornices and festively painted rooms. The basic dorms are out the back, along with a sizeable patio and a barbecue.

Beach Park Motor Inn MOTEL $$
(☑02-4226 1577; www.beachparkmotorinn.com.au; 16 Pleasant Ave; r $88-185; ❇☜) The friendly owners keep the slightly twee rooms in this white-brick establishment spick and span. It's in an urban setting a short walk from the beach.

Novotel Northbeach HOTEL $$$
(☑02-4226 3555; www.novotelnorthbeach.com.au; 2-14 Cliff Rd; r from $199; ❇@☜☲) Wollongong's flashiest joint has spacious and comfortable rooms featuring balconies with ocean or escarpment views.

🍴 Eating

★**Lee & Me** CAFE $
(www.leeandme.com.au; 87 Crown St; breakfast $11-16, lunch mains $13-19; ⊗7am-4pm Mon-Fri, 8am-4pm Sat & Sun) A cafe and art-and-clothing store in a two-storey, late-19th-century heritage building. There's nothing quite like dining on dishes like buttermilk-malt hotcakes (breakfast) or slow-braised pork belly, fresh peach and pistachio salad on the sunny balcony, then shopping on a full stomach.

Diggies CAFE, BAR $$
(☑02-4226 2688; www.diggies.com.au; 1 Cliff Rd; lunch mains $16-22, dinner mains $19-32; ⊗6.30am-4pm Sun-Thu, to 10pm Fri & Sat, later hours Sun summer) With a view to the rolling

Wollongong

waves, this is the perfect spot for feasting any time of the day. Friday and Saturday evening is tapas time, although more substantial mains are also possible. From 4pm Sunday afternoon during summer, cocktails and tunes are let loose on the deck.

★**Caveau** MODERN AUSTRALIAN **$$$**
(☏02-4226 4855; www.caveau.com.au; 122-124 Keira St; 7-course degustation $99, with wine $145; ⊗6-10.30pm Tue-Thu, to 11pm Fri & Sat) Sitting unpretentiously on Keira St, this lauded restaurant washed in a soft amber glow serves gourmet treats such as roasted lobster tails or scallop gnocchi. The menu changes with the seasons.

Lorenzo's Diner ITALIAN **$$$**
(☏02-4229 5633; www.lorenzosdiner.com.au; 119 Keira St; mains $35-45; ⊗noon-2.30pm & 6-9pm Thu & Fri, 6-9pm Tue, Wed & Sat) Seriously nice people run this upmarket modern Italian

restaurant. The food matches the excellent service. Bookings recommended.

🍷 Drinking

Hotel Illawarra   PUB
(www.hotelillawarra.com.au; cnr Market & Keira Sts; ⊙11am-late) Best suited to the cocktail-sipping crowd, this complex has the red-hued Amber Bar and the more lounge- and dance-bar Zenya Garden & Dance. The former has a generous 5pm-to-9pm happy hour.

Illawarra Brewery   BAR
(www.thebrewery.net.au; WIN Entertainment Centre, cnr Crown & Harbour Sts; ⊙11am-midnight Mon-Thu, 10am-1am Fri & Sat, 10am-midnight Sun) This slick bar has six house beers on tap, plus one that changes every season. It has also opened up its taps to other microbreweries from across the country and the result is a fabulous array of beers.

ℹ Information

Visitor Centre (📞1800 240 737; www.visitwollongong.com.au; 93 Crown St; ⊙9am-5pm Mon-Sat, 10am-4pm Sun)
NPWS Office (📞02-4223 3000; ground fl, State Government Office Block, Market St; ⊙9am-3pm Mon-Fri)

ℹ Getting There & Away

All long-distance buses leave from the **long-distance bus station** (📞02-4226 1022; cnr Keira & Campbell Sts).

Premier (📞13 34 10; www.premierms.com.au) has buses to Sydney ($18, two hours) and Eden ($69, eight hours). **Murrays** (📞13 22 51; www.murrays.com.au) travels to Canberra ($44.50, 3½ hours).

ℹ Getting Around

Bringing a bike on the train from Sydney is a great way to get around; a cycle path runs from the city centre north to Bulli and south to Port Kembla.

For taxis, call 📞02-4229 9311.

AROUND WOLLONGONG

South of the City

Just south of Wollongong, Lake Illawarra is popular for water sports, including windsurfing. There are good ocean beaches on the Windang Peninsula to the east of the lake. Further south is Shellharbour, a popular holiday resort, and one of the oldest towns along the coast. Its name comes from the number of shell middens (remnants of Aboriginal occupation) that the European colonists found here.

Illawarra Escarpment State Conservation Area

Rainforest hugs the edge of the ever-eroding sandstone cliffs of the escarpment, which rise to 534m at their peak at Mt Kembla. This discontinuous conservation area protects much of it. For wonderful views of the coast, you can drive up to the Mt Keira lookout (464m); take the freeway north and follow the signs. There are other lookouts at Bulli and Sublime Point.

The park is accessible from several roadside car parks; grab the excellent pamphlet from the National Parks & Wildlife Service (NPWS), with maps and details of walks.

North of the City

On the road to the Royal National Park, the Lawrence Hargrave Lookout at Bald Hill above Stanwell Park is a superb cliff-top viewing point. Hargrave, a pioneer aviator, made his first attempts at flying in the area early in the 20th century. His obsession has since been picked up by avid hang-gliders. To join in, HangglideOz (📞0417 939 200; www.hangglideoz.com.au; from $220) and Sydney Hang Gliding Centre (p182) offer tandem flights from $220.

Symbio Wildlife Gardens (📞02-4294 1244; www.symbiozoo.com.au; 7-11 Lawrence Hargrave Dr, Stanwell Tops; adult/child $27/15; ⊙9.30am-5pm) has more than 1000 cute and furry critters. Some are native, some are exotic and some are farm animals, but all are popular with kids.

You can hit the trails on the back of a horse at Darkes Forest Riding Ranch (📞02-4294 3441; www.horseridingnsw.net.au; 84 Darkes Forest Rd, Darkes Forest; 30/60min $40/55).

ROYAL NATIONAL PARK

The only thing preventing Wollongong from becoming a suburb of Sydney is this wonderful coastal park, which protects 15,091 hectares stretching inland from 32km of beautiful coast. Encompassing dramatic cliffs, secluded beaches, scrub and lush rainforest, it's the second-oldest national park in the world, having been gazetted in 1879.

The park has a large network of walking tracks, including the spectacular 26km (two-day) Coast Track. There are lots of beautiful beaches, but most are unpatrolled and rips can make them dangerous. Garie, Era, South Era and Burning Palms are popular surf beaches and Werrong Beach is 'clothing optional'. The side roads to the smaller beaches are closed at 8.30pm.

The sizeable town of Bundeena, on the southern shore of Port Hacking opposite Sydney's southern suburb of Cronulla, is surrounded by the park. From here you can walk 30 minutes towards the ocean to Jibbon Head, which has a good beach and interesting Aboriginal rock art. Bundeena is the starting point of the coastal walk.

🛌 Sleeping

Bush camping is allowed in several areas, but you must obtain a permit (adult/child $5/3) from the visitor centre, where you can get information about current usable camp sites.

Bonnie Vale Campground   CAMPGROUND $
(http://www.nationalparks.nsw.gov.au/Royal-National-Park/bonnie-vale/camping; Sea Breeze Lane; adult/child $14/7) This 74-space drive-in site near Bundeena is equipped with toilets, hot showers and picnic tables.

Beachhaven B&B   B&B $$$
(☑02-9544 1333; www.beachhavenbnb.com.au; r from $300; ❋ 🐾) Shaded by palms and with direct access to gorgeous Hordens Beach, this place has two swank rooms. Amenities include DVD players, antiques and a spa overlooking the sand.

Weemalah Cottage   COTTAGES $$$
(☑02-9542 0648; cottages $190-300) NPWS rents out this beautiful place by the river at Warumbul. Once kept for visiting dignitaries, this fully self-contained house has wide verandahs and sleeps eight.

ℹ Information

Visitor Centre (☑02-9542 0648; www.environment.nsw.gov.au/nationalparks; Farnell Ave; ⊙9am-4pm) Can assist with camping permits, maps and bushwalking details. The centre is

DON'T MISS

HERE'S TO THE VIEW

Built in 1886 and now heritage listed, the grand old **Scarborough Hotel** (☑02-4267 5444; www.scarborough-hotel.com.au; 383 Lawrence Hargrave Dr, Scarborough; mains $12-28; ⊙9am-4pm Sun-Fri, to 8pm Sat) boasts one of the best beer gardens in New South Wales, if not Australia. The ocean view from the wooden bench seats and tables is so spectacular it wouldn't matter if the beer was warm. It's not, thankfully, and the food gets thumbs up, too.

at Audley, 2km inside the park's northeastern entrance, off the Princes Hwy.

ℹ Getting There & Away

Cronulla National Park Ferries (☑02-9523 2990; www.cronullaferries.com.au; adult/child $6.30/3.15; ⊙hourly 8.30am-5.30pm) travels to Bundeena from Cronulla, which you can reach by train from Sydney. Hours are longer on weekdays and in summer.

KIAMA & AROUND

POP 12,817

Kiama's a large town with fine old buildings, magnificent mature trees, numerous beaches and crazy rock formations, but it's the blowhole that's the clincher.

◉ Sights & Activities

There's a small enclosed surf beach right in town, and **Bombo Beach**, 3km north of the centre, has a great beach and a CityRail stop near the sand.

Blowhole Point   LANDMARK
At its most dramatic when the surf's up, the water pounding the cliff explodes out of a gaping fissure in the headland. It's been drawing visitors for a century and is now floodlit at night. It's just off the main street.

Little Blowhole   LANDMARK
(off Tingira Cres, Marsden Head) It's only about half a metre wide, but it rivals its big brother, shooting water in a jet like a dragon snorting.

Saddleback Mountain   NATURE RESERVE
From the top you get a great view of the Illawarra Escarpment, the massive sandstone

rampart that separates the coastal plain from the Southern Highlands. From Manning St, turn right on to Saddleback Mountain Rd, keeping an eye out for the historic drystone walls lining the road.

Illawarra Fly NATURE RESERVE
(☑1300 362 881; www.illawarrafly.com.au; 182 Knights Hill Rd, Knights Hill; adult/child/family $25/10/64; ⊘9am-5pm) There are spectacular views from this 500m viewing tower above the rainforest canopy at the top of the escarpment, 25km west of town.

Minnamurra Rainforest Centre NATURE RESERVE
(☑02-4236 0469; admission car $12; ⊘9am-5pm, last entry 4pm) This impressive centre is on the eastern edge of **Budderoo National Park**, about 14km inland from Kiama. From the NPWS visitor centre you can take a 1.6km loop walk on a boardwalk through the rainforest following a cascading stream. Keep an eye out for water dragons and some of the most sociable lyrebirds in the country. A secondary 2.6km walk on a beautiful, but sometimes steep, track leads to the **Minnamurra Falls**. The visitor centre has a cafe.

Coastal Walk WALKING
This pretty 6km trail, with the requisite boulders, beaches, sea caves and cliff faces, stretches from Love's Bay in Kiama Heights to the northern end of Werri Beach.

🛏 Sleeping & Eating

Bellevue GUESTHOUSE $$
(☑02-4232 4000; bellevueaccommodation.com. au; 21 Minnamurra St; r from $140) This charming house hosts guests in luxury serviced apartments in a two-storey 1890s heritage manor. It has ocean views and is a short walk to the main street. Rates rise appreciably on weekends.

★ Kiama Harbour Cabins CABIN $$$
(☑02-4232 2707; Blowhole Point; 1-/2-/3-bedroom cabins from $210/225/285; ❇) In the best position in town, these cute cottages are neat as a pin and well equipped with barbecues on front verandahs that overlook the beach and the ocean pool.

Chachi's ITALIAN $$
(☑02-4233 1144; www.chachisrestaurant.com.au; 32 Collins St; mains $20-36; ⊘11.30am-2.30pm & 5.30-9pm Tue-Sat) Located in a historic strip of terraced houses, Chachi's is well loved among locals for its casual Italian alfresco

dining. Dishes might include crispy-skinned duck or veal masala. The menu changes with the seasons.

Seafood Co-op SEAFOOD $$
(☑02-4233 1800; Kiama Harbour) Fresh from the trawlers, this hidey-hole sells local tiger prawns and oysters ($22 per two dozen).

ℹ Information

Visitor Centre (☑1300 654 262, 02-4232 3322; www.kiama.com.au; Blowhole Point Rd; ⊘9am-5pm) On Blowhole Point.

ℹ Getting There & Around

Premier (☑13 34 10; www.premierms.com.au) buses run twice daily to Berry ($18, 30 minutes), Eden ($69, 7½ hours) and Sydney ($25, 2½ hours). **Kiama Coachlines** (☑02-4232 3466; www.kiamacoachlines.com.au) runs to Gerroa, Gerringong and Minnamurra (via Jamberoo).

Frequent **CityRail** (☑13 15 00; www.cityrail. info) trains run to Wollongong, Sydney and Bomaderry (Nowra).

If you're driving, take the beach detour via Gerringong and Gerroa and rejoin the highway either in Berry or just north of Nowra.

SHOALHAVEN COAST

The coastal beauty is undiminished in this region, with its great beaches, state forests and numerous national parks, including the huge (190,751-hectare) Morton National Park in the westerly ranges. You're still within striking distance of Sydney, so expect holiday spots to fill up and prices to explode on weekends and during school holidays.

Berry
POP 1690

Berry has metamorphosed from a small retiree kind of town into a popular inland stop on the South Coast. Is the chintz outweighing the heritage character these days? You decide. In any case, it has a plethora of great eating venues, an overdose of cafes (some good, some average), two pubs fit for shouting a round or two, and a smattering of heritage buildings.

◉ Sights & Activities

The town's short main street is worth a stroll for its National Trust–classified buildings and multitude of gift shops and cafes. Further afield, there are some good-quality vineyards in the rolling countryside around Berry.

Treat Factory
FOOD

(www.treatfactory.com.au; Old Creamery Lane; ☺9.30am-4.30pm Mon-Fri, 10am-4pm Sat & Sun) An old-school place that is chock-full of nostalgic lollies such as rocky road and liquorice.

Berry Museum
MUSEUM

(135 Queen St; ☺11am-2pm Sat, to 3pm Sun) **FREE** Near the post office, in an interesting 1884 bank building. Even if the exhibits don't appeal, it's a rare chance to see inside one of Berry's old buildings.

Jasper Valley Wines
WINERY

(www.jaspervalleywines.com; 152 Croziers Rd; ☺10am-5pm Fri-Sun) Located 5km south of Berry, and offers tastings and lunches.

Silos Estate
WINERY

(☑02-4448 6082; www.thesilos.com; B640 Princes Hwy, Jaspers Brush; mains $29-33; ☺lunch & dinner Thu-Sun) Offers tastings along with an acclaimed restaurant and boutique accommodation ($195 to $395).

✯ Festivals & Events

Berry Country Fair
AGRICULTURE

This popular art-and-craft market is held on the first Sunday of every month at the showgrounds.

Berry Celtic Festival
CULTURE

(www.berrycelticfestival.org.au; Berry Showground; adult/child $10/5) On the last Saturday in May the peace is shattered by the caber-tossers, haggis-hurlers and bagpipes.

🛏 Sleeping

Berry Hotel
HOTEL $

(☑02-4464 1011; www.berryhotel.com.au; 120 Queen St; s $50-75, d $80-100) This popular local watering hole has standard but large pub bedrooms with bathrooms down the hall. Its rear dining room serves grilled steaks and other pub grub. It organises tours of local wineries.

Village Boutique
MOTEL $$

(☑02-4464 3570; www.berrymotel.com.au; 72 Queen St; r $160-240; ❋❢❄) Large, comfortable rooms are the go at this upmarket place at the edge of the main strip. The tiny pool, just off reception, seems to work more as a water feature.

Bellawongarah at Berry
B&B $$$

(☑02-4464 1999; www.accommodation-berry.com.au; 869 Kangaroo Valley Rd, Bellawongarah; r/ste/cottages per 2 nights $400/520/500; ❋) Misty, magical rainforest surrounds this wonderful place, 8km from Berry on the mountain road leading to Kangaroo Valley. Asian art features in the main house, while nearby an 1868 Wesleyan church has been given a French provincial makeover and is rented as a self-contained cottage for two.

🍴 Eating

Coach House Restaurant
PUB $

(120 Queen St; pizzas $17.50, mains $21-32; ☺10am-late) The restaurant at the Berry Hotel offers a nice ambience and meals a cut above the usual pub grub. Sit in the large covered beer garden or grab a table in the 1860 Kangaroo Inn, a single-room brick building at the back.

Berry Woodfired Sourdough
BAKERY $$

(http://berrysourdoughcafe.com.au; Prince Alfred St; breakfast $5.50-17.50, lunch mains $16-26;

CANBERRA & SOUTHERN NEW SOUTH WALES BERRY

WORTH A TRIP

FITZROY FALLS

Water falling 81m makes a big roar and that's what you hear at this stunning spot in Morton National Park (www.nationalparks.nsw.gov.au; per vehicle $3). Even more spectacular is the view down the Yarrunga Valley from the sheer cliffs of the escarpment. There are various walks in the vicinity where, if you're very lucky, you might spot a platypus or a lyrebird. The visitor centre (☑02-4887 7270; www.environment.nsw.gov.au; ☺9am-5pm) has a cafe and good displays.

From either Nowra or Berry the road is a delight, heading through pretty Kangaroo Valley, where the historic town is hemmed in by the mountains. Then it's over castlelike Hampden Bridge, an ostentatious 1898 sandstone affair, before taking the steep climb up the escarpment.

8am-3pm Wed-Sun) Stock up on delicious bread or sit down for a light meal at this highly esteemed bakery that attracts foodies from far and wide. They also run the nearby Milkwood Bakery.

Hungry Duck
FUSION $$

(☑02-4464 2323; http://hungryduck.com.au; 85 Queen St; mains $17-34, 5-/9-course banquet $50/80; ⊙6-9.30pm Wed-Mon) ✐ This chic little red-and-black dining room is paired nicely with a contemporary Asian menu served tapas-style, although larger mains are available. There's a rear courtyard and kitchen garden where herbs are plucked direct to the plate. Fresh fish and meat are sourced locally and the eggs are from the chef's own chooks.

❶ Getting There & Away

Frequent trains go to Wollongong ($6.60, 75 minutes) with connections there to other South Coast towns and Sydney.

There are scenic roads from Berry to pretty Kangaroo Valley. **Premier** (☑13 34 10; www. premierms.com.au) has buses to Kiama ($18, 30 minutes), Nowra ($18, 20 minutes) and Sydney ($25, three hours, twice daily).

Nowra

POP 9257

Nowra, around 17km from the coast, is the largest town in the Shoalhaven area. Although there are prettier beach towns, it can be a handy regional base for Berry, 17km northeast, or the beaches of Jervis Bay, 25km southeast.

◎ Sights & Activities

The visitor centre produces a handy compilation of walks in the area. The relaxing **Ben's Walk** starts at the bridge near Scenic Dr and follows the south bank of the Shoalhaven River. North of the river, the circular 5.5km **Bomaderry Creek Walking Track** runs through sandstone gorges from a trailhead at the end of Narang Rd.

Shoalhaven Zoo
WILDLIFE RESERVE

(☑02-4421 3949; http://shoalhavenzoo.com. au; Rock Hill Rd, North Nowra; adult/child/family $20/10/50; ⊙9am-5pm) The 6.5-hectare park on the north bank of the Shoalhaven River is where you can kiss a cockatoo and meet other native animals. Head north from Nowra, cross the bridge and immediately turn left, then follow the signs. It has a fully catered **camp site** (adult/child from $10/6).

Meroogal
MUSEUM

(☑02-4421 8150; www.hht.net.au/museums/meroogal; cnr West & Worrigee Sts; adult/child $8/4; ⊙10.30am-3.30pm Sat) Intriguingly, this historic 1885 house contains the artefacts accumulated by four generations of women who have lived there.

Shoalhaven River Cruises
CRUISE

(☑0429 981 007; www.shoalhavenrivercruise.com; 2-/3hr cruise $29/45) Two hours upriver or three hours downriver, these cruises leave from the wharf just east of the bridge. Check the website for times.

🛏 Sleeping & Eating

Whitehouse
GUESTHOUSE $$

(☑02-4421 2084; www.whitehouseguesthouse. com; 30 Junction St; r $104-168; 🐾) A friendly family runs this beautifully restored guesthouse with comfortable en-suite rooms, some with spas. The light breakfast out on the wide verandah is a great way to start the day.

George Bass Motor Inn
MOTEL $$

(☑02-4421 6388; www.georgebass.com.au; 65 Bridge Rd; s/d from $119/139; ❄🐾) An unpretentious but well-appointed single-storey motor inn, the George Bass has clean and sunny rooms. The more expensive ones are slightly newer.

Tea Club
CAFE $

(☑02-4422 0900; www.teaclubnowra.com; 46 Berry St; breakfast $9-18, lunch $12-18; ⊙7.30am-3pm Mon-Sat) Nowra's bohemian set hangs out at this comfortable little cafe with art on the walls and a vast back garden. Try the chai, salads or fabulous Turkish-inspired 'whirling dervish'.

Red Raven
MODERN AUSTRALIAN $$

(☑02-4423 3433; 55 Junction St; mains $21-32; ⊙11.30am-2.30pm & 6pm-late Tue-Fri, 6pm-late Sat) Occupying the 1908 fire station, this BYO restaurant serves interesting Italian-influenced dishes, such as roasted kangaroo fillets with polenta chips.

❶ Information

NPWS Office (☑02-4423 2170; www.national-parks.nsw.gov.au; 55 Graham St)

Visitor Centre (☑02-4421 0778; www.shoal-haven.nsw.gov.au; cnr Princes Hwy & Pleasant Way)

SURF & TURF

East of Nowra, the Shoalhaven River meanders through dairy country in a system of estuaries and wetlands, finally reaching the sea at Crookhaven Heads, aka Crooky, where there's good surf. Greenwell Point, on the estuary about 15km east of Nowra, is a quiet, pretty fishing village specialising in fresh oysters. The little kiosk near the pier has fresh fish and chips.

On the north side of the estuary is Shoalhaven Heads, where the river once reached the sea but is now blocked by sandbars. Just north of the surf beach here is stunning Seven Mile Beach National Park, stretching up to Gerroa. It's an idyllic picnic spot.

Just before Shoalhaven Heads you pass through Coolangatta, the site of the earliest European settlement on NSW's south coast. Coolangatta Estate (☑02-4448 7131; www.coolangattaestate.com.au; r from $140; ☺winery 10am-5pm) is a slick winery with a golf course, a good restaurant and accommodation in convict-built buildings. Prices nearly double on the weekends.

ⓘ Getting There & Away

Premier (☑13 34 10; www.premierms.com.au) coaches stop on the run between Sydney ($25, three hours) via Berry ($18, 20 minutes), and Melbourne ($82, 14 hours) via Ulladulla ($19, one hour).

More than a dozen daily CityRail (☑13 15 00; www.cityrail.info) trains run from Sydney's Central or Bondi Junction stations to Kiama, from where there are onward connections to Nowra (Bomaderry; $8.60/4.30 per adult/child).

Jervis Bay

One of the most stunning spots on the South Coast, this large, sheltered bay is a magical amalgamation of snow-white sand, crystalline waters, national parks and frolicking dolphins. Seasonal visitors include hordes of Sydney holidaymakers (summer and most weekends) and migrating whales (May to November).

In 1995 the Aboriginal community won a land claim in the Wreck Bay area and now jointly administers Booderee National Park (p190) at the southern end of the bay. By a strange quirk this area is actually part of the Australian Capital Territory, not NSW.

Most of the development in Jervis Bay is on the western shore, around the settlements of Huskisson and Vincentia. The northern shore has less tourist infrastructure. Callala Bay, despite its close proximity to Huskisson, is cut off by the Currambene Creek – you have to drive back to the highway and head south (which is just the way the locals like it). Beecroft Peninsula forms the northeastern side of Jervis Bay, ending

in the dramatic sheer wall of appropriately named Point Perpendicular. Most of the peninsula is navy land but is usually open to the public.

◉ Sights & Activities

Huskisson (Huskie to her friends) is the centre for most tourist activities. South of Huskisson, Hyams Beach is an attractive stretch of sand that is said to be the whitest in the world. It's a little like walking on warm snow.

Jervis Bay National Park   PARK
(www.environment.nsw.gov.au) To reach Callala Bay, you have to pass through sections of Jervis Bay National Park, 4854 hectares of low scrub and woodland, which shelter the endangered eastern bristlebird. The bay itself is a marine park.

Lady Denman Heritage Complex   MUSEUM
(☑02-4441 5675; www.ladydenman.asn.au; Dent St; adult/child $10/5; ☺10am-4pm) Take a peek at the interesting historic collection as well as the 1912 *Lady Denman* ferry. Also, Timbery's Aboriginal Arts & Crafts sells work produced by one family of artisans. On the first Saturday of each month it hosts a growers market.

Dive Jervis Bay   DIVING, SNORKELLING
(☑02-4441 5255; www.divejervisbay.com; 64 Owen St; 1/2 dives $100/170) The marine park is popular with divers, offering the chance to get close to grey nurse sharks and fur seals. This reliable diving operator is a good choice.

Jervis Bay Kayaks
KAYAKING

(☑ 02-4441 7157; www.jervisbaykayaks.com; 13 Hawke St; kayak hire 3hr/day $60/75, guided half-/full-day tour $109/165) The guys here do rentals or guided sea-kayaking trips. Adventurers will appreciate the self-guided camping expeditions.

Huskisson Sea Pool
SWIMMING

(⊙ 7am-6pm Mon-Fri, 10am-5pm Sat & Sun) FREE Behind the pub, the pool has salt water but is more like an Olympic pool than the usual ocean pools.

Hire Au Go-Go
CYCLING

(☑ 02-4441 5241; http://hireaugogo.com; 1 Tomerong St; bike hire 1hr/day $19/60) Pathways around the water's edge can be explored on an electric bike.

Dolphin Watch Cruises
BOAT TOUR

(☑ 02-4441 6311; www.dolphinwatch.com.au; 50 Owen St; ⊙ dolphin-/whale-/seal-watching tour $35/60/80) Offers several dolphin-, seal- and whale-watching trips on its catamaran.

🛏 Sleeping

There's plenty of accommodation in Huskisson and Vincentia, but it still pays to book ahead. Prices skyrocket on weekends. Hyams Beach is a relaxing place to stay, but options are limited to mainly private rentals; try **Hyams Beach Real Estate** (☑ 02-4443 0242; www.hyamsbeachholidays.com.au; 76 Cyrus St, Hyams Beach).

Huskisson Beach Tourist Resort
CAMPGROUND $

(☑ 02-4441 5142; www.holidayhaven.com.au; Beach St; sites per 2 people $38-76, cabins $95-190; ⊛) Run by the Shoalhaven Council, this well-equipped camping ground has flash cabins and a great location right on the beach.

Jervis Bay Motel
MOTEL $$

(☑ 02-4441 5781; www.jervisbaymotel.com.au; 41 Owen St; d/f from $109/165; ⊛⊛) An old-fashioned motel that's been tarted up; you'll find pleasant decor and quality furnishings,

---

DON'T MISS

BOODEREE NATIONAL PARK

Occupying Jervis Bay's southeastern spit, sublime **Booderee National Park** (☑ 02-4443 0977; www.booderee.gov.au; 2-day car or motorcycle entry $11) offers good swimming, surfing and diving on both bay and ocean beaches. Much of it is heathland, with some forest, including small pockets of rainforest. Booderee means 'plenty of fish' and it's easy to see what a bountiful place this must have been for the Indigenous people. For personalised tours with an Aboriginal focus, talk to Wreck Bay identity **Uncle Barry** (☑ 0402 441 168).

There's a good **visitor centre** (☑ 02-4443 0977; www.booderee.gov.au; ⊙ 9am-4pm) at the park entrance with walking-trail maps and information on camping. Inside the park is **Booderee Botanic Gardens** (⊙ 8.30am-4pm), which is a branch of the Australian National Botanic Gardens in Canberra and includes some enormous rhododendrons as well as coastal plant species once used for food and medicine by local Indigenous groups.

There are many walking trails around the park. Keep an eye out for the 206 species of bird, 27 species of land mammal and 23 species of reptile. Amphibian enthusiasts can thrill to the 15 species of frog.

There are idyllic camping grounds at **Green Patch** (camp sites $11-22, plus per adult $5-11, per child $3-5) and **Bristol Point** (camp sites $11-22, plus per adult $5-11, per child $3-5). For a more secluded experience try the basic camping at **Caves Beach** (camp sites $7-12, plus per adult $5-11, per child $3-5). Book through the visitor centre or via the internet up to three weeks in advance at peak times. If you haven't booked, it's worth dropping by, as no-shows are common. There's a 24-hour self-registration system at the entrance to the park.

Surfing is good at Caves Beach, but the real drawcard is the **Pipeline** (aka Black Rock, Wreck Bay or Summercloud Bay), an A-grade reef break that produces 12ft tubes in optimal conditions.

The park is also home to the naval training base HMAS *Creswell*, which is off-limits to the public.

as well as lovely views from the (more expensive) upstairs rooms.

★ Paperbark Camp
CAMPGROUND $$$

(📞 1300 668 167; www.paperbarkcamp.com.au; 571 Woollamia Rd; d from $395; ⊘ closed mid-Jun–Aug) Camp in ecofriendly style in one of 12 luxurious solar-powered safari tents, with comfy beds, gorgeous en suites and wraparound decks. It's set in dense bush 3.5km from Huskisson; you can borrow kayaks to paddle up the creek to the bay.

Huskisson B&B
B&B $$$

(📞 02-4441 7551; www.huskissonbnb.com.au; 12 Tomerong St; r $195-245; 🖩 🛜) A quaint weatherboard with bright and airy eclectic rooms containing comfy beds and fluffy towels.

✕ Eating

Supply
CAFE $

(📞 02-4441 5815; www.supplyjervisbay.com.au; Shop 1, 54 Owen St; mains $10-17; ⊘ 7.30am-5pm Mon-Sat, to 3pm Sun) The best of Huskisson's cafes, Supply doubles as a deli. Grab a newspaper and settle into the smart surroundings for a satisfying breakfast.

Wild Ginger
ASIAN $$

(📞 02-4441 5577; www.wild-ginger.com.au; 42 Owen St; mains $31.50; ⊘ 4.30pm-late Tue-Sun) From the same people who brought you Seagrass Brasserie, this exciting new venture draws its inspiration primarily from Thailand, but you'll also come across dishes from Japan and Southeast Asia.

★ Seagrass Brasserie
SEAFOOD $$$

(📞 02-4441 6124; www.seagrass.net.au; 9 Hawke St; mains $34.50; ⊘ 6-9pm) This delightful beachy-but-classy restaurant offers a top-notch menu. Seafood dishes with Asian ingredients are the standouts.

Gunyah Restaurant
MODERN AUSTRALIAN $$$

(📞 02-4441 7299; 3-course meal $55; ⊘ 6.30-9pm) Sit under the canopy and watch the light change through the trees from the balcony of this acclaimed restaurant at Paperbark Camp. The focus is on local ingredients, although ordering 'roo has less appeal when there's a possibility of a live one walking past.

🍷 Drinking & Nightlife

Husky Pub
PUB

(📞 02-4441 5001; www.thehuskypub.com.au; Owen St) The funnest place in town has fabulous bay views from indoors and outside at the many picnic tables. There's live music most weekends.

ℹ Getting There & Around

Jervis Bay Territory (📞 02-4423 5244) Runs a bus around Jervis Bay communities, and from Huskisson to Nowra three times every weekday and once on Saturday and Sunday.

Nowra Coaches (📞 02-4423 5244; www.nowracoaches.com.au) Runs bus 733 around Jervis Bay and to Nowra (70 minutes) on Tuesday and Friday.

Ulladulla
POP 12,137

The harbour is the centre of life in this fishing-focused town that lets its hair down at Easter for the Blessing of the Fleet ceremony. While Ulladulla can be a bit, well, dull, it does have some beautiful beaches.

◉ Sights & Activities

Coastline
BEACH

North of the centre, gorgeous **Mollymook** stretches to over 2km of golden sand. **Narrawallee Beach**, the next one along, ends at a pretty kayak-friendly inlet. Both have beach breaks, although the serious surfers head for **Collers Beach** below the golf course, which offers left- and right-hand reef breaks and decent barrels. Immediately south of the harbour is a small beach with a large **ocean pool**.

Ulladulla's Oldest House
HISTORIC BUILDING

(📞 02-4455 6996; http://somethingsbrewing.com.au; 275 Green St; ⊘ 10am-5pm Tue-Fri, to 3pm Sat & Sun) FREE Dating back to 1850 (a mere blink of the eye when compared to local Indigenous history), this old house is now a speciality teashop, but gawkers are welcome.

Coomee Nulunga Cultural Trail
WALKING

This is a 700m walking trail established by the local Aboriginal Land Council. It begins near Lighthouse Oval (take Deering St east of the highway) and follows a path forged by the Rainbow Serpent (an important being in Aboriginal mysticism) from the headland through native bush to the beach.

🛏 Sleeping

For holiday-home rentals try **First National** (📞 02-4455 3999; www.firstnationalulladulla.com.au; The Plaza, 107 Princes Hwy).

Ulladulla Headland Tourist Park
CAMPGROUND $

(☑02-4455 2457; www.holidayhaven.com.au; South St; camp sites $26-44, cabins $82-250; ☎⚠) Not skimping on the 'park' part of the tourist-park equation, this headland property has a lovely leafy setting with ample ocean views. Facilities are good and well kept.

Ulladulla Lodge
HOSTEL $

(☑02-4454 0500; www.ulladullalodge.com.au; 63 Pacific Hwy; dm/d from $35/80) This guesthouse-style place attracts a mix of travellers, old and young alike. It's clean and comfy and guests have access to bikes, surfboards, bodyboards and a range of tour options.

Mollymook Shores
HOTEL $$

(☑02-4455 5888; www.mollymookshores.com. au; cnr Golf Ave & Shepherd St; r $120-180; ✳☎) If a leafy low-rise hotel right on Mollymook Beachfront sounds like your cup of tea, here it is. The owners are friendly, the suites have spas and the restaurant is well regarded (dinner Tuesday to Saturday).

Bannisters
HOTEL $$$

(☑02-4455 3044; www.bannisters.com.au; 191 Mitchell Pde, Mollymook; r $260-530, ste $395-1475; ✳@☎⚠) The ultimate extreme makeover: the bones of a 1970s concrete-block motel provide the basis of this hip, unassumingly luxurious place. Splash to the lip of the infinity pool for sublime views up the coast, or enjoy them from your balcony.

✗ Eating

Hayden's Pies
CAFE $

(☑03-4455 7798; 166 Princes Hwy; pies $4-7; ☺6.30am-5.30pm Mon-Fri, 7am-4.30pm Sat & Sun) From the traditional to the gourmet (Moroccan lamb or salmon and prawn) and vegetarian, this little pie shop is filled with crusty goodness and delicious smells.

★Bannisters Restaurant
SEAFOOD $$$

(☑02-4455 3044; www.bannisters.com.au; 191 Mitchell Pde; breakfast $15, dinner mains $28-48; ☺8-11am & 6pm-late) Elegantly situated on Bannister's Point, 1km north of town; famed UK chef Rick Stein's seafood fare matches the fine views. The catch of the day determines the menu, which is as it should be.

★Cupitt's Winery & Restaurant
MODERN AUSTRALIAN $$$

(☑02-4455 7888; www.cupittwines.com.au; 60 Washburton Rd; mains $28-35; ☺noon-2.30pm Wed, Thu & Sun, noon-2.30pm & 6-8.30pm Fri & Sat)

For a little piece of Provence make a pit stop at this glorious spot and enjoy some of the most respected cuisine this side of Sydney and wine tasting in the restored 1851 creamery. There's boutique accommodation in the vineyard.

ℹ Information

Visitor Centre (☑02-4455 1269; www.shoalhavenholidays.com.au; Princes Hwy; ☺9am-5pm)

ℹ Getting There & Away

Premier (☑13 34 10; www.premierms.com.au) coaches stop on the run between Sydney ($35, five hours) and Melbourne ($82, 12 hours) via Batemans Bay ($16, 45 minutes) and Nowra ($19, one hour).

Murramarang National Park

This beautiful 12,386-hectare coastal park (www.environment.nsw.gov.au; per car per day $7) begins just above Batemans Bay and extends to within 20km of Ulladulla. If you haven't seen a kangaroo in the wild yet, here's your chance. At dawn and dusk large numbers of them wander out of the eucalypt- and rainforests to the edges of lovely Durras Lake, while colourful parrots fill the trees.

Wasp Head, Depot, Pebbly and Merry Beaches are all popular with surfers and Myrtle Beach with nudists. We're not sure where nude surfers go. There are numerous walking trails snaking off from these beaches and a steep but enjoyable walk up Durras Mountain (283m).

At the north of the park, Murramarang Aboriginal Area encompasses the largest midden on the South Coast, its remains suggesting 12,000 years of continual occupation. A self-guided walking track has been laid out with interpretive displays.

⛏ Sleeping

NPWS has idyllic camp sites (www.environment.nsw.gov.au/NationalParks/; powered/unpowered sites $28/20) with showers, barbecues and flushing toilets at Depot Beach (☑02-4478 6582), Pebbly Beach (☑02-4478 6023) and Pretty Beach (☑02-4457 2019). Sites are scarce during school holidays; book ahead. It also rents tidy, self-contained forest and beachside cabins (forest/beach from $115/140)

CANBERRA & SOUTHERN NEW SOUTH WALES MURRAMARANG NATIONAL PARK at Depot Beach and Pretty Beach, sleeping between four and six people.

EcoPoint Murramarang Resort

CAMPGROUND $$

(☏ 02-4478 6355; www.murramarangresort.com.au; Mill Beach, Banyandah St, South Durras; camp sites per 2 people $28-50, villas $140-240; 🐾) This is a favourite hang-out of the marsupial mob. It is a big, modern place that has a row of Norfolk pines running between it and the beach. Posh extras such as camp sites with en suites and cabins with spa tubs are the norm.

Durras Lake North Holiday Park

CAMPGROUND $$

(☏ 02-4478 6072; www.durrasnorthpark.com.au; 57 Durras Rd, Durras North; camp sites per 2 people $25-60, cabins $65-225) This friendly holiday park has shady camp sites and cute cabins. It's very popular with kangaroos.

ⓘ Getting There & Away

The Princes Hwy forms the park's western edge, but it's 10km from the beaches. Many of the roads are pretty rough, but those to Durras, Durras Lake, Depot Beach and Durras North are all sealed, as is Mt Agony Rd to Pebbly Beach (but not Pebbly Beach Rd).

EUROBODALLA COAST

Meaning 'Land of Many Waters', this southern section of coast continues to celebrate all things blue. A fair bit of green gets a look in too, with segments of the disjointed Eurobodalla National Park spreading much of its length.

It's an area of sweet little townships, lakes, bays and inlets backed by spotted-gum forests and home to much native wildlife. Part of the Yuin homelands, it includes their sacred mountain, Gulaga.

Batemans Bay

POP 11,334

The good beaches and a luscious estuary in this fishing port have given it a leg-up to become one of the South Coast's largest holiday centres. There are plenty of activities on offer, but despite some fine exceptions the food scene is yet to take off.

◉ Sights & Activities

Beaches

BEACH

The closest beach to the town centre is **Corrigans Beach**. South of this a series of small beaches dot the rocky shore. There are longer beaches along the coast north of the bridge, leading into Murramarang National Park. Surfers flock to **Surf Beach**, **Malua Bay**, small **McKenzies Beach** (just south of Malua Bay) and **Bengello Beach**, which has waves when everywhere else is flat. For the experienced, the best surfing is at **Pink Rocks** (near Broulee) when a north swell is running. Locals say the waves are sometimes 6m high. Broulee itself has a wide crescent of sand, but there's a strong rip at the northern end.

Merinda Cruises

CRUISE

(☏ 02-4472 4052; Boatshed, Clyde St; 3hr cruise adult/child $28/15; ⏱11.30am) Cruises up the Clyde River Estuary from the ferry wharf just east of the bridge. No credit cards.

Region X

KAYAKING

(☏ 0400 184 034; http://regionx.com.au; kayak rental per 1hr $30, tours $50-80) Rent a kayak to explore nearby waterways or take one of the excellent paddling tours.

Bay & Beyond

KAYAKING

(☏ 02-4478 7777; www.bayandbeyond.com.au; kayak tours per person $50-120) Guided kayak trips along the coast and into the nearby estuaries.

Broulee Surf School

SURFING

(☏ 02-4471 7370; www.brouleesurfschool.com.au; adult/child $45/40) Learn to surf at nearby Broulee.

Soulrider Surf School

SURFING

(☏ 02-4478 6297; www.soulrider.com.au; 1hr adult/child $45/40) This surf school has a good reputation and a number of locations along the coast.

Surf the Bay Surf School

SURFING

(☏ 0432 144 220; www.surfthebay.com.au; group/private lesson $40/90) A well-regarded Broulee surf school.

Total Eco Adventures

WATER SPORTS

(☏ 02-4471 6969; www.totalecoadventures.com.au; 7/77 Coronation Dr, Broulee) Kayaking, snorkelling, stand-up paddling and surfing.

✪ Festivals & Events

Great Southern Blues & Rockabilly Festival MUSIC
(www.bluesfestival.tv) Grease up your quiff on the last weekend of October.

🛏 Sleeping

Batemans Bay's accommodation scene lacks quality at the upper end, although holiday apartments are profuse. Rates go up in the summer.

Alternatively, gather your mates and hire a houseboat. **Bay River Houseboats** (☑02-4472 5649; www.bayriverhouseboats.com.au; Wray St; 4 nights from $840-1360) and **Clyde River Houseboats** (☑02-4472 6369; www.clyderiver houseboats.com.au; 3 nights $700-1450) leases six-/10-berth boats from $840 for four nights (Monday to Friday).

Shady Willow Holiday Park HOSTEL, CAMPGROUND $
(☑02-4472 6111; www.shadywillows.com.au; cnr South St & Old Princes Hwy; powered sites $26, dm/d $28/58, caravans from $58; ❉🛜♨) Set amid static caravans and shady palms located close to the centre of town, this YHA has a rather boho ambience, which can attract or detract from the place depending on your disposition. Doubles sleep in a caravan and there is a cabin that accommodates groups of four.

Clyde River Motor Inn MOTEL $$
(☑02-4472 6444; www.clydemotel.com.au; 3 Clyde St; r/apt from $100/140; ❉🛜♨) An older motel on the river in the centre of town, this one's bathed in the sweet smell of jasmine. Rooms are clean and some have views. They also have some spacious townhouses and three-bedroom apartments.

Lincoln Downs HOTEL $$
(☑1800 789 250; www.lincolndowns.com.au; Princes Hwy; r from $115; ❉🛜♨) Excellent motel-style rooms, many of which overlook a private lake. There's also a resident peacock.

🍴 Eating

★Innes Boatshed FISH & CHIPS $
(1 Clyde St; fish & chips $15; ⊘9am-9pm Wed-Mon, to 3pm Tue) Around since the 1950s, this is one of the best-loved fish-and-chip joints on the South Coast. It also does sushi and oysters, and has some tables out the back on the decking.

North St CAFE $
(☑02-4472 5710; 5 North St; mains $10-18; ⊘8am-4pm Sun-Thu, to late Fri & Sat) This refreshingly funky little den has decent coffee and a tasty selection of breakfasts, salads, sandwiches and light lunches. It's a neat place for a wine too.

Blank Canvas MODERN AUSTRALIAN $$
(☑02-4472 5016; www.blankcanvasrestaurant.com.au; Annetts Arcade, Orient St; mains $15.50-23.50; ⊘noon-9pm Wed-Mon) Right on the water and with funky couches indoors, this cafe-by-day morphs into a more intimate dining experience in the evening. Try the coconut king prawn cocktail or the blue swimmer crab roulade. The restaurant is a block west of Orient St, from where it's signposted.

Starfish Deli AUSTRALIAN $$
(☑02-4472 4880; http://starfishdeli.com.au; 1 Clyde St; lunch mains $16-23, dinner mains $23-34; ⊘9am-9pm) Fish and chips, mussels and wood-fired pizzas are the mainstays at this waterfront place that seems to attract every hungry diner in town. Unless you don't mind waiting, booking ahead is a good idea for lunch and dinner in summer.

On the Pier SEAFOOD $$$
(☑02-4472 6405; onthepier.com.au; 2 Old Punt Rd; mains $27-35; ⊘6-10pm Mon & Tue, noon-2.30pm & 6-10pm Thu-Sun) Batemans Bay's most celebrated restaurant, with dishes such as crispy-skinned pork belly and grilled scallops. The seafood platter ($52 per person) is excellent.

🍷 Drinking & Nightlife

Bayview Hotel PUB
(☑02-4472 4522; www.bayviewhotel.com.au; 20 Orient St; ⊘10am-midnight) The only real pub in town offers a lively roster of bands, DJs and trivia nights.

ℹ Information

Visitor Centre (☑1800 802 528; www.eurobodalla.com.au; Princes Hwy; ⊘9am-5pm) Good for both the town and the wider Eurobodalla area.

ℹ Getting There & Away

The scenic Kings Hwy climbs the escarpment and heads to Canberra from just north of Batemans Bay.

Murrays (☑13 22 51; www.murrays.com.au) Services this route with daily runs to Canberra

($29.30, 2½ hours), Moruya ($13.10, one hour) and Narooma ($20.10, two hours).

Premier (☑13 34 10; www.premierms.com.au) Coaches stop on the run between Sydney ($45, six hours) and Melbourne ($73, 11 hours) via Ulladulla ($16, 45 minutes) and Moruya ($11, 30 minutes).

Mogo

POP 263

Mogo is a historic strip of wooden shops and houses almost entirely devoted to Devonshire teas, crafts and antiques.

Just off the highway is **Gold Rush Colony** (☑02-4474 2123; www.goldrushcolony.com. au; 26 James St; adult/child $20/12; ☉10am-5pm), a rambling recreation of a pioneer village, complete with free gold-panning. You can stay in **miners' cabins** (www.goldrushcolony. com.au; dm/d $26/130; ☒) inside the colony, giving you a good opportunity to play pioneer after dark.

Mogo Zoo (☑02-4474 4855; www.mogozoo.com.au; 222 Tomakin Rd, Mogo; adult/child $29.50/16; ☉9am-5pm), 2km east off the highway, is a small but interesting zoo where you can get close to the big cats. The stars of the show are the playful and rare white lions.

Moruya

POP 2531

Moruya, whose name means black swan, has a pleasant collection of Victorian buildings gathered around a broad river. There's a popular weekly **market** (☉9am-noon Sat) on the south side of Moruya Bridge. The best place to stay is **Post & Telegraph B&B** (☑02-4474 5745; www.southcoast.com.au/postandtel; cnr Page & Campbell Sts; s/d from $100/135), the beautifully restored old post office, which features polished floorboards, iron beds and verandahs overlooking gardens. Of the three rooms only one has an en suite.

★**River** (☑02-4474 5505; www.therivermoruya.com.au; 16b Church St; mains $30-36; ☉noon-2.30pm Wed-Sun, 6-9.30pm Wed-Sat; ☒), right on the the...you guessed it, is where fresh local ingredients mix liberally with international flavours on the ever-changing menu. It's popular, so book.

Moruya Airport (☑02-4474 2095; George Bass Dr) is 7km from town, near North Head. **Rex** (☑13 17 13; www.rex.com.au) flies here from Merimbula and Sydney at least daily. **Murrays** (☑13 22 51; www.murrays.com.au) bus-

es head to Canberra (from $34.70, 3½ hours) and Sydney (from $34.70, nine hours).

Moruya to Narooma

From Moruya the highway stays on its inland path, leaving a long stretch of little-visited coast to sections of **Eurobodalla National Park**. Nearly any turn-off towards the coast along here can be rewarding, especially if you're a surfer.

At **Moruya Heads** there's a good surf beach and views from Toragy Point. From here it's a 7km drive west along the river to Moruya, or south a dirt road heads through beautiful forest to **Congo**, a pretty and peaceful spot, where there's a **camp site** (☑02-4476 0800; adult/child $10/5) between the estuary and the surf beach. Congo is also the end of the **Bingi Dreaming Track**, a 14km walk following a spiritually significant Aboriginal route (pick up a brochure from the NPWS in Narooma). Keep an eye out for kangaroos, wallabies, bandicoots and goannas. The track starts further south at the incredible rock formations at **Bingi Point**.

North of Narooma the highway skirts a series of saltwater lakes (inlets, lagoons... call them what you will). The council operates **Dalmeny camp site** (☑02-4476 8596; powered/unpowered sites $26/23), close to **Brou Beach**. There's a free, basic **camp site** within the park at **Brou Lake**. **Potato Point** has a decent surf break.

Narooma

POP 2409

Sitting at the mouth of a tree-lined inlet and flanked by surf beaches, Narooma is a little seaside town and one of the prettiest such places along the coast. This is also the jumping-off point for Montague Island, one of the coast's most rewarding offshore excursions.

☉ Sights & Activities

★**Montague Island (Baranguba)**   NATURE RESERVE
Nine kilometres offshore from Narooma, this small, pest-free island is a spectacular nature reserve, home to many seabirds (shearwaters, sea eagles and peregrine falcons) and hundreds of fur seals. Little penguins nest here and although some remain year-round, there are more than 10,000 at their peak between September and February.

Baranguba, its Aboriginal name, translates as Big Brother, predating both the TV franchise and Orwell by around 8000 years. Sacred sites remain that only the local Yuin people may access.

The only way to see the island is via extremely interesting three-hour guided tours (☑1800 240 003; www.montagueisland.com.au; per person $120-155) conducted by NPWS rangers, which include climbing up the granite lighthouse (1881). Trips are dependent on numbers and weather conditions, so book ahead through the visitor centre. The boat voyage takes about 30 minutes and circumnavigates the island if the water's not too choppy. Take the afternoon tour for a better chance of seeing penguins.

NPWS offers the unforgettable opportunity to stay in the solar-powered lighthouse keepers' cottages (www.conservationvolunteers.com.au/volunteer/montague.htm; 2 nights s/d per person $690/810, r for 3 nights $1318-2058) on the proviso that you take part in conservation work while you're here. That might entail counting and weighing penguins, weeding, or planting trees. The cottages are beautifully renovated and very comfortable. Meals are included, but you'll be expected to help with the preparation. Rates are slightly cheaper out of whale season. Book well ahead.

The clear waters around the island are good for diving, especially from February to June. Island Charters Narooma (☑02-4476 1047; www.islandchartersnarooma.com; Bluewater Dr) offers diving (double dive $95), snorkelling ($75), whale watching (adult/child $77/60) and other tours. Attractions in the area include grey nurse sharks, seals and the wreck of the SS *Lady Darling*.

Beaches
BEACH

The water surrounding Narooma is so exceptionally clear that it's a constant struggle to resist leaping in. The best place for a sheltered swim is over the bridge in the netted swimming area at the south end of Bar Beach, below the breakwall. There's a surf club at Narooma Beach, but the breaks are better at Bar Beach when a southeasterly blows.

Bar Rock Lookout
LOOKOUT

If you fancy a stroll, there's a nice walk from Riverside Dr along the inlet to the ocean, and here you'll find excellent views. Just below the lookout is Australia Rock, a boulder with a bloody great hole in it that vaguely resembles the country (minus Tasmania, of course).

Wagonga Princess
CRUISE

(☑02-4476 2665; www.wagongainletcruises.com; adult/child $35/25; ⊙3hr cruise departs 1pm Sun, Wed & Fri Feb-Dec, daily Jan) A century old, this electric ferry takes a three-hour cruise up the Wagonga inlet, departing from Taylor's Boatshed.

🎊 Festivals & Events

Oyster Festival
FOOD

(www.narooma.org.au) Narooma has a shucking good time during this festival in mid-May.

🛏 Sleeping

Narooma YHA
HOSTEL $

(☑02-4476 3287; www.yha.com.au; 243 Princes Hwy; dm/d from $26/62; @) Although it was obviously once an old-style motel, this super-friendly establishment makes a great hostel. Each room has a bathroom, for starters. Free bikes and bodyboards are added bonuses.

Easts Narooma Shores Holiday Park
CAMPGROUND $$

(☑02-4476 2046; www.easts.com.au; Princes Hwy; sites $28-65, cabins $95-225; ❄@🛜🏊) More than 260 camp sites and 43 cabins occupy this lovely spot by the inlet. The friendly managers look after the place well and there's a big pool under the palm trees.

Whale Motor Inn
MOTEL $$

(☑02-4476 2411; www.whalemotorinn.com; 104 Wagonga St; d $125-215; ❄🛜🏊) Spot whales from your balcony (binoculars are to hand) at this upmarket motel with terrific views and nicely renovated rooms (though some of the bathrooms are a little last century). You can even make like a whale in the spa suites.

Horizon Holiday Apartments
APARTMENT $$

(☑02-4476 5200; www.horizonapartmentsnarooma.com.au; 147 Princes Hwy; 1-/2-bedroom apt from $129/179) Probably the pick of a fairly uninspiring bunch, these clean-lined modern apartments are well priced and some have partial ocean views.

🍴 Eating

The best eating options are on the marinas of Riverside Dr. They all have heart-melting views over the still, clear waters of the inlet – particularly romantic at sunset.

Narooma

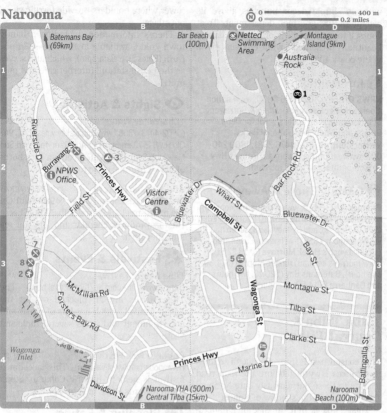

Taylor's Seafood FISH & CHIPS $
(Riverside Dr; mains $7-16; ☺noon-2.30pm & 6-9pm Tue-Sun) The takeaways are a little cheaper, but why miss out on the chance to consume the grilled fish and nongreasy chunky chips while gazing out over the water?

Na Siam THAI $$
(☏02-4476 5002; 1/26 Princes Hwy; mains $15-20; ☺noon-2.30pm & 5-9.30pm Tue-Sun, daily Dec-Apr) Better-than-average Thai cuisine on the main road through town.

Quarterdeck Marina SEAFOOD $$
(13 Riverside Dr; mains $22; ☺8am-3pm Thu-Mon) The only place on the inlet where the decor is even more captivating than the views. Enjoy the excellent breakfasts and seafood lunches under the gaze of dozens of tikis, Chairman Maos and autographed photos of 1950s TV stars.

★ **Whale Restaurant** MODERN AUSTRALIAN $$$
(☏02-4476 2411; www.whalemotorinn.com; 104 Wagonga St; mains $33; ☺6-9pm Tue-Sat) It might seem unlikely, but this hotel restaurant

with its simple decor punches above its weight in the gourmet department. Treat yourself to eye fillet steak or a rack of lamb – beautifully presented – while enjoying views of the coast. BYO wine.

ℹ Information

NPWS Office (☑02-4476 0800; www.nation-alparks.nsw.gov.au; cnr Graham & Burrawang Sts) Narooma is an access point for Deua, Gulaga and Wadbilliga National Parks.
Visitor Centre (☑02-4476 2881, 1800 240 003; www.eurobodalla.com.au; Princes Hwy; ⊙9am-5pm) Has a small museum.

ℹ Getting There & Away

Premier (☑13 34 10; www.premierms.com.au) has buses to Melbourne ($67, 10 hours) via Eden ($27, 2½ hours), and Sydney ($58, seven hours) via Wollongong ($56, five hours). Buses stop outside Lynch's Hotel. **Murrays** (☑13 22 51; www.murrays.com.au) runs to Moruya ($14.30, one hour), Batemans Bay ($20.10, two hours) and Canberra ($44.50, 4½ hours).

Tilba Tilba & Central Tilba

POP 391

The coastal road from Bermagui rejoins the Princes Hwy just before the loop road leading to these outrageously cute National Trust villages in the shadow of Gulaga.

Tilba Tilba is half the size of its singularly named neighbour, 2km down the road. Central Tilba sits in a nook of a valley that has remained virtually unchanged since the 19th century, when it was a gold-mining boomtown – except now the main street is jammed with visitors' cars on weekends. Strolling along Bate St, you'll find a string of cafes, and shops selling the sorts of things you'd expect to find in National Trust villages: fudge, boiled lollies, cheese, speciality teas, ice cream and crafts. Behind the pub, there's a short walk up to a water tower where boulders provide terrific views of Gulaga.

There's information, including a handy town guide, available at the **Bates Emporium** (Bates St; ⊙8am-5pm), which also serves as the petrol station, internet cafe and post office.

◎ Sights & Activities

Tilba Valley Wines   WINERY
(☑02-4473 7308; www.tilbavalleywines.com; 947 Old Hwy; ⊙10am-5pm Oct-Apr, 11am-4pm Wed-Sun May-Jul & Sep) This winery sits on the shores of Lake Corunna, close to Tilba.

ABC Cheese Factory   DAIRY FACTORY
(www.southcoastcheese.com.au; ⊙9am-5pm) On the main street at Central Tilba, ABC Cheese Factory produces cheddar and lets you see how they do it.

✿ Festivals & Events

Tilba Easter Festival   ARTS
(http://www.tilba.com.au/tilbafestival.html) The Tilba streets are all blocked off for the Easter festival, which has lots of music and entertainment and hosts several thousand visitors.

Cobargo Folk Festival   MUSIC
(www.cobargofolkfestival.com) This acclaimed festival is held in historic Cobargo, 20km south towards Bega, in February.

🛏 Sleeping & Eating

For information about the town and accommodation options, visit www.tilba.com.au.

Two-Story B&B   B&B $$
(☑02-4473 7290; www.tilbatwostory.com; Bate St; r from $150) This atmospheric 1894 former postmaster's residence has plenty of charm and a cosy log fire in winter. Some rooms have en suites and all have frilly floral decor. Cooked breakfast included.

WORTH A TRIP

MAGICAL MYSTERY BAY TOUR

South of Narooma, just before the turn-off to the Tilbas, take the road to gorgeously undeveloped **Mystery Bay** and the first pocket of **Eurobodalla National Park**. At the southern end of the main surf beach, a rock formation has created an idyllic **natural swimming pool**. There's a council-run **camp site** (☑0428 622 357; camp sites off-peak/peak $15/25) under the trees. It's so close to the beach you could boil a billy with your tootsies in the sand – well, almost.

THE MOTHER'S STORY

In Yuin tradition, Gulaga (Mt Dromedary, 806m) is the mother and Baranguba (Montague Island) and Najanuga (Little Dromedary) are her two sons. The sons wanted to head out exploring, but Gulaga thought that Najanuga was too young and kept him at her feet. Baranguba went out alone and was eventually cut off by the water.

These places are highly sacred and in 2006 the mountain was designated the first Area of Aboriginal Significance in Australia. The mountain now forms **Gulaga National Park** (4768 hectares) and is jointly managed by the Indigenous community and the NPWS. Its walking tracks are open to all people who treat the mountain with respect. Beginning at Pam's Store in Tilba Tilba you can follow an old **pack-horse trail**. The 11km return walk takes about five hours, but don't miss the loop walk at the summit. There's often rain and mist on the mountain, so come prepared. She's a woman's mountain and local lore has it that it's scornful men that get lost or return with grazes and sprained ankles.

Green Gables B&B **$$**
(☑02-4473 7435; www.greengables.com.au; 269 Corkhill Dr; r from $170) Try to resist the word 'delightful' when describing this gay-friendly B&B. The 1879 cottage offers three attractive rooms with either en suites or private bathrooms and views over the fields.

Bryn at Tilba B&B **$$**
(www.thebrynattilba.com.au; 91 Punkalla-Tilba Rd; r $170-220) Beautiful rooms with dark wood offset by white linen. You won't want to leave.

Premium Cheese Shop CAFE **$**
(☑02-4473 7387; www.southcoastcheese.com; 1 Bate St; mains $5-13; ⊙9am-5pm) Light meals and dozens of locally produced cheeses to take home with you.

ⓘ Getting There & Away

Premier (☑13 34 10; www.premierms.com. au) buses serve the Tilbas daily on the route between Sydney ($59, eight hours) via Narooma ($9, 25 minutes), and Eden ($25, two hours) and Merimbula ($23, 90 minutes).

SAPPHIRE COAST

Not to be outdone by Queensland's Gold Coast, the southernmost part of NSW considers itself precious too. The moniker is apt, with the coast's pristine water revelling in every shade of blue. You won't see a lot of it from the Princes Hwy, but you can feel confident that taking just about any road east will yield a bit of mostly unblemished coast set in rugged surrounds. This is the start of the traditional lands of the Yuin people.

Bermagui

POP 1473

South of the beautiful bird-filled Wallaga Lake and off the Princes Hwy, Bermagui is a pretty fishing port with a main street that hums to the sound of small-town contentment. The vibe is probably due to the eclectic mix of fisherfolk, surfers, alternative lifestylers and Indigenous Australians who call it home. In typical Aussie parlance it's invariably referred to as Bermie.

The purpose-built **information centre** (☑02-6493 3054; www.bermagui.net; Bunga St; ⊙10am-4pm) with its museum and discovery centre was the first sign that tourists had cottoned on to the place. Now there's a new whiz-bang **Fishermen's Wharf** (Lamont St), designed by renowned architect and resident Philip Cox, with all the temptations city visitors expect.

◉ Sights & Activities

There are several walks around Bermagui including a 6km trail north along the coast to **Camel Rock** and a further 2km to **Wallaga Lake**. The route follows **Haywards Beach**, a good surfing spot.

There's also good surfing at Camel Rock and Cuttagee beaches, or you could toss a mullet from the shops and hit **Shelly Beach**, a child-friendly swimming spot. A kilometre's wander around the point will bring you to the **Blue Pool,** a dramatic ocean pool built into the base of the cliffs.

🛏 Sleeping

For property lettings, see **Julie Rutherford Real Estate** (☏02-6493 3444; www.julierutherford.com.au).

Zane Grey Park CAMPGROUND **$**
(Bermagui Tourist Park; ☏02-6493 4382; www.zanegreytouristpark.com.au; Lamont St; powered/unpowered sites from $30/25, cabins $80-225) From its prime position on Dickson's Point, you could throw a frisbee from here into Horseshoe Bay.

★Bermagui Beach Hotel HOTEL **$$**
(☏02-6493 4206; www.bermaguibeachhotel.com.au; 10 Lamont St; dm $40, d/ste $90/125; ✱) At the beach end of the main street, this gorgeous old pub built in 1895 has nine suites, four of them with balcony views towards the beach and Gulaga. Stay here to tap into the local scene. The suites have spas.

Bermagui Motor Inn MOTEL **$$**
(☏02-6493 4311; www.acr.net.au/~bmi/; 38 Lamont St; s/d $99/115; ✱) Right in town, this motel may be a classic, but it's got new carpets, comfy beds and very friendly owners.

Harbourview Motel MOTEL **$$**
(☏02-6493 5213; www.harbourviewmotel.com.au; 56-58 Lamont St; s $130-175, d $140-185; 🛜) Good standard motel rooms close to the water.

🍴 Eating & Drinking

★Bluewave Seafoods FISH & CHIPS **$**
(☏02-6493 5725; www.bluewaveseafood.com.au; Fishermen's Wharf; fish & chips $12; ◷9am-7.30pm Mon-Wed, to 8pm Thu-Sun) Overlooking the marina, this smart takeaway joint is the reincarnation of the original fishermen's co-op. It has deck seats with a view to the trawlers and the lightly battered fish-and-chip box is the South Coast's best. Watch the seagulls!

Il Passaggio ITALIAN **$$**
(☏02-6493 5753; www.ilpassaggio.com.au; Fishermen's Wharf; pizzas $20, mains $27-35; ◷noon-2pm Wed & Thu, noon-2pm & 6-9.30pm Fri-Sun) This suitably hip place with green-felt walls and red-leather seating dishes up a short but authentic Italian menu. There are specials like veal saltimbocca alla Romana, and simpler dishes such as linguini with prawns, chilli, rocket and lemon prevail.

Mimosa Dry Stone MODERN AUSTRALIAN **$$$**
(☏02-6494 0164; www.mimosawines.com.au; 2845 Bermagui-Tathra Rd; mains $30-36, pizza $20-28; ◷noon-3pm Thu-Sun, plus 6-9pm Thu-Sun summer) Midway between Bermagui and Tathra, this winery has a respected restaurant in a stunning building that's often booked out months in advance for weddings. Ring ahead.

Mister Jones CAFE
(www.misterjones.com.au; 1/4 Bunga St; ◷7am-noon Mon-Sat) This anonymous little art studio–cafe would go unnoticed if it weren't for the coffee lovers sitting outside. Mister Jones (or the man purporting to be him) tops his cappuccinos with big chunks of chocolate. The art's cool too.

ℹ Getting There & Away

Premier (☏13 34 10; www.premierms.com.au) stops here once a day on the run between Sydney ($60, 10 hours) via Narooma ($13, 40 minutes), and Eden ($24, 1¾ hours) via Merimbula ($20, 45 minutes).

Bermagui to Merimbula

Mimosa Rocks National Park (www.environment.nsw.gov.au) is a wonderful 5802-hectare coastal park with dense and varied bush, sea caves, lagoons and 20km of beautiful coastline. Check out car-based **camp sites** (☏02-4476 2888; per adult/child $10/5) at Gillards Beach, Picnic Point and Aragunnu Beach. Walk-in camping at Middle Beach is especially lovely, passing under a canopy of tall eucalypts and palms to the deserted surf beach.

Sapphire Coast Ecotours (☏02-6494 0283; www.sapphirecoastecotours.com.au; adult $30-60, child $15-30) runs highly regarded walks exploring the park's varied ecosystems; there's a chance you'll be led by an Aboriginal guide.

South of the main beach at **Cuttagee**, Kullaroo St leads to secluded, bush-lined **Armands Bay**, the only clothing-optional beach on the Sapphire Coast.

Tathra (population 1526) is a sweet little beach town with the Bega River forming a dreamy, undeveloped lagoon at its north end. Dating from 1862, **Tathra Wharf** is the last remaining coastal steamship wharf in the state and a popular place for fishing. Despite offering disposable cups only, **Tathra Beach Pickle Factory** (2/37 Andy Poole Dr; snacks $4-10; ◷8am-2.30pm) is a very worthy grab-and-run deli-cafe with gourmet-food mags.

The 2654-hectare **Bournda National Park** (www.environment.nsw.gov.au; per car $7) has beautiful, empty surf beaches, rugged headlands and walking trails through heath, eucalyptus and tea tree. **Hobart Beach** (☑ 02-6495 5000; camp sites for 2 people $20, additional adult/child $10/5), in the park on the southern shore of peaceful **Wallagoot Lake**, is a great bush-break camp spot with 63 sites and well-maintained facilities.

Merimbula

POP 6873

Spread around the top end of a long, golden beach and an appealing inlet (which locals insist on calling a lake), Merimbula is in thrall to holidaymakers and retirees. The rather unappealing town centre plays second fiddle to the rather pretty inlet and surrounds. In summer, this is one of the few places on the far South Coast that really gets crowded.

◎ Sights

Nature Boardwalk   NATURE RESERVE
Make sure you don't miss this gorgeous addition to the town's natural highs. It follows the estuary 1.75km southwest of the causeway around mangroves, oyster farms and melaleucas. A plethora of birds, mammals and crustaceans are visible as you make your way along.

Merimbula Aquarium   AQUARIUM
(www.merimbulawharf.com.au; Lake St; adult/child $14.50/9; ☉10am-5pm) It might be small, but this aquarium displays the sorts of fish you'll find in the bay. There are 27 tanks and an Oceanarium for sharks and other predators. It's at the dead end of Lake St.

☀ Activities

With several wrecks in the area including the large *Empire Gladstone*, which sank in 1950, diving is especially popular.

Merimbula Marina   CRUISE
(☑ 02-6495 1686; www.merimbulamarina.com; Merimbula jetty; adult $45-69, child $20-40) The small kiosk here runs dolphin- and whale-watching cruises from mid-August to November and other scenic trips at other times of the year. There's also boat hire.

Coastlife Adventures   SURFING
(☑ 02-6494 1122; www.coastlife.com.au; group/private surf lessons $60/110, kayak tours from $60) Morning surf and stand-up paddle lessons

Merimbula

as well as marine kayak tours; the 3½-hour river-kayaking tour ($75) is our pick of the excursions.

Cycle n' Surf   CYCLING, SURFING
(☑ 02-6495 2171; www.cyclensurf.com.au; 1b Marine Pde; bicycle hire per hr/half-day/full day $10/20/30, body boards per half-/full day $10/25, surfboards per half-/full day $40/60) South of the lake, this place hires out bikes, bodyboards and surfboards, and carries out bike repairs.

WILDLIFE AROUND MERIMBULA

You can see whales off the coast near Merimbula from September to November, but there are other possibilities for land-based wildlife-watching as well.

Kangaroos and wallabies Head to Pambula-Merimbula Golf Course and Pambula Beach (follow the signs off the Princes Hwy along the road to Eden); sightings are possible throughout the day, but dusk (from 4.30pm) is the time for almost guaranteed sightings. Sometimes roos even hop down onto the beach itself.

Other native animals An impressive array of echidnas, kangaroos, dingoes, koalas, potoroos and native birds is housed at Potoroo Palace (02-6494 9225; www.potoroopalace.com; 2372 Princes Hwy; adult/child $17/10; 10am-4pm). It's 9km north of Merimbula on the road to Bega.

Waterbirds Walking trails through the Pambula wetlands are incorporated at Panboola (www.panboola.com; Pambula).

Merimbula Divers Lodge DIVING
(02-6495 3611; www.merimbuladiverslodge.com. au; 15 Park St; 1/2 shore dives $69/120 plus $55/99 per dive/day for equipment, PADI-certificate course $579) Offers basic instruction and snorkelling trips and is especially good for beginners.

🛏 Sleeping

Self-contained apartments are usually let on a weekly basis, particularly in summer when rates take a hike. See Getaway Merimbula & Eden (02-6495 2000; www.getawaymerimbula.com.au; The Promenade, Market St).

Wandarrah YHA Lodge HOSTEL $
(02-6495 3503; www.yha.com.au; 8 Marine Pde; dm/s/d/f from $28/55/69/135; @) This clean place, with a good kitchen and hanging-out areas, is near the surf beach and the bus stop. Pick-ups by arrangement, or let the staff know if you're arriving late.

Merimbula Beach Holiday Park CAMPGROUND $
(02-6495 3381; www.merimbulabeachholiday-park.com.au; 2 Short Point Rd; camp sites $29-57,

cabins $98-275; 🖥🏊) Away from the town centre but close to the surf action and vistas of Short Point Beach. Choose a leafy camping spot or a kid-friendly area by the pool.

Coast Resort APARTMENT $$
(02-6495 4930; www.coastresort.com.au; 1 Elizabeth St; 1-/2-/3-bedroom apt from $170/195/240; ❄🖥🏊) You could describe the decor of this huge upmarket apartment-style complex as ultramodern, although stark might be more apt. Still, comfort's not a problem and the two pools, tennis court and proximity to the beach are all very appealing.

Merimbula Lakeview Hotel MOTEL $$
(02-6495 1202; www.merimbulalakeview.com. au; Market St; r from $99; ❄🖥🏊) You could close your eyes and point anywhere in Merimbula and chances are that you'll end up facing a motel indistinguishable from any other. This waterfront establishment stands out for its location. It has moderately stylish rooms with all the motel trimmings. Come summertime, they're close to the hotel's beer garden...which may be good or bad.

🍴 Eating & Drinking

⭐ **Zanzibar** MODERN AUSTRALIAN $$
(02-6495 3636; http://zanzibarmerimbula. com.au; cnr Main & Market Sts; mains $25-33, 2-/3-course meals $65/80; 6-9pm Tue-Sat plus noon-2pm Thu & Fri) Don't leave town without treating yourself at this culinary gem, which prides itself on locally caught seafood and handpicked South Coast produce. There's so much here that's good, with options such as confit pork belly, black pudding and apple cauliflower, and that's just for starters.

Cantina SPANISH $$
(02-6495 1085; 56 Market St; tapas $7-15, mains $25-30; 11.30am-late Mon-Sat, 2.30-10pm Sun) This atmospheric place in the centre of town dishes up tapas plates, while the two-course lunch with a glass of wine for $25 is great value.

Waterfront Cafe CAFE, SEAFOOD $$
(02-6495 7684; www.thewaterfrontcafe.net.au; Shop 1, The Promenade; mains $19-30; 8am-10pm) One of few Merimbula eateries to take advantage of the town's lakeside location, the Waterfront is a local institution and recommended at any time of the day. Seafood dominates the menu and the oysters are among the best on the South Coast.

ℹ️ Information

NPWS Office (📞 02-6495 5000; www.environ-ment.nsw.gov.au; cnr Merimbula & Sapphire Coast Drs; ⏰ 9am-4pm Mon-Fri) Provides information on bushwalking.

Visitor Centre (📞 02-6495 1129; www.sap-phirecoast.com.au; cnr Market & Beach Sts; ⏰ 9am-5pm)

ℹ️ Getting There & Around

AIR

Merimbula Airport (MIM; 📞 02-6495 4211; www.merimbulaairport.com.au; Arthur Kaine Dr) is 1km out of town on the road to Pambula. **Rex** (📞 13 17 13; www.rex.com.au) flies daily to Melbourne (from $143, 90 minutes, one to two daily) and a couple of times weekly to Moruya.

BUS

Buses stop outside the Commonwealth Bank on Market St. **Premier** (📞 13 34 10; www.premierms.com.au) has two daily buses to Sydney ($69, 8½ hours) via Narooma ($25, two hours) and one to Melbourne ($58, 8¼ hours). **NSW TrainLink** (📞 13 22 32; www.nswtrainlink.info) runs a daily bus to Canberra ($40.20, four hours).

Eden

POP 3043

The first town north of the Victorian border, Eden's a little sleepy place where the only bustle you're likely to find is down at the wharf when the fishing boats come in. Pretty beaches run either side of the town's knobbly peninsula. In the hinterland, there are stirring beaches, national parks and wilderness areas.

For possibly thousands of years this bay has been the site of extraordinary interactions that have taken place between humans and whales. Migrating humpback whales and southern right whales pass so close to the coast that whale-watching experts consider this to be one of the best places in Australia for people to observe these magnificent creatures. Often they can be seen feeding or resting in Twofold Bay during their southern migration back to Antarctic waters.

👁 Sights & Activities

Killer Whale Museum MUSEUM
(www.killerwhalemuseum.com.au; 94 Imlay St; adult/child $9/2.50; ⏰ 9.15am-3.45pm Mon-Sat, 11.15am-3.45pm Sun) Established in 1931, the museum's main purpose is to preserve the skeleton of Old Tom, a killer whale and local legend.

Whale Lookout LOOKOUT
Among the many options to spot Moby and his mates is at the base of Bass St. When whales are spotted the Killer Whale Museum sounds a siren.

Cat Balou Cruises CRUISE
(📞 0427 962 027; www.catbalou.com.au; Main Wharf; adult/child $75/60) This crew operates 3½-hour whale-spotting voyages in October and November. At other times of the year, dolphins and seals can usually be seen during the two-hour bay cruise (adult/child $35/20).

Sapphire Coast Marine Discovery Centre HIKING, SNORKELLING
(📞 02-6496 1699; www.sapphirecoastdiscovery.com.au; Main Wharf; adult/child $7/2; ⏰ 10am-3pm Wed-Sat) See the sea through a rocky reef aquarium at this newish addition to town and sign up for a rocky shore ramble (adult/child $10/8) or group snorkelling trip ($25).

Ocean Wilderness KAYAKING
(📞 0405 529 214; www.oceanwilderness.com.au; 4/6hr tours from $85/130) Sea-kayaking trips through Twofold Bay and to Ben Boyd National Park and a full-day excursion to Davidson Whaling Station.

🎉 Festivals & Events

Whale Festival WHALES
(www.edenwhalefestival.com.au) Eden comes alive at the start of November with the annual Whale Festival, with the typical carnival, street parade and stalls plus some innovative local events such as the Slimy Mackerel Throw.

🛌 Sleeping

Great Southern Inn HOTEL $
(📞 02-6496 1515; www.greatsoutherninn.com.au; 121 Imlay St; dm/s/d from $30/70/90) This friendly place has good-value shared pub rooms and nicely renovated backpacker accommodation. The pub grub downstairs is hearty and the rear deck is a winner.

Eden Tourist Park CAMPGROUND $
(📞 02-6496 1139; www.edentouristpark.com.au; Aslings Beach Rd; unpowered/powered sites from $25/28, cabins from $70) Serenely situated on the spit separating Aslings Beach from Lake Curalo, this large, well-kept park echoes with birdsong from its sheltering trees.

★ **Seahorse Inn**   BOUTIQUE HOTEL **$$**
(☑ 02-6496 1361; www.seahorseinn.com.au; d $175-349; ❄ 🐾) At Boydtown, 6km south of Eden, the Seahorse Inn overlooks Twofold Bay. It's a lavish boutique hotel with all the trimmings.

Twofold Bay Motor Inn   MOTEL **$$**
(☑ 02-6496 3111; www.twofoldbaymotorinn.com. au; 164-166 Imlay St; r $110-180; ❄ 🐾 ☒) Substantial rooms, some with water views, are the norm at this centrally located motel. There's also a tiny indoor pool.

Crown & Anchor Inn   B&B **$$$**
(☑ 02-6496 1017; www.crownandanchoreden.com. au; 239 Imlay St; r $180-220; 🐾) Awesomely atmospheric, this historic house (1845) has been beautifully restored and furnished with the likes of four-poster beds and clawfoot baths. There's a lovely view over Twofold Bay from the back patio.

✖ Eating

The following eateries are located on the Main Wharf (253 Imlay St) at the bottom of town.

Taste of Eden   CAFE **$$**
(Main Wharf; mains $14-29; ⊘ 8am-3pm) With decor that has been pulled straight out of Davy Jones' locker, this brightly painted cafe serves delicious local seafood (among other dishes) without any airs or graces.

Wharfside Café   CAFE **$$**
(www.wharfsidecafe.com.au; Main Wharf; mains $11-27; ⊘ 8am-3pm) Decent breakfasts, strong coffees and tables that offer views of the harbour make this a good place to start the day or pass a lazy afternoon.

❶ Information

Visitor Centre (☑ 02-6496 1953; www.visit-eden.com.au; Mitchell St; ⊘ 9am-5pm Mon-Sat, 10am-4pm Sun)

❶ Getting There & Away

Premier (☑ 13 34 10; www.premierms.com.au) has two daily bus sevices that run to Wollongong ($69, eight hours) and Sydney ($71, nine hours), and one bus service to Melbourne ($58, eight hours). **NSW TrainLink** (☑ 13 22 32; www. nswtrainlink.info) runs a daily bus service to Canberra ($42.15, 4½ hours).

Ben Boyd National Park

The wilderness barely pauses for breath before starting again at 10,485-hectare Ben Boyd National Park. Boyd was an entrepreneur who failed spectacularly in his efforts to build an empire around Eden in 1850. This park protects some of his follies, along with a dramatic coastline peppered with isolated beaches. It's split into two sections, with Eden squeezed in between.

The southern section is accessed by mainly gravel roads (per vehicle $7) leading off sealed Edrom Rd, which leaves the Princes Hwy 19km south of Eden. At its southern tip, the elegant 1883 **Green Cape Lightstation** (☑ 02-6495 5555; www.nationalparks.nsw. gov.au; Green Cape Rd; cottages midweek/weekend from $200/280) copes with its isolation by gazing out at awesome views. There are **tours** (adult/child $7/5; ⊘ 1pm & 3pm Fri-Sun) or, if you want to share the seclusion, you can spend the night in a lavishly restored keepers' cottage (sleeps six).

Eleven kilometres along Edrom Rd there's a turn-off to the historic **Davidson Whaling Station** on Twofold Bay where you can have a picnic in the rustic gardens of **Loch Gaira Cottage** (1896). Not much whaling paraphernalia remains, but interpretive signs tell the story. It's hard to imagine that until 1929 the peace of this place was rent by the agonised groans of dying whales.

Further along is the turn-off for **Boyd's Tower**, an impressive structure indulgently built in the late 1840s with sandstone shipped from Sydney. It was intended to be a lighthouse, but the government wouldn't give Boyd permission to operate it.

The 31km **Light to Light Walk** links Boyd's wannabe lighthouse to the real one at Green Cape. There are **camp sites** (☑ 02-6495 5000; sites for 2 people $20, per additional adult/child $10/5) along the route at **Saltwater Creek** and **Bittangabee Bay**. Both have vehicle access.

The northern section of the park can be accessed from the Princes Hwy north of Eden. From Haycock Point, where there are good views, a walking trail leads to a headland overlooking the Pambula River. Another good – if short (1km) – walk is to the **Pinnacles**.

Melbourne & Coastal Victoria

Why Go?

From windswept beaches to cosmopolitan seaside towns and legendary surfing spots, Victoria's coastline has stunning vistas, cool-climate wineries and the culture-packed city of Melbourne. It's a diverse coast; fairy penguins march up and down beaches in the popular tourist destination of Phillip Island, while Victoria's west coast faces on to Bass Strait and attracts surfers and those searching for the iconic Twelve Apostles.

Heading up the southeast coast from the hiking paradise of Wilsons Promontory is a long, cruisy expanse of beach that meets up with a popular, activity-filled lakes system around Lakes Entrance (Australia's largest inland waterway system). There are more stunning national parks on the approach to the Victoria–New South Wales border.

Best Places to Eat

➡ Metung Galley (p271)
➡ Merrijig Kitchen (p256)
➡ MoVida (p226)
➡ Brae (p249)

Best Places to Stay

➡ Wilderness Retreat (p267)
➡ Adobe Mudbrick Flats (p277)
➡ Ovolo (p223)
➡ Beacon Point Ocean View Villas (p251)

When to Go
Melbourne

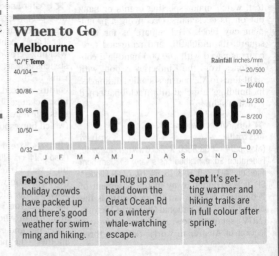

Feb School-holiday crowds have packed up and there's good weather for swimming and hiking.

Jul Rug up and head down the Great Ocean Rd for a wintery whale-watching escape.

Sept It's getting warmer and hiking trails are in full colour after spring.

MELBOURNE

POP 5.5 MILLION

Stylish, arty Melbourne is a city that's proud of its place as Australia's cultural capital. Coffee, food, art and fashion are taken seriously, but that doesn't mean they're only for those in the know; all you need to eat well, go bar-hopping and/or shopping is a bit of cash and a deft ability to find hidden stairways and explore graffiti-covered laneways.

In many ways, it's the indie scene that sets Melbourne's tone – it can be spotted mainly in the CBD, St Kilda, Fitzroy, Collingwood, Brunswick and Northcote, but ekes out a living in most nooks and crannies in the city's inner suburbs.

Splitting the northern suburbs of Fitzroy, Collingwood and Carlton from its southern sisters including Prahran and South Yarra is the very brown Yarra River. There's a slight cultural divide, too, though sport knows no boundaries and Melburnians are intoxicatingly loud-voiced about AFL football (footy), horse racing or cricket, depending on the season.

◎ Sights

◎ Central Melbourne

★**Federation Square** LANDMARK
(Map p214; www.fedsquare.com.au; cnr Flinders & Swanston Sts; 🚊1, 3, 5, 6, 8, 16, 64, 67, 72, 🚉Flinders St) While it's taken some time, Melburnians have finally come to embrace Federation Sq, accepting it as the congregation place it was meant to be – somewhere to celebrate, protest, watch major sporting events or hang out on its deckchairs. Occupying a prominent city block, 'Fed Square' is far from square: its undulating and patterned forecourt is paved with 460,000 hand-laid cobblestones from the Kimberley region, with sight-lines to Melbourne's iconic landmarks; its buildings are clad in a fractal-patterned reptilian skin.

★**Ian Potter Centre: NGV Australia** GALLERY
(Map p214; ☑03-8620 2222; www.ngv.vic.gov.au; Federation Sq; exhibition costs vary; ⊙10am-5pm Tue-Sun; 🚊1, 3, 5, 6, 8, 16, 64, 67, 72, 🚉Flinders St) FREE Hidden away in the basement of Federation Sq, the Ian Potter Centre is the other half of the National Gallery of Victoria (NGV), set up to showcase its impressive collection of Australian works. Set over three

levels, it's a mix of permanent (free) and temporary (ticketed) exhibitions, comprising paintings, decorative arts, photography, prints, sculpture and fashion. There's also a great museum gift shop. Free tours are conducted daily at 11am, noon, 1pm and 2pm.

Australian Centre for the Moving Image MUSEUM
(ACMI; Map p214; ☑03-8663 2200; www.acmi.net.au; Federation Sq; ⊙10am-6pm; 🚊1, 3, 5, 6, 8, 16, 64, 67, 72, 🚉Flinders St) FREE Managing to educate, enthrall and entertain in equal parts, ACMI is a visual feast that pays homage to Australian cinema and TV, offering an insight into the modern-day Australian psyche perhaps like no other museum can. Its floating screens don't discriminate against age, with TV shows, games and movies on-call – making it a great place to waste a day watching TV and not feel guilty about it. Free tours are conducted daily at 11am and 2.30pm.

★**Birrarung Marr** PARK
(Map p214; btwn Federation Sq & the Yarra River; 🚊1, 3, 5, 6, 8, 16, 64, 67, 72, 🚉Flinders St) The three-terraced Birrarung Marr is a welcome addition to Melbourne's patchwork of parks and gardens, featuring grassy knolls, river promenades, a thoughtful planting of indigenous flora and great viewpoints of the city and the river. There's also a scenic route to the Melbourne Cricket Ground (MCG; p213) via the 'talking' William Barak Bridge – listen out for songs, words and sounds representing Melbourne's cultural diversity as you walk.

★**Hosier Lane** STREET
(Map p214; Hosier Lane; 🚊75, 70) Melbourne's most celebrated laneway for street art, Hosier Lane's cobbled length draws camera-wielding crowds snapping edgy graffiti, stencils and art installations. Subject matter runs to the mostly political and counter-culture, spiced with irreverent humour; pieces change almost daily (not even a Banksy is safe here). Be sure to see Rutledge Lane (which horseshoes around Hosier), too.

Flinders Street Station HISTORIC BUILDING
(Map p214; cnr Flinders & Swanston Sts) If ever there was a true symbol of the city, Flinders Street Station would have to be it. Built in 1854, it was Melbourne's first railway station, and you'd be hard-pressed to find a Melburnian who hasn't uttered the phrase 'Meet me under the clocks' at one time or another (the popular rendezvous spot is

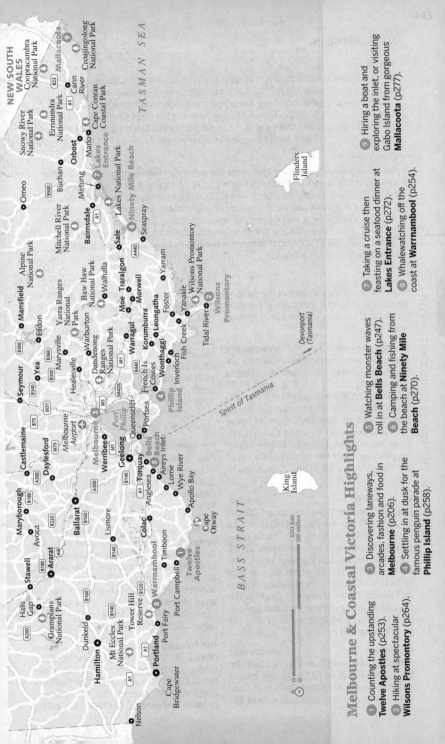

Melbourne & Coastal Victoria Highlights

① Counting the upstanding **Twelve Apostles** (p253).

② Hiking at spectacular **Wilsons Promontory** (p264).

③ Discovering laneways, arcades, fashion and food in **Melbourne** (p206).

④ Settling in at dusk for the famous penguin parade at **Phillip Island** (p258).

⑤ Watching monster waves roll in at **Bells Beach** (p247).

⑥ Camping and fishing from the beach at **Ninety Mile Beach** (p270).

⑦ Taking a cruise then feasting on a seafood dinner at **Lakes Entrance** (p272).

⑧ Whalewatching off the coast at **Warrnambool** (p254).

⑨ Hiring a boat and exploring the inlet, or visiting Gabo Island from gorgeous **Mallacoota** (p277).

MELBOURNE IN...

Two Days

Check out the Ian Potter Centre: NGV Australia (p206) and ACMI (p206) museums, then enjoy lunch at MoVida (p226). Join a walking tour to see Melbourne's street art (p220) then chill out at a **rooftop bar** until it's time to join an evening kayaking tour (p219) of the Yarra River. Day two, stroll along Birrarung Marr (p206) and into the Royal Botanic Gardens (p217), then head to the Queen Vic Market. Catch a tram to **St Kilda** and stroll along the beach before propping up a bar in lively **Acland St** for the evening.

One Week

Spend a couple of hours at the Melbourne Museum (p213) and then revive with a coffee at D.O.C (p228) in Lygon St. Head to **Fitzroy** and **Collingwood** and shop along **Gertrude St** before feasting at Cutler & Co (p228). Back in the city centre, wander through Chinatown and check out Ned Kelly's armour at the State Library before grabbing some dumplings for dinner. Spend the rest of the week shopping, cafe-hopping and people-watching in busy **Prahran** and **Windsor**. In winter, catch a footy game at the MCG (p213) before drinks at one of the city's **laneway bars**. Make sure to save time to hit Mamasita (p226) for tacos and the Tote (p234) in Collingwood for live music.

located at the front entrance of the station). Stretching along the Yarra, it's a beautiful neoclassical building topped with a striking octagonal dome.

Young & Jackson's
HISTORIC BUILDING

(Map p214; www.youngandjacksons.com.au; cnr Flinders & Swanston Sts; ⊙11am-late; 🚇Tourist Shuttle, 🚋City Circle, 1, 3, 5, 6, 8, 16, 64, 67, 72, 🚆Flinders St) Across the street from Flinders Street Station is a pub known less for its beer (served up since 1861) than its iconic nude painting of the teenaged *Chloe*, painted by Jules Joseph Lefebvre. Chloe's yearning gaze, cast over her shoulder and out of the frame, was a hit at the Paris Salon of 1875.

Block Arcade
ARCHITECTURE

(Map p214; www.theblockarcade.com.au; 282 Collins St; 🚋109) The top end of Collins St (aka the 'Paris end') is lined with plane trees, grand buildings and luxe boutiques, giving it its moniker. The Block Arcade, which runs between Collins and Elizabeth Sts, was built in 1891 and features etched-glass ceilings and mosaic floors. Doing 'the Block' (walking around the block) was a popular pastime in 19th-century Melbourne, as it was the place to shop and be seen.

Chinatown
NEIGHBOURHOOD

(Map p214; Little Bourke St, btwn Spring & Swanston Sts; 🚋1, 3, 5, 6, 8, 16, 64, 67, 72) Chinese miners arrived in search of the 'new gold mountain' in the 1850s and settled in this strip of Lit-

tle Bourke St, now flanked by traditional red archways. The **Chinese Museum** (Map p214; 🖋03-9662 2888; www.chinesemuseum.com.au; 22 Cohen Pl; adult/child $8/6; ⊙10am-5pm) here does a wonderful job of putting their experiences into context with five floors of displays, including artefacts from the gold-rush era, dealings under xenophobic White Australia policy and the stunning 63m-long, 200kg Millennium Dragon that bends around the building; in full flight it needs eight people just to hold up its head alone.

Parliament House
HISTORIC BUILDING

(Map p214; 🖋03-9651 8568; www.parliament.vic.gov.au; Spring St; ⊙tours 9.30am, 10.30am, 11.30am, 1.30pm, 2.30pm, 3.45pm Mon-Fri; 🚋City Circle, 86, 96, 🚆Parliament) The grand steps of Victoria's parliament (c 1856) are often dotted with slow-moving, tulle-wearing brides smiling for the camera, or placard-holding protesters doing the same. The only way to visit inside is on a tour, where you'll see exuberant use of ornamental plasterwork, stencilling and gilt full of gold-rush era pride and optimism. Building began with the two main chambers: the lower house (now the legislative assembly) and the upper house (now the legislative council).

Old Treasury Building
MUSEUM

(Map p214; 🖋03-9651 2233; www.oldtreasurybuilding.org.au; Spring St; ⊙10am-4pm, closed Sat; 🚋112, 🚆Parliament) **FREE** The fine neoclassical architecture of the Old Treasury (c 1862), designed by JJ Clarke, is a telling mix of hubris and functionality. The basement vaults were built to house the millions of pounds worth of loot that came from the Victorian goldfields and now feature multimedia displays telling stories from the gold rush. Also downstairs is the charmingly redolent reconstruction of the 1920s caretaker's residence, which beautifully reveals what life in Melbourne was like in the early part of last century.

Old Melbourne Gaol   HISTORIC BUILDING
(Map p214; ☑03-8663 7228; www.oldmelbournegaol.com.au; 337 Russell St; adult/child/family $25/14/55; ☺9.30am-5pm; ☒24, 30, City Circle) Built in 1841, this forbidding bluestone prison was in operation until 1929. It's now one of Melbourne's most popular museums, where you can tour the tiny, bleak cells. Around 135 people were hanged here, including Ned Kelly, Australia's most infamous bushranger, in 1880; one of his death masks is on display.

★ Queen Victoria Market   MARKET
(Map p214; www.qvm.com.au; 513 Elizabeth St; ☺6am-2pm Tue & Thu, to 5pm Fri, to 3pm Sat, 9am-4pm Sun; ☒ Tourist Shuttle, ☒19, 55, 57, 59) With over 600 traders, the Vic Market is the largest open-air market in the southern hemisphere and attracts thousands of shoppers. It's where Melburnians sniff out fresh produce among the booming cries of spruiking fishmongers and fruit-and-veg vendors. The wonderful deli hall (with art deco features) is lined with everything from soft cheeses, wines and Polish sausages to Greek dips, truffle oil and kangaroo biltong.

Koorie Heritage Trust   CULTURAL CENTRE
(Map p214; ☑03-8622 2600; www.koorieheritagetrust.com; 295 King St; gold-coin donation, tours $15; ☺9am-5pm Mon-Fri; ☒24, 30, ☒Flagstaff) ✐ Devoted to southeastern Aboriginal culture, this cultural centre displays interesting artefacts and oral history. Its gallery spaces show a variety of contemporary and traditional work, a model scar tree at the centre's heart, and a permanent chronological display of Victorian Koorie history. Behind the scenes, significant objects are carefully preserved; replicas that can be touched by visitors are used in the displays. It's in the process of relocating, so check the website for details.

Sea Life Melbourne Aquarium   AQUARIUM
(Map p214; ☑03-9923 5999; www.melbourneaquarium.com.au; cnr Flinders & King Sts; adult/child/family $38/22/93; ☺9.30am-6pm, last entry 5pm; ☒70, 75) This aquarium is home to rays, gropers and sharks, all of which cruise around a 2.2-million-litre tank, watched closely by visitors in a see-through tunnel. See the penguins in icy 'Antarctica' or get up close to one of Australia's largest saltwater crocs in the crocodile lair. Divers are thrown to the sharks three times a day; for between $210 and $300 you can join them. Admission tickets are cheaper online.

★ State Library of Victoria   LIBRARY
(Map p214; ☑03-8664 7000; www.slv.vic.gov.au; 328 Swanston St; ☺10am-9pm Mon-Thu, to 6pm Fri-Sun; ☒1, 3, 5, 6, 8, 16, 64, 67, 72, ☒Melbourne Central) A big player in Melbourne's achievement of being named Unesco City of Literature in 2008, the State Library has been at the forefront of Melbourne's literary scene since it opened in 1854. With over two million books in its collection, it's a great place to browse. Its epicentre, the octagonal **La Trobe Reading Room**, was completed in 1913; its reinforced-concrete dome was the largest of its kind in the world and its natural light illuminates the ornate plasterwork and the studious Melbourne writers who come here to pen their works. The library has several exhibitions on display, providing a fascinating story to Melbourne's history. Its most notable item is **Ned Kelly's armour**.

◉ Southbank & Docklands

Southbank, once a gritty industrial site, sits directly across the Yarra from Flinders St. Behind the Southgate shopping mall is the city's major arts precinct, including the NGV International and Arts Centre. Back down by the river, the promenade stretches to the Crown Casino & Entertainment Complex, a self-proclaimed 'world of entertainment', pulling in visitors 24/7. To the city's west lies Docklands.

NGV International   GALLERY
(Map p214; ☑03-8662 1555; www.ngv.vic.gov.au; 180 St Kilda Rd; exhibition costs vary; ☺10am-5pm Wed-Mon; ☒ Tourist Shuttle, ☒1, 3, 5, 6, 8, 16, 64, 67, 72) **FREE** Beyond the water-wall facade you'll find an expansive collection set over three levels, covering international art that

Melbourne

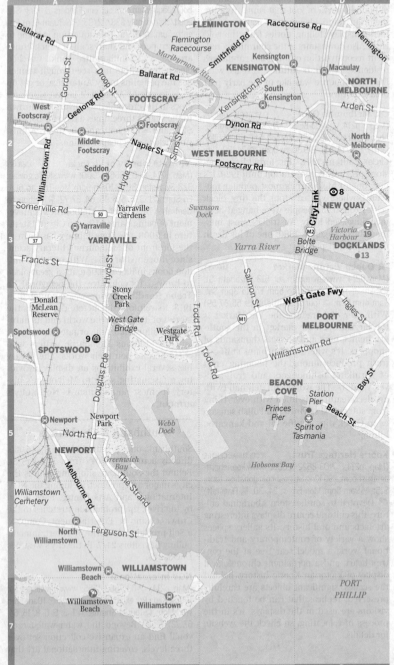

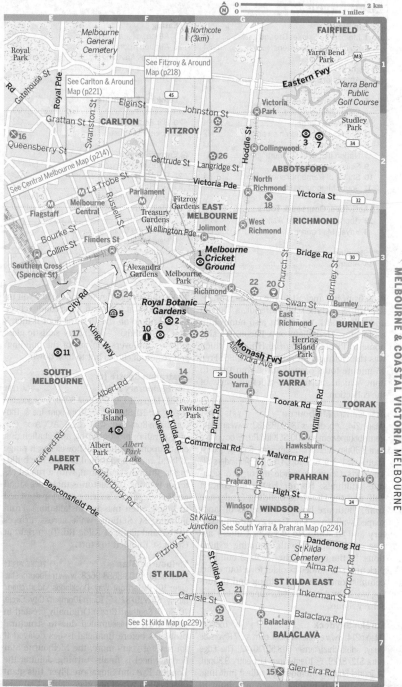

MELBOURNE & COASTAL VICTORIA MELBOURNE

0 — 2 km
N
0 — 1 miles

FAIRFIELD

Royal Park

Melbourne General Cemetery

Yarra Bend Park

M3

Eastern Fwy

Yarra Bend Public Golf Course

See Fitzroy & Around Map (p218)

Northcote (3km)

See Carlton & Around Map (p221)

Studley Park

34

Elgin St

45

Grattan St

CARLTON

Johnston St

Victoria Park

Swanston St

Gatehouse St

Royal Park

Royal Pde

Rd

16

Queensberry St

See Central Melbourne Map (p214)

FITZROY

27

Collingwood

3 7

ABBOTSFORD

Gertrude St

Langridge St

26

Hoddle St

La Trobe St

Parliament

Victoria Pde

North Richmond

Victoria St

32

Melbourne Central

Russell St

Fitzroy Gardens

EAST MELBOURNE

18

RICHMOND

Flagstaff

Treasury Gardens

Wellington Pde

West Richmond

Bourke St

Collins St

Flinders St

Jolimont

Bridge Rd

30

Southern Cross (Spencer St)

Alexandra Gardens

Melbourne Park

1 Melbourne Cricket Ground

Church St

Burnley St

City Rd

24

Richmond

22 20

Swan St

Burnley

5

Royal Botanic Gardens

East Richmond

BURNLEY

17

10 6 2

Kings Way

11

12 25

Herring Island Park

SOUTH MELBOURNE

Albert Rd

14

29

Monash Fwy

Alexandra Ave

SOUTH YARRA

South Yarra

Toorak Rd

Williams Rd

TOORAK

Gunn Island

4

Albert Park

Albert Park Lake

Queens Rd

St Kilda Rd

Fawkner Park

Punt Rd

Commercial Rd

Malvern Rd

Hawksburn

Toorak

ALBERT PARK

Kerferd Rd

Canterbury Rd

Chapel St

Prahran

PRAHRAN

High St

Toorak

24

Beaconsfield Pde

Windsor

WINDSOR

25

St Kilda Junction

See South Yarra & Prahran Map (p224)

Fitzroy St

ST KILDA

St Kilda Rd

Dandenong Rd

St Kilda Cemetery

Alma Rd

ST KILDA EAST

Inkerman St

Orrong Rd

21

Carlisle St

23

Balaclava Rd

Balaclava

BALACLAVA

See St Kilda Map (p229)

15

Glen Eira Rd

Melbourne

runs from the ancient to the contemporary. Key works include a Rembrandt, a Tiepolo and a Bonnard. You might also bump into a Monet, a Modigliani or a Bacon. It's also home to Picasso's *Weeping Woman*, which was the victim of an art heist in 1986. Free 45-minute tours occur hourly from 11am to 2pm, which alternate to different parts of the collection.

Arts Centre Melbourne   ARTS CENTRE

(Map p214; ☑ bookings 1300 182 183; www.artscentremelbourne.com.au; 100 St Kilda Rd; ⊗ box office 9am-8.30pm Mon-Fri, 10am-5pm Sat; ☐ Tourist Shuttle, ☐ 1, 3, 5, 6, 8, 16, 64, 67, 72, ☐ Flinders St) The Arts Centre is made up of two separate buildings: **Hamer Hall** (the concert hall) and the **theatres building** (under the spire). Both are linked by a series of landscaped walkways. The **George Adams Gallery** and **St Kilda Road Foyer Gallery** are free gallery spaces with changing exhibitions. In the foyer of the theatres building, pick up a self-guided booklet for a tour of art commissioned for the building and including works by Arthur Boyd, Sidney Nolan and Jeffrey Smart.

Eureka Skydeck   LOOKOUT

(Map p214; www.eurekaskydeck.com.au; 7 Riverside Quay; adult/child/family $18.50/10/42, The Edge extra $12/8/29; ⊗ 10am-10pm, last entry 9.30pm; ☐ Tourist Shuttle) Melbourne's tallest building, the 297m-high Eureka Tower, was built in

2006, and a wild elevator ride takes you up its 88 floors in less than 40 seconds (check out the photo on the elevator floor if there's time). The 'Edge' – a slightly sadistic glass cube – cantilevers you out of the building; you've got no choice but to look down.

**Australian Centre for
Contemporary Art**   GALLERY

(ACCA; Map p210; ☑ 03-9697 9999; www.accaonline.org.au; 111 Sturt St; ⊗ 10am-5pm Tue & Thu-Sun, 10am-8pm Wed; ☐ 1) **FREE** ACCA is one of Australia's most exciting and challenging contemporary galleries, showcasing a range of local and international artists. The building is, fittingly, sculptural, with a rusted exterior evoking the factories that once stood on the site, and a soaring interior designed to house often massive installations. From Flinders St Station, walk across Princes Bridge and along St Kilda Rd. Turn right at Grant St, then left to Sturt.

Melbourne Star   FERRIS WHEEL

(Map p210; ☑ 03-8688 9688; www.melbournestar.com; 101 Waterfront Way, Docklands; adult/child/family $32/19/82; ⊗ 10am-10pm; ☐ City Circle, 70, 86, ☐ Southern Cross) Originally erected in 2009, then disassembled due to structural problems before financial issues delayed it for several years more, the Melbourne Star Ferris wheel is finally turning. Joining the London Eye and Singapore Flyer, this giant observation wheel has glass cabins that take you up 120m for 360-degree views of the city, Port Philip Bay and even further afield to Geelong. Rides last 30 minutes.

East Melbourne & Richmond

East Melbourne's sedate wide streets are lined with grand double-fronted Victorian terraces and Italianate mansions. On the other side of perpetually clogged Punt Rd/Hoddle St (across from the Melbourne Cricket Ground) is the suburb of Richmond, which has some good pubs, a vibrant stretch of Vietnamese restaurants along Victoria St and clothing outlets along Bridge Rd.

★Melbourne Cricket Ground   STADIUM

(MCG; Map p210; ☑03-9657 8888; www.mcg.org.au; Brunton Ave; tour adult/child/family $20/10/50; ☺tours 10am-3pm; ☒Tourist Shuttle, ☒48, 70, 75, ☒Jolimont) With a capacity of 100,000 people, the 'G' is one of the world's great sporting venues, hosting cricket in the summer, and AFL footy in the winter – for many Australians it's considered hallowed ground. Make it to a game if you can (highly recommended), but otherwise you can still make your pilgrimage on non-match-day tours that take you through the stands, media and coaches' areas, change rooms and out onto the ground (though unfortunately not beyond the boundary).

National Sports Museum   MUSEUM

(Map p210; ☑03-9657 8856; www.nsm.org.au; MCG, Olympic Stand, Gate 3; adult/concession/family $20/10/50, with MCG tour $30/15/60; ☺10am-5pm) Hidden away in the bowels of the Melbourne Cricket Ground, this sports museum features five permanent exhibitions focusing on Australia's favourite sports and celebrates historic sporting moments. Kids will love the interactive sports section where they can test their footy, cricket or netball skills, among other sports.

Fitzroy Gardens   PARK

(Map p214; www.fitzroygardens.com; Wellington Pde, btwn Lansdowne & Albert Sts; ☒Tourist Shuttle, ☒75, ☒Jolimont) The city drops away suddenly just east of Spring St, giving way to Melbourne's beautiful backyard, the Fitzroy Gardens. The stately avenues lined with English elms, flower beds, expansive lawns, strange fountains and a creek are a short stroll from town.

The highlight is **Cooks' Cottage** (Map p214; ☑03-9419 5766; www.cookscottage.com.au;

adult/child/family $5/2.50/13.50; ☺9am-5pm), shipped brick by brick from Yorkshire and reconstructed in 1934 (the cottage actually belonged to the navigator's parents). It's decorated in mid-18th-century style, with an exhibition about Captain James Cook's eventful, if controversial, voyages to the Southern Ocean.

Fitzroy & Around

Fitzroy, Melbourne's first suburb, had a reputation for vice and squalor. Today, despite a long bout of gentrification, it's still where creative people meet up, though now it's more to 'do' lunch and blog about it before checking out the offerings at local 'one-off' boutiques and vintage shops.

Adjoining Collingwood is hipster central with Smith St and Gertrude St both Melbourne's streets of the moment. Smith St has some rough edges, though talk is more of its smart restaurants, cafes and boutiques rather than its down-and-out days of old. It's still a social spot for Aboriginal people.

To the north is the leafy residential area of North Fitzroy, which centres around the coolsie hang-out of Edinburgh Gardens. Further along is gentrified Northcote; its sleepy demeanour shifts once the sun goes down and fun-seekers hit High St.

Abbotsford Convent   HISTORIC SITE

(Map p210; ☑03-9415 3600; www.abbotsfordconvent.com.au; 1 St Heliers St, Abbotsford; tours $15; ☺7.30am-10pm; ☒200, 201, 207, ☒Victoria Park) **FREE** The nuns are long gone at this former convent, which dates back to 1861, so don't worry, no one will ask if you've been to Mass lately. Today its rambling collection of ecclesiastic architecture is home to a thriving arts community of galleries, studios, cafes and bars, spread over nearly 7 hectares of riverside land. Tours of the complex are run at 2pm every Sunday.

Carlton & Around

Lygon St reaches out through North Carlton to Brunswick. Here you'll find a vibrant mix of students, long-established families and newly arrived migrants. The central Brunswick artery, the traffic-clogged Sydney Rd, is packed with Middle Eastern restaurants and grocery shops. Lygon St in East Brunswick just keeps getting more fashionable, lined with quality restaurants and intimate bars.

Central Melbourne

MELBOURNE & COASTAL VICTORIA MELBOURNE

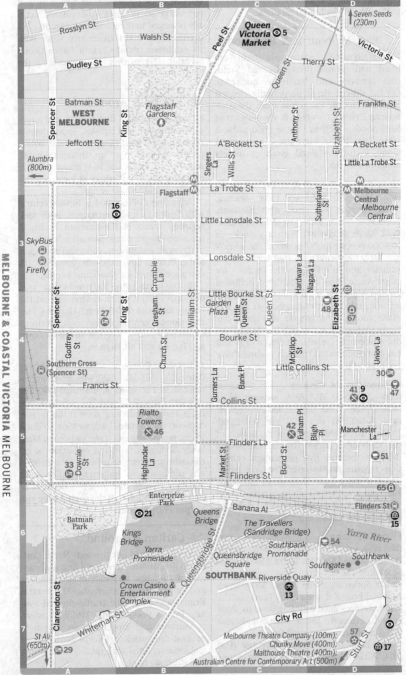

N 0 | 500 m
0 | 0.25 miles

CARLTON

Carlton Gardens North

Melbourne Museum

Royal Exhibition Building

RMIT

Queensberry St

Swanston St

Cardigan St

Earl St

Lygon St

Drummond St

Rathdowne St

Nicholson St

RMIT

Bowen St

Russell St

18 🏛

35 ✪

Mackenzie St

Victoria St

Carlton Gardens South

Gertrude St

La Trobe St

See Carlton & Around Map (p221)

Swanston St

◉ Melbourne Central

✪**State Library**
6 of Victoria

Davisons Pl

58 ✪

Exploration La

Little Lonsdale St

Spring St

St Vincents Hospital

Fitzroy St

Victoria Pde

Red Cape La

QV
Square

Artemis
La

Hayward La

Bennetts
La

Jones La

Lonsdale St

See Fitzroy & Around Map (p218)

37 ✪ **52** ⊗
⊗ **36**

CHINATOWN

11 🏛

59 ✪

Parliament Ⓜ

Parliament Gardens

St Patrick's Cathedral

10 ⊙

La Trobe Pl

Russell St

Coverlid Pl

61 ⊙

Little Bourke St

Exhibition St

45 ⊗
55 ⊙

34 ⊙ **62** ⊙

39 ⊗

Bourke St

20 🏛

Royal La

Russell Pl

49 🏛

Little Collins St

Alfred Pl

53 ⊗ **Parliament** Ⓜ

28 ⊙

32 ⊙

Cathedral Pl

St Andrews Pl

Melbourne
Town Hall

60 🏛
⊗

56 ✪

Collins St

Ⓜ **Parliament**

19 🏛

Treasury Pl

St Patrick's Cathedral ♰

City
Square

Regent Pl

63 ✪

George Pde

43 ⊗

Spring St

Treasury Gardens

Lansdowne St

Fitzroy Gardens

14 ⊙

Flinders La

ACDC
La

38 ⊗ ⊙
66 ⊗

25 ⊗

St Paul's
Cathedral

64 ⊙
22 🏛

♰

44 ⊗

50 ⊙

Flinders St

26 🏛

40 ⊗

31 ⊙

3 Hosier
⊙ **Lane**

ℹ **24** ⊗

Melbourne Visitor Centre

8 🏛

Wellington Pde

12 🏛

2 ⊙

Federation
Square

4 🏛

Ian Potter
Centre: NGV
Australia

Wellington Pde South

Princes
Bridge

23 ●

Birrarung
Marr **1** ⊙

Batman Ave

Jolimont Rd

St Kilda Rd

Boathouse Dr

Alexandra Gardens

Melbourne
Park

Melbourne Cricket
Ground (150m);
National Sports
Museum (150m)

Alexandra Ave

Queen
Victoria
Gardens

Central Melbourne

★ **Melbourne Museum**   MUSEUM
(Map p221; ☎13 11 02; www.museumvictoria.com.
au; 11 Nicholson St, Carlton; adult/child & student
$10/free, exhibitions extra; ☺10am-5pm; ▣Tourist Shuttle, ▣City Circle, 86, 96, ▣Parliament)
This museum provides a grand sweep of
Victoria's natural and cultural histories,
with exhibitions covering everything from
dinosaur fossils and giant squid specimens
to the taxidermy hall, a 3D volcano and an
open-air forest atrium of Victorian flora.
Become immersed in the legend of champion racehorse and national hero Phar Lap in
the Marvellous Melbourne exhibition. The
excellent **Bunjilaka**, on the ground floor,
presents Indigenous Australian stories and
history told through objects and Aboriginal voices with state-of-the-art technology.
There's also an **IMAX cinema** on site.

★ **Royal Exhibition
Building**   HISTORIC BUILDING
(Map p221; ☎13 11 02; www.museumvictoria.com.
au/reb; 9 Nicholson St, Carlton; tours adult/child
$5/3.50; ▣Tourist Shuttle, ▣City Circle, 86, 96,

🏛Parliament) Built for the International Exhibition in 1880, and winning Unesco World Heritage status in 2004, this beautiful Victorian edifice symbolises the glory days of the Industrial Revolution, the British Empire and 19th-century Melbourne's economic supremacy. It was the first building to fly the Australian flag, and Australia's first parliament was held here in 1901; it now hosts everything from trade fairs to car shows, as well as the biennial Melbourne Art Fair. Tours of the building leave from the Melbourne Museum at 2pm.

Royal Melbourne Zoo   ZOO

(☑03-9285 9300; www.zoo.org.au; Elliott Ave, Parkville; adult/child $30/13.20, children free on weekends/holidays; ☺9am-5pm; 🚊505, 🚌55, 🏛Royal Park) Established in 1861, this is the oldest zoo in Australia and the third oldest in the world. Today it's one of the city's most popular attractions. Set in spacious, prettily landscaped gardens, the zoo's enclosures aim to simulate the animals' natural habitats. Walkways pass through the enclosures: you can stroll through the bird aviary, cross a bridge over the lions' park or enter a tropical hothouse full of colourful butterflies. See the website for details about the zoo's other sites: Healesville Sanctuary (native critters) and Werribee Open Range Zoo (African savannah animals).

⊙ South Yarra, Prahran & Windsor

Chapel St's South Yarra strip still parades itself as a must-do fashion destination, but has seen better days; it's been taken over by chain stores, tacky bars and, come sunset, doof-doof cars. Prahran, however, has designer stores, bars and some refreshingly eclectic businesses. It is also the home of the **Prahran Market** (Map p224; www.prahranmarket.com.au; 163 Commercial Rd; ☺7am-5pm Tue, Thu & Sat, to 7pm Fri, 10am-3pm Sun; 🚊72, 78, 🏛Prahran), where the locals shop for fruit, veg and upmarket deli delights. Chapel St continues down to Windsor, a hive of cute cafes and vintage stores.

★Royal Botanic Gardens   GARDENS

(Map p210; www.rbg.vic.gov.au; Birdwood Ave, South Yarra; ☺7.30am-sunset, Children's Garden open Wed-Sun, closed mid-Jul–mid-Sep; 🚊Tourist Shuttle, 🚊1, 3, 5, 6, 8, 16, 64, 67, 72) **FREE** One of the finest botanic gardens in the world, the Royal Botanical Gardens are one of Melbourne's most glorious attractions. Sprawling beside the Yarra River, the beautifully designed gardens feature a global selection of plantings and specifically endemic Australian flora. Mini-ecosystems, such as a cacti and succulents area, herb garden and an indigenous rainforest, are set amid vast lawns. Take a book, picnic or frisbee – but most importantly, take your time.

Shrine of Remembrance   MONUMENT

(Map p210; www.shrine.org.au; Birdwood Ave, South Yarra; ☺10am-5pm; 🚊Tourist Shuttle, 🚊1, 3, 5, 6, 8, 16, 64, 67, 72) **FREE** Beside St Kilda Rd stands the massive Shrine of Remembrance, built as a memorial to Victorians killed in WWI. It was built between 1928 and 1934, much of it with depression-relief, or 'susso', labour. Its bombastic classical design is partly based on the Mausoleum of Halicarnassus, one of the seven ancient wonders of the world. Visible from the other end of town, planning regulations continue to restrict any building that would obstruct the view of the shrine from Swanston St as far back as Lonsdale St.

⊙ St Kilda & Around

Come to St Kilda for its sea breezes, seedy history and for a good old bit of people-watching. The palm trees, bay vistas, briny breezes and pink-stained sunsets are heartbreakingly beautiful. On weekends, the volume is turned up, the traffic crawls and the street-party atmosphere sets in.

Luna Park   AMUSEMENT PARK

(Map p229; ☑03-9525 5033; www.lunapark.com.au; 18 Lower Esplanade; single-ride adult/child $11/9, unlimited-rides $48/38; 🚊16, 96) It opened in 1912 and still retains the feel of an old-style amusement park, with creepy Mr Moon's gaping mouth swallowing you up as you enter. There's a heritage-listed 'scenic railway' (the oldest operating roller coaster in the world) and a beautifully baroque carousel with hand-painted horses, swans and chariots, as well as the full complement of gut-churning rides.

St Kilda Foreshore   BEACH

(Map p229; Jacka Blvd; 🚊16, 96) While there are palm-fringed promenades, a parkland strand and a long stretch of sand, St Kilda's seaside appeal is more Brighton, England, than *Baywatch*, despite 20-odd years of glitzy development. The kiosk at the end of **St Kilda Pier** (an exact replica of the

Fitzroy & Around

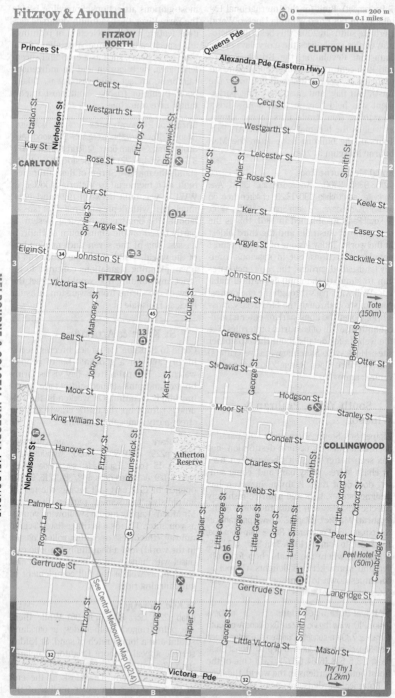

0 ————————— 200 m
0 ————————— 0.1 miles

FITZROY NORTH

Princes St

Queens Pde

Alexandra Pde (Eastern Hwy)

CLIFTON HILL

Cecil St

1

Cecil St

83

Station St

Nicholson St

Westgarth St

Westgarth St

Kay St

CARLTON

Fitzroy St

Brunswick St

Rose St

8

Young St

Napier St

Leicester St

Rose St

Smith St

15

Keele St

Kerr St

Spring St

Argyle St

14

Kerr St

Argyle St

Easey St

Sackville St

Elgin St

34

Johnston St

3

FITZROY

10

Johnston St

34

Victoria St

Young St

Chapel St

Tote
(150m)

Mahoney St

45

Bedford St

Bell St

John St

13

Greeves St

St David St

George St

Otter St

12

Kent St

Moor St

Moor St

Hodgson St

6

Stanley St

King William St

Condell St

COLLINGWOOD

2

Hanover St

Brunswick St

Atherton
Reserve

Charles St

Smith St

Nicholson St

Palmer St

Fitzroy St

Webb St

Little Oxford St

Oxford St

Royal La

45

Napier St

Little George St

George St

Little Gore St

Gore St

Little Smith St

7

Peel St

Cambridge St

5

16

9

11

Peel Hotel
(50m)

Gertrude St

4

Gertrude St

Langridge St

32

See Central Melbourne Map (p214)

Young St

Napier St

George St

Little Victoria St

Smith St

Mason St

Thy Thy 1
(1.2km)

Victoria Pde

32

Fitzroy & Around

original, which burnt down in 2003, a year short of its centenary) is as much about the journey as the destination.

◉ South Melbourne & Albert Park

There's something boastful about these seaside suburbs and their peaceful, upmarket environment (though come Grand Prix time, the noise is ramped up big time). Head to South Melbourne for its market (Map p210; www.southmelbournemarket.com.au; cnr Coventry & Cecil Sts; ⊙8am-4pm Wed, Sat & Sun, to 5pm Fri; 🚋96) famous for its dim sims, boutiquey homewares and top cafes.

Albert Park Lake   LAKE
(Map p210; btwn Queens Rd, Fitzroy St, Aughtie Dr & Albert Rd; 🚋96) Elegant black swans give their inimitable bottoms-up salute as you jog, cycle or walk the 5km perimeter of this constructed lake. Lakeside Dr was used as an international motor-racing circuit in the 1950s, and since 1996 the revamped track has been the venue for the Australian Formula One Grand Prix each March. Also on the periphery is the Melbourne Sports & Aquatic Centre, with an Olympic-size pool and child-delighting wave machine.

🏃 Activities

Cycling

Cycling maps are available from the Visitor Information Centre at Federation Sq and Bicycle Victoria (📞03-8376 8888; www. bv.com.au). The urban series includes the Main Yarra Trail (35km), off which runs the Merri Creek Trail (19km), the Outer Circle Trail (34km) and the Maribyrnong River Trail (22km). There are also paths taking you along Melbourne's beaches.

Melbourne Bike Share (📞1300 711 590; www.melbournebikeshare.com.au) offers free bike hire for the first half hour (or $2.80 per day) and is perfect for short trips around the city. Helmets are compulsory, and available either with the bike (but not always), or at 7-Eleven and IGA stores around the city for $5 ($3 refund on return). There are 51 bright-blue stations around the city.

Swimming

In summer, hit the sand at one of the city's popular beaches – St Kilda or Middle Park – with suburban beaches at Brighton (with its photogenic bathing boxes) and Sandringham. Public pools are also well loved, including Fitzroy Swimming Pool (Map p218; 📞03-9205 5180; 160 Alexandra Pde; adult/child $5/3; ⊙6am-8pm Mon-Fri, 8am-6pm Sat & Sun; 🚋112) and Prahran Aquatic Centre (Map p224; 📞03-8290 7140; 41 Essex St; adult/child $6/3; ⊙6am-7.45pm Mon-Fri, to 5pm Sat, 7am-5pm Sun; 🚋72, 78, 🚉Prahran).

Water Sports

Kayak Melbourne   KAYAKING
(Map p210; 📞0418 106 427; www.kayakmelbourne. com.au; tours $72-118; 🚋11, 31, 48) 🔱 Don't miss out on the chance to see Melbourne's Yarra River by kayak. These two-hour tours take you past Melbourne's newest city developments and explain the history of the older ones. Moonlight tours are most evocative and include a dinner of fish and chips. Tours usually depart from Victoria Harbour, Docklands – check the website for directions.

Kite Republic   KITEBOARDING
(Map p229; 📞03-9537 0644; www.kiterepublic. com.au; St Kilda Seabaths, 4/10-18 Jacka Blvd; 1hr lesson $90; ⊙10am-7pm) Offers kiteboarding lessons, tours and equipment; also a good source of info. In winter they can arrange snow-kiting at Mt Hotham. Also rents stand-up paddleboards (SUPs) and street SUPs.

Stand Up Paddle HQ
PADDLEBOARDING

(Map p229; ☑0416 184 994; www.supb.com.au; St Kilda Pier; per hour $25, 2hr penguin tour $130; ☎96) Arrange a lesson or hire out SUP equipment from St Kilda pier, or join one of their Yarra River or sunset St Kilda Penguin tours to visit a local penguin colony.

🍜 Tours

Aboriginal Heritage Walk
CULTURAL TOUR

(Map p210; ☑03-9252 2300; www.rbg.vic.gov.au; Royal Botanic Gardens, Birdwood Ave, South Yarra; adult/child $25/10; ⊙11am Tue-Fri and 1st Sun of the month; 🚌 Tourist Shuttle, ☎8) 🖉 The Royal Botanic Gardens are on a traditional camping and meeting place of the original Indigenous owners, and this tour takes you through their story – from songlines to plant lore, all in 90 fascinating minutes. The tour departs from the visitor centre.

Melbourne By Foot
WALKING TOUR

(☑0418 394 000; www.melbournebyfoot.com; tours $35 ; 🚉 Flinders St) 🖉 Take a few hours out with Dave and experience a mellow, informative 4km walking tour that covers laneway art, politics, and Melbourne's history and diversity. Tour includes a refreshment break. Highly recommended; book online.

Greeter Service
WALKING TOUR

(Map p214; ☑03-9658 9658; Melbourne Visitor Centre, Federation Sq; 🚉 Flinders St) 🖉 FREE Get your bearings on this free two-hour 'orientation tour', which departs Fed Sq daily at 9.30am (bookings required). It's run by the city's volunteer 'greeters'.

Melbourne Street Art Tours
WALKING TOUR

(☑03-9328 5556; www.melbournestreettours.com; tours $69; ⊙1.30-5pm Tue, Thu & Sat) 🖉 Three-hour tours exploring the street-art side of Melbourne. The tour guides are street artists themselves, so you'll get a good insight into this art form.

★✶ Festivals & Events

Melbourne isn't fussy about when it gets festive. Winter or summer are no excuse, with Melburnians joining like-minded types at outdoor festivals, and in cinemas, performance spaces or sporting venues year-round.

☀️ January

Australian Open
TENNIS

(www.australianopen.com; National Tennis Centre; ⊙Jan) The world's top tennis players and huge, merry-making crowds descend for Australia's Grand Slam tennis championship.

Midsumma Festival
GAY, LESBIAN

(www.midsumma.org.au; ⊙Jan-Feb) Melbourne's annual gay-and-lesbian arts festival features more than 100 events from mid-January to mid-February, with a Pride March finale.

❄️ February

St Kilda Festival
MUSIC

(www.stkildafestival.com.au; Acland & Fitzroy Sts; ⊙Feb) FREE This week-long festival ends in a suburb-wide street party on the final Sunday.

White Night
FESTIVAL

(http://whitenightmelbourne.com.au; ⊙Feb) FREE Melbourne's annual all-night event where the city is illuminated in colourful projections, forming a backdrop to free art, music and film.

Chinese New Year
CULTURAL

(www.chinatownmelbourne.com.au; Little Bourke St; ⊙Feb) Melbourne has celebrated the lunar new year since Little Bourke St became Chinatown in the 1850s.

❄️ March

Moomba
FESTIVAL

(www.thatsmelbourne.com.au; Alexandra Gardens; ⊙Mar) FREE A waterside festival famous locally for its wacky Birdman Rally, where competitors launch themselves into the Yarra in homemade flying machines.

Melbourne Food & Wine Festival
FOOD

(www.melbournefoodandwine.com.au; ⊙Mar) Market tours, wine tastings, cooking classes and presentations by celeb chefs take place at venues across the city (and state).

Australian Formula One Grand Prix
CAR RACING

(☑1800 100 030; www.grandprix.com.au; Albert Park; tickets from $55; ⊙Mar) The 5.3km street circuit around the normally tranquil Albert Park Lake is known for its fast surface. The buzz, both on the streets and in your ears, takes over Melbourne for four days of action.

❄️ April

Melbourne International Comedy Festival
COMEDY

(www.comedyfestival.com.au; Melbourne Town Hall; ⊙Mar-Apr) An enormous range of local and international comic talent hits town with four weeks of laughs.

Carlton & Around

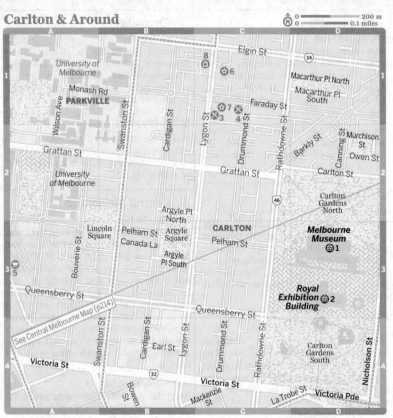

MELBOURNE & COASTAL VICTORIA MELBOURNE

☀ May

Melbourne Jazz JAZZ
(www.melbournejazz.com; ⊙ May-Jun) International jazz cats head to town and join locals for gigs at Hamer Hall, the Regent Theatre and the Palms at Crown Casino.

☀ July

Melbourne International Film Festival FILM
(MIFF; www.melbournefilmfestival.com.au; ⊙ Jul-Aug) Midwinter movie love-in brings out the black-skivvy-wearing cinephiles in droves.

☀ August

Melbourne Writers Festival LITERATURE
(www.mwf.com.au; ⊙ Aug) Yes, Melbourne is a Unesco 'city of literature', and it's proud of its writers and, indeed, readers. Beginning in the last week of August, the Writers Festival features forums and events at various venues.

September

AFL Grand Final AFL
(www.afl.com.au; MCG; ☉ Sep) It's easier to kick a goal from the boundary line than to pick up random tickets to the Grand Final, but it's not hard to get your share of finals fever anywhere in Melbourne (particularly at pubs).

Melbourne Fringe Festival ARTS
(www.melbournefringe.com.au; ☉ Sep-Oct) The Fringe showcases experimental theatre, music and visual arts.

October

Melbourne International Arts Festival ARTS
(www.melbournefestival.com.au; ☉ Oct) Held at various venues around the city, this festival features a thought-provoking program filled with Australian and international theatre, opera, dance, visual art and music events.

November

Melbourne Cup HORSE RACING
(www.springracingcarnival.com.au; ☉ Nov) Culminating in the prestigious Melbourne Cup, the Spring Racing Carnival is as much a social event as a sporting one. The Cup, held on the first Tuesday in November, is a public holiday in Melbourne.

December

Boxing Day Test CRICKET
(www.mcg.org.au; MCG; ☉ Dec) Boxing Day is day one of Melbourne's annually scheduled international Test cricket match, drawing out the cricket fans. Expect some shenanigans from Bay 13.

🛏 Sleeping

Stay in the city for good access to the main sights, or spread your wings and get to know an inner-city suburb such as grungy Fitzroy or seaside St Kilda.

🛏 Central Melbourne

★ Space Hotel HOSTEL, HOTEL $
(Map p214; ☎ 03-9662 3888; www.spacehotel.com.au; 380 Russell St; dm/s/d without bathroom from $28/70/99; ✽ @ ☂; ☐ City Circle, 24, 30) One of Melbourne's few genuine flashpackers, this sleek, modern and immaculate hotel has something for all demographics, all at very reasonable prices. Rooms have iPod docks and flat-screen TVs, while dorms have thoughtful touches like large lockers equipped with sensor lights and lockable adapters. A few doubles have en suites and balconies.

Melbourne Central YHA HOSTEL $
(Map p214; ☎ 03-9621 2523; www.yha.com.au; 562 Flinders St; dm/d $34/100; @ ☂; ☐ 70) This her-

---

MELBOURNE FOR CHILDREN

Melbourne's a great city for families, with plenty of stuff to keep the young ones entertained.

Children's Garden (Map p210; Royal Botanic Gardens, Birdwood Ave, South Yarra; ☉ 10am-4pm Wed-Sun, daily during Victorian school holidays, closed mid-Jul–mid-Sep) Has natural tunnels in the rainforest, a kitchen garden and water-play areas.

Collingwood Children's Farm (Map p210; www.farm.org.au; 18 St Heliers St, Abbotsford; adult/child/family $8/4/16; ☉ 9am-4.30pm; ☐ 200, 201, 207, ☒ Victoria Park) An organic, wholesome vibe with a bunch of farm animals close to the city.

Scienceworks (Map p210; ☎ 13 11 02; www.museumvictoria.com.au/scienceworks; 2 Booker St, Spotswood; adult/child $10/free, Planetarium & Lightning Room additional adult/child $6/4.50; ☉ 10am-4.30pm; ☒ Spotswood) Science fun in the western suburb of Spotswood.

ArtPlay (Map p214; ☎ 03-9664 7900; www.artplay.com.au; ☉ 10am-4pm Wed-Sun) Creative workshops in Birrarung Marr for two- to 13-year-olds, getting them sewing, painting and puppeteering.

Also fun and with activities for kids big and small: ACMI (p206), Melbourne Zoo (p217), Sea Life Aquarium (p209), National Sports Museum (p213) and Melbourne Museum (p213).

itage building has been totally transformed by the YHA gang: expect a lively reception, handsome rooms, and kitchens and common areas on each of the four levels. Entertainment's high on the agenda, and there's a fab restaurant called Bertha Brown on the ground floor and a grand rooftop area.

City Centre Budget Hotel HOTEL $

(Map p214; ☎03-9654 5401; www.citycentrebudgethotel.com.au; 22 Little Collins St; d shared/private bathroom $92/112; @ 📶; 🚆Parliament) Intimate, independent and inconspicuous, this 38-room budget hotel is a find. It's located at the city's prettier end, down a 'Little' street, up some stairs and inside an unassuming building. Rooms are no-frills yet neat and tidy, staff are ultra-friendly and there's free wi-fi, a laundry and communal kitchen on the pebbled rooftop.

Alto Hotel on Bourke HOTEL $$

(Map p214; ☎03-8608 5500; www.altohotel.com.au; 636 Bourke St; r from $158; P ❄ @ 📶; 🚋86, 96) 🍃 Environment-minded Alto has water-saving showers, energy-efficient lights and double-glazed windows, and in-room recycling is encouraged. Rooms are also well equipped, with good light and neutral decoration. Apartments (but not studios) have full kitchens and multiple LCD TVs, and some have spas. Freebies include organic espresso coffee, apples and access to a massage room. Guests can use an electric car at a rate of $17 per hour.

Adina Apartment Hotel APARTMENT $$

(Map p214; ☎03-8663 0000; www.adinahotels.com.au; 88 Flinders St; apt from $165; P ❄ 📶; 🚋City Circle, 70, 75) Quintessential Melbourne, these designer, cool, monochromatic warehouse-style loft apartments are extra large and luxurious. Ask for one at the front for amazing parkland views or get glimpses into Melbourne's lanes from the giant polished-floorboard studios, all with full kitchens. Also has apartments in **St Kilda** (Map p229; ☎03-9536 0000; 157 Fitzroy St; apt from $139) overlooking Albert Park.

Hotel Causeway HOTEL $$

(Map p214; ☎03-9660 8888; www.causeway.com.au; 275 Little Collins St; r incl breakfast from $170; ❄ @ 📶; 🚋86, 96) With a discreet entrance in the Howey Pl covered arcade, Causeway will appeal to those who've come to Melbourne to shop and bar-hop. It's intimate in scale, so don't expect the facilities of a big hotel. Rooms are boutiquey and feature luxurious linen, robes and slippers.

★Ovolo BOUTIQUE HOTEL $$$

(Map p214; ☎03-8692 0777; www.ovologroup.com; 19 Little Bourke St; r incl breakfast from $209; P ❄ @ 📶; 🚆Parliament) Melbourne's newest boutique hotel mixes hipster chic with a funky executive vibe. It's friendly, fun and loaded with goodies – there's a free minibar in each room, and free booze downstairs at the daily happy hour. Throw in a 'goodie bag' on arrival, Nespresso machine in the lobby and Le Patisserie breakfast pastries and you'll be wanting to move in permanently.

Crown Metropol HOTEL $$$

(Map p214; ☎03-9292 6211; www.crownhotels.com.au; 8 Whiteman St, Crown Casino; rooms from $295 ; ❄ @ 📶 🏊; 🚋96, 109, 112) The most boutique of Crown's hotels, guests here have access to the most extraordinary infinity pool in Melbourne, with 270-degree views over the city to the Dandenongs in the distance. The beautifully appointed luxe twin rooms are the least expensive on offer and sleep four.

Hotel Lindrum BOUTIQUE HOTEL $$$

(Map p214; ☎03-9668 1111; www.hotellindrum.com.au; 26 Flinders St; r from $250; P ❄ 📶; 🚋70, 75) One of the city's most attractive hotels, this was once the snooker hall of the legendary and literally unbeatable Walter Lindrum. Expect rich tones, subtle lighting and tactile fabrics. Spring for a deluxe room and you'll snare either arch or bay windows and marvellous Melbourne views. And yes, there's a billiard table – one of Lindrum's originals, no less.

Hotel Windsor HOTEL $$$

(Map p214; ☎03-9633 6000; www.thehotelwindsor.com.au; 111 Spring St; r from $175; ❄ @; 🚆Parliament) Sparkling chandeliers and a grand piano in the lobby set the scene for this opulent, heritage-listed 1883 building that's one of Australia's most famous and self-consciously grand hotels. It was still awaiting a controversial $260 million redevelopment at the time of research. Adding to its English quaintness is **high tea service** (Mon-Fri $69, Sat & Sun $89) and the historic Cricketers Bar, decked out in cricketing memorabilia.

Adelphi Hotel HOTEL $$$

(Map p214; ☎03-8080 8888; www.adelphi.com.au; 187 Flinders Lane; r from $250; ❄ @ 📶 🏊; 🚋3,

South Yarra & Prahran

Bar Economico (600m)

Aboriginal Heritage Walk (500m); Moonlight Cinema (500m);

Children's Garden (1.1km); Royal Botanic Gardens (1.3km); Shrine of Remembrance (1.3km)

Albany (600m)

CREMORNE

RICHMOND

Herring Island Park

Monash Fwy

Como Park

South Yarra

Toorak Rd

SOUTH YARRA

TOORAK

Hawksburn

PRAHRAN

Princes Gardens

Victoria Gardens

Prahran

Windsor

WINDSOR

Commercial Rd

Malvern Rd

High St

Dandenong Rd

ST KILDA

South Yarra & Prahran

5, 6, 16, 64, 67, 72) Under new ownership this discreet Flinders Lane property was one of Australia's first boutique hotels, and it's still rock 'n' roll. It's had a five-star makeover, and its cosy rooms have a distinctly glam European feel with design touches throughout. Thankfully its iconic rooftop pool, which juts out over Flinders Lane, remains.

📍 Fitzroy & Around

★ Nunnery   HOSTEL $
(Map p218; ☑ 03-9419 8637; www.nunnery.com.au; 116 Nicholson St, Fitzroy; dm/s/d incl breakfast $32/90/120; @�</; ☐96) Built in 1888, the Nunnery oozes atmosphere, with sweeping staircases and many original features; the walls are dripping with religious works of art and ornate stained-glass windows. You'll be giving thanks for the big comfortable lounges and communal areas. Next door to the main building is the Nunnery Guesthouse, which has larger rooms in a private setting (from $130). It's perennially popular, so book ahead.

Tyrian Serviced Apartments   APARTMENT $$$
(Map p218; ☑ 03-9415 1900; www.tyrian.com.au; 91 Johnston St, Fitzroy; r from $200; P✱@☎; ☐112) These spacious, self-contained mod-

ern apartments have a certain Fitzroy celeb appeal, which you'll feel from the moment you walk down the dimmed hallway to reception. Big couches, flat-screen TVs and balconies add to the appeal, and plenty of the neighbourhood restaurants and bars are right at your door.

📍 South Yarra, Prahran & Windsor

Back of Chapel   HOSTEL $
(Map p224; ☑ 03-9521 5338; www.backofchapel.com; 50 Green St, Windsor; dm incl breakfast $20-26, d $80; @; ☐78, 79) Twenty steps away from buzzing Chapel St, this clean backpackers in an old Victorian terrace has a prime location. It attracts a laid-back crew, and is popular with those on a working holiday. Reception closes at 5.30pm.

Albany   BOUTIQUE HOTEL $$
(Map p210; ☑ 03-9866 4485; www.thealbany.com.au; cnr Toorak Rd & Millswyn St, South Yarra; r $100-160; ✱@☎✱; ☐8) Proudly screaming fashion and rock 'n' roll, the Albany gives you the choice between fantastic refurbed rooms in an 1890s Victorian mansion, or cheap LA-style motel rooms, which are slightly shabby. There's a candy-pink rooftop pool and great location across from Fawkner Park, between the city and boutique South Yarra.

★ Art Series (The Cullen)   BOUTIQUE HOTEL $$$
(Map p224; ☑ 03-9098 1555; www.artserieshotels.com.au/cullen; 164 Commercial Rd, Prahran; r from $209; ✱@☎; ☐72, 78, 79, ⓡPrahran) The edgiest of the Art Series hotels, this one's decked out by the late grunge-painter Adam Cullen, whose vibrant and often graphic works provide visions of Ned Kelly shooting you from the glam opaque room/bathroom dividers. Rooms are classic boutique – ultra comfy but not big on space.

📍 St Kilda & Around

Base   HOSTEL $
(Map p229; ☑ 03-8598 6200; www.stayatbase.com; 17 Carlisle St; dm $26-38, d $90-120; P✱@☎; ☐3a, 16, 79, 96) Well-run Base has stream-lined dorms (each with en suite) and slick doubles. There's a floor set aside for female travellers complete with hair straighteners and champagne deals, and a bar and live music nights to keep the good-time vibe happening.

Hotel Barkly
HOTEL $

(St Kilda Beach House; Map p229; ☑03-9525 3371; www.stkildabeachhouse.com; 109 Barkly St; dm/d incl breakfast from $29/99; ❄@🏠; 🚌3, 67) Hotel Barkly is the party and you're on the guest list. Bright dorms are on the 1st floor; moody, though not luxurious, private rooms, some with balconies and views, are on the 2nd and 3rd floors. Below is a heaving pub, above is a happy, house-cranking bar. Noisy? You bet. But if you're up for it, there's definitely fun to be had.

Prince
HOTEL $$

(Map p229; ☑03-9536 1111; www.theprince. com.au; 2 Acland St; r incl breakfast from $185; P❄@🏠🏊; 🚌3a, 16, 79, 96, 112) Chic Prince has a dramatic lobby while rooms feature natural materials and a pared-back aesthetic. On-site 'facilities' take in some of the neighbourhood stars: **Aurora** (Map p229; ☑03-9536 1130; www.aurorasparetreat.com; 2 Acland St; 1hr massage from $120; ☺8.30am-8pm Mon-Fri, to 6pm Sat, 10am-7pm Sun; 🚌3a, 16, 96, 112) day spa, **Circa** restaurant, bars and band room, and breakfast is provided by **Acland St Cantina** downstairs. Be prepared for seepage of nightclub noise if you're staying the weekend. Free wi-fi is a bonus.

Hotel Tolarno
HOTEL $$

(Map p229; ☑03-9537 0200; www.hoteltolarno. com.au; 42 Fitzroy St; s/d/ste from $120/155/$230; ❄@🏠; 🚌3a, 16, 79, 96, 112) Tolarno was once the site of Georges Mora's seminal gallery, Tolarno. The fine-dining restaurant downstairs bears the name of Georges' well-known artist wife Mirka, as well as her original paintings. A range of rooms are on offer and all come eclectically furnished with good beds, bright and bold original artworks and free wi-fi.

✖ Eating

While the city has great dining options, be sure to venture out beyond its boundaries for innovative inner-city eats along Smith and Gertrude Sts in Collingwood/Fitzroy, or Acland and Fitzroy Sts in St Kilda.

Also keep an eye out on Twitter to track down the location of Melbourne's inner-city roaming fleet of diverse food trucks @wherethetruckat.

✖ Central Melbourne

Camy Shanghai Dumpling Restaurant
CHINESE $

(Map p214; 23-25 Tattersalls Lane; dumplings 10/20 pieces $5/7; ☺11.30am-3.30pm & 5-10pm Mon-Fri, noon-10pm Sat, noon-9pm Sun; 🚌3, 5, 6, 16, 64, 67, 72) A Melbourne institution. There's nothing fancy here; pour your own plastic cup of tea from the urn, then try a variety of dumplings (steamed or fried) with some greens and BYO booze. Put up with the dismal service and you've found one of the last places in town where you can fill up for under $10.

★ MoVida
SPANISH $$

(Map p214; ☑03-9663 3038; www.movida.com.au; 1 Hosier Lane; tapas $4-6, raciones $8-28; ☺noon-late; 🚌70, 75, 🚉Flinders St) MoVida sits in a cobbled laneway emblazoned with one of the world's densest collections of street art – it doesn't get much more Melbourne than this. Line up along the bar, cluster around little window tables or, if you've booked, take a table in the dining area for fantastic Spanish tapas and *raciones*.

Cumulus Inc
MODERN AUSTRALIAN $$

(Map p214; www.cumulusinc.com.au; 45 Flinders Lane; mains $21-38; ☺7am-11pm Mon-Fri, 8am-11pm Sat & Sun; 🚉City Circle, 48) One of Melbourne's best for any meal; it gives you that wonderful Andrew McConnell–style along with reasonable prices. The focus is on beautiful produce and simple but artful cooking: from breakfasts of sardines and smoked tomato on toast at the marble bar to suppers of freshly shucked *clair de lune* oysters tucked away on the leather banquettes. No reservations, so queues are highly probable.

Mamasita
MEXICAN $$

(Map p214; ☑03-9650 3821; www.mamasita.com. au; 1/11 Collins St; tacos from $5, shared plates from $19 ; ☺noon-late Mon-Sat, from 1pm Sun; 🚉City Circle, 11, 31, 48, 112) The restaurant responsible for kicking off Melbourne's obsession with authentic Mexican street food, Mamasita is still one of the very best – as evidenced by the perpetual queues to get into the place. The chargrilled corn sprinkled with cheese and chipotle mayo is a legendary starter, and there's a fantastic range of corn-tortilla tacos and 180 types of tequila. No reservations, so prepare to wait.

Cookie
THAI, BAR $$

(Map p214; ☑03-9663 7660; www.cookie.net.au; 1st fl, Curtain House, 252 Swanston St; mains from

$17.50; ⊙noon-late; 🚈3, 5, 6, 16, 64, 67, 72) Part Thai restaurant, part swanky bar, Cookie does both exceptionally well. Its all-Thai kitchen fires up authentic flavours with fusion twists to create some of the best Thai food in town. The bar is unbelievably well stocked with fine whiskies, wines and craft beers, and knows how to make a serious cocktail.

Gazi
GREEK $$

(Map p214; ☑03-9207 7444; www.gazirestaurant. com.au; 2 Exhibition St; shared plates from $10, mains $23; ⊙11.30am-11pm; 🚈48, 70, 75) The lastest offering from George Calombaris of *MasterChef* fame, this rebadged side project to the fancier Press Club (next door) is set in a cavernous industrial space with a menu inspired by Greek street food. Select from authentic shared starters and gourmet mini souvlakis filled with prawn or duck to wood-fire-spit mains. He also owns the East Brunswick eatery Hellenic Republic (☑03-9381 1222; www.hellenicrepublic.com.au; 434 Lygon St; mains $16-30; ⊙noon-4pm Fri, 11am-4pm Sat & Sun, 5.30pm-late Mon-Sun; 🛜; 🚈1, 8).

Pellegrini's Espresso Bar
ITALIAN, CAFE $$

(Map p214; ☑03-9662 1885; 66 Bourke St; mains $16-18; ⊙8am-11.30pm Mon-Sat, noon-8pm Sun; 🚇Parliament) The iconic Italian equivalent of a classic '50s diner, Pellegrini's has remained genuinely unchanged for decades. Pick and mix from the variety of homemade pastas and sauces; from the table out the back you can watch it all being thrown together from enormous, ever-simmering pots. In summer, finish with a glass of watermelon granita.

Hopetoun Tea Rooms
TEAROOM $$

(Map p214; ☑03-9650 2777; www.hopetountearooms.com.au; Block Arcade, 282 Collins St; dishes $13-21; ⊙8am-5pm) Since 1892 patrons have been nibbling pinwheel sandwiches here, taking tea (with pinkies raised) and delicately polishing off a lamington. Hopetoun's venerable status has queues almost stretching out the entrance of Block Arcade. Salivate over the window display while you wait.

★Vue de Monde
MODERN AUSTRALIAN $$$

(Map p214; ☑03-9691 3888; www.vuedemonde. com.au; Level 55, Rialto, 525 Collins St; degustation $200-250; ⊙reservations from noon-2pm Tue-Fri & Sun, 6-9.15pm Mon-Sat; 🚈11, 31, 48, 109, 112, 🚇Southern Cross) Sitting pretty in the old 'observation deck' of the Rialto, Melbourne's favoured spot for occasion dining has views to match its name. Visionary chef Shannon Bennett has moved away from its classic French style to a subtle Modern Australian theme that runs through everything from the decor to the menu.

Flower Drum
CHINESE $$$

(Map p214; ☑03-9662 3655; www.flower-drum. com; 17 Market Lane; mains $35-55; ⊙noon-3pm & 6-11pm Mon-Sat, 6-10.30pm Sun; 🛜; 🚈86, 96) The Flower Drum continues to be Melbourne's most celebrated Chinese restaurant. The finest, freshest produce prepared with absolute attention to detail keeps this Chinatown institution booked out for weeks in advance. The sumptuous, but ostensibly simple, Cantonese food (from a menu that changes daily) is delivered with the slick service you'd expect in such elegant surrounds.

Fitzroy & Around

Huxtaburger
BURGERS $

(Map p218; ☑03-9417 6328; www.huxtaburger.com. au; 106 Smith St, Collingwood; burgers from $8.50; ⊙11.30am-10pm Sun-Thu, to 11pm Fri & Sat; 🚈86) This American-style burger joint is a hipster magnet for its crinkle-cut chips in old-school containers, tasty burgers (veg options available) on glazed brioche buns and bottled craft beers. Cash only. Other branches in the City (Map p214; Fulham Pl, off Flinders Lane; ⊙11.30am-10pm Mon-Sat; 🚇Flinders St) and Prahran (Map p224; 201-209 High St; ⊙11.30am-10pm Sun-Thu, to 11pm Fri & Sat; 🚈6, 78, 79).

Gelato Messina
ICE CREAM $

(Map p218; www.gelatomessina.com; 237 Smith St, Fitzroy; 1 scoop $4; ⊙noon-11pm Sun-Thu, to 11.30pm Fri & Sat; 🚈86) Newly opened Messina is hyped as Melbourne's best ice-creamery. Its popularity is evident in the long queues of people waiting to wrap their smackers around smooth gelato like coconut and lychee, salted caramel and white chocolate, or pear and spiced rhubarb.

Charcoal Lane
MODERN AUSTRALIAN $$

(Map p218; ☑03-9418 3400; www.charcoallane. com.au; 136 Gertrude St, Fitzroy; mains $28-35; ⊙noon-3pm & 6-9pm Tue-Sat; 🚈86) 🌿 Housed in an old bluestone former bank, this training restaurant for Indigenous and disadvantaged young people is one of the best places to try native flora and fauna; menu items may include kangaroo burger with bush tomato chutney and wallaby tartare.

Weekend bookings advised. They also hold cooking masterclasses using native ingredients; check the website for details.

Vegie Bar
VEGETARIAN $$

(Map p218; ☑03-9417 6935; www.vegiebar.com.au; 380 Brunswick St, Fitzroy; mains $14-16; ☉11am-10.30pm Mon-Fri, from 9am Sat & Sun; ☝; ☐112) Its menu of delicious thin-crust pizzas, tasty curries and seasonal broths is perfectly suited to the cavernous warehouse decor with walls covered in band posters. Also has a fascinating selection of raw-food dishes, and plenty of vegan choices. Its fresh juices are popular, as are its yummy, cheap and original breakfasts.

Cutler & Co
MODERN AUSTRALIAN $$$

(Map p218; ☑03-9419 4888; www.cutlerandco.com.au; 55 Gertrude St, Fitzroy; mains $39-47; ☉noon-late Fri & Sun, 6pm-late Mon-Thu; ☐86) Hyped for all the right reasons, this is another of Andrew McConnell's restaurants and though its decor might be a little over-the-top, its attentive, informed staff and joy-inducing dishes (roast suckling pig, Earl Grey icecream and Moonlight Bay oysters, to name a few) have quickly made this one of Melbourne's best.

🍴 Carlton & Around

DOC Espresso
ITALIAN $$

(Map p221; ☑03-9347 8482; www.docgroup.net; 326 Lygon St, Carlton; mains $12-20; ☉7.30am-9.30pm Mon-Sat, 8am-9pm Sun; ☐205, ☐1, 8, 96) Run by third-generation Italians, DOC is bringing authenticity, and breathing new life, back into Lygon St. The espresso bar features homemade pasta specials, Italian microbrewery beers and *aperitivo* time, where you can enjoy a Negroni cocktail with complimentary nibble board (4pm to 7pm) while surrounded by dangling legs of meat and huge wheels of cheese behind glass shelves.

The **deli** (Map p221; ☑03-9347 8482; www.docgroup.net; 330 Lygon St; ☉9am-7pm) next door does great cheese boards and panini, while around the corner is their original **pizzeria** (Map p221; ☑03-9347 2998; www.docgroup.net; 295 Drummond St; pizzas around $13-18; ☉5-10.30pm Mon-Thu, noon-10.30pm Fri-Sun; ☐205, ☐1, 8), with excellent thin-crust pizzas and a convivial atmosphere.

Auction Rooms
CAFE $$

(Map p210; www.auctionroomscafe.com.au; 103-107 Errol St, North Melbourne; mains $14-20; ☉7am-5pm Mon-Fri, from 7.30am Sat & Sun; ☝; ☐57) This former auction house serves up some of Melbourne's best coffee, both espresso and filter, using ever-changing, house-roasted single-origin beans. Then there's its food, with a highly seasonal menu of creative breakfasts and lunches. From Queen Vic Market head west along Victoria St, then right at Errol.

Rumi
MIDDLE EASTERN $$

(☑03-9388 8255; www.rumirestaurant.com.au; 116 Lygon St, East Brunswick; mains $17-23; ☉6-10pm; ☐1, 8) A fabulously well-considered place that serves up a mix of traditional Lebanese cooking and contemporary interpretations of old Persian dishes. The *sigara boregi* (cheese and pine-nut pastries) are a local favourite, and tasty mains like meatballs are balanced with a large and interesting selection of vegetable dishes (the near-caramelised cauliflower and the broad beans are standouts).

🍴 St Kilda & Around

Lentil as Anything
VEGETARIAN $

(Map p229; www.lentilasanything.com; 41 Blessington St, St Kilda; by donation; ☉11am-9pm; ☝; ☐16, 96) Choosing from the organic, vegetarian menu is easy. Deciding what to pay can be hard. This unique not-for-profit operation provides training and educational opportunities for marginalised people, as well as tasty vegetarian food. Whatever you end up paying for your meal goes towards helping new migrants, refugees, people with disabilities and the long-term unemployed. Also at the **Abbotsford Convent** (Map p210; www.lentilasanything.com; 1 St Heliers St, Abbotsford; by donation; ☉9am-9pm; ☐Victoria Park).

Monarch Cake Shop
DESSERTS, EUROPEAN $

(Map p229; ☑03-9534 2972; www.monarchcakes.com.au; 103 Acland St, St Kilda; slice of cake $5; ☉8am-10pm; ☐96) St Kilda's Eastern European cake shops have long drawn crowds that come to peer at the sweetly stocked windows. Monarch is a favourite – its *kugelhopf* (marble cake), plum cake and poppyseed cheesecake can't be beaten. In business since 1934, not much has changed here with its wonderful buttery aromas and old-time atmosphere. Also does good coffee.

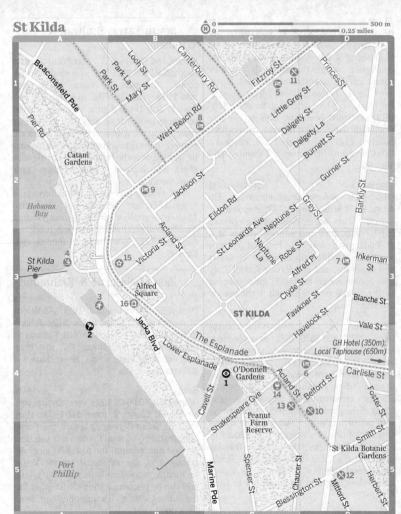

MELBOURNE & COASTAL VICTORIA MELBOURNE

St Kilda

◉ Sights
1 Luna Park	C4
2 St Kilda Foreshore	A4

◈ Activities, Courses & Tours
Aurora Spa Retreat	(see 9)
3 Kite Republic	A3
4 Stand Up Paddle HQ	A3

⊟ Sleeping
5 Adina Apartment Hotel St Kilda	C1
6 Base	D4
7 Hotel Barkly	D3
8 Hotel Tolarno	B1
9 Prince	B2

✦ Eating
10 Cicciolina	D4
11 Golden Fields	C1
12 Lentil as Anything	D5
13 Monarch Cake Shop	C4

⊟ Drinking & Nightlife
14 Vineyard	C4

✦ Entertainment
15 Esplanade Hotel	B3

⊟ Shopping
16 Esplanade Market	B3
Readings	(see 10)

St Ali
CAFE $$

(Map p210; ☑ 03-9689 2990; www.stali.com.au; 12-18 Yarra Pl, South Melbourne; dishes $10-28; ☻7am-6pm; ☐112) A hideaway warehouse conversion where the coffee is carefully sourced and guaranteed to be good. If you can't decide between house blend, speciality, black or white, there's a tasting 'plate' ($18). Awarded best food cafe in *The Age Good Cafe Guide 2013;* the corn fritters with poached eggs and haloumi are legendary. Off Clarendon St, between Coventry and York Sts.

Cicciolina
MEDITERRANEAN $$

(Map p229; www.cicciolinastkilda.com.au; 130 Acland St, St Kilda; mains $17-43; ☻noon-10pm; ☐16, 96) This warm room of dark wood, subdued lighting and pencil-sketches is a St Kilda institution. The inspired Modern Australian/Mediterranean menu is smart and generous, and the service warm. They take bookings only for lunch; for dinner eat early or while away your wait in the moody little back bar.

★Attica
MODERN AUSTRALIAN $$$

(Map p210; ☑ 03-9530 0111; www.attica.com.au; 74 Glen Eira Rd, Ripponlea; 8-course tasting menu $190; ☻6.30pm-late Wed-Sat; ☐67, ☒Ripponlea) Consistent award-winning Attica is a suburban restaurant that serves Ben Shewry's creative dishes degustation-style. Many dishes are not complete on delivery; staff perform minor miracles on cue with a sprinkle of this or a drop of that. 'Trials' of Shewry's new ideas take place at Tuesday night's Chef's Table ($125 per head). Booking several months in advance is essential. Follow Brighton Rd south out to Glen Eira Rd.

Golden Fields
MODERN ASIAN $$$

(Map p229; ☑ 03-9525 4488; www.goldenfields.com.au; 157 Fitzroy St, St Kilda; mains $32-70; ☻noon-midnight; ☐16, 96) Andrew McConnell has done it again. This chic eatery became famous for its New England lobster roll and for good reason – it's a testament to good things coming in small packages. Modern Asian subtleties can be found not only in the made-for-sharing dishes but also in the decor. Book a few weeks ahead for weekends, or score a spot at the long (non-bookable) bar, where you can glimpse the chefs in action.

✖ South Yarra, Prahran & Windsor

WoodLand House
MODERN AUSTRALIAN $$$

(Map p224; ☑ 03-9525 2178; www.woodlandhouse.com.au; 78 Williams Rd, Prahran; tasting menu from $115; ☻noon-3pm Thu, Fri & Sun, 6.30-9pm Tue-Sat; ☐6) Housed in a Victorian terrace of ample proportions, this was the former incarnation of Jacques Reymond, a local pioneer of degustation dining. After 15 years he handed over the reigns to two of his sous chefs, who learned everything they know from the man.

The tasting menu has shifted from its original French focus to an innovative Modern Australian direction incorporating quality local produce. Sunday lunch offers a good-value chef's set menu of four courses for $80.

✖ East Melbourne & Richmond

Thy Thy 1
VIETNAMESE $

(Map p210; ☑ 03-9429 1104; 1st fl, 142 Victoria St; mains from $9; ☻9am-10pm; ☐109, ☒North Richmond) Head upstairs to this Victoria St original (unchanged since 1987) for cheap and delicious Vietnamese. No corkage for BYO booze.

Baby
PIZZERIA $$

(Map p224; ☑ 03-9421 4599; www.babypizza.com.au; 631-633 Church St; mains $17; ☻7am-11pm; ☐70, 78, ☒East Richmond) Ignore the porno light feature (you won't notice it if you dine by day) and get into the food and vibe: delicious pizza, the occasional Aussie TV star and many, many trendy folk. It's busy, bold and run by restaurant king Christopher Lucas (Chin Chin), so it's quite brilliant. Even for a pizza joint.

🍷 Drinking & Nightlife

Melbourne's bars are legendary, and from laneway hideaways to brassy corner establishments, it's easy to locate a 'local' that will please the senses and drinking palate. Melbourne's live-music venues also have great front bars even if you're not keen on seeing a band.

🍸 Central Melbourne

★Bar Americano
COCKTAIL BAR

(Map p214; www.baramericano.com; 20 Presgrave Pl, off Howey Pl; ☻8.30am-1am; ☐11, 31, 48, 109, 112) A hideaway bar in a city alleyway, Bar

GAY & LESBIAN MELBOURNE

Melbourne's gay and lesbian community is well integrated into the general populace, but clubs and bars are found mostly in the Collingwood, Prahran and South Yarra areas.

Plenty of Melbourne venues get into the spirit during Midsumma Festival (p220). It has a diverse program of events, including the popular Midsumma Carnival at Alexandra Gardens and St Kilda's Pride March. Australia's largest GLBT film festival, the **Melbourne Queer Film Festival** (www.melbournequeerfilm.com.au), screens over 100 films from around the world each March.

For more local info, pick up a copy of the free weekly newspaper **MCV (Melbourne Community Voice)** or tune into **JOY 94.9FM** (www.joy.org.au).

Drinking & Nightlife

Kama Bar (Map p224; ☑ 03-9804 5771; www.facebook.com/kamaclub; 119 Commercial Rd, South Yarra; ☺ 5pm-late; ☷ 72) One of the few remaining gay venues along Commerical Rd, with regular DJs and drag shows.

Peel Hotel (Map p210; ☑ 03-9419 4762; www.thepeel.com.au; 113 Wellington St, Collingwood; ☺ 9pm-dawn Thu-Sat; ☷ 86) One of Melbourne's most famous gay venues, the Peel features a male crowd dancing to house music, retro and commercial dance. It's on Peel St, which runs east off Smith St.

Greyhound Hotel (Greyhound Hotel; Map p210; ☑ 03-9534 4189; www.ghhotel.com.au; cnr Carlisle St & Brighton Rd, St Kilda; ☷ 16, 67, 79) Expect drag-filled evenings from Thursday to Saturday and a nightclub with a state-of-the-art sound system.

Americano is a standing-room-only affair with black-and-white chequered floors complemented with classic 'do not spit' subway tiled walls and a subtle air of speakeasy. By day it serves excellent coffee but after dark it's all about the cocktails; they don't come cheap but they do come superb.

Lui Bar COCKTAIL BAR
(Map p214; www.vuedemonde.com.au; Level 55, Rialto, 525 Collins St; ☺ 5.30pm-midnight Mon, noon-midnight Tue-Fri, 5.30pm-late Sat, noon-evening Sun; ☷ 11, 31, 48, 109, 112, ☷ Southern Cross) One of the city's most sophisticated bars, Lui offers the chance to sample the views and excellent bar snacks (smoked ocean trout jerky!) without having to indulge in the whole Vue de Monde dining experience. Suits and jet-setters cram in most nights so get there early (nicely dressed), claim your table and order from the 'pop-up book' menu containing serious drinks like macadamia martinis – vacuum distilled at the bar.

Madame Brussels BAR
(Map p214; www.madamebrussels.com; Level 3, 59-63 Bourke St; ☺ noon-1am; ☷ 86, 96) Head here if you've had it with Melbourne-moody and all that dark wood. Although named for a famous 19th-century brothel owner,

it feels like a camp '60s rabbit hole you've fallen into, with much Astroturfery and staff dressed à la the country club. It's just the tonic to escape the city for a jug of Madame Brussels–style Pimms on the wonderful rooftop terrace.

Degraves Espresso CAFE
(Map p214; Degraves St; ☺ 7am-9pm Mon-Fri, 8am-9pm Sat, 8am-6pm Sun; ☷ 48, 70, 75, ☷ Flinders St) In atmospheric Degraves St, this institution is a good spot to grab a quick takeaway coffee and wander the laneways.

Ponyfish Island CAFE, BAR
(Map p214; www.ponyfish.com.au; under Yarra Pedestrian Bridge; ☺ 8am-1am; ☷ Flinders St) Laneway bars have been done to death; now Melburnians are finding new creative spots to do their drinkin'. Where better than a little open-air nook under a bridge arcing over the Yarra River? From Flinders St Station underground passage, head over the pedestrian bridge towards Southgate where you'll find steps down to people knocking back beers with toasted sangas or cheese plates.

Cherry BAR, LIVE MUSIC
(Map p214; www.cherrybar.com.au; AC/DC Lane; ☺ 6pm-3am Tue & Wed, 5pm-5am Thu-Sat, 2-6.30pm Sun; ☷ City Circle, 70, 75)

Melbourne's legendary rock 'n' roll bar is still going strong. Located down AC/DC Lane (yep, named after the band, who are homegrown heroes), there's often a queue, but once inside a welcoming, slightly anarchic spirit prevails. Live-music bands and DJs play rock 'n' roll seven nights a week, and there's a long-standing soul night on Thursdays.

Carlton Hotel   BAR

(Map p214; www.thecarlton.com.au; 193 Bourke St; ⊘4pm-late; ☒86, 96) Over-the-top Melbourne rococo gets another workout here and never fails to raise a smile. Check out the rooftop **Palmz** if you're looking for some Miami-flavoured vice, or just a great view.

Section 8   BAR

(Map p214; www.section8.com.au; 27-29 Tattersalls Lane; ⊘10am-late Mon-Fri, noon-late Sat & Sun; ☒3, 5, 6, 16, 64, 67, 72) Enclosed within a cage full of shipping containers and wooden-pallet seating, Section 8 remains one of the city's hippest bars. They do great hot dogs, including vegan ones. Run by the same folk and just next door is **Ferdydurke** (Map p214; ☑03-9639 3750; www.ferdydurke.com.au; Levels 1 & 2, 31 Tattersalls Lane, cnr Lonsdale St; ⊘noon-1am; ☏; ☒Melbourne Central), a gritty art space set over a couple of levels and a great place for a drink.

Alumbra   CLUB

(Map p210; ☑03-8623 9666; www.alumbra.com. au; Shed 9, Central Pier, 161 Harbour Esplanade; ⊘4pm-3am Fri & Sat, to 1am Sun; ☒Tourist Shuttle, ☒70, City Circle) Great music and a stunning location will impress – even if the Bali-meets-Morocco follies of the decor don't. If you're going to do one megaclub in Melbourne (and like the idea of a glass dance floor), this is going to be your best bet. It's in one of the old sheds jutting out into Docklands' Victoria Harbour.

East Melbourne & Richmond

Bar Economico   BAR

(Map p210; 438 Church St; ⊘5pm-late Wed-Sat, 2pm-late Sun; ☒70, 79, ☒East Richmond) The newspapered front windows might have you turning on your heel, but rest assured you're in the right place. With its menus on ripped cardboard boxes and caged bar, Economico is a kind of Central American dive bar specialising in rum-based cocktails – Wrong Island Iced Tea sums the place up nicely. Buy

your drink tickets from the booth first, then redeem them at the bar.

Carlton & Around

Seven Seeds   CAFE

(Map p221; www.sevenseeds.com.au; 114 Berkeley St, Carlton; ⊘7am-5pm Mon-Sat, 8am-5pm Sun; ☒19, 59) The most spacious of the Seven Seeds coffee empire; there's plenty of room to store your bike and sip a splendid coffee beside the other lucky people who've found this rather out-of-the-way warehouse cafe. Public cuppings are held Wednesday (9am) and Saturday (10am). They also have standing-room only **Traveller** (Map p214; www. sevenseeds.com.au; 2/14 Crossley St, Melbourne; ⊘7am-5pm Mon-Fri, 10am-5pm Sat; ☒86, 96) and **Brother Baba Budan** (Map p214; www. sevenseeds.com.au; 359 Little Bourke St; ⊘7am-5pm Mon-Sat, 9am-5pm Sun; ☏; ☒19, 57, 59).

Fitzroy & Around

★Naked for Satan   BAR

(Map p218; ☑03-9416 2238; www.nakedforsatan.com.au; 285 Brunswick St, Fitzroy; ⊘noon-midnight Sun-Thu, to 1am Fri & Sat; ☒112) Vibrant, loud and reviving an apparent Brunswick St legend (a man nicknamed Satan who would get down and dirty, naked because of the heat, in an illegal vodka distillery under the shop), this place packs a punch with its popular *pintxos* (Basque tapas; $2), huge range of cleverly named beverages and unbeatable roof terrace with wraparound decked balcony.

De Clieu   CAFE

(Map p218; 187 Gertrude St, Fitzroy; ⊘7am-5pm Mon-Sat, 8am-5pm Sun; ☒86) You'll find locals spilling out the door and perched on the window-sill seats on weekends at this funky cafe (pronounced 'clue') with its polished concrete floors and excellent coffee, courtesy of Seven Seeds. The all-day brunch menu features interesting cafe fare such as miso and broad-bean fritters, scrambled tofu and pork neck roti.

St Kilda & Around

Vineyard   BAR

(Map p229; www.thevineyard.com.au; 71a Acland St, St Kilda; ⊘10.30am-3.30pm Mon-Fri, 10am-3.30pm Sat & Sun; ☒3a, 16, 96) An old favourite, the Vineyard has the perfect corner position and a courtyard BBQ that attracts crowds of backpackers and scantily clad young locals who enjoy themselves so much they drown out the neighbouring roller coaster. Sunday afternoon sessions are big here.

Revolver Upstairs   CLUB

(Map p224; www.revolverupstairs.com.au; 229 Chapel St, Prahran; ⊙noon-4am Tue-Fri, 24hr Sat & Sun; ☷6, ☷Prahran) Rowdy Revolver can feel like an enormous version of your lounge room, but with 54 hours of nonstop music come the weekend, you're probably glad it's not. Live music, interesting DJs and film screenings keep the mixed crowd wide awake.

Local Taphouse   BAR

(Map p210; www.thelocal.com.au; 184 Carlisle St, St Kilda; ⊙noon-late; ☷16, 78, ☷Balaclava) Reminiscent of an old-school Brooklyn bar. Prop up to its dark-wood polished bar and scratch your head to decide which one of its 19 craft beers on tap or its impressive bottle list to order. There's a beer garden upstairs, while downstairs has chesterfield couches, an open fire and indoor bocce pit. It's also known for its live comedy nights.

Borsch, Vodka & Tears   BAR

(Map p224; www.borschvodkaandtears.com; 173 Chapel St, Windsor; ☷6, ☷Prahran) This place is *the* business for sampling vodka. The extensive list covers a range of clear, oak-matured, fruit-infused and traditional *nalewka kresowa* (made according to old Russian and Polish recipes); knowledgeable staff can help you choose your shot. Line your stomach with some excellent borsch or blintzes. There's another one in Elsternwick (☏03-9523 0969; www.afterthetears.net; 9b Gordon St; ⊙3pm-late Mon-Thu, from 1pm Fri & Sat, from 11am Sun; ☷67, ☷Elsternwick) with 140 types of vodka and contemporary Eastern European dishes.

☆ Entertainment

Cinemas

Astor   CINEMA

(Map p224; ☏03-9510 1414; www.astortheatre.net.au; cnr Chapel St & Dandenong Rd, Windsor; ☷5, 64, 78, ☷Windsor) See a double feature for the price of one. Screens a mix of recent releases, art-house films and classics in art deco surrounds.

Cinema Nova   CINEMA

(Map p221; ☏03-9347 5331; www.cinemanova.com.au; 380 Lygon St, Carlton; ☷Tourist Shuttle, ☷1, 8) The latest in art-house, docos and foreign films. Cheap Monday screenings.

Moonlight Cinema   CINEMA

(Map p210; www.moonlight.com.au; Gate D, Royal Botanic Gardens, Birdwood Ave, Melbourne; ☷8) Melbourne's original outdoor cinema, with the option of 'Gold Grass' tickets that include a glass of wine and a reserved beanbag bed.

Rooftop Cinema   CINEMA

(Map p214; www.rooftopcinema.com.au; Level 6, Curtin House, 252 Swanston St, Melbourne; ☷Melbourne Central) This rooftop bar sits at dizzying heights on top of the happening Curtain House. In summer it transforms into an outdoor cinema with striped deckchairs and a calendar of new and classic favourite flicks.

Theatre

Try Half Tix Melbourne (Map p214; www.halftixmelbourne.com; Melbourne Town Hall, 90-120 Swanston St, Melbourne; ⊙10am-2pm Mon, 11am-6pm Tue-Fri, 10am-4pm Sat; ☷Flinders St) for cheap tickets to the theatre. You need to front up at the Half Tix office in person on the day with cash.

La Mama   THEATRE

(Map p221; ☏03-9347 6948; www.lamama.com.au; 205 Faraday St, Carlton; ☷1, 8) La Mama is historically significant in Melbourne's theatre scene. This tiny, intimate forum produces new Australian works and experimental theatre, and has a reputation for developing emerging playwrights. It's a ramshackle building with an open-air bar. Shows also run at its larger Courthouse Theater at 349 Drummond St, so check tickets carefully for the correct location.

Melbourne Theatre Company   THEATRE

(MTC; Map p210; ☏03-8688 0800; www.mtc.com.au; 140 Southbank Blvd, Southbank; ☷1) Melbourne's major theatrical company stages around 15 productions each year, ranging from contemporary and modern (including many new Australian works) to Shakespearean and other classics. Performances take place in a brand-new, award-winning venue in Southbank.

Malthouse Theatre   THEATRE

(Map p210; ☏03-9685 5111; www.malthousetheatre.com.au; 113 Sturt St, Southbank; ☷1) The Malthouse Theatre Company often produces the most exciting theatre in Melbourne. Dedicated to promoting Australian works, the company has been housed in the

CURTAINS UP

Blockbuster musicals have the good fortune of playing in Melbourne's graceful old city-centre theatres:

Athenaeum (Map p214; ☑03-9650 1500; www.athenaeumtheatre.com.au; 188 Collins St; 🚊11, 31, 48, 112) The old dame dates back to the 1830s, with the Greek goddess of wisdom, Athena, sitting atop the facade, imbuing the theatre with classical gravitas.

Comedy Theatre (Map p214; ☑03-9299 9800; www.marrinertheatres.com.au; 240 Exhibition St; 🚊86, 96) This midsize 1920s Spanish-style venue is dedicated to comedy, theatre and musicals.

Her Majesty's (Map p214; ☑03-8643 3300; www.hmt.com.au; 219 Exhibition St; 🚊86, 96) On the outside Her Maj is red-brick Second Empire; on the inside it's 1930s Moderne. It's been the home of musicals and comedy since 1880 and is still going strong.

Princess Theatre (Map p214; ☑Ticketmaster 1300 111 011; www.marrinertheatres.com.au; 163 Spring St; 🚊86, 96) This gilded Second Empire beauty has a long and colourful history. It's reputed to have a resident ghost – that of singer Federici, who died as he descended through the stage trap in 1888 after playing Mephistopheles in the opera *Faust*. These days shows range from *Phantom of the Opera* to *Mary Poppins*.

Regent Theatre (Map p214; ☑03-9299 9500; www.marrinertheatres.com.au; 191 Collins St; 🚊11, 31, 48, 112) The opulent Regent, a rococo picture palace, was considered one of the most lavish theatres of its kind when it was built in 1929 with the advent of the talkies. Today it's used for blockbuster stage shows – still a fabulous opportunity to experience its elegant grandeur.

atmospheric Malthouse Theatre since 1990 (when it was known as the Playbox). From Flinders St Station walk across Princes Bridge and along St Kilda Rd. Turn right at Grant St, then left into Sturt.

Live Music

Melbourne still prides itself as Australia's home of rock 'n' roll with a plethora of sticky-carpeted venues scattered throughout town. Gig listings are covered in free street magazines **Beat** (www.beat.com.au) and the **Music** (www.themusic.com.au). Also tune in to independent radio stations **RRR** (102.7FM) and **PBS** (106.7FM) for the latest happenings.

The Tote   LIVE MUSIC
(Map p210; ☑03-9419 5320; www.thetotehotel. com; cnr Johnston & Wellington Sts, Collingwood; ⊙4pm-late Tue-Sun; 🚊86) One of Melbourne's most iconic live-music venues, not only does this divey Collingwood pub have a great roster of local and international underground bands, but one of the best jukeboxes in the universe. Its temporary closure in 2010 brought Melbourne to a stop, literally – people protested on the city-centre streets against the liquor licensing laws that were blamed for the closure.

Esplanade Hotel   LIVE MUSIC
(The Espy; Map p229; ☑03-9534 0211; www.espy. com.au; 11 The Esplanade, St Kilda; ⊙noon-1am Sun-Wed, to 3am Thu-Sat; 🚊16, 96) Rock-pigs rejoice. The Espy remains gloriously shabby and welcoming to all. A mix of local and international bands play nightly, everything from rock 'n' roll to hip hop either in the legendary Gershwin Room, the front bar or down in the basement.

Corner Hotel   LIVE MUSIC
(Map p210; ☑03-9427 9198; www.cornerhotel. com; 57 Swan St, Richmond; ⊙4pm-late Tue & Wed, noon-late Thu-Sun; 🚊70, 🚉Richmond) The band room here is one of Melbourne's most popular midsized venues and has seen plenty of loud and live action over the years, from Dinosaur Jr to the Buzzcocks. If your ears need a break, there's a friendly front bar. The rooftop has city views, but gets super-packed, and often with a different crowd from the music fans below.

Northcote Social Club   LIVE MUSIC
(☑03-9489 3917; www.northcotesocialclub.com; 301 High St, Northcote; ⊙4pm-late Mon & Tue, noon-late Wed-Sun; 🚊86, 🚉Northcote) The stage at this inner-north local has seen plenty of international folk just one album out from star status. Their homegrown line-up is also notable. If you're just after a drink, the front

bar buzzes every night of the week, and there's a large deck out back for lazy afternoons.

Bennetts Lane
JAZZ

(Map p214; ☑ 03-9663 2856; www.bennettslane. com; 25 Bennetts Lane, Melbourne; ☺ 9pm-late; 🚊 City Circle, 24, 30) Bennetts Lane has long been the boiler room of Melbourne jazz. It attracts the cream of local and international talent and an audience that knows when it's time to applaud a solo. Beyond the front bar, there's another space reserved for big gigs.

Classical Music

Melbourne Symphony Orchestra
CLASSICAL MUSIC

(MSO; ☑ 03-9929 9600; www.mso.com.au) The MSO has a broad reach: while not afraid to be populist (they've done sell-out performances with both Burt Bacharach and the Whitlams), it can also do edgy – such as performing with Kiss – along with its performances of the great masterworks of symphony. They perform regularly at venues around the city, including Melbourne Town Hall, the Recital Centre and Hamer Hall. Also runs a summer series of free concerts at the Sidney Myer Music Bowl.

Dance

Australian Ballet
DANCE

(Map p214; ☑ 1300 369 741; www.australianballet. com.au; 2 Kavanagh St, Melbourne; 🚊 1) Based in Melbourne and now more than 40 years old, the Australian Ballet performs traditional and new works at the State Theatre in the Arts Centre. You can take an hour-long Australian Ballet Centre Tour ($18, bookings essential) that includes a visit to the production and wardrobe departments as well as the studios of both the company and the school.

Chunky Move
DANCE

(Map p210; ☑ 03-9645 5188; www.chunkymove. com; 111 Sturt St, Melbourne; 🚊 1) This partially government-funded contemporary dance company performs internationally acclaimed pop-inspired pieces at its sexy venue behind the Australian Centre for Contemporary Art. They also run a variety of dance, yoga and Pilates classes; check the website. From Flinders St Station walk across Princes Bridge and along St Kilda Rd. Turn right at Grant St, then left into Sturt.

🔒 Shopping

The city's main department stores, **Myer** and **David Jones**, are both on the Bourke St Mall.

🔒 Central Melbourne

★ Craft Victoria Shop
CRAFT, DESIGN

(Craft Victoria; Map p214; ☑ 03-9650 7775; www. craft.org.au; 31 Flinders Lane; ☺ 10am-5pm Mon-Sat; 🚊 City Circle, 70, 75) This retail arm of Craft Victoria showcases the best of handmade, mainly by local Victorian artists. Its range of jewellery, textiles, accessories, glass and ceramics bridges the art/craft divide and makes for some wonderful mementoes of Melbourne. There are also a few galleries with changing exhibitions; admission is free.

City Hatters
ACCESSORIES

(Map p214; ☑ 03-9614 3294; www.cityhatters. com.au; 211 Flinders St; ☺ 9.30am-6pm Mon-Fri, 9am-5pm Sat, 10am-4pm Sun; 🚊 Flinders St) Located beside the main entrance to Flinders St Station, this is the most convenient place to purchase an iconic Akubra hat, kangaroo-leather sun hat or something a little more unique.

GPO
SHOPPING CENTRE

(Map p214; ☑ 03-9663 0066; www.melbournesgpo. com; cnr Elizabeth St & Bourke St Mall; ☺ 10am-6pm Mon-Thu & Sat, to 8pm Fri, 11am-5pm Sun; 🚊 19, 57, 59, 86, 96) This was once simply somewhere you went to buy a stamp, but a post-fire restoration has made for an atmospheric place to shop along its gallerias. It houses a three-storey concept store for European behemoth H&M.

Alice Euphemia
FASHION, JEWELLERY

(Map p214; Shop 6, Cathedral Arcade, 37 Swanston St; ☺ 10am-6pm Mon-Thu & Sat, to 7pm Fri, noon-5pm Sun; 🚊 Flinders St) Art-school cheek abounds in the Australian-made and designed labels sold here – Romance was Born, Karla Spetic and Kloke, to name a few. Jewellery sways between the shocking and exquisitely pretty, and their upstairs space hosts regular events and exhibitions.

🔒 Fitzroy & Around

★ Third Drawer Down
DESIGN

(Map p218; www.thirddrawerdown.com; 93 George St, Fitzroy; ☺ 11am-5pm Mon-Sat; 🚊 86) It all started with its signature tea towel designs (now found in MOMA in New York) at this 'museum of art souvenirs'. Third Drawer Down makes life beautifully unusual by stocking absurdist pieces with a sense of humour as well as high-end art by well-known designers.

Crumpler
ACCESSORIES

(Map p218; ☎03-9417 5338; www.crumpler.com; 87 Smith St, cnr Gertrude St, Fitzroy; ◷10am-6pm Mon-Sat, to 5pm Sun; ⌂86) Crumpler's bike-courier bags started it all, designed by two former couriers looking for a bag they could hold their beer in while cycling home. Its durable, practical designs now extend to bags for cameras, laptops and iPads, and can be found around the world.

Polyester Books
BOOKS

(Map p218; ☎03-9419 5223; www.polyester.com.au; 330 Brunswick St, Fitzroy; ◷10am-6pm Sun-Thu, to 9pm Fri & Sat; ⌂112) This unapologetic bookstore specialises in 'seriously weird shit', including literature, magazines and DVDs on topics ranging from satanic cult sex to underground comics and everything in between. It also stocks a great selection of music biographies and small-press zines.

Gorman
CLOTHING, ACCESSORIES

(Map p218; www.gormanshop.com.au; 235 Brunswick St, Fitzroy; ◷10am-6pm Mon-Thu & Sat, to 7pm Fri, 11am-5pm Sun; ⌂112) Lisa Gorman makes everyday clothes that are far from ordinary: boyish, but sexy, short shapes are cut from exquisite fabrics; pretty cardigans are coupled with relaxed, organic tees. You can find other branches elsewhere around town.

Carlton & Around

Readings
BOOKS

(Map p221; www.readings.com.au; 309 Lygon St, Carlton; ◷8am-11pm Mon-Fri, 9am-11pm Sat, 9am-9pm Sun; ⌂Tourist Shuttle, ⌂1, 8) A potter around this defiantly prospering indie bookshop can occupy an entire afternoon if you're so inclined. There's a dangerously

loaded (and good-value) specials table, switched-on staff and everyone from Lacan to *Charlie and Lola* on the shelves. Its exterior 'housemate wanted' board is legendary. Also in St Kilda (Map p229; ☎03-9525 3852; 112 Acland St; ⌂96) and the city centre (Map p214; State Library of Victoria, cnr La Trobe & Swanston Sts; ⌂Melbourne Central).

South Yarra, Prahran & Windsor

Chapel Street Bazaar
VINTAGE

(Map p224; ☎03-9521 3174; 217-223 Chapel St, Prahran; ◷10am-6pm; ⌂78, 79, ⌂Prahran) Calling this a 'permanent undercover collection of market stalls' won't give you any clue to what's tucked away here. This old arcade is a retro-obsessive riot. It doesn't matter if Italian art glass, vintage furniture or Noddy egg cups are your thing, you'll find it here. There's a mix of cluttered mayhem and well-organised boutiquey stalls.

Greville Records
MUSIC

(Map p224; www.grevillerecords.com.au; 152 Greville St, Prahran; ◷10am-6pm Mon-Thu & Sat, to 7pm Fri, noon-5pm Sun; ⌂78, 79) One of the last bastions of the 'old' Greville St, this fabulous music shop has such a loyal following that the great Neil Young invited the owners on stage during a Melbourne concert. It's now very much geared towards vinyl.

Fat
FASHION, ACCESSORIES

(Map p224; www.fat4.com; 272 Chapel St, Prahran; ◷10am-6pm Mon-Sat, 11am-5pm Sun; ⌂78, 79, ⌂Prahran) The Fat empire has changed the way Melbourne dresses, catapulting a fresh generation of designers into the city's consciousness, including Claude Maus, Dr

---

MELBOURNE'S BEST MARKETS

Meet local artists or stock up on fantastic original pieces at one of the following weekend markets.

Rose Street Artists' Market (Map p218; www.rosestmarket.com.au; 60 Rose St, Fitzroy; ◷11am-5pm Sat; ⌂112) One of Melbourne's best and most popular art-and-craft markets, in Fitzroy.

Camberwell Sunday Market (www.sundaymarket.com.au; Station St, Camberwell; by donation; ◷6am-12.30pm Sun; ⌂70, 72, 75, ⌂Camberwell) Located behind the corner of Burke and Riversdale Rds, this is where Melburnians come to offload their unwanted items and antique-hunters come to find them.

Esplanade Market (Map p229; www.esplanademarket.com; btwn Cavell & Fitzroy Sts; ◷10am-5pm Sun; ⌂96) Shop for toys, organic soaps and arts 'n' crafts with a seaside backdrop in St Kilda.

Denim, Kloke and Status Anxiety. There are also branches in the city centre (The Strand, 250 Elizabeth St; 19, 57, 59) in the city and **Fitzroy** (Map p218; 209 Brunswick St; 112).

❶ Information

DANGERS & ANNOYANCES

There are occasional reports of alcohol-fuelled violence in some parts of Melbourne's CBD, in particular King St late at night on weekends.

EMERGENCY

For police, ambulance or fire emergencies, dial 000.

There's a centrally located police station at 228 Flinders Lane, Melbourne.

INTERNET ACCESS

Most accommodation options have wi-fi and computer terminals, ranging from free to $10 per hour.

Otherwise wi-fi is available free at Federation Sq and Flinders St Station, as well as libraries throughout Melbourne – which also have terminals if you bring ID.

MEDIA

Melbourne's the *Age* (www.theage.com.au) covers local, national and international news. The *Herald Sun* (www.heraldsun.com.au) does the same in tabloid style.

MEDICAL SERVICES

Visitors from Belgium, Finland, Italy, Ireland, Malta, the Netherlands, Norway, New Zealand, Sweden and the UK have reciprocal health-care agreements with Australia and can access cheaper health services through **Medicare** (13 20 11; www.humanservices.gov.au/customer/dhs/medicare).

Travel Doctor (TVMC; 03-9935 8100; www.traveldoctor.com.au; Level 2, 393 Little Bourke St, Melbourne; 9am-5pm Mon, Wed & Fri, to 8.30pm Tue & Thu, to 1pm Sat; 19, 57, 59) specialises in vaccinations.

Royal Melbourne Hospital (03-9342 7000; www.rmh.mh.org.au; cnr Grattan St & Royal Pde, Parkville; 19, 59) is a public hospital with an emergency department.

MONEY

There are ATMs throughout Melbourne. Bigger hotels offer a currency-exchange service, as do most banks during business hours. There's a bunch of exchange offices on Swanston St.

POST

Melbourne GPO (Map p214; 13 13 18; www.auspost.com.au; 250 Elizabeth St, cnr Little Bourke St, Melbourne; 8.30am-5.30pm Mon-Fri, 9am-5pm Sat; 19, 57, 59) Poste restante available.

TOURIST INFORMATION

Melbourne Visitor Centre (MVC; Map p214; 03-9658 9658; www.melbourne.vic.gov.au/touristinformation; Federation Sq; 9am-6pm; ; Flinders St) Located at Federation Sq, the centre has comprehensive tourist information on Melbourne and regional Victoria, including excellent resources for mobility-impaired travellers. There's power sockets too for recharging phones etc. There's also a booth at Bourke St Mall, and City Ambassadors, dressed in red, wandering around the city who can help with info and directions.

USEFUL WEBSITES

Lonely Planet's website (www.lonelyplanet.com) has useful links. Other online resources:

Broadsheet Melbourne (www.broadsheet.com.au) Great source for reviews of the city's best eating, drinking and shopping spots.

That's Melbourne (www.thatsmelbourne.com.au) Downloadable maps, info and podcasts from the City of Melbourne.

Visit Victoria (www.visitvictoria.com.au) Highlights events in Melbourne and Victoria.

❶ Getting There & Away

AIR

Two airports serve Melbourne: **Tullamarine** (MEL; 03-9297 1600; www.melbourneairport.com.au) and **Avalon** (AVV; 03-5227 9100, 1800 282 566; www.avalonairport.com.au), located en route to Geelong. From Tullamarine, domestic and international flights are offered by **Qantas** (13 13 13; www.qantas.com), **Jetstar** (13 15 38; www.jetstar.com), **Virgin Australia** (13 67 89; www.virginaustralia.com) and **Tiger Air** (03-9034 3733; www.tigerairways.com). Presently only Jetstar serves Avalon.

BOAT

Spirit of Tasmania (Map p210; 1800 634 906; www.spiritoftasmania.com.au; adult/car one-way from $174/89) crosses Bass Strait between Melbourne and Devonport, Tasmania (11 hours) nightly; day sailings during peak season. It departs from Station Pier, Port Melbourne.

BUS, CAR & MOTORCYCLE

Long-distance buses depart from **Southern Cross Station's** (www.southerncrossstation.net.au; cnr Collins & Spencer Sts, Melbourne) main terminal. The **left-luggage facility** (03-9619 2588; during train service hours) at Southern Cross Station costs $12 for 24 hours.

V/Line (1800 800 007; www.vline.com.au) Around Victoria.

ⓘ HOOK TURNS

Many of the city's intersections require you to make a right-hand turn from the left lane so you don't block oncoming trams. When you see a 'Right Turn from Left Only' sign, get in the left lane and wait with your right indicator on; when the light turns green in the street you want to turn into, hook right and complete your turn.

Firefly (Map p214; ☑1300 730 740; www.fireflyexpress.com.au) To/from Adelaide, Canberra and Sydney.

Greyhound (☑1300 473 946; www.greyhound.com.au) Australia-wide.

TRAIN

Interstate trains arrive and depart from Southern Cross Station.

ⓘ Getting Around

TO/FROM THE AIRPORT
Tullamarine Airport

Inconveniently, there are no direct train or tram routes from Tullamarine airport to the city.

The most popular airport transport option is **Sky Bus** (Map p214; ☑03-9335 2811; www.skybus.com.au; adult/child one-way $17/6.50; ⓡ Southern Cross Station), a 24-hour express bus service from Southern Cross Station to Tullamarine Airport (20 to 30 minutes; departing every 10 minutes between 4.45am and 11.50pm, then every 20 to 30 minutes between midnight and 4.30am). It offers a free transfer service to several city hotels to/from Southern Cross Station (6am to 10.30pm Monday through Friday and 7.30am to 5.30pm on Saturday and Sunday); otherwise you'll need to catch onward transport or a taxi to your destination from Southern Cross.

Alternatively, budget travellers can chance their luck on Bus 901, departing Tullamarine's Terminal 1 to Broadmeadows Station (not the best place to hang out at night) from where you can catch the train to the city. It'll cost around $10 (including myki card) and take a minimum of 40 minutes (but expect longer); the last bus to/from the airport is around 11pm.

Taxis to Melbourne's city centre start from $50 (expect around $65 to $75, including surcharges and tolls, from midnight to 5am).

Drivers need to be aware that part of the main route into Melbourne from Tullamarine Airport is a toll road run by CityLink. You'll need to buy a Tulla Pass ($5.30); otherwise, take the Bell St

exit, then turn right onto Nicholson St and follow it all the way south to the city centre.

Avalon Airport

Sita Coaches (☑03-9689 7999; www.sita-coaches.com.au; adult/child $22/10) meets all flights in and out of Avalon, departing from Southern Cross Station (50 minutes).

BICYCLE

Numerous operators make it easy to pedal your way around town.

CAR & MOTORCYCLE
Car Hire

Rental-car agencies:

Avis (☑13 63 33; www.avis.com.au)

Budget (☑1300 362 848; www.budget.com.au)

Europcar (☑1300 131 390; www.europcar.com.au)

Hertz (☑13 30 39; www.hertz.com.au)

Rent a Bomb (☑13 15 53; www.rentabomb.com.au)

Thrifty (☑1300 367 227; www.thrifty.com.au)

Car Sharing

Car-sharing companies that operate in Melbourne include: **Flexi Car** (☑1300 363 780; www.flexicar.com.au), **Go Get** (☑1300 769 389; www.goget.com.au) and **Green Share Car** (☑1300 575 878; www.greensharecar.com.au). You rent the cars by the hour (from $14) or the day (from $80) and prices include petrol. They vary on joining fees (free to $40) and how they charge (insurance fees, per hour and per kilometre).

Parking

Most of the street parking is metered and if you overstay your metered time you'll probably be fined (between $72 and $144). Also keep an eye out for Clearway zones (prohibited kerb-side parking indicated by signs). Central city parking is around $5.50 per hour, and $3.20 per hour in the outer CBD.

Motorcyclists are allowed to park on the footpath.

Toll Roads

Both drivers and motorcyclists will need to purchase a toll pass if they're planning on using one of the two toll roads: **CityLink** (☑13 26 29; www.citylink.com.au), from Tullamarine Airport to the city and eastern suburbs, or **EastLink** (☑13 54 65; www.eastlink.com.au), which runs from Ringwood to Frankston. Pay online or via phone – but pay within three days of using the toll road to avoid a fine.

PUBLIC TRANSPORT

Flinders Street Station is the main metro train station connecting the city and suburbs. The

MELBOURNE & COASTAL VICTORIA MELBOURNE

'City Loop' runs under the city, linking the four corners of town.

An extensive network of trams covers every corner of the city, running north–south and east–west along most major roads. Trams run roughly every 10 to 20 minutes.

Check **Public Transport Victoria** (PTV; ☑1800 800 007; www.ptv.vic.gov.au; Southern Cross Station; ⓡ Southern Cross) for more information. Also worth considering is the free **City Circle Tram** (Tram 35; ☑13 16 38; www. ptv.vic.gov.au; ⊗10am-6pm Sun-Wed, to 9pm Thu-Sat; ⓐ 35), which loops around town, or the hop-on, hop-off **Melbourne Visitor Shuttle** (Tourist Shuttle; www.thatsmelbourne. com.au; daily ticket $5, children under 10 free; ⊗ 9.30am-4.30pm), which takes passengers to Melbourne's main sights.

Bicycles cannot be taken on trams or buses, but can be taken on trains.

Melbourne's buses, trams and trains use **myki** (www.myki.com.au), the controversial 'touch on, touch off' travel-pass system. It's not particularly user-friendly for short-term visitors, and you'll need to purchase a $6 plastic myki card and then put credit on it before you travel. Cards can be purchased from machines at stations, 7-Eleven stores or newsagents. Travellers are best advised to buy a myki Visitor Pack ($14), which gets you one day's travel and discounts on various sights; it's available only from the airport, Skybus terminal or the PTV Hub at Southern Cross Station.

The myki card can be topped up at 7-Eleven stores, myki machines at most train stations and at some tram stops in the city centre, costing $3.50 for two hours, or $7 for the day. Machines don't always issue change, so bring exact money. The fine for travelling without a valid myki card is $212 – ticket inspectors are vigilant and unforgiving.

TAXI

Melbourne's taxis are metered and require an estimated prepaid fare when hailed between 10pm and 5am. Toll charges are added to fares.

13 Cabs (☑13 22 27; www.13cabs.com.au)
Silver Top (☑13 10 08; www.silvertop.com.au)

AROUND MELBOURNE

The Dandenongs

On a clear day, you can see the Dandenong Ranges from Melbourne – conversely you can watch the sun set over the city from the lookout at the summit of 633m Mt Dandenong. A 35km day trip east of the city, there's good bushwalking and wildlife-spotting in the hills, or just go for a drive and stop for lunch at the quaint little villages of Olinda, Sassafras, Kallista or Emerald, where tea and scones is just about de rigueur.

Perennially popular **Puffing Billy** (☑03-9757 0700; www.puffingbilly.com.au; Old Monbulk Rd, Belgrave; return adult/child/family $59/30/119; ⓡ Belgrave) is an iconic restored steam train that toots its way through the ferny hills from Belgrave to Emerald Lake Park and Gembrook. You can hop-on and hop-off en route to enjoy a picnic or walk. Nearby, **Trees Adventure** (☑0410 735 288; www.treesadventure.com.au; Old Monbulk Rd, Glen Harrow Gardens; 2hr session adult/child $39/25; ⊗11am-5pm Mon-Fri, 9am-5pm Sat & Sun; ⓡ Belgrave) is a blast of tree-climbs, flying foxes and obstacle courses in a stunning patch of old-growth forest boasting sequoia, mountain ash and Japanese oak trees.

Dandenong Ranges National Park has many great walking tracks. The **Ferntree Gully** area has the popular **1000 Steps Track** up to One Tree Hill picnic ground (two hours return).

Drive up to **SkyHigh Mt Dandenong** (☑03-9751 0443; www.skyhighmtdandenong.com. au; 26 Observatory Rd, Mt Dandenong; vehicle entry $5; ⊗9am-10pm Mon-Thu, 9am-10.30pm Fri, 8am-11pm Sat & Sun; ⓐ 688) for amazing views over Melbourne and Port Phillip Bay from the highest point in the Dandenongs.

The **Dandenong Ranges & Knox visitors centre** (☑03-9758 7522; www.dandenongrangestourism.com.au; 1211 Burwood Hwy, Upper Ferntree Gully; ⊗1-5pm Mon, 9am-5pm Tue-Sat, 10.30am-2.30pm Sun; ⓡ Upper Ferntree Gully) is outside the Upper Ferntree Gully train station.

Queenscliff & the Bellarine Peninsula

Melburnians have been coming to the Bellarine Peninsula for its seaside village ambience for centuries. It has a good mix of family and surf beaches, diving and snorkelling, historic towns and relaxed wineries.

This stretch of coast not only joins up with the Great Ocean Road, but is just a short ferry trip over to the Mornington Peninsula.

Historic Queenscliff is a lovely spot, popular with day-tripping and overnighting Melburnians who come to stroll its heritage streetscapes and soak up its nautical

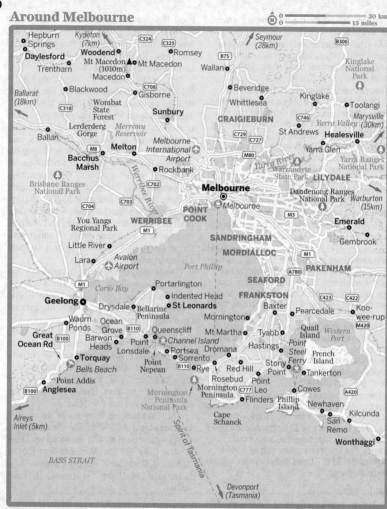

MELBOURNE & COASTAL VICTORIA QUEENSCLIFF & THE BELLARINE PENINSULA

atmosphere. The views across the Port Phillip Heads and Bass Strait are glorious.

🏃 Activities

Bellarine Peninsula Railway   TRAIN
(📞 03-5258 2069; www.bellarinerailway.com.au; Queenscliff train station; return adult/child/family $30/20/70; ⏱ departs 11am & 2.45pm Sun, plus Tue & Thu during school holidays) Run by a group of cheerful volunteer steam-train fanatics, the railway has beautiful heritage steam and diesel trains that ply the 1¾-hour return journey to Drysdale.

Sea-All Dolphin Swims   SNORKELLING
(📞 03-5258 3889; www.dolphinswims.com.au; Queenscliff Harbour; sightseeing adult/child $70/60, 3½hr snorkel $135/115; ⏱ 8am & 1pm Oct-Apr) Offers sightseeing tours and swims with seals and dolphins in Port Phillip Bay; seal sightings are guaranteed, dolphins are not always seen but there's a good chance.

✨ Festivals & Events

Queenscliff Music Festival   MUSIC
(📞 03-5258 4816; www.qmf.net.au; ⏱ late Nov) One of the coast's best festivals features big-name Australian musos with a folksy, bluesy bent.

ⓘ Information

Queenscliff Visitors Centre (☑ 03-5258 4843; www.queenscliffe.vic.gov.au; 55 Hesse St; ⏲ 9am-5pm) has plenty of brochures. There's free internet at the library next door.

ⓘ Getting There & Away

It's possible to catch a **V/Line** (☑ 13 61 96; www.vline.com.au) train from Melbourne to Geelong ($7.80, one hour), then a **McHarry's** (☑ 03-5223 2111; www.mcharrys.com.au) bus to Queenscliff (one hour), passing en route through Barwon Heads (30 minutes), Ocean Grove (45 minutes), Portarlington (45 minutes) and Point Lonsdale (55 minutes). A two-hour ticket costs $3.70, full-day is $7.10. Myki cards accepted.

The **Queenscliff–Sorrento Ferry** (☑ 03-5258 3244; www.searoad.com.au; one-way foot passenger adult/child $10/8, 2 adults & car $69; ⏲ hourly 7am-6pm) takes 40 minutes and runs till 7pm at peak times.

Mornington Peninsula

The Mornington Peninsula – the boot-shaped bit of land between Port Phillip and Western Port Bays – has been Melbourne's summer playground since the 1870s, when paddlesteamers ran down to Portsea. Today, the calm 'front beaches' on the Port Phillip Bay side are still a big magnet for family holidays at the bayside towns of Mornington, Rosebud, Dromana, Rye, Blairgowrie and Sorrento. The rugged ocean 'back beaches' facing Bass Strait offer challenging surfing and stunning walks along the coastal strip, part of Mornington Peninsula National Park.

Don't overlook a trip to the peninsula's interior; alongside lovely stands of native bushland, much of the undulating farmland has been replaced by vineyards and orchards – foodies love this region, where a winery lunch is a real highlight.

ⓘ Information

Peninsula Visitor Information Centre (☑ 03-5987 3078, 1800 804 009; www.visitmorningtonpeninsula.org; 359b Nepean Hwy, Dromana; ⏲ 9am-5pm) The main visitor information centre for the peninsula can book accommodation and tours. There are also visitor centres in Mornington (☑ 03-5975 1644; 320 Main St; ⏲ 9am-5pm) and Sorrento; the Mornington branch has useful regional information and a Mornington walking-tour map.

ⓘ Getting There & Around

Met trains (buy a Zones 1 & 2 ticket) run from Flinders St Station to Frankston station. **Portsea Passenger Service** (☑ 03-5986 5666; www.ptv.vic.gov.au) bus 788 runs from Frankston to Portsea ($2.50, 1½ hours) via Mornington, Dromana and Sorrento.

Inter Island Ferries (☑ 03-9585 5730; www.interislandferries.com.au; adult/child/bike return $24/12/8) runs between Stony Point and Cowes (Phillip Island) via French Island.

Queenscliff–Sorrento Car & Passenger Ferries (☑ 03-5258 3244; www.searoad.com.au; one-way foot passenger adult/child $10/8, 2 adults & car standard one-way/return $69/132; ⏲ hourly 7am-6pm, to 7pm Jan & long weekends) sails between Sorrento and Queenscliff.

Sorrento & Portsea

POP 1500

Historic Sorrento is the standout town on the Mornington Peninsula for its beautiful limestone buildings, ocean and bay beaches and buzzing seaside summer atmosphere. This was the site of Victoria's first official European settlement, established by an expedition of convicts, marines, civil officers and free settlers that arrived from England in 1803.

Grand 19th-century buildings include the Sorrento Hotel (1871), the Continental Hotel (1875) and Koonya (1878).

There are plenty of swimming and walking opportunities along Sorrento's wide, sandy beaches and bluffs. At low tide, the rock pool at the back beach is a safe spot for adults and children to swim and snorkel and the surf beach here is patrolled in summer.

Only 4km further west, tiny Portsea also has good back beaches and diving and watersports operators.

The small Sorrento visitors centre (☑ 03-5984 1478; cnr George St & Ocean Beach Rd) is on the main street.

👉 Tours

Two established operators run popular dolphin- and seal-swimming cruises from Sorrento Pier.

★ **Moonraker Charters**   DOLPHIN TOUR
(☑ 03-5984 4211; www.moonrakercharters.com.au; 7 George St; adult/child sightseeing $65/55, dolphin & seal swimming $125/115) Operates three-hour dolphin- and seal-swimming tours from Sorrento Pier.

LIQUID LUNCH

The Mornington Peninsula has developed into one of Victoria's great cool-climate wine regions. Most of the peninsula's 50-plus wineries are in the hills between Red Hill and Merricks and many have excellent cafes or restaurants attached. Some wineries to consider:

Montalto (☑03-5989 8412; www.montalto.com.au; 33 Shoreham Rd, Red Hill South; cafe mains $14-18, restaurant mains $35-39; ☺cellar door 11am-5pm, cafe noon-4pm Sat & Sun, restaurant noon-3pm daily, 6.30-11pm Fri & Sat) One of the Mornington Peninsula's best winery restaurants; the pinot noir and chardonnay here are terrific.

Port Phillip Estate (☑03-5989 4444; www.portphillipestate.com.au; 263 Red Hill Rd, Red Hill South; 2-/3-course meal from $68/85, cellar door mains $15-22; ☺cellar door 11am-5pm, restaurant noon-3pm Wed-Sun, 6.30-9pm Fri & Sat) Home of Port Phillip Estate and Kooyong wines, this award-winning winery has an excellent, breezy restaurant.

Red Hill Estate (☑03-5931 0177; www.redhillestate.com.au; 53 Shoreham Rd, Red Hill South; ☺cellar door 11am-5pm, restaurant noon-5pm daily, 6.30-11pm Fri & Sat) Red Hill Estate's signature pinot and sparkling wines are outstanding, while Max's Restaurant is one of the best on the peninsula.

Ten Minutes by Tractor (☑03-5989 6080; www.tenminutesbytractor.com.au; 1333 Mornington-Flinders Rd, Main Ridge; 5-/8-course tasting menu $109/139, 2-/3-course meal $69/89; ☺cellar door 11am-5pm, restaurant noon-3pm Wed-Sun, 6.30-9pm Thu-Sat) Another outstanding restaurant and a fine range of pinot noir, chardonnay and pinot gris. The unusual name comes from the three vineyards, which are each 10 minutes apart by tractor.

T'Gallant (☑03-5989 6565; www.tgallant.com.au; 1385 Mornington-Flinders Rd, Main Ridge; mains $16-32; ☺noon-3pm) Pioneered luscious pinot gris in Australia and produces the country's best. There's fine dining at La Baracca Trattoria, casual dining and pizza in Spuntino's Bar, and live music on weekends.

★**Polperro Dolphin Swims** DOLPHIN TOUR
(☑03-5988 8437; www.polperro.com.au; adult/child sightseeing $55/35, dolphin & seal swimming $130) Popular morning and afternoon dolphin- and seal-swimming tours from Sorrento Pier.

🛏 Sleeping & Eating

Sorrento Foreshore Camping Ground CAMPGROUND $
(☑03-5950 1011; Nepean Hwy; unpowered/powered sites $26/31, peak season $41/46; ☺Nov-May) Hilly, bush-clad sites between the bay beach and the main road into Sorrento.

Sorrento Beach House YHA HOSTEL $
(☑03-5984 4323; www.sorrento-beachhouse.com; 3 Miranda St; dm/d from $30/90) This purpose-built hostel situated in a quiet but central location maintains a relaxed atmosphere – the deck and garden are a great place to catch up with other travellers. Staff can also organise horse riding, snorkelling and diving trips.

Portsea Hotel HOTEL $$
(☑03-5984 2213; www.portseahotel.com.au; Point Nepean Rd; s/d from $85/105, s/d with bathroom from $135/175) Portsea's pulse is the sprawling, half-timber Portsea Hotel, an enormous pub with a great lawn and terrace area looking out over the bay. There's an excellent bistro (mains $24 to $39) and old-style accommodation (most rooms have shared bathroom) that increases in price based on sea views (weekend rates are higher).

Carmel of Sorrento GUESTHOUSE $$
(☑03-5984 3512; www.carmelofsorrento.com.au; 142 Ocean Beach Rd; d $130-220, apt from $210) This lovely old limestone house, right in the centre of Sorrento, has been tastefully restored in period style and neatly marries the town's history with contemporary comfort. There are three Edwardian-style suites with bathrooms and continental breakfast, and two modern self-contained units.

The Baths FISH & CHIPS $
(☑03-5984 1500; www.thebaths.com.au; 3278 Point Nepean Rd, Sorrento; fish & chips $10, restau-

rant mains $25-33; ⊙ noon-8pm) The waterfront deck of the former sea baths is the perfect spot for lunch or a romantic sunset dinner overlooking the jetty and the Queenscliff ferry. The menu has some good seafood choices and there's a popular takeaway fish and chippery at the front.

Smokehouse ITALIAN, PIZZERIA **$$**
(✆03-5984 1246; 182 Ocean Beach Rd, Sorrento; mains $20-34; ⊙6-9pm) Gourmet pizzas and pastas are the speciality at this local family favourite. Innovative toppings and the aromas wafting from the wood-fired oven hint at the key to its success.

Point Nepean & Mornington Peninsula National Parks

The peninsula's tip is marked by the scenic **Point Nepean National Park** (http://parkweb.vic.gov.au; Point Nepean Rd), originally a quarantine station and army base. There are long stretches of traffic-free road for excellent cycling, and walking trails leading to beaches. You can hire bikes at the visitor centre ($20 per day) or take the Point Transporter (adult/child/family return $8.70/6/22.90), a hop-on, hop-off bus service that departs the visitor centre six times daily.

Mornington Peninsula National Park covers the sliver of coastline between Portsea and Cape Schanck, where rugged ocean beaches are framed by cliffs and bluffs. You can walk all the way from Portsea to Cape Schanck (26km, eight hours) along a marked trail.

Built in 1859, **Cape Schanck Lightstation** (✆03-5988 6184; www.capeschancklighthouse.com.au; 420 Cape Schanck Rd; museum only adult/child/family $13.50/9.50/37, museum & lighthouse $16.50/10.50/44; ⊙10.30am-4pm) is a photogenic working lighthouse, with a kiosk, museum, information centre and regular guided tours. You can stay at **Cape Schanck B&B** (✆1300 885 259; www.capeschancklighthouse.com.au; 420 Cape Schanck Rd; d from $130) in the limestone keeper's cottage.

GREAT OCEAN ROAD

The Great Ocean Road (B100) is one of Australia's most famous road-touring routes. It takes travellers past world-class surfing breaks, through rainforest and calm seaside towns, and under koala-filled tree canopies. It shows off heathlands, dairy farms and sheer limestone cliffs and gets you up close and personal with the dangerous crashing surf of the Southern Ocean. Walk it, drive it, enjoy it.

MELBOURNE & COASTAL VICTORIA MORNINGTON PENINSULA

WORTH A TRIP

FRENCH ISLAND

It's only a 15-minute ferry ride from Stony Point on the Mornington Peninsula, but French Island feels a world away – it's two-thirds national park, virtually traffic-free and there's no mains water or electricity. The main attractions are bushwalking and cycling, taking in wetlands, one of Australia's largest **koala colonies**, and a huge variety of birds.

The island served as a penal settlement for prisoners serving out their final years from 1916 and you can still visit the original prison farm. A major industry here from 1897 to 1963 was chicory (a coffee substitute); visit the old **kilns** on Bayview Rd, where fourth-generation local Lois will whip you up chicory coffee or Devonshire tea in her rustic cafe.

The ferry docks at Tankerton, from where it's around 2km to the licensed **French Island General Store** (✆03-5980 1209; Lot 1, Tankerton Rd; bike hire $25; ⊙8am-6pm Mon-Sat, from 9am Sun), which also serves as post office, tourist information and bike-hire centre, and has accommodation ($110 per person). Bikes can also be hired at Tankerton Jetty.

French Island Biosphere Bus Tours (✆0412 671 241, 03-5980 1241; www.frenchislandtours.com.au; half-day adult/child $25/12, full day $49/22; ⊙Tue, Thu, Sun, plus Sat during school holidays) runs informative half-day tours with morning or afternoon tea. The full-day tour includes lunch.

You can camp for free at the basic **Fairhaven Camping Ground** (✆03-5986 9100; www.parkweb.vic.gov.au), but bookings (through Parks Victoria) are essential.

Inter Island Ferries (p241) runs a service between Stony Point and Tankerton (10 minutes, at least two daily, four on Tuesday, Thursday, Saturday and Sunday), continuing on to Phillip Island. You can reach Stony Point directly from Frankston on a Metlink train.

Great Ocean Road

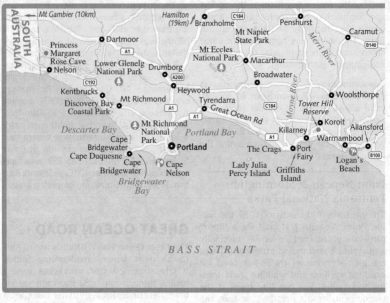

Mt Gambier (10km)
Hamilton (19km) Branxholme
Penshurst
Caramut
C184
B140
SOUTH AUSTRALIA
Princess
Margaret
Rose Cave
Nelson
Dartmoor
A1
Mt Napier
State Park
Mt Eccles
National Park
Macarthur
Lower Glenelg
National Park
Drumborg
A200
Broadwater
C192
Kentbrucks
Heywood
Discovery Bay
Coastal Park
Mt Richmond
Tyrendarra
Great Ocean Rd
C184
Tower Hill
Reserve
Woolsthorpe
A1
A1
Koroit
Allansford
Descartes Bay
Mt Richmond
National
Park
Portland Bay
Killarney
A1
Warrnambool
B100
Cape
Bridgewater
Cape Duquesne
Portland
The Crags
Port
Fairy
Logan's
Beach
Cape
Bridgewater
Cape
Nelson
Lady Julia
Percy Island
Griffiths
Island
Bridgewater
Bay
Merri River
Moyne River

BASS STRAIT

MELBOURNE & COASTAL VICTORIA GEELONG

Geelong

POP 216,000

⊙ Sights & Activities

Wander Geelong's revamped **waterfront**, and locate Jan Mitchell's 111 **painted bollards**. At **Eastern Beach**, stop for a splash about at the art deco **bathing pavilion**, opposite the promenade.

Geelong Art Gallery
GALLERY

(www.geelonggallery.org.au; Little Malop St; ⊙ 10am-5pm) FREE With over 4000 works in its collection this excellent gallery has celebrated Australian paintings such as Eugene von Guérard's *View of Geelong* and Frederick McCubbin's 1890 *A Bush Burial*. Also exhibits contemporary works and has free tours Saturday at 2pm.

National Wool Museum
MUSEUM

(☑03-5272 4701; www.geelongaustralia.com.au/nwm; 26 Moorabool St; adult/child/family $7.50/4/25; ⊙ 9.30am-5pm Mon-Fri, from 10am Sat & Sun) More interesting than it may sound, this museum showcases the importance that the wool industry had in shaping Geelong economically, socially and architecturally; many of the grand buildings in the area are former wool-store buildings, including the museum's 1872 bluestone building. There's a sock-making machine and a massive 1910 Axminster carpet loom that gets chugging on weekends.

Old Geelong Gaol
HISTORIC BUILDING

(☑03-5221 8292; www.geelonggaol.org.au; cnr Myers & Swanston Sts; adult/child $10/5; ⊙ 1-4pm Sat & Sun, daily school holidays) Built in 1849, HSM Prison Geelong may have closed its doors in 1991, but this old bluestone jail remains as terrifying as ever. You'll see its grim cells set over three levels, shower block, watchtowers and gallows. Each exhibit is accompanied by audio, explaining anything from contraband to crude homemade weapons to former cellmates such as Chopper Read (cell 39). **Ghost tours** (☑1300 856 668; www.geelongghosttours.com.au) are also run here.

Boom Gallery
GALLERY

(☑0417 555 101; www.boomgallery.com.au; 11 Rutland St, Newtown; ⊙ 8.30am-4pm Wed-Sat) Down an industrial street off Pakington St, Boom's warehouse space in an old wool mill shows contemporary works by Melbourne and local artists. It sells great design objects and jewellery, and the attached cafe does fantastic coffee and seasonal food.

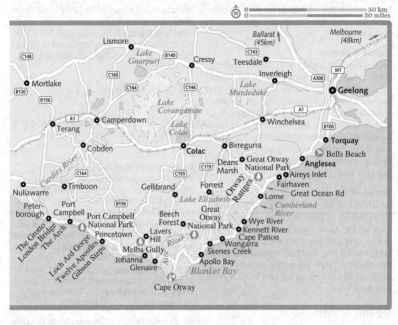

Sleeping

Irish Murphy's HOSTEL $
(☏ 03-5221 4335; www.irishmurphysgeelong.com.au; 30 Aberdeen St, Geelong West; dm/s/d $35/45/70; P ☎) Upstairs from an Irish pub, Geelong's only backpackers hostel is a family-owned affair with clean dorms, most of which only have two beds – a good deal. Plus guests get 20% off pub meals downstairs. It's a short walk from the city, Pakington St and Geelong station.

Gatehouse on Ryrie GUESTHOUSE $$
(☏ 0417 545 196; www.gatehouseonryrie.com.au; 83 Yarra St; d incl breakfast $95-130; P @ ☎) Geelong's best midrange choice, this guesthouse was built in 1897 with gorgeous timber floorboards throughout, spacious rooms (most with shared facilities) and a communal kitchen and lounge area. Breakfast is held in the glorious front room.

✖ Eating

Go! CAFE $
(www.cafego.com.au; 37 Bellarine St; mains from $10; ⊙ 7am-4pm Mon-Fri, 8am-4pm Sat; ☎) Go! is a local favourite for its fun, colourful atmosphere, good coffee and breakfasts. Head out to its lovely leafy courtyard.

Khan Curry Hut INDIAN $
(www.khancurryhut.com.au; 101-103 Ryrie St; mains from $10; ⊙ 5.30-10pm daily, noon-2.30pm Mon-Fri) Head to Khan for a cheap meal of authentic Indian flavours with fresh ingredients, including South Indian dishes.

★ **Jack & Jill** MODERN AUSTRALIAN $$$
(☏ 03-5229 9935; www.jackandjillrestaurant.com.au; 247 Moorabool St; tasting plates $32.50; ⊙ 6pm-late daily, noon-2.30pm Fri) Choose three small dishes from the menu of regional produce (perhaps parmesan-encrusted scallops, or a dish featuring ostrich) and they'll all be served to you on one plate. Upstairs has a rooftop beer garden with top craft beers. Roll the dice Fridays for free drinks between 5pm and 6.30pm. Also has regular live music.

♟ Drinking & Entertainment

★ **Little Creatures Brewery** BREWERY, BAR
(www.littlecreatures.com.au; cnr Fyans & Swanston Sts; ⊙ 11am-5pm Mon & Tue, to 9pm Wed-Fri, 8am-9pm Sat, 8am-5pm Sun; ☎) Geelong is the newest addition to the growing Little Creatures beer empire. Within an old red-brick wool mill and kitted out in an industrial warehouse feel, this is a cracking place to sample their brews with a thin-crust pizza (from $17). Tours of the brewery operate a

few times a day and include free tastings. Kids will love the sandboxes and room to run around.

Cartel Roasters CAFE
(www.coffeecartel.com.au; 6/21 Leather St, Breakwater; ⊗7am-4.30pm Mon-Sat; 🛜; 🖵61) An unexpected find in South Geelong's industrial backstreets, this hipster-haven coffeehouse roasts a range of African single-origins, to go with a menu of dude food. Tea lovers will be equally delighted with a refined tearoom serving leaves from around the world, set up by a certified 'tea master'. It's a 15-minute bus ride from the city.

Barwon Club LIVE MUSIC
(☑03-5221 4584; www.barwonclub.com.au; 509 Moorabool St; ⊗11am-late) The Barwon has long been Geelong's premier live-music venue, and has spawned the likes of Magic Dirt, Bored! and Warped, seminal bands in the 'Geetroit' rock scene. As well as catching local and international bands, it's a great pub for a beer.

ℹ Information

Pick up a copy of *What's On* or *Forte* for the local happenings in the area.

The **National Wool Museum Visitors Centre** (www.visitgreatoceanroad.org.au; 26 Moorabool St; ⊗9am-5pm; 🛜) has brochures on Geelong, Bellarine Peninsula and the Otways, plus free wi-fi. It also has a **visitor centre** (Princes Hwy; ⊗9am-5pm) on Geelong Rd at the service station near Little River for those bypassing Geelong and heading directly to the Great Ocean Road.

Geelong Library (www.grlc.vic.gov.au; 30-38 Little Malop St; ⊗8.30am-5pm Mon-Fri; 🛜) has free wi-fi and internet. Plans to relocate across the road in 2015.

ℹ Getting There & Away

AIR

Jetstar (☑13 15 38; www.jetstar.com) operates flights to/from Avalon Airport (p237).

BUS

Avalon Airport Shuttle (☑03-5278 8788; www.avalonairportshuttle.com.au) Meets flights at Avalon Airport from Geelong ($17, 35 minutes), and along the Great Ocean Road such as Lorne ($70, 1¾ hours).

Gull Airport Service (☑03-5222 4966; www.gull.com.au; 45 McKillop St) Runs 14 services a day between Geelong and Melbourne Tullamarine Airport ($30, 1¼ hours).

McHarry's Buslines (☑03-5223 2111; www.mcharrys.com.au) Frequent buses from Geelong station to Torquay ($3.70) and the Bellarine Peninsula ($3.50, 20 minutes).

V/Line has buses from Geelong station to Apollo Bay ($16.40, 2½ hours, four daily) via Torquay ($3.60, 25 minutes), Anglesea ($5.40, 45 minutes), Lorne ($10, 1½ hours) and Wye River ($12.40, two hours). On Monday, Wednesday and Friday a bus continues to Port Campbell ($28.60, five hours) and Warrnambool ($32.20, 6½ hours), with a bus transfer at Apollo Bay. Also runs to Ballarat ($8.80, 1½ hours, three or four daily).

GREAT OCEAN ROAD DISTANCES & TIMES

ROUTE	DISTANCE (KM)	DURATION
Melbourne to Geelong	75	1hr
Geelong to Torquay	21	13min
Torquay to Anglesea	16	13min
Anglesea to Aireys Inlet	10	10min
Aireys Inlet to Lorne	19	22min
Lorne to Apollo Bay	45	1hr
Apollo Bay to Port Campbell	96	1½hr
Port Campbell to Warrnambool	66	1hr
Warrnambool to Port Fairy	28	20min
Port Fairy to Portland	72	1hr
Melbourne to Portland	via Great Ocean Rd 440km/via Hamilton Hwy 358km	6½hr/4hr 10min

CAR

The 25km Geelong Ring Rd runs from Corio to Waurn Ponds, bypassing Geelong entirely. To get to Geelong itself stay on the Princes Hwy (M1).

TRAIN

V/Line (☑ 1800 800 007; www.vline.com.au) runs from **Geelong train station** (☑ 03-5226 6525; Gordon Ave) to Melbourne's Southern Cross station ($9, one hour, frequent). Trains also head to Warrnambool ($19, 2½ hours, three daily).

Torquay

POP 15,700

In the 1960s and '70s Torquay was just another sleepy seaside town. Back then surfing in Australia was a decidedly countercultural pursuit, and its devotees were crusty hippie drop-outs living in clapped-out Kombis, smoking pot and making off with your daughters. Since then surfing has become unabashedly mainstream and a huge transglobal business. The town's proximity to world-famous Bells Beach and status as home of two iconic surf brands – Rip Curl and Quiksilver, both initially wetsuit makers – ensures Torquay is the undisputed capital of Australian surfing.

☉ Sights & Activities

Two-hour surfing lessons start at around $60; try **Great Ocean Road Surf Tours** (☑ 1800 787 353; www.gorsurftours.com.au; 106 Surf Coast Hwy) or **Torquay Surfing Academy** (☑ 03-5261 2022; www.torquaysurf.com.au; 34a Bell St).

Surf World Museum   MUSEUM
(www.surfworld.com.au; Surf City Plaza; adult/child/family $12/8/30; ☉ 9am-5pm) The perfect starting point for those embarking on a surfing safari, this well-curated museum pays homage to Australian surfing: from Simon Anderson's ground-breaking 1981 thruster to Mark Richards' board collection and, most notably, Australia's Surfing Hall of Fame. It's full of great memorabilia (including Duke Kahanamoku's wooden longboard), videos and displays on surfing culture in the 1960s to '80s.

🛏 Sleeping & Eating

Bells Beach Backpackers   HOSTEL $
(☑ 03-5261 4029; www.bellsbeachbackpackers.com.au; 51-53 Surfcoast Hwy; dm/d $26/80; @ 🛜) On the main highway, this friendly backpackers does a great job of fitting into the fabric of this surf town with board hire, daily surf reports and a good collection of surf vids. Its basic rooms are clean and in good nick.

Torquay Foreshore Caravan Park   CAMPGROUND $
(☑ 03-5261 2496; www.torquaycaravanpark.com.au; 35 Bell St; powered sites $31-70, d cabins $99-280) Just behind Back Beach, this is the largest camping ground on the Surf Coast. It has good facilities and new premium-priced cabins with sea views.

Cafe Moby   CAFE $
(41 The Esplanade; mains $9-19; ☉ 7am-4pm; 🛜) This old weatherboard house on the Esplanade harks back to a time when Torquay was simple, which is not to say its meals are not modern: fill up on linguini or a honey-roasted lamb souvlaki. There's a whopping great playground in the back for kids.

❶ Information

Torquay Visitor Information Centre (www.greatoceanroad.org; Surf City Plaza, Beach Rd; ☉ 9am-5pm) Well-resourced tourist office next to Surf World Museum. Free wi-fi and internet available at the library next door.

❶ Getting There & Away

Torquay is 13 minutes south of Geelong on the B100.

McHarry's Buslines (☑ 03-5223 2111; www.mcharrys.com.au) Hourly from 9am to 8pm (around 5pm weekends) from Geelong to Torquay ($3.70, 30 minutes), arriving and departing Torquay from the corner of Pearl and Boston Sts (behind the Gilbert St shopping centre).

GREAT OCEAN ROAD TOURS

It's highly recommended you take your time along the Great Ocean Road (ideally a couple of nights to one week), but for those short on time, the following tours depart from Melbourne and often cover it in one whirlwind day.

Go West Tours (☑ 1300 736 551; www.gowest.com.au; tour $120)

Otway Discovery (☑ 03-9654 5432; www.otwaydiscovery.com.au; day trip $99)

Ride Tours (☑ 1800 605 120; www.ridetours.com.au; tour $195)

MELBOURNE & COASTAL VICTORIA TORQUAY

V/Line (☎1800 800 007; www.vline.com. au) Four times daily Monday to Friday (two on weekends) from Geelong to Torquay ($3.60, 25 minutes).

Torquay to Anglesea

About 7km from Torquay is **Bells Beach**. The powerful point break at Bells is part of international surfing folklore (it's here, in name only, that Keanu Reeves and Patrick Swayze had their ultimate showdown in the film *Point Break*). It's notoriously inconsistent, but when the long right-hander is working, it's one of the longest rides in the country. Since 1973, Bells has hosted the **Rip Curl Pro** (www.aspworldtour.com) every Easter – *the* glamour event on the world-championship ASP World Tour. The Rip Curl Pro regularly decamps to Johanna, two hours west, when fickle Bells isn't working.

Nine kilometres southwest of Torquay is the turn-off to spectacular **Point Addis**, 3km down this road. It's a vast sweep of pristine 'clothing-optional' beach that attracts surfers, nudists and swimmers. There's a signposted **Koorie Cultural Walk**, a 1km circuit trail to the beach through the **Ironbark Basin** nature reserve.

The **Surf Coast Walk** (www.visitgreatoceanroad.org.au/surfcoastwalk) follows the coastline from Jan Juc to near Aireys Inlet, and can be done in stages – the full route takes 11 hours. It's marked on the *Surf Coast Touring Map*, available from tourist offices.

Anglesea

POP 2300

Anglesea's **Main Beach** is the ideal spot to learn to surf, while sheltered **Point Roadknight Beach** is good for families. Check out the resident kangaroo population at the town's golf course, or hire a paddleboat and cruise up the Anglesea River.

🏃 Activities

Go Ride A Wave   SURFING
(☎1300 132 441; www.gorideawave.com.au; 143b Great Ocean Rd; 2hr lessons $65, board hire from $25; ◷9am-5pm) Long-established surf school that runs lessons and hires out boards, SUPs and kayaks.

🛏 Sleeping

Anglesea Backpackers   HOSTEL $
(☎03-5263 2664; www.angleseabackpackers.com; 40 Noble St; dm from $30, d $95-115, f $150; @) While most hostels like to cram 'em in, this simple, homely backpackers has just two dorm rooms and one double/triple, and is clean, bright and welcoming. In winter the fire glows warmly in the cosy living room.

Anglesea Rivergums   B&B $$
(☎03-5263 3066; www.anglesearivergums.com. au; 10 Bingley Pde; d $125-160; ❄) Tucked by the river with tranquil views, these two spacious, tastefully furnished rooms (a self-contained bungalow and a room attached to the house) are excellent value.

🍴 Eating

Red Till   CAFE $
(143a Great Ocean Rd; mains $10-20; ◷7am-4pm; 🛜) Across from the main beach, Red Till is decked out in eclectic retro style, with fantastic all-day breakfasts and the best coffee in town.

Locanda Del Mare   ITALIAN $$
(5 Diggers Pde; mains $19.50-25; ◷from 6pm Thu-Mon summer, from 6pm Thu-Sun winter) Don't be deceived by its ugly exterior – this authentic Italian restaurant hidden behind Anglesea's petrol station gets rave reviews, especially for its wonderful desserts.

ℹ Information

Visitor Centre (16/87 Great Ocean Rd; ◷9am-5pm) On the river, this information centre with useful info and maps is the first point of contact for many visitors along the Great Ocean Road.

ℹ Getting There & Away

V/Line has buses linking Anglesea with Geelong ($5.40, 45 minutes).

Aireys Inlet

POP 1200

Aireys Inlet is home to glorious stretches of sand, including long open beach that spans from **Fairhaven** to **Moggs Creek** and **Eastern View**. For a unique experience head along the beach on horseback with **Blazing Saddles** (☎03-5289 7322; www.blazingsaddlestrailrides.com; Lot 1, Bimbadeen Dr; 1/2½hr rides $45/100).

The **Split Point Lighthouse** (☎03-5263 1133; www.splitpointlighthouse.com.au; 45min tours adult/child/family $12/7/35; ⊙ hourly from 11am-2pm, summer holidays 10am-4pm), c 1891, has sensational 360-degree views from up top; you can climb up by booking a tour.

🛏 Sleeping

Cimarron B&B   B&B **$$**

(☎ 03-5289 7044; www.cimarron.com.au; 105 Gilbert St; d $150-175; 🛜) Built in 1979 from local timbers and using only wooden pegs and shiplap joins, Cimarron is an idyllic getaway with views over Point Roadknight. The large lounge area has book-lined walls and a cosy fireplace, while upstairs there are two unique, loft-style doubles with vaulted timber ceilings; otherwise there's a den-like apartment. Out back, it's all state park and wildlife. Gay friendly, but no kids.

Lightkeepers Inn   MOTEL **$$**

(☎ 03-5289 6666; www.lightkeepersinn.com.au; 64 Great Ocean Rd; d $130; 🛜🐾) Convenient for the shops, here you can expect clean motel rooms with extra-thick walls for peace and quiet.

🍴 Eating & Drinking

★ A La Grecque   GREEK **$$**

(☎ 03-5289 6922; www.alagrecque.com.au; 60 Great Ocean Rd; mains $28-38; ⊙ 9-11.30am, 12.30-2.30pm & 6-10pm daily Dec-Mar, Wed-Sun Apr-Nov, closed Jun-Aug) Be whisked away to the Mediterranean at this outstanding modern Greek taverna. Mezze such as cured kingfish with apple, celery and a lime dressing, and mains such as grilled baby snapper are sensational. Kosta, the host, ran Kosta's in Lorne for 27 years before decamping to Aireys.

Aireys Pub   PUB

(☎ 03-5289 6804; www.aireyspub.com.au; 45 Great Ocean Rd; ⊙ noon-late; 🛜) Established in 1904, this coastal pub is a survivor, twice burning to the ground, before closing its doors in 2011 only to be saved by a bunch of locals who chipped in to rescue it. Now it's better than ever, with a fantastic kitchen, roaring fire, sprawling beer garden, live music and its very own Aireys draught beer.

Lorne

POP 1000

Lorne has an incredible natural beauty, something you see vividly as you drive into town from Aireys Inlet. Old, tall gum trees line its hilly streets, and Loutit Bay gleams irresistibly. It's this beauty that has attracted visitors for centuries – Rudyard Kipling's 1891 visit led him to pen the poem 'Flowers': 'Gathered where the Erskine leaps/Down the road to Lorne.'

It gets busy; in summer you'll be competing with day-trippers for restaurant seats and lattes, but, thronging with tourists or not, Lorne is a lovely place to hang out.

⊙ Sights & Activities

Qdos Art Gallery   GALLERY

(☎ 03-5289 1989; www.qdosarts.com; 35 Allenvale Rd; ⊙ 9am-6pm daily Dec & Jan, 9am-5.30pm Thu-Mon Feb-Nov) **FREE** Amid the lush forest that backs on to Lorne, Qdos always has something interesting showing at its gallery, to go with its open-air sculpture garden. Refuel at the on-site cafe and treat yourself to a night in the accommodation (room including breakfast $250).

Erskine Falls   WATERFALL

(Erskine Falls Access Rd) Head out of town to see this lovely waterfall. It's an easy walk to the viewing platform or 250 (often slippery) steps down to its base, from which you can explore further afield or head back on up.

WORTH A TRIP

BRAE

Given the success chef Dan Hunter had at the Royal Mail Hotel in Dunkeld, the Birregurra tourism guys must've been licking their lips for several reasons when they heard he was moving to their town to open his new restaurant, **Brae** (☎ 03-5236 2226; www.braerestaurant.com; 4285 Cape Otway Rd, Birregurra; 8-course tasting plates per person $180; ⊙ noon-3pm Fri-Mon, from 6pm Thu-Sun).

Opening its doors at the time of research, Brae takes over from the much-loved Sunnybrae, with its farmhouse getting a refit by renowned architects Six Degrees, and using whatever is growing in its 30 acres of organic gardens. Reservations are essential, well in advance. Future plans include boutique accommodation on site.

It's located in the small historic town of Birregurra between Colac and Lorne.

Great Ocean Road National Heritage Centre
MUSEUM

(15 Mountjoy Pde; ⊙9am-5pm) Scheduled to open mid 2014, this museum will tell the story of the construction of the Great Ocean Road, built from 1919 to 1932 by mostly returned WWI soldiers using picks, shovels and crowbars.

✺ Festivals & Events

Falls Festival
MUSIC

(www.fallsfestival.com; 2-/3-/4-day tickets $320/390/433; ⊙28 Dec-1 Jan) A four-day knees-up over New Year's on a farm just out of town, this stellar music festival attracts a top line-up of international rock and indie groups. Past headliners include Iggy Pop, Kings of Leon and the Black Keys. Sells out fast, and tickets include camping.

🛌 Sleeping

Great Ocean Road Backpackers
HOSTEL $

(☑03-5289 1070; 10 Erskine Ave; dm/d $35/90; ❄☎) Tucked away in the bush among the cockatoos, koalas and other wildlife, this two-storey timber lodge has dorms and good-value doubles. Unisex bathrooms take some getting used to. Also has pricier A-frame cottages that come with kitchens and en suite.

Lorne Foreshore Caravan Park
CAMPGROUND $

(☑1300 364 797; www.lornecaravanpark.com.au; 2 Great Ocean Rd; powered sites $32-60, d cabins from $70) Book here for Lorne's five caravan parks. Of these Erskine River Park is the prettiest; it's on the left-hand side as you enter Lorne, just before the bridge. Book well ahead for peak-season stays.

🍴 Eating

Kafe Kaos
CAFE $

(52 Mountjoy Pde; lunch $8-15; ⊙8am-4.30pm; ☎) Bright and perky, Kafe Kaos typifies Lorne's relaxed foodie philosophy – barefoot patrons in boardies or bikinis tuck into first-class panini, bruschetta, burgers and chips, all-day breakfasts and a bar.

Lorne Beach Pavilion
MODERN AUSTRALIAN $$

(☑03-5289 2882; www.lornebeachpavilion.com.au; 81 Mountjoy Pde; ⊙8am-9pm) With its unbeatable spot on the foreshore, here life's literally a beach, especially with a cold beer in hand. Come at happy hour for 1kg of mussels for $10 and two-for-one cocktails. Cafe-

style breakfasts and lunches are tasty, while a more upmarket Modern Australian menu is on for dinner.

ℹ Information

Lorne Visitors Centre (☑1300 891 152; www.visitgreatoceanroad.org.au/lorne; 15 Mountjoy Pde; ⊙9am-5pm; ☎) Stacks of information, walking maps, fishing licences, bus tickets, accommodation booking, plus internet access and free wi-fi.

Cumberland River

Just 7km southwest of Lorne is Cumberland River. There's nothing here – no shops or houses – other than the wonderful **Cumberland River Holiday Park** (☑03-5289 1790; www.cumberlandriver.com.au; Great Ocean Rd; unpowered sites $37, en-suite cabins from $105). This splendidly located bushy camping ground is next to a lovely river and high craggy cliffs that rise on the far side.

Wye River

POP 140

The Great Ocean Road snakes spectacularly around the cliffside from Cumberland River before reaching this little town with big ideas.

🛌 Sleeping & Eating

Wye River Foreshore Camping Reserve
CAMPGROUND $

(☑03-5289 0412; sites $40; ⊙Nov-Apr) This camping ground offers powered beachside sites during summer.

★ Wye General
CAFE $$

(www.thewyegeneral.com; 35 Great Ocean Rd; dinner $15-26; ⊙8am-5pm Mon-Sat, to 4pm Sun) This cafe has marched into town and there's nothing general about it. From fantastic burgers and homemade sourdough to perfect coffee, this smart indoor-outdoor joint has polished-concrete floors, timber features and a sophisticated retro ambience that will impress.

Wye Beach Hotel
PUB $$

(☑03-5289 0240; www.wyebeachhotel.com.au; 19 Great Ocean Rd; mains $18-30, r $120-260; ⊙11am-11pm Mon-Fri, to late Sat; ☎) People come here for pub food on a verandah with some of the most stunning views of the coast. The hotel also has comfortable motel-style double rooms with great views. Rooms are well priced midweek.

Kennett River

Just 5km along from Wye River is Kennett River, which has some truly great koala-spotting in the town itself, and you'll also spot the furry creatures above the Great Ocean Road towards Apollo Bay. In town, just behind the caravan park, walk 200m up Grey River Rd and you'll see bundles of sleepy koalas clinging to the branches. Glow-worms light up the same stretch at night (take a torch).

The friendly Kennett River Holiday Park (☑ 03-5289 0272; www.kennettriver.com; 1-13 Great Ocean Rd; unpowered/powered sites $29/35, d cabins from $115; @ 🛜) is a bush park with free wireless internet and free barbecues.

Apollo Bay

POP 1800

One of the larger towns along the Great Ocean Road, Apollo Bay has a tight community of fisherfolk, artists and sea-changers.

Majestic rolling hills provide a postcard backdrop to the town, while broad, white-sand beaches dominate the foreground. It's also an ideal base for exploring magical Cape Otway and Otway National Park. It has some of the best restaurants along the coast and two lively pubs.

🏃 Activities

Mark's Walking Tours
WALKING TOUR
(☑ 0417 983 985; www.greatoceanwalk.asn.au/markstours; 2-3hr tours adult/child $50/15) Take a walk around the area with local Mark Brack, son of the Cape Otway Lighthouse keeper. He knows this stretch of coast, its history and its ghosts better than anyone around. Daily tours include shipwreck, historical, glow-worm and Great Ocean Walk tours. Minimum two people.

Apollo Bay Surf & Kayak
KAYAKING, SURFING
(☑ 0405 495 909; www.apollobaysurfkayak.com.au; 157-159 Great Ocean Rd; 2hr kayak tours $65, 1½hr surf lessons $60) Head out to an Australian fur-seal colony on a two-seated kayak. Tours (with full instructions for beginners) depart from Marengo beach (to the south of the town centre). Also offers surf lessons, plus boards, stand-up paddleboards and mountain bikes for hire. It also operates Walk 91 for the Great Ocean Walk.

Surf'n'Fish
DIVING
(☑ 03-5237 6426; www.surf-n-fish.com.au; 157 Great Ocean Rd) Authorised PADI dive centre that can arrange trips to Marengo reef and nearby wrecks, including SS *Casino*, which sank offshore in 1932. Rents out surfboards and fishing tackle, too.

🎉 Festivals & Events

Apollo Bay Music Festival
MUSIC
(☑ 03-5237 6761; www.apollobaymusicfestival.com; weekend pass $125, under-15 free; ⊙ late Feb) Three-day music festival spanning most genres, showcasing Aussie talent and international acts. Book accommodation well ahead.

🛏 Sleeping

YHA Eco Beach
HOSTEL $
(☑ 03-5237 7899; www.yha.com.au; 5 Pascoe St; dm from $35, d $95, f $119; @ 🛜) 🌱 This $3 million, architect-designed hostel is an outstanding place to stay, with ecocredentials, great lounge areas, kitchens, boules pit and rooftop terraces. Rooms are generic but spotless. It's a block behind the beach.

DON'T MISS

GREAT OCEAN WALK

The multiday Great Ocean Walk (www.greatoceanwalk.com.au) starts at Apollo Bay and runs all the way to the Twelve Apostles. It's possible to start at one point and arrange a pick-up at another (there are few public transport options). You can do shorter walks or the whole 104km trek over six days. Designated (and free) camp sites are spread along the Great Ocean Walk. Walk 91 (☑ 03-5237 1189; www.walk91.com.au; 157-159 Great Ocean Rd, Apollo Bay) arranges transport and equipment hire, and can take your backpack to your destination for you. GOR Shuttle (☑ 0428 379 278, 03-5237 9278) is a recommended shuttle service for luggage and walkers; it will pick you up when your walking's done.

THE WRECK OF THE LOCH ARD

The Victorian coastline between Cape Otway and Port Fairy was a notoriously treacherous stretch of water in the days of sailing ships, due to hidden reefs and frequent heavy fog. Of the many vessels that came to grief, the most famous wreck was that of the iron-hulled clipper *Loch Ard*, which foundered off Mutton Bird Island at 4am on the final night of its long voyage from England in 1878. Of 37 crew and 19 passengers on board, only two survived. Eva Carmichael, who couldn't swim, clung to wreckage and was washed into a gorge, where apprentice officer Tom Pearce rescued her. Tom heroically climbed the sheer cliff and raised the alarm but no other survivors were found. Eva and Tom were both 19 years old, leading to speculation in the press about a romance, but nothing actually happened – they never saw each other again and Eva soon returned back to Ireland (this time, perhaps not surprisingly) via steamship.

★ **Beacon Point Ocean View Villas**　　　　　　　VILLA $$
(☑ 03-5237 6196; www.beaconpoint.com.au; 270 Skenes Creek Rd; r from $160; ✳) With a commanding hill location among the trees, this wonderful collection of comfortable one- and two-bedroom villas is a luxurious yet affordable bush retreat. Most have sensational coast views, balconies and wood-fired heaters.

✖ Eating

Bay Leaf Café　　　　　　　　　　CAFE $
(☑ 03-5237 6470; 131 Great Ocean Rd; mains $10-16; ⊗ 8.30am-2.30pm) A local favourite for its innovative menu, good coffee, friendly atmosphere and boutique beer selection.

★ **Chris's Beacon Point Restaurant**　　　　　　GREEK $$$
(☑ 03-5237 6411; www.chriss.com.au; 280 Skenes Creek Rd; mains from $38; r incl breakfast $265; ⊗ 8.30-10am & 6pm-late daily, plus lunch Sat & Sun; ☎) Feast on memorable ocean views, deliciously fresh seafood and Greek-influenced dishes at Chris' hilltop fine-dining sanctuary among the treetops. Reservations recommended. You can also stay in its wonderful stilted villas. It's accessed via Skenes Creek.

❶ Information

Great Ocean Road Visitors Centre (☑ 1300 689 297; 100 Great Ocean Rd; ⊗ 9am-5pm; ☎) Heaps of info, an 'ecocentre' with displays, free wi-fi and bus bookings.

Around Apollo Bay

Hidden away in the Otways about 36km from Apollo Bay is the small town of For-rest, a hot spot for mountain-biking enthusiasts and home of the **Forrest Brewing Company** (☑ 03-5236 6170; www.forrestbrewing.com.au; Apollo Bay Rd, Forrest; 6-beer tasting pallet $10; ⊗ 10am-late Thu, 9am-late Fri-Sun, daily Dec-Jan), popular for beer tastings. **Otway Eco Tours** (☑ 0419 670 985; www.platypustours.net.au; adult/child $85/50) runs guided canoe trips at dusk and dawn to spot platypus in nearby **Lake Elizabeth**.

Accessed from either Lavers Hill or Beech Forest is the popular **Otway Fly** (☑ 03-5235 9200; www.otwayfly.com; 360 Phillips Track; adult/child $22.50/9; ⊗ 9am-5pm, last entry 4pm), an elevated steel walkway and zipline through the forest canopy.

Cape Otway

Cape Otway is the second most southerly point of mainland Australia (after Wilsons Promontory) and one of the wettest parts of the state. This coastline is particularly beautiful, rugged and dangerous. More than 200 ships met their demise between Cape Otway and Port Fairy between the 1830s and 1930s, which led to the 'Shipwreck Coast' moniker.

The turn-off for Lighthouse Rd, which leads 12km down to the lighthouse, is 21km from Apollo Bay. The **Cape Otway Lighthouse** (☑ 03-5237 9240; www.lightstation.com; Lighthouse Rd; adult/child/family $18.50/7.50/46.50; ⊗ 9am-5pm) is the oldest surviving lighthouse on mainland Australia and was built in 1848 by more than 40 stonemasons without mortar or cement; there's also **accommodation** (☑ 03-5237 9240; www.lightstation.com; d from $250) here. Keep your eyes peeled for koalas along the forested road en route.

🛏 Sleeping

Blanket Bay
CAMPGROUND $

(☑13 19 63; www.parkweb.vic.gov.au; sites from $20) Blanket Bay is one of those 'secret' campgrounds that Melburnians love to lay claim to discovering. It's serene (depending on your neighbours) and the nearby beach is beautiful. It's not really a secret; in fact, it's so popular during summer and Easter holidays that sites must be won by ballot (held August to October).

Bimbi Park
CAMPGROUND $

(☑03-5237 9246; www.bimbipark.com.au; 90 Manna Gum Dr; unpowered/powered sites $20/30, dm $45, d cabins $50-185; 🛜) 🐾 Down a dirt road 3km from the lighthouse is this character-filled caravan park with bush sites, cabins, dorms and old-school caravans. It's good for families, with plenty of wildlife, including koalas, horse rides ($45 per hour) and a rock-climbing wall. Good use of water-saving initiatives.

★ Great Ocean Ecolodge
LODGE $$$

(☑03-5237 9297; www.greatoceanecolodge.com; 635 Lighthouse Rd; r incl breakfast & activities from $370) 🐾 Reminiscent of a luxury African safari lodge, this mudbrick homestead stands among pastoral surrounds with plenty of wildlife. It's all solar-powered and rates go towards the on-site Conservation Ecology Centre (www.conservationecologycentre.org). It also serves as an animal hospital for local fauna, and operates a captive tiger-quoll breeding program, which you'll visit on a dusk wildlife walk with an ecologist.

Port Campbell National Park & the Twelve Apostles

The road levels out after leaving the Otways and enters narrow, relatively flat scrubby escarpment lands that fall away to sheer, 70m cliffs along the coast between Princetown and Peterborough – a distinct change of scene. This is Port Campbell National Park, home to the Twelve Apostles; it's the most famous and most photographed stretch of the Great Ocean Road. For aeons, waves and tides have crashed against the soft limestone rock, eroding, undercutting and carving out a fascinating series of rock stacks, gorges, arches and blowholes.

The Gibson Steps, hacked by hand into the cliffs in the 19th century by local landowner Hugh Gibson (and more recently replaced by concrete steps), lead down to feral Gibson Beach, an essential stop. This beach, and others along this stretch of coast, are not suitable for swimming because of strong currents and undertows – you can walk along the beach, but be careful not to be stranded by high tides or nasty waves. The lonely Twelve Apostles are rocky stacks that have been abandoned to the ocean by the retreating headland. Today, only seven apostles can be seen from the viewing platforms. Helicopters

HOW MANY APOSTLES?

The Twelve Apostles are not 12 in number, and, from all records, never have been. From the viewing platform you can clearly count seven Apostles, but maybe some obscure others? We consulted widely with Parks Victoria officers, tourist office staff and even the cleaner at the lookout, but it's still not clear. Locals tend to say 'It depends where you look from', which, really, is true.

The Apostles are called 'stacks' in geologic lingo, and the rock formations were originally called the 'Sow and Piglets'. Someone in the '60s (nobody can recall who) thought they might attract some tourists with a more venerable name, so they were renamed 'the Apostles'. Since apostles tend to come by the dozen, the number 12 was added some time later. The two stacks on the eastern (Otway) side of the viewing platform are not technically Apostles – they're Gog and Magog (picking up on the religious nomenclature yet?).

So there aren't 12 stacks; in a boat or helicopter you might count 11. The soft limestone cliffs are dynamic and changeable, constantly eroded by the unceasing waves – one 70m-high stack collapsed into the sea in July 2005 and the Island Archway lost its archway in June 2009. If you look carefully at how the waves lick around the pointy part of the cliff base, you can see a new Apostle being born. The labour lasts many thousands of years.

zoom around the Twelve Apostles, giving passengers an amazing view of the rocks. Try **12 Apostles Helicopters** (📞03-5598 8283; www.12apostleshelicopters.com.au; 15min flights $145), just behind the car park at the lookout.

Nearby **Loch Ard Gorge** is where the Shipwreck Coast's most famous tale unfolded when two young survivors of the wrecked iron clipper *Loch Ard* made it to shore.

Port Campbell

POP 400

This small, windswept town is poised on a dramatic, natural bay, eroded from the surrounding limestone cliffs, and almost perfectly rectangular in shape. It's a friendly spot with some great bargain accommodation options, and makes an ideal spot for debriefing after the Twelve Apostles. The tiny bay has a lovely sandy beach, the only safe place for swimming along this tempestuous coast.

🏃 Activities

A 4.7km **Discovery Walk**, with signage, gives an introduction to the area's natural and historical features. It's just out of town on the way to Warrnambool.

Port Campbell Touring Company   TOUR
(📞03-5598 6424; www.portcampbelltouring. com.au; half-day tours from $100) Runs Apostle Coast tours and walking tours including a *Loch Ard* evening walk.

Port Campbell Boat Charters   FISHING
(📞0428 986 366; per person from $50) Get up close and personal with the Twelve Apostles on a boat tour, as well as dive and fishing charters for groups.

🛏 Sleeping & Eating

Port Campbell Guesthouse   GUESTHOUSE $
(📞0407 696 559; www.portcampbellguesthouse. com; 54 Lord St; s/d incl breakfast from $40/70; ❄@) It's great to find a home away from home, and this historic cottage close to town has four cosy rooms and relaxed lounge and country kitchen. For added privacy there's a separate motel-style section up front with en-suite rooms. Its ultra-relaxed owner, Mark, is knowledgeable about the area.

Port Campbell Hostel   HOSTEL $
(📞03-5598 6305; www.portcampbellhostel.com. au; 18 Tregea St; dm/d from $28/70; @🤶) 🅿

This modern purpose-built double-storey backpackers has rooms with western views, a huge shared kitchen and an even bigger lounge and bar area. It's big on recycling and the toilets are ecofriendly, too. Offers bike hire and tours in the area.

12 Rocks Cafe Bar   CAFE $$
(19 Lord St; mains $20-36; ⊙9.30am-11pm) Watch flotsam wash up on the beach from this busy eatery, which has perfect beachfront views. Try a local Otways beer with a pasta or seafood main, or just duck in for a coffee.

❶ Information

Port Campbell Visitor Centre (📞1300 137 255; www.visit12apostles.com.au; 26 Morris St; ⊙9am-5pm) Stacks of regional information and interesting shipwreck displays – the anchor from the *Loch Ard* is out the front. Provides free use of binoculars for dusk-time penguin viewing at the Twelve Apostles.

❶ Getting There & Away

V/Line (📞13 61 96; www.vline.com.au) buses leave Geelong on Monday, Wednesday and Friday and travel through Port Campbell ($28.60, five hours) and onto Warrnambool ($6.80, 1 hour 20 minutes).

Port Campbell to Warrnambool

The Great Ocean Road continues west of Port Campbell, passing more rock stacks. The next one is the **Arch**, offshore from Point Hesse.

Nearby is **London Bridge**, which has indeed fallen down. It was once a double-arched rock platform linked to the mainland, yet it remains a spectacular sight nevertheless. In January 1990, the bridge collapsed leaving two terrified tourists marooned on the world's newest island – they were eventually rescued by helicopter. Nearby is the **Grotto**.

The **Bay of Islands** is 8km west of tiny **Peterborough**, where a short walk from the car park takes you to magnificent lookout points.

The Great Ocean Road ends near here where it meets the Princes Hwy, which continues through the traditional lands of the Gunditjmara people into South Australia.

Warrnambool

POP 28,100

Warrnambool was originally a whaling and sealing station – now it's booming as a major regional commercial and whale-watching centre. Its historic buildings, waterways and tree-lined streets are attractive, and there's a large student population that attends the Warrnambool campus of Deakin University.

◉ Sights & Activities

Southern right whales come to mate and nurse their bubs in the waters off Logan's Beach from July to September, breaching and fluking off **Logan's Beach Whale-Watching Platform**. It's a major tourist drawcard, but sightings are not guaranteed.

★**Flagstaff Hill Maritime Village** HISTORIC SITE
(☑03-5559 4600; www.flagstaffhill.com; 89 Merri St; adult/child/concession/family $16/6.50/12.50/39; ◎9am-5pm) The world-class Flagstaff Hill precinct is of equal interest for its shipwreck museum, heritage-listed lighthouses and garrison as it is for its reproduction of a historical Victorian port town. It also has the nightly **Shipwrecked** (adult/child/family $26/14/67), an engaging 70-minute sound-and-laser show telling the story of the *Loch Ard's* plunge.

Warrnambool Art Gallery GALLERY
(☑03-5559 4949; www.warrnambool.vic.gov.au; 165 Timor St; ◎10am-5pm Mon-Fri, noon-5pm Sat & Sun) FREE Small but worthwhile collection of rotating permanent artworks by prominent Australian painters, as well as temporary exhibits.

Rundell's Mahogany Trail Rides HORSE RIDING
(☑0408 589 546; www.rundellshorseriding.com. au; 1½hr beach rides $60) Get to know some of Warrnambool's quiet beach spots by horseback.

🛏 Sleeping

Warrnambool Beach Backpackers HOSTEL $
(☑03-5562 4874; www.beachbackpackers.com. au; 17 Stanley St; dm/d from $26/80; P@🛜) A short stroll to the beach, this hostel has all backpackers' needs, with a huge living area, kitchsy Aussie-themed bar, internet access, kitchen and free pick-up service. Its rooms are clean and good value, and you can hire surfboards and bikes. Vanpackers pay $12 per person to stay here.

Hotel Warrnambool PUB $$
(☑03-5562 2377; www.hotelwarrnambool.com. au; cnr Koroit & Kepler Sts; d incl breakfast shared/private bathroom from $110/140; P🌡🛜) Renovations to this historic 1894 hotel have seen rooms upgraded to the more boutique end of the scale, while keeping a classic pub-accommodation feel.

🍴 Eating & Drinking

Brightbird Espresso CAFE $
(www.brightbird.com.au; 157 Liebig St; mains $8-17; ◎7.30am-4pm Mon-Fri, 8.30am-2pm Sat) Polished-concrete floors, dangling light bulbs and single-origin coffees brewed by tattooed baristas bring a slice of inner-city Melbourne to the 'bool. All-day breakfasts encompass creative dishes to egg-and-bacon rolls.

Hotel Warrnambool PUB $$
(cnr Koroit & Kepler Sts; mains $18-24; ◎noon-late; 🛜) One of Vic's best coastal pubs, Hotel Warrnambool mixes pub charm with bohemian character and serves wood-fired pizzas among other gastro-pub fare.

ℹ Information

Warrnambool Library (25 Liebig St; ◎9.30am-5pm Mon & Tue, to 6pm Wed-Fri, 10am-noon Sat; 🛜) Free internet and wi-fi access.

Warrnambool Visitors Centre (☑1800 637 725; www.visitwarrnambool.com.au; Merri St; ◎9am-5pm) For the latest on whale sightings, bike maps and several walking maps. Also has bicycle hire ($30 per day).

ℹ Getting There & Away

Warrnambool is an hour's drive west of Port Campbell on the B100.

BUS

V/Line buses travel Monday, Wednesday and Friday from Geelong along the Great Ocean Road to Warrnambool ($32.20, 6½ hours).

V/Line and **Warrnambool Bus Lines** (☑03-5562 1866; www.transitsw.com.au) travel to Port Fairy ($4.20, 35 minutes), with V/Line continuing on to Portland ($11, 1½ hours).

Christian's Bus Co (☑03-5562 9432; www. christiansbus.com.au) runs on Tuesday, Friday and Sunday to Port Fairy ($4, departing 7.45am), continuing to Halls Gap ($25, 3¼ hours) and Ararat ($29.20, four hours).

TRAIN

V/Line (☎1800 800 007; www.vline.com.au; Merri St) trains run to/from Melbourne ($31, 3¼ hours, three or four daily) via Geelong ($22.20, 2½ hours).

Tower Hill Reserve

Tower Hill, 15km west of Warrnambool, is a vast caldera born in a volcanic eruption 35,000 years ago. Aboriginal artefacts unearthed in the volcanic ash show that Indigenous people lived in the area at the time and, today, the Worn Gundidj Aboriginal Cooperative operates the **Tower Hill Natural History Centre** (☎03-5565 9202; www.worngundidj.org.au; walks adult/child $18.95/8.80; ⊙9am-5pm Mon-Fri, 10am-4pm Sat, Sun & public holidays). The centre is housed within the UFO-like building designed by renowned Australian architect Robin Boyd in 1962. Bush walks led by Indigenous guides depart daily at 11am and include boomerang-throwing and bush-tucker demonstrations. The centre also sells handicrafts, artwork and accessories designed by the local Worn Gundidj community. It's one of the few places where you'll spot wild emus, kangaroos and koalas hanging out together.

There are excellent day walks, including the steep 30-minute **Peak Climb** with spectacular 360-degree views.

Port Fairy

POP 2600

Settled in 1833 as a whaling and sealing station, Port Fairy retains its historic 19th-century charm with a relaxed, salty feel, heritage bluestone and sandstone buildings, whitewashed cottages, colourful fishing boats and wide tree-lined streets. It has a rich and sometimes gloomy heritage that enraptures local history buffs. In 2012 it was voted the world's most liveable community, and for most visitors it's not hard to see why.

GREAT SOUTHWEST WALK

This 250km signposted loop begins and ends at Portland's information centre, and takes in some of the southwest's most stunning natural scenery, from the remote, blustery coast, through the river system of the Lower Glenelg National Park and back through the hinterland to Portland. The whole loop would take at least 10 days, but it can be done in sections. Maps are available from the Portland visitors centre and the Parks Victoria office and visitors centre in Nelson. See www.greatsouthwestwalk.com.

Sights & Activities

The visitors centre has brochures and maps that show the **Shipwreck Walk** and **History Walk**. On **Battery Hill** there are plenty of wallabies, a lookout point, and cannons and fortifications positioned here in the 1860s. Down below there's a lovely one-hour walk around **Griffiths Island** where the Moyne River empties into the sea. The island is connected to the mainland by a footbridge, and is home to a protected **muttonbird colony** (they descend on the town each October and stay until April) and a modest **lighthouse**.

Festivals & Events

★Port Fairy Folk Festival MUSIC
(www.portfairyfolkfestival.com; tickets $75-210; ⊙Mar) Australia's premier folk-music festival is held on the Labour Day long weekend in March. It includes an excellent mix of international and national acts, while the streets are abuzz with buskers. Accommodation can book out a year in advance.

Sleeping

Port Fairy YHA HOSTEL $
(☎03-5568 2468; www.portfairyhostel.com.au; 8 Cox St; dm $26-30, s/tw/d from $37/65/70; @) In the rambling 1844 home of merchant William Rutledge, this friendly, well-run hostel has a large kitchen, a pool table, free cable TV and peaceful gardens.

Seacombe House GUESTHOUSE $$
(☎03-5568 1082; www.seacombehouse.com.au; 22 Sackville St; r with shared/private bathroom $93/155; ❄📶) Built in 1847, historic Seacombe House has cosy (OK, tiny) rooms, but it offers all the atmosphere and romance you'd hope from this seafaring town. Modern motel rooms are available in its rear wing. It's above the acclaimed Stag restaurant.

Eating

Coffin Sally PIZZERIA $
(33 Sackville St; pizzas $9-19; ⊙4-10pm) Located within a former undertakers (relax, it was 100 years ago). Traditional thin-crust pizzas

are cooked in an open kitchen and wolfed down on streetside stools or in the dimly lit dining nooks out back next to an open fire.

Rocksalt CAFE **$$**
(☑ 03-5568 3452; 42 Sackville St; mains $12-34; ☺ 7.30am-4pm year-round & 6-8.30pm summer; 🛜) Homely, nonpretentious cafe with baked eggs, beans and chorizo for breakfast, steak sandwiches for lunch and pork belly for dinner.

★ **Merrijig Kitchen** MODERN AUSTRALIAN **$$$**
(☑ 03-5568 2324; www.merrijiginn.com; cnr Campbell & Gipps Sts; mains $30-38; ☺ 6-9pm Thu-Mon; 🛜) One of coastal Victoria's most atmospheric restaurants; warm yourself by the open fire and enjoy superb dining with a menu that changes according to what's seasonal. Delectable food with great service.

ℹ️ Information

Port Fairy Visitors Centre (☑ 03-5568 2682; www.visitportfairy-moyneshire.com.au; Bank St; ☺ 9am-5pm) Spot-on tourist information, walking tour brochures, V-Line tickets and bike hire (half-/full-day $15/25).

Port Fairy Library (www.corangamitelibrary. vic.gov.au; cnr Sackville & Bank Sts; ☺ 10am-1pm & 1.30-4.30pm Mon, Wed & Fri, to noon Sat; 🛜) Free wi-fi and internet.

ℹ️ Getting There & Away

V/Line (☑ 1800 800 007; www.vline.com.au) buses run three times daily weekdays (twice on Saturday and once on Sunday) to Portland ($7.80, 55 minutes) and Warrnambool ($4.20, 35 minutes).

Christian's Bus Co (p255) heads to Halls Gap ($21.60, 2½ hours) and Ararat ($27.20, 3¼ hours) Tuesday, Friday and Sunday around 8am.

Portland

POP 9800

Portland's claim to fame is as Victoria's first European settlement, founded as a whaling and sealing base in the early 1800s.

At the far end of the waterfront are several heritage bluestone buildings, including a small museum (☑ 03-5522 2266; Cliff St; adult/ child $3/2; ☺ 10am-noon & 1-4pm). At the other end **Portland Maritime Discovery Centre** (☑ 1800 035 567; Lee Breakwater Rd; adult/child $7/free; ☺ 9am-5pm) has excellent displays on shipwrecks and the town's whaling history.

There are some good beaches and surf breaks outside town.

DON'T MISS

CAPE NELSON LIGHTHOUSE

Cape Nelson Lighthouse is a wonderful spot for a bite to eat and some stunning views. Isabella's Cafe (☑ 03-5523 5119; ☺ 11am-4pm) takes pride of place at its blustering base and offers excellent deli-style food within its thick bluestone walls. Lighthouse tours (www. capenelsonlighthouse.com.au; adult/child $15/10; ☺ 11am & 2pm) get you high up, while those wanting to stay a while can book into a self-contained assistant lighthouse keepers' cottage (☑ 03-5523 5119; www.capenelsonlighthouse. com.au; d from $180).

🛌 Sleeping & Eating

Portland Holiday Village CARAVAN PARK **$**
(☑ 03-5521 7567; www.holidayvillage.com.au; 37 Percy St; unpowered/powered sites from $25/30, cabins from $89; ❄🛜) Centrally located caravan park with decent facilities.

Annesley House BOUTIQUE HOTEL **$$**
(☑ 0429 852 235; www.annesleyhouse.com.au; 60 Julia St; d from $145; ❄🛜) This recently restored former doctor's mansion (c 1878) has six very different self-contained rooms, some featuring clawfoot baths and lovely views. All have a unique sense of style.

Deegan Seafoods FISH & CHIPS **$**
(106 Percy St; mains $10; ☺ 9am-6pm Mon-Fri) This fish-and-chip shop famously serves up the freshest fish in Victoria.

ℹ️ Information

Portland Visitors Centre (☑ 1800 035 567; www.glenelg.vic.gov.au; Lee Breakwater Rd; ☺ 9am-5pm) Modern building on the waterfront, with a stack of suggestions of things to do and see.

ℹ️ Getting There & Away

V/Line (☑ 1800 800 007; www.vline.com.au) Buses to Port Fairy ($7.80, 55 minutes) and Warrnambool ($11, 1½ hours), departing from Henty St.

Nelson

POP 230

Tiny Nelson is the last vestige of civilisation before the South Australian border – just a general store, pub and a few accommoda-

CAPE BRIDGEWATER

Cape Bridgewater is a 21km detour off the Portland–Nelson Rd. The stunning 4km arc of Bridgewater Bay is perhaps Victoria's finest stretch of white-sand surf beach. The wind-farm-lined road continues on to Cape Duquesne, where walking tracks lead to a Blowhole and the Petrified Forest on the clifftop. A longer two-hour return walk takes you to a seal colony where you can see dozens of fur seals sunning themselves on the rocks.

Stay at friendly Sea View Lodge B&B (☑03-5526 7276; www.hotkey.net.au/~seaviewlodge; 1636 Bridgewater Rd; s/d incl breakfast $110/140; 🕿) or Cape Bridgewater Coastal Camp (☑03-5526 7247; www.capebridgewatercoastalcamp.com.au; Blowhole Rd; unpowered/powered sites $20/30, dm/d/house $25/50/150; ❋), which has sparkling dorms, self-contained houses and a huge camp kitchen. The coastal camp also runs fun Seals by Sea Tours (☑03-5526 7247; www.sealsbyseatours.com.au; adult/child $35/20; ⊘Aug-Apr).

tion places. It's a popular holiday and fishing spot at the mouth of the Glenelg River, which flows through Lower Glenelg National Park. Note that Nelson uses South Australia's 08 telephone area code.

🏃 Activities

Nelson River Cruises　　　　CRUISE
(☑0448 887 1225, 08-8738 4191; www.glenelgrivercruises.com.au; cruises adult/child $30/10; ⊘Sep-Jun) These leisurely 3½-hour cruises head along the Glenelg River, departing Nelson at 1pm several times a week; check the website for schedules. The tours include the impressive Princess Margaret Rose Cave (☑08-8738 4171; www.princessmargaretrosecave.com; adult/child/family $17.50/11.50/40; ⊘hourly tours 11am-4.30pm, reduced hours winter), with its gleaming underground formations; tickets for the cave cost extra.

★ Nelson Boat & Canoe Hire　　BOATING
(☑08-8738 4048; www.nelsonboatandcanoehire.com.au) Exploring the 65km stretch of scenic river along Lower Glenelg National Park on a multiday canoe trip or a houseboat is one of Victoria's best secrets. This outfit can rig you up for serious river-camping expeditions – canoe hire costs from $60 a day, or $45 a day for three days including waterproof barrels. Self-contained houseboats cost $410 for two nights. Also rents motorboats and paddles.

🛏 Sleeping & Eating

There are nine camp sites between Nelson and Dartmoor along the Glenelg River, which are popular with canoeists but are also accessible by road, with ablutions and

fireplaces (BYO firewood). Forest Camp South on the river is the nicest of these. Pre-arrange camping permits through Parks Victoria online.

★ Nelson Hotel　　　　　　PUB
(☑08-8738 4011; www.nelsonhotel.com.au; Kellett St; d/apt incl breakfast from $65/120, mains $17-35; 🕿) As real as outback pubs come, the Nelson Hotel (established in 1855) is an essential stop for a beer and friendly yarn with locals. It's got a character-filled front bar and bistro serving hearty meals, and rooms are basic, but comfortable. For more privacy, go for the fantastic attached studio.

ℹ Information

Nelson Visitors Centre (☑08-8738 4051; http://parkweb.vic.gov.au; internet per 30min $2.50; ⊘9am-5pm daily summer, Mon, Wed & Thu winter) Good info for both sides of the border. Internet access.

ℹ Getting There & Away

Nelson is 65km from Portland, and 4km from the South Australian border.

There's no public transport here, so you'll need your own wheels or walk here on the Great Southwest Walk.

GIPPSLAND & THE SOUTHEAST COAST

It may not be as well known as the Great Ocean Road to the west, but Victoria's southeast coast boasts easily the state's best beaches, pretty lakeside villages and Victoria's finest coastal national parks, typified by the glorious Wilsons Promontory.

Eastern Victoria (known as Gippsland and named for former New South Wales Governor George Gipps) also has some stirring detours that call you away from its equally stirring coast.

There's not much you *can't* do in Gippsland – swimming, surfing, fishing, camping and boating are all possible along the coast. Best of all, save for the intensely busy summer months, much of the coast is deserted for a good part of the year. The more active among you will relish the abundant cycling trails that follow the network of rail trails, or the chance to put on your hiking boots and head out into the most remote wilderness national parks in the state. More sedate (yet equally rewarding) activities include penguin- and wildlife-spotting, while there are ample opportunities to feast on the freshest seafood.

Phillip Island

POP 9406

Famous for the Penguin Parade and Grand Prix racing circuit, Phillip Island attracts a curious mix of surfers, petrol-heads, lovers of wildlife and international tourists making a beeline for those little penguins.

But the little island has plenty more to offer. At its heart, 100-sq-km Phillip Island is still a farming community, but along with the penguins, there's a large seal colony, abundant bird life around the Rhyll wetlands, and a healthy koala population. The rugged south coast has some fabulous surf beaches and the summer swell of tourists means there's a swag of family attractions, plenty of accommodation, and a buzzing if unexciting cafe and restaurant scene in the island capital, Cowes. Visit in winter, though, and you'll find a very quiet place where the local population of farmers, surfers and hippies go about their business.

◉ Sights & Activities

★ Penguin Parade   WILDLIFE RESERVE
(☑ 03-5951 2800; www.penguins.org.au; Summerland Beach; adult/child/family $23.80/11.90/59.50; ◎ 10am-dusk, penguins arrive at sunset) The Penguin Parade attracts more than half a million visitors annually to see the little penguins (*Eudyptula minor*), the world's smallest, and probably cutest of their kind. The penguin complex includes concrete amphitheatres that hold up to 3800 spectators who come to see the little fellas just after

sunset as they waddle from the sea to their land-based nests.

★ Seal Rocks & the Nobbies   WILDLIFE WATCHING
The Nobbies are a couple of large, craggy, offshore rocks at the island's southwestern tip. Beyond them are Seal Rocks, which are inhabited by Australia's largest fur-seal colony. The Nobbies Centre (☑ 03-5951 2852; www.penguins.org.au; ◎ 11am-1hr before sunset) FREE offers great views over the Nobbies and the 6000 distant Australian fur seals that sun themselves there. You can view the seals from boardwalk binoculars or use the centre's underwater cameras ($5). The centre also has some fascinating interactive exhibits, a kids' games room and a cafe.

★ Grand Prix Circuit   RACE TRACK
(☑ 03-5952 9400; Back Beach Rd) Even when the motorbikes aren't racing, petrol-heads love the Grand Prix Motor Racing Circuit, which was souped up for the Australian Motorcycle Grand Prix in 1989. The visitor centre (☑ 03-5952 9400; www.phillipisland-circuit.com.au; Back Beach Rd; ◎ 9.30am-5pm) FREE runs guided circuit tours (adult/child/family $19/10/44; ◎ tours 2pm), or check out the History of Motorsport Museum (adult/child/family $13.50/6.50/30). The more adventurous can cut laps of the track with a racing driver in hotted-up V8s ($295; bookings essential). Drive yourself in a go-kart around a scale replica of the track with Champ Karts (per 10/20/30min $30/53/68).

Phillip Island Chocolate Factory   CHOCOLATE FACTORY
(☑ 03-5956 6600; www.phillipislandchocolatefactory.com.au; 930 Phillip Island Rd; tours adult/child/family $15/10/45; ◎ 9am-6pm) Like Willy Wonka's, Panny's place has a few surprises. As well as free samples of handmade Belgian-style chocolate, there's a walk-through tour of the chocolate-making process, including a remarkable gallery of chocolate sculptures, from Michelangelo's *David* to an entire model village! Naturally, you can buy chocolate penguins, but most of the chocolate is prepackaged.

Churchill Island   FARM
(☑ 03-5956 7214; www.penguins.org.au; Phillip Island Rd, Newhaven; adult/child/family $11.30/5.65/28.25; ◎ 10am-5pm) Churchill Island, connected to Phillip Island by a bridge near Newhaven, is a working farm where Victoria's first crops were planted. There's

Southeast Coast Victoria

a historic homestead and garden here, and pleasant walking tracks looping around the island.

Koala Conservation Centre
ZOO

(☑03-5951 2800; www.penguins.org.au; 1810 Phillip Island Rd, Cowes; adult/child/family $11.30/5.65/28.25; ☺10am-5pm, extended hours in summer) From the boardwalks at the Koala Conservation Centre you're certain to see koalas chewing on eucalyptus leaves or dozing away – they sleep about 20 hours a day!

Beaches
BEACH

(boards per day $40) Excellent surf beaches bring day-tripping board riders from Melbourne, while there are calmer kid-friendly beaches on the island's north side, including Cowes. The island's south-side ocean beaches include spectacular Woolamai, which has rips and currents and is only suit-able for experienced surfers. Beginners and families can go to Smiths Beach, where Island Surfboards (☑03-5952 3443; www.islandsurfboards.com.au; lessons $60, surfboard hire per hr/day $12.50/40) offers surfing lessons and hires out gear.

☞ Tours

Go West
TOUR

(☑03-9485 5290, 1300 736 551; www.gowest.com.au; 1-day tour $130) One-day tour from Melbourne that includes lunch and iPod commentary in several languages. Includes entry to the Penguin Parade.

Wildlife Coast Cruises
BOAT TOUR

(☑03-5952 3501; www.wildlifecoastcruises.com.au; Rotunda Bldg, Cowes Jetty; seal-watching adult/child $72/49; ☺departures 2pm Fri-Wed May-Sep, 2pm & 4.30pm daily Oct-Apr) Runs a variety of

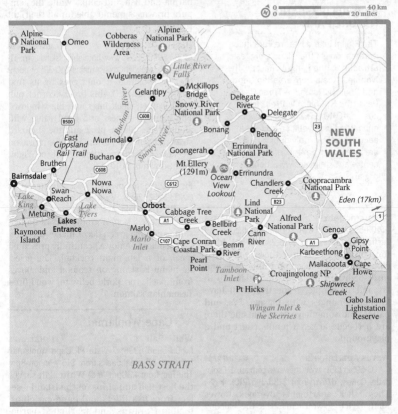

cruises including seal-watching, twilight and cape cruises; also runs a two-hour cruise to French Island (adult/child $30/20) and a full-day cruise to Wilsons Promontory ($190/140).

✱✱ Festivals & Events

Pyramid Rock Festival   MUSIC
(☉ New Year) This huge event, which coincided with New Year's festivities and featured some of the best Aussie bands, was cancelled in 2013 and it's unclear what the future holds for it.

**Australian Motorcycle
Grand Prix**   SPORT
(www.motogp.com.au; ☉ Oct) The island's biggest event – three days of bike action in October.

🛏 Sleeping

Most of the accommodation is in and around Cowes, although there are a few places in Rhyll and Newhaven, and B&Bs and numerous caravan parks are scattered around the island.

Island Accommodation YHA   HOSTEL $
(☎ 03-5956 6123; www.theislandaccommodation. com.au; 10-12 Phillip Island Rd, Newhaven; dm/d from $30/155; @ 🕏) 🕐 This large purpose-built backpackers has huge identical living areas on each floor, complete with table-tennis tables and cosy fireplaces for winter. Its rooftop deck has terrific views and its eco-credentials are excellent. Cheapest dorms sleep 12 and doubles are motel-standard.

ⓘ PHILLIP ISLAND NATURE PARK

The Phillip Island Nature Park incorporates four of the island's biggest attractions: the Penguin Parade, the Nobbies, Koala Conservation Centre and Churchill Island. A Three Parks Pass (the Nobbies Centre is free) costs $40.40/20.20/101 per adult/child/family, or you can buy tickets for each attraction individually. Passes are available from the information centre and online at www.penguins.org.au.

Surf & Circuit Accommodation
APARTMENT $$

(☑03-5952 1300; www.surfandcircuit.com; 113 Justice Rd, Cowes; apt $115-230; ❈❈) Ideal for families or groups, these eight spacious, modern and comfortable two- and three-bedroom units accommodate up to six and 10 people, respectively. All have kitchens, lounges with plasma TVs, and patios, and some have spas. Outside there are barbecue areas, a tennis court and a playground.

Waves Apartments
APARTMENT $$

(☑03-5952 1351; www.thewaves.com.au; 1 Esplanade, Cowes; d/tr/q from $180/195/210; ❈❈) These slick apartments overlook Cowes Main Beach so you can't beat the balcony views if you go for a beachfront unit. The modern, self-contained apartments come with spa, and balcony or patio.

✕ Eating

Regional Victoria's gastronomic revolution has yet to sweep Phillip Island and the places to eat here are surprisingly unexciting. Most of the eateries are in Cowes – the Esplanade and Thompson Ave are crowded with fish-and-chip shops, cafes and takeaways – but there are a few gems scattered around the island.

✕ Cowes

Madcowes
CAFE, DELI $

(☑03-5952 2560; www.madcowescafe.com.au; 17 The Esplanade, Cowes; mains $9-19; ⊘7am-4pm) This stylish cafe-foodstore looks out to the main beach and cooks up some of the heartiest breakfasts and light lunches on the island. Staples include chicken parma and fish and chips, while the tempura prawns is memorable for all the right reasons.

Hotel
AUSTRALIAN $$

(☑03-5952 2060; www.hotelphillipisland.com; 11-13 The Esplanade, Cowes; mains $10-32; ⊘noon-late) So cool that it only goes by its first name (like Cher...), this breezy corner pub is all leather, sleek lines and big windows. The menu is honest and good value with all-day tapas plates, pizza and the standard steak and chicken parma. Has live music on weekends. Its competition, the Isle of Wight, burnt down in 2010.

Fig & Olive at Cowes
MODERN AUSTRALIAN $$

(☑03-5952 2655; www.figandoliveatcowes.com.au; 115 Thompson Ave, Cowes; mains $24-38; ⊘9am-late Wed-Mon) A groovy mix of timber, stone and lime-green decor makes this a relaxing place to enjoy a beautifully presented meal, or a late-night cocktail. The eclectic menu is strong on seafood and moves from paella or pork belly to wood-fired Tasmanian salmon.

✕ Cape Woolamai

White Salt
FISH & CHIPS $

(☑03-5956 6336; 7 Vista Pl, Cape Woolamai; fish from $6, meal packs from $15; ⊘noon-8pm Thu-Tue, from 4.30pm Wed) White Salt serves the best fish and chips on the island – select from fish fillets and hand-cut chips, tempura prawns and marinated barbecue octopus salad with corn, pesto and lemon.

Curry Leaf
INDIAN $

(☑03-5956 6772; 9 Vista Pl, Cape Woolamai; mains $12-25; ⊘noon-8pm Wed-Mon; ☞) This cheery Indian restaurant and takeaway is popular for its piquant meat, seafood and vegetarian curries, samosas and aromatic biryani dishes.

ⓘ Information

Phillip Island Visitors Centre (☑1300 366 422; www.visitphillipisland.com; ⊘9am-5pm, to 6pm school holidays) Newhaven (895 Phillip Island Tourist Rd); Cowes (cnr Thompson & Church Sts) The main visitor centre for the island is on the main road at Newhaven, and there's a smaller centre at Cowes. Both sell the Three Parks Pass (adult/child/family $40.40/20.20/101), and the main centre has a free accommodation- and tour-booking service.

ⓘ Getting There & Away

By car, Phillip Island can only be accessed across the bridge at San Remo to Newhaven. From Melbourne take the Monash Fwy (M1) and exit at Pakenham, joining the South Gippsland Hwy at Koo Wee Rup.

BUS

V/Line (☎ 1800 800 007; www.vline.com. au) has train/bus services from Melbourne's Southern Cross station via Dandenong station or Koo Wee Rup ($12.40, two hours). There are no direct services.

FERRY

Inter Island Ferries (p241) runs between Stony Point on the Mornington Peninsula and Cowes via French Island (45 minutes). There are two sailings Monday and Wednesday, and three on Tuesday, Thursday, Friday, Saturday and Sunday.

ⓘ Getting Around

Ride On Bikes (☎ 03-5952 2533; www.rideon-bikes.com.au; 43 Thompson Ave, Cowes; day/week from $50/200; ⊙ 9am-6pm Mon-Fri, 9am-5pm Sat, 10am-4pm Sun) There's no public transport around Phillip Island but you can hire mountain bikes here.

South Gippsland

South Gippsland has plenty of gems along the coast between Inverloch and Wilsons Promontory – Venus Bay, Cape Liptrap Coastal Park and Waratah Bay are all worthy of exploration. Inland among the farming communities and vineyards are some beautiful drives through the Strzelecki Ranges, the Great Southern Rail Trail cycle path, and trendy villages like Koonwarra and Fish Creek.

Inverloch

Fabulous surf, calm inlet beaches and outstanding diving and snorkelling make Inverloch and the surrounding Bass Coast along the road to Cape Paterson a popular destination. Even with the inevitable holiday crowds it manages to maintain a down-to-earth vibe. Pencil in the popular Inverloch Jazz Festival (www.inverlochjazzfest.org.au; ⊙ Mar) on the Labour Day long weekend each March.

🏃 Activities

Offshore Surf School SURFING
(☎ 0407 374 743; www.offshoresurfschool.com.au; 32 Park St; 2hr lesson $60) If you want to learn

to catch a wave, the Offshore Surf School offers lessons at the main town surf beach.

🛌 Sleeping & Eating

Inverloch Foreshore Camping Reserve CAMPGROUND $
(☎ 03-5674 1447; www.inverlochholidaypark.com. au; cnr Esplanade & Ramsey Blvd; unpowered/powered sites from $26/30) Camping is a pleasure at this camp site set just back from the inlet beach and offering shade and privacy.

★ Moilong Express BOUTIQUE HOTEL $$
(☎ 0439 842 334; www.coastalstays.com/moilongexpress; 405 Inverloch-Venus Bay Rd; d $120) This quirky former railway train carriage, on a hillside property about 3km from Inverloch, has been converted into very comfortable accommodation. There's a kitchen, queen-sized bed, traditional wood panelling and an old railway station clock.

Red Elk Café CAFE $
(☎ 03-5674 3264; 27 A'Beckett St; mains $10-16.50; ⊙ 8.30am-3.30pm Mon-Fri, to 4pm Sat & Sun) In a weatherboard corner cottage, this new café and bar is a buzzing place for coffee and a hearty breakfast. Try the quinoa salad or the chicken-and-brie toasted roll.

Tomo JAPANESE $$
(☎ 03-5674 3444; www.tomos-japanese.com; 23 A'Beckett St; sushi from $4, mains $21-39; ⊙ noon-2pm & 6-9pm Wed-Sun, daily Dec-Feb) Modern Japanese cuisine prepared to perfection. Start with tender sushi or sashimi, but don't

---

GREAT SOUTHERN RAIL TRAIL

This 58km cycling and walking path (www.railtrails.org.au) follows the old rail line from Leongatha to Foster, passing through the villages of Koonwarra, Meeniyan, Buffalo and Fish Creek, where you can stop and refuel. The trail meanders through farmland with a few gentle hills, trestle bridges and occasional views of the coast and Wilsons Prom. The first section from Leongatha to Koonwarra is through the rolling open country of the region's dairy farms. The middle section from Koonwarra to Meeniyan and on to Foster is the most scenic section of the route, with plenty of bridges, eucalypt forest and fine views.

KOONWARRA

But a blip on the South Gippsland Hwy, culinary Koonwarra has made a name for itself thanks to a fine food store and an organic cooking school.

★ **Koonwarra Food, Wine & Produce Store** (☑ 03-5664 2285; www.koonwarrastore.com; cnr South Gippsland Hwy & Koala Dr; mains $12.50-24; ⊙ 8.30am-5.30pm) serves simple food with flair using organic, low-impact suppliers and products. The arrival of a Spanish chef has added tapas to the mix. Soak up the ambience in the wooded interior, or relax at a table in the shaded cottage gardens, home to the Outside Bit, a quirky little nursery.

Milly & Romeo's Artisan Bakery & Cooking School (☑ 03-5664 2211; www.milly-andromeos.com.au; Koala Dr; adult/child from $90/50; ⊙ 9.30am-4.30pm Thu & Fri, 8.30am-4.30pm Sat & Sun, longer hours in summer) is Victoria's first organic-certified cooking school. It carries the motto 'organic, seasonal, local' and offers short courses in making cakes, bread, traditional pastries, French classics and pasta, as well as running cooking classes for kids.

Koonwarra also has several good wineries nearby.

miss the *gyoza* (dumplings) or tempura tiger prawns.

❶ Information

Inverloch Visitor Centre (☑ 1300 762 433; www.visitbasscoast.com; 39 A'Beckett St; ⊙ 9am-5pm) Helpful staff can make accommodation bookings for free.

Bunurong Environment Centre & Shop (☑ 03-5674 3738; www.sgcs.org.au; cnr Esplanade & Ramsey Blvd; ⊙ 10am-4pm Fri-Mon, daily in school holidays) An abundance of books and brochures on environmental and sustainable-living topics. Also here is the Shell Museum ($2) with more than 6000 shells.

❶ Getting There & Away

V/Line (☑ 13 61 96; www.vline.com.au) trains depart daily from Melbourne's Flinders St and Southern Cross Stations for Dandenong, connecting with buses to Inverloch ($16.40, 3½ hours). A quicker option (2½ hours) is the V/Line coach with a change at gloriously named Koo Wee Rup.

If you're driving to Inverloch from Melbourne (148km), follow the signs to Phillip Island and Wonthaggi. The route via Leongatha, 27km northeast of Inverloch, is less picturesque but slightly quicker.

Bunurong Marine & Coastal Park

This surprising little marine and coastal park offers some of Australia's best snorkelling and diving, and a stunning, cliff-hugging drive between Inverloch and Cape Paterson. It certainly surprised the archaeological world in the early 1990s when dinosaur remains dating back 120 million years were discovered here. Eagles Nest, Shack Bay, the Caves and Twin Reefs are great for snorkelling. The Oaks is the locals' favourite surf beach. The Caves is where the dinosaur dig action is.

SEAL Diving Services (☑ 03-5174 3434; www.sealdivingservices.com.au; 7/27 Princes Hwy, Traralgon) has shore dives at Cape Paterson and boat dives in Bunurong Marine & Coastal Park.

Fish Creek

Travellers in the know have been stopping for a bite to eat at quirky Fish Creek on their way to the coast or the Prom for years, and these days it has developed into a bohemian little artists community with craft shops, galleries, studios, bookshops and some great cafes.

Celia Rosser Gallery (☑ 03-5683 2628; www.celiarossergallery.com.au; Promontory Rd; ⊙ 10am-4pm Fri-Sun) **FREE** is a bright art space featuring the works of renowned botanical artist Celia Rosser, and various visiting artists. The attached Banksia Café has a sunny deck.

The art deco **Fish Creek Hotel** (☑ 03-5683 2416; www.fishcreekhotel.com.au; Old Waratah Rd; mains $16-30; ⊙ noon-2pm & 6-9pm), universally known as the Fishy Pub (but also called the Promontory Gate Hotel), is an essential stop for a beer or bistro meal, and there's motel accommodation at the back.

Wilsons Promontory National Park

If you like wilderness bushwalking, stunning coastal scenery and secluded white-sand beaches, you'll absolutely love this place. 'The Prom', as it's affectionately known, is one of the most popular national parks in Australia and our favourite coastal park.

Wilsons Promontory was an important area for the Kurnai and Boonwurrung Aboriginal peoples, and middens have been found in many places, including Cotters and Darby Beaches, and Oberon Bay. The southernmost part of mainland Australia, the Prom once formed a land bridge that allowed people to walk to Tasmania.

Tidal River, 30km from the park entry, is the hub, and home to the Parks Victoria office, a general store, cafe and accommodation. The wildlife around Tidal River is remarkably tame: kookaburras and rosellas lurk expectantly (resist the urge to feed them), and wombats nonchalantly waddle out of the undergrowth.

Although there's a staffed entrance booth where you receive a ticket, entry is free. There's no fuel available at Tidal River.

⚡ Activities

There's more than 80km of marked walking trails here, taking you through forests, marshes, valleys of tree ferns, low granite mountains and along beaches backed by sand dunes. Even nonwalkers can enjoy much of the park's beauty, with car park access off the Tidal River road leading to gorgeous beaches and lookouts.

Swimming is safe from the beautiful beaches at Norman Bay (Tidal River) and around the headland at Squeaky Beach – the ultra-fine quartz sand here really does squeak beneath your feet!

If you're travelling light, you can hire camping equipment, including tents, stoves, sleeping bags and backpacks, from Wilsons Prom Hiking Hire (☑ 0400 377 993; http://wilsonspromhikinghire.com.au; 3670 Prom Rd, Yanakie).

☞ Tours

Bunyip Tours   BUS TOUR
(☑ 1300 286 947; www.bunyiptours.com; tours from $120; ⊙ Wed & Sun, plus Fri in summer) Proudly carbon-neutral, Bunyip Tours offers a one-day guided tour to the Prom from Melbourne, with the option of staying on another two days to explore by yourself.

TOP PROM WALKS

The Prom's delights are best discovered on foot. From November to Easter a free shuttle bus operates between the Tidal River visitors car park and the Telegraph Saddle car park (a nice way to start the Prom Circuit Walk). Here are six of the best:

Great Prom Walk This is the most popular long-distance hike, a moderate 45km circuit across to Sealers Cove from Tidal River, down to Refuge Cove, Waterloo Bay, the lighthouse and back to Tidal River via Oberon Bay. Allow three days, and coordinate your walks with tide times, as creek crossings can be hazardous.

Sealers Cove Walk The best overnight hike, this two-day walk starts at Telegraph Saddle and heads down Telegraph Track to stay overnight at beautiful Little Waterloo Bay (12km, four hours). The next day walk on to Sealers Cove via Refuge Cove and return to Telegraph Saddle (24km, seven hours).

Lilly Pilly Gully Nature Walk An easy 5km (two-hour) walk through heathland and eucalypt forests, with lots of wildlife.

Mt Oberon Summit Starting from the Mt Oberon car park, this moderate-to-hard 7km (two-hour) walk is an ideal introduction to the Prom, with panoramic views from the summit. The free Mt Oberon shuttle bus can take you to the Telegraph Saddle car park and back.

Little Oberon Bay An easy-to-moderate 8km (three-hour) walk over sand dunes covered in coastal tea trees with beautiful views over Little Oberon Bay.

Squeaky Beach Nature Walk Another easy 5km return stroll through coastal tea trees and banksias to a sensational white-sand beach.

Wilsons Promontory National Park

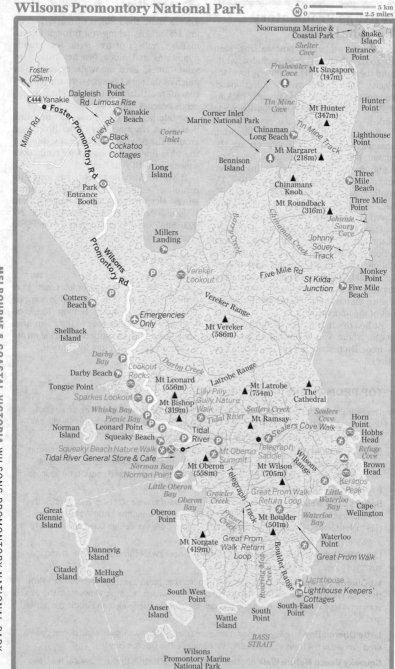

Nooramunga Marine &
Coastal Park
Snake
Island
Shelter
Cove
Entrance
Point

Foster
(25km)

Freshwater
Cove
Mt Singapore
(147m)

Duck
Point
Dalgleish
Rd   Limosa Rise

Tin Mine
Cove
Mt Hunter
(347m)
Hunter
Point

C444 Yanakie
Foster-Promontory Rd
Foley Rd
Yanakie
Beach

Corner
Inlet
Corner Inlet
Marine National Park
Chinaman
Long Beach

Tin Mine Track
Lighthouse
Point

Black
Cockatoo
Cottages

Mt Margaret
(218m)

Millar Rd

Long
Island
Bennison
Island

Three
Mile
Beach

Park
Entrance
Booth

Chinamans
Knob

Three Mile
Point

Wilsons Promontory Rd

Millers
Landing

Mt Roundback
(316m)

Chinaman Creek

Johnnie
Souey
Cove

Barry Creek

Johnny
Souey
Track

Vereker
Lookout

Five Mile Rd

St Kilda
Junction

Monkey
Point

Cotters
Beach

Vereker Range

Five Mile
Beach

Shellback
Island

Emergencies
Only

Mt Vereker
(586m)

Darby
Bay

Lookout
Rocks

Darby Creek

Latrobe Range

Darby Beach

Mt Leonard
(556m)

Mt Latrobe
(754m)

The
Cathedral

Tongue Point

Sparkes Lookout

Lilly Pilly
Gully Nature
Walk

Whisky Bay

Mt Bishop
(319m)

Sealers Creek

Mt Ramsay

Sealers
Cove

Horn
Point

Picnic Bay

Tidal River

Norman
Island

Leonard Point
Squeaky Beach

Tidal
River

Sealers Cove Walk

Hobbs
Head

Refuge
Cove

Squeaky Beach Nature Walk
Tidal River General Store & Cafe

Mt Oberon
Summit

Telegraph
Saddle

Wilsons Range

Brown
Head

Norman Bay
Norman Point

Mt Oberon
(558m)

Mt Wilson
(705m)

Kersops
Peak

Little Oberon
Bay

Oberon
Bay

Oberon Creek

Telegraph Track

Great Prom Walk
Return Loop

Little
Waterloo
Bay

Cape
Wellington

Great
Glennie
Island

Oberon
Point

Growler
Creek

Fraser Creek

Mt Boulder
(501m)

Waterloo
Bay

Dannevig
Island

Mt Norgate
(419m)

Great Prom
Walk Return
Loop

Boulder Range

Waterloo
Point

Great Prom Walk

Citadel
Island

McHugh
Island

Roaring Meg Creek

Lighthouse

South West
Point

Lighthouse Keepers'
Cottages

Anser
Island

Wattle
Island

South
Point

South-East
Point

BASS
STRAIT

Wilsons
Promontory Marine
National Park

First Track Adventures
ADVENTURE TOUR

(☑ 03-5634 2761; www.firsttrack.com.au) This Yarragon-based company organises customised bushwalking, canoeing and abseiling trips to the Prom for individuals and groups. Prices vary according to group size and activity.

🛏 Sleeping

Nothing beats a night at the Prom. The main accommodation base is at Tidal River, but there are 11 bush-camping (outstation) areas around the Prom, all with pit or compost toilets, but no other facilities; carry in your own drinking water. Overnight hikers need camping permits (adult/child $11.30/5.70 per night), which must be booked ahead through Parks Victoria.

🛏 Tidal River

Situated on Norman Bay and a short walk to a stunning beach, accommodation at Tidal River is justifiably popular. Book well in advance through Parks Victoria (p267), especially for weekends and holidays.

★ Lighthouse Keepers' Cottages
COTTAGE $

(☑ Parks Victoria 13 19 63; www.parkweb.vic.gov.au; 8-bed cottage $90-100, 20-bed $120-134) These isolated, heritage-listed 1850s cottages with thick granite walls are a real getaway, attached to a working lightstation on a pimple of land that juts out into the wild ocean. Kick back after the 19km hike from Tidal River and watch ships or whales passing by. The cottages have shared facilities, including a fully equipped kitchen.

Camp Sites
CAMPGROUND $

(unpowered sites per vehicle & 3 people $29.60-32.80, powered sites per vehicle & up to 8 people $49.30-54.70) Tidal River has 484 camp sites, but only 20 powered sites. For the Christmas school holiday period there's a ballot for sites (apply online by 30 June at www.parkweb.vic.gov.au).

Park Huts
CABIN $

(4-/6-bed huts from $72/109) If you're travelling tent-free, these cosy wooden huts are a decent budget option, with bunks and kitchenettes, but no bathrooms.

Park Cabins
CABIN $$

(d $186-207, additional adult/child $27/18) The spacious and private self-contained cabins sleep up to six people and have large, sliding-glass doors and a deck, and overlook the bush or river. The Lorikeet Units are equally comfortable, sleeping up to four people, but they're closer to the visitor centre and parking area.

★ Wilderness Retreat
SAFARI TENT $$$

(www.wildernessretreats.com.au; d $302.50, extra person $24.50) Nestled in bushland at Tidal River, these are the most expensive tents on the Prom. The luxury safari tents, each with their own deck, sleep up to four people and are pretty cool with a bathroom, queen-sized beds, heating and a communal tent kitchen. It's like being on an African safari with a kookaburra soundtrack.

🛏 Yanakie & Foster

The tiny, dispersed settlement of Yanakie offers the closest accommodation outside the park boundaries – from cabins and camping to luxury cottages. Foster, the nearest main town, has a backpacker hostel and several motels.

Prom Coast Backpackers
HOSTEL $

(☑ 0427 875 735; www.promcoastyha.com.au; 40 Station Rd; dm/d from $30/70; @) The closest backpacker hostel to the park is this friendly YHA in Foster. The cosy renovated cottage sleeps only 10 so it's always intimate.

Black Cockatoo Cottages
COTTAGE $$

(☑ 03-5687 1306; 60 Foley Rd, Yanakie; d $140-160, 6-person house $180) You can take in glorious views of the national park without leaving your very comfortable bed – or breaking the bank – in these private, stylish, black-timber cottages. There are three modern cottages and a three-bedroom house.

🍴 Eating

Tidal River General Store & Cafe
CAFE $

(mains $5-22; ⊙ 9am-5pm Sun-Fri, to 6pm Sat) The Tidal River general store stocks grocery items and some camping equipment, but if you're hiking or staying a while it's cheaper to stock up in Foster. The attached cafe serves takeaway food such as pies and sandwiches, as well as breakfast, light lunches and bistro-style meals on weekends and holidays.

ℹ Information

Parks Victoria (☑ 03-5680 9555, 13 19 63; www.parkweb.vic.gov.au; ⊙ 8.30am-4.30pm) The helpful visitor centre at Tidal River books all park accommodation, including permits for camping away from Tidal River.

ℹ Getting There & Away

There's no direct public transport between Melbourne and the Prom, but the **Wilsons Promontory Bus Service** (Moon's Bus Lines; ☑ 03-5687 1249) operates from Foster to Tidal River (via Fish Creek) on Friday at 4.30pm, returning on Sunday at 4.30pm (adult/child $8/4). This service connects with the V/Line bus from Melbourne at Fish Creek.

V/Line (☑ 13 61 96; www.vline.com.au) buses from Melbourne's Southern Cross Station travel direct to Foster ($19.80, three hours, four daily).

Port Albert

POP 250

This little old fishing village, 111km by road northeast of Tidal River, is developing a reputation as a trendy stopover for boating, fishing and sampling the local seafood. The town proudly pronounces itself Gippsland's first established port, and the many historic timber buildings in the main street dating from its busy 1850s era bear a brass plaque, detailing their age and previous use.

◉ Sights & Activities

Gippsland Regional Maritime Museum   MUSEUM
(☑ 03-5183 2520; Tarraville Rd; adult/child $5/1; ☉ 10.30am-4pm daily Sep-May, Sat & Sun Jun-Aug) The Gippsland Regional Maritime Museum, in the old Bank of Victoria (1861), will give you an insight into the highlights of Port Albert's maritime history, with stories of shipwrecks, the town's whaling and sealing days, and local Aboriginal legends.

Nooramunga Marine & Coastal Park   CANOEING, BOATING
You can hire boats and canoes from the Slip Jetty for cruising around the sheltered waters of the Nooramunga Marine & Coastal Park.

🛏 Sleeping & Eating

There's a caravan park at Seabank, about 6km northwest of Port Albert, and there are a few B&Bs in town.

Port Albert Hotel   MOTEL $
Sadly this historic timber hotel – which lay claim to being Victoria's oldest continually licensed pub (since 1842) – burned to

the ground in February 2014. No plans to rebuild were in place at the time of publication, but watch this space.

Port Albert Wharf   FISH & CHIPS $
(☑ 03-5183 2002; 40 Wharf St; mains from $7; ☉ 11am-7.30pm) The fish and chips here are renowned, perfectly presented and as fresh as you'd expect from a town built on fishing.

★**Wildfish**   SEAFOOD $$
(☑ 03-5183 2002; www.wildfish-restaurant.com. au; 40 Wharf St; lunch mains $8-17, dinner mains $26-36; ☉ noon-3pm & 6-8pm Thu-Sun) With a sublime harbourside location and the freshest local seafood, Wildfish is earning a well-deserved reputation for serving good food. By day it's a cafe offering coffee and sandwiches; by night the menu turns to thoughtful seafood dishes such as flake-and-scallop pie or tempura garfish fillets.

ℹ Getting There & Away

The closest public transport from Melbourne is the **V/Line** (☑ 13 61 96; www.vline.com.au) bus service to Yarram, 12km to the north of Port Albert. By road, take the South Gippsland Hwy and follow the signs to Port Albert along the Yarram–Port Albert Rd.

Gippsland Lakes

The beautiful Gippsland Lakes form the largest inland waterway system in Australia, with the three main interconnecting lakes – Wellington, King and Victoria – stretching from Sale to beyond Lakes Entrance. The lakes are actually saltwater lagoons, separated from the ocean by the Gippsland Lakes Coastal Park and the narrow coastal strip of sand dunes that is known as Ninety Mile Beach.

Sale

POP 12,800

Gateway to the Gippsland Lakes, Sale has plenty of accommodation, shops, restaurants and pubs, making it a good town-sized base for exploring the Ninety Mile Beach.

◉ Sights & Activities

Port of Sale   PORT
The Port of Sale is a redeveloped marina area in the town centre with boardwalks,

cafes and a canal leading out to the Gippsland Lakes.

Gippsland Art Gallery GALLERY
(☎03-5142 3372; www.wellington.vic.gov.au/gallery; Civic Centre, 68 Foster St; ⏰10am-5pm Mon-Fri, noon-4pm Sat & Sun) FREE Gippsland Art Gallery exhibits work by locally and nationally renowned artists and hosts touring exhibitions.

Sale Wetlands Walk WALKING
The Sale Wetlands Walk (4km, 1½ hours) is a pleasant wander around Lake Gutheridge (immediately east of where the Princes Hwy does a dogleg in the centre of Sale) and its adjoining wetlands, and incorporates an **Indigenous Art Trail** commemorating the importance of the wetlands to the local Kurnai community.

Sale Common BIRDWATCHING
Sale Common, a 300-hectare wildlife refuge with bird hides, an observatory, a waterhole, boardwalks and other walking tracks is part of an internationally recognised wetlands system. The best time to visit is early morning or late evening (wear some mosquito repellent), when you'll see lots of bird life. The visitor centre has a list of recorded species.

Sleeping & Eating

Cambrai Hostel HOSTEL $
(☎03-5147 1600; www.maffra.net.au/hostel; 117 Johnson St; dm per night/week $28/160; @) In Maffra, 16km north of Sale, this relaxed hostel is

WORTH A TRIP

WALHALLA

Enveloped by the green hills and forests of West Gippsland, 46km northeast of Moe, tiny Walhalla is one of Victoria's best-preserved and most charming historic gold-mining towns. Stringer's Creek runs through the centre of the township – an idyllic valley encircled by a cluster of sepia-toned historic buildings set into the hillsides.

The best way to see the town is on foot – take the **tramline walk** (45 minutes) that begins from opposite the general store soon after you enter town. Other good (and well-signposted) walks lead up from the valley floor. Among them, a trail leads to the **Walhalla Cricket Ground** (2km, 45 minutes return). Another trail climbs to the extraordinary **Walhalla Cemetery** (20 minutes return), where the gravestones cling to the steep valley wall and through their inscriptions tell a sombre yet fascinating story of the town's history.

During August the town lights up for the **Walhalla Vinter ljusfest** (Winter Lights Festival).

Walhalla Historical Museum (☎03-5165 6250; admission $2; ⏰10am-4pm), in the old post office, also acts as an information centre and books the popular two-hour **ghost tours** (www.walhallaghosttour.info; adult/child/family $25/20/75; ⏰7.30pm Sat, 8.30pm Sat during daylight saving) on Friday and Saturday nights.

A star attraction is the scenic **Walhalla Goldfields Railway** (☎03-5165 6280; www.walhallarail.com; return adult/child/family $20/15/50; ⏰from Walhalla station 11am, 1pm & 3pm, from Thomson Station 11.40am, 1.40pm & 3.40pm Wed, Sat, Sun & public holidays), a 20-minute ride between Walhalla Station and Thomson Station through forested gorge country and over restored trestle bridges.

Relive the mining past with guided tours of the **Long Tunnel Extended Gold Mine** (☎03-5165 6259; off Walhalla-Beardmore Rd; adult/child/family $19.50/13.50/49.50; ⏰1.30pm daily, plus noon & 3pm Sat, Sun & holidays), which explores Cohens Reef, once one of Australia's top reef-gold producers.

Camp for free at **North Gardens**, with toilets and barbecues, at the north end of the village, or anywhere along Stringer's Creek. Walhalla also has a handful of B&Bs and cottages.

The rebuilt historic **Walhalla Star Hotel** (☎03-5165 6262; www.starhotel.com.au; Main St; d incl breakfast from $175; ❄@📶) offers stylish boutique accommodation with king-size beds and sophisticated designer decor making good use of local materials such as corrugated-iron water tanks. There are good breakfasts, coffee and cake at the attached **Greyhorse Café** (mains from $5; ⏰10am-2pm).

BAIRNSDALE BYPASS?

Bustling Bairnsdale (population 11,820) is East Gippsland's commercial hub and the turn-off north for the Great Alpine Rd (B500) to Omeo or south to Paynesville and Raymond Island. There's better accommodation in Sale, Metung or Lakes Entrance. Otherwise, the only reason we can think to stop in the town itself is the **Krowathunkoolong Keeping Place** (☑ 03-5152 1891; 37-53 Dalmahoy St; adult/child $3.50/2.50; ☺ 9am-5pm Mon-Fri), a stirring and insightful Koorie cultural exhibition space that explores Kurnai life from the Dreaming until after European settlement. The exhibition traces the Kurnai people from their Dreaming ancestors, Borun the pelican and his wife Tuk the musk duck, and covers life at Lake Tyers Mission, east of Lakes Entrance, now a trust privately owned by Aboriginal shareholders. The massacres of the Kurnai from 1839 to 1849 are also detailed. For more information, try the **Bairnsdale Visitor Centre** (☑ 03-5152 3444, 1800 637 060; www.discovereastgippsland.com.au; 240 Main St; ☺ 9am-5pm). Bairnsdale lies 67km from Sale and 280km from Melbourne.

a budget haven and one of the few true backpackers in Gippsland. In a 120-year-old building that was once a doctor's residence, it has a licensed bar, an open fire and a pool table in the cosy lounge, a tiny self-catering kitchen and clean, cheerful rooms. The owners can sometimes arrange work in the region.

Quest Serviced Apartments   APARTMENT $$
(☑ 03-5142 0900; www.questapartments.com.au; 180-184 York St; studio/1-bedroom/2-bedroom apt $120/199/285; ❀ ☎ ☒) This reliable chain offers up modern, self-contained apartments that feel more luxurious than you'd expect for these prices. As such, it's streets ahead of most other motels around town.

Bis Cucina   CAFE $$
(☑ 03-5144 3388; 100 Foster St; breakfast & lunch $12-23, dinner $23-36; ☺ 8am-2pm daily, 6-8pm Fri, Sat & show nights) At the Wellington Entertainment Centre, Bis Cucina offers relaxed and attentive service combined with carefully chosen modern Australian cuisine with Mediterranean influences. This is a good choice for serious foodies, theatre-goers wanting a preshow meal, or those after just a coffee or lazy breakfast.

❶ Information

Wellington Visitor Information Centre (☑ 03-5144 1108; www.tourismwellington.com.au; 8 Foster St; ☺ 9am-5pm) Internet facilities and a free accommodation-booking service.

❶ Getting There & Away

V/Line (☑ 13 61 96; www.vline.com.au) has train and train/bus services between Melbourne and Sale ($24.60, three hours, six daily) via Traralgon.

Ninety Mile Beach

To paraphrase the immortal words of Crocodile Dundee: that's not a beach... *this* is a beach. Isolated Ninety Mile Beach is a narrow strip of sand backed by dunes and lagoons and stretching unbroken for more-or-less 90 miles (150km) from near McLoughlins Beach to the channel at Lakes Entrance – arguably Australia's longest single beach. The area is great for surf-fishing, camping and long beach walks, though the crashing surf can be dangerous for swimming, except where patrolled at Seaspray, Woodside Beach and Lakes Entrance.

Between Seaspray and Lakes Entrance, the **Gippsland Lakes Coastal Park** is a protected area of low-lying coastal shrub, banksias and tea trees, bursting with native wildflowers in spring. Permits for remote camping can be obtained from **Parks Victoria** (☑ 13 19 63; www.parkweb.vic.gov.au).

For a retro blast, head to **Seaspray** (population 316), which has somehow escaped the rampant development along the coast and is packed full of old holiday shacks – it's how Victorian coastal towns used to be in the 1970s.

On the road between Seaspray and Golden Beach, there are free **camp sites**, nestled back from the beach and shaded by tea trees – it's hard to get a spot over summer but at other times it's supremely peaceful. Some sites have barbecues and pit toilets, but you need to bring your own water and firewood. Hot showers are available at **Golden Beach** ($2).

Loch Sport (population 689) is a small, bushy town sprawling along a narrow spit of land with a lake on one side and the ocean on the other. There are some good swimming areas here for children. The **Marina Hotel** (☑03-5146 0666; Basin Blvd; mains $16-28; ☺noon-2pm & 6-9pm), perched by the lake and marina, has a friendly local-pub vibe, superb sunset views and decent seafood dishes on the bistro menu.

Lakes National Park

This narrow strip of coastal bushland surrounded by lakes and ocean is a beautiful and quiet little spot to set up camp.

Banksia and eucalypt woodland abound with areas of low-lying heathland and some swampy salt-marsh scrub. In spring the park is carpeted with native wildflowers and has one of Australia's best displays of native orchids. A loop road through the park provides good vehicle access, and there are well-marked walking trails. **Point Wilson**, at the eastern tip of the mainland section of the park is the best picnic spot and a popular gathering place for kangaroos. Industrial-strength mosquito repellent is a must here.

Emu Bight Camp Site (☑13 19 63; unpowered sites per 6 people $15) is the only camping area in the park, with pit toilets and fireplaces available; BYO water.

Metung

Curling around Bancroft Bay, little Metung is one of the prettiest towns on the Gippsland Lakes – besotted locals call it the Gippsland Riviera, and with its absolute waterfront location and unhurried charm, it's hard to argue with this.

Getting out on the water is easy enough: **Riviera Nautic** (☑03-5156 2243; www.rivieranautic.com.au; 185 Metung Rd; yachts & cruisers for 3 days from $1089) hires out boats and yachts for cruising, fishing and sailing on the Gippsland Lakes. At the visitor centre, **Slipway Boat Hire** (☑03-5156 2469) has small motor boats for hire from $60 for an hour to $175 a day, including fuel.

If you'd rather take it easy, cruise on board the **Director** (☑03-5156 2628; www.thedirector.com.au; 2½hr cruise adult/child/family $45/10/105; ☺3pm Tue, Thu & Sat) to Ninety Mile Beach and back.

At high noon pelicans fly in like dive-bombers for fish issued outside the Metung Hotel. Pelicans can tell time – or at least know when to get a good free feed.

🛏 Sleeping & Eating

The only budget accommodation is at the Metung Hotel. The nearest camping is up the road at Swan Reach.

Metung Holiday Villas　　CABIN $$
(☑03-5156 2306; www.metungholidayvillas.com; cnr Mairburn & Stirling Rds; cabins $150-250; ❄❄) Metung's former caravan park has reinvented itself as a minivillage of semiluxury cabins, and is one of the best deals in Metung.

McMillans of Metung　　RESORT $$$
(☑03-5156 2283; www.mcmillansofmetung.com. au; 155 Metung Rd; cottages $82-440, villas $88-367; ❄❄❄) This swish lakeside resort has

---

WORTH A TRIP

PAYNESVILLE & RAYMOND ISLAND

Paynesville, 16km south of Bairnsdale, is a relaxed little lakes town where life is all about the water. A good reason to detour down here is to take the flat-bottom ferry on the five-minute hop across to Raymond Island for some koala-spotting in a natural environment. There's a large colony of koalas here, mostly relocated from Phillip Island in the 1950s. The vehicle/passenger ferry operates every half-hour from 7am to 11pm and is free for pedestrians and bicycles.

Several operators hire out boats. **Aquamania** (☑0417 163 365; www.aquamania.com. au) organises boat tours, waterski and wakeboard instruction and operates a water taxi.

The popular **Paynesville Jazz Festival** happens on the last weekend in February.

Perched over the water and with an alfresco deck, **Fisherman's Wharf Pavilion** (☑03-5156 0366; 70 The Esplanade; lunch $8-24, dinner $22-43; ☺8am-3pm & 6-8pm Tue-Sun) is a sublime place for a breakfast of pancakes or quiche for lunch on a sunny day. By night it's a fine-dining steak-and-seafood restaurant, using fresh, local produce.

won stacks of tourism awards for its complex of English-country-style cottages set in 3 hectares of manicured gardens, its modern villas, private marina and spa centre.

⭐ Metung Galley
CAFE **$$**

(☎03-5156 2330; www.themetunggalley.com.au; 50 Metung Rd; lunch $9-15, dinner $19.50-34; ☺8am-4pm Tue, to late Wed-Fri, 7.30am-late Sat, to 4pm Sun) Felicity and Richard's city hospitality experience shines through at this friendly, innovative cafe. It serves up beautifully presented, quality food using local ingredients such as fresh seafood and Gippsland lamb (try the lamb 'cigars' with tzatziki).

Bancroft Bites
CAFE **$$**

(☎03-5156 2854; www.bancroftbites.com.au; 2/57 Metung Rd; lunch $8-22, dinner $20-34; ☺8am-3pm & 6-8pm Thu-Tue) This is another seriously good cafe-by-day, fine-dining-by-night place. Seafood chowder and glazed roast duck grace the contemporary menu.

Metung Hotel
PUB **$$**

(☎03-5156 2206; www.metunghotel.com.au; 1 Kurnai Ave; mains $25-33; ☺noon-2pm & 6-8pm) You can't beat the location overlooking Metung Wharf, and the big windows and outdoor timber decking make the most of the water views. The bistro serves top-notch pub food. The hotel also has the cheapest rooms in town ($85).

❶ Information

Metung Visitors Centre (☎03-5156 2969; www.metungtourism.com.au; 3/50 Metung Rd; ☺9am-5pm) Accommodation-booking and boat-hire services.

Lakes Entrance

With the shallow Cunninghame Arm waterway separating town from the crashing ocean beaches, Lakes Entrance basks in an undeniably pretty location, but in holiday season it's a packed-out tourist town with a graceless strip of motels, caravan parks, minigolf courses and souvenir shops lining the Esplanade. Still, the bobbing fishing boats, fresh seafood, endless beaches and cruises out onto the local lake system, including excursions to Metung, should easily win you over. There's plenty here for families and kids, and out of season there's an unhurried pace and accommodation bargains.

The town is named for the channel, artificially created in 1889 to provide ocean access from the lakes system and a harbour for fishing boats.

⊙ Sights & Activities

Beaches & Lakes
BEACH, LAKE

A long footbridge crosses the Cunninghame Arm inlet from the east of town to the ocean and Ninety Mile Beach. From December to Easter, paddle boats, canoes and sailboats can be hired by the footbridge on the ocean side. This is also where the Eastern Beach Walking Track (2.3km, 45 minutes) starts, taking you through coastal scrub to the entrance itself.

To explore the lakes, three operators along Marine Pde (on the back side of the town centre) offer boat hire (hire per 1/4/8hr $50/90/150).

Lakes Entrance

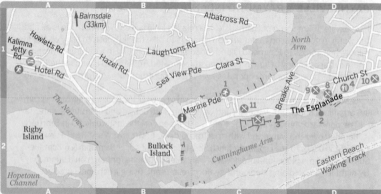

Lookouts
LOOKOUT

On the Princes Hwy on the western side of town, **Kalimna Lookout** is a popular viewing spot with coin-operated binoculars. For an even better view of the ocean and inlet, take the road directly opposite to **Jemmy's Point Lookout**.

Surf Shack
SURFING

(☑03-5155 4933; www.surfshack.com.au; 507 The Esplanade; 2hr lesson $50) Surfing lessons (gear provided) are run by the Surf Shack at nearby Lake Tyers Beach, around 10km from Lakes Entrance.

☞ Tours

Several companies offer cruises out on the lakes:

Lonsdale Cruises
CRUISE

(☑03-9013 8363; Post Office Jetty; 3hr cruise adult/child/family $50/25/120; ⊙1pm) ✎ Scenic eco-cruises out to Metung and Lake King on a former Queenscliff–Sorrento passenger ferry.

Peels Lake Cruises
CRUISE

(☑0409 946 292; www.peelscruises.com.au; Post Office Jetty; 4hr Metung lunch cruise adult/child $55/16, 2½hr cruise $41; ⊙11am Tue-Sun, 2pm Tue-Thu & Sat) This long-running operator has daily lunch cruises aboard the *Stormbird* to Metung and 2½-hour cruises on the *Thunderbird*.

Sea Safari
CRUISE

(☑0458 511 438; www.lakes-explorer.com.au; Post Office Jetty; 1hr/2hr cruise $15/25) ✎ These safaris aboard the *Lakes Explorer* have a focus on research and ecology, identifying and counting seabirds, testing water for salinity levels and learning about marine life.

🛏 Sleeping

Lakes Entrance has stacks of accommodation, much of it your typical motels, holiday apartments and caravan parks squeezed cheek-by-jowl along the Esplanade. Prices more than double during holiday periods (book ahead), but there are good discounts out of season.

Eastern Beach Tourist Park
CAMPGROUND $

(☑03-5155 1581; www.easternbeach.com.au; 42 Eastern Beach Rd; unpowered/powered sites from $26/31, cabins $105-185; @ 🛜 ⚐ 🐾) Most caravan parks in Lakes pack 'em in, but this one has space, grassy sites and a great location away from the hubbub of town in a bush setting back from Eastern Beach. A walking track takes you into town (30 minutes). New facilities are excellent, including a camp kitchen, barbecues and a kids' playground.

Kalimna Woods
COTTAGE $$

(☑03-5155 1957; www.kalimnawoods.com.au; Kalimna Jetty Rd; d $99-130, with spa $129-170; ❋) Retreat 2km from the town centre to Kalimna Woods, set in a large rainforest-and-bush garden, complete with friendly resident possums and birds. These self-contained country-style cottages with either spa or wood-burning fireplace are spacious, private and cosy.

Goat & Goose
B&B $$

(☑03-5155 3079; www.goatandgoose.com; 16 Gay St; d $160) Bass Strait views are maximised at this wonderfully unusual, multistorey, timber pole-framed house. The friendly owners

MELBOURNE & COASTAL VICTORIA GIPPSLAND LAKES

are long-time locals, and all the gorgeously quaint rooms have spas.

✗ Eating

With the largest fishing fleet in Victoria, Lakes Entrance is the perfect place to indulge in fresh seafood. You can sometimes buy shellfish (prawns, bugs etc) straight from local boats (look for signs) or try Ferryman's. Omega 3 (Shop 5, Safeway Arcade, Church St; ⊙9am-5pm) is the shopfront for the local Fishermen's Co-op, so the seafood is always fresh.

The best cafe strip is on the Esplanade and around the corner on Myer St, right opposite the Cunninghame Arm footbridge.

Six Sisters & A Pigeon   CAFE $
(☑03-5155 1144; 567 The Esplanade; mains $9-18; ⊙7am-3pm Tue-Sun; ☑) The name alone should guide you to this quirky, licensed cafe on the Esplanade opposite the footbridge. Good coffee; all-day breakfasts – Mexican eggs, French toast or Spanish omelettes; lunches of focaccias and baguettes; and light mains with an Asian-Italian influence.

★Ferryman's Seafood Cafe   SEAFOOD $$
(☑03-5155 3000; www.ferrymans.com.au; Middle Harbour, The Esplanade; lunch mains $19-23, dinner $22.50-43.50; ⊙10am-late, seafood sales 8.30am-5pm) It's hard to beat the ambience of dining on the deck of this floating cafe-restaurant, which will fill you to the gills with fish and seafood dishes, including good ol' fish and chips. The seafood platter is a great order. It's child-friendly, and downstairs you can buy fresh seafood, including prawns and crayfish.

Miriam's Restaurant   STEAKHOUSE, SEAFOOD $$
(☑03-5155 3999; www.miriamsrestaurant.com.au; cnr The Esplanade & Bulmer St; mains $25-39; ⊙6pm-late) The upstairs dining room at Miriam's overlooks the Esplanade, and the Gippsland steaks, local seafood dishes and casual cocktail-bar atmosphere are excellent. Try the epic 'Greek fisherman's plate' – half a kilo of local seafood for $55.

★The Boathouse   MODERN AUSTRALIAN $$$
(☑03-5155 3055; http://bellevuelakes.com; 201 The Esplanade; mains $38; ⊙6-9pm Tue-Sat) This much-awarded restaurant is Lakes Entrance's most celebrated kitchen. The atmosphere is refined and the emphasis is on creatively conceived seafood. Start with the Atlantic scallops with pea purée, pancetta and ocean foam.

ⓘ Information

Lakes Entrance Library (☑03-5153 9500; 18 Mechanics St; ⊙8.30am-5pm Mon-Fri) Free internet access.

Lakes Entrance Visitors Centre (☑03-5155 1966, 1800 637 060; www.discovereastgippsland.com.au; cnr Princes Hwy & Marine Pde; ⊙9am-5pm) Free accommodation- and tour-booking services. Also check out www.lakesentrance.com.

ⓘ Getting There & Away

V/Line (☑1800 800 007; www.vline.com.au) runs a train/bus service from Melbourne to Lakes Entrance via Bairnsdale ($34.20, 4½ hours, three daily).

Buchan

The sleepy village of Buchan in the foothills of the Snowy Mountains is famous for the spectacular and intricate limestone cave system at the Buchan Caves Reserve, open to visitors for almost a century. Underground rivers cutting through ancient limestone rock formed the caves and caverns, and they provided shelter for Aboriginal people as far back as 18,000 years ago. Parks Victoria (☑13 19 63; www.parks.vic.gov.au; tours adult/child/family $20.30/11.90/56.10, two caves $30.40/17.60/83.70; ⊙10am, 11.15am, 1pm, 2.15pm & 3.30pm, hours vary seasonally) runs guided cave tours daily, alternating between Royal and Fairy Caves. The rangers also offer hard-hat guided tours to the less-developed Federal Cave during high season. The reserve itself is a pretty spot with shaded picnic areas, walking tracks and grazing kangaroos.

🛌 Sleeping & Eating

Buchan Caves Reserve   CAMPGROUND $
(☑13 19 63; www.parks.vic.gov.au; unpowered/powered sites $23.40/30.20, d cabins $86.10, wilderness retreats d $181.50; ☒) You can stay right by the caves at this serene Parks Victoria camping ground edged by state forest. There are a couple of standard cabins, plus safari-style tents providing a 'luxury' wilderness experience (think comfortable queen-sized bed) without having to pitch your own tent.

Buchan Lodge   HOSTEL $
(☑03-5155 9421; www.buchanlodge.com.au; 9 Saleyard Rd; dm $25; 🛜) A short walk from the caves and the town centre, and just by the

SNOWY RIVER & ERRINUNDRA NATIONAL PARKS

These two isolated wilderness parks north of Orbost occupy most of Victoria's eastern corner between the alpine country and the coast. The parks are linked in the north by the mostly unsealed MacKillops Rd, making it possible to do a driving loop from Buchan to Orbost. In dry weather it's passable to conventional vehicles but check road conditions with Parks Victoria. Fierce bushfires raged through the corridor between the two parks during the 2013–2014 summer. Although most roads should be open again by the time you read this, the landscape's ashen hue will serve as a reminder of nature's power for years to come.

Snowy River National Park

Northeast of Buchan, this is one of Victoria's most isolated and spectacular national parks, dominated by deep gorges carved through limestone and sandstone by the Snowy River on its route from the Snowy Mountains in New South Wales to its mouth at Marlo. The entire 1145-sq-km park is a smorgasbord of unspoiled, superb bush and mountain scenery, ranging from alpine woodlands and eucalypt forests to rainforests. Abundant wildlife includes the rare brush-tailed rock wallaby.

On the west side of the park, the views from the well-signposted clifftop lookouts over Little River Falls and Little River Gorge, Victoria's deepest gorge, are awesome. From there it's about 20km to McKillops Bridge, a huge bridge spanning the Snowy River, making it possible to drive across to Errinundra National Park. The hilly and difficult Silver Mine Walking Track (15km, six hours) starts at the eastern end of the bridge.

There's free camping at a number of basic sites around the park, but the main site is McKillops Bridge, a beautiful spot with toilets and fireplaces.

Karoonda Park (☎ 03-5155 0220; www.karoondapark.com; 3558 Gelantipy Rd; s/d/tr $50/70/90, cabins per 6 people $115; ✳ @ ⛾), 40km north of Buchan on the road to Snowy River National Park, has comfortable backpacker and cabin digs. Activities available include abseiling, horse riding, wild caving, white-water rafting, mountain-bike hire and farm activities.

Errinundra National Park

Errinundra National Park contains Victoria's largest cool-temperate rainforest, but the forests surrounding the park are a constant battleground between loggers, and environmentalists who are trying to protect old-growth forests.

The national park covers an area of 256 sq km and has three granite outcrops that extend into the cloud, resulting in high rainfall, deep, fertile soils and a network of creeks and rivers that flow north, south and east. This is a rich habitat for native birds and animals, which include many rare and endangered species such as the potoroo.

You can explore the park by a combination of scenic drives, and short and medium-length walks. Mt Ellery has spectacular views; Errinundra Saddle has a rainforest boardwalk; and from Ocean View Lookout there are stunning views down the Goolengook River as far as Bemm River.

Frosty Hollow Camp Site (sites free) is the only camping area within the national park, on the eastern side. There are also free camping areas on the park's edges – at Ellery Creek in Goongerah, and at Delegate River.

Tours

Gippsland High Country Tours (☎ 03-5157 5556; www.gippslandhighcountrytours.com.au) ✐ offers easy, moderate and challenging five- to seven-day hikes in Errinundra, Snowy River and Croajingolong National Parks.

Snowy River Expeditions (☎ 03-5155 0220; www.karoondapark.com/sre; Karoonda Park; tours per day $150-275) is an established company running adventure tours including one-, two- and four-day rafting trips on the Snowy. Half- or full-day abseiling or caving trips are also available.

EAST GIPPSLAND RAIL TRAIL

The **East Gippsland Rail Trail** (www.eastgippslandrailtrail.com) is a 94km walking/cycling path along the former railway line between Bairnsdale and Orbost, passing through Bruthen and Nowa Nowa and close to a number of other small communities. The trail passes through undulating farmland, temperate rainforest, the Colquhoun Forest and some impressive timber bridges. On a bike the trail can comfortably be done in two days, but allow longer to explore the countryside and perhaps detour on the Gippsland Lakes Discovery Trail to Lakes Entrance. Arty **Nowa Nowa** is a real biking community, with a new mountain-bike park and trails leading off the main rail trail. There are plans to extend the trail from Orbost down to Marlo along the Snowy River.

If you don't have your own bike, **Snowy River Cycling** (0428 556 088; www.snowyrivercycling.com.au) offers self-guided tours with a bike (from $35), map and transfers ($35) plus luggage transport ($15). It also runs guided cycle adventures.

river, this welcoming pine-log backpackers is great for lounging about and taking in the country views. It boasts a big country-style kitchen, convivial lounge and has campfires out the back.

❶ Getting There & Away

Buchan is an easy drive 56km north of Lakes Entrance. **Buchan Bus 'n' Freight** (03-5155 0356) operates a service on Wednesday and Friday from Bairnsdale to Buchan ($18, one hour), linking with the train from Melbourne. At other times you'll need your own transport.

Orbost & Marlo

The town of Orbost services the surrounding farming and forest areas. Most travellers whiz through as the Princes Hwy passes just south of the town, while the Bonang Rd heads north towards the Snowy River and Errinundra National Parks. Marlo Rd follows the Snowy River south to Marlo and continues along the coast to Cape Conran.

Orbost visitor information centre (03-5154 2424; 39 Nicholson St; 9am-5pm) is in the historic 1872 Slab Hut. The impressive **Orbost Exhibition Centre** (03-5154 2634; www.orbostexhibitioncentre.org; Clarke St; adult/child $4/free; 10am-4pm Mon-Sat, 1-4pm Sun), next to the visitor centre, showcases works by local timber artists.

Just 15km south of Orbost, Marlo is a sleepy beach town at the mouth of the Snowy River. It's a lovely spot and the road continues on to Cape Conran before rejoining the highway. Aside from the gorgeous coast, the main attraction here is the **PS Curlip** (03-5154 1699; www.paddlesteamercurlip.com.au; adult/child/family $25/15/60; 10.30am Sat

& Sun, longer hours Dec & Jan), a recreation of an 1890 paddle steamer that once chugged up the Snowy River to Orbost. Buy tickets at the general store in town.

You can't beat an afternoon beer on the expansive wooden verandah of the **Marlo Hotel** (03-5154 8201; www.marlohotel.com.au; 17 Argyle Pde; d $140, with spa $130-160, mains $14-30). The boutique rooms here are above average for a pub and the restaurant serves local seafood such as gummy shark and king prawns.

Cape Conran Coastal Park

This blissfully undeveloped part of the coast is one of Gippsland's most beautiful corners, with long stretches of remote white-sand beaches. The 19km coastal route from Marlo to Cape Conran is particularly pretty, bordered by banksia trees, grass plains, sand dunes and the ocean.

Good walks include the nature trail, which meets up with the **East Cape Boardwalk**, where signage gives you a glimpse into how Indigenous people lived in this area. Following an Indigenous theme, take the West Cape Rd off Cape Conran Rd to **Salmon Rocks**, where there's an Aboriginal shell midden dated at more than 10,000 years old.

Cabbage Tree Palms, a short detour off the road between Cape Conran and the Princes Hwy, is Victoria's only stand of native palms – a tiny rainforest oasis.

🛌 Sleeping

Banksia Bluff Camping Area CAMPGROUND $
(03-5154 8438; http://conran.net.au; per person $30.20) Run by Parks Victoria, this excellent camping ground is right by the foreshore,

with generous sites surrounded by banksia woodlands offering shade and privacy. The camping ground has toilets, cold showers and a few fireplaces, but you'll need to bring drinking water. A ballot is held for using sites over the Christmas period.

Cape Conran Cabins CABIN $
(☑ 03-5154 8438; http://conran.net.au; 4 people from $161.90) These self-contained cabins, which can sleep up to eight people, are surrounded by bush and are just 200m from the beach. Built from local timbers, the cabins are like oversized cubby houses with lofty mezzanines for sleeping. BYO linen. An excellent option run by Parks Victoria.

Cape Conran Wilderness Retreat SAFARI TENT $$
(☑ 03-5154 8438; http://conran.net.au; d $181.50) Nestled in the bush by the sand dunes, these stylish safari tents are a great option for accommodation, run by Parks Victoria. All the simplicity of camping, but with comfortable beds and a deck outside your fly-wire door. Two-night minimum stay.

West Cape Cabins CABIN $$
(☑ 03-5154 8296; www.westcapecabins.com; 1547 Cape Conran Rd; d $175-215) Crafted from locally grown or recycled timbers, these self-contained cabins a few kilometres from the park are works of art. The timbers are all labelled with their species, and even the queen-sized bed bases are made from tree trunks. The outdoor spa baths add to the joy. The larger cottage sleeps eight. It's a 15-minute walk through coastal bush to an isolated beach.

Mallacoota

Isolated Mallacoota is a real gem – Victoria's most easterly town but an easy detour if you're heading along the coastal route between Melbourne and Sydney. It's snuggled on the vast Mallacoota Inlet and surrounded by the tumbling hills and beachside dunes of beautiful Croajingolong National Park. Those prepared to come this far are treated to long, empty surf beaches, tidal river mouths, and swimming, fishing and boating on the inlet. At Christmas and Easter Mallacoota is a busy family holiday spot but most of the year it's pretty quiet and very relaxed.

◉ Sights & Activities

Gabo Island ISLAND
On Gabo Island, 14km offshore from Mallacoota, the windswept 154-hectare Gabo Island Lightstation Reserve is home to seabirds and one of the world's largest colonies of little penguins – far outnumbering those on Phillip Island. Whales, dolphins and fur seals are regularly sighted offshore. The island has an operating lighthouse, built in 1862 and the tallest in the southern hemisphere, and you can stay in the old keepers' cottages here (contact Parks Victoria). Mallacoota Air Services (☑ 0408 580 806; return per 3 adults or 2 adults & 2 children $300) offers fast access to the island on demand, or you can get there by boat with Wilderness Coast Ocean Charters.

Mallacoota Hire Boats BOATING
(☑ 0438 447 558; Main Wharf, cnr Allan & Buckland Drs; motor boats per 2/4/6hr $60/100/140) Hire motor boats and fishing rods here.

Walks WALKING
There are plenty of great short walks around the town, the inlet, and in the bush. It's an easy 4km walk or cycle around the inlet to Karbeethong. From there the Bucklands Jetty to Captain Creek Jetty Walk follows the shoreline of the inlet past the Narrows. The Mallacoota Town Walk (7km, five hours) loops round Bastion Point, and combines five different walks.

Beaches BEACH
For good surf, head to Bastion Point or Tip Beach. There's swimmable surf and some sheltered waters at Betka Beach, which is patrolled during Christmas school holidays.

◉ Tours

Wilderness Coast Ocean Charters BOATING
(☑ 0417 398 068, 03-5158 0701) Runs day trips to Gabo Island ($70, minimum eight people; $70 each way if you stay overnight) and may run trips down the coast to view the seal colony off Wingan Inlet if there's enough demand.

MV Loch-Ard CRUISE
(☑ 03-5158 0764; Main Wharf; adult/child 2hr cruise $30/12) Runs several inlet cruises including wildlife spotting and a twilight cruise.

Porkie Bess CRUISE, FISHING
(☑ 0408 408 094; 2hr cruise $30, fishing trip $60) A 1940s wooden boat offering fishing trips

MELBOURNE & COASTAL VICTORIA MALLACOOTA

and cruises around the lakes of Mallacoota Inlet, and ferry services for hikers ($20 per person, minimum four people).

🛏 Sleeping

During Easter and Christmas school holidays you'll need to book well ahead and expect prices to be significantly higher.

Mallacoota Foreshore Holiday Park
CAMPGROUND $

(☑ 03-5158 0300; cnr Allan Dr & Maurice Ave; unpowered sites $20-29, powered $26-38; 🛜) Curling around the waterfront, the grassy sites here morph into one of Victoria's most sociable and scenic caravan parks, with sublime views of the inlet and its resident population of black swans and pelicans. No cabins, but the best of Mallacoota's many parks for campers.

★ Adobe Mudbrick Flats
APARTMENT $

(☑ 0409 580 0329, 03-5158 0329; www.adobeholidayflats.com.au; 17 Karbeethong Ave; d $75, q $90-170) 🖉 A labour of love by Margaret and Peter Kurz, these unique mudbrick flats in Karbeethong are something special. With an emphasis on recycling and ecofriendliness, the flats have solar hot water and guests are encouraged to compost their kitchen scraps. Birds, lizards and possums can be hand-fed outside your door. The array of whimsical apartments is comfortable, well-equipped and cheap. A real find.

★ Gabo Island Lighthouse
COTTAGE $$

(☑ 03-5161 9500, Parks Victoria 13 19 63; www.parkweb.vic.gov.au; up to 8 people $148-190) For a truly wild experience head out to stay at this remote lighthouse. Accommodation is available in the three-bedroom Assistant Lighthouse Keeper's residence. Watch for migrating whales in autumn and late spring. Pods of dolphins and seals basking on the rocks are also regular sightings. There's a two-night minimum stay, and a ballot for use during the Christmas and Easter holidays.

Karbeethong Lodge
GUESTHOUSE $$

(☑ 03-5158 0411; www.karbeethonglodge.com.au; 16 Schnapper Point Dr; d $110-220) It's hard not to be overcome by a sense of serenity as you rest on the broad verandahs of this early 1900s timber guesthouse, which gives uninterrupted views over Mallacoota Inlet. The large guest lounge and dining room have an open fire and period furnishings, and there's a mammoth kitchen if you want to prepare meals. The pastel-toned bedrooms are small but neat and tastefully decorated.

Mallacoota Wilderness Houseboats
HOUSEBOAT $$$

(☑ 0409 924 016; www.mallacootawilderness-houseboats.com.au; Karbeethong Jetty; 4 nights midweek from $750, weekly from $1200) These six-berth houseboats are not as luxurious as the ones you'll find on the Murray, but they are the perfect way to explore Mallacoota's waterways, and they are economical for a group or family.

🍴 Eating

Most visitors consider the best eating to be the fish you catch yourself; otherwise there are a few good places along Maurice Ave.

Croajingolong Cafe
CAFE $

(☑ 03-5158 0098; Shop 3, 14 Allan Dr; mains $6-14; ⏰ 8.30am-4pm Tue-Sun; 🛜) Overlooking the inlet, this is the place to read the newspaper over coffee, baguettes or a pancake breakfast.

VOLUNTEERING

Interested in doing some volunteer work? National parks and organic farms are two options for travellers.

Parks Victoria (www.parkweb.vic.gov.au) operates a program for volunteers at Wilsons Promontory National Park, Buchan Caves Reserve, Cape Conran and Croajingolong National Park during the Christmas and Easter holidays. Volunteers act as campground hosts for a minimum of two weeks and are involved in the day-to-day operations of the park assisting visitors and rangers. Volunteers camp for free; tents can be provided. Apply through Parks Victoria.

Willing Workers on Organic Farms (WWOOF; ☑ 03-5155 0218; www.wwoof.com.au; 2615 Gelantipy Rd, W Tree) is a national organisation with its base in East Gippsland. Volunteers work on organic farms that are members of the WWOOF association, in exchange for their meals and accommodation.

★**Lucy's** ASIAN **$$**
(📞03-5158 0666; 64 Maurice Ave; mains $10-22; ⊙8am-8pm) Lucy's is popular for delicious and great-value homemade rice noodles with chicken, prawn or abalone, as well as dumplings stuffed with ingredients from the garden. It's also good for breakfast.

Mallacoota Hotel PUB **$$**
(📞03-5158 0455; www.mallacootahotel.com.au; 51-55 Maurice Ave; mains $17-32; ⊙noon-2pm & 6-8pm) The local pub bistro serves hearty meals from its varied menu, with reliable favourites such as chicken parmigiana and Gippsland steak. Bands play regularly in the summer.

❶ Information

Mallacoota Visitors Centre (📞03-5158 0800; www.visitmallacoota.com.au; Main Wharf, cnr Allan & Buckland Dr; ⊙10am-4pm) Operated by friendly volunteers.

❶ Getting There & Away

Mallacoota is 23km southeast of Genoa (on the Princes Hwy). From Melbourne, take the train to Bairnsdale, then the V/Line bus to Genoa ($26.70, three hours, one daily). **Mallacoota–Genoa Bus Service** (📞1800 800 007) meets the V/Line coach on Monday, Thursday and Friday, plus Sunday during school holidays, and runs to Mallacoota ($3.40, 30 minutes).

Croajingolong National Park

Croajingolong is one of Australia's finest coastal wilderness national parks, recognised by its listing as a World Biosphere Reserve by Unesco (one of 12 in Australia). For remote camping, bushwalking, fishing, swimming and surfing, this one is hard to beat, with unspoiled beaches, inlets, estuaries and forests. The park covers 875 sq km, stretching for about 100km from Bemm River to the New South Wales border. The five inlets – Sydenham, Tamboon, Mueller, Wingan and Mallacoota (the largest and most accessible) – are popular canoeing and fishing spots.

The Wilderness Coast Walk, only for the well prepared and intrepid, starts at Sydenham Inlet by Bemm River and heads along the coast to Mallacoota. Thurra River is a good starting point, making the walk an easy-to-medium hike (59km, five days) to Mallacoota.

Croajingolong is a birdwatcher's paradise, with more than 300 recorded species (including glossy black cockatoos and the rare ground parrot), while the inland waterways are home to myriad waterbirds, such as the delicate azure kingfisher and the magnificent sea eagle. There are also many small mammals here, including possums, bandicoots and gliders, and some huge goannas.

Point Hicks was the first part of Australia to be spotted by Captain Cook and the *Endeavour* crew in 1770, and was named after his first Lieutenant, Zachary Hicks. There's a lighthouse here, open for tours and accommodation in the old cottages. You can still see remains of the SS *Saros*, which ran ashore in 1937, on a short walk from the lighthouse.

Access roads of varying quality lead into the park from the Princes Hwy. Apart from Mallacoota Rd, all roads are unsealed and can be very rough in winter, so check road conditions with Parks Victoria before venturing on, especially during or after rain.

🛏 Sleeping

Given their amazing beauty, the park's main camping grounds are surprisingly quiet, and bookings only need to be made for the Christmas and Easter holiday periods, when sites are issued on a ballot system.

There are four designated camp sites: Wingan Inlet and Shipwreck Creek can be booked through Parks Victoria (📞13 19 63; www.parkweb.vic.gov.au; unpowered sites $25.20); Thurra River and Mueller Inlet (unpowered sites $20) through Point Hicks Lighthouse. Shipwreck is the most accessible, 15km from Mallacoota, while Wingan has the prettiest setting.

The remote Point Hicks Lighthouse (📞03-5158 4268, 03-5156 0432; www.pointhicks.com.au; bungalows $100-120, cottages $330) has two comfortable, heritage-listed cottages and one double bungalow, which originally housed the assistant lighthouse keepers. The cottages sleep six people, and have sensational ocean views and wood-burning fireplaces.

❶ Information

Parks Victoria (📞13 19 63, Cann River 03-5158 6351, Mallacoota 03-5161 9500; www.parkweb.vic.gov.au) Contact offices in Cann River or Mallacoota for information on road conditions, overnight hiking, camping permits and track notes.

Brisbane & Around

Best Places to Eat

➡ Brew (p298)

➡ Gunshop Café (p299)

➡ George's Seafood (p299)

➡ Oceanic Gelati (p312)

Best Places to Stay

➡ Latrobe Apartment (p297)

➡ Limes (p296)

➡ Bowen Terrace (p296)

➡ Stradbroke Island Beach Hotel (p311)

➡ Casabella Apartment (p297)

Why Go?

Australia's most underrated city? Booming Brisbane is an energetic river town on the way up, with an edgy arts scene, pumping nightlife and great coffee and restaurants. Plush parks and historic buildings complete the picture, all folded into the elbows of the meandering Brisbane River.

Brisbanites are out on the streets: the weather is brilliant and so are the bodies. Fit-looking locals get up early to go jogging, swimming, cycling, kayaking, rock-climbing or just to walk the dog. And when it's too hot outside, Brisbane's subcultural undercurrents run cool and deep, with bookshops, globally inspired restaurants, cafes, bars and band rooms aplenty.

East of Brisbane is Moreton Bay, with its low-lying sandy isles (don't miss a trip to 'Straddie'), beaches and passing parade of whales, turtles and dolphins.

When to Go
Brisbane

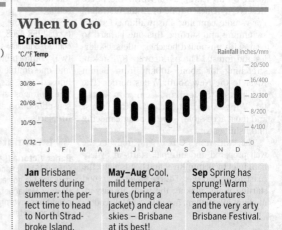

Jan Brisbane swelters during summer: the perfect time to head to North Stradbroke Island.

May–Aug Cool, mild temperatures (bring a jacket) and clear skies – Brisbane at its best!

Sep Spring has sprung! Warm temperatures and the very arty Brisbane Festival.

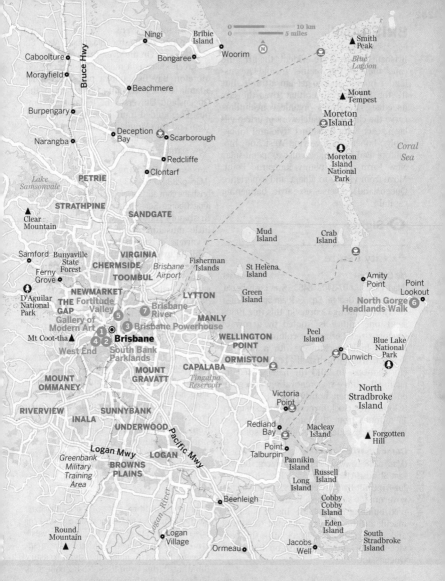

Brisbane & Around Highlights

1 Exploring the cavernous spaces of Brisbane's world-class **Gallery of Modern Art** (p283).

2 Finding a sunny patch of lawn or paddling at Streets Beach in Brisbane's **South Bank Parklands** (p283).

3 Catching some live comedy or some lunch by the river at the **Brisbane Powerhouse** (p283).

4 Checking out some bookshops, live bands and bars in Brisbane's **West End** (p303).

5 Spending a night on the tiles in Brisbane's heady **Fortitude Valley** (p303).

6 Roaming along the **North Gorge Headlands Walk** on North Stradbroke Island, spotting turtles, rays and dolphins offshore (p310).

7 Chugging up, down or across the **Brisbane River** on a ferry (p310).

BRISBANE

POP 2.15 MILLION

Brisbane's charms are evident: the arts, the cafes, the bars, the weather, the old Queenslander houses, the go-get-'em attitude. But it's the Brisbane River that gives the city its edge. The river's organic convolutions carve the city into a patchwork of urban villages, each with a distinct style and topography: bohemian, low-lying West End; hip, hilltop Paddington; exclusive, peninsular New Farm; prim, pointy Kangaroo Point. Move from village to village and experience Queensland's diverse, eccentric, happening capital.

◉ Sights

◎ City Centre

★**City Hall** LANDMARK
(Map p288; ✆07-3403 8463; www.brisbane.qld.gov.au; King George Sq; ◷10am-5pm) FREE Overlooking King George Sq, this fine 1930s sandstone edifice is fronted by a row of sequoia-sized Corinthian columns and has an 85m-high clocktower with a fabulous lookout, from which bells peal across the city rooftops. In 2013 the hall opened up again after three-year renovation. Free guided tours happen hourly from 10.30am to 3.30pm; free clocktower tours happen every 15 minutes from 10.45am to 4.45pm. Also here is the excellent Museum of Brisbane.

Commissariat Store Museum MUSEUM
(Map p288; www.queenslandhistory.org; 115 William St; adult/child/family $5/3/10; ◷10am-4pm Tue-Fri) Built by convicts in 1829, this former government storehouse is the oldest occupied building in Brisbane. Inside is an immaculate little museum devoted to convict and colonial history. Don't miss the convict 'fingers' and the exhibit on Italians in Queensland.

Roma Street Parkland PARK
(Map p288; www.romastreetparkland.com; 1 Parkland Blvd; ◷24hr) FREE This beautifully maintained, 16-hectare, 16-precinct downtown park is one of the world's largest subtropical urban gardens. Formerly a market and a railway yard, the park features native trees, a lake, lookouts, waterfalls, a playground, BBQs and many a frangipani. It's something of a maze: easy to get into, hard to get out.

City Botanic Gardens PARK
(Map p288; www.brisbane.qld.gov.au; Alice St; ◷24hr) FREE On the river, Brisbane's favourite green space is a mass of lawns, tangled Moreton Bay figs, bunya pines and macadamia trees descending gently from the Queensland University of Technology campus. Free guided tours leave the rotunda at 11am and 1pm Monday to Saturday. (Is it just us, or are things looking a tad shabby here? New signage please!).

Museum of Brisbane MUSEUM
(Map p288; ✆07-3339 0800; www.museumofbrisbane.com.au; Level 3, Brisbane City Hall, King George Sq; ◷10am-5pm) FREE Inside Brisbane's renovated City Hall, this great little museum illuminates the city from a variety of viewpoints, with interactive exhibits exploring both social history and the current cultural landscape. When we visited the three long-term exhibits were a fabulously kitsch display on Expo '88 ('We'll show the world!'), an exhibit on the history of the Brisbane River, and a display of panoramic photos of Brisbane from 1860 to today.

Parliament House HISTORIC BUILDING
(Map p288; www.parliament.qld.gov.au; cnr Alice & George Sts; ◷tours 1pm, 2pm, 3pm & 4pm non-sitting days) FREE With a roof clad in Mt Isa copper, this lovely blanched-white stone French Renaissance–style building dates from 1868 and occupies a suitably regal position overlooking the City Botanic Gardens. The only way to get a peek inside is on a free tour, which leave at the times listed above on demand (2pm only when parliament is sitting).

Treasury Building HISTORIC BUILDING
(Map p288; www.treasurybrisbane.com.au; cnr Queen & William Sts; ◷24hr) FREE At the western end of the Queen St Mall is the magnificent Italian Renaissance–style Treasury Building, dating from 1889. No tax collectors inside – just Brisbane's casino.

◎ South Bank

On South Bank, just over Victoria Bridge from the CBD, the Queensland Cultural Centre is the epicentre of Brisbane's cultural life. It's a huge compound that includes concert and theatre venues, four museums and the Queensland State Library.

★ **Gallery of Modern Art**   GALLERY
(GOMA; Map p288; www.qagoma.qld.gov.au; Stanley Pl; ☉10am-5pm Mon-Fri, 9am-5pm Sat & Sun) FREE All angular glass, concrete and black metal, must-see GOMA focuses on Australian art from the 1970s to today. Continually changing and often confronting, exhibits range from painting, sculpture and photography to video, installation and film. There's also an arty bookshop here, kids' activity rooms, a cafe and free guided tours at 11am and 1pm. Brilliant!

South Bank Parklands   PARK
(Map p288; www.visitsouthbank.com.au; Grey St; ☉dawn-dusk) FREE This beautiful smear of green – technically on the western side of the Brisbane River – is home to performance spaces, sculptures, buskers, eateries, bars, pockets of rainforest, BBQ areas, bougainvillea-draped pergolas and hidden lawns. The big-ticket attractions here are Streets Beach (p287), a kitsch artificial swimming beach resembling a tropical lagoon (packed on weekends); and the London Eye–style **Wheel of Brisbane** (Map p288; www.thewheelofbrisbane.com.au; Grey St; adult/child/family $15/10/42; ☉11am-9.30pm Mon-Thu, 10am-11pm Fri & Sat, 10am-10pm Sun), which offers 360-degree views from its 60m heights. Rides last around 10 minutes and include audio commentary (and air-con!).

Queensland Museum & Sciencentre   MUSEUM
(Map p288; www.southbank.qm.qld.gov.au; cnr Grey & Melbourne Sts; ☉9.30am-5pm) FREE The history of Queensland is given the once-over here, with interesting exhibits including a skeleton of the state's own dinosaur *Muttaburrasaurus* (aka 'Mutt'), and the *Avian Cirrus,* the tiny plane in which Queenslander Bert Hinkler made the first England-to-Australia solo flight in 1928. Have a snack to a whale soundtrack in the outdoor 'Whale Mall'.

Also here is the **Sciencentre** (adult/child/family $13/10/40), an educational fun house with over 100 hands-on, interactive exhibits that delve into life science and technology. Expect long queues during school holidays.

Queensland Art Gallery   GALLERY
(QAG; Map p288; www.qagoma.qld.gov.au; Melbourne St; ☉10am-5pm Mon-Fri, 9am-5pm Sat & Sun) FREE Duck into the QAG to see the fine permanent collection. Australian art dates from the 1840s to the 1970s: check out works by celebrated masters including Sir Sydney Nolan, Arthur Boyd, William Dobell and George Lambert. Free guided tours at 1pm.

Queensland Maritime Museum   MUSEUM
(Map p288; www.maritimemuseum.com.au; Stanley St; adult/child/family $12/6/28; ☉9.30am-4.30pm) On the southern edge of the South Bank Parklands is this quaint old museum, the highlight of which is the gigantic HMAS *Diamantina,* a restored WWII frigate that you can clamber aboard and explore.

◉ Fortitude Valley & New Farm

★ **Brisbane Powerhouse**   ARTS CENTRE
(Map p284; www.brisbanepowerhouse.org; 119 Lamington St, New Farm; ☉9am-5pm Mon-Fri, 10am-4pm Sat & Sun) FREE On the eastern flank of New Farm Park stands the Powerhouse, a once-derelict power station that's been superbly transformed into a contemporary arts centre. Inside the brick husk are graffiti remnants, pieces of old industrial machinery and randomly placed headphones offering sonic soundgrabs. The Powerhouse hosts a range of visual arts, comedy and music performances (many free), and has two restaurants with killer river views.

Chinatown   NEIGHBOURHOOD
(Map p292; Duncan St, Fortitude Valley) Brisbane's Chinatown occupies only one street (check out the Tang dynasty archway and the lions at the Ann St end), but it's just as flamboyant and flavour-filled as its Sydney and Melbourne counterparts. Glazed flat ducks hang behind steamy windows; aromas of Thai, Chinese, Vietnamese, Laotian and Japanese cooking fill the air. There are free outdoor movies during summer, and the whole place goes nuts during Chinese New Year festivities.

◉ Greater Brisbane

Mt Coot-tha Reserve   OUTDOORS
(www.brisbane.qld.gov.au; Mt Coot-tha Rd, Mt Coot-tha; ☉24hr) FREE A 15-minute drive or bus ride from the city, this huge bush reserve is topped by 287m Mt Coot-tha (more of a hill, really). On the hillsides you'll find the Brisbane Botanic Gardens, the Sir Thomas Brisbane Planetarium, walking trails and the eye-popping **Mt Coot-tha Lookout** (www.brisbanelookout.com; 1012 Sir Samuel Griffith Dr; ☉24hr) FREE. On a clear day you can see the Moreton Bay islands.

Greater Brisbane

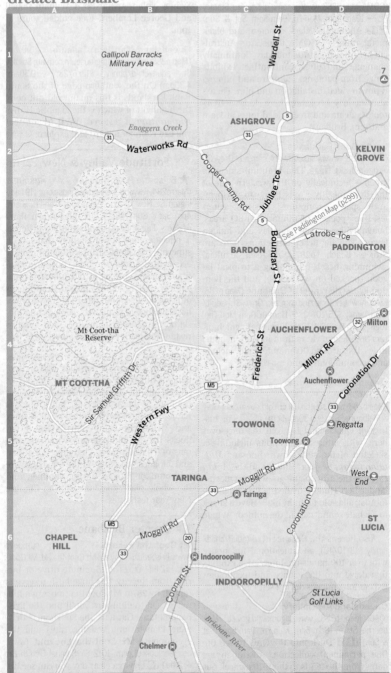

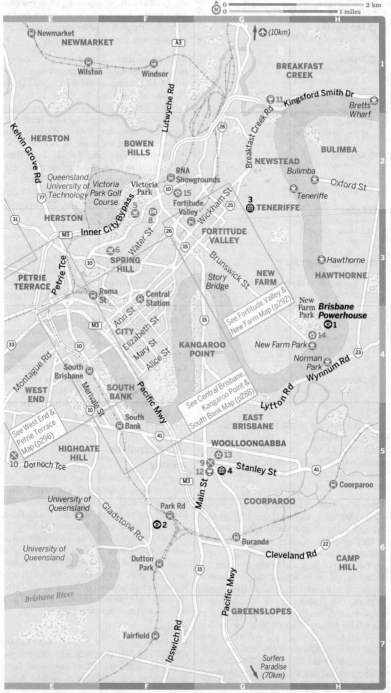

To get here via public transport, take bus 471 from Adelaide St in the city, opposite King George Sq ($4.80, 25 minutes). The bus drops you off at the lookout and stops outside the botanic gardens and planetarium en route.

Lone Pine Koala Sanctuary OUTDOORS
(🖉07-3378 1366; www.koala.net; 708 Jesmond Rd, Fig Tree Pocket; adult/child/family $33/22/80; ☻9am-5pm) About 12km south of the city centre, Lone Pine Koala Sanctuary occupies a patch of parkland beside the river. It's home to 130 or so koalas, plus kangaroos, possums, wombats, birds and other Aussie critters. The koalas are undeniably cute – most visitors readily cough up the $16 to have their picture snapped hugging one.

To get here catch bus 430 ($6.70, 45 minutes) from the Queen St bus station. Alternatively, **Mirimar II** (🖉0412 749 426; www.mirimar.com; incl park entry per adult/child/family $65/38/190) cruises to the sanctuary along

the Brisbane River, departing from the Cultural Centre Pontoon on South Bank next to Victoria Bridge. It departs daily at 10am, returning from Lone Pine at 1.45pm.

Brisbane Botanic Gardens GARDENS
(www.brisbane.qld.gov.au/botanicgardens; Mt Coot-tha Rd, Mt Coot-tha; ☻8am-5.30pm) **FREE** At the base of Mt Coot-tha, these 52-hectare gardens have a plethora of mini ecologies on display: cactus, bonsai and herb gardens, rainforests, arid zones... You'll feel like you're traversing the globe in all its vegetated splendour! Free guided walks are at 11am and 1pm Monday and Saturday; free minibus tours at 10.45am Monday to Thursday.

To get here via public transport, take bus 471 from Adelaide St in the city, opposite King George Sq ($4.80, 25 minutes).

Sir Thomas Brisbane Planetarium PLANETARIUM
(🖉07-3403 2578; www.brisbane.qld.gov.au/planetarium; Mt Coot-tha Rd, Mt Coot-tha; admission free, shows adult/child/family $15/9/40; ☻10am-4pm Tue-Fri & Sun, 11am-7.30pm Sat) At the entrance to the Brisbane Botanic Gardens at Mt Coot-tha is the newly renovated Sir Thomas Brisbane Planetarium, the biggest planetarium in Australia. The observatory has a variety of telescopes, and there are 10 regular outer-space shows inside the **Cosmic Skydome**, narrated by the likes of Harrison Ford and Ewan McGregor (bookings advised).

To get here via public transport, take bus 471 from Adelaide St in the city, opposite King George Sq ($4.80, 25 minutes).

🏃 Activities

Walking
Feel like stretching your legs? Pick up the self-guided *Brisbane City Walk* brochure from info centres, which weaves you through Roma Street Parkland, South Bank Parklands and the City Botanic Gardens.

Sadly the city's excellent **Riverwalk** pathway was destroyed by floods in 2011, but a stroll along the riverbanks remains rewarding. The new, more flood-resistant Riverwalk – including a section linking New Farm with the CBD – is being built at a cost of $72 million, and will be open in 2014.

Cycling
CityCycle BICYCLE RENTAL
(🖉1300 229 253; www.citycycle.com.au; hire per hr/day $2.20/165, first 30min free; ☻hire 5am-10pm, return 24hr) Brisbane's public bike-

share program has had a rocky start, but it's starting to win over the locals. Basically you subscribe via the website (per day/week/three months $2/11/27.50), then hire a bike (additional fee) from any of the 100-plus stations around central Brisbane. Good for short hops; pricey by the day. BYO helmet and lock (see the website for a list of bike shops where you can buy them).

Bicycle Revolution   BICYCLE RENTAL
(Map p296; www.bicyclerevolution.org.au; 294 Montague Rd, West End; per day/week $35/100; ⊙9am-5pm Mon, 9am-6pm Tue-Fri, 8am-2pm Sat) Friendly community shop with a handsome range of recycled bikes assembled by staff with reconditioned parts. Very 'hipster'.

Swimming

Streets Beach   SWIMMING
(Map p288; www.visitsouthbank.com.au; ⊙daylight hours) FREE A central spot for a quick (and free) dip is the artificial, riverside Streets Beach at South Bank. Lifeguards, hollering kids, beach babes, strutting gym-junkies, ice-cream carts – it's all here.

Centenary Pool   SWIMMING
(Map p284; ✆1300 332 583; www.brisbane.qld.gov.au; 400 Gregory Tce, Spring Hill; adult/child/family $5/3.60/15.20; ⊙5.30am-8pm Mon-Thu, 5.30am-7pm Fri, 7am-4pm Sat, 7am-2pm Sun)

This is the best pool in town and has been recently refurbished, with an Olympic-sized lap pool, a kids' pool and diving pool with a high tower.

Spring Hill Baths   SWIMMING
(Map p284; www.bluefitbrisbane.com.au; 14 Torrington St, Spring Hill; adult/child/family $5/3.60/15.20; ⊙6.30am-7pm Mon-Thu, 6.30am-6pm Fri, 8am-5pm Sat & Sun) Opened in 1886, this quaint heated 25m pool is encircled by cute timber change rooms. It's one of the oldest public baths in the southern hemisphere.

Climbing & Abseiling

You can make like Spiderman at the **Kangaroo Point Cliffs** (Map p288), on the southern banks of the Brisbane River at Kangaroo Point. The cliffs are floodlit until midnight or later.

Riverlife Adventure Centre   ROCK CLIMBING
(Map p288; ✆07-3891 5766; www.riverlife.com.au; Naval Stores, Kangaroo Point Bikeway, Kangaroo Point; ⊙9am-5pm) Near the 20m Kangaroo Point Cliffs, Riverlife runs rock-climbing sessions (from $49) and abseiling exploits ($39). They also offer kayaking river trips (from $39) and hire out bikes (per four hours $30), kayaks (per two hours $33) and in-line skates (per four hours $40).

BRISBANE IN...

Two Days

Start with breakfast in Brisbane's boho West End then saunter across to the South Bank Parklands (p283). Spend a few hours swanning around at the Gallery of Modern Art (p283), then grab some lunch at a riverside eatery and cool off with a swim at Streets Beach (p287). As the evening rolls in, jump on a ferry to the Brisbane Powerhouse (p283) in New Farm for a bite, a drink or perhaps a show.

On day two head downtown for a gander at the mix of old and new architecture, visiting the newly renovated City Hall (p282) – don't miss the Museum of Brisbane (p282) on the third floor – and the Treasury Building (p282), before ambling through the lush City Botanic Gardens (p282). Finish the day in Fortitude Valley: a brew at Alfred & Constance (p303), a noodle soup in Chinatown (p283), and a night of indulgences in the bars and clubs.

Four Days

On day three check out the rather French cafes in New Farm then scoot over to Paddington to check out the retro shops. Take a drive up to the lookout on top of Mt Coottha Reserve (p283) then meander away an hour or two in the Brisbane Botanic Gardens (p286). Dress up for dinner and drinks in the city: slake your thirst at Super Whatnot (p302) then eat in style at E'cco (p298).

On day four take a river cruise to Lone Pine Koala Sanctuary (p286). Recount the day's wildlife encounters over a beer and a steak at the Breakfast Creek Hotel (p304) then head back to the West End for beers and a live band.

Central Brisbane, Kangaroo Point & South Bank

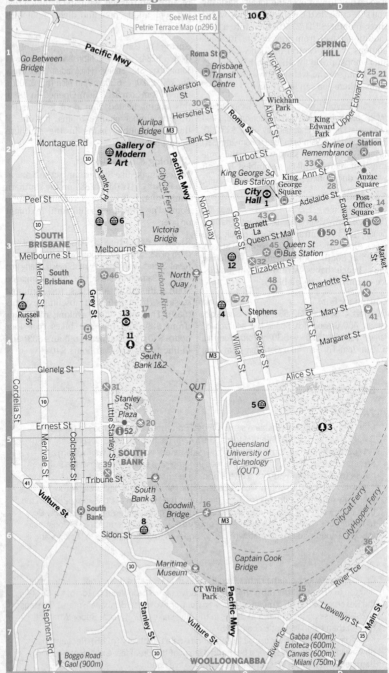

See West End & Petrie Terrace Map (p296)

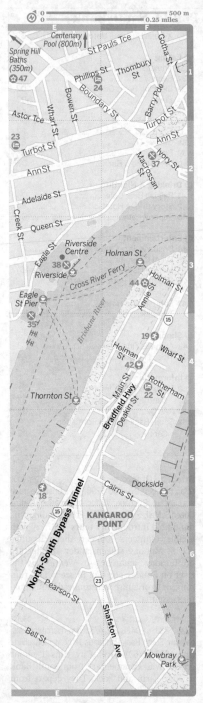

Story Bridge Adventure Climb

ADVENTURE TOUR

(Map p288; ☑1300 254 627; www.sbac.net.au; 170 Main St, Kangaroo Point; adult/child from $99/85) A Brisbane must-do, the bridge climb offers unbeatable views of the city – at dawn, day, twilight or night. The 2½-hour climb scales the southern half of the bridge, taking you 80m above the twisting, muddy Brisbane River below. Minimum age 10. Bridge abseiling expeditions are also available.

Urban Climb

ROCK CLIMBING, ABSEILING

(Map p296; ☑07-3844 2544; www.urbanclimb. com; 2/220 Montague Rd, West End; adult/child $18/16; ⊙noon-10pm Mon-Thu, noon-9pm Fri, 10am-6pm Sat & Sun) A large indoor climbing wall with 200-plus routes.

In-Line Skating

You can hire skates and equipment from Riverlife Adventure Centre (p287).

Planet Inline

SKATING

(Map p288; ☑07-3217 3571; www.planetinline.com; Goodwill Bridge; tours $15) Skaters reclaim the streets on Wednesday nights with Planet Inline skate tours, starting at 7.15pm from the top of the Goodwill Bridge ($15). Planet Inline also runs a Saturday-morning breakfast-club tour ($15), and Sunday-afternoon tours that differ each week and last about three hours ($15).

☞ Tours

CityCat

BOAT TOUR

(☑13 12 30; www.translink.com.au; one-way $5.60; ⊙5.25am-11.50pm) Ditching the car or bus and catching a sleek CityCat ferry along the river is the Brisbane sightseeing journey of choice! Stand on an open-air deck and glide under the Story Bridge to South Bank and the city centre. The ferries run every 15 to 30 minutes between the University of Queensland in the southwest to the Apollo Road terminal north of the city, stopping at 14 terminals in between, including New Farm Park, North Quay (for the CBD), South Bank and West End.

CitySights

GUIDED TOUR

(Map p288; www.citysights.com.au; day tickets per adult/child/family $35/20/80; ⊙9am-3.45pm) This hop-on-hop-off shuttle bus wheels past 19 of Brisbane's major landmarks, including the CBD, Mt Coot-tha, Chinatown, South Bank and Story Bridge. Tours depart every 45 minutes from Post Office Sq on Queen St.

BRISBANE & AROUND BRISBANE

Central Brisbane, Kangaroo Point & South Bank

The same ticket covers you for unlimited use of CityCat ferry services.

XXXX Brewery Tour TOUR
(Map p296; ☑ 07-3361 7597; www.xxxxbrewerytour.com.au; cnr Black & Paten Sts, Milton; adult/child $25/16; ⊙ hourly 11am-4pm Mon-Fri, 12.30pm, 1pm & 1.30pm Sat, 11am, noon & 12.30pm Sun) Feel a XXXX coming on? Grown-up entry to this brewery tour includes a few humidity-beating ales, so leave the car at home. Also on offer are beer-and-barbecue tours on Wednesday nights and Saturday during the day (adult/child $38/29), which include lunch. Book all tours in advance, online or by phone. The brewery is a 20-minute walk west from Roma St Station, or take the train to Milton Station. Wear enclosed shoes.

Brisbane Greeters GUIDED TOUR
(Map p288; ☑ 07-3006 6290; www.brisbanegreeters.com.au; Brisbane Visitor Information Centre, Queen St Mall; ⊙ 10am) FREE Free, small-group, hand-held introductory tours of Brizzy with affable volunteers. Tours are themed: public art on Monday, Queenslander architecture on Tuesday , churches on Wednesday, the river on Sunday etc. Call to see what's running, or to organise a customised tour. Bookings essential.

River City Cruises CRUISE
(Map p288; ☑ 0428 278 473; www.rivercitycruises.com.au; South Bank Parklands Jetty A; adult/child/family $25/15/60) River City runs 1½-hour cruises with commentary from South Bank to New Farm and back. They depart from

South Bank at 10.30am and 12.30pm (plus 2.30pm during summer).

Ghost Tours   TOUR
(📞 0401 666 441; www.ghost-tours.com.au; walking/coach tours from $30/50) 'Get creeped' on these 90-minute guided walking tours or 2½-hour bus tours of Brisbane's haunted heritage: murder scenes, cemeteries, eerie arcades and the infamous **Boggo Road Gaol** (Map p284; 📞 0411 111 903; www.boggoroadgaol.com; Annerley Rd, Dutton Park; historical tours adult/child/family $25/12.50/50, ghost tours adult/child over 12 $40/25; ⊘ historical tours 11am & 1pm Tue-Fri, 11am, 1pm & 3pm Sat, hourly 10am-1pm & 3pm Sun, night tours 7pm Thu, ghost tours 7.30pm Wed & Sun). Offers several tours a week; bookings essential.

⭐ Festivals & Events

Check out www.visitbrisbane.com.au for full listings of what's happening around town.

Brisbane International   TENNIS
(www.brisbaneinternational.com.au) A pro tennis tournament attracting the world's best, held in January at the Queensland Tennis Centre, just prior to the Australian Open (in Melbourne).

Chinese New Year   CULTURE
(www.chinesenewyear.com.au) Held in Fortitude Valley's Chinatown Mall (Duncan St)

in January/February. Firecrackers, dancing dragons and fantastic food.

Paniyiri Festival   CULTURE
(www.paniyiri.com) Greek cultural festival with dancing, food and music. Held in late May at Musgrave Park in the West End.

Brisbane Pride Festival   GAY & LESBIAN
(www.brisbanepridefestival.com.au) Brisbane's annual gay and lesbian celebration is held over four weeks in September (some events in June, including the fab Queen's Ball).

'Ekka' Royal Queensland Show   AGRICULTURAL
(www.ekka.com.au) Country and city collide in August for Queensland's largest annual event, the Ekka (formerly the Brisbane Exhibition, which was shortened to 'Ekka'). Baby animals, showbags, spooky carnies, shearing demonstrations, rides and over-sugared kids ahoy!

Brisbane Writers Festival   ARTS
(BWF; www.brisbanewritersfestival.com.au) The premier literary event in Queensland has been running for 50 years: words, books, and people who put words in books. Held in September.

Valley Fiesta   MUSIC
(www.valleyfiesta.com.au) Rock bands and DJs take over Fortitude Valley's Brunswick St and Chinatown malls for three days in October: Brisbane's biggest free music fest.

BRISBANE FOR CHILDREN

Out and about, swing by the South Bank Parklands (p283), which has lawns, BBQs, playgrounds and the slow-spinning Wheel of Brisbane (p283) – a real mind-blower for anyone under 15. The lifeguard-patrolled Streets Beach (p287) is here too, with a shallow section for really small swimmers. **New Farm Park** is another beaut spot by the river, with a series of treehouse-like platforms interlinking huge (and shady) Moreton Bay fig trees.

The Brisbane River is a big plus. Take a ferry ride around the bends of central Brisbane, or chug further afield to the Lone Pine Koala Sanctuary (p286) where the kids can cuddle up to a critter. If you're heading out Mt Coot-tha way, catch a starry show at the Sir Thomas Brisbane Planetarium (p286).

Too humid to be outside? The Queensland Museum (p283) runs some fab, hands-on programs for little tackers during school holidays. The incorporated Sciencentre has plenty of push-this-button-and-see-what-happens action. The Queensland Art Gallery (p283) has a Children's Art Centre which runs regular programs throughout the year, as does the State Library of Queensland (p308) and the Gallery of Modern Art (p283).

Day-care or babysitting options include **Dial an Angel** (📞 07-3878 1077, 1300 721 111; www.dialanangel.com) and **Care4Kidz** (📞 07-3103 0298; www.careforkidz.com.au). For info on current happenings pick up the free monthly magazine *Brisbane's Child* (www.brisbaneschild.com.au).

Fortitude Valley & New Farm

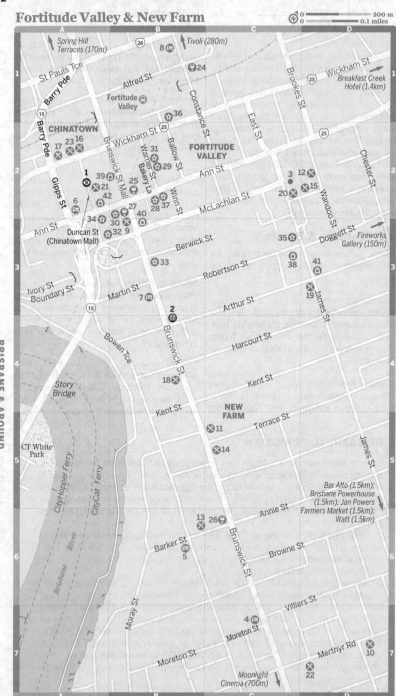

Fortitude Valley & New Farm

⊙ Sights
1 Chinatown.................................A2
Institute of Modern Art ....(see 33)
2 Philip Bacon Galleries B4

⊕ Activities, Courses & Tours
3 James St Cooking School.....................C2

⊜ Sleeping
4 Allender Apartments..........................C7
5 Bowen Terrace....................................B6
6 Bunk Backpackers...............................A2
7 Central Brunswick Apartments B3
8 Limes...B1

⊗ Eating
9 Brunswick Social.................................B3
10 Cafe Bouquiniste D7
11 Café Cirque C5
12 Campos..D2
13 Chouquette..B6
14 Himalayan Cafe...................................C5
15 James St Market..................................D2
16 Kuan Yin Tea House A2
17 Lust For Life..A2
18 Pintxo..B4
19 Sitar...D3
20 Spoon Deli Cafe....................................C2
21 Thai Wi-Rat..A2
22 The Smoke BBQ.....................................D7

23 The Vietnamese.......................................A2

⊙ Drinking & Nightlife
24 Alfred & Constance B1
25 Bowery...B2
Cru Bar & Cellar.............................(see 20)
26 Gertie's...C6
27 Press Club B2

⊛ Entertainment
28 Beat MegaClub B2
Birdees...(see 6)
29 Church...B2
30 Cloudland B2
31 Electric Playground..............................B2
32 Family..A3
33 Judith Wright Centre of
Contemporary Arts B3
34 Oh Hello...A3
35 Palace Centro C3
36 Wickham Hotel B1
37 Zoo..B2

⊚ Shopping
38 Blonde Venus..C3
39 Brisbane Valley Markets.......................B2
40 in.cube8r gallery..................................B3
41 Title...D3
42 Trash Monkey A2

Brisbane International Film Festival FILM
(www.biff.com.au) Twelve days of quality films flicker across Brisbane screens in November.

🛏 Sleeping

Brisbane has an excellent selection of accommodation options that will suit any budget. Many are beyond the business beds of the city centre, but they're usually within walking distance or have good public-transport connections.

🛏 City Centre

X-Base Brisbane Uptown HOSTEL $
(Map p288; ☑07-3238 5888; www.stayatbase.com; 466 George St; dm $22-36, d & tw $130-140; ❄@🛜) This purpose-built hostel near Roma St Station flaunts its youth with mod interiors, decent facilities and overall cleanliness. Each room has air-con, a bathroom and individual lockers, and it's wheelchair-accessible. The bar downstairs is one big party place – with live bands, DJs and open-mic nights. Also runs the colossal **X-Base Brisbane Central** (Map p288; ☑07-3211 2433; www.stayatbase.com; 398 Edward St; dm $27-33,

s/d/tw $55/70/70; ❄@🛜) and low-key **X-Base Brisbane Embassy** (Map p288; ☑07-3014 1715; www.stayatbase.com; 214 Elizabeth St; dm $31-35, d with/without bathroom $99/79; ❄@🛜).

Diamant Hotel BOUTIQUE HOTEL $$
(Map p288; ☑07-3009 3400; www.8hotels.com; 52 Astor Tce; d from $149; P❄🛜) Behind an ultra-mod black-and-white facade, seven-storey Diamant has compact, contemporary rooms with natty wallpaper and thoughtful touches (original artwork, iPod docks, free wi-fi). The bigger suites have kitchenettes and lounge areas, and there's a bar-restaurant on the ground floor. Parking $28.

Punthill Brisbane HOTEL $$
(Map p288; ☑07-3055 5777, 1300 731 299; www.punthill.com.au; 40 Astor Tce, Spring Hill; 1-/3-bed apt from $150/180; P❄🛜🐾) Melbourne's Punthill hotel chain has made a move north, serving up a slice of hip hotel style in Spring Hill. The lobby is full of retro bicycles and every balcony has a bird cage with a faux-feathered friend in it...but aside from these quirks, what you can expect is stylish suites (all taupe, charcoal, ivory and nice art) in a

BRISBANE GALLERY SCENE

The Gallery of Modern Art (p283; aka GOMA) and the Queensland Art Gallery (p283) in South Bank steal the show, but Brisbane also has a growing array of progressive smaller private galleries and exhibition spaces.

➜ The **Institute of Modern Art** (IMA; Map p292; www.ima.org.au; 420 Brunswick St, Fortitude Valley; ⊘ 11am-5pm Tue, Wed, Fri, Sat, to 8pm Thu) **FREE** in the Judith Wright Centre of Contemporary Arts in Fortitude Valley is an excellent noncommercial gallery with an industrial vibe. Risqué, emerging and experimental art for grown-ups: it's GOMA's naughty little cousin.

➜ The hip little artist-run **Queensland Centre for Photography** (Map p288; www.qcp. org.au; cnr Russell & Cordelia Sts; ⊘ 10am-5pm Wed-Sat, 11am-3pm Sun) **FREE** is the place to check out some ace Australian contemporary photography.

➜ **Milani** (Map p284; www.milanigallery.com.au; 54 Logan Rd, Woolloongabba; ⊘ 11am-6pm Tue-Sat) **FREE** is a superb gallery with cutting-edge Aboriginal and confronting contemporary artwork. If it looks closed it might not be: just turn the door handle.

➜ The estimable **Philip Bacon Galleries** (Map p292; www.philipbacongalleries.com.au; 2 Arthur St, Fortitude Valley; ⊘ 10am-5pm Tue-Sat) **FREE** has been around since 1974 and specialises in 19th-century and modern Australian paintings and sculpture.

➜ A fabulous warehouse space, **Fireworks Gallery** (Map p284; www.fireworksgallery. com.au; 52a Doggett St, Newstead; ⊘ 10am-6pm Tue-Fri, to 4pm Sat) **FREE** specialises in both Aboriginal art and offbeat contemporary ceramics, sculpture, weavings and canvases.

central location for competitive prices. Parking $25.

Urban Brisbane
HOTEL $$

(Map p288; ☏ 07-3831 6177; www.hotelurban.com. au; 345 Wickham Tce; d from $150; ❄ @ 🛜 🏊) Still looking sexy after a recent $10-million makeover, the Urban has stylish rooms with masculine hues, balconies and high-end fittings (super-comfy beds, big TVs, fuzzy bathrobes). There's also a heated outdoor pool, a bar, and lots of uniformed flight attendants checking in and out. Parking $15.

Inchcolm Hotel
HISTORIC HOTEL $$

(Map p288; ☏ 07-3226 8888; www.theinchcolm. com.au; 73 Wickham Tce; r $160-250; P ❄ 🛜 🏊) Built in the 1930s as doctors' suites, the heritage-listed Inchcolm (pronounced as per 'Malcolm') retains elements of its past (love the old elevator!), but the rooms have been overhauled. Those in the newer wing have more space and light; in the older wing there's more character. There's also a rooftop pool and in-house restaurant. Parking $30.

Soho Motel
MOTEL $$

(Map p288; ☏ 07-3831 7722; www.sohobrisbane. com.au; 333 Wickham Tce; r $115-160; P ❄ @ 🛜) This bricky 50-room joint a short hop from Roma St Station is better inside than it looks from the street, with smart, compact rooms

with little balconies. The owners are friendly and savvy, and pay attention to the little things: free wi-fi, 11am check-out, free parking, custom made furniture and plush linen. Good value for money.

Treasury
LUXURY HOTEL $$$

(Map p288; ☏ 07-3306 8888; www.treasury-brisbane.com.au; 130 William St; r from $230; P ❄ @ 🛜) Brisbane's most lavish hotel is behind the equally lavish exterior of the former Land Administration Building. Each room is unique and awash with heritage features; they have high ceilings, framed artwork, polished wood furniture and elegant furnishings. Perfect if plush and a little bit chintzy floats your boat. The best rooms have river views. Super-efficient staff; parking $20.

🛏 West End

Gonow Family Backpacker
HOSTEL $

(Map p296; ☏ 07-3846 3473; www.gonowfamily.com. au; 147 Vulture St; dm $18-30, d $69; P 🛜) These have to be the cheapest beds in Brisbane, and Gonow (which was only months old when we visited) is doing a decent job of delivering a clean, respectful, secure hostel experience despite the bargain-basement pricing. It's not a party place – you'll be better off elsewhere if you're looking party into the night. The upstairs rooms have more ceiling height.

Brisbane Backpackers Resort HOSTEL $
(Map p296; ☑ 07-3844 9956, 1800 626 452; www.
brisbanebackpackers.com.au; 110 Vulture St; dm $27-
34, tw/d/tr $110/120/135; [P] [✳] [@] [🛜] [🏊]) Is there
such a thing as 'backpacker kitsch'? If so, this
hulking hostel probably qualifies, with dubious marketing relating to 'bad girls' and what
they do and don't do... But if you're looking to
party, you're in the right place. There's a great
pool and bar area, and rooms are basic but
generally well maintained.

Petrie Terrace

Aussie Way Backpackers HOSTEL $
(Map p296; ☑ 07-3369 0711; www.aussieway-
backpackers.com; 34 Cricket St; dm/s/d/f/q
$26/55/68/78/104; [✳] [🛜] [🏊]) Set in a photo-
genic, two-storey timber Queenslander on
the appealingly named Cricket St, Aussie
Way feels more like a homely guesthouse
than a hostel, with spacious, tastefully furnished rooms and a fab pool for sticky Brisbane afternoons. The doubles in the second
building out the back are just lovely. All
quiet after 10.30pm.

Brisbane City YHA HOSTEL $
(Map p296; ☑ 07-3236 1004; www.yha.com.au; 392
Upper Roma St; dm from $39, tw & d with/without
bathroom from $122/103, f from $160; [P] [✳] [@]
[🛜] [🏊]) This immaculate, well-run hostel has
a rooftop pool and a sundeck with incredible river views. The maximum dorm size is
six beds (not too big); most have bathrooms.
Big on security, activities, tours and kitchen
space (lots of fridges). The cafe/bar has trivia nights and happy hours, but this is a YHA,
not party central. Parking $10.

Chill Backpackers HOSTEL $
(Map p296; ☑ 07-3236 0088, 1800 851 875; www.
chillbackpackers.com; 328 Upper Roma St; dm $29-
35, d/tr $89/105; [P] [✳] [@] [🛜]) This garish aqua
building on the CBD fringe has small, clean,
modern rooms, and there's a roof deck with

fab river views (just like the YHA up the
road, but from a slightly reduced altitude).
There are 150 beds here, but if they're full
the affiliated **Brisbane City Backpackers**
(Map p296; ☑ 07-3211 3221, 1800 062 572; www.cit-
ybackpackers.com; 380 Upper Roma St; dm $21-33,
s/tw/d/tr from $79/79/105/105; [P] [✳] [@] [🛜] [🏊]) is
a couple of doors away.

Spring Hill

Kookaburra Inn GUESTHOUSE $
(Map p288; ☑ 1800 733 533, 07-3832 1303; www.
kookaburra-inn.com.au; 41 Phillips St; s/tw/d without
bathroom from $65/80/80; [✳] [@] [🛜]) This small,
simple two-level guesthouse has basic rooms
with washbasin and fridge, and clean shared
bathrooms. The building itself is unremarka-
ble, but there's a lounge, kitchen and outdoor
patio. A decent budget option if you've done
dorms to death. Air-con in some doubles only.

Spring Hill Terraces MOTEL $
(Map p284; ☑ 07-3854 1048; www.springhillter-
races.com; 260 Water St; d $95-145, unit $175;
[P] [✳] [🛜] [🏊]) Offering good service, security
and a tiny pool (a pond?), Spring Hill Terraces has inoffensive motel-style rooms and
roomier terrace units with balconies and
leafy courtyards. A 10-minute walk from Fortitude Valley.

Fortitude Valley

Bunk Backpackers HOSTEL $
(Map p292; ☑ 07-3257 3644, 1800 682 865; www.
bunkbrisbane.com.au; cnr Ann & Gipps Sts; dm
$21-33, s $60, d/apt from $80/180; [P] [✳] [@] [🛜] [🏊])
This old arts college was reborn as a backpackers in 2006 – and the party hasn't
stopped! It's a huge, five-level place with
55 rooms (mostly eight-bed dorms), just
staggering distance from the Valley nightlife. There's also an inhouse bar (Birdees), a
Mexican cantina, and a few awesome apartments on the top floor.

BRISBANE FESTIVAL

Running over three weeks in September, the Brisbane Festival involves over 300 performances and 60-odd events, enticing 2000-plus artists from across the planet. Art exhibitions, dance, theatre, opera, symphonies, circus performers, buskers and vaudeville
acts generate an eclectic scene, with many free street events and concerts around town.

The festival is opened each year with a bang – literally. Staged over the Brisbane
River, with vantage points at South Bank, the city and West End, Riverfire is a massive
fireworks show with dazzling visual choreography and a synchronised soundtrack.

For more info see www.brisbanefestival.com.au.

West End & Petrie Terrace

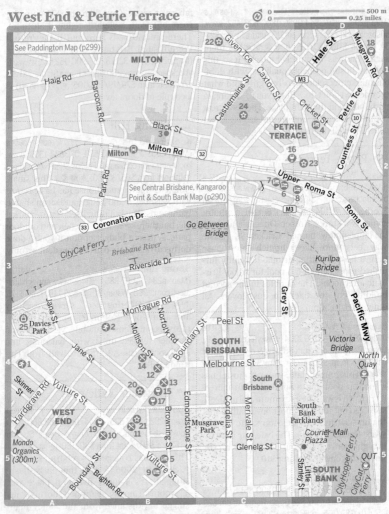

See Paddington Map (p299)

See Central Brisbane, Kangaroo Point & South Bank Map (p290)

BRISBANE & AROUND BRISBANE

Central Brunswick Apartments
APARTMENT $$

(Map p292; ☎07-3852 1411; www.centralbrunswickhotel.com.au; 455 Brunswick St; r $140-180; P❊☎) Emerging from the husk of an old brick brewery building, these 60 mod studio apartments are a hit with business bods. All have fully equipped kitchens, and there's an on-site gym, free wi-fi and rooftop BBQ. Parking $10 per night.

★Limes
BOUTIQUE HOTEL $$$

(Map p292; ☎07-3852 9000; www.limeshotel.com.au; 142 Constance St; d from $230; ❊☎) A slick slice of style in the Valley, Limes has 21 handsome rooms that make good use of tight space – each has plush furniture, kitchenettes and thoughtful extras (iPod docks, free wi-fi, free gym pass). The rooftop bar and cinema (!) are magic.

☐ New Farm

★Bowen Terrace
GUESTHOUSE $

(Map p292; ☎07-3254 0458; www.bowenterrace.com.au; 365 Bowen Tce; dm/s/d without bathroom $35/60/85, d/f with bathroom $99/145; P@☎) A beautifully restored, 100-year-old Queens-

West End & Petrie Terrace

lander, this quiet guesthouse offers TVs, bar fridges, quality bed linen and lofty ceilings with fans in every room. Out the back there's a deck overlooking the enticing pool. No air-con but real value for money, with far more class than your average hostel. The only downside is that the walls between rooms are a bit thin (built before TV was invented).

Allender Apartments　APARTMENT $$
(Map p292; 07-3358 5832; www.allenderapart-ments.com.au; 3 Moreton St; d $135, 1-bedroom apt $160-170;) Allender's apartments are a mixed bag. In the plain yellow-brick building are simply furnished but clean rooms. More attractive are the heritage apartments in the adjoining Fingal House, a 1918 Queenslander with polished timber floors, oak furniture and access to a private verandah or courtyard.

Kangaroo Point

Il Mondo　HOTEL $$
(Map p288; 07-3392 0111, 1300 665 526; www.ilmondo.com.au; 25 Rotherham St; r $160, 1-/3-bedroom apt $250/500;) In a brilliant location right near the Story Bridge, this postmodern-looking, seven-storey hotel has handsome rooms and apartments with minimalist design, high-end fixtures and plenty of space. The biggest apartments sleep six – good value for a full house.

Paddington & Around

Newmarket Gardens Caravan Park　CAMPGROUND $
(Map p284; 07-3356 1458; www.newmarketgar-dens.com.au; 199 Ashgrove Ave, Newmarket; un-powered/powered sites $39/41, on-site vans $56, budget r $66, cabins $125-150;) This upbeat caravan park doesn't have many trees (some of them are mangoes – beware falling fruit!), but it's just 4km north of the city, accessible by bus and train. There's a row of six simple budget rooms (no air-con), five tidy cabins (with air-con) and a sea of van and tent sites. Not much in the way of distractions for kids.

Casabella Apartment　APARTMENT $$
(Map p299; 07-3217 6507; www.casabella-apart ment.com; 211 Latrobe Tce, Paddington; apt $185;) The understorey of this fuchsia-coloured house at the quiet end of Paddo's main drag has been converted into a comfy self-contained unit. There are two bedrooms (sleeps three), warm Mediterranean colour schemes, recycled timber floors and lots of louvres to let the crossbreeze through (no air-con). Lovely! Free street parking.

★ Latrobe Apartment　APARTMENT $$$
(Map p299; 0448 944 026; www.stayz.com. au/77109; 183a Latrobe Tce, Paddington; apt from $200;) Underneath a chiropractor in affluent Paddington is this excellent two-bedroom apartment, sleeping four, with two bathrooms, polished floorboards, sexy lighting and a fabulous BBQ deck. It's

a sleek, contemporary design with quality everything: linen, toiletries, kitchenware, TV, iPod dock, leather lounge... Cafes and free parking up at street level.

✗ Eating

The city centre is the place for fine dining and coffee nooks. In Fortitude Valley you'll find cheap cafes and Chinatown. Nearby, New Farm has plenty of multicultural eateries, French-styled cafes and award winners. Eclectic West End is littered with bohemian cafes and cheap multicultural diners. South Bank swings between mainstream and pricey eats.

✗ City Centre

★ Brew
CAFE, WINE BAR $

(Map p288; ☑ 07-3211 4242; www.brewgroup.com. au; Lower Burnett La; mains $6-12; ☺ 7am-5pm Mon, to 10pm Tue & Wed, to 11.30pm Thu & Fri, 9am-11.30pm Sat, 9am-3pm Sun) You'd expect to find this kind of subcultural underground cafe in Seattle or Berlin...but Brisbane? Breaking new coffee-cultural ground in Queensland, Brew takes caffeine into the alleyways, serving simple food (tapas, pastas, sandwiches) to go with the black stuff. Wines and bottled beers if you feel like a different kind of brew.

Bleeding Heart Gallery
CAFE $

(Map p288; ☑ 07-3229 0395; www.bleedingheart. com.au; 166 Ann St; mains $5-10; ☺ 7am-5pm Mon-Fri; ☎) ✐ Set back from hectic Ann St in an 1865 servants' home (Brisbane's third-oldest building!), this spacious cafe/gallery has hippie vibes and hosts art exhibitions, occasional concerts and other events. All profits go into funding charitable community enterprises.

Bean
CAFE $

(Map p288; www.facebook.com/beanbrisbane; rear 181 George St; mains $9-15; ☺ 7am-6pm) One of Brisbane's new breed of hip laneway coffee shops, down a grungy, graffiti-spangled driveway off George St, surrounded by fire escapes, air-con units and construction cranes. You can grab a biscuit or a basic eggy breakfast here, but coffee is the main game. Live music Thursdays at 5pm.

Groove Train
CAFE $$

(Map p288; www.groovetrain.com.au; Riverside Centre, 123 Eagle St; mains $17-35; ☺ 7am-late) An orange and dark-wood bunker hunkered down by the Riverside ferry terminal, Groove

Train is long, low, lean and groovy. Watch the boats chug to-and-fro as you tuck into woodfired pizzas, wok fry-ups, burgers, calzones, risottos and big salads. Gets moody and bar-like at night.

Verve Cafe & Bar
ITALIAN $$

(Map p288; ☑ 07-3221 5691; www.vervecafe.com. au; 109 Edward St; mains $17-35; ☺ noon-late Mon-Fri, 5pm-late Sat & Sun) Subterranean Verve allegedly stocks Australia's biggest selection of ciders. But that's not why you're here. Well, it might be – but try some of the imaginative pastas, salads, risottos and pizzas before you start drinking. The sand crab and snapper risotto with lemon and fresh thyme is a winner. Radiohead on the stereo; arty, relaxed crowd.

★ E'cco
MODERN AUSTRALIAN $$$

(Map p288; ☑ 07-3831 8344; www.eccobistro.com; 100 Boundary St; mains $40-43; ☺ noon-3pm Tue-Fri, 6-10pm Tue-Sat; ✐) One of the finest restaurants in the state, award-winning E'cco is a culinary must! Menu masterpieces from chef Philip Johnson include liquorice-spiced pork belly with caramelised peach, onion jam and kipfler potatoes. The interior is suitably swish: all black, white and stainless steel.

Cha Cha Char
STEAKHOUSE $$$

(Map p288; ☑ 07-3211 9944; www.chachachar.com. au; Shop 5, 1 Eagle St Pier; mains $38-95; ☺ noon-11pm Mon-Fri, 6-11pm Sat & Sun) Wallowing in awards, this long-running favourite serves Brisbane's best steaks, along with first-rate seafood and roast game meats. The classy semicircular dining room in the Eagle St Pier complex has floor-to-ceiling windows and river views.

✗ South Bank

Piaf
FRENCH $$

(Map p288; ☑ 07-3846 5026; www.piafbistro.com. au; 5/182 Grey St; breakfast mains $7-16, lunch & dinner $18-26; ☺ 7am-late) A chilled-out but still intimate bistro with a loyal following, Piaf serves a small selection (generally just five mains and a few salads and other light options) of good-value, contemporary French-inspired food. French wines by the glass. No sign of Edith...

Ahmet's
TURKISH $$

(Map p288; ☑ 07-3846 6699; www.ahmets.com; Shop 10, 168 Grey St; mains $19-34, banquets per person $34-46; ☺ 11.30am-3pm & 6pm-late; ✐)

Paddington

On restaurant-lined Grey St, Ahmet's serves delectable Turkish fare amid a riot of colours and Grand Bazaar/Bosphorus murals. Try a *suçuk pide* (oven-baked Turkish bread with Turkish salami, egg, tomato and mozzarella). Deep street-side terrace and regular live music.

✗ West End

★ George's Seafood   FISH & CHIPS $
(Map p296; ☑07-3844 4100; 150 Boundary St; meals $8-10; ⊙9.30am-7.30pm Mon-Fri, 10.30am-7.30pm Sat & Sun) With a window full of fresh mudcrabs, Moreton Bay rock oysters, banana prawns and whole snapper, this old fish-and-chipper has been here forever. The $8 cod-and-chips is what you're here for – unbeatable!

Burrow   CAFE $
(Map p296; ☑07-3846 0030; www.theburrowwestend.com.au; 37 Mollison St; mains $10-20; ⊙7am-late Tue-Sun; 🐾) In the open-sided understorey of a shambling old Queenslander, casual Burrow is like a Baja California cantina crossed with a student share-house: laid-back and beachy with surf murals and wafting Pink Floyd. Try the hangover-removing El Desperados taco for breakfast – pulled pork, eggs and jalapeño salsa. Good coffee, too.

Paddington

🛏 Sleeping
1 Casabella Apartment A1
2 Latrobe Apartment A1

✗ Eating
3 Il Posto B2

🍸 Drinking & Nightlife
4 Lark C3

🛍 Shopping
5 Paddington Antique Centre B1
6 Retro Metro C2

Blackstar Coffee Roasters   CAFE $
(Map p296; 44 Thomas St; mains $6-12; ⊙7am-3pm Mon, to 5pm Tue-Fri, to late Sat, 8am-3pm Sun) A neighbourhood fave, West End's own bean roaster has excellent coffee, a simple breakfast menu (wraps, avocado on toast, eggs Benedict), wailing Roy Orbison and live jazz on Saturday evening. Try one of their cold-pressed coffees on a hot day.

★ Gunshop Café   CAFE, MODERN AUSTRALIAN $$
(Map p296; ☑07-3844 2241; www.thegunshopcafe.com; 53 Mollison St; mains $17-33; ⊙6.30am-2pm Mon, to late Tue-Sat, to 2.30pm Sun) With cool tunes, interesting art and happy staff, this

BRISBANE & AROUND BRISBANE

LOCAL KNOWLEDGE

PHILIP JOHNSON: HEAD CHEF AT E'CCO

Kitchens are great: there's always a melting pot of ideas. You work with different chefs, and things evolve over the years.

Claim to Fame

Winning *Gourmet Traveller's* Restaurant of the Year award in 1997. Some people say that's what helped put Brisbane's restaurant scene on the map. I hate to look at it like that but I think the rest of the country took notice: 'There must be some decent places to eat up there in Brisbane'. A well-known food critic said you couldn't eat north of Paddington – as in Paddington, Sydney. That changed a bit that year.

Cooking Style

Modern Australian, it has Italian influences, and there's always a bit of Asian in it owing to our proximity, plus a bit of Mediterranean.

Dining Scene in Brisbane

It's amazing. Brisbane is a city that has grown up in the last 15 years. I think for years we were considered playing second fiddle to Sydney and Melbourne, now I think we have great restaurants with top quality and service.

Other Favourite Restaurants

Something casual I love is Bar Alto (p304) at the Powerhouse.

---

peaceably repurposed gun shop has exposed-brick walls and an inviting back garden. The locally sourced menu changes daily, but regulars include smoked-chicken lasagne, a pulled-pork baguette and wild-mushroom risotto. Boutique beers, excellent Australian wines and afternoon pick-me-ups available.

Mondo Organics MODERN AUSTRALIAN **$$**
(Map p284; ☑07-3844 1132; www.mondo-organics.com.au; 166 Hardgrave Rd; mains $25-36; ⊙8.30-11.30am Sat & Sun, noon-2.30pm Fri-Sun, 6pm-late Wed-Sat) ✐ Using high-quality organic and sustainable produce, Mondo Organics earns top marks for its delicious seasonal menu. Recent hits include duck breast with fig, sage and strawberry; and potato and parmesan gnocchi with golden shallots, zucchini and salsa verde. See the website for details about the attached Mondo Organics Cooking School (three-hour classes are $110 to $140).

Little Greek Taverna GREEK **$$**
(Map p296; ☑07-3255 2215; www.littlegreektaverna.com.au; Shop 5, 1 Browning St; mains $15-30, banquets per person $35-42; ⊙11am-9pm; ⊞) Uptempo, eternally busy and in a prime West End location, the LGT is a beaut spot for a big Greek feast and some people watching. Launch into a prawn and saganaki salad or a classic lamb yiros, washed down with a sleep-defeating Greek coffee. Kid-friendly, too.

✗ Fortitude Valley & Chinatown

James St Market MARKET, SELF-CATERING **$**
(Map p292; www.jamesstmarket.com.au; 22 James St; ⊙8.30am-7pm Mon-Fri, 8am-6pm Sat & Sun) Paradise for gourmands, this small but beautifully stocked market has gourmet cheeses, a bakery/patisserie, fruit and veg, flowers and lots of quality goodies. The fresh seafood counter serves excellent sushi and sashimi. The **James St Cooking School** (Map p292; ☑07-3252-8850; www.jamesstcookingschool.com.au; 22 James St; 3hr class $135-155) is upstairs.

The Vietnamese VIETNAMESE **$**
(Map p292; ☑07-3252 4112; www.thevietnameserestaurant.com.au; 194 Wickham St; mains $10-20; ⊙11am-3pm & 5-10pm) Aptly if unimaginatively named, this is indeed the place in town to eat Vietnamese, with exquisitely prepared dishes served to an always crowded house. Go for something from the 'Chef's Recommendation' list: crispy beef strips with honey and chilli, or clay-pot prawns with oyster sauce. Great value for money.

Campos CAFE **$**
(Map p292; www.camposcoffee.com; 11 Wandoo St; mains $9-17; ⊙6.30am-4pm) Campos is a Sydney-based company, but that doesn't seem to bother the regulars here, who sidestep milk crates and stacks of cardboard boxes down

a little alley behind the James St Market for some of the best coffee in town. Food-wise it's substantial cafe fare (baked eggs; cherry, chocolate and coconut loaf; buttermilk pancakes). Takeaway bags of beans too.

Brunswick Social
DUMPLINGS, BAR $

(Map p292; ☑ 07-3252 3234; www.thebrunswicksocial.com; 351 Brunswick St; dumplings from $8; ☺ 6pm-late Wed, Thu, Sat & Sun, from 5pm Fri) Beat a retreat from the street down the stairs and into this sociable, funky dumpling house and late-night bar. A hip crew of Valley vixens and voyeurs eye each other over tapas-style plates of prawn-and-mushrom dumplings and BBQ pork buns. Drinks-wise, it's cocktails and craft beers: the 'Nu School Gimlet' (vodka, lime juice, lime marmalade and absinthe) will put a kink in your reality.

Lust For Life
CAFE $

(Map p292; ☑ 07-3852 5048; www.lustforlifetattoo.com; 176 Wickham St; items $5-12; ☺ 7am-3pm Mon-Fri, 10am-3pm Sat & Sun) Bagels, sandwiches, salads, organic juices, pastries, strong coffee and 'music your nanna hates' are on offer at Lust For Life, a quirky tattoo parlour that has morphed itself into a cafe and art gallery. Nibble a mango, almond and white-chocolate muffin as you wait to get inked.

Kuan Yin Tea House
CHINESE, VEGETARIAN $

(Map p292; ☑ 07-3252 4557; www.kuanyinteahouse.blogspot.com.au; 198 Wickham St; mains $6-12; ☺ 11.30am-7.30pm Mon, Wed & Thu, to 8pm Fri, to 5pm Sat, to 3pm Sun; ☑) Kuan Yin is a small, garish BYO place with faux-wood panelling and a bamboo-lined ceiling. Food-wise it's flavourful vegetarian noodle soups, dumplings and mock-meat rice dishes. Try the tofu salad. Great tea selection, too.

Thai Wi-Rat
THAI, LAOTIAN $

(Map p292; ☑ 07-3257 0884; 20 Duncan St; mains $11-18; ☺ 10am-4pm & 5-9.30pm) This modest, brightly illuminated hole-in-the-wall on the main Chinatown drag cooks up solid, chilli-heavy Thai and Laotian, including *pla dook yang* (grilled whole catfish). Takeaways available.

Spoon Deli Cafe
CAFE $$

(Map p292; ☑ 07-3257 1750; www.spoondeli.com.au; Shop B3, 22 James St; breakfast $7-20, mains $18-30; ☺ 6.30am-6pm Mon-Fri, 7am-5pm Sat & Sun) Inside James St Market, this upscale deli serves gloriously rich pastas, salads, soups and colossal paninis and lasagne slabs. The fresh juices are a liquid meal unto themselves. Walls are lined with deli produce: vinegars, oils, herbs and hampers. You'll feel hungry as soon as you walk in!

Sitar
INDIAN $

(Map p292; ☑ 07-3254 0400; www.sitar.com.au; 69 James St; mains $12-25; ☺ noon-2pm Sun-Fri, 6-9pm daily; ☑) Away from the fray on a quiet section of James St, Sitar occupies a lovely old white weatherboard Queenslander. Step inside for trad curries, dahls, naans and tandoori dishes, including plenty of gluten-free and vegetarian options. Love the psychedelic sitar player painting above the door.

✕ New Farm

Cafe Bouquiniste
CAFE $

(Map p292; 121 Merthyr Rd; mains $8-12; ☺ 7.30am-5pm Mon-Fri, 8.30am-5pm Sat, 8.30am-1pm Sun; ☑) Filling a tiny old side-street shopfront, this boho cafe and bookseller has buckets of charm (if not much space). The coffee is fantastic, service is friendly, and the prices are right for breakfast fare, toasted sandwiches, savoury tarts and cakes. Try the pumpkin, goat-cheese and sage tart.

Chouquette
CAFE, FRENCH $

(Map p292; ☑ 07-3358 6336; www.chouquette.com.au; 19 Barker St; items $2-10, 10 chouquettes $3.50; ☺ 6.30am-5pm Wed-Sat, to 12.30pm Sun; ☑) Some New Farmers say Chouquette is the best patisserie this side of Toulouse. We're not sure how many of them have actually been to Toulouse, but their argument holds up. Grab a nutty coffee and bag of the namesake *chouquettes* (small choux pastries topped with granulated sugar), a shiny slice of *tarte au citron* or a filled baguette. Sexy French-speaking staff.

Café Cirque
CAFE $

(Map p292; 618 Brunswick St; mains $14-17; ☺ 7am-4pm; ☑) One of the best breakfast spots (served all day) in town, buzzing Café Cirque serves rich coffee and daily specials, along with open-face sandwiches and gourmet salads for lunch. It's a skinny little room with foldback windows to the street.

Watt
MODERN AUSTRALIAN $$

(Map p284; ☑ 07-3358 5464; www.wattrestaurant.com.au; Brisbane Powerhouse, 119 Lamington St; mains $9-25; ☺ 9am-late Mon-Fri, 8am-late Sat & Sun) On the riverbank level of the Brisbane Powerhouse is casual, breezy Watt. Order up some duck salad with sweet chilli, rocket and orange; or a smoked ham-hock terrine with lentils and cornichons. Wines by the glass; DJ tunes on Sunday afternoons.

Himalayan Cafe NEPALESE $$
(Map p292; ☑07-3358 4015; 640 Brunswick St; mains $15-25; ☺5.30-10pm Tue-Sun; ☑) Awash with prayer flags and colourful cushions, this karmically positive, unfussy restaurant serves authentic Tibetan and Nepalese fare such as tender *fhaiya darkau* (lamb with vegies, coconut milk and spices). Repeat the house mantra: 'May positive forces be with every single living thing that exists'.

The Smoke BBQ BARBECUE $$
(Map p292; ☑07-3358 1922; www.thesmokebbq. com.au; 85 Merthyr Rd; mains lunch $15-21, dinner $25-37; ☺11.30am-2pm & 6-9pm Tue-Sat) The smell of hickory hangs heavy in the air of this small, buzzy restaurant plating up American-style BBQ. The menu includes tender short ribs, pulled pork and charcoal chicken (with vodka barbecue sauce), along with requisite sides like coleslaw, mac-and-cheese and fries. In-house joke: 'The trouble with BBQ is two or three days later you're hungry again'.

Pintxo SPANISH $$
(Map p292; ☑07-3333 2231; www.pintxo.com; 561 Brunswick St; tapas $9-14, share plates $16-28; ☺noon-3pm Sat & Sun, 5.30pm-late Wed-Sun) Grab a seat at the bar and choose your freshly prepared tapas as it glides past at this casual, paprika-red Spanish spot on Brunswick St. Shared plates are made to order, with authentic standouts like pancetta-wrapped shrimp, grilled chorizo with sweet potato and beef meatballs with manchego polenta. Wash it down with Spanish sangria, beers and wines by the glass.

Kangaroo Point & Around

Cliffs Cafe CAFE $
(Map p288; www.cliffscafe.com.au; 29 River Tce; mains $12-20; ☺7am-5pm) A steep climb up from the riverside, this cliff-top cafe has superb river and city-skyline views. It's a casual, open-air pavilion: thick burgers, battered barramundi and chips, salads, desserts and good coffee are the standouts.

Enoteca ITALIAN $$$
(Map p284; ☑07-3392 4315; www.1889enoteca. com.au; 10-12 Logan Rd, Woolloongabba; mains $36-42; ☺noon-2.30pm Tue-Fri & Sun, 6pm-late Tue-Sat) Simple and simply wonderful traditional Roman pasta, fish and meat dishes served in a gorgeous 1889 shopfront south of the city centre in Woolloongabba: one of the best restaurants in Brisbane. Even if you're not here for a meal (there's a little wine store here too) check out the lavish lead-lighting, marvellous marble bar and walk-around glass display cabinet full of Italian vino vessels.

Paddington

Il Posto ITALIAN $$
(Map p299; ☑07-3367 3111; www.ilposto.com. au; 107 Latrobe Tce; mains $20-29; ☺noon-4pm & 5.30pm-late Tue-Sun; ☑) Pizza and pasta just like they make in Rome, served on an outdoor piazza (or inside if it's too humid). Pizzas come either *rosse* or *bianche* (with or without tomato base), and are thin and crispy. Great staff, Peroni beer on tap, and kid-friendly too (also just like Rome).

Drinking & Nightlife

The prime drinking destination in Brisbane is Fortitude Valley, with its lounges, live-music bars and nightclubs (both straight and gay). Most clubs here are open Wednesday to Sunday nights; some are free, others charge up to $20. Dress nicely and bring your ID. In the CBD there's a bottoms-up after-work crowd, while the West End has cool bars full of inner-city funksters. New Farm has some hip bars, attracting a mostly neighbourhood crowd.

City Centre

★ Super Whatnot BAR
(Map p288; www.superwhatnot.com; 48 Burnett La; ☺3pm-late Tue-Sat) Trailblazing Super Whatnot is a funky, industrial laneway space, with a mezzanine floor and sunken lounge. Drinks: bottled boutique Australian beers and cocktails (try the cure-all Penicillin). Food: American-inspired bar snacks (hotdogs, mini burritos, nachos). Tunes: vinyl DJs Thursday to Saturday spinning funk, soul and hip-hop; live acoustic acts Wednesday. Winning combo!

Belgian Beer Cafe BAR
(Map p288; www.belgianbeercafebrussels.com.au; cnr Mary & Edward Sts; ☺11.30am-late) Wood-panelled walls and art-deco lights lend an old-world charm to this buzzing space. Out the back, the beer garden has big screens and big after-work egos. Lots of Hoegaarden and Leffe and high-end bistro fare. Ignore the '80s-era Stevie Wonder.

D'AGUILAR NATIONAL PARK

Suburban malaise? Slake your wilderness cravings at this 50,000-hectare **national park** (www.nprsr.qld.gov.au/parks/daguilar; 60 Mount Nebo Rd, The Gap), just 10km north-west of the city centre but worlds away. At the entrance the **Walkabout Creek Visitor Information Centre** (☑ 07-3512 2300; www.walkaboutcreek.com.au; wildlife centre adult/child/family $6.40/4.35/16; ⊙ 9am-4.30pm) has maps. Also here is the **South East Queensland Wildlife Centre**, where you can see a resident platypus, plus turtles, lizards, pythons and gliders. There's also a small walk-through aviary, and a cafe.

Walking trails in the park range from a few hundred metres to 13km, including the 6km Morelia Track at Manorina day-use area and the 4.3km Greene's Falls Track at Mt Glorious. Mountain biking and horse riding are also options. You can camp in the park too, in remote, walk-in bush **camp sites** (☑ 13 74 68; www.qld.gov.au/camping; per person $5.45).

To get here catch bus 385 ($6.70, 30 minutes) from Roma St Station; the last bus back to the city is at 4.48pm (3.53pm on weekends).

West End

Archive Beer Boutique
BAR
(Map p296; www.archivebeerboutique.com.au; 100 Boundary St; ⊙ 11am-late) Interesting beer, interesting people, interesting place: welcome to Archive, a temple of beer with many a fine frothy on tap (try the Evil Twin West Coast Red Ale). Check the bar made of books! Oh, and the food's good, too (steaks, mussels, pasta). Upstairs is **Loft West End** (Map p296; www.loftwestend.com), a sophisticated cocktail/food room.

The End
BAR
(Map p296; www.73vulture.com; 1/73 Vulture St; ⊙ 3pm-midnight) This mod-industrial shopfront conversion is a real locals' hangout, with hipsters, cheese boards, Morrissey on the turntable, DJs and live acoustic troubadours. The Blackstar mocha stout (caffeine courtesy of the local roaster) will cheer up your rainy river afternoon.

Lychee Lounge
COCKTAIL BAR
(Map p296; www.lycheelounge.com.au; 94 Boundary St; ⊙ 3pm-midnight Sun-Thu, 3pm-1am Fri & Sat) Sink into the lush furniture and stare up at the macabre doll-head chandeliers at this exotic Asian lounge bar, with mellow beats, mood lighting and an open frontage to Boundary St. Is this what a *real* opium den looks like?

Fortitude Valley

★ Alfred & Constance
BAR
(Map p292; www.alfredandconstance.com.au; 130 Constance St; ⊙ 10am-3am) Wow! Fabulously eccentric A&C occupies two old weatherboard houses away from the main Valley action. Inside, fluoro-clad ditch diggers, tattooed lesbians, suits and surfies roam between the tiki bar, rooftop terrace, cafe area and lounge rooms checking out the interior design: chandeliers, skeletons, surfboards, old hi-fi equipment... It's weird, and very wonderful.

Bowery
COCKTAIL BAR
(Map p292; www.thebowery.com.au; 676 Ann St; ⊙ 5pm-late Tue-Sun) The exposed-brick walls, gilded mirrors, booths and foot-worn floorboards at this long, narrow bar bring a touch of substance to the Valley fray. The cocktails and wine list are top-notch (and priced accordingly), and there's live jazz/dub Tuesday to Thursday. DJs spin on weekends.

Press Club
COCKTAIL BAR
(Map p292; www.pressclub.net.au; 339 Brunswick St; ⊙ 5pm-late Tue-Sun) Amber hues, leather sofas, ottomans, glowing chandeliers, fabric-covered lanterns... It's all rather glamorously Moroccan here (with a touch of that kooky cantina from *Star Wars*). Live music on Thursday (jazz, funk, rockabilly) and DJs on weekends.

Cru Bar & Cellar
WINE BAR
(Map p292; www.crubar.com; 22 James St; ⊙ 11am-late Mon-Fri, 10am-late Sat & Sun) A mind-pickling menu of hundreds of wines (by the glass, bottle or half-bottle) is on offer at this classy (and pricey) joint, with confidently strutting staff, a glowing marble bar and fold-back windows to the street.

GAY & LESBIAN BRISBANE

Brisbane can't compete with the extravagent G&L scenes in Sydney and Melbourne, but what you'll find here is quality rather than quantity.

For current entertainment and events listings, interviews and articles, check out Q News (www.qnews.com.au) and Queensland Pride (www.gaynewsnetwork.com.au). Major events on the calendar include the Queer Film Festival (www.bqff.com.au) held in April at the Brisbane Powerhouse, and the Brisbane Pride Festival (p291), which happens in September. Pride attracts around 25,000 people every year and peaks during Pride Fair Day held at New Farm Park mid-festival.

Brisbane's most enduring/endearing G&L venue is the Wickham Hotel (Map p292; www.thewickham.com.au; 308 Wickham St; ⊙10am-late) in Fortitude Valley, a classic old Victorian pub with good dance music, drag shows and dancers. Other good options in the Valley include the gay-friendly clubs Beat MegaClub (Map p292; www.thebeatmegaclub.com.au; 677 Ann St; ⊙9pm-5am Mon & Tue, 8pm-5am Wed-Sun) and Family (Map p292; www.thefamily.com.au; 8 McLachlan St; ⊙9pm-5am Fri-Sun); the latter hosts 'Fluffy' on Sundays, Brisbane's biggest gay dance party. Closer to the city, the Sportsman's Hotel (Map p288; www.sportsmanhotel.com.au; 130 Leichhardt St; ⊙1pm-late) is another perennially busy blue-collar gay venue.

Cloudland
CLUB

(Map p292; www.katarzyna.com.au/venues/cloudland; 641 Ann St; ⊙5pm-late Thu & Fri, noon-late Sat & Sun) Like stepping into a surreal cloud forest, this multilevel club has a huge plant-filled lobby with a retractable glass roof, a wall of water and wrought-iron birdcage-like nooks. Even if you're not a clubber, peek through the windows during the day: the interior design is astonishing!

Oh Hello
CLUB

(Map p292; www.ohhello.com.au; 621 Ann St; ⊙9pm-5am Thu-Sat) Oh hello! Fancy seeing you here! This convivial club is perfect if you like the idea of clubbing but find the reality a bit deflating. It's unpretentious (you can wear a T-shirt), there's a great selection of craft beers, and the cool kids here don't think too highly of themselves.

Birdees
CLUB

(Map p292; www.birdees.com.au; 608 Ann St; ⊙4pm-late Mon-Thu, noon-5am Fri & Sat, noon-late Sun) Part of the sprawling Bunk Backpackers complex, Birdees fills, predictably, with backpackers going berserk. Big fun. The Aviary room upstairs has comedy on Thursday nights.

Electric Playground
CLUB

(Map p292; www.electricplayground.com.au; 27 Warner St; ⊙9pm-5am Fri & Sat) The 1906 foundation stone of this old church says 'To the glory of God', but the new signage says, 'It's all about the music'. If you're not sure which one to believe, join the line to get inside,

where ungodly good times unwind late into Friday and Saturday nights. Even less pious is Church (Map p292; www.thechurchnightclub.com.au; 25 Warner St; ⊙9pm-5am Fri & Sat) next door, which keeps the same hours.

New Farm & Around

Gertie's
BAR

(Map p292; www.gerties.com.au; 699 Brunswick St, New Farm; ⊙4pm-midnight Tue-Fri, 3pm-midnight Sat, 2pm-midnight Sun) A sophisticated New Farm affair, Gertie's always seems to have groups of good-looking city girls sipping cocktails inside the fold-back windows (...do you think management pays them to sit there?). But even without the eye-candy, Gertie's – a moodily-lit corner bar with old soul on the stereo and retro photos on the walls – is a great place for a low-key drink or a bowl of pasta and a glass of wine.

Bar Alto
BAR

(Map p284; www.baralto.com.au; Brisbane Powerhouse, 119 Lamington St, New Farm; ⊙11am-late Tue-Sun) Inside the arts-loving Powerhouse, this snappy upstairs bar/restaurant has an enormous balcony with chunky timber tables overlooking the river – a mighty fine vantage point any time of day.

Breakfast Creek Hotel
PUB

(Map p284; www.breakfastcreekhotel.com; 2 Kingsford Smith Dr, Albion; ⊙10am-late) This historic 1889 pub is a Brisbane classic. Built in lavish French Renaissance style, it has various bars and dining areas (including a beer garden and an art-deco 'private bar' where you can drink beer tapped from a wooden keg). The stylish Substation No 41 bar serves cocktails and legendary steaks.

Petrie Terrace

Cabiria   BAR
(Map p296; www.cabiria.com.au; 6 The Barracks, 61 Petrie Tce; ⊙ 7-11am & noon-2.30pm Mon-Fri, 5pm-late Tue-Sat) Brisbane's old police barracks have been converted into a complex of quality bars and eateries, the pick of which is cool Cabiria. It's a skinny, dim-lit, moody room with big mirrors and shimmering racks of booze (35 different tequilas!). Awesome New York–style sandwiches, too.

Normanby Hotel   PUB
(Map p296; www.thenormanby.com.au; 1 Musgrave Rd; ⊙ 10am-3pm) A handsome 1889 redbrick pub on the end of Petrie Tce, with a beer garden under a vast fig tree. Goes nuts during 'Sunday Sessions' (boozy wakes for the weekend).

Paddington

Lark   BAR
(Map p299; ☑ 07-3369 1299; www.thelark.com.au; 1/267 Given Tce; ⊙ 4pm-midnight Mon & Wed-Fri, 1pm-midnight Sat, 1-10pm Sun) Inside an intimate, two-level brick terrace, Lark serves up artful drinks and inventive fusion fare. Tapas share plates ($11 to $28) involve hits like wagyu sliders and parmesan-crusted mushrooms, washed down with international wines, crafty beers and cocktails (go for the Cherry Bourbon Smash). What a lark!

Kangaroo Point & Around

Story Bridge Hotel   PUB
(Map p288; www.storybridgehotel.com.au; 200 Main St, Kangaroo Point; ⊙ 9am-late) Beneath the bridge at Kangaroo Point, this beautiful 1886 pub and beer garden is perfect for a pint after a long day exploring. Live jazz on Sundays (from 3pm); lots of different drinking and eating areas.

Canvas   WINE BAR
(Map p284; www.canvasclub.com.au; 16b Logan Rd, Woolloongabba; ⊙ 3pm-midnight Tue-Fri, 11.30am-late Sat & Sun) In the shadow of the Gabba cricket ground, Canvas is hip, compact and artsy. Step down off Logan St – an emerging eating/drinking/antiques hub – pause to

ogle the kooky mural, then order a 'Guerilla Warfare' cocktail from the mustachioed bartender.

☆ Entertainment

Most big-ticket international bands have Brisbane on their radar, and the city's nightclubs regularly attract top-class DJs. Theatres, cinemas and other performing-arts venues are among Australia's biggest and best.

Free entertainment street press includes **Time Off** (www.timeoff.com.au) and **Scene** (www.scenemagazine.com.au). Q News (p304) covers the gay and lesbian scene. The **Courier-Mail** (www.news.com.au/couriermail) newspaper also has daily arts and entertainment listings, or check the **Brisbane Times** (www.brisbanetimes.com.au).

Ticketek (Map p288; ☑ 13 28 49; www.ticketek.com.au; cnr Elizabeth & George Sts; ⊙ 9am-5pm) is a central booking agency that handles major events, sports and performances. Try **Qtix** (☑ 13 62 46; www.qtix.com.au) for loftier arts performances.

Cinemas

Palace Barracks   CINEMA
(Map p296; www.palacecinemas.com.au; 61 Petrie Tce, Petrie Terrace; adult/child $17.50/13; ⊙ 10am-late) Near Roma St Station in the Barracks Centre, the plush, six-screen Palace Barracks shows Hollywood and alternative fare, and has a bar.

Palace Centro   CINEMA
(Map p292; www.palacecinemas.com.au; 39 James St, Fortitude Valley; adult/child $17.50/13; ⊙ 10am-late) Palace Centro on James St screens

---

MOONLIGHT CINEMA

One of the best ways to spend a warm summer's night in Brisbane is with a picnic basket and some friends at an outdoor cinema. **Moonlight Cinema** (Map p284; www.moonlight.com.au; Brisbane Powerhouse, 119 Lamington Rd, New Farm; adult/child $16/12; ⊙ 7pm Wed-Sun) runs between December and February at New Farm Park near the Brisbane Powerhouse. New releases, indies and cult classics all get a screening from Wednesday to Sunday, flickering into life around 7pm. Tickets go on sale in the first week of November.

art-house films and has a French film festival in March/April.

Event Cinemas
CINEMA

(Map p288; www.eventcinemas.com.au; Level 3, Myer Centre, Elizabeth St; adult/child $17/12.50; ☉10am-late) On Queen St Mall; also shows mainstream blockbusters.

Live Music

Lock 'n' Load
LIVE MUSIC

(Map p296; www.locknloadbistro.com.au; 142 Boundary St, West End; ☉10am-late Mon-Fri, 7am-late Sat & Sun) This ebullient, woody, two-storey gastropub lures an upbeat crowd of music fans. Bands play the small front stage (jazz and originals). Catch a gig, then show up for breakfast the next morning (the grilled sardines go well with hangovers).

Hi-Fi
LIVE MUSIC

(Map p296; www.thehifi.com.au; 125 Boundary St, West End) This modern, minimalist rock room has unobstructed sight lines and a great line-up of local and international talent (from the Gin Blossoms to Suicidal Tendencies). Retro Vinyl bar is out the front.

Zoo
LIVE MUSIC

(Map p292; www.thezoo.com.au; 711 Ann St, Fortitude Valley; ☉7.30pm-late Wed-Sun) Going strong since 1992, the Zoo has surrendered a bit of musical territory to the Hi-Fi venue, but is still a grungy spot for rock, hip-hop, acoustic, reggae and electronic acts (lots of raw local talent).

Brisbane Jazz Club
JAZZ

(Map p288; ☑07-3391 2006; www.brisbanejazzclub.com.au; 1 Annie St, Kangaroo Point; ☉6.30-11pm Thu-Sat, 5.30-9.30pm Sun) Straight out of the bayou, this tiny riverside jazz shack has been Brisbane's jazz beacon since 1972. Anyone who's anyone in the scene plays here when they're in town. Cover charge $12 to $20.

Tivoli
MUSIC, COMEDY

(Map p284; www.thetivoli.net.au; 52 Costin St, Fortitude Valley) International notables (Nick Cave, Noel Gallagher) plus local success stories (Parkway Drive, The Cat Empire) regularly tread the boards at this elegant old art-deco stager built in 1917 (and tarted-up more recently). You're likely to catch some quality comedy here, too.

Performing Arts & Comedy

Brisbane Powerhouse
PERFORMING ARTS

(Map p284; www.brisbanepowerhouse.org; 119 Lamington St, New Farm) Nationally and internationally acclaimed theatre, music, comedy, dance... There are loads of happenings at the Powerhouse – many free – and the venue, with its cool bar-restaurants, enjoys a gorgeous setting overlooking the Brisbane River.

Judith Wright Centre of Contemporary Arts
PERFORMING ARTS

(Map p292; www.judithwrightcentre.com; 420 Brunswick St, Fortitude Valley; 🛜) A medium-sized creative space (300 seats max) for cutting-edge performances: contemporary dance and world music, Indigenous theatre, circus and visual arts.

Metro Arts Centre
THEATRE

(Map p288; www.metroarts.com.au; Level 2, 109 Edward St) This artsy downtown venue hosts community theatre, local dramatic pieces, dance and art shows. It's an effervescent spot for a taste of Brisbane's creative talent, be it offbeat, quirky, fringe, progressive or just downright weird.

Queensland Performing Arts Centre
PERFORMING ARTS

(QPAC; Map p288; www.qpac.com.au; Queensland Cultural Centre, cnr Grey & Melbourne Sts, South Bank; ☉box office 9am-8.30pm Mon-Sat) Brisbane's main high-arts performance centre comprises three venues and features concerts, plays, dance and performances of all genres: anything from flamenco to the Australian Ballet and *West Side Story* revivals.

Paddo Tavern
COMEDY

(Map p296; www.standup.com.au; 186 Given Tce, Paddington; ☉10am-late) If a carwash married its supermarket cousin, their first-born would probably look like this ugly Paddington pub, which has incongruously adopted a Wild West theme inside (stetsons, saddle seats, old rifles on the wall). But it's one of the best places in Brisbane to see stand-up comedy: check the website for listings.

Sport

Like most other Australians, Brisbanites are sports-mad. You can catch some interstate or international cricket at the Gabba (Brisbane Cricket Ground; Map p284; www.thegabba.org.au; 411 Vulture St, Woolloongabba), south of Kangaroo Point. The cricket season runs from October to March: if you're new to the game,

BRISBANE'S BEST MARKETS

Jan Powers Farmers Market (Map p284; www.janpowersfarmersmarkets.com.au; Brisbane Powerhouse, 119 Lamington St, New Farm; ⊙6am-noon 2nd & 4th Sat of month) Fancy some purple heirloom carrots or blue bananas? This fab farmers market, with more than 120 stalls, coughs up some unusual produce. Also great for more predictably coloured flowers, cheeses, coffees and fish. The CityCat ferry takes you straight there.

Davies Park Market (Map p296; www.daviesparkmarket.com.au; Davies Park, West End; ⊙6am-2pm Sat) Under a grove of huge Moreton Bay fig trees in the West End, this hippie riverside market features organic foods, gourmet breakfasts, herbs and flowers, bric-a-brac and buskers.

Brisbane Valley Markets (Map p292; www.brisbane-markets.com.au/brisbane-valley-markets.html; Brunswick St & Duncan St Malls, Fortitude Valley; ⊙8am-4pm Sat, 9am-4pm Sun) These colourful markets fill the Brunswick St Mall and the Duncan St (Chinatown) Mall in Fortitude Valley with a diverse collection of crafts, clothes, books, records, food stalls and miscellaneous works by budding designers.

try and get along to a Twenty20 match – cricket at its most explosive.

The Gabba is also a home ground for the Brisbane Lions, an **Australian Football League** (AFL; www.afl.com.au) team which dominated the league in the early 2000s (lately, not so much). Watch them in action, often at night under lights, between March and September.

Rugby league is also a massive spectator sport in Brizzy. The Brisbane Broncos, part of the **National Rugby League** (NRL; www.nrl.com.au) competition, play home games over winter at **Suncorp Stadium** (Map p296; www.suncorpstadium.com.au; 40 Castlemaine St, Milton) in Milton (between Petrie Terrace and Paddington).

Also calling Suncorp home are the Queensland Roar football (soccer) team, part of the **A-League** (www.aleague.com.au), attracting fat crowds in recent years. The domestic football season lasts from August to February.

🔒 Shopping

Queen St Mall and the **Myer Centre** in the CBD house big chain stores, upmarket outlets and the obligatory touristy trash.

🔒 City Centre

Archives Fine Books   BOOKS
(Map p288; www.facebook.com/archivesfinebooks; 40 Charlotte St; ⊙10am-7pm Mon-Fri, 9am-5pm Sat, 11am-5pm Sun) You could get lost in here for hours: rickety bookshelves, squeaky floorboards and upwards of half-a-million second-hand books.

🔒 West End

★**Egg Records**   MUSIC
(Map p296; www.eggrecords.com.au; 79 Vulture St; ⊙9.30am-5.30pm Mon-Fri, to 4pm Sat & Sun) This well-organised collection of LPs, CDs and fantastically kitsch memorabilia is a must-see for anyone with even the slightest hint of 'collector' in their DNA. Loads of second-hand vinyl and CDs, plus heavymetal T-shirts and a cavalcade of plasticky treasures featuring Doctor Who, *Star Wars* characters, Evel Knievel...awesome!

🔒 South Bank

Title   BOOKS
(Map p288; www.titlespace.com; 1/133 Grey St; ⊙10am-6pm Mon-Sat, to 4pm Sun) Offbeat and alternative art, music, photography and cinema books, plus vinyl, CDs and DVDs – a quality dose of subversive rebelliousness (just what South Bank needs!). Pick up that Woody Guthrie 100th-birthday *Centennial Collection* you've had your eye on. There's another branch in **Fortitude Valley** (Map p292; 60 James St; ⊙10am-6pm Mon-Sat, to 4pm Sun).

🔒 Fortitude Valley

★**in.cube8r gallery**   GIFTS, GALLERY
(Map p292; www.incube8r.com.au; 648 Brunswick St; ⊙10am-5pm Tue & Wed, 11am-6pm Thu & Fri, 10am-6pm Sat, 11am-3pm Sun) Supporting local talent, this artists' co-op features the work of 90 creative types, all of whom rent a wedge of space here to display and sell their wares.

Prints, kids' clothes, egg-carton lampshades, driftwood jewellery, ceramics, canvases, glasswear, earrings made of Lego – it's all here!

Trash Monkey
CLOTHING, ACCESSORIES

(Map p292; www.trashmonkey.com.au; 9/8 Duncan St; ☺10am-7pm Mon-Wed, to 9pm Thu-Sat, to 5pm Sun) Countercultural mayhem in the Valley! Goths, skaters, punks, alt-rockers and rockabilly rebels head here for their shoes, T-shirts, caps, nylon stockings, dress-up gear, socks, belts and beanies, much of which is spangled with tattoo-centric designs.

Blonde Venus
CLOTHING

(Map p292; www.blondevenus.com.au; Shop 3, 181 Robertson St; ☺10am-6pm Mon-Sat, 11am-4.30pm Sun) One of the top boutiques in Brisbane, Blonde Venus has been around for 20-plus years, stocking a well-curated selection of both indie and couture labels.

Paddington

Retro Metro
CLOTHING

(Map p299; 27 Latrobe Tce; ☺10am-5pm Mon-Sat, 11am-4pm Sun) A highlight of Paddington's boutique-lined main street, Retro Metro stocks a briliant selection of vintage gear: cowboy boots, suits, cocktail dresses, handbags, jewellery, vinyl, '80s rock T-shirts, sunglasses, vases, ashtrays and other interesting knick-knackery.

Paddington Antique Centre
ANTIQUES

(Map p299; www.paddingtonantiquecentre.com.au; 167 Latrobe Tce; ☺10am-5pm) The city's biggest antique emporium is inside a 1929 theatre, with over 50 dealers selling all manner of historic treasure/trash: clothes, jewellery, dolls, books, '60s Hawaiian shirts, lamps, musical instruments, toys and WWII German helmets.

ⓘ Information

EMERGENCY

Ambulance, Fire, Police (☏000) Brisbane's police HQ is at 200 Roma St in the city. There's another 24-hour station at the corner of Wickham St and Brookes St in Fortitude Valley.

Lifeline (☏13 11 14; www.lifeline.org.au) Crisis counselling.

RACQ (Map p288; ☏13 11 11; www.racq.com.au) Automotive roadside assistance.

INTERNET ACCESS

Brisbane Square Library (www.brisbane.qld.gov.au/; 266 George St; ☺9am-6pm Mon-Thu, 9am-7pm Fri, 10am-3pm Sat & Sun) Free internet terminals and wi-fi access.

IYSC (Level 1, 150 Adelaide St; ☺8.30am-6.30pm Mon-Fri, 10am-5pm Sat) Cheap downtown terminals.

State Library of Queensland (www.slq.qld.gov.au; Stanley Pl, South Bank; ☺10am-8pm Mon-Thu, 10am-5pm Fri-Sun) Quick 20-minute terminals or free wi-fi.

MEDICAL SERVICES

CBD Medical Centre (☏07-3211 3611; www.cbdmedical.com.au; Level 1, 245 Albert St; ☺7.30am-7pm Mon-Fri, 8.30am-5pm Sat, 9.30am-4pm Sun) General medical services and vaccinations.

Pharmacy on the Mall (☏07-3221 4585; www.pharmacies.com.au/pharmacy-on-the-mall; 141 Queen St; ☺7am-9pm Mon-Thu, 7am-9.30pm Fri, 8am-9pm Sat, 8.30am-6pm Sun)

Royal Brisbane & Women's Hospital (☏07-3636 8111; www.health.qld.gov.au/rbwh; cnr Butterfield St & Bowen Bridge Rd, Herston) Has a 24-hour casualty ward.

Travellers' Medical & Vaccination Centre (TMVC; ☏07-3815 6900; www.traveldoctor.com.au; 75a Astor Tce, Spring Hill; ☺8.30am-5pm Mon, Thu & Fri, 8.30am-8pm Tue, 9am-5pm Wed, 8.30am-noon Sat) Travellers' medical services.

MONEY

American Express (☏1300 139 060; www.americanexpress.com; 260 Queen St; ☺8.30am-4pm Mon-Thu, 9am-5pm Fri) Inside the Westpac bank.

Travelex (☏07-3210 6325; www.travelex.com.au; Shop 149F, Myer Centre, Queen St Mall; ☺9am-5pm Mon-Thu & Sat, 9am-8pm Fri, 10am-4pm Sun) Money exchange.

POST

Main Post Office (GPO; Map p288; www.auspost.com.au; 261 Queen St; ☺7am-6pm Mon-Fri, 10am-1.30pm Sat)

TOURIST INFORMATION

Brisbane Visitor Information Centre (Map p288; ☏07-3006 6290; www.visitbrisbane.com.au; Queen St Mall; ☺9am-5.30pm Mon-Thu, 9am-7pm Fri, 9am-5pm Sat, 10am-5pm Sun) Terrific one-stop info counter for all things Brisbane.

South Bank Visitor Information Centre (Map p288; www.visitsouthbank.com.au; Stanley St Plaza, South Bank; ☺9am-5pm) The low-down on South Bank, plus tours, accommodation and transport bookings and tickets to entertainment events.

ℹ Getting There & Away

The Brisbane Transit Centre – which incorporates Roma St Station in the same complex – is about 500m northwest of the city centre, and is the main terminus and booking point for all long-distance buses and trains, as well as Citytrain services. Central Station is also an important hub for trains.

AIR

Brisbane Airport (www.bne.com.au) is about 16km northeast of the city centre at Eagle Farm, and has separate international and domestic terminals about 2km apart, linked by the Airtrain (p309; between terminals per person $5).

Several airlines link Brisbane with the rest of the East Coast. The main players:

Qantas (www.qantas.com.au)

Virgin Australia (www.virginaustralia.com.au)

Jetstar (www.jetstar.com.au)

Tiger Airways (www.tigerairways.com.au)

BUS

Brisbane's main bus terminus and booking office for long-distance buses is the **Brisbane Transit Centre** (Map p288; www.brisbanetransitcentre.com.au; Roma St). Booking desks for **Greyhound** (www.greyhound.com.au) and **Premier Motor Service** (www.premierms.com.au) are here.

If you're up for a long haul, buses run between Brisbane and Sydney ($185, 16 to 18 hours), Melbourne ($210, 40 hours) and Cairns ($305, 30 hours).

Heading south to Byron Bay, there are four daily buses from Brisbane airport ($52, three hours) and the Brisbane Transit Centre ($38) on **Byron Easy Bus** (www.byroneasybus.com.au).

CAR & MOTORCYCLE

Brisbane has five major motorways (M1 to M5) run by **Queensland Motorways** (☑ 13 33 31; www.qldmotorways.com.au). If you're just passing through from north to south or south to north, take the Gateway Motorway (M1), which bypasses the city centre ($4.13 toll at the time of writing; see the website for payment options, in advance or retrospectively).

Car Hire

The major car-hire companies – **Avis** (www.avis.com.au), **Budget** (www.budget.com.au), **Europcar** (www.europcar.com.au), **Hertz** (www.hertz.com.au) and **Thrifty** (www.thrifty.com.au) – have offices at Brisbane Airport and in the city.

Smaller rental companies with branches near the airport (and shuttles to get you to/from there) include:

Ace Rental Cars (☑ 1800 620 408; www.acerentals.com.au; 330 Nudgee Rd, Hendra)

Apex Car Rentals (☑ 1800 121 029; www.apexrentacar.com.au; 400 Nudgee Rd, Hendra)

East Coast Car Rentals (☑ 1800 028 881; www.eastcoastcarrentals.com.au; 504 Nudgee Rd, Hendra)

TRAIN

Brisbane's main station for long-distance trains is Roma St Station (essentially the same complex as the Brisbane Transit Centre). For reservations and information contact the **Queensland Rail Travel Centre** (☑ 1800 872 467; www.queenslandrail.com.au; Concourse Level, 305 Edward St; ⊙ 8am-5pm Mon-Fri) at Central Station.

Long-distance services ex-Brisbane along the East Coast include the following:

NSW TrainLink Brisbane to Sydney

Spirit of Queensland Brisbane to Cairns

Sunlander Brisbane to Cairns via Townsville

Tilt Train Brisbane to Cairns

ℹ Getting Around

TO/FROM THE AIRPORT

Airtrain (www.airtrain.com.au) trains run every 15 to 30 minutes from 5.45am to 10pm from Brisbane Airport to Fortitude Valley, Central Station, Roma St Station (Brisbane Transit Centre) and other key destinations (one-way/return $16/30). There are also half-hourly services to the airport from Gold Coast Citytrain stops (one-way $37).

If you prefer door-to-door service, **Con-x-ion Airport Transfers** (www.con-x-ion.com) runs regular shuttle buses between the airport and CBD hotels (one-way/return $20/36); it also connects Brisbane Airport to Gold Coast and Sunshine Coast hotels: see the website for details.

A taxi into the centre from the airport will cost $35 to $45.

CAR & MOTORCYCLE

There is ticketed two-hour parking on many streets in the CBD and the inner suburbs. Heed the signs: Brisbane's parking inspectors take no prisoners. Parking is cheaper around South Bank and the West End than in the city centre, but is free in the CBD during the evening.

PUBLIC TRANSPORT

Brisbane's excellent public-transport network – bus, train and ferry – is run by **TransLink** (☑ 13 12 30; www.translink.com.au). There's a Translink **Transit Information Centre** at Central Station (on the corner of Edward St and Ann St), and another one at Roma St Station (Brisbane Transit Centre). The Brisbane Visitor Information Centre (p308) can also help with public transport info.

Fares Buses, trains and ferries operate on a zone system: most of the inner-city suburbs are in Zone 1, which translates into a single fare of $5.20/2.60 per adult/child. If travelling into Zone 2, tickets are $6.10/3.10. A Go Card will save you some money.

NightLink In addition to the services described in the following sections, there are also dedicated nocturnal NightLink bus, train and fixed-rate taxi services from the city and Fortitude Valley: see www.translink.com.au for details.

Boat

In addition to the fast CityCat (p289) services, Translink runs **Cross River Ferries**, connecting Kangaroo Point with the CBD, and New Farm Park with Norman Park on the adjacent shore (and also Teneriffe and Bulimba further north).

Free (yes free!) **CityHopper Ferries** zigzag back and forth across the water between North Quay, South Bank, the CBD, Kangaroo Point and Sydney St in New Farm. These additional services start around 6am and run till about 11pm. For Cross River Ferries, fares/zones apply as per all other Brisbane transport.

Bus

Translink runs Brisbane's bus services, including the free **City Loop** and **Spring Hill Loop** bus services that circle through the CBD and Spring Hill every 10 minutes on weekdays between 7am and 6pm.

The main stops for local buses are the underground **Queen St Bus Station** (Map p288) and **King George Sq Bus Station** (Map p288). You can also pick up many buses from the stops along Adelaide St, between George St and Edward St.

Buses generally run every 10 to 30 minutes Monday to Friday, from 5am till about 11pm, and with the same frequency on Saturday morning (starting at 6am). Services are less frequent at other times, and cease at 9pm Sunday and at midnight on other days.

Train

TransLink's fast **Citytrain** network has six main lines, which run as far north as Gympie on the Sunshine Coast and as far south as Varsity Lakes on the Gold Coast. All trains go through Roma St Station, Central Station and Fortitude Valley Station; there's also a handy South Bank Station.

The **Airtrain** service integrates with the City train network in the CBD and along the Gold Coast line.

Trains run from around 4.30am, with the last train on each line leaving Central Station between 11.30pm and midnight. On Sunday the last trains run at around 10pm.

Black & White (☑13 32 22; www.blackand-whitecabs.com.au)
Yellow Cab Co (☑13 19 24; www.yellowcab.com.au)

MORETON BAY ISLANDS

North Stradbroke Island

POP 2000

An easy 30-minute ferry chug from Cleveland, unpretentious 'Straddie' is like Noosa and Byron Bay rolled into one. There's a string of glorious powdery white beaches, great surf and some quality places to stay and eat (catering to Brisbane's naughty-weekend-away set). It's also a hot-spot for spying dolphins, turtles, manta rays and, between June and November, hundreds of humpback whales.

◉ Sights

At Point Lookout, the eye-popping North Gorge Headlands Walk is an absolute highlight. It's an easy 20-minute loop around the headland along boardwalks, with the thrum of cicadas as your soundtrack. Keep an eye out for turtles, dolphins and manta rays offshore.

There are several gorgeous beaches around Point Lookout. A patrolled swimming area, Cylinder Beach is popular with families and is flanked by Home Beach and the ominously named Deadman's Beach. Near the Headlands Walk, surfers and bodyboarders descend on Main Beach in search of the ultimate wave.

Fisher-folk take their 4WDs further down Main Beach (4WD permit required; $39.55 from Straddie Camping, p311) towards Eighteen Mile Swamp, continuing all the way down the east coast to Jumpinpin, the channel that separates North and South Stradbroke, a legendary fishing spot.

About 4km east of Dunwich, the tanin-stained Brown Lake is the colour of stewed tea, but is completely OK for swimming. About 4km further along this road, take the 2.6km (40-minute) bush track to Straddie's glittering centrepiece, swimmable Blue Lake, part of Naree Budjong Djara National Park (www.nprsr.qld.gov.au/parks/naree-budjong-djara): keep an eye out for forest birds, skittish lizards and swamp wallabies along the way.

North Stradbroke Island Historical Museum
MUSEUM

(☑07-3409 9699; www.stradbrokemuseum.com.au; 15-17 Welsby St, Dunwich; adult/child $3.50/1; ⊙10am-2pm Tue-Sat, 11am-3pm Sun) Once the 'Dunwich Benevolent Asylum' – a home for the destitute – this small but impressive museum describes shipwrecks, harrowing voyages and an introduction to the island's rich Aboriginal history (the Quandamooka are the traditional owners of Minjerribah, aka Straddie). Island artefacts include the skull of a sperm whale washed up on Main Beach in 2004, and the old Point Lookout lighthouse lens.

🏃 Activities

North Stradbroke Island Surf School
SURFING

(☑0407 642 616; www.northstradbrokeislandsurfschool.com.au; lesson from $50; ⊙daily) Small-group, 90-minute surf lessons in the warm Straddie waves.

Straddie Adventures
KAYAKING, SAND-BOARDING

(☑0417 741 963, 07-3409 8414; www.straddieadventures.com.au; ⊙daily) Hires out surfboards, snorkelling equipment and bicycles, and runs sea-kayaking trips (adult/child $60/45) and sand-boarding sessions ($30/25).

Manta Scuba Centre
DIVING

(☑07-3409 8888; www.mantalodge.com.au; 1 East Coast Rd, Point Lookout) Based at the YHA, Manta Scuba Centre runs snorkelling trips ($85), with a two-hour boat trip and all gear. A two-dive trip with all gear for certified divers is $196. Scuba courses start at $253; snorkel gear hire is $25.

Straddie Super Sports
BICYCLE RENTAL

(☑07-3409 9252; 18 Bingle Rd, Dunwich; ⊙8.30am-4.30pm Mon-Fri, 8am-3pm Sat, 9am-2pm Sun) Hires out mountain bikes (per hour/day $6.50/30) and has a huge range of fishing gear for sale.

👉 Tours

North Stradbroke Island 4WD Tours & Camping Holidays
DRIVING TOUR

(☑07-3409 8051; www.stradbroketourism.com; adult/child half-day $35/20, full day $85/55) Offers 4WD tours around the Point Lookout area, with lots of bush, beaches and wildlife. Beach fishing is $45/30 per adult/child.

Straddie Kingfisher Tours
DRIVING TOUR

(☑07-3409 9502; www.straddiekingfishertours.com.au; adult/child island pick-up $80/40, from Brisbane or Gold Coast $195/145) Operates six-hour 4WD and fishing tours; also has whalewatching tours in season. Ask about kayaking and sand-boarding options.

🛏 Sleeping

Almost all of the island's accommodation is in Point Lookout, strung along 3km of coastline. Most places require stays of more than one night, but this is often negotiable outside peak holiday times.

Straddie Camping
CAMPGROUND $

(☑07-3409 9668; www.straddiecamping.com.au; 1 Junner St, Dunwich; 4WD camp site from $16.50, unpowered/powered sites from $37/44, cabins from $115; ⊙booking office 8am-4pm) There are eight island campgrounds operated by this outfit, including two 4WD-only foreshore camps (permits required – $39.55 from Straddie Camping). The best of the bunch are grouped around Point Lookout: the camping grounds at **Adder Rock** and the **Home Beach** both overlook the sand, while the **Cylinder Beach** camping ground sits right on one of the island's best beaches. Book well in advance; good weekly rates.

Manta Lodge YHA
HOSTEL $

(☑07-3409 8888; www.mantalodge.com.au; 1 East Coast Rd, Point Lookout; dm/d $32/82; @ 🖢) This three-storey, lemon-yellow hostel has clean (if unremarkable) rooms and a great beachside location (who wants to sit around in a dorm anyway?). There are jungly hammocks out the back plus a dive school downstairs.

Straddie Views
B&B $$

(☑07-3409 8875; www.northstradbrokeisland.com/straddiebb; 26 Cumming Pde, Point Lookout; r from $150) There are two spacious downstairs suites in this B&B, run by a friendly Straddie couple. Cooked breakfast is served on the upstairs deck with fab sea views.

Stradbroke Island Beach Hotel
HOTEL $$$

(☑07-3409 8188; www.stradbrokehotel.com.au; East Coast Rd, Point Lookout; d from $235; ❋ ⛱) Straddie's only pub has 12 cool, inviting rooms with shell-coloured tiles, blonde timbers, high-end gadgets and balconies. Walk to the beach, or get distracted by the open-walled bar downstairs en route (serving breakfast, lunch and dinner; mains $15 to $36). Flashy three- and four-bed apartments also available.

Point Lookout

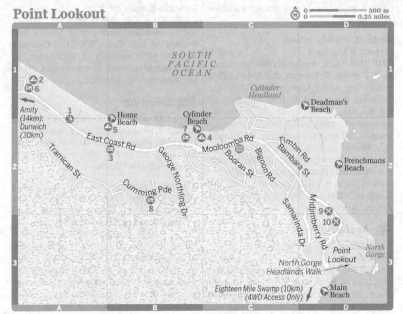

Point Lookout

Allure   APARTMENT $$$

(☎07-3415 0000, 1800 555 200; www.allurestrad-broke.com.au; 43 East Coast Rd, Point Lookout; apt from $216; ✳☞☎) These large ultramodern apartments are set in a leafy compound. Each villa (or 'shack' as the one-bedrooms are called) features lots of beachy colours, original artwork and an outdoor deck with barbecue. There isn't much space between villas, but they're cleverly designed with privacy in mind. Much cheaper for stays of more than one night.

✗ Eating

There are only a handful of dining choices around the island, mostly in Point Lookout. If you're staying for more than a few days it makes sense to bring supplies from the mainland. See also the Stradbroke Island Beach Hotel (p311).

★Oceanic Gelati   GELATI $

(☎07-3415 3222; 19 Mooloomba Rd, Point Lookout; gelati from $3; ☺9.30am-5pm) 'OMG! This is the best gelati ever!' So says one satisfied customer, and we're in complete agreement. Try the dairy-free tropical, cooling lemon or classic vanilla.

Island Fruit Barn   CAFE $

(16 Bingle Rd, Dunwich; mains $10-14; ☺7am-5pm Mon-Fri, to 4pm Sat & Sun; ☞) On the main road in Dunwich, Island Fruit Barn is a casual little congregation of tables with excellent breakfasts, smoothies, salads and sandwiches using top-quality ingredients. Order a spinach-and-fetta roll, then stock up in the gourmet grocery section.

Look   MODERN AUSTRALIAN $$

(☎07-3415 3390; www.beachbarcafe.com; 1/29 Mooloomba Rd; mains $22-38; ☺8am-3pm daily, 6-9pm Thu-Sat) The hub of the Point Lookout scene during the day, with funky tunes and breezy outdoor seating with water views. Lots of wines by the glass and smokin' chilli prawns.

ℹ️ Information

Although it's quiet most of the year, the island population swells significantly at Christmas, Easter and during school holidays: book accommodation or camping permits well in advance.

If you plan to go off-road, you can get information and buy a 4WD permit ($39.55) from Straddie Camping.

ℹ️ Getting There & Away

The hub for ferries to North Stradbroke Island is the seaside suburb of Cleveland. Regular **Citytrain** (www.translink.com.au) services run from Brisbane's Central and Roma St stations to Cleveland station ($9.50, one hour); buses to the ferry terminal meet the trains at Cleveland station ($4.80, 10 minutes).

Big Red Cat (☑07-3488 9777, 1800 733 228; www.bigredcat.com.au; return per vehicle incl passengers $149, walk-on adult/child $20/10; ☺5.15am-6pm Mon-Sat, 7am-7pm Sun) In a tandem operation with Stradbroke Ferries, the feline-looking Big Red Cat vehicle/passenger ferry does the Cleveland–Dunwich run around eight times daily (45 minutes).

Stradbroke Ferries (☑07-3488 5300; www.stradbrokeferries.com.au; return per vehicle incl passengers $149, walk-on adult/child $20/10; ☺5.15am-6pm Mon-Sat, 7am-7pm Sun) Teaming up with Big Red Cat, Stradbroke Ferries' passenger and passenger/vehicle services runs to Dunwich and back around 12 times daily (passenger ferries 25 minutes, vehicle ferries 45 minutes).

Gold Cats Stradbroke Flyer (☑07-3286 1964; www.flyer.com.au; Middle St, Cleveland; return adult/child/family $19/10/50) Gold Cats Stradbroke Flyer runs around a dozen return passenger-only trips daily between Cleveland and One Mile Jetty at Dunwich (30 minutes).

ℹ️ Getting Around

Straddie is big: it's best to have your own wheels to explore it properly. If not, **Stradbroke Island Buses** (☑07-3415 2417; www.stradbrokebuses.com) meet the ferries at Dunwich and run to Amity and Point Lookout (one-way/return $4.70/9.40). The last bus to Dunwich leaves Point Lookout at 6.20pm. There's also the **Stradbroke Cab Service** (☑0408 193 685), which charges around $60 from Dunwich to Point Lookout.

Straddie Super Sports (p311) in Dunwich hires out mountain bikes (per hour/day $6.50/30).

Moreton Island

POP 250

If you're not going further north in Queensland than Brisbane but want a slice of tropical paradise, slip over to blissful Moreton Island. About 95% of Moreton's cache of sandy shores, bushland, dunes and glorious lagoons is protected as the **Moreton Island National Park & Recreation Area** (www.nprsr.qld.gov.au/ parks/moreton-island). Off the west coast are the rusty, hulking Tangalooma Wrecks, which provide excellent snorkelling and diving.

◉ Sights & Activities

Check out the **dolphin feeding** which happens each evening around sunset at Tangalooma, halfway down the western side of the island. Around half-a-dozen dolphins swim in from the ocean and take fish from the hands of volunteer feeders. You have to be a guest of the Tangalooma Island Resort to participate, but onlookers are welcome. The resort also organises **whale-watching** cruises (June to October).

Just north of the resort, off the coast, are the famous **Tangalooma Wrecks** – 15 sunken ships forming a sheltered boat mooring and a brilliant snorkelling spot. You can hire snorkelling gear from the resort, or **Tangatours** (☑07-3410 6927; www.tangatours.com.au) runs two-hour **kayaking** and **snorkelling trips** ($79) around the wrecks as well as guided **paddleboarding** ($49) and dusk **kayaking** tours ($69).

Island **bushwalks** include a desert trail (two hours) leaving from the resort, as well as the strenuous trek up Mt Tempest (280m), 3km inland from Eagers Creek – worthwhile, but you'll need transport to reach the start.

☞ Tours

Adventure Moreton Island ADVENTURE TOUR (☑1300 022 878; www.adventuremoretonisland.com; 1-day tour from $129) Operated in cahoots with Tangatours at Tangalooma Island Resort, these tours offer a range of activities (paddle-boarding, snorkelling, sailing, kayaking, fishing etc), ex-Brisbane. Overnight resort accommodation packages are also available (including tour from $288).

Moreton Bay Escapes
ADVENTURE TOUR

(☏1300 559 355; www.moretonbayescapes.com.au; 1-day tour adult/child from $179/129, 2-day camping tour $309/179) 🏄 A certified ecotour, the one-day 4WD tour includes snorkelling or kayaking, sand-boarding, marine wildlife watching and a picnic lunch. Camp overnight to see more of the isle.

Dolphin Wild
ADVENTURE TOUR

(☏07-3880 4444; www.dolphinwild.com.au; adult/child/family incl lunch $125/75/325, snorkelling tour per adult/child additional $20/10) For a scenic trip around Moreton Bay, sign up for a one-day Moreton Island cruise with Dolphin Wild. Tours include boating around the bay, stopping at Moreton Island for snorkelling the Tangalooma Wrecks, lunch and a bit of beach time. Oh, and some dolphins! Tours depart Newport Marina in Scarborough, north of Brisbane.

🛏 Sleeping & Eating

Aside from the resort, there are a few holiday flats and houses for rent at Kooringal, Cowan Cowan and Bulwer: see listings at www.moretonisland.com.au.

There are also 10 national-park **camping grounds** (☏13 74 68; www.nprsr.qld.gov.au/experiences/camping; sites per person/family $6/21) on Moreton Island, all with water, toilets and cold showers; five of these are right are on the beach. Book online or by phone before you get to the island.

There's a small convenience store plus cafes, restaurants and bars at the resort; plus (expensive) shops at Kooringal and Bulwer; otherwise, bring food and drink supplies with you from the mainland.

Tangalooma Island Resort
HOTEL, APARTMENT $$$

(☏07-3637 2000, 1300 652 250; www.tangalooma.com; 1-night packages from $370; ✱@🅿🍽) This beautifully sited place has the island accommodation market cornered. There are abundant sleeping options, starting with simple hotel rooms. A step up are the units and suites, where you'll get beachside access and more contemporary decor. The apartments range from two- to four-bedroom configurations. The resort also has several eating options. Accommodation prices generally include return ferry fares and transfers.

❶ Information

There are no paved roads on Moreton Island, but 4WDs can travel along the beaches and cross-island tracks (regular cars not permitted). You can pick up maps from the ferry operators. Permits for 4WDs cost $43.60, valid for one month, and are available through ferry operators, online or via phone from the **Department of National Parks, Recreation, Sport & Racing** (www.nprsr.qld.gov.au). Ferry bookings are mandatory if you want to take a vehicle across.

Online, see www.visitmoretonisland.com.

❶ Getting There & Around

Several ferries operate from the mainland. To explore once you get to the island, bring a 4WD on one of the ferries or take a tour (most tours are ex-Brisbane, and include ferry transfers).

Tangalooma Flyer (☏07-3268 6333, shuttle bus 07-3637 2000; www.tangalooma.com; return adult/child $80/45) Fast passenger catamaran operated by Tangalooma Island Resort. It makes the 75-minute trip to the resort three times daily from Holt St Wharf in Brisbane. A shuttle bus (adult/child one way $21/10.50) scoots to the wharf from the CBD or airport; bookings essential.

Micat (www.micat.com.au; 14 Howard Smith Dr, Port of Brisbane; return passenger adult/child $50/35, vehicle incl 2 people $195-230) Vehicle ferries from Port of Brisbane to Tangalooma around eight times weekly (75 minutes); see the website for directions to the ferry terminal.

Moreton Island Tourist Services (☏07-3408 2661; www.moretonisland.net.au) 4WD taxi transfers around the island; one-way trips range from $50 to $220.

The Gold Coast

Best Places to Eat

➡ Providore (p325)

➡ Oskars (p329)

➡ BSKT Cafe (p326)

➡ Manolas Brothers Deli (p326)

➡ Borough Barista (p328)

Best Places to Stay

➡ Komune (p329)

➡ Vibe Hotel (p319)

➡ O'Reilly's Rainforest Retreat (p332)

➡ Mouses House (p333)

➡ Olympus Apartments (p318)

Why Go?

Boasting 35 beaches, 300 sunny days and four million visitors a year, the Gold Coast serves up a sexy Aussie cocktail of sun, surf and sand. It's no cliché to say that the beaches here are spectacular, with outstanding waves at Burleigh Heads, Currumbin and Kirra: it's one of the best places to learn to surf in Australia. Behind the beach is a shimmering strip of high-rise apartments, eateries, bars, clubs and theme parks. The party capital is Surfers Paradise, where the fun sucks you into a dizzying vortex and spits you back out exhausted. The hype diminishes drastically as you head south, with Broadbeach's sandy chic, Burleigh Heads' seaside charm and Coolangatta's laid-back surfer ethos. In the lush, subtropical hinterland, Lamington and Springbrook National Parks offer rainforest walks, waterfalls, sweeping views and cosy mountain retreats.

When to Go

Surfers Paradise

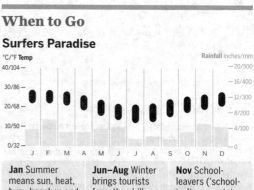

Jan Summer means sun, heat, busy beaches and the Big Day Out festival.

Jun–Aug Winter brings tourists from the chilly south chasing the sun.

Nov School-leavers ('schoolies') swarm into Surfers Paradise to party (avoid unless you're 18).

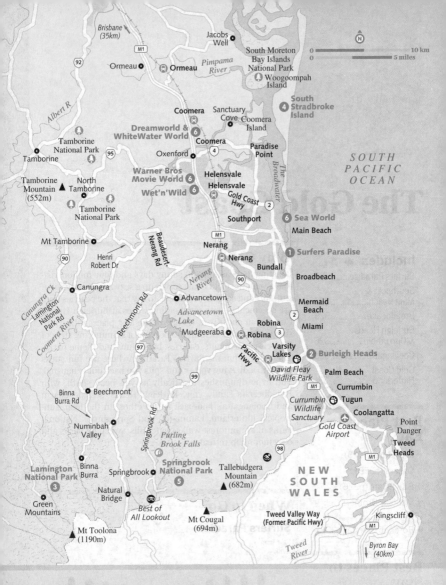

The Gold Coast Highlights

1 Drinking, dancing and watching the sun come up over the beach at **Surfers Paradise** (p317).

2 Getting up early to surf the point break at **Burleigh Heads** (p326).

3 Bushwalking through craggy gorges and rainforests in **Lamington National Park** (p332).

4 Beating a retreat from the crowds to a *looong* stretch of golden sand on **South Stradbroke Island** (p322).

5 Confirming the validity of the Best Of All Lookout's name in **Springbrook National Park** (p333).

6 Testing your nerve (and how long it's been since you had lunch) on the rollercoasters at the **Gold Coast theme parks** (p323).

ℹ Getting There & Away

AIR

Gold Coast Airport (www.goldcoastairport. com.au) is in Coolangatta, 25km south of Surfers Paradise. All the main Australian domestic airlines fly here, plus **Scoot** (www.flyscoot. com), **Air Asia** (www.airasia.com) and **Air New Zealand** (www.airnewzealand.com) flying in from overseas.

BUS

Greyhound (www.greyhound.com.au) and **Premier Motor Service** (www.premierms.com.au) run frequent daily services between Brisbane and the Gold Coast ($20, 1½ hours).

CAR & MOTORCYCLE

If you're driving, the Gold Coast is an easy one-hour hop south of Brisbane. Driving north, you'll cross the NSW/Queensland border at Tweed Heads: Coolangatta (the southern-most Gold Coast town) is immediately across the border.

TRAIN

Citytrain services run by TransLink (p309) connect Brisbane with Nerang, Robina and Varsity Lakes stations on the Gold Coast ($20.90, 75 minutes) roughly every half-hour. The same line extends north of Brisbane to Brisbane Airport (one-way Brisbane Airport to Varsity Lakes costs $36.10 and takes 1¾ hours).

ℹ Getting Around

TO/FROM THE AIRPORT

Gold Coast Tourist Shuttle (✆ 07-5574 5111, 1300 655 655; www.gcshuttle.com.au; one-way per adult/child $20/12) will meet your flight and drop you at most Gold Coast accommodation; book in advance. **Con-X-ion Airport Transfers** (✆ 1300 266 946; www.con-x-ion.com; one-way adult/child from $20/12) runs a similar service, with transfers available from Brisbane airport too (one-way adult/child $49/25). Both companies run transfers to the Gold Coast theme parks.

BUS

Surfside Buslines (www.surfside.com.au) – a subsidiary of Brisbane's main TransLink operation – runs regular buses up and down the Gold Coast, plus shuttles from the Gold Coast train stations into Surfers Paradise ($6.70) and beyond (including the theme parks).

Surfside (in conjunction with Gold Coast Tourist Shuttle) also offers a **Freedom Pass** including return Gold Coast Airport transfers and unlimited theme park transfers plus local bus travel for $71/36 per adult/child, valid for three days.

TAXI

Gold Coast Cabs (✆ 13 10 08; www.gccabs. com.au)

TRAM

By the time you read this, the new **Gold Coast Rapid Transit** (www.goldlinq.com.au) tram system might be operational, linking 16 stops over 13km between Southport and Broadbeach. Check the website for updates.

SURFERS PARADISE

POP 19,670

Some say the surfers prefer beaches elsewhere and paradise has been tragically lost, but there's no denying this wild and trashy party zone attracts a phenomenal number of visitors (20,000 per day!). Cashed-up tourists swarm to Surfers for a heady dose of clubs, bars, malls and maybe a bit of beach-time when the hangover kicks in. It's a sexy place: lots of shirtless, tattooed backpackers and more cleavage than the Grand Canyon. The beach itself is indeed a paradise, but if you're looking for cultural substance – with the notable exception of the Arts Centre – it's a case of 'Move along, nothing to see here'.

◉ Sights

SkyPoint Observation Deck   LOOKOUT
(www.skypoint.com.au; Level 77, Q1 Bldg, Hamilton Ave; adult/child/family $21/12.50/54.50; ◷ 7.30am-8.30pm Sun-Thu, to 11.30pm Fri & Sat) Surfers' sights are usually spread across beach towels, but for an eagle-eye view, zip up to this 230m-high observation deck near the top of Q1, the 27th-tallest building in the world! You can also tackle the **SkyPoint Climb** up the spire to 270m high (adult/child from $69/49).

Infinity   MAZE
(www.infinitygc.com.au; Chevron Renaissance, cnr Surfers Paradise Blvd & Elkhorn Ave; adult/child/family $25/17/70; ◷ 10am-10pm) Lose the kids for an hour (literally) inside Infinity, a walk-through maze cunningly disguised with elaborate audiovisual displays.

🏃 Activities

Cheyne Horan School of Surf   SURFING
(✆ 1800 227 873; www.cheynehoran.com.au; 2hr lesson $49, 3/5 lessons $129/189; ◷ 10am & 2pm) Learn to carve up the waves with former pro surfer Cheyne Horan. Board hire $30 per day.

Whales in Paradise   WHALE WATCHING
(✆ 07-5538 2111; www.whalesinparadise.com. au; cnr Cavill & Ferny Aves; adult/child/family

ⓘ SCHOOLIES ON THE LOOSE

Every year in November, thousands of teenagers flock to Surfers Paradise to celebrate the end of their high-school education in a three-week party known as 'Schoolies Week'. Although local authorities have stepped in to regulate excesses, boozed-up and drug-addled teens are still the norm. Time for a trip to Noosa?

For more info see www.schoolies.com.

$95/60/250; ⊘ Jun-Nov) Leaves central Surfers for 3½ hours of whale-watching action.

Jetboat Extreme   BOATING
(☑ 07-5538 8890; www.jetboatextreme.com.au; Ferny Ave; 1hr ride adult/child $59/38) Slide and spin across the water in a turbo-charged, twin-jet-powered, custom-built jet boat.

Balloon Down Under   BALLOONING
(☑ 07-5500 4797; www.balloondownunder.com; 1hr flights adult/child $299/240) Up, up and away on sunrise flights over the Gold Coast, ending with a champagne breakfast.

☞ Tours

Bunyip Bike Tours   CYCLING
(☑ 0447 286 947; www.bunyipbiketours.com.au; per person $49) Three-hour bike tours along Gold Coast beachfront trails. Hinterland tours also available.

Aqua Duck   BOAT
(☑ 07-5539 0222; www.aquaduck.com.au; 36 Cavill Ave, Surfers Paradise; adult/child/family $35/26/95; ⊘ 1hr tour every 75min 10am-5.30pm) Check out Surfers by land and water in a boat with wheels.

⁂ Festivals & Events

Big Day Out   MUSIC
(www.bigdayout.com) Huge international music festival in late January.

Tropfest   FILM
(www.tropfest.com/au/surfers-paradise) The biggest short film festival in the world hits screens in Surfers Paradise in February.

Quicksilver Pro Surfing Competition   SURFING
(www.aspworldtour.com) The world's best surfers hit the waves in mid-March in the first comp of the annual world tour.

Surfers Paradise Festival   FOOD, ARTS
(www.surfersparadisefestival.com) Food, wine and live music for four weeks in April.

Gold Coast Film Festival   FILM
(www.gcfilmfestival.com) Mainstream and left-of-centre flicks from all over the world on outdoor screens. In April.

Gold Coast Marathon   MARATHON
(www.goldcoastmarathon.com.au) Sweaty people running a really long way. In July.

Gold Coast 600   MOTORSPORTS
(www.surfersparadise.v8supercars.com.au) For three days in October the streets of Surfers are transformed into a temporary race circuit for high-speed V8 Supercars.

🛏 Sleeping

The **Gold Coast Accommodation Service** (☑ 07-5592 0067; www.goldcoastaccommodationservice.com) can arrange and book accommodation and tours.

Budds in Surfers   HOSTEL $
(☑ 07-5538 9661; www.buddsinsurfers.com.au; 6 Pine Ave; dm/tw/d/q from $28/70/70/90; @ 🛜 ☲) Laid-back Budds features tidy bathrooms, clean tiles, free wi-fi, a sociable bar and a beaut pool, all just a short hop from calm-water Budds Beach. Bike hire available.

Sleeping Inn Surfers   HOSTEL $
(☑ 07-5592 4455, 1800 817 832; www.sleepinginn.com.au; 26 Peninsular Dr; dm $28-32, d & tw $68-114; @ 🛜 ☲) This backpackers occupies an old apartment block away from the centre, so, as the name suggests, there's a chance you may get to sleep in. Pizza nights, barbecue nights and pick-ups in a vintage limo.

Backpackers in Paradise   HOSTEL $
(☑ 07-5538 4344, 1800 268 621; www.backpackersinparadise.com; 40 Peninsular Dr; d $80; @ 🛜 ☲) If you're in Surfers to wage war against sleep, this party backpackers is for you. Encircling a courtyard carpeted with astroturf, most rooms are freshly painted and have bathrooms. The bar does cheap dinners – fuel-up before you hit the town.

★ Olympus Apartments   APARTMENT $$
(☑ 07-5538 7288; www.olympusapartments.com.au; 62 Esplanade; 1br $100-160, 2br $150-300; 🛜 ☲) Great value for money and directly opposite the beach, this friendly, smallish high-rise has well-kept, spacious apartments with one or two bedrooms: mod furnishings, nice art, super-clean, and all facing the sea.

Vibe Hotel   HOTEL $$

(☑ 07-5539 0444, 13 84 23; www.vibehotels.com.au; 42 Ferny Ave; d $105-250; ❊ @ 🛜 ☒) Slick but affordable, this chocolate-and-green high-rise on the Nerang River is a vibrant gem amongst Surfers' bland plethora of hotels and apartments. The rooms are subtle-chic and the pool is a top spot for sundowners. The aqua-view rooms have Nerang River views.

Moorings on Cavill   APARTMENT $$

(☑ 07-5538 6711; www.mooringsoncavill.com.au; 63 Cavill Ave; 1/2br from $128/168; ❊ 🛜 ☒) This roomy, 73-apartment tower at the river end of Cavill Ave is great for families: the vibe is quiet and respectful. The location is close to the beach, the shops and the restaurants. Super-clean and managed with a smile.

Chateau Beachside Resort   APARTMENT $$

(☑ 07-5538 1022; www.chateaubeachside.com.au; cnr Elkhorn Ave & Esplanade; d/1-bedroom apt from $170/200; ❊ @ 🛜 ☒) Less Loire Valley, more Las Vegas, this seaside 'chateau' (actually an 18-storey tower) is an excellent choice. All the renovated studios and apartments have ocean views and the 18m pool is a bonus. Minimum two-night stay.

Artique   APARTMENT $$$

(☑ 07-5564 3100, 1800 454 442; www.artiqueresort.com.au; cnr Surfers Paradise Blvd & Enderley Ave; 1-/2-bedroom apt from $240/290; ❊ 🛜 ☒) One of several slick new apartment towers at Surfers' southern end, Artique (certainly not antique) features a curvy facade, glazed balustrades, muted charcoal-and-cream tones, classy kitchens and fountains. Minimum stays apply (usually three nights).

Q1 Resort   APARTMENT $$$

(☑ 1300 792 008, 07-5630 4500; www.q1.com.au; Hamilton Ave; 1-/2-/3-bedroom apt from $318/325/666; ❊ @ 🛜 ☒) Spend a night in the world's 27th-tallest building! It's a slick resort with a mod mix of metal, glass and fabulous wrap-around views. There's a lagoon-style pool and a fitness centre if the beach doesn't exhaust you. The very sassy French restaurant Absynthe (☑ 07-5504 6466; www.absynthe.com.au; mains $48; ⊙ 6-10pm Tue-Sat) is here, too.

🍴 Eating

Self-caterers will find supermarkets in the Chevron Renaissance Centre (www.chevronrenaissancecentre.com; cnr Elkhorn Ave & Surfers Paradise Blvd; ⊙ 7am-10pm Mon-Sat, 8am-8pm Sun) and Circle on Cavill (www.circleoncavill.com.au; cnr Cavill & Ferny Aves; ⊙ 7am-10pm Mon-Sat, 8am-8pm Sun) shopping centres.

Bumbles Café   CAFE $

(☑ 07-5538 6668; www.bumblescafe.com; 21 River Dr; mains $9-27; ⊙ 7am-3pm Fri-Wed, to 10pm Thu) Chilled-out, grey-painted corner cafe opposite shallow Budds Beach on the Nerang River. Order a FAT (fetta, avocado and tomato on toast) and enjoy a few minutes away from the fray.

Surfers Sandbar   MODERN AUSTRALIAN $

(www.facebook.com/surferssandbar; cnr Elkhorn Ave & Esplanade; mains $12-32; ⊙ 6.45am-late) The menu is predictable – burgers, fish and chips, pizza, steak sandwiches – but beachside prominence gives this cafe/bar the edge over most Surfers eateries. Forgo the pubby indoor space and chow-down on the terrace

---

THE GOLD COAST IN...

Two Days

Start with a beach swim before breakfast, then get dunked, rolled and spun a thousand different ways at one of the Gold Coast theme parks. Pull yourself together, grab some dinner in Surfers Paradise at Baritalia (p320) or Surfers Sandbar (p319) then hit the party scene along Orchid Ave.

Next day, hit the surf: book a lesson at Surfers Paradise or Currumbin, or head for the legendary big waves at Burleigh Heads or Coolangatta. Have lunch at Oskars (p329) overlooking Burleigh's beaut beach, then hang out with some native critters at Currumbin Wildlife Sanctuary (p327). Beachside beers at the Coolangatta Hotel (p331) await.

Three Days

With three days up your sleeve you can explore the hinterland. Skip Tamborine Mountain (unless Devonshire teas are your thing) and take a hike in Springbrook National Park (p333) (or just check out the waterfalls and lookouts you can drive right up to).

Surfers Paradise

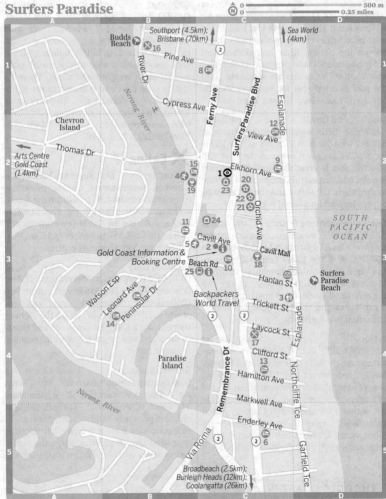

(you can hear lifesavers berating absent-minded swimmers across the street).

Baritalia   ITALIAN $$

(☏07-5592 4700; www.baritaliagoldcoast.com.au; Shop 15, Chevron Renaissance Centre, cnr Elkhorn Ave & Surfers Paradise Blvd; mains $15-35; ☺7.30am-late) This Italian bar and restaurant has a fab outdoor terrace and hip international staff. Go for the chilli seafood broth with Moreton Bay bugs, saffron and capers, or excellent pastas, pizzas and risotto. Decent wines by the glass and good coffee.

Matador   SPANISH $$

(☏07-5570 2007; www.matadortapasbar.com; Chevron Renaissance Centre, cnr Elkhorn Ave & Surfers Paradise Blvd; tapas from $6.50, mains $18-40; ☺4pm-late Mon-Fri, noon-late Sat & Sun) Small, bright and simple, this Spanish hole-in-the-wall is the pick of the Chevron Renaissance Centre eateries. It does a roaring trade in tapas (try the grilled prawns in serrano ham) and heftier mains, including an awesome Spanish marinara casserole.

Tandoori Place   INDIAN $$

(☏07-5538 0808, 1300 082 636; www.tandoori-place.com; 30 Laycock St; mains $15-19, banquets

Surfers Paradise

per person from $26; ⊙11.30am-2.30pm & 5pm-late) One of 17 (yes 17!) Tandoori Place restaurants in the Gold Coast area, this burgundy food room thankfully doesn't feel like part of a chain. On the vast menu you'll find seafood, chicken, lamb, beef and hot, hot, *hot* vindaloo roo. Kids welcome ('Children are nature's gift').

🍷 Drinking & Nightlife

Orchid Ave is Surfers' club strip. Cover charges are usually $10 to $20; Wednesday and Saturday are the big party nights. You can tag along with other boozy backpackers on club crawls organised by **Plan B Party Tours** (☑1300 721 570; www.planbtours.com; tickets $60): tickets get you into five clubs and take the hassle out of the experience. **Big Night Out** (www.goldcoastbackpackers.net; tickets $30) and **Wicked Club Crawl** (☑07-5504 7025; www.wickedclubcrawl.com.au; tickets $30-50) are similar (but with four clubs).

Helm Bar & Bistro BAR
(www.helmbarsurfers.com.au; 30-34 Ferny Ave; ⊙10am-9pm) Unless you like Irish pubs, this nautical-themed bar is the best drinking spot in town, perfect for a beer or six as the sun sets over the Nerang River. Good pizzas and steaks, too.

Beergarden BAR
(www.surfersbeergarden.com.au; Cavill Ave; ⊙10am-5am) Not so much a garden – more of a black-painted beer barn overlooking Cavill Ave. Steel yourself with a few cold ones before you hit the clubs, or catch live bands on Saturday nights or reggae on Sunday afternoons.

Sin City CLUB
(www.sincitynightclub.com.au; 22 Orchid Ave; ⊙9pm-late) This Vegas-style sin pit is the place for wrongdoings: sexy staff, big-name DJs and visiting celebs trying not to get photographed.

Shuffle CLUB
(www.platinumnightclub.com.au/shuffle-nightclub; Shop 15b, The Forum, 26 Orchid Ave; ⊙9pm-5am Fri & Sat) Shuffle into Shuffle for an intimate club experience, with dirty underground house and a backpacker-heavy crowd (less red carpet, more downmarket).

Vanity CLUB
(www.vanitynightclub.com.au; 26 Orchid Ave; ⊙5am-5pm) 'Because it's all about you' at Vanity, one of the glammest clubs in town, which digs deep into the sexy marketing book of tricks. Dress to the nines; no visible tatts.

☆ Entertainment

Arts Centre Gold Coast THEATRE, CINEMA
(☑07-5588 4000; www.theartscentregc.com.au;
135 Bundall Rd; ⊙box office 8am-9pm Mon-Fri,
9am-9pm Sat, 11am-7pm Sun) A bastion of culture and civility beside the Nerang River, the
Arts Centre has two cinemas, a restaurant, a
bar, the Gold Coast City Gallery and a 1200-
seat theatre, which hosts productions (comedy, jazz, opera, kids' concerts etc).

ℹ Information

Backpackers World Travel (☑07-5561 0634;
www.backpackerworldtravel.com; 6 Beach Rd;
⊙10am-6pm Mon-Fri, 10am-5pm Sat, to 4pm
Sun) Accommodation, tour and transport bookings and internet access.

Gold Coast Information & Booking Centre
(☑1300 309 440; www.visitgoldcoast.com;
Cavill Ave; ⊙8.30am-5pm Mon-Sat, 9am-4pm
Sun) The main GC tourist information booth;
also sells theme-park tickets and has public
transport info.

Post Office (www.auspost.com.au; Shop
165, Centro Surfers Paradise, Cavill Ave Mall;
⊙9am-5pm Mon-Fri)

Surfers Paradise Day & Night Medical Centre
(☑07-5592 2299; 3221 Surfers Paradise Blvd;
⊙6am-11pm) General medical centre and
pharmacy. Make an appointment or walk in.

ℹ Getting There & Away

Long-distance buses stop at the **Surfers Paradise Transit Centre** (10 Beach Rd). **Greyhound**
(☑1300 473 946; www.greyhound.com.au) and
Premier Motor Service (p359) have frequent
services to/from Brisbane ($20, 1½ hours),
Byron Bay ($30, 2½ hours) and beyond.

ℹ Getting Around

Car hire costs around $35 to $50 per day.

East Coast Car Rentals (☑07-5592 0444,
1800 028 881; www.eastcoastcarrentals.com.
au; 80 Ferny Ave; ⊙7am-6pm Mon-Fri, 8am-
5pm Sat, to 4pm Sun)

Red Back Rentals (☑07-5592 1655; www.red-
backrentals.com.au; Surfers Paradise Transit
Centre, 10 Beach Rd; ⊙8am-4.30pm Mon-Fri,
to 4pm Sat)

Scooter Hire Gold Coast (☑07-5511 0398;
www.scooterhiregoldcoast.com.au; 3269 Surfers Paradise Blvd; ⊙8am-5.30pm) Scooter hire
(50cc) from around $65 per day.

SOUTHPORT & MAIN BEACH

POP 28,320 & 3330

The northern gateway to the Gold Coast,
incongruously named Southport is a low-
key residential and business district. It's
sheltered from the ocean by a long sandbar
called the Spit, which is is home to one of
the big theme parks, Sea World.

Directly southeast is glorious, golden
Main Beach, where the apartment blocks
begin their inexorable rise towards Surfers.

◉ Sights

Main Beach Pavilion ARCHITECTURE
(Macarthur Pde, Main Beach; ⊙9am-5pm) The
lovely Spanish Mission–style Main Beach
Pavilion (1934) is a remnant from less
hectic times. Inside are some fabulous old
photos of the Gold Coast in pre-skyscraper
days.

OFF THE BEATEN TRACK

SOUTH STRADBROKE ISLAND

This narrow, 21km-long sand island is largely undeveloped – the perfect antidote to the
chaotic Gold Coast strip. At the northern end, the narrow channel separating it from
North Stradbroke Island is a top fishing spot; at the southern end, the Spit is only 200m
away. South Stradbroke was actually attached to North Stradbroke until a huge storm in
1896 blasted through the isthmus joining them. There's a resort here, plus three camping grounds, lots of wallabies and plenty of bush, sand and sea. And no cars!

The **Ramada Couran Cove Island Resort** (☑07-5597 9999; www.courancove.
com.au; South Stradbroke Island; d/ste from $210/250; ✴✳) is a luxe resort on the isle's
northwest side, with rooms on stilts by the water, restaurants, a spa, a private marina
and guided nature walks. Pre-booked ferry transfers (return adult/child $30/15) depart
three times daily from Runaway Bay Marina on Bayview St, 7km north of Southport.

For details on camping on the island – at Tipplers, North Currigee and South Currigee
camping grounds – incuding transport info, see www.mystraddie.com.au.

DON'T MISS

GOLD COAST THEME PARKS

The gravity-defying rollercoasters and waterslides at these American-style parks offer some seriously dizzy action – keeping your lunch down is a constant battle. Discount tickets are sold in most of the tourist offices on the Gold Coast; the VIP Pass (per person $110) grants unlimited entry to Sea World, Warner Bros Movie World and Wet'n'Wild.

A couple of tips: the parks can get insanely crowded, so arrive early or face a long walk from the far side of the car park. Also note that the parks don't let you bring your own food and drinks – load up on breakfast beforehand, or buy your lunch.

Dreamworld (☑ 1800 073 300, 07-5588 1111; www.dreamworld.com.au; Dreamworld Pkwy, Coomera; adult/child $95/75, online $90/70; ⊙ 10am-5pm) Home to the 'Big 8 Thrill Rides', including the Giant Drop and Tower of Terror II. Lots of kid-centric rides too. Get your photo taken with Aussie animals or a Bengal tiger at Tiger Island. Access to WhiteWater World is included in the ticket price.

Sea World (☑ 07-5588 2222, 13 33 86; www.seaworld.com.au; Seaworld Dr, The Spit, Main Beach; adult/child $83/50; ⊙ 9.30am-5.30pm) See polar bears, sharks, seals, penguins and performing dolphins at this aquatic park, which also has the mandatory rollercoasters and waterslides. Animal shows throughout the day.

Warner Bros Movie World (☑ 13 33 86, 07-5573 3999; www.movieworld.com.au; Pacific Hwy, Oxenford; adult/child $83/50; ⊙ 9.30am-5pm) Movie-themed shows, rides and attractions, including the Batwing Spaceshot, Justice League 3D Ride and Scooby-Doo Spooky Coaster. Batman, Austin Powers, Porky Pig et al roam through the crowds.

Wet'n'Wild (☑ 13 33 86, 07-5556 1660; www.wetnwild.com.au; Pacific Hwy, Oxenford; adult/child $60/35; ⊙ 10am-5pm) The ultimate waterslide here is the Kamikaze, where you plunge down an 11m drop in a two-person tube at 50km/h. This vast water park also has pitch-black slides, white-water rapids and wave pools.

WhiteWater World (☑ 1800 073 300, 07-5588 1111; www.whitewaterworld.com.au; Dreamworld Pkwy, Coomera; adult/child $95/75, online $90/70; ⊙ 10am-4pm) Connected to Dreamworld; features waterslide rides like the Temple of Huey, the Green Room and the Cave of Waves. You can learn to surf here too! Ticket price includes entry to Dreamworld.

Gourmet Farmers Market　MARKET
(☑ 07-5555 6400; www.facebook.com/marinamiragefarmersmarket; Marina Mirage, 74 Sea World Dr, Main Beach; ⊙ 7-11am Sat) On Saturday mornings, the spaces between boutiques at this flashy mall fill with stalls selling seasonal fruit and veg, baked goods, pickles, oils, vinegars, seafood, pasta and more...

Produce by the Pier　MARKET
(www.producebythepier.com.au; Broadwater Parklands, Southport; ⊙ 8am-2pm Sat) Fresh fruit and veg, coffee, flowers, wine and deli goods in the park by the Broadwater Parklands pier.

🏃 Activities

Opposite the entrance to Sea World, in the car park of Phillip Park, is the start of the **Federation Walk**, a 3.7km trail through littoral rainforest and connecting to the **Gold Coast Oceanway** (www.goldcoastcity.com.au/oceanway), a 36km walking/cycling trail running from here to Coolangatta.

Mariner's Cove in Main Beach can book water activities. Sift through the plethora of operators here at the **Mariner's Cove Tourism Information & Booking Centre** (☑ 07-5571 1711; www.marinerscovemarina.com.au; Mariner's Cove, 60-70 Seaworld Dr, Main Beach; ⊙ 8.30am-3.30pm Mon-Fri, 9.30am-2pm Sat & Sun).

Australian Kayaking Adventures　KAYAKING
(☑ 0412 940 135; www.australiankayakingadventures.com.au; half-day tour adult/child $95/75, sunset tours $55/45) Paddle out to underrated South Stradbroke Island and spot some dolphins, or take a dusk paddle around Chevron Island in the calm canals behind Surfers.

Gold Coast Watersports　PARASAILING
(☑ 0410 494 240; www.goldcoastwatersports.com; Mariner's Cove, 60-70 Sea World Dr, Main Beach; per person from $65) Daily parasailing jaunts.

Jet Ski Safaris　JET-SKIING
(☑ 0409 754 538, 07-5526 3111; www.jetskisafaris.com.au; Mariner's Cove, 60-70 Sea World Dr,

Southport & Main Beach

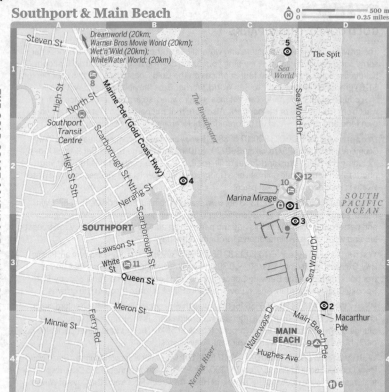

Southport & Main Beach

Main Beach; tour 30min/90min/2½hr per ski from $100/240/380) Jet-ski tours up and down the coast and out to South Stradbroke Island. No experience necessary; cheaper if you tandem on a ski with someone else.

Island Adventures
WHALE WATCHING

(☑07-5532 2444, 1300 942 537; www.tallship.com.au; Mariner's Cove, 60-70 Sea World Dr, Main Beach; 3hr tour adult/child from $99/69) Cruises to South Stradbroke Island and beyond in search of big wet mammals. Lots of add-on options and longer tours also available.

👉 Tours

Broadwater Canal Cruises
CRUISE

(☑0410 403 020; www.broadwatercanalcruises.com.au; Mariner's Cove, 60-70 Sea World Dr, Main Beach; 2hr cruise adult/child/family $22/15/60; ☺10.30am & 2pm) Runs slow-boat cruises around the Broadwater canals behind Surfers Paradise.

Gold Coast Helitours
SCENIC FLIGHTS

(☑07-5591 8457; www.goldcoasthelitours.com.au; 5min ride adult/child $65/55, 20min $190/140) Runs a range of helicopter flights over the Gold Coast in black-and-orange choppers.

🛏 Sleeping

Surfers Paradise YHA at Main Beach
HOSTEL $

(☑07-5571 1776; www.yha.com.au; 70 Sea World Dr, Main Beach; dm/d & tw $31/79; @ 🛜) In a great first-floor position overlooking the marina. There's a free shuttle bus, barbecue nights every Friday, and the hostel is within wobbling distance of the Fisherman's Wharf Tavern. Sky-blue dorms; very well organised.

Trekkers
HOSTEL $

(☑1800 100 004, 07-5591 5616; www.trekkersbackpackers.com.au; 22 White St, Southport; dm/d & tw $30/76; @ 🛜 ⛱) You could bottle the friendly vibes in this sociable old Queenslander and make a mint. The building is looking a bit tired, but the communal areas are homey and the garden is a mini-oasis.

Main Beach Tourist Park
CARAVAN PARK $

(☑07-5667 2720; www.gctp.com.au/main; 3600 Main Beach Pde, Main Beach; powered sites/cabins & villas from $45/125; ✴@🛜⛱) Just across the road from the beach and backed by high-rise apartments, this caravan park is a family favourite. It's a tight fit between sites, but the facilities are decent.

Harbour Side Resort
APARTMENT $$

(☑07-5591 6666; www.harboursideresort.com.au; 132 Marine Pde, Southport; 1-/2-bedroom apt $130/170; ✴@🛜⛱) 'Resort' is a bit of a stretch, and disregard the busy road: inside this facelifted, three-storey place you'll find motel-style units with well-equipped kitchens and a fab pool.

Palazzo Versace
RESORT $$$

(☑07-5509 8000, 1800 098 000; www.palazzoversace.com; Sea World Dr, Main Beach; d/ste from $415/500; ✴@⛱) A glitzy post-modern Roman apparition, the Palazzo Versace is pure extravagance, from the opulent rooms to the indulgent restaurants and bars. Everything, from the pool furniture to the bell-hops' belt buckles, is infused with over-the-top Versace glam. Staff are surprisingly un-snooty.

🍴 Eating

⭐Providore
CAFE $

(☑07-5532 9390; www.facebook.com/mirage-market; Shop 27, Marina Mirage, 74 Sea World Dr, Main Beach; mains $10-29; ☺7am-6pm Sun-Wed, to 10pm Thu-Sat) Floor-to-ceiling windows rimmed with Italian mineral water bottles, inverted desk lamps dangling from the ceiling, good-looking Euro tourists, wines by the glass, bread racks, cheese fridges and baskets overflowing with fresh produce: this excellent deli/cafe gets a lot of things right. Order some polenta and eggs and start your day with aplomb.

Peter's Fish Market
SEAFOOD, FISH & CHIPS $

(☑07-5591 7747; www.petersfish.com.au; 120 Sea World Dr, Main Beach; meals $9-16; ☺9am-7.30pm, cooking from noon) A no-nonsense fish market selling fresh and cooked seafood in all shapes and sizes (and at great prices), fresh from the trawlers moored out the front.

Sunset Bar & Grill
MODERN AUSTRALIAN $

(☑07-5528 2622; www.sunsetbarandgrill.com.au; Shop 31, Marina Mirage, 74 Sea World Dr, Main Beach; dishes $12-28; ☺7am-6pm Mon-Fri, to 7pm Sat & Sun) This umbrella-shaded, family-friendly place by the water serves reasonably priced (if predictable) steaks, salads, burgers and seafood dishes.

🍷 Drinking

Fisherman's Wharf Tavern
PUB

(☑07-5571 0566; Mariner's Cove, Main Beach; ☺10am-midnight) This boisterous harbour-side pub – on a pier out over the water – is a beers-from-10am kinda joint, and gets raucous on weekends (big Sunday sessions). The kitchen whips up reliable burgers and fish and chips, plus curries, steaks and salads.

ℹ Getting There & Away

Coaches stop at the **Southport Transit Centre** on Scarborough St, between North and Railway Sts. Catch local Surfside buses from outside the Australia Fair Shopping Centre on Scarborough St.

BROADBEACH

POP 4650

The decibel level tails off markedly directly south of Surfers Paradise in stylish Broadbeach, which offers chic cafes, shops and restaurants and a stretch of golden shore.

🏃 Activities

Brad Holmes Surf Coaching SURFING
(☑0418 757 539, 07-5539 4068; www.bradholmessurfcoaching.com; 90min lesson $75) Affordable one-on-one or group lessons at Broadbeach. Warm up with a t'ai-chi workout on the sand. Also caters to travellers with disabilities.

🛏 Sleeping

Hi-Ho Beach Apartments APARTMENT $$
(☑07-5538 2777; www.hihobeach.com.au; 2 Queensland Ave; 1-/2-bedroom apt from $100/130; ❋🖥❄) A top choice for location, close to the beach and cafes. You're not paying for glitzy lobbies here: it's standard, value-for-money, no-frills accommodation (a bit '90s decor-wise), but well managed, clean and quiet. Dig the Vegas-esque sign!

Wave APARTMENT $$$
(☑07-5555 9200; www.thewavesresort.com.au; 89-91 Surf Pde, Broadbeach; 1-/2-/3-bedroom apt from $290/405/480; ❋@🖥❄) Towering over glam Broadbeach, you can't miss this funky high-rise with its wobbly, wave-inspired facade. The plush pads here take full advantage of panoramic coastal views (especially good from the sky pool on the 34th floor). Minimum three-night stay.

🍴 Eating

⭐**Manolas Brothers Deli** DELI, CAFE $
(MBD; www.m-b-d.com.au; 19 Albert Ave; dishes $8-21; ❍6.30am-5pm) Busy but strangely unhurried, MBD is a brilliant sidestreet deli-cafe. Ceiling-high shelves overflow with produce – vats of oil, Mediterranean sea salt, olives and pasta – and the counter is packed with gourmet pies, quiches, tarts, imported cheeses, antipasti and cakes. Park yourself at the long central table and sip a 'Flu Fighter' juice (orange, carrot, ginger and parsley).

⭐**BSKT Cafe** CAFE $
(☑07-5526 6565; www.bskt.com.au; 4 Lavarack Ave, Mermaid Beach; mains $10-27; ❍7am-4pm Mon-Thu, to 10pm Fri-Sun; ☑) This hip corner cafe is 100m from Mermaid Beach, a quick jaunt south of Broadbeach. The brainchild of four buddies who obsess over service and organic ingredients, it's a mod-industrial affair with chunky timber tables, super staff and adventurous mains: try the quesadilla with goats cheese and sesame, or the 18-hour sticky pork with sour herb salad. Great coffee, too.

Beer Thai Garden THAI $$
(☑07-5538 0110; www.beerthaigarden.com.au; 2765 Gold Coast Hwy; mains $18-23; ❍5.30-10pm; ☑) With the best pad thai on the coast, Beer Thai Garden is right on the busy road but brims with atmosphere. Two affable elephants flank the entrance, and soft lighting brings an almost romantic vibe to the garden bar. Easy on the pocket, too.

Koi MODERN AUSTRALIAN, CAFE $$
(☑07-5570 3060; www.koibroadbeach.com.au; Wave Bldg, cnr Surf Pde & Albert Ave; mains breakfast $14-21, lunch & dinner $18-40; ❍7am-late) This cruisy cafe/bar is the pick of the eateries on Surf Pde. Fast-moving, black-clad wait staff shuffle out plates of risotto, pasta, gourmet pizza, tapas, seafood and Koi beans (with poached eggs, chorizo, crispy onion and balsamic reduction).

BURLEIGH HEADS & CURRUMBIN

POP 9200 & 2785

The true, sandy essence of the Gold Coast permeates the chilled-out surfie town of Burleigh Heads. With its cheery cafes and beachfront restaurants, famous right-hand point break, beautiful beach and little national park on the rocky headland, Burleigh charms everyone.

Beginner surfers should head to Currumbin Alley, 6km south of Burleigh. Currumbin itself is a sleepy little family-focused town, with safe swimming in Currumbin Creek.

◉ Sights

Burleigh Head National Park PARK
(www.nprsr.qld.gov.au/parks/burleigh-head; Goodwin Tce, Burleigh Heads; ❍24hr) FREE A walk around the headland through Burleigh Head National Park is a must for any visitor – it's a 27-hectare rainforest reserve with plenty of bird life and several walking trails. Great views of the Burleigh surf en route.

David Fleay Wildlife Park WILDLIFE RESERVE
(☑07-5576 2411; www.nprsr.qld.gov.au/parks/david-fleay; cnr Loman La & West Burleigh Rd, West Burleigh; adult/child/family $19/9/48; ❍9am-5pm) Opened by the doctor who first succeeded

Burleigh Heads

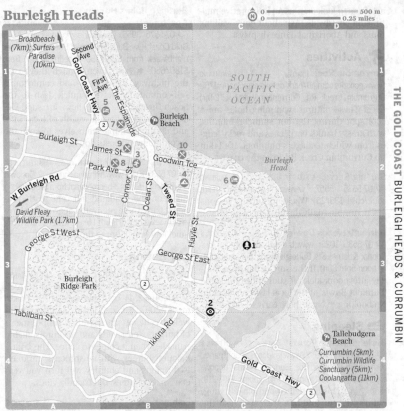

N 0 ⟶ 500 m
0 ⟶ 0.25 miles

Broadbeach (7km); Surfers Paradise (10km)

SOUTH PACIFIC OCEAN

Burleigh Beach

Burleigh Head

David Fleay Wildlife Park (1.7km)

Burleigh Ridge Park

Tallebudgera Beach

Currumbin (5km); Currumbin Wildlife Sanctuary (5km); Coolangatta (11km)

---

in breeding platypuses, this wildlife park has 4km of walking tracks through mangroves and rainforest and plenty of informative native wildlife shows throughout the day. It's around 3km inland from Burleigh Heads.

Currumbin Wildlife Sanctuary   WILDLIFE RESERVE
(☏1300 886 511, 07-5534 1266; www.cws.org.au; 28 Tomewin St, Currumbin; adult/child/family $49/33/131; ⊙8am-5pm) Currumbin Wildlife Sanctuary has Australia's biggest rainforest aviary, where you can hand-feed a technicolour blur of rainbow lorikeets. There's also kangaroo feeding, photo ops with koalas and crocodiles, reptile shows and Aboriginal dance displays. It's cheaper after 3pm. Coach transfers available (return from $15).

Jellurgal Cultural Centre   CULTURAL BUILDING
(☏07-5525 5955; www.jellurgal.com.au; 1711 Gold Coast Hwy, Burleigh Heads; ⊙8am-3pm Mon-Fri, 8am-4pm Sat, 9am-2pm Sun) ✔ FREE This new

Aboriginal cultural centre at the base of Burleigh's headland sheds some light on life here hundreds of years ago. There's lots of art and artefacts to look at, plus an interpretive multimedia boardwalk. Ask about daily walking tours and Aboriginal dance displays.

Activities

Currumbin Rock Pools
SWIMMING

(www.gcparks.com.au/park-details.aspx?park=1751; Currumbin Creek Rd, Currumbin Valley; ⊙24hr) **FREE** These natural swimming holes are a cool spot during the hot summer months, with grassy banks, barbecues and rocky ledges from which teenagers plummet. It's 14km up Currumbin Creek Rd from the coast.

Surfing Services Australia
SURFING

(☑07-5535 5557; www.surfingservices.com.au; adult/child $35/25) Weekend surfing lessons at Currumbin (daily during school holidays).

Burleigh Heads Bowls Club
LAWN BOWLS

(☑07-5535 1023; www.burleighbowls.org.au; cnr Connor & James Sts, Burleigh Heads; per person $4; ⊙noon-5pm Sun) If the surf is flat on a Sunday afternoon, kick off your shoes for some 'Barefoot Bowls' at the local lawn bowls club. No bookings, so get there early.

Sleeping

Burleigh Beach Tourist Park
CARAVAN PARK $

(☑07-5667 2750; www.goldcoasttouristparks.com.au; 36 Goodwin Tce, Burleigh Heads; unpowered/powered sites from $30/41, cabins $151-219; ❋@🡒☒) This council-owned park is snug, but it's well run and in a great spot near the beach. Aim for one of the three blue cabins at the front of the park.

Burleigh Palms Holiday Apartments
APARTMENT $$

(☑07-5576 3955; www.burleighpalms.com; 1849 Gold Coast Hwy, Burleigh Heads; 1-bedroom apt per night/week from $150/550, 2-bedroom apt from $180/660; ❋🡒☒) Even though they're on the highway, these large and comfortable self-contained units – a quick dash to the beach through the back alley – are solid value. The owners have a wealth of local info, and do the cleaning themselves to keep the accommodation costs down.

Hillhaven Holiday Apartments
APARTMENT $$

(☑07-5535 1055; www.hillhaven.com.au; 2 Goodwin Tce, Burleigh Heads; 2-bedroom apt from $180; @🡒) Right on the headland adjacent to the national park, these renovated apartments have great views of Burleigh Heads and the surf. It's quiet and only 150m to the beach.

Eating

★ Borough Barista
CAFE $

(www.facebook.com/pages/borough-barista/236745933011462; 14 The Esplanade, Burleigh Heads; mains $10-17; ⊙6am-2.30pm) A little open-walled caffeine shack with a simple menu of burgers and salads and an unmistakable panache when it comes to coffee. The grilled haloumi burger with mushrooms, caramelised onions and chutney will turn you vegetarian. Cool tunes and friendly vibes.

Fishmonger
SEAFOOD $

(☑07-5535 2927; 9 James St, Burleigh Heads; dishes $7-16; ⊙10am-7.30pm) This low-key

---

LOCAL KNOWLEDGE

LUKE EGAN: FORMER PRO SURFER

The Gold Coast is one of the top five surfing destinations in the world. The most unique thing about the Goldy is that the waves break mostly on sand, so for sandy bottoms we get some of the most perfect waves in the world.

Best Surf Beaches

The length of ride on the famous points of Burleigh Heads, Kirra, Rainbow Bay and Snapper Rocks make the Goldy a must for every passionate surfer.

Where to Learn

The waves at Greenmount Point and Currumbin allow first-timers plenty of time to get to their feet and still enjoy a long ride. Learning to surf at these two places would be close to the best place to learn anywhere in Australia, and probably the world.

Best Experience

There isn't a better feeling than being 'surfed out' – the feeling you have after a day of surfing. Even though I no longer compete on the world surfing tour I still surf every day like it's my last.

fish-and-chip shop has been here since 1948. Grab some takeaway and head for the beach.

Canteen Coffee
CAFE $

(☑ 0487 208 777; www.canteencoffee.com.au; 23 Park Ave, Burleigh Heads; items $3-8; ☺ 7am-4pm Mon-Fri, to 3pm Sat & Sun) In a twin-business pairing with **Canteen Kitchen** next door (a larger cafe: mains $14 to $20), this caffeine cranny casts another vote for Burleigh Heads as the Gold Coast's coffee capital. A double-shot flat white and a slab of carrot cake will jump-start your afternoon.

Elephant Rock Café
MODERN AUSTRALIAN, CAFE $$

(☑ 07-5598 2133; www.elephantrock.com.au; 776 Pacific Pde, Currumbin; mains $15-35; ☺ 7am-late Tue-Sat, to 4pm Sun & Mon) On the refreshingly under-developed Currumbin beachfront you'll find this breezy, two-tier cafe, which morphs from beach-chic by day into ultra-chic at night. Great ocean views and even better seafood linguini.

Oskars
SEAFOOD $$$

(☑ 07-5576 3722; www.oskars.com.au; 43 Goodwin Tce, Burleigh Heads; mains $38-43; ☺ 10am-midnight) One of the Gold Coast's finest, this *ooh-la-la* restaurant right on the beach serves award-winning seafood and has sweeping views up the coast to Surfers. Try the spanner crab soufflé and the satay spiced green prawns.

🍷 Drinking

Currumbin Beach Vikings SLSC
PUB

(☑ 07-5534 2932; www.currumbinslsc.com.au; 741 Pacific Pde, Currumbin; ☺ 7.30am-9.30pm) In an incredible position on Currumbin beach below craggy Elephant Rock, this surf pavilion is perfect for an afternoon beer. The menu is predictable, but the view will knock your socks off.

COOLANGATTA

POP 5200

A down-to-earth seaside town on Queensland's southern border, Coolangatta has quality surf beaches (including the legendary 'Superbank' break) and a tight-knit community. The Coolangatta Gold surf-lifesaving comp happens here every October. Follow the boardwalk north around Kirra Point to the suburb of Kirra itself, with a long stretch of beach and challenging surf.

🏃 Activities

Cooly Surf
SURFING

(☑ 07-5536 1470; www.surfshopaustralia.com.au; cnr Marine Pde & Dutton St, Coolangatta; ☺ 9am-5pm) Cooly Surf hires out surfboards (half/full day $30/45) and stand-up paddleboards ($40/55), and runs two-hour surf lessons ($45).

Gold Coast Skydive
SKYDIVING

(☑ 07-5599 1920; www.goldcoastskydive.com.au; tandem jump from $345) Plummet out of the sky from 12,000 feet up? Go on – you know you want to!

👉 Tours

Rainforest Cruises
CRUISE

(☑ 07-5536 8800; www.goldcoastcruising.com; 2hr cruise from $40) Cruise options ranging from crab-catching to surf 'n' turf lunches on rainforest cruises along the Tweed River.

🛏 Sleeping

★ Komune
HOTEL, HOSTEL $

(☑ 07-5536 6764; www.komuneresorts.com; 146 Marine Pde, Coolangatta; dm from $45, 1-/2-bedroom apt from $105/145, penthouse from $245; 🛜🏊) With beach-funk decor, a Bali-esque pool area and an ultra laid-back vibe, this eight-storey converted apartment tower is the ultimate surf retreat. There are budget dorms, apartments and a hip penthouse begging for a party.

Kirra Beach Tourist Park
CARAVAN PARK $

(☑ 07-5667 2740; www.goldcoasttouristparks.com.au; 10 Charlotte St, Kirra; unpowered/powered sites $30/37, cabins from $138; ❄@🛜🏊) Large council-run park with plenty of trees, wandering ibises, a camp kitchen and a heated swimming pool. Good-value self-contained cabins (with or without bathroom), and a few hundred metres to the beach.

Coolangatta Sands Hostel
HOSTEL $

(☑ 07-5536 7472; www.coolangattasandshostel.com.au; cnr Griffith & McLean Sts, Coolangatta; dm/d from $30/80; ❄@🛜) Above the boozy Coolangatta Sands Hotel, this hostel is a warren of rooms and corridors, but there's a fab wraparound balcony above the street (no booze allowed unfortunately – go downstairs to the pub).

Coolangatta YHA
HOSTEL $

(☑ 07-5536 7644; www.yha.com.au; 230 Coolangatta Rd, Bilinga; dm $27-34, s/d from $42/67; @🛜🏊) A *looong* 4km haul from the action in an industrial pocket next to the noisy

Coolangatta

airport, this YHA is redeemed by free breakfast, free transfers to Coolangatta and the beach across the road. You can also hire surfboards ($20 per day) and bikes ($25).

Meridian Tower
APARTMENT $$
(☎07-5536 9400; www.meridiantower.com.au; 6 Coyne St, Kirra; 1-/2-/3-bedroom apt per week from $815/930/1610; ❄️🐾🏊) This tall tower (the first in Kirra) opposite beautiful Kirra Beach has airy apartments with large north-facing balconies. It's a middle-of-the-road, family-friendly affair – not at all glam. Shorter stays possible outside of peak season.

Nirvana
APARTMENT $$$
(☎07-5506 5555; www.nirvanabythesea.com.au; 1 Douglas St, Kirra; 2-/3-bedroom apt from $205/365) Attaining some sort of salty nirvana across from Kirra Beach, this sleek new apartment tower comes with all the whistles and bells: two pools, gym, cinema room, ocean views and sundry salons.

✖ Eating

Burger Lounge
BURGERS $
(☎07-5599 5762; www.burgerlounge.com.au; cnr Musgrave & Douglas Sts, Kirra; mains $10-17; ⊗10am-9pm Thu-Tue, 11am-9pm Wed) Awesome bunfest in a triangular-shaped room at the base of the Nirvana apartment tower (fast-food

nirvana?). The chicken-and-mango-chilli burger is a winner! Lots of good beers, cocktails and wines, too, and sangria by the jug.

Earth 'n' Sea
PIZZERIA $$
(☎07-5536 3477; www.earthnseapizza.com.au; 72 Marine Pde, Coolangatta; mains $11-33; ⊗10am-9pm Mon-Fri, 8am-9pm Sat & Sun) An old-fashioned, family-friendly pizza and pasta restaurant on the main drag. Substance trumps style.

Bread 'n' Butter
TAPAS $$
(☎07-5599 4666; www.breadnbutter.com.au; 76 Musgrave St; tapas $13-22, pizzas$19-25; ⊗5.30pm-late) 🍴 Head upstairs to the Bread 'n' Butter balcony, where moody lighting and chilled tunes make this tapas bar perfect for a drink, some pizza or some tapas (or all three). Uses local and home-grown produce and recycles precisely 78% of waste. DJs spin on Friday and Saturday nights.

Bellakai
MODERN AUSTRALIAN, CAFE $$$
(☎07-5599 5116; www.facebook.com/bellakai.coolangatta; 82 Marine Pde, Coolangatta; mains $30-37; ⊗5am-late) From 5am until late, Bellakai plates up fine food. Start with black-tiger-prawn dumplings, followed by the fish of the day with kipfler potatoes, sesame greens and miso butter.

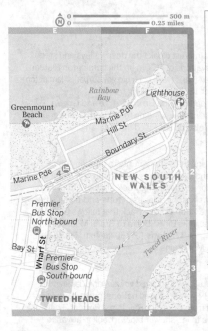

national parks here have subtropical jungle, waterfalls and wildlife. Springbrook National Park is the wettest place in southeast Queensland, with cool air and dense forest. Lamington National Park attracts birdwatchers and hikers; Tamborine Mountain lures the cottage weekend set.

🍷 Drinking

Coolangatta Hotel PUB
(www.thecoolyhotel.com.au; cnr Marine Pde & Warner St; ⊙10am-late) The hub of Coolangatta's nocturnal scene, this huge pub right across from the beach has live bands (Grinspoon, The Rubens, The Cat Empire), sausage sizzles, pool comps, trivia nights, acoustic jam nights and pub meals. Big Sunday sessions.

ℹ️ Information

Coolangatta Tweed Medical Centre (☎07-5599 3010, after hours 0413 511 443; 2 Griffith St, Coolangatta; ⊙8am-4.30pm Mon-Fri)

Post Office (www.auspost.com.au; cnr Griffith St & McLean St, Coolangatta; ⊙9am-5pm Mon-Fri)

ℹ️ Getting There & Away

The **Greyhound** (☎1300 473 946; www.greyhound.com.au) bus stop is in Warner St; **Premier Motor Service** (www.premierms.com.au) coaches stop on Wharf St.

GOLD COAST HINTERLAND

Inland from the surf and sand of the Gold Coast, the forested mountains of the McPherson Range feel a million miles away. The

👉 Tours

Bushwacker Ecotours ECOTOUR
(☎1300 559 355, 07-3848 8806; www.bushwackerecotours.com.au; tour adult/child from $125/95) Ecotours to the hinterland with rainforest walks in Springbrook National Park and around, departing the Gold Coast or Brisbane.

JPT Tour Group TOUR
(☎07-56301602; www.daytours.com.au; tour adult/child from $99/57) A variety of day tours ex-Brisbane or Gold Coast, including Lamington National Park via Tamborine Mountain and glow-worm tours to Natural Bridge.

Mountain Coach Company TOUR
(☎07-5524 4249, 1300 762 665; www.mountaincoach.com.au) Daily tours from the Gold Coast to Tamborine Mountain (adult/child $59/49), Lamington National Park ($84/54) and Springbrook National Park ($89/57). Transfer-only prices also available ex-Gold Coast (Tamborine Mountain adult/child $30/20; Lamington National Park $50/20).

Tamborine Mountain

This mountaintop rainforest community – comprising Eagle Heights, North Tamborine and Mt Tamborine – is 45km inland from the

WORTH A TRIP

LAMINGTON NATIONAL PARK

Australia's largest remnant of subtropical rainforest cloaks the deep valleys and steep cliffs of the McPherson Range, reaching elevations of 1100m on the Lamington Plateau. Here, the 200-sq-km Lamington National Park (www.nprsr.qld.gov.au/parks/lamington) is a Unesco World Heritage site and has over 160km of walking trails.

The two most accessible sections of the park are the Binna Burra and Green Mountains sections, both reached via long, narrow, winding roads from Canungra (not great for big campervans). Binna Burra can also be accessed from Nerang.

Sights & Activities

Bushwalks within the park include everything from short jaunts to multiday epics. For experienced hikers, the Gold Coast Hinterland Great Walk is a three-day trip along a 54km path from the Green Mountains section to the Springbrook Plateau. Other favourites include the excellent Tree Top Canopy Walk along a series of rope-and-plank suspension bridges at Green Mountains, and the 21km Border Track that follows the dividing range between NSW and Queensland and links Binna Burra to Green Mountains.

Walking guides are available from the ranger stations (⊙7.30am-4pm Mon-Fri, 9am-3.30pm Sat & Sun) at Binna Burra and Green Mountains.

Sleeping & Eating

Green Mountains Campground (☑13 74 68; www.nprsr.qld.gov.au/parks/lamington/camping.html; site per person/family $5.50/22) There's a tiered national parks camping ground on the left as you head down the hill from O'Reilly's Rainforest Retreat. There are plenty of spots for tents and caravans (and a toilet/shower block); book in advance.

O'Reilly's Rainforest Retreat (☑07-5502 4911, 1800 688 722; www.oreillys.com.au; Lamington National Park Rd, Green Mountains; s/d from $163/278, 1-/2-bedroom villa from $400/435; @☎⊛) This famous 1926 guesthouse has lost its original grandeur but retains a rustic charm – and sensational views! Newer luxury villas and doubles add a contemporary sheen. There are plenty of organised activities, plus a day spa, cafe, bar and restaurant (mains $25 to $40), open for breakfast, lunch and dinner.

Binna Burra Mountain Lodge (☑07-5533 3622, 1300 246 622; www.binnaburralodge.com.au; 1069 Binna Burra Rd, Beechmont; unpowered/powered site $28/35, safari tent from $55, d incl breakfast with/without bathroom $300/190, apt from $295) Stay in the lodge, in rustic log cabins, flashy new apartments or in a tent surrounded by forest in this atmospheric mountain retreat. The central restaurant (mains $20 to $40) serves breakfast, lunch and dinner, or there's a cafe-style Teahouse (mains $14 to $18) a few hundred metres up the road, open 9am to 3pm. Transport available.

Gold Coast, and has cornered the artsy-craftsy, Germanic-kitsch, chocolate/liqueur market in a big way. If this is your bag, Gallery Walk in Eagle Heights is the place to stock up.

◉ Sights & Activities

Tamborine National Park PARK
(www.nprsr.qld.gov.au/parks/tamborine) Queensland's oldest national park comprises 13 sections stretching across the 8km plateau, offering waterfalls and super views of the Gold Coast. Accessed via easy-to-moderate walking trails are Witches Falls, Curtis Falls, Cedar Creek Falls and Cameron Falls. The visitor centre in North Tamborine has maps.

Skywalk WALKING
(☑07-5545 2222; www.rainforestskywalk.com.au; 333 Geissman Dr, North Tamborine; adult/child/family $19.50/9.50/49; ⊙9.30am-4pm) Walk through the rainforest canopy at Skywalk, 30m above the ground. The path descends to the forest floor and leads to Cedar Creek. Look out for rare Richmond Birdwing butterflies.

⌂ Sleeping & Eating

Songbirds Rainforest Retreat HOTEL $$$
(☑07-5545 2563; www.songbirds.com.au; Lot 10, Tamborine Mountain Rd, North Tamborine; villas from $298) The classiest outfit on the hill. Each of the six plush Southeast Asian–inspired villas has a double spa with rainforest views.

St Bernards Hotel
PUB $$

(☑07-5545 1177; www.stbernardshotel.com; 101 Alpine Tce, Mt Tamborine; mains $20-32; ⊘10am-midnight) A woody old mountain pub with a large terrace and sweeping views.

Mt Tamborine Brewery
BREWERY $$

(☑07-5545 2032; www.mtbeer.com; 165 Long Rd, Eagle Heights; lunch mains $18-25; ⊘9.30am-5pm Mon-Thu, to late Fri-Sun) Beer boffins should head straight for this microbrewery for a Rainforest Lager or a tasting tray (four beer samples for $12). There's also a bistro.

❶ Information

Tamborine Mountain Visitor Information Centre (☑07-5545 3200; www.tamborinemt-ncc.org.au; Doughty Park, Main Western Rd, North Tamborine; ⊘10am-4pm Mon-Fri, 9.30am-4pm Sat & Sun) Info on Tamborine National Park.

Springbrook National Park

About a 40-minute drive west of Burleigh Heads, Springbrook National Park (www.nprsr.qld.gov.au/parks/springbrook) is a steep remnant of the Tweed Shield volcano that centred on nearby Mt Warning in NSW more than 20 million years ago. It's a wonderland for hikers; trails through cool-temperate, subtropical and eucalypt forests offer a mosaic of gorges, cliffs and waterfalls.

The park is divided into four sections. The 900m-high Springbrook Plateau section houses the strung-out township of Springbrook along Springbrook Rd, and receives the most visitors: it's laced with waterfalls, trails and eye-popping lookouts. The scenic Natural Bridge section, off the Nerang–Murwillumbah road, has a 1km walking circuit leading to a huge rock arch spanning a water-formed cave – home to a luminous colony of glow-worms. The Mt Cougal section, accessed via Currumbin Creek Rd, has several waterfalls and swimming holes (watch out for submerged logs and slippery rocks); while the forested Numinbah section to the north is the fourth section of the park.

◉ Sights & Activities

Best of All Lookout
LOOKOUT

(Repeater Station Rd, Springbrook) True to its name, the Best of All Lookout offers phenomenal views from the southern edge of the Springbrook Plateau to the lowlands below. The 350m trail from the carpark to the lookout takes you past a clump of gnarled Antarctic beech trees: you'll only find them around here and in northern NSW.

Purling Brook Falls
WATERFALL

(Forestry Rd, Springbrook) Just off Springbrook Rd, the Purling Brook Falls drop a rather astonishing 109m into the rainforest: check them out from the vertigo-inducing lookout.

Canyon Lookout
LOOKOUT

(Canyon Pde, Springbrook) Canyon Lookout affords views through the valley to Surfers Paradise. This is also the start of a 4km circuit walk to Twin Falls, which is part of Springbrook's longest trail, the 17km Warrie Circuit.

Goomoolahra Falls
WATERFALL

(Springbrook Rd, Springbrook) At the end of Springbrook Rd there's a lookout beside the 60m Goomoolahra Falls, with views across the plateau and all the way back to the coast.

🛏 Sleeping & Eating

Settlement Campground
CAMPGROUND $

(☑13 74 68; www.nprsr.qld.gov.au/parks/springbrook/camping.html; 52 Carricks Rd; per person/family $5.50/22) There are 11 grassy sites at this trim camping ground (the only one at Springbrook), which also has toilets and barbecues. Book ahead. The Gold Coast Hinterland Great Walk runs through here.

Mouses House
CHALET $$$

(☑07-5533 5192; www.mouseshouse.com.au; 2807 Springbrook Rd, Springbrook; r from $250, 2 nights from $430; ❄️ 📶) Linked by softly lit boardwalks, these 12 cedar chalets hidden in the misty woods are super-romantic mountain hideaways. Each has a spa and wood fire; breakfast, lunch and dinner hampers available.

Dancing Waters Café
CAFE $

(☑07-5533 5335; www.dancingwaterscafe.com; 33 Forestry Rd, Springbrook; dishes $6-18; ⊘10am-4pm) Next to the Purling Brook Falls car park, this affable tearoom serves healthy salads and light meals (fab toasted chicken sandwiches and homemade scones).

❶ Information

There's an unstaffed **visitor information centre** at the end of Old School Rd in the Springbrook Plateau section of the park, which has park maps.

Noosa &
the Sunshine Coast

Best Places to Eat

➡ Little Humid (p340)

➡ Berardo's (p340)

➡ Bohemian Bungalow (p355)

➡ Mooloolaba Fish Market (p349)

➡ Up Front Club (p356)

Best Places to Stay

➡ Secrets on the Lake (p353)

➡ Islander Noosa Resort (p338)

➡ YHA Halse Lodge (p338)

➡ Glass House Mountains Ecolodge (p343)

➡ Maroochydore Beach Motel (p348)

Why Go?

It's not called the Sunshine Coast for nothing: the 100 golden kilometres stretching from the tip of Bribie Island to the Cooloola Coast are aglow with glimmering coastlines, hot surf spots and a warm populace for whom smiles are de rigueur...and shoes démodé. Stylish Noosa boasts a sophisticated dining and resort scene, while Mooloolaba, with its popular beach, outdoor eateries and cafes, is a long-time favourite with holidaying Australian families.

The ethereal Glass House Mountains loom over the seascape, while further north, the Blackall Range offers a change of scenery with thick forests, lush pastures and quaint villages. The Sunshine Coast is also home to one of the world's great wildlife sanctuaries, the iconic Australia Zoo.

When to Go
Noosa

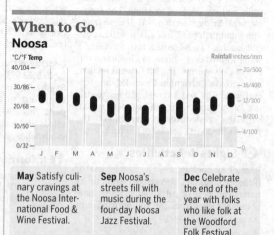

May Satisfy culinary cravings at the Noosa International Food & Wine Festival.

Sep Noosa's streets fill with music during the four-day Noosa Jazz Festival.

Dec Celebrate the end of the year with folks who like folk at the Woodford Folk Festival.

Noosa & the Sunshine Coast Highlights

1. Hiking the coastal track at **Noosa National Park** (p336).

2. Sampling gourmet beach fare in one of Noosa's **swish restaurants** (p338).

3. Surfing, sunning and lapping up the beach-cafe scene in **Mooloolaba** (p346).

4. Visiting the wild critters at **Australia Zoo** (p344).

5. Finding far-out treasures at the **Eumundi markets** (p354).

6. Donning flares, kaftans and wild, new-age hippie chic at the wonderful **Woodford Folk Festival** (p355).

7. Hiking to the summit of Mt Beerwah in the **Glass House Mountains National Park** (p343).

8. Canoeing and exploring the Cooloola Section of the **Great Sandy National Park** (p353).

ⓘ Getting There & Away

AIR

The Sunshine Coast's airport (Sunshine Coast Airport) is at Marcoola, 10km north of Maroochydore and 26km south of Noosa. **Jetstar** (☎13 15 38; www.jetstar.com.au) and **Virgin Blue** (☎13 67 89; www.virginblue.com.au) have daily flights from Sydney and Melbourne. **Tiger Airways** (☎03-9034 3733; www.tigerairways.com) has less frequent flights from Melbourne.

BUS

Greyhound Australia (☎1300 473 946; www.greyhound.com.au) has several daily services from Brisbane to Caloundra ($17, two hours), Maroochydore ($20, two hours) and Noosa ($22, 2½ hours). **Premier Motor Service** (☎13 34 10; www.premierms.com.au) also services Maroochydore and Noosa from Brisbane.

ⓘ Getting Around

Several companies offer transfers from the Sunshine Coast Airport and Brisbane to points along the coast. Fares from Brisbane cost $40 to $50 for adults and $20 to $25 for children. From Sunshine Coast Airport fares are around $20 to $30 per adult and $7 to $15 per child.

Sunbus (☎13 12 30; www.sunbus.com.au) buzzes frequently between Caloundra and Noosa, and has regular buses from Noosa to the train station at Nambour ($7, one hour) via Eumundi.

Col's Airport Shuttle (☎07-5450 5933; www.airshuttle.com.au)

Henry's (☎07-5474 0199; www.henrys.com.au)

Sun-Air Bus Service (☎07-5477 0888; www.sunair.com.au)

NOOSA

POP 14,000

Noosa is a swanky resort town with a stunning natural landscape of crystalline beaches and tropical rainforests. Designer boutiques and swish restaurants draw beach-elite sophisticates, but the beach and bush are still free, so glammed-up fashionistas simply share the beat with thongs, boardshorts and bronzed bikini bods baring their bits.

Noosa is undeniably developed but its low-impact condos and chichi landscape have been cultivated without losing sight of simple seaside pleasures. On long weekends and school holidays, however, bustling Hastings St becomes a slow-moving file of traffic.

The area has an amazing number of roundabouts and it's easy to get lost. Broadly speaking, Noosa encompasses three zones: Noosa Heads (around Laguna Bay and Hastings St), Noosaville (along the Noosa River) and Noosa Junction (the administrative centre).

◉ Sights

One of Noosa's best features, the lovely **Noosa National Park** (Map p339; www.noosanationalpark.com/), covering the headland, has fine walks, great coastal scenery and a string of bays with waves that draw surfers from all over the country. The most scenic way to access the national park is to follow the boardwalk along the coast from town. Sleepy koalas are often spotted in the trees near Tea Tree Bay and dolphins are commonly seen from the rocky headlands around Alexandria Bay, an informal nudist beach on the eastern side. Pick up a walking track map from the **Noosa National Park Information Centre** (☎07-5447 3522; ◉9.15am-4.45pm) at the entrance to the park.

For a panoramic view of the park, walk or drive up to **Laguna Lookout** from Viewland Dr in Noosa Junction.

The passage of the Noosa River that cuts into the **Great Sandy National Park** is poetically known as the 'river of mirrors' or the **Everglades**. It's a great place to launch a kayak and camp in one of the many **national park camping grounds** (www.nprsr.qld.gov.au; per person/family $5.45/21.80) along the riverbank.

🏃 Activities

Surfing & Water Sports

With a string of breaks around an unspoilt national park, Noosa is a fine place to catch a wave. Generally the waves are best in December and January but Sunshine Corner, at the northern end of Sunshine Beach, has an excellent year-round break, although it has a brutal beach dump. The point breaks around the headland only perform during the summer, but when they do, expect wild conditions and good walls at Boiling Point and Tea Tree on the northern coast of the headland. There are also gentler breaks on Noosa Spit at the far end of Hastings St, where most of the surf schools do their training.

Kite-surfers will find conditions at the river mouth and Lake Weyba are best between October and January, but on windy days the Noosa River is a playground for serious daredevils.

Merrick's Learn to Surf
SURFING

(☑0418 787 577; www.learntosurf.com.au; 2hr lesson $60; ☺9am & 1.30pm) Holds one-, three- and five-day surfing programs.

Adventure Sports Noosa
KITE-SURFING

(Map p341; ☑07-5455 6677; www.kitesurfaustralia. com.au; 203 Gympie Tce, Noosaville; kite-surfing 2½hr lesson $250) Also hires kayaks ($35 per half-day) and bikes ($19 for two hours).

Go Ride A Wave
SURFING

(☑1300 132 441; www.gorideawave.com.au; 2hr lesson $65, 2hr surfboard hire $25) Lessons and hire.

Noosa Stand Up Paddle
WATER SPORTS

(☑0423 869 962; www.noosastanduppaddle.com. au; Group SUP lesson $55; ☺lessons 9am, 11am, 1pm, 3pm) Learn stand-up paddling.

Noosa Longboards
SURFING

(Map p339; ☑07-5447 2828; www.noosalong-boards.com; 2/55 Hastings St, Noosa Heads; 2hr surfing lesson $60, surfboard hire from $40) Private and group lessons.

Canoeing & Kayaking

The Noosa River is excellent for canoeing; it's possible to follow it up through Lakes Cooroi-bah and Cootharaba and through the Cooloola Section of Great Sandy National Park.

Noosa Ocean Kayak Tours
KAYAKING

(☑0418 787 577; www.noosakayaktours.com; 2hr tour $66, kayak hire per day $55) Tours around Noosa National Park and along the Noosa River.

Kayak Noosa
KAYAKING

(Map p341; ☑07-5455 5651; www.kayaknoosa.com; 194 Gympie Tce, Noosaville; 2hr sunset kayak $55, half-/full-day guided kayak tour $90/145) Tours around Noosa National Park. Also hires out kayaks ($45 for two hours).

Adventure Activities

Noosa Ocean Rider
BOATING

(Map p341; ☑0438 386 255; www.oceanrider.com. au; Jetty 17, 248 Gympie Tce, Noosaville ; 1hr per person/family $70/$250) Thrills and spills on a very fast and powerful speedboat.

Bike On Australia
MOUNTAIN BIKING

(Map p339; ☑07-5474 3322; www.bikeon.com. au; tour from $80, bike hire per day $25) Hosts a variety of tours, including beach biking, self-guided and adventurous eco-jaunts.

Cruises

Gondolas of Noosa
BOATING

(Map p339; ☑0412 929 369; www.gondolasof-noosa.com) Romantic day or moonlit cruises along the Noosa River leave from the Shera-ton Jetty. Prices start from $150 for an hour.

Noosa Ferry
CRUISE

(Map p339; ☑07-5449 8442; per person $20) This ferry service has informative 90-minute round-trip cruises that run to Tewantin from the Sheraton Jetty. Book ahead for the two-hour Biosphere Reserve cruise ($45).

Horse Riding

Noosa Horse Riding
HORSE RIDING

(☑0438 710 530; www.noosahorseriding.com. au; Eumarella Rd, Lake Weyba; 1/2hr ride $65/95) Horse rides around (and in) Lake Weyba and the surrounding bush.

☞ Tours

Fraser Island
Adventure Tours
ADVENTURE TOUR

(☑07-5444 6957; www.fraserislandadventuretours. com.au; day tour from $145) Popular day trips to Eli Creek and Lake McKenzie pack as much punch as a two-day tour.

Discovery Group
DRIVING TOUR

(☑07-5449 0393; www.thediscoverygroup.com.au; day tour adult/child $175/120) Visit Fraser Is-land in a big black 4WD truck on tours that include a guided rainforest walk at Central Station and visits to Lakes Birrabeen and McKenzie. Also offers afternoon river cruis-es through the Everglades (from $79).

Offbeat Ecotours
ECOTOUR

(☑1300 023 835; www.offbeattours.com.au; day tour adult/child $155/100) Spirited day trips into the magnificent Noosa Hinterland with waterfall swimming, intimate encounters with ancient flora and a gourmet lunch.

★ Festivals & Events

Noosa Festival of Surfing
SURFING

(www.noosafestivalofsurfing.com/) A week of longboard action in March.

Noosa International Food & Wine Festival
FOOD, WINE

(www.noosafoodandwine.com.au) A three-day tribute to all manner of gastronomic de-lights, held each May.

Noosa Long Weekend FOOD, FASHION
(www.noosalongweekend.com) Ten-day festival of arts, culture, food and fashion in June/July.

Noosa Jazz Festival JAZZ
(www.noosajazz.com.au) Four-day event in early September.

🛏 Sleeping

Accommodation prices can rise between 50% and 100% in peak season. During these times most places require a minimum two- or three-night stay. Low-season rates are quoted.

For an extensive list of short-term holiday rentals, try Accom Noosa (Map p339; ✆07-5447 3444; www.accomnoosa.com.au; Shop 5/41 Hastings St, Noosa Heads).

★**YHA Halse Lodge** HOSTEL $
(Map p339; ✆07-5447 3377; www.halselodge.com.au; 2 Halse Lane; members/non-members dm $29/32, d $78/96; @🛜) This splendid colonial-era timber Queenslander is a legendary stop-over on the backpacker trail, and well worth the clamber up its steep drive. There are three- and six-bed dorms, doubles and a lovely wide verandah. The bar is a mix-and-meet bonanza and serves great meals ($10 to $15). Close to the Main Beach action.

Nomads Backpackers HOSTEL $
(Map p339; ✆07-5447 3355; www.nomadshostels.com; 44 Noosa Dr; dm from $26; @🛜🏊) One of the Nomad chain, this hostel has the usual trademarks: popular bar, central location and whoo-hoo atmosphere. You can't get less than an eight-bed dorm, but you'll be partying so hard it won't matter. If you remember to eat, Nomads do $5 meals that aren't as hideous as you might expect.

Noosa River Holiday Park CARAVAN PARK $
(Map p341; ✆07-5449 7050; www.sunshinecoastholidayparks.com; 4 Russell St; unpowered/powered site $34/42; 🛜) In a lovely spot on the banks of the Noosa River, this park has the closest camping facilities to Noosa. Keep in mind that they do so love their rules and regulations here.

Anchor Motel Noosa MOTEL $$
(Map p341; ✆07-5449 8055; www.anchormotelnoosa.com.au; 223 Weyba Rd; r from $120; ❄🛜🏊) Ship-shape rooms with plenty of space and the porthole windows requisite for a marine-themed establishment. Unlike many motels,

this is a social place, with guests mixing by the pool.

Noosa River Retreat APARTMENT $$
(Map p341; ✆07-5474 2811; www.noosariverretreat.com; 243 Weyba Rd; studios from $120; ❄@🛜🏊) Your buck goes a long way at this orderly complex with spick, span and spacious units. There's a central barbecue and laundry, and the corner spots are almost entirely protected by small, native gardens; traffic can be noisy in other units.

Noosa Sun Motel APARTMENT $$
(Map p341; ✆07-5474 0477; www.noosasunmotel.com.au; 131 Gympie Tce, Noosaville; r $130-220; ❄@🛜🏊) Uninspiring from the outside, but what lies within is most unexpected: modern, spacious and surprisingly stylish apartments replete with kitchenettes, free wi-fi and water views (cheaper units overlook the garden). Within walking distance of loads of eateries and shops.

Noosa Parade Holiday Inn APARTMENT $$
(Map p339; ✆07-5447 4177; www.noosaparadeholidayinn.com; 51 Noosa Pde; r from $110; ❄🛜🏊) The apartments are looking a little faded, but they're clean and comfortable, and a mere stroll from the treats of Hastings St.

Islander Noosa Resort RESORT $$$
(Map p341; ✆07-5440 9200; www.islandernoosa.com.au; 187 Gympie Tce; 2-/3-bedroom villas $210/260; ❄@🛜🏊) Set on 4 acres of tropical gardens, with a central tropical pool and wooden boardwalks meandering through the trees, this resort is excellent value. It's bright and cheerful and packs a cocktail-swilling, island-resort ambience that sits well with poolside idlers and families alike. The onsite Moondoggy's Cafe-Bar (open from 7am to 6pm) is famous for its breakfasts.

Emerald APARTMENT $$$
(Map p339; ✆07-5449 6100; www.emeraldnoosa.com.au; 42 Hastings St; 2-bedroom apt from $270; ❄@🛜🏊) The stylish Emerald has indulgent rooms bathed in ethereal white and sunlight. Expect clean, crisp edges and exquisite furnishings. All apartments are fully self-contained, but ask for a balcony with a view.

🍴 Eating

Noosa prides itself on being a foodie destination, with global and local flavours on offer everywhere from fine restaurants to

Noosa Heads

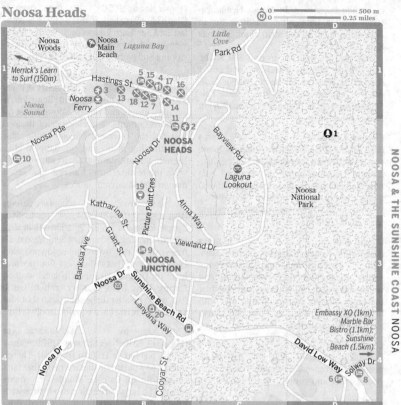

Noosa Heads

◎ Sights
1 Noosa National Park D2

⊕ Activities, Courses & Tours
2 Bike On Australia B2
Gondolas of Noosa .... (see 3)
3 Noosa Ferry B1
4 Noosa Longboards B1

⊜ Sleeping
5 Accom Noosa B1
6 Chez Noosa D4
7 Emerald B1
8 Flashpackers D4
9 Nomads Backpackers B3
10 Noosa Parade Holiday Inn A2
11 YHA Halse Lodge B2

⊗ Eating
12 Aromas B1

13 Bay Village Shopping Centre
Food Court B1
14 Berardo's B1
15 Bistro C B1
Cafe Le Monde .... (see 14)
Gaston .... (see 14)
Laguna Bakery .... (see 15)
16 Massimo's B1
17 Noosa Heads SLSC B1
18 Zachary's B1

⊜ Drinking & Nightlife
KB's .... (see 9)
19 Reef Hotel B2

⊜ Shopping
20 Noosa Fair Shopping Centre B3

ⓘ Information
Noosa Visitor Centre .... (see 17)
Palm Tree Tours .... (see 13)

beachside takeaways. In Noosa Heads, eateries clutter happening Hastings St; in Noosaville, head to the strip along Thomas St or Gibson St.

You can eat well for around $10 at the Bay Village Shopping Centre food court (Map p339; Hastings St, Noosa Heads). Self-caterers can stock up at the Noosa Fair Shopping Centre (Map p339; Lanyana Way) in Noosa Junction.

Elegant Eggplant   CAFE $
(Map p341; ☑07-5474 2776; www.eleganteggplant. com.au; 185 Gympie Tce, Noosaville; $9-15; ☺7am-2.30pm) Delicious takes on standard cafe fare (sangas, salads, ginormous breakfasts) using mostly local, organic ingredients. Wash it down with a smoothie or refreshing fresh juice cocktail.

Burger Bar   BURGERS $
(Map p341; 4 Thomas St; burgers $10-15; ☺11am-9pm; ⋰) This informal and quirky venue whips up hormone-free, vegetarian, and weird and wonderful between-bun delights; the lamb burgers (especially the one with brie cheese, lime slaw, and piccalilli sauce) are particularly divine.

Laguna Bakery   BAKERY $
(Map p339; ☑07-5447 2606; 3/49 Hastings St; pastries $2.50, coffee $3) Friendly bakery with strong coffee and yummy pastries to go.

Massimo's   GELATI $
(Map p339; 75 Hastings St; gelati $2-6; ☺9am-10pm) Definitely one of the best *gelaterias* in Queensland.

★Little Humid   MODERN AUSTRALIAN $$
(Map p341; ☑07-5449 9755; www.humid.com.au; 2/235 Gympie Tce, Noosaville; mains from $25; ☺lunch Wed-Sun noon-2pm, dinner Tue-Sun from 6pm) Extremely popular eatery that many locals regard as the best in town. It lives up to the hype, with toothsome treats including crispy-skin confit duck leg, sticky-pork belly with calamari, and creative vegie options. Definitely book ahead.

Aromas   CAFE $$
(Map p339; 32 Hastings St; breakfast $15-26, mains $13-36; ☺7am-11pm) This European-style cafe is unashamedly ostentatious, with chandeliers, faux-marble tables and cane chairs deliberately facing the street so patrons can see and be seen. There's the usual array of panini, cakes and light meals, but most folk come for the coffee and the atmosphere.

Noosa Heads SLSC   INTERNATIONAL $$
(Map p339; 69 Hastings St; mains $12-33; ☺breakfast Sat & Sun, lunch & dinner daily) Perfect beach views from the deck make for idyllic beer-sipping and (very good) pub-food chomping.

Berardo's   MODERN AUSTRALIAN $$$
(Map p339; ☑07-5447 5666; 52 Hastings St; mains $30-42; ☺from 6pm) Beautiful Berardo's is culinary utopia and one of Noosa's most famous restaurants. The elegance of its food matches the surrounds, an all-white affair with tinkling piano and sun-dappled chic. Ingredients are almost all locally-sourced, with interesting little touches like green mango and sugarcane sauces.

Thomas Corner   MODERN AUSTRALIAN $$
(Map p341; ☑07-5470 2224; cnr Thomas St & Gympie Tce; mains $16-33; ☺11.30am-11pm Mon-Fri, 9am-11pm Sat, 8.30am-11pm Sun) Casual alfresco diner run by locally-renowned chef David Rayner that's short on flourish and huge on flavour. All kinds of local seafood feature here, from spanner crab to cuttle fish, while meatier dishes like lamb shoulder and wagyu brisket are equally droolworthy.

Cafe Le Monde   MODERN AUSTRALIAN $$
(Map p339; 52 Hastings St; mains $15-39; ☺6am-9.30pm Sun-Thu, to 11.30pm Fri & Sat) There's not a fussy palate or dietary need that isn't catered for on Cafe Le Monde's enormous menu. The large, open-air patio buzzes with diners digging into burgers, seared tuna steaks, curries, pastas, salads and plenty more. Come for daily happy-hour drinks between 4pm and 6pm.

Zachary's   PIZZERIA $$
(Map p339; ☑07-5447 3211; www.zacharys.com.au; Upper Level, 30 Hastings St, Noosa Heads; pizzas from $16.50; ☺noon-late) Award-winning local stayer dishing up pizzas like Hoisin duck and 'posh chicken' (with cranberries and camembert), and all the classic faves. They also have a surprisingly extensive cocktail list; it's a great place to kick off a night on the town.

Gaston   MODERN AUSTRALIAN $$
(Map p339; 5/50 Hastings St; mains $17-25; ☺7am-midnight) Unpretentious, but with a menu that's up there with the best of them, Gaston is a (beautiful-) people-watching paradise. Gawk at the passing parade over superb-value lunch specials ($17 for a main and a drink) or dinner deals ($50 for two mains and a bottle of wine).

Noosaville

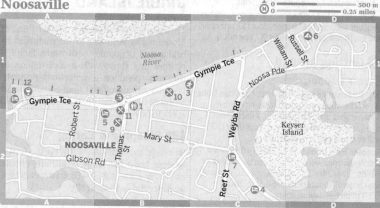

Noosaville

Activities, Courses & Tours
1 Adventure Sports Noosa B1
2 Kayak Noosa B1
3 Noosa Ocean Rider B1

Sleeping
4 Anchor Motel Noosa.............................C2
5 Islander Noosa Resort.......................... B2
6 Noosa River Holiday Park D1
7 Noosa River Retreat C2

8 Noosa Sun Motel...................................A1

Eating
9 Burger Bar B2
Elegant Eggplant ....(see 5)
10 Little Humid B1
11 Thomas Corner B2

Drinking & Nightlife
12 Noosa Yacht Club...................................A1

Bistro C MODERN AUSTRALIAN **$$**
(Map p339; ☑07-5447 2855; Hastings St; On the Beach Resort; mains $19-40; ⊙7.30am-11.30pm) The menu at this beachfront brasserie is an eclectic and delectable blend of everything that seems like a good idea at the time. The legendary egg-fried calamari is always a hit; for breakfast, do not go past the corn-and-chive griddle cake with bacon, spinach and avocado salsa ($22).

🍺 Drinking

KB's BAR
(Map p339; 44 Noosa Dr, Noosa Junction; ⊙5pm-midnight) Noosa's backpackers and other free spirits start their nightly revelries at this popular hostel bar (attached to Nomads Backpackers). Live rock fills every crevice several nights a week.

Noosa Yacht Club YACHT CLUB
(Map p341; Gympie Tce; ⊙10am-late Mon-Sat, 8am-late Sun) Everything you'd expect from a yacht club: cheap grog, water views and sociable salts.

Reef Hotel PUB
(Map p339; ☑07-5430 7500; 19 Noosa Dr; ⊙11am-midnight Sun-Thu, to 3am Fri & Sat) A little on the soulless side, decor-wise, but live music and cold bevvies make it all okay.

ℹ Information

Noosa Visitor Centre (Map p339; ☑07-5430 5000; www.visitnoosa.com.au; 61 Hastings St, Noosa Heads; ⊙9am-5pm)

Palm Tree Tours (Map p339; ☑07-5474 9166; www.palmtreetours.com.au; Bay Village Shopping Centre, Hastings St; ⊙9am-5pm) Very helpful tour desk that's been on the scene for over 20 years. Can book tours, accommodation and bus tickets.

Post Office (Map p339; 91 Noosa Dr)

ℹ Getting There & Away

Long-distance bus services stop at the Noosa Junction station on Sunshine Beach Rd. **Greyhound Australia** (☑1300 473 946; www.greyhound.com.au) has several daily bus connections from Brisbane ($22, 2½ hours) while **Premier Motor Service** (☑13 34 10; www.premierms.com.au) has one ($23, 2½ hours).

Most hostels have courtesy pick-ups.

Sunbus (☑13 12 30; www.sunbus.com.au) has frequent services to Maroochydore ($7, one hour) and the Nambour train station ($7, one hour).

ⓘ Getting Around

BICYCLE & SCOOTER

Bike On Australia (p337) rents out bicycles from several locations in Noosa including Nomads Backpackers and Flashpackers. Alternatively, bikes are delivered to and from your door ($35 or free if booking is over $100).

Scooter Hire Noosa (☑07-5455 4096; www. scooterhirenoosa.com; 13 Noosa Dr , Noosa Heads ; 2/4/24hr $35/45/59; ⊙8.30am-5pm) Big range of scooters from 50cc to 300cc in fun 'I'm on holiday!' colours.

BOAT

Noosa Ferry (Map p339; ☑07-5449 8442; www.noosaferry.com; Noosa Marina, Tewantin; one way adult/child/family $14/5/35, all-day pass $20/6/49) operates ferries between Noosa Heads and Tewantin every 30 minutes.

BUS

Sunbus has local services that link Noosa Heads, Noosaville, Noosa Junction and Tewantin.

CAR

All the big car-rental brands can be found in Noosa, or go with the locals at **Noosa Car Rentals** (☑0429 053 728; www.noosacarrentals.com.au). Car rentals in town start at about $50 per day.

BRIBIE ISLAND

POP 17,057

This slender island at the northern end of Moreton Bay is linked to the mainland by bridge and is popular with young families, retirees and those with a cool million or three to spend on a waterfront property. It's far more developed than Stradbroke or Moreton Islands, but there are still secluded spots to be found.

🛏 Sleeping & Eating

Bribie Island National Park on the north-western coast has some beautifully remote **camping areas** (☑13 74 68; www.nprsr.qld.gov. au; person/family $5.45/21.80).

Sylvan Beach Resort   RESORT **$$**
(☑07-3408 8300; www.sylvanbeachresort.com. au; 21-27 Sylvan Beach Esplanade; d from $175; ❊@🛜🌊) Cool and spacious beachside two- and three-bedroom units that all come with private balconies.

On The Beach Resort   APARTMENT **$$$**
(☑07-3400 1400; www.onthebeachresort.com. au; 9 North St, Woorim; 2-/3-bedroom apt from $205/275; ❊🌊) Weird building, stunning views. Out-luxes anything else on the is-land with superb service and great facili-ties including a saltwater pool and huge sundeck.

BIG THINGS OF THE SUNSHINE COAST

Fans of kitsch (and gigantism) will adore Australia's (in)famous Big Things. Hulking in offbeat nooks and along lonely highways across the country, these wonderfully bad-taste monuments honour everything from bananas to boxing crocs in supersized nov-elty architecture. The Big Thing craze kicked off in the 1960s...and it shows, with many of them rusting and teetering in glorious abandonment. While every state in Australia has at least one Big Thing, there's an unusually high concentration of the gaudy goliaths dotted around the Sunshine Coast. Keen on a quirky quest? You won't have to look too hard to find the looming likes of...

The Big Pineapple Arguably the most famous of Queensland's Big Things; in Woombye, near Nambour. One of the few Big Things that you can go inside.

The Big Macadamia Nut Happily crumbling away in the shadow of the Big Pineapple; Woombye.

The Big Cow Looming awkwardly over Yandina, in the Sunshine Coast Hinterland.

The Big Mower Woe betide the grass that sprouts near this 7m-high monster; in Beer-wah, not far from Australia Zoo.

The Big Pelican We dare you not to giggle at this guy's ginormous, goofball grin; in Noosaville on the Noosa River.

The Big Shell Frightful conch from the 1960s guarding a 'tropical lifestyle' store in Te-wantin, Noosa.

UNEXPECTED TREASURE: ABBEY MUSEUM

The impressive art and archaeology collection in the Abbey Museum (☑ 07-5495 1652; www.abbeymuseum.com; 63 The Abbey Pl, Caboolture, off Old Toorbul Point Rd; adult/child/family $8.80/5/19.80; ⊙ 10am-4pm Mon-Sat) spans the globe and would be at home in any of the world's famous museums. Once the private collection of Englishman John Ward, the pieces include neolithic tools, medieval manuscripts and even an ancient Greek footguard (one of only four worldwide), and will have you scratching your head in amazement. The church has more original stained glass from Winchester Cathedral than what is actually left in the cathedral. In June/July, make merry at Australia's largest medieval festival, held on the grounds.

The Abbey Museum is on the road to Bribie Island, 6km from the Bruce Hwy turn-off, where you'll find the Caboolture Warplane Museum (☑ 07-5499 1144; www.cabooolturewarplanemuseum.com; McNaught Rd, Hangar 104, Caboolture Airfield; adult/child/family $10/5/20; ⊙ 9am-3pm), with its collection of restored WWII warplanes, all in flying order.

Bribie Island SLSC AUSTRALIAN $$
(☑ 07-3408 2141; www.thesurfclubbribieisland.com.au; First Ave, Woorim; mains $14-29; ⊙ 10am-10pm) Sit on the deck and shovel in some good pub grub. Be there between noon and 3pm (from 11.30am weekends) for filling, tasty lunch specials ($14).

ⓘ Information

There is no 4WD hire on Bribie, and you'll need a **4WD permit** ($41.75 per week) to access the island's more off-track spots. Pick one up at **Gateway Bait & Tackle** (☑ 07-5497 5253; www.gatewaybaitandtackle.com.au; 1383 Bribie Island Rd, Ningi; ⊙ 5.30am-5.30pm Mon-Fri, 4.30am-6pm Sat, 4.30am-5pm Sun) or online (www.nprsr.qld.gov.au).

Bribie Island Visitor Information Centre (☑ 07-3408 9026; www.bribie.com.au; Benabrow Ave, Bellara; ⊙ 9am-4pm) Pick up 4WD maps and heaps of info.

ⓘ Getting There & Away

Frequent Citytrain services run from Brisbane to Caboolture from where **Bribie Island Coaches** (www.bribiecoaches.com.au) connects to Bribie Island; regular Brisbane Translink fares apply (one-way $13.90).

GLASS HOUSE MOUNTAINS

The volcanic crags of the Glass House Mountains rise abruptly from the subtropical plains 20km northwest of Caboolture. In Dreaming legend, these rocky peaks belong to a family of mountain spirits. It's worth diverting off the Bruce Hwy onto the slower Steve Irwin Way to snake your way through dense pine forests and green pastureland for a close-up view of these spectacular volcanic plugs.

The Glass House Mountains National Park is broken into several sections (all within cooee of Beerwah) with picnic grounds and lookouts but no camping grounds. The peaks are reached by a series of sealed and unsealed roads that head inland from Steve Irwin Way.

◉ Sights & Activities

A number of signposted walking tracks reach several of the peaks, but be prepared for some steep and rocky trails. Mt Beerwah (556m) is the most trafficked but has a section of open rock face that may increase the anxiety factor. The walk up Ngungun (253m) is more moderate and the views are just as sensational, while Tibrogargan (364m) is probably the best climb with a challenging scramble and several amazing lookouts from the flat summit. Rock climbers can usually be seen scaling Tibrogargan, Ngungun and Beerwah. Mt Coonowrin (aka 'crook-neck'), the most dramatic of the volcanic plugs, is closed to the public.

QPWS has compiled a list of organisations that offer eco-accredited tours of the Glass House Mountains; see www.nprsr.qld.gov.au/parks/glass-house-mountains/touroperators.html.

⌂ Sleeping & Eating

★ **Glass House Mountains Ecolodge** LODGE $$
(☑ 07-5493 0008; www.glasshouseecolodge.com; 198 Barrs Rd; r $112-185) ✈ This novel retreat overseen by a keen environmentalist is close

NOOSA & THE SUNSHINE COAST GLASS HOUSE MOUNTAINS

to Australia Zoo and offers a range of good-value sleeping options, including the cosy Orchard Room ($112) and the converted Church Loft ($175), each with polished floorboards and tremendous views of Mt Tibrogargan. Pick-ups available from Glass House Mountains station.

Glass on Glasshouse
B&B $$$

(☑ 07-5496 9608; www.glassonglasshouse.com.au; 182 Glasshouse-Woodford Rd; cottages from $295) Luxury woodsy cottages that live up to their name with floor-to-ceiling glass walls; the views to Mt Beerwah and Mt Coonowrin are gasp-inducing. Pampering touches like spa baths, fireplaces and free breakfasts make temper tantrums inevitable when it's time to leave.

Glasshouse Mountains Tavern
PUB $$

(10 Reed St, Glass House Mountains; mains $15-30; ☺ 10am-9pm Sun-Thu, to midnight Fri & Sat) The 'Glassy' cooks up good pub nosh. The open fire keeps things cosy during winter and a peppering of outdoor seating is great for a midday middy on sunny days.

CALOUNDRA

POP 20,220

Straddling a headland at the southern end of the Sunshine Coast, Caloundra is slowly shedding its retirement-village image without losing its sleepy seaside charm. Excellent fishing in Pumicestone Passage (the snake of water separating Bribie Island from the mainland) and a number of pleasant surf beaches make it a popular holiday resort for families and water-sports fans.

◉ Sights & Activities

Caloundra's beaches curve around the headland so you'll always find a sheltered beach no matter how windy it gets. Bulcock Beach, just down from the main street and pinched by the northern tip of Bribie Island, captures a good wind tunnel, making it popular with kite-surfers. There's a lovely promenade on the foreshore that extends around to Kings Beach, where there's a kiddie-friendly interactive water feature and a free saltwater swimming pool on the rocks. The coastal track continues around the headland towards Currimundi. Depending on the conditions, Moffat Beach and Dickey Beach have the best surf breaks.

Queensland Air Museum
MUSEUM

(☑ 07-5492 5930; www.qam.com.au; Caloundra Airport; adult/child/family $13/7/30; ☺ 10am-4pm) Plenty of planes to keep budding aviators happy for hours.

Caloundra Surf School
SURFING

(☑ 0413 381 010; www.caloundrasurfschool.com; lessons per person from $45) The pick of the surf schools, with board hire also available.

Blue Water Kayak Tours
KAYAKING

(☑ 07-5494 7789; www.bluewaterkayaktours.com; half-/full-day tours min 4 people $90/150, twilight tour $55) Energetic kayak tours across the channel to the northern tip of Bribie Island National Park.

Caloundra Cruise
CRUISE

(☑ 07-5492 8280; www.caloundracruise.com; Maloja Jetty; adult/child/family $20/10/52) Cruises (90 minutes) on a 1930s-style boat into Pumicestone Passage.

DON'T MISS

CREATURE FEATURE: AUSTRALIA ZOO

Just north of Beerwah is one of Queensland's, if not Australia's, most famous tourist attractions. Australia Zoo (☑ 07-5436 2000; www.australiazoo.com.au; Steve Irwin Way, Beerwah; adult/child/family $59/35/172; ☺ 9am-5pm) is a fitting homage to its founder, zany wildlife enthusiast, Steve Irwin. As well as all things slimy and scaly, the zoo has an amazing wildlife menagerie complete with a Cambodian-style Tiger Temple, the Asian-themed Elephantasia and the famous Crocoseum. There are macaws, birds of prey, giant tortoises, snakes, otters, camels and more crocs and critters than you can poke a stick at. Plan to spend a full day at this amazing wildlife park.

Various companies offer tours from Brisbane and the Sunshine Coast. The zoo operates a bus ($5) from towns along the coast, and a free bus from the Beerwah train station (bookings essential; see website).

Caloundra

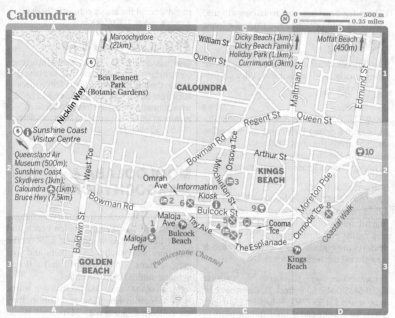

Sunshine Coast Skydivers SKYDIVING
(☑ 07-5437 0211; www.sunshinecoastskydivers.
com.au; Caloundra Airport; tandem jumps from
$249) Let your eyelids flap over stunning
views of Caloundra from a brain-squeezing
15,000ft.

🛏 Sleeping

There's often a minimum three- to five-night
stay in high season.

Caloundra Backpackers HOSTEL $
(☑ 07-5499 7655; www.caloundrabackpackers.com.
au; 84 Omrah Ave; dm/d $28/70; @ 🎧) Caloun-
dra's only hostel, this is a no-nonsense
budget option with a sociable courtyard,
book exchange, and BBQ and pizza nights.
Dorms aren't thrilling, but they're clean and
peaceful.

**Dicky Beach Family
Holiday Park** CARAVAN PARK $
(☑ 07-5491 3342; www.sunshinecoastholiday-
parks.com.au; 4 Beerburrum St; unpowered/pow-
ered site $37/41, cabin from $105; ❋🎧🏊) You
can't get any closer to Dicky, one of Caloundra's most popular beaches. The brick cabins are as ordered and tidy as the grounds
and there's a small swimming pool for the
kids.

Caloundra

City Centre Motel MOTEL $$
(☑ 07-5491 3301; www.caloundracitycentremo-
tel.com.au; 20 Orsova Tce; s/d/f $85/120/145;
🅿❋🎧) The closest motel to the city centre
holds no surprises. It's a small complex and
the rooms, although basic, are comfortable.

Rumba Resort RESORT $$$
(☑ 07-5492 0555; www.rumbaresort.com.au; 10
Leeding Tce; r from $240) This sparkling, resort-
white five-star playground is ultra trendy for

Caloundra. Staff are positively buoyant and the rooms and pool area live up to the hype.

✗ Eating

The Bulcock Beach esplanade is dotted with alfresco cafes and restaurants, all with perfect sea views.

Jow Noodles   ASIAN $
(☑07-5437 0072; 105-111 Bulcock St; mains $10-18; ☺lunch & dinner) Fresh and spicy noodles straight from the wok. It doesn't look like much, but the clattering kitchen and swarm of hungry traffic lends a fun atmosphere.

Saltwater at Kings   CAFE $$
(☑07-5437 2260; 8 Levuka Ave, Kings Beach; mains $21-38; ☺8am-11pm) Oooh er! Saltwater's playful menu offers 'sexy salads', 'voluptuous' mains and 'little teasers'. The orgasmic desserts are equally saucy. Perfect for lunch straight off the beach.

Jerome's Family Restaurant   ITALIAN $$
(☑07-5438 0445; 50 Bulcock St, Centrepoint Arcade; mains $14.50-27.50; ☺Tues-Fri 10am-9pm, 5-9pm Sat & Mon) Old-school Italian joint in homey surrounds and a hearty, dependable menu with all the favourites: pizza, pastas, steaks and seafood. Nothing cutting-edge, but its traditional feel is what makes it a local favourite.

La Dolce Vita   ITALIAN $$
(☑07-5438 2377; 10 Leeding Tce, Rumba Resort; mains $20-38; ☺7am-10pm Mon-Fri, 6.30am-11pm Sat & Sun) This modern Italian restaurant has a stylish black-and-white theme but it's best to sit outdoors behind the large glass-windowed booth for alfresco dining with gorgeous sea views.

☕ Drinking & Nightlife

CBX   PUB
(12 Bulcock St; ☺10am-midnight Sun-Thu, to 2am Fri & Sat) Live bands and DJs on weekends; pub meals available.

Kings Beach Tavern   PUB
(www.kingsbeachtavern.com.au; 43 Burgess St, Kings Beach; ☺10am-midnight Sun-Thu, to 2am Fri & Sat) Beer! Bistro meals! The decor is mod-soulless, but the pub does host loads of Aussie alternative musical acts; check website for gig guide.

ℹ Information

Sunshine Coast Visitor Centre (☑07-5478 2233; 7 Caloundra Rd; ☺9am-5pm) On the

roundabout at the town's entrance; there's another one at 77 Bulcock St.

ℹ Getting There & Away

Greyhound (☑1300 473 946; www.greyhound.com.au) buses from Brisbane ($17, two hours) stop at the **bus terminal** (Cooma Tce), a block back from Bulcock Beach. **Sunbus** (☑13 12 30; www.sunbus.com.au) has frequent services to Noosa ($8.20, 1½ hours) via Maroochydore ($4.60, 50 minutes).

MOOLOOLABA & MAROOCHYDORE

POP 11,064 & 16,757

Mooloolaba has seduced many a sea-changer with its sublime climate, golden beach and cruisy lifestyle. Take a morning walk on the foreshore and you'll find walkers and joggers, suntans and surfboards, and a dozen genuine smiles before breakfast.

Mooloolaba and Maroochydore, along with Alexandra Headland and Cotton Tree, are collectively known as 'Maroochy'. While Maroochydore takes care of the business end, Mooloolaba steals the show. Eateries, boutiques and pockets of resorts and apartments have spread along the Esplanade, transforming this once-humble fishing village into one of Queensland's most popular holiday destinations.

◎ Sights & Activities

There are good surf breaks along the strip – one of Queensland's best for longboarders is the **Bluff**, the prominent point at Alexandra Headland. **Pincushion** near the Maroochy River mouth can provide an excellent break in the winter offshore winds.

Diving to the wreck of the sunken warship, the **ex-HMAS Brisbane**, is also incredibly popular. Sunk in July 2005, the wreck lies in 28m of water and its funnels are only 4m below the surface.

Underwater World   AQUARIUM
(Map p347; ☑07-5458 6280; www.underwaterworld.com.au; The Wharf, Mooloolaba; adult/child/family $35/23/96; ☺9am-5pm) This is Queensland's largest tropical oceanarium, where you can swim with seals, dive with sharks or simply marvel at the ocean life outside the 80m-long transparent underwater tunnel. There's a touch tank, live shows and educational spiels to entertain both kids and adults.

Mooloolaba

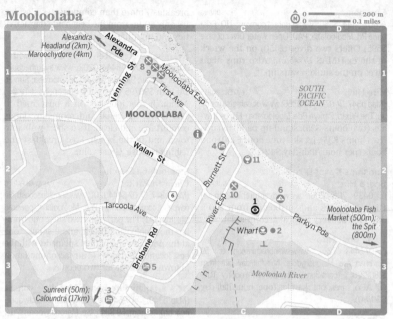

Mooloolaba

◎ Sights
1 Underwater World C2

☉ Activities, Courses & Tours
2 Canal Cruise C3
  Coastal Cruises .... (see 2)
  Hire Hut .... (see 2)
  Scuba World .... (see 2)
  Whale One .... (see 2)

⊜ Sleeping
3 Kyamba Court Motel B3
4 Landmark Resort C2
5 Mooloolaba Beach Backpackers B3

6 Mooloolaba Beach Caravan Park C2

⊗ Eating
7 Bella Venezia B1
8 Karma Waters B1
9 Lot 104 .... B1
10 Thai Seasons C2

☉ Drinking & Nightlife
11 Mooloolaba SLSC C2

⊛ Entertainment
  Club WT .... (see 2)

Big Pineapple   LANDMARK
(www.bigpineapple.com.au; 76 Nambour Connection Rd, Woombye) FREE Just 10km west of Maroochydore lies (OK, sprouts) the 16m-high Big Pineapple, possibly the most iconic of all Queensland's Big Things (see p342). You can climb it, shop in its shadow (markets every Saturday from 6.30am to 1pm), or toot around it on a little train.

Scuba World   DIVING
(Map p347; ☏ 1300 677 094; www.scubaworld.com.au; Mooloolaba Harbour (next to Underwater World); dives from $119; ☉ 9am-5pm Mon-Sat, 10am-4pm Sun) Arranges shark dives (certified/uncerti-fied divers $195/245) at Underwater World, coral dives off the coast and a wreck dive of the *Brisbane*. PADI courses available.

**Robbie Sherwell's XL
Surfing Academy**   SURFING
(☏ 07-5478 1337; www.robbiesherwell.com.au; 1hr lesson private/group $95/45) Dip a toe into Aussie surf culture at this long-established school.

Suncoast Kiteboarding   KITE-BOARDING
(☏ 0422 079 106; www.suncoastkiteboarding.com.au; 2hr lesson $180) At Cotton Tree, Noosa and Caloundra.

Sunreef
DIVING

(☏07-5444 5656; www.sunreef.com.au; 110 Brisbane Rd, Mooloolaba; PADI Open Water Diver course $595) Offers two dives ($150) on the wreck of the ex-HMAS *Brisbane*. Also runs night dives on the sunken warship.

Hire Hut
WATER SPORTS

(Map p347; ☏07-5444 0366; www.oceanjetski.com.au; The Wharf, Parkyn Pde, Mooloolaba) Hires kayaks (two hours $25), stand-up paddleboards (two hours $35), jet skis (one hour $150) and boats (per hour/half-day $42/75).

Sunshine Coast Bike & Board Hire
SURFING

(☏0439 706 206; www.adventurehire.com.au) Hires out bikes and surfboards from $30 a day. Free delivery to local accommodation.

Swan Boat Hire
BOATING

(☏07-5443 7225; www.swanboathire.com.au; 59 Bradman Ave, Maroochydore; half-/full-day hire from $180/270; ⊙6am-6pm) On the Maroochy River. Also hires out kayaks (one hour/half-day $20/80).

☞ Tours

Whale One
WHALE WATCHING

(Map p347; ☏1800 942 531; www.whaleone.com.au; The Wharf, Mooloolaba; adult/child/family $119/79/320) Whale-watching cruises between June and November.

Canal Cruise
BOAT TOUR

(Map p347; ☏07-5444 7477; www.mooloolabacanalcruise.com.au; The Wharf, Mooloolaba; adult/child/family $18/6/45; ⊙11am, 1pm & 2.30pm) These boat trips cruise past the McMansions preening beside the Mooloolah River.

Coastal Cruises
BOAT TOUR

(Map p347; ☏0419 704 797; www.cruisemooloolaba.com.au; The Wharf, Mooloolaba) Sunset ($25) and seafood lunch cruises ($35) through Mooloolaba Harbour, River and canals.

🛏 Sleeping

During school holidays, rates can double and most places require a minimum two- or three-night stay.

Mooloolaba Beach Backpackers
HOSTEL $

(Map p347; ☏07-5444 3399; www.mooloolababackpackers.com; 75 Brisbane Rd, Mooloolaba; dm/d $29/70; @🛜🌊) Some dorms have en suites, and although the rooms are a little drab, the amount of freebies (bikes, kayaks, surfboards, stand-up paddleboards and

breakfast) more than compensates. Besides, it's only 500m from the beachside day activities and nightlife.

Kyamba Court Motel
MOTEL $

(Map p347; ☏07-5444 0202; www.kyambacourtmotel.com.au; 94 Brisbane Rd, Mooloolaba; Sun-Fri s/d from $90/95, weekend tariffs apply; ❋🛜🌊) Although this motel is on a busy road, it also fronts the canal and rooms are large, comfortable and clean. It's a short walk into town and to the beach. Free breakfast and fishing rod use. Great value.

Mooloolaba Beach Caravan Park
CARAVAN PARK $

(Map p347; ☏07-5444 1201; www.sunshinecoastholidayparks.com.au; Parkyn Pde, Mooloolaba; powered site from $41) The park runs two sites; one fronting the Mooloolaba Beach, and a smaller one at the northern end of the Esplanade, with the best location and views of any accommodation in town. Prices are for two people.

★ Maroochydore Beach Motel
MOTEL $$

(Map p349; ☏07-5443 7355; www.maroochydorebeachmotel.com; 69 Sixth Ave, Maroochydore; s/d/f from $115/130/170; P❋@🌊) You've gotta love a theme motel, especially one as snazzy and spotless this one. There are 18 different rooms, including the Elvis Room (natch), the Egyptian Room and the Aussie room. The owners are lovely and helpful, and it's just 50m to the beach.

Maroochy River Resort
BUNGALOW $$

(☏07-5448 4911; www.maroochyriverbungalows.com.au; 38-46 David Low Way, Maroochydore; 1-/2-bedroom bungalows from $120/150) About 5km out from the centre of town, this natty collection of bungalows sits right on Eudlo Creek, a calm waterway where you can kayak, stand-up paddle and canoe (all equipment available to rent from the resort). The bungalows are welcoming, and have sweet locations either tucked within the resort gardens or right on the water's edge. Superlative value that just gets better the longer your stay.

Landmark Resort
RESORT $$

(Map p347; ☏07-5444 5555; www.landmarkresort.com.au; 11 Burnett St, Mooloolaba; studio/1-bedroom apt from $170/230; ❋@🛜🌊) Nothing compares to the ocean views from these breezy self-contained apartments. The resort sits above Mooloolaba's trendy eateries and is only 30m from the beach. There's a heated lagoon-style pool and a rooftop spa and barbecue.

Maroochydore

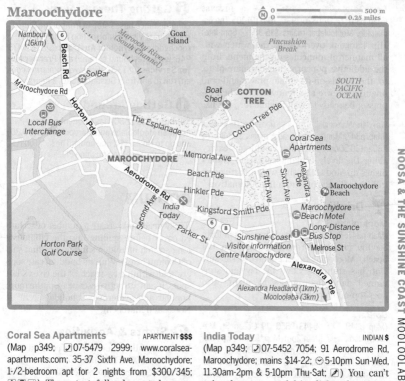

Coral Sea Apartments APARTMENT **$$$**
(Map p349; ☏07-5479 2999; www.coralsea-apartments.com; 35-37 Sixth Ave, Maroochydore; 1-/2-bedroom apt for 2 nights from $300/345; ✳@☒) These tastefully decorated apartments occupy a lovely spot close to Maroochy Surf Club and the beach. Balconies are big, breezy and have ocean views.

✗ Eating

★**Mooloolaba Fish Market** SEAFOOD **$**
(Lot 201, Parkyn Pde, Mooloolaba; fish & chips from $10, seafood platters $55; ⊙7am-8pm) This splashy, stinky and altogether atmospheric fish market is home to a variety of restaurants and takeaways all selling the freshest of fresh seafood (what else?) at a miscellany of prices.

Thai Seasons THAI **$**
(Map p347; ☏07-5444 4611; 10 River Esplanade, Mooloolaba; mains $10-15; ⊙6-10pm) It's affectionately known as 'dirty Thai', but don't be put off by the plastic outdoor setting and grubby exterior; this unpretentious restaurant dishes out the very best Thai food in town. If it's crowded, order takeaway and head for the picnic tables overlooking Mooloolaba's main beach.

India Today INDIAN **$**
(Map p349; ☏07-5452 7054; 91 Aerodrome Rd, Maroochydore; mains $14-22; ⊙5-10pm Sun-Wed, 11.30am-2pm & 5-10pm Thu-Sat; ☑) You can't miss the masses of fairy lights decorating this restaurant on Maroochydore's main drag. The menu is equally jazzy, with a humongous range of Indian favourites and lip-smacking regional specialties; there's also a very extensive vegetarian menu.

Bella Venezia ITALIAN **$$**
(Map p347; ☏07-5444 5844; 95 Esplanade, Mooloolaba; mains $25-42; ⊙noon-late) This understated, casually chic restaurant, with an all-Italian wine bar, spreads across an arcade cul-de-sac. The menu is high-end Oz-Italo and includes exquisite dishes such as Moreton Bay bug spaghetti.

Boat Shed SEAFOOD **$$**
(Map p349; ☏07-5443 3808; Esplanade, Cotton Tree; mains $21-37; ⊙9am-11.30pm Mon-Sat, to 5pm Sun) A shabby-chic gem on the banks of the Maroochy River, great for sunset drinks beneath the sprawling cotton tree. Seafood is the star of the menu; after dinner, roll back to the outdoor lounges for dessert and some seriously romantic stargazing.

Lot 104
FUSION **$$**

(Map p347; ☑07-5326 1990; 104/101-105 The Esplanade, Mooloolaba; mains $15-30; ☺6pm-late) Hip hangout overlooking the water with all manner of munchies on the menu, from the addictive popcorn chicken share-plate, to the hands-off-it's-mine prawn-and-crab linguini. They're also renowned for their espresso; be ready to wait a while for your fix.

Karma Waters
MODERN AUSTRALIAN **$$**

(Map p347; Mantra, Esplanade; mains $23-34; ☺7.30am-10.30pm) Another outdoor eatery along the lively esplanade, Karma Waters dishes up Mod Oz cuisine with a Portuguese influence. Loads of gluten-free alternatives.

🍷 Drinking

Mooloolaba SLSC
SURF CLUB

(Map p347; Esplanade, Mooloolaba; ☺10am-10pm Sun-Thu, to midnight Fri & Sat) Right on the beach, Mooloolaba's true-blue Aussie surf club has stunning views by day and suntanned dance-floor antics by night. Also does top-notch pub grub.

SolBar
CLUB

(Map p349; ☑07-5443 9550; 19 Ocean St, Maroochydore; ☺7.30am-2pm Mon & Tue, 7.30am-2pm & 5pm-1am Wed & Thu, 7.30am-3am Fri, 5pm-3am Sat, 2pm-1am Sun) SolBar is a godsend for city-starved indie fans. A constantly surprising line-up takes to the stages here, while punters enjoy an array of international beers and a less-surfy atmosphere than most other joints in town.

Club WT
CLUB

(Map p347; Wharf, Mooloolaba; ☺10am-3am Thu-Sat) It's loud, tacky and incredibly popular with backpackers and locals. Inside the otherwise family-friendly Wharf Tavern.

ℹ️ Information

The Mooloolaba Esplanade seamlessly morphs into Alexandra Pde along the beachfront at Alexandra Headland ('Alex' to the locals), then flows into Aerodrome Rd and the main CBD of Maroochydore. Cotton Tree is at the mouth of the Maroochy River.

Sunshine Coast Visitor Information Centre (Map p347; ☑1300 847 481; www.visitsunshinecoast.com.au; cnr Brisbane Rd & First Ave, Mooloolaba; ☺9am-5pm) Also has other branches throughout the region: Maroochydore (Map p349; cnr Sixth Ave & Melrose St; ☺9am-4pm); Sunshine Coast Airport (Marcoola; ☺airport hours)

ℹ️ Getting There & Away

Long-distance buses stop in front of the Sunshine Coast Visitor Information Centre in Maroochydore. **Greyhound Australia** (☑1300 473 946; www.greyhound.com.au) and **Premier Motor Services** (☑13 34 10; www.premierms.com.au) run to and from Brisbane ($20, 2 hours).

ℹ️ Getting Around

Sunbus (☑13 12 30) has frequent services between Mooloolaba and Maroochydore ($3.30) and on to Noosa ($7, one hour). The local bus interchange is at the Sunshine Plaza.

COOLUM

POP 7905

Rocky headlands create a number of secluded coves before spilling into the fabulously long stretch of golden sand and rolling surf of Coolum beach. With its budding cafe society, and within easy reach of the coast's hot spots, it's an attractive escape from the more popular and overcrowded holiday scene at Noosa and Maroochy.

👁️ Sights & Activities

For outstanding views of the coast, a hike to the top of Mt Coolum, south of town, is worth the sweat factor. Get all the details at the visitor centre (www.visitsunshinecoast.com.au; David Low Way, Coolum; ☺9am-3pm).

Coolum Surf School
SURFING

(☑0438 731 503; www.coolumsurfschool.com.au; 2hr lesson $55, 5-day package $200) Coolum Surf School will have you riding the waves in no time; they also hire out surfboards/bodyboards ($50/25 for 24 hours).

Skydive Ramblers
SKYDIVING

(☑07-5448 8877; www.skydiveforfun.com; jump from 6000/15,000ft $299/429) Skydive Ramblers will throw you out of a plane at a ridiculous height. Savour the coastal view before a spectacular beach landing.

🛏️ Sleeping

Villa Coolum
MOTEL **$**

(☑07-5446 1286; www.villacoolum.com; 102 Coolum Tce, Coolum Beach; r $89-99; ☀) Hidden behind a leafy verandah, these modest, good-value bungalows have spacious motel-style rooms; there's a large pool, and a pleasant garden to stroll through.

Coolum Beach Caravan Park CARAVAN PARK $

(☑07-5446 1474; 1827 David Low Way, Coolum; unpowered/powered site $37/41, cabin from $130) Location, location: the park not only has absolute beach frontage, but is also just across the road from Coolum's main strip.

Beach Retreat APARTMENT $$

(☑07-5471 7700; www.beachretreatcoolum.com; 1750 David Low Way, Coolum; d from $180-250; ✱@🛜🏊) With ocean views and within walking distance of the esplanade eateries, these spacious apartments are in a great spot. The central pool area is handy for rough beach weather. Rates get better the longer you stay.

✕ Eating

Coolum's esplanade has sprouted a string of outdoor cafes and restaurants. It's fun to wander along the strip before deciding where to eat.

My Place INTERNATIONAL $$

(☑07-5446 4433; 1768 David Low Way, Coolum; mains $17-26; ⊙7am-11pm) Opposite the boardwalk and boasting sensational ocean views, My Place can't be beaten for sunset cocktails, shared meze plates or summer alfresco dining.

Sunrise CAFE $$

(☑07-5471 7477; 1748 David Low Way; mains $16-28; ⊙Wed-Sun 7am-9pm) A cafe that goes above and beyond the usual snackery, with scrumptious mains including crispy-skin salmon in chilli jam and mussels dripping with garlic and cream. The beachfront views are easy to swallow, too.

Castro's Bar & Restaurant ITALIAN $$

(☑07-5471 7555; cnr Frank St & Beach Rd; mains $19-30; ⊙5pm-late) Not even vaguely Cuban, but this popular spot does enjoy a FIdel-like longevity thanks to imaginative wood-fired pizzas and mains including salmon risotto and big-serve pasta classics.

PEREGIAN & SUNSHINE BEACH

POP 3519 & 2298

Fifteen kilometres of uncrowded, unobstructed beach stretch north from Coolum to Sunshine Beach and the rocky northeast headland of Noosa National Park.

Peregian is the place to indulge in long solitary beach walks, to surf the excellent breaks and take in fresh air and plenty of sunshine; it's not uncommon to see whales breaking offshore.

A little further north, the laidback latte ethos of **Sunshine Beach** attracts Noosa locals escaping the summer hordes. Beach walks morph into bush trails over the headland; a stroll through the **Noosa National Park** takes an hour to reach Alexandria Bay and two hours to Noosa's Laguna Bay. Road access to the park is from McAnally Dr or Parkedge Rd.

🛏 Sleeping

Flashpackers HOSTEL $

(Map p339; ☑07-5455 4088; www.flashpackers-noosa.com; 102 Pacific Ave, Sunshine Beach; dm from $27, girls' dorm $34, d from $70, includes breakfast; ✱🛜🏊) Flashpackers challenges the notion of hostels as flea-bitten dives, with pristine dorm rooms and an airy tropical design. Thoughtful touches include full-length mirrors, ample wall sockets, free surfboard use and complimentary Friday night sausage sizzle.

Chez Noosa MOTEL $$

(Map p339; ☑07-5447 2027; www.cheznoosa.com. au; 263 Edwards St, Sunshine Beach; standard/deluxe unit from $110/120; ✱@🛜🏊) Right by Noosa National Park and set in aptly bushy gardens, the Chez is fantastic value for money. The self-contained units are basic but cute, and there's a heated pool and spa with an undercover BBQ area.

Peregian Court Resort APARTMENT $$

(☑07-5448 1622; www.peregiancourt.com; 380 David Low Way, Peregian Beach; 1/2 bedroom apt from $115/160, 2-night min stay; ✱🛜🏊) It's just a minute's walk to the beach from these clean, airy and altogether comfy resort-style apartments. Each has a fully-equipped kitchen, but the onsite, seabreezy BBQ area encourages alfresco feasting.

✕ Eating & Drinking

Baked Poetry Cafe CAFE $

(218 David Low Way, Peregian Beach Shopping Centre; dishes $10-16; ⊙9am-5pm Mon-Fri, to 4pm Sat & Sun) This minibakery and cafe is a local institution, known for great coffee and German sourdough bread. Try the *eier im glas*, a soft-boiled egg in a glass alongside a plate of bacon, grilled tomato and cheese.

Marble Bar Bistro BAR

(40 Duke St, Sunshine Beach; tapas $10-18.50; ⊙noon-late) Kick back in a cushioned lounge or perch yourself at one of the marble benches at this cruisy cocktail and tapas bar.

Embassy XO CHINESE $$

(☑07-5455 4460; 56 Duke St, Sunshine Beach; mains $25-39; ⊙5-10pm Tue-Sun) This chic, ambient restaurant is *not* your suburban Chinese takeaway. Dive right in with the exquisite banquet (from $55 per person) or weekend yum cha, or linger over the inventive menu with a Chinese beer or Shanghai Mule.

COOLOOLA COAST

Stretching for 50km between Noosa and Rainbow Beach, the Cooloola Coast is a remote strip of long sandy beach backed by the Cooloola Section of the Great Sandy National Park. Although it's undeveloped, the 4WD and tin-boat set flock here in droves so it's not always as peaceful as you might imagine. If you head off on foot or by canoe along the many inlets and waterways, however, you'll soon escape the crowds.

From the end of Moorindil St in Tewantin, the Noosa North Shore Ferry (☑07-5447 1321; www.noosacarferries.com; one way per pedestrian/car $1/6; ⊙5.30am-10.20pm Sun-Thu, 5am-12.20am Fri & Sat) shuttles across the river to Noosa North Shore. If you have a 4WD, you can drive along the beach to Rainbow Beach (and on up to Inskip Point to the Fraser Island ferry), but you'll need a permit (www.nprsr.qld.gov.au; per day/week/month $11/27.70/43.60). You can also buy a permit from the QPWS office (240 Moorindil St, Tewantin). Check the tide times!

On the way up the beach, you'll pass the Teewah coloured sand cliffs, estimated to be about 40,000 years old.

Lake Cooroibah

A couple of kilometres north of Tewantin, the Noosa River widens into Lake Cooroibah, which is surrounded by lush bushland. If you take the Noosa North Shore Ferry, you can drive up to the lake in a conventional vehicle and camp along sections of the beach.

⚡ Activities

Camel Company CAMEL RIDING

(☑0408 710 530; www.camelcompany.com.au; Beach Rd, Tewantin; safari adult/child from $60/45) Beach and bush safaris on board your very own dromedary.

Noosa Equathon HORSE RIDING

(☑07-5474 2665; www.equathon.com; Beach Rd, Noosa North Shore; 2hr beach ride $175) Intimate horse rides led by triple Olympian Alex Watson. Also runs overnight rides, starting at $350 per person.

🛏 Sleeping

Gagaju Bush Camp HOSTEL $

(☑07-5474 3522; http://gagaju.tripod.com; 118 Johns Rd, Tewantin; dm $15; @) The refreshingly feral Gagaju Bush Camp is a riverside eco-wilderness camp with basic dorms constructed out of recycled timber. There's a somewhat hands-off managerial approach, unless a good party is involved! Don't forget to bring food and mozzie repellent. A courtesy shuttle runs to and from Noosa twice a day.

Noosa North Shore Retreat RETREAT $

(☑07-5447 1225; www.noosanorthshoreretreat.com.au; Beach Rd; unpowered/powered site from $20/30, cabin/r from $75/145; ❋@☒) They've got everything here, from camping and vinyl 'village tents' to shiny motel rooms and cottages. Ditch your bags, then head out for a paddle around the lake, a bushwalk or a bounce on the jumping pillow. The retreat also houses the Great Sandy Bar & Restaurant, open weekends for lunch and dinner (mains $15 to $25).

Lake Cootharaba & Boreen Point

Cootharaba is the biggest lake in the Cooloola Section of Great Sandy National Park, measuring about 5km across and 10km in length. On the western shores of the lake and at the southern edge of the national park, Boreen Point is a relaxed little community with several places to stay and to eat. The lake is the gateway to the Noosa Everglades, offering bushwalking, canoeing and bush camping.

From Boreen Point, an unsealed road leads another 5km to Elanda Point.

MONTVILLE & KENILWORTH

It's hard to imagine that the chintzy mountain village of Montville with its fudge emporiums, Devonshire tearooms and cottage crafts began life under the dramatic name of Razorback – until you arrive at the town's spectacular ridge-top location 500m above sea level. To work off that excess fudge, take a rainforest hike to Kondalilla Falls in Kondalilla National Park, 3km northwest of town. After a refreshing swim, check for leeches!

Secrets on the Lake (☑07-5478 5888; www.secretsonthelake.com.au; 207 Narrows Rd; midweek/weekend from $205/255; ❋) is a romantic hideaway where boardwalks through the foliage lead to magical, wooden treehouses with sunken spas, log fires and stunning views of Lake Baroon.

From Montville, head to the tiny village of Mapleton and turn left on the Obi Obi Rd. After 18km, you reach Kenilworth, a small country town in the pretty Mary River Valley. Kenilworth Country Foods (☑07-5446 0144; www.kenilworthcountryfoods.com.au; 45 Charles St; ☺9am-4pm Mon-Fri, 10am-3pm Sat & Sun) is a boutique cheese factory with creamy yoghurt and wickedly good cheese. If you plan to camp in the Kenilworth State Forest or Conondale National Park you'll need a permit (☑13 74 68; www.nprsr.qld.gov.au; per person $5.45). The Kenilworth Showgrounds has camping (no permit required) for $15 per vehicle, with power, water and $1 showers.

Otherwise, head northeast on the Eumundi–Kenilworth Rd for a scenic drive through rolling pastureland dotted with traditional old farmhouses and floods of jacarandas. After 30km you reach the Bruce Hwy near Eumundi.

🏃 Activities

Kanu Kapers
KAYAKING
(☑07-5485 3328; www.kanukapersaustralia.com; 11 Toolara St, Boreen Point; half-/full-day guided tour $155/185, 1-day self-guided tour $75) Paddle into the placid Everglades.

Discovery Group Canoe Safari
BOATING
(☑07-5449 0393; www.thediscoverygroup.com.au; 3-day/2-night self-guided canoeing safari $155) Canoe and camp your way down the Everglades over three days. They also run afternoon cruises on-board a purpose-built boat ($79).

🛏 Sleeping & Eating

Lake Cootharaba Motel
MOTEL $
(☑07-5485 3127; www.cootharabamotel.com; 75 Laguna St, Boreen Point; r $95-130; ❋) A quaint and tidy spot that's less motel than lakeside retreat, this is a great base for visiting the Everglades or simply splashing about on Cootharaba. There are only five rooms; be sure to book ahead.

Boreen Point Camping Ground
CAMPGROUND $
(☑07-5485 3244; Esplanade, Boreen Point; unpowered/powered site $22/28) On the river, this quiet, simple camping ground is dominated by large gums and native bush.

Apollonian Hotel
PUB $
(☑07-5485 3100; 19 Laguna St, Boreen Point; mains $12-30; ☺10am-midnight) This is a gorgeous old pub with sturdy timber walls, shady verandahs and a beautifully preserved interior. The pub grub is tasty and popular. Plan to be there (and do book ahead) for the famous Sunday spit-roast lunch.

Great Sandy National Park: Cooloola Section

The Cooloola Section of Great Sandy National Park covers more than 54,000 hectares from Lake Cootharaba north to Rainbow Beach. It's a varied wilderness area with long sandy beaches, mangrove-lined waterways, forest, heath and lakes, all featuring plentiful bird life, including rarities such as the red goshawk and the grass owl, and lots of wildflowers in spring.

The Cooloola Way, from Tewantin up to Rainbow Beach, is open to 4WD vehicles unless there's been heavy rain – check the situation with the rangers before you set out. Most people prefer to bomb up the beach, though you're restricted to a few hours either side of low tide. You'll need

WORTH A TRIP

THE MAJESTIC

About 10km northwest of Eumundi, the little village of Pomona sits in the shadow of looming Mt Cooroora (440m) and is home to the wonderful Majestic Theatre (☑ 07-5485 2330; www.majestictheatre.com.au; 3 Factory St, Pomona; ticket $15, meal deal $27; ⊙ screening 7.30pm Tue-Fri), billed as the only authentic silent movie theatre in the world. It's one of the only places where you can see a silent movie accompanied by the original Wurlitzer organ soundtrack. They've been screening the iconic *The Son of the Sheikh* (first Thursday of each month) for the last 25 years!

a permit (www.nprsr.qld.gov.au; per day/week/month $11/27.70/43.60).

The best way to see Cooloola is by boat or canoe along the numerous tributaries of the Noosa River. Boats can be hired from Tewantin and Noosa (along Gympie Tce), Boreen Point and Elanda Point on Lake Cootharaba.

There are some fantastic walking trails starting from Elanda Point on the shore of Lake Cootharaba, including the 46km Cooloola Wilderness Trail to Rainbow Beach and a 7km trail to an unstaffed QPWS information centre at Kinaba.

The QPWS Great Sandy Information Centre (☑ 07-5449 7792; 240 Moorindil St, Tewantin; ⊙ 8am-4pm) can provide information on park access, tide times and fire bans within the park. The centre also issues car and camping permits for both Fraser Island and the Great Sandy National Park, but these are best booked online at www.nprsr.qld.gov.au.

The park has a number of camping grounds (☑ 13 74 68; www.nprsr.qld.gov.au; per person/family $5.45/21.80), many of them along the river. The most popular (and best-equipped) camping grounds are Fig Tree Point (at the northern end of Lake Cootharaba), Harry's Hut (about 4km upstream) and Freshwater (about 6km south of Double Island Point) on the coast. You can also camp at designated zones on the beach if you're driving up to Rainbow Beach. Apart from Harry's Hut, Freshwater and Teewah Beach, all sites are accessible by hiking or river only.

EUMUNDI

POP 1790

Sweet little Eumundi is a quaint highland village with a quirky New Age vibe greatly amplified during its famous market days.

The historic streetscape blends well with modern cafes, artsy boutiques, silversmiths and crafty folk doing their thing. Once you've breathed Eumundi air, don't be surprised if you feel a sudden urge to take up beading or body painting.

⊙ Sights & Activities

★ Eumundi Markets   MARKET
(80 Memorial Dr; ⊙ 8am-1.30pm Wed, 7am-2pm Sat) The Eumundi markets attract thousands of visitors to their 300-plus stalls and have everything from hand-crafted furniture and jewellery to homemade clothes and alternative healing booths. Local produce and hot meals also go down a right treat.

Tina Cooper Glass   GALLERY
(www.tinacoopergallery.com; 93 Memorial Dr; ⊙ 9am-4pm Wed & Sat, 10am-3pm Fri & Sun) Beautiful glass sculptures and other works of art are on display here. Often has in-shop glassblowing exhibitions.

Murra Wolka Creations   GALLERY
(☑ 07-5442 8691; www.murrawolka.com; 39 Memorial Dr; ⊙ 9am-4.30pm Mon-Fri) Buy boomerangs and didgeridoos hand-painted by Indigenous artists at this Aboriginal-owned-and-operated gallery.

🛏 Sleeping & Eating

Hidden Valley B&B   B&B $$
(☑ 07-5442 8685; www.eumundibed.com; 39 Caplick Way; r $175-195; ⊛ ⊠) This not-so-hidden retreat is on 1.5 hectares of land, only 400m from Eumundi on the Noosa road. Inside this attractive Queenslander, you can choose a themed room to match your mood: Aladdin's Cave, the Emperor Suite or the Hinterland Retreat.

Harmony Hill Station   B&B $$
(☑ 07-5442 8685; www.eumundibed.com; 81 Seib Rd; carriage $155; ⊠) Perched on a hilltop in a 5-hectare property, this restored and fully

self-contained 1912 purple railway carriage is the perfect place to relax or romance. Share the grounds with grazing kangaroos, watch the sunset from Lover's Leap, share a bottle of wine beneath a stunning night sky...or even get married (the owners are celebrants!).

Joe's Waterhole   PUB $
(☏07-5442 8144; www.liveatjoes.com; 85 Memorial Dr; meals $10; ☺10am-9pm Sun-Thu, to 11.30pm Fri & Sat) Pub grub and heaps of local/international music acts in down-home, knees-up surrounds.

Bohemian Bungalow   INTERNATIONAL $$
(☏07-5442 8679; www.bohemianbungalow.com.au; 69 Memorial Dr; mains $19-30; ☺8am-3pm & 5.30-9pm Thu-Sat, 8am-3pm Wed & Sun) Whimsical fare in this gorgeous white Queenslander includes hearty mains with oddball names like 'Flying South for the Winter' (homemade gnocchi with confit duck) and share plates like 'This Little Piggy Went to Paris' (pâté, pâté, pâté). They also whip up lovely coffees, gourmet pizzas and fine brekkies.

Imperial Hotel   PUB $$
(☏07-5442 8811; Memorial Dr; mains $16-32; ☺10am-7pm Mon & Tue, to 9pm Wed, to 11pm Thu-Sat, to 6pm Sun) This utterly gorgeous colonial-style pub serves up fine favourites (steak, local seafood) on back-in-time verandahs and classy dining rooms. Also has great beers on tap and live music.

ⓘ Information

Discover Eumundi Heritage & Visitor Centre (☏07-5442 8762; Memorial Dr; ☺10am-4pm Mon-Fri, 9am-3pm Sat, 10am-2pm Sun) Also houses the museum (admission free).

ⓘ Getting There & Away

Sunbus (☏13 12 30; www.sunbus.com.au) runs hourly from Noosa Heads ($4.50, 45 minutes) and Nambour ($5.90, 40 minutes). A number of tour operators visit the Eumundi markets on Wednesdays and Saturdays.

SUNSHINE COAST HINTERLAND

Inland from Nambour, the Blackall Range forms a stunning backdrop to the Sunshine Coast's popular beaches a short 50km away. A relaxed half- or full-day circuit drive from the coast follows a winding road along the razorback line of the escarpment, passing through quaint mountain villages and offering spectacular views of the coastal lowlands. The villages (some suffering from an overdose of kitschy craft shops and Devonshire tearooms) are worth a visit, but the real attraction is the landscape, with its lush green pastures and softly folded valleys and ridges, and the waterfalls, swimming holes, rainforests and walks in the national parks. Cosy cabins and B&Bs are popular weekend retreats, especially during winter.

ⓖ Tours

Plenty of tour companies operate through the hinterland and will pick up from anywhere along the Sunshine Coast.

Storeyline Tours   TOUR
(☏07-5474 1500; www.storeylinetours.com.au; from $25) Runs small-group tours to the Eumundi Markets (Wednesdays and Saturdays, from $25) and various Hinterland villages.

WOODSTOCK DOWN UNDER

The famous Woodford Folk Festival (www.woodfordfolkfestival.com) features a huge diversity of over 2000 national and international performers playing folk, traditional Irish, Indigenous and world music, as well as buskers, belly dancers, craft markets, visual-arts performances, environmental talks and Tibetan monks. The festival is held on a property near the town of Woodford from 27 December to 1 January each year. Camping grounds are set up onsite with toilets, showers and a range of foodie marquees, but prepare for a mud bath if it rains. The festival is licensed so leave your booze at home. Tickets cost around $133 per day ($163 with camping) and can be bought online, at the gate or the festival office (☏07-5496 1066). Check online for updated programs.

Woodford is 35km northwest of Caboolture. Shuttle buses run regularly from the Caboolture train station to and from the festival grounds.

Boomerang Tours TOUR
([✓]1300 287 626) Organises personalised tours of the Hinterland, taking in national parks, waterfalls and the Eumundi Markets. Includes sausage-sizzle lunch.

Maleny

POP 3442

Perched high in the rolling green hills of the Blackall Range, Maleny is an intriguing melange of artists, musicians and creative souls, the ageing hippie scene, rural 'tree-changers' and co-op ventures. Its bohemian edge underscores a thriving commercial township that has moved on from its timber and dairy past without yielding (much) to the tacky heritage developments and ye olde tourist-trap shoppes of nearby mountain villages. The town has a strong community and is heavily into all matters green.

Sights & Activities

Mary Cairncross Scenic Reserve OUTDOORS
(www.mary-cairncross.com.au; 148 Mountain View Rd) Mary Cairncross Scenic Reserve is a lovely rainforest shelter spread over 55 hectares just out of town. Walking tracks snake through the rainforest and there's a healthy population of bird life and unbearably cute pademelons.

Maleny Dairies TOUR
([✓]07-5494 2392; www.malenydairies.com; 70 McCarthy Rd; $9; ⊙10.30am & 2.30pm Mon-Sat) Cute dairy tours that take in the milking pit, a handmilking demonstration, factory gawk and baby-calf-petting-fest; you get to sample the in-house delights at the end.

Sleeping

Morning Star Motel MOTEL $
([✓]07-5494 2944; www.morningstarmotel.com; 2 Panorama Pl; r $88-110) The rooms at this comfortable and clean motel have outstanding coastal views and deluxe suites have spas. Wheelchair accessible.

Maleny Lodge B&B $$
([✓]07-5494 2370; www.malenylodge.com.au; 58 Maple St; r from $159-260; [📶][❄]) This B&B is a gracious 1905 residence with cushy, four-poster beds and lashings of stained wood and antiques. There's an open fire for cold winter days and an open pool house for warm summer ones. Prices include cooked breakfast.

Maleny Tropical Retreat B&B $$$
([✓]07-5435 2113; www.malenytropicalretreat.com; 540 Maleny Montville Rd; cabin from $210, r from $235-275) Leafy and private, this is definitely one for the romantics. Choose between a self-contained cabin with fireplace and spa, or one of three luxurious B&B rooms with private verandahs and exquisite mountain views. There's a two-night minimum stay on weekends; breakfast is included.

Eating

Maple St is chockas with cafes, restaurants and cute little eating/drinking nooks. Almost everything everywhere will be organic, sustainable and sensitive to allergy and ethical concerns.

Up Front Club CAFE $
([✓]07-5494 2592; 31 Maple St; dishes $12-26; ⊙7.30am-10pm) This cosy co-op cafe injects funk by the bucketful into Maleny's main strip, with organic breads, dahl, tofu and even something for the carnivores. Live music on the weekends includes reggae, folk and spontaneous jam-a-thons.

Monica's Cafe CAFE $
(11/43 Maple St; mains $8.50-20; ⊙7am-4pm Mon-Fri, 7.30am-2am Sat & Sun) Ever-changing blackboard specials boast hearty dishes and innovative salads. Sit outside to rubberneck at the fascinating parade, take a seat indoors at the long wooden table or clomp upstairs to the more private mezzanine.

Sweets on Maple DESSERTS $
(39 Maple St; home-made fudge 100g from $5; ⊙9.30am-4.30pm Mon-Fri, 10am-3.30pm Sat & Sun) There are a lot of ye olde lolly shops in this neck of the woods, but Sweets on Maple licks them all. The old-fashioned sweets parlour lures in passer-bys with the crazy-making smell of fresh-baking fudge, and keeps them there with flavours including chocolate chilli and Frangelico with lime. Divine.

Information

There's a small **visitor centre** ([✓]07-5429 6043; www.malenycommunitycentre.org; 23 Maple St; ⊙10am-3pm) at the Maleny Community Centre.

Fraser Island & the Fraser Coast

Best Places to Eat

➡ Waterview Bistro (p366)

➡ Muddy Waters Cafe (p368)

➡ Bayaroma Cafe (p363)

➡ Rosie Blu (p371)

➡ Mammino's (p369)

Best Places to Stay

➡ Kingfisher Bay Resort (p375)

➡ Debbie's Place (p365)

➡ Beachfront Tourist Parks (p362)

➡ Flashpackers (p362)

➡ Colonial Village YHA (p362)

Why Go?

Nature lovers, rejoice! World Heritage–listed Fraser Island is the world's largest sand island, a mystical, at times eerie, land of giant dunes, ancient rainforests, luminous lakes and wildlife including Australia's purest strain of dingo. Across the calm waters of the Great Sandy Strait, the mellow coastal community of Hervey Bay is the gateway to Fraser Island. From July to October, migrating humpback whales stream into the bay before continuing on to Antarctica. Further south, tiny Rainbow Beach is a laid-back seaside village and an alternative launching pad to Fraser. Fishing, swimming, boating and camping are hugely popular along this stretch of coastline.

Inland, agricultural fields surround old-fashioned country towns steeped in history. Bundaberg, the largest city in the region, overlooks the sea of waving cane fields that fuel its eponymous rum, a fiery, gut-churning spirit guaranteed to scramble a few brain cells.

When to Go
Bundaberg

Jun–Jul Bring your brolly to Maryborough's Mary Poppins Festival.

Jul–Nov Watch humpback whales; optimal sighting time is August to October.

Nov–Mar Spy on turtles laying eggs in the sand at Mon Repos.

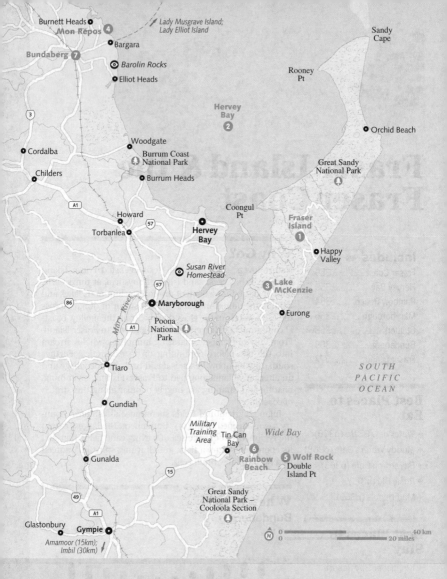

Fraser Island & the Fraser Coast Highlights

① Cruising up the beach 'highway', hiking through the rainforest and camping under the stars on **Fraser Island** (p372).

② Watching the whales play in **Hervey Bay** (p359).

③ Cooling off in the pristine, clear-blue water of the white-sand-fringed freshwater **Lake McKenzie** (p375) on Fraser Island.

④ Witnessing turtles take their first flipper-stumble down the beach at **Mon Repos** (p370).

⑤ Diving with sharks at **Wolf Rock** (p365) off Rainbow Beach.

⑥ Copping an eyeful of the coloured sand cliffs at **Rainbow Beach** (p364).

⑦ Sampling 'liquid gold' at the **rum distillery** (p369) in Bundaberg.

ⓘ Getting There & Away

AIR
Qantas (🖉13 13 13; www.qantas.com.au) and **Virgin Blue** (🖉13 67 89; www.virginblue.com.au) fly to Bundaberg and Hervey Bay.

BUS
Greyhound Australia (🖉1300 473 946; www.greyhound.com.au) and **Premier Motor Service** (🖉13 34 10; www.premierms.com.au) both have regular coach services along the Bruce Hwy with stops at all the major towns. They also detour off the highway to Hervey Bay and Rainbow Beach.

TRAIN
Queensland Rail (🖉1800 872 467; www.travel-train.com.au) has frequent services between Brisbane and Rockhampton passing through the region. Choose between the high-speed *Tilt Train* or the more sedate *Sunlander*.

FRASER COAST

The Fraser Coast runs the gamut from coastal beauty, beachfront national parks and tiny seaside villages to agricultural farms and sugarcane fields surrounding old-fashioned country towns.

Hervey Bay

POP 76,403

Named after an English Casanova, it's no wonder that Hervey Bay's seductive charms are difficult to resist. Its warm subtropical climate, long sandy beaches, calm blue ocean and a relaxed and unpretentious local community lure all sorts of travellers to its shores, from backpacking travellers to families and sea-changing retirees. Throw in the chance to see majestic humpback whales frolicking in the water and the town's convenient access to the World Heritage–listed Fraser Island, and it's easy to understand how Hervey Bay has gone from sleepy fishing village to come-hither tourist hotspot.

Fraser Island shelters Hervey Bay from the ocean surf and the sea here is shallow and completely flat – perfect for kiddies and postcardy summer-holiday pics.

◉ Sights

Reef World   AQUARIUM
(🖉07-4128 9828; Pulgul St, Urangan; adult/child $18/9, shark dive $50; ☺9.30am-4pm) A small aquarium stocked with some of the Great Barrier Reef's most colourful characters, in-cluding a giant 18-year-old groper. You can also take a dip with lemon, whaler and other non-predatory sharks.

Vic Hislop's Shark Show   SHARK EXHIBIT
(🖉07-4128 9137; 553 The Esplanade, Urangan; adult/child $17/8; ☺8.30am-5.30pm) For an informative, but slightly kitsch and often controversial peek at what hides beneath the sea visit the acclaimed Sharkman's collection of all things toothy. If the newspaper clippings of gruesome shark attacks don't make you shudder maybe the 5.6m frozen Great White in the freezer will!

Fraser Coast Discovery Sphere   MUSEUM
(🖉07-4197 4207; www.frasercoastdiscoverysphere.com.au; 166 Old Maryborough Rd, Pialba; adult/child/family $7.50/5.50/20.50; ☺10am-4pm) Loads of educational activities inspired by the region. Ideal for kids and curious adults.

Wetside Water Education Park   PARK
(www.widebaywater.qld.gov.au/quicklinks/wetsidewatereducationpark; The Esplanade, Scarness; ☺10am-6pm daily, night show 7pm Sat) On hot days, this wet spot on the foreshore can't be beaten. There's plenty of shade, fountains, tipping buckets and a boardwalk with water infotainment. Opening hours vary so check the website for updates.

🏃 Activities

Whale Watching
Whale-watching tours operate out of Hervey Bay every day (weather permitting) during the annual migrations between late July and early November. Sightings are guaranteed from August to the end of October (with a free return trip if the whales don't show). Off season, many boats offer dolphin-spotting tours. Boats cruise from **Urangan Harbour** out to Platypus Bay and then zip around from pod to pod to find the most active whales. Most vessels offer half-day tours for around $120 for adults and $70 for children, and most include breakfast or lunch. Tour bookings can be made through your accommodation or the information centres.

Spirit of Hervey Bay   WHALE WATCHING
(🖉1800 642 544; www.spiritofherveybay.com; ☺8.30am & 1.30pm) The largest vessel with the greatest number of passengers.

MV Tasman Venture   WHALE WATCHING
(🖉1800 620 322; www.tasmanventure.com.au; ☺8.30am & 1.30pm) One of the best, with underwater microphones and viewing

Hervey Bay

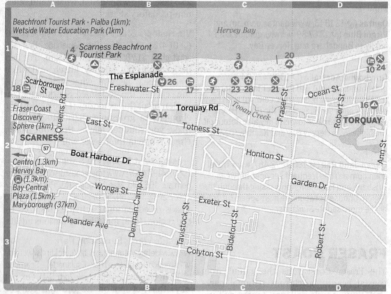

Hervey Bay

◎ Sights
1 Reef World	H2
2 Vic Hislop's Shark Show	G1

◉ Activities, Courses & Tours
3 Aquavue	C1
Blue Dolphin Marine Tours	(see 5)
Colonial Village YHA	(see 13)
4 Enzo's on the Beach	A1
5 Freedom Whale Watch	H2
6 Krystal Klear	H3
MV Tasman Venture	(see 5)
7 Nomads	C1
Spirit of Hervey Bay	(see 5)

⊜ Sleeping
8 Alexander Lakeside B&B	E1
9 Arlia Sands Apartments	E1
10 Australis Shelly Bay Resort	D1
11 Bay B&B	F1
12 Boat Harbour Resort	G3
13 Colonial Village YHA	G3
14 Flashpackers	B2
15 Grange Resort	F1
16 Happy Wanderer Village	D2
17 La Mer Beachfront Apartments	B1
18 Mango Eco Hostel	A1
19 Quarterdecks Harbour Retreat	G3
20 Torquay Beachfront Tourist Park	C1

⊗ Eating
21 Bayaroma Cafe	C1
22 Black Dog Café	B1
23 Café Tapas	C1
24 Coast	D1
Enzo's on the Beach	(see 4)
25 Pier Restaurant	G1
Simply Wok	(see 23)

◉ Drinking & Nightlife
26 Hoolihan's	B1
27 Liquid Lounge	G1

◉ Entertainment
28 Viper	C1

windows. Whale sightings are guaranteed during the high season; you will get a free subsequent trip if the whales don't show up.

Blue Dolphin Marine Tours WHALE WATCHING
(☏ 07-4124 9600; www.bluedolphintours.com.au) Skipper Pete has almost 30 years of marine mammal experience, making him the ideal receptacle for the many questions this up-close whale-watching trip will generate.

Freedom Whale Watch WHALE WATCHING
(☑ 1300 879 960; www.freedomwhalewatch.com.au) Watch the whales from three levels on a 58m catamaran.

Fishing

MV Fighting Whiting FISHING
(☑ 07-4124 3377; www.fightingwhiting.com.au; adult/child/family $70/35/175) Keep your catch on these calm water tours. Sandwiches, bait and all fishing gear included.

MV Princess II FISHING
(☑ 07-4124 0400; adult/child $150/100) Wet your hook with an experienced crew who've been trolling these waters for more than two decades.

Cruises

Krystal Klear CRUISE
(☑ 07-4124 0066; www.krystalkleer.com.au; 5hr tour adult/child $90/50) Cruise on a 40ft glass-bottomed boat, the only one in Hervey Bay. Includes snorkelling, coral viewing and an island barbecue.

Water Sports

Aquavue WATER SPORTS
(☑ 07-4125 5528; www.aquavue.com.au; The Esplanade, Torquay) Hires out paddle-boards, kayaks and aqua-trikes ($20 per hour), catamarans ($50 per hour) and jet skis ($50 per 15 minutes). Also runs guided Fraser Island jet-ski tours from $250.

Enzo's on the Beach WATER SPORTS
(☑ 07-4124 6375; www.enzosonthebeach.com.au; The Esplanade, Scarness) Kite-surfing (two-hour lesson $130) and paddle-boarding (per hour/two hours $30/40). Also hires out kayaks (from $20 per hour) and surf-skis ($15 per hour).

Scenic Flights

Fraser Coast Microlites SCENIC FLIGHT
(☑ 1800 811 728; flight from $125-250) Ditch the metal shell to soar over islands and lakes on 20-, 30-, 45- and 70-minute flights. Book ahead.

Other Activities

Skydive Hervey Bay SKYDIVING
(☑ 0458 064 703; www.skydiveherveybay.com.au) Tandem skydives from $325 at 12,000ft with up to 45 mouth-flapping seconds of freefall.

Susan River Homestead HORSE RIDING
(☑ 07-4121 6846; www.susanriver.com; Hervey Bay–Maryborough Rd) Horse-riding packages (adult/child $250/160) include accommodation, all meals and use of the on-site swimming pool and tennis courts. Day-trippers can canter off on two-hour horse rides (adult/child $85/75).

✾ Festivals & Events

Hervey Bay Whale Festival WHALE
(www.herveybaywhalefestival.com.au) Celebrates the return of the whales in August.

🛏 Sleeping

★ Flashpackers HOSTEL $
(☎ 07-4124 1366; www.flashpackersherveybay.com; 195 Torquay Tce, Torquay; dm $25-30, d $70; ❉ 🛜🖵) This is the new standard for backpacker accommodation in Hervey Bay. Comfortable, spacious dorm and en suite rooms, with reading lights, numerous power sockets, walk-in communal fridge, spotless communal areas and showers with power. Set a street back from the beach.

Beachfront Tourist Parks CARAVAN PARK $
(☎ Pialba 07-4128 1399, Scarness 07-4128 1274, Torquay 07-4125 1578; www.beachfronttouristparks.com.au; unpowered/powered site $25/36) Fronting Hervey Bay's exquisitely long sandy beach, all three of these shady parks live up to their name, with fantastic ocean views; the Torquay site is in the heart of the action.

Colonial Village YHA HOSTEL $
(☎ 07-4125 1844; www.yha.com.au/hostels/qld/fraser-capricorn-coasts/hervey-bay; 820 Boat Harbour Dr, Urangan; dm/d/cabin from $27/56/72; ❉🖵@) This excellent YHA is set on eight hectares of tranquil bushland, close to the marina and only 50m from the beach. It's a lovely spot, thick with ambience, possums and parrots. Facilities include a spa, tennis and basketball courts and a sociable bar.

Mango Eco Hostel HOSTEL $
(☎ 07-4124 2832; www.mangohostel.net; 110 Torquay Rd, Scarness; dm/d $28/60; 🅿❉🛜) This small, locally-run hostel is an old-school travellers' haunt. Intimate and loaded with character, it sleeps guests in a four-bed dorm room and two very homey doubles. The wraparound verandah and outdoor dining area add to the cosy, tropical atmosphere.

Happy Wanderer Village CARAVAN PARK $
(☎ 07-4125 1103; www.happywanderer.com.au; 105 Truro St, Torquay; unpowered/powered site from $30/35, cabin/studio/villa from $69/89/121; ❉🛜🖵) The manicured lawns and profuse gum-tree cover at this large park make for great tent sites.

Bay B&B B&B $$
(☎ 07-4125 6919; www.baybedandbreakfast.com.au; 180 Cypress St, Urangan; s $100, d $125-140; ❉@🖵🐾) This great-value B&B is run by a friendly, well-travelled Frenchman, his wife and their dog... Guest rooms are in a comfy annexe out the back, and the Bay's famous breakfast is served in a tropical garden. Families can take over the separate fully self-contained unit.

Quarterdecks Harbour Retreat APARTMENT $$
(☎ 07-4197 0888; www.quarterdecksretreat.com.au; 80 Moolyyir St, Urangan; 1-/2-/3-bedroom villas $185/225/290; ❉🛜🖵) These excellent villas are stylishly furnished with a private courtyard, all the mod cons and little luxuries such as fluffy bathrobes. Backing onto a nature reserve, it's quiet apart from the wonderful bird life, and only a cooee from the beach. The accommodation and tour packages are great value.

Australis Shelly Bay Resort APARTMENT $$
(☎ 07-4125 4533; www.shellybayresort.com.au; 466 The Esplanade, Torquay; 1-/2-bedroom unit $180/195; ❉@🖵) The bold, cheerful self-contained units at this complex are clean and spacious. All rooms have water views, and with the beach just across the road, this is one of the best options in town. Good discounts on multiple-night stays.

Alexander Lakeside B&B B&B $$
(☎ 07-4128 9448; www.herveybaybedandbreakfast.com.au; 29 Lido Pde, Urangan; r $140-150, ste $160-170; ❉@🛜) This warm and friendly B&B offers lakeside indulgence, where turtles come a-visiting in the morning. There's a heated lakeside spa, two spacious rooms with en suites and two luxury self-contained suites.

La Mer Beachfront Apartments APARTMENT $$
(☎ 07-4128 3494; www.lamer.com.au; 396 The Esplanade, Torquay; 1/2 bedroom from $150/180; ❉🛜🖵) With colours this bold, you'll think you're in the Med. The rainbow scheme continues indoors but it's actually quite pleasant. The apartments are large, comfortable and have fully equipped kitchens. Choose between poolside or beachfront units.

Arlia Sands Apartments APARTMENT $$
(☎ 07-4125 4360; www.arliasands.com.au; 13 Ann St, Torquay; 1/2 bedroom from $135/145; ❉🖵) These self-contained units may not be super-characterful, but they're comfortable, sport plush furniture and spacious modern bathrooms. It's off the main drag yet close to the beach and shops and is *très* quiet.

A WHALE OF A TIME

Every year, from July to early November, thousands of humpback whales cruise into Hervey Bay's sheltered waters for a few days before continuing their arduous migration south to the Antarctic. Having mated and given birth in the warmer waters off northeast Australia, they arrive in Hervey Bay in groups of about a dozen (known as pulses), before splitting into smaller groups of two or three (pods). The new calves utilise the time to develop the thick layers of blubber necessary for survival in icy southern waters, by consuming around 600L of milk daily.

Viewing these majestic creatures is simply awe-inspiring. You'll see these showy aqua-acrobats waving their pectoral fins, tail slapping, breaching or simply 'blowing', and many will roll up beside the whale-watching boats with one eye clear of the water...making those on board wonder who's actually watching whom.

Boat Harbour Resort APARTMENT **$$**

(✆ 07-4125 5079; www.boatharbourresort.net; 651-652 Charlton St, Urangan; studio from $120, bungalow from $150; ❄ 🐕 🖥) Close to the marina, these timber studios and cabins are set on attractive grounds. The studios have sizeable decks out the front and the roomy villas are great for families.

Grange Resort RESORT **$$$**

(✆ 07-4125 2002; www.thegrange-herveybay.com.au; 33 Elizabeth St, Urangan; 1-/2-bedroom villas $155/230; ❄ 🐕 🖥) Reminiscent of a stylish desert resort with fancy split-level condos and filled with life's little luxuries, this place is close to the beach and to town.

✗ Eating

⭐ **Bayaroma Cafe** CAFE **$**

(✆ 07-4125 1515; 428 The Esplanade, Torquay; breakfast $10-22, mains $9.50-20; ◷ 6.30am-3.30pm) Famous for its coffee, all-day breakfasts and people-watching pole position, Bayorama has a jam-packed menu that truly has something for everyone (even vegetarians!). Attentive, chirpy service is an added bonus.

Enzo's on the Beach CAFE **$**

(www.enzosonthebeach.com.au; 351a The Esplanade, Scarness; mains $8-20; ◷ 6.30am-5pm) This shabby-chic beachside cafe is the place to fill up on sandwiches, wraps, salads and coffees before working it off on a hire kayak or kite-surfing lesson.

Café Tapas TAPAS **$**

(✆ 07-4125 6808; 417 The Esplanade, Torquay; tapas $9; ◷ 11am-midnight) This sleek venue has all the cool-kid accoutrements: upmarket artwork, dim lighting, red couches and low tables flickering with coloured lights. Come

for Asian-inspired tapas; linger longer for cocktails and music.

Simply Wok ASIAN **$$**

(✆ 07-4125 2077; 417 The Esplanade, Torquay; mains $14-23; ◷ 7am-10pm) Noodles, stir-fries, seafood and curries will satisfy any cravings for Asian cuisine, and there's a nightly (from 5pm to 9pm) all-you-can-eat hot buffet for $16.90.

Black Dog Café FUSION **$$**

(✆ 07-4124 3177; 381 The Esplanade, Torquay; mains $15-37; ◷ lunch & dinner) Groovy, man. The very Zen menu features twists on sushi, Japanese pancakes, burgers, schnitzel, seafood salads and vegan options.

Coast FUSION **$$**

(✆ 07-4125 5454; 469 The Esplanade, Torquay; mains $21-60; ◷ Tues & Wed 5pm-late, Thurs-Sun 11.30am-late) Gourmet grub for the discerning diner prepared to splurge. Fancy meat and seafood dishes get the Asian/Middle Eastern fusion touch; desserts like the pumpkin cheesecake go beyond the realms of the superlative adjective.

Pier Restaurant SEAFOOD **$$**

(✆ 07-4128 9699; 573 The Esplanade, Urangan; mains $20-40; ◷ from 6pm Mon-Sat) Although sitting opposite the water, the Pier makes little use of its ocean views. But an interesting seafood menu – including macadamia/coconut crumbed prawns, chilli bugs and crabs – makes it a deservedly popular spot.

🍸 Drinking & Nightlife

Hoolihan's PUB

(382 The Esplanade, Scarness; ◷ 11am-2am) Like all good Irish pubs, Hoolihan's is wildly popular, especially with the backpacker crowd.

Liquid Lounge
CAFE

(577 The Esplanade, Urangan; coffee from $3.50; ⊙ Fri-Wed 8.30am-6.30pm, Thu 7.30am-4.30pm) Strong, good coffees and chatty service from passionate staff. Great location to boot.

Viper
CLUB

(410 The Esplanade, Torquay; ⊙ 10pm-3am Wed, Fri & Sat) This new club is a rough diamond with cranking music and an energetic crowd, especially during summer.

ℹ Information

Hervey Bay covers a string of beachside suburbs – Point Vernon, Pialba, Scarness, Torquay and Urangan – but behind the flawless beachfront and pockets of sedate suburbia, the outskirts of town dissolve into a sprawling industrial jungle.

Hervey Bay Visitor Information Centre (☑ 1800 811 728; www.visitfrasercoast.com; Cnr Urraween & Maryborough Rds) Helpful and well-stocked with brochures and information. On the outskirts of town.

ℹ Getting There & Away

AIR

Hervey Bay airport is on Don Adams Dve, just off Booral Rd. **Qantas** (☑ 13 13 13; www.qantas.com.au) and **Virgin Blue** (☑ 13 67 89; www.virginblue.com.au) have daily flights to/from destinations around Australia.

BOAT

Boats to Fraser Island leave from River Heads, about 10km south of town, and Urangan's Great Sandy Straits Marina. Most tours leave from Urangan Harbour.

BUS

Buses depart **Hervey Bay Coach Terminal** (☑ 07-4124 4000; Central Ave, Pialba). **Greyhound Australia** (☑ 1300 473 946; www.greyhound.com.au) and **Premier Motor Service** (☑ 13 34 10; www.premierms.com.au) have several services to/from Brisbane ($69, 5½ hours), Maroochydore ($47, 3½ hours), Bundaberg ($24, 1½ hours) and Rockhampton ($87, six hours).

Tory's Tours (☑ 07-4128 6500; www.torystours.com.au) has twice daily services to Brisbane airport ($75).

Wide Bay Transit (☑ 07-4121 3719; www.widebaytransit.com.au) has hourly services from Urangan Marina (stopping along The Esplanade) to Maryborough ($8, one hour) every weekday, with fewer services on weekends.

ℹ Getting Around

CAR

Hervey Bay is the the best place to hire a 4WD for Fraser Island. Try any of the following for starters:

Aussie Trax (☑ 07-4124 4433; www.fraserisland4wd.com.au; 56 Boat Harbour Dr, Pialba)

Fraser Magic 4WD Hire (☑ 07-4125 6612; www.fraser4wdhire.com.au; 5 Kruger Ct, Urangan)

Safari 4WD Hire (☑ 07-4124 4244; www.safari4wdhire.com.au; 102 Boat Harbour Dr, Pialba)

Hervey Bay Rent A Car (☑ 07-4194 6626; www.herveybayrentacar.com.au; 5 Cunningham St, Torquay) Also rents out scooters ($30 per day).

Rainbow Beach

POP 1103

Gorgeous Rainbow Beach is a tiny town at the base of the Inskip Peninsula with spectacular multicoloured sand cliffs overlooking its rolling surf and white sandy beach. The town's friendly locals, relaxed vibe and convenient access to Fraser Island (only 10 minutes by barge) and the Cooloola Section of the Great Sandy National Park has made this a rising star of Queensland's coastal beauty spots.

⊙ Sights

The town is named for the coloured sand cliffs, a 2km walk along the beach. The cliffs arc their red-hued way around Wide Bay, offering a sweeping panorama from the lighthouse at Double Island Point to Fraser Island in the north.

A 600m track along the cliffs at the southern end of Cooloola Dr leads to the Carlo Sandblow, a spectacular 120m-high dune.

🏃 Activities

Bushwalking & Camping

The Cooloola Section of the Great Sandy National Park has a number of national park camp sites (www.nprsr.qld.gov.au; per person/family $5.45/21.80), including a wonderful stretch of beach camping along Teewah Beach. Book camping and 4WD permits (www.nprsr.qld.gov.au; per day/week/month $11/27.70/43.60) online.

Bushwalking tracks in the national park (maps from the QPWS office on Rainbow Beach Rd) include the 46.2km Cooloola Wilderness Trail, which starts at Mullens car park (off Rainbow Beach Rd) and ends near Lake Cooloola.

Camping on the beach is one of the best ways to experience this part of the coast, but if you don't have camping gear **Rainbow Beach Hire-a-Camp** (☏07-5486 8633; www.rainbow-beach-hire-a-camp.com.au; per day/night from $30/50) can hire out equipment, set up your tent and camp site, organise camping permits and break camp for you when you're done.

Diving

Wolf Rock, a congregation of volcanic pinnacles off Double Island Point, is regarded as one of Queensland's best scuba-diving sites. The endangered grey nurse shark is found here all year round.

Wolf Rock Dive Centre   DIVING
(☏0438 740 811, 07-5486 8004; www.wolfrockdive.com.au; 20 Karoonda Rd; double dive charter from $220) High-adrenalin dives for experienced divers at Wolf Rock.

Kayaking

Rainbow Beach Dolphin View Sea Kayaking   KAYAKING
(☏0408 738 192; www.rainbowbeachsurfschool.com; Shop 1, 6 Rainbow Beach Rd; 3hr tour per person $70) Just like the name says, this mob offers dolphin-spotting kayak tours.

Skydiving & Paragliding

Skydive Rainbow Beach   SKYDIVING
(☏0418 218 358; www.skydiverainbowbeach.com; 2400/4200m dives $299/369) Soft landings on the beach.

Rainbow Paragliding   PARAGLIDING
(☏07-5486 3048, 0418 754 157; www.paraglidingrainbow.com; glides $180) Exhilarating tandem flights over the colourful cliffs.

Surfing

There's a good surf break at Double Island Point.

Rainbow Beach Surf School   SURFING
(☏0408 738 192; www.rainbowbeachsurfschool.com; 3hr session $60) Surfing lessons.

🔾 Tours

Surf & Sand Safaris   DRIVING TOUR
(☏07-5486 3131; www.surfandsandsafaris.com.au; per adult/child $75/40) Half-day 4WD tours through the national park and along the beach to the coloured sands and lighthouse at Double Island Point.

Dolphin Ferry Cruises   CRUISE
(☏0428 838 836; www.dolphinferrycruises.com.au; 3hr cruise adult/child $30/15; ⊙departs 7am) Cruise across the inlet to Tin Can Bay to hand-feed wild Indo-Pacific dolphins and scout for dugong...all before checkout time.

🛏 Sleeping

⭐**Debbie's Place**   B&B $
(☏07-5486 3506; www.rainbowbeachaccommodation.com.au; 30 Kurana St; d/ste from $99/109, 3-bedroom apt from $260; ✻🐾) Inside this beautiful timber Queenslander dripping with pot plants, the charming rooms are fully self-contained, with private entrances and verandahs. The effervescent Debbie is a mine of information and makes this a cosy home away from home.

Pippies Beach House   HOSTEL $
(☏07-5486 8503; www.pippiesbeachhouse.com.au; 22 Spectrum St; dm/d $22/65; ✻@🐾) With only 12 rooms, this small, relaxed hostel is the place to catch your breath between outdoor pursuits. Free breakfast, wi-fi and boogie boards sweeten the stay; be there Monday, Wednesday or Friday for a boomerang-painting workshop!

Dingo's Backpacker's Resort   HOSTEL $
(☏1800 111 126; www.dingosresort.com; 20 Spectrum St; dm $24; ✻@🐾) This party hostel with bar has live music, karaoke and face-painting nights, a chill-out gazebo and cheap meals nightly.

Rainbow Sands Holiday Units   MOTEL $
(☏07-5486 3400; www.rainbowsands.com.au; 42-46 Rainbow Beach Rd; d $95, 1-bedroom apt $125; ✻🐾) Perfectly pleasing low-rise, palm-fronted complex with standard motel rooms and self-contained units with full laundries for comfortable longer stays.

Fraser's on Rainbow   HOSTEL $
(☏07-5486 8885; www.frasersonrainbow.com; 18 Spectrum St; dm/d from $25/75; @🐾) Roomy dorms in a converted motel give you somewhere to sleep off any carousing at its popular outdoor bar.

Rainbow Beach Holiday Village   CARAVAN PARK $
(☏07-5486 3222; www.rainbowbeachholidayvillage.com; 13 Rainbow Beach Rd; unpowered/powered site from $30/37, villa from $100; ✻🐾) Popular beachfront park.

✖ Eating

Self-caterers will find a supermarket on Rainbow Beach Rd.

Waterview Bistro   MODERN AUSTRALIAN **$$**
(📞07-5486 8344; Cooloola Dr; mains $26-35; ⊙11.30am-11.30pm Wed-Sat, to 6pm Sun) Sunset drinks are a must at this swish restaurant with sensational views of Fraser Island from its hilltop perch. Get stuck into the signature seafood chowder ($22), or try the lunch special ($19, glass of wine included).

Rainbow Beach Hotel   PUB **$$**
(1 Rainbow Beach Rd; mains $18-35; ⊙ lunch & dinner) The spruced-up pub is bright, airy and brings to mind all things plantation, with ceiling fans, palm trees, timber floors and cane furnishings. The restaurant serves up traditional pub grub; scope the street scene from the upstairs balcony.

❶ Information

QPWS (Rainbow Beach Rd; ⊙8am-4pm)

Rainbow Beach Visitor Centre (📞07-5486 3227; www.rainbowbeachinfo.com.au; 8 Rainbow Beach Rd; ⊙7am-5.30pm)

Shell Tourist Centre (36 Rainbow Beach Rd; ⊙6am-6pm) Located at the Shell service station; tour bookings and barge tickets for Fraser Island.

❶ Getting There & Around

Greyhound (📞1300 473 946; www.greyhound.com.au) has several daily services from Brisbane ($49, five hours), Noosa ($32, three hours) and Hervey Bay ($26, two hours). **Premier Motor Service** (📞13 34 10; www.premierms.com.au) has less-expensive services. **Cooloola Connections** (📞07-5481 1667; www.coolconnect.com.au) runs a shuttle bus to Rainbow Beach from Brisbane Airport ($135, three hours) and Sunshine Coast Airport ($95, two hours).

Most 4WD-hire companies will also arrange permits, barge costs (per vehicle $100 return) and hire out camping gear. Some recommended companies:

All Trax 4WD Hire (📞07-5486 8767; www.fraserisland4x4.com.au; Rainbow Beach Rd, Shell service station; per day from $170)

Rainbow Beach Adventure Centre 4WD Hire (📞07-5486 3288; www.adventurecentre.com.au; 66 Rainbow Beach Rd; per day from $180) Also rents trail bikes.

Maryborough

POP 26,000

Born in 1847, Maryborough is one of Queensland's oldest towns, and its port was the first shaky step ashore for thousands of 19th-century free settlers looking for a better life in the new country. Heritage and history are Maryborough's specialities, the pace of yesteryear reflected in its beautifully restored colonial-era buildings and gracious Queenslander homes.

This charming old country town is also the birthplace of Pamela Lyndon ('PL') Travers, creator of the umbrella-wielding Mary Poppins. The award-winning film *Saving Mr Banks* tells Travers' story, with early-1900s Maryborough in a starring role.

◉ Sights

Portside   HISTORIC SITE
(101 Wharf St; ⊙10am-4pm Mon-Fri, to 1pm Sat & Sun) In the historic area beside the Mary River, Portside has 13 heritage-listed buildings, parklands and museums. Today's tidy colonial-era buildings and landscaped gardens paint a different story from Maryborough's once-thriving port and seedy streets filled with sailors, ruffians, brothels and opium dens. The **Portside Centre** (📞07-4190 5730; cnr Wharf & Richmond Sts; ⊙10am-4pm), located in the former **Customs House**, has interactive displays on Maryborough's history. Part of the centre but a few doors down, the **Bond Store Museum** also highlights key periods in Maryborough's history. Downstairs is the original packed-earth floor and even some liquor barrels from 1864.

Mary Poppins Statue   MONUMENT
On the street in front of the neoclassical **former Union Bank** (birthplace of Mary Poppins creator, PL Travers) is a life-size statue of the acerbic character Travers created rather than the saccharine Disney version.

Brennan & Geraghty's Store   MUSEUM
(64 Lennox St; adult/family $5.50/13; ⊙10am-3pm) This National Trust–classified store traded for 100 years before closing its doors. The museum is crammed with tins, bottles and packets, including early Vegemite jars and curry powder from the 1890s.

GOLD, WOOD, STEAM & SONG: GYMPIE & THE MARY VALLEY

Gympie's gold once saved Queensland from near-bankruptcy, but that was in the 1860s and not much has happened here since. History buffs will find a large collection of mining equipment and functioning steam-driven engines at the **Gympie Gold Mining & Historical Museum** (www.gympiegoldmuseum.com.au; 215 Brisbane Rd; adult/child/family $10/5/25; ⊙9am-3pm). There's also the **Woodworks Forestry & Timber Museum** (www.woodworksmuseum.com.au; cnr Fraser Rd & Bruce Hwy; admission $5; ⊙10am-4pm Mon-Sat) on the Bruce Hwy south of town. The highlight of the museum (and perhaps the lowlight of the logging industry) is a cross-section of a magnificent kauri pine that lived through the Middle Ages, Columbus' discovery of America and the Industrial Revolution, only to be felled in the early 20th century.

After the summer rains, the Mary Valley around here is lush and scenic. If you don't have a car, explore the valley on a 1923 steam train, the **Valley Rattler** (☎07-5482 2750; www.thevalleyrattler.com). Schedules and prices are ever-changing; see website for updates.

Amamoor is the site of the annual **Gympie Music Muster** (www.muster.com.au), a six-day country-music hoedown held annually in August.

Gympie Cooloola Tourism (www.cooloola.org.au; Lake Alford, Bruce Hwy, Gympie; ⊙9am-4.30pm) has a wealth of information on sights and activities along the entire Fraser Coast.

Greyhound (p322) and **Premier** (☎13 34 10; www.premierms.com.au) have numerous daily services to Gympie from Brisbane, Noosa, Bundaberg and Hervey Bay. **Traveltrain** (☎1800 872 467; www.traveltrain.com.au) operates the *Tilt Train* and the *Sunlander* from Brisbane to Gympie on their way to Rockhampton and Cairns.

Maryborough Military & Colonial Museum
MUSEUM

(☎07-4123 5900; www.maryboroughmuseum.org; 106 Wharf St; adult/couple/family $5/8/10; ⊙9am-3pm) Check out the only surviving three-wheeler Girling car, originally built in London in 1911. There's also a replica Cobb & Co coach and one of the largest military libraries in Australia.

Queens Park
PARK

With a profusion of glorious trees, including a banyan fig that's more than 140 years old, this is a pleasant spot for a picnic.

Maryborough Heritage City Markets
MARKET

(cnr Adelaide & Ellena Sts; ⊙8am-1.30pm Thu) Market fun made all the more entertaining by the firing (1pm) of the historic Time Cannon, a town crier and rides (adult/child $3/2) on the Mary Ann steam loco through Queen's Park.

🏃 Activities

Tea with Mary
TOUR

(☎1800 214 789; per person $13) Tour the historic precinct with a Mary Poppins–bedecked guide who spills the beans on the town's past; book through the visitor centre.

Guided Walks
WALKING TOUR

(⊙9am Mon-Sat) **FREE** Free guided walks depart from the City Hall to take in the town's many sites.

Ghostly Tours & Tales
TOUR

(☎1800 811 728; tours incl dinner $65; ⊙6pm, last Saturday of the month) Get spooked on a torch-lit tour of the city's grisly murder sites, opium dens, haunted houses and cemetery. Tours begin from the Maryborough Post Office in Bazaar St.

🎉 Festivals & Events

Mary Poppins Festival
CULTURAL

(www.marypoppinsfestival.com.au) A supercalifragilisticexpialidocious festival celebrating PL Travers and the famous Miss Poppins. Every June/July over the school holidays.

🛏 Sleeping

Ned Kelly's Motel
MOTEL $

(☎07-4121 0999; www.nedkellymotel.com.au; 150 Gympie Rd; s/d $49/79, cabins from $89; ❋ ≋) Basic, budget and beside the highway. But there's a pool, laundry and mammoth Ned Kelly statue out the front: what more do you need?

FRASER ISLAND & THE FRASER COAST MARYBOROUGH

Eco Queenslander BOUTIQUE HOTEL **$$**
(📞0438 195 443; www.ecoqueenslander.com; 15 Treasure St; per couple $140) 🏄 You won't want to leave this lovely converted Queenslander with comfy lounge, full kitchen, laundry and a cast-iron bathtub. Sustainable features include solar power, rainwater tanks, energy-efficient lighting and bikes for you to use. Minimum two-night stay.

Tin Peaks B&B B&B **$$**
(📞07-4123 5294; www.tinpeaks.com.au; 54 Berallan Dve; d incl breakfast $135; ✳@🛜🐾) Spacious self-contained cottage that comes over all rustic (with a random hint of nautical), but has all the mod-cons you need. The huge verandah and warm furnishings make it just like home, but better. Six minutes from the CBD.

🍴 Eating & Drinking

Toast CAFE **$**
(📞07-4121 7222; 199 Bazaar St; dishes $6-12; ⊗6am-4pm Mon-Sat, to 2.30pm Sun) Stainless-steel fittings, polished cement floors and coffee served in paper cups stamp a metro-chic seal on this groovy cafe.

★Muddy Waters Cafe SEAFOOD **$$**
(📞07-4121 5011; 103 Wharf St, Portside; mains $15-32; ⊗9.30am-3pm Mon-Wed, 9.30am-9.30pm Thu, 9.30am-3pm & 6-9.30pm Fri & Sat) The shady riverfront deck and the summery menu at this classy cafe will keep you happy with tempting seafood dishes such as citrus-and-vodka-cured salmon and beer-battered fish.

Lounge 1868 BAR
(116 Wharf St; ⊗6pm-late Fri & Sat) Ambient watering hole in the historic Customs House Hotel with a whopping great beer garden and small but sophisticated menu (mains are $12 to $17).

ℹ️ Information

The **Maryborough/Fraser Island visitor centre** (📞1800 214 789; www.visitfrasercoast.com; Kent St; ⊗9am-5pm Mon-Fri, to 1pm Sat & Sun) in the 100-year-old City Hall is extremely helpful and has free copies of comprehensive self-guided walking tours. Speak with them about inclusive tickets to Portside's museums and attractions.

ℹ️ Getting There & Away

Both the *Sunlander* ($75, five hours) and the *Tilt Train* ($75, 3½ hours) connect Brisbane with the Maryborough West station, 7km west of the centre. It's connected to the centre via shuttle bus.

Greyhound Australia (📞1300 473 946; www.greyhound.com.au) and **Premier Motor Service** (📞13 34 10; www.premierms.com.au) have buses to Gympie ($29, one hour), Bundaberg ($39, three hours) and Brisbane ($65, 4½ hours).

Wide Bay Transit (📞07-4121 4070; www.widebaytransit.com.au) has hourly services (fewer on weekends) between Maryborough and Hervey Bay ($8, one hour), departing from outside City Hall in Kent St.

Childers

POP 1410

Surrounded by lush green fields and rich red soil, Childers is a charming little town, its main street lined with tall, shady trees and lattice-trimmed historical buildings. Backpackers flock here for fruit-picking and farm work. Sadly, Childers is best known for the 15 backpackers who perished in a fire in the Palace Backpackers Hostel in June 2000.

👁 Sights & Activities

There is a moving memorial for the deceased backpackers and some fantastic art at the **Childers Palace Memorial & Art Gallery.** (72 Churchill St; ⊗9am-5pm Mon-Fri, to 3pm Sat & Sun)

The Old Pharmacy (90 Churchill St; ⊗9am-3.30pm Mon-Fri) was an operational apothecary's shop between 1894 to 1982, and also functioned as the town dentist, vet, optician and local photographer.

The lovely, 100-year-old **Federal Hotel** has swingin' saloon doors, while a bronze statue of two romping pig dogs sits outside the **Grand Hotel**.

On the last weekend in July, Childers' main street is swamped with street performers, musicians, dancers, and food and craft stalls during its annual **Festival of Cultures**, which draws over 50,000 people.

🛏 Sleeping & Eating

Sugarbowl Caravan Park CARAVAN PARK **$**
(📞07-4126 1521; www.sugarbowlchilders.com; Bruce Hwy; powered site $29, cabin $90; @🐾) A 10-minute walk out of town is this clean and green spot favoured by many seasonal pickers. The owners can help arrange work, and transport to job-sites. Rates are for two people; prices drop for longer stays.

Mango Hill B&B
B&B $$

(📞07-4126 1311; www.mangohillcottages.com; 8 Mango Hill Dr; s/d incl breakfast $100/130; 🖾) For warm, country hospitality, the cute cane-cutter cottages at Mango Hill B&B, 4km south of town, are decorated with hand-made wooden furniture, country decor and comfy beds that ooze charm and romance. There's an organic winery on-site.

Vietnamese Mini Resturant
VIETNAMESE $

(📞07-4126 1144; 108 Churchill St; mains from $11; ⊙lunch & dinner) That there's a Vietnamese restaurant way out in Childers may come as a shock, but the fact that it's not half bad may be even more surprising. Definitely worth a stop.

Kapé Centro
CAFE $

(65 Churchill St; mains $10-18; ⊙9am-3pm) Kapé Centro in the old post office building dishes up light meals, salads and pizzas.

Mammino's
ICE CREAM $

(115 Lucketts Rd; ice-cream cups $5; ⊙9am-5pm) On your way out of town, take a detour to Mammino's for wickedly delicious, home-made macadamia ice cream. Lucketts Rd is off the Bruce Hwy just south of Childers.

❶ Information

Childers Visitor Information Centre (📞07-4126 3886; ⊙9am-4pm Mon-Fri, to 3pm Sat & Sun) Beneath the Childers Palace Memorial & Art Gallery.

❶ Getting There & Away

Childers is 50km southwest of Bundaberg. **Greyhound Australia** (📞1300 473 946; www.greyhound.com.au) and **Premier Motor Service** (📞13 34 10; www.premierms.com.au) both stop at the Shell service station north of town and have daily services to/from Brisbane ($86, 6½ hours), Hervey Bay ($17, one hour) and Bundaberg ($24, 1½ hours).

Burrum Coast National Park

The Burrum Coast National Park covers two sections of coastline on either side of the little holiday community of Woodgate, 37km east of Childers. The Woodgate section of the park begins at the southern end of The Esplanade, and has attractive beaches, abundant fishing and the **NPRSR camping ground** (www.nprsr.qld.gov.au; per person/family $5.15/20.60) at Burrum Point, reached by a 4WD-only track. Several walking tracks start at the camping ground or Acacia St in Woodgate. There are more isolated bush-camping areas in the Kinkuna section of the park, a few kilometres north of Woodgate; you'll need a 4WD to reach them. Book camping permits online at www.nprsr.qld.gov.au.

Woodgate Beach Tourist Park
CARAVAN PARK $

(📞07-4126 8802; www.woodgatebeachtouristpark.com; 88 The Esplanade; unpowered/powered site $28/32, cabin $60-110, beachfront villa $135; ❄ @) Close to the national park and opposite the beach.

Bundaberg
POP 69,805

Despite boasting a sublime climate, coral-fringed beaches and waving fields of sugar cane, 'Bundy' is still overlooked by most travellers. Hordes of backpackers flock here for fruit-picking and farm work; other visitors quickly pass through on their way to family summer holidays at the nearby sea-side villages.

This is the birthplace of the famous Bundaberg Rum, a mind-blowingly potent liquor bizarrely endorsed by a polar bear but as iconically Australian as Tim Tams and Vegemite.

◉ Sights & Activities

Bundaberg Rum Distillery
DISTILLERY

(📞07-4131 2999; www.bundabergrum.com.au; Avenue St; self-guided tour adult/child $14/7, guided tour $25/12; ⊙10am-3pm Mon-Fri, until 2pm Sat & Sun; tours run on the hour) Bundaberg's biggest claim to fame is the iconic Bundaberg Rum – you'll see the Bundy Rum polar bear on billboards and bumper stickers all over town. Tours follow the rum's production from start to finish and include a tasting for the over-18s. Wear closed shoes.

Bundaberg Barrel
BREWERY

(📞07-4154 5480; www.bundaberg.com; 147 Bargara Rd; adult/child $12/5; ⊙9am-4.30pm Mon-Sat, 10am-3pm Sun) Bundaberg Ginger Beer is not quite as famous as Bundy Rum, probably because it's nonalcoholic. Visit the Barrel to see how the ginger is mushed, crushed, brewed and fermented.

Bundaberg Regional Arts Gallery   GALLERY

(07-4130 4750; www.brag-brc.org.au; 1 Barolin St; 10am-5pm Mon-Fri, 11am-3pm Sat & Sun) This small (and vividly purple) gallery has surprisingly good exhibitions.

Hinkler Hall of Aviation   MUSEUM

(www.hinklerhallofaviation.com; Mt Perry Rd, Botanic Gardens; adult/child/family $18/10/38; 9am-4pm) This modern museum has multimedia exhibits, a flight simulator and informative displays chronicling the life of Bundaberg's famous son Bert Hinkler, who made the first solo flight between England and Australia in 1928.

Alexandra Park & Zoo   PARK, ZOO

(Quay St) FREE Lovely sprawling park with plenty of shady trees, flower beds and swaths of green lawn for a lazy picnic, right beside the Burnett River. There's also a small zoo for the littlies.

Bundaberg Aqua Scuba   DIVING

(07-4153 5761; www.aquascuba.com.au; 239 Bourbong St; diving courses from $349) Dive shop that runs courses.

Burnett River Cruises   CRUISE

(0427 099 009; www.burnettrivercruises.com.au; School Lane, East Bundaberg; 2½hr tour adult/child $25/10) The *Bundy Belle*, an old-fashioned ferry, chugs at a pleasant pace to the mouth of the Burnett River. See website or call for tour times.

🛏 Sleeping

There are plenty of midrange motels on the Bundaberg–Childers Rd into town. Bundaberg's hostels cater to working backpackers, and most can arrange harvest work.

Bigfoot Backpackers   HOSTEL $

(07-4152 3659; www.footprintsadventures.com.au; 66 Targo St; dm from $24; P) Comfortable and friendly central hostel that also runs fabulous turtle tours to Mon Repos. Fresh paint, happy staff and and a relaxed vibe raise this above its competitors. There are ample fruit-picking opportunities available.

Federal Backpackers   HOSTEL $

(07-4153 3711; www.federalbackpackers.com.au; 221 Bourbong St; dm from $25) One for the workers, this hostel isn't exactly sparkling, but it is social. There's a lively bar on-site, and staff can help out with finding work and transport to jobs.

Cellblock Backpackers   HOSTEL $

(07-4154 3210; cnr Quay & Maryborough Sts; dm per night/week from $28/165, d $70; @) Housed in a former jail – some might say aptly – this is a place for hardened travellers only. The rooms don't have windows (of course), but will do in a crisis. You'll forget about its shortcomings over a few drinks at the very happening poolside bar.

★ Inglebrae   B&B $$

(07-4154 4003; www.inglebrae.com; 17 Branyan St; r incl breakfast $120-150;) For old-world English charm in a glorious Queenslander, this delightful B&B is just the ticket. Polished timber and stained glass seep from the entrance into the rooms, which come with high beds and small antiques.

Bundaberg Spanish Motor Inn   MOTEL $$

(07-4152 5444; www.bundabergspanishmotorinn.com; 134 Woongarra St; s/d $95/105;) In a quiet side street off the main drag, this Spanish hacienda–style motel is great value. Units are self-contained and all rooms overlook the central pool.

Burnett Riverside Motel   MOTEL $$

(07-4155 8777; www.burnettmotel.com.au; 7 Quay St; d $150-200;) This modern pit stop is popular with conferences and travelling business folk, and the good facilities and popular H2O restaurant set it apart

---

TURTLE TOTS

Mon Repos, 15km northeast of Bundaberg, is one of Australia's most accessible turtle rookeries. From November to late March, female loggerheads lumber laboriously up the beach to lay eggs in the sand. About eight weeks later, the hatchlings dig their way to the surface, and under cover of darkness emerge en masse to scurry as quickly as their little flippers allow down to the water.

The **Mon Repos visitor centre** (07-4153 8888; 271 Bourbong St) has information on turtle conservation and organises nightly tours (adult/child $10.55/5.55) from 7pm during the season. Bookings are mandatory and can be made through the Bundaberg Visitor Centre (p372) or online at www.bookbundabergregion.com.au.

Bundaberg

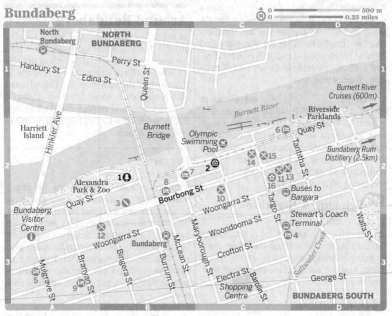

Bundaberg

from just about every other option in town. There's a gym, a sauna and fine river views.

🍴 Eating

Rosie Blu   DELI **$**
(☑07-4151 0957; 90a Bourbong St; mains $9-19; ☺8am-4pm Mon, 8.30am-4pm Tue-Fri, 8am-1.30pm Sat) Locals congregate en masse at this cute little spot, which isn't shy with its portions of gourmet sandwiches, salads and hot lunches dished up at lightning speed.

Spicy Tonight   FUSION **$**
(☑07-4154 3320; 1 Targo St; dishes $12-20; ☺11am-2.30pm & 5-9pm Mon-Sat, 5-9pm Sun)

Bundaberg's saucy little secret combines Thai and Indian cuisine with hot curries, vindaloo, tandoori and a host of vegetarian dishes.

Teaspoon   CAFE **$**
(10 Targo St; mains $5-10; ☺8am-5pm Mon-Sat) Great coffee and astonishingly cheap breakfasts ($7!).

Indulge   CAFE **$**
(80 Bourbong St; dishes $9-18; ☺8.30am-4.30pm Mon-Fri, 7.30am-12.30pm Sat) Delicious pastries and a fancy menu built around local produce.

Alowishus Delicious CAFE $

(207-4154 2233; 176 Bourbong St; coffees from $3, mains $9.50-22; ⊙7am-5pm Mon-Wed, 7am-9pm Thu, 7am-11pm Fri, 8am-11pm Sat, 9am-10pm Sun) Finally! A cafe open at night! Pop in for creative coffees, wholesome tucker and a massive range of pastries.

Les Chefs INTERNATIONAL $$

(207-4153 1770; 238 Bourbong St; mains $27; ⊙lunch Tue-Fri, dinner Mon-Sat) The most popular restaurant in town serves enormous plates of international fare. The large menu includes chicken enchiladas, grilled fish, veal schnitzel and yummy desserts. It gets very busy; book ahead. BYO.

🍷 Drinking & Nightlife

Central Hotel CLUB

(18 Targo St; ⊙11.30am-9pm Tue & Wed, to 3am Thur-Sat) Strut your stuff on the dance floor at Bundy's hottest nightclub. Pretty young things and the backpackers crowd are here every weekend.

ℹ️ Information

Bundaberg Visitor Centre (207-4153 8888, 1300 722 099; www.bundabergregion.org; 271 Bourbong St; ⊙9am-5pm)

ℹ️ Getting There & Around

AIR

The **Bundaberg Airport** (Airport Drive) is about 6km southwest of the centre. There are several daily flights to Brisbane with **Qantaslink** (213 13 13; www.qantas.com.au).

BUS

The coach terminal is on Targo St. Both **Greyhound Australia** (21300 473 946; www.greyhound.com.au) and **Premier Motor Service** (213 34 10; www.premierms.com.au) have daily services connecting Bundaberg with Brisbane ($87, seven hours), Hervey Bay ($24, 1½ hours) and Rockhampton ($50, four hours).

Duffy's Coaches (21300 383 397) have numerous services every weekday to Bargara ($5, 35 minutes), leaving from the back of Target on Woongarra St.

TRAIN

Run by **Queensland Rail** (21800 872 467; www.traveltrain.com.au), *Sunlander* ($89, seven hours, three weekly) and *Tilt Train* ($89, five hours, Sunday to Friday) travel from Brisbane to Bundaberg on their respective routes to Cairns and Rockhampton.

Around Bundaberg

In many people's eyes, the beach hamlets around Bundaberg are more attractive than the town itself. Some 25km north of the centre is **Moore Park** with wide, flat beaches. To the south is the very popular **Elliot Heads** with a nice beach, rocky foreshore and good fishing. Locals and visitors also flock to Mon Repos to see baby turtles hatching from November to March.

Bargara

POP 6893

Some 16km east of Bundaberg, the cruisy beach village of **Bargara** is a picturesque little spot with a good surf beach, a lovely esplanade and a few snazzy cafes. Recent years have seen a few high-rises sprout up along the foreshore but the effect is relatively low-key. Families find Bargara attractive for its clean beaches and safe swimming, particularly at the 'basin', a sheltered artificial rock pool.

In a great location opposite the esplanade, **Kacy's Bargara Beach Motel** (207-4130 1100; www.bargaramotel.com.au; 63 Esplanade; d from $139, 2-bedroom apt from $199; ✻ 🛜 🐕) offers a range of accommodation from pleasant motel rooms to self-contained apartments. Downstairs is the tropically themed **Kacy's Restaurant and Bar** (mains $17-40; ⊙breakfast & dinner daily, lunch Fri-Sun).

FRASER ISLAND

The local Butchulla people call it K'Gari or 'paradise', and not for no reason. Sculpted from wind, sand and surf, the striking blue freshwater lakes, crystalline creeks, giant dunes and lush rainforests of this gigantic sandbar form an enigmatic island paradise unlike any other in the world. Created over hundreds of thousands of years from sand drifting off the East Coast of mainland Australia, Fraser Island is the largest sand island in the world (measuring 120km by 15km), and the only place where rainforest grows on sand.

Inland, the vegetation varies from dense tropical rainforest and wild heath to wetlands and wallum scrub, with 'sandblows' (giant dunes over 200m high), mineral streams and freshwater lakes opening on to long sandy beaches fringed with pounding

SAND SAFARIS: EXPLORING FRASER ISLAND

The only way to explore Fraser Island (besides walking) is with a 4WD. For most travellers, there are three transport options: tag-along tours, organised tours or 4WD hire. This is a fragile environment; bear in mind that the greater the number of individual vehicles driving on the island, the greater the environmental damage.

Tag-Along Tours

Popular with backpackers, tag-along tours see groups of travellers pile into a 4WD convoy and follow a lead vehicle with an experienced guide and driver. Rates hover around $350 to $400; be sure to check if yours includes food, fuel, alcohol, etc.

Advantages Flexibility; you can make new friends fast.

Disadvantages If your group doesn't get along it's a loooong three days. Inexperienced drivers get bogged in sand all the time, but this can be part of the fun.

Recommended operators include the following:

Colonial Village YHA (07-4125 1844; www.yha.com.au/hostels/qld/fraser-capricorn-coasts/hervey-bay) Hervey Bay.

Dropbear Adventures (1800 061 156; www.dropbearadventures.com.au) Ex-Hervey Bay, Rainbow Beach and Noosa.

Fraser Roving (07-4125 6386; www.fraserroving.com.au) Hervey Bay.

Fraser's on Rainbow (07-5486 8885; www.frasersonrainbow.com) Rainbow Beach.

Pippies Beach House (07-5486 8503; www.pippiesbeachhouse.com.au) Rainbow Beach.

Nomads (07-5447 3355; www.nomadsfraserisland.com) Noosa.

Organised Tours

Most organised tours cover Fraser's hotspots: rainforests, Eli Creek, Lakes McKenzie and Wabby, the coloured Pinnacles and the *Maheno* shipwreck.

Advantages Minimum fuss, expert commentary.

Disadvantages During peak season you could share the experience with 40 others.

Among the many operators:

Cool Dingo Tours (07-4120 3333; www.cooldingotour.com; 2-/3-day tour from $325/395) Overnight at lodges with the option to stay extra nights on the island.

Fraser Experience (07-4124 4244; www.fraserexperience.com; 1-/2-day tour $180/327) Small groups and more freedom with the itinerary.

Fraser Explorer Tours (07-4194 9222; www.fraserexplorertours.com.au; 1-/2-day tour $175/319) Highly recommended.

4WD Hire

You can hire a 4WD from Hervey Bay, Rainbow Beach or on Fraser Island itself. All companies require a hefty bond, usually in the form of a credit-card imprint, which you *will* lose if you drive in salt water – don't even think about running the waves!

When planning your trip, reckon on covering 20km an hour on the inland tracks and 40km an hour on the eastern beach. Most companies will help arrange ferries, permits and camping gear. Rates for multiday rentals start at around $185 a day.

Advantages Complete freedom to roam the island and escape the crowds.

Disadvantages You may tackle beach and track conditions that even experienced drivers find challenging.

There are rental companies in Hervey Bay (p359) and Rainbow Beach (p364). On the island, **Aussie Trax** (07-4124 4433; www.fraserisland4wd.com.au) hires out 4WDs from $230 per day.

Fraser Island

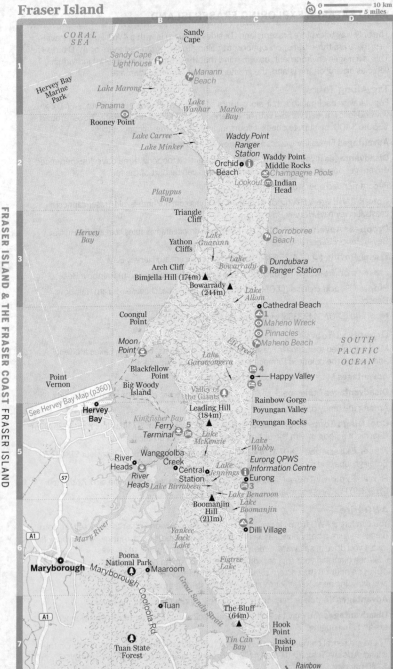

0 ——— 10 km
0 ——— 5 miles

CORAL SEA

Sandy Cape

Sandy Cape Lighthouse

Manann Beach

Hervey Bay Marine Park

Lake Marong

Panama

Lake Wanhar

Marloo Bay

Rooney Point

Lake Carree

Lake Minker

Waddy Point Ranger Station

Waddy Point
Middle Rocks
Champagne Pools

Orchid Beach

Lookout

Indian Head

Platypus Bay

Hervey Bay

Triangle Cliff

Corroboree Beach

Yathon Cliffs

Lake Gnaronn

Lake Bowarrady

Dundubara Ranger Station

Arch Cliff
Bimjella Hill (174m)

Bowarrady (244m)

Lake Allom

Coongul Point

Cathedral Beach

1

Maheno Wreck

Pinnacles

Moon Point

Eli Creek

Maheno Beach

SOUTH PACIFIC OCEAN

Lake Garawongera

Blackfellow Point

Big Woody Island

Point Vernon

See Hervey Bay Map (p360)

Happy Valley
4
6

Valley of the Giants

Rainbow Gorge
Poyungan Valley
Poyungan Rocks

Hervey Bay

Kingfisher Bay

Leading Hill (184m)

Ferry Terminal
5

Lake McKenzie

Lake Wabby

River Heads

Wanggoolba Creek

Central Station

Lake Jennings

Eurong QPWS Information Centre

Eurong
3

River Heads

Lake Birrabeen

Boomanjin Hill (211m)

Lake Benaroon

Lake Boomanjin

Mary River

Yankee Jack Lake

Dilli Village
2

Maryborough

Poona National Park

Maaroom

Maryborough Cooloola Rd

Figtree Lake

A1

Tuan

Great Sandy Strait

The Bluff (64m)

Hook Point

Inskip Point

A1

Tuan State Forest

Tin Can Bay

Rainbow Beach (3km)

Tiaro

Fraser Island

surf. The island is home to a profusion of bird life and wildlife including the famous dingo, while offshore waters teem with dugong, dolphins, sharks and migrating humpback whales.

Once exploited for its natural resources, sand and timber, Fraser Island joined the World Heritage list in 1992. The majority of the island is protected as part of the Great Sandy National Park.

This island utopia, however, is marred by an ever-increasing volume of 4WD traffic tearing down the beach and along sandy inland tracks. With over 360,000 people visiting the island each year, Fraser can sometimes feel like a giant sandpit with its own peak hour and congested beach highway.

Before crossing via ferry from either Rainbow Beach or Hervey Bay, ensure that your vehicle has suitably high clearance and, if camping, that you have adequate food, water and fuel. Driving on Fraser looks pretty relaxed in the brochures, but a sudden tide change or an unseen pothole can set your wheels spinning perilously.

Sights & Activities

Starting at the island's southern tip, where the ferry leaves for Inskip Point on the mainland, a high-tide access track cuts inland, avoiding dangerous Hook Point, and leads to the entrance of the Eastern Beach's main thoroughfare. The first settlement is Dilli Village, the former sand-mining centre; Eurong, with shops, fuel and places to eat, is another 9km north. From here, an inland track crosses to Central Station and Wanggoolba Creek (for the ferry to River Heads).

Right in the middle of the island is the ranger centre at Central Station, the starting point for numerous walking trails. From here you can walk or drive to the beautiful McKenzie, Jennings, Birrabeen and Boomanjin Lakes. Lake McKenzie is spectacularly clear and ringed by white-sand beaches, making it a great place to swim;

Lake Birrabeen sees fewer tour and backpacker groups.

About 4km north of Eurong along the beach, a signposted walking trail leads across sandblows to the beautiful Lake Wabby, the most accessible of Fraser's lakes. An easier route is from the lookout on the inland track. Lake Wabby is surrounded on three sides by eucalypt forest, while the fourth side is a massive sandblow that encroaches on the lake at about 3m a year. The lake is deceptively shallow and diving is very dangerous.

As you drive up the beach, you may have to detour inland to avoid Poyungan and Yidney Rocks during high tide before you reach Happy Valley, with places to stay, a shop and bistro. About 10km north is Eli Creek, a fast-moving, crystal-clear waterway that will carry you effortlessly downstream. About 2km from Eli Creek is the rotting hulk of the Maheno, a former passenger liner blown ashore by a cyclone in 1935 as it was being towed to a Japanese scrap yard.

Roughly 5km north of the Maheno you'll find the Pinnacles, an eroded section of coloured sand cliffs, and about 10km beyond, Dundubara, with a ranger station and excellent camping ground. Then there's a 20km stretch of beach before you come to the rock outcrop of Indian Head. Sharks, manta rays, dolphins and (during the migration season) whales can often be seen from the top of this headland.

Between Indian Head and Waddy Point, the trail branches inland, passing Champagne Pools, which offers the only safe saltwater swimming on the island. There are good camping areas at Waddy Point and Orchid Beach, the last settlement on the island.

Many tracks north of this are closed for environmental protection.

Kingfisher Bay Resort (☑07-4194 9300; www.kingfisherbay.com) can organise scenic helicopter flights, or go for a jaunt with Air Fraser Island (☑07-4125 3600; www.airfraseris-land.com.au; return flight from $135).

Sleeping & Eating

★ Kingfisher Bay Resort   RESORT $$
(☑07-4194 9300, 1800 072 555; www.kingfish-erbay.com; Kingfisher Bay; d $188, 2-bedroom villa $228; ✳ @ ☲) ◢ This elegant eco-resort has hotel rooms with private balconies and sophisticated two- and three-bedroom timber villas elevated to limit their environmental

impact. The villas and spacious holiday houses are gorgeous; some have spas on their private decks. There's a three-night minimum stay in high season. The resort has restaurants, bars and shops and operates daily ranger-guided, eco-accredited tours of the island (adult/child $160/110).

Fraser Island Beachhouses   CABIN $$
(📞 07-4127 9205, 1800 626 230; www.fraserisland-beachhouses.com.au; Eurong Second Valley; studio/house from $150/300; minimum stays apply; 🖳) Top option for those wanting their own space without sand or tents. The sunny, self-contained units are kitted out with polished wood, cable TVs and ocean views; there are four categories of beach house, with prices varying by size and location.

Eurong Beach Resort   RESORT $$
(📞 07-4120 1600, 1800 111 808; www.eurong.com.au; Eurong; r $135, 2-bedroom apt $185; 🟦 @ 🖳) Bright, cheerful Eurong is the main resort on the East Coast and a solid option for most budgets. Choose from simple motel rooms and comfortable, self-contained apartments. There's a pub-style restaurant (open for breakfast, lunch and dinner; mains $18 to $40), a bar, two pools, tennis courts and a petrol station.

Fraser Island Retreat   CABIN $$
(📞 07-4127 9144; www.fraserisretreat.com.au; Happy Valley; cabin per 2 nights $330; @ 🛜 🖳) The retreat's nine timber cabins (sleeping up to four people) offer some of the best-value accommodation on the island. The cabins are airy, nestled in native foliage and close to the beach. There's a camp kitchen, restaurant and shop – which sells fuel – on-site.

Sailfish on Fraser   APARTMENT $$$
(📞 07-4127 9494; www.sailfishonfraser.com.au; d from $230-250, extra person $10; 🖳) Any notions of rugged wilderness will be forgotten quick smart at this plush, indulgent retreat. These two-bedroom apartments (which sleep up to six people) are cavernous and classy, with spas, mod cons, an alluring pool and 4WD washing area.

Camping
Supplies on the island are limited and costly. Before arriving, stock up well and be prepared for mosquitoes and March flies.

Camping permits are required at NPRSR camping grounds and any public area (ie along the beach). The most developed **NPRSR camping grounds** (📞 13 74 68; www.nprsr.qld.gov.au; per person/family $5.45/21.80), with coin-operated hot showers, toilets and BBQs, are at Waddy Point, Dundubara and Central Station. Campers with vehicles can also use the smaller camping grounds with fewer facilities at Lake Boomanjin, Ungowa and Wathumba on the western coast. Walkers' camps are set away from the main camping grounds along the Fraser Island Great Walk trail. The trail map lists the camp sites and their facilities. Camping is permitted on designated stretches of the eastern beach, but there are no facilities. Fires are prohibited except in communal fire rings at Waddy Point and Dundubara – bring your own firewood in the form of untreated, milled timber.

Dilli Village Fraser Island   CAMPGROUND $
(📞 07-4127 9130; camp site per person $10, bunkroom/cabin $40/100) Managed by the University of the Sunshine Coast, Dilli Village offers good sites on a softly sloping camp ground.

Cathedrals on Fraser   CARAVAN PARK $
(📞 07-4127 9177; www.cathedralsonfraser.com.au; Cathedral Beach; 'wilderness site' $29, unpowered/powered site $39/45, cabin with/without bathroom $220/180; @) Spacious, privately run park with abundant, flat, grassy sites that's a hit with families.

❶ Information
A 4WD is necessary if you're driving on Fraser Island. General supplies and expensive fuel

---

FRASER ISLAND GREAT WALK

The Fraser Island Great Walk is a stunning way to experience this enigmatic island. The trail undulates through the island's interior for 90km from Dilli Village to Happy Valley. Broken up into seven sections of around 6km to 16km each, plus some side trails off the main sections, it follows the pathways of Fraser Island's original inhabitants, the Butchulla people. En route, the walk passes underneath the rainforest canopies, circles around some of the island's vivid lakes and courses through shifting dunes.

Visit www.nprsr.qld.gov.au for maps, detailed information and updates on the track.

ⓘ DEALING WITH DINGOES

Despite its many natural attractions and opportunities for adventure, there's nothing on Fraser Island that gives a thrill comparable to your first glimpse of a dingo. Believed to be among the most genetically pure in the world, the dingoes of Fraser are sleek, spry and utterly beautiful. They're also wild beasts that can become aggressive at the drop of a hat (or a strong-smelling foodsack), and while attacks are rare, there are precautions that must be taken by every visitor to the island:

➡ However skinny they appear, or whatever woebegone look they give you, never feed dingoes. Dingoes that are human-fed quickly lose their shyness and can become combative and competitive. Feeding dingoes is illegal and carries heavy fines.

➡ Don't leave any food scraps lying around, and don't take food to the lakes: eating on the shore puts your food at 'dingo level', an easy target for scroungy scavengers.

➡ Stay in groups, and keep any children within arm's reach at all times.

➡ Teasing dingoes is not only cruel, but dangerous. Leave them alone, and they'll do same.

➡ Dingoes are best observed at a distance. Pack a zoom lens and practice some shush, and you'll come away with some brilliant photographs...and all your limbs intact.

are available from stores at Cathedral Beach, Eurong, Kingfisher Bay, Happy Valley and Orchid Beach. There are public telephones at these locations and at most camping grounds.

The main ranger station, **Eurong QPWS Information Centre** (☏ 07-4127 9128) is at Eurong. Others can be found at **Dundubara** (☏ 07-4127 9138) and **Waddy Point** (☏ 07-4127 9190). Offices are often unattended as the rangers are out on patrol.

The 4WD **Fraser Island Taxi Service** (☏ 07-4127 9188) operates all over the island. Bookings are essential, as there's only one cab for the whole island!

If your vehicle breaks down, call the **tow-truck service** (☏ 0428 353 164, 07-4127 9449) in Eurong.

PERMITS

You must purchase permits from **NPRSR** (☏ 13 74 68; nprsr.qld.gov.au) for vehicles (per day/week/month $11/27.70/43.60) and camping (per person/family $5.45/21.80) before you arrive. Permits aren't required for private camping grounds or resorts. Permit issuing offices:

Great Sandy Information Centre (☏ 07-5449 7792; 240 Moorinidil St; ⏱ 8am-4pm) Near Noosa.

Marina Kiosk (☏ 07-4128 9800; Buccaneer Ave, Urangan Boat Harbour, Urangan; ⏱ 6am-6pm)

Maryborough QPWS (☏ 07-4121 1800; Cnr Lennox & Alice Sts; ⏱ 9am-4.30pm Mon-Fri)

Rainbow Beach QPWS (☏ 07-5486 3160; Rainbow Beach Rd; ⏱ 8am-4pm)

River Heads Information Kiosk (☏ 07-4125 8485; ⏱ 6.15am-12.30pm & 1.30-4pm) Ferry departure point at River Heads, south of Hervey Bay.

ⓘ Getting There & Away

AIR

Air Fraser Island (☏ 07-4125 3600; www.air fraserisland.com.au) charges from $135 for a return flight (30-minute round trip) to the island's eastern beach, departing Hervey Bay airport.

BOAT

Vehicle ferries connect Fraser Island with River Heads, about 10km south of Hervey Bay, or further south at Inskip Point, near Rainbow Beach.

Fraser Island Barges (☏ 07-4194 9300, 1800 227 437; www.fraserislandferry.com.au) makes the crossing (vehicle and four passengers $160 return, 30 minutes) from River Heads to Wanggoolba Creek on the western coast of Fraser Island. It departs daily from River Heads at 8.30am, 10.15am and 4pm, and returns from the island at 9am, 3pm and 5pm.

Kingfisher Bay Ferry (☏ 07-4194 9300, 1800 227 437; www.fraserislandferry.com) operates a daily vehicle and passenger ferry (pedestrian adult/child return $50/25, vehicle and four passengers return $160, 50 minutes) from River Heads to Kingfisher Bay, departing at 6.45am, 9am, 12.30pm, 3.30pm, 6.45pm and 9.30pm (Friday and Saturday only) and returning at 7.50am, 10.30am, 2pm, 5pm, 8.30pm and 11pm (Friday and Saturday only).

Coming from Rainbow Beach, **Manta Ray** (☏ 07-5486 3935) has two ferries making the 15-minute crossing from Inskip Point to Hook Point on Fraser Island continuously from about 6am to 5.30pm daily (vehicle return $110).

Capricorn Coast & the Southern Reef Islands

Best Places to Eat

➡ Ferns Hideaway (p391)

➡ Tree Bar (p381)

➡ Ginger Mule (p387)

➡ Saigon Saigon (p388)

➡ Megalomania (p390)

Best Places to Stay

➡ Svendsen's Beach (p392)

➡ LaLaLand Retreat (p381)

➡ Surfside Motel (p390)

➡ Criterion (p387)

➡ Workmans Beach
Camping Area (p380)

Why Go?

The stretch of coastline that straddles the tropic of Capricorn is one of the quietest and most lovely lengths of the East Coast. While local families flock to the main beaches during school holidays, the scene is uncrowded for most of the year, and even in high season you needn't travel far to find a deserted beach.

The stunning powdery white sand and turquoise waters of the Capricorn Coast fit the holiday-brochure image perfectly. The pristine islands of the southern Great Barrier Reef offer some of the best snorkelling and diving in Queensland, and the opportunities for wildlife spotting – from turtle hatchlings to passing whales – are plentiful. Unspoilt beaches and windswept national parks can be found along the entire coastline.

Inland, you'll find bustling Rockhampton – Capricornia's economic hub and the capital of cattle country, with all the steakhouses, rodeos and gigantic hats to prove it.

When to Go
Rockhampton

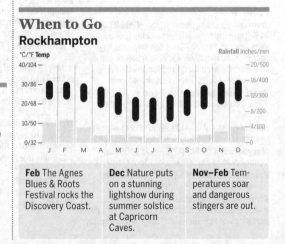

°C/°F **Temp**

Rainfall inches/mm

40/104 —

30/86 —

20/68 —

10/50 —

0/32 —

— 20/500

— 16/400

— 12/300

— 8/200

— 4/100

— 0

J F M A M J J A S O N D

Feb The Agnes Blues & Roots Festival rocks the Discovery Coast.

Dec Nature puts on a stunning lightshow during summer solstice at Capricorn Caves.

Nov–Feb Temperatures soar and dangerous stingers are out.

AGNES WATER & TOWN OF 1770

POP 1815

Surrounded by national parks and the Pacific Ocean, the twin coastal towns of Agnes Water and Town of 1770 are among Queensland's most appealing – and least hectic – seaside destinations. The tiny settlement of Agnes Water has the East Coast's most northerly surf beach, while the even tinier Town of 1770 (little more than a marina!) marks Captain Cook's first landing in the state; the hamlet is known as 'The Birthplace of Queensland'. The 'Discovery Coast' is popular for surfing, boating, and fishing away from the crowds. To get here, turn east off the Bruce Hwy at Miriam Vale, 70km south of Gladstone. It's another 57km to Agnes Water and a further 6km to the Town of 1770.

Capricorn Coast & Southern Reef Islands Highlights

① Diving the spectacular underwater coral gardens of **Heron Island** (p385) and **Lady Elliot Island** (p384).

② Playing castaway on the coral cays of the **Southern Reef Islands** (p384).

③ Tucking into a huge steak in Australia's beef capital, **Rockhampton** (p386).

④ Crawling through black holes and tight tunnels in the **Capricorn Caves** (p387).

⑤ Hiking through lush rainforest at **Byfield** (p391).

⑥ Surfing and chilling at Queensland's most northerly surf beach, **Agnes Water** (p379).

⑦ Claiming a tropical beach for the day on **Great Keppel Island** (p391).

⊙ Sights

Miriam Vale Historical Society Museum MUSEUM
(☑ 07-4974 9511; Springs Rd, near cnr Captain Cook Dr, Agnes Water; adult/child $3/free; ☺ 1-4pm Mon & Wed-Sat, 10am-4pm Sun) The museum displays extracts from Cook's journal and the original telescope from the first lighthouse built on the Queensland coast.

⋆ Activities & Tours

The action around here happens on and in the water. Agnes Water is Queensland's northernmost **surf beach**. A surf life-saving club patrols the main beach and there are often good breaks along the coast. If you're looking for boating, Round Hill Creek at the Town of 1770 is a calm anchorage. There's also good **fishing** and **mudcrabbing** upstream, and the southern end of the Great Barrier Reef is easily accessible from here. Charter boats are available for fishing, surfing, snorkelling and diving trips out to the Reef.

1770 Larc Tours TOUR
(☑ 07-4974 9422; www.1770larctours.com.au; adult/child $155/95) 🍃 Ride the world's most peculiar ecotourism chariot (a hot pink amphibious military vehicle) on adventurous seven-hour tours around Bustard Head and Eurimbula National Park. They also run hour-long afternoon tours (adult/child $38/17) and sandboarding safaris ($120).

ThunderCat 1770 ADVENTURE TOUR
(☑ 0411 078 810; tours from $70) Go wave-jumping on a surf-racing craft, slingshot over the waves on the Tube Rider Xpress or – best of all – bounce and spin through the water in a sumo suit. For those less in need of an adrenaline hit, explore calmer waterways on a Wilderness Explorer ecotour.

Lady Musgrave Cruises CRUISE
(☑ 07-4974 9077; www.1770reefcruises.com; Captain Cook Dr, Town of 1770; adult/child $185/85; ☺ departs daily 8.30am) This family-owned company has excellent day trips to Lady Musgrave Island. Groups spend five hours at the island, and cruises include coral viewing in a semi-submersible, lunch, morning and afternoon tea and snorkelling gear. For an extra cost you can go diving or reef fishing. Island camping transfers are also available for $340 per person.

Reef 2 Beach Surf School SURFING
(☑ 07-4974 9072; www.reef2beachsurf.com; Agnes Water Shopping Centre, Agnes Water) Learn to surf on the gentle breaks of the main beach with this highly acclaimed surf school. A three-hour group lesson is $17 per person; surfboard hire is $20 for four hours.

1770 Liquid Adventures KAYAKING
(☑ 0428 956 630; www.1770liquidadventures.com.au) Paddle off on a spectacular twilight kayak tour. For $55, you ride the waves off 1770, before retiring to the beach for drinks and snacks as the sun sets – keep an eye out for dolphins. You can also rent kayaks for $35 (two hours).

Scooteroo MOTORCYCLING
(☑ 07-4974 7697; www.scooterootours.com; 21 Bicentennial Dr, Agnes Water; 3hr chopper ride $75) Straddle a chopper and vroom off on an irreverent and engaging 50km ride around the area. Anyone with a car licence can ride the gear-less bikes. Wear long pants and closed-in shoes; they'll supply the tough-guy leather jackets (with flames on them, of course).

Lazy Lizard Surf School SURFING
(☑ 0488 177 000; 31 Starfish St, Agnes Water) The Lazy Lizard offers lessons for smaller groups of up to 12 people ($22 for four hours).

Fishing FISHING
You can rent a dinghy (half day $75, full day $110) at Town of 1770's small marina; ask for Poppy Bob. He'll also get you set up with everything you need to dip a line. If you don't want to go it alone, **Hooked on 1770** (☑ 07-4974 9794; www.1770tours.com; half-/full-day tour $150/220) runs charter tours.

⋆ Festivals

Agnes Blues & Roots Festival MUSIC
(www.agnesbluesandroots.com.au; SES Grounds, Agnes Water) Top names and up-and-coming Aussie acts crank it up in the last weekend of February.

⊨ Sleeping

Workmans Beach Camping Area CAMPGROUND $
(Workmans Beach, Springs Rd, Agnes Water; sites per person $6) Why doesn't every coastal town have one of these? Workmans Beach is a council-run camping ground with spacious sites in gorgeous beachside surrounds; if you're really smitten, you can stay up to 44 days. Facilities are limited but for those

who can exist without whiz-bang mod-cons, you won't find anything lacking. You can't book sites; just turn up, and good-humoured council blokes will knock on your van/tent at an ungodly hour of the morning.

Cool Bananas
HOSTEL **$**

(☑ 1800 227 660, 07-4974 7660; www.coolbananas. net.au; 2 Springs Rd, Agnes Water; dm $26, $140 weekly; @) This good-humoured, Balinese-themed backpackers has roomy six- and eight-bed dorms, open and airy communal areas, and is only a five-minute walk to the beach and shops. Otherwise, you can laze the day away in a hammock in the tropical gardens.

1770 Southern Cross Tourist Retreat
HOSTEL **$**

(☑ 07-4974 7225; www.1770southerncross.com; 2694 Round Hill Rd, Agnes Water; dm/d incl breakfast $25/85; @ 🛜 🛏) There's an enlightened approach to budget accommodation at this bushland retreat, with a fish-filled, swimmable lake, Buddhist statues and meditation areas ideal for pensive reflection (or sleeping off a hangover). The dorms are superb. It's 2.5km out of town, and is connected by a courtesy bus.

1770 Camping Ground
CARAVAN PARK **$**

(☑ 07-4974 9286; www.1770campingground.com. au; Captain Cook Dr, Town of 1770; unpowered/powered site $33/37) A large but peaceful park with sites right by the beach and plenty of shady trees.

★ LaLaLand Retreat
RETREAT **$$**

(☑ 07-4974 9554; www.lalalandholiday.com.au; 61 Bicentennial Dve, Agnes Water; cottage $100-240; P ❄ 🛏) The colourful cottages at this vibrant guesthouse on the road into town are set in attractive bushland scrub and each sleeps up to five people. There is an excellent lagoon-style pool, wheelchair access and a sense of being removed from civilisation. Call for deals on rates.

Agnes Water Beach Club
APARTMENT **$$**

(☑ 07-4974 7355; www.agneswaterbeachclub.com. au; 3 Agnes St, Agnes Water; 1-/2-bedroom apt from $145/200; ❄ @ 🛏) Brand-new luxury apartments with excellent facilities in a great location.

✖ Eating

Agnes Water Bakery
BAKERY **$**

(Endeavour Plaza, Agnes Water; pies $5; ☺ from 6am) Do. Not. Miss. This. The pies here are above and beyond the offerings of most city bakeries, let alone those in a sleepy seaside village, with gourmet stuffings including the magnificent Tandoori chicken. Sweet treats and, surprisingly, coffees, are equally divine. It gets packed, so get in early.

Bustards
CAFE **$**

(7 Agnes St, Agnes Water; mains $12-25; ☺ breakfast, lunch & dinner) The hottest breakfast spot in Agnes Water is close to the main beach and rightfully popular for its locally sourced seafood and light lunches. Charming and laid-back.

★ Tree Bar
MODERN AUSTRALIAN **$$**

(☑ 07-4974 7446; 576 Captain Cook Dr, Town of 1770; mains $19-34; ☺ breakfast, lunch & dinner) This little salt-encrusted waterfront diner has plenty of charm and an atmospheric bar. Local seafood is a winner here, though breakfasts (from $8) are pretty damned fine as well.

Deck
INDIAN **$$**

(☑ 07-4974 9157; 384 Captain Cook Dr, Captain Cook Holiday Village, Town of 1770; mains $20-32; ☺ dinner Tue-Sun) Stupendous Indian fare that's not afraid to dip its toe in a vat of chillis. Lovely, palm-rustling surrounds make it even easier to swallow.

Yok Attack
THAI **$$**

(☑ 07-4974 7454; Endeavour Plaza, Agnes Water; mains $17-25.50; ☺ lunch & dinner Mon-Sat) This simple Thai restaurant is very popular with the locals and is highly recommended by repeat customers.

Agnes Water Tavern
PUB **$$**

(☑ 07-4974 9469; 1 Tavern Rd, Agnes Water; mains $15-30; ☺ lunch & dinner) Pleasant multipurpose pub with plenty of outdoor seating. Lunch and dinner specials daily.

🛍 Shopping

1770 Markets
MARKET

(SES Grounds, Town of 1770) Mellow markets with chatty stallholders flogging everything from edibles to antiques. Held the second and fourth Sunday of the month from 8am to noon.

ℹ Information

The **Agnes Water visitor centre** (☑ 07-4902 1533; 71 Springs Rd, Town of 1770; ☺ 9am-5pm Mon-Fri, to 4pm Sat & Sun) is staffed by above-and-beyond volunteers who even leave information and brochures out overnight, just in case a lost soul blows into town. Next door, the **Agnes Water Library** (☑ 07-4902 1515; 71 Springs Rd, Town of 1770; ◷ 9am-4.30pm Mon-Fri) has free internet access (half an hour, book in advance).

ⓘ Getting There & Away

BUS

A handful of **Greyhound** (☑ 1300 473 946; www. greyhound.com.au) buses detour off the Bruce Hwy to Agnes Water; daily services include Bundaberg ($25, 1½ hours) and Cairns ($217, 21 hours). **Premier Motor Service** (☑ 13 34 10; www.premierms.com.au) also goes in and out of town.

EURIMBULA & DEEPWATER NATIONAL PARKS

South of Agnes Water is Deepwater National Park, an unspoiled coastal landscape with long sandy beaches, freshwater creeks, good fishing spots and two camping grounds. It's also a major breeding ground for logger-head turtles, which dig nests and lay eggs on the beaches between November and February. You can watch the turtles laying and see hatchlings emerging at night between January and April, but you need to observe various precautions: the Agnes Water visitor centre has more info, or see www.nprsr.qld. gov.au/parks/deepwater.

The northern park entrance is 8km south of Agnes Water and is only accessible by 4WD. It's another 5km to the basic camping ground at Middle Rock (no facilities) and a further 2km to the Wreck Rock camping ground and picnic area, with rain and bore water and composting toilets. Wreck Point

can also be accessed from the south by 2WD vehicles via Baffle Creek.

The 78-sq-km Eurimbula National Park, on the northern side of Round Hill Creek, has a landscape of dunes, mangroves and eucalypt forest. There are two basic camping grounds, one at Middle Creek with toilets only and the other at Bustard Beach with toilets and limited rainwater. The main access road to the park is about 10km south-west of Agnes Water.

You must obtain permits for all camping grounds from the NPRSR (☑ 13 74 68; www.nprsr.qld.gov.au; permit per person/family $5.45/21.80).

GLADSTONE

POP 31,778

Unless you've got an industry fetish, Gladstone, with its busy port, power station and alumina refineries, is rather uninspiring. You might want to head straight for the marina (Bryan Jordan Dr), the main departure point for boats to the southern coral cay islands of Heron, Masthead and Wilson on the Great Barrier Reef. If there's anything happening in town, it's on at the port end of Gondoon St.

◉ Sights & Activities

If you have some time to spare before or after island hopping, drive up to the Auckland Point Lookout for views over Gladstone harbour, the port facilities and shipping terminals. A brass tablet on the lookout maps the harbour and its many islands.

ART DETOUR

Cedar Galleries (☑ 07-4975 0444; www.cedargalleries.com.au; Bruce Hwy, Calliope; ◷ 9am-4pm Thu-Sat, 8am-4pm Sun) is a tranquil artists' bush retreat where you can watch painters and sculptors at work in the rustic slab-hut studios. To unleash your creative genius you can take art & craft classes with visiting artists (call ahead to book) or just browse the gardens and the gallery. There's also a cafe, a beautiful handcrafted wedding chapel, kids' jumping castle, a winery cellar door and a herd of friendly alpacas. The complex runs a weekly farmers' market every Sunday (from 8am to noon); the friendly bazaar is the ideal spot for stocking up on gourmet goodies, freshly baked bread, local wines and handmade gifts. Having too much fun to move on? Cedar Galleries has limited farmstay accommodation available (studio $100 first night, $60 subsequent nights).

This old-school Aussie artists' colony (25km south of Gladstone) is signposted off the Bruce Hwy, 7km southeast of Calliope.

CURTIS ISLAND

Curtis Island, just across the water from Gladstone, can't be confused with a resort island. Apart from swimming, fishing and lolling about on the dunes, its main drawcard is the annual appearance of rare flatback turtles on its eastern shores between October and January. Camping permits can be booked via **NPRSR** (☑13 74 68; www.nprsr.qld.gov. au; permit per person/family $5.45/21.80) or you can stay with the friendly folks at **Capricorn Lodge** (☑07-4972 0222; capricornlodge@bigpond.com; lodgings from around $80). They have a corner store and a liquor licence. Curtis Ferry Services (p384) connects the island with Gladstone every day bar Tuesday and Thursday.

Toondoon Botanic Gardens GARDENS
(☑07-4977 6899; Glenlyon Rd; ☺7am-6pm Mon-Fri, 9am-6pm Sat & Sun Oct-Mar, 7am-5.30pm Mon-Fri, 8.30am-5.30pm Sat & Sun Apr-Sep) **FREE**
More than 80 hectares of rainforest, lakes and Australian native plants. There's a visitor centre, an orchid house, and free guided tours between February and November. About 7km south of town.

**Calliope River
Historical Village** HISTORIC SITE
(☑07-4975 7883; www.calliooperiverhistoricalvillage.com; Dawson Hwy, Calliope; admission $5; ☺10am-4pm) If you are in the area, **market days** (8am to 1pm, seven times a year; ask the visitor centre or see website for dates) at the Calliope River Historical Village, 26km south of Gladstone, are hugely popular, attracting over 3000 people. Wander around the village's restored heritage buildings and browse the 200-plus stalls of goodies.

Lake Awoonga LAKE
Created by the construction of the Awoonga Dam in 1984, Lake Awoonga is a popular recreational area 30km south of Gladstone. Backed by the rugged **Castle Tower National Park**, the barramundi-stocked lake has landscaped picnic areas, a cafe, barbecues, walking trails and bird life. You can hire watercraft from **Lake Awoonga Boat Hire** (☑07-4975 0930; tinnies half-day $80, kayaks per hour $15) and snooze lakeside at **Lake Awoonga Caravan Park** (☑07-4975 0155; www.lakeawoonga.net.au; Lake Awoonga Rd, Benaraby; 2 people unpowered/powered site $26/34, cabins from $70).

☞ Tours

Gladstone's big-ticket industries, including the alumina refineries, aluminium smelter, power station and port authority, open their doors for free **industry tours**. The one- or 1½-hour tours start at different times on dif- ferent days of the week depending on the industry. Book at the visitor centre.

Various charters offer fishing, diving and sightseeing cruises to the Swains Reef and Bunker Island groups. Try **MV Mikat** (☑0427 125 727; www.mikat.com.au), **Capricorn Star Cruises** (☑07-4978 0499; www.capricornstarcruises.citysearch.com.au) or **Kanimbla Charters** (☑1800 677 202; www.kanimblacharters.net.au).

⊨ Sleeping

Gladstone Backpackers HOSTEL $
(☑07-4972 5744; www.gladstonebackpackers.com. au; 12 Rollo St; dm/d $25/70; @ ☱) Friendly, family-run place in an old Queenslander, with a large kitchen, clean bathrooms and an airy outside deck. There's free use of bicycles and free pick-ups from the all transport depots.

**Barney Beach
Accommodation Centre** CARAVAN PARK $
(☑07-4972 1366; www.barneybeachaccommodationcentre.com.au; 10 Friend St; powered site $39, cabin for 2 people $155-220; ✳@☱) About 2km east of the city centre and close to the foreshore, this is the most central of the caravan parks. It's large and tidy, with a good camp kitchen and excellent self-contained accommodation. There are complimentary transfers to the marina for guests visiting Heron Island.

Harbour Sails Motel MOTEL $$
(☑07-4972 3456; www.harboursails.com.au; 23 Goondoon St; r from $150; ✳☞☱) Sparkling, modern and central motel with the classy **Brass Bell Restaurant** attached (mains $22 to $34).

Auckland Hill B&B B&B $$$
(☑07-4972 4907; www.ahbb.com.au; 15 Yarroon St; s/d incl breakfast $175/235; ✳☱) This sprawling, comfortable Queenslander has six spacious rooms with king-sized beds. Each is differently decorated: there's a spa suite and

one with wheelchair access. Breakfasts are hearty and the mood is relaxed.

✖ Eating & Drinking

Gladstone Yacht Club
PUB $$

(☑07-4972 2294; www.gyc.com.au; 1 Goondoon St; mains from $22; ☺noon-2pm & 6-8.30pm Mon-Thu, 11.30am-2.30pm & 5.30-9pm Fri & Sat, 11.30am-2pm & 6-8.30pm Sun) The yacht club is a popular place for winin' and dinin', and with very good reason. The steak, chicken, pasta and seafood are tasty and generous, there are daily buffet specials and you can eat on the deck overlooking the water.

Tables on Flinders
SEAFOOD $$$

(☑07-4972 8322; 2 Oaka La; mains from $38; ☺lunch Tue-Fri, dinner Tue-Sat) If you feel like a Gladstone splurge, this is the place to do it, with exquisite local seafood including fresh mudcrab, bugs and prawns dominating the pricey menu.

❶ Information

Gladstone City Library (☑07-4976 6400; 39 Goondoon St; ☺9am-5.45pm Mon-Fri, to 3pm Sat & Sun) Free internet access but you must book in advance.

Visitor Centre (☑07-4972 9000; Bryan Jordan Dr; ☺8.30am-4.30pm Mon-Fri, 9.30am-4.30pm Sat & Sun) Located at the marina, the departure point for boats to Heron Island.

❶ Getting There & Away

AIR

Qantas (☑13 13 13; www.qantas.com.au) and **Virgin** (☑13 67 89; www.virginaustralia.com) operate flights to and from Gladstone Airport, which is 7km from the city centre.

BOAT

Curtis Ferry Services (☑07-4972 6990; www. curtisferryservices.com.au; return adult/child/ family $30/22/from $84) has regular services to Curtis Island five days per week. The service leaves from the Gladstone marina and stops at Farmers Point on Facing Island en route. Transport to other nearby islands can be arranged on request.

You can also access the islands with various charter operators.

If you've booked a stay on Heron Island, the resort operates a launch (one way adult/child $50/25, two hours), which leaves the Gladstone marina at 11am daily.

BUS

Greyhound Australia (☑1300 473 946; www. greyhound.com.au) has several coach services from Brisbane ($143, 10 hours), Bundaberg ($44, 3 hours) and Rockhampton ($21, 1½ hours). The terminal is at the BP service station on the Dawson Hwy, about 200m southwest of the centre.

TRAIN

Queensland Rail (☑07-3235 1122, 1800 872 467; www.queenslandrail.com.au) has frequent north- and southbound services passing through Gladstone daily. The *Tilt Train* stops in Gladstone from Brisbane ($119, 5 hours) and Rockhampton ($39, one hour).

SOUTHERN REEF ISLANDS

If you've ever had 'castaway' dreams of tiny coral atolls fringed with sugary white sand and turquoise-blue seas, you've found your island paradise in the southern Great Barrier Reef islands. From beautiful Lady Elliot Island, 80km northeast of Bundaberg, secluded and uninhabited coral reefs and atolls dot the ocean for about 140km up to Tryon Island, east of Rockhampton.

Several cays in this part of the Reef are excellent for snorkelling, diving and just getting back to nature – though reaching them is generally more expensive than reaching islands nearer the coast. Some of the islands are important breeding grounds for turtles and seabirds, and visitors should be aware of precautions to ensure the wildlife's protection, outlined in the relevant NPRSR information sheets.

Camping is allowed on Lady Musgrave, Masthead and North West national park islands, and campers must be totally self sufficient. Numbers are limited, so it's advisable to apply well ahead for a camping permit. Contact **NPRSR** (☑13 74 68; www.nprsr.qld.gov. au; permit per person/family $5.45/21.80).

Access is from Town of 1770 and Gladstone.

Lady Elliot Island

On the southern frontier of the Great Barrier Reef, Lady Elliot is a 40-hectare vegetated coral cay popular with divers, snorkellers and nesting sea turtles and seabirds. Divers can walk straight off the beach to explore an ocean-bed of shipwrecks, coral gardens, bommies (coral pinnacles or outcroppings) and blowholes, and abundant marine life including barracuda, giant manta rays and harmless leopard sharks.

Lady Elliot Island is not a national park, and camping is not allowed; your only option is the low-key **Lady Elliot Island Resort** (☑1800 072 200; www.ladyelliot.com.au; per person $147-350). Accommodation is in tent cabins, simple motel-style units or more expensive two-bedroom, self-contained suites. Rates include breakfast and dinner, snorkelling gear and some tours.

The only way to reach the island is in a light aircraft. Resort guests are flown in from Bundaberg, the Gold Coast and Hervey Bay; flights are booked through the hotel. The resort also manages day trips; see their website for updates and info.

Lady Musgrave Island

Wannabe castaways look no further. This tiny, 15-hectare cay, 100km northeast of Bundaberg, sits on the western rim of a stunning, turquoise-blue reef lagoon renowned for its safe swimming, snorkelling and diving. A squeaky white-sand beach fringes a dense canopy of pisonia forest brimming with roosting bird life, including terns, shearwaters and white-capped noddies. Birds nest from October to April while green turtles nest from November to February.

The uninhabited island is part of the Capricornia Cays National Park and there is a NPRSR camping ground on the island's west side; you must be totally self-sufficient and bring your own water. Numbers are limited to 40 at any one time, so apply well ahead for a permit with the **NPRSR** (☑13 74 68; www.nprsr.qld.gov.au; per person/family $5.45/21.80). Bring a gas stove; fires are not permitted on the island.

Day trips to Lady Musgrave depart from the Town of 1770 marina.

Heron & Wilson Islands

With the underwater reef world accessible directly from the beach, Heron Island is famed for superb scuba diving and snorkelling, although you'll need a fair amount of cash to visit. A true coral cay, it is densely vegetated with pisonia trees and surrounded by 24 sq km of reef. There's a resort and research station on the northeastern third of the island; the remainder is national park.

Heron Island Resort (☑1300 863 248; www.heronisland.com; d/suite/beach house from

> **ⓘ STINGERS**
>
> The potentially deadly chironex box jellyfish and irukandji, also known as sea wasps or marine stingers, occur in Queensland's coastal waters north of Agnes Water (and occasionally further south) from around October to April, and swimming is not advisable during these times. Fortunately, swimming and snorkelling are usually safe around the reef islands throughout the year; however, appearances of the rare and tiny (1cm to 2cm across) irukandji have been recorded on the outer Reef and islands. For more information on stingers and treatment, see p507.

$419/669/909) has comfortable accommodation that is suited to families and couples; the Point Suites have the best views. Meal packages are extra, and guests will pay $50/25 (one way) per adult/child for launch transfer, $291 by seaplane, or $395 for helicopter transfer. All are from Gladstone.

Wilson Island (☑1300 863 248; www. wilsonisland.com; per couple $1100), also part of a national park, is an exclusive wilderness retreat with six permanent 'tents' and solar-heated showers. There are excellent beaches, superb snorkelling and, during the season, turtle-watching. The only access is from Heron Island and to get here, you'll need to buy a combined Wilson-Heron package and spend at least two nights on Wilson Island. Transfers between Wilson and Heron are included in the tariff.

North West Island

Behind North West's uninspiring name is a national park that's proving evermore popular with campers, walkers and those seeking a slice of seclusion. At 106 hectares, this is the second-biggest cay on the reef, and despite a dubious past (North West was once a guano mine and home to a turtle-soup cannery), is now an important site for nesting green turtles and birds; every October, hundreds of thousands of wedge-tailed shearwaters descend on the island to nest, squabble and scare the wits out of campers with their creepy nighttime howls.

There's a limit of 150 campers on the island at any one time; camping is closed from January 26 until Easter each year (day trips allowed year-round). There's no scheduled service to North West, but **Curtis Ferry Services** (📞 07-4972 6990; www.curtisferryservices.com.au) can arrange a drop-off. **NPRSR** (📞 13 74 68; www.nprsr.qld.gov.au) has more info on getting to the island, camping and essentials.

ROCKHAMPTON

POP 61,724

Welcome to Rockhampton ('Rocky' to its mates), where the hats, boots and utes are big...but the bulls are even bigger. With over 2.5 million cattle within a 250km radius of Rockhampton – it's called Australia's Beef Capital for a reason – it's no surprise the smell of bulldust hangs thick in the air. This sprawling country town is the administrative and commercial centre of central Queensland, its wide streets and fine Victorian-era buildings reflecting the region's prosperous 19th-century heyday of gold and copper mining and the beef-cattle industry.

Straddling the tropic of Capricorn, Rocky can be aptly scorching; it's 40km inland, lacks coastal sea breezes and summers are often unbearably humid. The town has a smattering of attractions but is best seen as the gateway to the coastal gems of Yeppoon and Great Keppel Island. Stay in the old part of town to enjoy some charming walks along the Fitzroy River.

◉ Sights & Activities

★ Botanic Gardens & Zoo
GARDENS
(📞 07-4932 9000; Spencer St; ⊙ 6am-6pm) FREE Just south of town, these gardens are a beautiful oasis, with impressive figs, tropical and subtropical rainforest, landscaped gardens and lily-covered lagoons. The formal Japanese garden is a zen-zone of tranquillity, the **cafe** (open 8am to 5pm) serves tea and cakes under a giant banyan fig, and the awesome **free zoo** (open 8.30am to 4.30pm) has koalas, wombats, dingoes, apes, a walk-through aviary and tonnes more.

Tropic of Capricorn
LANDMARK
(Gladstone Rd) Attitude on the latitude! Straddle the tropic of Capricorn at the visitor centre on Gladstone Rd; it's marked by a huge spire.

Quay Street
STREET
In town, wander down this historic streetscape, with its grand sandstone Victorian-era buildings dating back to the gold-rush days. You can pick up leaflets that map out walking trails around Rockhampton from the visitor centres.

Rockhampton City Art Gallery
GALLERY
(📞 07-4936 8248; www.rockhamptonartgallery.com.au; 62 Victoria Pde; ⊙ 10am-4pm) FREE Boasting an impressive collection of Australian paintings, this gallery includes works by Sir Russell Drysdale, Sir Sidney Nolan and Albert Namatjira. Contemporary Indigenous artist Judy Watson also has a number of works on display.

Dreamtime Cultural Centre
CULTURAL CENTRE
(📞 07-4936 1655; www.dreamtimecentre.com.au; Bruce Hwy; adult/child $14/6.50; ⊙ 10am-3.30pm Mon-Fri, tours 10.30am) An easily accessible insight into Aboriginal and Torres Strait Islander heritage and history. The excellent 90-minute tours are hands on (throw your own boomerangs!) and appeal to all ages. About 7km north of the centre.

Heritage Village
MUSEUM
(📞 07-4936 8680; Bruce Hwy; adult/child/family $10.50/6.80/30.50; ⊙ 9am-4pm) An active museum of replica historic buildings with townsfolk at work in period garb. There's also a visitor centre here. It's 10km north of the city centre.

Kershaw Gardens
GARDEN
(📞 07-4936 8254; via Charles St; ⊙ 6am-6pm) FREE Just north of the Fitzroy River, this excellent botanical park is devoted to Australian native plants. Its attractions include artificial rapids, a rainforest area, a fragrant garden and heritage architecture.

Archer Park Rail Museum
MUSEUM
(📞 07-4922 2774; www.rockhamptonregion.qld.gov.au; Denison St; adult/child/family $8/5/26; ⊙ 9am-4pm Sun-Fri) This museum is housed in a former train station built in 1899. Through photographs and displays it tells the station's story, and that of the unique Purrey steam tram. Take a ride on the restored tram (the only remaining one of its kind in the world!) every Sunday from 10am to 1pm.

Mt Archer
MOUNTAIN
This mountain (604m) has walking trails weaving through eucalypts and rainforest abundant in wildlife. A brochure to the park is available from the visitor centres.

☞ Tours

Little Johnny's Tours and Rentals TOUR
(📞 0414 793 637; www.littlejohnnysrentals.com)
Runs trips to many nearby attractions like
Byfield and the Capricorn Caves, and also
does minibus runs between Rockhampton
Airport and Yeppoon.

✦ Festivals & Events

Beef Australia AGRICULTURAL
(www.beefaustralia.com.au) Held every three
years, this is a huge exposition of all things
beefy.

Jazz on Quay Festival JAZZ
(www.jazzonquay.com.au) Held each spring
along the Fitzroy River.

🛏 Sleeping

The northern and southern approach roads
to Rocky are lined with numerous motels
but if you want to stroll the elegant palm-
lined streets overlooking the Fitzroy, choose
somewhere in the old centre, south of the
river.

Rockhampton Backpackers HOSTEL $
(📞 07-4927 5288; www.rockhamptonbackpackers.
com.au; 60 MacFarlane St; dm/d $22/60; ❋ @ ☎)
A YHA member, Rocky Backpackers has a
spacious lounge and dining area, plus varied types of accommodation. They do it all,
from arranging tours and courtesy pickups
from the bus station to selling coach tickets.
There's also free bike hire.

Southside Holiday Village CARAVAN PARK $
(📞 07-4927 3013; www.sshv.com.au; Lower Dawson
Rd; site unpowered/powered $30/38, cabin $72-93,
villa $103-120; ❋ @ 🛜 ☎) One of the city's best
caravan parks, with neat, self-contained cabins and villas, large grassed camp sites and
a good kitchen. Prices are for two people.
It's about 3km south of the centre on a busy
main road.

Criterion HOTEL $$
(📞 07-4922 1225; www.thecriterion.com.au; 150
Quay St; r $60-85, motel r $130-160; ❋) The Cri-
terion is Rockhampton's grandest old pub,
with an elegant foyer and function room, a
friendly bar and a great bistro (Bush Inn).
Its top two stories have dozens of period
rooms; the rooms have showers, although
the toilets are down the hall. They also have
a number of 4½-star motel rooms.

Coffee House MOTEL, APARTMENT $$
(📞 07-4927 5722; www.coffeehouse.com.au; 51
William St; r $160-189; ❋ ❋ ☎) The Coffee House
features beautifully appointed motel rooms,
self-contained apartments and spa suites.
There's a popular, stylish cafe-restaurant–
wine bar on site.

🍴 Eating & Drinking

⭐ Ginger Mule STEAKHOUSE $
(📞 07-4927 7255; 8 William St; mains from $10;
⊙ 11.30am-midnight Wed & Thu, to 2am Fri, 4pm-
2am Sat) Rocky's coolest eatery bills itself
as a tapas bar, but everyone's here for one
thing: steak! And bloody (or chargrilled)
good steak it is too. They have regular

CAPRICORN CAVES

In the Berserker Range, 24km north of Rockhampton near the Caves township, the
amazing **Capricorn Caves** (📞 07-4934 2883; www.capricorncaves.com.au; 30 Olsens
Caves Rd; adult/child $27/14; ⊙ 9am-4pm) are not to be missed. These ancient caves
honeycomb a limestone ridge, and on a guided tour through the caverns and labyrinths
you'll see cave coral, stalactites, dangling fig-tree roots and little insectivorous bats. The
highlight of the one-hour 'cathedral tour' is the beautiful natural rock cathedral where a
recording of 'Amazing Grace' is played to demonstrate the cavern's incredible acoustics.
Every December, traditional Christmas carol singalongs are held in the cathedral. Also
in December, around the summer solstice (1 December to 14 January), sunlight beams
directly through a 14m vertical shaft into Belfry Cave, creating an electrifying light show.
If you stand directly below the beam, reflected sunlight colours the whole cavern with
whatever colour you're wearing.

Daring spelunkers can book a two-hour 'adventure tour' ($75) which takes you
through tight spots with names such as 'Fat Man's Misery'. You must be at least 16 years
old for this tour.

The Capricorn Caves complex has barbecue areas, a pool, kiosk, and **accommodation** (unpowered/powered site $30/35, cabin from $140).

late-week meals specials (including $10 steaks); pop down early or prepare to battle for a table. Morphs into a cocktail bar late in the evenings.

Saigon Saigon ASIAN $

(☑07-4927 0888; www.saigonbytheriver.com; Quay St; mains $12-20; ◷11.30am-2.30pm & 5-9pm Wed-Mon) This two-storey bamboo hut overlooks the Fitzroy River and serves pan-Asian food with local ingredients like kangaroo and crocodile served in a sizzling steamboat. Not up for reptile? The menu is as intricate as the restaurant exterior's neon light display. There are lots of vegetarian options, too.

Steakhouse 98 SEAFOOD, STEAKHOUSE $$

(☑07-4920 1000; www.98.com.au; 98 Victoria Pde; mains $18-46; ◷breakfast daily, lunch Mon-Fri, dinner Mon-Sat) In Rocky, it's all about the steak. And this licensed dining room doesn't disappoint with its Mod Oz takes on beef, as well as kangaroo, lamb and seafood. Sit inside or on the terrace overlooking the Fitzroy River. Attached to the Motel 98.

Pacino's ITALIAN $$

(☑07-4922 5833; cnr Fitzroy & George Sts; mains $25-40; ◷dinner Tue-Sun) This stylish Italian restaurant oozes Mediterranean warmth with its wooden tables and potted fig trees. Pricey, though consistently popular for favourites such as osso bucco and pasta cooked a dozen different ways.

Heritage Hotel PUB $$

(☑07-4927 6996; www.theheritagehotel.com.au; cnr William & Quay St; meals $20-30; ◷ noon-3pm & 6-9pm Tue-Fri, 6-9pm Mon & Sat) This pub with sugarspun iron-lattice balconies has a cocktail lounge with river views and outdoor tables. The steak-heavy menu features other grilled meats billed under names like 'baaaah' and 'cluck cluck'. You'll work it out.

★ Great Western Hotel PUB

(☑07-4922 1862; www.greatwesternhotel.com.au; cnr Stanley & Denison Sts; ◷10am-2am) Yeehaw! Looking like a spaghetti-western film set, this 1862 pub is home to Rocky's cowboys and 'gals. Out the back there's a rodeo arena where every Wednesday and Friday night you can watch brave cattlefolk being tossed in the air by bucking bulls and broncos. Touring bands occasionally rock here; you can get tickets online.

ⓘ Information

Rockhampton Library (☑07-4936 8265; 230 Bolsover St; ◷9am-5.30pm Mon, Tue, Thu, Fri, to 8pm Wed, to 4.30pm Sat) Free internet access, but you need to book.

Tropic of Capricorn Visitor Centre (☑1800 676 701; Gladstone Rd; ◷9am-5pm) Helpful centre on the highway right beside the tropic of Capricorn marker, 3km south of the centre. Its sister branch is the Rockhampton visitor centre (☑1800 805 865; 208 Quay St; ◷8.30am-

RINGERS & COWBOYS: FARM STAYS

Kick up some red dust on a fair-dinkum Aussie outback cattle station and find out the difference between a jackeroo, a ringer, a stockman and a cowboy. On a farm stay, you'll be immersed in the daily activities of a working cattle station, riding horses and motor-bikes, mustering cattle, fencing, and cooking damper and billy tea over a campfire. Before you know it you'll find yourself looking for a ute and a blue dog to go with your RM Williams boots and Akubra hat.

Myella Farm Stay (☑07-4998 1290; www.myella.com; Baralaba Rd; 2/4 days $260/480, day trips $120; ❄@☎), 125km southwest of Rockhampton, gives you a taste of the outback on its 10.6-sq-km farm. The package includes bush explorations by horseback, motorcycle and 4WD, all meals, accommodation in a renovated homestead with polished timber floors and a wide verandah, farm clothes and free transfers from Rockhampton. You get to do bushie stuff like fix fences, dowse for water and help care for orphaned joeys at the station's kangaroo rehab centre.

The Kroombit Lochenbar Cattle Station (☑07-4992 2186; www.kroombit.com.au; dm $27, d with/without bathroom $86/78, 2-day & 2-night package per person incl room, meals & activities $280; ❄@☎) offers several farm-stay packages to choose from and you can pitch a tent or stay in bush-timber or upmarket cabins. While soaking up the Aussie experience you can learn to crack a whip, throw a boomerang or loop a lasso, and earn your spurs on a mechanical bucking bull. Rates include meals and pick-up from nearby Biloela.

4.30pm Mon-Fri, 9am-4pm Sat & Sun) in the beautiful former Customs House in central Rocky. Both centres also serve as branches for the NPRSR.

ℹ️ Getting There & Away

AIR

Qantas (📞13 13 13; www.qantas.com.au) and **Virgin** (📞13 67 89; www.virginaustralia.com) connect Rockhampton with various cities. The airport is about 6km from the centre of town.

BUS

Greyhound Australia (📞1300 473 946; www.greyhound.com.au) has regular services from Rocky to Mackay ($60, four hours), Brisbane ($155, 11 hours) and Cairns ($195, 17 hours). All services stop at the **Mobil roadhouse** (91 George St). **Premier Motor Service** (📞13 34 10; www.premierms.com.au) operates a Brisbane–Cairns service, stopping at Rockhampton.

Young's Bus Service (📞07-4922 3813; www.youngsbusservice.com.au; 171 Bolsover St) travels to Yeppoon and Mt Morgan ($6.40 one way) Monday to Friday. Buses depart from Bolsover St, outside the police station.

TRAIN

Queensland Rail (📞1800 872 467; www.queenslandrailtravel.com.au) runs the *Tilt Train*, which connects Rockhampton with Brisbane (from $135, 8 hours, Sunday to Friday) and Cairns (from $322, 16 hours, twice weekly). Rocky's a great gateway to Queensland's dusty interior: hop the twice-weekly *Spirit of the Outback* to bush towns including Longreach (from $145, 14 hours) or Emerald (from $75, five hours). The train station is 450m southwest of the city centre.

ℹ️ Getting Around

Sunbus (www.sunbus.com.au) runs a reasonably comprehensive city bus network operating all day Monday to Friday and Saturday morning; pick up a timetable at the visitor centre. Otherwise, there's always **Rocky Cabs** (📞13 10 08).

YEPPOON

POP 13,500

Pretty little Yeppoon is a small seaside town with a long beach, a calm ocean and an attractive hinterland of volcanic outcrops, pineapple patches and grazing lands. The handful of quiet streets, sleepy motels and beachside cafes attracts Rockhamptonites beating the heat, and tourists heading for Great Keppel Island only 13km offshore.

👁 Sights & Activities

Cruises and the ferry to Great Keppel Island depart from the Keppel Bay Marina at Rosslyn Bay, just south of Yeppoon.

Cooberrie Park   WILDLIFE RESERVE

(📞07-4939 7590; www.cooberriepark.com.au; Woodbury Rd; adult/child/family $25/15/65; ⏱10am-3pm, animal show 1pm) About 15km north of Yeppoon, Cooberrie Park is a small wildlife sanctuary on 10 hectares of bushland. You can see kangaroos, wallabies and peacocks wandering freely through the grounds. You can also feed the critters and, for an extra cost, hold a furry koala or some slithering reptiles.

Funtastic Cruises   CRUISE

(📞0438 909 502; www.funtasticcruises.com; full-day cruise adult/child/family $98/80/350) Funtastic Cruises operates full-day snorkelling trips on board its 17m catamaran, with a two-hour stopover on Great Keppel Island, morning and afternoon tea, and all snorkelling equipment included. It can also organise camping drop-offs to islands en route.

Sail Capricornia   CRUISE

(📞0402 102 373; www.sailcapricornia.com.au; full-day cruise incl lunch adult/child $115/75) Sail Capricornia offers snorkelling cruises on board the *Grace* catamaran, as well as sunset ($55) and three-day ($499) cruises.

🛏 Sleeping

There are beaches, caravan parks, motels and holiday units along the 19km coastline running south from Yeppoon to Emu Park. A fairly complete listing can be found at www.yeppooninfo.com.au.

Coral Inn Flashpackers   HOSTEL $

(📞07-4939 2925; www.flashpackers.net.au; 14 Maple St; dm $29, d from $90; 🅿❄@🛜🐾) Reef-bright colours and vibrant communal spaces make Coral Inn a difficult place to leave. All rooms have en suites, and there's a great communal kitchen. Parking is an extra $5, and there's absolutely no smoking anywhere on the property.

Beachside Caravan Park   CARAVAN PARK $

(📞07-4939 3738; Farnborough Rd; unpowered/powered site $25/30-34) This basic but neat little camping ground north of the town centre commands a wonderful, totally beachfront location. It has good amenities and grassed sites with some shade but no cabins or on-site vans. Rates are for two people.

Surfside Motel
MOTEL $$

(☑07-4939 1272; 30 Anzac Pde; r $110-140; ❋@
� ❖ ❄) Across the road from the beach and close to town, this 1950s strip of lime-green motel units epitomises summer holidays at the beach. And it's terrific value – the rooms are spacious and unusually well equipped, complete with toaster, hair dryer and free wi-fi.

Driftwood Units
UNIT $$

(☑07-4939 2446; www.driftwoodunits.com.au; 5-7 Todd Ave; unit $120-140; ❋❋) Driftwood has huge self-contained units at motel prices with absolute beach frontage. Great for families, or anyone in need of a seaside slowdown. If you're too lazy to stagger a few steps to the beach, there's a nice saltwater pool on-site.

While Away B&B
B&B $$

(☑07-4939 5719; www.whileawaybandb.com.au; 44 Todd Ave; s/d incl breakfast $115/140-155; ❋) With four good-sized rooms and an immaculately clean house with wheelchair access, this B&B is a perfect, quiet getaway. There are complimentary nibbles, tea, coffee, port and sherry as well as generous breakfasts.

✕ Eating & Drinking

Flour
CAFE $

(☑07-4925 0725; 9 Normanby St; pastries $3.50, breakfast $8.50; ☉8am-3pm Mon-Fri, to 2pm Sat) Adorable smalltown cafe with big-city breakfasts and melt-in-mouth cakes. Loads of gluten-free options, and without a doubt the best coffee for miles.

Thai Take-Away
THAI $$

(☑07-4939 3920; 24 Anzac Pde; mains $14-32; ☉6-10pm) A deservedly popular Thai BYO restaurant where you can sit outside on the sidewalk, catch a sea breeze, and satisfy those chilli and coconut cravings. There's a large selection of seafood dishes and snappy service.

Strand Hotel
PUB $$

(☑07-4939 1301; Normanby St; mains from $14; ☉11.30am-2.30pm & 5.30-9pm Mon-Fri, 8am-9pm Sat & Sun) This is upmarket pub food with classic/exotic pizzas ($14 to $24) and fantastic steaks ($28 to $41). It's famous for its Sunday evening (6pm to 7.30pm) *parrilla*, an Argentinian barbecue, with music to match.

Megalomania
FUSION $$

(☑07-4939 2333; Arthur St; mains $22-36; ☉noon-3pm & 5.30-9pm Tue-Sat, to 3pm Sun) An urban-island feel permeates Yeppoon's best restaurant, which serves up Oz-Asian fusion cuisine with interesting takes on local seafood. Loll beneath the fig tree or clink silverware in the indoor woodsy surrounds.

Footlights Theatre Restaurant
COMEDY

(☑07-4939 2399; www.footlights.com.au; 123 Rockhampton Rd; dinner & show $51) Footlights Theatre Restaurant hosts a three-course meal and a two-hour comedy-variety show every Friday and Saturday night.

ℹ Information

The **Capricorn Coast visitor centre** (☑1800 675 785; www.capricorncoast.com.au; Ross Creek Roundabout; ☉9am-5pm) has plenty of information on the Capricorn Coast and Great Keppel Island, and can book accommodation and tours.

Yeppoon library (☑07-4939 3433; 78 John St; ☉9am-5pm Mon, Tue, Thu & Fri, to 8pm Wed, to 4pm Sat) has free internet access; bookings essential.

ℹ Getting There & Away

Yeppoon is 43km northeast of Rockhampton. **Young's Bus Service** (☑07-4922 3813; www. youngsbusservice.com.au) runs frequent buses from Rockhampton ($6.40 one way) to Yeppoon and down to the Keppel Bay Marina.

If you're heading for Great Keppel or the Reef, some ferry operators will transport you between your accommodation and Keppel Bay Marina. If you're driving, there's a free day car park at the marina. For secure undercover parking, the **Great Keppel Island Security Car Park** (☑07-4933 6670; 422 Scenic Hwy; per day from $15) is on the Scenic Hwy south of Yeppoon, by the turn-off to the marina.

AROUND YEPPOON

The drive south from Yeppoon and Rosslyn Bay passes three fine headlands with good views: Double Head, Bluff Point and Pinnacle Point. After Pinnacle Point, the road crosses Causeway Lake, a saltwater inlet that's a top spot for estuary fishing. Emu Park (population 2021), 19km south of Yeppoon, is the second-largest township on the coast, but there's not much here, apart from more good views and the Singing Ship

BYFIELD

The staggeringly beautiful Byfield National Park is a diverse playground of mammoth sand dunes, thick semi-tropical rainforest, wetlands and rocky pinnacles. It's superb Sunday-arvo driving terrain, with plenty of hiking paths and isolated beaches to warrant a longer stay. There are five camping grounds (☑ 13 74 68; www.nprsr.qld.gov.au; per person/family $5.85/21.80) to choose from (pre-book). Nine Mile Beach and Five Rocks are on the beach and you'll need a 4WD to access them. When conditions are right, there's decent surf at Nine Mile.

Get to know the rainforest on a silent, electric boat cruise with Waterpark Eco-Tours (☑ 07-4935 1171; www.waterparkecotours.com; 201 Waterpark Creek Rd; 2-3hr tour $25, cabins $120), run out of a working tea-tree plantation.

Byfield Mountain Retreat (☑ 07-4935 1161; www.byfieldmountainretreat.com; 216 Arnolds Rd; per night/week $220/1200) is set on 66 acres of rich rainforest with heady hinterland views. The home sleeps 12, and there's a log fire, walking trails and king-sized beds. The retreat is attached to Nob Creek Pottery (☑ 07-4935 1161; www.nob-creekpottery.com.au; 216 Arnolds Rd; ⊙ 10am-4pm) FREE, a working pottery and gallery showcasing hand-blown glass, woodwork and jewellery; the handmade ceramics are outstanding.

Signposted just north of Byfield, Ferns Hideaway (☑ 07-4935 1235; www.ferns hideaway.com; 67 Cahills Rd, Byfield; unpowered site per person $15, cabins $150; ❀ ❁) is a secluded bush oasis with cabins, a camping ground, canoeing and nature walks. The homestead has a cosy restaurant (mains $20-38; ⊙ lunch Fri & Sun, lunch & dinner Sat), replete with a log fire, hearty, heartwarming meals and live music on the weekends.

Byfield General Store (☑ 07-4935 1190; Byfield Rd; ⊙ 8am-6pm Wed-Mon) has fuel, basic grocery supplies and a simple courtyard cafe serving pies, sandwiches and highly recommended burgers. It doubles as an information centre.

The park is a 40km drive north from Yeppoon. North of Byfield, the Shoalwater Bay military training area borders the forest and park, and is strictly off limits.

memorial to Captain Cook – a curious monument of drilled tubes and pipes that emit mournful whistling and moaning sounds in the breeze. Emus Beach Resort (☑ 07-4939 6111; www.emusbeachresort.com; 92 Pattison St, Emu Park; dm $25-28, d/tr/q $80/95/105; ❀ @ ❁) is a superlative hostel, with a pool, kitchen, barbecue and a travel booking service; it also offers tours to the local crocodile farm. Otherwise, Bell Park Caravan Park (☑ 07-4939 6202; www.bellparkcaravanpark.com.au; Pattinson St; unpowered/powered site $25/30, cabin $107) is just stone's throw from the beach.

Emu Park Pizza & Pasta (☑ 07-4938 7333; Hill St; pizzas $12-24; ⊙ 4.30-9pm) is an unprepossessing place, but the pizzas attract locals from Yeppoon.

Situated 15km along the Emu Park–Rockhampton road, the Koorana Crocodile Farm (☑ 07-4934 4749; www.koorana.com.au; Coowonga Rd; adult/child $27/12; ⊙ tours 10.30am & 1pm) can only be explored via the informative guided tours. After watching the man-eaters splash and dash frighteningly around, get your feeble human revenge by sampling croc kebabs, croc ribs or a croc pie at the restaurant.

GREAT KEPPEL ISLAND

Great Keppel Island is a stunning island with rocky headlands, forested hills and a fringe of powdery white sand lapped by clear azure waters. Numerous 'castaway' beaches ring the 14-sq-km island, while natural bushland covers 90% of the interior. A string of huts and accommodation options sits behind the trees lining the main beach but the developments are low-key and relatively unobtrusive. Only 13km offshore, and with good snorkelling, swimming and bush walking, Great Keppel is an easily accessible, tranquil island retreat.

The kiosk at Great Keppel Island Holiday Village has a few essentials, but if you want to cook, bring your own supplies.

Great Keppel Island

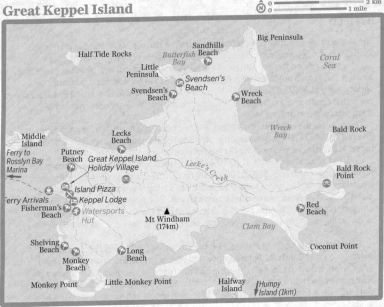

N   0 _____ 2 km
     0 _____ 1 mile

Map labels:
Big Peninsula
Half Tide Rocks
Sandhills Beach
Butterfish Bay
Little Peninsula
Svendsen's Beach
Svendsen's Beach
Wreck Beach
Coral Sea
Middle Island
Lecks Beach
Wreck Bay
Bald Rock
Ferry to Rosslyn Bay Marina
Putney Beach
Great Keppel Island Holiday Village
Leeke's Creek
Bald Rock Point
Island Pizza
Ferry Arrivals
Fisherman's Beach
Keppel Lodge
Watersports Hut
Mt Windham (174m)
Red Beach
Clam Bay
Shelving Beach
Long Beach
Coconut Point
Monkey Beach
Monkey Point
Little Monkey Point
Halfway Island
Humpy Island (1km)

◉ Sights

The beaches of Great Keppel rate among Queensland's best. Take a short stroll from Fisherman's Beach, the main beach, and you'll find your own deserted stretch of white sand. There is fairly good coral and excellent fish life, especially between Great Keppel and Humpy Island to the south. A 30-minute walk south around the headland brings you to Monkey Beach, where there's good snorkelling. A walking trail from the southern end of the airfield takes you to Long Beach, perhaps the best of the island's beaches.

There are several bushwalking tracks from Fisherman's Beach; the longest and perhaps the most difficult leads to the 2.5m 'lighthouse' near Bald Rock Point on the far side of the island. It's about three hours return.

⚡ Activities & Tours

Watersports Hut
WATER SPORTS
(☏ 07-4925 0624; Putney Beach; ⊙ Sat & Sun & school holidays) The Watersports Hut on the main beach hires out snorkelling equipment, kayaks and catamarans, and runs tube rides.

Freedom Fast Cats
CRUISE
(☏ 07-4933 6888; www.freedomfastcats.com; Keppel Bay Marina, Rosslyn Bay; adult/child from $75/48) Operates a range of island tours, from glass-bottomed boat viewing to snorkelling and boom-netting.

🛏 Sleeping

★ Svendsen's Beach
CABIN $$
(☏ 07-4938 3717; www.svendsensbeach.com; cabins per 3 nights per person $330) 🌿 This secluded boutique retreat has two luxury tent-bungalows on separate elevated timber decks overlooking lovely Svendsen's Beach. It's an eco-friendly operation, run on solar and wind power; there's even a bush-bucket shower. It's the perfect place for snorkelling, bushwalking and romantic getaways. Transfers from the ferry drop-off on Fisherman's Beach are included in the tariff.

Great Keppel Island Holiday Village
HOSTEL, CABIN $$
(☏ 07-4939 8655; www.gkiholidayvillage.com.au; dm $35, s & d tent $90, cabin $150, house from $230) The village offers various types of good budget accommodation (dorms, cabins, decked tents), as well as entire houses. It's a friendly, relaxed place with shared bathrooms, a decent communal kitchen and barbecue area.

Snorkelling gear is free and they run motorised canoe trips to top snorkelling spots.

Keppel Lodge GUESTHOUSE **$$**
(☑07-4939 4251; www.keppellodge.com.au; Fisherman's Beach; d per person $65-75, house $520-600; @☞) A pleasant open-plan house with four large bedrooms (with bathrooms) branching from a large communal lounge and kitchen. The house is available in its entirety – ideal for a group booking – or as individual suites.

✖ Eating

Bring all supplies; there is only one restaurant and no supermarkets on the island.

Island Pizza PIZZERIA **$**
(☑07-4939 4699; The Esplanade; dishes $6-30; ☺varies) This friendly place prides itself on its gourmet pizzas with plenty of toppings. Check blackboard for opening times.

ℹ Getting There & Away

Freedom Fast Cats (☑07-4933 6888; www.freedomfastcats.com) departs from the Keppel Bay Marina in Rosslyn Bay (7km south of Yeppoon) for Great Keppel Island each morning, returning that same afternoon (call ahead for exact times). The return fare is $52/33/150 per adult/child/family. If you've booked accommodation on the island, check that someone will meet you on the beach to help with your luggage.

OTHER KEPPEL BAY ISLANDS

Although you can make day trips to the fringing coral reefs of Middle Island or Halfway Island from Great Keppel Island (ask your accommodation or at Great Keppel Island Holiday Village), you can also camp (per person/family $5.85/21.80) on several national park islands, including Humpy Island, Middle Island, North Keppel Island and Miall Island. Take your own supplies and water. For information and permits contact the NPRSR (☑13 74 68; www.nprsr.qld.gov.au) or Rosslyn Bay Marine Parks (☑07-4933 6595).

The otherwise glamorous Pumpkin Island was temporarily renamed XXXX Island, after being leased until 2015 by the Queensland brewing giant; at the time of research unless you have any luck with a 'specially marked' box of beer, you are not allowed to visit.

From Rosslyn Bay, Funtastic Cruises (☑0438 909 502; www.funtasticcruises.com; cruise adult/child $98/80) offers day cruises exploring the islands and can also provide drop-offs and pick-ups for campers.

Whitsunday Coast

Best Places to Eat

➡ Mr Bones (p411)
➡ Spice n Flavour (p398)
➡ Fish D'vine (p410)
➡ Jochheims Pies (p416)
➡ Kevin's Place (p399)

Best Places to Stay

➡ Qualia (p414)
➡ Whitsunday Island camping grounds (p416)
➡ Platypus Bushcamp (p402)
➡ Kipara (p408)
➡ Fernandos Hideaway
   (p410)

Why Go?

Speckling the calm waters of the Coral Sea, the superlative Whitsunday Islands are one of Australia's greatest natural attractions. Opal-jade waters and pure-white beaches fringe the forested domes of these 'drowned mountains', where you can camp in secluded bays, laze in resorts, snorkel, dive or island-hop through the archipelago. Beneath the shimmering seas, tropical fish swarm through the world's largest coral garden in the Great Barrier Reef Marine Park. The gateway to the islands, Airlie Beach, is a happening backpacker hub with a continuous parade of tanned, happy faces zinging between boats, beaches and banging nightclubs.

South of Airlie, Mackay is a typical coastal Queensland town with palm-lined streets framed by art deco buildings. There's not a lot to do here, but Mackay is a handy base for trips to Finch Hatton Gorge and Eungella National Park – lush hinterland oases where platypuses cavort in the wild. To the north, Bowen has secret beaches and historical street art.

When to Go
Mackay

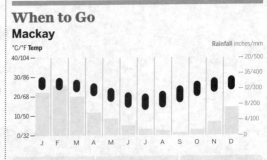

Jun–Oct The perfect time to enjoy sunny skies, calm days, mild weather and stinger-free seas.

Aug Sailboats skim across the water, and parties are held during Airlie Beach Race Week.

Sep–Oct Optimal conditions for kayaking around the islands.

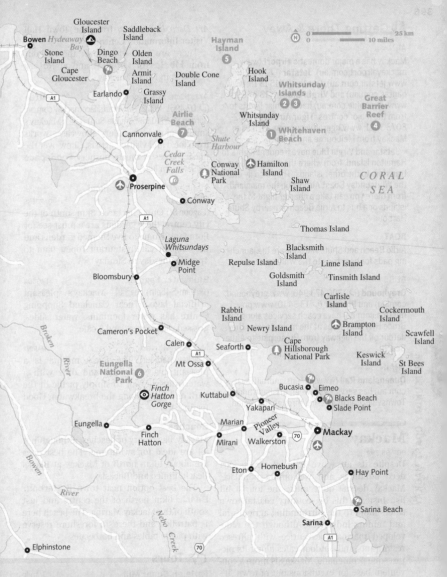

Whitsunday Coast Highlights

1 Being dazzled by the bright-white silica sand at stunning **Whitehaven Beach** (p415).

2 Sailing through the magnificent aquamarine waters of the **Whitsunday Islands** (p403).

3 Camping under the stars, hiking nature trails and making like an island castaway in the **Whitsunday Islands National Park** (p407).

4 Diving and snorkelling the fringing reefs or the outer **Great Barrier Reef** (p404).

5 Sipping cocktails by the pool at the luxurious tropical island resort of **Hayman Island** (p415).

6 Waiting patiently for a glimpse of a shy platypus and walking in the misty rainforest at **Eungella National Park** (p401).

7 Getting wet, swilling beer and partying hard in fun-lovin' **Airlie Beach** (p408).

ℹ️ Getting There & Away

AIR

Mackay has a major domestic **airport** (www.mackayairport.com.au). **Jetstar** (☎13 15 38; www.jetstar.com.au), **Qantas** (☎13 13 13; www.qantas.com.au) and **Virgin Blue** (☎13 67 89; www.virginblue.com.au) have regular flights to/from the major centres. **Tiger Airways** (☎02-8073 3421; www.tigerairways.com.au) flies to Mackay from Melbourne and Sydney.

Jetstar and Virgin Blue have frequent flights to Hamilton Island, from where there are boat/air transfers to the other islands. They also fly into the Whitsunday Coast Airport on the mainland; from there you can take a charter flight to the islands or a bus to Airlie Beach or nearby Shute Harbour.

BOAT

Airlie Beach and Shute Harbour are the launching pads for boat trips to the Whitsundays.

BUS

Greyhound (☎1300 473 946; www.greyhound.com.au) and **Premier** (☎13 34 10; www.premierms.com.au) have coach services along the Bruce Hwy with stops at the major towns. They detour off the highway from Proserpine to Airlie Beach.

TRAIN

Queensland Rail (www.queenslandrailtravel.com.au) has services between Brisbane and Townsville/Cairns passing through the region.

Mackay

POP 85,399

Despite its attractive tropical streets, art deco buildings and welcoming populace, Mackay doesn't quite make the tourist hit list. Instead, this big country coastal town caters more to the surrounding agricultural and mining industries. Although the redeveloped marina does entice with alfresco restaurants and outdoor cafes along its picturesque promenade, Mackay is more a convenient base for excursions out of town. It's only a 1½-hour drive to the Whitsundays, a short flight or charter boat to the pretty Cumberland Islands and a scenic jaunt past the sugar-cane fields to Pioneer Valley and Eungella National Park.

👁 Sights

Mackay's impressive art deco architecture owes much to a devastating cyclone in 1918, which flattened many of the town's buildings. Enthusiasts should pick up a copy of *Art Deco in Mackay* from the Town Hall Visitor Information Centre.

There are good views over the harbour from Mt Basset Lookout and at Rotary Lookout in North Mackay.

Artspace Mackay
GALLERY

(☎07-4961 9722; www.artspacemackay.com.au; Gordon St; ⏱10am-5pm Tue-Sun) FREE Mackay's small regional art gallery showcases works from local and visiting artists. Chew over the masterpieces at onsite noshery Foodspace (⏱9am-3pm Tue-Sun).

Mackay Regional Botanical Gardens
GARDENS

(Lagoon St) On 33 hectares, 3km south of the city centre, these gardens are a must-see for flora fans. Home to five themed gardens and the Lagoon cafe/restaurant (open 9am to 4pm Wednesday to Sunday).

Bluewater Lagoon
LAGOON

(⏱9am-5.45pm) FREE Mackay's pleasant artificial lagoon near Caneland Shopping Centre has water fountains, water slides, grassed picnic areas and a cafe.

Mackay Marina
MARINA

(Mackay Harbour) The lively marina is a pleasant place to wine and dine with a waterfront view, or to simply picnic in the park and stroll along the breakwater. Good fishing, too.

Beaches

Mackay has plenty of beaches, although not all are ideal for swimming. The best ones are about 16km north of Mackay at Blacks Beach, Eimeo and Bucasia.

The best option near town is Harbour Beach, 6km north of the centre and just south of the Mackay Marina. The beach here is patrolled and there's a foreshore reserve with picnic tables and barbecues.

👉 Tours

Farleigh Sugar Mill
TOUR

(☎07-4959 8360; 2hr tour adult/child $25/13; ⏱9.30am & 1pm May-Dec) In the cane-crushing season, you can see how sugar cane is turned into sweet crystals. Dress appropriately for a working mill: long sleeves, long pants, enclosed shoes. Morning/afternoon tea included.

Reeforest Adventure Tours
CULTURAL TOUR

(☎1800 500 353; www.reeforest.com) Offers a wide range of junkets, including a platypus

Central Mackay

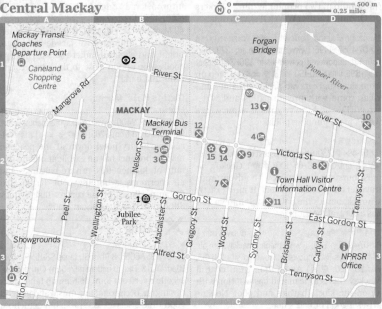

and rainforest ecosafari and two-day Eungella tours.

Heritage Walk WALKING
(☎07-4944 5888; ⏱9am Wed May-Sep) FREE
Weekly wandering (1½ to two hours) that takes in the sights and secrets of ye olde Mackay. Leaves from the visitor centre at the Old Town Hall, Sydney St.

✦ Festivals

Wintermoon Folk Festival MUSIC
(www.wintermoonfestival.com) Folk and world-music lovefest every May.

🛌 Sleeping

There are plenty of motels strung along busy Nebo Rd, south of the centre. The budget options (from around $110 for a double) post their prices out front and tend to suffer from road noise.

★Stoney Creek Farmstay FARM STAY $
(☎07-4954 1177; www.stoneycreekfarmstay.com; Peak Downs Hwy; dm/livery stable/cottage $25/100/145) 🐾 This bush retreat (32km south of Mackay) is a down'n'dirty option in the best possible way. Stay in an endearingly ramshackle cottage, the rustic livery stable or the charismatic Dead Horse Hostel, and forget all about the mod-cons for

Central Mackay

◉ Sights
1 Artspace Mackay	B2
2 Bluewater Lagoon	B1

🛏 Sleeping
3 Coral Sands Motel	B2
4 Gecko's Rest	C2
5 International Lodge Motel	B2

✗ Eating
6 Austral Hotel	A2
7 Burp Eat Drink	C2
8 Comet Coffee	D2
Foodspace	(see 1)
9 Kevin's Place	C2
10 Maria's Donkey	D2
11 Oscar's on Sydney	C2
12 Spice n Flavour	C2

🍷 Drinking & Nightlife
13 Ambassador Hotel	C1
14 Gordi's Cafe & Bar	C2

✪ Entertainment
15 Tryst	C2

🛍 Shopping
16 Markets	A3

a while: this is deadset bush livin'. Three-hour horse rides cost $95 per person. The owners will pick you up if you ring ahead (minimum of two people). Willing Workers on Organic Farms (WWOOFs) welcome.

Mackay Marine Tourist Park   CARAVAN PARK $
(07-4955 1496; www.mmtp.com.au; 379 Harbour Rd; unpowered/powered site $30/34, budget cabin $95, villa $110-150; ✳@☎☎) A step up from the usual caravan parks: all cabins and villas come with private patios and widescreen TVs, and you've gotta love anywhere with a giant jumping pillow.

Gecko's Rest   HOSTEL $
(07-4944 1230; www.geckosrest.com.au; 34 Sydney St; dm/d/f $28/65/100; ✳@) Gecko's almost bursts at the seams with adventurous travellers and mine workers. It ain't exactly schmick, but it's the only hostel in town and has a central location.

The Park Mackay   CARAVAN PARK $
(07-4952 1211; www.theparkmackay.com.au; 284 Farrellys Rd; unpowered/powered site $31/33, villa $85-120; @☎) About 7km from central Mackay, this is a clean and basic option with an on-site kiosk, barbies and pool. No surprises – good or bad – here.

Coral Sands Motel   MOTEL $$
(07-4951 1244; www.coralsandsmotel.com.au; 44 Macalister St; r $130-165; ✳☎☎) One of Mackay's better midrange options, the Coral Sands boasts ultra-friendly management and large rooms in a central location. It's a bit tropi-kitsch, but with the river, shops, pubs and cafes so close to your doorstep, you won't care.

Ocean Resort Village   RESORT $$
(1800 075 144; www.oceanresortvillage.com.au; 5 Bridge Rd; studio/family unit/2br unit from $90/100/135; ✳☎) This is a good-value beachside resort set amid tropical gardens. The cool, shady setting has two pools, barbecue areas, half-court tennis and the occasional possum drop-in. The village is located 4km southeast of the town centre (take Gordon to Goldsmith to Bridge).

> ### ⓘ SUMMER STING: WHERE TO SWIM?
>
> The presence of marine stingers means swimming in the sea isn't advisable between October and May unless you wear a stinger suit. In Airlie Beach, the gorgeous lagoon (p408) on the foreshore provides year-round safe swimming.

International Lodge Motel   MOTEL $$
(07-4951 1022; www.internationallodge.com.au; 40 Macalister St; r from $120; P✳☎) Hidden behind an unimpressive facade are clean, bright and cheerful motel rooms. This is a good-value option close to the city's restaurants and bars.

Clarion Hotel Mackay Marina   LUXURY HOTEL $$$
(07-4955 9400; www.mackaymarinahotel.com; Mulherin Dr; d from $285; ✳@☎☎) This welcoming luxury hotel down at the peaceful marina precinct has an excellent on-site restaurant, kitchenettes, private balconies and an enormous swimming pool. It's located 6.5km northeast of the centre. Take Sydney St north across the Forgan Bridge.

🍴 Eating

Maria's Donkey   TAPAS $
(07-4957 6055; 8 River St; tapas $8-15; ☉ noon-10pm Wed & Thu, to midnight Fri-Sun) Quirky, energetic riverfront joint dishing up tapas, jugs of sangria, occasional live music and general good times. Service is erratic, but somehow, that's part of the charm.

Comet Coffee   CAFE $
(0423 420 195; 43 Victoria St; sandwiches $7-9; ☉ 5.30am-3pm Mon-Fri, 9am-noon Sat & Sun) Mackay's best drop is served in an old garage in the quiet end of town. Rifle through the magazine collection and munch on a magnificent muffin or pastrami-pickle-Swiss-cheese sanga.

Oscar's on Sydney   FUSION $
(07-4944 0173; cnr Sydney & Gordon Sts; mains $10-23; ☉ 7am-5pm Mon-Fri, to 4pm Sat, 8am-4pm Sun) The delicious *poffertjes* (Dutch pancakes with traditional toppings) are still going strong at this very popular corner cafe, but don't be afraid to give the other dishes a go. Top spot for breakfast.

★ Spice n Flavour   INDIAN $$
(07-4999 9639; 162 Victoria St; mains $15-25, banquets per person from $35; ☉ 11.30am-2.30pm Mon-Fri, 5.30pm-late daily) Chilli lovers disappointed by what passes for 'hot' in other Indian restaurants will get their fill of mouth-burning here (by request). All the favourites and some more exotic tastes are on the menu, and they offer drink-pairing advice for the unsure. Come what may, you must try the mango beer.

Kevin's Place
ASIAN $$

(☑07-4953 5835; 79 Victoria St; mains $16-27; ☺lunch & dinner Mon-Fri, dinner Sat) Sizzling, spicy Singaporean dishes and efficient, revved-up staff combine with the building's colonial ambience and the tropical climate to create a Rafflesesque experience.

Austral Hotel
PUB $$

(☑07-4951 3288; 189 Victoria St; mains $19-36, steaks $24-47; ☺noon-2.30pm & 6-9pm) So many steaks. Such little time.

Burp Eat Drink
MODERN AUSTRALIAN $$$

(☑07-4951 3546; www.burp.net.au; 86 Wood St; mains from $33; ☺11.30am-3pm & 6pm-late Tue-Fri, 6pm-late Sat) A swish Melbourne-style restaurant in the tropics, Burp has a small but tantalising menu. Sophisticated selections include pork belly with scallops, kaffir-lime-crusted soft shell crab, plus some serious steaks.

🍷 Drinking & Nightlife

Gordi's Cafe & Bar
PUB

(85 Victoria St) Gordi's is a street-side watering hole known locally as the unrivalled pre-party or post-work meeting place.

Ambassador Hotel
BAR

(☑07-4953 3233; www.ambassadorhotel.net.au; 2 Sydney St; ☺5pm-late Thu, 4pm-late Fri-Sun) Art deco outside, wild'n'crazy inside. Multilevel carousing, including Mackay's only rooftop bar.

Sails Sports Bar
BAR

(☑07-4955 3677; Mulherin Dr, Mackay Harbour; ☺10am-midnight) This themed bar can get rowdy at night, but it's a great place on Sunday arvo with live music and a marina outlook.

Tryst
CLUB

(99 Victoria St; ☺10pm-4am Thu-Sat) Frenetic dance club hosting a mix of resident and guest-star DJs.

🛍 Shopping

Markets
MARKET

They like their markets in Mackay, with a surprisingly varied bunch of bazaars selling everything from bric-a-brac to one-off duds to organic fruit. Try the Mackay Showgrounds Markets (Saturdays from 7.30am, Milton St), Twilight Markets (first Friday of the month from 5pm to 9pm, Mackay Surf Club) and the Troppo Market (second Sunday of the month from 7.30am, Mt Pleasant Shopping Centre carpark).

ℹ Information

The train station, airport, botanic gardens and visitor centre are about 3km south of the city centre. Mackay Harbour, 6km northeast of the centre, is dominated by a massive sugar terminal, while the adjacent marina has a smattering of waterfront restaurants.

Mackay Visitor Centre (☑1300 130 001; www.mackayregion.com; 320 Nebo Rd; ☺9am-5pm Mon, 8.30am-5pm Tue-Fri, 9am-4pm Sat & Sun) About 3km south of the centre. Internet access.

NPRSR Office (☑07-4944 7818; www.nprsr.qld.gov.au; 30 Tennyson St; ☺8.30am-4.30pm Mon-Fri) For camping permits.

Town Hall Visitor Information Centre (☑07-4957 1775; 63 Sydney St; ☺9am-5pm Mon-Fri, to noon Sat) Info and internet access.

ℹ Getting There & Away

AIR

The airport is about 3km south of the centre of Mackay.

Jetstar (☑13 15 38; www.jetstar.com.au), **Qantas** (☑13 13 13; www.qantas.com.au) and **Virgin Blue** (☑13 67 89; www.virginblue.com.au) have flights to/from Brisbane. **Tiger Airways** (☑02-8073 3421; www.tigerairways.com.au) has direct flights between Mackay and Melbourne/Sydney.

BUS

Buses stop at the **Mackay Bus Terminal** (cnr Victoria & Macalister Sts), where tickets can also be booked. **Greyhound** (☑1300 473 946; www.greyhound.com.au) travels up and down the coast. Sample one-way adult fares and journey times: Airlie Beach ($30, two hours), Townsville ($67, 6 hours), Cairns ($113, 13 hours) and Brisbane ($213, 17 hours).

Premier (☑13 34 10; www.premierms.com.au) is less expensive than Greyhound but has less services.

TRAIN

The **Queensland Rail** (☑1800 872 467; www.traveltrain.com.au) *Tilt Train* connects Mackay with Brisbane ($260, 13 hours), Townsville ($125, 5½ hours) and Cairns ($200, 12 hours). The slower *Sunlander* does the same: Brisbane (economy seat/sleeper $140/240, 17 hours). The train station is at Paget, 5km south of city centre.

❶ Getting Around

Major car-rental firms have desks at the Mackay Airport: see www.mackayairport.com.au/travel/car-hire for listings.

Mackay Transit Coaches (✆ 07-4957 3330; www.mackaytransit.com.au) has several services around the city, and connects the city with the harbour and northern beaches; pick up a timetable from one of the visitor centres or look online. **Ocean Breeze Transfers** (www.ocean-breeze-transfers.com.au) run between the city and airport: book in advance.

For a taxi, call **Mackay Taxis** (✆ 13 10 08).

Mackay's Northern Beaches

The coastline north of Mackay is made up of a series of headlands and bays sheltering small residential communities with holiday accommodation.

At Blacks Beach, the beach extends for 6km, so stretch those legs and claim a piece of Coral Sea coast for a day. Of the several accommodation options, **Blue Pacific Resort** (✆ 07-4954 9090; www.bluepacificresort.com.au; 26 Bourke St, Blacks Beach; studio $165-180, 1-2br unit $180-265; ✼🖥🕿✳) has bright, cheerful units directly on the beach. All rooms have self-catering facilities.

Close by is **Blacks Beach Holiday Park** (✆ 07-4954 9334; www.mackayblacksbeach-holidaypark.com.au; 16 Bourke St, Blacks Beach; unpowered/powered site $30/35, villa $140-180; P✼✳), with tent sites overlooking a gloriously long stretch of beach.

At the north end of Blacks Beach, the four-star **Dolphin Heads Resort** (✆ 07-4944 4777; www.dolphinheadsresort.com.au; Beach Rd, Dolphin Heads; d $160-220; ✼@🖥✳) has 80 comfortable, motel-style units overlooking an attractive (but rocky) bay.

North of Dolphin Heads is Eimeo, where the **Eimeo Pacific Hotel** (Mango Ave, Eimeo; ⏰10am-10pm) crowns a headland commanding magnificent Coral Sea views. It's a great place for a beer.

Bucasia is across Sunset Bay from Eimeo and Dolphin Heads, but you have to head all the way back to the main road to get up there. The recently upgraded **Bucasia Beachfront Caravan Resort** (✆ 07-4954 6375; www.bucasiabeach.com.au; 2 The Esplanade; powered site $30-45; ✳🖥) has a selection of sites, some of which enjoy absolute beachfront views.

Sarina

POP 5730

In the foothills of the Connors Range, Sarina is a service centre for the surrounding sugarcane farms and home to CSR's Plane Creek sugar mill and ethanol distillery. It's also a nice little fishing spot: ask the locals for their favourite place to wet a hook.

The **Sarina Tourist Art & Craft Centre** (✆ 07-4956 2251; www.sarinatourism.com; Railway Sq, Bruce Hwy; ⏰9am-5pm) showcases locally made handicrafts and assists with visitor information.

Sarina Sugar Shed (✆ 07-4943 2801; www.sarinasugarshed.com.au; Railway Sq; adult/child $21/11; ⏰tours 9.30am, 10.30am, noon & 2pm Mon-Sat) is the only miniature sugar-processing mill and distillery of its kind in Australia. After the tour, enjoy a complimentary tipple at the distillery.

The town centre straddles the Bruce Hwy. The **Tramway Motel** (✆ 07-4956 2244; www.tramwaymotel.com.au; 110 Broad St; d from $125, unit $180-200; ✼🖥✳), north of the centre, has clean, bright units. For a dining experience with a difference, head to the Diner (11 Central St; mains $4-6; ⏰4am-6pm Mon-Fri, to 10am Sat), a rustic roadside shack that has served tucker to truckies and cane farmers for decades. Take the turn-off to Clermont in the centre of town and look for the tin shack on your left, just before the railway crossing.

Around Sarina

There are a number of low-key beachside settlements a short drive east from Sarina. Clean, uncrowded beaches and mangrove-lined inlets provide excellent opportunities for relaxing, fishing, beachcombing and spotting wildlife such as nesting marine turtles.

Sarina Beach

On the shores of Sarina Inlet, this laid-back coastal village boasts a long beach, a general store/service station and a boat ramp at the inlet.

★**Fernandos Hideaway** (✆ 07-4956 6299; www.sarinabeachbb.com; 26 Captain Blackwood Dr; s/d/ste $130/140/160; ✼✳) is a Spanish hacienda–style B&B perched on a rugged headland. It offers magnificent coastal views and absolute beachfront. In the living room there's a stuffed lion, a suit of armour and an eclectic assortment of souvenirs from the eccentric owner's global travels.

Sarina Beach Motel (☎07-4956 6266; www.sarinabeachmotel.com; 44 Owen Jenkins Dve; d $135-160; ❀ ❋) is located at the northern end of the Esplanade. Most rooms have beach frontage. Its restaurant is open nightly.

Armstrong Beach

Armstrong Beach Caravan Park (☎07-4956 2425; 66 Melba St; unpowered/powered site $21-50) is a lovely coastal spot just a few kilometres southeast of Sarina. Prices are for two people.

Pioneer Valley

Travelling west, Mackay's urban sprawl gives way to the lush greenness of beautiful Pioneer Valley, where the unmistakable smell of sugar cane wafts through your nostrils as loaded cane trains busily work their way along the roadside. The first sugar cane was planted here in 1867 and today almost the entire valley floor is planted with the stuff. The route to Eungella National Park, the Mackay–Eungella Rd, branches off the Peak Downs Hwy about 10km west of Mackay and follows the river through vast fields of cane to link up with the occasional small town or steam-belching sugar mill.

About 17km west of the small town of Mirani is the **Pinnacle Hotel** (www.pinnaclehotel.com.au; Eungella Rd , Pinnacle; mains $10-20). The pub has accommodation (camp sites $10 to $20, doubles $50), an outdoor cafe, and live music on Sunday afternoons. Try a Pinnacle Pie or regret it for the rest of your days.

Another 10km further down the road is the turn-off for Finch Hatton Gorge, part of Eungella National Park, and 1.5km past the turn-off is the pretty township of **Finch Hatton**.

From Finch Hatton, it's another 18km to Eungella, a quaint mountain village overlooking the valley. The last section of this road climbs suddenly and steeply with several incredibly sharp corners – towing a large caravan is not recommended.

Eungella

Pretty little Eungella (*young*-gulluh, meaning 'land of clouds') sits perched on the edge of the Pioneer Valley. There's a general store with snacks, groceries and fuel, plus a couple of accommodation and eating options. Lively markets are held on the first Sunday of each month (April to December) from 9am at the town hall.

The tidy little **Eungella Mountain Edge Escape** (☎07-4958 4590; www.mountainedgeescape.com.au; North St; 1/2br cabin $115/135; ❀) has three self-contained wooden cabins perched on the edge of the escarpment. Wonderful views, predictably, are to be had here.

Eungella Chalet (☎07-4958 4509; www.eungellachalet.com.au; Chelmer St; 1/2br cabin $115/155; ❋) exudes rustic charm in a once-grandiose kind of way. The chalet is perched on the edge of a mountain and the views are spectacular. The cabins are large and spacious but furnishings are quite dated. There's a small bar, a dining room and live music most Sunday afternoons.

Explorers' Haven (☎07-4958 4750; www.eungella.com; unpowered/powered site $25/30; @❀) is a small and very basic camping ground located just north of the township, right on the edge of the escarpment. You'll need to self-register on arrival. Prices are for two people. Luxury cabin accommodation may be available; contact the park in advance.

If it's open, the **Hideaway Cafe** (☎07-4958 4533; Broken River Rd; dishes $4-10; ⊙9am-4pm) is worth a stop; sit on the picturesque little balcony and enjoy a decent home-cooked dish.

Eungella National Park

Stunning Eungella National Park is 84km west of Mackay, covering nearly 500 sq km of the Clarke Range and climbing to 1280m at Mt Dalrymple. The mountainous park is largely inaccessible except for the walking tracks around Broken River and Finch Hatton Gorge. The large tracts of tropical and subtropical vegetation have been isolated from other rainforest areas for thousands of years and now boast several unique species including the orange-sided skink and the charming Eungella gastric-brooding frog, which incubates its eggs in its stomach and gives birth by spitting out the tadpoles.

Most days of the year, you can be pretty sure of seeing a platypus or two in the Broken River. The best times are the hours immediately after dawn and before dark, but you must remain patient, silent and still. Platypus activity is at its peak from May to August, when the females are fattening themselves up in preparation for gestating their young. Other river life you're sure to see are large northern snapping turtles and brilliant azure kingfishers.

Finch Hatton Gorge

About 27km west of Mirani, just before the town of Finch Hatton, is the turn-off to Finch Hatton Gorge. The last 2km of the 10km drive from the main road are on unsealed roads with several creek crossings that can become impassable after heavy rain. A 1.6km walking trail leads to Araluen Falls, with its tumbling waterfalls and swimming holes, and a further 1km hike takes you to the Wheel of Fire Falls, another cascade with a deep swimming hole.

A brilliantly fun and informative way to explore the rainforest here is to glide through the canopy with Forest Flying (07-4958 3359; www.forestflying.com; $60). The skyhigh guided tours see you harnessed to a 350m-long cable and suspended up to 25m above the ground; you control your speed via a pulley system. Bookings are essential, and you must weigh less than 120kg.

The following places are signposted on the road to the gorge:

Platypus Bushcamp (07-4958 3204; www.bushcamp.net; Finch Hatton Gorge; camp site $7.50, dm/d $25/75) is a true-blue bush retreat hand-built by Wazza, the eccentric owner. The basic huts have barely-there walls, with the rainforest at your fingertips. A creek with platypuses and great swimming holes runs next to the camp, and the big open-air communal-kitchen-eating area is the heart of the place. There are wonderful hot bush showers and a cosy stone hot tub. Bring your own food and linen. WWOOFers welcome.

The only luxury accommodation in Eungella National Park is the Rainforest B&B (07-4958 3099; www.rainforestbedandbreakfast.com.au; 52 Van Houweninges Rd; cabin $300). There's a touch of Balinese to this rainforest retreat with its garden sculptures, wooden cabin and romantic decor. A freshly-baked, complimentary afternoon tea awaits on your arrival. Rates go down the longer the stay.

The self-contained cabins at Finch Hatton Gorge Cabins (07-4958 3281; www.finchhattongorgecabins.com.au; d $95; ✳) are quite basic but have wonderful views of the forest. The cabins can sleep up to five people.

Broken River

Broken River, 5km south of Eungella, is home to a rightfully renowned platypus-viewing platform (near the bridge): it's reputedly one of the most reliable spots on earth to catch these meek monotremes at play. Bird life is also prolific. There are some excellent walking trails between the Broken River picnic ground and Eungella. Maps are available from the information office (by the platform), which is rarely staffed.

For accommodation, you have the choice of camping or cabins. Broken River Mountain Resort (07-4958 4000; www.brokenrivermr.com.au; d $130-190; ✳@🛜🐾) has comfortable cedar cabins ranging from small, motel-style units to a large self-contained lodge sleeping up to six. There's a cosy guest lounge with an open fire and the friendly Possums Table Restaurant & Bar (mains $22.50-35.50; ⊙ breakfast & dinner). The name is well-deserved: a family of possums dines on the balcony here every night. The resort organises several (mostly free) activities for its guests, including spotlighting, birdwatching and guided walks, and can arrange shuttle transfers for longer walks.

Fern Flat Camping Ground (www.nprsr.qld.gov.au; per person/family $5.45/21.80) is a lovely place to camp, with shady sites adjacent to the river where the platypuses play. Prepare to be spied on by nosy scrub turkeys, and serenaded by morning birds! This is a walk-in camping ground and is not vehicle accessible. Self-register camp sites are about 500m past the information centre and kiosk.

Crediton Hall Camping Ground (www.nprsr.qld.gov.au; per person/family $5.45/21.80), 3km after Broken River, is accessible to vehicles. Turn left into Crediton Loop Rd and turn right after the Wishing Pool circuit track entrance. The camping ground has toilets.

❶ Getting There & Away

There are no buses to Eungella or Finch Hatton, but Reeforest Adventure Tours (p396) runs day trips from Mackay and will drop off and pick up those who want to linger; however, tours don't run every day and your stay may wind up longer than intended.

WHITSUNDAY COAST EUNGELLA NATIONAL PARK

Cumberland Islands

There are about 70 islands in the Cumberland group, sometimes referred to as the southern Whitsundays. Almost all the islands are designated national parks. Apart from Keswick Island – home to the sophisticated and secluded Keswick Island Guest House (☑ 07-4965 8002; www.keswick-islandguesthouse.com.au; s/d from $360/550; ☎) – there's no formal accommodation in the Cumberlands.

Brampton Island is well-known for its nature walks, and was until recently the home of a posh resort. Carlisle Island is connected to Brampton by a narrow sand-bar and, during low tide, it may be possible to walk between the two. Scawfell Island is the largest in the group; on its northern side, Refuge Bay has a safe anchorage and a camping ground.

Camp-site availability, bookings and permits for the Cumberland Islands and the nearby Sir James Smith Island group can be found online at www.nprsr.qld.gov.au or at the Mackay visitor centre (p399).

Facilities on all islands are limited and access can be difficult unless you have your own boat or can afford to charter one (or a seaplane); ask for more info at the Mackay visitor centre.

Cape Hillsborough National Park

Despite being so easy to get to, this small coastal park, 50km north of Mackay, feels like it's at the end of the earth. Ruggedly beautiful, it takes in the rocky, 300m-high Cape Hillsborough and Andrews Point and Wedge Island, which are joined by a causeway at low tide. The park features rough cliffs, a broad beach, rocky headlands, sand dunes, mangroves, hoop pines and rainforest. Kangaroos, wallabies, sugar gliders and turtles are common, and the roos are likely to be seen on the beach in the evening and early morning. There are also the remains of Aboriginal middens and stone fish traps, accessible by good walking tracks. On the approach to the foreshore area there's also an interesting boardwalk leading out through a tidal mangrove forest.

Smalleys Beach Campground (www.nprsr.qld.gov.au; site per person/family $5.45/21.80) is a small, pretty and grassed camping ground hugging the foreshore and absolutely jumping with kangaroos. There's no self-registration here; book permits online.

Cape Hillsborough Nature Resort (☑ 07-4959 0152; www.capehillsboroughresort.com.au; 51 Risley Pde; unpowered/powered site $29/34, fishing hut $65-75, cabin $65-135; ✳ @ ☎) is in a quiet spot on a long stretch of beach. There's nothing fancy about the joint, but once you see kangaroos on their magical morning beach hops, things like shiny surrounds somehow matter less.

THE WHITSUNDAYS

The Whitsunday group of islands off the northeast Queensland coast is, as the cliché goes, a tropical paradise. The 74 islands that make up this arresting archipelago are really the tips of mountain tops jutting out from the Coral Sea, and from their sandy fringes the ocean spreads towards the horizon in beautiful shades of crystal, aqua, blue and indigo. Sheltered by the Great Barrier Reef, there are no crashing waves or deadly undertows, and the waters are perfect for sailing.

Of the numerous stunning beaches and secluded bays, Whitehaven Beach stands out for its pure white silica sand. It is undoubtedly the finest beach in the Whitsundays, and possibly one of the finest in the world.

Airlie Beach, on the mainland, is the coastal hub and major gateway to the islands. Only seven of the islands have tourist resorts, catering to every budget and whim: choose from the basic accommodation at Hook Island to the exclusive luxury of Hayman Island. Most of the Whitsunday Islands are uninhabited, and several offer back-to-nature beach camping and bushwalking.

✦ Activities

Sailing

What could be better than sailing from one island paradise to another? There are plenty of sailing tours itching to get your landlubber feet on deck, but if you've got salt water in your veins, a bareboat charter might be more your style. A bareboat charter lets you rent a boat without skipper, crew or provisions. You don't need formal qualifications, but you (or one of your party) have to prove you can competently operate a vessel.

Expect to pay between $500 to $1000 a day in the high season (September to January) for a yacht sleeping four to six people. A booking deposit of $500 to $750 and a security bond of between $200 and $2000 is payable before departure and refunded after the boat is returned undamaged. Bedding is usually supplied and provisions can be provided at extra cost. Most companies have a minimum hire period of five days.

It's worth asking if the company belongs to the Whitsunday Bareboat Operators Association, a self-regulatory body that guarantees certain standards. Also check that the latest edition of David Colfelt's *100 Magic Miles of the Great Barrier Reef* is stowed on board.

There are a number of bareboat charter companies around Airlie Beach: Charter Yachts Australia (☑1800 639 520; www.cya.com.au; Abel Point Marina); Cumberland Charter Yachts (☑1800 075 101; www.ccy.com.au; Abel Point Marina); Queensland Yacht Charters (☑1800 075 013; www.yachtcharters.com.au; Abel Point Marina); Whitsunday Escape (☑1800 075 145; www.whitsundayescape.com; Abel Point Marina); and Whitsunday Rent A Yacht (☑1800 075 000; www.rentayacht.com.au; 6 Bay Terrace, Shute Harbour).

If you want to know why those old salts at the bar keep smiling into their drinks, learn to sail at the Whitsunday Marine Academy (☑07-4946 5782; www.explorewhitsundays.com; 4 The Esplanade), run by Explore Whitsundays, or the Whitsunday Sailing Club (☑07-4946 6138; www.whitsundaysailingclub.com.au; Airlie Point).

Diving

Dreamy diving experiences abound at spectacular sites such as Black, Knuckle, Fairy, Bait and Elizabeth Reefs. However, the fringing reefs around the islands (especially on their northern tips) are often more colourful and abundant than most of the walls on the outer reef, and there's usually a greater variety of softer coral.

Costs for open-water courses with several ocean dives start at around $600 and generally involve two or three days' tuition on the mainland, with the rest of the time diving the reef. Check that the Great Barrier Reef Marine Park levy and any other additional costs are included in the price. Whitsunday Dive Adventures (☑07-4948 1239; www.whitsundaydivecentre.com; 16 Commerce Close, Cannonvale; PADI course $599) is a good place to start.

A number of sailing cruises include diving as an optional extra. Prices start from $75 for introductory or certified dives. Ferry operator Cruise Whitsundays (☑07-4946 4662; www.cruisewhitsundays.com; intro dive from $119) offers dives on day trips to the reef.

Most of the island resorts also have dive schools and free snorkelling gear.

Kayaking

Paddling with dolphins and turtles is one of the best ways to experience the Whitsundays. Salty Dog Sea Kayaking (☑07-4946 1388; www.saltydog.com.au; Shute Harbour; half-/full-day trip $80/130) offers guided tours and kayak rental ($50/70 per half-/full day), plus a brilliant six-day kayak/camping expedition ($1490) that's suitable for beginners.

The Ngaro Sea Trail combines kayaking trails with island bushwalks for a modern-day walk (and paddle) in the local Ngaro people's footsteps. Visit www.nprsr.qld.gov.au/parks/whitsunday-ngaro-sea-trail for info and itinerary ideas.

☞ Tours

Not everyone has the time or the money to sail, and must rely on the faster catamarans to whisk them around the islands on a day trip.

Most day trips include activities such as snorkelling or boom-netting with scuba diving as an optional extra. Most of the cruise operators run out of Abel Point Marina but those that run from Shute Harbour do coach pick-ups from Airlie Beach and Cannonvale. You can take a public bus to Shute Harbour.

Following are some of the day trips on offer; bookings can be made at any Airlie Beach tour agent:

Cruise Whitsundays CRUISE
(☑07-4946 4662; www.cruisewhitsundays.com; Shingley Dr, Abel Point Marina; full-day cruise from $99) As well as operating as a ferry, Cruise Whitsundays offers trips to Hardy Reef, Whitehaven Beach and various islands including Daydream and Long. Or you can grab a daily Island Hopper pass (adult/child $120/59) and make your own itinerary. It also operates a popular day trip aboard the Camira (adult/child $189/99 including lunch and all drinks), a catamaran that takes in Whitehaven Beach.

Voyager 4 Island Cruise BOAT TOUR
(☑07-4946 5255; www.wiac.com.au; adult/child $140/80) A good-value day cruise that in-

Whitsunday Islands

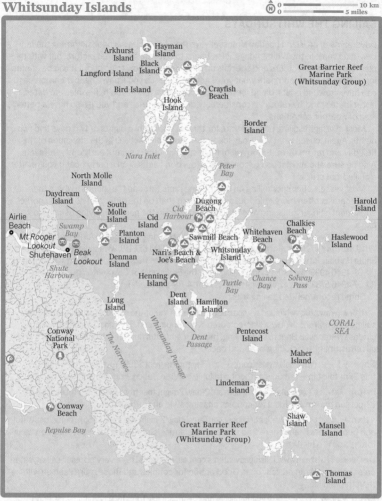

cludes snorkelling at Hook Island, beach-combing and swimming at Whitehaven Beach, and checking out Daydream Island. Add a scenic flight for $60.

Ecojet Safari
TOUR

(☏07-4948 2653; www.ecojetsafari.com.au; per person $190, 2 people per jet ski) Explore the islands, mangroves and marine life of the northern Whitsundays on these three-hour, small-group jet-ski safaris.

Ocean Rafting
BOAT TOUR

(☏07-4946 6848; www.oceanrafting.com.au; adult/child/family $129/81/384) Visit the 'wild'

side of the islands in a very fast, big yellow speedboat. Swim at Whitehaven Beach, regain your land legs with a guided national park walk or snorkel the reef at Mantaray Bay and Border Island.

Big Fury
BOAT TOUR

(☏07-4948 2201; adult/child/family $130/70/350) Speeds out to Whitehaven Beach on an open-air sports boat followed by lunch and snorkelling at a secluded reef nearby.

Air Whitsunday
SCENIC FLIGHTS

(☏07-4946 9111; www.airwhitsunday.com.au; Terminal 1, Whitsunday Airport) Offers a range of

SAILING THE WHITSUNDAYS

Daydreams of an island holiday almost always feature a white sailboat skimming the fantasy-blue seas. In the Whitsundays, it isn't hard to put yourself in that picture, but with the plethora of charters, tours and specials on offer, deciding how to go about it can be confusing. Before booking, compare what you'll get for the price you'll pay. Cheaper companies can have crowded boats, bland food and cramped quarters. If you're flexible with dates, last-minute stand-by rates can considerably reduce the price and you'll also have a better idea of weather conditions.

Most overnight sailing packages are for three days and two nights or two days and two nights. Again, check what you'll pay for. Some companies set sail in the afternoon of the first day and return by mid-morning of the last, while others set out early and return late. Also be sure about what you're committing to – don't set sail on a party boat if you're after a chilled-out cruise.

Most vessels offer snorkelling on the fringing reefs (around the islands), where the softer coral is often more colourful and abundant than on the outer reef. Check if snorkel equipment, stinger suits and reef taxes are included in the package. Diving usually costs extra.

Once you've decided, book at one of the many booking agencies in Airlie Beach such as **Whitsundays Central Reservation Centre** (☎1800 677 119; www.airliebeach.com; 259 Shute Harbour Rd) or a management company such as **Whitsunday Sailing Adventures** (☎07-4946 4999; www.whitsundaysailing.com; The Esplanade) or **Explore Whitsundays** (☎07-4946 5782; www.explorewhitsundays.com; 4 The Esplanade).

Some recommended sailing trips:

Camira (www.cruisewhitsundays.com; day trip $189) One of the world's fastest commercial sailing catamarans is now a lilac-coloured Whitsunday icon. This good-value day trip includes Whitehaven Beach, snorkelling, morning and afternoon tea, a barbecue lunch and all refreshments (including wine and beer).

Solway Lass (www.solwaylass.com; 3-day/3-night trip from $559) You get a full three days on this 28m tallship – the only authentic tallship in Airlie Beach. Popular with backpackers.

Prima Sailing (www.primasailing.com.au; 2-day/2-night tour from $360) Fun tours with a 12-person maximum. Ideal for couples chasing style and substance.

Atlantic Clipper (www.atlanticclipper.com.au; 2-day/2-night trip from $455) Young, beautiful and boozy crowd...and there's no escaping the antics. Snorkelling (or recovering) on Langford Island is a highlight.

Derwent Hunter (www.tallshipadventures.com.au; day trip $175) A very popular sailing safari on a timber gaff-rigged schooner. Good option for couples and those more keen on wildlife than the wild life.

Whitehaven Xpress (www.whitehavenxpress.com.au; day trip $160) Locally owned and operated for over a decade, the Xpress rivals the bigger operators for its Hill Inlet and Whitehaven tours.

SV Domino (www.aussieyachting.com; day trip $150) Takes a maximum of eight guests to Bali Hai island, a little-visited 'secret' of the Whitsundays. Includes lunch and a good two-hour snorkel.

Crewing

Adventurous types might see the 'Crew Wanted' ads posted in hostels or at the marina and dream of hitching a ride on the high seas. In return for a free bunk, meals and a sailing adventure, you get to hoist the mainsail, take the helm and clean the head. You could have the experience of a lifetime – whether good or bad depends on the vessel, skipper, other crew members (if any) and your own attitude. Think about being stuck with someone you don't know on a 10m boat several kilometres from shore before you actually find yourself there. Be sure to let someone know where you're going, with whom and for how long.

tours, including day trips to Hayman Island ($245) and Whitehaven ($240).

🛏 Sleeping

Resorts

Rates quoted are standard, but hardly anyone pays them. Most travel agents will put together a range of discounted package deals combining air fares, transfers, accommodation and meals.

Camping

NPRSR (www.nprsr.qld.gov.au) manages the Whitsunday Islands National Park camping grounds on several islands for both independent campers as well as groups on commercial trips. Camping permits (per person/family $5.45/21.80) are available online or at the NPRSR booking office in Airlie Beach.

You must be self-sufficient and are advised to take 5L of water per person per day plus three days' extra supply in case you get stuck. You should also have a fuel stove as wood fires are banned on all islands.

Get to your island with Whitsunday Island Camping Connections – Scamper (☑ 07-4946 6285; www.whitsundaycamping.com. au). It leaves from Shute Harbour and can drop you at South Molle, Denman or Planton Islands ($65 return); Whitsunday Island ($105 return); Whitehaven Beach ($155 return); and Hook Island ($160 return). Camping transfers include complimentary 5L water containers. You can also hire camp kits ($40 first night; $20 subsequent nights) which include a tent, gas stove, Esky and more.

ℹ Information

Airlie Beach is the mainland centre for the Whitsundays, with a bewildering array of accommodation options, travel agents and tour operators. Shute Harbour, about 12km east of Airlie, is the port for some day-trip cruises and island ferries, while most of the yachts and other cruise companies berth at Abel Point Marina about 1km west of Airlie Beach.

David Colfelt's *100 Magic Miles of the Great Barrier Reef – The Whitsunday Islands* has been referred to as the 'bible to the Whitsundays'. It contains an exhaustive collection of charts with descriptions of boat anchorages in the area, articles on the islands and resorts and features on diving, sailing, fishing, camping and natural history.

Visit the NPRSR (p411) in Airlie Beach for camping permits and info.

Whitsundays Region Information Centre (☑ 1300 717 407; www.whitsundaytourism. com; ☺ 10am-5pm) On the Bruce Hwy at the southern entry to Proserpine.

ℹ Getting There & Around

AIR

The two main airports for the Whitsundays are at Hamilton Island and Proserpine (Whitsunday Coast). Airlie Beach is home to the small Whitsunday Airport, about 6km from town.

BOAT

Cruise Whitsundays (☑ 07-4946 4662; www. cruisewhitsundays.com; one-way adult/child from $36/24) provides ferry transfers to Daydream, Long and South Molle Islands and to the Hamilton Island Airport.

BUS

Greyhound (☑ 1300 473 946; www.greyhound. com.au) and **Premier** (☑ 13 34 10; www.premierms.com.au) detour off the Bruce Hwy to Airlie Beach. **Whitsunday Transit** (☑ 07-4946 1800; www.whitsundaytransit.com.au) connects Proserpine, Cannonvale, Abel Point, Airlie Beach and Shute Harbour.

Whitsundays 2 Everywhere (☑ 07-4946 4940; www.whitsundaytransfers.com) operates airport transfers from both Whitsunday Coast (Proserpine) and Mackay Airports to Airlie Beach.

Proserpine

POP 3390

There's no real reason to linger in this industrial sugar-mill town, which is the turn-off point for Airlie Beach and the Whitsundays. However, it's worth stopping at the helpful Whitsundays Region Information Centre (p407) just south of town for information about the Whitsundays and surrounding region.

If you do find yourself in Proserpine with time to spare, head to Colour Me Crazy (☑ 07-4945 2698; 2b Dobbins Lane; ☺ 8.30am-5.30pm Mon-Fri, to 3.30pm Sat, 9.30am-2.30pm Sun), an eye-popping labyrinth of out-there jewellery, clothing and homewares.

Proserpine's Whitsunday Coast Airport is 14km south of town, serviced from Brisbane and some other capitals by Jetstar (☑ 13 15 38; www.jetstar.com.au) and Virgin Blue (☑ 13 67 89; www.virginblue.com.au).

In addition to meeting all planes and trains, Whitsunday Transit (☑ 07-4946 1800; www.whitsundaytransit.com.au) has eight scheduled bus services running daily from Proserpine to Airlie Beach. One way/return from

WHITSUNDAY COAST PROSERPINE

the airport costs $18/36, and from the train station it's $12.10/24.20.

Airlie Beach

POP 7868

Like olives, oysters and Vegemite, Airlie Beach is a love-or-hate affair. A good-time town of the highest order, the mainland gateway to the Whitsundays is loud, brash and busy, a total contrast to the tranquil ocean glittering just metres offshore. Despite a backdrop of jungle-clad hills and Airlie's proximity to obvious natural wonders, those in search of serenity will find it only once anchors are aweigh; those after wildlife need look no further than the frenzied backpacker bars lining the recently renovated main drag. That said, the town does offer some respite from the party pace in the form of a lovely swimming lagoon and the amble-worthy landscaped foreshore.

Abel Point Marina, where the Cruise Whitsundays ferries depart from and where many of the cruising yachts are moored, is about 1km west along a pleasant boardwalk, while many other vessels leave from Shute Harbour (about 12km east); most cruise companies run courtesy buses into town.

🏃 Activities

There are seasonal operators in front of the Airlie Beach Hotel that hire out jet skis, catamarans, windsurfers and paddle skis.

Lagoon SWIMMING
(Shute Harbour Rd) FREE Take a dip year-round in the stinger-croc-tropical-nasties-free lagoon in the centre of town.

Tandem Skydive Airlie Beach SKYDIVING
(☑07-4946 9115; www.skydiveairliebeach.com.au; from $249) Jump out of a plane from 8000, 10,000, 12,000 or 14,000ft up.

Fishing FISHING
Grab a cheap handline and have a go at catching your own dinner. Popular spots in Airlie include the rock walls by the sailing club in Cannonvale, the Airlie Beach Marina and the fishing pontoon in Shute Harbour.

🕝 Tours

See the Whitsundays Tours section (p404) for details of tours throughout the islands.

Whitsunday Crocodile Safari TOUR
(☑07-4948 3310; www.proserpineecotours.com; adult/child $120/60) Spy on wild crocs, explore secret estuaries and eat bush tucker.

✨ Festivals & Events

Airlie Beach Race Week SAILING
(www.airlieraceweek.com) Sailors from across the world descend on Airlie for the town's annual regatta, held in August.

🛌 Sleeping

Airlie Beach is a backpacker haven, but with so many hostels, standards vary and bedbugs are a common problem. Most of the resorts have package deals and stand-by rates that are much cheaper than those advertised. Try the **Whitsundays Central Reservation Centre** (☑1800 677 119; www.airliebeach.com; 259 Shute Harbour Rd) for accommodation ideas and specials, or the usual suspects online.

★**Kipara** RESORT $
(www.kipara.com.au; 2614 Shute Harbour Rd; private room/cabin/villa from $60/95/105; ❋@🕿🏊) Tucked away in lush, green environs, this budget resort makes it easy to forget you're only 2km from the frenzy of town. Mega-clean, outstanding value, helpful staff and regular wildlife visits make this one of Airlie's best options. Long-term rates also available.

Bush Village Budget Cabins HOSTEL $
(☑1800 809 256; www.bushvillage.com.au; 2 St Martins Rd; dm from $32, d $80; P❋@🏊) Among the best budget accommodation options in town. Dorms and doubles are in 17 self-contained cabins set in leafy gardens. There's off-street parking and it's close to the supermarket.

Nomads Backpackers HOSTEL $
(☑07-4999 6600; www.nomadsairliebeach.com; 354 Shute Harbour Rd; dm/d $23/88; ❋@🕿🏊) Set on a 3-hectare leafy lot with volleyball and a pool, Nomads feels a bit more 'resorty' than many of the other hostels in town. Accommodation is nothing special, though tent sites are nice and shady, and private rooms have TV, fridge and kitchenette.

Seabreeze Tourist Park CARAVAN PARK $
(☑07-4946 6379; www.theseabreezepark.com.au; 234 Shute Harbour Rd; camp site $14, caravan site from $30, cabin/villa from $90/130; P❋@🕿🏊🐾) Grassy and sprawling with fresh

Airlie Beach

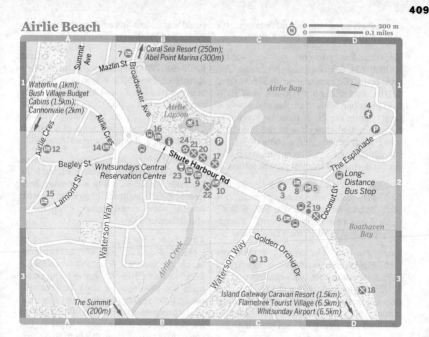

ocean views and a nice kicked-back feel. Camp sites are shady, while the new timber Bali Villas offer an exoticism most caravan parks are decidedly lacking.

Beaches Backpackers HOSTEL $
(☏ 07-4946 6244; www.beaches.com.au; 356 Shute Harbour Rd; dm/d $22/70; ❄@🛜🏊) You must at least enjoy a drink at the big open-air bar, even if you're not staying here. If you

do choose to hang your hat, bring earplugs and your biggest party boots. Not one for the serenity set.

Backpackers by the Bay HOSTEL $
(☏ 07-4946 7267; www.backpackersbythebay.com; 12 Hermitage Dr; dm/d & tw $25/68; ❄@🏊) A low-key alternative to the seething party-hostel cluster downtown, with tidy rooms, hammocks, a good pool and a distinct lack

of skull-clanging tunes and whoops. It's about a 10-minute walk from Airlie's centre.

Magnums Backpackers
HOSTEL $

(📞1800 624 634; www.magnums.com.au; 366 Shute Harbour Rd; camp site/van site $22/24, dm/d $22/56, share cabin per person $24; 🌸@🛜) A loud party bar, loads of alcohol and a bevy of pretty young things...it must be Magnums. Forget the tent sites close to the bar – you won't sleep unless you're comatose. Once you get past the hectic reception, you'll find simple dorms in a tropical garden setting.

Airlie Beach YHA
HOSTEL $

(📞07-4946 6312; airliebeach@yha.com.au; 394 Shute Harbour Rd; dm $26.50, d $69; 🌸@🛜) Central and reasonably quiet with a sparkling pool and great kitchen facilities.

Flametree Tourist Village
CARAVAN PARK $

(📞07-4946 9388; www.flametreevillage.com.au; 2955 Shute Harbour Rd; unpowered/powered site $21/27, cabin from $79; 🌸@🛜🌸) The spacious sites are scattered through lovely, bird-filled gardens and there's a good camp kitchen and barbecue area. It's 6.5km west of Airlie.

Waterview
APARTMENT $$

(📞07-4948 1748; www.waterviewairliebeach. au; 42 Airlie Cres; studio/1-bedroom unit from $135/150; 🌸🛜) An excellent choice for location and comfort, this boutique accommodation overlooks the main street and has gorgeous views of the bay. The rooms are modern, airy and spacious and have kitchenettes for self-caterers.

Coral Sea Resort
RESORT $$

(📞1800 075 061; www.coralsearesort.com; 25 Ocean View Ave; d/1-bedroom apt/2-bedroom apt from $185/330/410; 🌸@🛜🌸) At the end of a low headland overlooking the water, just west of the town centre, Coral Sea Resort has one of the best positions around. Many rooms have stunning views.

Whitsunday Organic B&B
B&B $$

(📞07-4946 7151; www.whitsundaybb.com.au; 8 Lamond St; s/d $155/185-210) 🍃 Rooms are comfortable, but it's the organic-everything (garden, walks, breakfasts, wines) that everyone comes here for. You can book a healing essential-oil massage, meditate in the garden tepee or just indulge in all things *om*.

Sunlit Waters
APARTMENT $$

(📞07-4946 6352; www.sunlitwaters.com; 20 Airlie Cres; studios from $92, 1-bedroom apt $115; 🌸🌸) These large studios have everything you could want, including a self-contained kitchenette and great views from the balconies.

Club Crocodile
HOTEL $$

(📞07-4946 7155; www.clubcroc.com.au; 240 Shute Harbour Rd; d from $110; 🅿🌸🌸) On the road between Cannonvale and Airlie Beach is this excellent budget option that's really popular with domestic tourists and young families. The Olympic-sized swimming pool is the hub of the action and even features a waterfall.

Airlie Waterfront Backpackers
HOSTEL $$

(📞1800 089 000; www.airliewaterfront.com; 6 The Esplanade; dm $25-33, d & tw with/without bathroom $130/60) Flashpackin' good-times, with coveted ocean views, squeaky-clean rooms and flatscreen TVs.

Airlie Beach Hotel
HOTEL $$

(📞1800 466 233; www.airliebeachhotel.com. au; cnr The Esplanade & Coconut Gr; motel s/d $135/145, hotel r $179-289; 🌸🛜🌸) The motel units are looking a bit tired, but the sea-facing hotel rooms are clean and spacious. With three restaurants and a bottle shop on site and a perfect downtown location, you could do far worse than stay here.

Water's Edge Resort
APARTMENT $$$

(📞07-4948 2655; www.watersedgewhitsundays. com.au; 4 Golden Orchid Dr; 1-bedroom apt $225-275, 2-bedroom apt $275-350; 🌸🌸) Its Balinese theme, wet-edge pools and languid tropical vibe (gently) scream 'Holidays!' Cool, creamy pastel rooms, top-notch facilities and fecund gardens keep up the dreamy feel; you'll easily forget you're just minutes from town.

Airlie Waterfront B&B
B&B $$$

(📞07-4946 7631; www.airliewaterfrontbnb.com.au; cnr Broadwater Ave & Mazlin St; d $242-285; 🌸@) Absolutely gorgeous views and immaculately presented from top to toe, this sumptuously furnished B&B oozes class and is a leisurely five-minute walk into town along the boardwalk. Some rooms have a spa.

🍴 Eating

The **Airlie supermarket** (277 Shute Harbour Rd) is the main self-catering option in the centre of town.

Fish D'vine
SEAFOOD $

(📞07-4948 0088; 303 Shute Harbour Rd; mains $14-28; ⏱5pm-late) Pirates were definitely onto something: this fish-and-rum bar is shiploads of fun, serving up all things nibbly from Neptune's realm and lashings and lashings of rum (over 200 kinds of the stuff).

Harry's Corner
CAFE $

(☑ 07-4946 7459; 273 Shute Harbour Rd; mains $6.70-17.50; ☺ 7am-3pm) Come for the all-day breakfasts, giant in scope and mammoth in portion. Harry's also serves up open Danish sandwiches, filled bagels and good salads.

Denman Cellars Beer Cafe
TAPAS $

(☑ 07-4948 1333; Shop 15, 33 Port Dr; mains $12-26; ☺ 11am-10pm Mon-Fri, 8am-11pm Sat & Sun) Solid mod-Oz food including lamb meatballs, very small shared seafood tapas and a stock breakfast menu pales in comparison to the beer menu (over 700 brews!).

Whitsunday Sailing Club
PUB $

(☑ 07-4946 6138; Airlie Point; mains $14-32; ☺ noon-2.30pm & 5.30-8.30pm Mon-Fri, 11am-2.30pm & 5.30-8.30pm Sat & Sun) Sit outside on the terrace for a substantial meal, a drink and wonderful ocean views. Steak, schnitzel and seafood choices offer few surprises.

Marino's Deli
DELI $

(Whitsunday Shopping Centre, Cannonvale; dishes $8-23.50; ☺ 7.30am-8pm Mon-Sat) Great takeaway pasta and antipasto offerings.

★ Mr Bones
PIZZERIA, TAPAS $$

(☑ 0416 011 615; Lagoon Plaza, 263 Shute Harbour Rd; shared plates $12-17, pizza $15-23; ☺ 9am-9pm Tue-Sat) Mr Bones is the new standard bearer in Airlie Beach for hip, affordable dining. It's rightfully gaining repute for its perfect thin-based pizzas – try the prawn and harissa – while the 'not pizzas' (appetisers including the lip-licking blackened fish skewers with pineapple and mint salsa) are also spectacular.

Village Cafe
CAFE $$

(☑ 07-4946 5745; 366 Shute Harbour Rd; mains $19.95-29.50; ☺ 7.30am-9pm) Village Cafe is always busy with hungover backpackers and those chasing good coffee, and the breakfasts at this place are just the tonic to get the day started. Order a 'hot rock' and cook your protein of choice to perfection on a sizzling volcanic slab that's been heated for 12 hours.

Deja Vu
FUSION $$

(☑ 07-4948 4309; Golden Orchid Dr; lunch $19-25, dinner $27.50-34.50; ☺ noon-2.30pm & 6-9pm Wed-Sat, noon-2.30pm Sun) Rated as one of Airlie's best, this Polynesian-themed restaurant concocts dishes with all kinds of international influences. Aim to be in town for weekly gastro-event The Long Sunday Lunch (eight courses per person costs $44.50). Bookings are required here.

🍷 Drinking & Nightlife

It's said that Airlie Beach is a drinking town with a sailing problem. The bars at Magnums and Beaches, the two big backpackers in the centre of town, are always crowded, and are popular places to kick off a ribald evening.

Phoenix Bar
BAR

(390 Shute Harbour Rd; ☺ 7pm-3am) Dance'n'DJ hotspot with drink specials and free pizzas nightly (from 6pm to 8pm).

Paddy's Shenanigans
IRISH PUB

(352 Shute Harbour Rd; ☺ 5pm-3am) As one would expect.

Mama Africa
CLUB

(263 Shute Harbour Rd; ☺ 10pm-5am) Just a stumble across the road from the main party bars, this African-style safari nightclub throbs a beat that both hunter and prey find hard to resist.

ℹ️ Information

The main drag is stacked with privately run tour agencies. Check out their noticeboards for stand-by rates on sailing tours and resort accommodation. Internet and wi-fi access is widely available.

NPRSR (☑ 13 74 68; www.nprsr.qld.gov.au; cnr Shute Harbour & Mandalay Rds; ☺ 9am-4.30pm Mon-Fri) For camping permits and info.

ℹ️ Getting There & Away

AIR

The closest major airports are Whitsunday Coast (Proserpine) and Hamilton Island.

Whitsunday Airport (☑ 07-4946 9180), a small airfield 6km east of Airlie Beach, is midway between Airlie Beach and Shute Harbour.

BOAT

Transfers between Abel Point Marina and Daydream and Long Islands are provided by **Cruise Whitsundays** (☑ 07-4946 4662; www.cruise-whitsundays.com), as are airport transfers from Abel Point Marina to Hamilton Island.

See the Getting There & Away sections of individual islands for more details.

BUS

Greyhound (☑ 1300 473 946; www.greyhound.com.au) and **Premier Motor Service** (☑ 13 34 10; www.premierms.com.au) buses detour off the Bruce Hwy to Airlie Beach. There are buses between Airlie Beach and all the major centres along the coast, including Brisbane ($232, 19 hours), Mackay ($30, two hours), Townsville ($46, 4 hours) and Cairns ($92, 9 hours).

Long-distance buses stop on The Esplanade, between the sailing club and the Airlie Beach Hotel.

Whitsunday Transit (☑ 07-4946 1800; www. whitsundaytransit.com.au) connects Proserpine (Whitsunday Airport), Cannonvale, Abel Point, Airlie Beach and Shute Harbour. Buses operate from 6am to 10.30pm.

ⓘ Getting Around

Airlie Beach is small enough to cover by foot. Most cruise boats have courtesy buses that will pick you up from wherever you're staying and take you to either Shute Harbour or Abel Point Marina. To book a taxi, call **Whitsunday Taxis** (☑ 13 10 08).

Most of the major car-rental agencies are represented here: offices line Shute Harbour Rd.

Conway National Park

The mountains of this national park and the Whitsunday Islands are part of the same coastal mountain range. Rising sea levels following the last ice age flooded the lower valleys, leaving only the highest peaks as islands, now cut off from the mainland.

The road from Airlie Beach to Shute Harbour passes through the northern section of the park. Several walking trails start from near the picnic and day-use area. About 1km past the day-use area, there's a 2.4km walk up to the Mt Rooper lookout, with good views of the Whitsunday Passage and islands. Further along the main road, towards Coral Point and before Shute Harbour, there's a 1km track leading down to Coral Beach and The Beak lookout. This track was created with the assistance of the Giru Dala, the traditional custodians of the Whitsunday area, and a brochure available at the start of the trail explains how the local Aborigines use plants growing in the area.

To reach the beautiful Cedar Creek Falls, turn off the Proserpine–Airlie Beach road on to Conway Rd, 18km southwest of Airlie Beach. It's then about 15km to the falls; the roads are well signposted.

Long Island

Long Island has some of the prettiest beaches in the Whitsundays and 13km of walking tracks. The island stretches 9km long by 1.5km wide; a 500m-wide channel separates it from the mainland. Day-trippers can use the facilities at Long Island Resort.

🛏 Sleeping

National Park Camp Site　　　CAMPGROUND $
(www.nprsr.qld.gov.au; per person/family $5.45/21.80) Basic camping at Long Island's Sandy Bay (not to be confused with the Sandy Bay camping ground at nearby South Molle).

Paradise Bay　　　BUNGALOW $$$
(☑ 07-4946 9777; www.paradisebay.com.au; 3-night packages, d from $1500) 🗲 This secluded eco-friendly lodge comprises 10 spacious bungalows made from Australian hardwood. In the name of peace and tranquillity, no children or motorised water sports are allowed, and there's no internet either. The tariff is inclusive of sailing tours, food and house wines; helicopter transfers are an extra $760 per bungalow.

Long Island Resort　　　RESORT $$$
(☑ 1800 075 125; www.oceanhotels.com.au/longisland; d incl all meals $230-380; ❄ @ ☎) A resort for everyone – yep, the kids are more than welcome here. Sitting on Happy Bay at the north of the island, Long Island Resort is a comfortable place with three levels of accommodation, the best being those on the beachfront. There are some fabulous short walks and plenty of activities to keep all age groups busy: who doesn't love mini-golf?

ⓘ Getting There & Around

Cruise Whitsundays (☑ 07-4946 4662; www. cruisewhitsundays.com) connects Long Island Resort to Shute Harbour by frequent daily services. The direct trip takes about 20 minutes, and costs adult/child $36/24.

Hook Island

The 53-sq-km Hook Island, second-largest of the Whitsundays, is predominantly national park and rises to 450m at Hook Peak. There are a number of good beaches dotted around the island, and some of the region's best diving and snorkelling locations. Many travellers come here enticed by the low prices and have left disappointed because it's not what they expected. If you want luxury, don't come to Hook Island...try Hayman instead!

There are national-park camping grounds (www.nprsr.qld.gov.au; per person/

WHITSUNDAY COAST CONWAY NATIONAL PARK

family \$5.45/21.80) at Maureen Cove, Steen's Beach, Curlew Beach and Crayfish Beach. Although basic, they provide some wonderful back-to-nature opportunities.

Hook Island Wilderness Resort (📞 07-4946 5255; www.hookislandresort.com; camp site per person \$10, dm \$35, d with/without bathroom \$150/100; ❄ ☎) is an extremely basic place: the only stars it rates are the ones twinkling overhead. But if you don't mind roughing it and value snorkelling (and a wonderful beachfront location) over style, give it a go. The resort is open erratically: be sure to check the website before making plans.

Transfers are arranged when you book your accommodation. Otherwise, **Whitsunday Island Camping Connections – Scamper** (📞 07-4946 6285; www.whitsundaycamping.com.au) can organise drop offs to the camping grounds (minimum four people) for around \$160 per person return.

South Molle Island

The largest of the Molle group of islands at 4 sq km, South Molle is virtually joined to Mid Molle and North Molle Islands. Apart from the resort area and golf course at Bauer Bay in the north, the island is all national park and is crisscrossed by 15km of walking tracks, with some superb lookout points. The highest point is Mt Jeffreys (198m), but the climb up **Spion Kop** will reward you with fantastic sunset views. The track to Spion Kop passes an ancient Ngaro stone quarry – look out for an area of shattered rock spilling down the hillside.

There are national park **camping grounds** (📞 13 74 68; www.nprsr.qld.gov.au; per person/family \$5.45/21.80) at Sandy Bay in the south and at Paddle Bay near the resort.

Adventure Island Resort (📞 1800 466 444; www.koalaadventures.com; 2 nights/3 days Sail and Stay package \$379; ❄ @ ☎) is *the* party place to stay, but there are plenty of daytime activities to keep you busy too, including archery, bushwalking, fish feeding, sailing, paddling and snorkelling. The resort is the sole domain of those cruising on the *Pride of Airlie,* which stops at South Molle for two nights on its three-day 'Sail and Stay' trip. The journey also includes Whitehaven Beach.

Day-trippers and campers can get to South Molle with Whitsunday Island Camping Connections (\$65 return; p413).

Daydream Island

Daydream Island, just over 1km long and 200m wide, would live up to its name a bit more if it wasn't quite so busy; one could be forgiven for mistaking it for a floating theme park. The closest resort to the mainland, it's a very popular day-trip destination suitable for everybody, especially busy families, swinging singles and couples looking for a romantic island wedding.

The large **Daydream Island Resort & Spa** (📞 1800 075 040; www.daydreamisland. com; d from \$310; ❄ ☎ ☎) is surrounded by beautifully landscaped tropical gardens, with a stingray-, shark- and fish-filled lagoon running through it. It has tennis courts, a gym, catamarans, windsurfers, three swimming pools and an open-air cinema all included in the tariff. There are five grades of accommodation and most package deals include a buffet breakfast. There's also a club with constant activities to keep children occupied, and they'll love the **stingray splash** (\$38) and fish-feeding sessions. The resort occupies the entire island, so it's not the place to head if you're seeking isolation.

Cruise Whitsundays (📞 07-4946 4662; www.cruisewhitsundays.com; one-way adult/child \$36/24) connects Daydream Island to Abel Point Marina and Shute Harbour with frequent daily services.

Hamilton Island

POP 1209

Hamilton can come as a shock for the first-time visitor, with swarms of people and heavy development making it more like a busy town rather than a castaway island. Though not everyone's idea of a perfect getaway, it's hard not to be impressed by the sheer range of accommodation options, restaurants, bars and activities – there's something for everyone. Day-trippers can use some resort facilities, including tennis courts, squash courts, a gym, a golf driving range and a mini-golf course.

From **Catseye Beach**, in front of the resort, you can hire windsurfers, catamarans, jet skis and other equipment, and go parasailing or waterskiing.

A few shops by the harbour organise dives and certificate courses; you can take a variety of cruises to other islands and the outer reef. Half-day fishing trips cost around \$190 per person with fishing gear supplied.

There are a few **walking trails**, the best being the clamber up to Passage Peak (239m) on the northeastern corner of the island. Hamilton also has day care and a Clownfish Club for kids.

🛏 Sleeping

Hamilton Island Resort RESORT $$$
(☑13 73 33; www.hamiltonisland.com.au; d from $340; ❄ @ 🛜 ⚐) Hamilton Island Resort has options ranging from hotel rooms to self-contained apartments and penthouses. The rates listed in the following reviews are for one night, although almost everyone stays for at least three when the cheaper package deals come into effect.

Qualia RESORT $$$
(☑1300 780 959; www.qualia.com.au; d from $975; ❄ @ 🛜 ⚐) The ultra-luxe Qualia is set on 12 hectares, with modern villas materialising like heavenly tree houses in the leafy hillside. The resort has a private beach, two restaurants, a spa and two swimming pools.

Beach Club RESORT $$$
(www.hamiltonisland.com.au/BeachClub; d from $595; ❄ @ 🛜 ⚐) Flanking the main resort complex, the Beach Club has terraced rooms with absolute beachfront positions.

Whitsunday Holiday Homes APARTMENT $$$
(☑13 73 33; www.hihh.com.au; from $288; ❄ @ 🛜 ⚐) Private accommodation ranging from three-star apartments to family-friendly houses and five-star luxury digs. Rates include your own golf buggy for high-brow hooning. There's a four-night minimum stay in some properties.

BEST WHITSUNDAY ISLAND RESORTS...

Only seven of the islands have resorts, but each has its own unique flavour and style. Do you want partying or pampering? Eco or extravagant? Check the list below...

...for ecotourism

➡ Paradise Bay (p412) is an exclusive ecoresort with a conscience. It has just 10 simple hardwood bungalows and implements 'Earth-kind' sustainable operations without compromising on luxury.

...for luxury

➡ Qualia (p414) on Hamilton Island is divine. Guests stay in luxurious pavilions among the trees and feast on Coral Sea views from their own private plunge pool.

➡ Hayman Island Resort (p415) epitomises old-fashioned luxury with a focus on sensory/gustatory indulgence and impeccable service. It also has a whopping big pool.

...for families

➡ Daydream Island Resort & Spa (p413) is always buzzing with activity. There's fun stuff for all age groups on and off the water. With a kiddies club, an open-air cinema and plenty of restaurants, cafes and a pool bar, neither you or your young charges will be bored.

➡ Long Island Resort (p412) may be less glitzy than others, but still has plenty of activities to keep the kids busy while you laze on the beach or lounge beside the pool with pink cocktail in hand.

...for romance

➡ Paradise Bay (p412) is not only an ecoresort, it's a honeymoon hotspot. It's exclusive and intimate but don't expect glitzy-glam – this is simple, nature-based elegance.

...for fun

➡ Adventure Island Resort (p413) on South Molle Island carries the Airlie Beach party crowd into the wee hours, with DJs, hot bands and nightly shenanigans. The island has fantastic bushwalks to cure those nasty hangovers so, come nightfall, you can start all over again. The resort is for those on a 'Sail and Stay' package (travelling on the *Pride of Airlie*).

Palm Bungalows CABIN $$$

(www.hamiltonisland.com.au/palm-bungalows; d from $340; ✱@🛜🏊) These attractive individual units behind the resort complex are closely packed but buffered by lush gardens. Each has a double and single bed and a small patio.

Reef View Hotel HOTEL $$$

(www.hamiltonisland.com.au/reef-view-hotel; d from $360; ✱@🏊) Four-star hotel popular with families.

✗ Eating

The main resort has a number of restaurants, but the marina also offers plenty of choice. There's also a supermarket for self-caterers.

Manta Ray Cafe CAFE $$

(✑07-4946 8213; Marina Village; mains $17-30; ⏱10.30am-9pm) Wood-fired gourmet pizzas are a favourite here.

Marina Tavern PUB $$

(✑07-4946 8839; Marina Village; mains from $17.50; ⏱11am-midnight) Drop in for a decent pub feed or a drink.

Bommie Restaurant MODERN AUSTRALIAN $$$

(✑07-4948 9433; mains $38-50; ⏱6pm-midnight Tue-Sat) Upmarket Mod-Oz cuisine with water views as exclusive as the prices. It's within the resort complex.

Romano's ITALIAN $$$

(✑07-4946 8212; Marina Village; mains $33-40; ⏱6pm-midnight Thu-Mon) Popular Italian restaurant with a deck jutting over the water.

Mariners Seafood Restaurant SEAFOOD $$$

(✑07-4946 8628; Marina Village; mains $38-48; ⏱6pm-late Sat-Wed) While the emphasis is on seafood, grills are also available.

♟ Drinking & Nightlife

Some of the bars in the resort and harbourside offer nightly entertainment; try the popular Boheme's Nightclub (Marina Village; ⏱9pm-late Thu-Sat).

ℹ Getting There & Away

AIR

Hamilton Island Airport is the main arrival centre for the Whitsundays, and is serviced by Qantas (✑13 13 13; www.qantas.com.au), Jetstar (✑13 15 38; www.jetstar.com.au) and Virgin Blue (✑13 67 89; www.virginblue.com.au).

BOAT

Cruise Whitsundays (✑07-4946 4662; www.cruisewhitsundays.com) connects Hamilton Island Airport and the marina with Abel Point Marina and Shute Harbour in Airlie Beach ($48).

ℹ Getting Around

There's a free shuttle-bus service operating around the island from 7am to 11pm.

You can hire a golf buggy (per one/two/three/24 hours $45/55/60/85) to whiz around the island.

Hayman Island

The most northern of the Whitsunday group, little Hayman is just 4 sq km in area and rises to 250m above sea level. It has forested hills, valleys and beaches and a five-star resort.

An avenue of stately date palms leads to the main entrance of the recently refurbished One&Only Hayman Island Resort (✑07-4940 1838; www.hayman.com.au; r incl breakfast $590-8000; ✱@🏊), one of the most gilded playgrounds on the Great Barrier Reef with its hectare of swimming pools, landscaped gardens and exclusive boutiques.

Resort guests must first fly to Hamilton's Great Barrier Reef Airport before being escorted to Hayman's fleet of luxury cruisers (one way adult/child $145/72.50) for a pampered transfer to the resort.

Lindeman Island

Lovely little Lindeman was once home to a busy Club Med resort; these days, it's only nature photographers and hikers who provide any semblance of bustle, making independent treks for the varied island tree life and the sublime view from Mt Oldfield (210m). Lindeman is mostly national park, with empty bays and 20km of impressive walking trails. Boat Port is the best spot for camping.

Whitsunday Island

Whitehaven Beach, on Whitsunday Island, is a pristine 7km-long stretch of blinding sand (at 98% pure silica, said sand is some of the whitest in the world), bounded by lush tropical vegetation and a brilliant blue sea. From Hill Inlet at the northern end of the beach, the pattern of dazzling sand through the turquoise and aquamarine water paints a magical picture. There's excellent snorkelling from its southern end. Whitehaven is one of Australia's most beautiful beaches.

There are national-park **camping grounds** (☑13 74 68; www.nprsr.qld.gov.au; adult/family $5.45/21.80) at Dugong, Nari's and Joe's Beaches in the west; at Chance Bay in the south; at the southern end of Whitehaven Beach; and Peter Bay in the north.

Whitsunday Island Camping Connections (p407) can get you there from $105 return.

Other Whitsunday Islands

The northern islands are undeveloped and seldom visited by cruise boats. Several of these – Gloucester, Saddleback and Armit Islands – have national-park camping grounds. The NPRSR (p411) office in Airlie Beach can issue camping permits and advise you on which islands to visit and how to get there.

Bowen

POP 10,260

Bowen is a classic reminder of the typical small Queensland coastal towns of the 1970s: wide streets, low-rise buildings, wooden Queenslander houses and laid-back, friendly locals. What makes Bowen stand out from other similar northern towns is its 24 colourful murals, all depicting various events and facets of the region's history. The large, detailed artworks are scattered on walls throughout the centre of town; grab a walking map and more info at the visitor centre.

The foreshore, with its landscaped esplanade, picnic tables and barbecues is a focal point, and there are some truly stunning beaches and bays northeast of the town centre.

Bowen gets busy during fruit-picking season (April to November). The famous Bowen mango unsurprisingly hails from here.

Keep an eye out for the 'Bowenwood' sign on the town's water tower; Baz Luhrmann's epic movie *Australia* was shot here in 2007 and the locals are still a little star-struck.

🛏 Sleeping & Eating

Bowen Backpackers　　　　　HOSTEL $
(☑07-4786 3433; www.bowenbackpackers.net; Herbert St; dm from $20; ❄ @) Located at the beach end of Herbert St (past the Grandview Hotel), this is the place to stay if you're working in the surrounding fruit farms. Rooms are neat and reasonably spacious. Ring ahead, as it sometimes closes in the off-season.

Barnacles Backpackers　　　　HOSTEL $
(☑07-4786 4400; www.barnaclesbackpackers. com; 18 Gordon St; dm from $30; ❄) Clean, hostel that can help with fruit-picking jobs.

Bowen Arrow Motel　　　　　MOTEL $$
(☑07-4786 2499; www.bowenarrowmotel.com.au; 18512 Bruce Hwy; d $115; ❄ ❄) Come for the wordplay, stay for the friendly service. Intimate (there are only 12 rooms) and clean with free wi-fi and a great little pool/spa.

Rose Bay Resort　　　　　RESORT $$
(☑07-4786 9000; www.rosebayresort.com.au; 2 Pandanus St; r $150-300; ❄ @ ❄) In a beautiful location right on the beach, these spacious studios and comfy units will ensure plenty of quiet time. Minimum two-night stay.

Jochheims Pies　　　　　BAKERY $
(49 George St; pies $4.60; ⏰5.30am-3.30pm Mon-Fri, to 12.30pm Sat) They've been keeping Bowen bellies full of homemade pies and baked treats since 1963; try a Hugh Jackman ('hunky beef') pie; the actor was a regular here during the filming of *Australia*.

Cove　　　　　CHINESE, MALAY $$
(☑07-4791 2050; Coral Cove Apartments, Horseshoe Bay Rd; mains $17-28.50; ⏰lunch & dinner Tue-Sun) The spectacular views of the Coral Sea from the timber deck demand a long lunch, or at least a sunset drink before dinner. The menu features an interesting fusion of Chinese and Malay dishes.

❶ Information

Tourism Bowen (☑07-4786 4222; www. tourismbowen.com.au; ⏰8.30am-5pm Mon-Fri, 10.30am-5pm Sat & Sun) Just look for the humongous mango about 7km south of Bowen on the Bruce Hwy.

There's also an **information booth** (Santa Barbara Pde; ⏰10am-5pm Mon-Fri, open sporadically Sat & Sun) in town.

❶ Getting There & Away

BUS

Long-distance bus services stop outside **Bowen Travel** (☑07-4786 1611; 40 Williams St) where you can book tickets for bus journeys. **Greyhound Australia** (☑1300 473 946; www.greyhound.com.au) and **Premier** (☑13 34 10; www. premierms.com.au) are two companies that have frequent buses running to/from Airlie Beach ($23, 1½ hours) and Townsville ($26, four hours).

Townsville to Mission Beach

Best Places to Eat

➡ Wayne & Adele's Garden of Eating (p424)
➡ Sweatshop (p422)
➡ Monsoon Cruising (p440)
➡ Benny's Hot Wok (p423)
➡ Fish Bar (p438)

Best Places to Stay

➡ Shambhala Retreat (p428)
➡ Noorla Heritage Resort (p431)
➡ Jackaroo Hostel (p437)
➡ Bungalow Bay Koala Village (p428)
➡ Coral Lodge (p422)

Why Go?

In between the tourist magnets of Cairns and Airlie Beach, Townsville is a 'real' city with a pulse. Although North Queensland's largest urban centre is often bypassed by visitors, it has a surprising number of attractions: a palm-lined beachfront promenade, gracious 19th-century architecture and a host of cultural and sporting venues and events. Magnetic Island's national park, beaches, walking trails and wildlife are a quick ferry ride away.

North of Townsville, the Great Green Way wends past small sugar towns including Ingham, Cardwell, Tully and Innisfail; a stop offers the chance to experience true far northern country hospitality. Mission Beach, about half an hour east of Tully, is a laid-back village that ironically attracts thrillseekers by the busload, all keen on the region's skydiving, white-water rafting and water sports. Forested Hinchinbrook Island and the lovely Dunk Island are top choices for the less adrenaline-addled.

When to Go
Townsville

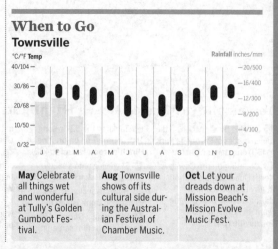

May Celebrate all things wet and wonderful at Tully's Golden Gumboot Festival.

Aug Townsville shows off its cultural side during the Australian Festival of Chamber Music.

Oct Let your dreads down at Mission Beach's Mission Evolve Music Fest.

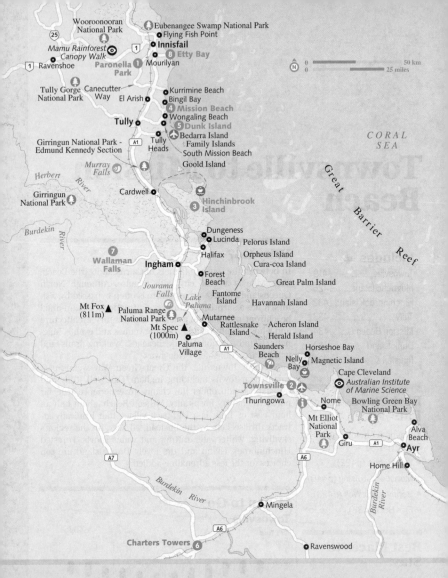

Townsville to Mission Beach Highlights

1 Hearing the story behind the ruined castles of **Paronella Park** (p439) on a day or night tour.

2 Cheering on the Cowboys, North Queensland's National Rugby League team, or National Basketball League team, the Crocodiles, in **Townsville** (p419).

3 Tackling the 32km-long Thorsborne Trail on pristine **Hinchinbrook Island** (p432).

4 Skydiving onto a sandy landing at **Mission Beach** (p435).

5 Having a secluded beach to yourself on **Dunk Island** (p439).

6 Watching a *Ghosts After Dark* outdoor film screening in the gold-rush town of **Charters Towers** (p426).

7 Slipping, sliding and schlepping down to Australia's highest single-drop waterfall, **Wallaman Falls** (p431).

8 Watching wild cassowaries wander along the beach at picturesque **Etty Bay** (p439).

TOWNSVILLE & AROUND

North Queensland's largest city is an ideal base for coastal, inland and offshore day trips.

Townsville

POP 189,931

Sprawling beneath a brooding red hill, Townsville is an underrated spot with a lot to offer: excellent museums, a huge aquarium, world-class diving, two major sporting teams, vibrant nightlife and an endless esplanade. A pedestrian-friendly city, it's easy to take in its sights on foot: grand, refurbished 19th-century buildings offer loads of landmarks, and if you get lost the friendly locals will be only too happy to lend a hand... or shout you a beer. Townsville has a lively, young populace, with thousands of students and armed forces members intermingling with old-school locals, fly-in-fly-out mine workers and summer-seekers lapping up the average 320 days of sunshine per year.

Townsville is only 350km from Cairns, but is much drier than its tropical rival: if 'Brownsville' is baking your bones, the splendid beaches of Magnetic Island are but a ferry jaunt away.

◎ Sights & Activities

The compact city centre is easy to get about on foot.

★ **Reef HQ Aquarium**　　　AQUARIUM
(www.reefhq.com.au; Flinders St E; adult/child $26.50/12.80; ◎9.30am-5pm) Townsville's excellent aquarium is a living reef on dry land. A staggering 2.5 million litres of water flow through the coral-reef tank, home to 130 corals and 120 fish species. The backdrop of the predator exhibit is a replica of the bow of the SS *Yongala*, which sank in 1911 off the coast of Townsville during a wild cyclone, killing all 122 passengers onboard; it wasn't located until 1958. Kids will love seeing, feeding and touching turtles at the turtle hospital. Talks and tours throughout the day focus on different aspects of the reef and the aquarium.

Castle Hill　　　LOOKOUT
Hoof it up this striking 286m-high red hill (an isolated pink granite monolith) that dominates Townsville's skyline for stunning views of the city and Cleveland Bay. Walk up via the rough 'goat track' (2km one way) from Hillside Cres. Otherwise, drive via Gregory St up the narrow, winding 2.6km Castle Hill Rd. A signboard up top details short trails leading to various lookout points.

Museum of Tropical Queensland　　　MUSEUM
(www.mtq.qm.qld.gov.au; 70-102 Flinders St E; adult/child $15/8.80; ◎9.30am-5pm) Not your everyday museum, the Museum of Tropical Queensland reconstructs scenes using detailed models with interactive displays. At 11am and 2.30pm, you can load and fire a cannon, 1700s-style; galleries include the kid-friendly MindZone science centre and displays on North Queensland's history from the dinosaurs to the rainforest and reef.

Billabong Sanctuary　　　WILDLIFE RESERVE
(www.billabongsanctuary.com.au; Bruce Hwy; adult/child $30/19; ◎9am-4pm) 🍴 Just 17km south of Townsville, this eco-certified wildlife park offers up-close-and-personal encounters with Australian wildlife – from dingoes to cassowaries – in their natural habitat. You could easily spend all day at the 11-hectare park, with feedings, shows and talks every half-hour or so.

Botanic Gardens　　　GARDENS
(◎sunrise-sunset) FREE Townsville's botanic gardens are spread across three locations: each has its own character, but all have tropical plants and are abundantly green. Closest to the centre, the formal, ornamental **Queens Gardens** (cnr Gregory & Paxton Sts) are 1km northwest of town at the base of Castle Hill.

Cultural Centre　　　CULTURAL CENTRE
(☏07-4772 7679; www.cctownsville.com.au; 2-68 Flinders St E; ◎9.30am-4.30pm) Showcases the history, traditions and customs of the Wulgurukaba and Bindal people. Call for guided-tour times.

Perc Tucker Regional Gallery　　　GALLERY
(www.townsville.qld.gov.au/facilities/galleries/perc-tucker; cnr Denham & Flinders Sts; ◎10am-5pm Mon-Fri, to 2pm Sat & Sun) Contemporary art gallery in a stately 1885-built former bank. Exhibitions focus on North Queensland artists.

Maritime Museum of Townsville　　　MUSEUM
(www.townsvillemaritimemuseum.org.au; 42-68 Palmer St; adult/child $6/3; ◎10am-3pm Mon-Fri, noon-3pm Sat & Sun) One for the boat buffs, with a gallery dedicated to the wreck of the *Yongala* and exhibits on North Queensland's naval industries. Tours of decommissioned patrol boat HMAS *Townsville* are available.

Townsville

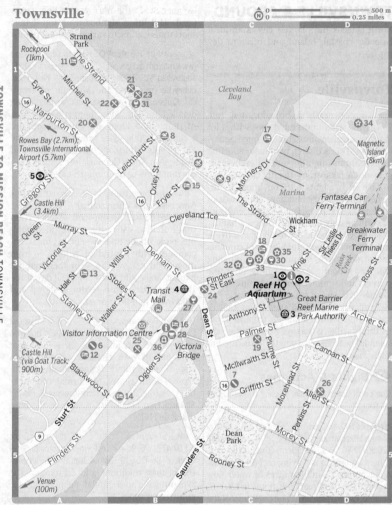

Strand

SWIMMING, OUTDOORS

Stretching 2.2km, Townsville's waterfront is interspersed with parks, pools, cafes and playgrounds – with hundreds of palm trees providing shade. Walkers and joggers take to the path from first light while beachgoers take over by mid-morning, and evening strollers are at it by late afternoon. Its golden-sand beach is patrolled and protected by two stinger enclosures.

At the northern tip is the **rock pool** (⊘24hr) FREE, an enormous artificial swimming pool surrounded by lawns and sandy beaches. Alternatively, head to the chlorin-ated safety of the heritage-listed, Olympic-sized swimming pool, **Tobruk Memorial Baths** (www.townsville.qld.gov.au; adult/child $5/3; ⊘5.30am-7pm Mon-Thu, to 6pm Fri, 7am-4pm Sat, 8am-5pm Sun). There's also a fantastic **water playground** (⊘10am-8pm Dec-Mar, to 6pm Sep-Nov, Apr & May, to 5pm Jun-Aug) FREE for the kids.

Skydive Townsville

SKYDIVING

(☏07-4721 4721; www.skydivetownsville.com.au; tandem jump from $395) Hurl yourself from a perfectly good plane and land right on the Strand.

Townsville

Woodstock Trail Rides HORSE RIDING
(☑ 07-4778 8888; www.woodstocktrailrides.com.
au; Jones Rd; 90min/half-day ride $80/100, cattle
muster $175) Situated 43km south of Towns-
ville, this huge property has full- and half-
day horse-riding trips as well as **cattle
musters** for aspiring cowboys and cowgirls.
Transfers for full-day rides and cattle musters are included from Townsville. Bookings
essential.

👉 Tours

Kookaburra Tours GUIDED TOUR
(☑ 0448 794 798; www.kookaburratours.com.au)
Highly recommended day trips in Townsville and further afield, with enthusiastic,
informed commentary. Options include
'Heritage and Highlights' city tours (adult/
child $40/18), Wallaman Falls (adult/child
$125/55), rainforest tours (adult/child $125/
55) and Aboriginal cultural tours (adult/
child $140/65).

Townsville Ghost Tours GUIDED TOUR
(☑ 0404 453 354; www.townsvilleghosttours.com.
au) Five spooky options, from city haunts
aboard the 'ghost bus' (from $65) to an over-
night trip to Ravenswood ($250 including
meals and accommodation).

🎊 Festivals & Events

The city has a packed calendar of festivals
and events, including home games of its
revered sporting teams, the **North Queensland Cowboys** (www.cowboys.com.au; ⊙ season
Mar-Sep) National Rugby League team and
the **Crocodiles** (www.crocodiles.com.au; ⊙ season mid-Oct–Apr) National Basketball League
team. If you don't believe how popular basketball can be in Australia, you will when
you see locals driving around with croc tails
hanging out of their car boots.

Townsville 400 MOTOR SPORTS
(www.v8supercars.com.au) V8 Supercars roar
through a purpose-built street circuit each
July during the V8 Supercar Championship.

**Australian Festival of
Chamber Music** MUSIC
(www.afcm.com.au) Townsville gets cultural
during this internationally renowned festival each August.

🛏 Sleeping

Townsville fills to capacity during festivals
and events, so it's wise to book ahead. Midrange motels and self-catering units stretch
along the Strand, while international chains

and backpacker places cluster in the city centre and around Palmer St.

Reef Lodge
HOSTEL $

(☑07-4721 1112; www.reeflodge.com.au; 4 Wickham St; dm $22-26, d with/without bathroom $80/62; ✴@🕲) The cruisy atmosphere at Townsville's best – and most central – hostel extends from Buddhist sculptures and hammocks strewn through the garden to a nerdishly compelling '80s video-game room.

Coral Lodge
B&B $

(☑07-4771 5512; www.corallodge.com.au; 32 Hale St; s/d without bathroom $70/90, units from $85; ✴) If you're looking to stay in a charming, old-fashioned Aussie home (with a three-legged cat), this century-old property can't be beat. Upstairs self-contained units are like having your own apartment while downstairs guest rooms share bathrooms. The welcoming owners will pick you up from the bus, train or ferry.

Civic Guest House
HOSTEL $

(☑07-4771 5381; www.civicguesthousetownsville. com.au; 262 Walker St; dm from $24, d from $58; @🕲) Recently renovated, and oh how it sparkles. A contender for cleanest hostel on earth, the Civic lives up to its name with friendly staff and a laid-back clientele. Free transport to/from the ferry or bus station.

Rowes Bay Caravan Park
CARAVAN PARK $

(☑07-4771 3576; www.rowesbaycp.com.au; Heatley Pde; unpowered/powered site $26/36, cabin with/without bathroom from $98/65, villa $105; ✴@🕲) Leafy park directly opposite Rowes Bay's beachfront. Brand-new villas are smaller than cabins but spiffier.

Orchid Guest House
GUESTHOUSE $

(☑07-4771 6683; www.orchidguesthouse.com. au; 34 Hale St; dm $27, s with/without bathroom $75/55, d $85/65; ✴) Not one for the party set, but a godsend to those looking for somewhere cheap and cheerful to lay their head. Weekly rates available for working backpackers.

Grand Northern Hotel
HOTEL $

(☑07-4771 6191; www.gnhotel.com.au; 500 Flinders St; s with/without air-con $70/60, d & tw with/without air-con $80/70; P✴) Swill and sleep at this historic 1901 pub in Townsville's bustling centre. It's not exactly a tranquil haven, but for those who like to be in the thick of it all, the GN can't be beat. All rooms share facilities.

Historic Yongala Lodge Motel
MOTEL $$

(☑07-4772 4633; www.historicyongala.com.au; 11 Fryer St; motel r $99-105, 1-bedroom apt $115-120; ✴🕲✖) Built in 1884, this lovely historic building is but a short stroll from the Strand and city centre. The rooms and apartments are small but good value. The excellent restaurant (mains $20 to $38, open for dinner Monday to Saturday) is long-loved by locals.

Holiday Inn
HOTEL $$

(☑07-4729 2000; www.townsville.holiday-inn.com; 334 Flinders St; d $110-189; ✴🕲✖) Nicknamed the 'sugar shaker', this 20-storey, 1976-built circular building (the city's tallest) is a Townsville icon. Its rooms are much more contemporary than the exterior suggests, and there's a great rooftop pool with unrivalled views over the city.

Aquarius on the Beach
HOTEL $$

(☑1800 622 474; www.aquariusonthebeach.com. au; 75 The Strand; d $110-150; ✴@🕲✖) The spectacular balcony views impress almost as much as the size of this place, the tallest building on the Strand. Don't be put off by the dated facade – this is one of the better places around, and the service is faultless.

Mariners North
APARTMENT $$$

(☑07-4722 0777; www.marinersnorth.com.au; 7 Mariners Dr; 2-/3-bedroom apt from $259/405, min stay two nights; ✴🕲✖) Self-contained, absolute oceanfront apartments have generous living areas, big bathrooms and brilliant balconies overlooking Cleveland Bay and out to Maggie. Free gym use.

✖ Eating

Palmer St is Townsville's premier dining strip, offering a diverse range of cuisines: wander along and take your pick. Perpendicular to the Strand, Gregory St has a clutch of cafes and takeaway joints. Many of Townsville's bars and pubs also serve food.

★ Sweatshop
CAFE $

(☑0435 845 237; www.thesweatshop.com.au; 181 Flinders St; jaffles $7, burgers $12; ⊙7.30am-4pm Mon-Wed, to 8pm Thu, to midnight Fri & Sat, 9am-3pm Sun) Hipsters in Townsville? Who'd a-thunk it? This tongue-in-cheek art space serves simple, high-quality food and the best coffee ($3.50) in Townsville. Chow down on fresh-baked treats and gawk at an ever-evolving gallery showcasing local talent.

Benny's Hot Wok   ASIAN $$

(07-4724 3243; 17-21 Palmer St; mains $14-32; 5pm-late daily, yum cha 10.30am -2.30pm Sun) Famous in FNQ for its staggering range of pan-Asian options – from freshly made sushi and sashimi to Peking duck rolls, steaming laksas and sizzling Mongolian lamb – Benny's is also a top spot for a cocktail and a catch-up.

Cafe Bambini   CAFE $

(46 Gregory St; mains $11.50-20; 5.30am-5pm Mon-Fri, 6.30am-4pm Sat & Sun;) With four locations strewn around town, this local success story cooks up some of the best (all-day!) breakfasts in Townsville, while lunches are fresh and filling.

Summerie's Thai Cuisine   THAI $

(07-4420 1282; 232 Flinders St; lunch special $12.50, dinner mains from $17; 11.30am-2.30pm & 5.30-10pm) Authentic Thai food that gets the thumbs up from coconut-curry-crazed locals. The name of specialty dish 'Heaven on Earth' (slow-cooked coconut prawns with crunchy greens) is definitely not false advertising.

Souvlaki Bar   GREEK $

(Shops 3 & 4, 58 The Strand; mains $6.50-17.50; 10.30am-9pm Mon-Fri, to 10pm Sat & Sun) Hellenic heaven, with juicy gyros, meze galore and home-made honey puffs all vying for tummy space.

BLOWIN' IN THE WIND

Queensland is The Sunshine State, known for its sultry climate and year 'round holiday weather; an old slogan went as far as claiming it was 'Beautiful one day, perfect the next'. But up in the far north, a dark cloud looms – literally – on the horizon between November and April each year. Cyclones – known elsewhere as hurricanes or typhoons – are a part of life in the tropics, with an average of four or five forming each season. While it's rare for these cyclones to escalate into full-blown destructive storms, big ones do come a'crashing: in February 2011, Cyclone Yasi smashed into the coast around Mission Beach with winds estimated at up to 300km/h, ripping through the towns of Tully and Cardwell and islands including Dunk, Bedarra and Hinchinbrook. Hundreds of homes along the coast between Innisfail and Ingham were severely damaged, banana plantations and cane fields flattened and areas of national park rainforest pummelled. Amazingly, there were no deaths or serious injuries.

Here are a few cyclonic facts to blow your hair back:

➡ Tropical cyclones are rated by their intensity in categories. A Category 1 storm blows gales of less than 125km/h, a Category 2 has destructive winds of 125km/h to 164km/h, cyclones from Category 3 (165km/h to 224km/h) to Category 5 (over 280km/h) are unsurprisingly billed as 'severe'.

➡ During the season, keep a sharp ear out for cyclone predictions and alerts. If a cyclone watch or warning is issued, stay tuned to local radio and monitor the **Bureau of Meteorology** website (www.bom.gov.au) for updates and advice. Locals tend to be complacent about cyclones, but will still buy out the bottle shop when a threat is imminent!

➡ Cyclone names are given in alphabetical order, alternating between male and female, from a seasonal list of 104 names compiled by the Bureau of Meteorology Tropical Cyclone Warning Centre. Names must not offend or be controversial, but it was a different story in the old days, when storms were frequently named after irksome politicians, mythological creatures and mothers-in-law.

➡ Yasi was a shocker, but the worst cyclone to hit the far northern coast was Category 5 Cyclone Mahina, which hit Bathurst Bay on Cape York in March 1899. More than 400 people were killed, including 100 Indigenous Australians and hundreds of workers on pearler fleet vessels. Mahina still holds the record for the world's greatest-ever storm surge (between 13m and 14.6m); on a nearby island, dolphins were found atop 15m-high cliffs!

Harold's Seafood
SEAFOOD $

(cnr The Strand & Gregory St; meals $4-10; ⊘ lunch & dinner) This takeaway joint has bug burgers of the Moreton Bay variety.

Wayne & Adele's Garden of Eating
MODERN AUSTRALIAN $$

(☑07-4772 2984; 11 Allen St; mains from $19; ⊘6.30-10pm Mon, 6.30-11pm Thu-Sat, noon-3pm Sun) For those who like a side serving of quirky with their grub, you can't miss mains like 'Don't Lose Your Tempeh' (curried vego tempeh fritter with kaffir-lime gado-gado salad) or 'Goat in a Boat' (Moroccan goat pie on date dahl). The purple courtyard is as flamboyant as the menu.

Absolute Tea
TEAHOUSE $$

(☑07-4721 2311; 269 Flinders St; tea per pot from $4.90, high tea $25; ⊘9.30am-3.30pm Wed-Sun) Ignore the sweat trickling down your neck and imagine yourself a lady (or gentleman) at this refined tropical tea-room. Take High or Devonshire Tea, opt for an elegant luncheon or just sip your way through 100 types of tea.

Longboard Bar & Grill
MODERN AUSTRALIAN $$

(☑07-4724 1234; The Strand, opposite Gregory St; mains $15-34; ⊘11.30am-3pm & 5.30pm-late) This waterfront eatery plies a lively crowd with grillhouse favourites such as sticky barbecue pork ribs, steaks and buffalo wings. Ignore the incongruous surf theme and be sure to pack a bib.

Cbar
CAFE $$

(The Strand, opposite Gregory St; mains $16-32; ⊘7am-10pm; ☑) Dependable and delicious, with an all-day dining menu that caters to

the grazers (antipasto $18) and the gluttons (huge battered fish burgers $17).

🍷 Drinking & Nightlife

It must be the sunny climate because Townsville sure loves a sip. Most nightlife concentrates around Flinders St East, while Palmer St and the Strand offer lower-key spots. Check listings in Thursday's edition of the *Townsville Bulletin*. Opening hours tend to vary according to the season and the crowds, and nightclubs generally stay open until 5am.

Heritage Bar
BAR

(www.heritagebar.com.au; 137 Flinders St E; ⊘5pm-2am Tue-Sat) A surprisingly chic craft bar with suave 'mixologists' delivering creative cocktails to a cool crowd looking for something more than a beer-barn swillfest. Also has a sophisticated bar menu for tipsy nibbles: don't miss Oyster Overdose ($11.50 per dozen) on Monday to Thursday afternoons.

Brewery
BREWERY

(252 Flinders St; ⊘11.30am-midnight Mon-Sat) Brews are made on-site at this stunningly restored 1880s former post office. Soak up a Townsville Bitter or Bandito Loco with a meal at its refined **restaurant** (mains $17 to $36).

Coffee Dominion
CAFE

(cnr Stokes & Ogden Sts; ⊘6am-5pm Mon-Fri, 7am-1pm Sat & Sun) 🍃 Eco-conscious establishment roasting beans from the Atherton Tableland to Zambia. If you don't find a blend you like, invent your own and they'll grind it fresh.

Seaview Hotel
PUB

(cnr The Strand & Gregory St; ⊘10am-midnight) Renowned for its Sunday beer-garden sessions and prime position on the Strand, the Seaview serves ice-cold schooners and has live music and entertainment. Its immense **restaurant** (mains $21 to $44) serves steaks on a par with the size of the premises.

Molly Malones
PUB, CLUB

(87 Flinders St E; ⊘11.30am-1am Mon & Tue, to 2am Wed, to 3am Thu, to 5am Fri, 5pm-5am Sat, 5pm-1am Sun) This boisterous Irish pub stages live music on Friday and Saturday nights, or you can shake it on the dance floor at its adjacent nightclub, **The Shed** (⊘8pm-3am Sun-Thu, to 5am Fri & Sat).

> ### ⓘ DANGER: STINGERS & CROCS
>
> From around late October to May, swimming in coastal waters is inadvisable due to the presence of box jellyfish, irukandji and other marine stingers. Only swim where there is a patrolled stinger net.
>
> Saltwater crocodiles inhabit the mangroves, estuaries and open water. Warning signs are posted around the waterways where crocodiles might be present. Pay heed, as these signs are not just quirky props for your holiday snaps: crocs are faster and more clever than you might think!

GREAT BARRIER REEF TRIPS FROM TOWNSVILLE

The Great Barrier Reef lies further offshore than from Cairns and Port Douglas, hence fuel costs push up the prices. On the upside, it's less crowded (and suffers fewer effects from crowds). Trips from Townsville are dive-oriented; if you just want to snorkel, take a day trip that just goes to the reef – the *Yongala* is for diving only. The *Yongala* is considerably closer to Alva Beach near Ayr, so if your main interest is wreck diving, you may want to consider a trip with Alva Beach–based Yongala Dive (p430).

The visitor centre has a list of Townsville-based operators offering Professional Association of Diving Instructors (PADI)–certified learn-to-dive courses with two days' training in the pool, plus at least two days and one night living aboard the boat. Prices start at about $615; you'll need to obtain a dive medical (around $60). A couple of popular options:

Adrenalin Dive (☑ 07-4724 0600; www.adrenalinedive.com.au; 252 Walker St) Day trips to the *Yongala* (from $220) and Wheeler Reef (from $280), both including two dives. Also offers snorkelling (from $180) on Wheeler Reef as well as live-aboard trips and dive-certification courses.

Remote Area Dive (RAD; ☑ 07-4721 4424; www.remoteareadive.com.au; 16 Dean St) Runs day trips (from $220) to Orpheus and Pelorus Islands. Also live-aboard trips and dive courses.

☆ Entertainment

Flynns   LIVE MUSIC
(101 Flinders St E; ⊘ 5pm-late Tue-Sun) A jolly Irish pub that doesn't try too hard to be Irish. Wildly popular for its $8 jugs and live music every night except Wednesdays, when karaoke takes over.

Consortium   CLUB
(159 Flinders St E; ⊘ 9pm-5am Tue & Thu-Sun) Resident DJs, DJ comps and events like foam parties and RNB bashes make this big city–style venue Townsville's brashest nightclub.

Jupiters Casino   CASINO
(www.jupiterstownsville.com.au; Sir Leslie Thiess Dr; ⊘ 10am-2am Sun-Thu, to 4am Fri & Sat) For a waterside flutter.

🛍 Shopping

Cotters Market   MARKET
(www.townsvillerotarymarkets.com.au; Flinders St Mall; ⊘ 8.30am-1pm Sun) Around 200 craft and food stalls, as well as live entertainment.

Strand Night Market   MARKET
(www.townsvillerotarymarkets.com.au; The Strand; ⊘ 5-9.30pm 1st Fri of month May-Dec) Browse the stalls on the Strand for curios, crafts and knick-knacks.

ℹ Information

Australia Post (Shop 1, Post Office Plaza, Sturt St; ⊘ 8.30am-5.30pm Mon-Fri)

Internet Den (277 Flinders St; per 90min $5; ⊘ 8am-10pm) Full-service internet cafe with super-fast computers.

Visitor Information Centre (☑ 07-4721 3660; www.townsvilleholidays.info; cnr Flinders & Stokes Sts; ⊘ 9am-5pm Mon-Fri, to 1pm Sat & Sun) Extensive visitor information on Townsville, Magnetic Island and nearby national parks. There's another branch on the Bruce Hwy 10km south of the city.

ℹ Getting There & Away

AIR

From **Townsville Airport** (www.townsvilleairport.com.au), **Virgin Blue** (☑ 13 67 89; www.virginblue.com.au), **Qantas** (☑ 13 13 13; www.qantas.com.au) and **Jetstar** (☑ 13 15 38; www.jetstar.com.au) fly to Cairns, Brisbane, the Gold Coast, Sydney, Melbourne, Mackay and Rockhampton, with connections to other major cities.

BUS

Greyhound Australia (☑ 1300 473 946; www.greyhound.com.au) has three daily services to Brisbane ($270, 23 hours), Rockhampton ($136, 12 hours), Airlie Beach ($45, 4½ hours), Mission Beach ($41, 3¾ hours) and Cairns ($60, six hours). Buses pick up and drop off at the Breakwater Ferry Terminal.

Premier Motor Service (☑ 13 34 10; www.premierms.com.au) has one service a day to/from Brisbane and Cairns, stopping in Townsville at the Fantasea car ferry terminal.

CAR

Major car-rental agencies are represented in Townsville and at the airport.

TRAIN

Townsville's **train station** (Charters Towers Rd) is 1km south of the centre.

The Brisbane–Cairns *Sunlander* travels through Townsville three times a week. Journey time between Brisbane and Townsville is 24 hours (one-way from $140); contact **Queensland Rail** (☑ 1800 872 467; www.traveltrain.com.au).

ⓘ Getting Around

TO/FROM THE AIRPORT

Townsville Airport is 5km northwest of the city centre in Garbutt. A taxi to the centre costs about $20. The **Airport Shuttle** (☑ 1300 266 946; www.con-x-ion.com; one way/return $10/18) services all arrivals and departures,

with pick-ups and drop-offs throughout the central business district (bookings essential).

BUS

Sunbus (☑ 07-4771 9800; www.sunbus.com. au) runs local bus services around Townsville. Route maps and timetables are available at the visitor information centre and online.

TAXI

Taxis congregate at ranks across town, or call **Townsville Taxis** (☑ 13 10 08; www.tsvtaxi. com.au).

Magnetic Island

POP 2500

'Maggie', as she's affectionately called, is a 'real' island. Permanent residents live and work here and some even make the daily commute to Townsville. Over half of this mountainous, triangular-shaped island's 52

RAVENSWOOD & CHARTERS TOWERS

You don't have to venture too far inland for a taste of the dry, dusty Queensland outback – a stark contrast to the verdant coast. This detour is easily accessible on a day trip from Townsville, but it's worth staying overnight if you can.

Along the Flinders Hwy, a turn-off at Mingela, 88km southwest of Townsville, leads 40km south to the tiny gold-mining village of Ravenswood (population 350), with a couple of gorgeous turn-of-the-20th-century pubs with basic (shared-bathroom) accommodation.

A further 47km west along the Flinders Hwy from Mingela is the historic gold-rush town of Charters Towers (population 8234). The 'towers' are its surrounding tors (hills). William Skelton Ewbank Melbourne (WSEM) Charters was the gold commissioner during the rush, when the town was the second-largest, and wealthiest, in Queensland. With almost 100 mines, some 90 pubs and a stock exchange, it became known simply as 'the World'.

Today, a highlight of a visit to the Towers is strolling past its glorious facades recalling the grandeur of those heady days, and listening to locals' ghost stories.

History oozes from the walls of the 1890 Stock Exchange Arcade, next door to the Charters Towers visitor centre (☑ 07-4761 5533; www.charterstowers.qld.gov.au; 74 Mosman St; ⊙ 9am-5pm). The visitor centre has a free brochure outlining the One Square Mile Trail of the town centre's beautifully preserved 19th-century buildings. The centre books all tours in town, including those to the reputedly haunted Venus Gold Battery, where gold-bearing ore was crushed and processed from 1872 to 1973.

Come nightfall, panoramic Towers Hill, the site where gold was first discovered, is the atmospheric setting for a free open-air cinema showing the 20-minute film *Ghosts After Dark* – check seasonal screening times with the visitor centre.

In-town accommodation includes the period-furniture-filled former pub, the Royal Private Hotel (☑ 07-4787 8688; www.royalprivate-hotel.com; 100 Mosman St; d without bathroom $55, d with bathroom from $95; ※ ☎). A venture to Charters Towers is incomplete without scoffing one of the award-winning pies at Towers Bakery (114 Gill St; pies from $4; ⊙ 5am-3pm Mon-Fri, to 1pm Sat).

Greyhound Australia (☑ 1300 473 946; www.greyhound.com.au) has four weekly services between Townsville and Charters Towers ($38, 1¾ hours).

The Queensland Rail (☑ 1800 872 467; www.traveltrain.com.au) *Inlander* train runs twice weekly between Townsville and Charters Towers ($35, three hours).

sq km is national park, with scenic walks and abundant wildlife, including one of Australia's largest concentrations of wild koalas. Inviting beaches offer adrenalin-pumping water sports or just the chance to bask in the sunshine, and the granite boulders, hoop pines and eucalypts are a fresh change from the clichéd tropical-island paradise.

Sights & Activities

There's one main road across the island, which goes from Picnic Bay, past Nelly and Geoffrey Bays, to Horseshoe Bay. Local buses ply the route regularly.

Picnic Bay

Picnic Bay was once home to the ferry terminal (now at Nelly Bay), and its erstwhile hustle and bustle has been replaced by serenity-seekers and the elegant curlew, whose spooky cries seem to carry all the way to Townsville (which there are great views of from here). There's a stinger net during the season (November to May) and the swimming is superb.

Nelly Bay

Your time on Maggie will begin and end here if you come by ferry. There's a wide range of eating and sleeping options and a decent beach. There's a children's playground towards the northern end of the beach and good snorkelling on the fringing coral reef.

Arcadia

Arcadia village has the island's major concentration of shops, eateries and accommodation. Its main beach, Geoffrey Bay, has a reef at its southern end (reef walking at low tide is discouraged). By far its prettiest beach is Alma Bay cove, with huge boulders tumbling into the sea. There's plenty of shade, along with picnic tables and a children's playground here.

If you head to the end of the road at Bremner Point, between Geoffrey Bay and Alma Bay, at 5pm you can have wild rock wallabies – accustomed to being fed at the same time each day – literally eating out of your hand.

Radical Bay & the Forts

Townsville was a supply base for the Pacific during WWII, and the forts were designed to protect the town from naval attack. If you're going to do just one walk, then the forts walk (2.8km, 1½ hours return) is a must. It starts near the Radical Bay turn-off, passing lots of ex-military sites, gun emplacements and false 'rocks'. At the top of the walk is the observation tower and command post, which have spectacular coastal views, and you'll almost certainly spot koalas lazing about in the treetops. Return the same way or continue along the connecting paths, which deposit you at Horseshoe Bay (you can catch the bus back).

Nearby Balding Bay is Maggie's unofficial nudie beach.

Horseshoe Bay

Horseshoe Bay, on the north coast, is the best of Maggie's accessible beaches. You'll find water-sports gear for hire, a stinger net, a row of cafes and a fantastic pub.

Bungalow Bay Koala Village has a wildlife park (www.bungalowbay.com.au; adult/child $19/12; ⊙2hr tours 10am, noon & 2.30pm), where you can cuddle crocs and koalas.

Pick up local arts and crafts at Horseshoe Bay's market (⊙9am-2pm second and last Sun of month), which sets up along the beachfront.

Tours

Pleasure Divers   DIVING
(☑07-4778 5788; www.pleasuredivers.com.au; 10 Marine Pde, Arcadia; open-water course per person $349) Three-day PADI open-water courses, as well as advanced courses and *Yongala* wreck dives.

Tropicana Tours   DRIVING TOUR
(☑07-4758 1800; www.tropicanatours.com.au; full day adult/child $198/99) If you're time-poor, this full-day tour with guides takes in the island's best spots in its stretch 4WD. Price includes close encounters with wildlife, lunch at a local cafe and a sunset cocktail. Shorter tours are also available.

Horseshoe Bay Ranch   HORSE RIDING
(☑07-4778 5109; www.horseshoebayranch.com.au; 38 Gifford St, Horseshoe Bay; 2hr ride $100) Gallop dramatically into the not-so-crashing surf on this popular bushland-to-beach two-hour tour. Pony rides for littlies are available too (20 minutes, $20).

Magnetic Island Sea Kayaks   KAYAKING
(☑07-4778 5424; www.seakayak.com.au; 93 Horseshoe Bay Rd, Horseshoe Bay; tours from $60) ✐

Join an eco-certified morning or sunset tour, or go it alone on a rented kayak (single/double per day $75/150).

Providence V CRUISE
(📞0427 882 062; www.providencesailing.com.au) Snorkel, boom-net and simply indulge sailing-off-into-the-sunset fantasies on Maggie's only tallship. Two-hour sails from $65 per person.

🛏 Sleeping

🛌 Picnic Bay

Tropical Palms Inn MOTEL $$
(📞07-4778 5076; www.tropicalpalmsinn.com.au; 34 Picnic St; unit from $100; ❄ ⊛) With a terrific little swimming pool right outside your front door, the self-contained motel units here are bright and comfortable. Reception rents 4WDs (from $75 per day).

🛌 Nelly Bay

Base Backpackers HOSTEL $
(📞1800 242 273; www.stayatbase.com; 1 Nelly Bay Rd; camping per person $12, dm $25-30, d with/without bathroom from $120/70; @ 🛜 ⊛) If sleep is a dirty word, then step right up. Base is famous for wild full-moon parties, but things can get raucous any time, thanks to the infamous on-site Island Bar. Sleep/food/transport package deals are available.

★ Shambhala Retreat RETREAT $$
(📞0448 160 580; www.shambhala-retreat-magnetic-island.com.au; 11 Barton St; d from $105; ❄ ⊛) 🍃 Serenity now. This green-powered property consists of three tropical units complete with Buddhist wall hangings and tree-screened patios for spying on local wildlife. Two have outdoor courtyard showers; all have fully-equipped kitchens, large bathrooms and laundry facilities. Minimum stay is two nights.

Island Leisure Resort RESORT $$
(📞07-4778 5000; www.islandleisure.com.au; 4 Kelly St; d buré from $189/f buré from $229; ❄ 🛜 ⊛) Self-contained, Polynesian-style cabins (*burés*) give this by-the-beach spot an extra-tropical feel. Private patios allow guests to enjoy their own piece of paradise: a lagoon pool and barbie area beckon social souls.

🛌 Arcadia

Hotel Arcadia HOTEL $
(📞07-4778 5177; www.hotelarcadia.com.au; 7 Marine Pde; r $99-145; ❄ @ ⊛) Formerly Magnums, the Hotel Arcadia has been upgraded from salacious to surprisingly swish. It hasn't lost its fun feel, though, and its on-site bistro and bar, the **Island Tavern** (mains $19.50-28; ⊙bistro 11am-8pm, bar noon-3am), keeps punters happy with cheap jugs, live music and cane-toad races every Wednesday night. Two awesome pools.

Arcadia Beach Guest House GUESTHOUSE $$
(📞07-4778 5668; www.arcadiabeachguesthouse.com.au; 27 Marine Pde; dm $35-40, safari tent $55, d without bathroom $85-100, d with bathroom $130-160; ❄ 🛜 ⊛) So much to choose from! Will you stay in a bright, beachy room (named after Magnetic Island's bays), a safari tent or dorm? Go turtle-spotting from the balcony, rent a canoe, a Moke or a 4WD...or all of the above? Free ferry pick-ups.

🛌 Horseshoe Bay

Bungalow Bay Koala Village HOSTEL $
(📞07-4778 5577, 1800 285 577; www.bungalowbay.com.au; 40 Horseshoe Bay Rd; unpowered/powered site per person $12.50/15, dm $28, d with/without bathroom $90/74; ❄ @ ⊛) 🍃 Not only a resort-style, YHA-associated hostel but a nature wonderland with its own wildlife park. Less than five minutes' walk from the beach, A-frame bungalows are strewn throughout leafy grounds backing onto national park. Cool off at the breezy outdoor bar, go coconut bowling on Thursdays, or tuck into a curry at the on-site **restaurant** (mains $15.50-24; ⊙lunch & dinner).

Shaws on the Shore APARTMENT $$$
(📞07-4778 1900; www.shawsontheshore.com.au; 7 Pacific Dr; 1-/2-/3-bedroom apt $175/265/320; ❄ 🛜 ⊛) These great-value, self-contained apartments are just a literal stagger from the beach. Private balconies overlook the bay, and inside, they're cool, clean and welcoming.

🍴 Eating & Drinking

Several hotels and hostels have restaurants and bars that are at least as popular with locals as they are with guests and visitors. Opening hours can fluctuate according to the season and the crowds.

Seafood is, unsurprisingly, the chomp of choice on Maggie.

Picnic Bay

Picnic Bay Hotel
PUB **$**

(The Esplanade; mains $11-26; ☺R&R Cafe Bar 9am-late) Settle in for a drink, with Townsville's city lights sparkling across the bay. Its **R&R Cafe Bar** has an all-day grazing menu and huge salads, including Cajun prawn.

Nelly Bay

Man Friday
MEXICAN, INTERNATIONAL **$$**

(✐07-4778 5658; 37 Warboy St; mains $14-39; ☺dinner Wed-Mon; ✐) Chow down on classy Mexican favourites in an incongruous but idyllic fairy-lit garden. Bring your own wine, and be sure to book ahead.

Le Paradis
FRENCH **$$**

(✐07-4778 5044; cnr Mandalay Ave & Sooning St; restaurant mains $23-40; ☺restaurant from 6pm, cafe from 11am) This fully-licenced restaurant offers a range of French-inspired eats, including divine garlic butter escargot. The attached cafe sells fresh baguettes and the usual burgery/fish-and-chipsy fare.

Arcadia

Arcadia Night Market
MARKET **$**

(RSL Hall, Hayles Ave; ☺5.30-8pm Fri) Small but lively night market, with licenced bar and plenty of cheap eats to chow through.

Caffè dell' Isola
ITALIAN **$$**

(7 Marine Pde; mains from $15; ☺breakfast & lunch Tue, Thu & Sun, breakfast, lunch & dinner Wed, Fri & Sat (& daily during school holidays)) Order pineapple on your pizza at your peril at this authentic Italian cafe, where the crust is crispy and the tastes are traditional. Or indulge your sweet tooth with a gelato instead: there are more than 20 fruity flavours to choose from.

Horseshoe Bay

Noodies on the Beach
MEXICAN **$**

(✐07-4778 5786; 2/6 Pacific Dr; from $10; ☺10am-10pm Mon-Wed & Fri, 8am-10pm Sat, 8am-3pm Sun; P) You can't help but love a joint which hands out free sombreros with jugs of margarita. Noodies dishes up fine Mexican food, but is arguably more famous for its coffee – reputedly the best on Maggie – and has a book exchange to boot.

Marlin Bar
PUB **$$**

(3 Pacific Dr; mains $16-24; ☺lunch & dinner) You can't leave Maggie without enjoying a cold one by the window as the sun sets across the bay at this popular seaside pub. The meals are on the large side and (surprise!) revolve around seafood.

Barefoot
MODERN AUSTRALIAN **$$**

(✐07-4758 1170; www.barefootartfoodwine.com.au; 5 Pacific Dr; mains from $20; ☺lunch & dinner Thu-Mon) Sophisticated without being standoffish, this restaurant/art gallery has an extensive wine list, fresh seafood platters and gourmet desserts.

ℹ Information

There's no official visitor information centre on Magnetic Island, but Townsville's visitor information centre has info and maps, and can help find accommodation. Maps are also available at both ferry terminals in Townsville and at the terminal at Nelly Bay.

Most businesses take EFTPOS, and ATMs are scattered throughout the island, including one at the **post office** (Sooning St, Nelly Bay; ☺9am-5pm Mon-Fri, to 11am Sat).

ℹ Getting There & Away

All ferries arrive and depart Maggie from the terminal at Nelly Bay.

Sealink (✐07-4726 0800; www.sealinkqld.com.au) operates a frequent passenger ferry between Townsville and Magnetic Island (adult/child return $32/16), which takes around 20 minutes. Ferries depart Townsville from the Breakwater Terminal on Sir Leslie Thiess Dr.

Fantasea (✐07-4796 9300; www.magneticislandferry.com.au; Ross St, South Townsville) operates a car ferry crossing eight times daily (seven on weekends) from the south side of Ross Creek, taking 35 minutes. It costs $178 (return) for a car and up to three passengers, and $29/17 (adult/child return) for foot passengers only. Bookings are essential and bicycles are transported free.

Both Townsville terminals have car parking.

ℹ Getting Around

BICYCLE

Magnetic Island is ideal for cycling, although some of the hills can be hard going. Most places to stay rent bikes for around $20 per day, though many offer them free to guests.

BUS

Sunbus (www.sunbus.com.au/sit_magnetic_island) ploughs between Picnic Bay and Horseshoe Bay, meeting all ferries and stopping at

ORPHEUS ISLAND

Forget about Orpheus in the Underworld: here, it's all about the underwater. Part of the Palm Islands group, Orpheus is surrounded by magnificent fringing reef that's home to a mind-blowing collection of fish (1100 species) and a mammoth variety of both hard and soft corals. While the island is great for snorkellers and divers year 'round (pack a stinger suit in summer), seasonal treats like manta-ray migration (August to November) and coral spawning (mid-November) make the trip out here all the more worthwhile.

The island itself is mostly national park, and is formed out of ancient volcanic rock. There is scattered rainforest, but Orpheus is mainly blanketed in dry woodland trees such as Moreton Bay ash and acacias. While the island shelters a miscellany of birds and reptiles, it is also home to a surprising number of goats; the animals were released on Orpheus in the 19th century as part of a madcap scheme to provide food for potential shipwreck survivors. At one stage, the hardy ruminants numbered more than 4000; these days, QPWS keep the numbers down with regular control programs.

Accommodation on Orpheus comes in two flavours: splurge or scrimp. The luxurious **Orpheus Island Resort** (☎07-4777 7377; www.orpheus.com.au; d $900-2800) offers minimalistic island-chic in the form of ultra-classy suites and villas; gourmet meals, water-sports equipment and some tours are included in the price. Otherwise, pitch your tent at any of the island's three bush camping sites at Yank's Jetty, Pioneer Bay or South Beach. The first two have toilets and picnic tables; the last is totally without facilities. You'll need to be self-sufficient, so bring all water and a fuel stove. Get permits from **NPRSR** (www.nprsr.qld.gov.au).

The resort offers helicopter transfers (ex-Townsville/Cairns $275/550); otherwise, ask around the town of Lucinda to arrange a boat ride over.

major accommodation places. A day pass covering all zones is $7.20.

MOKE & SCOOTER

Moke and scooter rental places abound. You'll need to be over 21, have a current international or Australian driver's licence and leave a credit-card deposit. Scooter hire starts at around $35 per day, Mokes about $75. Try **MI Wheels** (☎07-4758 1111; www.miwheels.com.au; 138 Sooning St, Nelly Bay) for a classic Moke or 'topless' car, or **Roadrunner Scooter Hire** (☎07-4778 5222; 3/64 Kelly St, Nelly Bay) for scooters and trail bikes.

Ayr & Around

POP 8885

On the delta of the mighty Burdekin River 90km southeast of Townsville, Ayr is the commercial centre for the rich farmlands of the Burdekin Valley. The town and its surrounds are devoted to the production and harvesting of sugar cane, melons and mangoes. Find out more at the **Burdekin visitor centre** (☎07-4783 5988; www.burdekintourism.com.au; Plantation Park, Bruce Hwy; ⊙9am-4pm) on the southern side of town.

Yongala Dive (☎07-4783 1519; www.yongaladive.com.au; 56 Narrah St, Alva Beach) does dive trips ($259 including gear) out to the *Yongala* wreck from Alva Beach, 17km northeast of Ayr. It only takes 30 minutes to get out to the wreck from here, instead of a 2½-hour boat trip from Townsville. Book ahead for backpacker-style accommodation at its onshore **dive lodge** (dm/d $25/60; @), with free pick-ups from Ayr.

NORTH OF TOWNSVILLE

As you leave Townsville, you also leave the Dry Tropics. The scorched-brown landscape slowly gives way to sugar-cane plantations lining the highway and tropical rainforest shrouding the hillsides.

Waterfalls, national parks and small villages hide up in the hinterland, including **Paluma Range National Park** (part of the Wet Tropics World Heritage Area); visitor centres in the area have leaflets outlining walking trails, swimming holes and camping grounds.

The region north of Townsville was hardest hit by Cyclone Yasi in February 2011 (and by Cyclone Larry in 2006), with damage to the coastline, islands, national parks and farmland. Much of the damage has been cleaned up, while some areas are still recovering.

Ingham & Around

POP 4767

Ingham is the proud guardian of the 120-hectare Tyto wetlands (Tyto Wetlands Information Centre; ☑ 07-4776 4792; www.tyto.com. au; cnr Cooper St & Bruce Hwy; ☺ 8.45am-5pm Mon-Fri, 9am-4pm Sat & Sun), which has 4km of walking trails and attracts around 230 species of birds, including far-flung guests from Siberia and Japan. The locals – hundreds of wallabies – love it too, converging at dawn and dusk. There's an art gallery and library on-site.

The poem which inspired the iconic Slim Dusty hit 'Pub With No Beer' (1957) was written in the Lees Hotel (☑ 07-4776 1577; www.leeshotel.com.au; 58 Lannercost St; s/d from $88/105, meals from $12; ☺ meals lunch & dinner Mon-Sat; ❋ ☜) by Ingham canecutter Dan Sheahan, after American soldiers drank the place dry. You'll spot the pub – which today has rooms, meals and even beer – by the mounted horseman on the roof.

Noorla Heritage Resort (☑ 07-4776 1100; www.hotelnoorla.com.au; 5-9 Warren St; s $69-169, d $79-179; ❋ ☜ ☷) was once the domain of Italian canecutters. These days, Ingham's wonderful 1920s art deco guesthouse has magnificently restored high-ceilinged rooms, plus cheaper container-style rooms in the garden. A photo montage of local stories lines the walls, bringing its history to life, as do the stories told around its aqua-tiled, guest-only bar.

The Australian Italian Festival (www.australianitalianfestival.com.au) celebrates the fact that 60% of Ingham residents are of Italian descent, with pasta flying, wine flowing and music playing over three days. Check the website for festival dates.

Ingham is the jumping-off point for the majestic Wallaman Falls, the longest single-drop waterfall in Australia at 305m. Located in Girringun National Park, 51km southwest of the town (the road is sealed except for the last 10km), the falls look their best in the Wet, though they are spectacular at any time. A steep but very worthwhile walking track (2km) takes you to the bottom. The camping ground (www.nprsr.qld.gov.au; per person/family $5.45/21.80) has barbecues and showers, plus regular wildlife visits, including – for those who can sit quietly and still – the occasional bobbing platypus in the swimming hole. Pick up a leaflet from the Tyto Wetlands Information Centre.

Mungalla Station (☑ 07-4777 8718; www.mungallaaboriginaltours.com.au; 2hr tour adult/child $52/30) ✈, 15km east of Ingham, runs insightful Aboriginal-led tours, including boomerang throwing and stories from the local Nywaigi culture. It's worth the extra cash to experience the traditional Kupmurri (adult/child incl tour $102.50/60) lunch of meat and vegies that are wrapped in banana leaves and cooked underground in an earth 'oven'. If you have a self-contained caravan or a campervan, you can camp (per van $10) overnight.

Cute little Lucinda, 27km northeast of Ingham, attracts happy-snappers gawking at the town's 5.76km-long jetty. The roofed structure, with a continuous conveyor belt running its length, is the world's longest bulk sugar-loading jetty, allowing enormous carrier ships to dock. Public access is off limits but it's an impressive sight nonetheless. Hinchinbrook Marine Cove (☑ 07-4777 8377; www.hinchinbrookmarinecove.com.au; 1 Denney St; d $125, bungalow $150, townhouse $195, cafe dishes $7-18, restaurant mains $22-32; ☺ cafe 7am-6pm, restaurant dinner Wed-Sat; ❋ ☷) overlooks a busy little fishing port, and has the area's best accommodation, plus a cafe and restaurant. Lucinda is also a top fishing spot: ask locals for the best place to wet your line.

Greyhound Australia (☑ 1300 473 946; www.greyhound.com.au; Townsville/Cairns $39/52) and Premier (☑ 13 34 10; www.premierms.com. au; Townsville/Cairns $26/34) buses stop in Ingham on their Cairns–Brisbane runs.

Ingham sits along the Queensland Rail (☑ 1800 872 467; www.traveltrain.com.au) Brisbane–Cairns train line.

Cardwell & Around

POP 1250

Most of the Bruce Hwy runs several kilometres inland from the coast, so it comes as something of a shock to see the sea lapping right next to the road as you pull into the small town of Cardwell – the closest access point to Hinchinbrook Island. Poor Cardwell took a beating from Cyclone Yasi, with many of the town's older homes smashed and the new marina switched to spin cycle.

◉ Sights & Activities

Cardwell Forest Drive   OUTDOORS

From the town centre, this scenic 26km round trip through the national park is chockas with lookouts, walking tracks and picnic areas signposted along the way. There are super swimming opportunities at **Attie Creek Falls**, as well as the aptly named **Spa Pool**, where you can sit in a rock hollow as water gushes over you.

Cardwell's visitor centre has brochures detailing other walking trails and swimming holes in the park.

Historic Cardwell Post Office & Telegraph Station MUSEUM
(53 Victoria St; ⊙10am-1pm Mon-Fri, 9am-noon Sat) FREE Check out the original postal room and old telephone exchange at this wooden building (built in 1870), which has survived cyclones and termites.

Girringun Aboriginal Art Centre GALLERY
(www.art.girrungun.com.au; 235 Victoria St; ⊙8.30am-5pm Mon-Thu, to 2pm Fri) ◢ Traditional woven baskets are among the works for sale at this corporation of Aboriginal artists.

🛏 Sleeping & Eating

Cardwell Beachcomber Motel & Tourist Park CARAVAN PARK $
(⊉07-4066 8550; www.cardwellbeachcomber. com.au; 43a Marine Pde; unpowered/powered site $27/34, motel d $98-125, cabins & studios $95-115; ❋@�⍾) This large park took a thrashing in Yasi, but is back in action with new poolside cabins, cute studios and modern oceanview villas. A surprisingly swish **restaurant** (mains from $25; ⊙breakfast daily, lunch & dinner Mon-Sat) dishes up seafood, steaks and whizbang pizzas.

Kookaburra Holiday Park CARAVAN PARK $
(⊉07-4066 8648; www.kookaburraholidaypark. com.au; 175 Bruce Hwy; unpowered/powered site $22/29, dm/s/d without bathroom $25/45/50, cabin without bathroom $65, unit $85-105; ❋@⍾) Well-run park that lends guests fishing rods, prawn nets and crab pots to catch dinner.

Cardwell Central Backpackers HOSTEL $
(⊉07-4066 8404; www.cardwellbackpackers.com. au; 6 Brasenose St; dm $20; @�⍾) Friendly hostel catering mostly to seasonal workers (management can help find jobs), but accepts overnighters. Free internet and pool table.

Mudbrick Manor B&B $$
(⊉07-4066 2299; www.mudbrickmanor.com.au; Lot 13, Stony Creek Rd; s/d $90/120; ❋⍾) As the name suggests, this family home is hand-built from mud bricks (and timber and

stone). Huge, beautifully appointed rooms congregate around a fountained courtyard. Rates include hot breakfast; book at least a few hours ahead for delicious three-course dinners (per person $30).

Seaview Cafe FAST FOOD $
(87 Victoria St; ⊙24hr) A famous stopover for hungry drivers, the cavernous Seaview dishes up local flavours in the form of crab sangas ($11), barra burgers ($9.90) and a mammoth all-day breakfast ($16.80). It ain't fancy, but it gets the job done nicely.

ℹ Information

The **Rainforest & Reef Centre** (⊉07-4066 8601; www.greatgreenwaytourism.com/rain-forestreef.html; 142 Victoria St; ⊙8.30am-5pm Mon-Fri, 9am-1pm Sat & Sun), next to Cardwell's jetty, has a truly brilliant interactive rainforest display and detailed info on Hinchinbrook Island and other nearby national parks.

ℹ Getting There & Away

Greyhound Australia (⊉1300 473 946; www. greyhound.com.au) and **Premier** (⊉13 34 10; www.premierms.com.au) buses on the Brisbane–Cairns route stop at Cardwell. Fares to Cairns are $48, to Townsville $36.

Cardwell is on the Brisbane–Cairns train line; contact **Queensland Rail** (⊉1800 872 467; www.traveltrain.com.au) for details.

Boats depart for Hinchinbrook Island from Port Hinchinbrook Marina, 2km south of town.

Hinchinbrook Island

Australia's largest island national park is a holy grail for walkers and those wanting to spend a bit of alone time with nature. Granite mountains rise dramatically from the sea; rugged Mt Bowen (1121m) is the 399-sq-km island's highest peak. The mainland side is dense with lush tropical vegetation, while long sandy beaches and tangles of mangrove curve around the eastern shore. Hinchinbrook's rainforest sustained considerable damage during Cyclone Yasi.

Hinchinbrook's highlight is the **Thorsborne Trail** (also known as the East Coast Trail), a 32km coastal track from Ramsay Bay past Zoe Bay, with its beautiful waterfall, to George Point at the southern tip. **NPRSR camp sites** (⊉13 74 68; www.nprsr.qld. gov.au; per person $5.45) are interspersed along the route. It's recommended that you take three nights to complete the challenging trail; return walks of individual sections are

PALUMA RANGE NATIONAL PARK

As the southern gateway to the Wet Tropics World Heritage Area, Paluma Range National Park and the little village of Paluma offer a leafy respite from the tedium of the Bruce Hwy. Running almost all the way from Ingham to Townsville, the park is divided in two parts, the Mt Spec section and the northern Jourama Falls section.

Mt Spec

The Mt Spec part of the park (61km north of Townsville or 40km south of Ingham) is a misty Eden of rainforest and eucalypt trees crisscrossed by a variety of walking tracks. This range of habitats houses an incredibly diverse population of birds, from golden bowerbirds to black cockatoos.

From the northern access route of the Bruce Hwy, take the 4km-long partially-sealed Spiegelhauer Rd to Big Crystal Creek; from there, it's an easy 100m walk from the car park to Paradise Waterhole, a popular spot with a sandy beach and lofty mountain views. There's an NPRSR camping ground (www.nprsr.qld.gov.au; per person/family $5.45/ 21.80) here with gas barbecues, toilets and drinking water; be quick, as sites get snapped up quickly.

The southern access route (Mt Spec Rd) is a sealed, albeit twisty, road that writhes up the mountains to Paluma village. Beware: though you may have come up here 'just for a drive', the village's cool air and warm populace may change your mind. Stay overnight at the Paluma Rainforest Inn (☑ 07-4770 8688; www.rainforestinnpaluma.com; 1 Mt Spec Rd; d $125; ❄), a true rainforest haven that sports 50 varieties of rhododendrons in its gardens.

En route to Paluma, be sure to stop off at Little Crystal Creek, a picturesque swimming hole with a cute stone bridge, picnic area and waterfalls.

Jourama Falls

Waterview Creek tumbles down these eponymous falls and other cascades past palms and umbrella trees, making this section a fine place for a picnic and a perambulation. It's a steep climb to the lookout; keep your eyes peeled for kingfishers, freshwater turtles and endangered mahogany gliders on the way up. The NPRSR camping ground (www.nprsr.qld.gov.au; per person/family $5.45/ 21.80) has cold showers, gas barbecues, water (treat before drinking) and composting toilets.

This part of the park is reached via a 6km sealed road (though the creek at the entrance can be impassable in the Wet), 91km north of Townsville and 24km south of Ingham. Be sure to fuel up before veering off the highway.

also possible. This is no tiptoe through the tulips, but a real-life wilderness adventure, with hungry native beasts (including crocs), saber-toothed mossies, and very rough patches. You'll have to draw your own water.

As only 40 walkers are allowed to traverse the trail at any one time, NPRSR recommends booking a year ahead for a place during the high season and six months ahead for other dates. Cancellations are not unheard of, so it's worth asking if you've arrived without a booking.

Hinchinbrook Island Cruises (☑ 07-4066 8601; www.hinchinbrookislandcruises.com.au) runs a service from Cardwell to Hinchinbrook's Ramsay Bay boardwalk (one way $90, one hour). It also operates a cruise to Zoe Bay as well as water taxis for the region

and island transfers: book through Cardwell's Rainforest & Reef Centre (p432).

Thorsborne Trail walkers can pick up a one-way transfer back to the mainland with Hinchinbrook Wilderness Safaris (☑ 07-4777 8307; www.hinchinbrookwildernesssafaris.com.au; $50), from George Point at the southern end of the trail.

Tully

POP 2500

It may look like just another sleepy sugarcane village, but Tully is a burg with a boast, calling itself the 'Wettest town in Australia'. A gigantic golden gumboot at Tully's entrance is as high as the waters rose (7.9m) in 1950: climb the spiral staircase to the viewing

TULLY RIVER RAFTING

The Tully River provides thrilling white water year-round thanks to Tully's trademark bucket-downs and the river's hydroelectric floodgates. Rafting trips are timed to coincide with the daily release of the gates, resulting in grade-four rapids foaming against a backdrop of stunning rainforest scenery.

Day trips with **Raging Thunder Adventures** (✆07-4030 7990; www.ragingthunder. com.au; standard/'xtreme' trip $189/215) or **R'n'R White Water Rafting** (✆07-4041 9444; www.raft.com.au; $189) include a barbecue lunch and transport from Tully or nearby Mission Beach. Transfers from Cairns are an extra $10.

platform up top to get a sense of just how much that is! The **Golden Gumboot Festival** (www.tullygumbootfestival.com), held each May, celebrates the soak with a parade and lashings of entertainment. And while boggy **Babinda** challenges Tully's claim, the fact remains that all that rain ensures plenty of raftable rapids on the nearby Tully River.

The **Tully Visitor & Heritage Centre** (✆07-4068 2288; Bruce Hwy; ⊙8.30am-4.45pm Mon-Fri, 9am-2pm Sat & Sun) has a brochure outlining a self-guided **heritage walk** around town, with 17 interpretative panels (including one dedicated to Tully's UFO sightings), and **walking trail** maps for the nearby national parks. The centre also has free internet and a book exchange.

Book at the visitor centre for 90-minute **Tully Sugar Mill Tours** (adult/child $17/11; ⊙daily late Jun-early Nov). Tour times depend on seasonal conditions; wear closed shoes and a shirt with sleeves.

The Indigenous operators of **Ingan Tours** (✆1300 728 067; www.ingan.com.au; adult/child $120/60) visit 'sacred story places' on their full-day 'Spirit of the Rainforest' tours (Tuesdays, Thursdays and Saturdays).

Practically all accommodation in Tully is geared for banana workers, with cheap weekly rates and help finding farm work – try the excellent **Banana Barracks** (✆07-4068 0455; www.bananabarracks.com; 50 Butler St; dm with/without bathroom $28/24, bungalows $30-40; @ 🛜 🏊) bang in the town centre, which is also the hub of Tully's nightlife, with an on-site **nightclub** (⊙Thu-Sat).

Tully's pubs serve hearty meals (except Sundays), while **Joe's Pizza Parlour** (✆07-4068 1996; 46 Butler St; pizzas from $12; ⊙dinner, days vary) has thick-crust old-school pizzas.

Greyhound Australia (✆1300 473 946; www.greyhound.com.au) and **Premier** (✆13 34 10; www.premierms.com.au) buses stop in town on the Brisbane–Cairns route; fares to Cairns/Townsville are $29/$39. Tully is

also on the **Queensland Rail** (✆1800 872 467; www.traveltrain.com.au) Brisbane–Cairns train line.

Mission Beach

POP 4000

Less than 30km east of the Bruce Hwy's rolling sugar-cane and banana plantations, the hamlets that make up greater Mission Beach are hidden amongst World Heritage rainforest. The rainforest extends right to the Coral Sea, giving this 14km-long palm-fringed stretch of secluded inlets and wide, empty beaches the castaway feel of a tropical island.

The frightfully powerful Cyclone Yasi made landfall at Mission Beach in 2011, stripping much of the rainforest and vegetation bare. However, the communities here recovered quickly – within two weeks, water and power was restored and most businesses and tourist operators were running normally.

Although collectively referred to as Mission Beach or just 'Mission', the area comprises a sequence of individual villages strung along the beach. **Bingil Bay** lies 4.8km north of **Mission Beach proper** (sometimes called North Mission). **Wongaling Beach** is 5km south; from here it's a further 5.5 kilometres south to **South Mission Beach**. Most amenities are in Mission proper and Wongaling Beach; South Mission Beach and Bingil Bay are mainly residential.

Mission is one of the closest access points to the Great Barrier Reef, and the gateway to Dunk Island. There are plenty of opportunities for on-foot exploring here: walking tracks fan out around Mission Beach, with Australia's highest density of cassowaries (around 40) roaming the rainforest. While Mission's coastline seems to scream 'toe dip!', don't just fling yourself into the water any old where: stick to the swimming enclosures, lest you have a nasty encounter with a marine stinger...or croc.

🏃 Activities

Adrenalin junkies flock to Mission Beach for extreme and water-based sports, including white-water rafting on the nearby Tully River. If you've got your own board, Bingil Bay is one of the rare spots inside the reef where it's possible to surf, with small but consistent swells of around 1m.

Stinger enclosures at Mission Beach and South Mission Beach provide safe year-round swimming.

The visitor centre has heaps of information on the many superb walking tracks in the area.

Skydiving   SKYDIVING
Mission Beach is rightfully one of the most popular spots in Queensland for skydiving. Two outfits will take you up: **Jump the Beach** (🖉 1300 800 840; www.jumpthe-beach.com.au; 9000/11,000/14,000ft tandem jump $284/345/369) and **Skydive Mission Beach** (🖉 1300 800 840; www.skydivemission-beach.com; 9000/11,000/14,000ft tandem dive $249/310/334). Both use the beach to cushion your landing.

Big Mama Sailing   SAILING
(🖉 0437 206 360; www.bigmamasailing.com; adult/child from $65/40) Hit the water on an 18m ketch with passionate boaties Stu, Lisa and Fletcher. Choose from a 2.5hr sunset tour, barbecue lunch cruise or full day on the reef.

Calypso Dive   DIVING
(🖉 07-4068 8432; www.calypsodive.com.au) Calypso runs reef dives (from $264, including gear), wreck dives of the *Lady Bowen* ($225), and PADI open-water courses ($625). Otherwise, snorkel the reef ($169) or take a jet-ski tour around Dunk Island (from $224).

**Mission Beach
Adventure Centre**   WATER SPORTS
(🖉 0429 469 330; Seaview St, Mission Beach) This little rainbow hut by the beach runs the gamut of water and beach sports, from kayak (single/double per hour $15/30) to stand-up board hire (per hour $15). Its **cafe** (dishes $5-8) is famed for its hot dogs.

Coral Sea Kayaking   KAYAKING
(🖉 07-4068 9154; www.coralseakayaking.com; half-/full-day tour $80/128) Knowledgable full-day guided tours to Dunk Island; easygoing bob-arounds on the half-day option.

Fishin' Mission   FISHING
(🖉 0427 323 469; www.fishinmission.com.au; half-/full-day trip $140/230) Chilled-out reef-fishing charters with local pros.

**Mission Beach Tropical
Fruit Safari**   FOOD TASTING
(🖉 07-4068 7099; www.missionbeachtourism.com; Mission Beach Visitor Centre, Porter Promenade; adult/family $8/20; ⊙ 1-2pm Mon & Tue) Get to know (and taste) weird and wonderful local tropical fruits.

🎊 Festivals & Events

Markets   MARKET
Local arts, crafts, jewellery, tropical fruit, home-made gourmet goods and more overflow from stalls at the **Mission Beach Markets** (Porter Promenade; ⊙ 8am-1pm 1st & 3rd Sun of month). Even more wonderful stuff, including hand-made log furniture, is up for grabs at the **Mission Beach Rotary Monster Market** (Marcs Park, Cassowary Dr, Wongaling Beach; ⊙ 8am-12.30pm last Sun of month Apr-Nov).

Mission Evolve Music Fest   MUSIC
(www.missionevolve.com.au) Two days of live music in October featuring blues, roots, soul, funk and DJs from around Far North Queensland.

🛏 Sleeping

The visitor centre has a list of booking agents for holiday rentals. Hostels have courtesy bus pick-ups.

🛏 South Mission Beach

Sea-S-Ta   GUESTHOUSE $$$
(🖉 07-4088 6699; www.sea-s-ta.com.au; 38 Kennedy Esplanade; per night $350, 2-night min stay) Awkward name, amazing place. This self-contained holiday house is a great option for groups looking to stay and play in Mission. The bright, Mexico-inspired hacienda sleeps six, and comes with *mucho* extras, from juicers to his'n'hers slippers. Rates go down the longer you stay.

🛏 Wongaling Beach

★**Scotty's Mission Beach House**   HOSTEL $
(🖉 1800 665 567; www.scottysbeachhouse.com.au; 167 Reid Rd; dm $25-29, d $71; ❋ @ 🛜 🞩) Clean, comfy rooms (including girls-only dorms

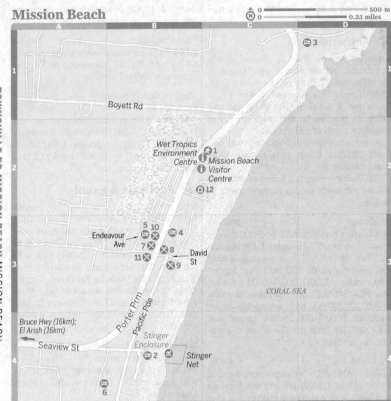

Mission Beach

with Barbie-pink sheets!) are grouped around Scotty's grassy, social pool area. Out front, **Scotty's Bar & Grill** (mains $10-30; ⊙ dinner), open to nonguests, has something happening virtually every night, from fire-twirling shows to pool comps and live music. Classic backpackery good times, ahoy!

Dunk Island View
Caravan Park   CARAVAN PARK **$**
(☎07-4068 8248; www.dunkislandviewcaravan-park; 21 Webb Rd; unpowered/powered site $28/38, 1-/2-bedroom unit $98/128; ❄ 🛜 🏊 🐾) Wake to fresh sea breezes at this clean and congenial spot just 50m from the beach. Everything you'd want from a caravan park, with the bonus of a new on-site cafe (fish and chips $8).

Hibiscus Lodge B&B   B&B **$$**
(☎07-4068 9096; www.hibiscuslodge.com.au; 5 Kurrajong Cl; r $115-155; ℗) Wake to the sound of birds chirping and, more than likely, spot a cassowary or two during breakfast (an

absolute must) on the rainforest-facing deck of this lovely B&B. With only three (very private) rooms, bookings are essential. No kids.

Licuala Lodge
B&B **$$**

(☑ 07-4068 8194; www.licualalodge.com.au; 11 Mission Circle; s/d/t incl breakfast $99/135/185; 🎐 💌) Chummy B&B with a guest kitchen, wonderful verandah and cassowary gatecrashers. Don't be alarmed by the teddy bears in your bedroom.

🛏 Mission Beach

Mission Beach Retreat
HOSTEL **$**

(☑ 07-4088 6229; www.missionbeachretreat. com.au; 49 Porter Promenade; dm $22-25, d $56; ❄ @ 🎐 💌) Bang in the centre of town with the bonus of being beachfront, this is an easy, breezy backpacker spot that's hard not to like.

Mission Beach Ecovillage
CABIN **$$**

(☑ 07-4068 7534; www.ecovillage.com.au; Clump Point Rd; d $135-220; ❄ 🎐 💌) With its own banana and lime trees scattered around its tropical gardens and a direct path through the rainforest to the beach, this 'ecovillage' makes the most of its environment. Bungalows cluster around a rocky pool, and deluxe cottages have private spas. There's a licensed restaurant (mains $18.50; ☺ dinner Wed-Sat).

Rainforest Motel
MOTEL **$$**

(☑ 07-4068 7556; www.missionbeachrainforest-motel.com.au; 9 Endeavour Ave; s/d $98/119; ❄ @ 🎐 💌) A charming little gem, this motel is not only great value, but friendly and well-appointed to boot. Close to the shops but tucked away behind lush greenery. Free bikes available.

Castaways Resort & Spa
RESORT **$$$**

(☑ 07-4068 7444; www.castaways.com.au; Pacific Pde; d $165-215, 1-/2-bedroom unit $265/345; ❄ @ 🎐 💌) Castaways' cheapest rooms don't have balconies, so it's worth splashing out a bit more for one of the 'Coral Sea' rooms with an extended deck and day bed. The units are small, but perks include two elongated pools, a luxurious spa (www.driftspa. com.au) and stunning beach views from its tropical-style bar/restaurant (mains $12-32; ☺ breakfast, lunch & dinner). Come on Tuesdays for tropical high tea.

Sejala on the Beach
CABIN **$$$**

(☑ 07-4088 6699; www.sejala.com.au; 26 Pacific Pde; d $260; ❄ 💌) Three huts (request one facing the beach) with rainforest showers, decks with private BBQs and loads of character. Romance central.

🛏 Bingil Bay

★ Jackaroo Hostel
HOSTEL **$**

(☑ 07-4068 7137; www.jackaroohostel.com; 13 Frizelle Rd; camp site $15, dm/d incl breakfast $24/58; P @ 🎐 💌) Run by globetrotting brothers Robert and Jade, this timber pole-frame retreat high in the rainforest has it all, and then some. Jungly surrounds, a sparkling pool, airy rooms and the breezy terrace tempt you to linger longer; the outdoor cinema and free surfboard hire cement the deal.

Sanctuary
CABIN **$$**

(☑ 1800 777 012, 07-4088 6064; www.sanctuaryat-mission.com; 72 Holt Rd; dm $35, s/d hut $65/70, cabin $145/165; ☺ mid-Apr–mid-Dec; @ 🎐 💌) ✐ Reached by a steep 600m-long rainforest walking track from the car park (4WD pickup available), you can sleep surrounded only by flyscreen on a platform in simple huts, or opt for en suite cabins whose showers have floor-to-ceiling rainforest views. Tramp the walking tracks, take a yoga class ($15), indulge in a massage (per hour $80), and cook in the self-catering kitchen or dine on wholesome fare at the restaurant (mains $19-33; ☺ 7.30am-8.30pm; ✐). Eco-initiatives include its own sewerage system, rainwater harvesting and biodegradable detergents. Not suitable for kids under 11.

🍴 Eating & Drinking

The majority of bars and/or restaurants are clustered in Mission Beach proper along Porter Promenade and its adjoining spider's web of tiny walkways and arcades. There's a small supermarket here, and a huge Woolworths supermarket at Wongaling Beach (look for the giant cassowary), which also has a handful of eateries, bars and bottle shops.

🍴 Wongaling Beach

Millers Beach Bar & Grill
PUB **$**

(☑ 07-4068 8177; 1 Banfield Pde; $10-38; ☺ 3pm-late Tue-Fri, noon-late Sat & Sun) So close to the beach you'll be picking sand out of your beer, Millers has a rockin' little courtyard custom-made for lazy loitering. Graze on $10 pizzas (4pm to 6pm daily), attack a giant steak, or just devour the view of Dunk Island over a cocktail.

★ **Cafe Rustica** ITALIAN $$

(☑ 07-4068 9111; 24 Wongaling Beach Rd; mains $18-25; ⊙ 5pm-late Wed-Sat, 10am-late Sun; ☑) This contemporary corrugated-iron beach shack is home to delicious home-made pastas and crispy-crust pizzas; they also make their own gelato and sorbet. Be sure to book ahead.

✗ Mission Beach

★ **Fish Bar** SEAFOOD $

(☑ 07-4088 6419; Porter Promenade; $10-17; ⊙ 10am-midnight) For socialising and scarfing, this place is tough to top. It's laid-back yet lively, with an equally zingy menu that includes buckets of prawns (lunch $10) and pig on a spit ($13). Live music on Sundays.

New Deli CAFE, DELI $

(Shop 1, 47 Porter Promenade; mains $8-16; ⊙ 9.30am-6pm Mon-Fri; ☑) Stock up on goodies for a gourmet picnic at this aromatic gourmet deli/cafe where most produce is organic and everything is home-made, including scrumptious biscuits.

Zenbah INTERNATIONAL $

(☑ 07-4088 6040; 39 Porter Promenade; mains $9-25; ⊙ 10am-1.30am Fri & Sat, to midnight Sun-Thu) The colourful chairs on the sidewalk mark Zenbah as the vibrant little eatery/hangout

it is. The food ranges from Middle Eastern to Asian all the way back to pizza, and you can digest it all to a backdrop of live tunes on Fridays and Saturdays. Free courtesy bus.

Early Birds Cafe CAFE $

(Shop 2, 46 Porter Promenade; mains $6-15; ⊙ 6am-3pm Thu-Tue; ☑) Early Birds' all-day tropical Aussie Brekkie ($13.50) of bacon and eggs, grilled tomato and banana, toast, and tea or coffee is perfect after a morning swim.

Garage Bar & Grill MODERN AUSTRALIAN $$

(☑ 07-4088 6280; 41 Donkin Lane; meze plate $17; ⊙ 9am-late; ❄ ☑) This super-social spot on Mission's 'Village Green' serves delicious 'sliders' (mini burgers), free-pour cocktails ($14), good coffee, cakes and tapas. Wash it all down with some toe-tappin' live music.

✗ Bingil Bay

Bingil Bay Cafe CAFE $$

(29 Bingil Bay Rd; mains $14-23; ⊙ 6.30am-10pm; ☑) Everything is groovy at this lavender landmark, from the eclectic menu to the mellow vibes emanating from the porch. Breakfast is a highlight, or just grab a coldie and immerse yourself in the art displays, live music and hey-dude buzz.

THE CASSOWARY: ENDANGERED NATIVE

Looking like something out of *Jurassic Park*, a flightless prehistoric bird struts through the rainforest. It's as tall as a grown man, has three razor-sharp, dagger-style clawed toes, a bright-blue head, red wattles (the lobes hanging from its neck), a helmet-like horn and shaggy black feathers similar to an emu's. Meet the cassowary, an important link in the rainforest ecosystem. It's the only animal capable of dispersing the seeds of more than 70 species of trees whose fruit is too large for other rainforest animals to digest and pass (which acts as fertiliser). You're most likely to see cassowaries in the wild around Mission Beach, Etty Bay and the Cape Tribulation section of the Daintree National Park. They can be aggressive, particularly if they have chicks. Do not approach them; if one threatens you, don't run – give the bird right-of-way and try to keep something solid between you and it, preferably a tree.

It is estimated that there are 1000 or less cassowaries in the wild north of Queensland. An endangered species, the cassowary's biggest threat is loss of habitat, and most recently the cause has been natural. Tropical Cyclone Yasi stripped much of the rainforest around Mission Beach bare, threatening the struggling population with starvation. The birds are also exposed to the elements and more vulnerable to dog attacks and being killed by cars as they venture out in search of food.

Next to the Mission Beach visitor centre, there are cassowary conservation displays at the Wet Tropics Environment Centre (☑ 07-4068 7197; www.wettropics.gov.au; Porter Promenade; ⊙ 10am-4pm), staffed by volunteers from the Community for Cassowary & Coastal Conservation (C4; www.cassowaryconservation.asn.au). Proceeds from gift-shop purchases go towards buying cassowary habitat. The website www.savethecassowary.org.au is also a good source of info.

❶ Information

The efficient **Mission Beach visitor centre** (☑ 07-4068 7099; www.missionbeachtourism.com; Porters Promenade; ☺ 9am-4.45pm Mon-Sat, 10am-4pm Sun) has reams of info in multiple languages.

The **Mission Beach Information Station** (www.missionbeachinfo.com; 4 Wongaling Shopping Centre, Cassowary Dr, Wongaling Beach; internet 20min/hr $2/5; ☺ 9am-7pm) can also help with tour bookings, and has internet booths.

❶ Getting There & Around

Greyhound Australia (☑ 1300 473 946; www.greyhound.com.au) and **Premier** (☑ 13 34 10; www.premierms.com.au) buses stop in Wongaling Beach next to the 'big cassowary'. Fares with Greyhound/Premier are $23/19 to Cairns, $41/46 to Townsville.

Sugarland Car Rentals (☑ 07-4068 8272; www.sugarland.com.au; 30 Wongaling Beach Rd, Wongaling Beach; ☺ 8am-5pm) rents small cars from $35 per day.

Mission Beach Adventure Centre (p435) rents bikes ($10/20 for a half-/full day).

Or call a **taxi** (☑ 13 10 08).

Dunk Island

Dunk Island is known to the Djiru Aboriginal people as Coonanglebah (the island of peace and plenty). They're not wrong: this is pretty much your ideal tropical island, with lush jungle, white sand beaches and blue water.

Walking trails crisscross (and almost circumnavigate) Dunk: the circuit track (9.2km) is the best way to have a proper stickybeak at the island's interior and abundant wildlife. There's good snorkelling over bommies at Muggy Muggy and great swimming at Coconut Beach.

The island's resort is closed due to cyclone damage, though camping (Map p478; ☑ 0417 873 390; per person $5.15) has reopened.

Mission Beach Dunk Island Water Taxi (☑ 07-4068 8310; www.missionbeachwatertaxi.com; Banfield Pde, Wongaling Beach; adult/child return $35/18), departing from Wongaling Beach, makes the 20-minute trip to Dunk Island.

Mission Beach to Innisfail

The road north from Mission Beach rejoins the Bruce Hwy at El Arish (population 442), home to not much bar a golf course and the memorabilia- and character-filled El Arish Tavern (38 Chauvel St), built in 1927.

From El Arish, you can take the more direct route north by continuing straight along the Bruce Hwy, with turn-offs leading to beach communities including exquisite Etty Bay, with its wandering cassowaries, rocky headlands, rainforest, large stinger enclosure and a superbly sited caravan park.

Alternatively, detour west via the Old Bruce Hwy, also known as Canecutter Way (www.canecutterway.com.au). Mena Creek is home to the enchanting ruins of two once-grand castles at the five-hectare Paronella Park (☑ 07-4065 0000; www.paronellapark.com.au; Japoonvale Rd; adult/child $40/20; ☺ 9am-7.30pm). Built in the 1930s as a whimsical entertainment centre for the area's hard-working folk, the mossy Spanish ruins now have an almost medieval feel, and walking trails lead through rambling gardens past a waterfall and swimming hole. Take the 45-minute daytime tour and/or one-hour night tour to hear the full, fascinating story. Admission includes both tours, as well as one night at its powered camping ground; otherwise book in to one of the sweet little cabins (d shared bathroom $85; ✢). Tickets to Paronella Park are valid for one year.

Innisfail & Around

POP 8262

Sitting pretty just 80km south of the Cairns tourism frenzy, Innisfail is a textbook example of a laid-back, far northern country town. Fisherfolk ply the wide Johnstone River, tractors trundle down the main street, and locals are equally proud of their magnificent art deco architecture and born-and-bred footy (rugby league) hero Billy Slater.

Beachside Flying Fish Point is 8km northeast of Innisfail's town centre, while national parks, including the Mamu Rainforest Canopy Walkway, are within a short drive.

❂ Sights & Activities

**Mamu Rainforest
Canopy Walkway** VIEWPOINT
(www.nprsr.qld.gov.au/parks/mamu; Palmerston Hwy; adult/child $20/10; ☺ 9.30am-5.30pm, last entry 4.30pm) ❂ About 27km along the Palmerston Hwy (signposted 4km northwest of Innisfail), this canopy-level rainforest walkway gives you eye-level views of the fruits, flowers and birds, and a bird's-eye perspective from its 100-step, 37m-high tower.

Allow at least an hour to complete the 2.5km, wheelchair-accessible circuit.

The Palmerston Hwy continues west to Millaa Millaa, passing the entrance to the Waterfalls Circuit.

Wooroonooran National Park PARK
The Palmerston (Doongan) section of this national park is home to some of the oldest surviving rainforest in Australia; NPRSR (www.nprsr.qld.gov.au) has details of camping grounds and walking trails.

Art Deco Architecture ARCHITECTURE
(www.artdeco-innisfail.com.au) Following a devastating 1918 cyclone, Innisfail rebuilt in the art deco style of the day, and 2006's Cyclone Larry resulted in many of these striking buildings being refurbished. Pick up a free, comprehensive town walk brochure from the visitor centre, detailing over two dozen key points of interest.

🎊 Festivals & Events

Foodie fun during the Feast of the Senses (www.feastofthesenses.com.au) in March includes food stalls, farm tours and markets.

🍽 Sleeping & Eating

Innisfail's hostels primarily cater to banana pickers who work the nearby plantations; weekly rates average about $185 (dorm). The Backpackers Shack (☑07-4061 7760; www.backpackersshack.com; 7 Ernest St; ▣✳@) and Codge Lodge (☑07-4061 8055; www.codgelodge.com; 63 Rankin St; dm $30; ✳@🛜✼) are good options. The visitor centre has a full list.

Drop by the Innisfail Fish Depot (51 Fitzgerald Esplanade; ◷8am-6pm Mon-Fri, 9am-4pm Sat, 10am-4pm Sun) for fresh-as-it-gets fish to throw on the barbie and organic cooked prawns by the bagful ($18 to $20 per kilo).

Flying Fish Tourist Park CARAVAN PARK $
(☑07-4061 3131; www.ffpvanpark.com.au; 39 Elizabeth St, Flying Fish Point; unpowered/powered site $28/33, cabin $60-95, villa $105-115; ✳@🛜✼) Fish right off the beach across the road from this first-rate park, or organise boat rental through the friendly managers.

Barrier Reef Motel MOTEL $$
(☑07-4061 4988; www.barrierreefmotel.com.au; Bruce Hwy; s/d $110/120, unit $150-170;

✳@🛜✼) The best place to stay in Innisfail, this comfortable motel next to the visitor centre has airy, tiled rooms with large bathrooms. Self-caterers should nab one of the units with kitchenettes; otherwise head to the restaurant (mains $28-30.50; ◷breakfast & dinner; ☝) or just have a drink at the bar.

Monsoon Cruising SEAFOOD $
(☑0427 776 663; 1 Innisfail Wharf; mains $12-17.50; ◷10am-5pm Wed-Sat Mar-Dec; ☝) Everything is locally sourced and/or organic aboard this moored cruiser – from bread baked fresh to black tiger prawns straight off the trawlers.

Flying Fish Point Cafe CAFE $
(9 Elizabeth St, Flying Fish Point; mains $12-21; ◷7.30am-8pm) Come hungry to finish the huge seafood baskets of battered and crumbed fish, barbecued calamari, wonton prawns, tempura scallops and more.

Oliveri's Continental Deli DELI $
(www.oliverisdeli.com.au; 41 Edith St; sandwiches $8-9; ◷8.30am-5.15pm Mon-Fri, to 12.30pm Sat; ☝) An Innisfail institution offering goodies like 60-plus varieties of European cheese, ham and salami, and scrumptious sandwiches.

Roscoe's ITALIAN $$
(☑07-4061 6888; 3b Ernest St; mains $22-36, buffets $18-42; ◷11.30am-1.30pm & 5.30-9.30pm) Popular local haunt for its buffets, complete with home-made desserts like tiramisu.

ℹ Information

The visitor centre (☑07-4061 2655; www.cassowarycoasttourism.com.au; cnr Eslick St & Bruce Hwy; ◷9am-5pm Mon-Fri, 10am-12.30pm Sat & Sun) gives out discount vouchers for many of the area's attractions.

ℹ Getting There & Away

Bus services operate once daily with Premier (☑13 34 10; www.premierms.com.au) and several times daily with Greyhound Australia (☑1300 473 946; www.greyhound.com.au) between Innisfail and Townsville (4½ hours) and Cairns (1½ hours).

Innisfail is on the Cairns–Brisbane train line; contact Queensland Rail (☑1800 872 467; www.traveltrain.com.au) for information.

Cairns & the Daintree Rainforest

Includes ➡

Best Places to Eat

Best Places to Stay

Why Go?

Tropical, touristy Cairns is an unmissable stop on any East Coast traveller's itinerary. Experienced divers and first-time toe-dippers swarm to the steamy city for its easy access to the Great Barrier Reef, while those more interested in submerging themselves in boozy good times are well-served by a barrage of bars and clubs. For day-trippers, the Atherton Tableland – home to cooler climes, volcanic-crater lakes, jungly waterfalls and gourmet food producers – is just a short and scenic drive away.

The winding road from Cairns to ritzy Port Douglas offers spectacular coastal vistas, but it's north of the Daintree River that the adventure really begins. The magnificent Daintree National Park stretches up the coast, with rainforest tumbling right onto white-sand beaches; don't be so awestruck by the stunning surrounds that you forget to keep an eye out for crocs! Further up, the Bloomfield Track from Cape Tribulation to Cooktown is one of Australia's great 4WD journeys.

When to Go
Cairns

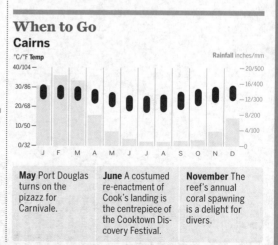

May Port Douglas turns on the pizazz for Carnivale.

June A costumed re-enactment of Cook's landing is the centrepiece of the Cooktown Discovery Festival.

November The reef's annual coral spawning is a delight for divers.

Cairns & the Daintree Rainforest Highlights

1 Diving, snorkelling and swimming among the fish, turtles and anemones in the multicoloured corals of the **Great Barrier Reef**, from Cairns (p445) or Port Douglas (p463).

2 Taking an Aboriginal-guided walk and swimming in the crystal-clear waters of **Mossman Gorge** (p474).

3 Riding the Skyrail cable car through the rainforest to the market town of **Kuranda** (p458) and returning to Cairns by scenic railway.

4 Barra fishing, barbecuing or watching the sunset

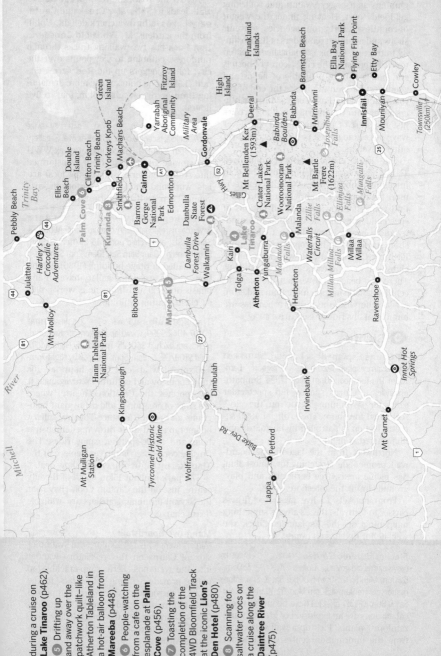

CAIRNS

POP 165,860

Cairns has come a long way since its beginnings as a boggy swamp and rollicking goldfields port. Heaving under the weight of countless resorts, tour agencies, souvenir shops and a million reminders of its proximity to the reef, Cairns is unabashedly geared towards tourism. The city's scores of hostels and hotels ring to a jumble of hellos and goodbyes: for many, Cairns is the end of the road after a long East Coast jaunt; for others flying into the international airport, it's just the start of the adventure. Whichever way you're going, it's a perfect place to meet other travellers.

Old salts claim Cairns (pronounced 'Cans') has sold its soul, but it does have an infectious holiday vibe. The city centre is more boardshorts than briefcases, and you'll find yourself throwing away all notions of speed and schedules here, thanks to humidity and a hearty hospitality that can turn a short stroll into an impromptu social event. Fittingly, Cairns is awash with bars, nightclubs, eateries and cafes suiting all budgets. There's no beach in town, but the magnificent Esplanade Lagoon more than makes up for it; otherwise, the northern beaches are but a local bus ride or easy drive away.

🅞 Sights

★ **Cairns Esplanade & Lagoon** WATERFRONT
(www.cairnsesplanade.com.au; ⊙ lagoon 6am-10pm Thu-Tue, noon-10pm Wed) FREE Sunbathers flock to Cairns' shallow but spectacular saltwater swimming lagoon on the city's reclaimed foreshore. The artificial 4800-sq-metre lagoon is patrolled by lifeguards and illuminated at night.

Northwest from the lagoon, the boardwalk promenade, stretching for almost 3km, has picnic areas, free barbecues and playgrounds lining the foreshore.

From markets to live gigs, free fitness classes to festivals, there's always something happening on the Esplanade. Check the website for updates on events.

Flecker Botanic Gardens GARDENS
(www.cairns.qld.gov.au; Collins Ave; ⊙ 7.30am-5.30pm Mon-Fri, 8.30am-5.30pm Sat & Sun, information centre 9am-4.30pm Mon-Fri, 10am-2.30pm Sat & Sun; 🚍 131) FREE These beautiful tropical gardens are an explosion of greenery and rainforest plants. Pick up a walks brochure from the information centre or ask about

free guided walks. There's a great cafe and a new, well-camouflaged visitor centre (it's made of mirrors!).

Across the road, the **Rainforest Boardwalk** leads to **Saltwater Creek** and **Centenary Lakes**, a birdwatcher's delight. Uphill from the gardens, **Mt Whitfield Conservation Park** has two walking tracks through rainforest, climbing to viewpoints over the city; follow joggers up the **Red Arrow circuit** (1.5km, one hour) or the more demanding **Blue Arrow circuit** (6.6km, four to five hours).

Tanks Arts Centre GALLERY, THEATRE
(www.tanksartscentre.com; 46 Collins Ave; ⊙ gallery 10am-4pm Mon-Fri) Three gigantic, ex-WWII fuel-storage tanks have been transformed into studios, galleries showcasing local artists' work and an inspired performing-arts venue. There's a lively **market day**.

Cairns Regional Gallery GALLERY
(www.cairnsregionalgallery.com.au; cnr Abbott & Shields Sts; adult/child under 16 $5/free; ⊙ 9am-5pm Mon-Fri, 10am-5pm Sat, 10am-2pm Sun) In a colonnaded heritage building (1936), exhibitions at this acclaimed gallery have an emphasis on local and Indigenous works, plus excellent visiting exhibitions.

Tjapukai Cultural Park CULTURAL CENTRE
(🖉 07-4042 9999; www.tjapukai.com.au; Kamerunga Rd; adult/child $40/25, Tjapukai by Night adult/child $109/59; ⊙ 9am-5pm, Tjapukai by Night 7pm-9.30pm) Allow at least three hours at this Indigenous-owned cultural extravaganza. It incorporates the Creation Theatre, where the story of creation is told using giant holograms and actors, a Dance Theatre, gallery, boomerang- and spear-throwing demonstrations and turtle-spotting canoe rides. The fireside corroboree is the centrepiece of the **Tjapukai by Night** dinner-and-show deal.

The park is about 15km north of the city centre, just off the Captain Cook Hwy near the Skyrail terminal; transfers are available (extra charge).

Mangrove Boardwalk BOARDWALK
(Airport Avenue) FREE Explore the swampier side of Cairns on this revelatory wander into the wetlands. Eerie snap-crackle-slop noises provide a fitting soundtrack to the spooky surrounds, which are signposted with informative guides to the weird lifeforms scurrying in the mud below you. Bring mosquito repellant. It's just before the Cairns Airport.

Crystal Cascades & Lake Morris
WATERFALL, LAKE

About 14km from Cairns, the Crystal Cascades are a series of beautiful waterfalls and (croc-free) pools. The area is accessed by a 1.2km (30-minute) pathway. Crystal Cascades is linked to Lake Morris (the city's reservoir) by a *steep* rainforest **walking trail** (allow three hours return); it starts near the picnic area.

Reef Teach
INTERPRETIVE CENTRE

(☑ 07-4031 7794; www.reefteach.com.au; 2nd fl, Main Street Arcade, 85 Lake St; adult/child $18/9; ⏰ lectures 6.30-8.30pm Tue-Sat) 🍴 Before heading out to the reef, take your knowledge to greater depths at this excellent and informative centre, where marine experts explain how to identify specific types of coral and fish and how to treat the reef with respect.

Centre of Contemporary Arts
GALLERY, THEATRE

(CoCA; www.centre-of-contemporary-arts-cairns.com.au; 96 Abbott St; ⏰ 10am-5pm Mon-Sat) **FREE** CoCA houses the **KickArts** (www.kickarts.org.au) galleries of local contemporary visual art, as well as the **JUTE Theatre** (www.jute.com.au; CoCA, 96 Abbott St) and the **End Credits Film Club** (www.endcredits.org.au). Their wonderful gift shop is full of local artworks and jewellery.

🏃 Activities

Innumerable tour operators run adventure-based activities from Cairns, most offering transfers to/from your accommodation.

★ NQ Watersports
WATERSPORTS

(☑ 0411 739 069; www.nqwatersports.com.au; B-finger, Pier Marina; jet-ski croc tours solo/tandem $190/260) It's a world first: croc-spotting tours...on a jet ski! Zip down Trinity Inlet to cop an eyeful of salties up-close, while nesting eagles soar dramatically overhead. The company also offers parasailing ($90), jetskiing sans-crocs ($90) and bumper tubing ($35).

AJ Hackett Bungee & Minjin
BUNGEE JUMPING

(☑ 1800 622 888; www.ajhackett.com; McGregor Rd; bungee jumps $169, minjin swings $89, bungee & minjin swing combos $225; ⏰ 10am-5pm) Bungee jump from the purpose-built tower or swing from the trees on the minjin (a harness swing).

ⓘ DANGER: STINGERS & CROCS

From around late October to May, swimming in coastal waters is inadvisable due to the presence of box jellyfish, irukandji and other marine stingers. Only swim where there is a patrolled stinger net.

Saltwater crocodiles inhabit the mangroves, estuaries and open water. Warning signs are posted around the waterways where crocodiles might be present. Pay heed, as these signs are not just quirky props for your holiday snaps: crocs are faster and cleverer than you might think!

Fishing Cairns
FISHING

(☑ 0448 563 586; www.fishingcairns.com.au) Arranges river, reef and game fishing trips.

Cable Ski
WATERSPORTS

(☑ 07-4038 1304; www.cableskicairns.com.au; Captain Cook Hwy; adult/child per hr $39/34, per day $69/64; ⏰ 10am-6pm) Learn to waterski, wakeboard or kneeboard without the boat at this water-sports park near the Skyrail.

👉 Tours

An astounding 600-plus tours drive, sail and fly out of Cairns each day. You can book at any of the zillions of agencies lining the city streets.The following is but a small taste of what's on offer.

Great Barrier Reef

Reef trips generally include transport, lunch and snorkelling gear. Many have diving options including introductory dives requiring no prior experience. When choosing a tour, consider the vessel (catamaran or sailing ship), its capacity (from six to 300 people), what extras are offered and the destination. The outer reefs are more pristine; inner reef areas can be patchy, showing signs of damage from humans, coral bleaching and crown-of-thorns starfish. In most cases you get what you pay for. Some operators offer the pricier option of a trip in a glass-bottomed boat or semi-submersible.

The majority of boats depart from the Pier Marina and Reef Fleet Terminal at about 8am, returning at around 6pm. A number of operators also offer multiday liveaboard trips, which include specialised dive

Cairns

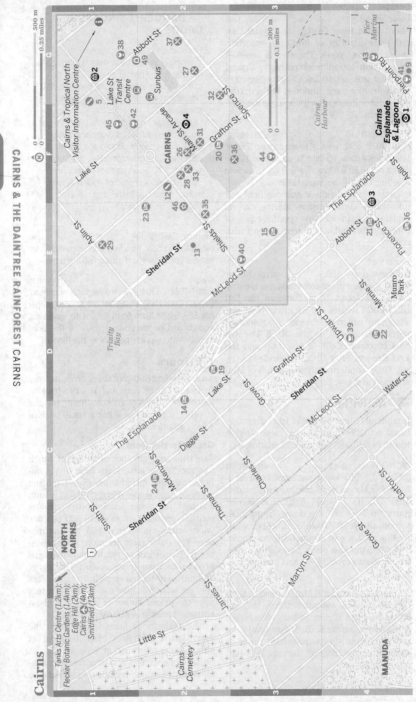

CAIRNS

NORTH CAIRNS

MANUNDA

Cairns Esplanade & Lagoon

Cairns & Tropical North Visitor Information Centre

Lake St Transit Centre

Cairns & Tropical North Visitor Information Centre

Tanks Arts Centre (1.2km);
Flecker Botanic Gardens (1.4km);
Edge Hill (2km);
Cairns (4km);
Smithfield (13km)

Trinity Bay

Cairns Harbour

Pier Marina

Cairns Cemetery

opportunities such as night diving. Dive-course companies also offer tours.

Cod Hole, near Lizard Island, is one of Australia's premier diving locations; extended live-aboard trips are mainly for keen certified divers.

Coral Princess
CRUISE

(☎1800 079 545, 07-4040 9999; www.coralprin-cess.com.au) Three- to seven-night cruises between Cairns, Pelorus Island and Lizard Island return (from $1347 per person, twin share).

Reef Daytripper
SAILING

(☎07-4036 0566; www.reefdaytripper.com.au; adult/child/family from $139/100/425) Small-group, personalised catamaran trips to Upolu Reef on the outer Great Barrier Reef.

Passions of Paradise
DIVING, SNORKELLING

(☎1800 111 346, 07-4041 1600; www.passions.com. au; adult/child $139/89) Sexy catamaran taking you to Michaelmas Cay and Paradise Reef for snorkelling or diving.

Great Adventures
BOAT TOUR

(☎07-4044 9944; www.greatadventures.com.au; 1 Spence St, Reef Fleet Terminal; adult/child trips from $84/42) Runs half and full day trips to Green Island and the outer Great Barrier Reef on fast catamarans. Diving add-ons, glass-bottomed boat and semi-submersible tours available.

Silverswift
DIVING, SNORKELLING

(☎07-4044 9944; www.silverseries.com.au; adult/child from $196/146) Popular catamaran trips that offer snorkelling/diving on three outer reefs.

Sunlover
DIVING, SNORKELLING

(☎07-4050 1333; www.sunlover.com.au; adult/child/family $190/80/460) Fast family-friendly catamaran rides to a snorkelling pontoon on the outer Moore Reef. Options include semi-submersible trips and helmet diving.

Scenic Flights
Great Barrier Reef
Helicopters
SCENIC FLIGHTS

(☎07-4081 8888; www.gbrhelicopters.com.au; flights from $159-599) Huge range of helicopter flights, including a 10-minute soar above Cairns city ($159), a 15-minute flight from Green Island ($239) and an hour-long reef and rainforest trip ($599, ex-Cairns).

Cairns

Cairns Seaplanes SCENIC FLIGHTS
(☑ 07-4031 4307; www.cairnsseaplanes.com; 2/3 Abbott St; 30-minute flights from $269) Scenic reef flights, including to Green Island.

White-Water Rafting

The thrill level of white-water rafting down the Barron, Russell and North Johnstone Rivers is hitched to the season: the wetter the weather, the whiter the water. The Tully River has rapids year-round.

Trips are graded according to the degree of difficulty, from armchair rafting (Grade 1) to white-knuckle (Grade 5).

Foaming Fury RAFTING
(☑ 07-4031 3460, 1800 801 540; www.foamingfury. com.au) Full-day trips on the Russell River ($200) or half-day on the Barron ($124); family rafting options available.

Raging Thunder RAFTING
(☑ 07-4030 7990; www.ragingthunder.com.au; adult/child from $74/47) Full-day Tully trips (standard trip $199, 'xtreme' trip $229) and half-day Barron trips ($133).

Ballooning & Skydiving

Hot Air Cairns BALLOONING
(☑ 07-4039 9900; www.hotair.com.au/cairns; 30-minute flights from $235) Balloons take off from Mareeba to take in dawn over the Atherton Tablelands. Prices include return transfers from Cairns.

Skydive the Reef Cairns SKYDIVING
(☑ 1800 800 840; www.skydivethereefcairns. com.au; 51 Sheridan St; tandem jumps 14,000ft $334) See the reef from a whole new perspective.

City Tours

Cairns Discovery Tours GUIDED TOUR
(✆07-4028 3567; www.cairnsdiscoverytours.com;
adult/child $69/35; ⊙Mon-Sat) Half-day afternoon tours run by horticulturists; they includes the botanic gardens and Palm Cove. Northern-beaches transfers are an extra $5.

Atherton Tableland

Food Trail Tours FOOD TOUR
(✆07-4041 1522; www.foodtrailtours.com.au; adult/child from $159/80; ⊙ Mon-Sat) Taste your way around the Tableland visiting farms producing macadamias, tropical-fruit wine, cheese, chocolate and coffee.

On the Wallaby OUTDOORS
(✆07-4033 6575; www.onthewallaby.com; day/ overnight tours $99/169) Excellent activity-based tours including cycling, hiking and canoeing.

Uncle Brian's Tours OUTDOORS
(✆07-4033 6575; www.unclebrian.com.au; tours $119; ⊙ Mon-Wed, Fri & Sat) Lively small-group day trips covering forests, waterfalls and lakes.

Captain Matty's Barefoot Tours OUTDOORS
(✆07-4055 9082; www.barefoottours.com.au; tours $85) Fun full-day jaunt around the Tablelands with swimming stops at waterfalls and a natural waterslide.

Cape Tribulation & the Daintree

After the Great Barrier Reef, Cape Trib is the region's next most popular day trip – usually including a cruise on the Daintree River. Access is via a well-signposted sealed road, so don't discount hiring your own vehicle, especially if you want to take your time.

Billy Tea Bush Safaris ECOTOUR
(✆07-4032 0077; www.billytea.com.au; day trips adult/child $185/135) ⚲ Exciting day ecotours to Cape Trib.

Tropics Explorer OUTDOORS
(✆1800 801 540, 07-4031 3460; www.tropicsexplorer.com.au; day tours from $99) Fun Cape Trib trips; overnight tours available.

Cape Trib Connections OUTDOORS
(✆07-4032 0500; www.capetribconnections.com; day trips adult/child $119/99) Includes Mossman Gorge, Daintree River, Cape Tribulation Beach and Port Douglas. Also runs overnight tours.

Cooktown & Cape York

Adventure North Australia DRIVING TOUR
(✆07-4028 3376; www.adventurenorthaustralia. com; 1-day tours adult/child $250/200) Has 4WD trips to Cooktown via the coastal route, returning via the inland route. Also two- and three-day tours, fly-drive and Aboriginal cultural tours.

CAIRNS & THE DAINTREE RAINFOREST CAIRNS

DIVE COURSES

Cairns is the scuba-diving capital of the Great Barrier Reef and a popular place to attain Professional Association of Diving Instructors (PADI) open-water certification. There's a staggering number of courses to choose from, from budget four-day courses that combine pool training and reef dives to five-day courses that include two days' pool theory and three days' living aboard a boat, diving less-frequented parts of the reef. Many operators are multilingual.

All operators require you to have a dive medical certificate, which they can arrange (around $60). A reef tax ($40 to $80) is payable as well. Many operators also offer advanced courses for certified divers. Dive schools include the following:

Cairns Dive Centre (✆07-4051 0294; www.cairnsdive.com.au; 121 Abbott St) A long-running operator affiliated with Scuba Schools International (SSI) rather than PADI. There are live-aboard courses (four/five days $640/780) and day tours ($180).

Deep Sea Divers Den (✆07-4046 7333; www.diversden.com.au; 319 Draper St) Long-established school running multiday live-aboard courses and trips from $445.

Pro-Dive (✆07-4031 5255; www.prodivecairns.com; cnr Grafton & Shields St) One of Cairns' most experienced operators, offering a comprehensive, five-day learn-to-dive course incorporating a three-day live-aboard trip ($825).

✸✸ Festivals & Events

Cairns Festival
FESTIVAL

(www.festivalcairns.com.au; ⊙Aug-Sept) The Cairns Festival takes over the city with a packed program of performing/visual arts, music and family events.

🛏 Sleeping

Cairns is a backpacker hotspot, with around 40 hostels ranging from intimate converted houses to hangar-sized resorts. Dozens of midrange, virtually identical motels line up along Sheridan St.

For families or groups, it's worth checking out Cairns Holiday Homes (www.cairnsholidayhomes.com.au). Workers and backpackers sticking around for a while will be well-served by Cairns Sharehouse (☑07-4041 1875; www.cairns-sharehouse.com; 17 Scott St; s per week from $155, d per person per week from $120; ✱❀☎⊠), with almost 200 long-stay rooms strewn across the city. The Accommodation Centre (☑1800 807 730, 07-4051 4066; www.accomcentre.com.au) has information on a wide range of options.

Most tour operators also pick up and drop off at accommodation at Cairns' northern beaches.

★ Tropic Days
HOSTEL $

(☑1800 421 521, 07-4041 1521; www.tropicdays.com.au; 26-38 Bunting St; camp sites $12, tents $16, dm $26-27, d without bathroom $64-74; ✱@☎⊠) Tucked behind the Showgrounds (with a courtesy bus into town), Cairns' best hostel has a tropical garden with hammocks, pool table, bunk-free dorms and a relaxed feel. Nonguests can book for Monday night's croc, emu and roo barbecue ($12 including a didgeridoo show).

Gilligan's
HOSTEL $

(☑07-4041 6566; www.gilligansbackpackers.com.au; 57-89 Grafton St; dm $25-37, d $130; ✱@☎⊠) The 'G spot' is pricey, impersonal and very loud, but all rooms at this flashpacker resort have en suites and most have balconies; higher-priced rooms come with fridges and TVs. It has several bars plus nightly entertainment, a beauty salon and a gym to work off all that beer.

Cairns Girls Hostel
HOSTEL $

(☑07-4051 2016; www.cairnsgirlshostel.com.au; 147 Lake St; dm/tw $20/48; @☎) Sorry lads! This white-glove-test-clean, female-only hostel is one of the most accommodating budget stays in Cairns.

Njoy Travellers Resort
HOSTEL $

(☑07-4031 1088; www.njoy.net.au; 141 Sheridan St; dm/s/d from $19/40/56; P✱❀@☎⊠) Fun and easygoing spot with a lagoon pool and licensed communal areas. Also offers free shuttle buses to the marina every morning and free dinner vouchers.

Cairns Central YHA
HOSTEL $

(☑07-4051 0772; www.yha.com.au; 20-26 McLeod St; dm $25-30, s/d/f $40/80/117; ✱@⊠) Bright, spotless and professionally staffed. Free pancakes for breakfast!

Dreamtime Travellers Rest
HOSTEL $

(☑07-4031 6753, 1800 058 440; www.dreamtimehostel.com; cnr Bunda & Terminus Sts; dm $24-26, s/d from $55/60; @☎⊠) This hostel at the edge of the city combines friendly staff with cosy rooms in an old Queenslander. Cheap pizza, fire twirling and barbecue nights make your stay all the sweeter.

Lake Placid Tourist Park
CARAVAN PARK $

(☑07-4039 2509; www.lakeplacidtouristpark.com; Lake Placid Rd; powered sites $31, cabins from $50, cottage with en suite from $110; P✱❀☎⊠) Close enough to enjoy the spoils of the Big Smoke (it's a 15-min drive from the CBD) but far enough to revel in rainforesty repose, this spot overlooks the aptly named Lake Placid. Easy access to Skyrail, Kuranda Scenic Railway and the northern beaches.

Floriana Guesthouse
GUESTHOUSE $

(☑07-4051 7886; www.florianaguesthouse.com; 183 The Esplanade; s/d/studio $69/79/130; ✱@☎⊠) Cairns-of-old still exists at this enchanting guesthouse, which retains its original polished floorboards and art deco fittings. The swirling staircase leads to 10 individually decorated rooms; all have en suites.

Northern Greenhouse
HOSTEL $$

(☑07-4047 7200; www.northerngreenhouse.com.au; 117 Grafton St; dm/tw/apt $28/95/140; P✱@☎⊠) It fits into the budget category with dorm accommodation and a relaxed attitude, but this friendly place is a cut above, with neat studio-style apartments with kitchens and balconies. The central deck, pool and games room are great for socialising. Free breakfast and Sunday barbie.

Reef Palms
APARTMENTS $$

(☑1800 815 421; www.reefpalms.com.au; 41-7 Digger St; apt $120-180; ✱@☎⊠) The crisp, white interiors of Reef Palms' apartments will have you wearing your sunglasses inside. All rooms have kitchen facilities; larger ones include a lounge area and a spa. Good for couples and families.

Acacia Court
HOTEL **$$**

(☑ 07-4051 1501; www.acaciacourt.com; 223-227 The Esplanade; d $120-170; P✳❄⊚☰) A stroll along the Esplanade from town, this waterfront high-rise's beachy touches and a choice of ocean or mountain views make it great value for money. Most rooms have private balconies and its famous buffet restaurant Charlie's is downstairs.

Shangri-La
HOTEL **$$$**

(☑ 07-4031 1411; www.shangri-la.com/cairns; Pierpoint Rd; r from $270; P✳❄⊚☰) In an unbeatable waterfront setting towering over the marina, Shangri-La is Cairns' top hotel, a super-swish five-star that ticks all the boxes for views, facilities (including a gym and pool bar) and service. Off-season rates available online.

Hotel Cairns
HOTEL **$$$**

(☑ 07-4051 6188; www.thehotelcairns.com; cnr Abbott & Florence Sts; d $195-265; ✳❄☰) There's a true tropical charm to this sprawling bonewhite hotel, built in traditional Queenslander 'plantation' style. Rooms have an understated elegance and the huge 'tower' rooms and suites offer luxury touches including private balconies. Check the website for special deals.

✖ Eating

There's something to tickle every tastebud here: pubs dish up some surprisingly fab (and cheap) fare; the Esplanade has an overwhelming variety of chowhouses; the Pier Marketplace's boardwalk is lined with international restaurants and a random wander around the city streets (Grafton Street especially) throws up everything from Indian to Bavarian to hipster cuisine. Check the *Cairns Post* every Wednesday for restaurant coupons and specials.

Lillypad
CAFE **$**

(☑ 07-4051 9565; 72 Grafton St; dishes $10-14; ☉7am-3pm; ✐) With humungous feasts from crepes to wraps and a truckload of vegetarian options, this is one of the best-value options in town. It's a little bit hippy, and a whole lot busy: you'll probably have to wait a while. Don't miss the fresh juices.

Caffiend
CAFE **$**

(78 Grafton St; dishes from $12; ☉ Tues-Sat 7.30am-3pm, Sunday 8am-2pm; 🛜) Down the graffitied alleyway and bang! You're in Melbourne! Superb coffee, all-day breakfast, gourmet lunches, art galore and the occasional live gig: what's not to love?

Corea Corea
KOREAN **$**

(upstairs, Orchid Plaza, 58 Lake St; dishes from $9.50; ☉10am-9pm) Disregard the empty-mall atmosphere at Orchid Plaza and dig into the spicy, sizzling Korean dishes at this massively popular haunt.

Voodooz Cajun Kitchen
CAJUN **$**

(☑ 07-4051 3493; 5/12 Spence St; dishes from $9.50; ☉ noon-midnight, closed Tues) A little bit of the South up north, Voodooz serves up bewitching belly-busters including Po-Boy sandwiches, Creole jambalaya and seafood gumbo. Live music and cocktails (including The Hurricane) add to the N'Orleans feel.

Fusion Organics
CAFE **$**

(www.fusionorganics.com.au; cnr Aplin & Grafton Sts; dishes $4-19.50; ☉7am-3pm Mon-Fri, to 2pm Sat; ✐) In the courtyard of a 1921 redbrick former ambulance station, Indian chefs spice up Fusion's organic, allergy-free fare, including quiches, frittata, filled breads and 'detox' juices.

Meldrum's Pies in Paradise
BAKERY **$**

(97 Grafton St; pies $4.70-5.90; ☉7am-5pm Mon-Fri, to 2.30pm Sat; ✐) A Cairns institution, Meldrum's bakes 40 inventive varieties of the humble Aussie pie – from chicken and avocado to pumpkin gnocchi or tuna mornay.

Night Markets
FOOD COURT **$**

(The Esplanade; dishes $10-15; ☉5-11pm daily) The Night Markets have a cheap, busy Asian-style food court.

Ochre
MODERN AUSTRALIAN **$$**

(☑ 07-4051 0100; www.ochrerestaurant.com.au; 43 Shields St; mains $23-37; ☉noon-3pm & 6-10pm Mon-Fri, 3-10pm Sat & Sun; ✐) The menu at this innovative restaurant utilises native Aussie fauna (such as croc with native pepper, or roo with quandong-chilli glaze) and flora (like wattle-seed damper loaf or lemon myrtle panacotta). Can't decide? Try a tasting plate.

Green Ant Cantina
MEXICAN **$$**

(☑ 07-4041 5061; www.greenantcantina.com; 183 Bunda St; mains $15-40; ☉6pm-late daily; ✐)

Behind the railway station, this little slice of alternative Mexico is worth seeking out for its homemade quesadillas, enchiladas and Corona-battered tiger prawns. Stick around after eating and try the Green Ant brews (there are seven). Open-mic night on Sundays.

Charlie's   SEAFOOD $$

(☑07-4051 5011; 223-227 The Esplanade; buffet $23.50; ☺6-10.30pm daily) It's not the fanciest place in town, but Charlie's (at Acacia Court) is famous for its nightly all-you-can-eat seafood buffet. Fill your plate over and over with prawns, oysters, clams or hot food, and shamelessly scoff it all on the poolside terrace.

Fetta's Greek Taverna   GREEK $$

(☑07-4051 6966; www.fettasgreektaverna.com.au; 99 Grafton St; dishes $13-25; ☺11.30am-3pm Mon-Fri, 5.30pm-late daily) The white walls and blue-accented windows do a great job evoking Santorini. But it's the classic Greek dishes that are the star of the show here. The $35 set menu goes the whole hog – dip, saganaki, mousakka, salad, grilled meats, calamari, baklava AND coffee. Yes, you can break your plate.

Marinades   INDIAN $$

(☑07-4041 1422; 43 Spence St; mains $14-30, lunch sets $10-12; ☺11am-2.30pm, 6-10pm Tue-Sun; ☑) The pick of Cairns' Indian restaurants for its *long* menu of aromatic dishes, such as lobster marinated in cashew paste and Goan prawn curry.

Perrotta's at the Gallery   MEDITERRANEAN $$

(☑07-4031 5899; 38 Abbott St; mains $14-36; ☺8.30am-11pm daily; ☑) This chic spot adjoining the Cairns Regional Gallery tempts you onto its covered deck for tasty breakfasts, good coffees, and an inventive Med-inspired menu.

Self-Catering

For fresh fruit, veg and other local treats, hit the frenzied, multicultural Rusty's Markets (www.rustysmarkets.com.au; 57 Grafton St; ☺5am-6pm Fri-Sat, to 3pm Sun), or for groceries, try the Cairns Central Shopping Centre (www.cairnscentral.com.au; McLeod St; ☺9am-5.30pm Mon-Wed, Fri & Sat, to 9pm Thu, 10am-4.30pm Sun).

🍸 Drinking & Entertainment

Cairns has a reputation as the party capital of the north, and there are loads of going-out options available. Many venues are multipurpose, offering food, alcohol and some form of entertainment, and you can always find a beer garden or terrace to enjoy balmy evenings.

The website www.entertainmentcairns.com and the *Time Out* section in Thursday's *Cairns Post* list the hotspots and gig guides. Can't decide? Try Cairns Ultimate Party (☑07-4041 0332; www.ultimatepartycairns.com; per person $35; ☺Tues & Sat nights), a wild-n-crazy bus tour that takes in five suitably frenetic venues over six hours.

★ Salt House   BAR

(www.salthouse.com.au; 6/2 Pierpoint Rd; ☺9am-2am Fri-Sun, noon-midnight Mon-Thu) Next to Cairns' yacht club, Salt House is the city's most sought-after bar. Killer cocktails are paired with occasional live music or DJs hitting the decks. Its restaurant serves up excellent modern Australian food.

Flying Monkey Cafe   CAFE

(☑0411 084 176; 154 Sheridan St; coffee $3.50; ☺6.30am-3.30pm Mon-Fri, 7am-noon Sat) Fantastic coffee, ever-changing local art exhibitions, colourful buskers and a beyond-affable staff make the Monkey a must-do for caffeine-and-culture hounds.

Court House Hotel   PUB

(38 Abbott St; ☺9am-late) Housed in Cairns' gleaming-white former courthouse (1921), this pub is now a buzzing watering hole with polished timber bar and heaps of outdoor nooks. Live music in the beergarden all weekend.

Pier Bar & Grill   BAR

(www.pierbar.com.au; Pier Marketplace; ☺11.30am-late) A local institution for its waterfront location and well-priced meals. The Sunday session is a must, at the very least for the $5 wood-fired pizzas.

Grand Hotel   PUB

(www.grandhotelcairns.com; 34 McLeod St; ☺10am-10pm Mon-Thu, 10am-midnight Fri & Sat, 11am-8pm Sun) This laidback haunt is worth a visit just so that you can rest your beer on the bar – an 11m-long carved crocodile! Great place to loiter with the locals.

The Jack   BAR

(☑07-4051 2490; www.thejack.com.au; cnr Spence & Sheridan Sts; ☺til late daily) The huge beer garden with barrels for tables, big screens and a music stage is the stand-out at this vaguely Irish-themed pub attached to a hostel (dorms from $19).

Woolshed Chargrill & Saloon BAR
(www.thewoolshed.com.au; 24 Shields St; ⊘til late daily) An eternal backpacker magnet, where young travellers, dive instructors and the occasional locals get hammered and dance on tables.

PJ O'Briens IRISH PUB
(cnr Lake & Shields Sts; ⊘til late daily) It has sticky carpets and reeks of stale Guinness, but Irish-themed PJ's packs 'em in with party nights, pole dancing and dirt-cheap meals.

The Reef Hotel Casino CASINO, BAR
(www.reefcasino.com.au; 35-41 Wharf St; ⊘9am-5am Fri & Sat, to 3am Sun-Thu) In addition to table games and pokies, Cairns' casino has three restaurants and four bars, including Vertigo Cocktail Bar & Lounge, with free live music, ticketed shows and a massive sports bar (free movies twice a week). Check out the upstairs wildlife dome.

12 Bar Blue JAZZ
(✆07-4041 7388; 62 Shields St; ⊘7pm-late Wed-Sun) Intimate bar with jazz, blues and swing. Songwriter open-mic night takes place on Thursdays, and general jam-a-thon on Sundays.

🛍 Shopping

Cairns offers the gamut of shopping, from high-end boutiques to garish souvenir barns.

The huge Cairns Central Shopping Centre (www.cairnscentral.com.au; McLeod St; ⊘9am-5.30pm Mon-Wed, Fri & Sat, to 9pm Thu, 10am-4.30pm Sun) has a couple of supermarkets plus a huge range of speciality stores selling everything from books to bikinis. Woolworths (103 Abbott St; ⊘9am-9pm daily) is another CBD option for items such as sunscreen and SIM cards.

Head to the Night Markets (www.night markets.com.au; The Esplanade; ⊘4.30pm-midnight) if your supply of 'Cairns Australia' T-shirts is running low, or you need your name on a grain of rice.

ℹ Information

INTERNET ACCESS
Dedicated internet cafes are clustered along Abbott St between Shields and Aplin Sts.

POST
Post Office (✆13 13 18; www.auspost.com.au; Shop 115, Cairns Central Shopping Centre; ⊘9am-5pm Wed-Fri, to noon Sat)

THE BAMA WAY

From Cairns to Cooktown, you can see the country through Aboriginal eyes along the Bama Way (www.bamaway.com.au). Bama (pronounced Bumma) means 'person' in the Kuku Yalanji and Guugu Yimithirr languages, and highlights include tours with Aboriginal guides, such as the Walker Family tours on the Bloomfield Track, and Willie Gordon's enlightening Guurrbi Tours in Cooktown. Pick up a Bama Way map from visitor centres.

TOURIST INFORMATION
The government-run **Cairns & Tropical North Visitor Information Centre** (✆1800 093 300; www.cairns-greatbarrierreef.org.au; 51 The Esplanade; ⊘8.30am-6pm Mon-Fri, 10am-6pm Sat & Sun) offers impartial advice, books accommodation and tours and houses an interpretive centre.

Other useful contacts:

Cairns Discount Tours (✆07-4055 7158; www.cairnsdiscounttours.com.au) Knowledgeable booking agent specialising in last-minute deals.

Far North Queensland Volunteers (✆07-4041 7400; www.fnqvolunteers.org; 68 Abbott St) Arranges volunteer positions with nonprofit community groups.

Royal Automobile Club of Queensland (RACQ; ✆07-4042 3100; www.racq.com.au; 537 Mulgrave Rd, Earlville) Maps and information on road conditions state-wide, including Cape York. For 24-hour recorded road-report service, call 1300 130 595.

ℹ Getting There & Away

AIR
QANTAS (✆13 13 13; www.qantas.com.au), **Virgin Australia** (✆13 67 89; www.virginaustralia.com) and **Jetstar** (✆13 15 38; www.jetstar.com.au) arrive and depart the **Cairns Airport** (www.cairnsairport.com) with flights to/from all Aussie capital cities and large regional centres. There are international flights to/from places including China, Papua New Guinea and New Zealand.

Skytrans (✆1300 759 872; www.skytrans.com.au) services Cape York with regular flights to Coen, Bamaga and Lockhart River, as well as Burketown and Normanton in the Gulf and Mount Isa.

Hinterland Aviation (✆07-4040 1333; www.hinterlandaviation.com.au) has one to four flights daily to/from Cooktown (one-way from $125, 40 minutes).

BUS

Cairns is the hub for Far North Queensland buses.

Greyhound Australia (☑1300 473 946; www.greyhound.com.au) Has four daily services down the coast to Brisbane (from $300, 29 hours) via Townsville ($60, six hours), Airlie Beach ($93, 11 hours) and Rockhampton ($195, 18 hours). Departs from Reef Fleet Terminal, at the southern end of The Esplanade.

Premier (☑13 34 10; www.premierms.com.au) Runs one daily service to Brisbane ($205, 29 hours) via Innisfail ($19, 1½ hours), Mission Beach ($19, two hours), Tully ($26, 2½ hours), Cardwell ($30, three hours), Townsville ($55, 5½ hours) and Airlie Beach ($90, 10 hours). Cheaper bus passes are available. Departs from Cairns Central Station.

Trans North (☑07-4095 8644; www.transnorthbus.com; Cairns Central Rail Station) Has five daily bus services connecting Cairns with the Tablelands, including Kuranda ($8, 30 minutes, four daily), Mareeba ($18, one hour, one to three daily) and Atherton ($23.40, 1¾ hours, one to three daily). Departs from Cairns Central Rail Station; buy tickets when boarding.

John's Kuranda Bus (☑0418 772 953) Runs a service ($5, 30 minutes) between Cairns (departs Lake St Transit Centre) and Kuranda two to five times daily.

Sun Palm (☑07-4087 2900; www.sunpalmtransport.com.au) Runs northern services from Cairns to Port Douglas ($40, 1½ hours) via Palm Cove and the northern beaches (from $20). Departs from the airport and CBD.

Country Road Coachlines (☑07-4045 2794; www.countryroadcoachlines.com.au) Runs a daily bus service between Cairns and Cooktown ($81) and Cape Tribulation ($50) on either the coastal route (Bloomfield Track via Port Douglas/Mossman) or inland route (via Mareeba), depending on the day of departure and the condition of the track. Departs from the Reef Fleet Terminal.

CAR & MOTORCYCLE

All major car-rental companies have branches in Cairns and at the airport, with discount car and campervan-rental companies proliferating throughout town and on the Cook Highway just north of the airport turn-off. Daily rates start at around $45 for a late-model small car and around $80 for a 4WD. The big operators like Hertz and Europcar are located in Cairns Square (cnr Shields & Abbott Sts), or try the cheaper **Cairns Older Car Hire** (☑07-4053 1066; www.cairnsoldercarhire.com; 410 Sheridan St; per day from $35) or **Rent-a-Bomb** (☑07-4031

4477; www.rentabomb.com.au; 144 Sheridan St; per day from $30).

Wicked Campers (☑07-4031 1387; www.wickedcampers.com.au; 75 Sheridan St) and **Hippie Camper Hire** (☑1800 777 779; www.hippiecamper.com; 432 Sheridan St) have Cairns branches.

If you're in for the long haul, check hostels, www.gumtree.com.au and the big noticeboard on Abbott St for used campervans and ex-backpackers' cars.

Alternatively, hire a Harley ($190 to $260) from **Choppers Motorcycle Tours & Hire** (☑0408 066 024; www.choppersmotorcycles.com.au; 150 Sheridan St), or smaller bikes/scooters from $95/$75 a day. Also offers motorcycle tours, from one hour to a full-day ride to Cape Trib.

TRAIN

The *Sunlander* departs Cairns' **train station** (Bunda St) on Tuesday, Thursday and Saturday for Brisbane (one-way from $200, 31½ hours): contact **Queensland Rail** (☑1800 872 467; www.traveltrain.com.au).

The Kuranda Scenic Railway (p460) runs daily services.

❶ Getting Around

TO/FROM THE AIRPORT

The airport is about 7km north of central Cairns; many accommodation places offer courtesy pick-ups. Sun Palm (p454) meets all incoming flights and runs a shuttle bus (adult/child $12/6) to the CBD. You can also book airport transfers with them to/from Cairns' northern beaches ($20), Palm Cove ($20) and Port Douglas ($40). A trip to the CBD with **Black & White Taxis** (☑13 10 08; www.blackandwhitetaxis.com.au) is around $25.

BICYCLE & SCOOTER

Bike Man (☑07-4041 5566; www.bikeman.com.au; 99 Sheridan St; per day/week $15/60) Hire, sales and repairs.

Cairns Scooter & Bicycle Hire (☑07-4031 3444; www.cairnsbicyclehire.com.au; 47 Shields St; scooters/bikes per day from $85/25) Zip around on a nifty-fifty or take it slow on a pushie. Also sells used scooters.

BUS

Sunbus (☑07-4057 7411; www.sunbus.com.au) runs regular services in and around Cairns from the Lake Street Transit Centre, where schedules are posted. Useful routes include: Flecker Botanic Gardens/Edge Hill (bus 131), Holloways Beach and Yorkeys Knob (buses 112, 113, 120), and Trinity Beach, Clifton Beach and Palm Cove (buses 110, 111). Most buses heading north go via Smithfield. All are served by the late-running night service (N). Heading south, Bus 140 runs as far south as Gordonvale. Single tickets from $2.30.

TAXI

Black & White Taxis (p454) have a rank near the corner of Lake and Shields Sts, and one outside Cairns Central Shopping Centre.

AROUND CAIRNS

The city and its northern beaches have plenty to keep you entertained, but nearby islands and highlands make great side trips.

Babinda & Around

South of Cairns, a lush pocket of rainforest offers a rewarding trip for walkers and wildlife watchers. The surrounding towns and settlements also provide enchanting glimpses into the area's heritage.

Babinda

POP 1069

On the Bruce Hwy, 60km south of Cairns, Babinda is a small working-class town that leads 7km inland to a rainforest park called the Babinda Boulders, where a photogenic creek rushes between 4m-high granite rocks. It's croc-free, but here lurks an equal danger: highly treacherous waters. Legend has it that a young Aboriginal woman threw herself into the then-still waters after being separated from her love; her anguish caused the creek to rise up, becoming the surging, swirling torrent it is today. Almost 20 visitors have lost their lives at the Boulders. Swimming is permitted in calm, well-marked parts of the creek, but pay heed to signs where even thoughts of a toe-dip are prohibited. Walking tracks give you the close – but safe – access you need for obligatory gasps and photographs.

The free Babinda Boulders Camping Ground (two-night maximum) has toilets, cold showers and free barbecues.

Nearby, you can kayak the clear waters of Babinda Creek with Babinda Kayak Hire (☑07-4067 2678; www.babindakayakhire.com. au; 330 Stager Rd; half-/full-day including pick-ups $42/63).

Drop into Babinda's little blue visitor centre (☑07-4067 1008; www.babindainfocentre. com.au; cnr Munro St & Bruce Hwy; ☺9am-4pm) for more info.

Wooroonooran National Park

Part of the Wet Tropics World Heritage Area, the rugged rainforest in the Josephine Falls section of Wooroonooran National Park creeps to the peak of Queensland's highest mountain, Mt Bartle Frere (1622m). It provides an exclusive environment for a number of plant and animal species. The car park for Josephine Falls – a spectacular series of waterfalls and pools – is signposted 6km off the Bruce Hwy, about 10km south of Babinda, followed by a steep paved 600m walk through the rainforest and along a mossy creek.

The falls are at the foot of the Bellenden Ker Range. The Mt Bartle Frere Summit Track (15km, two days return) leads from the Josephine Falls car park to the summit. The ascent is for fit and well-equipped walkers only; rain and cloud can close in suddenly. Get a trail guide from the info centre or contact the NPRSR (☑13 74 68; www.nprsr.qld. gov.au). Camping (per person $5.45) is permitted along the trail; book ahead.

Cairns' Northern Beaches

Despite what some brochures may infer, Cairns city is sans-beach. But just 15 minutes, a Sunbus ticket or a foot on the gas will bring you to a string of lovely beach communities, all with their own distinct character: Yorkeys Knob is popular with sailors (though a proposed mega-casino could change that vibe), Trinity is big with families and Palm Cove is a swanky honeymoon haven.

All beaches can be reached via well-marked turnoffs on the Cook Highway.

Yorkeys Knob

Yorkeys Knob is a low-key settlement that's known for its Half Moon Bay, home to 200 bobbing boats. The 'Knob' part of the name still elicits nudges and chortles from easily amused locals; others wonder where the apostrophe went.

Kite Rite (☑07-4055 7918; www.kiterite.com. au; Shop 9, 471 Varley St; per hr $79) offers kite- and windsurfing instruction, including gear hire, and a two-day certificate course ($499).

A block or so back from the beach, Villa Marine (☑07-4055 7158; www.villamarine. com.au; 8 Rutherford St; d $89-159; ❋ ☎ ☒) is the best-value spot in Yorkeys. Friendly owner Peter makes you feel at home in the retro-style, single-storey self-contained apartments arranged around a pool.

Yorkeys Knob Boating Club (☎07-4055 7711; www.ykbc.com.au; 25-29 Buckley St; mains $17-29.50; ☺noon-3pm & 6-9pm daily, 8-10am Sat & Sun; ☝) is a diamond find: try the fresh seafood basket ($22.50) or the local catch of the day ($24); oysters are $10 a dozen on Saturdays.

Trinity Beach

Trinity Beach, with its many dining and drinking options and long stretch of sheltered sands, make it a favourite for holiday-makers.

Self-contained apartments are just footsteps from the beach at **Castaways** (☎07-4057 6699; www.castawaystrinitybeach.com.au; cnr Trinity Beach Rd & Moore St; 1-/2-bedroom apt $132/165; ❉☒), which has three pools, spas, tropical gardens and good stand-by rates.

The beachside **L'Unico Trattoria** (☎07-4057 8855; www.lunico.com.au; 75 Vasey Esplanade; mains $16-44; ☺noon-late daily; ☝) serves stylish Italian cuisine, including bugs with garlic, chilli and white wine, homemade four-cheese gnocchi and wood-fired pizzas.

Fratelli on Trinity (☎07-4057 5775; 47 Vasey Esplanade; mains from $15; ☺7-11.30am & noon-4.30pm Thu-Sun, 5.30pm-late daily) is a cute little beach shack, but don't let its easy-breezy feel fool you into thinking the food is anything less than top-class: the pastas are superb and dishes like slow-cooked lamb shoulder and garlic, and rosemary rolled pork belly roast might even distract you from the million-dollar views.

Palm Cove

More intimate than Port Douglas and more upmarket than its southern neighbours, Palm Cove is essentially one big promenade along the paperbark-lined Williams Esplanade, with a gorgeous stretch of white-sand beach and top-notch restaurants luring sun-lovers out of their luxury resorts.

🏃 Activities

Beach strolls, shopping and leisurely swims will be your chief activities here, but there's no excuse for not getting out on the water.

Palm Cove Watersports　KAYAKING
(☎0402 861 011; www.palmcovewatersports.com; kayak hire per hour $33) Organises 1½-hour early-morning sea-kayaking trips ($56) and half-day paddles to nearby Double Island (adult/child $96/74).

Beach Fun & Co　WATERSPORTS
(☎0411-848 580; www.tourismpalmcove.com; Williams Esplanade) Hires catamarans ($50 per hour), jet skis (per 15 minutes single/double $60/80), paddle boats ($30) and SUP boards ($30), and organises jet-ski tours around Double Island and Haycock – aka Scout's Hat – Island (single/double from $140/200). Fishing boats start from $100 for two hours.

🛌 Sleeping

Most of Palm Cove's accommodation has a minimum two-night stay.

Palm Cove Camping Ground　CAMPGROUND $
(☎07-4055 3824; 149 Williams Esplanade; unpowered/powered sites $19/27) The only way to do Palm Cove on the cheap, this council-run beachfront camping ground is right near the jetty, and has a barbecue area and laundry.

Silvester Palms　APARTMENTS $$
(☎07-4055 3831; www.silvesterpalms.com.au; 32 Veivers Rd; 1-/2-/3-bedroom apt from $100/140/150; ❉☎☒) These bright self-contained apartments are an affordable alternative to Palm Cove's city-sized resorts.

★**Reef House Resort**
& Spa　BOUTIQUE HOTEL $$$
(☎07-4080 2600; www.reefhouse.com.au; 99 Williams Esplanade; d from $279; ❉@☎☒) Once the private residence of an army brigadier, Reef House is more intimate and understated than most of Palm Cove's resorts. The whitewashed walls, wicker furniture and big beds romantically draped in muslin all add to the air of refinement. The Brigadier's Bar works on a quaint honesty system; complimentary punch is served by candlelight at twilight.

Peppers Beach Club & Spa　HOTEL $$$
(☎1300 737 444, 07-4059 9200; www.peppers.com.au; 123 Williams Esplanade; d from $200; ❉@☎☒) Step through the opulent lobby at Peppers and into a wonder-world of swimming pools – there's the sand-edged lagoon pool and the leafy rainforest pool and swim-up bar – tennis courts and spa treatments. Even the standard rooms have private balcony spas, and the penthouse suites (from $550) have their own rooftop pool.

✕ Eating & Drinking

Palm Cove has some fine restaurants and cafes strung along the Esplanade. All resorts have swish dining options open to non-guests.

Surf Club Palm Cove   LICENSED CLUB $$
(☑07-4059 1244; 135 Williams Esplanade; meals $14-30; ☺6pm-late) A great local for a drink in the sunny garden bar and bargain-priced seafood, plus decent kids' meals.

El Grecko   GREEK $$
(☑07-4055 3690; www.elgrekostaverna.com.au; level 1, Palm Cove Shopping Village, Williams Esplanade; meze from $14, mains $24-30; ☺5.30-10.30pm; ☑) Souvlaki, spanakopita and moussaka are among the staples at this lively taverna. Good meze platters; belly dancing Friday and Saturday nights.

Apres Beach Bar & Grill   BAR, BISTRO $$
(☑07-4059 2000; www.apresbeachbar.com.au; 119 Williams Esplanade; mains $23-39; ☺7.30am-late daily) The most happening place in Palm Cove, with a zany interior of old motorcycles, racing cars and a biplane hanging from the ceiling, and regular live music. Big on steaks of all sorts, too.

Beach Almond   ASIAN $$$
(☑07-4059 1908; www.beachalmond.com; 145 Williams Esplanade; mains $28-59; ☺11am-3pm Sat & Sun, 6-10pm daily) A rustic beach house near the jetty is the setting for Palm Cove's most inspired dining. Black-pepper prawns, Singaporean mud crab and Balinese barra are among the fragrant, fresh innovations.

Nu Nu   MODERN AUSTRALIAN $$$
(☑07-4059 1880; www.nunu.com.au; 123 Williams Esplanade; mains $24-80; ☺11.30am-late Thurs-Mon) With one of the highest profiles on the coast, you'll need to book way ahead at the designer Nu Nu. Try something from the Mod Oz/Asian/Med menu, or throw in the towel and let the chef decide (six-course tasting menu $110, $175 with paired wines).

❶ Information

Commercially run tour-booking companies are strung along Williams Esplanade; the Cairns & Tropical North Visitor Information Centre (p453) in Cairns can help with bookings.

Paradise Village Shopping Centre (113 Williams Esplanade) has a post office (with internet access, $4 per hour), small supermarket and newsagent.

Ellis Beach

Ellis Beach is the last (and possibly best) of the northern beaches and the closest to the highway, which runs right past it. The long sheltered bay is a stunner, with a palm-fringed, patrolled swimming beach and stinger net in summer.

Daily events at **Hartley's Crocodile Adventures** (☑07-4055 3576; www.crocodileadventures.com; adult/child $33/17.50; ☺8.30am-5pm daily) ✐ include tours of this croc farm, along with feedings, 'crocodile attack' shows, and boat cruises on its lagoon. The park is just up the highway in Wangetti Beach.

Ellis Beach Oceanfront Bungalows (☑1800 637 036, 07-4055 3538; www.ellisbeach.com; Captain Cook Hwy; unpowered sites $32, powered sites $35-41, cabins without bathroom $95-115, bungalows $155-190; ❋@❋) is a beachfront slice of paradise, with camping, cabins and contemporary bungalows, all of which enjoy widescreen ocean views.

Ellis Beach Bar 'n' Grill (Captain Cook Hwy; mains $15-28; ☺8am-8pm daily) has good food, great views, live music Sundays from 1pm and pinball.

Islands off Cairns

Green Island

This beautiful coral cay is only 45 minutes from Cairns and has a rainforest interior with interpretive walks, a fringing white-sand beach and snorkelling just offshore. You can walk around the island in about 30 minutes.

The island and its surrounding waters are protected by their national- and marine-park status. **Marineland Melanesia** (☑07-4051 4032; www.marinelandgreenisland.com.au; adult/child $18/8) has an aquarium with fish, turtles, stingrays and crocodiles, plus a collection of Melanesian artefacts.

Luxurious **Green Island Resort** (☑07-4031 3300, 1800 673 366; www.greenislandresort.com.au; ste $650-750; ❋@❋) has stylish split-level suites, each with a private balcony. Island transfers are included. It is partially open to day trippers, meaning anyone can enjoy the restaurants, bars, ice-cream parlour and watersports facilities.

Great Adventures (p447) and **Big Cat** (☑07-4051 0444; www.greenisland.com.au; adult/child from $84/42) run day trips, with optional glass-bottomed boat and semi-submersible tours.

Alternatively, hop aboard **Ocean Free** (☑ 07-4052 1111; www.oceanfree.com.au; adult/child from $140/95), spending most of the day offshore at Pinnacle Reef, with a short stop on the island.

Fitzroy Island

A steep mountaintop rising from the sea, Fitzroy Island has coral-strewn beaches, woodlands and walking tracks, one of which ends at a now-inactive lighthouse. The most popular snorkelling spot is around the rocks at Nudey Beach, which, despite its name, is not officially clothing-optional. Unlike the rest of the island, Nudey actually has some sand on it.

The **Fitzroy Island Turtle Rehabilitation Centre** (www.saveourseaturtles.com.au; adult/child $5.50/2.20; ☺ tours 2pm daily) looks after sick and injured sea turtles before releasing them back into the wild. Daily educational tours (maximum 15 guests) visit the new turtle hospital. Book through the Fitzroy Island Resort.

You can pitch a tent at the **Fitzroy Island Camping Ground** (☑ 07-4044 6700; camp sites $32), run by the Fitzroy Island Resort. It has showers, toilets and barbecues; advance bookings essential.

Tropi-cool accommodation at the **Fitzroy Island Resort** (☑ 07-4044 6700; www.fitzroyisland.com; studio/cabin $195/369, 1 & 2 bedroom ste $350-515; ❋ ☀) ranges from sleek studios and beachfront cabins through to a luxurious self-contained apartment ($650). Its restaurant, bar and kiosk are open to day trippers.

Raging Thunder (p448) runs day trips from Cairns. Bounce off the ocean trampoline!

Frankland Islands

If the idea of hanging out on one of five uninhabited coral-fringed islands with excellent snorkelling and stunning white sandy beaches appeals – how can it not? – cruise out to the Frankland Group National Park.

Camping is available on the rainforesty High and Russell Islands; contact the **NPRSR** (☑ 13 74 68; www.nprsr.qld.gov.au; permit $5.45) for advance reservations and seasonal restrictions.

Frankland Islands Cruise & Dive (☑ 07-4031 6300; www.franklandislands.com.au; adult/child from $149/79) run excellent day trips which include a cruise down the Mulgrave River, snorkelling gear and tuition and lunch. Guided snorkelling tours with a marine biologist and diving packages are also offered. Transfers for campers to/from Russell Island are available. Boats depart from Deeral; transfers from Cairns and the northern beaches cost $16 per person.

You'll need to organise your own boat or charter to reach High Island.

Atherton Tableland

Climbing back from the coast between Innisfail and Cairns is the fertile food bowl of the far north, the Atherton Tableland. Quaint country towns, eco-wilderness lodges and luxurious B&Bs dot greener-than-green hills between patchwork fields, pockets of rainforest, spectacular lakes and waterfalls, and Queensland's highest mountains: Bartle Frere (1622m) and Bellenden Ker (1593m).

Four main roads lead in from the coast: the Palmerston Hwy from Innisfail, the Gillies Hwy from Gordonvale, the Kennedy Hwy from Cairns, and Rex Range Rd between Mossman and Port Douglas.

ℹ Getting There & Around

There are bus services to the main towns from Cairns (generally three services on weekdays, two on Saturday and one on Sunday), but not to the smaller towns or all the interesting areas *around* the towns, so it's worth hiring your own wheels.

Trans North (p454) has regular bus services connecting Cairns with the Tableland, departing from Cairns Central Rail Station and running to Kuranda ($8, 30 minutes), Mareeba ($18, one hour), Atherton ($23.40, 1¾ hours) and Herberton/Ravenshoe ($31/36, two/2½ hours, Mondays, Wednesdays, Fridays).

John's Kuranda Bus (☑ 0418 772 953) runs a service between Cairns and Kuranda two to five times daily ($5, 30 minutes).

Kuranda

POP 3000

Hidden in the rainforest, the artsy, alternative market town of Kuranda is the Tableland's most popular day trip.

◉ Sights & Activities

Walking trails wind around the village – the visitor centre has maps, or just get Kuranda-zen with it all and go with the flow. During the Wet, the mighty, must-see Barron Falls are in full thunder; they're just a quick tootle down Barron Falls Road (Skyrail and the railway have lookouts too).

Markets
MARKETS

Follow the clouds of incense down to the Kuranda Original Rainforest Markets (www.kurandaoriginalrainforestmarket.com.au; Therwine St; ⊗9.30am-3pm). Operating since 1978, they're still the best place to see artists at work and hippies at play. Pick up everything from avocado ice cream to organic lingerie and sample local produce like honey and fruit wines.

Across the way, the more touristy Heritage Markets (www.kurandamarkets.com.au; Rob Veivers Dr; ⊗9.30am-3.30pm) overflow with souvenirs and crafts, such as ceramics, emu oil, jewellery, clothing and bottles of incredibly hot sauce.

Rainforestation
ZOO

(☑07-4085 5008; www.rainforest.com.au; Kennedy Hwy; adult/child $44/22; ⊗9am-4pm) An enormous tourist park west of town with a wildlife section, rainforest/river tours aboard an amphibious WWII Army Duck and an interactive Aboriginal experience.

Wildlife Sanctuaries & Zoos
WILDLIFE SANCTUARIES

Kuranda's rainforest twitters, growls and snaps with all manner of creatures, and the town itself is home to a handful of zoos and sanctuaries. The visitor centre has a full list; try these ones for starters.

If you can wake 'em from their gum-leaf coma, you can cuddle a koala (there are wombats and wallabies too) at the Koala Gardens (☑07-4093 9953; www.koalagardens.com; Heritage Markets, Rob Veivers Dr; adult/child $17/8.50, koala photos extra; ⊗9.45am-4pm daily). The Australian Butterfly Sanctuary (☑07-4093 7575; www.australianbutterflies.com; 8 Rob Veivers Dr; adult/child/family $19/9.50/47.50; ⊗9.45am-4pm daily) is Australia's largest butterfly aviary: you can see butterflies being bred in the lab on a half-hour tour. Birdworld (☑07-4093 9188; www.birdworldkuranda.com; Heritage Markets, Rob Veivers Dr; adult/child $17/8.50; ⊗9am-4pm) is home to 80 species of free-flying native and exotic birds. Combination tickets for all three cost $46/23 per adult/child.

Kuranda Riverboat
CRUISE

(☑07-4093 7476; www.kurandariverboat.com; adult/child/family $15/7/37; ⊗hourly 10.45am-

DON'T MISS

WATERFALLS CIRCUIT

Take in four of the Tableland's most picturesque waterfalls on this leisurely 15km circuit. Start by swinging on to Theresa Creek Rd, 1km east of Millaa Millaa on the Palmerston Hwy. Surrounded by tree ferns and flowers, the Millaa Millaa Falls, 1.5km along, are easily the best for swimming and have a grassy picnic area. Almost ridiculously picturesque, the spectacular 12m falls are reputed to be the most photographed in Australia. Zillie Falls, 8km further on, are reached by a short walking trail that leads to a lookout peering down (with some vertigo) on the falls from above. The next, Ellinjaa Falls, have a 200m walking trail down to a rocky swimming hole at the base of the falls. A further 5.5km down the Palmerston Hwy there's a turn-off to Mungalli Falls.

2.30pm) Hop aboard for a 45-minute calmwater cruise along the Barron River. Located behind the train station; buy tickets on board.

🛏 Sleeping

Kuranda Rainforest Park
CARAVAN PARK $

(☑07-4093 7316; www.kurandarainforestpark.com.au; 88 Kuranda Heights Rd; unpowered/powered sites from $28/30, s/d without bathroom $30/60, cabins $95-105; 🐾🏊) This well-tended park lives up to its name, with grassy camping sites enveloped in rainforest. The basic but cosy 'backpacker rooms' open onto a tin-roofed timber deck, cabins come with poolside or garden views, and there's a restaurant serving local produce on site. It's a 10-minute walk from town via a forest trail.

★Cedar Park Rainforest Resort
ECO RESORT $$

(☑07-4093 7892; www.cedarparkresort.com.au; 250 Cedarpark Road; s/d from $125/145; @🏊) ✐ Set deep in the bush (a 20-minute drive from Kuranda), this unusual property is part Euro-castle, part Aussie-bush-retreat. In lieu of TV, visitors goggle at wallabies, peacocks and dozens of native birds; there's also a spa, creek access, fireplace, a gourmet restaurant and free port wine.

CAIRNS & THE DAINTREE RAINFOREST ATHERTON TABLELAND

Kuranda Hotel Motel MOTEL $$
(☑07-4093 7206; www.kurandahotel.com.au; cnr Coondoo & Arara Sts; s/d $95/100; ❄❄) Locally known as the 'bottom pub', the back of the Kuranda Hotel Motel has spacious '70s-style motel rooms. Open for lunch daily and dinner Thursday to Saturday.

✖ Eating

★Petit Cafe CREPERIE $
(www.petitcafekuranda.com; Shop 35, Kuranda Original Rainforest Markets; crepes $10-17) Duck out the back of the original markets for a mouth-watering range of crepes with savoury or sweet fillings. Winning combinations such as macadamia pesto and feta cheese will entice *le* drool.

Kuranda Coffee Republic CAFE $
(10 Thongon St; coffee $3.50-5.50; ☺8am-4pm Mon-Fri, 9am-4pm Sat & Sun) Food is basically limited to biscotti, but who cares when the coffee's this good? You can see – and smell – the locally grown beans being roasted on site.

Annabel's Pantry BAKERY $
(Therwine St; pies $4.50-5; ☺10am-3pm daily; ☑) With around 25 pie varieties, including kangaroo and veggo.

Frogs CAFE $$
(Heritage Markets; mains $14-36; ☺9.30am-4pm daily; ☎☑) Frogs has been a stayer on the Kuranda eat-scene since 1980: even the local water dragons hang out here. Relaxed and casual with a menu including gourmet salads and tasting platters of roo, emu, croc, barra and tiger prawns (the eponymous frogs get a reprieve).

❶ Information

The **Kuranda visitor centre** (☑07-4093 9311; www.kuranda.org; Centenary Park; ☺10am-4pm) is centrally located in Centenary Park.

❶ Getting There & Away

Those who believe in the journey as much as the destination are in luck here.

Winding 34km from Cairns to Kuranda through picturesque mountains and 15 tunnels, the **Kuranda Scenic Railway** (☑07-4036 9333; www.ksr.com.au) line was built between 1886-91: workers dug tunnels by hand, and battled sickness, steep terrain and hostile Aboriginals. Today, the 1¾-hour pleasure trip costs $49/25 per adult/child one way, and $79/37 return. Trains depart from Cairns at 8.30am and

9.30am daily, returning from the pretty Kuranda station at 2pm and 3.30pm.

At 7.5km, **Skyrail Rainforest Cableway** (☑07-4038 5555; www.skyrail.com.au; Cnr Cook Hwy & Cairns Western Arterial Rd; adult/child one way $47/23.50, return $71/35.50; ☺9am-5.15pm) is one of the world's longest gondola cableways, skimming the jungle canopy for a true bird's-eye view of the rainforest. There are two stops on the 90-minute ride; both offer spectacular views and interpretive panels.

Combination Scenic Railway and Skyrail deals are available.

You can also get to Kuranda with **Trans North** (☑07-4095 8644; www.transnorthbus.com; one way $8) and **John's Kuranda Bus** (☑0418 772 953; one way $5).

Mareeba

POP 10,181

This town revels in a 'wild west' atmosphere, with local merchants selling leather saddles, handcrafted bush hats and the oversized belt buckle of your bronco-bustin' dreams. July's Mareeba Rodeo (www.mareebarodeo.com.au) is one of Australia's biggest and best, with bull riding, a 'beaut ute' muster and boot scootin' country music.

Once the heart of Australia's largest tobacco growing region, Mareeba now turns its soil to more wholesome produce, with organic coffee plantations, distilleries, a mango winery, and abundant fruit and nut crops. Food Trail Tours (www.foodtrailtours.com.au; adult/child $159/80 from Cairns) visits food and wine producers in and around Mareeba; alternatively, self-drive to Mt Uncle Distillery (☑07-4086 8008; www.mtuncle.com; 1819 Chewko Rd, Walkamin; ☺10am-4.30pm daily) to wet your whistle with local liqueurs. The Mareeba Wetlands (☑07-4093 2514; www.mareebawetlands.org; adult/child $15/7.50; ☺10am-4.30pm April-Jan) is a 20-sq-km sanctuary harbouring more than 200 bird species: over 12km of walking trails criss-cross the park. Safari tours (from $38) depart during the week, or you can take a 30-minute eco-cruise (adult/child $15/7.50) or paddle in a canoe ($15 per hour). The on-site Jabiru Safari Lodge (☑07-4093 2514; www.jabirusafarilodge.com.au; cabins per person incl breakfast $109-179, all inclusive $215-285) has solar-powered tented cabins and a spa. Take the Pickford Rd turn-off from Biboohra, 7km north of Mareeba.

The Mareeba Heritage Museum & Tourist Information Centre (☑07-4092 5674; www.mareebaheritagecentre.com.au; Centenary Park, 345 Byrnes St; ⊘ 8am-4pm) FREE has heaps of info.

Atherton

POP 7288

Atherton is a spirited country town that makes a decent base for exploring the delights of the southern Tablelands. It also offers year-round picking jobs: the Atherton Tableland Information Centre (☑ 07-4096 7405; www.athertontablelands.com.au; cnr Main & Silo Rds) has work info.

Thousands of Chinese migrants came to the region in search of gold in the late 1800s, but all that's left of Atherton's Chinatown is the corrugated iron Hou Wang Temple (www.houwang.org.au; 86 Herberton Rd; adult/child $10/5; ⊘ 11am-4pm Wed-Sun). Admission includes a guided tour.

Crystal Caves (☑ 07-4091 2365; www.crystalcaves.com.au; 69 Main St; adult/child $22.50/10; ⊘ 8.30am-5pm Mon-Fri, to 4pm Sat, 10am-4pm Sun, closed Feb) is a gaudy mineralogical museum that houses the world's biggest amethyst geode (more than 3m high and weighing 2.7 tonnes). Crack a geode and take home your own glittery, gazillion-year-old souvenir.

The Barron Valley Hotel (☑ 07-4091 1222; www.bvhotel.com.au; 53 Main St; s/d without bathroom $40/60, s/d with bathroom $60/85; ❉ 🛜) is a Heritage-listed art deco beauty, with tidy rooms and a restaurant serving hearty meals (mains $18 to $35).

Millaa Millaa

POP 600

The dairy community of Millaa Millaa is the gateway to the Tablelands from the south and the closest village to the Waterfalls Circuit. Information is available at www.millaamillaa.com.au.

The village's heart is its only pub, Millaa Millaa Hotel (☑ 07-4097 2212; 15 Main St; s/d $80/90, mains $15-27; ⊘ 10am-9pm), which serves mountain-sized meals and has six spick-and-span motel units.

At the Falls Teahouse (☑ 07-4097 2237; www.fallsteahouse.com.au; Palmerston Hwy; bunks from $35, d incl breakfast $120; ⊘ teahouse 10am-5pm daily), you might like to warm your bones by the fireplace, or soak up rolling farmland views on the back verandah as you hoe into dishes like pan-fried barra and local beef pies (meals $7 to $23). It's at the intersection of the Millaa Millaa Falls turn-off.

About 6km southeast of the village, the bio-dynamic Mungalli Creek Dairy (☑ 07-4097 2232; www.mungallicreekdairy.com.au; 254 Brooks Rd; meals $18; ⊘ 10am-4pm, closed Feb) serves up tasting platters of creamy yoghurt and cheese.

Malanda & Around

POP 2053

Round these parts, 'Malanda' has been a by-word for 'milk' ever since 560 cattle made the 16-month overland journey from New South Wales in 1908. There's still a working dairy here, and the town is surrounded by rainforest. Locals cool off in the shady, croc-free Malanda Falls.

Guided rainforest walks (per person $16; ⊘ 9.30am, 11.30am Sat & Sun; bookings essential), led by members of the Ngadjonji community, can be organised through Malanda's visitor centre (☑ 07-4096 6957; www.malandafalls.com; Malanda-Atherton Rd, across from Malanda Falls; ⊘ 9.30am-4.30pm daily). Or head on up to the Malanda Dairy Centre (☑ 07-4095 1234; www.malandadairycentre.com; 8 James St; tours adult/child $10.50/6.50; ⊘ tours at noon Thu-Tue, call to confirm) for 40-minute factory tours, which include a cheese platter or a milkshake. If you're not yet languishing in a lacto-haze, its licenced cafe (mains from $15; 🍴) has great grub.

About 10km from Malanda, tiny Tarzali has accommodation options including the wonderful Canopy (☑ 07-4096 5364; www.canopytreehouses.com.au; Hogan Rd, Tarzali, via Malanda; d $229-379; 🛜) 🍴, with timber pole-houses tucked into a patch of old-growth rainforest and loads of inquisitive wildlife to watch. Two-night minimum stay.

Yungaburra

POP 1150

Home to a colony of platypuses, tiny Yungaburra is one of the unassuming gems of the Tableland. Queensland's largest National Trust village with 18 Heritage-listed buildings, its boutique accommodation and stunning surrounds have made it a popular weekend retreat for those in the know.

The 500-year-old Curtain Fig tree, sign-posted 3km out of town, is a must-see for its gigantic, otherworldly aerial roots that hang down to create an enormous 'curtain'.

Day trippers descend on the village to hunt through crafts and produce at the vibrant Yungaburra Markets (www.yungaburramarkets.com; Gillies Hwy; ⊘ 7.30am-12.30pm, 4th Saturday of the month). In late October, the

Tablelands Folk Festival (www.tablelandsfolk festival.org; tickets $55, camping $22.50) features music, workshops and poetry readings.

If you're very quiet, you might be lucky enough to catch a glimpse of a timid monotreme at the **platypus viewing platform** on Peterson Creek. Dusk and dawn give you your best chance, but it's worth stopping any time.

★**On the Wallaby** (07-4095 2031; www.onthewallaby.com; 34 Eacham Rd; camping $10, dm/d with shared bathroom $24/55; @) is a homey hostel with handmade timber furniture and mosaics, spotless rooms – and no TV! Nature-based **tours** ($40) include night canoeing; tour packages and transfers (one-way $30) are available from Cairns.

Nick's Restaurant (07-4095 9330; www. nicksrestaurant.com.au; 33 Gillies Hwy; mains $8.50-36.50; 11.30am-3pm Sat & Sun, 5.30-11pm Tue-Sun) has been serving it up Swiss-style since 1986. Costumed staff, piano-accordion serenades and impromptu yodelling provide an apt backdrop for a menu that spans schnitzels to smoked pork loin. Vegos are catered for, too.

Yungaburra's **visitor centre** (07-4095 2416; www.yungaburra.com; Maud Kehoe Park; 9am-5pm) has a complete list of B&Bs, including beautiful retreats in the nearby countryside.

Lake Tinaroo

Tinaroo was allegedly named after a prospector stumbled across a deposit of alluvial tin there and, in a fit of excitement, shouted 'Tin! Hurroo!'. The excitement hasn't died down since, with locals fleeing the swelter of the coast for boating, waterskiing and lazy shoreline lolling.

Barramundi fishing is permitted year-round, though you'll need to pick up a permit (weekly $7.45), available from local businesses and accommodation. Or you might like to head out for a fish, a barbie or glass of wine during a sunset cruise aboard a super-comfy 'floating lounge room' skippered by **Lake Tinaroo Cruises** (0457 033 016; www.laketinaroocruises.com.au; 2/4hr boat charters $200/300).

The 28km **Danbulla Forest Drive** winds its way through rainforest and softwood plantations along the north side of the lake. There are five **Queensland Parks camping grounds** (13 74 68; www.nprsr.qld.gov. au; permits $5.45) in the Danbulla State For-

est. All have water, barbecues and toilets; advance bookings are essential. Otherwise, **Lake Tinaroo Holiday Park** (07-4095 8232; www.laketinarooholidaypark.com.au; 3 Tinaroo Falls Dam Rd; unpowered/powered sites $27/31, cabins $89-129;) has mod-cons, rents out boats ($90 per half-day) and canoes ($10 per hour) AND has a giant jumping pillow!

Crater Lakes National Park

Part of the Wet Tropics World Heritage Area, the two mirror-like, croc-free crater lakes of **Lake Eacham** and **Lake Barrine** are easily reached by sealed roads off the Gillies Hwy. Camping is not permitted.

Lake Barrine is the largest of the lakes, and is cloaked in thick old-growth rainforest; a 5km walking track around its edge takes about 1½ hours. The **Lake Barrine Rainforest Tea House** (07-4095 3847; www. lakebarrine.com.au; Gillies Hwy; mains $7.50-18; 9am-3pm daily) sits out over the lakefront; book downstairs for 45-minute **lake cruises** (adult/child $16/8; 9.30am, 11.30am, 1.30pm). A quick scamper from the teahouse brings you to the grand **twin Kauri Pines**, 1000-year-old giants over 45m tall.

Lake Eacham's clear waters are ideal for swimming and turtle-spotting. There are sheltered picnic areas, a pontoon and boat ramp. The 3km lake-circuit track is an easy one hour walk. Stop by the **Rainforest Display Centre** (McLeish Rd; 9am-1pm Mon, Wed & Fri) for information on the history of the timber industry and replanting of the rainforest.

Crater Lakes Rainforest Cottages (07-4095 2322; www.craterlakes.com.au; Lot 17, Eacham Close, Lake Eacham; d $240;) has four themed timber cottages, each in their own private patch of rainforest and filled with romantic treats. For something a little more earthy, the **Lake Eacham Tourist Park** (07-4095 3730; www.lakeeachamtouristpark.com; Lakes Dr; unpowered/powered sites $22/25, cabins $90-110; @) has shady campsites and cute cabins.

PORT DOUGLAS TO THE DAINTREE

Be pampered in Port Douglas, explore the wilderness of the Daintree Rainforest, or journey to rough-and-ready Cooktown.

Port Douglas

POP 4772

Back in the 1960s, Port Douglas was a sleepy fishing village with a laidback population of 100; come the '80s and the construction of the Sheraton Mirage mega-resort, and 'Port' morphed into a flashy playground for the big-hair, big-money set. These days, the town has settled somewhere between the two extremes: unhurried yet upmarket, it's a sophisticated alternative for those looking to escape Cairns' hectic tourist scene. Port's white-sand beach, Four Mile, is mere steps away from the main streets (Macrossan and Davidson), and the Great Barrier Reef is less than an hour offshore.

◉ Sights & Activities

Four Mile Beach   BEACH
Backed by palms, this broad stretch of squeaky sand reaches as far as you can squint. There's a swimming enclosure in front of the surf life-saving club. In ye olde days, planes used to land on Four Mile, so firm is its sand.

For a fine view over the beach, follow Wharf St and the steep Island Point Rd to **Flagstaff Hill Lookout**.

★**Wildlife Habitat Port Douglas**   ZOO
(☑07-4099 3235; www.wildlifehabitat.com.au; Port Douglas Rd; adult/child $32/16; ◎8am-5pm) There's no shortage of wildlife tourist parks in north Queensland, but this one is up there with the best. The sanctuary endeavours to keep and showcase native animals in enclosures that mimic their natural environment, while allowing you to get up close to koalas, kangaroos, crocs, cassowaries and more. Tickets valid for three days. It's 4km from town; head south along Davidson St.

Come early to have **Breakfast with the Birds** (adult/child breakfast incl admission $47/23.50; ◎8-10.30am) or book in for **Lunch with the Lorikeets** (adult/child incl admission $47/23.50; ◎noon-2pm).

St Mary's by the Sea   CHURCH
(6 Dixie St) FREE Worth a peek inside (when it's not overflowing with wedding parties), this quaint, nondenominational, white timber church was built in 1911.

Ballyhooley Steam Railway   MINIATURE TRAIN
(www.ballyhooley.com.au; adult/child day pass $10/5; ◎Sun) Kids will get a kick out of this cute miniature steam train. Every Sunday (and some public holidays), it runs from the little station at Marina Mirage to St Crispins station. A round trip takes about one hour; discounts are available for shorter sections.

Port Douglas Yacht Club   SAILING
(☑07-4099 4386; www.portdouglasyachtclub.com. au; 1 Spinnaker Cl) Free sailing with club members every Wednesday afternoon (WAGS): sign on from 4pm.

Diving Courses   DIVING
Several companies offer PADI open-water certification as well as advanced dive certificates, including **Blue Dive** (☑0427 983 907; www.bluedive.com.au; 4- to 5-day open-water courses from $760). For one-on-one instruction, learn with **Tech Dive Academy** (☑07-3040 1699; www.tech-dive-academy.com; 4-day open-water courses from $1090).

Port Douglas Boat Hire   BOATING
(☑07-4099 6277; Berth C1, Marina Mirage) Rents dinghies (per hour $33) and canopied, family-friendly pontoon boats (per hour $43) plus fishing gear.

Wind Swell   WATERSPORTS
(☑0427 498 042; www.windswell.com.au; 6 Macrossan St) Kite surfing and stand-up paddle boarding for everyone from beginners to high flyers: lessons begin at $50. Find them in action at the southern end of Four Mile Beach at the park or drop into their shop on Macrossan St.

Golf   GOLF
The **Sheraton Mirage** (www.miragecountryclub.com.au) and **Paradise Links** (www.paradiselinks.com.au) resorts have prestigious, pricey, golf courses. The **Mossman Golf Club** (www.mossmangolfclub.com.au), 20 minutes north of Port, is considerably cheaper.

Historical Walks   WALKING
Download DIY historical walks through Port Douglas, Mossman and Daintree from the **Douglas Shire Historical Society** (www.douglashistory.org.au).

☞ Tours

Port Douglas is a hub for tours, and many based out of Cairns also pick up from here, including some white-water rafting and hot-air ballooning trips. Conversely, many of the following tours departing from Port Douglas also offer pick-ups from Cairns and Cairns' northern beaches.

Port Douglas

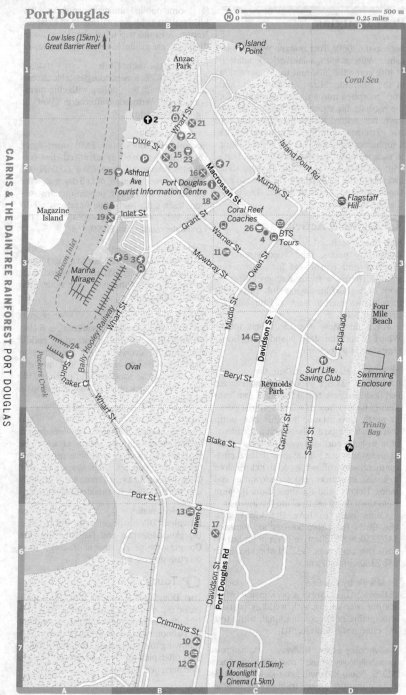

Low Isles (15km);
Great Barrier Reef

Coral Sea

Island Point

Anzac Park

Dixie St

Wharf St

Macrossan St

Port Douglas Tourist Information Centre

Ashford Ave

Magazine Island

Inlet St

Dickson Inlet

Marina Mirage

Coral Reef Coaches

BTS Tours

Island Point Rd

Murphy St

Flagstaff Hill

Warner St

Grant St

Mowbray St

Owen St

Mudlo St

Packers Creek

Bally Hooley Railway

Spinnaker Cl

Wharf St

Oval

Davidson St

Beryl St

Reynolds Park

Garrick St

Sand St

Esplanade

Four Mile Beach

Surf Life Saving Club

Swimming Enclosure

Trinity Bay

Blake St

Wharf St

Port St

Craven Cl

Davidson St

Port Douglas Rd

Crimmins St

QT Resort (1.5km);
Moonlight Cinema (1.5km)

Port Douglas

Great Barrier Reef

The outer reef is closer to Port Douglas than it is to Cairns, and the unrelenting surge of visitors has had a similar impact on its condition here. You will still see colourful corals and marine life, but it is patchy in parts.

Most day tours depart from Marina Mirage. Tour prices usually include reef tax, snorkelling, transfers from your accommodation, lunch and refreshments.

An introductory, controlled scuba dive, with no certification or experience necessary, costs around $250, with additional dives around $50; certified divers will pay around $260 for two dives with all gear included.

Several operators visit the Low Isles, a small group of islands surrounded by beautiful coral reef just 15km offshore; you've got a great chance for spotting turtles here.

Quicksilver   CRUISE
(☑07-4087 2100; www.quicksilver-cruises.com; adult/child $219/110) Major operator with fast cruises to Agincourt Reef. Try an 'ocean walk' helmet dive ($155) on a submerged platform. Also offers scenic helicopter flights from the pontoon on the reef ($159, minimum two passengers).

Sailaway   SAILING, SNORKELLING
(☑07-4099 4772; www.sailawayportdouglas.com; adult/child $215/130) Popular sailing and snorkelling trip to the Low Isles that's great for families. Also offers 90-minute twilight sails ($50) off the coast of Port Douglas.

Sail Tallarook   SAILING
(☑07-4099 4070; www.sailtallarook.com.au; adult/child half-day sail $99/75) Historic 30-metre yacht. Sunset cruises ($50, Tuesday and Thursday) include cheese platters; BYO drinks.

Reef Sprinter   SNORKELLING, BOATING
(☑07-4099 6127; www.reefsprinter.com.au; adult/child $120/100) Superfast 15-minute trip to the Low Isles for snorkelling (and no seasickness!).

The Daintree & Around

There are 4WD tours from Cairns via Port Douglas to Cooktown and Cape York.

Reef & Rainforest Connections   ECOTOUR
(☑07-4035 5566; www.reefandrainforest.com.au; adult/child from $177/115) Runs a flagship, 12-hour Cape Trib and Mossman Gorge trip.

BTS Tours   OUTDOORS
(☑07-4099 5665; www.btstours.com.au; 49 Macrossan St; Daintree adult/child $160/115, Mossman Gorge $72/40) Tours to the Daintree Rainforest and Cape Trib, including canoeing, swimming and rainforest walks.

Fishing

Reef-, river- and land-based fishing charters operate regularly out of Port Douglas. Fishing gear and bait is included.

Tropical Fishing & Eco Tours   FISHING, TOURS
(☑07-4099 4272; www.fishingecotours.com; fishing trips from $100, inlet tours from $40) For fishing, inlet tours or charter.

Fishing Port Douglas   FISHING

(☑0409 610 869; www.fishingportdouglas.com.
au; share/sole charter per half day from $90/320)
Fishing on the river and reef.

River Cruises & River Snorkelling

Back Country Bliss
Adventures   SNORKELLING

(☑07-4099 3677; www.backcountryblissadven-
tures.com.au; trips $80) Drift-snorkel down the
Mossman River. Expect to see turtles and
freshwater fish. Kid-friendly.

Lady Douglas   RIVER CRUISES

(☑07-4099 1603; www.ladydouglas.com.au; 1½hr
cruises adult/child $30/20) Paddlewheeler run-
ning four daily croc-spotting tours (including sunset cruise) along the Dickson Inlet.

Bike Tours

Bike N Hike Adventure Tours   BIKE TOUR

(☑0416 339 420; www.bikenhiketours.com.
au; tours from $88) Bounce down the aptly
named Bump Track (an old Aboriginal
trail) on a cross-country tour ($128, 7.30am
to 11.30am Tuesday and Thursday, 1.30pm
to 5.30pm Sunday) or a berserk night tour
($88, 6.30pm to 8.30pm nightly).

✵ Festivals & Events

Port Douglas Carnivale   CARNIVAL

(www.carnivale.com.au; ☉May) This 10-day festival includes a colourful street parade, live
music, and lashings of good food and wine.

Porttoberfest   BEER FESTIVAL

(Port Douglas Marina; ☉late October) The tropical
take on Octoberfest, with live music, German
food and beer. See www.visitportdouglasdain-
tree.com.au/events for annual updates.

🛏 Sleeping

Port Douglas is swimming in accommodation, mainly in self-contained apartments or
upmarket resorts just out of town.

ParrotFish Lodge   HOSTEL $

(☑07-4099 5011; www.parrotfishlodge.com; 37-39
Warner St; dm $25-32, d with/without bathroom
$110/80; ❋@✿≋) Energetic backpackers with
a bar, live tunes and lots of freebies, including
breakfast, bikes and pick-ups from Cairns.

Dougies   HOSTEL $

(☑07-4099 6200; www.dougies.com.au; 111 Davidson St; campsites per person $15, dm $26, d $68;
❋@✿≋) It's easy to hang about Dougies'
sprawling grounds in a hammock by day
and move to the bar at night. If you can sum-

mon the energy, bikes and fishing gear are
available for rent. Free pick-up from Cairns
on Monday, Wednesday and Saturday.

Pandanus Caravan Park   CARAVAN PARK $

(☑07-4099 5944; www.pandanuscp.com.au; 97-107
Davidson St; 2-person unpowered/powered sites
$38/44, 2-person cabins $80-110; ❋@✿≋) Five
minutes' stroll from the beach, this park has a
good range of cabins and free gas barbecues.

Port O' Call Lodge   HOSTEL $

(☑07-4099 5422; www.portocall.com.au; cnr Port
St & Craven Cl; dm $38, d $85-129; ❋@✿≋) 🖉
Low-key hostel on solar/wind energy with
en suite rooms and a good-value bar/bistro.

Tropic Sands   APARTMENTS $

(☑07-4099 6166; www.tropicsands.com.au; 21
Davidson St; d from $89; ❋@≋) Schmick open-
plan rooms with fully equipped kitchens
and private balconies in a beautiful colonial-
style building. No kids; two-night minimum.

★Pink Flamingo   BOUTIQUE HOTEL $$

(☑07-4099 6622; www.pinkflamingo.com.au; 115
Davidson St; r $125-195; ❋@✿≋❋) Flam-
boyantly painted rooms, private courtyards
(with hammocks, outdoor baths and outdoor
showers) and an al fresco bar make the Pink
Flamingo Port Douglas' hippest digs. Outdoor
movie nights, gym and bike rental on offer.

Birdsong Bed & Breakfast   B&B $$

(☑07-4099 1288; www.portdouglasbnb.com;
6188 Captain Cook Hwy; d/apt from $135/249;
℗❋✿≋) Posh open-plan B&B set on
sprawling tropical grounds. Induce delu-
sions of grandeur as you ogle the private
heli-pad and gawp at the in-house movie
theatre. Rates go down the longer you stay.

Turtle Cove Beach Resort   GAY RESORT $$

(☑07-4059 1800; www.turtlecove.com; Captain Cook
Hwy; d/suite from $154/277; ℗❋@≋) Mega-
popular gay/lesbian resort with absolute
beach frontage and a clothing-optional beach.
Located 15 minutes south of Port. No kids.

★QT Resort   RESORT $$$

(☑07-4099 8900; www.qtportdouglas.com.au; 87-
109 Port Douglas Rd; d $240-260, villa $290-410;
❋@✿≋) Upmarket retro-kitsch decor and
a DJ spinning lounge beats in the bar may
make you forget you're in Queensland. Restaurant, Bazaar, serves up a quality buffet
spread and stylish rooms have flat-screen TVs
and plush beds.

(Continued on page 473)

PATRICK DANCEL / GETTY IMAGES ©

The Great Barrier Reef

Each year, more than 1.5 million visitors come to this World Heritage–listed area that stretches across 2000km of coastline. Diving and snorkelling are just some of the ways to experience this wonderful and rich ecosystem. There's also sailing, scenic flights and idyllic days exploring the reef's gateway towns and stunning islands.

Contents

➡ **Gateways to the Reef**

➡ **Top Reef Encounters**

➡ **Nature's Theme Park**

Above Aerial view of the Great Barrier Reef

Gateways to the Reef

There are numerous ways to approach Australia's massive undersea kingdom. You can head to a popular gateway town and join an organised tour, sign up for a multiday sailing or diving trip exploring less-travelled outer fringes of the reef, or fly out to a remote island, where you'll have the reef largely to yourself.

The Whitsundays

Home to turquoise waters, coral gardens and palm-fringed beaches, the Whitsundays have many options for reef-exploring: base yourself on an island, go sailing or stay on Airlie Beach and island-hop on day trips.

Cairns

The most popular gateway to the reef, Cairns has dozens of boat operators offering day trips with snorkelling as well as multiday reef explorations on live-aboard vessels. For the uninitiated, Cairns is a good place to learn to dive.

Port Douglas

An hour's drive north of Cairns, Port Douglas is a laid-back beach town with dive boats heading out to over a dozen sites, including more pristine outer reefs, such as Agincourt Reef.

Townsville

Australia's largest tropical city is far from the outer reef (2½ hours by boat) but has some exceptional draws: access to Australia's best wreck dive, an excellent aquarium, marine-themed museums, plus multiday live-aboard dive boats departing from here.

Southern Reef Islands

For an idyllic getaway off the beaten path, book a trip to one of several remote reef-fringed islands on the southern edge of the Great Barrier Reef. You'll find fantastic snorkelling and diving right off the island.

AUSCAPE / UIG / GETTY IMAGES ©

1. Clownfish 2. Airlie Beach (p408) 3. Reef HQ Aquarium (p419), Townsville

ULLA LOHMANN / GETTY IMAGES ©

WILL GRAY / GETTY IMAGES ©

TANYA PUNTTI / GETTY IMAGES ©

1. Whitehaven Beach (p415) 2. Helicopter scenic flight over Whitsunday Islands (p403) 3. Snorkelling, Cairns (p445)

Top Reef Encounters

Donning a mask and fins and getting an up-close look at this marine wonderland is one of the best ways to experience the Great Barrier Reef. You can get a different take aboard a glass-bottomed boat tour, on a scenic flight or on a land-based reef walk.

Diving & Snorkelling

The classic way to see the Great Barrier Reef is to board a catamaran and visit several different coral-rich spots on a long day trip. Nothing quite compares to that first underwater glimpse, whether diving or snorkelling.

Semi-submersibles & Boats

A growing number of reef operators (especially around Cairns) offer semi-submersible or glass-bottomed boat tours, which give cinematic views of coral, rays, fish, turtles and sharks – without you ever having to get wet.

Sailing

You can escape the crowds and see some spectacular reef scenery aboard a sailboat. Experienced mariners can hire a bareboat, others can join a multiday tour – both are easily arranged from Airlie Beach or Port Douglas.

Reef Walking

Many reefs of the southern Great Barrier Reef are exposed at low tide, allowing visitors to walk on the reef top (on sandy tracks between living coral). This can be a fantastic way to learn about marine life, especially if accompanied by a naturalist guide.

Scenic Flights

Get a bird's-eye view of the vast coral reef and its cays and islands from a scenic flight. You can sign up for a helicopter tour (offered from Cairns) or a seaplane tour (particularly memorable over the Whitsundays).

Sea turtle

Nature's Theme Park

Home to some of the greatest biodiversity of any ecosystem on earth, the Great Barrier Reef is a marine wonderland. You'll find 30-plus species of marine mammals along with countless species of fish, coral, molluscs and sponges. Above the water, 200 bird species and 118 butterfly species have been recorded on reef islands and cays.

Common fish species include dusky butterfly fish, which are a rich navy blue with sulphur-yellow noses and back fins; large graphic turkfish, with luminescent pastel coats; teeny neon damsels, with darting flecks of electric blue; and six-banded angelfish, with blue tails, yellow bodies and tiger stripes. Rays, including the spotted eagle ray, are worth looking out for.

The reef is also a haven to many marine mammals, such as whales, dolphins and dugongs. Dugongs are listed as vulnerable, and a significant number of them live in Australia's northern waters; the reef is home to around 15% of the global population. Humpback whales migrate from Antarctica to the reef's warm waters to breed between May and October. Minke whales can be seen off the coast from Cairns to Lizard Island in June and July. Porpoises and killer and pilot whales also make their home here. One of the reef's most-loved inhabitants is the sea turtle. Six of the world's seven species (all endangered) live on the reef and lay eggs on the islands' sandy beaches in spring or summer.

(Continued from page 466)

Hibiscus Gardens
RESORT $$$

(☑07-4099 5995; www.hibiscusportdouglas.com. au; 22 Owen St; d $155-385; ﹡@☎) Balinese influences of teak furnishing and fixtures and plantation shutters give this stylish resort an exotic ambience. Their day spa is renowned as one of the best in town.

✖ Eating

For a town its size, Port Douglas has some incredibly sophisticated dining options. Advance reservations are recommended and essential for really popular places. For self-catering, there's a large Coles (11 Macrossan St) supermarket in the Port Village shopping centre.

Mocka's Pies
BAKERY $

(☑07-4099 5295; 9 Grant St; pies $4.50-6; ☺8am-4pm) Institution serving amazing Aussie pies with exotic ingredients such as crocodile, kangaroo and barra.

The Beach Shack
MODERN AUSTRALIAN $$

(☑07-4099 1100; www.the-beach-shack.com.au; 29 Barrier St, Four Mile Beach; mains $16.50-29; ☺11.30am-3pm & 5.30-10pm; ☑) There'd be an outcry if this locals' favourite took its macadamia-crumbed eggplant (with grilled and roast veggies, goat's cheese and wild rocket) off the menu. But it's the setting that makes it really worth heading to the southern end of Four Mile: a lantern-lit garden with sand underfoot. Good fish, sirloins and blackboard specials, too.

On the Inlet
SEAFOOD $$

(☑07-4099 5255; www.portdouglasseafood.com; 3 Inlet St; mains $24-40; ☺noon-11.30pm) Jutting out over Dickson Inlet, tables spread out along a huge deck where you can await the 5pm arrival of George the 250kg groper, who comes to feed most days. Take up the bucket-of-prawns-and-a-drink deal ($18 from 3.30pm to 5.30pm).

Salsa Bar & Grill
MODERN AUSTRALIAN $$

(☑07-4099 4922; www.salsaportdouglas.com.au; 26 Wharf St; mains $20-37; ☺noon-3pm & 5.30-9.30pm; ☑) Salsa is a stayer on Port's fickle scene. Try the Creole jambalaya (rice with prawns, squid, crocodile and smoked chicken) or the roo with tamarillo marmalade. Also has outstanding cocktails.

Han Court
CHINESE $$

(☑07-4099 5007; 85 Davidson Street; mains from $16) If Port's fancy fusion/Mod Oz/culinary-

buzzword-du-jour menus are wearing you out, head to Han for good comfort food. They've been in town forever, and dish up familiar, tasty staples, such as honey chicken and black-bean beef, on a candlelit deck.

★ Sassi Cucina e Bar
ITALIAN $$$

(☑07-4099 6744; cnr Wharf & Macrossan Sts; mains $26-49; ☺noon-10pm) Scrimp, save, steal to splurge on an authentic Italian feast at this legendary local. Owner-chef Tony Sassi's spin on seafood is world-renowned, but the taste of absolutely anything off the menu will linger longer than your Four Mile tan.

2 Fish
SEAFOOD $$$

(☑07-4099 6350; www.2fishrestaurant.com.au; 7/20 Wharf St; mains $29-40; ☺11.30am-3pm & 5.30-10pm daily) There's a lot more seafood here than the modest name would infer: over a dozen types of fish, from coral trout to red emperor and wild barramundi, are prepared in a variety of innovative ways.

Flames of the Forest
FINE DINING $$$

(☑07-4099 5983; www.flamesoftheforest.com.au; Mowbray River Rd; dinner with show, drinks & transfers from $180) This unique experience goes way beyond the traditional concept of 'dinner and a show', with diners escorted deep in to the rainforest for a truly immersive night of theatre, culture and gourmet cuisine. Bookings essential.

☗ Drinking & Nightlife

Drinking and dining go hand in hand in Port Douglas and the local clubs and hotels all serve up inexpensive pub-style meals.

Tin Shed
LICENSED CLUB

(www.thetinshed-portdouglas.com.au; 7 Ashford Ave; ☺10am-10pm) Port Douglas' Combined Services Club is a rare find: bargain dining on the waterfront, and even the drinks are cheap.

Iron Bar
PUB

(☑07-4099 4776; www.ironbarportdouglas.com. au; 5 Macrossan St; ☺11am-3am) Incongruous, wacky outback decor sets the scene for a wild night out: after polishing off a slab o'steak (mains $17 to $30), head upstairs for a flutter on the cane-toad races ($5) or dance to the live tunes.

Court House Hotel
PUB

(☑07-4099 5181; cnr Macrossan & Wharf Sts; ☺11am-late) Commanding a prime corner location, the 'Courty' is a lively local, with bands on weekends. Meals ($20 to $30) available.

Whileaway Bookshop Cafe
CAFE

(2/43 Macrossan St; ⊙6am-6pm) For smart coffees in literary surrounds.

Port Douglas Yacht Club
LICENSED CLUB

(www.portdouglasyachtclub.com.au; 1 Spinnaker Cl; ⊙bar 4-10pm Mon-Fri, noon-10pm Sat & Sun) There's a spirited nautical atmosphere at the PDYC. Inexpensive meals are served nightly.

☆ Entertainment

Moonlight Cinema
CINEMA

(www.moonlight.com.au/port-douglas/; 87-109 Port Douglas Rd, QT Resort, Port Douglas; tickets adult/child $16/12; ⊙Jun-Oct) Bring a picnic or hire a bean bag for outdoor movie screenings.

🛍 Shopping

Port Douglas Markets
MARKET

(Anzac Park, Macrossan St; ⊙8am-1pm Sun) These markets are treasure without the trash, with handmade arts, crafts and jewellery, plus local tropical fruits and produce.

❶ Information

The **Port Douglas Tourist Information Centre** (✆07-4099 5599; www.infoportdouglas.com.au; 23 Macrossan St; ⊙8am-6.30pm) has maps and makes tour bookings.

The *Port Douglas & Mossman Gazette* comes out every Thursday, and has heaps of local info, gig guides and more.

❶ Getting There & Away

The 70km coast-hugging drive between Cairns and Port Douglas is one of the loveliest in the whole country. For those sans-wheels, there are many bus options, including the following:

Coral Reef Coaches (✆07-4098 2800; www.coralreefcoaches.com.au) connects Port Douglas with Cairns ($40, 1¼ hours) via Cairns airport and Palm Cove.

Sun Palm (p474) has frequent daily services between Port Douglas and Cairns ($40, 1½ hours) via the northern beaches and the airport.

Country Road Coachlines (✆07-4045 2794; www.countryroadcoachlines.com.au) has a bus service between Port Douglas and Cooktown on the coastal route via Cape Tribulation three times a week ($70), weather permitting.

❶ Getting Around

Port Douglas Bike Hire (✆07-4099 5799; www.portdouglasbikehire.com.au; cnr Wharf & Warner Sts; per day from $19) Has high-performance bikes for hire as well as tandems ($32 per day). Free delivery and pick-up.

Sun Palm (✆07-4087 2900; www.sunpalm-transport.com.au) Runs in a continuous loop every half-hour (7am to midnight) between Wildlife Habitat and Marina Mirage.

For vehicle hire, the major international rental chains are represented here, or try a local company like **Paradise Wheels** (✆07-4099 6625; www.paradisewheels.com.au) or **Port Douglas Car Hire** (✆07-4099 4999; www.portdouglas-carhire.com). Many places don't let you take cars off-road: check before hiring. It's the last place before Cooktown where you can hire a 4WD.

Mossman

POP 1733

Mossman – only 20km north of Port – is a pleasant, unpretentious town with a sugar mill and cane trains. Mossman is an obligatory stop on a visit to Mossman Gorge, and it's also a good place to stock up on petrol and supplies if you're heading north.

◎ Sights & Activities

★ Mossman Gorge
GORGE

(✆07-4099 7000; www.mossmangorge.com.au; Mossman Gorge Centre; Dreamtime walk adult/child $50/25; ⊙8am-6pm) In the southeast corner of Daintree National Park, 5km west of Mossman town, Mossman Gorge forms part of the traditional lands of the Kuku Yalanji Indigenous people. Carved by the Mossman River, the gorge is a boulder-strewn valley where sparkling water washes over ancient rocks. Walking tracks loop along the river to a refreshing swimming hole – take care, as the currents can be swift. There's a picnic area here but no camping. The complete circuit back to the entrance takes about an hour.

Book in for one of the 1½-hour Indigenous Kuku-Yalanji Dreamtime Walks through the slick new on-site centre, which also houses an art gallery and bush-tucker restaurant.

Janbal Gallery
GALLERY

(✆07-4098 3917; www.janbalgallery.com.au; 5 Johnston Rd; ⊙10am-5pm Tue-Sat) Browse and buy the art at this Aboriginal-run gallery, or create your own masterpiece (canvas, boomerang or didgeridoo) under the guidance of artist-in-residence, Binna.

🛏 Sleeping & Eating

Mossman Motel Holiday Villas
VILLAS $$

(✆07-4098 1299; www.mossmanmotel.com.au; 1-9 Alchera Drive; villas $120-210; P ✳ @ 🛜 🛋) Fantastic-value villas on landscaped grounds complete with rock waterfall and pool.

Silky Oaks Lodge   LUXURY RESORT $$$
(☑07-4098 1666; www.silkyoakslodge.com.au; Finlayvale Rd; studio treehouse/garden treehouse/ deluxe treehouse/riverhouse $400/500/630/800; ✳@🖥❄🖳) This international resort woos honeymooners and stressed-out execs with hammocks, rejuvenation treatments and polished-timber cabins complete with spa baths. Its stunning Treehouse Restaurant & Bar (mains $36-44; ⏰breakfast 7-10am, lunch noon-2.30pm, dinner 6-8.30pm) is open to interlopers.

Mojo's   MODERN AUSTRALIAN $$
(☑07-4098 1202; www.mojosbarandgrill.com.au; 41 Front St; mains $18-45; ⏰11.30am-2pm Mon-Fri, 6pm-late Mon-Sat; 🖊) Mojo's has a menu that's more Montmartre than Mossman – elegant fare includes fried brie with truffle-honey walnuts and pork-belly spring rolls.

ℹ️ Information

NPRSR (☑13 74 68; www.nprsr.qld.gov.au) has information on the Daintree National Park up to and beyond Cape Tribulation.

ℹ️ Getting There & Away

BTS (☑07-4099 5665; www.portdouglasbus. com; 49 Macrossan St, Port Douglas) has return shuttles from Port Douglas to Mossman Gorge (adult/child return $26/16, 8.30am and 11.30am).

THE DAINTREE

The Daintree represents many things: a river, a rainforest national park, a reef, a village, and the home of its traditional custodians, the Kuku Yalanji people. It encompasses the coastal lowland area between the Daintree and Bloomfield Rivers, where the rainforest meets the coast. It's an ancient but fragile ecosystem, once threatened by logging and development but now largely protected as a World Heritage Area.

Daintree River to Cape Tribulation

Part of the Wet Tropics World Heritage Area, the region from the Daintree River north to Cape Tribulation is extraordinarily beautiful and famed for its ancient rainforest, sandy beaches and rugged mountains.

The length of Cape Tribulation Rd is scattered with places to stay and eat. There's no mains power north of the Daintree River – electricity is supplied by generators or, increasingly, solar power. Shops and services are limited, and mobile-phone reception is largely nonexistent.

The Daintree River ferry (car/motorcycle/ bicycle & pedestrian one way $13/5/1; ⏰6am-midnight, no bookings) carries people and their cars across the river about every 15 minutes.

Cow Bay & Around

👁 Sights & Activities

On the steep, winding road between Cape Kimberley and Cow Bay is the Walu Wugir-riga Lookout (Alexandra Range Lookout), with an information board and sweeping views over the range and the Daintree River inlet that are especially breathtaking at sunset.

Not far beyond the lookout, the award-winning Daintree Discovery Centre (☑07-4098 9171; www.daintree-rec.com.au; Tulip Oak Rd; adult/child/family $32/16/78, valid seven days; ⏰8.30am-5pm) takes you high into the forest canopy with its aerial walkway, including climbing up a 23m tower used to study carbon levels. A small theatre runs films on cassowaries, crocodiles, conservation and climate change. The (included) audio guide offers an excellent Aboriginal tour.

The white-sand Cow Bay Beach lies at the end of the sealed Buchanan Creek Rd (also called Cow Bay Rd, or simply 'the road to the beach') and rivals any coastal paradise.

Also known as Jungle Bugs & Butterflies, the Daintree Entomological Museum (☑07-4098 9045; www.daintreemuseum.com.au; Turpentine Rd; adult/child $10/5; ⏰10am-5pm) displays a large private collection of local and exotic bugs, butterflies and spiders.

Book ahead for a walk with Cooper Creek Wilderness (☑07-4098 9126; www. ccwild.com; Cape Tribulation Rd; guided walks $55-250). Bring your togs for the day walks (departing 9am, 2pm and 3pm), which take you through Daintree rainforest and include a dip in Cooper Creek. Night walks (departing at 8pm) focus on spotting nocturnal wildlife. There's also a full day tour including lunch and a river cruise ($130).

Cape Tribulation Wilderness Cruises (☑0457 731 000; www.capetribcruises.com; Cape Tribulation Rd; adult/child from $28/20) has one-hour mangrove cruises where you can go in search of crocodiles.

🛏 Sleeping & Eating

The best-value accommodation in the area is at Daintree Rainforest Bungalows

WORTH A TRIP

DAINTREE VILLAGE

You may be racing to the beaches of Cape Trib, but for lovers of local wildlife, it's worth taking the 20km detour to tiny Daintree village (population 146).

Croc-spotting and birdwatching cruises on the Daintree River are the village's main attraction. Numerous operators run trips – try Crocodile Express (☑07-4098 6120; www.crocodileexpress.com; 1hr cruises adult/child $25/13; ☺daily from 8.30am), or Daintree River Wild Watch (☑07-4098 7068; www.daintreeriverwildwatch.com.au; 2hr cruises adult/child $55/35), which has informative sunrise bird-watching cruises and sunset photography nature cruises. Those short on time can take a one-hour cruise on a covered boat with Bruce Belcher's Daintree (☑07-4098 7717; www.daintreerivercruises.com; 1hr cruises adult/child $27/12).

The 15 boutique 'banyans' (treehouses) of Daintree Eco Lodge & Spa (☑07-4098 6100; www.daintree-ecolodge.com.au; 20 Daintree Rd; banyans from $215-598; ☀@☀☀) 🌿 sit high in the rainforest a few kilometres south of the village. Nonguests are welcome at its superb Julaymba Restaurant (mains $26.50-40; ☺breakfast, lunch & dinner), where the menu makes tasty use of local produce, including bush tucker ingredients.

Daintree Riverview (☑0409 627 434; www.daintreeriverview.com; 2 Stewart St; unpowered/powered sites per person $10/15, cabins $99-130) is a less pricey option, with waterside camping, good-value cabins and a lovely deck overlooking the river.

Tick off another of Australia's 'Big Things' – and try a Barra Burger – at the Big Barra (☑07-4098 6186; 12 Stewart St; mains $18, burgers from $7; ☺9am-5pm). Their homemade ice cream ($5.50) comes in exotic local flavours including soursop and black sapote.

No fuel is available in Daintree village.

(☑07-4098 9229; www.daintreerainforestbungalows.com; Lot 40, Spurwood Rd; d $110). Its free-standing wooden cabins are simple but stylish, with en suites and covered decks overlooking the rainforest. Minimum stay is two nights.

Also in the Cow Bay area, Epiphyte B&B (☑07-4098 9039; www.rainforestbb.com; 22 Silkwood Rd; s/d/cabins from $75/110/135) is situated on a 3.5-hectare property with individually styled rooms with en suites and their own verandahs. The spacious cabin has a patio, kitchenette and sunken bathroom. From the front deck of the house you can kick back with views of imposing Thornton Peak (1975m). Rates include breakfast.

The boutique motel rooms at Daintree Rainforest Retreat Motel (☑07-4098 9101; www.daintreeretreat.com.au; 1473 Cape Tribulation Rd; r $110-240, cabin $550; ☀) have tropical colour schemes and glossy woodwork. Some have kitchenettes, or guests can dine at its restaurant Tree Frogs (mains $15-40; ☺dinner Mon-Sat).

The Cow Bay Hotel (☑07-4098 9011; Cape Tribulation Rd; mains $14-30; ☺11am-3pm & 6-9.30pm), adjacent to the turn-off to the beach, is the only real pub in the whole Daintree region. Down towards the beach on Buchanan Creek Rd, the jungly Crocodylus Village (☑07-4098 9166; www.crocodyluscapetrib.com; Buchanan Creek Rd; dm $25 d $75-110; @☀☀) hostel also has a restaurant and bar that are open to the public. It organises activities in-

cluding half-day kayaking trips and two-day sea-kayaking tours to Snapper Island.

There are no agonising decisions at Daintree Ice Cream Company (☑07-4098 9114; Lot 100, Cape Tribulation Rd; ice creams $6; ☺11am-5pm), an all-natural ice-cream producer – you get a cup of four exotic flavours that change daily. Hustle it off on a 20-minute orchard walk.

Just south of Cooper Creek, Rainforest Village (☑07-4098 9015; www.rainforestvillage.com.au; ☺7am-7pm) sells groceries, ice and fuel, and has a small camping ground (unpowered/powered sites $22/28) with hot showers and a camp kitchen.

At the crescent-shaped Thornton Beach, the licensed Cafe on Sea (☑07-4098 9118; Cape Tribulation Rd; mains $12-25; ☺9am-4pm) is only a towel-length back from the sand.

Cape Tribulation

This little piece of paradise retains a frontier quality, with low-key development, road signs alerting drivers to cassowary crossings and crocodile warnings.

The rainforest tumbles right down to two magnificent, white-sand beaches – Myall and Cape Trib – separated by a knobby cape. The village of Cape Tribulation marks the end of the road and the beginning of the 4WD-only coastal route along the Bloomfield Track.

⊙ Sights & Activities

Beaches & Waterholes   SWIMMING

Long walks on the swathes of Cape Tribulation Beach or Myall Beach are a favourite pastime and you can swim safely outside stinger season, though heed warning signs and local advice about croc sightings. A couple of boardwalks run through the mangroves.

If you're a bit wary, take a dip in the clear, croc-free swimming hole (admission by gold coin donation) next to Mason's Store.

Bat House   WILDLIFE CENTRE

(☎07-4098 0063; www.austrop.org.au; Cape Tribulation Rd; admission $5; ☉10.30am-3.30pm Tue-Sun) A nursery for injured or orphaned fruit bats (flying foxes), run by conservation organisation Austrop, which also welcomes forest rehabilitation and planting volunteers for a minimum of one week.

Mt Sorrow   HIKING

Fit walkers should start early for the Mt Sorrow Ridge walk (7km, five to six hours return, start no later than 10am); it's strenuous but worth it. The start of the marked trail is 150m north of the Kulki picnic area car park.

☞ Tours

Most tours offer free pick-ups from local accommodation.

Jungle Surfing   ZIPLINE, HIKING

(☎07-4098 0043; www.junglesurfing.com.au; zipline $90, night walks $40, combo $120; ☉night walks 7.30pm) Get right up into the rainforest on an exhilarating flying fox (zipline) zoom through the canopy, stopping at five tree platforms. Guided night walks follow zany biologist-guides, who shed light on the dark jungle. Rates include pick-up from Cape Trib accommodation (self-drive not allowed).

Cape Trib Exotic Fruit Farm   FARM TOUR

(☎07-4098 0057; www.capetrib.com.au; Lot 5, Nicole Dr; tour adult/child $25/12.50; ☉2pm Sun, Tue & Thu Jun-Oct) Bookings are essential for tours of these magnificent tropical orchards and a tasting of 10 of the 100-plus seasonal organic fruits grown here. It also has a couple of stunning private cabins.

Cape Trib Horse Rides   HORSE RIDING

(☎07-4098 0030; www.capetribhorserides.com.au; per person $89; ☉8am & 1.30pm) Leisurely rides along the beach.

D'Arcy of the Daintree   DRIVING

(☎07-4098 9180; www.darcyofdaintree.com.au; tours adult/child from $129/77) Entertaining 4WD trips up the Bloomfield Track to Wujal Wujal Falls and as far as Cooktown and down Cape Tribulation Rd.

Mason's Tours   WALKING, DRIVING

(☎07-4098 0070; www.masonstours.com.au; Mason's Store, Cape Tribulation Rd) Longtimer Lawrence Mason conducts interpretive walks (groups up to five people two hours/half day $300/500) through the rainforest; 4WD tours up the Bloomfield Track to Cooktown are also available (groups up to five people half/full day $800/1250).

Ocean Safari   SNORKELLING

(☎07-4098 0006; www.oceansafari.com.au; adult/child $123/79; ☉9am & 1pm) Ocean Safari leads

CAIRNS & THE DAINTREE RAINFOREST CAPE TRIBULATION

DAINTREE NATIONAL PARK: THEN & NOW

The greater Daintree Rainforest is protected as part of Daintree National Park. The area has a controversial history: despite conservationist blockades, in 1983 the Bloomfield Track was bulldozed through lowland rainforest from Cape Tribulation to the Bloomfield River, and the ensuing international publicity led indirectly to the federal government nominating Queensland's wet tropical rainforests for World Heritage listing. The move drew objections from the Queensland timber industry and the state government but, in 1988, the area was inscribed on the World Heritage List, resulting in a total ban on commercial logging in the area.

World Heritage listing doesn't affect land ownership rights or control and, since the 1990s, efforts have been made by the Queensland Government and conservation agencies to buy back and rehabilitate freehold properties, adding them to the Daintree National Park and installing visitor interpretation facilities. Sealing the road to Cape Tribulation in 2002 opened the area to rapid settlement, triggering the buy-back of hundreds more properties. Coupled with development controls, these efforts are now bearing the fruits of forest regeneration. Check out Rainforest Rescue (www.rainforestrescue.org.au) for more information.

Cape Tribulation Area

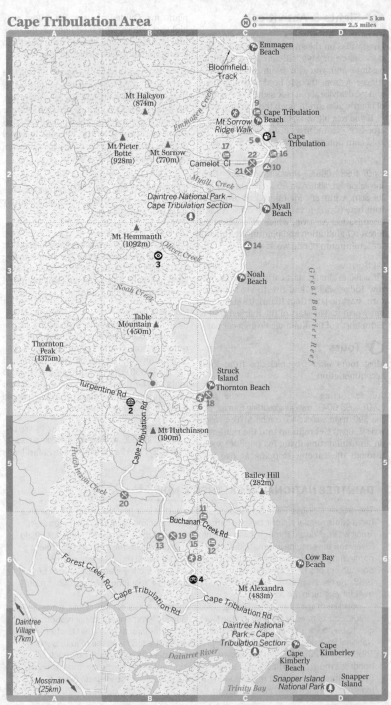

CAIRNS & THE DAINTREE RAINFOREST

Cape Tribulation Area

small groups (25 people maximum) on snorkelling cruises to the Great Barrier Reef, just half an hour offshore.

Paddle Trek Kayak Tours   KAYAKING
(📞 07-4098 0062; www.capetribpaddletrek.com.au; kayak hire per hour $16-55, trips $69-79) Guided sea-kayaking trips and kayak hire.

🛏 Sleeping & Eating

Cape Trib Beach House   HOSTEL $
(📞 07-4098 0030; www.capetribbeach.com.au; Lot 7, Rykers Rd; dm $26-32, d $80, cabins $130-230; ❄@🛜🏊) Rainforest huts house dorms through to en suite timber cabins. There's a tidy communal kitchen as well as an open-deck licensed restaurant and bar.

PK's Jungle Village   HOSTEL $
(📞 07-4098 0040; www.pksjunglevillage.com; Cape Tribulation Rd; unpowered sites per person $15, dm $25-28, d $95-125; ❄@🛜🏊) PK's is a long-standing backpacker hub. You can reach My-

all Beach by boardwalk, and its Jungle Bar is the entertainment epicentre of Cape Trib.

Cape Tribulation Camping   CAMPGROUND $
(📞 07-4098 0077; www.capetribcamping.com.au; Cape Tribulation Rd; unpowered & powered sites from $40; @) Beachfront spot with a nightly communal fire and friendly managers and kayaking guides (kayak hire from $20 per hour).

★ Cape Trib Exotic Fruit Farm Cabins   CABIN $$
(📞 07-4098 0057; www.capetrib.com.au; Lot 5, Nicole Dr; d $190) 🍃 Amid the orchards of Cape Trib Exotic Fruit Farm, these two pole cabins have timber floors, ceilings and decks, and electric Eskies. Rates include breakfast hampers filled with tropical fruit from the farm. Minimum stay two nights; book in advance.

Rainforest Hideaway   B&B $$
(📞 07-4098 0108; www.rainforesthideaway.com; 19 Camelot Cl; d $130-140) 🍃 This B&B was single-handedly built by its owner, artist and sculptor 'Dutch Rob' – even the furniture is handmade. A sculpture trail winds through the property; rates include breakfast.

Mason's Store & Cafe   CAFE, SELF-CATERING $
(Cape Tribulation Rd; mains $15; ⊙10am-4pm Sun-Thu, to 7pm Fri & Sat) Dishes up good fish and chips and huge steak sandwiches. The store sells some groceries and takeaway alcohol.

Whet Restaurant & Cinema   AUSTRALIAN, INDIAN $$
(📞 07-4098 0007; www.whet.net.au; 1 Cape Tribulation Rd; mains $17.50-33; ⊙11.30am-3pm & 5.30-9.30pm) Cape Trib's coolest address, offering trendy Mod-Oz and Indian (Fridays) cuisine. Movies ($10) are at 2pm, 4pm and 8pm.

IGA Supermarket   SUPERMARKET
(📞 07-4098 0015; PK's Jungle Village; ⊙8am-6pm) The Daintree's largest supermarket.

ⓘ Information

Stop in at **Mason's Store** (📞 07-4098 0070; Cape Tribulation Rd; ⊙8am-6pm) for info on the region, including Bloomfield Track conditions.

NORTH TO COOKTOWN

There are two routes to Cooktown from the south: the coastal route from Cape Tribulation via the 4WD-only Bloomfield Track, and the inland route, which is sealed all the way via Peninsula Developmental Rd and Cooktown Developmental Rd.

CAIRNS & THE DAINTREE RAINFOREST CAPE TRIBULATION

Inland Route

The inland route runs along the western side of the Great Dividing Range for 332km (about 4½ hours' drive) from Cairns to Cooktown.

The historical township of Mt Molloy (population 274) marks the start of the Peninsula Developmental Rd, about 40km north of Mareeba. Since its mining heyday, the town centre has shrivelled to comprise a pub, bakery, post office and a cafe that serves up jaw-crackingly massive burgers that have twice been recognised as the 'world's best'. The road continues north via Mt Carbine to the Palmer River Roadhouse, where you'll find fuel, camping and meals. The Palmer River gold rush (1873–83) occurred about 70km west of here; there are still pockets of miners trying their luck in them thar hills.

It's another 15km to Lakeland at the junction of the Peninsula Developmental Rd and the Cooktown Developmental Rd. Head west and you're on your way to Laura and Cape York (4WD and forward planning essential); continue straight northeast and it's another 80km to Cooktown.

Some 30km shy of Cooktown, the spooky Black Mountain National Park, with thousands of stacked, square, black granite boulders formed 260 million years ago, marks the northern end of the Wet Tropics World Heritage Area. The eerie mountain is cloaked in mystery and legend: ask a local for their take on the place!

Coastal Route

The legendary 4WD-only Bloomfield Track connecting Cape Tribulation to Cooktown traverses creek crossings, diabolically steep climbs and patchy surfaces. It can be impassable for weeks on end during the Wet, and even in the Dry you should check road conditions, as creek crossings are affected by tide times. It's unsuitable for trailers.

The track is a contentious one: bulldozed through pristine forest in the early '80s, it was the site of battles between environmental protestors and police. Some locals still seek a staged closure over the next decade or so.

It's 8km from Cape Trib to Emmagen Creek, from where the road climbs and dips steeply and turns sharp corners. This is the most challenging section of the drive. The road then follows the broad Bloomfield River before crossing it 30km north of Cape Trib.

Turn left immediately after the bridge to see the Bloomfield Falls. Crocs inhabit the river and the site is significant to the Indigenous Wujal Wujal community, just north of the river. The local Walker Family (☑07-4040 7500; www.bamaway.com.au; adult/child $25/12.50; ⊙ by reservation) runs highly recommended half-hour walking tours of the falls and surrounding forest.

About 5km north of Wujal Wujal, the Bloomfield Track Takeaway & Middleshop (☑07-4060 8174; dishes from $10; ⊙ 8am-10pm Tue-Sat, to 8pm Sun & Mon) serves food and has fuel, fishing tackle and groceries.

North of Bloomfield, several walks begin from Home Rule Rainforest Lodge (☑07-4060 3925; www.home-rule.com.au; Rossville; unpowered sites per adult/child $10/5, r adult/child $25/15), at the end of a bumpy 3km driveway. Spotless facilities include a communal kitchen; meals are available as well as canoe hire. Home Rule is ground zero for the weekend-long Wallaby Creek Festival (www.wallabycreekfestival.org.au; ⊙ Sep), with roots, blues and Indigenous music on two stages.

It's only another 9km to the welcoming Lion's Den Hotel (☑07-4060 3911; www.lionsdenhotel.com.au; 398 Shiptons Flat Rd, Helenvale; unpowered/powered sites per person $12/28, s/d $45/65, d safari tents $80; ※ ≋). This iconic watering hole with genuine corrugated, graffiti-covered decor dates back to 1875 and still attracts a steady stream of travellers and local characters. There's fuel and ice-cold beer, and its restaurant (mains from $20; ⊙ breakfast, lunch & dinner) serves up excellent pub grub.

David Attenborough has spent time at the Mungumby Lodge (☑07-4060 3158; www.mungumby.com; Helenvale; s/d $260/279; ⛳ ≋) ✐ – you'll see why as you explore its rainforest walks and nearby waterfall. En suite bungalows are scattered among the lawns and mango trees. Rates include breakfast, lunch, dinner and nature tours are available.

About 4km north, the Bloomfield Track meets the sealed Cooktown Developmental Rd, from where it's 28km to Cooktown.

Cooktown

POP 2339

At the southeastern edge of Cape York Peninsula, Cooktown is a small place with a big history: for thousands of years, Waymbuurr was the place the local Guugu Yimithirr and Kuku Yalanji people used as a meeting ground, and it was here that on 17 June 1770,

Lieutenant (later Captain) Cook beached the *Endeavour*. The *Endeavour* had earlier struck a reef offshore from Cape Tribulation, and Cook and crew spent 48 days here while they repaired the damage – making it the site of Australia's first, albeit transient, non-Indigenous settlement.

Cooktown is a hotspot for history hounds, those looking to work on banana plantations and folks who believe that happiness is a fishing rod and an Esky full of beer.

◉ Sights

Cooktown hibernates during the Wet, and many attractions and tours close or have reduced hours. The main street, Charlotte St, has some beautiful 19th-century buildings.

Grassy Hill LOOKOUT
Be sure you get to the top of this 162m-high knoll come dusk/dawn: with 360-degree views of the town, river and ocean, the view is spectacular! Cook himself climbed this hill looking for a passage out through the reefs. Drive up or walk via a steep path from town or bush trail via Cherry Tree Bay: walkers need minimum 20 minutes to ascend.

Nature's Powerhouse INTERPRETIVE CENTRE
(☑ 07-4069 6004; www.naturespowerhouse.com. au; off Walker St; admission by donation; ⊗ 9am-5pm) This environmental centre is home to two excellent galleries: the Charlie Tanner Gallery, with pickled and preserved creepy-crawlies, and the Vera Scarth-Johnson Gallery, displaying botanical illustrations of the region's native plants.

The centre doubles as Cooktown's official visitor centre and is at the entry to Cooktown's 62-hectare Botanic Gardens (off Walker St; ⊗ 24hr) **FREE**, one of Australia's oldest.

James Cook Museum MUSEUM
(☑ 07-4069 5386; cnr Helen & Furneaux Sts; adult/child $10/3; ⊗ 9.30am-4pm) Built as a convent in 1889, Cooktown's finest historical building houses well-preserved relics from Cook's time in the area, including journal entries and the cannon and anchor from the *Endeavour*, retrieved from the sea floor in 1971, plus displays on local Indigenous culture.

Bicentennial Park PARK
Bicentennial Park is home to the much-photographed bronze Captain Cook statue. Nearby, the Milbi Wall is a 12m-long mosaic that spans creation stories to European contact with the local Gungarde (Guugu Yimithirr) people, to recent attempts at reconciliation. Sitting just out in the water from Bicentennial Park is the rock marking the spot where Cook ran aground and tied up to a tree (part of the original tree is on display at the James Cook Museum).

Cooktown's wharf is one of Queensland's sweetest fishing spots.

TOURS FROM COOKTOWN

Although the reef is not far away, there are no regularly scheduled dive or snorkelling trips. Water-based tours depart from the wharf.

★ **Guurrbi Tours** (☑ 07-4069 6043; www.guurrbitours.com; tours 2/4hr $95/120, self-drive $65/85; ⊗ Mon-Sat) Nugal-warra family elder Willie Gordon runs revelatory tours that use the physical landscape to describe the spiritual landscape. The morning Rainbow Serpent tour involves some walking, bush tucker and rock-art sites, including a birthing cave. The afternoon Great Emu tour is shorter and visits three rock-art sites. Self-drivers meet near the Hopevale Aboriginal Community.

Maaramaka Walkabout Tours (☑ 07-4060 9389; irenehammett@hotmail.com; tours 1/2hr $84/42) Aboriginal cultural stories, rainforest walks and bush tucker in a gorgeous setting near Hopevale.

Cooktown Barra Fishing Charters (☑ 0408 036 887; half-/full day $120/220, minimum two people) Fishing and heli-fishing trips, plus croc-spotting, bird-watching, mud-crabbing and eco tours.

Cooktown Tours (☑ 1300 789 550; www.cooktowntours.com) Two-hour town tours (adult/child $55/33) and half-day trips to Black Mountain and the Lion's Den Hotel (adult/child $110/77).

Saratoga Fishing & Hunting Adventures (☑ 07-4069 6697; www.capeyorksafaris.com) Fishin' and piggin' up the Cape York Peninsula.

✦ Festivals & Events

Cooktown Discovery Festival HISTORICAL
(www.cooktowndiscoveryfestival.com.au; ⊙Queen's
birthday weekend) Commemorates Cook's landing in 1770 with costumed re-enactment,
grand parade and Indigenous events.

⌂ Sleeping & Eating

Cooktown has plenty of accommodation,
including several caravan parks, but book
ahead in the Dry. See www.tourismcapeyork.
com for more options, including B&Bs.

Pam's Place Hostel &
Cooktown Motel HOSTEL, MOTEL $
(☑07-4069 5166; www.cooktownhostel.com; cnr
Charlotte & Boundary Sts; dm/s/d $27.50/55/60,
motel d $100; ❉@☂❉) Cooktown's YHA-
associated hostel offers the cheapest sleeps
in town. Friendly managers can help find
harvest work.

Seaview Motel MOTEL $$
(☑07-4069 5377; www.cooktownseaviewmotel.
com.au; 178 Charlotte St; d $99-175, townhouses
$235; ❉☂❉) A great location opposite the
wharf, with modern rooms (some with pri-
vate balconies). Includes breakfast.

Sovereign Resort Hotel HOTEL $$$
(☑07-4043 0500; www.sovereign-resort.com.au; cnr
Charlotte & Green Sts; d $180-220, tr & q $210-280;
❉@☂❉) Nicknamed 'the Half-Sovereign'
following cyclone damage in 1949, these are
now Cooktown's swishest digs, with tropical-
style rooms and gorgeous gardens. Dine fine
at the smart **Balcony Restaurant** (☑07-4069
5400; Sovereign Resort , cnr Charlotte & Green Sts;
mains $25-33; ⊙7-9.30am & 6-10pm) or kick back
at the low-key **Cafe-Bar** (mains $11-23; ⊙11am-
8pm; ☑).

Verandah Cafe CAFE $
(Walker St; mains $8-18; ⊙10am-2.30pm; ☑) At-
tached to Nature's Powerhouse at the entrance to the botanic gardens, the deck of this
cafe is a serene setting for tea and scones or
dishes like gado gado with coconut damper.

Gill'd & Gutt'd FISH & CHIPS $
(☑07-4069 5863; Fisherman's Wharf, Webber Esplanade; mains $7-12; ⊙11.30am-9pm) Fish and
chips on the waterside wharf.

Cooktown Bowls Club LICENSED CLUB $$
(☑07-4069 5819; Charlotte St; mains $15-25;
⊙11.30am-2.30pm Wed-Fri, 5.30-10pm daily; ☑)
Big bistro meals. Join the locals in social
bowls Wednesday and Saturday afternoons.

Restaurant 1770 MODERN AUSTRALIAN $$$
(☑07-4069 5440; 7 Webber Esplanade; breakfast
$19, lunch & dinner mains $30-39; ⊙7.30-9.30am,
11.30am-2pm & 6-9.30pm Tue-Sat; ☑) Opening
on to a waterside deck, try the fresh local fish
but save space for mouth-watering desserts.

ℹ Information

Cooktown Travel Centre (☑07-4069 5446;
113 Charlotte St) Information and bookings for
tours, transport and accommodation.
Tourist Information Centre (☑07-4069 6004;
www.naturespowerhouse.com.au; Walker St;
⊙9am-5pm) Housed in the Nature's Powerhouse complex.

ℹ Getting There & Around

Cooktown's airfield is 7.5km west of town along
McIvor Rd. **Hinterland Aviation** (☑07-4040
1333; www.hinterlandaviation.com.au) has one
to four flights daily to/from Cairns (one-way
from $125, 40 minutes).
  Country Road Coachlines (☑07-4045 2794;
www.countryroadcoachlines.com.au) runs a
daily bus service between Cairns and Cooktown
($81) on either the coastal route (Bloomfield
Track, via Port Douglas) or inland route (via
Mareeba), depending on the day of departure
and the condition of the track.

Lizard Island

The five islands of the Lizard Island Group
cluster just 33km off the coast about 100km
north from Cooktown. The continental main
island, Lizard Island, has a dry, rocky, mountainous terrain and spectacular fringing
reef for snorkelling and diving. Most of the
island is national park, with plenty of wildlife – including 11 different species of lizard –
and 24 glistening white beaches.
  Accommodation is either five-star luxury
at *ultra*-exclusive **Lizard Island Resort**
(☑1300 863 248; www.lizardisland.com.au; Anchor
Bay; d from $1520; ❉@☂❉), or bush camping
at the island's **camping grouns** (☑13 74 68;
www.nprsr.qld.gov.au; per person $5.45). Bring all
supplies as there are no shops on the island.
  Flying is the easiest way to reach Lizard Island; book all air transfers to/from
Cairns (return $650, $590 for resort guests)
through the resort. Flight time is one hour.
  Daintree Air Services (☑1800 246 206,
07-4034 9400; www.daintreeair.com.au) has full-
day tours from Cairns at 8am ($750). The
trip includes gourmet lunch, snorkelling
gear, transfers and a local guide.

Understand East Coast Australia

East Coast Australia Today

When most people think 'Australia', the East Coast is what springs to mind: big cities, photogenic beaches, coral reefs and rolling surf. But in reality most of Australia – the 'outback' – is a vast desert. Turning its back on the sun-baked interior, the East Coast is a celebration of life on the edge – a long, fertile strip of land where most Aussies live, work and play.

Best on Film

Australia (director Baz Luhrmann; 2008) Sweeping Aussie epic beautifully shot in NSW and Queensland.
The Castle (director Rob Sitch; 1997) Hit comedy gleefully playing with Aussie stereotypes.
Picnic at Hanging Rock (director Peter Weir; 1975) Disquieting film about schoolgirls 'absorbed' into the mysterious Victorian landscape.
Lantana (director Ray Lawrence; 2001) Mystery for grown-ups: a meditation on love, truth and grief.
Two Hands (director Gregor Jordan; 1999) Vicious humour in Sydney's criminal underworld.

Best in Print

The Tree of Man (Patrick White; 1955) Profound story of early pioneers living in the bush.
Johnno (David Malouf; 1975) A coming-of-age tale set in 1940s Brisbane.
Oscar and Lucinda (Peter Carey; 1988) Man Booker Prize winner: how to relocate a glass church.
The Secret River (Kate Grenville; 2005) Of 19th-century convict life around Sydney.
The Bodysurfers (Robert Drewe; 1983) Sexy tales from Sydney's sandy suburbia.

The Big Wet Continues

Much of Australia was wracked by drought for the first decade of this century, a period tragically defined by the apocalyptic 2009 'Black Saturday' bushfires in Victoria. But this all ended in 2011 with record rainfalls across New South Wales and Queensland. These rains were followed by category-five Cyclone Yasi, which dumped further rain across Queensland.

The drought was over, but flood waters inundated dozens of towns, affecting 1 million sq km (roughly the size of France and Germany combined). The Brisbane River broke its banks, flooding vast stretches of Australia's third-largest city. Flooding also hit Victoria, with crops devastated and thousands of livestock drowned. Coal production was affected, crop and livestock losses mounted and tourism took a big hit – costing the nation $5.6 billion.

Then, in early 2013, southeast Queensland suffered another blow, this time from the tail end of Tropical Cyclone Oswald, which immersed Bundaberg and parts of Brisbane in river water. Residents of low-lying suburbs wrung themselves dry and started rebuilding (again...).

Later in 2013, savage bushfires in the Blue Mountains behind Sydney blazed for weeks, part of an outbreak of more than 100 fires across NSW that burned out almost 300,000 acres of forest and destroyed around 250 homes.

Meanwhile, Out on the Reef

For many climatologists these natural disasters are just part of the growing pattern of human-induced climate change wreaking havoc on Australia's weather.

Climate change remains a hot topic along the East Coast (no pun intended) – particularly when it comes to Queensland's biggest tourist attraction, the Great Barrier Reef. Marine researchers predict disastrous consequences for the reef as sea temperatures rise. Some estimates place the reef's near-total devastation within the next 50 years. This destruction is unthinkable on many fronts – not least of which are the catastrophic economic consequences: the reef generates an estimated $4 billion in annual tourism revenue.

Economic Ebbs & Flows

Natural disasters aside, Australia has done comparatively well on the economic front of late. The commodities-powered country was one of the only OECD nations to avoid recession during the global financial crisis. Unemployment was expected to reach 8% to 10% during the GFC but didn't even hit 6%. But with a cooling Chinese economy (one of Australia's major export markets), the mining boom that kept Australia afloat during the GFC has also slowed, and a growing budget deficit now faces the new conservative Liberal-National coalition federal government.

Despite these harsh and dramatic environments (both natural and fiscal), Australia remains a desirable destination for immigrants, and the nation boasts one of the world's highest living standards. In the UN's Human Development Index, Australia consistently appears in the world's top five countries for its high levels of education, health care, democratic freedoms, safety and security, and life expectancy. Australians enjoy a high per-capita income, and Melbourne, Sydney and Brisbane regularly top the charts on 'World's Most Liveable Cities' lists.

Quality-of-living indexes notwithstanding, some Australians remain anxious about the future. House prices have soared in the last 20 years, with many Aussies overextending themselves or abandoning the dream of owning their own home. During the GFC, growth in Australian housing prices stalled (and even regressed in some areas). The market showed hints of recovery in 2013, but some economists warn that home values remain overinflated by 20% or more in some locations, including the big East Coast cities.

This Sporting Life

Nowhere in Australia are sporting passions so divisive and heartfelt as the East Coast. This is a battleground: East Coast sports fans must choose to align themselves either with rugby league (the dominant code in Queensland, NSW and the ACT) or Australian rules football (dominant in Victoria and the rest of Australia). The mutual loathing north and south of the Murray River is palpable. Confusingly for everyone involved, in 2012 the Sydney Swans won the Australian Football League (Aussie rules) championship final in Melbourne, and the Melbourne Storm won the National Rugby League final in Sydney. Strange days indeed...

POPULATION: **17,809,059**

AREA: **2,902,073 SQ KM**

GDP: **AUD$1.09 TRILLION**

GDP GROWTH: **3%**

INFLATION: **2.2%**

UNEMPLOYMENT: **4.8%**

if East Coast Australia were 100 people

60 born in Australia
4 born in England
4 born in China
2 born in New Zealand
2 born in India
28 born elsewhere

belief systems
(% of population)

50 Christian
14 Agnostic
4 Buddhist

4 Islamic
2 Hindu
26 other

population per sq km

SYDNEY MELBOURNE BRISBANE

≈ 346 people

History

By Michael Cathcart

Australia is an ancient continent – rocks here have been dated back beyond the Archean eon 3.8 billion years ago. Its Indigenous people have been here more than 50,000 years. Given this backdrop, 'history' as we describe it can seem somewhat fleeting...but it sure makes an interesting read!

Intruders Arrive

Michael Cathcart presents history programs on ABC TV, is a broadcaster on ABC Radio National and teaches history at the Australian Centre, University of Melbourne.

By sunrise, the storm had passed. Zachary Hicks was keeping sleepy watch on the British ship *Endeavour* when suddenly he was wide awake. He summoned his captain, James Cook, who climbed into the brisk morning air to a miraculous sight. Ahead of them lay an uncharted land of wooded hills and gentle valleys. It was 19 April 1770. In the coming days, Cook began methodically to draw the first European map of Australia's eastern coast. He was mapping the end of Aboriginal supremacy.

Two weeks later Cook led a party of men onto a narrow beach. As they waded ashore, two Aboriginal men stepped onto the sand and challenged the intruders with spears. Cook drove the men off with musket fire. For the rest of that week, the Aboriginal people and the intruders watched each other warily.

When the *Endeavour* reached the northern tip of Cape York, blue ocean opened up to the west. Cook and his men could smell the sea route home. And on a small, hilly island ('Possession Island'), Cook raised the Union Jack. Amid volleys of gunfire, he claimed the eastern half of the continent for King George III.

Cook's intention was not to steal land from the Indigenous Australians. In fact he rather idealised them. 'They are far more happier than we Europeans', he wrote. 'They think themselves provided with all the necessaries of Life and that they have no superfluities.'

Convict Beginnings

Eighteen years later, in 1788, the English were back to stay. They numbered 751 ragtag convicts and children, and around 250 soldiers, officials and their wives. This motley 'First Fleet' was under the command of a

TIMELINE	60,000 BC	43,000 BC	3000 BC
	Although the exact start of human habitation in Australia is still uncertain, according to most experts this is when Aborigines first arrived on the continent.	A group of Indigenous Australians sits down in the Nepean Valley near current-day Sydney and makes some stone tools. Archaeological sites like this have been found across Australia.	The last known large immigration to the continent from Asia occurs. Over 250 languages are spoken among the myriad groups living in Australia.

humane and diligent naval captain, Arthur Phillip. By a small cove, in the idyllic lands of the Eora people, Phillip established a British penal settlement. He renamed the place after the British Home Secretary, Lord Sydney.

Robert Hughes' bestseller, *The Fatal Shore* (1987), depicts convict Australia as a terrifying 'Gulag' where Britain tormented rebels, vagrants and criminals. But other historians point out that powerful men in London saw transportation as a scheme for giving prisoners a new and useful life. Indeed, with Phillip's encouragement, many convicts soon earned their 'ticket of leave', a kind of parole that gave them the freedom of the colony and the right to seek work on their own behalf.

However, the convict system could also be savage. Women (who were outnumbered five to one) lived under constant threat of sexual exploitation. Female convicts who offended their gaolers languished in the depressing 'female factories'. Male reoffenders were cruelly flogged, and could even be hanged for minor crimes, such as stealing. In 1803 English officers established a second convict settlement at Hobart in Van Diemen's Land (later called Tasmania). Soon male reoffenders filled the grim prison at Port Arthur on the beautiful and wild coast. Others endured the senseless agonies of Norfolk Island in the remote Pacific.

At first Sydney and these smaller colonies depended on supplies brought in by ship. Anxious to develop productive farms, the government granted land to soldiers, officers and emancipated convicts. After 30 years of trial and error, their farms began to flourish.

Land

Each year, settlers pushed deeper into the Aboriginal territories in search of pasture and water for their stock. These men became known as squatters (because they 'squatted' on Aboriginal lands), and many held this territory with a gun. In the USA the conflict between settlers and indigenous people formed the basis for a rich mythology known as 'the

---

Vestiges from a Convict Past

Hyde Park Barracks Museum (p58), Sydney

St Thomas Anglican Church (p132), Port Macquarie, NSW

Trial Bay Gaol (p136), South West Rocks, NSW

Commissariat Store Building (p282), Brisbane

Argyle Cut (p51), Sydney

50,000 YEARS BEFORE COOK

Little is known about how the first people came to Australia. Even the dates are broadly debatable and seem measured more in geological rather than human terms: 50,000 to 70,000 years ago. What is known is that people came to the continent from Asia during times when the Earth was much cooler and water levels much lower. This made it possible for them to walk across the Torres Strait from New Guinea. Migrations are thought to have occurred at various times since, with the last major one 5000 years ago. By Cook's arrival in 1770, the continent had a rich and varied culture of Indigenous communities.

Regis St Louis

AD 1607	1770	1776	1788
Spanish explorer Luis Torres manages to sail between Australia and New Guinea and not discover the rather large continent to the south. The strait bears his name today.	English captain James Cook maps Australia's East Coast in the scientific ship *Endeavour*. He then runs aground on the Great Barrier Reef near a place he names Cape Tribulation.	The 13 British colonies in the US declare independence, leaving the King's government without a place to ship convicts. Authorities turn their attention to the vast Australian continent.	The Eora people of Bunnabi discover they have new neighbours; 11 ships arrive bearing soldiers and convicts, and drop anchor in what the new arrivals call Botany Bay.

Wild West'. But in Australia the conflict has largely passed from white memory, so white historians now disagree about the extent of the violence. However, Indigenous Australians still recount how their waterholes were poisoned and their people massacred. Some of the most bitter struggles occurred in the remote mining districts of central Queensland. In Tasmania the impact of settlement was so devastating that, today, no 'full blood' Indigenous Tasmanians survive; all of the island's Aboriginal people are of mixed heritage.

On the mainland many of the squatters reached a truce with the defeated Indigenous people. In remote regions it became common for Aboriginal people to take low-paid jobs on farms, working on sheep and cattle stations as drovers, rouseabouts, shearers and domestics. In return, those lucky enough to be working on their traditional lands adapted their cultures to the changing circumstances. This arrangement continued in outback pastoral regions until after WWII.

The handsome blue-and-white Southern Cross flag flown at the Eureka stockade in 1854 has since become a symbol of union movements in Australia.

BURKE & WILLS

The Great Northern Expedition was an attempt to cross Australia from Melbourne to the Gulf of Carpentaria, and was funded by the colonial government. Despite a sad lack of experience, Robert O'Hara Burke was chosen to lead the 19-man expedition with William 'Jack' Wills his deputy. As 10,000 onlookers cheered them on, the group set off for the 3200km journey from Melbourne in August 1860. They were spectacularly unprepared – bringing with them such ephemera as heavy wooden tables, rockets, flags and a Chinese gong, as well as two years' worth of rations. All in all, they brought more than 20 tonnes of supplies, loaded onto 26 camels, 23 horses and six wagons. Overburdened, they moved at a snail's pace, taking nearly two months to cover some 750km (the mail run took about 10 days), and the road was littered with discarded items. They also reached the hottest parts of Australia in the middle of summer. With temperatures soaring above 50°C, the group ran into serious troubles – equipment malfunctions, incessant quarrelling, resignations and dismissal of expedition members.

Growing frustrated, Burke split the group and made a dash for the coast with three others (Wills, Charles Gray and John King) in December. The main group stayed behind, ordered by Burke to wait three months before returning south. Burke calculated he could make it to the coast and back in two months. In fact it took over four months, and when they finally came near the coast, mangrove swamps prevented them from actually reaching the ocean. They returned to base camp (Gray died along the way), only to discover the group had packed up and headed south just hours earlier. The three then set off for a pastoral settlement near Mt Hopeless. Burke and Wills perished. King was rescued by Aboriginal people and nursed back to health. He was the only expedition member to make the full crossing and return alive.

Regis St Louis

1824	1835	1844–45	1871
The government establishes the brutal penal colony of Moreton Bay, a place of blood, sweat and tears. A second penal colony, Brisbane, follows two years later.	John Batman arranges the 'purchase' of 2500 sq km from people of the Dutigalla tribe for flour and trinkets. Melbourne is established on the north bank of the Yarra River.	The first guidebook to Australia is written in the form of a journal by Ludwig Leichhardt. It chronicles his party's exploration from Brisbane almost to Darwin. In 1848, he vanishes without a trace.	Aboriginal stockman Jupiter discovers gold in Queensland and the rush is on. Within 10 years Brisbane has made its fortune from both gold and wool.

Gold & Rebellion

Transportation of convicts to eastern Australia ceased in the 1840s. This was just as well: in 1851 prospectors discovered gold in New South Wales and central Victoria. The news hit the colonies with the force of a cyclone. From every social class, young men and some adventurous women headed for the diggings. Soon they were caught up in a great rush of prospectors, entertainers, publicans, sly-groggers, prostitutes and quacks from overseas. In Victoria the British governor was alarmed – both by the way the Victorian class system had been thrown into disarray, and by the need to finance law and order on the goldfields. His solution was to compel all miners to buy an expensive monthly licence, in the hope that the lower orders would return to their duties in town.

But the lure of gold was too great. In the reckless excitement of the goldfields, the miners initially endured the thuggish troopers who enforced the government licence. But after three years the easy gold at Ballarat was gone, and miners were toiling in deep, water-sodden shafts. They were now infuriated by a corrupt and brutal system of law that held them in contempt. Under the leadership of a charismatic Irishman named Peter Lalor, they raised the flag of the Southern Cross and swore to defend their rights and liberties. They armed themselves and gathered inside a rough stockade at Eureka, where they waited for the government to make its move.

In the predawn of Sunday 3 December 1854, a force of troopers attacked the stockade. In 15 terrifying minutes, they slaughtered 30 miners and lost five soldiers. The story of the Eureka stockade is often told as a battle for nationhood and democracy – as if a true nation must be born out of blood. But these killings were tragically unnecessary. The eastern colonies were already in the process of establishing democratic parliaments, with the full support of the British authorities. In the 1880s Lalor himself became speaker of the Victorian parliament.

The gold rush also attracted boatloads of prospectors from China. The Chinese prospectors endured constant hostility from whites, and were the victims of ugly race riots on the goldfields at Lambing Flat (now called Young) in NSW in 1860–61. Chinese precincts developed in the backstreets of Sydney and Melbourne and, by the 1880s, popular literature indulged in tales of Chinese opium dens, dingy gambling parlours and oriental brothels. But many Chinese went on to establish themselves in business and particularly in market gardening. Today the busy Chinatowns of Sydney and Melbourne, and the ubiquitous Chinese restaurants in country towns, are reminders of Chinese vigour.

Revered by many as the great Australian novel, Patrick White's *Voss* (1957) was inspired by the story of the Prussian explorer Leichhardt. It's a psychological tale, a love story and an epic journey over the Australian desert.

Written in 1895 by AB 'Banjo' Paterson, 'Waltzing Matilda' is widely regarded as Australia's unofficial national anthem. Some say the song paid homage to striking sheep shearers during the 1890s labour uprisings.

1891	1901	1915	1918
A shearers' strike around Barcaldine, Queensland, establishes a labour legend; the confrontation leads to the birth of the Australian Labor Party.	The Australian colonies federate; a new national parliament meets in Melbourne. The White Australia policy is passed, which bans non-Europeans from immigrating.	In line with Australia's close ties to Britain, Australian and New Zealand troops (the Anzacs) join the Allied invasion of Turkey at Gallipoli. The Anzac legend is born.	The Great War ends. From a country of 4.9 million, 320,000 were sent to war in Europe and almost 20% were killed. Cracks appear in Australian–British relations.

Gold and wool brought immense investment and gusto to Melbourne, Sydney and a swath of Queensland. By the 1880s they were stylish modern cities, with gaslights in the streets, railways and that great new invention: the telegraph. In fact, the southern capital became known as 'Marvellous Melbourne', so opulent were its theatres, hotels, galleries and fashions.

Meanwhile, the huge expanses of Queensland were remote from the southern centres of political and business power. It was a tough, raw frontier colony, in which money was made by hard labour – in mines, in the forests and on cattle stations. In the coastal sugar industry, southern investors grew rich on a plantation economy that exploited tough Pacific Island labourers (known as 'Kanakas'), many of whom had been kidnapped from their islands.

The most accessible version of the Anzac legend is Peter Weir's epic film *Gallipoli* (1981), with a cast that includes a fresh-faced Mel Gibson.

Nationhood

On 1 January 1901 Australia became a federation. When the bewhiskered members of the new national parliament met in Melbourne, their first aim was to protect the identity and values of a European Australia from an influx of Asians and Pacific Islanders. Their solution was what became known as the White Australia policy. It became a racial tenet of faith in Australia for the next 70 years. For those who were welcome to live in Australia (ie whites), this was to be a model society, nestled in the skirts of the British Empire.

Just one year later, white women won the right to vote in federal elections. In a series of radical innovations, the government introduced a broad social-welfare scheme and protected Australian wage levels with import tariffs. Its mixture of capitalist dynamism and socialist compassion became known as 'the Australian settlement'.

War & the Great Depression

The hard-fought biennial 'Ashes' Test cricket series between Australia and England has been played since 1882. Despite long periods of dominance by both sides, the ledger stands at 32 series wins to Australia, 31 to England.

Living on the edge of this forbidding land, and isolated from the rest of the world, most Australians took comfort from the idea that they were still a part of the British Empire. When war broke out in Europe in 1914, thousands of Australian men rallied to the Empire's call. They had their first taste of death on 25 April 1915, when the Australian and New Zealand Army Corps (the 'Anzacs') joined British and French troops in an assault on the Gallipoli Peninsula in Turkey. It was eight months before the British commanders acknowledged that the tactic had failed, but by then 8141 young Australians were dead. Soon the Australian Imperial Force was fighting in the killing fields of Europe. By the time the war ended, 60,000 Australian men had been slaughtered. Ever since, on 25 April, Australians have gathered at war memorials around the country and at Gallipoli for the sad and solemn services of Anzac Day.

1928	1929	1937	1941
Reverend John Flynn starts the Royal Flying Doctor Service in Cloncurry, Queensland – an invaluable service that now has networks around the country.	The Great Depression: thousands go hungry as the economy crashes. Unemployment peaks at 28% in 1932 – one of the highest rates in the industrialised world (second only to Germany).	Cane toads are released into the wild to control pests damaging Queensland's sugarcane fields. The action proves disastrous, creating a plague that spreads to other states.	The Japanese bomb Townsville. The war in the Pacific is on. Hundreds of thousands of Australian troops pour out to battlefields worldwide; thousands of American troops pour in and drink a lot of beer.

Australia careered wildly through the 1920s, continuing to invest in immigration and growth, until the economy collapsed into the abyss of the Great Depression in 1929. Unemployment brought its shame and misery to one in three houses. For those who were wealthy – or who had jobs – the Depression was hardly noticed. In fact, the fall in prices actually meant that the purchasing power of their income was enhanced.

Heroes

In the midst of the hardship, sport brought escape to a nation in love with games and gambling. Champion racehorse Phar Lap won an effort-less and graceful victory in the 1930 Melbourne Cup (the race that stops a nation). In 1932 the great horse travelled to the racetracks of America, where he mysteriously died. In Australia the gossips insisted that the horse had been poisoned by envious Americans. And the legend was es-tablished of a sporting hero cut down in his prime.

The year 1932 also saw accusations of treachery on the cricket field. The English team, under its aloof captain Douglas Jardine, employed a violent new bowling tactic known as 'Bodyline'. Jardine's aim was to unnerve Australia's star batsman, the devastating Donald Bradman. The bitterness of the tour became part of the Australian legend. And Brad-man batted on – achieving the unsurpassed career average of 99.94 runs.

WWII

As the economy began to recover, the whirl of daily life was hardly damp-ened when Australian servicemen sailed off to Europe for a new war, in 1939. Though Japan was menacing, Australians took it for granted that the British navy would keep them safe. In December 1941 Japan bombed the US Fleet at Pearl Harbor. Weeks later the 'impregnable' British naval base in Singapore crumbled, and soon thousands of Australians and other Al-lied troops were enduring the savagery of Japan's prisoner-of-war camps.

As the Japanese swept through Southeast Asia and into Papua New Guinea, the British announced that they could not spare any resources to defend Australia. But the legendary US commander General Douglas MacArthur saw that Australia was the perfect base for American opera-tions in the Pacific. In a series of savage battles on sea and land, Allied forces gradually turned back the Japanese advance. Importantly, it was the USA, not the British Empire, that came to Australia's aid. The days of the British alliance were numbered.

Peace, Prosperity & Multiculturalism

As the war ended, a new slogan rang through the land: 'Populate or Per-ish!' The Australian government embarked on an ambitious scheme to attract thousands of immigrants. With government assistance, people

Best History Museums

The Rocks Discov-ery Museum (p53), Sydney

Museum of Sydney (p58), Sydney

Melbourne Museum (p216), Melbourne

Queensland Museum (p283), Brisbane

National Museum of Australia (p174), Canberra

1956	1962	1969	1970s
The summer Olympics are held in Melbourne – the first time the games are held in the southern hemisphere. Australia places third in the medal tally behind the USSR and the USA.	Indigenous Australians gain the right to vote in federal elections – but they have to wait until 1967 to receive full citizenship, which happens overwhelm-ingly in a nationwide referendum.	Setting the political scene in Queensland for the next 21 years, Joh Bjelke-Petersen becomes premier. His political agenda was widely described as 'development at any price'.	Inflation, soaring inter-est rates and rising un-employment bring the golden postwar days to an end. As house prices skyrocket, home ownership becomes out of reach for many.

flocked from Britain and from non-English-speaking countries. They included Greeks, Italians, Slavs, Serbs, Croatians, Dutch, Poles, Turks and Lebanese among others. These 'new Australians' were expected to assimilate into a suburban stereotype known as 'the Australian way of life'.

This was the great era of the nuclear family in which Australians basked in the prosperity of a 'long boom'. Many migrants found jobs in manufacturing, where companies such as General Motors and Ford operated with generous tariff support. At the same time, there was growing world demand for Australia's primary products: metals, wool, meat and wheat. In time, Australia even became a major exporter of rice to Japan.

This era of growth and prosperity was dominated by Robert Menzies, the founder of the modern Liberal Party and Australia's longest-serving prime minister. Menzies had an avuncular charm, but he was also a vigilant opponent of communism. As the Cold War intensified, Australia and New Zealand entered a formal military alliance with the USA – the 1951 Anzus security pact. And when the USA hurled its righteous fury into a civil war in Vietnam, Menzies committed Australian forces to the conflict. The following year Menzies retired, leaving his successors a bitter legacy. The antiwar movement split Australia.

There was a feeling among artists, intellectuals and the young that Menzies' Australia had become a dull, complacent country, more in love with American popular culture and British high arts than with its own talents and stories. Australia, they said, had 'an inferiority complex'. In an atmosphere of youth rebellion and newfound nationalism, Australians began to embrace their own history and culture. The arts blossomed. Universities flourished. A distinctive Australian film industry made iconic movies, mostly funded by government subsidies.

At the same time, increasing numbers of white Australians believed that Indigenous Australians had endured a great wrong that needed to be put right – and from 1976 until 1992, Indigenous Australians won major victories in their struggle for land rights. Australia's imports from China and Japan increased – and the White Australia policy became an embarrassment. It was officially abolished in the early 1970s, and Australia became a leader in the campaign against the racist 'apartheid' policies of white South Africa.

By the 1970s, more than one million migrants had arrived from non-English-speaking countries, filling Australia with new languages, cultures, foods and ideas. At the same time, China and Japan began to outstrip Europe as Australia's major trading partners. As Asian immigration increased, Vietnamese communities became prominent in Sydney and Melbourne. In both those cities a new spirit of tolerance and diversity known as 'multiculturalism' became a particular source of pride.

Before Europeans arrived, Australia contained an estimated 750,000 Indigenous people, scattered among 600 to 700 Aboriginal nations. Among them, they spoke at least 250 Indigenous languages and dialects.

1972	1975	1992	2000
The Aboriginal Tent Embassy is erected on the lawns of Parliament House in Canberra. Over the next decades it serves as a reminder that Indigenous peoples have been denied sovereignty to their land.	The Great Barrier Reef Marine Park is created. It later becomes a World Heritage Site, which angers Queensland Premier Joh Bjelke-Petersen, who intended to explore for oil on the reef.	After 10 years in the courts, the landmark Mabo decision is delivered by the High Court, effectively recognising Indigenous land rights across the country.	Sydney hosts the summer Olympics: a triumph of spectacle and goodwill. Aboriginal runner Cathy Freeman lights the flame at the opening ceremony and wins gold in the 400m event.

MABO & TERRA NULLIUS

In May 1982 Eddie Mabo led a group of Torres Strait Islanders in a court action to have traditional title to their land on Mer (Murray Island) recognised. Their argument challenged the legal principle of *terra nullius* (literally, 'land belonging to no one') and demonstrated their unbroken relationship with the land over a period of thousands of years. In June 1992 the High Court found in favour of Eddie Mabo and the Islanders, rejecting the principle of *terra nullius* – this became known as the Mabo decision. The result has had far-reaching implications in Australia ever since, including the introduction of the *Native Title Act* in 1993.

Alan Murphy

New Challenges

Today Australia faces new challenges. In the 1970s the country began dismantling its protectionist scaffolding. New efficiency brought new prosperity. At the same time, wages and working conditions, which were once protected by an independent tribunal, became more vulnerable as egalitarianism gave way to competition. And after two centuries of development, the strain on the environment was starting to show – on water supplies, forests, soils, air quality and the oceans.

Under the conservative John Howard, Australia's second-longest-serving prime minister (1996–2007), the country grew closer than ever to the USA, joining the Americans in their war in Iraq. The government's harsh treatment of asylum seekers, its refusal to acknowledge the reality of climate change, its anti-union reforms and the prime minister's lack of empathy with Indigenous Australians dismayed more liberal-minded Australians. But Howard presided over a period of economic growth that emphasised the values of self-reliance and won him continuing support in middle Australia.

In 2007 Howard was defeated by the Labor Party's Kevin Rudd, an ex-diplomat who immediately issued a formal apology to Indigenous Australians for the injustices they had suffered over the past two centuries. Though it promised sweeping reforms in environment and education, the Rudd government found itself faced with a crisis when the world economy crashed in 2008; by June 2010 it had cost Rudd his position. New prime minister Julia Gillard, along with other world leaders, now faced three related challenges – climate change, a diminishing oil supply and a shrinking economy. These difficulties and dwindling party support for Gillard saw her ousted by a resurgent Rudd in 2013. Rudd's Labor subsequently lost the 2013 federal election, handing over the reins to Tony Abbott, at the helm of the right-wing Liberal–National Party coalition.

Reading Australian History

The Fatal Shore, Robert Hughes (1986)

History of Queensland, Raymond Evans (2007)

Burke's Soldier, Alan Attwood (2003)

Birth of Melbourne, Tim Flannery (2004)

2008	2009	2011	2013
On behalf of parliament, prime minister Kevin Rudd delivers a moving apology to Australia's Aboriginal people for laws and policies that 'inflicted profound grief, suffering and loss'.	A record-breaking heatwave generates the catastrophic 'Black Saturday' bushfires in Victoria. Over 170 people die; property damage totals around $1 billion.	Powerful floods inundate vast areas of Queensland, including Brisbane, killing 35 people and causing billions of dollars of damage. Cyclone Yasi follows weeks later, devastating parts of north Queensland.	Federal elections oust prime minister Kevin Rudd (a Queenslander) from office, after he was ousted as PM by Julia Gillard in 2009, then reinstated a few months before the 2013 election.

Climate Change & the Great Barrier Reef

By Terry Done & Paul Marshall

The Great Barrier Reef (GBR) is one of the world's most diverse coral-reef ecosystems. It is also the world's largest, an archipelagic edifice so vast that it can be viewed from space. But, like coral reefs all around the world, the GBR is facing some big environmental challenges.

The Reef

The reef's ecosystem includes the sea-floor habitats between the reefs, hundreds of continental islands and coral cays, and coastal beaches, headlands and estuaries. The 2900 reefs (ranging from less than 1km to 26km in length) that make up the GBR system support truly astounding biological diversity, with over 1500 species of fish, over 400 species of reef-building coral, and hundreds of species of mollusc (clams, snails, octopuses), echinoderm (sea stars, bêches-de-mer, sea urchins), sponge, worm, crustacean and seaweed. The GBR is also home to marine mammals (dolphins, whales, dugongs), dozens of species of bird, and six of the planet's seven species of sea turtle. The GBR's 900 or so islands range from ephemeral, unvegetated or sparsely vegetated sand cays to densely forested cays and continental islands.

At the Crossroads

These are tough times in which to be a coral reef. In the last three decades the GBR has endured more severe cyclones than in the whole of the last century (and more can be expected in the changed climate of the 21st century); recurrent outbreaks of coral-devouring crown-of-thorns starfish; two major coral-bleaching events caused by unusually hot water temperatures; and record-breaking floods that washed huge volumes of fresh water, sediments, fertilisers and other farm chemicals into the sea, triggering blooms of light-blocking plankton and disrupting the ecological relationships that keep coral reefs vibrant and resilient.

With all this going on, it's no surprise that a bit of web surfing could give the impression that the GBR is suffering more than other reefs around the world. But the plethora of information about risks to the reef simply reflects the amount of research, government investment and national commitment to tackling the challenge rather than pretending that everything is OK. It is an unfortunate reality that damaged reefs are easier to find now than they were 30 years ago. But the GBR is still one of the best places in the world to see coral reefs, especially if you have one of the hundreds of accredited tourism operators show you around. A recent study by the volunteer reef-monitoring group Reef Check Australia found that the amount of coral at 70% of dive sites monitored between 2001 and 2011 either remained the same or increased. Like every reef around the world, the GBR is in trouble – but in this case scientists, reef managers, coastal residents and even visitors are joining forces to help the reef through the challenges of the century ahead.

Eroding the Foundations

Overshadowing the future of coral reefs is climate change. Global warming is a serious problem for these iconic ecosystems, even though they have evolved in warm water, and thrive in clear, shallow seas along the equator and as far north and south as the Tropics of Cancer and Capricorn.

The main building blocks of coral reefs are 'stony' or 'hard' corals, and about 400 of the world's 700 or so species occur on the GBR. The secret of their success as reef builders – and their Achilles heel in a warming world – is symbiosis between the coral and tiny single-celled plants called zooxanthellae that live within their tissues. Thanks to bright sunlight and warm waters, the zooxanthellae are photosynthetic powerhouses that produce sugars and other carbohydrates needed by the coral (a colony of polyps) to grow its tissues, produce sperm and eggs, and build the colony's communal limestone skeletons. These skeletons – occupied by thousands of polyps and capable of growing several metres high and across in many different shapes – are an evolutionary bonanza in that they provide a rigid framework to orient the polyps to best utilise the sunlight and to use their stinging tentacles to catch passing pinhead-sized crustaceans that corals need nutritionally. Over thousands of years, the corals produce the reef framework, lagoon sands, coral beaches and coral islands that are the foundation for the entire coral-reef ecosystem. But now, as temperatures approach levels not seen for thousands of years, these foundations are at risk.

Changing Environments & Coral Bleaching

The idyllic symbiosis between coral and zooxanthellae evolved to perfectly match the environmental conditions of the past. But corals don't like change, and they are currently being hit with rates of change unparalleled for at least 400,000 years.

Bright sunlight and warm waters are required to support coral reefs, but it's a fine line between warm enough and too warm. Around the turn of the last century (mainly 1998 and 2002 for the GBR, as late as 2010 elsewhere), spikes in water temperatures caused the densely packed zooxanthellae to go into metabolic overdrive, producing free radicals and other chemicals that are toxic to the coral host. The corals' response was to expel their zooxanthellae, to rid themselves of the

THE GREAT BARRIER REEF MARINE PARK

Established in 1975, the 360,000-sq-km Great Barrier Reef Marine Park (about the same size as Italy) is one of the best-protected large marine systems on the planet. About 30% of the park is closed and the remainder is open to commercial and recreational fishing. There are a handful of coastal cities along the reef's southern half (notably Cairns, Townsville, Mackay and Gladstone), some with ports to service cattle and sugar export, and mineral export and import. Shipping lanes traverse its length and breadth, and ore carriers, cargo ships and cruise liners must use local marine pilots to reduce the risk of groundings and collisions.

Australia is internationally recognized for its leading management and protection of the Great Barrier Reef: the marine park is inscribed on the World Heritage List and has an envied program of management led by the Great Barrier Reef Marine Park Authority. But there is an aura of pessimism across the reef-science world, and the elephant in the room is climate change. For comprehensive information and educational tools at all levels, see www.gbrmpa.gov.au and www.coralwatch.org.

REEF GEOLOGY

Unlike mainland Australia, today's Great Barrier Reef (GBR) is relatively young, geologically speaking. Its foundations formed around 500,000 years ago, northern Australia was by then surrounded by tropical waters, as Australia drifted gradually northward from the massive South Pole land mass that was Gondwana. The GBR grew and receded several times in response to changing sea levels. Coastal plains that are now the sea floor were occupied by Indigenous Australians only 20,000 years ago, when the ice-age sea level was 130m lower than it is today. As the icecaps contracted, seas flooded continental shelves and stabilised near their current levels about 6000 to 8000 years ago. Corals settled atop high parts of the Queensland shelf, initiating the unique combination of biological and geological processes that have built the reef ecosystem we see today.

damaging toxins. Water temperatures must return to normal before the small numbers of remaining zooxanthellae start to reproduce and thus reinstate the corals' live-in food factory. But if the heat wave persists for more than a few weeks, the highly stressed corals succumb to disease and die, their skeletons soon becoming carpeted with fine, shaggy algal turfs. A 2013 study found that about 10% of GBR coral deaths over the last three decades followed these episodes, known as coral bleaching. And an important reality is that climate change isn't occurring in isolation: this study also highlighted that storm waves and outbreaks of the coral-eating crown-of-thorns starfish are big killers of corals (each around 40%). The effects are cumulative, and with projections of an increase in the severity of cyclones and the frequency of coral-bleaching events, we are likely to see more incidents of broad-acre coral death under a changing climate.

It takes one to two decades for a healthy coral reef to bounce back after being wiped out. So far, damaged GBR sites have shown remarkable resilience to damaging events, but the future might not be so rosy, as more frequent events driven by climate change repeatedly decimate reefs before they can fully recover. In other parts of the world, some reefs have suffered the added insults of decades of pollution and overfishing. By those means, former coral areas have become persistent landscapes of rubble and seaweed.

Worry Globally, Act Locally

Floating in the warming waters of the GBR, feeling the immensity of the reef and the problem that is climate change, it's easy to feel that action is futile. But science is showing that local efforts can make a difference. Reducing the amount of nutrients (from fertilisers) that enter GBR waters may increase the tolerance of corals to warmer seas, decrease crown-of-thorns outbreaks and help corals maintain dominance over seaweeds. State and federal governments are therefore working with farmers to improve practices and reduce the losses of chemicals and valuable soil into the reef, and their efforts have already begun to deliver encouraging results.

Science also suggests that those fishing practices that maintain abundant herbivorous fish on the reefs may also be vital in keeping corals in the ascendancy. Fishing is carefully regulated, making the GBR a rare example of a coral-reef system that maintains a healthy coral-seaweed balance while still delivering sustainable seafood. There is no commercial use of fish traps or spears, and responsible fishing practices adopted by most fishers in the GBR also mean that sharks are still a common sight (although more work needs to be done to secure the future of these important predators). Bottom trawling for prawns (shrimp) has been dramatically scaled back over recent decades, with associated improvements in the health of the soft-seabed communities between reef outcrops. Other issues on the radar for the GBR include ship groundings, dredging and port expansion.

The GBR tourism industry is a world leader in sustainable, eco-friendly and climate-friendly practices. Visiting the reef with an eco-accredited tourism business is not only a great way to experience the beauty and wonder of coral reefs; it's also one of the best things you can do to help the GBR, a small part of your fare directly supporting reef research and management.

Beyond the Corals...

Coral reefs are more than just corals, and our worries about a warming climate extend to the multitude of critters that call these ecosystems home. Green and loggerhead turtles bury their eggs at the back of coral-island beaches, the warm sand incubating the developing embryos. The sex of the hatchlings is determined by the temperature the eggs experience: cooler temperatures cause eggs to develop into male hatchlings; warmer eggs become females. Turtle researchers are worried that a warmer world could create an imbalance in the sex ratio, putting extra strain on already depleted turtle populations. For turtles the risks don't stop there. Rising sea levels (predictions are as much as 1.1m higher by the end of this century) put many nesting areas at greater risk of deadly flooding. Turtles will need to find higher ground for nesting, but in many coastal areas natural barriers or urban development limit their options.

For coral-reef fish, sea-level change might not be a big issue, but changes in ocean temperature have the potential to affect the timing and success of important processes such as reproduction. There is also growing evidence that fish might be prone to the effects of ocean acidification, which is the direct result of increased absorption of CO_2 by the world's seas. The upside to this process is that it has kept the atmosphere from warming even faster. But the pH of seawater is important to a wide range of chemical and biological processes, including the ability of fish to find their home reef and to avoid predators.

Climate change is also altering ocean currents, making life difficult for animals that rely on the timing and location of water movements for their survival. Scientists have already observed mass deaths of seabird chicks on remote islands as a result of their parents having to travel too far to find the schools of fish they need to feed their flightless young. Plankton, too, are vulnerable to changing chemistry and currents, with potential flow-on effects through entire food chains. Corals don't escape the effects of ocean acidification, either. More-acidic water makes it more

GET INVOLVED

You can help the reef in practical ways during your visit. You can report sightings of important reef creatures or send in information about any problems you encounter directly to the Great Barrier Reef Marine Park Authority by contributing to the Eye on the Reef Program (go to www.gbrmpa.gov.au or get the free Eye on the Reef smartphone app). If you're around for long enough (or time your visit right), you could undertake some training and become a Reef Check volunteer (see www.reefcheckaustralia.org). If turtles are your passion, see www.seaturtlefoundation.org for opportunities to volunteer with them. If you're a resident, look out for www.seagrasswatch.org, and if you like fishing, combine your fishing with research at www.info-fish.net.

difficult for corals to build their skeletons, leading to slower growth or more fragile structures.

The Future

In the best traditions of good science, its practitioners are a sceptical lot, but you won't find a credible coral-reef expert who will say that climate change isn't a serious issue. Where scientists may differ is about the rate at which and the extent to which reefs and their mind-boggling biodiversity may adjust or adapt.

You might have heard it said that 'the climate has changed before and we still have corals'. While this has a grain of truth, the reality is that previous episodes of rapid climate change caused mass extinctions that took millions of years to get over. Playing on the Australian tendency to believe that 'she'll be right, mate', those who deny that climate change is happening have tried to portray the science as uncertain, biased and even wrong. But the solid body of science indicates that climate change is real, it is already under way, and coral reefs are right in the firing line. Certainly we should energetically debate the best ways of tackling this problem, but there can be no room for equivocation: we have to act with urgency and decisiveness at local, national and global levels if we are to give coral reefs a fighting chance of providing future generations with the wonderful experiences we can still enjoy.

If humans continue to pollute the atmosphere with greenhouse gases at present rates, we will likely overtax any realistic capacity of coral-reef ecosystems to cope. All around the world, coral reefs are proving themselves to be the 'canary in the coalmine' of climate change. The worldwide reduction in reef assets that occurred when heat waves swept equatorial regions in 1998 was unprecedented in scale, providing a wake-up call to reef scientists, reef managers and the community at large about what the future holds. Like polar zones, coral reefs are sentinel systems that will continue to show us the impacts of climate change on the natural world (and the millions of humans who depend on these ecosystems). But the ending to the climate-change story is still being written. Concerted action can yet avoid the worst-case scenario for reefs. And when visitors and residents choose to avoid and reduce sources of pressure on corals and other reef creatures, they buy coral reefs important time to adapt – and, hopefully, to cope – until society takes the necessary action to control its impacts on the climate.

Food & Wine

Australians once proudly survived on a diet of 'meat and three veg'. Fine fare was a Sunday roast; lasagne was exotic. Fortunately, the country's cuisine has evolved, and these days Australian gastronomy is keen to break rules, backed up by top chefs, world-renowned wines, excellent coffee and a burgeoning craft-beer scene. All along the East Coast you'll find incredible seafood, from humble fish-and-chippers to fine-dining restaurants overlooking the ocean, while fantastic food markets and hip cafe culture make for top-notch culinary exploring.

Mod Oz (Modern Australian)

The phrase Modern Australian (Mod Oz) has been coined to classify contemporary Australian cuisine: a melange of East and West; a swirl of Atlantic and Pacific Rim; a flourish of authentic French and Italian.

Immigration has been the key to this culinary concoction. An influx of immigrants since WWII, from Europe, Asia, the Middle East and Africa, introduced new ingredients and new ways to use staples. Vietnamese, Japanese, Fijian – no matter where it's from, there are expat communities and interested locals keen to cook and eat it. You'll find Jamaicans using Scotch bonnet peppers and Tunisians making tajine.

As the Australian appetite for diversity and invention grows, so does the food culture surrounding it. Cookbooks and foodie magazines are best-sellers and Australian celebrity chefs – highly sought overseas – reflect Australia's multiculturalism in their backgrounds and dishes.

If all this sounds overwhelming, never fear. The range of food in Australia is a true asset. You'll find that dishes are characterised by bold and interesting flavours and fresh ingredients. All palates are catered for along the East Coast: the chilli-metre spans gentle to extreme, seafood is plentiful, meats are full flavoured, and vegetarian needs are considered (especially in the cities). For prices ranges, see p511.

Local Delicacies

Australia's size and diverse climate – from the tropical north to the temperate south – mean that there's an enormous variety of produce on offer.

Seafood connoisseurs prize Sydney rock oysters and scallops from Queensland. Rock lobsters (aka crayfish) are fantastic and fantastically expensive; mud crabs, despite the name, are a sweet treat. Another odd-sounding delicacy is 'bugs' – like shovel-nosed lobsters without a lobster's price tag; try the Balmain and Moreton Bay varieties. Aussie prawns are also superb, particularly the school prawns or the eastern king (Yamba) prawns found along northern New South Wales.

Aussies love their seafood, but they've not lost their yen for a hefty chunk of steak. Rockhampton is the beef capital of Australia, while lamb from Victoria's lush Gippsland is also highly prized.

Queensland's fertile fields are dappled with banana and mango plantations, orchards and vast seas of sugar cane. In summer, mangoes are so plentiful that Queenslanders actually get sick of them. The macadamia, a buttery native nut, grows throughout southeastern Queensland – you'll

Vegemite: you'll either love it or hate it. For reference, Barack Obama diplomatically called it 'horrible'. It's certainly an acquired taste, but Australians consume more than 22 million jars of the stuff each year.

find them tossed in salads, crushed in ice cream and petrified in sticky cakes.

There's a small but brilliant farmhouse-cheese movement in Australia, hampered by the fact that all the milk must be pasteurised. Despite this, the results can be spectacular. Keep an eye out for goat's cheese from Gympie and anything from the boutiquey Kenilworth Country Foods (p353) and **Witches Chase Cheese Company** (www.witcheschasecheese. com.au; 165 Long Rd, Eagle Heights; ⊙10am-4pm).

Coffee Culture

Coffee has become an Australian addiction. There are Italian-style espresso machines in every cafe, boutique roasters are all the rage and, in urban areas, the qualified barista is ever-present (there are even barista-staffed cafes attached to petrol stations). Sydney and Melbourne have given rise to a whole generation of coffee snobs, the two cities duking it out for bragging rights as Australia's coffee capital. The cafe scene in Melbourne is particularly artsy; the best way to immerse yourself in it is by wandering the city centre's cafe-lined laneways. Beyond the big cities, you'll be able to find a decent coffee in most towns, but you might struggle in rural areas.

Foodie Touring Hot Spots

The vine-covered Hunter Valley produces far more than just wine. Among the rolling hillsides, you'll find farmhouse cheeses, smoked fish and meats, seasonal produce (figs, citrus, peaches, avocados), Belgian-style chocolate, boutique beer, olives and much more. For a memorable assemble-your-own picnic, it doesn't get much better than this.

In the Atherton Tableland in north Queensland, you can get a first-hand look at the nation's best coffee-growing plantations. Even better, you'll get to sample the good stuff, plus coffee liqueur and dark chocolate–coated coffee beans.

Further north, the Daintree offers gustatory temptations of a different sort. You can sample delectable ice cream made from freshly picked fruits grown in the surrounding orchards, or feast on tropical fruit grown at the Cape Trib Exotic Fruit Farm (p477).

Wine Country

Dating from the 1820s, the **Hunter Valley** (a few hours north of Sydney) is Australia's oldest wine region. The Hunter is home to over 120 wineries: a mix of boutique, family-run outfits and large-scale commercial vintners. The Lower Hunter is known for shiraz and unwooded semillon. Upper Hunter wineries specialise in cabernet sauvignon and shiraz, with forays into verdelho and chardonnay. The area around Canberra also sustains a growing number of excellent wineries.

To the south, Victoria has more than 500 wineries. Just northeast of Melbourne, the **Yarra Valley** is a patchwork of vines producing fine pinot noir, peachy chardonnay and crisp sparkling. Further south, the hills

---

The Cook's Companion by Stephanie Alexander is the bible of Australian cooking, with nearly 1000 recipes across 12 chapters, spicing things up with touches of folklore and literary quotations.

Foodie Websites

www.urbanspoon. com: restaurant reviews country-wide

grabyourfork. blogspot.com: gastronomic journeys around Sydney

www.melbournegastronome. com: in-depth restaurant and bar reviews

www.eatingbrisbane.com: the Bris-vegas eating scene

www.lifestylefood. com.au Thousands of recipes, cooking videos, tips and techniques

---

THE AUSSIE BARBECUE

The iconic Australian barbecue (BBQ or barbie) is a near-mandatory cultural experience. In summer locals invite their mates around at dinnertime and fire up the barbie, grilling burgers, sausages (snags), steaks, seafood, and vegie, meat or seafood skewers (if you're invited, bring some meat and cold beer). Year-round the BBQ is wheeled out at weekends for quick-fire lunches. There are also coin-operated and free BBQs in parks around the country – a terrific, traveller-friendly option.

BYO

If a restaurant is 'BYO', it means you can bring your own alcohol. If it also sells alcohol, you can usually only bring your own bottled wine (no beer, no cask wine) and a 'corkage' charge is added to your bill. The cost is either per person or per bottle, and can be up to $20 per bottle in fine-dining places.

and valleys of the **Mornington Peninsula** and **Bellarine Peninsula** produce beautiful early-ripening pinot noir, subtle, honeyed chardonnay, pinot gris and pinot grigio.

There's even a wine region in Queensland – the **Granite Belt**, two hours southwest of Brisbane – which has been carving out a name for itself in recent years. The neighbouring towns of Stanthorpe and Ballandean are gateways to this understated region.

Most wineries are open to visitors, with free tastings, though some keep limited hours (opening only on weekends).

Beer, Breweries & Bundaberg

As the Australian public develops a more sophisticated palate, local beers are rising to the occasion, with a growing wealth of microbrews available. The default options (Carlton, VB, XXXX and Tooheys) are passable if you're dry on a hot day, but for something more flavourful, look for some of the following labels:

Blue Sky Brewery (www.blueskybrewery.com.au) Hits from this award-winning Cairns brewery include a crisp lager (the FNQ) and a traditional Czech-style Pilsner.

Burkes Brewing Company Best known for its Hemp Premium Ale, a sweet golden beer brewed (legally, apparently) through hemp filters. From Brisbane.

James Squire (www.maltshovel.com.au) A Sydney brewer with wide distribution and a range of craft beers; the IPA is a winner.

Mountain Goat (www.goatbeer.com.au) Brewed in the Melbourne suburb of Richmond (not particularly mountainous); the English-style Hightale Ale makes a perfect pint.

Mt Tamborine Brewery (www.mtbeer.com) Producing some of Queensland's best microbrews: top picks include Belgian-style ale, a hops-loving IPA and a rich imperial stout.

Piss (www.pi55.com) Once you're past the puns, it's an excellent, rich lager. From Victoria.

St Arnou (www.st-arnou.com.au) A micro-micro brewery in NSW; look for the excellent Belgian-style white beer, St Cloud.

You'll also encounter Bundaberg Rum (www.bundabergrum.com.au) almost everywhere on the East Coast – a fecund potion from Bundaberg in Queensland, bottles of which are incongruously emblazoned with a polar bear.

Farmers Markets

Local farmers markets are terrific places to sample the culinary riches of the region, support local growers and enjoy the congenial air (live music, friendly banter, free food sampling). You'll find fruit, vegies, seafood, nuts, meat, bread and pastries, liqueurs, wine, coffee and much more in markets all along the East Coast. For locations, check out the **Australian Farmers Market Association** (www.farmersmarkets.org.au) website.

The *Australian Wine Annual* by Jeremy Oliver is a must-read. Oliver profiles more than 300 wineries, with notes on thousands of wines. His picks – wine of the year, top 100 and best under $20 – make a handy cheat-sheet when selecting a bottle.

Top Food Markets

Sydney Fish Market (p61) A big fish in a big pond: trading second only to Tokyo.

Prahran Market (p217) One of Melbourne's finest produce markets.

Noosa Farmers Market (www.noosafarmersmarket.com.au) A splendid Sunday market that brings a huge number of vendors.

Byron Farmers Market (p163) A community treasure.

Jan Power's Farmers Market (p307) Riverside in Brisbane.

Sport

Whether they're filling stadiums, glued to the big screen at the pub or on the couch in front of the TV, Australians invest heavily in sport – both fiscally and emotionally. The federal government kicks in more than $300 million every year – enough cash for the nation to hold its own against formidable international sporting opponents. Despite slipping to 10th spot on the 2012 London Olympics medal tally, Australia is looking forward to redemption at the 2016 Rio Olympics.

Sporting Obsessions

All three East Coast states can stake legitimate claims to the title of Australia's sporting mecca (even Canberra has pro teams and more than its fair share of sports-mad residents). The object of passion, however, varies from state to state. In New South Wales and Queensland it's the gladiatorial arena of rugby league, while down south, Victoria is a smouldering cauldron of Australian rules football. Cricket unifies everyone and is a nationwide obsession in summer.

But these sports are hardly the only games in town. Australians love all sport, from basketball and car racing (the Aussie Formula One Grand Prix happens in Melbourne every March) to tennis, soccer, horse racing, netball, surfing, even bull-riding – when competition is afoot, the roaring crowds will appear (case in point: Brisbane's Australia Day Cockroach Races attract upwards of 7000 cheering fans each year).

Australian Rules Football

Australia's most attended sport, and one of the two most watched, is Australian Rules football (Aussie Rules). While traditionally embedded in the Victorian culture and identity, the **Australian Football League** (AFL; www.afl.com.au) has expanded its popularity across the country, including rugby-dominated NSW and Queensland. Long kicks, high marks and brutal collisions whip crowds into frenzies and the roar of 50,000-plus fans yelling 'Baaall!!!' upsets dogs in backyards for miles around.

'Footy' in Australia can mean a number of things: in NSW and Queensland it's usually rugby league, but the term is also used for Australian rules football, rugby union and soccer.

During the season (March to September) Australians go footy-mad, entering tipping competitions, discussing groin and hamstring strains and savouring the latest in loutish behaviour (on and off the field). It all culminates on the last Saturday in September, when Melbourne hosts the AFL grand final – the whole city goes berserk. Around 100,000 fans pack into the Melbourne Cricket Ground and millions more watch on TV.

Some teams – notably Essendon, Richmond and Port Adelaide – run Indigenous programs to promote the sport in Aboriginal communities across the country, and all teams recruit Indigenous players, praising their unique vision (kicking into a space for a teammate to run into) and skills.

Rugby

While Melburnians refuse to acknowledge it (or do so with a scowl akin to that directed at an unfaithful spouse), there are other versions of 'footy' in Australia. The **National Rugby League** (NRL; www.nrl.com) is the most popular sporting competition north of the Murray River. The competition, which parallels the Aussie Rules season from March to September, features 16 teams – 10 from NSW, three from Queensland, and one each from ACT, New Zealand and Victoria. To witness an NRL game is to appreciate all of Newton's laws of motion – bone-crunching!

One of the most anticipated events in the league calendar (apart from the grand final in September) is the **State of Origin** series held in June or July, when all-star players from Queensland take on their counterparts from NSW in explosive state-against-state combat. At last count, NSW had suffered a long run of humiliating defeats to their Queensland arch-rivals, the 'Maroons' (eight losses in a row from 2006 to 2013).

Rugby union, run by **Australian Rugby Union** (www.rugby.com.au), is almost as popular as rugby league. Historically, union was an amateur sport played by upper-class blokes from prestigious British public-school systems, while league was associated with working-class communities of northern England. The ideological divide carried over to Australia, where it has remained to a large degree over the past century.

The national union team, the Wallabies, won the Rugby World Cup in 1991 and 1999 and was runner-up in 2003, but it hasn't made the final since. In between world cups, annual **Bledisloe Cup** matches between Australia and arch-rivals New Zealand (the world-beating 'All Blacks') draw huge crowds. Bledisloe matches form part of the annual southern-hemisphere **Rugby Championship** (www.sanzarrugby.com) played between Australia, New Zealand, South Africa and Argentina.

Australia, South Africa and New Zealand also field rugby union teams in the super-popular **Super 15s** (www.superxv.com) competition, which includes five Australian teams: the Waratahs (Sydney), the Reds (Brisbane), the Brumbies (Australian Capital Territory), the Force (Perth) and the Rebels (Melbourne).

Russell Crowe spent part of his childhood in Sydney. Today he's part-owner of the Rabbitohs, the 100-year-old South Sydney team in the National Rugby League.

Cricket

The Aussies dominated both Test and one-day cricket for much of the noughties, holding the No 1 world ranking for most of the decade. But the subsequent retirement of once-in-a-lifetime players like Shane Warne and Ricky Ponting has sent the team into an extended 'rebuilding' phase. Series losses in 2009, 2011 and 2013 to arch-enemies England caused nationwide misery, but redemption came in 2014 when Australia demoralised England 5-0 – things are looking up! This biennial showdown is known as 'The Ashes', the trophy for which is a tiny terracotta urn containing the ashen remnants of an 1882 cricket bail (the perfect Australian BBQ conversation opener: ask a local what a 'bail' is).

It's said by some cynics that more Australians know cricket legend Don Bradman's Test batting average (99.94) than know the year Captain Cook first bobbed around the coast (1770).

FOOTY LINGO

Baaall! Short for 'Holding the ball!' – requesting that the umpire penalise a player; a lamentable position for a player to be caught in.

Carn! 'Come on', as in 'Carn the Blues!'

Drop kick Term of verbal abuse (not a kicking technique).

Had a blinder Played particularly well.

Take a screamer To mark (catch) the ball spectacularly (most spectacularly at altitude atop another player's shoulders).

White maggots Umpires (traditionally clad in white).

Note that saying you're 'rooting' for a team will always elicit a smile from Australians (if you're 'rooting' in Australia you're most probably having sex). To 'barrack for', on the other hand, means to cheer for your team.

SURF'S UP!

Australia has been synonymous with surfing ever since the Beach Boys enthused about 'Australia's Narrabeen', one of Sydney's northern beaches, in *Surfin' USA*. Other East Coast surfing hot spots such as Bells Beach, the Pass at Byron Bay, and Burleigh Heads on the Gold Coast resonate with international surfers. Iron man and surf-lifesaving competitions are also held on beaches around the country, attracting dedicated fans to the sand.

Quite a few Australian surfers have attained world-champion status. Legendary names include Mark Richards, Tom Carroll, 2012 champ Joel Parkinson, 2013 champ Mick Fanning, Wendy Botha, seven-time champion Layne Beachley and 2012 champ (and five-time winner) Stephanie Gilmore.

Despite the Australian cricket team's bad rep for sledging (verbally dressing down one's opponent), cricket is still a gentleman's game. Take the time to watch a match if you never have – such tactical cut-and-thrust, such nuance, such grace... For current info, see www.espncricinfo.com.

Soccer

Australia's national soccer team, the Socceroos, qualified for the 2006 and 2010 World Cups after a long history of almost-but-not-quite getting there. The Socceroos have also qualified for the 2014 World Cup in Brazil – national pride in the team is at an all-time high! The national **A-League** (www.a-league.com.au) has enjoyed increased popularity in recent years, successfully luring a few big-name international players to bolster the home-grown talent pool.

Tennis

Every January in Melbourne, the **Australian Open** (www.australian open.com) attracts more people to Australia than any other sporting event. The men's competition was last won by an Australian, Mark Edmondson, back in 1976 – and while Lleyton Hewitt has been Australia's great hope for the last decade, the former world No 1's best playing days are behind him (but he looks set for a career as a commentator). In the women's game, Australian Sam Stosur won the US Open in 2011 and has been hovering around the top-10 player rankings ever since.

The first Australian cricket team to tour England was 100% Victorian Aboriginal – in 1868. The subsequent 'whiteness' of the sport in Australia meant that this achievement was unheralded until quite recently.

Swimming

Girt by sea and pockmarked with pools: Australians can swim. Australia's greatest female swimmer, Dawn Fraser, won the 100m freestyle gold at three successive Olympics (1956–64), plus the 4 x 100m freestyle relay in 1956. Australia's greatest male swimmer, Ian Thorpe (aka Thorpie or the Thorpedo), retired in 2006 aged 24 with five Olympic golds swinging from his neck. In early 2011, Thorpe announced his comeback, his eye fixed on the 2012 London Olympics – but he failed to make the team in the trials, and clambered out of the pool again to finish his autobiography.

Horse Racing

Australian's love to bet on the 'nags' – in fact, betting on horse racing is so mainstream and accessible that it's almost a national hobby!

Australia's biggest race – the 'race that stops a nation' – is the **Melbourne Cup** (www.racingvictoria.net.au), which occurs on the first Tuesday in November. The most famous Melbourne Cup winner was the New Zealand–born Phar Lap, who won in 1930 before dying of a mystery illness (suspected arsenic poisoning) in America. Phar Lap is now a prize exhibit in the Melbourne Museum. The British-bred (but Australian trained) Makybe Diva is a recent star, winning three cups in a row before retiring in 2005.

Survival Guide

Deadly & Dangerous

If you're the pessimistic type, you might choose to focus on the things that can bite, sting, burn, freeze or drown you in Australia. But chances are the worst you'll encounter are a few pesky flies and mosquitoes. Splash on some insect repellent and boldly venture forth!

OUT & ABOUT

At the Beach

Around 80 people per year drown on Australia's beaches, where pounding surf and rips (strong currents) can create serious hazards. If you happen to get caught in a rip and are being taken out to sea, swim parallel to the shore until you're out of the rip, then head for the beach – *don't* try to swim back against the rip; you'll only tire yourself.

Bushfires

Bushfires happen regularly across Australia. In hot, dry and windy weather and on total-fire-ban days, be extremely careful with naked flames (including cigarette butts) and don't use camping stoves, campfires or BBQs. Bushwalkers should delay trips until things cool down. If you're out in the bush and you see smoke, take it seriously: find the nearest open space (downhill if possible). Forested ridges are danger-ous places to be. Always heed the advice of authorities.

Coral Cuts

Coral can be extremely sharp; you can cut yourself by merely brushing against the stuff. Thoroughly clean cuts and douse with antiseptic to avoid infection.

Heat

Very hot weather is common in Australia and can lead to heat exhaustion or more severe heatstroke (resulting from extreme fluid depletion). When arriving from a temperate or cold climate, remember that it takes two weeks to acclimatise.

Unprepared travellers die from dehydration each year in remote Australia. Always carry sufficient water for any trip (driving or hiking), and let someone know where you're going and when you expect to arrive. Carry communications equipment, and if in trouble, stay with your vehicle rather than walking for help.

Sun Exposure

Australia has one of the highest rates of skin cancer in the world. Monitor exposure to sunlight closely: ultraviolet (UV) exposure is greatest between 10am and 4pm, so avoid skin exposure during these times. Wear a wide-brimmed hat and a long-sleeved shirt with a collar, and always use 30+ sunscreen, applied 30 minutes before exposure, and repeated regularly, to minimise sun damage.

THINGS THAT BITE & STING

Crocodiles

The risk of crocodile attack in tropical Far North Queensland is real, but it is entirely avoidable with common sense. Crocs aren't a risk in Victoria, New South Wales or southern Queensland (south of Rockhampton). 'Salties' are estuarine crocodiles that can grow to 7m. They inhabit coastal waters and are mostly seen in the tidal reaches of rivers, though on occasion they're spotted on beaches and in freshwater lagoons. Always heed advice, such as warning signs. Don't assume it's safe to swim if there are no signs: if you're not sure, don't swim.

If you're away from popular beaches anywhere north of Mackay, avoid swimming in rivers, waterholes and estuaries. Don't clean fish or prepare food near the water, and camp at least 50m away from waterways. Crocodiles are particularly mobile and dangerous around breeding season (October to March).

Jellyfish

Jellyfish – including the potentially deadly box jellyfish and Irukandji – occur in Australia's tropical waters. It's unwise to swim north of Agnes Water between November and May unless there's a stinger net. 'Stinger suits' (full-body Lycra swimsuits) prevent stinging, as do wetsuits. Swimming and snorkelling are usually safe around Queensland's reef islands throughout the year; however, the rare (and tiny) Irukandji has been recorded on the outer reef and islands.

Wash stings with vinegar to prevent further discharge of remaining stinging cells, then rapidly transfer the victim to a hospital. Don't attempt to remove the jellyfish tentacles.

Marine Animals

Marine spikes and poisonous spines – including those on sea urchins, stingrays, scorpion fish and stonefish – can cause severe local pain. If this occurs, immediately immerse the affected area in hot water (as hot as can be tolerated) and seek medical care.

Blue-ringed octopuses and Barrier Reef cone shells can be fatal – don't pick them up. If someone is stung, apply a pressure bandage, monitor breathing and conduct mouth-to-mouth resuscitation if breathing stops. Seek immediate medical care.

Mosquitoes

'Mozzies' can be a problem just about anywhere in Australia. Malaria isn't present, although dengue fever is a danger in northern Queensland, particularly during the wet season (November to April). Most people recover in a few days, but more severe forms of the disease can occur. To minimise bites:

→ Wear loose, long-sleeved clothing.

→ Apply repellent with minimum 30% DEET on exposed skin.

→ Use mosquito coils.

→ Sleep under fast-spinning ceiling fans.

Sharks

Despite extensive media coverage, the risk of shark attack in Australia is no greater than in other countries with extensive coastlines. Check with surf-lifesaving groups about local risks.

Snakes

There's no denying it: Australia has plenty of venomous snakes. Most common are brown and tiger snakes, but few species are aggressive: unless you're messing around with or accidentally standing on one, you're unlikely to be bitten. About 80% of bites occur on the lower limbs: wear protective clothing (such as gaiters) when bushwalking. If bitten, apply an elastic bandage (or improvise with a T-shirt). Wrap firmly around the entire limb – but not so tightly that you cut off the circulation – and immobilise with a splint or sling; then seek medical attention. Don't use a tourniquet, and don't try to suck out the poison.

Spiders

Australia has poisonous spiders, although deaths are extremely rare. Common species:

→ Funnel-web: a deadly spider found in New South Wales (including Sydney). Apply pressure to bites and immobilise before transferring to hospital.

→ Redback: live throughout Australia. Bites cause increasing pain followed by profuse sweating. Apply ice and transfer to hospital.

→ Whitetail: blamed for causing slow-healing ulcers. If bitten, clean bite and seek medical assistance.

→ Huntsman: a disturbingly large spider that's harmless, though seeing one can affect your blood pressure (and/or underpants).

Ticks

The common bush tick (found all along the East Coast) can be dangerous if lodged in the skin and undetected. Check your body (and those of children and dogs) every night if walking in tick-prone areas. Remove by dousing the tick with methylated spirits or kerosene and levering it out intact. See a doctor if bites become infected (tick typhus cases have been reported here).

MAINTAINING PERSPECTIVE

Australia's plethora of poisonous and biting critters is impressive, but don't let it put you off. There's approximately one shark-attack and one croc-attack fatality per year here. Blue-ringed-octopus deaths are rarer – only two in the last century. Jellyfish do better – about two deaths annually – but you're still more than 100 times more likely to drown. Spiders haven't killed anyone in the last 20 years. Snake bites kill one or two people per year, as do bee stings, but you're about a thousand times more likely to perish on the nation's roads.

Directory A–Z

Accommodation

The East Coast is a route that is well trodden with plenty of accommodation options to suit all budgets: hotels, motels, guesthouses, B&Bs, hostels, pubs and caravan parks. There are also less conventional possibilities, such as farmstays, house-boats and yachts.

Reviews are listed in budget order and then by preference, from most to least desirable.

B&Bs

Bed-and-breakfast (B&B) options include restored miners cottages, converted barns, rambling old houses, upmarket country manors, beachside bungalows and simple bedrooms in family homes. Tariffs are typically in the midrange bracket but can be much higher.

Tourist offices can usually give you a list of options. Good online information:

B&B and Farmstay Far North Queensland (www. bnbnq.com.au)

B&B and Farmstay NSW & ACT (www.bedandbreak-fastnsw.com.au)

Hosted Accommodation Australia (www.austral-ianbedandbreakfast.com.au)

OZ Bed and Breakfast (www.ozbedandbreakfast.com)

Camping & Caravanning

If you want to explore the East Coast on a shoestring, camping is the way to go.

PRICES

Camping in national parks can cost from nothing to $15 per person – nights spent around a campfire under the stars are unforgettable. Tent sites at private camping and caravan parks cost around $20 to $30 per couple per night (slightly more with electricity). Many of these outfits also hire out cabins with kitchenettes, running from $60 to $170 per night sleeping one to six people. Note that all camping and cabin rates quoted in reviews are for two people.

NATIONAL PARKS

National parks and their camping areas are admin-istered state by state, with bookings often handled online.

New South Wales (www. environment.nsw.gov.au/na-tionalparks)

Queensland (www.nprsr.qld. gov.au)

Victoria (www.parkweb.vic. gov.au)

MAJOR CHAINS

If you intend to do a lot of caravanning or camping, joining a major chain will save you some money:

Big 4 (www.big4.com.au)

Discovery Holiday Parks (www.discoveryholidayparks. com.au)

Top Tourist Parks (www. toptouristparks.com.au)

Farmstays

Many coastal and hinterland farms offer a bed for the night and the chance to see rural Australia at work. At some you sit back and watch other people raise a sweat, while others like to get you involved in day-to-day activities. Check out **B&B Australia** (www.babs.com.au) (under family holidays/farm-stays) and **Willing Workers on Organic Farms** (WWOOF; www.wwoof.com.au). Regional and town tourist offices should also be able to tell you what's available in their area.

Hostels

Backpackers are highly social, low-cost fixtures on the East Coast. There are staggering numbers of them, ranging from family-run

BOOK YOUR STAY ONLINE

For more accommodation reviews by Lonely Planet authors, check out http://lonelyplanet.com/hotels/. You'll find independent reviews, as well as recommen-dations on the best places to stay. Best of all, you can book online.

SLEEPING PRICE RANGES

The following price indicators refer to a double room with bathroom in high season (December to February down south, June to September up north):

$ less than $100

$$ $100–200

$$$ more than $200

Expect to pay $20 to $50 more in expensive areas (notably Sydney) and during school and public holidays.

places in converted houses to huge, custom-built resorts replete with bars, nightclubs and party propensity. Standards range from outstanding to awful, and management from friendly to scary.

Dorm beds typically cost $25 to $35, with single rooms sometimes available (around $60) and doubles costing $70 to $100.

The following are useful organisations with annual memberships (around $45) that yield lodging and other discounts:

Base Backpackers (www. stayatbase.com)

Nomads (www.nomadsworld. com)

VIP Backpackers (www. vipbackpackers.com)

YHA (www.yha.com.au)

Hotels

Hotels along the East Coast are generally of the business or luxury-chain variety (midrange to top end): comfortable, anonymous, mod con–filled rooms in multistorey blocks. For these hotels we quote 'rack rates' (official advertised rates – usually more than $150 a night), though significant discounts can be offered when business is quiet.

Motels

Drive-up motels offer comfortable midrange accommodation and are found all over the East Coast. They rarely offer a cheaper rate for singles, so are better value for couples or groups of three. You'll mostly pay between $100 and $150 for a simple room with kettle, fridge, TV, air-con and bathroom.

Pubs

Hotels along the East Coast – the ones that serve beer – are commonly known as pubs (from the term 'public house'). Generally, rooms are small and weathered, with a long amble down the hall to the bathroom. They're usually central and cheap – singles/ doubles with shared facilities cost from $50/80, more if you want a private bathroom – but if you're a light sleeper, avoid booking a room above the bar and check whether a band is playing downstairs that night.

Rental Accommodation

If you're on the East Coast for a while, then a rental property or room in a shared flat or house will be an economical option. Delve into the classified-advertisement sections of the daily newspapers; Wednesday and Saturday are usually the best days. Noticeboards in universities, hostels, bookshops and cafes are also useful.

RESOURCES

City Hobo (www.cityhobo. com) Matches your personality with your ideal big-city suburb.

Couch Surfing (www.couch-surfing.com) Connects spare couches with new friends.

Flatmate Finders (www.flat-matefinders.com.au) Long-term share-accommodation listings.

Stayz (www.stayz.com.au) Holiday rentals.

Useful websites for discounted or last-minute accommodation include the following:

Wotif.com (www.wotif.com.au)

Lastminute.com (www. au.lastminute.com)

Quickbeds.com (www. quickbeds.com.au)

Children

If you can survive the long-haul distances, travelling Australia's East Coast with the kids can be a real delight. There's oodles of interesting stuff to see and do, both indoors and outdoors.

Practicalities

Accommodation Most motels supply cots; many also have playgrounds and swimming pools, as well as child-minding services. Many B&Bs, on the other hand, market themselves as child-free sanctuaries.

Change Rooms & Breastfeeding All cities and major towns have public rooms where parents can breastfeed or change nappies (diapers). Most Australians have a relaxed attitude about breastfeeding or nappy changing in public.

Child Care If you want to leave Junior behind for a few hours, licensed child-care agencies have places set aside for casual care (check the *Yellow Pages*), and many of the larger hotels have contacts.

Child Safety Seats Under newish national laws, safety restraints are compulsory for all children up to seven years old. Major hire-car companies will supply and fit child safety seats, charging a one-off fee of around $25. Phone taxi companies in advance to organise child safety seats.

Concessions Discounts for children apply for such things as accommodation, admission fees, and air, bus and train transport, with some discounts as high as 50% of the adult rate. However, the definition of 'child' can vary from under 12 to under 18 years.

Eating Out Many cafes and restaurants offer kids' meals, or will provide small serves from the main menu. Some also supply high chairs.

PRACTICALITIES

Currency The Australian dollar comprises 100 cents. There are 5c, 10c, 20c, 50c, $1 and $2 coins, and $5, $10, $20, $50 and $100 notes.

DVDs Australian DVDs are encoded for region 4, which includes Mexico, South America, Central America, New Zealand, the Pacific and the Caribbean.

Newspapers Leaf through the daily *Sydney Morning Herald*, Melbourne's *Age*, Brisbane's *Courier-Mail* or the national *Australian* newspapers.

Radio Tune in to ABC radio; at www.abc.net.au/radio.

Smoking Banned on public transport, in pubs, bars and eateries, and in some public outdoor spaces.

TV The main free-to-air TV channels are the government-sponsored ABC, multicultural SBS and the three commercial networks – Seven, Nine and Ten – plus numerous additional channels from these main players.

Weights and measures Australia uses the metric system.

Health Care Australia has high-standard medical services and facilities, and items such as baby formula and disposable nappies are widely available.

Resources Lonely Planet's *Travel with Children* contains plenty of useful information. Online, check out www.webchild.com.au.

to full-time students worldwide, yields discounts on accommodation, transport and admission to various attractions.

Seniors Travellers over 60 with some form of identification (eg a Seniors Card – www.seniorscard.com.au) are often eligible for concession prices.

Customs Regulations

For comprehensive information on customs regulations, contact the **Australian Customs & Border Protection Service** (02-6275 6666, 1300 363 263; www.customs.gov.au).

There's a duty-free quota of 2.25L of alcohol, 50 cigarettes and dutiable goods up to $900 per person.

Prohibited goods include drugs (all medicines must be declared), wooden items and food – Australia is very strict on this, so declare all food items, even leftover edibles taken from the plane.

Discount Cards

Students The **International Student Identity Card** (ISIC; www.isic.org), available

Electricity

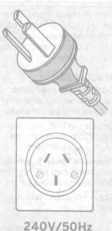

240V/50Hz

Embassies & Consulates

The **Department of Foreign Affairs & Trade** (www.dfat.gov.au) lists all foreign missions in Australia. Most are in Canberra; many countries also have consular offices in Sydney and Melbourne.

Canadian Embassy Canberra (02-6270 4000; www.australia.gc.ca; Commonwealth Ave, Yarralumla); Sydney (02-9364 3000; www.canadainternational.gc.ca; Level 5, 111 Harrington St; Circular Quay)

Chinese Embassy (02-6273 4780; http://au.china-embassy.org/eng; 15 Coronation Dr, Yarralumla, ACT)

Dutch Embassy Canberra (02-6220 9400; www.netherlands.org.au; 120 Empire Circuit, Yarralumla); Sydney (02-9387 6644; Level 23, Westfield Tower 2, 101 Grafton St, Bondi Junction)

French Embassy Canberra (02-6216 0100; www.ambafrance-au.org; 6 Perth Ave, Yarralumla); Sydney (02-9268 2400; Level 26, 31 Market St, Sydney)

German Embassy Canberra (02-6270 1911; www.canberra.diplo.de; 119 Empire Circuit, Yarralumla); Sydney (02-9328 7733; www.sydney.diplo.de; 13 Trelawney St, Woollahra); Melbourne (03-9864 6888; www.melbourne.diplo.de; 480 Punt Rd, South Yarra)

Irish Embassy (02-6214 0000; www.embassyofireland.au.com; 20 Arkana St, Yarralumla, ACT)

Japanese Embassy Canberra (02-6273 3244; www.au.emb-japan.go.jp; 112 Empire Circuit, Yarralumla); Sydney (02-9250 1000; Level 12, 1 O'Connell St, Sydney)

New Zealand Embassy Canberra (02-6270 4211; www.nzembassy.com; Commonwealth Ave, Yarralumla); Sydney (1300 559 535; Level 10, 55 Hunter St, Sydney)

UK Embassy Canberra (☎02-6270 6666; www. ukinaustralia.fco.gov.uk; Commonwealth Ave, Yarralumla); Sydney (☎02-9247 7521; www. ukinaustralia.fco.gov.uk; Level 16, 1 Macquarie Pl, Sydney; ⓇCircular Quay); Melbourne (☎03-9652 1600; Level 17, 90 Collins St, Melbourne)

US Embassy Canberra (☎02-6214 5600; canberra. usembassy.gov; 1 Moonah Pl, Yarralumla); Sydney (☎02-8278 1420; Level 10, MLC Centre,19-29 Martin Pl, Sydney); Melbourne (☎03-9526 5900; Level 6, 553 St Kilda Rd, Melbourne)

Food

For detailed foodie info, see the Food & Wine chapter (p499).

Gay & Lesbian Travellers

Australia's East Coast – Sydney especially – is a popular destination for gay and lesbian travellers. The legendary annual **Sydney Gay & Lesbian Mardi Gras** (www.mardigras.org.au) in February-March draws huge numbers of visitors, as does Melbourne's **Midsumma Festival** (www.midsumma. org.au; ⊙Jan-Feb) in January-February.

In general, Australians are open-minded about homosexuality, but the further out of the cities you get, the more likely you are to run into homophobia. Same-sex acts are legal in all states, but the age of consent varies.

Gay and lesbian magazines include *DNA*, *Lesbians on the Loose (LOTL)* and the Sydney-based *SX*. In Melbourne look for *MCV*; in Queensland look for *Queensland Pride*.

Resources

Gay & Lesbian Tourism Australia (Galta; www.galta. com.au) General info.

Same Same (www.same-same.com.au) News, events and lifestyle features.

Health

Although there are plenty of hazards in Australia, few travellers should experience anything worse than sunburn or a hangover. If you do fall ill, health-care standards are high.

Availability & Cost of Health Care

Facilities Australia has an excellent health-care system. It's a mixture of privately run medical clinics and hospitals alongside a system of public hospitals funded by the Australian government.

Medicare This system covers Australian residents for some health-care costs. Visitors from countries with which Australia has a reciprocal health-care agreement are eligible for benefits specified under the Medicare program. Agreements are currently in place with Finland, Italy, Malta, the Netherlands, Norway, Sweden and the UK – check the details before departing these countries. For further details, visit www.humanservices.gov.au/ customer/enablers/medicare/

medicare-card/new-arrivals-and-visitors-to-australia.

Medications Painkillers, antihistamines for allergies, and skincare products are widely available at chemists throughout Australia. You may find that medications readily available over the counter in some countries are only available in Australia by prescription. These include the oral contraceptive pill, some medications for asthma and all antibiotics.

In Remote Areas In remote locations there may be a significant delay in emergency services reaching you. Don't underestimate the vast distances between most major outback towns; an increased level of self-reliance and preparation is essential. Consider taking a wilderness first-aid course, such as those offered by **Wilderness First Aid Consultants** (www. equip.com.au). Take a comprehensive first-aid kit and ensure that you have adequate means of communication. Australia has extensive mobile-phone coverage, but additional radio communication is important for remote areas. The **Royal Flying Doctor Service** (RFDS; www.flyingdoctor.net) provides a back-up for remote communities.

Health Insurance

Health insurance is essential for all travellers; see Insurance (p512).

Vaccinations

The **World Health Organization** (WHO; www.who.int/ wer) recommends that all travellers be covered for diphtheria, tetanus, measles, mumps, rubella, chicken pox and polio, as well as hepatitis B, regardless of their destination.

If you're entering Australia within six days of having stayed overnight or longer in a yellow fever–infected country, you'll need proof of yellow-fever vaccination. For a full list of these countries visit **Centers for Disease Control & Prevention** (www. cdc.gov/travel).

EATING PRICE RANGES

The following price indicators refer to a typical main course:

$ less than $15

$$ $15–32

$$$ more than $32

Tap Water

Tap water in Australia is generally safe to drink. Water taken from streams, rivers and lakes should be treated before drinking.

Resources

There's a wealth of travel-health advice online: **Lonely Planet** (www.lonelyplanet.com) is a good place to start. The **World Health Organization** (WHO; www.who.int/wer) publishes *International Travel and Health*, revised annually and available free online. **MD Travel Health** (www.mdtravelhealth.com) provides complete travel-health recommendations for every country, updated daily.

Insurance

Worldwide travel insurance is available at www.lonelyplanet.com/travel_services. You can buy, extend and claim online anytime – even if you're already on the road.

Level of Cover A good travel-insurance policy covering theft, loss and medical problems is essential. Some policies specifically exclude designated 'dangerous activities' such as scuba diving, white-water rafting and even bushwalking (hiking). Make sure your policy covers you for your activity of choice.

Health You should check if your insurer will pay doctors or hospitals directly rather than requiring you to pay on the spot and claim later. If you have to claim later, keep all documentation. Check that the policy covers ambulances and emergency medical evacuations by air.

Internet Access

There are fewer internet cafes around these days than there were five years ago (thanks to the advent of iPhones/iPads and wi-fi), but you'll still find them in most sizeable towns. Hourly costs range from $6 to $10. Most youth hostels have both

internet computers and wi-fi, as do many hotels and cara-van parks. Most public libraries have internet access (but generally it's provided for research, not for travellers to check Facebook).

If you're bringing your tablet or laptop, check with your Internet Service Provider (ISP) for access numbers you can dial into in Australia. Major Australian ISPs include the following:

Dodo (☑13 36 36; www.dodo.com)

iinet (☑13 19 17; www.iinet.net.au)

iPrimus (☑13 17 89; www.iprimus.com.au)

Optus (☑1800 780 219; www.optus.com.au)

Telstra BigPond (☑13 76 63; www.bigpond.com)

Wi-Fi

It's still rare in remote Australia, but wireless internet access is increasingly the norm in Australia's big-city accommodation, with cafes, bars, libraries and even some public gardens providing wi-fi access (often free for customers/guests). For locations, visit www.freewifi.com.au.

Telstra, Optus, Vodafone and other big carriers sell mobile broadband devices with a USB connection that work with most laptops and allow you to get online just about anywhere in the country. Prices are around $80 for 30 days of access (cheaper for long-term fixed contracts).

Legal Matters

Most travellers will have no contact with Australia's police or legal system; if they do, it's most likely to be while driving.

Driving There's a significant police presence on East Coast Australian roads. Police have the power to stop your car, see your licence (you're required to carry it), check your vehicle for roadworthiness, and insist that

you take a breath test for alcohol (and sometimes illicit drugs). The legal limit is 0.05 blood-alcohol content. If you're over you'll be facing a court appearance, a fine and/or suspension of your licence.

Drugs First-time offenders caught with small amounts of illegal drugs are likely to receive a fine rather than go to jail, but the recording of a conviction against you may affect your visa status.

Visas If you remain in Australia beyond the life of your visa, you'll officially be an 'overstayer' and could face detention and then be prevented from returning to Australia for up to three years.

Arrested? It's your right to telephone a friend, lawyer or relative before questioning begins. Legal aid is available only in serious cases; for Legal Aid office info see www.nationallegalaid.org. However, many solicitors do not charge for an initial consultation.

Money

In this book, prices are listed in Australian dollars.

ATMs & Eftpos

ATMs ATMs proliferate in cities, but don't expect to find them everywhere, certainly not off the beaten track or in small towns. Most ATMs accept cards issued by other banks (for a fee) and are linked to international networks.

Eftpos Most service stations, supermarkets, restaurants, cafes and shops have Electronic Funds Transfer at Point of Sale (Eftpos) facilities, allowing you to make purchases and even withdraw cash with your credit or debit card. Just don't forget your PIN (Personal Identification Number)!

Fees Remember that withdrawing cash via ATMs or Eftpos may incur significant fees – check the costs with your bank first.

Credit Cards

Credit cards such as Visa and MasterCard are widely accepted for everything from

TAX REFUNDS FOR TRAVELLERS

If you purchase new or secondhand goods with a total minimum value of $300 from any one supplier no more than 30 days before you leave Australia, you are entitled under the Tourist Refund Scheme (TRS) to a refund of any Goods & Services Tax paid (GST, which is one 11th of the purchase price). The scheme only applies to goods you take with you as hand luggage or wear onto the plane or ship. The refund is valid for goods bought from more than one supplier, but only if at least $300 has been spent at each. For more information, contact the **Australian Customs & Border Protection Service** (02-6275 6666, 1300 363 263; www.customs.gov.au).

a hostel bed to a restaurant meal to an adventure tour, and are essential for hiring a car. They can also be used for cash advances at banks and from ATMs, though these transactions incur immediate interest. Diners Club and American Express (Amex) are not as widely accepted.

Contact numbers for lost credit cards:

American Express (1300 132 639; www.americanexpress.com.au)

Diners Club (1300 360 060; www.dinersclub.com.au)

MasterCard (1800 120 113; www.mastercard.com.au)

Visa (1800 450 346)

Debit Cards

A debit card allows you to draw money directly from your home bank account using ATMs, banks or Eftpos machines. Any card connected to the international banking network (Cirrus, Maestro, Plus and Eurocard) should work with your PIN. Expect substantial fees. Companies such as Travelex offer debit cards (Travelex calls them 'Cash Passport' cards) with set withdrawal fees and a balance you can top up from your personal account while on the road.

Exchanging Money

Changing foreign currency or travellers cheques is usually no problem at banks throughout Australia, or at licensed

moneychangers such as Travelex or AmEx in cities.

Tipping

Tipping isn't traditonally part of Australian etiquette, but it's increasingly the norm to tip around 10% for good service in restaurants, and a few dollars for porters (bellhops) and taxi rides.

Travellers Cheques

The ubiquity and convenience of internationally linked credit- and debit-card facilities in Australia means that travellers cheques are virtually redundant – both AmEx and Travelex will cash travellers cheques, as will major banks. In all instances present your passport for identification when cashing them.

Opening Hours

Business hours vary from state to state, but use the following as a guide:

Banks 9.30am to 4pm Monday to Thursday, to 5pm Friday

Bars 4pm to late

Cafes 7am to 5pm

Nightclubs 10pm to 4am Thursday to Saturday

Post Offices 9am to 5pm Monday to Friday; some also 9am to noon Saturday

Pubs 11am to midnight

Restaurants noon to 2.30pm and 6pm to 9pm

Shops 9am to 5pm Monday to Saturday

Supermarkets 7am to 8pm

Photography

Availability & Printing Digital cameras, memory sticks and batteries are sold prolifically in cities and urban centres. Try electronics stores (Dick Smith, Tandy) or the larger department stores. Many internet cafes, camera stores and large stationers (Officeworks, Harvey Norman) have printing and CD-burning facilities. Cheap, disposable underwater cameras are available at most beach towns.

Etiquette As in any country, politeness goes a long way when taking photographs; ask before taking pictures of people. For Indigenous Australians, photography can be highly intrusive: photographing cultural places, practices and images, sites of significance and ceremonies may also be a sensitive matter. Always ask first.

Resources Check out Lonely Planet's *Travel Photography* guide.

Post

Australia Post (www.auspost.com.au) is efficient and reliable. Posting standard letters or postcards within the country costs 60c. International rates for airmail letters up to 50g are $2.60. Postcards cost $1.70.

Public Holidays

Public holidays vary from state to state (and sometimes year to year). The following is a list of the main national and state public holidays; check locally for precise dates.

National

New Year's Day 1 January

Australia Day 26 January

Easter (Good Friday to Easter Monday inclusive) late March or early April

Anzac Day 25 April

Queen's Birthday Second Monday in June in all states except Western Australia

Christmas Day 25 December

Boxing Day 26 December

Australian Capital Territory

Canberra Day Second Monday in March

Bank Holiday First Monday in August

Labour Day First Monday in October

New South Wales

Bank Holiday First Monday in August

Labour Day First Monday in October

Queensland

Labour Day First Monday in May

Royal Queensland Show Day (Brisbane) Second or third Wednesday in August

Victoria

Labour Day Second Monday in March

Melbourne Cup Day First Tuesday in November

School Holidays

Key times when prices are highest and much accommodation is booked out in advance:

➡ Christmas holiday season (mid-December to late January)

➡ Easter (March–April)

➡ Shorter (two-week) school-holiday periods generally fall in mid-April, late June to mid-July, and late September to mid-October.

Safe Travel

Australia is a relatively safe place to visit – in terms of crime and war, at any rate – but take reasonable precautions. Sydney, the Gold Coast, Cairns and Byron Bay all get dishonourable mentions when it comes to theft: don't leave hotel rooms or cars unlocked or valuables visible through car windows. See p506 for more.

Bushfires, floods and cyclones regularly decimate parts of most states and territories: pay attention to warnings from local authorities.

Telephone

Regular Australian phone numbers have a two-digit area code followed by an eight-digit number.

Australia's main telecommunications companies:

Telstra (☎13 22 00; www.telstra.com.au) The main player – landline and mobile phone services.

Optus (☎1800 780 219; www.optus.com.au) Telstra's main rival – landline and mobile phone services.

Vodafone (☎1300 650 410; www.vodafone.com.au) Mobile phone services.

Virgin (☎1300 555 100; www.virginmobile.com.au) Mobile phone services.

Mobile Phones

Numbers Local numbers with the prefix 04xx belong to mobile phones.

Networks Australia's digital network is compatible with GSM 900 and GSM 1800 (used in Europe) but generally not with networks in the USA or Japan.

Reception The East Coast generally gets good reception, but service can be haphazard or nonexistent in the interior.

New Accounts To get connected, just buy a starter kit, which may include a phone or, if you have your own phone, a SIM card (under $10) and a prepaid charge card. Purchase recharge vouchers at convenience stores and newsagents.

Local Calls

Calls from private phones cost 15c to 30c, while local calls from public phones cost 50c; both involve unlimited talk time. Calls to mobile phones attract higher rates and are timed.

International Calls

To call overseas from Australia, dial 0011 or 0018, the country code and the area code (without the initial 0). So, for a London number you'd dial 0011-44-171, then the number.

If dialling Australia from overseas, the country code is 61 and you need to drop the 0 (zero) in the area code.

Area codes within Australia:

State/Territory	Area Code
ACT	02
NSW	02
VIC	03
QLD	07

Phonecards & Public Phones

Phonecards can be bought at newsagents, hostels and post offices for a fixed dollar value ($10, $20 etc) and can be used with any public or private phone by dialling a toll-free access number and then the PIN on the card.

GOVERNMENT TRAVEL ADVICE

The following government websites offer travel advisories and information on current hot spots.

Australian Department of Foreign Affairs & Trade (DFAT; www.smartraveller.gov.au)

British Foreign & Commonwealth Office (www.gov.uk/fco)

Government of Canada (www.travel.gc.ca)

US State Department (www.travel.state.gov)

Most public phones use phonecards; some also accept credit cards. Old-fashioned coin-operated public phones are increasingly rare (and if you do find one, chances are the coin slot will be gummed up or vandalised).

Toll-Free & Reverse-Charges Calls

Toll-free numbers (prefix 1800) can be called for free. Calls to numbers beginning with 13 or 1300 are charged at the rate of a local call.

To make a reverse-charge (collect) call within Australia, dial 1800-REVERSE (1800 738 3773) from any public or private phone.

Time

Australia is divided into three time zones:

Eastern Standard Time (Greenwich Mean Time plus 10 hours) Queensland, New South Wales, Victoria and Tasmania.

Central Standard Time (half-hour behind Eastern Standard Time) Northern Territory, South Australia.

Western Standard Time (two hours behind Eastern Standard Time) Western Australia.

Note that Queensland remains on Eastern Standard Time all year, while most of Australia switches to daylight-saving time over the summer (October to early April), when clocks are wound forwards one hour.

Toilets

Toilets in Australia are sit-down Western style (though you mightn't find this prospect too appealing in some remote outback pit stops). See www.toiletmap.gov.au for public-toilet locations.

Tourist Information

Tourist information is provided in Australia by various regional and local offices – often volunteer-staffed info centres in key tourist spots. Each state also has a government-run tourist organisation ready to inundate you with information:

Queensland Holidays (www.queenslandholidays. com.au)

Visit New South Wales (www.visitnsw.com)

Visit Victoria (www.visitvictoria.com)

The **Australian Tourist Commission** (ATC; www. australia.com) is the country-wide government body charged with luring foreign visitors. For ATC branches in other countries visit www. tourism.australia.com.

Travellers with Disabilities

Disability awareness in Australia is reasonably high. Legislation requires that new accommodation must meet accessibility standards and tourist operators must not discriminate. Facilities for wheelchairs are improving in accommodation, but there are still many older establishments where the necessary upgrades haven't been made.

Resources

Accessible Tourism (www. australiaforall.com) Good site for accessibility information.

Australian Tourist Commission (ATC; www.australia. com) Publishes detailed, downloadable information for people with disabilities, including travel and transport tips and contact addresses of organisations in each state.

Deaf Australia (www.deafau. org.au)

National Disability Service (☑07-3357 4188; www.nds. org.au) The national industry association for disability services.

National Information Communication & Awareness Network (Nican; ☑TTY 1800 806 769, TTY 02-6241 1220; www.nican.com.au) Australia-wide directory providing information on access, accommodation, sporting and recreational activities, transport and specialist tour operators.

Vision Australia (www. visionaustralia.org.au)

Visas

All visitors to Australia need a visa. Only New Zealand nationals are exempt: they sheepishly receive a 'special category' visa on arrival. The main visa categories for travellers are as follows:

eVisitor (651) A three-month visa (free) for many European passport holders.

Electronic Travel Authority (ETA; 601) A three-month visa (free) for citizens of 34 countries, including Brunei, Canada, Hong Kong, Japan, Malaysia, Singapore, South Korea and the USA.

Tourist Visa (600) A three-, six- or 12-month visa ($115) for citizens of countries other than those listed above, or for people from the above countries who want to stay longer than three months.

Detailed information and application forms are available on the website of the **Department of Immigration and Border Protection** (www.immi.gov.au). For info on working visas, see Work (p515).

Volunteering

Lonely Planet's *Volunteer: A Traveller's Guide to Making a Difference Around the World* provides useful information about volunteering.

Resources

Conservation Volunteers Australia (www.conservation-volunteers.com.au) Nonprofit organisation involved in tree planting, walking-track construction, and flora and fauna surveys.

Go Volunteer (www.govolunteer.com.au) National website listing volunteer opportunities.

i to i Volunteering (www.i-to-i.com) Conservation-based volunteer holidays in Australia.

Reef Check (www.reefcheck-australia.org) Train to monitor the health of the Great Barrier Reef.

Sea Turtle Foundation (www.seaturtlefoundation.org) Volunteer opportunities in sea-turtle conservation.

Volunteering Australia (www.volunteeringaustralia.org) Support, advice and volunteer training.

Volunteering Qld (www.volunteeringqld.org.au) Volunteering info and advice across Queensland.

Willing Workers on Organic Farms (WWOOF; www.wwoof.com.au) 'WWOOF-ing' is where you do a few hours' work each day on a farm in return for bed and board, often in a family home. As the name states, the farms are supposed to be organic (including permaculture and biodynamic growing), but that isn't always so. Some places aren't even farms – you might help out at a pottery or do the books at a seed wholesaler. Whether participants in the scheme have a farm or just a vegie patch, most are concerned to some extent with alternative lifestyles. Most places have a minimum stay of two nights. You can join online or through various WWOOF agents (see the website for details) for a fee of $65. You'll get a membership number and a booklet that lists participating enterprises. If you need these posted overseas, add another $5.

Women Travellers

Australia is generally a safe place for women travellers, although the usual sensible precautions apply. Avoid hitchhiking and walking alone late at night in any of the major cities and towns. And if you're out on the town, always keep enough money aside for a taxi back to your accommodation. Solo women should be wary of staying in basic pub accommodation unless it looks safe and well managed.

Work

If you come to Australia on a tourist visa then you're not allowed to work for pay. You'll need one of the following visas:

Working Holiday Visa (417) – for citizens of Belgium, Canada, Republic of Cyprus, Denmark, Estonia, Finland, France, Germany, Hong Kong, Republic of Ireland, Italy, Japan, Republic of Korea, Malta, Netherlands, Norway, Sweden, Taiwan and the UK.

Work and Holiday Visa (462) – for citizens of Argentina, Bangladesh, Chile, Indonesia, Iran, Malaysia, Thailand, Turkey, the USA and Uruguay.

Both visas cost $365; see www.immi.gov.au for more info.

Finding Work

Backpacker magazines, newspapers and hostel notice-boards are good for sourcing local work opportunities. Casual work can often be found during peak season in tourist hubs, such as Cairns, the Gold Coast and the resort towns along the Queensland coast.

Seasonal fruit-picking (harvesting) relies on casual labour, and there is something to be picked, pruned or farmed somewhere in Australia year-round (just don't expect to make a fortune).

Other casual employment options include factory work, labouring, bar work and waiting on tables. People with computer, secretarial, nursing and teaching skills can find work temping in the major cities (via employment agencies – see the listings following).

Resources

Career One (www.careerone.com.au) General employment site; good for metropolitan areas.

Grunt Labour (www.gruntlabour.com) Specialises in mining, manufacturing and agricultural-based recruitment, plus seasonal fruit-picking.

Harvest Trail (www.jobsearch.gov.au/harvesttrail) Harvest jobs around Australia.

Seek (www.seek.com.au) General employment site; good for metropolitan areas.

Travellers at Work (www.taw.com.au) Excellent site for working travellers in Australia.

Workabout Australia (www.workaboutaustralia.com.au) Gives a state-by-state breakdown of seasonal work opportunities.

Taxes

If you're earning money in Australia, you'll be paying tax in Australia and will have to lodge a tax return. See the website of the **Australian Taxation Office** (ATO; www.ato.gov.au) for info on how to do this, including getting a payment summary from your employer, timing and dates for lodging returns, and receiving your notice of assessment.

As part of this process you'll need to apply for a **Tax File Number** (TFN) to give your employer. Without it, tax will be deducted at the maximum rate from your wages. Apply online via the Australian Taxation Office; it takes up to four weeks to be issued.

Transport

GETTING THERE & AWAY

Australia's East Coast is a long way from just about everywhere – getting there usually means a long-haul flight. Flights, tours and rail tickets can be booked online at lonelyplanet.com/bookings.

Entering Australia

Arrival in Australia is usually straightforward and efficient, with the usual customs declarations. There are no restrictions for citizens of any particular foreign countries entering Australia – if you have a current passport and visa, you should be fine.

Air

High season (with the highest prices) for flights into Australia is roughly over the country's summer (December to February); low season generally tallies with the winter months (June to August), though this is actually peak season in the tropical north. Australia's international carrier is **Qantas** (www.qantas.com.au), which has an outstanding safety record (...as Dustin Hoffman said in *Rainman*, 'Qantas never crashed').

International Airports

On the East Coast of Australia, most international flights head to Sydney, Melbourne or Brisbane, though Cairns and the Gold Coast also receive international flights.

Brisbane Airport (www.bne.com.au)

Cairns Airport (www.cairnsairport.com)

Gold Coast Airport (www.goldcoastairport.com.au)

Melbourne Airport (MEL; 03-9297 1600; www.melbourneairport.com.au)

Sydney Airport (www.sydneyairport.com.au)

Sea

It is possible (if not straightforward) to travel between Australia and Papua New Guinea, Indonesia, New Zealand and the Pacific islands by hitching rides or crewing on yachts – usually you have to at least contribute towards food. Ask around at marinas and sailing clubs in places like Coffs Harbour, Great Keppel Island, Airlie Beach, the Whitsundays and Cairns. April is a good time to look for a berth in the Sydney area.

Alternatively, **P&O Cruises** (www.pocruises.com.au) operates holiday cruises between Brisbane, Melbourne or Sydney and destinations in New Zealand and the Pacific. Even more

---

CLIMATE CHANGE & TRAVEL

Every form of transport that relies on carbon-based fuel generates CO_2, the main cause of human-induced climate change. Modern travel is dependent on aeroplanes, which might use less fuel per kilometre per person than most cars but travel much greater distances. The altitude at which aircraft emit gases (including CO_2) and particles also contributes to their climate change impact. Many websites offer 'carbon calculators' that allow people to estimate the carbon emissions generated by their journey and, for those who wish to do so, to offset the impact of the greenhouse gases emitted with contributions to portfolios of climate-friendly initiatives throughout the world. Lonely Planet offsets the carbon footprint of all staff and author travel.

QANTAS AIRPASS

Qantas offers a discount-fare **Walkabout Air Pass** for passengers flying into Australia from overseas with Qantas or American Airlines. The pass allows you to link up around 80 domestic Australian destinations for less than you'd pay booking flights individually. See www.qantas.com.au for more information.

alternatively, some freighter ships allow passengers to travel on board as they ship cargo to/from Australia: see websites such as www.freighterexpeditions.com.au and www.freightercruises.com for options.

GETTING AROUND

Air

East Coast Australia is well serviced by airlines big and small.

Hinterland Aviation (www.hinterlandaviation.com.au) Flies between Cairns and Cooktown.

Jetstar (www.jetstar.com.au) Budget offshoot of Qantas; has extensive service.

Qantas (www.qantas.com.au) Services across Australia.

Regional Express (Rex; www.regionalexpress.com.au) Connects Melbourne, Sydney and Townsville with small regional airports.

Skytrans (www.skytrans.com.au) Serves northern Queensland, flying from Cairns to Bamaga (tip of Australia) and Mt Isa among other obscure locations.

Tiger Airways (www.tigerair.com) Budget offshoot of Singapore Airlines. Serves multiple East Coast destinations from Melbourne to Cairns.

Virgin Australia (www.virginaustralia.com.au) Service throughout Australia.

Bicycle

Whether you're hiring a bike to ride around a city or wearing out your sprockets on a long-distance haul, the East Coast is ideal for cycling. There are bike paths in most cities, and in the country you'll find thousands of kilometres of good (and not too hilly) roads. Many touring cyclists carry camping equipment, but it's feasible to travel from town to town staying in hostels, hotels or caravan parks.

Legalities Bicycle helmets are compulsory, as are white front lights and red rear lights for riding at night.

Weather The Aussie summer cooks! Always carry plenty of water. Wear a helmet with a peak (or a cap under your helmet), use sunscreen and avoid cycling in the middle of the day. Beware summer northerlies that can make a north-bound cyclist's life hell. It can get very cold in Victoria and inland New South Wales, so pack appropriate clothing.

Bicycle Hire

Rates charged by most rental outfits for road or mountain bikes range from $10 to $15 per hour and $25 to $50 per day. Security deposits can range from $50 to $200, depending on the rental period.

Buying a Bicycle

For a new road or mountain bike in Australia, your bottom-level starting price will be around $600. With all the requisite on-the-road equipment (panniers, helmet, lights etc) you're looking at upwards of $1700.

To sell your bike (or buy a secondhand one), try hostel noticeboards or online at **Trading Post** (www.tradingpost.com.au), **Gumtree** (www.gumtree.com.au) or **Bike Exchange** (www.bikeexchange.com.au).

Resources

The national cycling body is the **Bicycle Federation of Australia** (www.bfa.asn.au). Each state and territory also has a cycling organisation that can help with local information and put you in touch with touring clubs include the following:

Bicycle Network Victoria (www.bicyclenetwork.com.au)

Bicycle NSW (www.bicyclensw.org.au)

Bicycle Queensland (www.bq.org.au)

Pedal Power ACT (www.pedalpower.org.au)

BIKE MELBOURNE & BRISBANE

Both Melbourne and Brisbane have inexpensive public bike-sharing schemes that allow speedy access to bikes across town. The two systems vary slightly, but basically you either subscribe online or pay a one-off fee at one of the many dozens of bike stations. You can then borrow a bike for up to 24 hours, and return it to any bike station. Sometimes a helmet will accompany the bike, but it's a good idea to have your own (and a lock).

For details, including info on places that sell helmets, go online:

Melbourne (⌨1300 711 590; www.melbournebikeshare.com.au)

Brisbane (www.citycycle.com.au)

For more information, see Lonely Planet's *Cycling Australia*.

Bus

East Coast Australia's bus network is reliable, but not the cheapest for long hauls. Most buses have air-con and toilets; all are smoke-free. There are no separate classes on buses (very democratic). Book seats at least a day ahead (a week or two during summer). Small towns eschew formal bus terminals for an informal drop-off/pick-up point, usually outside a post office or shop.

Bus Companies

In addition to the companies below, **V/Line** (www.vline.com.au) offers bus connections to complement its train services.

Coachtrans (www.coachtrans-online.com.au) Connects Brisbane with Queensland's Gold Coast and Sunshine Coast.

Firefly Express (www.firefly-express.com.au) Runs between Sydney, Canberra, Melbourne and Adelaide.

Greyhound Australia (www.greyhound.com.au) Extensive nationwide network.

NSW TrainLink (www.nswtrainlink.info) Coach and train services in New South Wales.

Premier Motor Service (www.premierms.com.au) Greyhound's main competitor on the East Coast. Has fewer daily services but usually costs a little less.

Bus Passes

Bus passes are a good option if you plan on multiple stopovers. Book online or phone at least a day ahead to reserve a seat.

Greyhound (www.greyhound.com.au) offers myriad money-saving passes – check the website for comprehensive info. Options include the following:

Kilometre Pass Gives you go-anywhere flexibility, plus the choice to backtrack. Choose from 1000km ($188) up to 25,000km ($2499). Valid for 12 months.

Mini Traveller Pass Up to 90 days of one-direction travel along a dozen popular routes – including Cairns to Melbourne ($472) and Sydney to Brisbane ($150) – stopping as often as you like.

Micro Pass Set route between Sydney and Melbourne via Canberra ($110). Valid for 10 days.

Premier Motor Service (www.premierms.com.au) offers several passes for one-way travel along the East Coast, including a six-month pass between Melbourne and Cairns ($345) and a three-month pass between Sydney and Brisbane ($90).

Costs

The following are typical, non-discounted, one-way bus fares for some popular East Coast routes:

ROUTE	FARE	TIME (HR)
Melbourne-Canberra	$90	8
Melbourne-Sydney	$100	12
Sydney-Byron Bay	$150	14
Sydney-Brisbane	$180	16
Brisbane-Airlie Beach	$230	19
Brisbane-Cairns	$295	29
Townsville-Cairns	$60	5½

Car & Motorcycle

The best way to see the East Coast is by car – it's certainly the only way to access interesting out-of-the-way places without taking a tour.

Motorcycles are popular, as the climate is ideal for

bikes for much of the year. A fuel range of 350km will easily cover fuel stops along the coast. The long, open roads here are really made for large-capacity machines above 750cc.

Driving Licence

To drive in Australia you'll need to hold a current driving licence issued in English from your home country. If the licence isn't in English, you'll also need to carry an **International Driving Permit**, issued in your home country.

Automobile Associations

The national **Australian Automobile Association** (AAA; ☑ 02-6247 7311; www.aaa.asn.au) is the umbrella organisation for the various state associations.

The state organisations have reciprocal arrangements with other states and with similar organisations overseas – including AAA in the USA and RAC or AA in the UK. Bring proof of membership with you.

NRMA (☑ 13 11 22; www.mynrma.com.au) Covers NSW and the Australian Capital Territory.

RACQ (☑ 13 19 05; www.racq.com.au) Covers Queensland.

RACV (☑ 13 72 28; www.racv.com.au) Covers Victoria.

Car Hire

There are plenty of car-rental companies, big and small, ready to put you behind the wheel. The main thing to remember is distance – if you want to travel far, you'll need unlimited kilometres.

Larger car-rental companies have drop-offs in major cities and towns. Smaller local firms are sometimes cheaper but may have restrictions. The big firms sometimes offer one-way rentals, which may not cost extra. Most companies require drivers to be over the age of 21, though in some cases it's 18 and in others

TRANSPORT

Brisbane to Cairns via the Bruce Hwy

Total Distance = 1705km

93 Distance (km) between towns

Mossman (75km)
44 ✪ CAIRNS
88
Ravenshoe (94km)
25 ● Innisfail
52
● Tully
96
Ingham ●
A1 110
● Townsville
A6 87
Charters Towers (135km)
● Ayr
115
Bowen ●
66
Airlie Beach (36km)
Proserpine ●
123
● Mackay
70
Clermont (274km)
332
Emerald (270km)
A1
Yeppoon (40km)
A4
● Rockhampton
171
33
●Gladstone
Calliope ● 19
Bundaberg (53km)
155
3
Childers ● 33
57 ●Hervey Bay
Maryborough ● 34
89
● Gympie
60
Noosa (21km)
Nambour ● 6
Kingaroy (164km)
17
104
Toowoomba (128km)
✪ BRISBANE

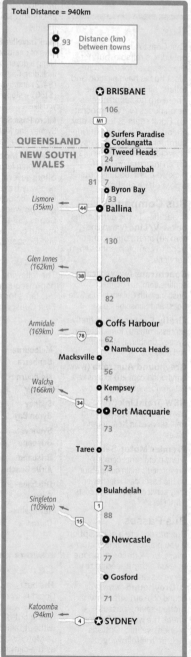

Sydney to Brisbane via the Pacific Hwy

Total Distance = 940km

93 Distance (km) between towns

✪ BRISBANE
106
M1
QUEENSLAND
● Surfers Paradise
● Coolangatta
NEW SOUTH WALES
● Tweed Heads
24
● Murwillumbah
81
7 ● Byron Bay
Lismore (35km)
44 33
● Ballina
130
Glen Innes (162km)
38 ● Grafton
82
Armidale (169km)
● Coffs Harbour
78 62
● Nambucca Heads
Macksville ●
56
Walcha (166km)
● Kempsey
34 41
●● Port Macquarie
73
Taree ●
73
● Bulahdelah
Singleton (109km)
1
15 88
● Newcastle
77
● Gosford
71
Katoomba (94km)
4 ✪ SYDNEY

Sydney to Melbourne via the Princes Hwy

Total Distance = 1041km

Distance (km) between towns: 93

SYDNEY
93
Wollongong — 28
Kiama
47
Nowra
68
Canberra (144km)
Ulladulla
48
Batemans Bay
69
Narooma
Cooma (101km)
77
Bega
35
Pambula — Merimbula
Eden — 19
57

NSW

VICTORIA Genoa
Bombala (85km) — 47 — Mallacoota (23km)
Cann River
Bemm River (23km)
75
Orbost — Marlo (15km) & Cape Conran (34km)
59
Lakes Entrance — Metung (10km)
Omeo (120km) — 36
Bairnsdale
69
Sale — Yarram (72km)
49
Traralgon — Yarram (60km)
31
Moe
28 — Leongatha (56km)
Warragul
72
Dandenong
34
MELBOURNE

25. Typical rates are from $40/60/80 per day for a small/medium/large car.

The usual big international companies all operate in Australia (Avis, Budget, Europcar, Hertz, Thrifty). The following websites offer last-minute discounts:

Carhire.com (www.carhire.com.au)

Drive Now (☎1300 547 214; www.drivenow.com.au)

Webjet (www.webjet.com.au)

CAMPERVANS

Companies for campervan hire – with rates from around $90 (two-berth) or $150 (four-berth) per day, usually with minimum five-day hire and unlimited kilometres – include the following:

Apollo (☎1800 777 779; www.apollocamper.com)

Britz (☎1800 331 454; www.britz.com.au)

Hippie Camper (☎1800 777 779; www.hippiecamper.com)

Jucy Rentals (☎1800 150 850; www.jucy.com.au)

Maui (☎1300 363 800; www.maui.com.au)

Mighty Cars & Campers (☎1800 670 232; www.mightycampers.com)

Spaceships (☎1300 132 469; www.spaceshipsrentals.com.au)

Travelwheels (☎1800 289 222; www.travelwheels.com.au)

Wicked Campervans (☎1800 246 869; www.wickedcampers.com.au)

4WDS

Having a 4WD enables you to get right off the beaten track and revel in the natural splendour that many travellers miss. Something midsized like a Nissan X-Trail costs around $100 to $150 per day; for a Toyota Land Cruiser you're looking at around $150 up to $200, which should include unlimited kilometres. Check insurance conditions carefully, especially the excess, as they can be onerous.

The major car-hire companies have 4WD rentals, or try Apollo or Britz.

ONE-WAY RELOCATIONS

Relocations are usually cheap deals, although they don't allow much time flexibility. Most of the large hire companies offer deals, or try the following operators:

Drive Now (☑1300 547 214; www.drivenow.com.au)

imoova (☑1300 789 059; www.imoova.com)

Relocations2Go (☑1800 735 627; www.relocations2go. com)

Transfercar (☑02-8011 1870; www.transfercar.com.au)

Purchase

If you plan to stay several months and do plenty of driving, buying a car will probably work out to be cheaper than renting one. You can buy from a car dealer, a private seller or from the dedicated

---

SHARE A RIDE

Ride-sharing is a good way to split costs and environmental impact with other travellers. As with hitching, there are potential risks: meet in a public place before hitting the road, and if anything seems off, don't hesitate to back out. Hostel noticeboards are good places to find ads; also check these online classifieds:

Catch a Lift (www. catchalift.com)

Coseats (www.coseats. com)

Jayride (www.jayride. com.au)

Need A Ride (www. needaride.com.au)

---

travellers' car markets you'll find in Sydney and Cairns.

REGISTRATION & LEGALITIES

When you buy a vehicle in Australia, you need to transfer the registration into your own name within 14 days. Each state has slightly different requirements and different organisations that do this. Similarly, when selling a vehicle you need to advise the state or territory road transport authority of the sale and change of name.

In NSW, Queensland and Victoria, the buyer and seller need to complete and sign a transfer-of-registration form. In the ACT there's no form, but the buyer and seller need to co-sign the reverse of the registration certificate.

Note that it's much easier to sell a car in the same state in which it's registered, otherwise you (or the buyer) must re-register it in the new state, which can be a hassle.

It's the buyer's responsibility to ensure the car isn't stolen and that there's no money owing on it: check the car's details with the **Personal Property Securities Register** (☑1300 007 777; www.ppsr.gov.au).

ROADWORTHY CERTIFICATE

Sellers are required to provide a roadworthy certificate when transferring registration in the following situations:

ACT Once the vehicle is six years old; annual inspection record also required for vehicles running on gas.

NSW Once the vehicle is five years old.

Queensland Safety Certificate required for all vehicles; certificate also required for vehicles running on gas.

Victoria Certificate of roadworthiness required for all vehicles.

If the vehicle you're considering doesn't have a roadworthy certificate, it's worth

---

having a roadworthiness check done by a mechanic before you buy it. The state automobile associations have lists of licenced vehicle testers.

ROAD TRANSPORT AUTHORITIES

For more information about processes and costs:

Rego ACT (☑13 22 81; www. rego.act.gov.au) ACT.

Transport, Roads & Maritime Services (☑13 27 01; www.rta.nsw.gov.au) NSW.

Department of Transport & Main Roads (www.tmr.qld. gov.au) Queensland.

VicRoads (☑13 11 71; www. vicroads.vic.gov.au) Victoria.

CAR MARKETS

Sydney and Cairns are particularly good places to buy cars from backpackers who have finished their trips: try hostel noticeboards. There are also a couple of big backpacker car markets in Sydney. It's possible these cars have been around Australia several times, so it can be a risky option:

Kings Cross Car Market (☑1800 808 188; www.car market.com.au; 110 Bourke St, Woolloomooloo; ⊙9am-5pm)

Sydney Travellers Car Market (www.sydneytravel lerscarmarket.com.au; Level 2, Kings Cross Car Park, Ward Ave, Kings Cross; ⊙9am-4.40pm; ▣Kings Cross)

Insurance

Third-Party Insurance In Australia, third-party personal-injury insurance is included in the vehicle-registration cost, ensuring that every registered vehicle carries at least minimum insurance. We recommend extending that minimum to at least third-party property insurance – minor collisions can be amazingly expensive.

Rental Vehicles When it comes to hire cars, understand your liability in the event of an accident. You can pay an additional daily amount to the rental company that will reduce your liability in the event of an accident from upwards of $3000 to a few hundred dollars.

Road Rules

Australians drive on the left-hand side of the road; all cars are right-hand drive.

Give Way If an intersection is unmarked (unusual) and at roundabouts, you must give way to vehicles entering the intersection from your right.

Speed Limits The general speed limit in built-up and residential areas is 50km/h (sometimes 60km/h). Near schools, the limit is usually 25km/h around school drop-off and pickup times. On the highway it's 100km/h or 110km/h. Police have speed radar guns and cameras and are fond of using them in strategic locations.

Seatbelts & Car Seats Seatbelt use is compulsory. Children up to the age of seven must be belted into an approved safety seat.

Drink Driving Random breath-tests are common. If you're caught with a blood-alcohol level of more than 0.05%, expect a court appearance, a fine and the loss of your licence. Police can randomly pull any driver over for a breathalyser or drug test.

Mobile Phones Using a mobile phone while driving is illegal (excluding hands-free technology).

Fuel

Diesel and unleaded fuel is available from service stations. LPG (gas) is also available in populated areas but not always at more remote service stations. On main East Coast highways there's usually a small town or petrol station every 50km or so.

Prices vary from place to place, but at the time of writing unleaded was hovering between $1.40 and $1.60 in the cities. Out in the country, prices soar – in outback Queensland you can pay as much as $2.20 per litre.

Parking

One of the big problems with driving around big cities

TOLL ROADS

There are a handful of toll roads on the East Coast – mostly on major freeways around Melbourne, Sydney and Brisbane. Ensure you pay tolls online or you'll face hefty fines – whether you're travelling in your own vehicle or in a rental. Unless you've organised a toll pass ahead of time, you usually have two or three days to pay after driving the toll road.

New South Wales Pay tolls by signing up for a pass online: www.roam.com.au, www.myRTA.com or www.roamexpress.com.au.

Queensland Pay tolls online: www.govia.com.au.

Victoria Pay tolls by signing up for a pass online: www.citylink.com.au.

like Sydney and Melbourne (or popular tourist towns like Byron Bay) is finding somewhere to park. Even if you do find a spot there's likely to be a time restriction, a meter (or ticket machine) or both. Parking fines range from about $50 to $120 and if you park in a clearway your car will be towed away or clamped – always check the signs.

In the cities there are large car parks where you can park all day for $20 to $40.

Road Hazards & Precautions

➡ Be wary of driver **fatigue**; driving long distances (particularly in hot weather) can be utterly exhausting. Falling asleep at the wheel is not uncommon. On a long haul, stop and rest every two hours or so – do some exercise, change drivers or have a coffee.

➡ Unsealed road conditions vary wildly and cars perform differently when braking and turning on dirt. Don't exceed 80km/h on **dirt roads**; if you go faster you won't have time to respond to a sharp turn, stock on the road or an unmarked gate or cattle grid. If you're in a rental car, check your contract to ensure you're covered for driving on unsealed roads.

➡ Australia has few multi-lane highways, although there are stretches of divided road (four or six lanes) in busy areas such as the toll roads in Sydney, Melbourne and Brisbane. **Two-lane roads**, however, are the only option for many routes.

➡ **Roadkill** is a huge problem in Australia. Many Australians avoid travelling once the sun drops because of the risks posed by nocturnal animals on the roads.

Kangaroos are common on country roads, as are cows and sheep in the unfenced outback. Kangaroos are most active around dawn and dusk and often travel in groups: if you see one hopping across the road, slow right down, as its friends may be just behind it.

If you hit and kill an animal, pull it off the road, preventing the next car from having a potential accident. If the animal is only injured, wrap it in a towel or blanket and call the relevant wildlife rescue line:

Department of Environment & Heritage Protection (☏1300 130 372; www.ehp.qld.gov.au) Queensland

NSW Wildlife Information, Rescue & Education Service (WIRES; ☏1300 094 737; www.wires.org.au)

Wildlife Victoria (☏1300 094 535; www.wildlifevictoria.org.au)

Hitching

Hitching is never entirely safe in any country in the world, and we don't recommend it. Travellers who decide to hitch should understand that they are taking a small but potentially serious risk. Those who do choose to hitch will be safer if they travel in pairs and let someone know where they are planning to go.

Local Transport

Brisbane, Melbourne and Sydney all have public-transport systems utilising buses, trains, ferries and/or trams. Larger regional towns and cities have their own local bus systems. Sizeable towns also have taxis. There's almost no service north of Cairns, so your only option is to join a tour or hire a car.

By the time you read this, the new **Gold Coast Rapid Transit** (www.goldlinq.com.au) tram system might be operational, linking 16 stops over 13km between Southport and Broadbeach. Until then, local buses are your best bet.

Tours

Several backpacker and tour bus companies operate along the coast. These trips are economically priced and can be more fun than conventional buses: the buses are usually smaller and you'll meet other travellers.

AAT Kings (☏1300 556 100; www.aatkings.com) Big coach company (popular with the older set) with myriad tours all around Australia.

Adventure Tours Australia (☏1800 068 886; www.adventuretours.com.au) Affordable, young-at-heart tours in all states.

Autopia Tours (☏03-9391 0261; www.autopiatours.com.au) Three-day trips from Melbourne to Sydney.

Oz Experience (☏1300 300 028; www.ozexperience.com) Backpacker buses covering central, northern and eastern Australia.

Train

Train travel is a comfortable option for short- or long-haul sectors along the East Coast, but it's also a few dollars more than travelling by bus and it may take a few hours longer.

Rail services within each state (and sometimes extending interstate) are run by that state's rail body:

NSW TrainLink (☏13 22 32; www.nswtrainlink.info) In NSW, operates from Sydney south to Canberra and Melbourne and along the coast north to Brisbane (but *not* Byron Bay).

Queensland Rail (☏1800 872 467; www.queenslandrail.com.au)

Sydney Trains (☏13 15 00; www.sydneytrains.info) Covers the NSW coast around Sydney and as far north as Newcastle; also to the Blue Mountains.

V/Line (www.vline.com.au) Connects Victoria with NSW, South Australia and the ACT.

Costs

Children, students and backpackers can generally secure a discount on standard fares. If you can stretch your budget to a sleeper cabin, we highly recommend it (sleeping upright in a seat surrounded by the snoring proletariat isn't always a great way to travel). Note that cheaper fares are generally nonrefundable with no changes permitted. Some typical fares:

Brisbane–Cairns Adult/child seated from $269/135; from $349/215 in a cabin

Sydney–Canberra Adult/child seated $57/28

Sydney–Brisbane Adult/child seated $130/65; cabin $271/180

Sydney–Melbourne Adult/child seated $130/65; cabin $271/180.

Reservations

During national holidays, school holidays and weekends, book your seat a week or two in advance if possible. Many discount fares require you to reserve well in advance.

Rail Passes

Coverage of the East Coast by rail isn't bad, and several useful passes are sold. **Rail Australia** (www.railaustralia.com.au) has information on passes available from the various rail companies, including the following:

Austrail Flexipass Available only to international visitors; allows long-distance travel across Australia on specific services over a three-/six-month period ($722/990).

Backtracker Pass Available only to international visitors; permits travel on the NSW TrainLink network. There are four versions: 14 days/one/three/six months ($232/275/298/420).

East Coast Discovery Pass Allows travel with unlimited stops over a designated route in one direction in a six-month period. The entire Melbourne to Brisbane route costs $220. You can buy shorter segments, such as Sydney to Brisbane ($130).

Queensland Explorer Pass Three/six months' unlimited travel on the Queensland rail network ($390/550).

Behind the Scenes

SEND US YOUR FEEDBACK

We love to hear from travellers – your comments keep us on our toes and help make our books better. Our well-travelled team reads every word on what you loved or loathed about this book. Although we cannot reply individually to your submissions, we always guarantee that your feedback goes straight to the appropriate authors, in time for the next edition. Each person who sends us information is thanked in the next edition – the most useful submissions are rewarded with a selection of digital PDF chapters.

Visit **lonelyplanet.com/contact** to submit your updates and suggestions or to ask for help. Our award-winning website also features inspirational travel stories, news and discussions.

Note: We may edit, reproduce and incorporate your comments in Lonely Planet products such as guidebooks, websites and digital products, so let us know if you don't want your comments reproduced or your name acknowledged. For a copy of our privacy policy visit lonelyplanet.com/privacy.

OUR READERS

Many thanks to the travellers who used the last edition and wrote to us with helpful hints, useful advice and interesting anecdotes: Antti Huotari, Bert Ruitenberg, Christoph Boneberg, Dirk Latijnhouwers, Donald Bruce Telfer, Henk Groenewoud, Hilary Winchester, Jalscha Stadler, Jonathan Boyle, Keith Hillier, Laura Pearce, Loeki Bouwmans, Marvin Minaldi, Nick Hough, Stephen Crawford, Sue Erskine, Victoria Walker

AUTHOR THANKS

Charles Rawlings-Way

Huge thanks to Maryanne for the gig, and to my highway-addled co-authors, who covered a helluva lot of kilometres in search of the perfect review. Thanks also to the all-star in-house LP production staff, and in Brisbane thanks to Christian, Lauren, Rachel, Brett and all the kids. Special thanks as always to Meg, my road-trippin' sweetheart, and our daughters Ione and Remy who provided countless laughs, unscheduled pit-stops and ground-level perspectives along the way.

Meg Worby

Thanks to Maryanne for this one and for all the gigs: it's been a pleasure working with you. More than ever, thanks to the in-house team at LP: you guys are great at what you do. In Brisbane, a massive thank you to Lauren, Christian, Orlando, Ilaria and the Goodies for your generosity, soulful company and high-rollin' insider tips on Brisvegas. To our little daughters, Ione and Remy, thanks for crawling over every inch of South Bank with us! And to Charles: 'proper job' (Brisbane's a long way from Devon, but you made it seem like home).

Peter Dragicevich

I owe a great debt of thanks to David Mills and Barry Sawtell, Michael Woodhouse, Tony and Debbie Dragicevich, Tim Moyes, and Maureen and Peter Day for all their help during the research of this book. But above all, I'd like to thank Maryanne Netto for her dedication to this title and her faith in me.

Anthony Ham

Thanks to Maryanne Netto for sending me to such wonderful places – your legacy will endure. To David Andrew for so many wise wildlife tips. And to every person I met along the road – from knowledgeable and patient tourist office staff to other travellers. And to Marina, Carlota and Valentina – home is wherever you are.

Trent Holden & Kate Morgan

A huge thanks to the lovely Maryanne Netto for giving us the chance to research our home town – a great gig. We'd like to thank both of our families, especially Tim and Larysa, Gary and Heather, for all of your help, not to mention a place to crash at times! Shout out to Shaun at Port Fairy Motors for your help in getting us back on the road quick smart in a time of chaos. To Linda Bosidis, Caro Cooper, Jane Ormond, Paul and Max Waycott, Alex and Mat Forsman, cheers for great insider tips and suggestions. Finally big thanks to Tasmin Waby, Glenn van der Knijff and all of the in-house staff who worked hard on this book during a tough transitional time.

Tamara Sheward

Backslapping g'days and goodonyas to the multitude of Queenslanders (and a few non-Smart State ring-ins) who helped with the large but lovely challenge of covering the almost-2000km from FNQ to the Sunshine Coast. Everyone from visitor info centre staff to pub-propper-uppers proved that with sunny climes come equal dispositions. Extra big shout-out to 1770: we'll be back, and we will be annexing. *Dušan moj ljubav, ti si najbolji avanturista i muž na svetu*; Masha, are you ready for this?

ACKNOWLEDGMENTS

Climate map data adapted from Peel MC, Finlayson BL & McMahon TA (2007) 'Updated World Map of the Köppen-Geiger Climate Classification', *Hydrology and Earth System Sciences*, 11, 163344.

Illustration pp84-5 by Javier Zarracina.

Cover photograph: Surfers at Queenscliff, Sydney, Oliver Strewe, Getty Images ©.

THIS BOOK

This 5th edition of Lonely Planet's *East Coast Australia* guidebook was researched and written by Charles Rawlings-Way, Meg Worby, Peter Dragicevich, Anthony Ham, Trent Holden, Kate Morgan and Tamara Sheward. The previous edition was coordinated by Regis St Louis. This guidebook was commissioned in Lonely Planet's Melbourne office, and produced by the following:

Commissioning Editor
Maryanne Netto

Destination Editor
Tasmin Waby

Product Editor
Alison Ridgway

Senior Cartographer
Julie Sheridan

Book Designer
Katherine Marsh

Senior Editors
Catherine Naghten, Karyn Noble

Assisting Editors
Sarah Bailey, Michelle Bennett, Nigel Chin, Rosie Nicholson, Ross Taylor

Assisting Cartographers
Mick Garrett, James Leversha

Cover Researcher
Naomi Parker

Thanks to Anita Banh, Imogen Bannister, Laura Crawford, Noirin Hegarty, Briohny Hooper, Kate James, Elizabeth Jones, Martine Power, Averil Robertson, Angela Tinson, Glenn van der Knijff

Index

Map Pages **000**
Photo Pages 000

Map Legend

Sights

- Beach
- Bird Sanctuary
- Buddhist
- Castle/Palace
- Christian
- Confucian
- Hindu
- Islamic
- Jain
- Jewish
- Monument
- Museum/Gallery/Historic Building
- Ruin
- Sento Hot Baths/Onsen
- Shinto
- Sikh
- Taoist
- Winery/Vineyard
- Zoo/Wildlife Sanctuary
- Other Sight

Activities, Courses & Tours

- Bodysurfing
- Diving
- Canoeing/Kayaking
- Course/Tour
- Skiing
- Snorkelling
- Surfing
- Swimming/Pool
- Walking
- Windsurfing
- Other Activity

Sleeping

- Sleeping
- Camping

Eating

- Eating

Drinking & Nightlife

- Drinking & Nightlife
- Cafe

Entertainment

- Entertainment

Shopping

- Shopping

Information

- Bank
- Embassy/Consulate
- Hospital/Medical
- Internet
- Police
- Post Office
- Telephone
- Toilet
- Tourist Information
- Other Information

Geographic

- Beach
- Hut/Shelter
- Lighthouse
- Lookout
- Mountain/Volcano
- Oasis
- Park
- Pass
- Picnic Area
- Waterfall

Population

- Capital (National)
- Capital (State/Province)
- City/Large Town
- Town/Village

Transport

- Airport
- Border crossing
- Bus
- Cable car/Funicular
- Cycling
- Ferry
- Metro station
- Monorail
- Parking
- Petrol station
- Subway station
- Taxi
- Train station/Railway
- Tram
- Underground station
- Other Transport

Note: Not all symbols displayed above appear on the maps in this book

Routes

- Tollway
- Freeway
- Primary
- Secondary
- Tertiary
- Lane
- Unsealed road
- Road under construction
- Plaza/Mall
- Steps
- Tunnel
- Pedestrian overpass
- Walking Tour
- Walking Tour detour
- Path/Walking Trail

Boundaries

- International
- State/Province
- Disputed
- Regional/Suburb
- Marine Park
- Cliff
- Wall

Hydrography

- River, Creek
- Intermittent River
- Canal
- Water
- Dry/Salt/Intermittent Lake
- Reef

Areas

- Airport/Runway
- Beach/Desert
- Cemetery (Christian)
- Cemetery (Other)
- Glacier
- Mudflat
- Park/Forest
- Sight (Building)
- Sportsground
- Swamp/Mangrove